The Economics of
European Integration

Својим синовима Јовану и Николи,
посвећујем све на свету *изузев* ове књиге
која је безвредна у односу на
љубав, срећу и наду коју пружају.

Στους υιούς μου, Γιάννη και Νικόλαο,
αφιερώνω τα πάντα στον κόσμο *εκτός* από αυτό το βιβλίο
που δεν είναι τίποτα μπροστά
στην αγάπη, την ευτυχία και την ελπίδα που προσφέρουν.

Ai miei figli, Jovan e Nikola
dedico ogni cosa, *tranne* questo libro,
che non vale tutto l'amore, la felicità e la speranza
che mi danno.

To my sons, Jovan and Nikola,
I dedicate everything in the world *except* this book
which is worthless compared with
the love, happiness and hope that they provide.

The Economics of European Integration

Limits and Prospects

Miroslav N. Jovanović

Economic Affairs Officer, United Nations Economic Commission for Europe, Geneva, Switzerland

Edward Elgar
Cheltenham, UK • Northampton, MA, USA

© Miroslav N. Jovanović, 2005

All rights reserved. No part of this publication may be reproduced, stored in a retrieval system or transmitted in any form or by any means, electronic, mechanical or photocopying, recording, or otherwise without the prior permission of the publisher.

Published by
Edward Elgar Publishing Limited
Glensanda House
Montpellier Parade
Cheltenham
Glos GL50 1UA
UK

Edward Elgar Publishing, Inc.
136 West Street
Suite 202
Northampton
Massachusetts 01060
USA

A catalogue record for this book
is available from the British Library

ISBN 1 84376 691 4 (cased)

Printed and bound in Great Britain by MPG Books Ltd, Bodmin, Cornwall

> How good and pleasant it is when brothers live together in unity.
> Psalms 133:1

Contents

Preface and acknowledgements   xi
List of abbreviations and acronyms   xvii

1   The Origin, Evolution and Prospects for the European Union   **1**

1	Introduction	1
2	The Marshall Plan	3
3	Unity of the West	6
4	European Coal and Steel Community	7
5	Political cooperation	9
6	European Economic Community	10
7	European Free Trade Association	14
8	EEC and Britain	15
9	Luxembourg Agreement	16
10	The first enlargement	17
11	Eurosclerosis	20
12	The Single European Act	22
13	The Maastricht Treaty	25
14	Northern enlargement	31
15	Treaty of Amsterdam	32

16	*Acquis communautaire*	34
17	Preparations for the future: *Agenda 2000* and the Lisbon Council	35
18	Treaty of Nice	36
19	The topsy-turvy future or permanent disillusionment	39
20	Federal future of Europe or what?	54
21	Priorities	59
22	Conclusion	62

2 Monetary Integration — 89

1	Introduction	89
2	Traditional model	91
3	Costs and benefits	100
4	Parallel currencies	107
5	European Union	109
6	European Monetary Union	119
7	Achievements, problems and outlook	128
8	Britain and the euro	134
9	Conclusion	141

3 Fiscal Policy and the Budget — 147

1	Introduction	147
2	Fiscal policy	148
3	A bit of history	154
4	Direct taxes	163
5	Indirect taxes	178
6	Future challenges	187
7	Conclusion	189
8	Budget of the European Union	193

4 Common Agricultural Policy — 209

1	Introduction	209
2	Distinctiveness of agriculture	210
3	Objectives	213
4	Implementation	215
5	Operation and consequences	218
6	Reforms	255
7	Common Fisheries Policy	260
8	Conclusion	262

5	**Competition Policy**	**267**
1	Introduction	267
2	Competition, efficiency and location	269
3	European Union	313
4	Conclusion	343
6	**Industrial Policy in Manufacturing and Services**	**352**
1	Introduction	352
2	Industrial policy issues	353
3	European Union	383
4	Services	408
5	Conclusion	421
7	**Trade Policy**	**431**
1	Introduction	431
2	Theory of customs unions	432
3	Why countries integrate	463
4	World Trade Organisation and international trade	468
5	Non-tariff barriers	481
6	The European Union in world trade	497
7	Preferred partners	554
8	Conclusion	558
8	**Spatial Location of Production and Regional Policy**	**568**
1	Introduction	568
2	Issues	570
3	Theories of location	572
4	Cities	581
5	Clusters	584
6	History and expectations	595
7	War and the location of firms	605
8	Wrapping up the theory of location	607
9	Regional policy	610
10	Objectives and justification	617
11	Instruments	622
12	Impact of integration	624
13	European Union	637
14	Conclusion	651

9 Capital Mobility — 666

1. Introduction — 666
2. Factor mobility and trade — 667
3. Foreign direct investment — 670
4. Transnational corporations — 688
5. Intervention — 715
6. Transnational corporations and international economic integration — 720
7. European Union — 723
8. Conclusion — 748

10 Mobility of Labour — 755

1. Introduction — 755
2. Country of origin — 756
3. Country of destination — 758
4. European Union — 760
5. Conclusion — 769

11 Social Policy — 771

1. Introduction — 771
2. Social policy issues — 773
3. Unemployment — 775
4. European Union — 777
5. Conclusion — 788

12 Environment Policy — 792

1. Introduction — 792
2. Issues — 793
3. European Union — 795
4. Conclusion — 805

13 Transport Policy — 808

1. Introduction — 808
2. European Union — 810
3. Conclusion — 820

14	**Eastern Enlargement**	**822**
1	Introduction	822
2	Economic structure of the accession countries	823
3	Entry criteria	826
4	Costs and benefits	828
5	Disillusionment	844
6	Cost of enlargement	846
7	Conclusion	847
15	**Conclusion**	**851**
Bibliography		863
Index		907

Preface and Acknowledgements

Created by the Treaty of Rome[1] in 1957, the European Union (EU) established a full customs union in 1968. This was, indeed, a great achievement in economic integration as it took place well before the deadline stipulated in the treaty (1970). The first EU enlargement in 1973 followed this early success. Then came a period of Eurosclerosis and Europessimism in the 1970s and early 1980s. The EU received an antidote in the form of the Single Market Programme (1985–92). The objective of this 'technical' programme was to remove non-tariff barriers on internal trade, open up the internal market, stimulate competition and, hence, increase welfare in the region. The next logical step to consolidate these and earlier achievements in European integration was to eliminate exchange rate fluctuations and to move the EU towards economic and monetary union. That step came with the Maastricht Treaty (1991). European economic, monetary and certain aspects of political integration gained momentum. The European Monetary Union (eurozone) started for the 12 EU member countries in 1999, while the euro notes replaced their national currencies in 2002. The European Council in Lisbon (2000) set a new strategic and ambitious goal for the decade: to make the EU 'the most competitive and dynamic knowledge-based economy in the world capable of sustainable economic growth with more and better jobs and greater social cohesion'.[2]

The eastern bloc fell apart in 1989 and with it went several composite countries. This provided a rare opportunity to redesign Europe. The Treaty of Nice (2001) paved the legal and organisational way for the eastern enlargement of the EU in 2004, when EU membership increased from 15 to 25 countries; several more countries are in line to join.

The EU was an attractive and long-lasting institution for countries to join in an attempt to shape a common European future. The EU, with different degrees of success, provided a fairly flexible foundation for a relatively smooth absorption of certain changes brought by various economic, political and organisational challenges and opportunities. The EU was changing, adapting, expanding in scope and coverage, and it survived. However, has the European integration exhausted itself? Are there limits to European economic integration? Has the EU reached the ceiling? The answer to these questions is negative. For example, if some projects had a fairly limited success, if they are more aspirational than operational (at the moment), even if some of them fail, that does not mean that the idea of European integration is weak or perhaps moribund. On the contrary. There are many other areas, dimensions and speeds for European integration that may preserve the continent's unity along with its diversity.

The objective of this book is to look into the origin, evolution, operation, problems, successes, failures and possible prospects for *economic* integration in Europe through the EU. Economic integration of some of the oldest nations in the world with different organisational traditions and history, full of secular conflicts and rivalries, is a tremendously difficult, but potentially highly rewarding political and economic task. Economic integration between relatively small and medium-sized countries can be recommended and defended with the same arguments that are used for the integration of various regions within a single country. Just as one can always enhance the integration of various regions within a single country and exploit unexplored opportunities for national economic integration, one can do the same in a group that comprises various countries. In pure economic theory and taken to the limit, this process could continue until the whole world is integrated. However, there are mainly political limits to doing this on the national level. There are also mainly political limits to further integration in a group that integrates different countries. The main one is the protection of regional and national sovereignty and, hence, distinctiveness.

The term 'European Union' is used throughout the book as the organisational habitat for the European integration. The one exception is the first chapter on the origin, evolution and prospects for European integration from the European Coal and Steel Community, to the European Economic Community, the European Communities and finally to the EU.

The book is organised as follows. Chapter 1 traces the origin, evolution and prospects for the EU. It starts with the ideas for European integration as a means for West European reconciliation following the Second World War. A relatively modest beginning with a sectoral integration (coal and steel) was extended to a wider economic integration in the European Economic Community. Once economic integration started, the process continued to expand in spite of hiccups. European integration grew from the economic sphere to new areas such as foreign policy, security and defence. It also included an ever-increasing number of member countries.

Monetary integration is the subject of Chapter 2. Monetary domain is, together with trade and competition, the first area where the impact of real integration is felt and tested. An overview of the theory of optimum currency areas precedes the discussion of monetary integration in the EU. Consideration of monetary integration as conceived in the Maastricht Treaty criteria reveals that the eurozone has potential, but also a degree of fragility. However, the political determination of the participating countries to stick to this project is so strong and clear that it will continue at least in the medium term. This is in spite of coordination difficulties as almost half of the 25 EU member countries are in the eurozone, while the other half are out of it either by choice or by ineligibility.

Chapter 3 deals with fiscal policy and the budget. Once tariffs and quotas are removed on intra-EU trade, the illusion is that such trade is free. Not quite. Differences in taxes may contribute to the distortion of internal trade and factor flows. Although there were certain achievements in the approximation of taxes in the EU, there is immense room for improvement. Consideration of the EU budget reveals that, apart from agriculture, the budget does not play a significant role in many aspects of EU economic policy. This is particularly important because of the lack of influence on EU macroeconomic stabilisation. Following the EU eastern enlargement in 2004, very tough, complicated and controversial negotiations are expected to define the new EU financial perspective that will set the EU spending for the 2007–13 period. In any case, in 2004 the EU entered into a much more difficult phase of integration than most people imagine.

The Common Agricultural Policy (CAP), covered in Chapter 4, is, together with trade and competition, the oldest major economic area in which the EU exerts significant influence. The CAP was based on political compromise between France and Germany, it consumes the bulk of the EU budget, distorts trade and is in need of an overhaul. However, historically, agriculture has been a very special social and economic activity in Europe for several millennia. Hence, it may be unfair, unnecessary and harmful to assess the needs, accomplishments and effects of this sector by employing unconditional free trade criteria. None the less, external factors, such as negotiations about liberalisation of trade under the auspices of the World Trade Organisation (WTO), continue to push for the reform in the EU farm policy.

Chapters 5, 6 and 7, respectively, on competition, industrial and trade policy, form an integral part of this book. The division of certain topics among those chapters is arbitrary. For example, consideration of non-tariff barriers is placed in the trade chapter, although it could easily fit into the other two. The EU has greatly expanded its involvement in competition matters (state aids or restrictive business practices), which has an impact on industrial policy. Within industrial policy, technology policy shapes the comparative advantage of the EU, which in turn, has an impact on competition and trade. The EU is one of the largest international traders. As such, it exerts an influence on international trade flows and negotiations within the WTO and its predecessor, the General Agreement on Tariffs and Trade (GATT). The EU has a passion for preferential (that is, discriminatory) trade agreements. It has considerable discretionary power to differentiate among its trade partners by offering or not offering different types of trade and cooperation agreements. Although member countries of the EU are members of the WTO, which promotes multilateralism, the EU 'rewards' its foreign friends with special bilateral trade agreements.

Spatial location of production and regional policy (Chapter 8) is relevant because one of the most important and challenging questions in economics is where will economic activity locate in the future? In addition, in a monetary union, balance of payments disequilibria are replaced by regional discrepancies. A country or an economic group cannot be considered as well integrated if regional disparities do not have at least a tendency to narrow. There are still large regional gaps in the EU(15), but the EU budget is still too small to reduce them. This problem is accentuated with the eastern enlargement, that is, the entry of Central and East European countries which have an average GDP per capita well below the EU average. In addition, the solution to the 'regional problem' is important for the cohesion of the group. An interesting finding is that while certain member countries give up their national regional policies as inefficient, the EU is expanding its role in this area.

Chapters 9 and 10 discuss factor mobility. Capital mobility (foreign direct investment) is still highly concentrated in the 'core' EU countries, although certain EU-rim countries such as Spain show that if the infrastructure and a certain type of labour are provided, this may give foreign investors the incentive to locate production in a peripheral EU country. Labour mobility in the EU is quite low because of various social barriers. Any such mobility tends to come from third countries.

The rest of the book covers relatively small, although expanding, policies of the EU. Chapter 11 addresses social policy, which at the EU level is nothing like the national policy. EU social policy is carried out in part through the European Social Fund, which gives support to the vocational training of the unemployed. Although the objectives of the European Social Charter are noble, its provisions may introduce additional rigidities in the labour market, which would be very undesirable in a situation of relatively high and persisting unemployment and when the business community demands a higher degree of flexibility in labour markets. Demographical trends are such that there will be serious labour shortages in the EU from 2010 for several decades. Controlled immigration may be one of the solutions to this problem.

The environment policy of the EU (Chapter 12) is relatively novel, but it is expanding in scope and coverage. All EU policies and projects must take into account their consequences on the environment. Chapter 13 is devoted to transport policy. Although the Treaty of Rome advocates a common EU transport policy, this has not been evident for a very long time, which is one of the big disappointments in the process of European integration. There are certain signs that the policy is getting off the ground, but problems arise from a lack of financial resources for large pan-European infrastructural projects. Following the experience with the Channel Tunnel, the private sector is very wary of similar projects in the future, while governments are lukewarm to such proposals as they struggle to keep their budget deficits under control.

The eastern enlargement is altering the EU almost beyond recognition (see Chapter 14). The EU has an unprecedented opportunity to reshape Europe and make it a better and safer region. However, the EU is no longer what it was 30, 20 or even 10 years ago. From a relatively 'generous' common market (later Single European Market) regarding expenditure on agriculture and other policy areas such as cohesion, the EU has become a much more demanding and costly place to be in as far as the *acquis communautaire*[3] is concerned. At the same time, EU spending has become tight and thrifty. Hence the 'promised land' the Central and East European countries expected from the EU at the time (1989) when they aspired to join is not at all what they got at entry in 2004. It may take the EU at least a decade or a generation to 'digest' all the economic, political and organisational dimensions that the eastern enlargement brings with it.

The conclusion of the book is that there is much room for reform and improvement in European economic integration. The constraints come from the political sphere where certain vested interests and national and European elites, rightly or wrongly, preserve certain parts of national sovereignty, while on the EU level, they do certain things (monetary integration) for which there is a lack of large-scale popular enthusiasm and support. They fail to explain convincingly to the people that in economic integration sovereignty is most often pooled, rather than given up.

I hope that this book will be of interest to economists concerned with international economics, integration and European studies. If it is also of interest to others, such as those specialising in economic development, international business and management, as well as policy makers, then this is to be welcomed.

My involvement in European economic integration began when I was studying the topic at the University of Amsterdam (1980–81). That period was followed by work in other subjects, such as industrial policy, foreign direct investment and the geography of production. However, an interest in European integration has always been present, although in the first half of the 1980s, during the period of Eurosclerosis, I did wonder whether my choice of specialisation was wise.

Over the years I have profited from the intellectual capital of many friends and colleagues. There are several to whom I owe a special debt of gratitude for various kinds of assistance and encouragement in the preparation of this book. Je tiens à remercier tout particulièrement Marinette Payot qui m'a beaucoup aidé sans que je le sache. Others include Marc-Aurel Battaglia, Luis Biedma, Martine Campoy, Victoria Curzon Price, Anthony Donnarumma, Sandra Dučič, Dencho Georgiev, Monique Ferrand, Cristina Giordano, Eric Fiechter, Eckhard Freyer, Dragoš Kalajić, Oskar Kovač, Philip Kuruvilla, Alexandar Rado, Marina Rossi, Dušan Sidjanski, Constantine Stephanou, Rolf Traeger, Henri Tyrman, Joanna Wheeler and James Wiltshire. Jovan and Nikola Jovanović assisted considerably with the figures. Luke Adams was enthusiastic about this project from the outset, while Margaret Pugh edited the text superbly. Alison Stone efficiently prepared the text for print.

I am very grateful to all of them. The usual disclaimer applies here: I alone am responsible for all shortcomings and mistakes. In addition, the expressed views are only my own and have nothing to do with the organisation in which I work.

Notes

1. The Treaty of Rome has been altered by the Single European Act (1987) and the treaties of Maastricht (1992), Amsterdam (1997) and Nice (2001), respectively. Throughout this book reference is made to the latest consolidated version of the Treaty of Rome (2002) available at the following web address: http://europa.eu.int/eur-lex/pri/en/oj/dat/2002/c_325/c_32520021224en00010184.pdf.
2. European Council, Lisbon 2000, Presidency Conclusions, §5.
3. The existence and operation of the EU is based on law. The whole body of the established EU laws, policies and practices is called the *acquis communautaire* or the EU patrimony. It is widely estimated that the *acquis* consisted of about 80 000 pages of legal acts in 2004. The ever-evolving and -expanding *acquis* was enlarged by 2348 new regulations in 2003 alone. However, most of the regulations have a limited time duration.

Abbreviations and Acronyms

AASM	Associated African States and Madagascar
ACP	African, Caribbean and Pacific
ASEAN	Association of South-East Asian Nations
CAP	Common Agricultural Policy
CCC	Community Customs Code
CEEC	Committee of European Economic Cooperation
CET	common external tariff
CIF	cost, insurance and freight
CMEA	Council for Mutual Economic Assistance
COCOM	Coordinating Committee on Multilateral Export Controls
Coreper	Comité des Représentants Permanents
DG	Directorate-General
EAGGF	European Agricultural Guidance and Guarantee Fund
EBRD	European Bank for Reconstruction and Development
EC	European Community
ECB	European Central Bank
ECOFIN	Economic and Financial Committee
ECSC	European Coal and Steel Community
ECU	European Currency Unit
EDC	European Defence Community
EDF	European Development Fund

EEA	European Economic Area – also European Environment Agency
EEC	European Economic Community
EFTA	European Free Trade Association
EIB	European Investment Bank
EMI	European Monetary Institute
EMS	European Monetary System
EMU	economic and monetary union
EPC	European Political Community
ERDF	European Regional Development Fund
ERRF	European Rapid Reaction Force
ERM	Exchange Rate Mechanism
ESF	European Social Fund
EU	European Union
Euratom	European Atomic Energy Community
EURES	European Employment Services
FAO	Food and Agriculture Organisation (UN)
FAST	Forecasting and Assessment in Science and Technology
FDI	foreign direct investment
FIRA	Foreign Investment Review Agency (Canada)
FSC	Foreign Sales Corporation
GATS	General Agreement on Trade in Services
GATT	General Agreement on Tariffs and Trade
GDP	gross domestic product
GSP	generalised system of preferences
HHI	Hirschman–Herfindahl Index
IGC	intergovernmental conference
IIT	intra-industry trade
IMF	International Monetary Fund
MA	Multilateral Agreement on Investment
MCA	monetary compensatory amount
MFA	Multi-Fibre Agreement
MFN	most favoured nation
MITI	Ministry for International Trade and Industry
MNE	multinational enterprise
MRA	Mutual Recognition Agreement
NAFTA	North American Free Trade Agreement
NAIRU	non-accelerating inflation rate of unemployment
NATO	North Atlantic Treaty Organisation
NGO	non-governmental organisation
NRF	NATO Reaction Force
NTB	non-tariff barrier

OECD	Organisation for Economic Cooperation and Development
OEEC	Organisation for European Economic Cooperation
PHARE	Poland, Hungary: Assistance for Economic Restructuring
PPS	purchasing power standard
PSE	producer support equivalent
PSI	production specialisation index
SCP	structure–conduct–performance
R&D	research and development
SITC	Standard International Trade Classification
SME	small and medium-sized enterprise
Stabex	Stabilisation of Export Earnings from Agricultural Commodities
TACIS	Technical Assistance for the Commonwealth of Independent States
TNC	transnational corporation
TRIM	trade-related investment measure
TRIPS	Trade-Related Intellectual Property Rights
TSI	trade specialisation index
UK	United Kingdom
UN	United Nations Centre on Transnational Corporations
UNCTAD	UN Conference on Trade and Development
UNCTC	UN
UNECE	UN Economic Commission for Europe
US	United States
USSR	Union of Soviet Socialist Republics
VAT	value-added tax
VCR	video cassette recorder
WEU	Western European Union
WTO	World Trade Organisation

> Anyone who hears and obeys these teachings of mine
> is like a wise person who built a house on solid rock.
> Rain poured down, rivers flooded, and winds beat against that house.
> But it did not fall, because it was built on solid rock.
> Matthew 7:24–5

1 The Origin, Evolution and Prospects for the European Union

1. Introduction

The concept of European integration has been a topic for discussion among European intellectuals since the early 1920s.[1] The idea, however, can be traced back to the Middle Ages. At the start of the 14th century, Dante Alighieri argued in his book *On Monarchy* in favour of a supranational power that would respect diversity between different peoples and their traditions, while Pierre Dubois had the idea of a Christian Republic. In 1849, Victor Hugo was in favour of a pan-European integration in which nations of the continent would not lose their individuality. Richard Coudenhove-Kalergi argued in 1923 for the creation of a Pan-European Union. An emerging 'European movement' assembled about 2000 participants from 24 countries in a Congress in Vienna in 1926. They approved the Pan-European Manifesto that was, among other things, in favour of a customs union, common currency, military alliance and the protection of national minorities. Aristide Briand, the French foreign minister, was in charge of the Government Memorandum on organisation of the federal union in Europe in 1930, at the time when Adolf Hitler scored his first electoral victories. The memorandum considered issues such as a common market; customs union; free movement of goods, capital and people; and a community of European people (Sidjanski, 2000, pp. 7–9).

Altiero Spinelli and Ernesto Rossi, although deported to the island of Ventotene (west of Naples) in 1941, founded the European Federalist Movement and secretly circulated the Ventotene Manifesto. At its first meeting in Milan in 1943, the movement established a structure and strategy for action. To avoid international anarchy and safeguard freedom in Europe, they claimed, one needs to establish a federal Europe to which nation states should transfer certain sovereign rights in the common interest of all Europeans (Sidjanski, 2000, p. 10). Following the Second World War, the British and Americans would restore nation states in their old form. As was often the case in the past, this would again permit the British and now the Americans to shape the European continent in a pattern and form that would serve their own economic and geopolitical interests. Therefore, this had to be resisted. According to the Manifesto, federalists must snatch the opportunity created by the turmoil and uncertainty that would accompany the end of the war in order to establish a European Federation.

In Nazi Germany in March 1943, Carl Friedrich Goerdeler circulated within the German resistance movement a secret paper on European unification. He proposed that an economic union with a permanent council should be created immediately after the war, and political union would follow. There should be a European ministry of the economy, a European army and a European ministry for foreign affairs. A democratic Germany should join the integration process with France. If Germany were integrated in a democratic community, this would prevent it from undertaking another military adventure (Sidjanski, 2000, p. 11).

The Second World War left many deep scars in Europe. These included not only the destruction of a large part of the population and production potential, but also the presence of foreign troops in many countries. There was also a danger that after their joint elimination of Nazism, the confronting forces of the Red Army and the armies of the West would create an open conflict between East and West. That was clearly seen by Winston Churchill, who called for a closing of the ranks in the West. In a speech in Zurich on 19 September 1946 he said: 'I am going to say something that will astonish you. The first step in the recreation of the European family must be a partnership between France and Germany' (Jansen, 1975, p. 7). It was a revival of many earlier visions that cooperation between former adversaries could defuse potential conflicts in the future.

Intellectuals on the European continent continued to develop the integration idea after the Second World War. The European Federalist Union was created in Paris in 1946. This multiparty movement was matched by the creation of similar partisan movements among the Christian democrats and socialists. Political issues were supplemented by the establishment of the European League for Economic Cooperation on the initiative of Paul van

Zeeland in 1947. The League prepared studies on issues such as capital mobility, monopolies, enterprises and currencies. In the same year, the Hague Congress considered two prominent reports dealing with possible ways for European integration. The first one was on federalist issues, by Denis de Rougemont, and the second on economic issues, by Maurice Allais. All these activities by European intellectuals and government officials point to the fact that ideas about European integration were sincere and that post-Second World War regional integration was a real prospect.[2]

Declassified documents by the United States (US) government reveal that the US intelligence community ran a covert operation during the 1950s and 1960s to build a momentum for a united Europe. It funded and directed the European Federalist Movement, the most important federalist organisation at the time. In 1958, for example, it provided over half of the movement's funds.[3]

This chapter is structured as follows. Section 2 starts with a survey of first ideas about European integration and the Marshall Plan. This is followed by sections on the expansion in the unity of Western Europe (Section 3) and the creation of the European Coal and Steel Community (Section 4). Section 5 examines political cooperation. The next step in integration was the establishment of the European Economic Community (Section 6) and the European Free Trade Association (Section 7). Sections 8 and 9 deal with the EEC and Britain, and the Luxembourg Agreement, respectively. European integration led to the enlargement of the European Economic Community (1973) (Section 10). A period of Eurosclerosis (1974–84) (Section 11) was changed by the Single European Act (1987) (Section 12). The Maastricht Treaty (1992) (Section 13) paved the way for economic and monetary union (eurozone). Section 14 examines the northern enlargement. The treaties of Amsterdam (1997) (Section 15) and Nice (2001) (Section 18), respectively, reformed the institutions and enabled the European Union to expand eastwards. The *acquis communautaire* is examined in Section 16, and *Agenda 2000* and the Lisbon Council in Section 17. Sections 19–21 present views about the possible structure, direction and potentially federal future of European integration and Section 22 concludes. Appendix 1A outlines the structure and operation of the institutions of the European Union.

2. The Marshall Plan

The mistrust and apprehension between the East and the West reduced contact between the two blocs, which basically was taking place only within the United Nations (UN), and in particular its regional organisation, the

Economic Commission for Europe, created in Geneva in 1947, with the aim of fostering contacts among all European countries that would help with the economic reconstruction of the region. The Cold War increased the gap between the two blocs, and their respective countries tried to find their own way in their political, military and economic recovery and development.

Poverty and hardship of a large part of the population tend to instigate social upheavals, and such a situation led to the build-up of the left-wing parties in the post-war period in France, Italy and Greece. Harsh winter conditions (1946–47) and the following dry summer led to a shortage of food. The aggregate production in Western Europe was small. Domestic consumption absorbed almost everything that was produced. There was little export surplus that might have covered the growing demand for imports. The leader of the Western world, the US, realised that there should be a consolidation of the social system in Western Europe by means of a recovery programme. Such a programme would inject on a one-off basis a large amount of aid into the West European economies. The expectation was that it would help Western Europe recover and grow as a significant market for American goods, services and interests.

In May 1947, three young economists who were working for the US Department of State, Harold van Cleveland, Ben Moore and Charles Kindleberger, wrote to George Kennan, Director of Policy Planning Staff, calling for a 'Coordinated European Recovery Programme' directed 'toward a strong and economically integrated Europe'. Among the 'top secret' documents from that time, there was also a 'Report of the Special "Ad Hoc" Committee of the State–War–Navy Coordinating Committee', in April 1947, which sought a 'reintegration of these countries into healthy regional and world trading and production systems' (Machlup, 1979, p. 10). It was in America's strategic interest to have reliable partners in Europe, rather than unpredictable adversaries.

In June 1947, US Secretary of State George Marshall gave a speech at Harvard University announcing the European Recovery Programme (known as the Marshall Plan). The plan basically revealed American readiness to help the reconstruction of *all* European countries subject to two conditions:

- European countries had to prepare jointly a reconstruction programme; and
- they needed to agree about the amount of the financial-aid package, as well as each country's share in it.

The message of the plan to the Europeans was that they had to integrate in some way if they wanted to get aid from America. Such a stance by the US was based on the top secret documents that argued in favour of European integration (Machlup, 1979, pp. 10, 186), as the Americans did not have confidence in some 20 atomised states in Western Europe. US aid was not offered on a bilateral, but rather on a continental basis.

In July 1947, the foreign ministers of France and Britain invited their counterparts from all European countries, with the exception of Spain, to a conference in Paris to discuss the drafting of a joint reconstruction programme. Poland and Czechoslovakia were the only countries from the East that initially accepted the invitation. However, they both subsequently declined because of the Soviet fear that the Marshall aid programme was an American Trojan horse which would destabilise the Soviet zone of influence. The Paris conference consequently took place with the participation of 16 West European countries.[4] These countries established a Committee of European Economic Cooperation (CEEC) which was supposed to prepare the principles of the reconstruction programme and suggest the necessary means to implement it. The programme was prepared and submitted to the US government in September 1947.

In April 1948, the US government approved the European Recovery Programme (the Marshall Plan). During the tenure of the programme (1948–52), the US spent about $15 billion. The biggest single users of the programme funds were Britain (about 23 per cent), France (about 20 per cent) and the western zones of occupied Germany (about 10 per cent). The Marshall funds had an enormous stimulating effect on the recovery of West European countries from their post-war economic disarray. Marshall aid was not conditional in any way, but in fact almost all the funds were spent by the recipients in the US because that was the only country able to provide the goods required.[5]

The member countries of the CEEC discussed the possibility of establishing a permanent organisation with the aim of fostering economic cooperation among the member countries. Subsequently, they established the Organisation for European Economic Cooperation (OEEC) in April 1948. During the negotiations there were, basically, two schools of thought. The British thought that the OEEC ought to be an organisation with minimum authority, just enough to satisfy the American demands. In contrast, the French argued that the OEEC needed to have a wider authority. The British approach prevailed in the final agreement as the balance of the European leadership tipped over to the British side. It should be remembered that Britain was still an important partner in the victory over the Nazis and one of the three parties that had divided up the world in Yalta (1945), as well as a large colonial power. There are ancient rivalries between France and Britain, but one may find here the first overt contemporary bone of contention between Britain (and, perhaps, the Scandinavian states), on the one hand, and France and the other continental European states (which would subsequently create the European Community) on the other.

3. Unity of the West

The creation of various economic, political and defence organisations in Eastern and Western Europe reinforced the division of Europe into two blocs. Britain, France and the Benelux countries dealt with questions of mutual assistance in the event of an attack on any of those countries. In March 1948 they[6] established in Brussels the Western European Union (WEU) which obliges the contracting parties to collectively defend themselves in the case of an armed attack.[7]

Fearing that Western Europe might in the long term become too independent (or become communist) in the political and military field, the US decided to continue its military presence in Europe.[8] The US invited the Benelux countries, Britain, Canada, Denmark, France, Iceland, Italy, Norway and Portugal to unite in their defence efforts, and the North Atlantic Treaty Organisation (NATO) was established in April 1949. An armed attack on any NATO member country would be taken as an attack on all NATO countries.[9] West European countries accepted the American proposition[10] since that meant a partial reduction in the tax burden on the domestic taxpayers. Italy was included in NATO from its inception, although it is not an Atlantic state. The US had a paramount vision about the question of defence. The Americans, as well as the French, wanted to include Italy in the family of West European states, although it was a member of the Axis, in order to avoid its isolation, which would create fertile soil for any communist onslaught. In addition, Italy could provide a strategic contribution to the south flank of the Alliance. The defence club of the West now had an intercontinental dimension. Meanwhile, the WEU, as a European defence institution, went into hibernation.

Economic cooperation of the West European countries in the post-war period took place within the OEEC. Defence was organised first by the Dunkirk Treaty (1947) of Britain and France (against Germany), then the WEU (against Germany and the then Soviet Union), and next NATO (against the Soviet bloc). Political cooperation, as the third pillar of Western unity, was ignored – but not for long.

Political cooperation also started to develop in Europe. The Hague was the site of the European Congress in May 1948 for the consideration of issues linked with the creation of a united Europe. The congress was, in essence, to take up two approaches to that issue. The first was the unionists' (minimalists') model. The British and the Scandinavians (the Protestants) argued that European unity could be achieved through intergovernmental consultations. The second, the federalist model, was favoured by the French (the Catholics). The federalists wanted a more formal organisation of European political cooperation: a political institution with real and supranational powers. The subsequent debate led to the creation of the Council of Europe. The Statute of the Council, according to the British–Scandinavian model, was signed in London in 1949, but its headquarters was, and still is, in Strasbourg.[11]

The Council of Europe is mainly occupied with issues relating to human rights, freedom of the media, health, law and human mobility. The real basis for a political union within the Council of Europe was modest, since it excluded the defence issues, while the participation of neutral states precluded the possibility of a common foreign policy. The principle of unanimity in the Council made it difficult to agree on important problems.

The Yalta division of the world found a special partnership in the eastern part of Europe, too. The Soviet Union wanted to consolidate its grip in the East and created political (Cominform, 1947), economic (Comecon, 1949) and defence (Warsaw Pact, 1955) alliances there. The Warsaw Pact was created only after the entry of West Germany into NATO.

4. European Coal and Steel Community

The rivalry between Germany and France brought about three open wars between the two countries in modern history.[12] France wanted to take advantage of the favourable political circumstances following the Second World War. After all, France was a part of the Allied forces that had defeated the Nazis. Germany was occupied, and its discredited political and moral position gave France an opening to shape and direct events in Western Europe without Britain, albeit with some support from the US.

The occupation of West Germany could not last for ever. Therefore, the Western Allies established the International Ruhr Authority in 1949. Its aim was to control the production and distribution of coal, coke and steel in the Ruhr region, in order to control West German heavy industry. The economy of West Germany started to recover, and there were certain signs that the country was looking for greater independence. The questions that the Allies were facing were, on the one hand, how to permit the development of the mighty West German manufacturing base in order to create a strong shield to withstand the first blow in the event of armed conflict with the Eastern bloc and, on the other hand, how to prevent the situation of a powerful West Germany again destabilising peace and security in Europe. The solution was found in the Schuman Plan.

The UN Economic Commission for Europe was asked by the French government to prepare a report on trends in European steel production. The conclusion of the report was that the national investment plans in European countries in the area of steel production were proportionately larger than would be justified by demand. Therefore, uncoordinated national investment in this industry would create overproduction (Economic Commission for Europe, 1949). Jean Monnet, a senior officer of the French government in the field of planning, made good use of these conclusions. He drafted a plan for the establishment of the European Coal and Steel Community (ECSC). The political responsibility for its presentation was taken by the French foreign minister, Robert Schuman (Sidjanski, 1998, p. 6).

Robert Schuman presented this plan for the creation of the ECSC on 9 May 1950. Instead of opting for the first federalist action that would embrace all economic aspects, Schuman and Monnet were realistic in restricting it to a limited area: the production of coal and steel.[13] In Schuman's words: 'The solidarity in the production thus established will make it plain that any war between France and Germany becomes not merely unthinkable, but materially impossible' (Jansen, 1975, p. 36). In this unprecedented international cooperation project, France was ready to sacrifice some of its sovereignty to a supranational[14] body, the ECSC, which would manage a part of France's economy, in order to obtain partial control of West German heavy industry. Konrad Adenauer, the West German chancellor, saw a chance for his country to improve its subordinate position in the post-war period and to regain equality with other states, so he accepted the plan.

The Schuman Plan was one of the biggest turning points in French history. In the past, France had always been looking for allies against Germany, either in the east (Poland and Russia) or in the south (Serbia). After the Second World War any partnership with those countries was out of the question, at least during the Cold War division of Europe. Since coal and steel were the most important levers of economic growth and conventional warfare at the time, France decided to abandon a part of its sovereignty in those industries in order to penetrate the most important manufacturing industries in its former and secular mortal enemy, Germany.

Italy and the Benelux countries accepted the negotiations with France and West Germany concerning sectoral integration; they signed the Treaty of Paris, which created the ECSC on 18 April 1951. The single original text of the treaty was written in French and deposited in the French government archives.

The objectives of the ECSC are stated in the Preamble of the Paris treaty. They include the maintenance of peace (mentioned three times in the Preamble), a substitution of old rivalries, an avoidance of bloody conflicts and a determination to raise the standard of living. The ECSC was expected to contribute to economic expansion, the growth of employment and a rising standard of living in the member states (Article 2). The principles of the ECSC are given in Article 3. They include a regular supply in the common market, equal access to the sources of production for consumers in the Community, the prohibition of price discrimination and the need for an orderly expansion and modernisation of production.

The High Authority is charged with implementing the Paris treaty (Article 8). It may: facilitate investment programmes (Article 54), establish a system of production quotas in the case of manifest crisis (Article 58), influence prices (Article 60), outlaw agreements that prevent, restrict or distort competition within the common market and authorise in advance any transaction that might directly or indirectly bring about a consolidation of industry (Articles 65 and 66), inspired by the French desire to block a reconcentration of West German coal and steel industries. The treaty was to last for a period of 50 years from its entry into force (Article 97). After ratification, the Paris treaty became effective on 23 June 1952.[15]

During the Paris treaty negotiations, objections were raised that the ECSC and its executive body, the High Authority, would avoid democratic control. A compromise was found in the creation of another body, the Council of Ministers, which was supposed to serve as a link between all national governments and the High Authority (Articles 26–8).

5. Political cooperation

At about the same time that the ECSC was created, the international political stage was burdened with worrying events. The Korean War (1950–53) increased the possibility of a conflict between the East and the West, particularly in Europe. The US demanded from its European allies that they increase their defence efforts. The US also wanted to rearm West Germany – a proposition that was unpalatable to the Europeans, since it was only five years since the end of the Second World War.

René Pleven, the French prime minister, offered a plan for the creation of the European Defence Community (EDC) in October 1950. The EDC would integrate the armed forces of all NATO members, including those of West Germany, and it would empower the West European minister for defence to be in charge of that force. The EDC treaty was signed in May

1952, but the French parliament failed to ratify it, so the whole project broke down. The reasons for the failure of the EDC could be found in the awkward situation in which the countries were supposed to have a common defence policy, but without having a common foreign policy. The other reason, no less important, was French involvement in Indochina (1946–54) where it had a significant deployment of troops. If a European army were to be created in those circumstances, then it would consist mainly of soldiers from West Germany! France could not accept that.[16]

The foreign ministers of the six ECSC countries wanted to consider the notion of European political cooperation. They met in Paris in June 1953 to discuss the creation of a European Political Community (EPC), the aim of which would be to fill the gap in political cooperation among the six countries. Final agreement was reached in Baden-Baden in August 1953. This attempt at political cooperation among some of the West European countries was, again, torpedoed by the French parliament, which failed to ratify it on account of the existence of a supranational element, the rearming of West Germany and the absence of Britain from the scheme.

The relative success in the creation of the ECSC was not followed by progress in other social fields in Western Europe. Cooperation in the defence field failed (EDC) and remained within NATO. As for the area of politics, collaboration remained within the Council of Europe because of the collapse of the EPC. In a situation when most of Western Europe was in an impasse, the 'rescue' came from Britain.

In 1954, Anthony Eden, the British foreign secretary, proposed to rearm West Germany, but within the framework of the WEU (Britain, France and the Benelux). Paris was where, in October, a multitude of agreements prompted several profound political changes. It was decided to cease the occupation of West Germany; to welcome Italy and West Germany into the WEU; to limit production of military goods in West Germany; and to retain troops of the Western Allies (US, Britain and France) in West Germany. One of the differences between NATO and the WEU is that the former organisation demanded the continued presence of a predetermined, but minimal, number of troops. To control West Germany's rearmament, stricter control was needed, as provided by the WEU (Jansen, 1975, p. 53).

6. European Economic Community

The West European experience regarding regional integration in the post-Second World War period points to the fact that the political union of Western Europe might be realised in the long term.[17] What was left for the integration in the short and medium terms was the economy. Having their own experience of economic integration, the Benelux countries[18] proposed to the ECSC partners in 1955 an integration of the economic activities that were most closely linked with coal and steel: transport and energy.

The foreign ministers of the ECSC countries met in Messina in June 1955 in order to consider the Benelux proposal. Paul-Henri Spaak (of Belgium) was appointed to lead an intergovernmental committee with the task of preparing a report on the possible avenues for integration. Spaak's committee invited the British to join the talks, although Britain still argued along the minimalist's line in favour of a free trade area and within the framework of the OEEC. The ECSC countries argued that profound economic integration was inconceivable within the framework of the OEEC. Britain left the discussions in November, so only the six ECSC countries continued the talks. The Spaak Report claimed that there was a need for the creation of a common market among the six countries, with one exception: atomic energy needed to be covered by a special, sectoral agreement.

During the drafting of the common market agreement, numerous problems arose:

- France feared that its manufacturing industry would not be able to withstand open competition from other partner countries. This would come as a consequence of the elimination of tariffs and quotas on internal trade. A compromise was found in the inclusion of agriculture into the agreement, as well as in the avoidance of sensitive issues related to monetary integration. The customs union for the West German manufacturing industry would be as significant as the inclusion of agriculture was supposed to be for France.
- France, as a traditionally protectionist country, demanded a high rate of common external tariff (CET), while the Netherlands as a traditionally free-trading country, wanted a low one. The agreement was that the CET would be the arithmetic average of tariffs in the six countries.
- The association of colonies was one of the most contested issues. With the exception of Luxembourg, all of the negotiating countries were once colonial powers. They would be reluctant to give up those 'special' relations with their colonies or former colonies. The tone of the discussion was set by France, which did not want the application of the CET to the African Francophone countries. On the matter of tariffs and quotas France wanted these countries to be treated as if they were a part of France. These territories received aid from France, which wanted to share the burden with the new Community and, in particular, with West Germany. Only after West Germany,

although reluctantly, agreed to this French request, as well as the inclusion of agriculture into the final arrangement, did the French accept the West German demand for a customs union (tariff and quota-free trade) in the future community.
- Atomic energy was the only area for sectoral integration. There was a fear that the conventional European sources of energy might be depleted. The development, operation and closure of units that produce atomic energy needed large investment. France wanted to reduce the influence of the US on Western Europe in this (and other) spheres. A European atomic energy integration organisation would give France a chance to have additional control of nuclear research and production of energy in West Germany.

The foreign ministers of the six countries accepted the Spaak Report in Venice in May 1956 and decided that the Spaak Committee should prepare the agreements for the creation of a common market and an atomic energy community. Britain decided not to take part in the final negotiations and proclaimed in October, as before, that it was interested above all in a free trade area. After a number of consultations, the treaty that established the European Economic Community (EEC) was signed on 25 March 1957 in Rome, hence its name, the Treaty of Rome. The originals were written in four official languages (Dutch, French, German and Italian).

The Preamble to the Treaty of Rome states that its founders are resolved to preserve and strengthen peace (mentioned only once) and liberty, and called on other people of Europe who shared their ideals to join in their efforts. The Preamble also calls for the improvement of the living and working conditions in the EEC, harmonious development of the regions, a common commercial policy and a progressive abolition of restrictions on international trade. The *objectives* of the treaty are (Article 2):[19] the promotion of a continuous, harmonious, sustainable and balanced development through the EU; a high level of employment and social protection; equality between men and women; sustainable and non-inflationary growth; a high degree of competitiveness; raising the standard of living and quality of life; protection and improvement of the quality of the environment; and economic and social cohesion and solidarity among the member states.

The *means* to achieve those objectives are: the creation of a common market and an economic and monetary union and by implementing common policies (Article 2); the elimination of customs duties and quantitative restrictions on intra-group trade; the freedom of movement for goods, persons, services and capital (four freedoms of movement) in the internal market; the assurance of an undistorted competition in the internal market;

the establishment of a common commercial policy towards third countries; the adoption of common policies in agriculture and transport; the promotion of coordination of policies regarding employment, the environment, competitiveness of industry, and research and technological development; a policy in the social sphere comprising a European Social Fund; contribution to education and training, as well as the attainment of a high level of health protection (Article 3). Any discrimination on grounds of nationality is outlawed (Article 39): this refers, of course, to the nationals of the member states. The Treaty of Rome was concluded for an unlimited period of time (Article 312).

The economic arguments in favour of the creation of the EEC included a positive impact through increased competition on efficiency in production and employment of resources; an extension of markets demanded by specialisation and economies of scale; an expansion of research and development (R&D) and the creation of new or improved goods, services and technologies; a reduction in risk and uncertainty; a tendency towards factor-price equalisation; and an improvement in production and distribution management.

There is a supranational institution in the EEC. The Council of Ministers is empowered to reach decisions by a simple or qualified majority vote, while acting on a proposal by the Commission. The Commission is an independent body that initiates and implements decisions of the Council of Ministers. There is also a consultation and co-decision process with the European Parliament and consultations with the Economic and Social Committee and with the Committee of the Regions. The Court of Justice is charged to implement the Treaty of Rome throughout the EEC. The treaty was ratified during 1957 and it came into force on 1 January 1958. The structure and operation of the various institutions are given in Appendix 1A.

The treaty establishing the European Atomic Energy Community (Euratom) was concluded at the same time and place as the one that created the EEC. The task of Euratom is: to create conditions for the speedy establishment and growth of nuclear industries (Article 1); to promote R&D in the field; to set uniform safety standards; to facilitate investment; to ensure a regular and equitable supply of ores and nuclear fuels; to exercise the right of ownership regarding special fissile materials; to create a common market in specialised materials and equipment; and to foster progress in the peaceful uses of nuclear energy (Article 2). The Euratom Treaty was concluded for an unlimited period of time (Article 208).

West Germany was licensed to carry out R&D in nuclear energy, but exclusively for peaceful purposes. It could obtain the nuclear material solely through Euratom. This gave Euratom an unrestricted right to inspect all West German R&D in nuclear energy. But what is 'peaceful' R&D in nuclear energy? Even if R&D is carried out with the best intentions, the result may be totally different from the desired or intended one.

7. European Free Trade Association

Having seen that the ECSC countries were determined to persist with an overall economic integration, in 1956 Britain proposed the creation of a free trade area for manufactured goods in the OEEC. The ECSC countries rejected the proposal since it was one-sided. Britain would obtain free access to its manufactured goods in the market of the 'group of six' without giving reciprocal access to farm goods from the continent in its domestic market.

As a response to the creation of the EEC, Britain gathered together the 'other six' countries;[20] they signed the Stockholm Convention, thus creating the European Free Trade Association (EFTA). The small secretariat (only about 70 people) did not have any supranational authorities, and it was the only body of EFTA. Agriculture was excluded from the arrangement, so the whole business referred to manufactured goods only. This was not very popular in those countries with a relatively developed agricultural and fisheries sector, such as Denmark, Norway and Portugal. Apart from the elimination of tariffs on internal trade, there was almost no other intervention by EFTA. Market forces were left to do the job of integration. There were no common policies whatsoever. Therefore, the history of EFTA appears to be without significance or event. The important thing, that is, market-induced specialisation, happened at such a micro level as to escape the commentator's eye (Curzon Price, 1988, p. 100). However, the group was successful in economic terms. Their average GDP per capita was always (significantly) higher than the same indicator in the EEC.

As a purely commercial arrangement (tariff- and quota-free internal trade in manufactured goods), EFTA did not have any grand expectations regarding integration compared to the EEC. The reasons are simple. The EFTA countries are in geographical terms very dispersed, they were at different levels of development and, most importantly, they traded much more with the EEC countries than with their partners in EFTA. From the outset, the aim of EFTA was not to create strong integration links among its members, but rather to find a mutually satisfactory cohabitation with the EEC. In other words, the free trade area among the seven EFTA countries was only a means to an end, rather than an objective in itself (Curzon Price, 1987, p. 4). Since the EFTA countries intended to neutralise the impact of the creation of the EEC on EFTA trade, it appears that EFTA succeeded in its aim.

Just one year after the establishment of EFTA, Britain (the most important EFTA member country) submitted its application for full membership of the EEC. Britain realised that it had to be a part of a stronger and larger economic group, especially as EFTA appeared to be stillborn. It had a kind of negative identity: members of EFTA were regarded as being 'not-yet-in-the-EEC'.

The creation of the two economic blocs (the EEC and EFTA) in Western Europe revealed that the OEEC had failed in its efforts to promote economic cooperation in the region. So the US tried to maintain some kind of economic unity, as well as to shape and direct Western Europe as a region. Therefore, the US, Britain, France and West Germany signed an agreement in 1960 (taking effect in 1961) concerning the transformation of the OEEC into the Organisation for Economic Cooperation and Development (OECD) and an increase in its membership to 20 countries (including the US and Canada). The objective of the OECD was to achieve the highest sustainable economic growth and employment; promotion of free trade; and support of development in the poor non-member countries. The means to achieve these objectives were consultations (the OECD is the main international forum for discussion about the economic matters of the mainly highly developed countries), exchange of macroeconomic information and coordination of economic policies and forecasts.

8. EEC and Britain

Until the end of the 1950s it seemed that Britain would be neither ready nor willing to accept the 'rules of the game' of the EEC. The reasons could be found in the unacceptability of supranationality, ties with the Commonwealth, membership of EFTA and a system of farm prices (which allowed much higher prices in the EEC than in Britain). The British economy, however, did not develop at a satisfactory pace compared with the other EFTA or EEC countries. A boost to the economy could come from access to a larger market. This was why the Tory prime minister, Harold Macmillan, decided in July 1961 to begin negotiations with the EEC for full British membership. The application was warmly welcomed by the Benelux countries already in the EEC, as well as by the US. The Benelux countries wanted to see Britain in the EEC as a counterbalance to French political supremacy and West German industrial dominance. The favourable stance of the US could be found in its desire to close the ranks among West European allies.

The EEC Council of Ministers accepted the British application, and negotiations began. However, many observers questioned British sincerity regarding entry into the EEC. Weeks and months were lost during negotiations on questions of relatively marginal importance such as the import of cricket equipment from India or kangaroo meat from Australia (Jansen, 1975, pp. 91–2). Jean Monnet told a British delegation that 'There is one thing you British will never understand: an idea; and there is one thing you are supremely good at grasping: a hard fact. We will build Europe without you, but then you will come and join us' (Dent, 1997, p. 42). French president Charles de Gaulle unexpectedly announced at a press conference in Paris in January 1963 that Britain was not yet ready to join the EEC. This was de Gaulle's first veto for British entry.

The negative French attitude towards British entry, in spite of the favourable stance of West Germany and the US, indicated the complex and calculated nature of relations in the EEC. France did not want a British presence, since in the absence of Britain, France had the monopoly regarding political action in Western Europe. As for West Germany, more time needed to elapse before it became a positive force in European and international relations. This complex and difficult structure of views and interests regarding values and objectives, forms and consequences of choices, and levels and shapes of action, as well as about the present and the future, between France and Britain were even more obvious in 2003 on the (global) subject of the military action against Iraq. This issue will be discussed towards the end of this chapter.

9. Luxembourg Agreement

The six West European countries all belonged to the three organisations: the ECSC, the EEC and Euratom. Each one had its own Commission (High Authority in the ECSC), Council of Ministers, Parliament and Court of Justice. In order to avoid the unnecessary duplication of organs a Merger Treaty was signed in Brussels in April 1965. This treaty (taking effect in July 1967) brought together the bodies of the three distinct Communities into the common organs of the European Community (EC). Indeed, the three Communities had had common parliaments and courts of justice since 1958.

The work of the Council of Ministers is based on the proposals of the European Commission. The Commission was most active at that time in the field of agriculture. Hence, the Council of Ministers received three proposals in April 1965. The first one dealt with the financing of the Common Agricultural Policy (CAP), the second referred to the creation of EC financial resources, while the third argued in favour of a larger democratic control of the EC's expenditure by the Community's Parliament. France wanted to strengthen the CAP, but was against the increase in the powers of the Community's institutions. Since there was no compromise by July 1965, the EC entered its deepest crisis since its creation. France left its chair empty in the Council of Ministers. In a press conference (his favourite way of communication),[21] de Gaulle stated in September 1965 that French sovereignty belonged to the French people. The message was that France no longer wanted to accept the majority vote (supranationality) as the mechanism for decision making in the Council of Ministers.

After seven months of conflict between the Council of Ministers and France, a compromise settlement was reached on 29 January 1966 in Luxembourg (the Luxembourg Agreement) about the decision-making process in the Council of Ministers. This agreement about disagreement had two important points:

- When very important interests of one or more countries were at stake, and decisions based on the proposal from the Commission could be reached by a majority vote, the members of the Council of Ministers would endeavour to reach a solution acceptable to all member countries, bearing in mind their common interest, as well as the interests of the EC, and all that in light of Article 2 of the Treaty of Rome.
- In view of the former point, the French delegation considered that when very important interests were at stake, negotiations had to continue until a unanimous agreement could be reached.

The Luxembourg Agreement, which was a 'compromise to differ', meant the virtual end of the undemocratic (but operationally very useful and flexible) principle of outvoting in international relations. On the one hand, any minister could declare that the issue at stake was of vital importance for his/her country, while on the other, the European Commission (as an independent body of the EC) became more prudent in preparing proposals for the Council of Ministers. In addition, one may find in the Luxembourg Agreement the origin of the opt-out possibility for a country from a plan that it did not like (for example, Britain and monetary union) and the 'value' of an exit option while bargaining for better political terms of trade.

10. The first enlargement

With regard to the elimination of tariffs and quotas on internal trade, the Treaty of Rome was implemented much faster and more smoothly than envisaged in the treaty. All tariffs for EC internal trade were eliminated on 1 July 1968, a year and a half before the Treaty of Rome deadline. At the same time, the Community introduced the CET in its external trade. This was the first big achievement in the EC's integration efforts. Another provision of the Treaty of Rome that was also implemented was the association of non-European countries and territories which had 'special' relations with the EC member countries (Article 182). The association of these countries with the EC started in 1963, when 18 African countries and the EEC signed an agreement on trade and aid in Yaoundé, Cameroon (Yaoundé Convention). The Second Yaoundé Convention was signed in 1969.

A relatively unsatisfactory performance of the British economy in the second half of the 1960s caused the government in office (Labour) to revive the idea of accession to the EC since it might bring important economic benefits (free and secure access to a large, rich and growing market). Britain submitted its second application for membership to the EC in May 1967. With the exception of France, all the EC member countries warmly welcomed the British desire to enter the Community. British entry would reduce French political dominance in the EC. However, because of the British balance of payments problems and still desirous of keeping Britain out of the EC, de Gaulle held a press conference in November 1967 where he stated that the British economy was still too weak to join the EC, and he shut the door on British entry into the Community for the second time.

The French policy of national independence and the priority of national over other interests, followed by de Gaulle (but not by some other French politicians), were disliked by the US. Michel Poniatowski, the French minister of the interior, as well as others subsequently discovered and argued that the well-known anarchist, 'left-wing' Student Revolution[22] of May 1968 was instigated by the American secret services. Their goal was to undermine de Gaulle's authority because of his 'political incorrectness' in cases which included: an attempt to return to the gold standard in order to avoid the hegemony of the dollar; France's exit from NATO; an independent French nuclear programme; openness towards Eastern Europe; dismantling of the 'Iron Curtain'; the creation of the European Union from the Atlantic Ocean to the Urals; and a policy of neutrality in the Arab–Israeli conflict.

During the heyday of anarchist demonstrations in Paris (29 May 1968), de Gaulle went to Baden-Baden to visit his old friend General Jacques Massu, who was the head of the French military contingent there. Apparently de Gaulle asked for military support against the anarchist demonstrators: he got it on condition that he would accord clemency to OAS[23] members and release General Raoul Salan from prison. De Gaulle returned from

Baden-Baden so encouraged and motivated that he immediately addressed the nation on the radio. He announced that he would decisively defend the state order. His three-minute speech immediately provoked crowds of counter-demonstrators, a million or so in Paris alone, to go out on the streets and cheer de Gaulle. Among the leaders of these anti-anarchy demonstrations was André Malraux, a legendary patriot, one of the leaders of the resistance movement and the minister for culture.

In the parliamentary elections in June 1968, de Gaulle increased his support, while the socialists and communists were heavily defeated. Encouraged by this victory, de Gaulle asked the French in 1969 to vote on his state reforms, principally devolution (more powers to regions).[24] Even though the voters failed to accept de Gaulle's proposal by only a very small margin, he took this as a vote of no confidence and resigned in April 1969.

De Gaulle's withdrawal from public life enabled the Hague Summit (December 1969) of the presidents and prime ministers of the EC countries to revisit the opening of negotiations with Britain about entry into the EC, on the basis of the 1967 application which had never been withdrawn. Denmark, Ireland and Norway also submitted applications for entry. Encouraged by the success of integration, as well as the growing insistence of other countries to join the EC, Pierre Werner was commissioned to prepare a report on economic and monetary union in the EC.

The biggest stumbling blocks for the EC during negotiations with Britain were agriculture, financing of the EC budget and relations with the Commonwealth. Most of British trade before EC entry was with non-European countries where, among other products, Britain purchased food at much lower prices than those prevailing in the Community. With respect to financial matters, the Community budget was financed by tariffs on imports and direct contributions by the member countries dating from the creation of the EC up until 1970. The Council of Ministers decided in April 1970 that the EC needed to change the previous system and get its 'own resources'. The EC started raising finance from levies charged on imports of agricultural goods, proceeds from the CET and direct contributions by the member states, totalling up to 1 per cent of value-added tax.

The agreement endorsing the entry of Britain, Denmark, Ireland and Norway into the EC (ECSC, EEC and Euratom) was signed in January 1972 after lengthy and difficult negotiations. The agreement stipulated a five-year transition period, quotas for imports of food (butter and cheese from New Zealand) to Britain, the British contribution to the EC budget (because of the disproportionately large share of trade with the non-EC countries) and the association of the countries and territories with 'special' relations with the new members.

Britain, Denmark and Ireland supported the Accession Agreement, but this failed to get the support of the Norwegians in a referendum. The British and the Danes accepted the EC accession on the false assumption that the EC business was all about economics, and not about politics, which is the root of subsequent opt-outs for these two countries from new legislation. In any case, the EC acquired three new members on 1 January 1973. On the same date the Brussels series of bilateral agreements of July 1972 between the EC and the rest of the EFTA countries on a free trade area for manufactured products came into effect, as Britain and Denmark left EFTA on the day of their entry into the EC. The small EFTA countries stepped part way into the EC.[25] This had been a long-held desire of Austria, since Article 4 of its State Treaty does not permit an economic partnership with West Germany, although in the post-Cold War era, there has been a more liberal interpretation of its provision.

At the time of the British entry into the EC, the Tories (the Conservative Party) were in office. However, the Labour Party, which had submitted the application for entry, was not satisfied with the terms of entry, and promised voters that it would renegotiate. The Labour Party had a national programme for the production of coal and steel which wanted to keep the ECSC out of that business in Britain. After they came to office, the Accession Agreement was renegotiated, but the results of the year-long negotiations had not revised the original agreement in any important way. In the national referendum in June 1975, the British voted in favour of remaining in the EC. The EC offered benefits to every member country. In the case of the three big states, these were most obvious: Britain received EC finances from the regional fund, France benefited from the CAP, while West Germany gained from the EC's internal free trade.

The group of developing countries with which the EC has 'special' relations expanded to African, Caribbean and Pacific countries after the British entry, which was reflected in 1975 when the Yaoundé Agreements were replaced by an extended agreement signed in Lomé (Togo).

11. Eurosclerosis

The Treaty of Rome envisaged a transition period of 12 years. The EC would be fully established by the end of 1969. It specified the means and deadlines for the elimination of tariffs on internal trade and the introduction of the CET. After 1970, the Treaty of Rome was not a precise guide for the future of the EC, which was one of the contributing factors that led the EC into Eurosclerosis.

The decision to start negotiations with Britain about entry into the EC was reached during the Hague Summit in 1969. Two years later, in 1971, the same group met in Paris and prepared the grounds for British entry. It became obvious that the summits of heads of states or governments were quite an effective forum for the resolution of problems, as well as for the guidance of the EC. During the 1974 Paris Summit, the participants agreed to formalise their meetings (at least twice a year) under the name of the European Council.[26]

The European Council became the highest institution of the EC although it was not mentioned either in the Treaty of Rome or the Treaty of Paris, which empowered only the Council of Ministers to pass all the important laws in the EC. The introduction of the European Council pushed the organisational developments in the EC towards the strengthening of intergovernmental decision making and away from the community method (supranationality). The problem with such a structure was and is that the Council of Ministers tended to pass on very important decisions to the European Council, which sometimes had to deal with certain technical issues (such as decisions about production or import quotas). These negotiations are often linked with national and political horse-trading, conducted in the small hours of the morning, which reflect transient issues and sometimes do not have very much in common with the real long-term interests of the EC.

The EC aimed to expand the coverage of its (common) economic policies outside trade and agriculture. During the turmoil the international currency markets (1972–79), the majority of the EC national currencies had a common floating rate of exchange against the US dollar. At the same time, there was an energy crisis coupled with two large external shocks that came from sharp increases in oil prices. The EC countries were preoccupied with their short-term national problems which pushed EC integration down the list of priorities.

The European Monetary System (EMS), created in 1979, established a stricter system for the common float (for the participating countries) by reducing the margins of fluctuations and by providing the system with relatively generous short-term financial assistance. The objective was to influence the EC countries, by a sophisticated exchange rate method, to apply coordinated and comparable economic policies. Apart from those changes and the largely unnoticed entry of Greece[27] into the EC on 1 January 1981, the 1970s and the first half of the 1980s were quite uneventful. On the economic front, productivity was sluggish and labour costs were increasing, so the EC producers were at a competitive disadvantage relative to their principal rivals in the US and Japan. At that time the EC lacked a clear vision about its future, so the mood during these years was often referred to as 'Eurosclerosis'. None the less, a wake-up call came when it became obvious that the original Treaty of Rome was not a good blueprint for the future of the EC after 1969, when the economic performance of the US and Japan (as well as a few newly industrialised countries) seriously threatened the effectiveness of the EC economy.

12. The Single European Act

In spite of a tariff- and quota-free trade within the EC, the still excessive non-tariff barriers (NTBs) were segmenting national markets within the EC, which seriously jeopardised the ability of the EC manufacturing and services industries to profit fully from economies of scale and potential increase in their international competitiveness in relation to both the US and Japan, as well as newly industrialised countries. In addition, Article 115 of the original Treaty of Rome permitted the Commission to authorise the member countries in economic difficulties to adopt protective measures. These usually took the form of quotas against Japanese cars, or textiles from the developing countries. Article 115 enabled those EC nations in difficulty to block imports from the non-EC countries through another EC country which was not in trouble. This resulted in (sometimes) large differences in prices of identical goods sold in different EC member states. The consequence was a negative impact on the spatial allocation of resources and the integration of the region. Something had to be done about this.

Strong transnational business groups were looking for a large and vibrant unified European market. Wisse Dekker, chief executive officer of Philips and Per Gyllenhammer and chief executive of Volvo, set up the Roundtable of European Industrialists in 1983. Under the auspices of this powerful business group, Dekker produced a proposal for the creation of a single market in Europe. This move anticipated the official plan prepared by Lord Cockfield.

The White Paper (Cockfield Report or Single Market Programme) of June 1985 offered the Programme for the Completing of the Internal Market.[28] This supply-side-oriented 'technical' programme included 282 legislative proposals and a timetable for their completion by the end of 1992.

Since the classical way of economic integration among countries through the elimination of tariffs and quotas on internal trade was exhausted in 1968, the objective of the White Paper was to oust NTBs and create a genuine and homogeneous frontier-free internal market. This was an ambitious task. It has not yet been achieved even in the federal and developed countries such as Switzerland, where a free circulation of goods, services, people and capital has not been fully realised because of the diversity of regulations in the constituent cantons. Canada is another example: it has a free trade deal with the US which liberalises trade between the two countries; however, public procurement policies among Canadian provinces remain important trade barriers within the country. The internal situation in Australia is similar to that of Canada.

At about the same time as the White Paper was delivered, and after a few years of delay from the planned target, the EC finalised negotiations with Spain and Portugal about accession. On 1 January 1986, the EC was enlarged by the two new (southern) members and became the Community of 12 countries.

The intention of the Single Market Programme was to increase the competitiveness of EC goods, services and factors in relation to American and Japanese rivals through a change in internal rules, rather than subsidies. The programme was a kind of EC antidote to Eurosclerosis. The Single Market Programme, a reader-unfriendly document, mentioned the removal of physical, technical and fiscal barriers.[29] Since the programme was widely accepted throughout all segments of the EC, it represented the end of lethargy and Eurosclerosis in the EC. It was the biggest boost to the integration process since the signing of the Treaty of Rome. However, the programme was not an aim in itself; it was merely a step towards another goal: economic and political union.

The main aspects of the Single Market Programme include the following six features:

- removal of NTBs for internal trade (including Article 115[30] from the original Treaty of Rome);
- increased competition;
- promotion of cooperation among firms in R&D;
- unification of factor markets through full liberalisation of factor (labour and capital) mobility;
- monetary integration; and
- social protection (Social Charter).

A smooth implementation of the Single Market Programme required a change in the decision-making process of the EC. This led to the first, although relatively modest, reform of the Treaty of Rome. The alteration was brought about by the Single European Act (signed in February 1986) which came into force on 1 July 1987. What the act basically did was to speed up the implementation of the Single Market Programme. Except for fiscal matters, rights of employees and free movement of persons (where unanimity remained the rule), the act increased the importance of majority vote in the Council of Ministers for measures that were supposed to implement the programme. This overturned the Luxembourg Agreement. The original spirit of the community method of voting from the Treaty of Rome was revived. The act set only a framework for change, rather than the course of change.

There are two basic methods of work in the EU: the community and the intergovernmental methods. The Union may always remain a hybrid institution which is partly run by the first and partly by the second method:

- *Community method*: Proposals and plans come from the European Commission (guarantor of the common interest), then go through the European Parliament to the Council of Ministers. The Council decides sometimes unanimously, other times through qualified majority and at times it co-decides with the European Parliament.
- *Intergovernmental method*: Governments directly negotiate among themselves and then decide. The process lacks both an independent institution that has the right to initiate and secure a common interest, as well as any parliamentary debate and vote. This method has always existed and has produced certain, although changeable, alliances. It has been growing in importance since the Treaty of Maastricht (1992).

The European Commission gained in importance through the Single European Act because it had to prepare proposals for the Council of Ministers to carry out the Single Market Programme. As for the decisions linked to the creation of the Single European Market, the Council of Ministers acquired new powers. It may act on a qualified majority basis, after consultations with the European Parliament and the Economic and Social Committee, with the exception of measures that deal with taxation, rights of employees and issues dealing with the mobility of people (Articles 93 and 95, respectively, of the Treaty of Rome). For those three issues, unanimity, or the veto power of each member state, was introduced at the request of Britain. Other matters that were officially raised in EC legislation by the act include: the formal inclusion of the European Council in the EC structure, which is supposed to meet at least twice a year (Article 2 of the Single European Act) (there were no provisions about what the Council is supposed to do); an endeavour to jointly formulate and implement an EC foreign policy (Article 30 of the Single European Act); and the addressing of environmental issues (Articles 174–6 of the Treaty of Rome).

The Single European Act shifted the balance of power from the national governments towards the EC, from the intergovernmental to the community method of running the Community. This exacerbated concern in some of the member countries about the transfer of national sovereignty to a relatively distant and appointed bureaucracy which lacks political accountability. The relative concentration of decision-making authority about economic issues had certain benefits. Fragmented economic policies and distinct national currencies would not improve the lot, for example, of most of the federal states in the US. The EC had to go ahead. The step following the Single Market Programme 'had' to be towards a monetary union.

13. The Maastricht Treaty

Political cooperation (and federalism), one of the necessary conditions for monetary union[31] in the EC, had two basic proponents. While Germany and Italy were in favour of a fast federalisation of the EC through such means as a common defence policy,[32] other member countries were considering a more gradual process. The preference for gradualism stemmed from the fact that the EC countries are among the oldest in the world with long-standing and well-established systems of administration and politics. This would be difficult to change over a relatively short period of time.

Ideas about political cooperation and union in the EC were plentiful, but in reality there was little progress. The most controversial matters dealt with a common foreign policy and defence, as well as the powers of the European Parliament (since it would not be realistic to expect the Parliament and the Commission to play the same role as they did in the area of agriculture). In spite of the name, potential European Political Union would not create a single government, but it would increase the power of the European Parliament to reduce the 'democratic deficit' of the EC's institutions.

After the overhaul of the former East Germany and once the memories of the Second World War had faded away with a new generation of politicians, a reunited Germany (October 1990) could, in the longer term, present a mighty power that could do something independently. Therefore, throughout the post-war period France aimed to tie Germany into an arrangement that would prevent Germany going its own way, particularly in the field of security and foreign policy. These objectives first started to materialise with the ECSC. Although the Franco-German axis was and still is the backbone of European integration, relations between the two countries were not free of strain.

Tensions between France and Germany were obvious in the case of the potential enlargement of the EC. France wanted to reduce the number of new entrants, while Germany was in favour of 'eastern' expansion. Germany wanted future enlargement of the EC to embrace the Scandinavian and East European countries,[33] not only for stability on its eastern border and as a buffer against turmoil in the former Soviet Union, but more importantly because these countries would view EC affairs from a German perspective. At least that was the German hope at the start of the 1990s. The potential menace of other (American) perspectives on European and global affairs by Central and East European countries was not appreciated. In addition, some Germans asked why they should pay through the various EC funds more to Greece or Spain than, say, to Poland?

Another conflicting point was French apprehension regarding the secession rights of Croatia and Slovenia. From the start, however, Germany succeeded in pushing through that issue at the end of 1991 and 'forced' the other 11 EC states to accept a *fait accompli*.[34] The recognition of those two countries for the political establishment (European elite) of the EC was, in fact, of secondary importance. The newly independent countries could be the Czech Republic and Slovakia, or the Baltic states. What mattered primarily in Maastricht was the fact that it was the 'vote' of 11 EC countries on the question: did they recognise Germany as a great European power, a potential leader of the EU, or not? The answer in Maastricht was yes.

After a period of active diplomacy, frantic negotiations and horse-trading, the European Council, at its meeting in Maastricht on 9 and 10 December 1991, reached a settlement about European Union. France's major goal to bring Germany into a single currency (in 1999) was fulfilled, as were its defence and foreign policy arrangements. Germany obtained agreement that the monetary policy of the EU would be German inspired and that the European Parliament would increase its powers. The southern countries, led by Spain, got the Cohesion Fund. The Dutch were able to push through the Social Chapter. Britain obtained from Maastricht two opt-outs: one from the single currency and the other from the Social Chapter.[35]

Because of these important exceptions, from the outset the treaty was not a tidy arrangement. The final agreement, just as any other major deal in the EU, was as hard to understand as it was tough to reach. The two exceptions from the Maastricht Treaty are good examples which show that Britain still thinks it is different from other EU countries. Britain, as usual, wanted the Maastricht Summit to do as little as possible. The Treaty on European Union was signed in Maastricht (hence the Maastricht Treaty) on 7 February 1992.

The Maastricht Treaty that established the EU is just like the Single European Act, a reader-unfriendly crowd of amendments and additions to the EEC, the ECSC and the Euratom treaties. It expands the scope of the activities of the EU beyond its original economic affairs. Substantively, the Maastricht Treaty consists of three basic parts (pillars): the revised Treaty of Rome, which includes terms for economic and monetary union (EMU); defence and foreign policy; and justice and home affairs.

No matter how it is interpreted, the Maastricht Treaty is basically about economic and monetary union. This is spelt out both in the Preamble and in Articles B and G, respectively. Unlike the supply-side-oriented and 'technical' Single Market Programme, EMU touches on political issues. Although it may be masked behind technicalities, it deals with a single currency and, hence, the political sovereignty of the EU nations. EMU was an expected development following the completion of the internal market. A 'free' flow of goods, services and factors in the EU market, together with an efficient structural and spatial allocation of resources, needs to be supported by stability in exchange rates. Monetary integration seeks to serve as a replacement for a deep(er) political union which did not take solid shape in the treaty. EMU is to be achieved in three stages:

- During the first stage, there must be a reinforcement in the coordination of economic and monetary policies of the member countries.
- The second stage started in January 1994 with the establishment of the European Monetary Institute (EMI) in Frankfurt. The EMI is to coordinate the EU members' monetary policies and prepare the conditions for the final stage. The central banks of the member states need to become independent before the end of the second stage when the EMI would be transformed into an independent European Central Bank (ECB).[36]
- The Council of Ministers would decide by a qualified majority, not later than 31 December 1996, whether a majority (at least seven) of the EU countries fulfil the five conditions necessary for the third stage of EMU.[37] If a country fails one (or, perhaps, two conditions), but makes good progress, it may be allowed into the EMU. Should the Council be unable to decide on the beginning of the third stage, the Maastricht Treaty stipulates that it would begin on 1 January 1999 for the countries that fulfil the necessary conditions for EMU. Those countries would irrevocably fix their exchange rates and the European Currency Unit (ECU), under the name of the 'euro', would replace the national currencies in 2002. The ECB would follow its primary commitment of price stability and, consequently, set interest rates and conduct foreign exchange operations. In addition, the ECB would support economic growth and employment. The ECB would report regularly to the EU's finance ministers (Economic and Financial Committee (ECOFIN) meetings would issue broad economic policy guidelines) and to the European Parliament.

The second basic part of the Maastricht Treaty is the provisions on the common foreign and security policy (Preamble and Articles B and J, respectively). The undefined role of the European Council that came out of the Article 2 of the Single European Act was clarified in the Maastricht Treaty (Article D). The job of the European Council is to provide the EU with the necessary impetus for its development, as well as to define the necessary political guidelines. Applied to the foreign and security policy, the EU members 'shall define and implement a common foreign and security policy' (Article J.1) which would lead to 'the eventual framing of a common defence policy, which might in time lead to a common defence' (Article B). A common defence policy is the objective of the EU, not a commitment. So a minimalist or non-federal (British) view prevailed. The European Council is in charge of the definition of 'the general principles and general guidelines for the common foreign and security policy . . . The Council shall act unanimously' (Article J.8). The governments of the member states would have to follow the common line. All this is supposed 'to deepen the solidarity between their peoples while respecting their history, their culture and their traditions' (Preamble).

As for the security and common defence policy which might in time lead to common security, the EU is allowed to request the WEU, 'which is an integral part of the development of the Union, to elaborate and implement decisions and actions of the Union which have defence implications' (Article J.4). On French insistence, the WEU is subordinated to the EU (the WEU became the Union's defence wing), while what Britain got out of the deal was the wording that the defence policy would not run counter to the interests of NATO. It was not only Britain that still wanted the involvement of NATO in the EU's defence. Some other countries, such as Germany, wanted American involvement (and taxpayers' money) in defence matters, since that brings savings for the EU's taxpayers.[38] When the eastern bloc disappeared, German money would be better spent on the reunification of the eastern part of the country, although certain defence efforts need to be made because of the uncertainties that may come from the distant southeast and south. In addition, the US sometimes declares its intention to cut expenditure, including that for defence. The Americans want to see the EU more reliant on its own defence. In addition, an event that made many in NATO question American commitment to the Alliance was when the US unilaterally withdrew from the naval blockade in the Adriatic Sea in 1994.

The third major part of the treaty refers to close cooperation in justice and home affairs (Preamble and Articles B and K, respectively). Interior ministers will work together on issues such as crime, terrorism, drugs, immigration, visas, asylum and frontier rules. The decisions should be taken unanimously.

Apart from the three basic 'pillars' of the EU, the Maastricht Treaty brought in a number of interesting features to the Union. One of them is subsidiarity, as a basic federalist principle that is increasingly advocated by the EU's institutions. It is mentioned in the Preamble and Articles B and G. On subsidiarity, the Treaty says that the EU would take action 'only if and in so far as the objectives of the proposed action cannot be sufficiently achieved by the Member States and can therefore, by reason of scale or effects of the proposed action, be better achieved by the Community' (Article G). As the EU becomes bigger and more diverse in size and deeper in scope, it may be costlier to implement decisions. Hence, there may be certain economies of scale in the taking of some decisions at EU level. So, the EU needs to be involved only in those affairs which the member states cannot deal with satisfactorily from a common standpoint. In some cases the local level is better placed and informed to handle certain matters. It is also more accountable and has superior insight into what the electors want and taxpayers are willing to pay. In other cases, for example pollution, because of cross-country spillovers, local or regional authorities may overlook these effects, but the EU should not.

The EU does not take action automatically. It would act only when the benefits of the action exceed its cost. If applied to the limit, the principle of subsidiarity which defines the border between the national and supranational issues would change the EU out of recognition (just think of the British and, perhaps, French reactions in the event of a further transfer of national sovereignty). Therefore, there could be more talk about it than real action.

Since subsidiarity is an ambiguous term (it means different things to different people), it can be interpreted in a number of ways: from a liberal to a dirigiste viewpoint. Ideally, subsidiarity would mean taking a decision on the most appropriate level and as close as possible to those it affects. But can any one person unquestionably discern what can be done better independently on a local level and what collectively, as well as satisfy an outright majority of the people? The diplomats may argue that to implement subsidiarity may be only the exception in the EU's affairs, while the powers of the member states would be the rule. None the less, the subsidiarity principle masks its real substance. That is, the potential for the continuous expansion and centralisation of powers of the EU's institutions, even though the original intention is to limit the EU from acquiring too much influence. The history of EU integration shows a continuous expansion and deepening in the EU jurisdiction which culminated in the creation of a single currency and a supranational European Central Bank.

The European Parliament increased its authority too. In the new decision-making procedure (Articles 251 and 252 of the Treaty of Rome) for the measures that relate to the single market, environment, research, trans-European networks, health, consumer protection, education and culture, the Parliament may reject the draft law put forward by the Council of Ministers. The Council may reject the amendments to the law by the Parliament. In either case, the two sides form a Conciliation Committee. If the committee finds a compromise, then both the Parliament and the Council of Ministers have to endorse it. If there is no compromise, the law cannot be passed. This procedure, explained in detail below, increased the power of Parliament at the expense of the Council of Ministers. It gave an effective veto power to the European Parliament, which emerged as the biggest institutional winner from the Maastricht deal. On the other hand, the institutional status of the European Commission was weakened by the Maastricht Treaty. The right of initiative, the basis of its overall authority, was diluted in the monetary policy field to the right to make recommendations.

Other matters that were mentioned in the Maastricht Treaty are: the rights of citizens of the EU to live and work anywhere in the Union; the entitlement of EU citizens while travelling outside of the EU to receive diplomatic and consular services from the representatives of any of the EU member countries; and the right to vote and stand for election in the local and EU elections in any of the member countries. The EU is to contribute to the establishment and development of trans-European networks in the areas of transport, telecommunications and energy infrastructure. A Cohesion Fund is to support environment and trans-European network projects in the member countries with a below-average GDP per capita. A Committee of the Regions was added to the EU structure for consultative purposes. A Social Protocol, from which Britain opted out, licensed the EU to regulate on working conditions, employment rights for men and women and workers' participation. The EU is to contribute and encourage (but not legislate) in the areas of cross-border cooperation in education, culture and health.

The final provisions of the Maastricht Treaty provide a safety valve if things go wrong. An intergovernmental conference (IGC) was to be convened in 1996 to examine and, if necessary, revise the objectives of the Treaty (Article N). Any European state may apply to become a member of the EU. If admitted, it must join the whole Union (Article O). This means that new entrants have to accept some four decades of the EU's legislation (no opt-outs) and to align their policies with the EU during the adjustment period. The treaty was concluded for an unlimited period of time (Article Q) and was to enter into force on 1 January 1993, or failing that, on the first day following the day of the last ratification of a signatory state (Article S). The treaty deadline was not honoured, and it finally entered into force on 1 November 1993 when the last parliament – that of Britain – ratified it. On that date, the EC officially became the EU.

14. Northern enlargement

The European Economic Area (EEA) quietly entered into force on 1 January 1994. It was conceived in 1990 as a vehicle for keeping potential new entrants (the EFTA countries) from applying, but it ended up being a waiting room for the new enlargement. The EEA, the world's biggest free trade area with over 370 million consumers, is in essence the virtual entry of the EFTA countries minus Switzerland[39] into the EU, but excluding agriculture, energy, external trade, coal and steel, and foreign and security policy. Within the EEA, which is served by an independent EEA Court of Justice, the participating countries enjoy free mobility of goods, services, capital and people (four freedoms), but only for internally produced goods and services.

From the EEA, the small EFTA countries achieved free entry for their manufactured goods to the largest market in the world, which would increase competition for their businesses and, hence, bring efficiency gains. The EU obtained secure access to wealthy consumers and assistance in resisting domestic protectionist appeals. The EFTA countries have always had a liberal trade policy for their manufactured goods. The EEA was to an extent, stillborn, since Austria, Finland, Norway and Sweden all applied for full membership of the EU in order to get a say in the EU's law-making. These applications were welcomed by the EU as the Union needed net contributors to its budget.[40] Austria, Finland and Sweden entered into the EU on 1 January 1995. Norway's voters, however, rejected the deal.

Lack of popular enthusiasm for the Maastricht Treaty was reserved not only for monetary affairs. In foreign policy, for example, which is supposed to be agreed unanimously (Article J.8) and which ought 'to deepen the solidarity between their peoples while respecting their history, their culture and their traditions' (Preamble), the EU has, in some cases, done quite the opposite. One of the most obvious cases is the dispute between Greece and the Former Yugoslav Republic of Macedonia (FYR Macedonia). The whole affair revealed the difficulty of creating and implementing a common EU foreign policy.

After the breakup of the former Yugoslavia (1992), the 'Republic of Macedonia'[41] had claims not only on Macedonia (the northern Greek province) in its name and constitution, but it also usurped Macedonian, that is, Greek symbols because it lacked its own. The Maastricht Treaty stands for solidarity among the EU states 'while respecting their history, their culture and their traditions'. Instead of showing solidarity with an EU member country on whose province a newly created and foreign state had certain claims in the constitution, the other EU member countries allied against Greece and pressurised it to accept something that runs contrary to one of the most glorious parts of Greek history, spirit, culture, tradition and territory. What a splendid hypocrisy and implementation of the Maastricht Treaty.

Since negotiations between Athens and Skopje did not lead anywhere, Greece introduced unilateral economic sanctions against the FYR Macedonia in February 1994. The European Commission and other member countries were pressing Greece to revoke the measure on the grounds that it violated the free flow of goods. There was no similar pressure on Skopje, which is, after all, outside the EU. However, when Germany introduced identical unilateral sanctions against Serbia and Montenegro in 1991, although there were no territorial and other claims on Germany or any other state, the European Commission expressed no concern that such a unilateral measure would prevent the free flow of goods. However, when a small country such as Greece did the same thing, that did cause concern. Are small countries 'really' being consulted about certain problems in the EU and is their stance 'respected'?[42]

15. Treaty of Amsterdam

Intergovernmental conferences are not only legal, but also operational necessities. The EU is constantly outgrowing its old treaties and adding new functions and new members. These conferences provide occasional opportunities to redesign the EU. There were seven IGCs before the Treaty of Amsterdam. The first one began in 1950 and culminated in the signing of the Treaty of Paris, which created the ECSC; the second began in 1955 in Messina and resulted in the Treaty of Rome; the third was initiated in 1970 in order to revise Article 203 of the Treaty of Rome on the financing of the budget; the fourth started in 1985 and led to the Single European Act; the fifth and the sixth started simultaneously in 1990. One dealt with the extension of the Single European Market to economic and monetary union, while the other focused on political union. They both produced the Maastricht Treaty. The seventh IGC started in Turin in 1996 with the goal of making the EU more manageable in the decades to come once it increases, or even doubles, the number of member countries.

'Any European state may apply to become a Member of the Union' (Article O of the Maastricht Treaty).[43] Together with the Preamble of the Treaty of Rome, this was an open invitation and the only Maastricht Treaty-based (sufficient) condition for a country to be considered for full membership of the EU. In addition, the EU set several other, necessary, economic and political requirements for entry. These were formally defined during the European Council in Copenhagen (1993). The potential candidate country must fulfil three conditions. It must have:

- a functioning market economy,
- a democratic political system and
- accept, implement and enforce the *acquis communautaire*.

Following almost half a century of invitations to the countries behind the Iron Curtain to join the free and democratic world, as well as almost a decade of painful economic transition towards a market-type economic system, the EU called an IGC in 1996 to pave the way for the eastern enlargement of the EU. The conference was supposed to establish institutional arrangements for the EU enlargement. However, the issue was so thorny that the subsequent Treaty of Amsterdam (signed on 2 October 1997; entered into force on 1 May 1999) postponed the decision about these crucial institutional issues.

In spite of much greater expectations, in particular regarding the structure of the existing or the creation of new EU institutions in the light of the approaching enlargement, the Treaty of Amsterdam introduced several important innovations into the EU:

- *Justice and home affairs*: The Schengen Agreement on common visas for third-country citizens was incorporated into the EU (bar Britain and Ireland).
- *Employment and social policy*: A new employment chapter is supposed to promote (undefined) cooperation among member countries to create jobs. Maastricht's Social Chapter is included in the treaty.
- *Foreign policy*: The EU needs to cooperate with the WEU, which may be integrated into the EU in the future if all countries agree.
- *Subsidiarity and flexibility*: The EU should do only those things that cannot be better done at national or lower levels. A flexibility clause permits some countries to adopt a common policy even if the others do not want it. There is a possibility of constructive abstention (Article J.13).[44] Abstention shall not prevent the adoption of common decisions. If member states exercising their abstention right represent more than one-third of the votes of the qualified majority, the decision cannot be adopted.
- *Openness and information*: All EU citizens and legal subjects have the right of access to EU documents (Article 255 of the Treaty of Rome).
- *Other issues of doubtful merit*: These concerned the protection of state-owned savings banks, confirming Strasbourg as the seat of the European Parliament, and the protection of animal rights.

The rationale for flexibility is a kind of insurance against problems in the future. The principal EU procedure that all move together at the same speed or not at all ('one-size-fits-all') may seem unworkable in an EU of 25 or more countries. The bigger and the more diverse the EU becomes, the harder it will be to join forces to launch a new policy or project. Monetary union was one example of this flexibility, the Schengen Agreement was another, common defence and foreign policy may be next. It is still unclear whether this flexible approach would keep countries together in the EU or may prove to be a way to drive them apart. The voters, if they are asked, may prefer EU *à la carte*.[45] Such flexibility may further complicate the legal structure and operation of the EU, but that may be what voters seek and are ready to pay for. However, the voters need to be well informed in advance about the consequences of their choice.

The most important issue of the new institutional structure and voting weights, for which the conference was convened after all, was deferred until the start of the enlargement negotiations with new candidate countries. In this light, the Treaty of Amsterdam was a rather modest achievement. The major part of its substance may look more like a party's political manifesto than a constitutional document. Following the experience of the Maastricht Treaty, countries became hesitant about ceding more of their national sovereignty and paid more attention to national public opinion.

16. *Acquis communautaire*

The existence and operation of the EU is based on law. The whole body of the established EU laws, policies and practices are called the *acquis communautaire*[46] or the EU patrimony. It is widely estimated that the *acquis* consisted of about 80 000 pages of legal acts in 2004. The ever-evolving and expanding *acquis* was enlarged by 2348 new regulations in 2003 alone. However, most of the regulations have a limited time duration.

Almost half a century of (too) activist approach left the EU overregulated. This situation may be re-examined. However, the European Commission need not be the only culprit for the abundance of regulation. Many legal instruments are introduced at the request of member states, the Council of Ministers, the European Parliament and the Economic and Social Committee, as well as a variety of pressure groups, rather than on the independent initiative of the Commission. Such a way of running EU business clearly increases the perception of relevance and influence of the European Commission, but at the same time adds to the relentless growth of EU regulation.

When one looks at the size and scope of the *acquis communautaire*, a question comes to mind: are European economies capable of change within this (rigid) framework? The European Council in Lisbon (2000) set a new strategic goal for the decade: to make the EU 'the most competitive and dynamic knowledge-based economy in the world capable of sustainable economic growth with more and better jobs and greater social cohesion' by 2010.[47] The Lisbon process may perhaps be acknowledged by those directly concerned with certain projects, but not necessarily by public opinion. There may be too much hot air, too many texts, too many projects, but nothing is yet tangible.

17. Preparations for the future: *Agenda 2000* and the Lisbon Council

In order to prepare for the expected eastern enlargement, in 1997 the European Commission presented *Agenda 2000 for a Stronger and Wider Union* as its medium-term plan of action for the 2000–06 period. It is a blueprint for the reform of the EU in order to prepare itself for the eastern enlargement. *Agenda 2000* refers to major challenges, as most of the accession economies have a much lower GDP per capita than the EU average. Prior to this enlargement, the EU had to reform both its CAP and its budget as the newcomers have on average a much larger farm sector and they would bring large regional disequilibria into the EU.

Agenda 2000 included a decision to keep the limit for spending for all EU activities at the level of 1.27 per cent of total GDP of the EU(15). It stated that annual aid from the EU per member country should not pass the limit of 4 per cent of a country's GDP. It also earmarked €45 billion for the 2000–06 period (a kind of mini-Marshall Plan) as a pre-entry aid to the accession countries. As far as EU environmental standards are concerned, it stated that this issue is a major challenge for the accession countries which would require huge investment. In addition, *Agenda 2000* is firmly opposed to allowing 'derogations' (opt-outs) from the *acquis communautaire* to any new entrant. Such an option would prevent the new members from exercising their right to participate fully in the EU decision-making process and to enjoy benefits of full membership of the EU. In addition, the EU would have to reform its institutions and decision-making procedures in order to accommodate enlarged membership.

In general, few were satisfied with the ideas presented in *Agenda 2000*. For example, France wanted to keep high subsidies in the farm sector;

Spain opposed reductions in regional assistance; Britain sought to guard its special budgetary rebate hard won in the mid-1980s; while Germany wanted to reduce its net budgetary contribution. Of course, accession countries expected more aid and easier EU entry conditions.

In addition to the preparations for the eastern enlargement, the EU wanted to prepare and change its economy to face the new challenges and opportunities that would spring from domestic and international markets and technology. Britain and Spain were behind the ambitious goal set by the European Council in Lisbon (2000). This rests on the liberal aspirations and ideas of deregulation that would make the EU economy more flexible and dynamic. Other EU countries did not quite realise what they agreed to. The European councils usually set political targets which include deadlines. This tends to be the straight forward part of the exercise. Then comes the slow and cumbersome part when both the European Commission and the national governments legislate and implement policies. Most governments at least try to protect their national interests during this phase. If the principal competitor, the US economy, slows down (because of the huge trade deficit), the EU may feel less urgency to make painful reforms in its structured labour and product markets. Table 1.1 outlines the basic features of the Single European Market and Lisbon strategies.

18. Treaty of Nice

Negotiations for EU entry started with several Central and East European countries and Cyprus in March 1998. Therefore, institutional conditions for EU enlargement had to be devised. Negotiations culminated at the European Council in Nice (December 2000) and the signature of the Treaty of Nice (26 February 2001). No matter how it is interpreted, this was one of the turning points in EU history. It was about the distribution of power and influence in the enlarged EU.

The European Council dealt with Amsterdam 'leftovers'[48] and not only provided institutional changes for enlargement, but also rearranged the structure of power within the EU. In Nice, this balance of power was shifted towards the bigger countries. There are two dangers from such an outcome: first, it may turn the EU towards the G-8 type of model where the largest powers dominate; and second, there is no 'independent' institution to make proposals based on the common interest. However, if this method in the decision-making process entirely replaces the community method, then it may herald the end of the EU as we know it.

Table 1.1   Strategies: Single European Market and Lisbon strategy for 2010

	Single European Market	Lisbon
Ultimate aim	Integration and growth	Growth Social cohesion Employment
Intermediate objectives	Cuts on costs of cross-border transactions for products and services	Advances in education and innovation Increase in R&D spending Liberalisation of service industries Increase in labour force participation and employment rates
Means	Elimination of border controls Harmonisation and approximation of laws	Definition of common targets Performance reporting and benchmarking Joint monitoring
Instruments	EU directives Enforcement by case law of courts	Mostly national (spending, taxation, regulation)

Source: Sapir et al. (2003, p. 85).

One may argue that the Treaty of Nice brought the following innovations:

- *Rebalance of votes in the Council of Ministers*: A shift in the voting weights within the Council of Ministers towards larger countries at the expense of smaller ones; some commentators call this a 'major power grab'.
- *The European Commission*: Larger countries will no longer have two commissioners in an enlarged EU from November 2004; from that time, each country will have only one commissioner. When the EU increases to 27 member countries or more, the number of commissioners will be less than the number of countries. The number of commissioners and a system of rotation of member country appointees following the principle of equality will be set by the unanimous decision of the Council of Ministers.
- *Flexibility (enhanced cooperation or variable geometry)*: A group of eight countries or more may pursue deeper integration in certain policy fields. This would mean that an 'inner circle' or 'hard core'

(pioneer group; advance group; *avant garde*; or coalition of the able and willing) of countries may move faster in select policy areas than the rest of the EU. Examples of this flexibility or multispeed EU include the single currency and the passport-free Schengen travel area.
- *Majority voting*: Political integration is advanced as member countries give up the right to veto decisions in 29 new areas.

The Treaty of Nice is popularly portrayed as an act that allowed the new EU enlargement, but the 15 EU member countries first preserved their influence in the new voting structure. After enlargement, however, that will change substantially. The EU voting allotments and procedures changed drastically as a result of the Treaty of Nice. As is often the case, the devil is in the detail. The new voting arrangement was 'hidden' in Declaration 20 on the enlargement of the EU annexed to the Final Act. There is now a triple test:

- Smaller states (apart from Poland, Central and East European countries are small) have proportionally more voting power than larger countries. The post-enlargement Poland-led eastern bloc of ten countries would have the largest voting weight.
- If a new policy is to be adopted, then it must have the support of a majority of member states. The ten new countries would need only three votes from any of the EU(15) to push through new policies.
- The final requirement is the 'killer': new policies must have the support of states that represent 62 per cent of the EU's expanded population of 452 million.[49] The ten new countries combined have only 16 per cent. Hence, while the Central and East European countries can certainly play a major part in setting or blocking the policy agenda, they cannot necessarily force anything through – and nor can any other country.

This all puts the EU on track for a train wreck as far as quick action is concerned. No bloc, indeed no two blocs, would be able to force through any policy, but virtually any single bloc would have the ability to veto any policy. And there is no shortage of topics that would face harsh clashes of interest.

The struggle in Nice was not about whether to enlarge the EU, but rather about the distribution of power and influence in the enlarged EU. The treaty would make the eastern enlargement somehow easier, but enlargement itself was still not a *fait accompli*. The treaty did not touch the thorny issues such as the CAP, budgetary allocations and labour mobility, which were left for later. (See Chapter 14 for a detailed consideration of the EU eastern enlargement.)

The biggest success of the Treaty of Nice was that it opened up institutional possibilities for enlargement. Germany acquired the same number of votes as other 'big' countries, in spite of the fact that it has both a larger population and a bigger economy. However, the biggest failure of the treaty was that regarding institutional reform: the new baroque arrangement for the operation of the Council of Ministers is more complex than ever before.

The decision-making process and counting the winning vote is much more complicated. To obtain a majority decision, several obstacles have to be overcome – a formula guaranteed to prevent the introduction of new policies. Therefore, the EU (*acquis communautaire*) may stay in the future as it is now, since it will be hard to introduce new and radical changes that would please all or even the winning majority. Hence, one of the goals of the European Council in Nice to bring the EU closer to the people by making decision making more comprehensible, transparent and efficient has not been achieved. This may further enlarge the gulf that already exists between citizens and the EU institutions.

Ireland, which represents 2 per cent of the EU population, was the only EU country to hold a referendum on the Treaty of Nice. In a popular vote the Irish rejected the treaty in 2001. They were voting principally to preserve the country's neutrality (against the new defence dimension of the EU) and against the 'Brussels meddling' in the national economy. It is not that the Irish or others are 'bad' Europeans. The issue is that there are different ideas and expectations concerning the common EU venture. Nevertheless, following a political uproar and pressure to accept the treaty, the Irish endorsed it in a second referendum in 2002. Without this endorsement, the EU enlargement could not legally take place.

The key procedure in the EU is/was that *all* member countries should try to move together or not at all (one-size-fits-all).[50] This was not always easy to achieve even among the 15 member states before the eastern enlargement, and it is unlikely to be more so in an enlarged EU. So, would 'flexibility' make the enlarged EU of almost 30 countries more manageable?[51] Would flexibility, that is, a multispeed organisation of the EU, make it more viable? Would it strengthen the EU or make it weaker?

19. A topsy-turvy future or permanent disillusionment

EASTERN ENLARGEMENT

At the start of the 1990s there were, basically, two equally divided EU groups of countries regarding enlargement. The 'deepeners' preferred the consolidation of integration before any new members are admitted into the club. They were strongest in France, Italy and Spain (the Catholic tier). The Protestant 'wideners', led by Britain and supported by Germany and Scandinavia, argued in favour of expansion of the EU. These countries perceive the EU in a liberal way, which would dilute Latin activism. The wideners have had the edge as Austria, Finland and Sweden quietly joined the EU in 1995 (if there was any public debate about this enlargement, it went unnoticed).

At about the same time Germany wanted to see some of the East European transition countries join the EU, because it expected that these new member countries would tend to see the Union's affairs in a German (hopefully, Franco-German) way. The southern EU countries were concerned with the possible entry of some of the Central and East European countries, since they may be democratic (but poor) and would compete with the EU's Club Med ('olive belt' or 'southern axis') for regional aid from EU funds. France and Spain would also like to see a 'balanced' approach between the potential eastern enlargement of the EU and the policy of openness towards the southern Mediterranean countries.

European integration is too important to be left only to the 'exclusive' club of the EU(15). The EU accepted this fact and adapted to expand in order to survive as an open institution. Therefore, bilateral entry negotiations started in March 1998 with the Czech Republic, Estonia, Hungary, Poland and Slovenia, as well as with Cyprus. Two years later, in March 2000, bilateral entry negotiations started with Bulgaria, Latvia, Lithuania, Romania and Slovakia, as well as with Malta.

One may wish to recall here the Copenhagen criteria (1993) for EU entry. The potential candidate country must have a functioning market economy; a democratic political system; and be willing, able and ready to accept, implement and enforce the *acquis communautaire*. The problem is that apart from the Czech Republic and Slovakia, not a single transition country had a fully functioning market economy even before they became centrally planned countries. Hence, the EU entry had to be well prepared. Regarding a stable democratic political system, the candidate countries were making significant progress. As far as the *acquis communautaire* is concerned, there were worries that the candidate countries may have difficulties in accommodating this condition, particularly regarding competition and environmental issues. The fourth, tacit, requirement is that an enlargement should not imperil the EU's financial resources, nor should widening of the EU risk deepening of the integration process. As most of the accession countries are on a much lower level of per capita GDP than the EU average, this would require a rearrangement of EU finances and expenditure.

The overriding goal of the EU is to safeguard the efficient operation of its Single European Market. This means that a multispeed EU needs to be avoided as much as possible. Thus, there could be a sufficiently long pre-accession period tailored to the individual conditions of each accession country in order to absorb the *acquis communautaire*. This would eliminate the need for the unnecessary post-entry transition period. However, all this was highly speculative as the *acquis communautaire* would be different in the year 2004 and later from what it was in 1998 or 2000 when negotiations started. In 2003 alone, the *acquis communautaire* was 'enriched' by 2348 new regulations. To make matters worse, more and tougher rules are on the horizon. It is true that most of them have limited time duration. However, the new member countries have a race against ever-shifting goalposts. This would not be a problem for Cyprus as *Agenda 2000* does not expect any major obstacle regarding the adoption, implementation and enforcement of the *acquis communautaire* in the southern part of the country.[52]

The Convention on the Future of Europe that dealt with the constitutional reform of the EU raised new doubts among the accession countries, which feared that the accession would be made subject to new conditions or that something was being plotted against them. Expectation fatigue was taking its toll. None the less, the European Commission considered that Cyprus, the Czech Republic, Estonia, Hungary, Latvia, Lithuania, Malta, Poland, Slovakia and Slovenia would be ready for EU membership from May 2004. Bulgaria and Romania have 2007 as their indicative date for accession (European Commission, 2002a, pp. 33–4). The other Balkan countries may subsequently follow.

A last-minute internal reform deal (principally agreed between France and Germany) on the future of the CAP and the budget made the eastern enlargement relatively cheap for the EU in budgetary terms. The net annual cost of eastern enlargement for the EU would be €3.4 billion in the 2004–06 period. This issue will be elaborated further in the chapter on the eastern EU enlargement.

A near absence of public debate in the EU about this enlargement leaves most people in ignorance about the tectonic political and economic changes that this involves. For most people this is a remote abstraction and a *fait accompli*. Enlargement should not be done 'on the quiet' as was the case with the eurozone. This was an important reason for the Irish rejection of the Treaty of Nice in 2001, and can serve as an argument that the enlargement process is proceeding too fast and that public opinion is not supporting it. Ireland was the only EU country to offer its citizens the privilege of consulting them directly on the Treaty of Nice; the rest, that is, 98 per cent of EU citizens, were not given the opportunity to express themselves directly on this crucial issue.

AWKWARD TIMES, OR A CLUMSY INSTITUTION

The European Union is increasingly becoming an awkward institution to be in. The Union finds ways to interfere directly not only in the composition of democratically elected governments of its member states even before they err, but also in the leadership of individual national parties. Democracy in the EU and respect for others are in certain cases reduced to a simple and definite acceptance of decisions by 'others' (recall the Irish referendum regarding the Treaty of Nice).

The EU introduced diplomatic sanctions against Austria in February 2000 because the coalition government of Wolfgang Schüssel (People's Party) included Jörg Heider's right-wing Freedom Party because of its anti-immigration, pro-Nazi and anti-EU platform during the October 1999 elections. This was the first time that the EU as a whole criticised domestic policies or attempted to influence the composition of a member country's government – even before the new government had put a foot wrong. The sanctions were in the form of freezing bilateral contacts with Austria. Even though Austria had broken no EU rules the intention, based on moral objections and subjective criteria, was to send a strong signal throughout Europe against the rise of nationalist parties that may put EU cohesion at risk. During the period of these bilateral sanctions, Heider stepped down from the leadership of his party. Subsequently, an EU report by the 'three wise men' recommended in September 2000 that the sanctions should be lifted as soon as possible. This suggestion was accepted, since such sanctions could lead to a nationalistic 'uprising' in Austria and could be counterproductive to EU enlargement. None the less, the 14 ostracisers created an important precedent for sweeping interference in a member's domestic politics. It was unusual as no EU country had ever made similar demands when larger EU countries included communists or post-fascists in their governments. In addition, the move towards 'nationalism' in Austria and later on in France (and elsewhere in the EU) was not peculiar to these two countries alone – it is a general trend in Europe. In addition, certain EU accession countries were far more right wing than either Austria or France.

Mindful about the disturbing effects of the response to the success of the Freedom Party in Austria in 1999, the 14 EU countries did not threaten France with the introduction of bilateral sanctions following the election achievements of Jean-Marie Le Pen (National Front) and his entry into the second round of presidential elections in France in 2002. Sick and tired of the ideological consensus among the ruling parties (any differences in their programmes evaporated), of being disdained by the patrician national elite and of constant transfer of powers to Brussels, voters supported a right-wing politician who opposed the entire system (Le Pen was anti-EU, anti-common currency, anti-globalisation and anti-immigration). Le Pen received 20 per cent of the votes. This occurred during a period of relative economic prosperity. Le Pen's electoral victories were most evident in the border regions. Interestingly, these are the areas where the experience of integration and the EU is most evident. Hence, the neo-liberal theories that economic prosperity brings happiness and satisfaction did not hold water in this case.[53] Prosperity is necessary, but people need a sense of a common perception of the future. They need to be asked by or involved in the system in order to contribute to the creation of such a perspective. The issue and power of nationalism[54] was seriously misjudged by the elite, which is also why the Dutch right-wing politician Pim Fortyn[55] had such success in the 2002 elections.

Denmark is often referred to as a 'Euro-sceptical' country. Part of the reason for the protection of sovereignty may be found in its history. Danes proudly emphasise that they have the oldest European royal family. Denmark was a significant European power during the 18th century. It controlled much of Scandinavia, Schleswig-Holstein and Iceland. However, since that time, it has lost every war it has fought, and has shrunk in size. Danes voted 'no' to the Treaty of Maastricht in 1992. The question is whether the no vote of 50.7 per cent in a country that represents 2 per cent of EU citizens justifies the right of veto in the EU.[56] To persuade them to change their mind, the EU granted the Danes four opt-outs: from the monetary union; from any defence issue; from cooperation in justice and home affairs; and from EU citizenship. In the second referendum in 1993, the Danes approved the treaty.

François Mitterrand, the late French president, once said that 'if you ask a specific question in a referendum you will always get an answer to a completely different one' (*The Economist*, 27 September 2003, p. 34). If this is applied to the Swedish rejection of the eurozone in the 2003 referendum, it is apparent that the national elite did not trick the Swedish voters regarding the eurozone. The voters did not reject the euro to the same extent as they declared the case unproven, in particular regarding rigidities that impede national economies.

A FRANCO-GERMAN 'INTEGRATION ENGINE' AND BRITAIN

There are various alliances within the EU. The principal Franco-German alliance (at times including the Low Countries) tends to be weakened by others that still do not have a strong economic or political muscle. None the less, the Scandinavian countries harmonise their posture, Spain and

Portugal often act together, while Britain allies with anyone that wants to slow down the process of integration. A possible eastern EU tier of a group of countries with similar histories and goals may add an important new factor that may contribute to the watering down of the leading Franco-German integration axis. This may slow down the entire integration process. This is just what Britain wanted in the post-Second World War period from outside the EU and what it did from within it after entry in 1971. Britain, basically, wants to be at the heart of the EU decision-making process, but without being overcommitted, in order to leave generous room for its own manoeuvres.[57] To put it bluntly: France and Germany make unhedged bets on Europe, while Britain has always been hedging them.

The Franco-German friendship suffered upsets, sometimes quite serious,[58] but always emerged safe and sound. This relationship is not automatic. It is maintained and built on a constant political choice and will to build an effective EU. These two countries have fully realised that it may be better to be united than to stand against each other. At the same time, ever since the Roman legions departed from the shores of southern England in AD 410 (after 367 years of occupation), Britain has always been somewhat semi-detached from and suspicious about Europe.

The French political class has always been the best educated in and most resolute about Europe. It comes as no surprise that the EU is built in a way that echoes French interests and traditions.[59] Britain has always seen the EU as a Franco-German 'plot'. As such, it accepted the EU as something inevitable, rather than something to be enthusiastic about. Even though there were occasional attempts to include the British in this 'inner core', the Franco-German duo never evolved into a *ménage à trois* with the British. The problem is not only that even after more than three decades in the EU, Britain cannot clearly decide whether it wants to be a full participant in the EU venture, but also that France and Germany are too close to allow a third country to come between them.

France has realised that in a wider EU its economic and political weight would diminish, while Germany could become even more influential. The myth about the grandeur of France in the EU is being seriously shaken by the rising political power of Germany after reunification. It seemed throughout the 1990s that France has manipulated rather than created events.

Britain has always tried to maintain a certain balance of power on the European continent and to profit from it. Britain did not care who won on the continent, as long as nobody did over a long-term period. Britain always managed to be 'in between' the others and to profit from such a situation. For example, around the time of the US-led war against Iraq in 2003, the British government was between Europe and the US, between the UN and the US, between the BBC reports and the hidden true reasons and agenda for war, as well as between the Palestinians and the US (roadmap for peace plan). Earlier, and to put it in very simple terms, when France tried to create and hold an empire, Britain plotted against it and, together with Russia, Austria and Prussia, contributed to Napoleon's defeat in 1815. Before that, Britain defeated Spain on the high seas in 1805. Britain was also between Russia and the Middle East (in favour of Turkey). In 1854–55, Britain fought the Crimean War against Russia. However, in 1915–16, Britain with France, Australia and New Zealand unsuccessfully attempted the invasion of Turkey (Dardanelles Strait – Gallipoli) in order to relieve the Turkish pressure on Russian forces in the Caucasus and to control the straits. When Germany sought supremacy in two world wars, Britain joined France and Russia against Germany. Then in 2004, Britain was between Turkey and a number of EU states that had serious doubts about the Turkish credentials for EU eligibility. Lasting friendship, durable alliances, lifelong understanding and enduring gratitude in international relations simply do not exist. They have never existed in the long term. What exists and lasts is only the politics of national self-interest. That is simply the basic geopolitical law. But the object of this interest can easily change and fall into disfavour rather quickly, according to the interest of the moment. Opponents of such a geopolitical view would argue that all the mentioned relations exist, but they may be slightly altered because of 'temporary emphasis'.[60]

Slow growth, unemployment and protectionist pressures often provide a fertile soil for introverted and nationalist policies. Those policies may be supported by currency speculation, as occurred in September 1992 when Britain and Italy suspended their membership of the exchange rate mechanism of the EMS, while Spain devalued the peseta. A bigger shock took place at the end of July 1993 with the actual demise of the exchange rate mechanism of the EMS[61] and the EU's federal dreams (at least for some time in the future). The EU was pushed back to the reality of the present, rather than trying to imagine its future. France thought of the EU as a club of like-minded peers. It was immensely disappointed when Germany refused to cut its interest rate and put its national interest first. When major national issues are at stake, EU solidarity is still fragile. The wide increase in fluctuation margins seemed to slow down the Maastricht Treaty's aim to introduce the euro in the relatively near future. The reunification of Germany was the major instigator of the Maastricht Treaty, as well as the reason for the treaty's half-hearted implementation.

Germany has already achieved economic dominance in Europe. A strong Franco-German relationship still exists. This was exemplified by a joint action to escape the eurozone fiscal rules[62] in 2003 (the two countries do not always work for the benefit of the entire EU). Even though this special relation between the two countries still exists, it is being modified. The (temporary) emerging London–Madrid–Rome partnership in 2003 (on the issue of the war in Iraq) may merely reposition rather than replace the Paris–Berlin alliance. The Franco-German partnership is still necessary for the stability of Europe, but not sufficient. Germany is now locked in the EU for some time to come, but the question still remains as to how it will use its clout in EU affairs in the future. Would this be 'European Germany', or 'German Europe'?

As a rule, when France and Germany and perhaps another larger EU country reach agreement about an issue during the very last minutes of negotiations and horse-trading, then they draw others into the deal. It remains to be seen how this type of EU integration engine would operate following the eastern enlargement.

Germany is a crucial power factor at the heart of an expanding EU. However, there is a key policy dilemma facing Germany as a potentially 'expanding regional power' over the coming decades. It deals with demographical trends. If Germany does not accept approximately 350 000 immigrants per year, it could shrink from 82 to 60 million people by 2050 (Messerlin, 2001, p. 255).

'COMMON' FOREIGN, SECURITY AND DEFENCE POLICY

An internationally or globally important issue is that the EU countries, contrary to the US, have faith in a 'social contract'.[63] This was obvious in different attitudes towards the Kyoto Protocol on Global Warming (1997) or the International Criminal Court (2002). The US has such an awesome political, economic and military power that it may not need (or may easily ignore) international institutions as they only constrain unilateral acts and room for manoeuvre. Does international law apply to the weak but not the strong? The EU can exert the only substantial international pressure towards such ends, in particular as the US appears to be a 'rogue state' on issues of global warming and the International Criminal Court. If the EU collapses in dysfunctional paralysis, everyone may become weaker, poorer and may suffer. The EU is at present in no-man's-land. It is powerful enough not to be the American pawn, but it is too divided to be an impressive counterbalance or an equal partner.

On foreign policy issues, for example Iraq, EU countries were more unwilling than ever to speak with one voice. In fact only Britain and France have strong international clout as they sit on the UN Security Council. However, neither speaks for the EU, but rather for its own national interest, as was obvious during the US-led war against Iraq (2003). If past enlargements can give some indication, it may take a generation before such a change is absorbed and organisationally digested, and before there is functional coordination throughout the EU. If this proves to be true, then this is great news for the US.

A major split in EU foreign and security policy occurred in January 2003, just before the war with Iraq. Eight European states (Britain, the Czech Republic, Denmark, Hungary, Italy, Poland, Portugal and Spain) declared in a joint letter from foreign ministers their support for the US position. The country holding the EU presidency and the official speaker for the EU (Greece) was unaware of this letter before it was made public, and neither the commissioner for external relations (Chris Patten), nor the European Council's foreign policy chief (Javier Solana) were informed.[64] Bulgaria and Romania also aligned with the US. The 'American EU' encircled the 'Franco-German EU'. The EU geopolitical shift in Europe since 2001 became obvious. Instead of supporting a united Europe under the EU umbrella as before, the US prefers to see a divided EU which cannot endanger or challenge the global American primacy.

France and Germany were strongly opposed to the war in Iraq. The Americans were irritated by this because they believed that the disagreement was a betrayal of gratitude for the long-standing American support to Europe. The French, the Germans and very many other Europeans were equally antagonistic as they thought that such American behaviour was a betrayal of what the Americans preached about respect for the legitimacy of the established international order and organisations, about law and democracy, and about just causes for war approved by the UN.

Henry Kissinger wrote half a century ago that:

> [T]he distinguishing feature of a revolutionary power is not that it feels threatened – such feeling is inherent in the nature of international relations based on sovereign states – *but that nothing can reassure it*. Only absolute security – the neutralization of the opponent – is considered a sufficient guarantee, and thus the desire of one power of absolute security means absolute insecurity for all others. . . . But it is the essence of a revolutionary power that it possesses the courage of its convictions, that it is willing, indeed eager, to push its principles to their ultimate conclusion. (Kissinger, 1957, pp. 2–3)

Paul Krugman later commented: 'Why don't the usual rules apply? Because a revolutionary power, which does not regard the existing system as legitimate, doesn't feel obliged to play by the rules' (2003, p. 16).[65]

The official *casus belli* was the existence of a massive arsenal of weapons of mass destruction that could be used by Iraq at very short notice. However, neither the UN inspectors before the war, nor the occupation force inspectors, one year following the war, could corroborate either their existence or even active programmes to produce such weapons.[66] Paul Wolfowitz, the US deputy defense secretary, publicly claimed that 'the real motive was that Iraq is "swimming" in oil'.[67] Oil is a resource in finite supply. No major oil fields have been discovered since the mid-1970s. Is war in Iraq only a pilot project (Krugman, 2003, pp. 6–7)? Is it only one stop on the way towards other oil-rich countries, including Russia?

The American media-led[68] militant democracy was reinforced by the country's militarised diplomacy. In this new situation there is a rise in the power of the Pentagon (the military) and decline in the authority of the State Department (diplomacy). Many Europeans are suspicious about such a change and they think that the 2003 attack on Iraq was a return to the times of Bismarck. Armed 'missionaries', even if they 'export democracy', are rarely popular.

The EU's common foreign and security policy failed the test on this important issue. This sent a warning signal to France, Germany and the EU institutions that foreign policy in an enlarged EU cannot easily be conducted as was formerly the case. A foreign and security policy (if there is any) of the enlarged EU may be subject to strong American influence and guidance. Several EU member countries (Holland, Italy, Portugal and Spain), as well as most of the accession countries drew similar conclusions. The issue of Iraq was not important in all this. What was at the heart of the matter was that they did not have enough confidence in the Franco-German hub of the EU. They sent a powerful signal that they did not want to be part of an EU formulated by France and Germany alone. Most of these countries are not convinced that either France or Germany would put European interests ahead of their own. In addition, the formerly socialist countries still have misgivings regarding Germany. They want a longer-term American presence in Europe.

In order to play a greater global role and contribute more to international security, the EU agreed in Helsinki in 1999 to build a 60 000 strong European Rapid Reaction Force (ERRF) (Euro-army) by mid-2003, but these original plans were subsequently scaled down. The force would be assembled for operations from voluntary contributions from member states within 60 days' notice and be able to sustain its operations for at least one year. The mission of this force, according to the Treaty of Nice (Article 1 §2), has to be compatible with NATO and its duties would include peacekeeping, peacemaking, humanitarian and rescue tasks. It is to complement, rather than to compete with NATO. It would be involved in missions where NATO does not intend to be involved. This occurred for the first time in March 2003 when the 350-strong EU force took over operations[69] from NATO in FYR Macedonia. Britain and France, Europe's biggest military powers, were working closely and continuously on EU defence issues in spite of a parallel row over Iraq. In addition, a replacement of NATO by the EU forces could take place in Bosnia from 2005. Notwithstanding all this, the question remains: is a common security and defence policy possible without a common foreign policy? And vice versa?

Because of NATO's lack of strategic capability, the EU wants to have free access to NATO planning capability. The EU hopes to use shared NATO assets such as surveillance and telecommunications systems. However, there is the issue of Turkey. As a member of NATO, but not the EU, Turkey could block operations by vetoing the use of NATO assets. Although the EU will not be able to match the US military potential for quite some time, it could still make a meaningful contribution to the global peace efforts by playing its strongest card and using the American greatest (current) weakness. This includes trade, aid, monitoring by international institutions and, even, peacekeeping.

The newcomers from Central and Eastern Europe are joining NATO even though it may soon be defunct in its present form. Its founder and primary patron, the US, is losing interest in it and prefers to take unilateral action. Since the end of the Cold War, NATO may be losing some of its geopolitical relevance and purpose. As Russia has embraced democracy, US priorities are shifting away from Europe. Germany, as a regional power, is interested in the stability of the region. So, of what real value is NATO now to the US? The answer is not very clear even though NATO was involved in 2003, albeit a long way from home, in Afghanistan.

NATO operates on the basis of consensus. The US is a country that has awesome global influence, unknown since the days of the ancient Roman Empire, and can dare to act unilaterally. International institutions may only constrain such actions and introduce a certain level of predictability in international relations.[70]

The 2003 war with Iraq in effect became a global referendum on US power. Both those that sided with the US, as well as those that did not, paid a high price. American allies suffered war casualties and increased tension and mistrust with other countries, while those that did not side with the US will not get contracts for the reconstruction of Iraq. Overall, the US problem has perhaps been the inability to understand its dependence on the 'others'.[71]

Central and Eastern European countries wanted US involvement in their defence, but in future they may get the EU instead.[72] None the less, quite a few Europeans support NATO as they perceive this organisation with its US presence as a counterweight to the Franco-German core in the EU.

In 2002, the US proposed the creation of a NATO Reaction Force (NRF). If this proposal is accepted in practice, this would link NATO more closely to US foreign policy goals and actions. This would also spoil a plan to create a distinct European defence identity from the US. This European project has run into trouble for several reasons. First, the question of funding: the combined budgets of the EU countries are half of that in the US. Tight budgetary constraints and slow growth do not permit an increase in expenditure. The amount in question would involve an additional €25 billion over 15–20 years. The issues are who will foot the bill; and how to convince voters and taxpayers that the EU should provide security outside its region. According to a report commissioned by the British government, many of the requirements for the force will not be met before 2008 or 2010.[73] Second, the involvement of countries that consider themselves to be neutral (Austria, Finland, Ireland and Sweden). Third, the disagreement between Britain and France about the level and scope of coordination with NATO.

One has to bear in mind that the NRF and the ERRF are different animals. While the NRF is conceived to be NATO's tool for a military offensive, the ERRF would not be involved in warfare, but rather its mission would be to discourage others from doing so and to provide peace-keeping missions. The NRF would be 20 000 strong. It has to be ready to accompany American forces anywhere in the world at short notice. To have forces at this level of readiness requires a base at least three times as large (a total of 60 000 people in the army, navy and air force). If one recalls that the average wealthy European country spends about $80 000 per soldier a year (the US spends $200 000; Britain spends $155 000) the cost of this force would be stupendous.[74] No senior official either from the EU or from NATO has mentioned the (new) source of finance for these projects; where the money would come from is far from clear. Italy and Spain, great supporters of the US-led military attack on Iraq, sent few forces to support the war effort. The question may then be: why spend money on creating a force that the EU would never agree to send anywhere? Given the continuing involvement and the size of the EU peacekeeping forces in the former Yugoslavia and in Afghanistan (and soon perhaps in Iraq), as well as the need for troop rotation, most European troops would be involved in peacekeeping missions, rather than in readiness for fresh combat.

More good news for the US is that the EU(15) (with the exception of Britain) thought that it would accept new member countries that presumably held a 'European' view of international events. As a gesture of goodwill, the European Council in Copenhagen (2002) created an additional new and special 'cash-flow facility' for the year 2004 and for budgetary compensation for the 2004–06 period.[75] The Polish benefit from this additional windfall 'subsidy' (which would go directly into the Polish budget) would be €1 billion.[76] At about the same time, Poland announced that it would purchase US-built F-16 fighter jets ($3.5 billion), rather than EU-made Gripens or Mirages.[77] In addition, and much to the irritation of

France, the accession countries openly and actively sided with the US in the 2003 war against Iraq (Poland and the Czech Republic sent troops from the outset). The EU is deeply divided on such a crucial foreign policy issue.[78] Is a common foreign policy feasible in the near or in the distant future? Bearing in mind how easy it would be to block any new initiative in the enlarged EU, what should be the way forward in the EU? Is it to start again from the beginning? Should the original core of France and Germany with the Benelux be recreated? There is a certain precedence in creating such 'coalitions of the willing' that move at a faster speed than the rest of the EU (Schengen; the eurozone).

Who runs EU foreign policy? The European Commission's external affairs manager (Chris Patten) or the high representative nominated by the EU member governments (Javier Solana)? Should these two jobs be integrated? Would this produce a kind of EU foreign policy 'Kaiser'? If there is a common EU foreign policy, it may be introduced in stages, just as was the case with the eurozone (recall that it took 30 years for the EU to create a single European currency). A transition to the final phase of a common foreign and defence policy may take a decade or a generation. At the end of such a period the decision ought to be unanimous.

THE BALKANS

Most of EU foreign policy actions, funds, time and energy from the start of the 1990s were spent on the Balkans, in particular with respect to the consequences of the violent break-up of the former Yugoslavia and the attempts to stabilise and reconstruct the countries in the region following the wars. However, certain basic principles and directions were badly dented. For example, the UN, NATO and EU military forces and police were sent to Bosnia and Herzegovina from the early 1990s together with international administrators (with the full authority of colonial governors).[79] Their mission was to force the Muslims, Serbs and Croats to live *together*. The same type of administration was sent to Kosovo and Metohia in 1999 (some 150 km east of Bosnia) in order, basically, to *separate* the Albanians and Serbs there.[80]

Distrust, fear, intolerance and lack of self-discipline are deep and destructive sentiments and types of behaviour. Even an old complacent democracy and welfare state such as Britain cannot resolve such difficulties easily. An obvious case in point is Northern Ireland. Harsh ethnic and religious violence provoked the government to build a kilometre-long wall (named with Stalinist irony the 'Peace Wall') in Belfast in 1969. This wall outlived the 28-year-old Berlin Wall (dismantled in 1989). Such walls may be required only when relations between people break down. There are some 20 such walls in Northern Ireland. They separate the Protestant and Roman Catholic districts. Simon Jenkins wrote about this problem that '"Ethnic cleansing", notably west of the River Bann, has differed from that in Kosovo only in its longevity'.[81] Apparently British governments like walls and divisions: they left them in India, the Middle East and in Cyprus, and there are new ones in the Balkans. Jenkins also wrote:

> [That British ministers] travel the world telling Israelis and Palestinians, Serbs and Albanians, Sunnis and Shias how to get on with each other is hypocrisy on a truly imperial scale . . . The wall in the Springmartin Road area of Belfast is almost a thousand yards long and 20ft high. Would Mr Blair like to be photographed in front of that for The Jerusalem Post? These monuments of intolerance and fear are the starkest admission of the failure of democracy.[82]

None the less, fragmentation has become the default mode of Western intervention: Yugoslavia, Afghanistan, and perhaps soon in Iraq and the looming conflicts in the Caucasus region.

Following civil wars during the 1990s, sanctions and NATO military intervention, the EU countries jointly wanted to pacify the region and try to put it on the long road towards EU membership. One of the principal means was the Stability Pact for Southeastern Europe. This is a joint initiative by a number of international institutions and countries which include the EU, NATO, the OECD, the WEU, the World Bank, the International Monetary Fund, the European Bank for Reconstruction and Development, the Council of Europe, the US, Canada, Japan and Turkey, as well as countries of the region.[83] The objective of the stability pact, launched in Sarajevo in July 1999 with a score of top world leaders in attendance, is to prepare countries in the region for speedier integration into the Euro-Atlantic institutions. It was hoped by many that this could become a kind of the Marshall Plan for Southeast Europe. The main instrument comes from Brussels in the form of Stabilisation and Association Agreements. The pact's complex structure of 'working tables' that deal with three core areas (economic reform; democracy and human rights; and security cooperation) was cumbersome. In addition, little new money was promised. Funds would come from the existing aid programmes. All this created 'fears that the West will fail to honour its high-level political pledges' (*European Voice*, 20 January 2000, p. 12). These worries turned out subsequently to be true. The 'Pact has not fulfilled its aim of giving a clear sense of direction to the region's governments or to aid donors' (*Financial Times*, 9 January 2002, p. 12). The first regional funding conference was held in Brussels in March 2000. Pledges were in excess of $2.5 billion, but disbursement[84] of funds has been unwieldy and slow.[85]

In March 2003, the Committee of Ministers of the Council of Europe[86] invited Serbia and Montenegro to join this political organisation. Remember that the Council of Europe (Strasbourg) is an organisation that includes democratic countries of Europe that stand for the respect of civil and political liberties, freedom of speech, respect of law and the like. For many years the Council of Europe (all EU countries are members of this Council) has demanded that Serbia and Montenegro should alter and improve their laws, political practices, access to the media and the like, as well as to respect EU requirements.[87] Incidentally, this invitation to join coincided with fully blown martial law in Serbia, that is, at a time when civil liberties were suspended following the assassination of the prime minister.

The European Council has reiterated that it supports the EU perspective of all Balkan countries. However, the speed of the approach and the eventual EU entry depend on the individual country. This is relevant in the light of the reform and improvement in the operation of the public administration, legal system and fight against organised crime and corruption, as well as economic reforms.

DISILLUSIONMENT

European integration has been led so far largely by an economic doctrine. Political concerns started to feature higher on the agenda from the mid-1980s, while constitutional matters were neglected. This is why the national elites and governments treated Europeans to a large extent as consumers, rather than as citizens.

The disillusionment problem regarding European integration is perhaps less to do with the fact that the European elite decides the shape, extent and direction of European integration. The problem lies much more in the fact that this elite disdains[88] voters and does not try enough to explain and convince the electorate that European integration is for the good of all in the long term. There is an obvious distrust by a significant part of the electorate versus a distant, alienated and unaccountable patrician elite that imposes rules. If this elite occasionally holds a referendum on certain crucial national interests regarding European integration, it may easily run as many referendums on the same issue as necessary, until it gets the required outcome. This gives an illusion of democracy, but in fact the decision has already been made. The European and national elites have to work very hard indeed to win the hearts, minds and confidence of the people for further projects in European integration. A vague promise that economic benefits outweigh the costs is no longer as safe a bet as once it was.

20. Federal future of Europe or what?

A discussion about the future course of Europe and the EU often turns around federalism. This is an often misinterpreted and misunderstood concept. Federalism for Germany means a rational division of powers among different levels of government. This is a structure in which federal entities are not absorbed into a centralised state, but keep their autonomy, while competences handed to the central authority are clearly delimited.[89] For the English, federalism means just the opposite: a country gives up its autonomy to a single central power (a super-state). In these conditions it is hard for the countries to understand each other.[90]

Within the debate about the future of the EU one may distinguish two broad lines of argument:

- *Federalists* stand for a single foreign policy; tax harmonisation; more EU power over national budgets; an elected EU president; a single EU constitution that replaces all existing EU treaties; and a preference for the 'community method' in decision making.
- *Sovereignty defenders (minimalists, non-federalists or Eurosceptics)* argue in favour of a national foreign policy; more national freedom to run state budgets; national governments to appoint the president of the Council of Ministers; a non-political European Commission; more powers to national parliaments to supervise and control the EU; and no more powers to the European Parliament. Article 308 of the Treaty of Rome, which allows the possibility of allocating new powers to the EU, should be deleted.

While Britain would like to see the development of the EU along its preferred lines of common law and informal unwritten constitution, countries that tilt towards a federal EU have different motives for such a concept. Germany would like to see a federal model as a way to soothe the sleeping demons. Germany knows full well that if it wanted to do something alone, it would immediately face an anti-German coalition. Therefore, Germany still needs France in the project. France would like to use the federal model to 'control' its German neighbour; Italy would like to use it as a way out of its knotty political system; Spain may be in favour of federalism in order to modernise and gain respectability; while small countries see a federal model as a means to curb the might of big countries and the return of the type of politics that existed between the two world wars, when their fate was decided in London, Paris or Munich. No country, however, sees the EU primarily as a means to sponsor a liberal type of citizenship.

According to the principles set by Denis de Rougemont at the Montreux Congress (1947) to federate means to unite heterogeneous elements, but without any organisational hegemony. The goal of federation is to create and maintain a communication set-up and to sustain uniqueness and individual qualities of each minority, region or state.[91] It should be done in a spirit of democracy, liberty, free choice and agreement, which would eliminate uniformity and rigidity. What states can do, the federal authority must not do. The federal process is quite slow, but this is the price to be paid for its existence and progress (Sidjanski, 2000, pp. 15–16). Sidjanski later commented:

> the federal approach can be seen as an attitude towards others and society, a method and an approach to reality, an outlook and a style of social organization and behaviour. It is not a rigid model to categorize different societies, but a system of structures and adequate processes that rely on basic principles. It is also a dynamic method, which often works by progressive adjustments. (Sidjanski, 2001, p. 3)

> Federalism appears to be an appropriate counterweight to globalisation and the most appropriate form of social organization, to assemble Europeans into a union that guarantees national, regional and local identities with the necessary interdependence and the affirmation of a European identity. (Sidjanski, 2001, p. 2)

There are no ideal forms of federalism. The organisational structures based on federal principles do not form a hierarchical order as observed in centralised states. The formation of a federation depends on the existing political cultures and institutions, and proceeds to redistribute tasks and authorities in an optimal way according to the capabilities of the constituent units (subsidiarity). The federal model is always open to change, and it should respond to changes in the integration process. There are different functioning federal models, including those in Germany, Switzerland, Russia and the US. However, the diversity in forms and practices of federalism is a serious warning against the reproduction of any one model (Sidjanski, 2001, pp. 5–27).[92]

The issue is not delineation between national sovereignty and federalism. The EU already has certain federal powers. Sovereignty will always have to be shared between states and the common institutions. The principal constitutional questions for the EU are:

- How much power will EU institutions have relative to the EU member countries in order to protect legitimacy and to preserve the efficiency of the government? That is: how centralised should the EU be?
- How should power be divided among various EU institutions?

Both the European Commission and the Council of Ministers are hybrid bodies. The European Commission is half administration and half executive body, while the Council of Ministers is half executive and half legislative institution, which is why many people have problems understanding them. In order to be accepted, prosperous and effective, the EU must be democratically accountable, legitimate, relevant and intelligible, otherwise the EU may become a supranational bureaucracy instead of a supranational democracy.

Whenever the EU encountered an important issue or when it tried to shape a certain future event, it called an IGC to propose the course of and means for action. However, over time these conferences might have outlived their usefulness. They also gave the impression that diplomats plot behind the backs of EU citizens. The treaties of Maastricht, Amsterdam, Nice and others were negotiated and agreed upon behind closed doors.

The European Council in Nice (2000) triggered a wide-ranging debate about the future of the EU. The same Council decided in Laeken (2001) to convene a European Convention to pave the way for the future reform of the EU structure. Such a wide discourse is crucial as complexity is an exponential, not a proportional, function of the number of EU member countries. This was the first time that citizens could expect a vigorous and extensive debate about the future of the EU from the start of a certain project.

For the first time the elected representatives (largely parliamentarians) of 28 countries (EU members and candidates) were brought together under the chairmanship of Valéry Giscard d'Estaing, to discuss and draft a possible constitution for Europe. The convention[93] started work in Brussels in March 2002. One task was to suggest an institutional and operational set-up for an EU comprising about 30 member countries. Another task was to state the purpose of the EU, so that people could understand its relevance to their well-being and feel more enthusiastic about its activities.

The convention sought consensus, not unanimity. It tackled questions such as: who will be the future government of Europe? Who will control that government? Will there be a directly elected president of the EU? How to manage the EU(25) economy when half of its members use the euro, while the other half does not? In any case although the various delegates may have reached agreement, that did not mean that the proposed text of the Draft Constitutional Treaty would be acceptable to the governments of the day. None the less, the proposal would carry certain political weight.

Rather than a six-month rotating presidency (perceived as inefficient), the convention proposed the creation of the post of chairman of the European Council with a mandate of two and a half years (renewable for one further term). This person would chair and drive the work of the European Council (heads of state and/or government), prepare its work agenda and represent the EU abroad. The candidate for this post would come from the ranks of past or serving EU leaders. This new organisational structure may, but not necessarily will, provoke a power struggle between the president of the European Council and the president of the European Commission.

As of 2009, the size of the European Commission would be reduced to 15 voting commissioners including its president. Even though these ideas provoked discontent (small countries deem that this system would favour big countries), the strongest argument on the side of the d'Estaing camp is that the opposition did not put forward any viable alternative.

The legislative Council of Ministers would vote according to the new formula for a qualified majority from 2009. The Byzantine system of weighted votes agreed in Nice would be replaced by the double majority technique: a law is passed if: (i) a majority of member countries which represent (ii) at least 60 per cent of the EU(25) total population support it.

A new post of EU minister of foreign affairs was also proposed, the post to be anchored within both the Commission and the Council. Other existing EU institutions would be largely unchanged. However, as law making is simplified in the Council of Ministers, the European Parliament would gain in importance because of its co-decision and veto power.

Even though there is a reference to subsidiarity and proportionality as a check on the power of the EU institutions, the text of the Draft Constitutional Treaty shows that the EU is increasing its intervention and coordination powers not only over the Single European Market and trade, but also on a host of policies which include foreign affairs and security, monetary affairs, agriculture, fisheries, industry, education, employment, social issues, transport, energy, R&D, and even space (Chapter III, §10). The Constitutional Treaty would likely increase the EU law-making activity in several ways. It would expand sole and shared EU competences, it would lower the threshold for the qualified majority decisions and it would enlarge the number of areas subject to qualified majority voting.

The convention submitted its Draft Constitutional Treaty to the European Council in Thessaloniki in June 2003. The Council welcomed the draft and called for an IGC to finalise it by the end of 2003. Not everyone was happy about the Draft Constitutional Treaty, and the text was clarified and modified during the Brussels Council in December 2003. Certain countries, including Poland and Spain, wanted to add a reference to the European Christian heritage, while France opposed that because of its desire to pursue multicultural principles. However, the biggest problem and battle related to voting rights in the enlarged EU. If nothing is done about current voting rights, Poland and Spain with a combined population just below Germany's 82 million, would together have 54 votes compared with

Germany's 29. The Draft Treaty replaced this by a system in which at least 13 (a half) of the 25 member states which include at least 60 per cent of the EU population have an upper hand. Poland and Spain would have less influence in the proposed system.

Even though the EU has a long history of pulling victory from the jaws of defeat, deeply entrenched positions by France and Germany on one side and Poland and Spain on the other made it impossible for the Brussels Council to approve the Draft Constitutional Treaty. The summit and the IGC collapsed on 13 December 2003. From the beginning, the handling and building of the EU(25) caused more trouble than expected. The benevolence of the new members cannot be taken for granted. One can just imagine the complications regarding future negotiations over agriculture or the budget.

Just a few days after the Brussels Council, the leaders of Austria, Britain, France, Germany, the Netherlands and Sweden (net contributors to the EU budget) sent a letter to the European Commission's president, suggesting that future EU expenditure should be pegged at about 1 per cent of EU GDP for the future financial period, 2007–13. The political message was clear. Spain, the biggest recipient of EU funds, and Poland, the biggest new gainer, as 'bad boys' were warned not to expect generosity in the future. The consequence may be a slower convergence between rich and less fortunate EU countries.

Following the collapse of this Brussels Council, ideas for a two-speed EU resurfaced. France and Germany, together with a select group of like-minded countries, would form the pioneering core (presumably the original six members of the EU), while others would join this group as and when they could. As such, Central and Eastern European countries would have much more in common with one another than with the rest and they could be grouped together. If this happens, it may be much easier for the US to manipulate Europe towards its own ends. However, the EU may use financial bait to reward loyalty to Europe.

There are certain political signs that the European elite should perhaps not push the federalist agenda too far at the current political moment as it may meet resistance. The ratification procedure of the Maastricht Treaty did not go smoothly at all. Although all member countries ratified the treaty, in most of them it provoked heated debate. Indeed, the winning majority for the ratification in most countries was very slim.[94] A popular and overwhelming support for the Maastricht Treaty and, hence, for monetary union (eurozone) was not obtained. The elite thought that the plan was too complicated to be explained to the man in the street. In Denmark, the first national referendum on the treaty was rejected. In practice that could mean the exclusion of Denmark from the EU.[95] After obtaining opt-outs from the eurozone and foreign and security policies, Denmark held a second referendum and a (slim) majority in favour was obtained. Ireland also held a second referendum on the Treaty of Nice. This may be a sign to the integration enthusiasts to slow down and reflect more carefully before undertaking further grand steps.

The 'minimalists bloc' (Britain, Austria and the Scandinavian states) may easily block any mounting federalisation and potential creation of a European 'superstate'. In addition, this stance may easily be bolstered by the ten new member countries which tend to be anti-federalist. This may undercut the new large-scale EU federal intentions, as Poland demonstrated during the final negotiations on the Draft Constitutional Treaty at the end of 2003.

Since the future developments of the EU depend on a plethora of volatile multinational political factors, its future is hard to predict. Various 'dimensions' of the EU are still vague, including the external, defence and social dimensions. Even the term 'Union' is unclear. It may be easier to point to problems in the ongoing development of the EU than to suggest solutions acceptable to everybody. The EU is, indeed, rich in diversity. This should not be very surprising since, for example, even the EU member states themselves have changed. Belgium has transformed itself since the 1970s from a unitary into a federal state. Only the future will tell how that development will end up in Belgium, or in Italy (highly developed northern 'Padania'), or in Britain (oil-rich Scotland). Hence a federal approach to the future development of the EU according to the principles set by de Rougemont may have the highest potential for success.

21. Priorities

The goal for the EU set by the Lisbon Council (2000) is to make the EU 'the most competitive and dynamic knowledge-based economy in the world'[96] by 2010. Fine words and aspirations, no doubt. Unfortunately, this aim produced little more than hot air. In order to provide 'food for thought', to contribute to discussions and to assist in the policy making, the European Commission commissioned a report from eight academics. Under the chairmanship of André Sapir, the group produced *An Agenda for a Growing Europe* (2003). In order to achieve and maintain sustainable growth, the study group recommended among other things that the EU should use its funds more wisely than was the case in the past. The EU should spend about half of its budget on growth-stimulating activities such as research, higher education, infrastructure projects and institution building in the new Central and East European member countries. The only way to do this and to remain within the current budgetary limits is to scrap the CAP and regional funds. Fiscal systems should stimulate investments in innovation. In addition, the Stability Pact should have greater flexibility. No wonder that such suggestions were highly controversial to some commissioners, while some observers thought that such suggestions were politically naive because of the entrenched interests. But perhaps that was the objective of this report: to provoke a wide-ranging debate about the future direction of the EU.

In the coming decade or two the EU will be occupied with several broad strategic projects which include the following:

- *Protection of the Single European Market*: The creation of the Single European Market was the objective for the 1985–92 period. Following that, ongoing goals include making rules more transparent and effective, as well as removing the remaining and potentially new market distortions. These areas include competition, taxation, ecology and, especially, services (which account for about 70 per cent of EU GDP) in order to deliver continuously the full benefits of the Single European Market to the citizens and make the EU 'the most competitive and dynamic knowledge-based economy in the world'.
- *Eurozone, growth, unemployment and demography*: The eurozone is the biggest risk the EU has ever taken as it was created well before a political union. It is also a mission that may transform both the political and economic scenery of Europe. One of the basic features of national sovereignty, the currency, was pooled among 12 EU member countries even in the absence of a political union.

    As with many other projects the EU elite conceived the eurozone. It is the most ambitious project in Europe since the Bolshevik revolution (1918). No currency has circulated in Europe so widely since the Roman Empire (44BC to 476AD). The introduction of the euro in January 1999 (conversion of national currencies into the euro was achieved relatively painlessly during the first months of 2002) was the biggest currency innovation since the introduction of the US dollar in 1792. However, unlike in the US, there is no fiscal element in the deal. Automatic fiscal transfers as built-in stabilisers do not exist. The 12 eurozone countries have a cap on the national budget deficit of only 3 per cent of GDP (which is not always enforced). This was a serious limitation for the conduct of macroeconomic policy in both Germany and France from 2002. This limit on the budget deficit may be relaxed and replaced by a balanced budget requirement over the course of the economic cycle.

Challenges and problems include an acceleration in the rate of growth; a reduction in the rate of unemployment, in particular structural unemployment; immigration; an enlarged public sector; and tax harmonisation.

A looming problem relates to an ageing population and extra demands on public pension funds. This issue will put great pressure on national public finances when the 'baby boom' generation starts to retire around the year 2010. Public pension schemes will become one of the principal economic imbalances as are imbalances in trade or capital flows.

- *Institutional and operational aspects*: The IGC failed to accept the Draft Constitutional Treaty in 2003. However, the EU leaders agreed on the Treaty in June 2004. Now there is a laborious and uncertain ratification of the text in the member countries. Some of them intend to have referendums. Positive outcome cannot be guaranteed in all cases. If all member countries do not ratify the Treaty, then there would be another IGC which would determine what to do next.
- *Public security*: Following the terrorist attacks in Madrid on 11 March 2004 and on the World Trade Center in New York on 11 September 2001,[97] as well as permanent instability in the Middle East, security has continued to gain additional importance in the EU.
- *Enlargement*: Enlargement to 25, 27 or more than 30 countries, as well as the problems linked with transition, the adjustment period and a relentless narrowing of wide gaps will consume considerable time, energy and funds. In certain cases this may be a tough task for the newly arrived countries as the EU is evolving – it may be a race with a moving target. Additionally, the EU ought to ensure that its (over)extension does not jeopardise its inner cohesion.
- *Popular support*: Notwithstanding the above issues, the principal priority for the elite in the EU is to win and retain the hearts, minds and confidence of EU citizens to support integration. It has to re-establish a feeling for the popular mood. The elite should try to create and maintain the popular notion that European integration is necessary, desirable for everyone in the long run and that the EU really matters.

22. Conclusion

The European Union is at an important turning point. On the international political front, it had difficulties in its attempts to calm the neighbouring problem in the Balkans throughout the 1990s and it is not faring any better in the Middle East (although other organisations did not fare much better either). Before and during the US- (and British-) led war against Iraq (2003) the EU was completely divided regarding a common stance on this globally grave political and defence issue.

In the economic field the EU cannot create new jobs and reduce unemployment while it has an ambitious plan Lisbon (2000) to become for the decade. The eurozone was the Union's major undertaking during the 1990s. Since then, the EU member countries have been trying hard to stick to tough macroeconomic criteria prescribed by the Maastricht Treaty and the Stability Pact, which prevents governments from overborrowing. At the same time, the EU is enlarging eastwards. This is another major risk for the EU to take because of the large gap in economic development, the staggering costs of the *acquis communautaire* for the new member countries and different ideas about common actions and policies, all of which may introduce tensions and divisions in the enlarged EU(25). The goodwill of the new member countries regarding all EU policies and actions cannot be taken for granted (as Poland demonstrated in 2003 with respect to the Draft Constitutional Treaty). The EU may face a bumpy road in the foreseeable future.

During their term of office as president of the European Commission, Roy Jenkins in the 1970s and Jacques Delors in the 1980s selected as the major subject of their presidency the European Monetary System and the Single European Market, respectively. Romano Prodi sought a new direction for the start of the new century: security and stability in Europe (particularly in the Balkans) or 'governance' of Europe, but progress is unsatisfactory. However, Prodi inherited the ambitious idea of enlargement. During his term the EU finalised negotiations with ten new states which joined the EU in 2004. In addition, during his term, two other important events took place: reform of the internal organisation of the European Commission and a relatively smooth introduction of the euro notes and coins in 12 eurozone countries. The principal subject for José Manuel Durão Barroso may be to push the Lisbon strategy.

Predictions about future political events are uncertain, risky, problematical and thankless, and are always subject to harsh criticism. Politics is very difficult, which is why among all the arts it has advanced least since the times of ancient Greece and Rome. If mistakes are made now, they may well be the consequence of ignorance or lack of knowledge about historical events and accumulated experience, including, for example, the centralisation of power and the eventual decay of ancient Rome; the style of rule and proclivities of the medieval papacy that brought about the rise of protestantism; interventions during the Crusades (and the fight with Saladin) or in the Balkan civil wars; or the fragmentation of the Holy Roman Empire, Austria-Hungary or the Soviet bloc, and the like.

If the declared goal is that the EU does not want to cause loss of national sovereignty, then it is not clear what the EU is trying to achieve. The EU created a customs union that is broad and which is getting broader. It created a single currency within the eurozone which is not as extensive as the customs union, but is sufficiently rooted to be seen as a success for now. The next steps must involve taxation and foreign policy. Once those are gone from the national level, so is sovereignty. If the ability to levy taxes, mint money and make war are taken away from states, they have lost their sovereignty.

The Treaty of Nice changed the voting system in the enlarged EU, which complicated and slowed down the introduction of new policies and reaction to new challenges, while facilitating the blocking of new initiatives. In addition, the EU limited its total expenditure in advance of enlargement. Some welcomed the eastern enlargement as they consider that this would dilute the EU into an extended free trade area. Others are depressed because they think that enlargement is being done in a rush, without fully prepared candidates and without a duly consolidated EU. Although there is a Draft Constitutional Treaty that is supposed to simplify the organisation and operation of the EU, its acceptance is postponed for the future.

Appendix 1A   Institutions

In order to accomplish its mandate, the EU has institutions that perform legislative, executive, supervisory, consultative and judiciary tasks. The basic seven institutions of the EU are the European Commission, the Council of Ministers, the European Parliament, the European Council, the Court of Justice, the Court of Auditors and the European Central Bank. The two advisory institutions are the Economic and Social Committee and the Committee of the Regions. There is also the European Investment Bank.

When the Merger Treaty (signed in 1965) came into effect in 1967, the EU unified the thus far separate institutions of the ECSC, the EEC and Euratom into the single body of the European Communities. It needs to be kept in mind that the Parliament and the Court of Justice were common for all three Communities from 1958. The objective of the merger was to bring one step closer the creation of a single Community that would have one treaty which would replace the treaties of Paris and Rome.

EUROPEAN COMMISSION

The European Commission was conceived to play a central role in the EU structure. It is half administrative and half executive body which has a vested interest in the centralisation of EU affairs. The European Commission's assigned tasks are to initiate and execute the Union's policy, to defend the EU's interests in the Council of Ministers and to guard the treaties of the Union.

The *initiation* of EU policies is perhaps the most important function in the whole system of the Union. The European Commission formulates recommendations or delivers opinions. The former refer to specific cases, while the latter deal with general policy guidelines. During the formulation of its proposal, the Commission has to make sure that it is impartial. In reality, the Commission does not look after national interests; however, in the decision-making process it makes a note of national sensibilities. Its proposal must conform with the interests of the entire EU and no favour is to be granted to the benefit of a member state or a group of states unless this complies with the objectives of the EU. As such, it *defends* the Union's interests. The Commission also makes sure that the legal acts and policies are consistent. Before drafting its proposal, the Commission has thorough consultations and exchanges of views with the political leaders of the member countries, employers and labour organisations. Once the guidelines of the policy are in place, the discussions continue with high-ranking experts and national civil servants in order to work out technical details of the piece of law to be submitted to the Council of Ministers as a proposal for a decision about an issue.

As the *executive* arm of the EU, the European Commission carries out the tasks that come from the treaties and that are mandated by the Council of Ministers. The Commission directly legislates issues that relate to trade, agriculture, competition (restrictive business practices, monopolies and subsidies) and safeguard clauses.[98] In addition, the Commission administers the Union's funds.

As the *guardian* of the treaties, the European Commission makes sure that the provisions of the treaties are observed, implemented and enforced. It is authorised to investigate any suspected infringement. The most numerous violations of the Union's law have been in the fields of the internal market, agriculture and the environment. Although they were infringements of the law, the largest number came from delays in the national implementation of the EU's legislation or a difference in the interpretation of EU law between the Commission and the member states that had to be settled by the Court of Justice.

Each EU member country delegates one commissioner to the European Commission. This body has 25 commissioners with a five-year renewable term in office.[99] The conditions for the selection of a commissioner are competence and capability to act exclusively in conformity with the interests of the EU. The commissioner must be free and independent from any other interests, including those of his/her country of origin.

Commissioners are appointed on the basis of an agreement of the governments of the member countries. They are not elected; nor do they campaign or make public their views about their job. They are not subject to control by the voters. Hence, their mandate is constitutional, not popular. Once appointed by their governments, the commissioners become independent and they cannot be dismissed from their office. In theory, the head of the Commission is appointed (not elected) on the basis of the agreement of the European Council, but this choice has to be confirmed by the European Parliament.[100] He/she must accept the government's nominees for the Commission and may not influence their choice, but may reward able appointees with important portfolios.

The Commission is responsible to the European Parliament which needs to approve the full Commission and, once appointed, the Parliament may dismiss the Commission only as a body (this has not happened so far). None the less, once dismissed, the 'old' Commission remains in office until a new one is appointed. Each member country may block the decision of the Parliament by failing to nominate a commissioner, but in fact all involved in the process try to cooperate. The Treaty of Nice enhanced the powers of the president of the European Commission, who has the right to request the resignation of a commissioner, subject to the Commission's approval.

A ceiling on the number of commissioners is set once the EU reaches 27 member states. At that stage, the European Council will unanimously decide on the number of commissioners, which shall be less than 27. The nationality of the commissioners will then be determined by a system of rotation that will be fair to all countries. A contributory factor to some of the institutional troubles in EU bodies may lie in the number of commissioners. At the time of the creation of the EU in 1957 there were nine commissioners, while now they number 25.

The theoretical independence of commissioners from national interests and their work during their mandate entirely for the benefit of the EU may have another side. Lord Cockfield, the commissioner (appointed in 1984) in charge of the internal market, gave an account of bargaining within the European Commission: 'The agreement I made with my colleagues from the South was that in return for their support for my Internal Market

Programme, I would support them in their demands that the Structural Funds should be doubled' (Cockfield, 1994, p. 45). It is clear that when such things take place within the European Commission, which must be neutral in its policy concerning specific national interests, one can only imagine the amount of tough bargaining that takes place in the Council of Ministers or the European Council, where representatives defend their national interests.[101]

The European Commission is a unified body and it acts accordingly. Although each commissioner is in charge of one or a few portfolios, he/she does not have the same degree of liberty of action as a counterpart in a national ministry. In the decision-making process there are basically three procedures:

- For straightforward matters, the Commission uses the written procedure. The file with the issue and the proposed decision about it is sent to each commissioner. If there are no disputes within a week (the usual time period) or another specified period, the proposal is taken to be accepted.
- For routine matters which do not imply political issues, such as agriculture, the Commission may authorise one of its members to take the decision on behalf of the Commission. None the less, the discretionary right in this case is very limited, since only delicate and important subjects are considered at the Commission's weekly meeting.
- All decisions of the Commission are reached collectively. The influence of the Commission on the shaping of events was amplified with the expiry of the transition period (end of 1969) set in the Treaty of Rome. Since events after that date were not regulated by the treaty, the Commission was given greater opportunity to direct the life and affairs of the EU after that date.

The Commission has 17 directorates-general (DGs) for various policies and six for external relations. In addition there are general and internal services. The European Commission's staff numbers some 19 000 officials.[102] The Commission is located in Brussels, but some of its departments operate in Luxembourg.

The tasks and authority of the European Commission are often misunderstood, questioned and criticised. This is because the Commission is initiator of laws and policies, investigator, prosecutor, judge, jury and executioner all at the same time. The 'normal' democratic principle of separation of power (legislation–execution) does not exist in any palpable way within the appointed European Commission. This contributed to the deplorable administration and corruption that led to the resignation of the Commission in 1999.

Many people question the wisdom of surrendering additional sovereign rights to such a supranational administration. The community method in the decision-making process in which the European Commission leads in EU affairs is being silently, but forcefully, replaced by an intergovernmental method. Since the Treaty of Maastricht (1992) the European Commission has lost much of its authority. The EU relied largely on the European Council to provide guidance and to settle problems, and the principal moving force became the agreement among EU member governments. Following this type of intergovernmental accord, the Commission has less influence. In any case, the Commission no longer has personalities and leaders of the calibre of Walter Hallstein (1958–67) and Jacques Delors (1985–95).

The resignation of the European Commission of Jacques Santer in March 1999 exemplifies the sense of responsibility of the members of the executive branch. Following this resignation, the EU functioned without the European Commission for eight months – an absence that was barely noticed by European citizens. In order to restore its credibility the Commission, as well as politicians, should explain its functions more thoroughly to EU citizens to convince them of the need for this institution.

COUNCIL OF MINISTERS

While the European Commission is a common institution of the EU, the Council of Ministers is an intergovernmental body. The dialogue between the Council of Ministers and the European Commission was supposed to be the moving spirit of the EU. Since the appointment of both bodies, they have been criticised on the grounds that there was a lack of accountability. The usual or classical separation of powers was not respected with the EU institutions. This often reappears in discussions as the existence of the 'democratic deficit' (Stephanou, 1997, p. 108). The European Parliament is the only directly elected institution of the EU. Under the terms of the Maastricht Treaty, the Parliament was granted co-decision powers with the Council of Ministers, thus introducing a certain amount of democratic control into the EU's affairs. All the Union's institutions fall under the legal control of the Court of Justice.

The Council of Ministers, together with the European Council, are the only bodies of the EU with directly delegated representatives of the governments of all member countries. The composition of the Council of Ministers varies. It does not have a fixed membership like the European Commission. It can include various ministers, but only one from each country with the right to vote. When the Council of Ministers considers farming issues, it is composed of the national ministers of agriculture; when transport issues are at stake, the national ministers of transport are present and so on. Since various councils tend to reach decisions that can be quite costly, the representatives from the national ministries of finance are often present. None the less, the Council of Foreign Ministers is somehow supposed to be the most senior Council of the EU. The presidency of the Council of Ministers rotates in alphabetical order every six months, and the Council's headquarters is in Brussels.

The Council of Ministers is the Union's legislative body. It acts only on the basis of a proposal from the European Commission. If there is no such proposal, the Council and, hence, the EU is stymied. The Commission drafts a proposal which may be amended as a result of comments from Parliament. The amended proposal is then passed on to the Council of Ministers, and the dialogue between the Council and the Commission begins. The Council upholds national interests, while the Commission stands for those of the Union. During the dialogue they try to find joint solutions to problems. If the Council wants to alter a proposal, its members have to act unanimously. In other cases, only the Commission has the right to amend its proposal. The Council of Ministers may adopt the proposal as it stands; modify the proposal and accept it unanimously; or fail to reach a decision. This kind of decision making has often been criticised. The Council has been accused of 'lavish legislation' (*acquis communautaire*) behind closed doors as if it were a Politburo in a communist country and that is not accountable to anybody, hence the 'democratic deficit'.

The primary sources of EU law are the treaties of Paris, Rome, Maastricht, Amsterdam and Nice, the Merger Treaty and the Single European Act, as well as all the treaties that led to the various enlargements of the EU. The secondary sources of law are created by the Council of Ministers, the European Parliament and the European Commission. After consultations with the European Parliament, the Economic and Social Committee and the Committee of the Regions (on regional matters), the European Commission submits a proposal to the Council of Ministers which co-decides with the European Parliament. This co-decision element was introduced by the Single European Act and extended by the Maastricht Treaty. The objective is to eliminate the 'democratic deficit' in the Council of Ministers. In this co-decision process the Council and the Parliament deliver the following four types of legal acts (Article 249 of the Treaty of Rome):

- *Regulations* are compulsory and general in their application. They are to be directly implemented in all of the member countries. They overrule the national law if it existed.

- *Directives* are compulsory regarding the final outcome, but the member countries have the freedom to select how they are implemented.
- *Decisions* are binding for the subjects (governments, associations, enterprises, individuals and so on) that they refer to.
- The implementation of *Recommendations* and *Opinions* is not compulsory.

Decisions in the Council of Ministers are taken by unanimous, simple or qualified majority vote. If majority vote is permitted, then the decision binds all the countries, even those that voted against the proposal in question. While the Council usually tries to take into account the interests of all member countries, find a compromise and act unanimously, since the Single European Act (1987) and the subsequent treaties, majority rule has been introduced for an increasing number of issues. Majority rule in some cases may act as a buffer against obstruction and in certain cases can facilitate and hasten a unanimous decision. Although the (qualified) majority vote has potential risks, it introduced a certain degree of flexibility in the decision-making procedure, as well as the willingness to compromise. Under the Luxembourg Agreement (1966), a unanimous vote was required each time a member country declared that an issue was in its vital interest, but it was not necessary to define that interest. The Single European Act and subsequent treaties reintroduced the majority vote procedure for a number of issues, mainly dealing with the creation of a Single European Market. However, the resolution of the Maastricht Treaty to create 'an ever closer union' (Preamble) may not be achieved in a satisfactory way if the vital interests of one or more nations in the EU are damaged.

The Committee of Permanent Representatives (Coreper)[103] assists the Council of Ministers in its work. Coreper is composed of the ambassadors of the EU member countries. It is included in all phases of decision preparation and making. If possible, Coreper makes the decisions and the Council of Ministers simply endorses them. In fact, most decisions (80–90 per cent) are agreed on below the Coreper level in various working groups. However, crucial decisions are settled by national ministers.

Unanimous decisions by the Council of Ministers are still required in the following areas:[104]

- taxation;
- common foreign and security policy;
- police and judicial cooperation in criminal matters;
- asylum and immigration policy; and
- economic and social cohesion policy.

When qualified majority rule is permitted in the Council of Ministers, then the four large countries, Britain, France, Germany and Italy, have ten votes each. Spain has eight, while the smaller countries, Belgium, Greece, the Netherlands and Portugal, have five each. Austria and Sweden have four votes each. Others, Denmark, Finland and Ireland, have three votes each, while Luxembourg has two. The total is 87 votes, and the qualified majority is 62. This means that the four largest countries, plus Spain, need to consider the interests of at least two or more small countries (Table 1A.1). The principle is that the qualified majority takes into account the interests of about 70 per cent of the EU's population. The blocking minority is 25 votes (two large and one or two small countries, with the exception of Luxembourg; for instance the olive oil-producing countries: Spain, Italy, Greece and Portugal). The meetings of the Council of Ministers are relatively frequent and often long; they are not pure formalities as similar meetings in various international organisations often are; and they involve hard negotiations and horse-trading.

France fought tooth and nail in Nice to maintain parity with Germany within this 'management board'. However, in order to keep this formal parity, France was 'forced' to consent to the introduction of a demographical standard into the definition of the blocking minority. Germany gained power, because since the blocking majority is based on population size, this gives Germany an obvious edge.

The Treaty of Nice is popularly portrayed as an act that allowed the new EU enlargement. However, the EU(15) member countries first preserved their influence in the new voting structure. The EU voting allotments and procedures changed as a result of the Treaty of Nice and the enlargement (Table 1A.1). As is often the case, the devil is in the detail. The new voting arrangement was 'hidden' in Declaration 20 on the enlargement of the EU, annexed to the Final Act. There is now a triple test in the voting structure:

- Smaller states (apart from Poland, Central and East European countries are small) have proportionally more voting power than larger countries. The post-enlargement Poland-led eastern bloc of ten countries would have the largest voting weight.
- If a new policy is to be adopted, then it must have the support of a majority of member states. The ten new countries would need only three votes from any of the EU(15) to push through new policies.
- The final requirement is the 'killer': new policies must have the support of states that represent 62 per cent of the EU's expanded population of 452 million.[105] The ten new countries combined have only 16 per cent. Hence, while the Central and East European countries can certainly play a major part in setting or blocking the policy

Table 1A.1 Voting weights in the Council of Ministers after the eastern enlargement

Country	Council of Ministers votes		Population in 2002 (m)
	Until May 2004	From May 2004	
Germany	10	29	82.4
Britain	10	29	58.7
France	10	29	58.5
Italy	10	29	57.8
Spain	8	27	41.1
Netherlands	5	13	16.1
Greece	5	12	11.0
Belgium	5	12	10.3
Portugal	5	12	10.3
Sweden	4	10	8.9
Austria	4	10	8.3
Denmark	3	7	5.4
Finland	3	7	5.2
Ireland	3	7	3.9
Luxembourg	2	4	0.4
New member countries			
Poland	8	27	38.2
Czech Republic	5	12	10.2
Hungary	5	12	10.2
Slovakia	3	7	5.4
Lithuania	3	7	3.5
Latvia	3	4	2.3
Slovenia	3	4	2.0
Estonia	3	4	1.4
Cyprus	2	4	0.7
Malta	2	3	0.4
Total EU(25)	124	321	452.6
Romania	6	14	21.9
Bulgaria	4	10	7.9
Total EU(27)	134	345	482.4

Source: Eurostat (2004).

agenda, they cannot necessarily force anything through – and nor can anyone else.

This all puts the EU on track for a train wreck as far as quick action is concerned. No bloc, indeed no two blocs, would be able to force through any policy, but almost any single bloc would have the ability to veto any policy. And there is no shortage of topics that would face harsh clashes of interest. Hence, one may predict that the basic policy structure of the EU (*acquis communautaire*) would remain as it is for quite some time to come.

EUROPEAN PARLIAMENT

The European Parliament is the only EU institution that is directly elected. In spite of this, it is puzzling that for more than a quarter of a century, it had only a consultative role, the right to dismiss the European Commission and to accept or reject the Union's budget (which it did a few times). Although the opinions of the Parliament could be legally disregarded, in most cases both the European Commission and the Council of Ministers respected its views. It often takes a long time for a parliament to gain importance in the governing process, but the wait usually proves fruitful in the long term. This was the case with the European Parliament.

The expansion-of-authority process of the European Parliament started with the Single European Act. It was reinforced in the Treaty of Amsterdam and the Maastricht Treaty (Articles 251 and 252 of the Treaty of Rome). The Parliament was given the right to co-decide with the Council of Ministers on matters relating to the conduct of the internal market, mobility of labour and capital, trans-European infrastructure networks, consumer protection, research, environment, health, cultural matters, and the like.[106] The decision-making scheme of the EU is shown in Figure 1A.1.

If an act is to be adopted it has to be initiated by the European Commission, which has to send its proposal to the Parliament for the first reading. After the European Parliament has reported back to the Council of Ministers, the Council then has to adopt a common position that is relayed to the Parliament for a second reading. Regarding the common position, the Parliament may:

- approve it,
- not take a decision,
- propose amendments or
- reject it.

If the Parliament approves the common position, then the act is adopted. The 'double signature' symbolises the co-decision process between the Parliament and the Council of Ministers. This is supposed to provide some democratic supervision. If it fails to take a decision, the Council is allowed to accept the act. In the case when the Parliament proposes amendments to the common position, the Council may accept them within three months. If the Council fails to do that, it may, together with the Parliament, convene a meeting of the Conciliation Committee (composed of an equal number of

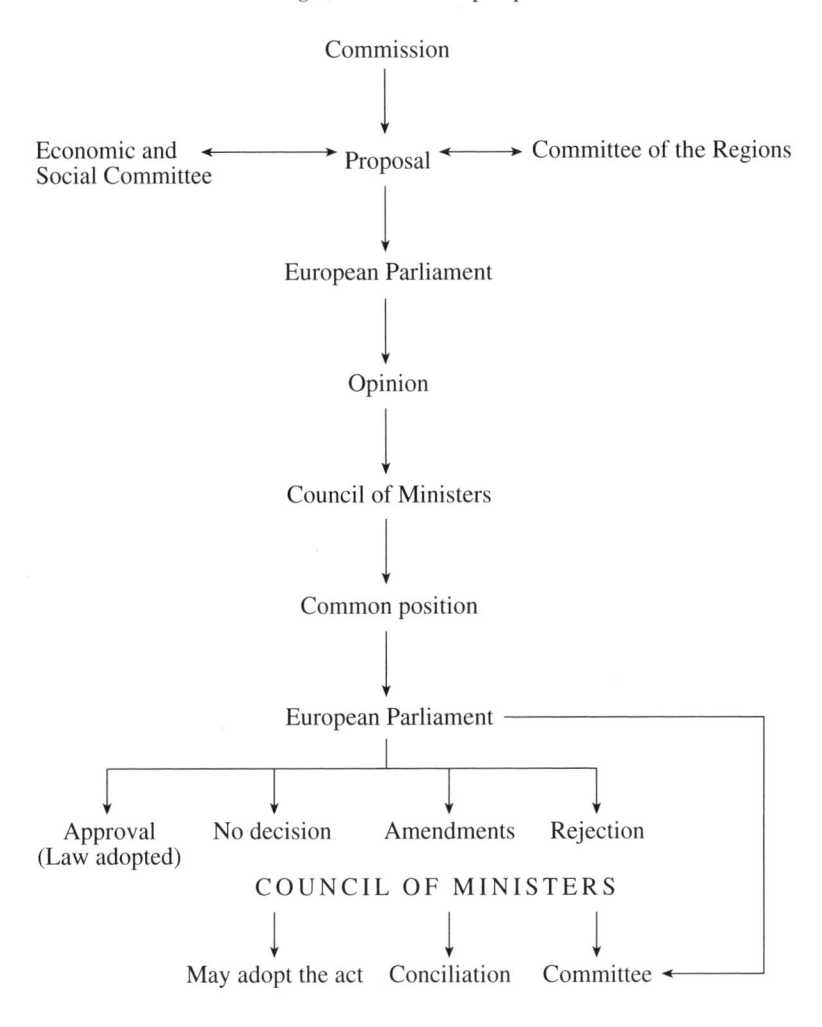

```
                           Commission
                               │
                               ▼
Economic and    ──────▶    Proposal    ◀──────  Committee of the Regions
Social Committee
                               │
                               ▼
                       European Parliament
                               │
                               ▼
                            Opinion
                               │
                               ▼
                       Council of Ministers
                               │
                               ▼
                        Common position
                               │
                               ▼
                       European Parliament ──────────────────┐
                               │                              │
        ┌──────────────┬───────┴───────┬──────────────┐      │
        ▼              ▼               ▼              ▼      │
    Approval       No decision     Amendments     Rejection  │
  (Law adopted)                                              │
                       COUNCIL OF MINISTERS                  │
                               │                              │
                ┌──────────────┼──────────────┐              │
                ▼              ▼              ▼              │
        May adopt the act  Conciliation   Committee ◀────────┘
```

1. Parliament and the Council have six weeks to agree on the common text, failing that, the act is not acepted.

2. After the failure of the conciliation procedure, the Council may adopt its first common position within six weeks, but the Parliament may overrule that within six weeks by an absolute majority vote.

Figure 1A.1   The decision-making process in the European Union

representatives of the Council and the Parliament) with the task of reaching an agreement on a common text. The same procedure is also possible in the case when the common position is rejected by the Parliament. The conciliation process is supported by the European Commission, which helps both the Council and the Parliament to modify their positions. Both the Parliament and the Council have six weeks to approve the common text of the act in question. If one of the two bodies fails to do that or if there is no agreement on the common text, the proposed act is not adopted. However, there is one more provision that is heavily contested by the Parliament. After the failure of the conciliation procedure, the Council of Ministers may within six weeks confirm its previous common position (which may include some of the Parliament's amendments) and adopt the act. The Parliament can still overrule the Council's decision by an absolute majority of its members if it acts within six weeks after the Council's decision. In practice, however, this may not be possible because of absenteeism. The amendments of the Parliament require a majority vote of the entire Parliament (not just those that are present and voting). Often barely more than half of the members of the Parliament bother to attend the meetings, so many amendments fail.

The new powers of the Parliament may alter the agenda of its sessions. Over the years, the Parliament has dissipated its time and energy on issues that it does not control: the killing of kangaroos in Australia; animal welfare; globalisation; violence in the West Bank; vote rigging in Zimbabwe; human rights in Chile, Salvador, Sudan, and so on.[107] None the less, the new co-decision, cooperation and the dialogue between the Parliament and the Council of Ministers may steadily develop into a new and important feature of the Union's set-up.

Following the eastern enlargement, 453 million EU(25) citizens are represented by 732 members in the European Parliament. Each member country has a quota in the Parliament that depends on the size of the population. Germany, as the most populous country, has 99 representatives; France, Italy and Britain have 72 each; Spain 50 and so on.

The European Parliament was directly elected for the first time in June 1979. Before that, it was composed of the members of the national parliaments. The members of the European Parliament do not sit in national groups, but rather according to their political orientation. The European People's Party and European Democrats (268 members) and the Socialists (200 members) are the largest political groups during the 2000–2004 term.[108] No matter how one looks at the distribution of the seats, neither the centre-right nor the socialists can dominate. However, unlike in national parliaments, there is neither majority, nor opposition. There is no ruling government and opposition that face each other in the European Parliament. This Parliament is supposed to solve problems, rather than help a political party survive in office. It is in effect a forum, not a true parliament. In a complex EU politics and law-making procedure, no drama captures the headlines as is the case in national parliaments, which is why the general public have a poor understanding of the Parliament's role, significance, operation, powers and influence.

The Parliament has 17 committees that prepare the work of the plenary sessions. It sits in Strasbourg, but for historical reasons there are two other working venues: the secretariat is in Luxembourg, while various committees meet in Brussels.

EUROPEAN COUNCIL

As European integration becomes deeper and wider, as well as more and more political in all its aspects, the European Council is invoked to operate at the highest political level. The European Council is a kind of glorified version of the Council of Ministers. Although there is a continuous problem that big countries dominate in this EU body, the former's advantage is that it arrives at major political decisions that concern the EU. If they need to be enshrined in Union law, these decisions are passed on to other EU institutions in order to proceed with the usual law-making agenda which provides directions for the future.

Although the European Council has been in operation since the early 1970s and was *de facto* the supreme body of the EU, it was introduced *de jure* into the Union's structure in the Single European Act (1987). The Council is made up of heads of government (head of state in the case of France) and the president of the European Commission. Its work is assisted by the foreign ministers. The role of the European Council was reinforced by the Maastricht Treaty (Article D). Its function is to provide the EU with the necessary impetus for development, and to lay down general political guidelines for the future. The meetings of the Council are free of any formalities and take place at least twice a year (in practice it meets three to four times or whenever necessary).

Matters discussed include not only EU business, but also intergovernmental issues. The country holding the Union's rotating (in alphabetical order) presidency has a ceremonial, but no real power; it is the first among equals for only six months. However, it can set the agenda by choosing what the Council discusses. The six-month rotating presidency is too short to create either consistency or continuity in EU visions and policies. It is not open to wider public understanding and appreciation of what the EU is about. Hence, the future institutional structure of the EU may address this issue.

COURT OF JUSTICE

The structure of the European Union is complex indeed. To implement the Union's law (*acquis communautaire*) may sometimes be difficult and costly in political and financial terms. Therefore, the Court of Justice has to intervene whenever the implementation of the primary or secondary law of the EU comes into question.[109] The Court is supposed to provide interpretations of the Union's law and, when asked, may give its opinion about an issue. When delivered, that opinion becomes binding.

The Court has one judge per member state and eight advocates-general appointed according to the agreement of the member countries for six years. They sit in Luxembourg. Since everyone affected by EU legislation has the right to file charges to the Court, the task of the advocates-general is to conduct a preliminary investigation of the case and give their non-binding, but highly respected (although not always accepted)[110] opinion to the judges. Court hearings are public, but the discussions about the judgments and the majority vote system for making judgments is always closed to the public. Outside the chamber for deliberation, there is no dissenting minority among the judges. They are unanimous in their views. Judgments in a particular case are signed by all participating judges in order to avoid possible trouble for them after the expiry of their term of office.

For the execution of its decisions, the Court relies on the administration of the member countries on which the ruling applies. In order to make sure that its decisions are implemented, the Court has the capacity to impose serious fines on member states that do not carry out their obligations. The matters that appear most often in the Court relate to agriculture, competition, the internal market and social issues. The Court of Justice represents the highest legal authority in the EU. There are no appeals against its judgments. A judge can be dismissed from the Court only by the unanimous vote of his or her colleagues.

The Court of Justice is assisted in its work by the Court of First Instance, which has one judge per member state. This court deals mainly with cases brought by individuals. This new court was introduced in the Union's structure under the Single European Act and started operation in 1989. Its job is to speed up the judicial process by relieving the workload of the Court of Justice. The Maastricht Treaty reinforced its role. Its jurisdiction covers competition issues, charges by individuals and firms (but not states) against EU institutions and disputes between the EU and its staff. Appeals against judgments of the Court of First Instance may be filed in the Court of Justice.

COURT OF AUDITORS

The ever-expanding resources that the EU disposes of (its budget for 2003 was €100 billion) demand an accurate auditing of those resources. The EEC and Euratom, on the one hand, and the ECSC, on the other, had separate auditing boards. Both of them were merged by a treaty into the Court of Auditors in 1975. The new Court started its operation two years later in Luxembourg. In order to ensure sound financial management, this Court monitors the EU accounts and examines the legality and regularity of the revenue and expenditure. According to the Treaty of Nice, the Court has one national from each EU member state, appointed for a renewable period of six years. This Court scrutinises the inflow and outflow of resources in all bodies of the EU, as well as the Union's budget. At the end of each fiscal year, the Court of Auditors publishes its annual report. The statements of that report provide influential guidelines for the collection of revenue and for expenditure from the Union's funds.

EUROPEAN CENTRAL BANK

The European Monetary Institute was established in 1994 in Frankfurt. It started to prepare the ground for the single currency, the euro, which was introduced in 1999. In the same year the EMI was transformed into an independent European Central Bank, which is in charge of the monetary policy of member countries that participate in the eurozone.

The key task of the ECB is straightforward: price stability (Article 105 of the Treaty of Rome). The ECB is independent of political intrusion and it may not bail out prodigal governments. Monetary union eliminated risks and costs that are built-in currency fluctuations. The single currency brings transparency and downward convergence in prices through the countries that use it. This would facilitate, improve and stimulate trade, investment and integration throughout the EU.

OTHER INSTITUTIONS

Economic and Social Committee

The Economic and Social Committee is only a consultative body in the EU's structure. It is located in Brussels and has 222 members, between six and 24 nationals per member state (depending on the size of the country).

The number of members may not exceed 350 following enlargement. It is composed of representatives of the various components of organised civil society: employers, employees and various interest groups (agriculture, consumers, environment, transport and others). They are appointed for a four-year term in their private capacity by the Council of Ministers. Opinions of the committee provide a blend of views of various groups that may be affected by the decisions of the EU. As such, they provide a helpful input to the European Commission and the Council of Ministers during the preparation of the Union's laws. Apart from its consultative role, the committee has not yet found or established any other place in the structure of the EU.

Committee of the Regions

Local authorities in a number of EU countries are exerting or gaining increasing influence in the countries' legislative process. The Maastricht Treaty reacted to these developments by creating the Committee of the Regions. This committee gives an opportunity to the regional authorities of the member countries to be involved in the Union's legal matters. It has to be consulted on proposals that have a bearing on the regions. The number of members is limited to 350. It is located in Brussels and still needs to earn a certain respect and status in the Union's structure. Since the regional authorities have gained influence in the governing structure of the member countries, they also have a chance to wield a certain influence in the future or in the EU.

European Investment Bank

The European Investment Bank (EIB) raises funds on the capital markets to finance investment projects which contribute to the development of the EU. The EIB is allowed to grant loans to third countries if the projects are of relevance to the EU. These projects include roads, ports or railways, or its loans may be seen as a part of development aid. It was established in 1958 and operates from Luxembourg. It is a non-profit-making lender that granted loans totalling €172 billion over the five-year period, 1998–2003.

CONCLUSION

From the long-term standpoint, the Union's system has demonstrated its viability and endurance. Figure 1A.2 presents the organisational scheme of the Union's institutions. The EU is a fully recognised international organisation since most of the countries in the world have diplomatic relations

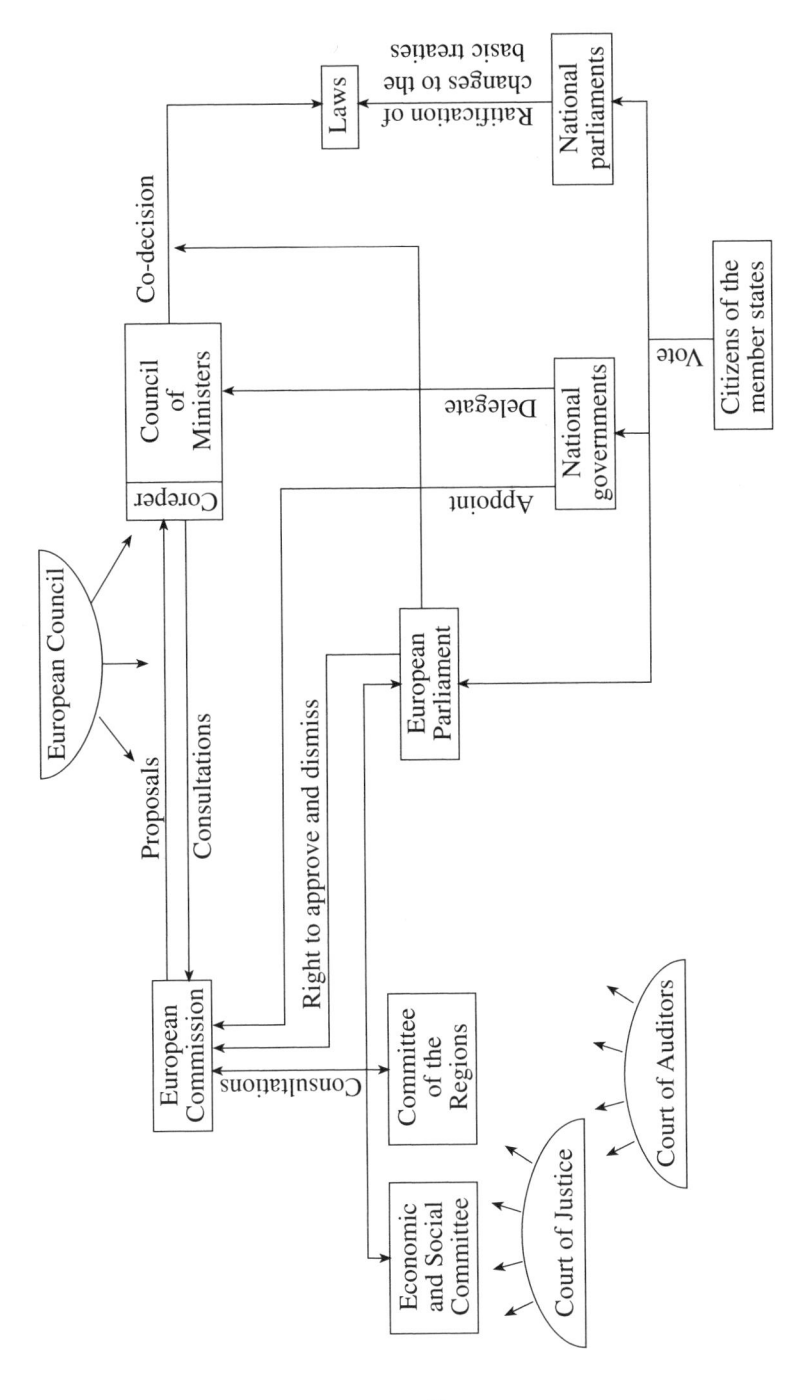

Figure 1A.2 Operation of the institutions of the European Union

with it. An increasing number of countries aim to join the EU. The Union takes part in the annual summits of the most important developed market economies (G-8). As the Union's business and membership expand, additional powers are given to already existing bodies, and new ones are being created. These additional powers were most evident in the case of the European Parliament.

The powers within the EU institutions have shifted over time. Because of the decline in the community method of decision making in favour of the intergovernmental method, the European Commission has lost its central role. The rise in importance of the European Council since 1972 and in particular since 1992, as well as of the Council of Ministers since the Treaty of Nice, is offset by an increase in importance of the European Parliament. It remains for the Parliament to demonstrate, in practice, that it can meet the challenges assigned to it in the EU structure. None the less, the operation of the EU following enlargement needs to provide evidence that the enlarged EU is 'manageable'.

The evolving and changing EU institutions are located at the following sites:

- European Commission: Brussels (certain departments such as Eurostat in Luxembourg)
- European Parliament: Strasbourg and Brussels
- European Court of Justice: Luxembourg
- European Food Safety Authority: Brussels
- European Maritime Safety Agency: Brussels
- European Aviation Safety Agency: Brussels
- European Court of Auditors: Luxembourg
- European Investment Bank: Luxembourg
- Translation Centre for the Bodies of the European Union: Luxembourg
- European Agency for Reconstruction: Thessaloniki
- European Centre for the Development of Vocational Training: Thessaloniki
- European Central Bank: Frankfurt
- European Environment Agency: Copenhagen
- European Agency for the Evaluation of Medicinal Products: London
- European Police Office (Europol): The Hague
- European Monitoring Centre for Drugs and Drug Addiction: Lisbon
- Agency for Health and Safety at Work: Bilbao
- Office for Harmonisation in the Internal Market (Trade Marks and Designs): Alicante

- Community Plant Variety Office: Angers (France)
- European Training Foundation: Turin
- European Foundation for the Improvement of Living and Working Conditions: Dublin
- European Monitoring Centre on Racism and Xenophobia: Vienna

Notes

1. The Roman Empire (1st century BC to the 5th century AD) fulfilled many goals regarding integration of the European continent, although it covered parts of northern Africa and the Middle East too. There was a common currency, free trade, common defence, foreign policy and legal system, as well as certain autonomy of the regions. After the decline of the Roman Empire, Charlemagne (742–814) was able to create and maintain a partial integration of Europe at the beginning of the 9th century. In post-classical history, Napoleon succeeded, through military conquest, in integrating a large part of Europe during the 1809–12 period. During the 20th century, Hitler tried to do the same during 1939–45.
2. The interested reader is invited to consult Sidjanski (2000 and 2001) for a penetrating political analysis of the origin and possible future of European integration.
3. A. Evans-Pritchard, 'Euro-federalists financed by US spy chiefs', *Daily Telegraph*, 19 September 2000.
4. Austria, Belgium, Britain, Denmark, France, Greece, the Netherlands, Ireland, Iceland, Italy, Luxembourg, Norway, Portugal, Sweden, Switzerland and Turkey.
5. Sweden was another country, but its supply capacities were limited.
6. The original five member countries were joined by West Germany and Italy in 1954, as well as Spain and Portugal in 1988.
7. An armed attack is a wider notion than a war, since a (classical) war has its established rules.
8. This presence continued and is alive and well even after the demise of the communist bloc and the withdrawal of the Soviet forces in 1990.
9. However, NATO does not have a clear-cut answer to the problem of armed conflict between its members. For example, Turkey often claims sovereignty over certain Greek islands (for example, Imia and Gavdos). These unfounded expansionist claims have been on the verge of provoking armed conflict several times. Tensions have been defused (temporarily?) only after excessive pressure from the US on the two countries.
10. Greece (location) and Turkey (location and the contribution in manpower) entered NATO in 1951; West Germany joined in 1954 (the unified Germany joined in 1990), Spain in 1982, while the Czech Republic, Hungary and Poland did so in 1999. Bulgaria, Estonia, Latvia, Lithuania, Romania, Slovakia and Slovenia joined in 2004. (Weapons manufacturers expect to make billions of dollars and euros in new arms sales to these countries as they are obliged to follow and keep NATO standards.)
11. Strasbourg is in the heart of Europe. Since 1648 this city has changed hands five times between the French and the Germans and is marked by the culture of both nations.
12. The Franco-Prussian war (1870–71) and the two world wars.
13. The low-profile, sectoral approach to integration in the areas of coal and steel was relatively easy to negotiate. There were a limited number of production facilities, they were relatively large, and there was a high degree of cartelisation of business. Control over this production can be exercised in an easier and more effective way than in other production fields with many competitors and an easy entry and exit from business. In any case, the sectoral approach was a good training ground for the pan-economic integration that came in the following years.

14. This expression entered discussions about international relations, never to leave it.
15. The Treaty of Paris expired in 2002. According to a protocol to the Treaty of Nice (2002) all ECSC assets and liabilities were transferred to the European Community.
16. The territorial controversies between France and West Germany were finally settled in 1957 when France returned Saarland. Since 1945 that part of Germany had been in the French occupation zone. It was economically attached to France, from 1948 until its handover.
17. The experience of Germany in the creation of a political union may be instructive here. The German customs union (*Zollverein*), led by Prussia, was set up in 1834. It was only after the war with France, in 1871, that political union came about.
18. The Belgian, Dutch and Luxembourg governments signed a convention on the creation of a customs union in 1944. It was implemented in 1948.
19. All references to the articles in the Treaty of Rome relate to the consolidated version of the Treaty Establishing the European Community as published in the *Official Journal of the European Communities* C 325/33 of 24 December 2002, unless otherwise stated. This version of the treaty includes changes that were brought to the original Treaty of Rome by subsequent treaties.
20. Apart from Britain there were Denmark and Norway, as well as the neutral countries: Austria, Sweden and Switzerland. Portugal joined the group a little later, but took part in the establishment of the organisation. Iceland joined in 1970. Finland became an associate member in 1961, and entered the group in 1986 as a full member.
21. De Gaulle grasped well the power and influence of mass media.
22. It took 'students' more than a month to attract workers to join.
23. De Gaulle took tentative steps towards allowing self-determination for Algeria in 1959. Certain French army generals argued that 'Algeria must stay French!'. They created the Secret Army Organisation (*Organisation de l'Armée Secrète* – OAS), which was opposed to Algerian independence. The OAS used violent methods to promote its cause; it carried out numerous killings of civilians in Algeria and in France, including attempts to assassinate de Gaulle.
24. Other reforms referred to the economic and political system. One of these included the system of workers' 'participation' in the running of companies and distribution of profits. This was expected to be an alternative to the system of liberal capitalism. De Gaulle's economic advisers were inspired by the Roman Catholic social principles presented in the *Rerum Novarum* (1891), the encyclical of Pope Leo XIII on capital and labour, which argued in favour of reconciliation, rather than Marxist-type conflict between social classes.
25. The small countries, members of EFTA, had an interest in staying out of the EC since they did not have to accept the CET of the Community which was at a higher level than their own tariffs on external trade, and they did not take part in the CAP, which in some cases (for example, Switzerland or Finland) offered smaller subsidies to the farm sector than was the case in the EFTA countries. In addition, the costs of staying outside the EC would have meant sacrificing the chance to influence the economic policies of the new generation in the EC. However, this view is based on an assumption that small countries are, in reality, asked for their opinion and, more importantly and optimistically, that the opinion is (highly) valued. We shall see later whether this is, in fact, the case.
26. The European Council should not be confused with the Council of Europe (the European 'talking-shop' in Strasbourg).
27. The reason for this enlargement and the entry of a relatively poor country relative to the rest of the group was political. The EC wanted to consolidate democracy in Greece following the military rule and to expand and to show that there were an increasing number of countries that shared its values.
28. Lord Arthur Cockfield was the commissioner who was the author of many legal acts that brought about the Single Market Programme. Dissatisfied with such initiatives, the government of Margaret Thatcher did not reappoint him for another term in 1989.
29. The European Parliament estimated *annual* losses for the EC coming from the NTBs (internal costs). From an incomplete EC internal market, the losses were €12 billion from

frontier formalities, €40 billion from diverse national standards and technical regulations, €40 billion from discriminatory practices (domestic-firms' preference) during public procurement and, in addition to all that, €10 billion because of high production costs (meagre economies of scale) arising from the limited size of national markets (*European File*, No. 17, 1987).

30. Authorisations based on Article 115 of the original Treaty of Rome came to an end in 1993.
31. In a monetary union where the money supply is jointly and centrally controlled, a country in economic difficulties is not able to devalue its currency or to 'inflate' its way out of economic trouble. Therefore, smooth political cooperation in the group is a necessary condition for its existence and survival.
32. The relatively slow progress in the federalisation of Western Europe is different from the history of the US. In the *initial* days of the US, it was the young member states that transferred foreign, defence and tax policies to Washington, DC. These are federal rights that the EC states have been very slow to cede to a central authority.
33. The desire to have political and economic stability and environmental security on Germany's eastern border, as well as a discouragement of migration, plays a role in the German policy towards the new 'democracies' in the East.
34. During the final negotiations in Maastricht, and the horse-trading phase, Germany offered to support the British opt-out from the single currency arrangement, but in return requested and got British backing for the instant and *unconditional* recognition of the independence of Germany's Nazi-period ally, Croatia. (Germany does not forget its former loyal allies!)
35. The British argument against the inclusion of the social issues in the deal was that it would make the EU producers uncompetitive.
36. There would be, in fact, the European System of Central Banks. It would be composed of the ECB and the central banks of the member states.
37. The five necessary criteria that a country needs to fulfil are: (1) a high degree of price stability (inflation within the margin of 1.5 per cent of the three best-performing EU countries); (2) a sound public financial position (budget deficit of less than 3 per cent of GDP); (3) a national debt of less than 60 per cent of GDP; (4) the observance of the 'normal' fluctuation margins (no devaluation within the EU's exchange rate mechanism for at least two past years); and (5) the durability of convergence of economic policies, which needs to be reflected in long-term interest rate levels (interest rate needs to be within the 2 per cent margin of the three best-performing EU countries).
38. The WEU is beset by several crucial problems. Unlike NATO, the WEU does not have an integrated military command; it does not have as efficient a command, control and communication system as NATO has; and the WEU has no airlift for moving troops and hardware to match that of the Americans. To create an entirely European system would cost money which the taxpayers in the EU would not want to pay.
39. The Swiss voted against it in a referendum in 1992.
40. The neutrality of most of the EFTA countries was seen to be an obstacle to those countries joining the EU. None the less, the concept became quite flexible (except in Switzerland) after the dissolution of the East European bloc.
41. The Slav Macedonia, a communist invention mainly of the 1940s, has *never* existed before, either as a state or as a religious entity; the very existence of the nation is highly controversial. Those who are interested in this issue are invited to consult Message No. 868.014 of 26 December 1944 by the US Secretary of State.
42. The European Commission took Greece to the EU Court of Justice in order to exert additional pressure on that country to lift its embargo on FYR Macedonia. The Court, however, refused the Commission's request for an interim emergency ruling that would force Greece to lift its embargo in June 1994. This was a serious blow to the Commission as it was not able to convince the Court that the sanctions caused damage to the EU. Tensions between Athens and Skopje were defused, at least for the time being, by a deal in September 1995. Greece lifted its embargo in return for a change of flag and an alteration in FYR Macedonia's constitution.

43. The unresolved question is what is a European state? Is it a state that is a member of the UN Economic Commission for Europe (including, among others, the US, Canada, Turkmenistan and Uzbekistan)? Does religion matter?
44. Similar references may also be found in the Treaty of Maastricht in Articles J.4§5 and K.7, respectively.
45. The comment by the Italian statesman Massimo Taparelli Marchese d'Azeglio (1798–1866): 'We have made Italy, now we must make Italians', does not readily apply to international arrangements that integrate countries. Even in contemporary Italy there are still strong regional feelings, not to mention the divide between the *terroni* (those that live or come from the south) and the *polentoni* (those from the prosperous north). An old saying says that there is little to hold Italy together – except perhaps the national soccer team. Most Italians continue to identify themselves first and foremost with their home town.
46. The *acquis communautaire* is a clear demand for harmonisation. The Treaty of Westphalia (1648) ended the Thirty Years' War. The treaty established the principle that the states are free to do whatever they like within their own borders (for example, choice of religion). Only those measures that have external implications concern foreigners. This principle gained definitive form and was enshrined with the creation of the UN in 1945. However, this principle was strongly undermined when NATO attacked Yugoslavia in 1999, an attack that was not authorised by the UN. No similar attacks were undertaken against Turkey (Kurds, Cyprus), China (Tibet) or Russia (Chechnya) or certain parts of the Middle East. The UN was also bypassed by the American-led coalition which attacked Iraq in 2003.
47. European Council, Lisbon 2000, Presidency Conclusions, §5.
48. Issues such as the size of the European Commission, balance of power, voting weights and the qualified majority in the Council of Ministers were 'leftovers' because it was impossible to solve them in Amsterdam.
49. Bulgaria and Romania are not included. Even if they were, this would not alter the general picture.
50. One-size-fits-all policies in Europe may become increasingly inappropriate in a highly diversified EU. This may wreck individuality. The Irish and Danish demonstrated that clearly when given a referendum on important EU matters.
51. Imagine how simple it would be for almost 30 councillors to decide where to go, for example, for dinner. And then, imagine the ease with which they may decide about monetary or any other policy.
52. European Commission (1997a), p. 54.
53. Terrorists do not necessarily need to be desperate individuals from slums. As the 11 September 2001 attack on the World Trade Center in New York exemplified, terrorists are numerous and widespread, highly educated, from well-to-do families, prepared, organised and coordinated over a long period of time.
54. Nationalism is understood here in the sense of positive patriotism, rather than in the harmful and negative sense of chauvinism. Unfortunately, the political left has been quite successful over the past century in altering and misrepresenting the positive meaning of the term 'nationalism', which to many may have acquired the negative and politically unacceptable meaning of chauvinism.
55. Fortyn was assassinated shortly after his election success.
56. A less paralysing procedure in the future may include a provision that a treaty is accepted after it is ratified by two-thirds of the member states.
57. Britain perceives itself to be part of a wider 'Atlantic Community'.
58. Examples include German unification (1990) when France had concerns about the might of a neighbour with 82 million inhabitants; French frustration at Germany's rushed recognition of Croatia in 1991; the French row regarding the German-inspired Stability Pact for the single currency; German objections to the French nuclear tests in the Pacific in 1995; German hostility to the French president of the European Central Bank; German worries about the French hesitations concerning the eastern enlargement; current concerns are about relations with the US and the like.

59. 'Everyone and everything in France sees the state as a nurturing and bountiful mother who will forgive their failings. As Alexis de Tocqueville once feared, it saves them the trouble of thinking for themselves, and from the burden of making their own way in life' (*Financial Times*, 12 April 2002, p. 15).
60. In spite of Poland's staunch support for the US in the Iraq war and the fact that it is very low on the list of countries likely to pose any terrorist threat, Poland and the US had a row in 2004. The US demanded that Polish citizens should obtain travel visas.
61. The need for Germany to obtain funds to finance the reintegration of its eastern part increased interest rates. Germany placed its national interest ahead of the EU's by refusing to cut interest rates, and produced a currency crisis. To ease the strain, a way out was found in an increase in the earlier margins for the fluctuations of the currencies participating in the exchange rate mechanism of the EMS. They were widened from ±2.25 per cent to ±15 per cent on either side of the central parity. The 'dirty float' began. A condition for the establishment of EMU is that 'normal' (without a definition) fluctuation margins for currencies need to be observed for at least two years. However, what is 'normal' in a situation when the exchange rate mechanism of the EMS remained only in name? As long as currencies are allowed to move against one another, the genuine Single European Market will not be secure.
62. The finance ministers breached the Stability and Growth Pact in November 2003 by voting not to impose sanctions on France and Germany for perpetually breaking the 3 per cent deficit cap. The European Commission took the Council of Ministers to the Court of Justice in January 2004 because of that. The real issue in this case was not whether this pact is sensible or not (it isn't), but whether the Council of Ministers has the right to abandon a procedure which is necessary for legal certainty. This is not only a legal, but also a political question about who guides the EU – the national governments (through the Council of Ministers) or the European Commission which stands for the common EU interest? The power struggle between the two EU institutions and worsening atmosphere between the two are obvious.
63. European and American values differ. In general, the Europeans tend to search more for public rather than private solutions to certain problems than do the Americans (a deregulated, US-type social and economic model is not something that most Europeans are striving for because of the possible wide social inequalities); international norms are more respected by the Europeans than the Americans (environment is a good example as Europe prefers a word of law, rather than one of power); many Americans look at the EU with six weeks of annual leave and public holidays converted into extended weekends as the last bastion of socialism; there is also a rejection of capital punishment in Europe. All this contributes to the opinion that there may be a wide set of issues on which Europe and America may seriously continue to disagree in the future.
64. *Stratfor*, 'Europe: splintering on Iraq war shatters common policy', 30 January 2003.
65. According to the Bush doctrine of unilateral and preventive war goals of any war are the same: to shape the political future. The means are always the same: to kill 'enough' enemy in order to break his will to fight and resist.
66. P. Krugman, 'Where's the apology?', *New York Times*, 30 January 2004.
67. George Wright, 'Wolfowitz: Iraq war was about oil', *The Guardian*, 4 June 2003.
68. Unlike politicians, journalists, particularly anchors, have never been elected by popular vote. As they are not elected (normally every four years) one may question their legitimacy in certain situations.
69. These were basically surveillance operations in the belligerent Albanian-populated areas.
70. The US may have the status of a 'New Rome' that is, ready, willing and able to send legions to conquer and discipline the barbarians.
71. The US depends on Canada and Mexico for the security of its land border, it needs Europe to track down terrorist cells of the Islamic diaspora, North Korea can be contained only with the assistance of China, Japan and South Korea, while it has to count on the cooperation of India to prevent the collapse of the Pakistani government and the fall of its nuclear weapons into the hands of terrorists (*Financial Times*, 24 December 2003).

72. The Central and East European countries fear the future actions of Russia. These are, however, only *opinions*. None the less, one has to bear in mind *hard facts*. It has always been Russia that was attacked by the West over the past two centuries: first by Napoleon and then during two world wars. At the same time, Russia is losing confidence in the West, in particular in the US. The US promised Russia that no NATO forces would move into East Germany following German reunification; that the post-communist countries would not become part of NATO; and that no foreign forces would be stationed inside the borders of the new NATO members. These promises were not honoured (*Stratfor*, 8 March 2003). Is this a reflection of what King Richard II said in 1381 to calm the peasant rebellion that threatened London? He promised the rebels that he would end the repression of the peasants by the nobility, as soon as the menace passed, he said: 'Villeins ye are, and villeins ye shall remain'. That is to say: promises to little people do not count. Following the 2003 attack on resource-rich Iraq, are resource-rich Iran and then resource-rich Russia next on the list?
73. *Financial Times*, 19 November 2001, p. 15.
74. B. Posen, 'Europe cannot advance on two fronts', *Financial Times*, 24 April 2003.
75. European Council, Copenhagen 2002, Presidency Conclusions, Annex I.
76. *Bulletin Quotidien Europe*, 15 December 2002.
77. *Financial Times*, 27 January 2003.
78. To what extent were the national democratic procedures respected in both wars against Serbia (1999) and Iraq (2003)? Did the national parliaments have any say over this intervention which was planned many months in advance? Parliaments could be excluded from these deliberations only in the case of a surprise attack on a NATO member country. Were the international procedures in the UN Security Council followed?
79. In the semi-protectorate status of Bosnia and Herzegovina, the international administrators directly control and rule over the police, army, state administration, finance, education, media, privatisation and judiciary. They desire even wider authority (what else is left?), but they do want to have a declared or formal full protectorate. The reason is that in the current situation the international administration may easily pass on the responsibility for the appalling economic and political situation to the local 'nationalistic' and 'warmongering' political parties. The locally elected politicians decide on very few things (and even those are always fully verified), but they are blamed by the international administrators for all the problems. Paradoxically, it may seem that the country does not need democracy, but rather, rule by international experts!
80. On 11 March 2001 Afghanistan's ruling Taleban Muslims blew up two giant Buddha statues in defiance of international diplomatic efforts to save them. This provoked a huge worldwide rage. Little is, however, known about similar actions by the Albanian Muslims in Kosovo. This Serbian province has been ruled by the UN mission since June 1999. Security has been provided by tens of thousands of NATO forces equipped with the state of the art military hardware and logistics. Since the UN rule, the Albanian Muslims militants burned, bombed and destroyed 115 Christian Orthodox churches and monasteries that originate mostly from 14th and 15th century. Thirty of those churches and monasteries were destroyed in an organised and well-coordinated action in front of the NATO military forces only on 17 and 18 March 2004. Most of those churches and monasteries represented 'precious and irreplaceable heritage of our civilisation' (*Bulletin Quotidien Europe*, 3 April 2004, p. 3).
81. Simon Jenkins 'Britain's Berlin Wall', *The Times*, 10 November 1999.
82. Simon Jenkins, 'The Good Friday agreement is brain-dead', *The Times*, 22 October 2003.
83. 'Too many cooks spoil the broth.'
84. *Financial Times*, 'Brussels loses battle over aid to Yugoslavia', 18 July 2001, p. 2.
85. Another controversial political initiative known as 'Asphalt for Democracy' in 2000 was supposed to help Serbia to change the government of Slobodan Milošević.
86. The Council of Europe should not be confused with the European Council which is an EU institution.
87. Serbia and Montenegro were under constant pressure, even political blackmail. For

many years the people suffered sticks but were offered very few carrots. The country even sent two presidents (Slobodan Milošević and Milan Milutinović) to The Hague tribunal which has no precedent in the history of international affairs. No matter what the Serbs have done, nothing was good enough for years. However, since the start of the civil war in the former Yugoslavia, Serbia and Montenegro have had over 1 million refugees. This is more than all the countries in the region combined at any time since 1991. For this mass expulsion of Serbs from Croatia, Bosnia and Herzegovina, as well as from Kosovo and Metohia, The Hague tribunal has not tried anyone. Certain Serbs were indicted instantly, even during their military operations, while most of the others were indicted just after those operations. However, it took the tribunal over a decade after the committed crime against the Serbs to start indicting Croats and Muslims in 2004. This was, perhaps, to avoid the criticism that it is not even handed. The Tribunal publicly stated that Franjo Tudjman, the former wartime president of Croatia, and Alija Izetbegović, the former wartime president of Bosnia and Herzegovina and the leader of the Islamic population, were both under investigation for their crimes. In both cases these public statements were made for the first time only a few days *after* their deaths in 1999 and 2003, respectively.

88. Do you still remember the ratification of the Treaty of Nice or the popular 'enthusiasm' for the introduction of the euro?
89. The roots of the German preference for federalism lie partly in the Middle Ages when what is now Germany comprised a score of kingdoms, states, principalities and free cities. At the time of Germany's 'integration' in 1871, there were 25 self-governing entities.
90. *Bulletin Quotidien Europe*, 7 March 2001, p. 4.
91. Firefighters have the right to strike in Britain, however the German constitution does not allow such a possibility. If a harmonised model is imposed throughout the EU, this may create substantial damage to the established industrial relations in each country. Certain common benchmarks may initially be superior to fixed and uniform standards.
92. Switzerland is a multilingual and culturally diverse federation. It may provide a number of lessons for the reformers of the EU. The Swiss democracy is very close to the hearts of the people. If there is a petition signed by at least 50 000 voters opposing a law three months after its adoption in the parliament, the law must be put to a national referendum. If it fails to be approved by the majority, it is thrown out. The government is therefore very careful in its legislative activities. In order to alter the constitution, reformers must obtain at least 100 000 signatures. Once put to the popular vote this proposal must receive a double majority: a majority of both voters and cantons.
93. Certain observers looked at this convention as a modest version of the gathering that created the US Constitution in Philadelphia in 1787. However, the US convention had 50 participants, they were all men (predominantly slave owners) and they met in secret. Some think that the lack of flexibility in the US Constitution contributed to the American Civil War, others admire this constitution. None the less, until just a few decades ago the US Constitution overlooked racism and still permits capital punishment, which has long been abolished in EU countries.
94. In France, for example, it was 'only' 51 per cent, with some 3 per cent of votes invalid.
95. There are no provisions to deal with the expulsion of a member country from the EU (it is neither allowed nor prohibited by the treaty). However, in theory, it could happen. The countries that want to go ahead with a deal could draft and accept a new treaty that could leave the dissenting country outside the club. By implication, that may continue until those presumably weak, unwilling, poor or small countries are all excluded. Ultimately the 'ideal' union would consist only of a single country. Alternatively, ostracism was known and practised in ancient Greece. Those that were powerful and dangerous to the state (rather than the weak) were expelled from the city for five to ten years.
96. European Council, Lisbon 2000, Presidency Conclusions, §5.
97. This was not the first foreign attack on US soil. The British invaded and set fire to Washington, DC in 1814.

98. A safeguard clause was embodied in Article 115 in the original Treaty of Rome. Authorisations based on this article came to an end in 1993 once the Single European Market was established.
99. Prior to the eastern enlargement in May 2004, the 'big' EU countries (Britain, France, Germany, Italy and Spain) delegated two commissioners each, while the other countries had only one each.
100. France and Germany decided independently in June 1994 that the new head of the Commission was to be the then prime minister of Belgium Jean Luc Dehaene. They thought that the other EU countries would go along with their choice. This arrogant attitude irritated many other member countries, although Britain was the most vocal and blocked that choice, not necessarily because they were not happy about the candidate, but more importantly because of the distorted procedure. A compromise candidate was later found in the then prime minister of Luxembourg, Jacques Santer.
101. Some 24000 Italian farmers exceeded their EU-set milk-production quotas. They were fined a total of €1.3 billion by the Commission in 2003. The terms of payment of this fine were special: the farmers will pay annual interest-free instalments until the end of 2017, which means that they will pay approximately a third less than if they were forced to settle the fine straight away (*Financial Times*, 3 June 2003).
102. Although this number may seem large, it is often much smaller than some of the important ministries in the EU's member countries. A large part of the Commission's staff is in the translation service since all the documents need to be published in all of the 21 official languages of the EU, hence the size of the translation and interpretation service. The proponents of rationalisation suggest that if the operation of the UN can be handled in six languages or if EFTA uses only one language for its business (English – a language that is not the official language of any of its member countries), the EU may start to think along these lines too. It needs to be borne in mind that many of the EU's affairs are carried out through the administrations of the member countries which need to be informed in a timely and punctual way. Hence, the need for an efficient translation service.
103. The French acronym Coreper (*Comité des Représentants Permanents*) for this body is often used even in English.
104. Britain is the most vocal defender of the national veto in the EU. The British 'red lines' that cannot be crossed are in the areas of taxation, EU budget, social security, foreign policy and judicial cooperation.
105. Bulgaria and Romania are not included. Even if they were, this would not alter the general picture.
106. The Parliament has the right of consent regarding the application of new member countries and important international agreements. It was withholding or stalling its assent to agreements with countries that had a poor record of human rights.
107. A discussion about the existence of aliens in outer space was on the Parliament's proposed agenda in January 1994, until a last-minute withdrawal.
108. Turnout in the elections for the European Parliament was 56 per cent in 1994, 49 per cent in 1999, while it was 45 per cent in 2004, the lowest ever. Real democracy is not about elections and voting every four or five years. Democracy is what happens between elections. It involves an ongoing process of consultation, negotiation, compromises and adjustments. Explanations of voters' apathy might be the perception that the Parliament is too far away from the man in the street and that it has complex and unfathomable procedures.
109. Supremacy of EU law over national law was established by the Court of Justice in 1964 (*Costa v. ENEL* case) when it rejected the argument that a national court has a duty to apply national law that was both inconsistent with and adopted later than the Treaty of Rome.
110. The Continental Can case (1973) is an example.

> For wisdom is a shelter as money is a shelter,
> but the excellence of knowledge is that wisdom gives life to those who have it.
> Ecclesiastes 7:12

2 Monetary Integration

1. Introduction

Monetary policy is central for overall economic strategy in an economic and monetary union (EMU) because of its control over the money stock. The control over the rate of inflation contributes to the creation of conditions necessary for sustained economic growth. As monetary policy is one of the most sensitive economic policies, the treaties establishing the EU made special reference to these issues. In fact, the Maastricht Treaty is almost entirely about EMU. This is because integration of monetary policies in the EU is necessary not only for the stability of rates of exchange and prices (and their transparency), balance of payments and investment decisions, but also for the protection of the already achieved level of integration, as well as for the motivation for further integration in the future.

Relatively small countries may have, in certain cases, an incentive to integrate their money in order to avoid the monetary domination of large countries. The joint money may overcome the disadvantage (vulnerability to external shocks) of atomised currencies and under certain theoretical conditions it may become a rival to the money of larger countries in international currency markets. A common currency among the integrated countries may become an outward symbol, but it is not a necessary condition for a successful EMU.

A monetary system between countries should be distinguished from a monetary union. Countries in a monetary system link their currencies together and act as a single unit in relation to third currencies. A monetary union among countries is an ambitious enterprise. It exists if there is either a single money (*de jure* EMU) or an irrevocable fixity among the rates of exchange of the participating countries together with a free mobility of goods, services and factors (*de facto* EMU). This prevents any alterations in the rates of exchange as indirect methods of non-tariff protection or as a subsidy to exports. It also means that the member countries should seek recourse to the capital markets in order to find funds to cover their budget deficit. Within an EMU, it should be as easy, for example, for a Frenchman to pay a German within Europe, as it is for a Welshman to pay an Englishman within the United Kingdom (Meade, 1973, p. 162).

An economic and monetary union requires the following elements:

- centralisation of monetary policy;
- a single central bank or a system of central banks that control stabilisation policies;
- convertibility (at least internal) of the participating countries' currencies;
- unified performance on the international financial markets;
- capital market integration;
- identical rates of inflation;
- harmonisation of fiscal systems;
- replacement of balance of payments disequilibria with regional imbalances;
- similar levels of economic development or a well-endowed fund for transfers of real resources to the less-developed regions and those under external shocks; and
- continuous consultation about and coordination of economic policies among the participating countries, as well as the adjustment of wages on the union level.

There may exist, also, a pseudo exchange rate union (Corden, 1972). In this kind of union, member countries fix the exchange rates of their currencies and freely accept each other's money. However, since there is no pooling of foreign reserves and no central monetary authority, such a union is not stable. Since there is no mechanism to coordinate national policies, an individual member country may choose to absorb real resources from the union partners by running a balance of payments deficit with them. In addition, such a country may change the effective exchange rates of other members by creating a deficit in the union's balance of payments with the rest of the world. A full EMU is not vulnerable to such instability. Foreign exchange rates are pooled and monetary policy is operated by a single monetary authority. In a pseudo exchange rate union, there is imperfect coordination of national monetary policies, but in a full EMU the problem is solved by policy centralisation (Cobham, 1989, p. 204).

This chapter is structured as follows. It starts with the traditional single-criterion theory of monetary integration (Section 2). A superior, that is, cost–benefit model, further develops these theoretical concepts in Section 3. Parallel currencies (Section 4) are presented before the analysis of the past monetary arrangements in the EU (Section 5). The eurozone, that is, monetary unification based on the Maastricht Treaty, is the subject matter of Section 6. Section 7 spells out the achievements, problems and outlook for the eurozone. A separate Section 8 deals with the British quandary regarding the eurozone. The conclusion, Section 9, is that the creation of the eurozone is the greatest achievement in the history of European integration. However, there is a note of caution. The whole enterprise is primarily based on political considerations. Thus, it needs to pass the test of time.

2. Traditional model

EXCHANGE RATE REGIMES

Both flexible and fixed exchange rates have their virtues and vices. The benefits of a flexible exchange rate include its free floating according to demand and supply. This improves the spatial and industrial allocation of resources and in liberal societies removes the need for government interference. There is no need whatsoever for foreign currency reserves, because balance of payments disequilibria are adjusted automatically. A country is free to pursue independently its national priorities regarding inflation, employment and interest rate targets. Any possible mistake in economic policy may be straightened out by continuous and smooth changes in rates of exchange. If there is an external shock, flexible exchange rates offer a fast short-term adjustment policy instrument.

There are, of course, several arguments against free floating. The most serious one is that this rate of exchange divides the economies of different countries. As such, it reduces the benefits of economies of scale and lower costs of goods and services, and also influences spatial location of firms in a suboptimal way. The floating rates of exchange stimulate speculation, uncertainty and instability. All the alleged criticisms about a smooth adjustment without the need for changes in reserves were disproved during the 1970s. Any change in the rate of exchange would have an impact on home prices. Its repercussions would be swifter in the countries which have a relatively greater degree of openness. There is, however, another problem with the floating rate of exchange: overshooting. Although some changes in economic policy have been announced but not yet implemented, the floating rates of exchange move and overshoot their long-run equilibrium.

The objections to fixed exchange rates are a mirror image of the virtues of the flexible rates. They include the following. Fixed exchange rates do not permit every country to pursue independently its own policy choices and goals regarding employment and inflation. Countries have to subordinate their monetary policy to the requirements of the external balance. When the time comes for adjustment in the rate of exchange, it may be relatively large and disruptive in relation to the smooth, potentially frequent and small changes in the exchange rate in the case of the free float. The system of fixed rates of exchange requires reserves of foreign currencies for intervention in the currency market in order to defend the fixed parity. These funds may be derived from alternative productive uses.

The arguments in favour of fixed rates of exchange are those which justify the introduction of a single currency in a country. This system stimulates cooperation and integration among countries and under certain conditions contributes to an efficient spatial distribution of resources, as opposed to floating rates which encourage 'economic nationalism' and disintegration. The most important feature of fixed rates of exchange is that they bring stability; prices are less inflationary and more transparent and comparable; the spatial allocation of resources is improved because decisions about investment are not delivered exclusively on the basis of short-term market signals; uncertainty is reduced and trade flows are stabilised. All this stimulates economic integration among countries, which is why the establishment of the Single European Market in 1993 'needed' to be followed by a monetary union.

There is no general rule about which system of exchange rates is better. If a country has a balance of payments deficit, then it has to restore competitiveness. This can be done by a reduction in private and public consumption, so it requires cutting wages directly, or devaluation, which in turn cuts wages indirectly. But the choice of the exchange system here plays no role at all. Reductions in real income are necessary under either exchange rate system.

It is a formidable task to offer a definite conclusion about the 'correct' system of exchange rates. The above choices contrast costs against benefits of a particular system. In practice, the choice may often be between the costs of one system and the costs of another. In such a situation it comes as no surprise that economists cannot be unanimous. In an EMU, small countries can overcome their disadvantage, which stems from their relatively small economic size, and thus these countries can create an area of economic stability. They may also reap the fruits of economic cooperation in an area where expectations may have a significant degree of accuracy.

Discussion about the exchange rate regimes (fixed, floating or managed) sheds light only on one side of a country's monetary policy in an international context. The other side deals with domestic monetary policy and market rigidities or flexibility. Linkages between national money supply and rates of interest, as well as price levels and price control, factor mobility and flexibility in wages, must also be considered. Otherwise, the debate may be pointless.

In its highest form, monetary integration means that everybody within an EMU is free to use their own currency for any kind of payment to partners. The minimum definition of monetary integration is absence of restrictions, while the maximum definition requires the use of a single currency (Machlup, 1979, p. 23). Monetary integration may exist even without the integration of markets for goods (and services) and the integration of goods markets may exist without monetary integration. The former case is exemplified by countries in the West African Monetary Union which have a single currency, the CFA (*Communauté financière africaine franc*), and a similar monetary policy to France (their former colonial master), but there is little real integration of markets for goods, services and factors among them. The latter case may be found in the European Free Trade Association, where member countries have integrated their markets for manufactured goods, but there is no formal integration of the monetary policy among them.

FACTOR MOBILITY

The traditional single criterion model of monetary integration started with the theory of optimum currency areas. This theory was a purely academic exercise during the 1960s, and interest in it was not revived until the early 1990s. This was prompted by the intention to bolster the European Monetary System (EMS) introduced in 1979, as well as by the break-up of formerly federal states in Central and Eastern Europe, in particular the former Soviet Union. These developments created problems of how to handle the new and separate currencies in most of the newly independent or newly created states, which are 'small' and have their own national currency for the first time in their history.

The theory of optimum currency areas was started by Mundell (1961). Economic adjustment can take place on international and national levels.

On the international level, the basic issue of adjustment is whether the countries with trade deficits will accept inflation or deflation in their respective economies. On the national level, the pace of inflation in countries that have a single currency, but several regions, is regulated by the desire of the central authorities to permit unemployment in regions with a deficit. If the objective is the achievement of a greater degree of employment and stable prices in a world where there is more than one currency area, then this requires floating exchange rates based on regional rather than national currencies. For Mundell, a region is the optimum currency area as people and factors move easily within it. Factor mobility is the criterion that determines a region. Within the currency areas factors are mobile, while between them, factors are immobile. Fluctuating rates of exchange are the adjustment mechanism between various currency areas, while factor mobility is the equilibrating mechanism within them.

Factor mobility as the criterion for an optimum currency area should be considered carefully. The difficulty with this model is that a region may be an economic unit, while the domain of a currency is an expression of national sovereignty which seldom coincides with a region.[1] In addition, factor mobility may change over time. Strong integration of goods and factor markets can tighten the budget constraint. Borrowing today implies higher taxes tomorrow. If factors (labour and capital) are free to move, this may give incentives to mobile factors to move to lower-tax jurisdictions which would erode the tax base in a high-tax country. Investors know that today's ability to borrow from a government is limited by its capability to tax tomorrow, and also its ability to tax tomorrow is restricted by factor mobility. Hence, investors will reduce or refuse their lending to governments threatening to exceed their borrowing capacity. The higher the integration of factor markets, the sooner this takes place (Eichengreen, 1993a, p. 1335). The governments also know the likely reactions of firms (and workers) and are therefore careful not to run large public deficits. Otherwise, they risk the departure of both firms and employable labour elsewhere.

Mobility of capital is sensitive to the degree of economic activity and the outlook for economic prosperity. In the 19th century, labour and capital were flowing towards the Americas and Australia as the areas of promising development which needed those factors most. During the 'golden' 1960s, however, labour and capital were flowing towards the growing developed and relatively rich regions and countries.

Labour is not a homogeneous factor. Its full mobility may exist only in relatively small geographical areas or within a very specialised professional category. The experience of the EU(6) provides the best proof of this. The flow of labour in the EU in the 1960s and up to the mid-1970s came mostly from workers from the Mediterranean countries that were not members of the EU (with the exception of Italy). Those labour flows may not be taken as intra-EU labour mobility. In addition, migration rates are lower in Europe than they are in the US. This is not only between European states, but also within them. 'The elasticity of migration with respect to interregional wage differences is at least five times as large for the US as for Britain' (Eichengreen, 1993b, p. 132). The gap in this type of responsiveness between the US and other European countries is bigger. The implication is that labour mobility is a less powerful labour market stabiliser (adjustment mechanism) in Europe than is the case in the US. In addition, EU governments may tax personal income at high(er) rates without any great danger that this would provoke emigration.

Regions within a single country grow at different rates. The same holds for countries in an EMU. These developments cause strain which is exacerbated if there are fewer opportunities for adjustment, such as factor mobility and fiscal compensations. However, it would not have been sensible for northern Italy (for example, Padania) to have a separate currency, thus creating a separate economy from the southern (Mafia-ridden, subsidy-consuming and Vatican-dominated) part of the country. The cost of such monetary disintegration could be relatively high. However, quite a number of 'Padanians' have a very different opinion about the issue.

OPENNESS

The second major approach focused attention on the degree of openness of a country (McKinnon, 1963). Commodities in a country may be distributed between tradables and non-tradables. The ratio between these goods determines the degree of its openness to trade. As a rule, the smaller the country, the greater the relative degree of its trade interaction with other countries. A high degree of openness embodies relatively high specialisation of a country and it may be taken as the criterion for the optimum currency area.

When the tradable goods represent a significant part of home consumption (unless most of the consumer's goods are imported), then changing the rate of exchange would not change a country's real wages. Such a country (presumably small) is advised to enter into an EMU for it may not be an optimum currency area as a single unit (Corden, 1972). The greater a country's openness, the smaller the chances for the effective independent use of exchange rates as an instrument for economic stabilisation.

Relatively small economies are advised to link their currencies with the currency of their major trading partner. This is the case when former colonies link their currency to that of their former master (for example, the

CFA franc zone) or when some of the transition economies of Central and Eastern Europe linked their currencies to the German mark, as was the case during the 1990s. The second piece of advice to small economies which conduct a significant part of their trade among themselves is to link their currencies together. In the case of a single currency all financial dealings may be simpler. This is part of the reason why the 50 federal states in the US may not be able to separately issue and operate their own currencies in an efficient way.[2] A similar observation may be applied to the 16 federal states in Germany or the 23 Swiss cantons. Further evidence can be found in the serious problems in handling monetary affairs in most of the independent states that emerged from the former Soviet Union. Whether such advice is unconditionally applicable to all EU countries is debatable among economists.

If small open economies operate near full employment, then internal fiscal measures are advised for the adjustment of the balance of payments. Fixed exchange rates will be more productive in this case than flexible ones as they would have a less damaging effect on prices. A variation in the exchange rate will elicit a small response to the change in the level of imports because of high dependency on imports. Therefore, a variation in the rate of exchange should be much higher than in those countries which are relatively less open.

An alteration in the exchange rate will have a direct and significant impact on real income. Consumers and trade unions will demand indexation of wages with a resulting change in prices and the exchange rate. If money illusion exists, that is, the impression that changes in nominal (money) wages are identical to changes in real income, then a change in the exchange rate may be an effective means for adjusting the balance of payments. However, money illusion is not a long-term phenomenon. It is no longer even a short-term event. An alteration in the exchange rate may not be effectively employed for the adjustment of balance of payments independently of other instruments. Flexible rates of exchange may be an efficient means for the adjustment in relatively large economies which are linked by small trade relations.

The assumptions in this model are that the equilibrium in the balance of payments is caused by microeconomic changes in demand and supply and, also, that prices in the outside world are stable. The argument about the relative stability of prices in the outside world cannot be substantiated for the period lasting for about three decades since the early 1970s. When prices in the outside world are fluctuating, this is directly conveyed to home prices through a fixed exchange rate. The openness of an economy may be the criterion for an optimum currency area if the outside world is more stable than the economic situation in a small open economy. Fixed exchange rates may force small open economies to pursue a more rigorous economic policy than under the fluctuating exchange rates regime which permits a policy of monetary 'indiscipline'. If money illusion does not exist, then the possibility of altering the exchange rate as an adjustment instrument becomes meaningless.

The Benelux countries and Denmark have participated in the EMS since its creation. Other small European countries (for example, Austria, Finland, Norway, Sweden and Switzerland) initially decided to stay out of the EMS and manage their exchange rates unilaterally, although these countries paid close attention to the developments in the EMS. The argument of openness fails to explain why small EU countries such as Denmark and Sweden still have national control over their exchange rate in spite of strong trade relations with the member countries of the EMU (introduced into the EU in three stages by the Maastricht Treaty). In addition, it fails to explain why relatively large countries such as Germany and France opted for the EMU and the euro, while Britain is still out of it. The basic flaw of the optimum currency area theory is that it fails to distinguish between the case for fixed exchange rates and the situation when separate states join together in a common currency (McKinnon, 1994, p. 61).

DIVERSIFICATION

The third major contribution stated that countries whose production is diversified do not have to change their terms of trade with foreign countries as often as the less-diversified countries (Kenen, 1969). An external shock in the form of a reduction in foreign demand for a country's major export item may have a relatively smaller impact on the diversified country's employment than on a specialised country's economy and employment. Finally, links between home and foreign demand, as well as export and investment, are weaker in the diversified country than in a specialised one. Large and frequent exchange rate changes are not necessary for a diversified country because of the overlap in the reduction and increase in demand for various export goods. This overlap may keep the proceeds from exports at a relatively stable average level. In conclusion, Kenen suggested that fixed rates of exchange are suitable for diversified countries. Diversification is his criterion for the optimum currency area.

Diversification helps the stabilisation of home investment and adjustment of the economy to external shocks. The US may be the closest example of such an economy. The continued wide acceptance and use of the US dollar as an international currency reflect in part the essential structural properties of the US economy that change slowly over time. These include the size of the US economy and its diversification and openness. Countries with specialised economies and relatively low levels of diversification have a need to belong to currency areas with flexible rates of exchange. Such countries are more vulnerable to external shocks than are diversified economies. Examples may be found in Denmark, Iceland, New Zealand and most of the African countries.

Regarding the EU, one may note and expect that the structure of the economies of the member countries may change, even radically alter, as the result of the EMU (and eastern enlargement). If transactions costs and exchange rate risk are important for commerce, then the EMU would promote competition and trade. This would also influence specialisation and spatial location of firms and industries. Hence, at least in theory, the past structure of the national economies and historical data may not be appropriate benchmarks for the comparisons of future business cycles and industry-specific external shocks. Empirically, Frenkel and Rose (1998, p. 1023) found that 30 years of data from 20 industrialised countries provide a strong positive relationship between the degree of bilateral trade intensity and the cross-country bilateral correlation of business cycles.

While McKinnon deals with internal shocks to an economy, Kenen considers external ones. Kenen's argument may be weakened in the situation where the reduction in foreign demand occurs during a general fall in demand during recession. This reduces total demand, so a country's diversification does not help much in mitigating the fall in the demand for exports.

OTHER STRANDS

Coordination of economic policies can be a criterion for an EMU (Werner, 1970). Economic policies which are not coordinated among countries may be a major reason for the disturbance in the equilibrium of the balance of payments. Coordination of economic, in particular monetary policies, from a supranational centre requires political will on the part of the participating countries. A declaration towards such an objective was made in the Maastricht Treaty.

One criterion for monetary integration may be a similar rate of inflation among the potential member countries (Fleming, 1971). Diverging ratios of employment to inflation among these countries will cause hardship and disagreements about the necessary policy tools. Countries with a balance of payments surplus would be driven to accept a higher rate of inflation than when they are free to choose this ratio. Conversely, countries with deficits may be asked to tolerate a higher rate of unemployment than they would be willing to accept if they were free to choose it.

An optimum currency area may be defined as a region in which no part insists on creating money and having a monetary policy of its own (Machlup, 1979, p. 71). A monetary union which imposes minimum costs on the participating countries may be called an optimum currency area (Robson, 1983, p. 143). An optimum currency area may be alternatively defined as an area in which the net benefits of integration (for example, increase in welfare in the form of greater stability in prices and smaller disturbances coming from abroad) outweigh the costs (restraint to individual uses of monetary and fiscal policies) (Grubel, 1984, p. 39). This is to say that 'the last recruit conferred more benefits than costs on existing members, but the next one will do the reverse' (Maloney and Macmillen, 1999, p. 572).

An optimum currency area aims at identifying a group of countries within which it is optimal to have fixed exchange rates while, at the same time, keeping a certain flexibility in the exchange rate with the third countries (Thygesen, 1987, p. 163). Very small currency conversion costs and openness are likely to make the EU an optimal currency area, while high levels of government spending will make it less likely (Canzoneri and Rogers, 1990, p. 422). An optimum currency area may also be defined as one that attains the macroeconomic objectives of internal balance (low unemployment and inflation) and external balance (a sustainable position in the balance of payments) (Tavlas, 1993a, p. 32).

The notion of an optimum currency area is more theoretical than practical. An eternal trilemma (impossible trinity) in open economies is how to solve three basic issues. One cannot have perfectly mobile capital, monetary independence and a fixed exchange rate all at the same time (although it is possible to have any two of these elements). If a government or a monetary authority of an EMU wants free capital mobility and fixed exchange rates, it has to give up monetary autonomy. If it wants monetary autonomy and free capital mobility, it has to have a floating exchange rate. If it wants fixed exchange rates and monetary autonomy, it has to restrict capital mobility.

A region may be an economic unit which does not necessarily coincide with the domain of a currency. An optimum currency area may be able to sustain itself on its own. Its definition may ask for liberalisation of all economic activities within it and its protection against the outside world. Despite their relevant arguments, these definitions can hardly be applied to countries in the real world, since the states are constituted in a suboptimal way, so that full economic efficiency (regardless of the external world) can seldom, if ever, be achieved.

The EU may not be an optimum currency area according to these criteria. There is a relatively low labour mobility and wages are quite rigid if there is a need and pressure to move downwards. If this is what really matters for the success of an EMU, then the cost of it may be unacceptably high. A single criterion theoretical model has a narrow scope. Therefore, it is unable to present the costs and benefits of an EMU. The next task is to amend this shortcoming.

3. Costs and benefits

ISSUES

A more practical and fruitful way to analyse an EMU is to study the optimum economic policy area, rather than the optimum currency area. A single state becomes increasingly ineffective as an independent policy-making unit in modern times of continuous changes in technology, relatively easy and cheap dissemination of information and frequent market changes. This is true for all countries in the world, but it is not true for all of them equally. Therefore, not all of them seek international solutions to their national problems. In a situation where economic problems assume global proportions there is only one optimum policy area: the world (Panić, 1988, pp. 317–30). The most pressing international economic problems cannot be solved by countries acting in isolation. The solutions to these problems can be found in coordinated national economic management. A system of safeguards which would include assistance in the form of transfer of (real) resources to the countries which experience temporary difficulties is an essential feature for the survival of an efficient multilateral system of trade and payments.

The shortcomings of the traditional single criterion and optimum currency model of international monetary integration may be overcome by the 'new theory' of monetary integration that relies on the cost–benefit model. This model offers more satisfactory policy implications. The costs which may be incurred by a country's participation in monetary integration may be traced to the losses of a country's right to alter independently its rate of exchange, its ratio between inflation and unemployment and its ability to handle regional development policy, as well as its seigniorage. Monetary integration brings a number of benefits. These include a dismissal of the exchange problems within the group of countries in the arrangement, an increase in influence in monetary affairs and an increase in monetary stability. The larger the integrated area, the larger the gains. Both the costs and the benefits of monetary integration are analysed next.

COSTS

First, the creation of a supranational body to conduct monetary policy (money supply, rate of interest and rate of exchange) in an EMU may be perceived as a significant loss of the participating countries' national sovereignty. This is the first cost, which may provoke adverse political, as well as psychological, consequences in countries that take part in the arrangement. The most sensitive issue may be the loss of the right to alter independently the rate of exchange. The loss occurs fully against the currencies of partner countries and partially against other countries. A right, often used selfishly, is gone. However, the gains here come from the pooling of the monetary policies of the member countries that can exercise a much greater leverage over their monetary policy in comparison to the situation prior to monetary integration.

When policy makers want to adjust the balance of payments by means of alterations in a country's rate of exchange, then the most critical issue is the fall in real wages. Labour may accept a fall in real wages under the condition that the other alternative is (longer-term) unemployment. A reduction in the rate of exchange introduces an increase in the price for imported goods, as well as for some home-produced goods and services. The impact of the devaluation depends on the openness of a country. A reduction in real wages brings an advantage in the cost of labour and a relative decrease in the price of export goods and services in the short run. This classical scenario may be seriously questioned. Money illusion no longer has a significant impact on labour. Every increase in inflation and corresponding fall in real wages, under the assumption that there is no change in productivity, encourages labour and concerned trade unions to demand an increase in wages. The short-term cost advantage of devaluation is eroded by such increases.

Devaluation as an instrument of economic policy may not alone eliminate deficits in the balance of payments. The government may state that its policy objective is not to use devaluation in the fight against inflation. Such a policy goal may act as an important incentive to firms to resist higher costs because their goods and services would become uncompetitive on the foreign and, potentially, home market, if trade were free. A recession may be another, although less desirable, cure for inflation. Shrinking markets give firms incentives to keep prices low, while rising unemployment forces trade unions to resist increases in wages.

Exchange rates started to float in the early 1970s and did so for a decade. The experience has provided sufficient evidence that a country's autonomy in a situation of floating exchange rates is overstated. The reason is that a majority of countries are small and open. This leads to the conclusion that the sole use of the exchange rate as the adjustment mechanism of the balance of payments is of limited significance. Fiscal policy[3] and labour mobility are necessary supplements. The devaluation of a national currency is a sign of failure to manage the economy soundly and carefully according to sharp, but widely accepted and applied international standards. The standards of international economic prudence show that it is the national bureaucracy which is the only loser from the deprivation of the right to devalue the national currency. Therefore, the loss of autonomy in the management of a country's rate of exchange as a policy instrument is of little real significance.

If, however, the rate of exchange of a group of countries such as the EU is fixed to an anchor currency such as the German mark, as was the case in the EMS until August 1993, the situation can change. If international capital markets are free, the loss of autonomy in the fixing of the exchange market does not matter as long as the business cycles match one another. If the cycles differ, as has been the case in the EU, partner countries may be reluctant to follow the monetary policy of the anchor currency, since it may not match the necessary policy actions of the other participating countries.

The correlation of business cycles among countries depends on the depth of their economic integration, particularly integration in trade. If a common currency among countries assists in promotion of trade, as it is widely claimed, then this may contribute to synchronising business cycles.

Second, it was argued that floating rates of exchange permit unconstrained choices between unemployment and inflation in a country. On these grounds, countries may seem to be free to pursue their own stabilisation policies. An EMU constrains the independent national choice of the rates of inflation, unemployment and interest rate. This national choice, as a second cost of monetary integration, is constrained by the choice and influence of other partner countries. A loss of the right to deal independently may significantly jeopardise national preferences regarding the possible choices. The country with relatively low inflation and a balance of payments surplus may, in accordance with its economic and political strength, impose its own goals on other partner countries, because this country has much less pressure to adjust than the other countries.

A common currency levels the competitiveness of the group in the monetary field. If a region's factor productivity is lower than the average in the group, then the regional/country authorities will have to 'tolerate' unemployment. Labour mobility (outflow) may be a solution to the problem. The higher the labour mobility, the more diversified the output pattern, and the more flexible prices and wages, the smoother the adjustment. Applied to the EU, only the relative diversification of the economic structure may pass the test for a smooth adjustment. Other macroeconomic criteria (labour mobility and flexible wages) do not fare well at all.

This consideration has been examined with geometric rigour by de Grauwe (1975). It was proved that countries differ regarding the position of their Phillips curves, rates of productivity growth and the preferences of governments between unemployment and inflation. These are the differences that explain why, in the absence of an EMU, rates of inflation among countries will be equal only by accident. For a smooth operation of an EMU, the condition is not only balanced growth but also equal unemployment rates, otherwise the EMU may not survive without inter-country compensatory transfer of resources. The mere integration of economic policy goals may not be effective without agreement on the means to achieve the agreed targets. If countries cope with a common problem and employ different tools, the outcome of harmonisation of economic policy objectives may only do more harm than good.

The Phillips curve suggests that there is a measurable, inverse relation between unemployment and inflation (for example, see Figure 2.3, below). The government could reduce unemployment by means of a demand stimulus such as an increase in budget deficit while the price for this policy is increased inflation. In Milton Friedman's model, the rate of unemployment is independent of the rate of inflation. The followers of this school criticise Phillips curve theory for not seeing that continuous inflationary policy provokes changes in expectations about future inflation. They argue that there is only one rate of unemployment at which prices (inflation) and wages are constant: the natural rate of unemployment or the non-accelerating inflation rate of unemployment (NAIRU).

No matter what a government does, the rate of unemployment may not fall below the national NAIRU. It is like a speed limit for an economy. However, this rate is not constant over time. It is determined by real factors which include minimum wage legislation, tax policy, dole money, labour mobility, the level of education and impetus for vocational training, payroll taxes[4] and demographic factors, as well as the choice between work and leisure. In another words, the NAIRU is determined by the structure of the labour market, rather than by the amount of demand. Most of these factors are influenced by economic policy. Every attempt to lower the rate of unemployment below the NAIRU by means of monetary expansion would only accelerate inflation. Hence, the loss of this economic policy choice is also of limited significance.

The main way to reduce unemployment is to reduce the NAIRU. This can be done by reducing social security benefits below the minimum wage for unskilled labour, shortening the time during which these benefits apply, providing incentives for vocational training and by control over the demands of trade unions. Economic policy should be active in combating unemployment. The long-term unemployed have obsolete experience and training which makes them less attractive to potential employers. These unemployed compete less vigorously on the labour market and put less downward pressure on wages. The NAIRU increases with the expansion of the long-term unemployed. Economic policy should withdraw social benefits from those who refuse vocational training and/or jobs with the exception of anyone beyond an agreed age. The problem of the EU and its member countries is that they have not dealt with the long-term unemployed. These countries handed out relatively generous benefits for long periods to the unemployed. Almost half of the unemployed in the EU are out of work for over a year, while in the US the proportion is about 10 per cent.

The Canadian experience during 1950–62 with a fluctuating rate of exchange is illustrative. Canada wanted monetary independence in relation to the US. Theoretical arguments (illusions) about greater national independence and freedom regarding employment policy in a flexible exchange rate situation seemed attractive. Canadian hopes were high. At the end of this period a mismanaged government intervention succeeded in destabilising prices in Canada and growth stagnated. The decision to abandon flexible exchange rates showed that the benefits in the stability of employment and economic independence are smaller than the cost paid in economic instability and efficiency. Given the contemporary capital market integration among open economies, significant differences in real interest rates among different countries may not exist. Hence, an open economy may not rely independently on this instrument of economic policy. In a situation where two or more currencies are close substitutes and where there exists free capital mobility, the central banks of these countries cannot conduct independent monetary policies even under fluctuating exchange rates. Small open economies may be advised to link their monetary policies to those of their major partners in trade and investment.

Third, a serious problem in a monetary union may be traced in the inflow of capital into the prosperous regions. The regions losing this capital expect a compensatory public action including transfers from the prosperous ones. Those countries which feel that their destiny is to be losers from an EMU would not enter into such an arrangement. The system of transfers may be a bribe to these regions/countries to participate. When there are budget deficits and expenditure cuts, the funds for transfers may not be found easily. None the less, the gainers may be quite happy to compensate the losers and protect the net gains from integration.

Fourth is the loss of seigniorage. This comes from the national currency held abroad (also called the inflation tax).[5] Instead of selling debt, a government may print money and, hence, raise revenue in order to cover its budget deficit. The government taxes (inflation tax) the holders of cash held by the public and the commercial banks' low-interest-bearing deposits/reserves held at the central bank.[6] In an EMU, inflating a national way out of economic crisis is not possible. Therefore, a country in need is supposed to reduce its debt or to sell more reserves, or both.

To sum up, an EMU introduces significant losses in the constitutional autonomy of participating states, but real autonomy to conduct independent monetary policy for a small open country in the situation of convertibility, synchronised economic cycles and openness for trade and investment will remain almost intact.

BENEFITS

The benefits of monetary integration are numerous, but generally intuitive in their nature. They are barely quantifiable and non-economists have difficulty in comprehending their character and significance. The principal gains from monetary integration are the following:

- The most important benefit that an EMU brings to its participants is an improvement in integration of markets for goods, services and factors.
- Prices are transparent and directly comparable. This boosts competition and specialisation in tradable goods and services. Spatial and industrial location of resources is improved.
- In a situation of stable prices, interest and exchange rates, internal trade and investment flows are not volatile, as there is no exchange rate risk and uncertainty.
- Transaction[7] and hedging costs are significantly reduced.
- There are gains from an additional trade.
- Investors may decide with a high degree of long-term confidence. There are no intra-union controls for direct investment. For example, without a single currency, a German investor may look at an investment project in Belgium as a riskier one than the same project in Germany.
- By unifying monetary and coordinating fiscal policies, the participating countries are led to fewer distortions while combating macroeconomic disequilibria. This introduces both a greater internal monetary stability and an increase in influence in international monetary affairs. This contributes to economic growth and dynamic gains.
- The pooling of national reserves of foreign currencies is also advantageous for the members of an EMU. By internalising their 'foreign' trade, these countries reduce their demand for foreign currency reserves. Such reserves may not be necessary for trade within the

group, but they may still be needed for trade with third countries. Anyway, there are certain economies in the use of reserves. Their level is reduced and overhead costs are spread on the participating countries. These funds can easily be spent on or invested in alternative and more productive uses.

This is an expectation in theory. A single currency in the EU was likely to save on the exchange reserves of the member states.[8] In practice, countries still hold official reserves, which may be a hangover from the Bretton Woods system of fixed exchange rates. However, that system fell apart three decades ago. Therefore, the need to hold reserves ought to be reduced, perhaps significantly. None the less, global foreign exchange reserves are still there without a declining tendency. The reason is that countries still need such reserves to close transitory gaps in the demand and supply of foreign exchange.

The net effect of monetary integration may not be easily and directly quantified. Let us assume the reverse case. There were tremendous costs from the monetary disintegration of countries such as the former Soviet Union or the former Yugoslavia. Just imagine the losses of the monetary disintegration of the US or Germany where each federal state independently handles its own currency. If there is no control group of similar non-integrated countries, then there is no yardstick against which one may compare the relative performance of the countries which created an EMU.

The costs which may be brought by monetary integration in the form of an increase in prices or unemployment are relatively easily identifiable, borne by the few and perhaps of a short-term nature. If this nature is not short term, then an indefinite intra-union system of transfer of resources is a necessary condition for the survival of the scheme. The benefits which accrue from monetary integration are long term in nature, they come in small amounts to everybody and they are hard to quantify with any precision. Moreover, these benefits create the potential for new capital formation (a permanent growth bonus) which may accelerate growth of output in the long run.

The 'new theory' of monetary integration suggests that there are somewhat fewer costs (loss of autonomy to handle domestic macroeconomic policies) and somewhat more benefits (gains in credibility in the fight against inflation) associated with monetary integration (Tavlas, 1993b, p. 682). The benefits of an EMU are larger the greater the intra-union factor mobility, the more diversified the economies, the higher the flexibility of wages, the greater the internal trade and the greater the synchronisation of economic cycles among the member countries. The EU can pass most of these tests, except for labour mobility and flexibility of wages.

4. Parallel currencies

Is an irrevocable fixity of exchange rates a sufficient condition for monetary integration or is the introduction of a single currency necessary in an EMU? Suppose that there are various currencies in an EMU which are tied by a fixed exchange rate. If there is an increase in the supply of any of these currencies, then convertibility may be maintained only by intervention, either in the form of the absorption of this currency by the monetary authorities or by a reduction in demand (restriction in transactions). The first method represents monetary expansion, while the other is an act of disintegration.

A common currency may be an outward symbol, but is not a necessary condition for a successful EMU. Capital mobility and irrevocably fixed exchange rates of currencies in an EMU may create a single currency *de facto* in everything except, possibly, in name, while a single currency will create a monetary union *de jure*. Ultimately a single currency will be necessary, because it makes the irrevocable fixity of exchange rates of the participating currencies completely credible. Many international pledges towards fixed exchange rates have broken down.[9] As soon as markets question the commitment of the participants in the deal, this leads them to start speculating. In addition, a single money will eliminate possible conversion charges; prices in the area will be fully transparent and comparable; and there will be external benefits (such as the introduction of a 'better' symmetry in the international monetary system). Individual participating countries will not have even the remote possibility of finding their way out of economic difficulties by using the means of devaluation and/or inflation.

An evolutionary approach to the introduction of an EMU may be that a common currency exists side by side with currencies of the member countries. Once agents are used to dealing with the common currency, it may gradually replace the money of the participating countries. This is the case with parallel currencies. An important issue here is that the new, parallel currency ought to be linked to the pace of economic activity, otherwise price stability can be threatened. In addition, it may bring an extra complication in the monetary affairs among the integrated countries. A gradual convergence among the currencies will cause the participating currencies to yield an identical return. They will become perfect substitutes. A full monetary unification can take place.

Gradual monetary integration suffers from a serious flaw: a lack of credibility. During the transition phase, participating countries may find a way to step out temporarily from the arrangement. A system that permits some, even though remote, autonomy in the national monetary policy in a situation of free capital mobility is subject to speculative attacks (the most obvious example in the EU took place in July 1993). On the one hand, the longer the transition to a single currency, the greater the fragility of the system. On the other, a fast acceptance of a single money can provoke harsh regional disequilibria for which the countries may not be prepared (for example, a lack of stabilisers such as well-endowed regional funds). Policy makers need to balance the two sides before they decide. They also have to take into account the German experience. Unemployment increased in the former East Germany after reunification with the Western part of the country in 1990. It resulted directly from an instant merger of the two economies that were on a very different level of development before they were ready for a full EMU. Should the same be repeated in the EU? If one member country is in economic expansion, while the other one is in recession, they need different monetary policy countermeasures. How to reconcile this in the absence of effective built-in stabilisers or automatic transfer of sufficient funds?

The above theoretical model about parallel currencies has two caveats. It ignores network effects and switching costs (Dowd and Greenaway, 1993a, p. 1180). For example, after the break-up of the former Soviet Union (1992), the rouble was a currency which did not fit well into the new realities. Certain newly independent states continued to use roubles because of network effects, that is, because most of their trading partners were using them. In addition, the switching costs from one currency to another are quite high. At the limit, it is perhaps better to use only one money because of the network effects, conversion charges and switching costs. If the benefits of a single currency outweigh these costs, welfare is maximised and it is justified, from the economic point of view, in switching to a single currency. According to a view from the start of the 1990s, in the case of the EU, the German mark would be the best option as the EU common currency. The mark had the biggest existing network, while the Bundesbank had greater credibility than any of the existing central banks in the EU (Dowd and Greenaway, 1993b, p. 243).

The currencies of member countries in an EMU are perfect substitutes. On the one hand, it would be meaningless to speak here about a parallel currency, since any parallel currency would be indistinguishable from national currencies in everything but name. The concept of a parallel currency becomes meaningful only in the intermediate stage of an EMU, when different currencies are not perfect substitutes because of transaction costs and/or exchange rate expectations. Reductions in exchange rate variability diminish the usefulness of a parallel (basket) currency as an instrument for risk diversification, unless transaction costs in the parallel (common) currency decline by more than the transaction costs in the component currencies. On the other hand, a parallel currency is unlikely to develop in a case where national currencies are only very imperfect substitutes, because of high conversion costs. Widespread use of a parallel currency alongside national currencies can therefore be expected only under a high degree of monetary integration (Gros, 1989, p. 224).

A common currency may replace national currencies after some period of adjustment. Stability in the monetary sphere may be a result. However, the new and single currency in the area would not solve the problem of the budget deficits of member countries that would be revealed, in part, as regional disequilibria.

Gresham's law says that in a situation of two currencies (in his example, gold and silver coins) circulating side by side in the economy, then 'the bad money will drive out the good', except where there is a fixed exchange rate between the two moneys. This result has not materialised in certain instances.[10]

5. European Union

BACKGROUND

Integration in the EU has advanced at a pace faster than envisaged in the Treaty of Rome. The customs union was fully established among the founding member countries in 1968, a year and a half ahead of schedule. This was one of the most significant initial achievements of the group.

After the initial success in the establishment of a customs union, the EU contemplated the establishment of an EMU. There were two schools of thought about how to implement this idea. They were the 'monetarists' and the 'economists'. The first school (Belgium, France and Luxembourg) argued that a promising EMU requires an irrevocable fixity of exchange rates of the participating countries from the outset. The member countries will, then, be driven to coordinate their economic policies in order to mitigate and, eventually, eliminate the discrepancies in their economies, necessary for a full EMU. They also argued in favour of a well-endowed fund for the support of adjustments of the balance of payments. Complete freedom of capital movements should be permitted only after the establishment of a full EMU. Finally, they felt that supranationality should be on a relatively low level.

The school of 'economists' (Germany and the Netherlands) argued that fixed exchange rates for a group of countries that are at relatively different levels of development is a formidable task. They argued that the coordination of economic policies should be the primary task, because it would bring economic harmonisation among the participating countries. They argued in favour of a free movement of capital from the outset and felt that fixed exchange rates could be introduced only after the fulfilment of the above conditions.

The Werner Report (1970) was offered as the blueprint for EMU in the EU. The report required fixed exchange rates and free mobility of capital. Thus, it represented a compromise between the two schools. Super-optimism (EMU by 1980) was not rewarded because the report overestimated the will of the member states to abandon their monetary authority in favour of a supranational body, in particular in the light of the turmoil on the currency markets during the 1970s. This approach may also have failed because it wanted to fix rates of exchange without prior monetary reform among the member countries.

EUROPEAN MONETARY SYSTEM

The early 1970s were characterised by significant turbulence on the international monetary scene. Currencies were fluctuating, so this state of affairs endangered the functioning of trade flows in the EU. The Council of Ministers asked the member governments not only to follow the ±2.25 per cent margins of fluctuation in relation to the dollar, but also to reduce the level of fluctuation among their respective currencies. This created the 'European snake' (common margins of fluctuation). If one plotted the daily fluctuations of the currencies of the EU member states, then one would get a snake-like ribbon. The width of the snake depended on the fluctuation of the strongest and the weakest currencies, remaining always within the ±2.25 per cent fluctuation margins of the dollar tunnel. The creation of the 'snake' was mainly a European reaction to the erratic behaviour of the dollar on the international money market.

The main feature of the 'snake' was intervention. When the sum of the fluctuations in the 'snake' exceeded the margins, intervention was supposed to take place (the strongest currency should purchase the weakest one). The dollar tunnel disappeared in 1973, so the 'snake' found itself in the lake. The currencies in the 'snake' were entering and leaving the system quite often. This introduced uncertainty in trade relations in the EU. Apart from external pressures which the 'snake' was unable to resist, an internal shortcoming (different national monetary policies) also played a role. Something should have been done about that.

The member countries of the EU wanted not just to preserve the already achieved level of economic integration, but also to add to it. A further step was the creation of the EMS. The approach was completely different from the one which established the 'snake'. Instead of preparing various economic plans for political consideration, the EU member countries first delivered their political decision about the establishment of the system, and then reached agreement about the technical/operational details of the system. The EMS was introduced in 1979.

The objectives of the EMS were:

- to stabilise exchange rates through closer monetary cooperation among the member countries;
- to promote further integration of the group; and
- to contribute to the stabilisation of international monetary relations.

The key role in the EMS was played by the European Currency Unit (ECU). The ECU was basically a 'cocktail' of fixed proportions of currencies of EU member countries. The share of every currency in the ECU depended on the economic potential of the country (aggregate GDP), its share in intra-EU trade and the need for short-term monetary support. The composition of the ECU is presented in Table 2.1. Alterations in the composition of the ECU may occur every five years or when the share of each currency changes by at least 25 per cent in relation to the originally calculated value. In addition, the composition of the ECU can be changed when the currency of a new member country enters the 'basket'. The currency composition of the ECU was 'frozen' by Article 118 of the Treaty of Rome (as revised by the Maastricht Treaty), which is why the currencies of Austria, Finland and Sweden are not included in the basket.

The exchange rate mechanism (ERM) of the EMS has been at the centre of controversy since its inception. Every currency in the EMS had its own central rate versus other partner currencies and the ECU. In relation to the partner currencies in the system individual currencies could fluctuate within a ±2.25 per cent band. The exceptions were the Italian lira, the Spanish peseta and the British pound which were permitted to float within a ±6 per cent limit.[11] When a currency reached its limit (upper or lower) of fluctuation in relation to another EMS partner currency, then intervention in the national currency of one of the two central banks is compulsory. Intervention within the margins of fluctuation may be either in the national currencies of the EMS members or in dollars.[12]

The fluctuation of each EMS currency against the ECU was slightly stricter. The Commission has individualised each currency's margin of fluctuation. It was strictest for the German mark (±1.51 per cent) and widest for the Irish pound (±2.22 per cent) (the currencies under the 'special treatment' had wider margins of fluctuation than the standard ones in relation to the ECU).

Table 2.1   Composition of the ECU (%)

Currency	Weight in the 'basket'			
	1979–84	1984–89	1989–94	1995
1 German mark	33.0	32.0	30.1	32.7
2 French franc	19.8	19.0	19.0	20.8
3 Pound sterling	13.3	15.0	13.0	11.2
4 Dutch guilder	10.5	10.1	9.4	10.2
5 Belgian franc	9.3	8.2	7.6	8.4
6 Italian lira	9.5	10.2	10.15	7.2
7 Spanish peseta	–	–	5.3	4.2
8 Danish krone	3.1	2.7	2.45	2.7
9 Irish pound	1.1	1.2	1.1	1.1
10 Portuguese escudo	–	–	0.8	0.7
11 Greek drachma	–	1.3	0.8	0.5
12 Luxembourg franc	0.4	0.3	0.3	0.3
Total	100.0	100.0	100.0	100.0

Source: European Monetary Institute (1996).

There was an implicit objective behind the relatively strict margins of fluctuation for currencies in the EMS: to drive member countries to accept similar economic policies and to converge. This convergence does not necessarily aim at averaging out the economic performance criteria. Although the EMS has not produced full convergence of the macroeconomic indicators of the member countries, it seemed for quite some time that it was heading towards the desired outcome. The best signal was that most member countries remained in the EMS despite strains.

In order to prevent frequent interventions, the EMS has introduced an early-warning system in the form of a divergence indicator. The divergence threshold was ±75 per cent of a currency's fluctuation in relation to the ECU. The role of this indicator was ambiguous. As soon as the divergence threshold was reached, the countries in question were not formally required to do anything, even to consult. Therefore, this innovation has not played an important role in the EMS. None the less, consultation and cooperation of the monetary authorities of the EU member countries have compensated, at least in part, for this shortcoming.

The strongest arguments for the non-participating countries to join the ERM of the EMS seemed to be predominantly political. It was not conducive to integration for them to remain aloof from one of the most significant achievements of the EU at that time. In addition, and more importantly, the creation of a genuine internal market for goods, services and factors would be incomplete without a single market for money.

The EMS funds for exchange market interventions were relatively well endowed. The very-short-term financing facility for compulsory interventions provides the participating central banks with an unlimited amount of partner currency loans. None the less, the Bundesbank did not accept in practice intervention without limits. The short-term monetary support disposed of ECU14 billion for the finance of temporary balance of payments deficits, while the medium-term support facility disposes of ECU11 billion (but the use of this mechanism was subject to certain conditions).

A country with a better performance in inflation, balance of payments, employment and growth than other countries has least pressure to adjust and, in relation to its size and weight, it may call the tune in the shaping of other countries' economic variables. Hence, Germany was able to dominate within the EMS. The system operated asymmetrically in formulating the monetary policies of other member countries as they had to bear the adjustment burden. Since inflation was reduced and other monetary variables were generally aligned among most member countries, the EMS operated in a more symmetric way before the reunification of Germany in October 1990.[13]

The EMS could sometimes slow down the rate of economic adjustment of a member country. When countries borrow on the international financial markets, such markets do not consider exclusively the creditworthiness (reserves, deficits, experience in adjustments and outlooks) of the borrowing country. These markets also consider membership of the EMS and its possibilities for financial support. In this indirect way, financial markets take into account the reserves of other EMS countries. The markets believe that the partner countries will help the borrowing country in financial difficulties. This was a recognition of the relative success of the EMS. However, it may prevent a country accepting greater monetary discipline. A government may employ a more ruthless method of eroding the real burden of debt and use inflation. In any case, a country which follows a policy of a relative monetary undiscipline will reduce domestic reserves and lose creditworthiness in the long run. Foreign creditors may reasonably demand higher interest rates which usually deter investment and, hence, reduce the future economic potential of the country. An agreed limitation for national borrowing needs to be a part of an EMU.

Apart from funds for exchange market interventions, other EMS adjustment mechanisms include home price and income alterations, rates of interest and control of capital flows, as well as increased cooperation and exchange of information. Controls of internal trade flows are, of course, prohibited.

The rates of exchange in the EMS were semi-fixed. The EMS did not have as its goal the petrification of exchange rates among member countries. The adjustments of the central rates may take place either every five years or according to needs. When all other mechanisms for intervention were used up, the country in question could ask for permission to change the central rate of its currency. The Council of Ministers usually decided about these changes during the weekend (when the financial markets are closed). The effects of realignments (or devaluations) may be eroded by inflation. So, the best and, surely, the hardest way for the stability of the system is that the deficit countries increase productivity above the EU average.

In spite of its relative rigidity, the EMS made the rates of exchange quasi-flexible. If a currency was experiencing difficulties that could not be solved by intervention, then the system permitted adjustments (revaluations and devaluations) of the central rate of exchange. This kind of adjustment has happened relatively often during the first years of the existence of the EMS.

A change of the central rate of a currency (devaluation) was still a permitted means for the restoration of competitiveness among EMS member countries. In a distant scenario without national currencies, even *de facto*, the restoration of national competitiveness could be achieved by an increase in productivity, reduction in wages or by labour migration to the advanced regions or all of these. The US is an example where wages are flexible and labour is highly mobile. At the same time a single currency has a smooth internal performance. The US interregional adjustments are eased by a system of implicit federal government transfers of real resources. The federal government spends much and taxes little in the backward or ill-performing states/regions, while it does the reverse in the advanced states/regions.[14] A similar mechanism does not (yet) exist in the EU, which, with its vast internal market, does not yet have economic stabilisers on the American scale that are intended to ease the adjustment troubles of both countries and regions within them. There are, however, growing structural funds in the EU. The adjustment requires not only the transfer of real resources, but also measures to enhance mobility of factors from low- to high-productivity regions. On this account, the EU has so far failed. Hence, because of relatively low labour mobility, EU countries will be able to sustain relatively high taxes on people's income.

All member countries of the EU have exchanged for ECUs 20 per cent of their gold reserves (the role of gold was partly reaffirmed)[15] and 20 per cent of their dollar reserves with the European Monetary Institute (until 1994, the European Fund for Monetary Cooperation). These assets were swapped on a revolving quarterly basis for ECUs. Hence the ECU was not a newly created reserve asset which was an addition to the existing stocks of reserves such as the special drawing rights. The creation of the ECU transformed a part of the existing reserve assets into another asset. The amount of ECUs issued changed every quarter in relation to the changes in member countries' volume of reserves, the price of gold and the dollar exchange rate.

The ECU was used as:

- an accounting unit for intervention;
- a means of settlement among central banks;
- a part of international financial reserves;
- a basis for the calculation of the divergence indicator;
- a unit for the store of value (because of its relative stability); and
- a unit for financial transactions and statistics of the EU administration.

There were, also, ECU-denominated bonds. Many banks opened personal accounts in ECUs and offered an interest rate which was a weighted average of interest rates of the participant countries in the ECU. They also offered travellers' cheques denominated in ECUs. Interest rate differentials reflect mainly differences in the national rates of inflation. Once the exchange rates start to move with inflation differentials, the profitability of holding ECUs was expected to diminish.

The ECU used by the monetary authorities was the official ECU, while businesses and the public used the private or commercial ECU. Nevertheless, the ECU market was not fragmented. All dealings were in a single ECU, as the definition of both was the same. A central bank could hold ECUs. If the national currency comes under pressure, the bank could sell ECUs and purchase the national currency. This might be a cheaper and less notable way of intervention than a direct borrowing of other currencies to buy domestic when the exchange rate was falling. The major reason for the relative spread in the use of private ECUs was the demand of business for simplifying transactions and, possibly, avoiding capital controls where they existed. The ECU was attractive because of its greater stability in relation to its components. Apart from the intra-firm trade, firms did not have great incentives to use the ECU when the rates of exchange were not stable (since they may have wished to exploit the difference in prices). Non-EU investors preferred to deal in a single currency rather than several different ones. The market value of the ECU was not directly influenced by the value of the dollar as it was not incorporated in the ECU basket as is the case with the special drawing rights. Therefore, dollar holders could buy ECUs and hedge against the dollar exchange risk.

A shock came in September 1992. The demand for funds to cover the excessive costs of the reunification of Germany put pressure on its budget. In order to contain this inflationary pressure, Germany raised interest rates. At about the same time, the US wanted to revive demand by cutting interest rates. The dollar became cheaper, while the German mark became dearer. The divergency prompted speculation that hit the weaker currencies hard in the EMS. Currency market speculation forced Britain, followed by Italy, to suspend their membership in the ERM. The EMS was on the brink of a breakdown. In this situation, a single EU currency would evade such a crisis. Britain gained certain benefits from the 25 per cent depreciation in the value of the pound in the following months. For example, Philips moved the manufacturing of cathode tubes from the Netherlands to Britain. Likewise, Hoover relocated the production of vacuum cleaners from France to Britain.

Adjustments in the rates of exchange together with capital controls were used by some countries in the EMS, for example Italy and France, to control the domestic monetary system more easily than through other, relatively harsh means, such as recession. They were able to follow, to an extent and for some time, a different course in the national macroeconomic variables from their foreign partners. Capital, one of the major lubricants of the economy, was 'forced' to remain at home. In addition, an outflow of capital pushes up interest rates. This slows down the economy, perhaps at a moment when it needs to grow. However, the problem is that capital controls retard structural adjustments that need to take place in any case. Although a short-term effect of controls may bring certain policy successes, the long-term costs of the structural transformation increase, which is why an interest rate policy may be a preferred policy means.

Capital controls are effective ways to manage monetary affairs in a situation where money markets expect adjustments in the exchange rate.[16] Then, controls drive holders to keep (in the country) the currency that is about to be devalued. Controls may be permanent or temporary (as emergency measures to prevent speculative capital flows). In the absence of capital controls, devaluation of weak currencies cannot be postponed; however, controls make the delay of devaluation possible. None the less, delays increase uncertainty about the rate of exchange in the future and, hence, jeopardise investment decisions. With capital controls, a relatively modest increase in the national rate of interest will achieve the desired monetary policy effect. Without capital controls, the only instrument that can be used with the same effect is a sudden and, usually, large increase in interest rates. The main defence of capital controls is not found in the fact that they are cost free, but rather that they are less costly than the movements of exchange and interest rates that would occur without these controls (Folkerts-Landau and Mathieson, 1989, p. 8).

The removal of the remaining capital controls in the EU in 1995 was one of the notable achievements of the Single Market Programme. It made residents of the EU sensitive to differences in interest rates. Transnational corporations (TNCs), including banks, as major beneficiaries of the dismantling of capital controls, were able to easily and swiftly change and diversify the currency composition and maturity of their financial portfolios. By doing so, TNCs and other money holders may jeopardise the objective of monetary policy of individual member countries in a situation with easy and cheap currency substitution. An increase in the national rate of interest in order to reduce the supply of money and 'cool' the economy will have the opposite effect. Increased interest rates will suddenly attract an inflow of foreign capital and increase the national supply of money. Such swift changes are not very likely in the flow of goods (and services.) Conversely, if the intention of the national government is to stimulate home economic activity by a reduction in interest rates, the effect of such a policy will be the opposite from the one intended. Capital will fly out of the country to locations where rates of interest are higher. Without capital controls, investors speculate about which currency is to be devalued next. Enormous capital flows can destabilise exchange rates. With a daily trade of about $1.2 trillion on foreign-exchange markets and with more than one currency in the market, it is possible to gamble. No national intervention can triumph over the speculators. This happened in the EU in the summers of 1992 and 1993. The grand dreams of an EMU in the relatively medium term were, in fact, pushed further into the future.

In the situation with huge and rapid capital movements, a monetary union with the major trading partners may offer a promising degree of insulation against harmful features of international capital mobility. A separate currency and independent setting of the rate of exchange may move in a way obstructive to the economy. As such it may become in itself a source of shocks to the economy.

Without capital controls, large differences in the rate of interest among the EMS countries cannot be sustained. In the new situation, the EU member countries have no other rational choice but to pool their national monetary policies and cooperate. Any increase in monetary instability among EU currencies will provoke the mobility of funds in the search for a greater profit in the short run or a greater security in the long run, thus making it impossible to maintain EMS parities without even greater harmonisation of national monetary policies (Panić, 1991). The Bundesbank was calling the tune in the EMS. In that situation a pooling of monetary policies among the countries of the EU can increase the sovereignty of smaller countries because they would, in the new situation, have some say in the EU monetary policy-making process from within. Although national central banks may become increasingly independent from their national governments, they need to enhance their reliance on other national central banks in the EU.

A reduction in the variance of economic indicators among countries may illustrate their economic convergence. The narrowing of the differences in the performance criteria among countries does not necessarily mean that their standards of living are becoming more equal. Membership of the EMS may be used by the national government as a convincing argument during the pursuance of a prudent national economic policy in the fight against the opposition. The EMS has introduced convergence in domestic monetary policies and inflation rates, but it has not been fully backed up by corresponding progress in the fiscal sector and external balance.

A mere convergence in the rate of inflation and other monetary variables may not be enough for the smooth operation of the single EU market. The EMS was not able to increase significantly the use of the ECU, the role of the European Fund for Monetary Cooperation was marginalised and the present form of the system was unable to bring about spontaneous monetary integration. Those objectives might be achieved if there was a common European Central Bank, a system of central banks or a common monetary authority. This did not happen before the implementation of the Maastricht Treaty because of a fear that the monetary issues would be passed on to a remote bureaucracy. Every government was afraid of losing monetary sovereignty: the right to cheat on its citizens, firms and other holders of its money without a promise to convert paper money into gold. Another fear was that they might not be able to pursue their own stabilisation policy. These anxieties were not well founded. In order to carry on with the national stabilisation, balance of payments, regional, industrial and other policies, governments still have at their disposal taxes, certain subsidies, some procurement and certain budget deficits. The only (severe) restrictions to their sovereignty to choose stabilisation policies were that they could not employ exchange rate changes and have a different rate of inflation from their partner countries.

It must always be borne in mind that in an EMU, the national governments still have a chance to tax and spend in the way they think is most appropriate. Budget deficits are still possible, but subject to only one condition: expenditure must be financed by borrowing (on commercial terms) rather than by printing domestic money. For example, borrowing and expenditure of the cantons in Switzerland and provinces in Canada are not subject to constraints. The *Länder* in Germany restrict borrowing only to the extent that it is necessary to finance investment. The federal states and local governments in the US are not allowed to run deficits (this is an American version of the Stability and Growth Pact). Only in Australia does the federal government continuously supervise state debts.

The freedom to tax and spend in an EMU, however, is not absolute. As soon as a country's national finances jeopardise the stability of the union, such as excess imports that depress the value of a common currency, the union's authority may intervene. It may impose limits on the borrowing from the central bank and other sources, ceilings on the budget deficit, a request for non-interest-bearing deposits and impose fines. In a single-currency area, foreign debt has to be serviced by export earnings. The national debt, however, does not present an immediate real burden on the economy because it represents a transfer between present and future generations.

There may be a temptation for a country in a monetary system to run a budget deficit for quite some time according to current needs. Although governments are often safer borrowers in relation to private ones,[17] capital markets will increase interest rates to heavy borrowers when their creditworthiness is jeopardised. Big budget deficits keep long-term interest rates on a higher level than would otherwise be the case. This reduces the size and effectiveness of the cuts in short-term interest rates. The governments of the EU countries generally failed to do this during the 1980s, hence the lack of power in employing fiscal policy to prop up recovery in the 1990s. If a state in federations such as the US and Canada increases its borrowing, then the value of government bonds falls throughout the country. In this case, the federal government can step in to correct the distortion. However, such a well-developed corrective mechanism does not yet exist in the EU.

6. European Monetary Union

Monetary unions were often, but not always, created as a part of the process of political unification among countries.[18] Economic reasons for an EMU include enhanced monetary stability, improved spatial and industrial allocation of resources, boosted competition because of transparent prices, deepened integration, reduced transaction costs, access to wider markets, gains from economies of scale and from trade, as well as gains that come from harmonisation of policies. Non-economic reasons such as geographical proximity, common language, culture, history and religion contributed to monetary unification. The break-ups of monetary unions are foremost found in political factors. Once the political unity among the participating countries dissolves, it is most likely that the monetary union will vanish (Bordo and Jonung, 1999, pp. 24–5). Hence, the political will and the firm promise and determination to respect fully a common currency system explains the rise and fall[19] of monetary unions. Interestingly enough, the Irish break-up with sterling had no noted effect on trade between Britain and Ireland.

The main argument in favour of a common central bank is that it reduces uncertainties and conflicts about and among national monetary policies. It does so by providing a forum in which national views can be represented and problems resolved. In the absence of a common central bank, national conflicts are resolved by market forces with adverse externalities for efforts to promote greater stability of exchange rates (Folkerts-Landau and Mathieson, 1989, p. 15). Therefore, within a common central bank the national sovereignty may be increased in comparison to the previous situation. Independent central banks, such as the judiciary, are constitutional institutions since they are not accountable to the elected government or parliament. Their autonomy comes from a general consensus about long-term economic objectives and from the fact that their instruments may be badly abused by the political majority of the day (Vaubel, 1990, p. 941).

Even though the experts are not subject to great political pressure to court popular opinion, a question still remains: do the appointed central bankers (a part of the elite) possess a knowledge about the country's long-term needs that is superior to that held by the governments that represent the voting public? The same question also applies to the entire national elite. Does it foster the necessary dialogue and cooperation with the general public? Does the general public have the relevant information and clarification by the experts and by the elite to understand and evaluate how a certain decision factors into the national interest? Does the general public have the knowledge to identify and assess the importance and character of crucial decisions for the shape and direction of the national interest? Does the general public have the time and interest to bother with these issues? Voter apathy is becoming common. Is this a reaction to being treated with disdain by the remote and arrogant elite? Or is this situation created deliberately? People need to hold on to their jobs, to have two part-time jobs because of the general uncertainty (possible unemployment or terrorist attacks), because of their mortgages, savings for their old age and/or the education of their children. Hence, they pass on these decisions to the elite. They know that the elite will get what it wants in the end. And all this has a democratic sugar-coating.

During the discussions that led to the Maastricht Treaty, there were two extreme possibilities for the final shape of the EU Central Bank and a number of intermediary ones. One extreme was the model of Germany's Bundesbank. It was independent from the government in the conduct of monetary policy and possibly, therefore, quite successful. The Bundesbank ensured stable prices, high employment, balanced foreign trade, as well as a constant and reasonable economic growth. The other extreme was the Bank of France, in which the government had a full stake. Thus France wanted to see a kind of 'accountability' (transparency in operations and reporting) of the EU Central Bank to public bodies. As Germany was the engine of EU monetary stability until 1992–93, the Maastricht Treaty opted for this kind of central bank for the EU. Many EU member countries preferred to see a 'German-influenced' EU bank, rather than the continuation of the prevailing system that is 'German controlled'. In the system with binding rules and procedures, the smaller EU countries may be represented on the bank's board where they could, at least to an extent, shape policy from within.

The Delors Report (1989) gave an impetus to the creation of the EMU. It envisaged the EMU in three stages. Its wise approach was not to state any specific date apart from mid-1990 for the beginning of the first stage. During the first stage, the member countries would strengthen the coordination of their economic and monetary policies. The removal of the remaining capital controls would require this in any case. All countries would enter the ERM of the EMS. Stage two would be marked by the creation of the European Central Bank (a system of central banks or a monetary authority). The major macroeconomic indicators would be set for all member countries including the size and financing of the budget deficit. In addition, the margins of fluctuation in the ERM would be narrowed. The first two stages would not be fully stable, as there would be the potential for speculative attacks. In the last stage of the creation of the EMU, a common central bank would be the only authority responsible for the conduct of monetary policy throughout the EU. Exchange rates among the national currencies would be permanently fixed without any fluctuations. A single currency would emerge. It may be a necessary condition for a genuine single market where a national competitiveness would not be influenced by the individual alterations in exchange rates. This was the blueprint for the finalisation of the Maastricht Treaty.

In 1990, the British proposed an alternative plan that would introduce a 'hard ECU' as the 13th currency at that time, in stage two, as a parallel currency. It would be an additional anti-inflationary control on governments that aim to ease national monetary policy. It would be issued by the central bank in exchange for deposits of national currencies. The 'hard ECU' would be managed in such a way that each national central bank would compensate the Union's central bank for any losses caused by devaluation of its currency and that any inflating national central bank would buy back its national currency with, for example, dollars or yen. Wide acceptability of the 'hard ECUs' would prevent national central banks from inflating. The problem with this plan was that the British saw it as an end in itself, not as a vehicle towards a single currency of the EU. This plan received little support during negotiations over EMU.

After the currency disturbances of September 1992 when Britain and Italy left the ERM, a new and bigger shock took place at the end of July 1993 with the actual demise of the ERM of the EMS. Germany's need to obtain funds to finance the reintegration of its eastern region increased interest rates. The country placed its national interest ahead of the concerns of the EU by refusing to cut interest rates.[20] This produced a currency crisis. To ease the strain, a way out was found in an increase in the margins for the fluctuations of the currencies participating in the ERM. They were widened from ±2.25 per cent to ±15 per cent from the central parity. The 'dirty float' began. The EMS revealed its fragility. However, a step back from the EMU path was a preferable action to total suspension of the EMS. The widening of opportunities to fluctuate within the ERM increased the room for differences in the national economic policies. Even though this was a possibility, it was not exercised. Countries endeavoured to keep the exchange rate of their currencies within the 'old' margins of fluctuation. None the less, the mere existence of the permitted wider margins for fluctuations introduced an element of uncertainty.

A condition for the establishment of the EMU is that 'normal' (without a definition) fluctuation margins for currencies need to be observed for at least two years. However, what was 'normal' in the situation when the ERM remained only in name? The wide increase in fluctuation margins made a mockery of the Maastricht Treaty's intentions to introduce a single currency in the relatively near future. One needs to remember, however, that annual exchange rate movements of ±15 per cent are quite common outside the EU (for example, the dollar).

The Maastricht Treaty is in essence mostly about the EMU. This is voiced both in the Preamble and in Article B, as well as in Articles 2 and 98–124, of the Treaty of Rome (as amended by the Maastricht Treaty). This was an expected step after the establishment of a free internal market in 1993. For a free flow of goods and services, as well as for an efficient sectoral and geographical allocation of resources, a necessary condition is a degree of stability in exchange rates and a removal of conversion costs.

According to the Maastricht Treaty, EMU is to be achieved in three stages. During the first, there was a reinforcement of coordination of economic and monetary policies of the member countries. The second stage started in January 1994 with the establishment of the European Monetary Institute in Frankfurt. This took place in an unsettled exchange rate environment. The European Monetary Institute was to coordinate the EU members' monetary policies and prepare the conditions for the final stage. The central banks of the member states need to become independent before the end of the second stage when the EMI would be transformed into an independent European Central Bank (ECB). In fact, there would be a European System of Central

Banks, which would be composed of the ECB and the central banks of the member states (Article 107 of the Treaty of Rome).

The ECB is supposed to be very tough on inflation. However, this policy could cost the EU countries hundreds of thousands of existing and new jobs. Perhaps this may be partly true, but the primary source of the EU unemployment problem is not necessarily in a looser monetary or fiscal policy (although both of them were made inflexible by the Maastricht criteria for EMU), but rather in reforms of labour markets and the welfare system. Politicians might have realised somehow belatedly that the only 'soft' option for economic adjustment needs to come from flexibility in labour markets.

According to the Treaty of Rome (Article 105 as amended by the Maastricht Treaty), the ECB has to:

- keep prices stable;[21]
- define and implement the monetary policy;
- conduct foreign-exchange operations;
- hold and manage official foreign reserves of the member states; and
- promote the smooth operation of the payments system.

There was a chance that Frankfurt would take the major part of trade in the EU single currency if the pound stayed out of this project. Having an EMU whose major financial markets are off-shore would be, on the surface, an unusual arrangement. However, London has already become the market where trading in the German mark, Europe's most important currency (before the introduction of the euro), took place. Hence, its position on the financial markets should not be seriously threatened.

The siting of London as the principal European financial market need not be jeopardised by the location of the ECB in Frankfurt. The US Federal Reserve is based in Washington, DC, while the principal financial centre is New York. London continues to have big advantages over Frankfurt. The chief institutional investors are located in London; regulation is rather light; and there is a cluster of accumulated talent, knowledge, experience and expertise in finance. More people work in the City of London in finance than constitute the entire population of Frankfurt.[22]

The Council of Ministers was supposed to decide by a qualified majority whether a majority (at least eight) of the EU countries fulfil all of the following five necessary criteria for the third stage of EMU (Article 121 of the Treaty of Rome and Protocol on the Convergence Criteria of the Maastricht Treaty):

- a high degree of price stability (inflation within the margin of 1.5 per cent of the three best-performing EU countries);

- sound public financial position (budget deficit of less than 3 per cent of GDP);[23]
- a national debt of less than 60 per cent of GDP;[24]
- the observance of the 'normal' fluctuation margins (no devaluation within the EU exchange rate mechanism for at least two preceding years); and
- a durability of convergence of economic policies that needs to be reflected in the long-term interest rate levels (interest rate has to be within the 2 per cent margin of the three best-performing EU countries).

The final decision about the eligibility of the countries was to be taken in 1998. If a country fails one (or, perhaps, two conditions), but if it makes good progress on these issues, it may be let into the EMU. If the Council is not able to decide about the beginning of the third stage, the Maastricht Treaty stipulated that it would begin on 1 January 1999 for the countries which fulfil the necessary conditions for the EMU. These countries would irrevocably fix their exchange rates and the ECU would subsequently replace the national currencies under the name of the euro. This was expected to unleash the full potential of the genuine Single European Market. The ECB would follow its primary commitment of price stability and, consequently, set interest rates and conduct foreign-exchange operations. In addition, the ECB would support economic growth and employment. The ECB would report regularly to the EU finance ministers (meetings of ECOFIN, which would issue broad economic policy guidelines) and to the European Parliament. In any case, the implementation of the five criteria for the third stage of the EMU, if carried out strictly, would have a certain deflationary effect on the economy of the EU.

There are two theoretical types of deflation (a general fall in the level of prices):

- 'Good deflation' is the consequence of improvements in technology (faster computers or more fuel efficient engines) as this permits the production of better new goods at lower costs.
- 'Bad deflation' is that which creates production overcapacity: the market is flooded with goods that it cannot absorb. Prices fall, but producers neither hire new workers nor invest in new equipment. Consumers are accustomed to falling prices and postpone purchases. Hence, producers have even less revenue. The breakdown of the relation between supply and demand is at the heart of bad deflation.

The immense analytical and policy problem is that the two types of deflation often take place at the same time and within the same industry. Signals can be mixed, so policy advice and actions may be confused and damaging. The way to tackle the deflationary economy is to ensure a sustained demand (consumer spending). Leapfrogging in technology and/or expansion in demand can tackle this problem. With its 'culture' of relentless innovation, the American economy has a degree of resistance to deflationary pressure.

Deflation may easily be cured if the central bank prints more money and passes it to the banks. With this extra cash, banks issue more loans, the rate of interest falls, there is more investment by firms and spending by the population, the economy picks up and the price level stops falling. That is how it works in theory. Suppose now that the economy is in such bad shape that a decline in interest rate towards zero is not enough to revive the economy and to push it towards prosperity. This situation is known as a liquidity trap. There is extra money in the economy, but these funds rest idle. There is no point in lending money if there is no reward (profit) for doing so. Hence, the monetary policy becomes ineffective. If the expectation is that prices would fall further in the future, then consumers would postpone their purchases. This would further depress the current demand.

Falling prices also mean falling incomes and capacity utilisation, as well as rising unemployment. Firms may find that they have to pay their fixed interest rates from a dwindling cash flow, while families have to pay a fixed mortgage out of shrinking income (the real value of debt rises). The indebted cut their spending. All this further discourages both borrowing and spending by the private sector. In order to balance its books, the government may borrow until the investors have faith in the government's ability to repay its debt. At the point at which debt grows faster than revenue and when there is no credible scenario that the budget can come under control, creditors would not lend money to such a government. Then, the government may both increase taxes and cut social spending, which became a well-accepted way of life (pensions, health care and education) and a part of the social contract in Europe. All this would hit hard the middle class and those in need.

One strategy to fight deflation can be to announce an inflation target by a credible[25] central bank and to flood the economy with money. A certain, but small, inflation may always be welcome in the countries that use the euro. The reason for this type of controlled inflation is simple. It is the inflexibility in prices and nominal wages to downward pressure. If inflation is non-existent or if it is very low, real wages and prices in weak industries will remain high. This would trigger bankruptcies and job losses. Germany and France are the main victims of very low inflation. The employed in these two countries have relatively high wages and high prices prevail in the production of non-tradable goods and services.[26] Labour market reforms, including a reduction in welfare benefits, are also one of the policy choices. However, the political process for this is thorny and highly uncertain.

The Maastricht convergence criteria for the eurozone are arbitrary. Economic theory suggests other conditions for an EMU. These include flexibility in labour markets, factor (labour) mobility, openness, diversification and fiscal transfers. The Maastricht criteria could be met once the countries are *in* the EMU; however, before such union takes place it may be extremely hard to do so. 'The Maastricht treaty has it back to front. . . . On balance the Maastricht convergence criteria are *obstacles* to a monetary union in Europe' (de Grauwe, 1994, pp. 159–61). The question is whether the difficult road towards a durable EMU as structured by the Maastricht Treaty is becoming impossible.[27]

In the rush to meet the Maastricht criteria for the third stage of the EMU, governments introduced additional (temporary) taxes, took on austerity measures and, consequently, restrained flexibility of fiscal policy. The consequences were numerous industrial actions, as well as high taxation as an obstacle to employment.

The 1998 decision was that Austria, Belgium, Finland, France, Germany, Ireland, Italy, Luxembourg, the Netherlands, Portugal and Spain satisfied the Maastricht criteria for the EMU. Even if some countries such as Belgium and Italy (later, also, Greece) had excessive public debt, they were judged to have made sufficient progress towards the satisfaction of this criterion. Greece subsequently fulfilled the same conditions and joined the eurozone group in 2001. Britain, Denmark and Sweden chose to stay detached from participation in the eurozone.

A single currency is favourable for the US economy (there are no harmful effects in the sense of restraints to the national macroeconomic policy obvious in the eurozone) because it has three features that are still missing in the EU:

- wage flexibility (non-existent in the EU);
- relatively high mobility of labour (non-existent in the EU, even within the EU member countries); and
- automatic fiscal transfers from the central government (non-existent in the EU).

As shown in Figures 2.1 and 2.2, the Maastricht convergence criteria for the EMU were applied in a relaxed way. If the EMU took place only

Monetary integration 127

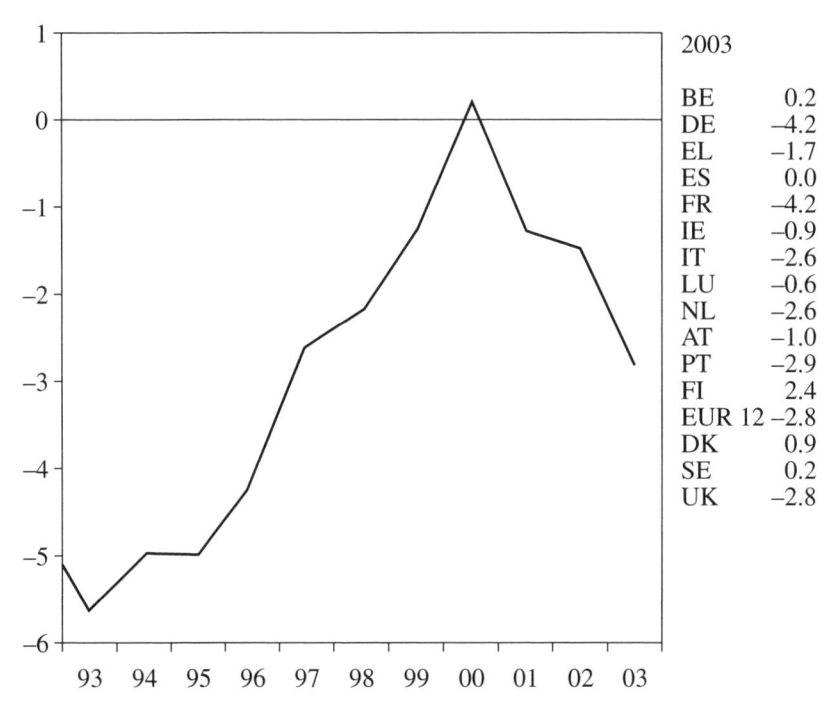

% of GDP

	2003
BE	0.2
DE	−4.2
EL	−1.7
ES	0.0
FR	−4.2
IE	−0.9
IT	−2.6
LU	−0.6
NL	−2.6
AT	−1.0
PT	−2.9
FI	2.4
EUR 12	−2.8
DK	0.9
SE	0.2
UK	−2.8

Source: European Commission Economic and Financial Affairs (2003).

Figure 2.1 General government balance as per cent of GDP, 1993–2003

among the select group of countries that strictly fulfilled the Maastricht criteria, the excluded countries would face divergence, rather than convergence in certain macroeconomic variables, because they have been left out of the arrangement. Exchange rates between the full eurozone countries and those that are outside could be volatile.[28] This would have an adverse impact on trade flows in the Single European Market of the EU.

As so much political capital had been invested in the EMU, it took place as planned in the Maastricht Treaty, but it was based on a flexible and generous interpretation of the Maastricht criteria. Hence, there may be certain doubts about the stability and endurance of the system. Policy makers should always think about a contingency plan in the event of tensions and if things go wrong or, indeed, very wrong with the EMU in the years to come. However, this has not taken place and there are no contingency plans.

% of GDP

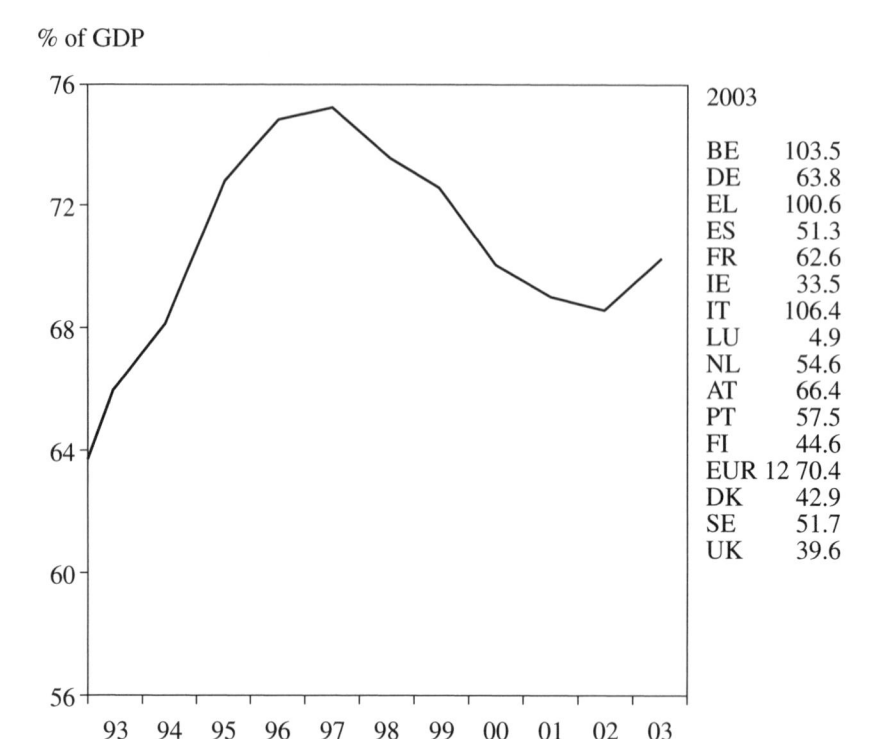

	2003
BE	103.5
DE	63.8
EL	100.6
ES	51.3
FR	62.6
IE	33.5
IT	106.4
LU	4.9
NL	54.6
AT	66.4
PT	57.5
FI	44.6
EUR 12	70.4
DK	42.9
SE	51.7
UK	39.6

Source: European Commission Economic and Financial Affairs (2003).

Figure 2.2 General government debt as per cent of GDP, 1993–2003

7. Achievements, problems and outlook

The officially declared and planned schedule for the introduction of the euro as a new European über-currency followed the expected timetable:

- February 1996: start of the banknote competition;
- December 1996: winning design selected;
- Mid-1998: start of printing;
- January 1999: scheduled start of the EMU (stage three); one-for-one conversion of the ECU for the (virtual currency) euro; irrevocable fixation of the rate of exchange of the currencies in the EMU;
- Mid-2001: currency delivered to EMU central banks;

- January 2002: euro notes and coins (real currency) enter circulation *alongside* national currencies, which will no longer be legal tender six months after the introduction of the euro;[29]
- July 2002: the euro is the only legal tender in the eurozone countries.

Although many had serious doubts not only about the EMU, but also about its timetable, the implementation of the eurozone among the 12 EU member countries was, indeed, the greatest achievement in EU history. In addition, it was one of the greatest monetary achievements since the existence of written history, in particular because it involved paper money and the whole enterprise took place without political integration among countries.

The objective of the Stability and Growth Pact (1997) is to keep the EMU on track by means of a sustainable fiscal policy. This was needed to stabilise the debt/GDP ratios at reasonable levels following years of rising public debt. If one or several governments borrow recklessly, no limits on borrowing would give them a chance for a free ride in the eurozone. As a result, all eurozone countries would pay a price for such irresponsible national policy as interest rates would increase throughout the zone. Therefore, the reasoning behind the pact was to shield the ECB from national pressures to reduce debt through inflation.

The German-inspired idea of the Stability and Growth Pact was generally accepted by the EU politicians. It was disputed only when its application brought national economic pain. The pact limits the eurozone member countries' deficit to 3 per cent of GDP and threatens any member country that exceeds this limit with relatively heavy fines. Germany wanted to have automatic fines for any eurozone country that has a budget deficit of over 3 per cent. However, France argued that sanctions for excessive borrowing of member states must be a political matter. The final agreement was that the Council of Ministers (excluding the country being hit) may penalise the country with a fine of up to 0.5 per cent of its GDP by a qualified majority vote. Countries in deep recession are exempt from fines, that is if their economies shrink by over 2 per cent. Even though the threat of fines exists in theory, it is hard to imagine that they would be implemented in practice. One cannot fine a state as if it were a tipsy driver. States must never be humiliated. This stance is something that questions the credibility of the system. Perhaps certain non-pecuniary sanctions such as a reduction in the voting right or weight for a limited period of time may need to be considered.

When a country's budget is in the deficit zone covered by the Stability and Growth Pact, the European Commission has three types of involvement (see also Articles 101 and 104 of the Treaty of Rome):

- If a country's deficit moves towards the 3 per cent limit, the European Commission may just note the problem.
- If it comes close to the 3 per cent limit, it may warn the government of the country in question.
- If the limit is broken, a complicated fining procedure may begin.

The European Commission issued the first warning to a eurozone country on 30 January 2003: to Germany, the country that is the biggest European economy and, ironically, the country that insisted on the introduction of the pact. Later on, the Commission warned France, Italy and Portugal (see data in Figure 2.1). While Germany and Portugal made tough spending cuts in order to try to reduce the budget deficit below 3 per cent in 2004, France was facing falling government revenue and rising unemployment. Hence, to reduce the budget deficit below the 3 per cent norm would have been a tough task for 2004 and beyond. The Commission's president, Romano Prodi, told *Le Monde* (17 October 2002) 'I know very well that the Stability Pact is stupid, like all decisions that are rigid. The Stability Pact is imperfect, we need a more intelligent mechanism and more flexibility.' This gave certain hints that the European Commission may yield to the demands of big countries (Germany, France and Italy which together account for three-quarters of the eurozone economy), even though the (small) countries that have made unpopular and tough macroeconomic measures are reluctant to give Germany and France a 'get out of jail free' card.

Most of these deficits arose because of cyclical factors (growth rates were lower than expected), rather than because of reckless national spending. Hence, revenues were falling and were not meeting the budgetary outlays. Growth prospects are such that Germany cannot expect to balance its budget by 2006 as requested by the Commission. This is adding to the strain in the eurozone's Stability and Growth Pact. Is a solution to the problem to relax the 3 per cent limit? Would this introduce a precedent: when the rules governing the eurozone become inconvenient, ought they to be rewritten? Would this put at risk the credibility of the eurozone?

Eurozone finance ministers breached the Stability and Growth Pact in November 2003 by voting not to impose sanctions on France and Germany for continually breaking the 3 per cent deficit cap. France and Germany tried to avoid the rules with impunity. Because of this, the European Commission took the Council of Ministers to the Court of Justice in January 2004. The issue in this case was not whether the pact is sensible or not (it isn't), but the real issue is whether the Council of Ministers has the right to abandon a procedure which is necessary for legal certainty. This is not only a legal, but also a political question about who guides the EU – the national governments (through the Council of Ministers) or the European Commission, which stands for the common EU interest? The power struggle and worsening atmosphere between the two EU institutions are obvious.

The Stability and Growth Pact created a source of conflict within the EU. However, in reality national borrowing on the capital market may not significantly increase interest rates for all countries. Hence, this may be a weak argument against the pact. However, a stronger argument against it is this: if a country has a slow growth or is in recession and if its budgetary deficit is near 3 per cent of GDP, the pact may force that country to tighten its budgetary policy and restrain the economy at the very time when it needs loosening. Some argue that the pact has been a 'stupid idea' as markets could offset the profligate spenders by charging an extra premium on loans without damaging the others. Others say that the pact is necessary to enforce fiscal rigour. Is the construction of an EMU to be a learning-by-doing process? Or is this type of learning more appropriate for a primary school? The markets and voters may punish fast unwanted experiments and painful errors.

Modern nations have many (social) responsibilities towards their citizens, which are stretched during recessions when there is a greater expectation and demand for the social system to operate. The Stability and Growth Pact was blind to this issue. The new altered arrangement should treat countries in a different and flexible way. A budget deficit should be treated as a target over the business cycle that allows certain flexibility on both sides. If a country's target is a 50 per cent debt to GDP ratio, then simple maths implies that this country can maintain an average annual budget deficit of 2 per cent (assuming that the nominal annual average GDP growth rate is 4 per cent).[30]

Although the pact reduces the room for manoeuvre for autonomous national budgetary policy, this may need to be the price, at least in the current circumstances, for the credibility of the new common paper übercurrency. Lest it be forgotten, this credibility is based on a promise, a credible promise for the time being, to pay. But it is still an international promise which ought to be tested over time and, especially, during lean times. History is full of promises that were not honoured. The future problem for governments is related to the issue of how to honour international promises and, at the same time, to please the domestic voters. As long as governments are sovereign (no political union), the EMU will be capable of breaking up.

The eurozone countries have few instruments to combat recession. There are no ample, automatic and preset funds at the EU level to act as anti-recession stabilisers, while member government expenditure is severely limited by the Stability and Growth Pact. The MacDougall Report (1977) suggested that a workable EMU may need a common budget equal to the size of 7.5 per cent of the EU's GDP. The usual annual EU budget that is equal to about 1 per cent of the EU's GDP is too small to act as a real and effective built-in stabiliser.

While all countries occasionally face the same problem in recessions, none of the developed countries imposed a numerical target for its budget deficit. Why should the eurozone be an exception? The reason is the risk of default (and the consequent massive capital outflow). However, in mature democracies such dangers are remote. The political cost of governments failing to maintain solvency is high. Voters would quickly oust such governments. In addition, huge debts are not created out of 'thin air'. It takes years to accumulate large debts. The members of the eurozone have solid political institutions that would steer them away from budgetary disasters. Viewed in a political light, the Stability and Growth Pact is a vote of no confidence by the EU regarding the strength of the democratic institutions in the member states.[31]

Doubts have been raised as to whether market forces can replace fiscal policy in an EMU. That is, whether citizens of the participating countries can diversify their risk in such a way that their consumption patterns are non-stochastic. The view that the EMU can provide a consumption smoothing by way of private capital mobility and that no fiscal intervention is necessary, presupposes the existence of two conditions (Demopoulos and Yannacopoulos, 2001):

- *Capital markets are efficient*: that is, all agents cannot simultaneously improve their welfare.
- *Risk sharing is complete*: this means that agents can transfer their wealth across all states so that their consumption levels are identical in all of them.

Markets are, however, incomplete. Asset holders may diversify their risk through stock markets, but wage earners cannot do that. In addition, information is asymmetric. Not everyone may observe, understand and appreciate properties of all goods, and there are also transaction costs. This all limits the ability of agents to transfer wealth across markets. Optimum allocation of risk without a matching distribution of wealth may benefit the rich who hold well-diversified assets, but not the poor who have no such distribution. Therefore, in a world of perfect markets, equal probability beliefs by agents and equitable distribution of income, all risks can be shared through markets. Fiscal transfers of funds across regions are not required. In all other cases, consumption cannot be equalised by markets alone. Therefore, a transfer of funds is necessary for the survival of an EMU.

The great problem and a serious test, even a time bomb, that is looming in Europe is linked to pensions. Chancellor Otto von Bismarck first introduced the prevailing pay-as-you-go pension system in Germany in 1889. This system can work nicely as long as the number of active workers greatly outnumbers the retired. This was the case during the Bismarck days: at that time retirement age was 70 years, while life expectancy was 48.[32]

A vast majority of pension liabilities are unfunded.[33] Current pensions come out of current tax income (pay-as-you-go system). This level varies from around half in Britain (a highly developed privately funded pension system for households) to over 90 per cent in Italy.[34] The ongoing burden on taxpayers is immense, which is an alarming fact for public spending. Demographic trends show that the 'baby-boom' generation will retire en masse around the year 2010. The pressure on the pension funds would significantly increase for several decades to come. This important and expanding imbalance would put a strain on EMU rules.[35] Certain countries would find it impossible to pay state guaranteed pensions without raising budget deficits or raising taxes to insupportable levels. However, this is only half of the problem. Another half is that governments are unable to do anything about this! At least not at the moment. Alain Juppé lost his job as French prime minister in 1997 because of the reform of pensions that provoked a wave of strikes in 1995, the worst since 1968. The same thing happened earlier to the first government of Silvio Berlusconi in Italy: pension reforms provoked strikes, so the government left office in 1994. Strikes, for example that brought French cities to a virtual standstill in May and June 2003, illustrated trade unions' determination to resist changes in the pension system. Similar reforms were also bitterly resisted in Germany, Italy and Austria.

The national annual public expenditure on pensions as a share of GDP in the EU(15) countries is high. Although this ratio is the highest in Austria and Italy (14.6 and 14.2 per cent, respectively) and lowest in Ireland and Britain (3 and 5.3 per cent, respectively), most of the other EU(15) countries have a ratio of about 11 per cent of GDP.[36] Even if an additional increase in public expenditure on pensions of 3 to 5 per cent of GDP is spread over several decades, it would create a serious challenge for the sustainability of public finances. However, this is only part of the story. Another additional difficulty and, perhaps, greater demand would come from the expenditure for health care and other old-age-related outlays. This risk has not yet been fully realised or explained – perhaps because there are no obvious or easy and sweet answers to this problem. Hence, an additional 'danger' is in a liberal complacency which comes from a lack of insight as to how dire the fiscal outlook actually is. The profound crisis that is looming may challenge, destabilise and damage the very basic values on which the contemporary quality of life in Europe is based.

So what to do in a situation in which the population is ageing while there are falling birth rates? Possibly there are measures such as various types of direct and indirect subsidies to people to have more children; raising the age for regular and early retirement; incentives to those who want to continue to work after the retirement age; encouragement to participate in private pension schemes; larger worker and employer contributions; subsidies for savings for old age; and immigration. Some of these measures are highly unpopular and strongly resisted.

When given an opportunity to vote on the crucial issue of their country's participation in the eurozone, Swedish voters did not approve entry in a 2003 referendum. The voters did not so much reject the euro as declare the case unproven, in particular regarding rigidities that impede the national economies.

8. Britain and the euro

The issue of whether Britain should join the eurozone and accept the euro causes much political controversy and is a great research challenge. On the technical side, economists examine the pros and cons of the issue, which will have deep consequences for the shape and direction of the British economy. Eurozone entry would represent the end of 1000 years of British monetary independence. Politicians must grasp the strength and depth of these (often ambiguous) arguments, and then evaluate and select the desired, preferred or possible course of action. However, it ought to be clear from the outset that there are no clear-cut suggestions for Britain regarding the eurozone.

One of the first questions to ask in this long and heated debate is what is in the national interest of Britain? Is it growing together (deeper integration) with EU partners? Or is it drifting apart from them?

- If a deeper union with EU partners is in the British interest, then 'growing together' is the outcome of common policies with EU partners, including monetary policy. In this case, it may be a smart move to join the eurozone fast and to abandon the pound.
- If it is in the British interest to join the eurozone, but in some undefined time in the future, then the policy of staying aloof may

Monetary integration

carry a significant cost. As with any new policy, eurozone participants are still formulating the rules. From the outside, Britain and its Bank of England would have little influence on the ECB. However, if Britain were an insider, it would have a direct and significant weight and influence in the shaping of eurozone events. An obvious example is a possible revision of the Stability and Growth Pact. Here, public spending on long-term investment projects should be looked at in a different light from other public expenditure. This would resolve the controversy between a short-run need for flexibility and a longer-run demand for fiscal discipline. If Britain continues to 'wait and see', the eurozone rules will be shaped and consolidated without a British input from within. This could make British entry into the eurozone much harder in the future.[37]

- If it is in the British interest not to join, the situation resolves itself. The pound will continue to be independent.

Could Britain live in a larger family of countries with a single monetary policy? Is the British economy so very different from others in Europe? Could a one-size-fits-all interest rate be acceptable in and favourable for Britain? The British economy has some important particularities:

- Shocks, such as those in 1979–80 (oil prices) and around 1992 (recession), were relatively better absorbed by Britain than by the other major EU economies such as France and Germany (Figures 2.3 to 2.7). Basically, the first consequences of these shocks were the acceleration in the rates of unemployment and inflation everywhere. Over time, Britain, France and Germany were all able to decelerate inflation to very similar rates. However, regarding unemployment, the situation is different. Unemployment was only a transitory event in Britain, which was able to reduce the unemployment rate in 2002 to the 1975 level. Developments in France and Germany show a very different story: unemployment became a permanent feature and doubled in both countries in the 1975–2002 period. This suggests that labour markets, particularly wages, are rigid in both France and Germany. Adjustment does not lead to reduced wages, but rather to increased unemployment. There is a general consensus that the British labour market is more flexible than those in the major countries on the continent. If British macroeconomic policy was more successful relative to those in France and Germany, should Britain abandon its pound and accept the euro as the currency of the 'less successful' partners? Would this mean that Britain may have less influence over its economy from within the eurozone than from

without? Or is going forward with the rest of the EU a much more important national goal?
- The public infrastructure in Britain is crumbling compared to that in a number of EU countries, and a doubling of public investment in infrastructure may be necessary. Borrowing these funds may be a fairer way to finance projects than through current taxation. Borrowing spreads the cost to the people who will benefit from the investment in the years, even decades, to come. A common EU limit on borrowing may be a policy constraint in Britain.
- The British housing market is highly responsive to changes in rates of interest. A single pan-eurozone rate of interest may be harmful for Britain.
- Britain (Scotland) is a significant oil exporter, so the pound is a petro-currency. As such it is much more sensitive to actual and expected changes in the price of oil than is the euro. As long as the exchange rate of the dollar (in which the price of oil is denominated) remains volatile and as long as Britain remains a significant oil exporter, this potential over-reaction of the pound on the exchange market will remain.
- An ageing population in Europe will increase public expenditure for pensions. In Britain these schemes are privately funded to a much larger extent than elsewhere in the EU. Hence, Britain would be less affected than the rest of the EU regarding this problem. Therefore a one-size-fits-all monetary and fiscal policy may be problematic for Britain.
- At the heart of the eurozone policy is a single basic target: low inflation. It is difficult to coordinate national policies in order to achieve and sustain this policy goal. All other desired objectives such as reduction in unemployment, economic stability, investment and growth are supposed to come about as side-effects. They are subject to 'soft' coordination. It may be quite demanding and problematical to coordinate national macroeconomic policies with the demands of the ECB. These difficulties would be amplified because the participating countries have different sizes and causes of budget deficits, diverse priorities and policy targets, as well as distinct ideas about the causes of and remedies for their economic problems.
- Asymmetric transmission of shocks within the eurozone may remain a common factor for quite some time in the future. This may hit certain regions particularly hard as there are no (or if there are, they are weak and slow) automatic stabilisers. Perhaps one should consider more carefully before entering into a monetary union with countries in which there is a wide discrepancy in the above elements.

- This is very important not only for Britain, but also for the countries in Central and Eastern Europe.
- But what are the real and significant costs of remaining outside the eurozone? Are they in lost additional trade, reduced competition and slower growth? Frenkel and Rose (1998) argued that currency unions expand trade. Prices are becoming transparent, competition intensifies, there is more specialisation and productivity increases. 'Countries that use the same currency tend to trade disproportionately . . . *countries with the same currency trade over three times as much as countries with different currencies*' (Rose, 2000, p. 17).[38] If this were true, then the eurozone countries should have improved their performance since the introduction of the euro in 1999. However, this has not yet been observed to any significant degree. In fact, 'productivity growth has deteriorated substantially in the EU since 1995, precisely when one would have expected the looming currency union to have had a powerful positive effect'.[39] If large currency areas are so important, then one may expect to find that larger European countries are richer per capita than the smaller ones. The evidence, however, does not support such an expectation.

Bearing all this in mind, Britain may perhaps face less integration and more asymmetric shocks in the eurozone. Therefore, costs of eurozone membership may be potentially high for Britain (de Grauwe, 2002, p. 8). However, one may credibly argue that each and every country has its peculiarities, that there are important costs and significant benefits (see Section 3, above) that come from monetary integration. In any case, 12 EU countries took a *political* decision to take part in the eurozone. It is up to the other EU countries to evaluate whether it is a shrewd move to join the 'innermost core' of EU integration or to stay in the outer 'circles'.

In order to assess the possibility of joining the eurozone, as well as the costs and benefits of such a policy move, in 2003 the British government devised five 'tests':

- economic convergence with the eurozone;
- sufficient flexibility to adapt;
- impact on jobs;
- effect on financial services; and
- influence on foreign direct investment (FDI).

After publishing 18 detailed studies and a lengthy assessment on British membership of the eurozone in 2003, the Treasury's answer was 'not yet'. Martin Wolf wrote, 'Never in human history can so many have written so much for so small a result' (*Financial Times*, 9 June 2003). If only Britain had approached the CAP with such rigour before it joined the EU in 1971. If Britain retains these five tests for future reference and use regarding the eurozone, these criteria would become a barrier to eurozone entry – implying that Britian is not serious about joining.

Long-term potentials and gains such as lower currency volatility, deeper capital markets, price transparency, greater competition and increased trade should be compared with the costs of a partial loss of monetary sovereignty to set short-term interest rates. This would affect the influence on the level of output, in particular if the national cycle is out of step with the rest of the eurozone. The British economy is strongly linked with the rest of the EU economy. More than half of its trade is with the eurozone countries (there may be savings in transaction costs). Eurozone entry may be a favourable move to reinforce these ties, and national trade, productivity and wealth may increase.

Whether to join the eurozone is a tantalising issue for Britain. If the prize in the form of a more dynamic and stable economy that attracts FDI is tempting enough, then the government should commit itself to overcoming obstacles as soon as possible, but perhaps without a fixed timetable. Obviously, the decision to join the eurozone is linked with as many risks as there are in the choice to stay outside it.

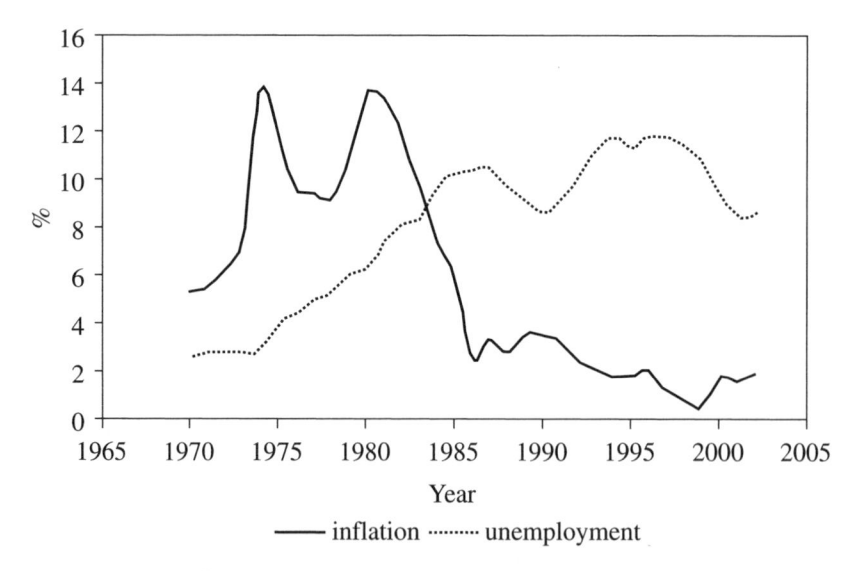

Source: UNECE (2003).

Figure 2.3 Inflation and unemployment in France, 1970–2002

Monetary integration 139

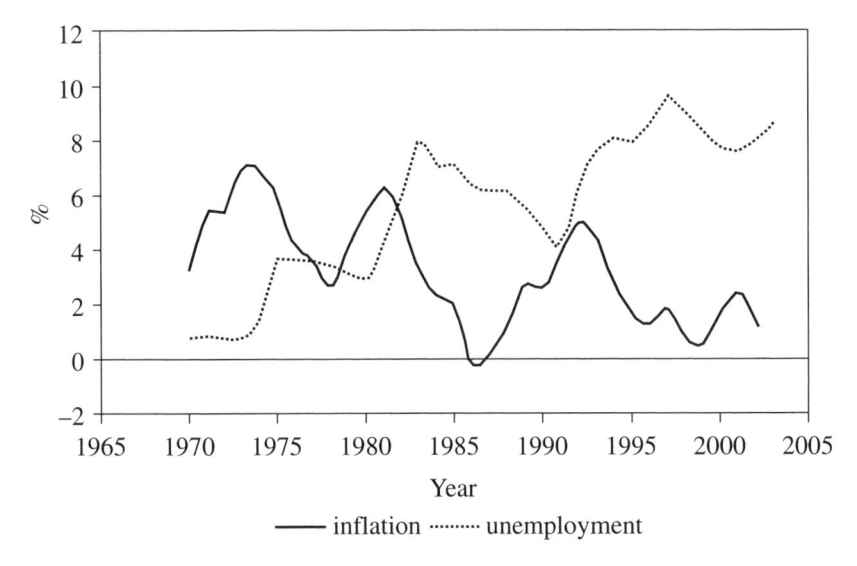

Source: UNECE (2003).

Figure 2.4   Inflation and unemployment in Germany, 1970–2002

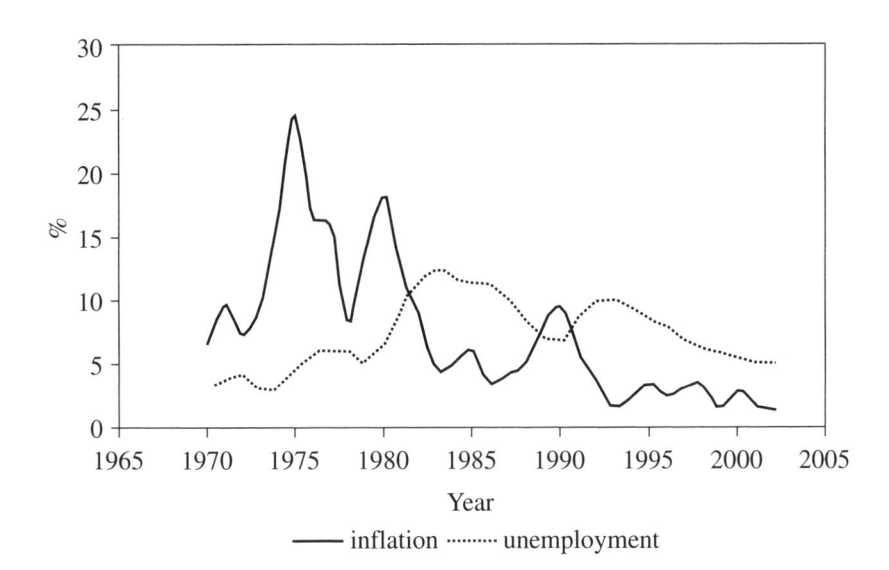

Source: UNECE (2003).

Figure 2.5   Inflation and unemployment in the UK, 1970–2002

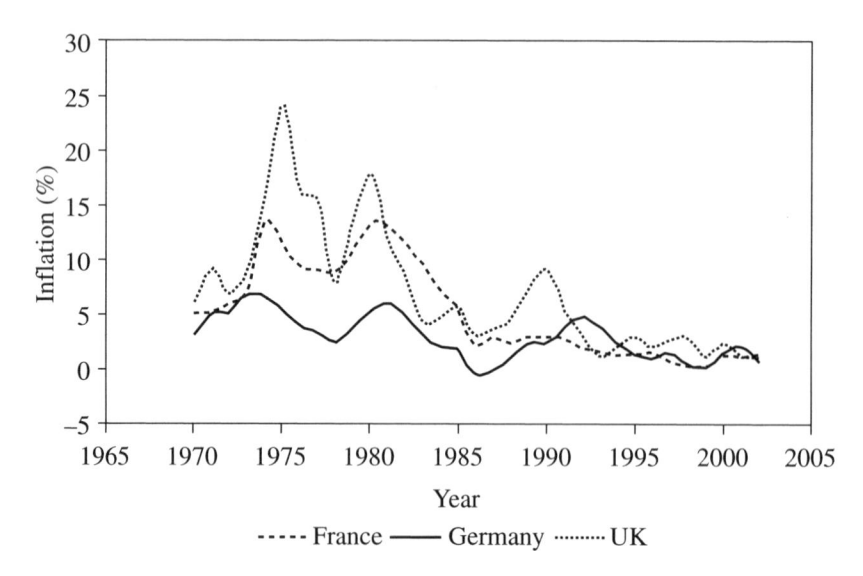

Source: UNECE (2003).

Figure 2.6 Inflation in France, Germany and the UK, 1970–2002

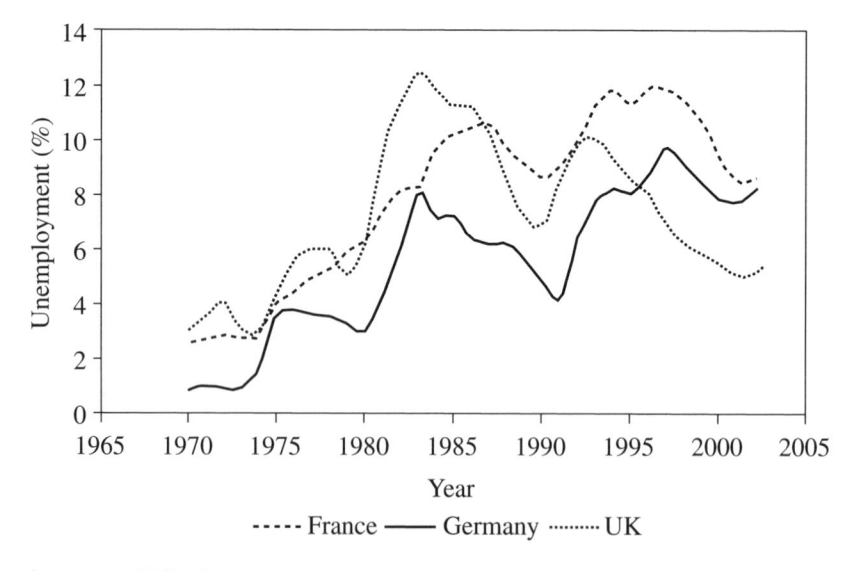

Source: UNECE (2003).

Figure 2.7 Unemployment in France, Germany and the UK, 1970–2002

9. Conclusion

The rationale for common economic policies exists in the case where the EU is better placed to do certain things than are the member countries (subsidiarity). One can hardly think of a better example of this than are the cases of monetary and trade/competition policies. An EMU promotes and strengthens integration. The politicians in the eurozone countries succeeded in creating the EMU with the euro as an über-currency that may rival the dollar. This introduced both monetary stability in economic relations among the participating countries and rigidities regarding monetary and fiscal policy. However, a mere EMU is not the end of the story. Fiscal harmonisation and budgetary coordination could be the next step, as this would contribute to the full effectiveness of the stabilisation and growth policy.

Monetary integration is a field where genuine economic integration among countries is tested.[40] Hence, the creation of the eurozone among the 12 EU countries is not only great, it is the greatest achievement in the history of the EU. The EU countries supplemented the customs union and the Single European Market with the EMU,[41] which would secure and enhance growth and trade flows. Policy priority in the eurozone is to keep inflation very low. All other beneficial outcomes (investment, employment, growth) are implicitly supposed to come as a byproduct of stable prices.

Even though the creation of the eurozone is a very important step towards completing the Single European Market, the eurozone has always been an essentially political, rather than a predominantly economic project. Never before have so many countries entered into a monetary union with so little progress towards a political union. As long as governments are sovereign (no political union), the eurozone will be capable of breaking up. Therefore, the eurozone is the greatest achievement but also the biggest risk the EU has ever taken. It is also a mission that may transform both the political and economic scenery of Europe.

As was the case with many other major projects, the eurozone was conceived by the EU elite. It is the most ambitious project in Europe since the Bolshevik revolution (1918). No currency has circulated in Europe so widely since the Roman Empire. The introduction of the euro in January 1999 was the biggest currency innovation since the introduction of the US dollar in 1792. However, unlike in the US, there is no fiscal element in the deal: automatic fiscal transfers as built-in stabilisers are absent. The 12 eurozone countries have a cap on the national budget deficit of only 3 per cent of GDP. This has been a serious limitation for the conduct of macroeconomic policy in both Germany and France from 2002. The Stability and Growth Pact is too rigid for the stabilisation policy over an economic cycle, hence certain rules may be altered in the future.

Although the EU does not have either high mobility of labour or flexibility in wages (this may provoke high adjustment costs and unemployment), an EMU is welcome not only because of the Single European Market, but also because of external factors. There are serious doubts about the future stability and value of the dollar because of the rising American foreign debt (over $2.3 trillion or over a quarter of total US GDP in 2003). The US has a huge and growing budget and trade deficits, the biggest in the history of the planet. Projections are that such deficits will continue as far as the eye can see. The officially projected budget deficit for 2004 is $521 billion (the 2002 official projection for 2004 was $14 billion). Increased spending, primarily for defence and homeland security, contributes to this deficit. But the biggest reason is the fall in revenues that comes almost entirely from personal income tax and corporate profit tax (mostly paid by the richest 5 per cent of families). This plunge in tax collection from the wealthy is partly due to the Bush administration's tax cuts and probably also due to tax avoidance and evasion. Even a severe reduction in the non-defence and homeland security-related spending would not make a significant reduction in the deficit.[42] In addition, the growing reliance on short-term borrowing from the rest of the world must be closely watched. The US needed $1.5 billon of foreign capital a day to finance its current account deficit in 2003. A strong alternative currency such as the euro (if it is credible and widely accepted) is most welcome. Portfolio switching into the euro may keep its value high. If this happens, or better, once this takes place, there will be considerable fluctuations in the exchange rate between the dollar and the euro.

The current strength of a currency on the international market is not a sign of national economic virility.[43] A superior and more sophisticated measure is how the economy responds and adjusts to changes; how it reforms its structure; how it overcomes rigidities; and how this affects prospects for future growth. A reduction in the value of a currency on the currency market may concern the national economy only if it pushes up prices of imported goods and services to the extent that this translates into domestic inflation. A currency's long-term value is based on economic fundamentals and the political stability of the issuing country.

The reunification of Germany was the major instigator of the Maastricht Treaty, as well as the reason for the treaty's good and bad implementation points. The eurozone became too rigid to adjust to disequilibrating shocks such as the reunification of Germany and the consequent budget deficits. The high German interest rates (because of the decision to pay for the reunification[44] by borrowing, rather than by raising taxes) and the need of other EU economies in recession to get cheap loans, produced the upheaval that speculators desired. The exchange rate crisis of 1993 was a good reminder to policy makers that markets cannot be avoided. Capital markets will always test the resolve of governments to defend the narrow bands of the exchange rate. While economies are in recession, governments will not enter such a contest. The wreckage of the ERM of the EMS is one of the symbols of the evident 'weakness' of governments and the power of markets.

The eurozone is and will be subject to institutional tests. The ECB will be tested in times of economic difficulties as there may be a perception that it is not able to act decisively because it has to be mindful of each component nation. In addition, budget deficits in the major eurozone countries will challenge the rules and the credibility of the zone. This will be compounded by a hard test around the year 2010 with the arrival of an increased demand for pension funds. The eurozone should pass the hardest test: that of time. There are a number (particularly in America) who question the long-term viability of the scheme.

Intra-eurozone exchange rate risk is eliminated, but a single European capital market is not guaranteed. National government bonds (for example, German and Italian) in euros may not become perfect substitutes. Differences in default risk and national tax treatment mean that the bond market will remain fragmented, although less than was the case before the introduction of the euro.

One of the expected consequences of the creation of the eurozone is that member countries have similar prices for traded goods. However, there are still large differences in prices for non-tradable goods and services (rents, catering, building materials). The primary reason is a difference in wage levels which reflects different levels in development. Economic convergence over the coming decades will have a certain impact on the convergence of prices in industries that produce non-tradable goods and services.

Increased heterogeneity in the EU(25) following the eastern enlargement will be one of the big tests for the coordination of EU policies.[45] Half of the EU will be inside the eurozone, while the other half will be outside. The structure of the economy in Britain and countries in Central and Eastern Europe is such that they may easily be subject to asymmetric shocks relative to the eurozone. Policy coordination problems may become tough.

Notes

1. Separate countries may, *de facto*, share a common currency. For example, Estonia's Law on Security for the Estonian Kroon (1992), Clause 2, directly linked the exchange rate of the kroon to the German mark. The Estonian central bank was forbidden to devalue the kroon. However, devaluation could take place, but only if the law was changed, for which

the usual parliamentary procedure was necessary. There have been no cases so far in history where authorisation for the devaluation of a national currency has been loudly trumpeted by a parliament.
2. Some Californians may argue, perhaps rightly, that this is not so in the case of their own state.
3. The impact of fiscal policy for the fast fine tuning of the economy should not be exaggerated. A country's fiscal policy is almost as a rule an annual event. It passes through a long parliamentary procedure. Therefore, it is the monetary policy that is continuously at hand to equilibrate the economy. Fiscal policy is not a replacement, but rather a less-flexible supplement.
4. If payroll taxes are high, firms are less willing to hire new or even keep existing staff.
5. Estimates are that the annual seigniorage revenue of the US is between $11 and $15 billion (Tavlas, 1997, p. 712). *The Economist* estimated that the annual American seigniorage may be worth some 0.1 per cent of American GDP (14 November 1998, p. 107).
6. If a government cannot or does not want to tax businesses and individuals, it may print money and tax everybody through inflation. Keynes wrote about such an inflation tax that 'a government can live for a long time . . . by printing money. The method is condemned, but its efficacy, up to a point, must be admitted. . . . so long as the public use the money at all, the government can continue to raise resources by inflation' (Keynes, 1923, p. 23).
7. Businesses in the EU yearly convert several trillion ECUs at an annual cost for the conversion charges of over €15 billion or about 0.4 per cent of the EU's GDP (*European Economy*, 1990a, p. 63). This is the only cost of the monetary non-union that may be relatively easy to quantify.
8. The official foreign currency reserves in the eurozone were €227 billion at the end of 1999. They were €233 billion in January 2000, €244 billion in January 2001, €245 billion in January 2002, €198 billion in January 2003 and €160 at the end of November 2003. An obvious reduction in these reserves due to the creation of the monetary union in 1999 was not observed.
9. De Gaulle once said: 'Treaties, you see, are like girls and roses: they last while they last' (Macleod et al., 1998, p. v).
10. In the early 1980s, firms in the former Yugoslavia were permitted to sell their home-made durable goods to domestic private buyers for hard currency. These buyers received price rebates and priority in delivery. Due to shortages and accelerating inflation, domestic private hard-currency holders increased their purchases in order to hedge against inflation. Growth of this type of home trade relative to 'normal' trade in the (sinking) domestic currency has been increasing. The discrimination of home firms against the domestic currency has been spreading. Firms were happy because they received hard currency without the effort required to export, while consumers were happy because they were able to get what they wanted. Subsequently, the domestic sales for hard currency were banned because they reduced the effectiveness of the domestic monetary policy. This is an example of where a weak domestic currency (prior to state intervention) was crowded out from domestic trade by a relatively strong foreign currency (the German mark). Hard currency was not, however, driven out of Yugoslav private savings. About 80 per cent of these savings were in foreign hard currency in Yugoslav banks. This was the way to protect savings from rising home inflation and negative interest rates on savings in the home currency. A new restatement of Gresham's law had in this case the reverse meaning: good money drove out the bad.
11. In 1990, however, 11 years after the creation of the EMS, the special (±6 per cent floating band) treatment for the Italian lira ended.
12. Greece and Portugal did not participate in the ERM as those countries were at a lower level of development relative to the 'core' EU countries, so they wanted time for a gradual adjustment. This made the EMS incomplete even in its first phase. A few other countries were out of the ERM, but they joined this part of the EMS later.
13. Belgium and Luxembourg have shared a monetary union since 1921. It has worked relatively well. One reason for such an operation is that one partner dominates the

14. A one-dollar reduction in per capita income of a US region causes a reduction in the payment of federal taxes by about 34 cents and, at the same time, an increase in transfers of about 6 cents. Between one-third and one-half of the initial one-dollar shock is absorbed by the federal government (Sala-i-Martin and Sachs, 1992, p. 216).
15. The US is trying to persuade central banks to keep reserves in US dollars as those reserves may bring interest. However, the US dollar may easily fluctuate ±20 per cent a year relative to other major currencies. Many central bankers think that the reserves need to be kept in assets that are subject to much greater discipline than is the US dollar.
16. An alternative policy instrument could be (interest-free, one-for-one) deposit requirements.
17. An appraisal of the relative safety of a borrower introduces many problems. The value of assets in the private sector is determined by the net present value of the stream of profit that those assets earn. As for the public assets, there are many that do not yield a financial return (military camps, for example). Their value can be assessed in an indirect way through replacement costs.
18. Exceptions included small states such as Andorra (with Spain), Monaco (with France), Liechtenstein (with Switzerland), Luxembourg (with Belgium), and San Marino and the Vatican (both with Italy). In addition, Ireland shared currency with Britain for quite some time.
19. Austro-Hungarian Empire, Czechoslovakia, the Soviet Union and Yugoslavia.
20. Solidarity in the EU is still quite fragile when major national interests are in question. The Bretton Woods currency system collapsed because of similar reasons. Countries refused to forgo control over the domestic money supply for the sake of external equilibrium.
21. The goal of the ECB is to keep annual inflation over the medium term at the rate of at most 2 per cent.
22. *Financial Times*, 21 November 1997, *The Economist*, 21 November 1998, p. 76.
23. The budget-deficit condition provoked most criticism. A country with a heavy public debt has good reason to have episodes of inflation: it is to reduce the real burden of its debt. Paul de Grauwe argued that France had been more successful than Germany in keeping the domestic budget deficit low over the past 25 years. Yet the franc was weak, while the mark was strong. A low budget deficit is not sufficient to ensure a strong currency. Other factors such as monetary policy are necessary. During the same period France had higher inflation than Germany. Tough monetary policy, rather than strict adherence to the 3 per cent budget-deficit criterion, would make the euro strong (*Financial Times*, 11 July 1997).
24. While annual budget deficits may occur depending on the business cycle, the overall national debt may need to be controlled in a different way from that proposed in the Maastricht Treaty. Instead of putting a cap on public debts (and on the budget deficit) which are, indeed, at various levels among the EU countries, a more effective way may be to install instruments that discourage trends of growing debts and deficits, and that encourage their continuous reduction.
25. Competence and credibility are crucial elements for the success of this policy. They are very hard to gain, but easy to lose. Even highly competent institutions such as the Bank of Japan or the World Bank have made wrong predictions in certain cases.
26. H. Sinn, 'A shot of inflation would be good for Europe', *Financial Times*, 20 May 2003.
27. In 1912 the blueprint for *Titanic* looked perfect. It was said to be unsinkable. In EMU's case, even the blueprint was full of holes (*The Economist*, 27 July 1996, p. 14).
28. Once the euro replaced the national currencies, the biggest part of the internal EU trade was transacted in euros. Hence, 'international' trade will be smaller. Policy makers in the EU *may* pay less attention to exchange rates than they usually do. If the policy goal is internal stability, rather than stability in the exchange rate, cooperation between the major international players may be weak and the result may be an instability in the currency market.

29. Conversion of the national currencies into euros was achieved relatively painlessly over the first few months of 2002.
30. Paul de Grauwe, 'The pact should be replaced and not mourned', *Financial Times*, 27 November 2003.
31. Paul de Grauwe, 'Europe's instability pact', *Financial Times*, 25 July 2002, p. 11.
32. *The Economist*, 27 September 2003, p. 72.
33. It is very hard to approximate this ratio, but most research would estimate that it is about 85 per cent.
34. The interested reader should consult the Commission of the European Communities (2002a, pp. 31–2).
35. Pensions are becoming one of the principal economic imbalances. However, they are not studied as much as imbalances in trade and in capital flows.
36. Economic Policy Committee (2000, p. 27).
37. Had Britain been a member of the EU from the outset, the EU farm policy would look very different. Perhaps the decades long and sterile reforms, plus certain costs of this policy, would have been avoided.
38. In fact, subsequent research pointed to the fact that Rose's estimates relied overwhelmingly on currency unions that involve small and/or poor countries. Other econometric methods give positive estimates on the impact of the euro on trade within a range of between 4 and 16 per cent (Micco et al., 2003, p. 318).
39. M. Wolf, 'The benefits of euro entry will be modest', *Financial Times*, 12 May 2003, p. 17.
40. This subject is challenging both for policy makers and for researchers as it combines the most difficult macroeconomic issues. At the same time it is annoying as there are no *ex ante* counterfactual situations against which one may measure costs and benefits of monetary integration.
41. The emu is a large flightless bird.
42. P. Krugman, *New York Times*, 27 January 2004 and 3 February 2004.
43. During the first two years of its life, the euro was weaker than its creators would have liked it to be. It lost about a third of its value relative to the dollar. This trend was reversed in 2003 mainly because of the huge US trade deficit of $491 billion in that year. The value of the dollar declined, while that of the euro soared (obstructing EU exports).
44. The net annual fiscal transfers from the western part of Germany to the eastern part of the country were about €75 billion throughout the 1990s. They will be necessary for another decade. The danger is that such 'gifts' may ruin local incentives for entrepreneurship and self-reliant adjustment; it may also create a structurally dependent economy as is the case with the Italian Mezzogiorno.
45. It may be an easy matter for 25 or 27 (or even more) persons to agree about where to go, say, to the cinema, but imagine the same number of finance ministers trying to reach agreement about the common rate of interest.

> Render therefore unto Caesar the things which are Caesar's,
> and unto God the things that are God's.
> Matthew 22:21

3. Fiscal Policy and the Budget

1. Introduction

It is a regular assumption in the standard theory of customs unions that by the elimination of tariffs and quotas, trade within an integrated area becomes free (but for the existence of the common external tariff). It is also commonly assumed that foreign trade is fostered by relative differences in national production functions and resource endowments. This is just an illusion. Tariff and quota systems are not the only obstacles that distort the free flow of trade in goods and services (as well as factor mobility). Fiscal measures such as taxes and subsidies also create distortions in trade and they influence spatial and industrial allocation of resources. The focus of the White Paper (1985) and the Single Market Programme was mostly on the elimination of frontier controls. After the creation of a genuine Single European Market in the EU in 1993 and the EMU (achieved in 1999 for the 12 eurozone countries), attention needs to be directed towards tax harmonisation.

The basic questions in this process include the following: what are the taxation principles? What is the historical experience in tax harmonisation? What is economically necessary and politically feasible? Should taxes and subsidies be identical throughout the EU? Should they be set independently by each country and markets allowed to equilibrate trade flows and allocation of factors and, supposedly, introduce approximation in taxes at the end of the process? Should national preferences coming from a variety of geographical or social reasons be reflected in tax diversity among the EU countries? What are the lessons from fiscal federalism?

This chapter deals with fiscal policy and the budget of the EU and is structured as follows. Section 2 starts with fiscal policy issues and principles. Section 3 outlines a part of tax history in federal[1] states such as Switzerland, Germany, the US and Britain. Direct and indirect taxes are the subject matter of Sections 4 and 5, respectively. Future challenges are discussed in Section 6, while Section 7 concludes the discussion about tax policy. A brief analysis of the EU budget is contained in Section 8. The overall conclusion is that there is considerable room for improvement in the field of fiscal and budgetary integration; however, deeply rooted national interests and practices will prevent any rapid and large-scale moves in this area.

2. Fiscal policy

INTRODUCTION

The right to tax is at the very heart of a country's national sovereignty. Certain government revenue is always necessary for the operation of the state administration and for the conduct of select policies. The fiscal policy of a country deals with the influence and consequences of the demand, size, revenues and expenditure of the public sector. Taxation and fiscal policy are often used to affect and shape the basic economic variables, including:

- setting the stage, rules and incentives for the 'economic game' (permissions, bans, competition, taxes, subsidies, corporate governance, intellectual property, dispute settlement and so on);
- achieving and maintaining macroeconomic and political stability and having a long-term vision and programme on how to reach this goal and maintain it over time;
- affecting economic stabilisation (reduction in the fluctuation of macroeconomic variables around desired, planned or possible levels) and combatting cyclical disturbances;
- having an effect on equity in the distribution of national wealth and income among regions, sectors, firms, classes, age groups, family status groups and persons;

- influencing allocation of resources (spatial and sectoral; investment and organisation of firms);
- supervising and directing the volume and composition of expenditure, consumption and investment;
- motivating and sustaining savings;
- improving general microeconomic capacity (education, infrastructure, information, forecasting, institutions);
- influencing the provision of a range of goods and services;[2]
- managing the pattern and extent of employment of resources;
- reflecting strategic behaviour of national government;[3]
- reducing and eliminating tax evasion and tax fraud;
- initiating certain actions; and
- owning and using certain assets.

As such, the fiscal policy shapes and directs the level and form of operation of markets for goods, services and factors.

Fiscal policy is concerned with the creation and adjustment of a system of taxes that is required to finance the necessary and chosen level and direction of public expenditure (intervention). This system should be equitable and efficient. Ideally:

- it ought to keep the budget in balance over an economic cycle;
- it ought to interfere as little as possible with the private sector business decisions in normal situations; and
- it ought to be in certain harmony with basic international tax standards.

As one of the oldest sovereign rights, fiscal policy is deeply entrenched in the state structure. It is a long-drawn-out and difficult process to alter fiscal policy in a democratic society. Fiscal, including budgetary procedures are slow, long and rather complex.

A prudent fiscal policy ought to ensure that the government at all its levels (local, regional and central) is involved in and spends only on those activities where it can use resources in a better way than the private sector. Taxes ought to be high enough to cover that cost, but levied in a way that distorts the economy as little as possible. However, there are some valid social cases for distortion such as conservation of energy and control of pollution. The problem that must be avoided is to resist the burdening of too narrow a tax base, otherwise tax rates would be high and distorting.

Fiscal policy has a direct (blunt) effect on income of factors, as well as on consumption of goods and services. This is in contrast to monetary policy, which does the same thing, but in an indirect (fine-tuning) way through financial markets. By a simple change in transfers and rates of taxes and subsidies, the fiscal authority may directly affect expenditure and consumption. However, the problem with fiscal policy is that its impact is gradual. In normal circumstances, this policy has to pass through a long and rigid parliamentary procedure. Therefore, fiscal policy changes may take place once (or only a few times) a year. Monetary policy may do the same job as fiscal policy, but in a discreet manner and, potentially, much faster. By changing interest or exchange rates, a government may react swiftly to emerging crises and opportunities. Such a quick reaction is not always possible with fiscal policy. 'Fiscal policy is like a tanker, it cannot promptly change course' (Baldwin and Wyplosz, 2003, ch. 14). Hence the need for the coordination of fiscal and monetary policies in an EMU. If they work one against the other, neither would be effective and the result may be damaging.

A tax ratio relates tax revenues to the GDP of a country. This ratio has been increasing over time, for which there are at least three reasons:

- the welfare state has increased social care transfers, which are financed mostly by social security levies;
- economic development and an increase in opportunities have had their impact on the growth of taxable incomes. Taxpayers have been climbing into higher brackets, so these proceeds have increased; and
- inflation has increased nominal tax revenues and devalued their real value.

These trends in the EU may change around the year 2010 and beyond when the baby-boom generation starts to retire en masse. An ageing population and the related needs and social obligations (pensions, health and other care) will increase the demand for such types of transfer over the coming decades. Tough budgetary rules in the eurozone may alter (perhaps reduce) certain transfers for social care. At the same time, enlarged demand for social services would exert a strong opposite pressure. In addition, the introduction of the euro and monetary stability with a very low inflation rate are reducing the devaluation of the real value of tax revenues.

TAXATION PRINCIPLES

In designing tax systems, governments customarily consider three basic indicators of taxpayers' ability to pay (wealth): what people and firms own; what they spend; and what they earn. The traditional principles of taxation deal with fairness, certainty, convenience and efficiency. They were established by Adam Smith (1839, pp. 371–2) and have stood the test of time remarkably well.

- *Fairness (equality or inequality)*: 'The subjects of every state ought to contribute towards the support of the government, as nearly as possible, in proportion to their respective abilities; that is in proportion to the revenue which they respectively enjoy under the protection of the state' (Smith, 1839, p. 371). It is of primary importance that any tax must be fair. Citizens ought to be taxed both in proportion to their ability to pay and relative to 'benefits received' from the state. However, there are widely dispersed government services such as security. The criteria of benefits received and ability to pay are often impossible to differentiate. When government services grant identifiable benefits to some taxpayers and not to others (customs protection of a domestic car manufacturer by tariffs and quotas), and when it is reasonable to expect the user (monopolist) to bear an acceptable part of the cost, financing the benefits (customs service), at least partly, is seen to be fair. Evidently, this does not apply to such public services as welfare assistance to the poor and needy.
- *Clarity and certainty*: 'The tax which each individual is bound to pay ought to be certain and not arbitrary. The time of payment, the manner of payment, the quantity to be paid, ought all to be clear and plain to the contributor, and to every other person' (Smith, 1839, p. 371). The consequence of uncertain and arbitrary application of taxes produces a lack of confidence in the public system. Inflation, in particular high inflation, may move people to higher taxable income brackets. Rising tax bills on inflated values may endanger fairness in imposing taxes. Therefore, a respected tax system ought to be clear and certain. People and firms must know who and what is being taxed and how tax legislation is enacted.
- *Convenience*: 'Every tax ought to be levied at the time or in the manner in which it is most likely to be convenient for the contributor to pay it. . . . Taxes on consumable goods . . . paid by the consumer . . . little and little, as he has occasion to buy the goods' (Smith, 1839, pp. 371–2). Convenience and compliance ought to ease the obligations of taxpayers and the work of tax authorities. Income tax may be deducted automatically on payday.
- *Efficiency*: 'Every tax ought to be contrived as both to take out and to keep out of the pockets of people as little as possible over and above what it brings into the public treasury' (Smith, 1839, p. 372). Levying may require a great number of officers; frequent visits and intensive investigations may create unnecessary trouble and officers'

salaries may eat up much of the collected taxes. The fiscal system should not impede the free flow of goods, services and factors, domestically or internationally.

Further basic principles have been added to the Smith list over time:

- *Source*: Smart taxes ought to be other than taxes on trade and company profits. These two types of taxes are the most distorting. Unfortunately, they are also the most common in the developing world. Taxes on trade (both export and import) prevent specialisation, while loophole-ridden taxes on company profits distort investment decisions. Sales taxes (for example, value-added tax) may be the most attractive alternative.
- *Tax elasticity*: This deals with an automatic response of taxes to changing economic conditions without adjustments in tax rates. High elasticity, however, creates inequities during periods of rapid inflation by pushing people into higher tax-rate brackets, although the value of their income is failing to keep pace with rising prices. The large nominal revenues then encourage government spending just when the growing tax burdens discourage taxpayers from working, saving and investing. This situation may worsen a state of economic stagnation accompanied by inflation. In such instances, the tax levy has become too elastic.
- *No retroactivity*: Taxpayers must have confidence in the law as it existed at the time when they entered into a transaction.
- *Neutrality*: The primary purpose of taxes is to raise revenue, not to micromanage the economy with subsidies and penalties. A tax should not cause people to change their economic behaviour. Suppliers and buyers of a good or service ought to be indifferent about being taxed in any of the integrated countries.

FISCAL FEDERALISM

Harmonisation of the fiscal system among countries has two meanings. First, the lower form of fiscal harmonisation may be equated with cooperation among countries. These countries exchange information and/or enter into loose agreements about ways and types of taxation. Second, in its higher meaning, fiscal harmonisation means the standardisation of mutual tax systems regarding methods, types and rates of taxes and tax exemptions (Prest, 1983, p. 61).

Fiscal federalism deals with the design of an agreed and optimal system of cooperation, coordination and sharing fiscal rights and responsibilities between different levels of local, regional, state and federal governments. At the EU level, it may also imply the creation of a supranational fiscal authority (subsidiarity). However, this should be measured and adjusted to the merits and costs of economies of scale in joint action, as well as the availability of information and their understanding on different levels of government.

Revenue decentralisation favours a smaller size of the (central) government proceeds. This shifts public revenue from taxes to user charges. The advantage of such a policy choice is that users may choose to use or not to use certain services. If users decide to use those services, they have to pay for them directly.

The integration of fiscal policies in an EMU refers to the role of public finance and the part played by the budget. It studies the rationale, structure and impact of fiscal (tax and budgetary) systems of the integrated countries. Integration of fiscal policies implies not only a harmonisation of national systems of taxes and subsidies, but also issues such as public expenditure; transfers (redistribution) within and between countries, regions, economic sectors and individuals; combat of cyclical disturbances; stabilisation policy; and tax evasion. The highest type of fiscal integration among countries represents a unified system of taxes and subsidies, as well as the existence of a single budget that is empowered to cope with all economic issues of common concern. This has, however, only been achieved in centralised federal states.

In a general case, fiscal federalism is complicated by the existence of different currencies that take part in the venture and that are not irrevocably linked through the fixed exchange rate. If an EMU is to conduct an effective stabilisation policy it should be endowed with the power to tax and borrow, as well as to spend. This implies that its budget may be not only in balance, but more importantly, in temporary deficit or surplus over an economic cycle. An EMU may not necessarily directly tax firms and individuals, but it may tax member governments. In order to maximise welfare, the EMU needs to decide about the preferred distribution of functions among distinct governments (principles of subsidiarity, cooperation or competition). It should also act upon that decision and divide public goods and services into those that ought to be provided commonly and those that should be supplied at a national or local level. In addition, applied to an EMU, fiscal federalism needs to take care of a certain transfer of resources from prosperous countries/sectors to needy ones, as well as to promote mobility of resources.

Fiscal neutrality among the integrated countries refers to a situation in which a supplier or a consumer of a good or service is indifferent about being taxed in any of the integrated countries. This is an important prerequisite for the efficient spatial and sectoral allocation of resources and for the operation of an EMU.[4] The fiscal authorities should be quite cautious while assessing taxes and spending tax receipts. If they tax a significant part of profit or income, then they may destroy incentives for business, work, savings and investment. They may stimulate factors to move to geographical or professional locations where they can maximise net returns. Taxation can, however, be a powerful tool for the direction of certain business activities towards desired spatial or professional locations, but there may also be a capital flight towards tax havens. A high tax policy may find a certain social justification (for example, equity), although it may be questionable from an efficiency standpoint. The above scenario depends on the sensitivity of factors to taxation. If this sensitivity and responsiveness are relatively low (as is the case with the mobility of labour in the EU), then the local authorities may tax income at higher rates in the knowledge that this is unlikely to provoke a large-scale emigration.

The member countries of an EMU may basically finance a common budget according to the principles of benefit and ability to pay. First, the principle of benefit is based on the rule of clear balances or *juste retour* (a fair return). Those who obtain concessions from the budget expenditure ought to contribute to these public funds in proportion to the benefits they receive. Second, economic benefits of integration accrue to the participating countries not only through the transfers of (common) public funds. The most important gains come from a secure long-term freedom for intra-group trade and investment, mobility of factors, specialisation, acceleration in economic activity and the like. Such a neo-classical expectation may not require 'corrective measures' since all countries and regions benefit from integration in the medium and long terms.[5] However, in the case of imperfect markets and economies of scale, this expectation may not materialise. In this situation, the principle of the ability to pay features highly. Individual contributions and receipts from the common budget in a given period do not have to be equal. Net contributions reflect a country's ability to pay. However, a nominal net contributory position of a country can be more than compensated by various spillovers that stem from membership of an EMU. Therefore, the *juste retour* principle may get a new dimension: it is a discreet but continuous economic growth throughout a group with a flow of resources from the rich and thriving to the less-well-off member countries and those in (temporary) need.

3. A bit of history

The purpose of this section is to refer briefly to a few historical examples that relate, in part, to the issue of international tax harmonisation which may have a federal dimension. Most of these select stories refer to a 'forced' imposition of taxes by foreigners. Some of them may seem (indeed they are) extreme. The reason why they were selected was simply to make a point for the EU. These examples may provide a part of the answer to the question of why tax harmonisation or unification among countries is a very delicate and difficult matter. For example, the Duke of Alva (Fernando Álvarez de Toledo), the Spanish governor-general, was the last foreigner to try to impose a tax on the Dutch. That was in the 16th century. His action, together with the Roman Catholic Inquisition, provoked an 80-year war (1567–1648). The following examples relate to Switzerland, Germany, the US and Britain.

SWITZERLAND

Around the 10th century, the area that is now known as Switzerland consisted of a collection of small states ruled by dukes, counts, bishops and abbots, as well as a number of independent small city-states. The Holy Roman Emperor Rudolf I of the Habsburg dynasty attempted to claim feudal rights in Switzerland in 1276. His authority would present a threat to the traditional liberties of the Swiss. To resist Rudolf's aggression, the three central forest cantons (Uri, Schwyz and Unterwalden) concluded a secret deal concerning mutual defence in 1291. During the 14th century Zurich, Glarus, Bern, Lucerne and Zug entered this league. Other cantons joined later.

Although nominally under the Habsburg family early in the 14th century, the Swiss opposed the Habsburgs in the Welf-Waiblingen disputes. The Habsburgs sent punitive expeditions into the mountains and triggered nearly a century of warfare. Unable to cope with the freedom-loving, strong and belligerent Swiss mountaineers, the Habsburgs abandoned their attempts to acquire the region in 1474. However, the Holy Roman Emperor Maximilian I attempted in 1499 to cancel various Swiss rights and to tax them. A war followed and the mountaineers defeated him. The subsequent Treaty of Basle (1499) gave Switzerland virtual independence.

New cantons continued to join the confederation. There was no chief of state or attempt by any one canton to impose authority on another, even though there were religious and other differences.[6] The Helvetic[7] confederation was loose, but its army was one of the strongest in Europe at that time. Because of their skill and bravery in war, Swiss mercenaries became famous throughout Europe.[8] Their services were in demand, appreciated and well paid, and occasionally they were even on different sides of the same conflict. In the course of the wars between Italy and France in the early

16th century, Swiss troops, fighting with the French as mercenaries, were able to annex the Italian districts and towns that later formed the canton of Ticino. The Swiss troops then fought against the French, but were defeated in 1515. This prompted Switzerland to follow a neutral policy in international affairs.

Swiss bank secrecy has been protecting deposits for over three centuries. Geneva bankers were known as the French king's bankers. The first known text on bank secrecy dates back to 1713. The Great Council of Geneva adopted banking regulations which stipulated the bankers' obligation to 'keep a register of their clients and their transactions. They are, however, prohibited from revealing this information to anyone other than the client concerned, except with the expressed agreement of the City Council'. Switzerland then became and remained a political and financial asylum for those fleeing the political upheavals that have been present in Europe since 1789.

The first big clients in Swiss banks were the kings of France, who greatly valued the discretion of their money lenders. The Geneva bankers were actually Protestants. Many of them were French citizens, chased out of France following the repeal of the Edict of Nantes by Louis XIV in 1685. Putting behind them the discrimination and bullying they suffered in France, they financed the French kings from Geneva. The French kings were the best clients for loans at the time – they were fund hungry, but they had the ability to repay loans. Discretion was of the utmost importance in these delicate matters. It should not be known publicly that the French Roman Catholic king borrowed money from 'heretic' Protestants. Business is business – on both sides.[9]

The Great Depression led to stricter foreign exchange controls in Germany in 1931. Hitler introduced a law whereby the penalty for any German with capital abroad was capital punishment. The Gestapo began to spy on Swiss banks, and when three Germans who had deposits in Switzerland were sentenced and executed, the Swiss government was persuaded to reinforce bank secrecy. The federal banking law (1934) stated that bank secrecy fell within the criminal domain, and any banker who infringed this law was thereafter punishable by imprisonment. Clients' secrecy was reinforced.

Switzerland did not have a direct tax on revenue until the time of the Second World War. That event was dramatic enough to justify the introduction of the much resisted Federal Tax for Defence (*Impôt pour la Défense Nationale*). Solidarity during times of war has been one of the principal integration factors in Switzerland since the creation of the country in 1291. The newly introduced tax was envisaged to stay only until the end of the war. However, as time passed, the population became accustomed to the tax (which is still a solidarity tax since two-thirds are redistributed to the cantons according to their needs) and accepted its renewal when the government decided to call it the Direct Federal Tax (*Impôt fédéral direct*) after the war, provided that it would remain limited in time. This limitation to ten-year periods is still in force, and despite the government's wish to abolish it, it is most likely to be retained lest the whole tax bill is rejected when it is presented for approval to voters at the end of 2004.

Before the Direct Federal Tax was introduced, the Swiss cantons and communes were the only administrations that had the power to tax. They levied independently direct local taxes on persons and firms (the communal tax is a percentage of the cantonal tax, but each commune is free to set that percentage). The Swiss federation did not aim to restrict the freedom of the cantons. One of the objectives was to be rid of the burden presented by any emperor who tried to squeeze a share of their gains in business through various tolls. The Swiss were and remained businessmen who wanted to see value added to anything they were paying for. Apparently, creating an association among the cantons was economically more efficient than depending on an emperor for security. This type of democracy seemed cheaper and more effective.

Thus, it is not difficult to understand why the Swiss continue to value highly their tax, banking and other national legacies and why it was hard to enter into a deal with the EU (or anyone else) concerning taxation of non-resident deposits.

GERMANY

It took many centuries to unify the German nation and state. Larger-scale unification was started by Charlemagne (742–814), the King of Franks (768–814) and the Emperor of the Romans (800–814). His empire was the origin of his successors from Saxony. The Holy Roman Empire (800–1806) was a loose confederation in Europe. The borders of this empire shifted greatly throughout its history because of wars, alliances and marriages, but its principal area was always that of the German states. Even though its character and population were German, its aspirations were a universal rule in the West. Germany became a 'belated nation' because of internal quarrels and rivalries not only among kingdoms, principalities and a number of free cities, but also because of religious tensions. Put together, this prevented German integration. From the 10th century the rulers of the Holy Roman Empire were elected German kings, who usually sought, but did not always receive, imperial coronation by the popes in Rome. In any case, before the French Revolution, the Germans never had a unified state of their own.

Friedrich Barbarossa (1122–90) saw himself as the successor of the Roman emperors who claimed to be the 'lords of the world'. As such he considered that he had an absolute right to levy taxes. His grandson, Friedrich II (1194–1250) had his court in Palermo (Sicily). He was a powerful promoter of Roman law, and took a different approach to taxation from his grandfather. He applied the Byzantine emperor Justinian's (483–565) principle *'Quod omnes tangit, ab omnes approbari debet'*[10] (what concerns all, should be approved by all). This meant that the royal families in various German states were not allowed to levy taxes without the consent of the nobility.

Modern absolutism in Europe started at the end of the 15th century and did well for more than two centuries. It marked the emergence of nation states and brought, at the time, modern principles of sovereignty. Its best example was the French king Louis XIV (1643–1715). His declaration *'L'état, c'est moi'* (I am the state) sums up the concept neatly. Bavaria, Brandenburg, Hanover and Saxony started to develop into centres in their own right in Germany. The family of Hohenzollern[11] was granted Brandenburg (Berlin) in the 15th century, and they acquired a number of additional, geographically unconnected territories to the west. Eastwards was Prussia, which they inherited as a Polish duchy in 1618 and transformed into an independent kingdom in 1701. Gradually, all the Hohenzollern lands together became known as the kingdom of Prussia.

The origin of German patriotism (some call it nationalism) can be traced to the Romantic Movement in the late 18th century. It was a response to the export of French Enlightenment ideas and invasions by Napoleon. For 16 years (1799–1815) the German states fought five wars against the well-trained and integrated armies of revolutionary and Napoleonic France. As there had never been a unified German state, the Germans experienced in practice the French example of what a unified state could achieve. As far as Austria was concerned, it was relatively sizeable as a state, but largely un-German. Marriages and wars caused Austria to include 'states' and territories that were not German speaking. The only large 'German' state was Prussia.

The Congress of Vienna (1815) replaced the Holy Roman Empire of more than 240 states with the German Confederation. This was a loose association of 39 sovereign states. Many Germans hoped for a free unified nation state and liberal type of government similar to the British model. They wanted a constitution guaranteeing popular representation, trial by jury and free speech. These ideas also appealed to the various peoples incorporated in the Austrian Empire. Austria, Britain, Prussia and Russia formed the Quadruple Alliance to suppress, by force if necessary, any threat to the Vienna arrangement. However, later on Prussia outsmarted the others, principally Austria, by instituting a customs union among most of the German states apart from Austria.

Friedrich List (1789–1846) was a prominent intellectual and practical proponent of the economic unification of Germany. In 1820, together with Frankfurt merchants and industrialists, he founded the German Trade and Business Union, which strived for the abolition of the 39 tax (customs) frontiers that existed among the German states and for the introduction of a unified German customs area. On the basis of this intellectual input, Prussia encouraged neighbouring states to join this low tax alliance, which gradually developed into a customs union, the *Zollverein* (1834–71). List also planned a train network for all of Germany and in 1834 founded the Leipzig–Dresden Train Company, which started providing rail transport services a year later. In theoretical terms, he put forward the 'theory of productive forces', which defended infant industry protection. List saw this to be an element leading to a free trade (no-duty) area in Mitteleuropa.

This all had a strong impact on economic development. Germany's industrial output, principally in Prussia, was lower than that in Britain in the 1850s, but its rate of growth was faster. Prussia wanted to secure the new German lands along the Rhine. This was done by a carefully crafted major tax reform and by lowering customs duties. Karl Friedrich von Stein, Karl August von Hardenberg and Wilhelm von Humboldt, together with List, influenced reforms in Prussia. They sought to crack the old feudal intra-German barriers and to create a modern society of free citizens. Strong cultural, linguistic and patriotic feelings about unifications were always present, but it was principally the economic interest that was at the very heart of German unification.

The *Zollverein* was the principal factor that brought 39 German states closer together. It allowed trade among them by lowering taxes. These were originally set by each country at a very high rate. Before 1848 the Austrian emperors (but not their foreign minister, Clemens von Metternich) did not conceive that the *Zollverein* could lead to a larger political role for Prussia. However, Metternich and his successors pushed for Austria to join the *Zollverein* in order to dominate the group and to turn it into a high tariff area, but Prussia prevented this on economic and political grounds. In addition, Prussia concluded a free trade agreement with France in 1861. Austrian products made behind a high tariff wall could not compete easily on such a large 'liberal' trading market.

In 1861, the Prussian parliament granted the government additional funds for reforms, but a year later it refused to do so without a reduction of compulsory military service from three to two years. King William I would not yield to that request as he feared that conservative values would be insufficiently inculcated in the recruits. For the very same reason, the liberal-dominated parliament insisted on shortening the term of military service. As a compromise deal, they named Otto von Bismarck (1815–98) as prime minister. He proceeded to collect the additional taxes on the basis of the 1861 budget, arguing that the constitution did not provide for the case of an impasse, hence he would have to apply the preceding year's budget.[12] To justify the increase in the army, he warned that 'the great questions of the day [German unification] will not be settled by speeches and majority decisions . . . but by blood and iron'.

Public opinion began to shift to Bismarck's side in 1864, when he used the expanded Prussian army, in alliance with Austria, to extract the provinces of Schleswig and Holstein from Denmark. In 1866 he intensified a Prusso-Austrian quarrel over the abysmal running of these territories by Austria. This escalated into a brief and victorious war with Austria. Some smaller German states that allied with Austria were also crushed. Bismarck incorporated Schleswig-Holstein and Hanover into Prussia. During the same year, he also united all north and central German states into the North German Confederation which was under the Prussian leadership. Faced with these achievements, the Prussian parliament bowed to Bismarck and retroactively sanctioned his financial improvisations of the past four years.

Not sufficiently pleased with these accomplishments, Bismarck's next ambition was to make Prussia the great power in Europe. In order to do this, it would be necessary to defeat France, a feat that was accomplished in 1870.[13] He wanted to use the strength of the consequent national enthusiasm to bring the reluctant south German states into a united Germany. Bismarck had not only established Prussia as the great continental power, but also provoked patriotic enthusiasm and attracted the southern German states to join the North German Confederation, thus forming the German Empire (*Deutsches Reich*). On 18 January 1871, King William I of Prussia was proclaimed in Versailles by all the states of Germany to be their emperor. Germany was a united country on a federal basis and the Second Reich had been created.

Having sufficiently enlarged Prussia, the Iron Chancellor, as Bismarck was called, worked for peace. During his 19 years of governing, Bismarck continued to encourage the Industrial Revolution through technical universities and tax incentives. Advanced industrial technology was applied from 1850 in the iron production in the Ruhr and Saar regions and stimulated through tax incentives. Regarding social care, he introduced the prevailing pay-as-you-go pension system in 1889.

UNITED STATES

At the end of the Seven Years' War (1756–63) France was expelled both from North America and from India. In both regions Britain became the pre-eminent power and supreme on the high seas. However, the war left Britain with a sizeable debt and costly responsibilities to govern the newly gained land in North America. In order to make the colonies pay for a part of the empire's defence expenses (in particular, the British forces stationed in the colonies) and to raise revenue, parliament passed the Stamp Act (1765) without any debate. The colonists had to buy and use specially stamped paper for all official documents and newspapers. This act provoked strong opposition throughout North America. The colonists regarded this to be a violation of their right not to be taxed without representation: no representation, no taxation! The protest, which included a boycott of British goods, was so strong that trade between Britain and North America came to a halt. The British parliament rescinded the Stamp Act in 1766, not because of the North American protest to taxation, but rather at the request of the economically depressed British traders.

The objective of the Tea Act (1773) was to rescue the British East India Company from bankruptcy and to demonstrate the power of the British parliament to tax the colonies. The tax on tea shipped to the colonies in North America was reduced so that the East India Company's tea could be sold there at a lower price than was the price of smuggled tea. The colonists, however, refused to buy the English tea. They viewed the Tea Act as a violation of their constitutional right not to be taxed without representation. In addition, this could easily lead to the monopoly of the East India Company as local traders could be put out of business. This led a group of Bostonians to protest against this tax. They would not permit the unloading of three British ships that arrived in Boston in November 1773 with 342 chests of tea. The royal governor of Massachusetts, Thomas Hutchinson, however, would not let the tea ships return to England until the duty had been paid. On the evening of 16 December 1773 a group of Bostonians boarded the ships and dumped the tea into Boston Harbour (the 'Boston Tea Party'). When the government of Boston refused to pay for the destroyed tea, the British closed the port until the compensation was paid. In addition, the British parliament passed the Coercive Acts (1774), a series of laws designed to punish the province of Massachusetts and to demonstrate parliament's sovereignty. This led to the first armed conflicts and, eventually, to the American revolution.

The US federal law of 1791, sponsored by the head of the federalists and secretary of the treasury Alexander Hamilton, imposed an excise duty on whisky. This provoked a number of riots in 1794 known as the 'Whiskey Rebellion'. The burden of this excise duty fell largely on western Pennsylvania, which was at the time one of the chief whisky-producing regions of the country. Many grain farmers were also distillers. They depended almost totally on whisky as a source of income. They considered the law to be an attack on their basic economic interest and liberty. Their resistance to the collection of excise duty assumed grave proportions. The federal authorities issued arrest warrants for a large number of non-compliant distillers in the spring of 1794. The riots that followed brought damage to property and the death of one federal officer. In August 1794, President George Washington ordered the insurgents to disperse and requested the governors of Pennsylvania and a few other states to mobilise their troops. There were also negotiations with representatives from western Pennsylvania. However, all was in vain, and Washington ordered a military action in October 1794. The operation was swift as there was almost no resistance. The Whiskey Rebellion is interesting and important as it reflected the strong local preferences and because it provided a test (the first of its kind in the US) about the strengths and limits of the federal government's authority.

BRITAIN

Imposition of new taxes in our times, even within a single complacent democratic country or a federation, is neither easy nor untroubled. The British government under Margaret Thatcher introduced a poll tax (the 'community charge'). As a government with a free market ideology, the rationale for the poll tax was found in the argument that people do not pay for goods on the market in proportion to their income and wealth. There is a strong market tendency to have the same price for an identical good or service throughout the market: one good, one price. Therefore, it would be a market-neutral policy for each person to pay the same tax, rather than pay in proportion to his/her income or wealth. Hence, according to this ultra-liberal doctrine everyone should pay an equal tax – equal voting weight, equal taxation – regardless of income. It was called the poll tax.

The poll tax is not only economically flawed, but also socially unjust. The purchase of goods and services on the market is, under normal conditions, voluntary. However, the payment of tax is obligatory. The government has coercive powers to charge a tax on a person's very existence no matter the need of that person for the public service. This regressive tax has not been seriously considered by London for over 600 years. One of the reasons was that a similar tax in 1381 sparked the Peasants' Revolt. In order to calm the insurgence, King Richard II promised to end the repression of peasants by the nobility. Once the menace had passed, the king reneged on his promise and commented: 'Villeins ye are, and villeins ye shall remain'; that is, promises to little people do not count.

The poll tax was supposed to be the flagship of Mrs Thatcher's government. It was first introduced in Scotland in 1989 and a year later in England. There was a strong 'don't pay' campaign in Scotland even though this was punishable by law. The Scots felt that the poll tax was anti-Scottish and that it had been imposed on them by the English majority in London. It was outrageous and in breach of the Treaty of Union which was supposed to ensure that no taxes were imposed on Scotland which were not also levied on England. In addition, large-scale but peaceful protests in Scotland were ignored by the government in London. However, the 'don't pay' campaign later inspired about 15 million British people to refuse to pay the tax. Many people switched to supporting Labour because they detested the tax, even though senior Labour politicians did little to oppose it. The violent and wide-scale anti-poll tax riots, particularly in Trafalgar Square in London, forced the government to renounce the poll tax on 21 March 1990 and this contributed to Mrs Thatcher's resignation six months later.

Models of society differ among countries. These national choices need not be transposed to others, particularly not by bullying. These models depend on habits, mentality, history and social priorities, choices and values. Citizens in some countries hold the usefulness and efficiency of the government in high esteem, while in others this respect is much lower for various reasons, for example corruption. Therefore, it comes as no surprise that Britain insists that unanimity in EU tax matters should be preserved. According to Britain (and some other countries, such as Austria and Luxembourg, which do not express themselves as forcibly), there should be no changes whatsoever in EU tax matters without the full consent of all EU member countries. Therefore, it is not surprising that the EU has no power to levy taxes.

4. Direct taxes

The issue that needs to be addressed next is the classification of taxes. According to their base, taxes may be levied on income and wealth (direct taxes) and consumption (indirect taxes). *Direct taxes* are charges on income of firms and individuals (factor returns), as well as property ownership, and are effective at the end of the production process. They have an impact on the mobility of factors and any change has a direct impact on taxpayers' purchasing power. They include corporation tax, income tax and tax on wealth. *Indirect taxes* are applied to consumption. They affect movements of goods and services. Any alteration of these taxes changes the price of goods and services. Local governments traditionally depend most heavily on property taxes, while state governments rely on sales and income taxes.

In addition, a federal government can create money. It does not have to raise enough proceeds from its tax system to balance its budget.

CORPORATE TAXES

The international aspect of corporate taxation refers to the taxation of transnational corporations (TNCs). Differences in corporate taxes among countries in which a free capital mobility is permitted may endanger the efficient spatial and sectoral allocation of resources if capital owners tend to maximise their net profits in the short run. Other things being equal, capital would flow to and locate in countries or regions with a relatively low level of corporate taxes (although this is only one, allegedly minor, variable that influences investment decisions). TNCs decide on their trans-border location not only according to the production-efficiency criteria, but also according to others that include differences in market growth, trade regime, competition, tax rates, subsidies, general stability and so on.

Two issues should be stated from the outset. The first one deals with high taxes. If this type of tax burden shows that there is a high-quality infrastructure, trained labour and educated management, this may be an indication that the location may be attractive for a TNC. If low taxes mean that these services are at a low level then, depending on the industry and strategic goals of a TNC, foreign and domestic investors may not find this an attractive location to go to or to be in. The second issue concerns subsidies. If in a free market situation a firm, domestic or foreign (TNC), finds a location in geographical space or in an industry to be attractive profit-wise, then it will locate there without any subsidy. Subsidies to firms to locate in an already determined place are not necessary. If public subsidies are offered at all, are they a sign of a lack of business appeal (lack of competitive attraction) of the location in question? However, the empirical evidence about the impact of taxes and subsidies on the geographical location of firms is still inconclusive.

Corporate taxes may be collected according to several methods: the classical, integrated, dual and imputation systems. Their basic features are as follows:

- A *classical* (or a *separate*) method represents one extreme. According to this method, a firm is taken as a separate entity, distinct from its shareholders. Corporations are taxed irrespective of whether profits are distributed. At the same time, shareholders' income is taxed notwithstanding the fact that the corporation has already paid taxes on its profit.

- An *integrated* method represents another extreme which is relevant for theoretical considerations. Here, a corporation is viewed as a collection of shareholders. Corporate tax is eliminated while shareholders pay tax on their portion of corporate profits. Hence, personal income tax and corporate tax are integrated in full. However, it is very hard to implement this system because of the practical problems of allocating corporate income to possibly thousands of shareholders.
- The *dual* (two-rate, split-rate) method falls between the two extremes. A corporation pays tax at a lower rate if profits are distributed than in the case when they are not.
- *Imputation* is another intermediate system for taxing corporations. In contrast to the dual system, however, relief is provided here at the shareholder level. Corporations pay taxes just as in the classical system, while shareholders receive credit, usually in the year they receive dividends, for the tax already paid by the corporation.

Computation of corporate profits has provoked much controversy. The authorities of several states in the US[14] apply a *unitary* (formulary apportionment) method for the taxation of TNCs. This arbitrary and controversial method was inspired, in part, by the problem of transfer pricing (manipulation of the cost of imported inputs and exported output). A TNC derives its income not only from the place of its residence, but also from the operation of its subsidiaries. The rationale for the unitary method of taxation is that profits of the TNC accrue from its global operations, so that a TNC needs to be taken as a single unit. The tax authorities, in particular in California, extend beyond the confines of their state's geographical jurisdiction. Because of an increasing diversity and volume of international transactions and the globalisation of business activities, it is hard to assess exactly the individual affiliate's contribution to the overall profit of a TNC (UNCTAD, 1993, p. 209).

If the unitary method is applied, then the tax authorities relate sales, assets and/or payroll expenditure of the affiliate under their jurisdiction to the TNC's worldwide sales, assets and/or payroll outlays. The business community adamantly and rightly disputes such a mechanical view that averages the global operations of a TNC across the board. Profit uniformity at all stages of production and trade, as well as at all international locations, does not prevail. The cost-plus or resale-minus method of taxation that exists elsewhere may be a superior tax choice.

In a 'globalised' international economy there may be continuous multi-jurisdictional conflicts regarding the taxation of TNCs. The national tax authorities take a semi-arbitrary unitary method and assess the share of global profits of the TNC that should be taxed within the confines of their jurisdiction. This approach contrasts sharply with the traditional separate accounting rules (arm's-length method) of tax assessment among distinct fiscal authorities because it is not (necessarily) arbitrary. Although the unitary method has elicited support from certain intellectuals, the business community is adamantly opposed to it. This opposition not only comes from the increased administrative costs for the TNCs, but it also runs contrary to the US constitutional provision that the federal government (not the ones in the constituting states) is in charge of foreign commerce.

If the unitary principle is applied in only one or a few (but not all) locations where a TNC operates, the following two cases are possible. First, if the operation of the affiliate is more profitable than the average overall profitability of the TNC, then the local authority that applies the unitary method of corporate taxation would collect less tax than it could by the application of the cost-plus method. Second, if business operations of the affiliate are less profitable than the average-universal profitability of the TNC, then the local tax office will collect more tax than under the alternative collection method. The second case directly harms the profitability of the affiliate, reduces corporate funds for potential investment and, hence, reduces the long-term interests of the host country. In 1994, after 17 years of legal battle, the US Supreme Court decided in favour of California with respect to the unitary method of taxation (Barclays Bank lost the case). The Court held that unitary taxation did not violate the foreign commerce clause. The implications of the decision are not fully clear. If profitability of a TNC is higher in California than elsewhere in the world, that company may benefit from unitary tax assessment. As of 1986, California allowed taxpayers to choose between unitary tax assessment and the 'water's edge' method (taxation of income within the confines of the US, rather than worldwide income). This is a system close to the universally accepted arm's-length method.

Unitary taxation offers the advantage of being location neutral. It also discourages tax evasion and flight. The problem and difficulty is, however, how to arrive at the unitary taxation in practice. The problems of technical tax assessment and tax base determination are formidable. The first victim in this process may be tax autonomy. Hence, changes in any tax system are very slow indeed. If a 'correct' unitary taxation is the final goal, then it should be arrived at multilaterally by all tax authorities.

The principal disadvantages of the unitary method of taxation are the following:

- The method of calculation is the most significant objection.[15] The formula used to determine the allotment of profit to be taxed by a specific tax authority could easily have certain arbitrary elements. The main distortion that is brought by unitary taxation is that it is

different from the standard arm's-length taxation principle. In addition, states using the unitary method adopt a formula favourable to themselves. Many states use different formulas (more distortions) and the outcome is the creation of a potentially higher aggregate taxable income than the aggregate economic income.
- Data that use tax authorities to assess the portion of the global profit that ought to be taxed within their tax jurisdiction may be neither sufficient nor fully reliable. Collection of data and reporting obligations may easily be (very) different among different countries. In these circumstances, it may be difficult to assess the 'global business' and the 'local profit' of a company to be taxed.
- An international consensus in these matters is necessary. Unfortunately, this is very hard to achieve. An extremely long period of time is necessary for this. A predetermined global formula for taxation may be a possible solution to this problem. However, these pre-arranged formulas have flaws as they do not pay attention to the specific facts, circumstances, merits, business efficiency and risks in each particular case and location.[16] The result is that in many cases there could be overtaxation, while in others there could be undertaxation (Sadiq, 2001, p. 283).

The arm's-length method of taxation is the accepted international norm even though it may not be the most astute approach. This is because such a method creates a simulated world in which each and every transaction is treated as if it were between independent firms. The argument for a unitary method of taxation is based on the idea that a TNC is one company. Therefore, it ought to be taxed in that way. Internal transactions, including transfer pricing within a TNC, need not be made in an arm's-length way (that is, as if the transaction was between independent firms).

The main goal of corporate taxation is not to increase the price of goods and services, but rather to capture a part of the firm's profit. Frequent changes in the corporation-tax systems should be avoided, because they increase uncertainty and the administrative burden on firms. Unless they are favourable for business, these variations distort the decision-making process concerning investment and may have a long-term negative effect on capital that would withdraw or reduce investment in these geographical locations.

A firm may pass on the tax burden to consumers in the form of higher prices for its goods and services or to its employees, by reduced wages, or a combination of the two. By passing on the tax burden, it may reduce, in part or in full, the impact of the tax on its profit. The possibility for the passing on of the tax burden depends on the idiosyncrasies of the goods/services and the labour market. If a firm is free to set its prices, then it depends on competition if this passing on is possible. If prices are regulated, then the way of passing on the tax burden is different. Suppose that the prices do not rise. A firm may reduce the quality of its output in order to save profits. In the opposite case when prices do not fall, a firm may improve the quality of its output and after-sales service in order to increase its competitiveness and save or increase its market share.

The importance of the distribution of the tax burden between individuals and firms may be analysed in the following example. Suppose that P_d stands for the price paid by consumers. If one imposes a tax of t dollars per unit of output on the suppliers (firms), then the price P_s which they receive is:

$$P_s = P_d - t. \tag{3.1}$$

The condition for equilibrium is:

$$P_s(q) = P_d(q) - t. \tag{3.2}$$

Assume that one imposes the same tax of t dollars per unit of purchased good on the buyers. The price paid by consumers is:

$$P_d = P_s + t. \tag{3.3}$$

The condition for equilibrium in this case is:

$$P_d(q) = P_s(q) + t. \tag{3.4}$$

Note that the two conditions for equilibrium, (3.2) and (3.4), are the same. Thus the quantity, P_s and P_d in equilibrium is independent of whether the tax is levied on demanders (individuals) or suppliers (firms). The volume of government revenue does not change. What changes is the composition of revenue, which may provoke heated political debate. These equations are obviously not understood by many tax authorities.

The integrationist school argues that income has to be taxed as a whole in spite of differences in its source, and that all taxes are ultimately borne by the people. In contrast, the absolutist school argues that firms are separate legal entities that need to be taxed in their own capacity (under the assumption that they do not pass on the tax burden either to their employees or to consumers). Another reason for the separate treatment of corporations is that they use government services without fully paying for them. This has an impact on the reduction of costs of operation. Tax authorities can use their policy to regulate investment of firms and to control their monopoly position. On these grounds, tax instruments can influence the behaviour of the business sector.

If private capital flows are a significant feature of economic relations among countries, some of these countries may find an incentive to negotiate tax treaties in order to avoid double taxation and, possibly, achieve tax neutrality. Tax neutrality between investment in home country A and foreign country B is achieved when firms are indifferent (other things being equal) between investing, producing, buying and selling in either country. This means that a tax should not cause people to change their economic behaviour. In this case, the foreign country's tax equals the corporate tax plus the withholding tax (tax on the transfer of profits). If under a condition of free capital mobility country A's firm finds country B's taxes equal to country A's, then there is tax neutrality between these two countries.[17] If this is not the case and if other conditions are equal, investment may flow to the country that has relatively lower taxes.

Cooperation among the tax authorities in partner countries may be necessary for the smooth operation of the economies of the integrated countries. This demand is amplified if the desired goals are free mobility of capital, free competition, efficient spatial and sectoral allocation of resources, 'fairness' in the distribution of revenues among the member countries and the elimination of administrative difficulties. This is of special importance in a situation of fixed exchange rates and free capital mobility. Measures to reduce the risks of tax evasion can take the form of a generalised withholding tax to all EMU residents and/or a commitment of banks to disclose information about interest received by the union residents. Therefore, the need to create conduit companies, as intermediary subsidiaries that take advantage of tax treaties in order to reduce withholding taxes, can be eliminated. As tax harmonisation deals with difficult and deeply rooted national customs, the EU has not put the harmonisation issue aside, but it did not press member countries on this issue in an aggressive way. The Single European Market and the eurozone are expected to perform the sophisticated, behind-the-scenes market-led pressure on countries to approximate taxes, as the high-tax countries, other things being equal, would lose market competitiveness of their goods and services, and also be less attractive geographical locations for foreign direct investment.

Tax competition generally lowers taxes, while tax harmonisation may, in general, make them rise. If let alone, tax competition may provoke a 'race to the bottom' in order to attract business to locate in specific places and countries. However, this scenario depends on the assumption that the firms care only about taxes when they select the location for their operations. In addition, low taxes may be too low from both the business and the social standpoints. Business and the social infrastructure may be poor and unattractive.

Hence, relatively higher tax locations may be preferred by firms to low tax areas. At the same time, authorities in these locations may safely presume that the majority of firms may not go elsewhere only because of high(er) local taxes. If there are benefits in the agglomeration of businesses and clustering of firms (strong functional intra-industry production links), then tax rates may safely be different between the cluster (centre) and its periphery. If, however, taxes are harmonised between the two regions or countries, then both may suffer. The centre would have to reduce taxes and, consequently, social and business services. The periphery would need to increase taxes and bankrupt many local firms. The tax base would shrink further.

Competition between countries to attract TNCs to locate within their confines is driving down tax rates.[18] However, this has a side-effect. Governments find it increasingly difficult to raise revenue from businesses. Hence, there is an intensified pressure to increase taxes on individuals in the same locations, particularly if they are not mobile. Otherwise the social programmes may not continue.

Capital income has a high degree of mobility. This has become more pronounced since the introduction of the euro in 1999. However, the taxation of income from savings is a sensitive issue. The European Commission would like to reduce 'harmful' tax competition among the EU member countries regarding income from non-resident savings. A withholding tax may find a certain rationale as Germany[19] and Scandinavian states forgo quite a bit of tax revenue as their wealthy citizens and institutions (pension funds) save in non-resident accounts, primarily in Luxembourg and Britain. However, an argument against this tax cites the logistical nightmare of administering it and distributing proceeds. In addition, it would give incentives to place holdings in non-EU financial centres such as the Channel Islands (UK), Switzerland and elsewhere. Jersey, Guernsey and the Isle of Man are not members of the EU. They have no obligation to align their fiscal system with that of the EU. Therefore, Luxembourg would never accept an accord which excludes the Channel Islands. A common tax of, for example, 20 per cent in the EU would mean an immediate capital flight from Luxembourg to the Channel Island banks.

After a 14-year process of negotiations (horse-trading and blackmailing[20]) over the taxation of income from savings, the EU agreed on rules to crack down on tax fraud and tax evasion in 2003. According to this deal, from 2005 12 EU countries would start exchanging information on the savings of non-residents. Hence, each EU member country will be able to tax its citizens on non-resident savings in the EU. Austria, Belgium and Luxembourg were exempt from the obligation to exchange information because of the secrecy provisions in their banking systems, but they will have to levy a withholding tax instead. Three-quarters of these proceeds will be transferred to the saver's country of origin, while the rest would remain in the country in which the funds were saved. The tax rate would rise from 15 per cent in 2005 to 35 per cent in 2010. In order to prevent capital flight from the EU to 'easier' tax regimes such as Andorra, the Channel Islands, Liechtenstein, Monaco and Switzerland[21] will have to either exchange information or impose a tax. Switzerland agreed to apply the same withholding tax as sharing account information violates clients' right to secrecy.[22] However, this may play into the hands of tax evaders, money launderers, arms traders, drug and human smugglers and terrorists who need to hide their money. If the elimination of tax evasion and money laundering is the principal policy objective, it seems that the exchange and sharing of information on bank accounts among governments are the most effective policy tools.

CORPORATE TAXES IN THE EUROPEAN UNION

The basic treaties of the EU are relatively short on tax provisions. There are just a few articles in the Treaty of Rome that refer to the general issue of taxation. Article 90 stipulates that imported products from the partner countries may not be taxed more highly than comparable domestic goods. This has introduced the principle of destination for VAT, as well as non-discrimination in EU internal commerce. Article 91 introduced tax neutrality. It states that any repayment of tax on the goods exported to the EU partner countries may not exceed the taxes actually paid on the good in question. Article 93 requires unanimity in harmonisation of indirect taxes. This harmonisation of taxes may go only as far as 'is necessary to ensure the establishment and functioning of the internal market'. Article 94 authorises the Council of Ministers to approximate laws that directly affect the establishment or operation of the common market. The decision about this must be unanimous. Article 95 §2 excludes fiscal matters from the majority voting procedure. The unanimity principle has prevented rapid progress in the approximation of fiscal matters in the EU.

Table 3.1 illustrates, in a simplified way, differences in corporate tax systems in the EU, candidate countries, Switzerland, the US and Japan. The table does not take into account any of the complex and different surtaxes, surcharges, local taxes, credits, exemptions, special treatment of small and medium-sized enterprises (SMEs) and the like, that apply in nearly all countries. The differences in systems and rates of corporate taxes point at the distortions of tax neutrality for investment in the EU (and outside it). Therefore, the European Commission considered proposing a single corporate tax rate for the EU, but stepped back from the idea.

Table 3.1 Systems and rates of corporate taxes in the EU(25), candidate countries, Switzerland, the US and Japan in 2003

Country	System	Rate (%)
1. Austria	Classical	34
2. Belgium	Classical	33
3. Denmark	Classical	30
4. Finland	Imputation	29
5. France	Imputation	34
6. Germany	Classical	25
7. Greece	Corporate tax	35 (no tax on shareholder)
8. Ireland	Classical	12
9. Italy	Imputation	34
10. Luxembourg	Classical	22
11. Netherlands	Classical	29
12. Portugal	Partial exemption	30
13. Spain	Partial imputation	35
14. Sweden	Classical	28
15. United Kingdom	Imputation	30
16. Cyprus	Classical	10 (25% on public corporate bodies)
17. Czech Republic	Modified classical	31 (additional 5% on income over 1 million kounas)
18. Estonia	Tax on distribution	26 (on distributed profit only)
19. Hungary	Classical	18
20. Latvia	Corporate tax	15 (no tax on shareholder)
21. Lithuania	Corporate tax	15
22. Malta	Imputation	35
23. Poland	Classical	27
24. Slovakia	Classical	25
25. Slovenia	Classical	25
26. Bulgaria	Classical	23.5
27. Romania	Classical	25
28. Turkey	Corporate tax	30 (tax on distributions 5.5 or 16%)
29. Switzerland	Classical (federal)	8.5 (cantonal taxes are important and different)
30. United States	Classical	15–35
31. Japan	Classical	28–37.5

Source: International Bureau of Fiscal Documentation (2003).

A special committee proposed a minimum tax rate (30 per cent) and a maximum rate (40 per cent) that could be introduced in the EU countries. The proposed rates may be meaningful only if the tax base is also harmonised.[23] The problem has been identified, but a solution that could be transformed into EU law is not always easy to find. In theory, a TNC is ready to pay relatively higher corporate taxes in country A if it supplies the business sector with educated labour, infrastructure, lower social contributions, even trade protection, relative to country B where the corporate tax rate is lower.

The objective of tax harmonisation or equalisation of corporate tax rates in the EU is to introduce an identical 'tax distortion' across the EU (to level the tax playing field). However, the corporate tax distorts another important variable for firms, related to the form and level of financing. A corporate tax 'punishes' enterprises that raise their capital through equity, rather than debt. This is because interest payments can be deducted from taxable profits, while the return on equity cannot. Possibly the best solution would be to eliminate corporate taxes. Taxes on corporate profit could be collected from shareholders' income and/or on corporate cash flow before the interest is paid (not as now, after the deductions for the interest payments). This would be in line with a tendency to avoid taxes that hurt capital formation and investment. In addition, if dividends get special tax treatment, then wealthy people who get most of their income from dividends may easily end up paying lower tax rates than ordinary people who work for a living.

Differences in corporate taxation may distort investment decisions and the operation of the Single European Market. The Ruding Committee (1992) reaffirmed this observation, but recommended that the existing system of corporate taxation is retained. That is to say, the state in which profits of a TNC originate should continue to tax them in full (that is, both distributed and retained profits should be taxed). If the profits are transferred to the parent country, this state should exempt them from taxation or allow a tax credit for the taxes already paid in the country where they were made. This reflects the difficulty of harmonising taxes on the international level. It seems that tax reform within countries needs to precede tax reform between them.[24]

Juridical double taxation arises when a single economic income is taxed twice. If a firm (TNC) operates in two countries, its profit may be taxed by the two national tax authorities. It is often forgotten that what matters for TNCs is not the fact that profits are taxed twice, but rather the level of total taxation. If the profit of country A's TNC earned in country B has been taxed by country B, then country A may exempt this TNC from taxes on that part of its income earned in country B. Another method of solving this problem is that country A provides credit to its TNCs on taxes paid in country B.

In this case the tax burden on country A's corporation operating in country B is the same as that made from purely home operations in country A, provided that country B's taxes are lower or equal to those in country A.

The solution to the double taxation problem may also be found elsewhere. One possible solution is the unitary method of collection of corporate taxes (with all its controversies). A second is the profit-split method. Income of the distinct affiliates of a TNC is split in relation to the functions they perform and in relation to the associated risk. The difference between the profit-split and the unitary methods is that the former applies a functional analysis that is unique to each transaction, while the latter averages out all transactions. A third potential solution is the mutual agreement procedure where the national tax authorities discuss and try to correct tax discrepancies. In fact, they try to find an acceptable way of applying an existing method. The EU Arbitration Convention provided for binding arbitration related to the adjustment of profits of associated enterprises. A fourth answer may be found in advance-pricing agreements. This is, again, the application of an existing method. A TNC may acquire an advance agreement from the tax authority on the system for the allocation of its profit. This method represents a departure from the usual tax procedure (tax audits may take place even a few years after a transaction has taken place) since it refers to unknown future evolution (UNCTAD, 1993, pp. 207–10).

THE ARBITRATION CONVENTION

The objective of the 1990 EU Convention on the Elimination of Double Taxation in Connection with the Adjustment of Profits of Associated Enterprises (90/436/EEC), or the EU Arbitration Convention, is to eliminate double taxation of profits in connection with the adjustment of transfers of profits between associated enterprises. The convention came into force in January 1995 for a period of five years.

Transnational corporations operating within the Single European Market need to know that their profits will not be exposed to double taxation. The Arbitration Convention provides for independent arbitration (dispute resolution) where two EU member states are unable to resolve a disagreement as to the proper allocation of taxable profits in transfer pricing cases. It will help to ensure that enterprises doing business within the Single European Market are not exposed to double taxation of their profits. Such disagreements can arise from differing interpretations of the 'arm's-length principle', the internationally agreed tax standard for determining prices at which associated enterprises (TNCs) transfer goods, services, finance and intangible assets between each other.

Double taxation hinders a free flow of trade, capital and investment, so it is desirable to avoid it wherever possible. When the double taxation problem arises, the firm affected presents its case to the tax authorities concerned. If these authorities cannot solve the problem satisfactorily, they endeavour to reach mutual agreement with the authorities of the member state where the associated firm is taxed. If no agreement can be reached, the authorities present the case to an advisory commission, which suggests a way of solving the problem. Although the tax authorities may subsequently adopt, by mutual agreement, a solution different from that suggested by the advisory commission, they are bound to adopt the commission's advice if they cannot reach agreement. The commission consists of a chairman, two representatives from each of the tax authorities concerned and an even number of independent members.

In May 1999, before the expiration of the convention, the EU member states signed a protocol to extend its application for an additional five years. However, not all the member states ratified the protocol. This means that the EU Arbitration Convention has not been in force since 2000. However, informal application of the convention is currently possible to some extent, pending its entry into force. According to a survey prepared by the EU Joint Transfer Pricing Forum, several states have accepted a taxpayer request to initiate a mutual agreement procedure under the EU Arbitration Convention and are willing to participate in the arbitration procedure, provided that there is agreement with the other member state involved in the dispute. It should be noted that the positions of the member states regarding the informal application of the Arbitration Convention differ substantially.

Parallel to the process of ratification of the extension protocol, the EU member states have, within the framework of the EU Joint Transfer Pricing Forum, agreed to give the highest priority to finding practical solutions for a more uniform application of the convention. The aim is to work on the basis of consensus to reach non-legislative improvements to practical procedural problems such as deadlines, suspension of tax collection, interest charges, advisory committee establishment and operation.

PERSONAL INCOME TAX

Differences in personal income taxes between countries and different regions within them may have effects on the mobility of labour. Actual labour mobility depends on a number of factors that include the chances of finding employment, improved standards of living, social obstacles, social security benefits and immigration rules. Differences in personal income taxes may be neither the most decisive nor the only incentive for labour to move. This is generally the case throughout the EU. As labour has a very low propensity to migrate, the local authorities can retain rather high taxes on personal income without fearing that this would create incentives for a massive emigration from the region. The difference in personal income tax rates has a certain sway only for the migration of the upper-middle class and the rich.

It is a generally accepted principle that taxes are applied in those countries in which income originated. In addition, most countries tax the global income of their residents, but with foreign tax relief. A person originating in country A who works for part of the year in country B and the rest of the year in country A would pay income tax on pay earned in country B and ask for tax credit while paying income tax in country A for the rest of the taxable income. This person's tax payment would be the same as if the whole income had been earned in country A, unless country B's income tax is higher than that in country A.

Personal income tax is taken to be one of the most genuine rights of a state. There is little chance of this tax being harmonised in either the eurozone or an EMU. The EU is fully aware of this issue, so it has few ambitions in the sphere of personal income taxation. On the one hand, a potential for free mobility of labour in the EU may provide a behind-the-scenes pressure for harmonisation of national personal income taxes. On the other hand, such pressure is not great because of the still considerable social obstacles[25] to moving from one country to another.

A notable exception has often been the taxation of income of frontier and migrant workers. Tax agreements generally avoid double taxation, both in the country of destination (where the income was earned) and the country of origin (where the income maker resides). Troublesome issues remain regarding deductions, allowances and applicable rates. Granting an allowance to a non-resident worker may involve a concession. This would be the case when the country of residence offers the same allowance. Generally, there is full taxation in the country of residence with a credit for tax paid in the source country (Cnossen, 1986, p. 558).

The European Commission adopted a Communication on Undeclared Work in 1998. This communication encourages cooperation across the EU and the formulation of joint policies based on examples of best practice in combatting the 'underground economy' (that is not taxed by the government). This feature highlights the extent of the problem and outlines the Commission's approach. According to a Commission study, undeclared work represents between 7 and 16 per cent of the EU's GDP. This is a significant increase from 5 per cent during the 1970s. Although it is difficult to assess the precise extent of the underground economy, the report classifies the EU countries into three main groups. In the first group, the level of underground activity is relatively low at about 5 per cent of GDP. This group includes the Scandinavian countries, Ireland, Austria and the Netherlands. At the other extreme are countries where the underground economy exceeds 20 per cent of GDP, such as Italy and Greece. The other member countries lie between these two extremes.

The communication issued by the European Commission defines undeclared work as paid activity which is lawful in nature, but is neither notified to the public authorities nor taxed. It estimates that it is equal to 10 to 28 million jobs or 7 to 19 per cent of total declared employment. The communication perceives undeclared work as a common problem for all member states and argues that it should be tackled jointly through the exchange of good practice and, where appropriate, coordinated action at EU level. Undeclared work, which is mainly prevalent in labour-intensive, low-profit sectors and in business and innovative services, harms the career prospects and working conditions of those engaged in it and deprives the state of receipts needed to finance the provision of public services. The reduction in receipts means a drop in the level of services the state can offer. This creates a vicious circle as the government raises taxes to continue to provide these services. Hence, there are more incentives for undeclared work. Engagement in undeclared work is particularly harmful for workers who are officially inactive, as it deprives them of training opportunities and the development of a career profile, thus ultimately harming their future employability.

The factors that contribute to the existence of undeclared work include high taxes and social contributions, heavy regulatory and administrative burdens, inappropriate labour market legislation, cultural acceptance and the existence of easy opportunity. What is necessary to combat this situation is a combination of measures aimed at reducing the advantages of being in the undeclared economy, such as awareness-raising campaigns, tighter controls and stronger sanctions, as well as the adaptation of inappropriate legislation and the reduction of burdens on and obstacles to business.

The level, nature, consequences and causes of undeclared work have also been the subject of European Commission reports in the past. There are still difficulties in reaching a common definition and obtaining reliable data on the level of undeclared activity and the individuals involved in it. The wide margin in the estimated size of the underground economy as a percentage of GDP bears witness to these difficulties. Undeclared work is of particular concern because it is particularly prevalent in the sectors which the Commission seeks to target for job creation (labour-intensive services such as domestic services). It causes possible distortions of competition in the internal market and loss of revenue to the state, thus reducing the ability to provide services. Undeclared work is particularly difficult to combat, because it is often either based on a consensual exchange of the two parties involved or perceived as a matter of economic necessity. The European Commission is now hoping to build on the exchange of best practice in order to design measures to help combat this problem.

5. Indirect taxes

Indirect taxes are levied on the production and consumption of goods and services. They influence the retail price, and hence affect patterns of trade and consumption. Indirect taxes are ultimately paid by the final consumer. Sales and turnover taxes, excise duties and tariffs are the basic indirect taxes. In contrast with direct taxes, indirect taxes are seldom progressive. The principles for the levying of these taxes will be considered before the analysis of indirect taxes.

PRINCIPLES OF DESTINATION AND ORIGIN

Tax authorities are aware of the possible impact that indirect taxes have on trade in goods and services. Therefore, they introduced a safety device in the form of the destination and origin principle for taxation. This is of great importance to those countries that integrate. According to the principle of destination, taxes on goods are applied in the country of their consumption. This is the norm accepted in the World Trade Organisation. However, according to the principle of origin, taxes apply in the country of their production.

The *destination principle* states that consumption of all goods in one destination should be subject to the same tax, irrespective of the origin of their production. This principle removes tax distortions on competition between goods on the consuming country's market. The goods compete on equal tax conditions. This principle does not interfere with the location of production. It is widely accepted in international trade relations even though it requires the existence of fiscal frontiers among countries. The problem is that this principle may give the illusion that it stimulates exports and acts as a quasi-tariff on imports. This issue will be discussed shortly.

The *origin* or *production principle* asserts that all goods produced in one country should be taxed in that country, despite the possibility that these goods may be exported or consumed at home. If the production tax on good X in country A is lower than the same tax on the same good in country B, then if exported at zero transport and other costs, good X produced in country A will have a tax advantage in country B's market over country B's home-made good, X. This introduces a distortion that interferes with the spatial location of production between the countries. For allocational neutrality, a harmonised rate of tax, between countries, is a necessary condition.

Even within a customs union or a common market, there may exist fiscal frontiers if the member countries accept the principle of destination. The fiscal authorities of each country should know where and when they are entitled to tax consumption of goods or services. The origin principle may have an advantage, for it does not require fiscal frontiers. This conserves scarce resources.

Taxes levied according to the destination and origin principles differ regarding their revenue impact. These two principles determine to which government the proceeds accrue. A full economic optimisation cannot be achieved if there are different tax rates levied on various goods. Suppose that country A levies a VAT at the rate of 25 per cent on cars only, while the partner country B applies a uniform tax at the rate of 10 per cent on all goods. Suppose that both countries apply the destination principle for tax collection. In this case, the production in either country would be maximised because it would not be affected by the tax. Consumption would, however, be distorted. The relative consumer prices would be distorted because cars are dearer relative to clothes in country A, than they are in country B. Consequently, country A's consumers buy fewer cars and more clothes than they would do otherwise. The opposite tendency prevails in country B. In this case, trade between the two countries would not be optimal. Conversely, suppose that the two countries collect taxes according to the origin principle. In this case, trade would be optimised, for the relative consumer prices would be the same in each country. But, although trade is optimised, tax would still distort the maximisation of production. This is because producer prices, net of tax, would be reduced in a disproportionate way. Country A producers would be stimulated to produce clothes, rather than cars, while the opposite tendency would prevail in country B. Once indirect tax is not levied at a uniform rate on all goods, the choice is between the destination principle, which maximises production but does not optimise trade, and the origin principle, which optimises trade but does not maximise production (Robson, 1987, pp. 122–3).

The principle of destination offers a chance for tax evasion that is unavailable (if the records are not faked) with the origin principle. If taxes differ, then a consumer may be tempted to purchase a good in the state in which the relative tax burden is lower and consume it in the country where the tax burden is relatively higher. Consumers may easily purchase goods in one country and send or bring them to another one, or order these goods from abroad. This tax evasion depends on the differences in taxation, cost of transport and cooperation of buyers and sellers who do not inform the tax authorities if they know that the objective of certain purchases is tax evasion. The revenue effect of a standard tax at a rate of 40 per cent in a country where tax evasion is widespread (for example, the 'olive-oil belt' or Club Med countries of the EU) may be much smaller than the revenue impact of the same tax at a rate of 10 per cent in the country where tax evasion is not a common practice.

The tax system in the US relies on corporate and personal income taxes applied using the origin principle. The tax authorities in the EU countries rely upon consumption taxes with the application of the destination principle.[26] If the Europeans export goods to the US, they may have an advantage embodied in the difference in the tax systems. The US may contemplate the introduction of a border tax adjustment. This step may involve an addition to or reduction in the taxes already paid in Europe. The objective would be to keep competition in the US market on the same tax footing.

While the origin principle does not involve visible border tax adjustment, the destination principle includes it to the full extent of the tax. The long-run effect of either principle is, however, the same. In general equilibrium, any short-run advantage by one country will be eliminated in the long run by changes in the rate of exchange and domestic prices (Johnson and Krauss, 1973, p. 241). The US is a net importer of manufactured goods from Europe and Japan. It is advantageous, however, for the US to have these two exporting countries administer taxes on a destination, rather than origin basis (Hamilton and Whalley, 1986, p. 377). This is correct in the short run. In the long-run general equilibrium, the operation of exchange rates and factor prices (Johnson–Krauss law) would, presumably, eliminate any short-run (dis)advantage to these countries.

The new theory of trade and strategic industrial policy disputes the Johnson–Krauss argument. In a real situation with imperfect markets (increasing returns to scale, externalities and the economies of learning) and when the economic system is non-ergodic, once the production of, for example, aircraft or fast trains starts at a very restricted number of locations in the world, it perpetuates itself at that or those few locations. There is no room in the world even for three producers of wide-body passenger aircraft. In this case, the exchange rate argument (Johnson–Krauss) is of little help for the small and medium-sized countries.

Both the destination and the origin principles are imperfect. The destination principle for taxation is able to accomplish efficiency in the location of production, but not efficiency in trade. The origin principle has an inverse effect. If taxes are applied according to this principle, then trade may be efficient, but the location of production may not be efficient.

SALES AND TURNOVER TAXES

Sales and turnover taxes are payments to the government that are applied to all taxable goods and services except those subject to excise duties. Turnover tax is applied during the process of production, while if the tax is applied during sales to the final consumer it is called a sales tax. There are two methods for the collection of the sales tax. One is the cumulative multistage cascade method, while the other is called VAT. Apart from these two multiphase methods for the collection of the sales tax, there is also a one-stage method, applied only once, either at the stage of production or at the wholesale or retail sales phase. The following analysis will deal with the multiphase methods.

CUMULATIVE MULTISTAGE CASCADE METHOD

According to the cumulative multistage cascade method for the collection of sales tax, the tax is applied every time goods and services are transferred against payment. The tax base includes the aggregate value of goods that includes previously paid taxes on raw materials and inputs. The levying and collection of this tax are relatively simple, the tax burden may appear to be distributed over a larger number of taxpayers and the rate of sales tax applied by this method is relatively lower than the rate applied by the VAT method.

Firms may be stimulated by this method of collection of sales tax to integrate vertically in order to pay tax only at the last stage of the production process. This may have a favourable impact on the expansion of the business activities of firms (diversification). It may, however, cause a misallocation of resources. This artificial vertical integration may erode the advantages of specialisation and the efficiency of numerous SMEs if the vertically integrated firm ceases to use their output or if it absorbs them.

VALUE-ADDED TAX

This method of collection of sales tax is applied every time a good or service is sold, but it applies only on the value that is added in the respective phase of production, which is the difference between the price paid for inputs and the price received for output (hence, value added). The application of VAT starts at the beginning of the production process and ends up in the retail sale to the final consumer. VAT avoids double or multiple taxation in the previous stages of production (addition of value). Every taxpayer has to prove to the tax authorities, with an invoice, that the tax has been paid in the previous stages of production. Hence, there is a kind of self-regulating mechanism.

At the early stages of economic development, countries have relatively simple tax systems which apply only to a few goods and services. As countries develop, they tend to introduce a tax system that is more sophisticated, with a wider and more neutral tax base and coverage, and more efficient. Taxes on international trade (exports and imports) should be replaced by sales taxes that are collected by the VAT method. A relatively low rate of tax applied according to this method can raise a high return. It does not distort the economy, because it is neutral to the production mix of home and imported factors. In addition, it does not discriminate between production for home and foreign markets. VAT is neutral regarding the vertical integration of firms, so specialised SMEs may remain in business. If sales tax is collected according to the VAT method, then it would be harder to evade it in comparison to the situation where tax is collected only at the retail stage.

VAT based on the principle of destination is accepted in the EU as the method for the collection of sales tax. The method is harmonised, but there is a wide range of differences in the rates of this tax among EU countries. If the objective is to have a single rate of this tax, then there is considerable room for improvement in the future. The elimination of fiscal frontiers in the EU in 1993 and the creation of the Single European Market placed a certain market pressure on tax authorities to 'align' national VAT rates and prices, otherwise firms would lose business, in particular in the frontier regions. The creation of the eurozone (1999) and the introduction of the euro in circulation in 2002 added to this pressure.

A White Paper (European Communities, 1985) proposed the setting up of the EU Clearing House System. Its role would be to ensure that the VAT collected in the exporting member country and deducted in the importing member country was reimbursed to the latter. The crucial feature in this system would play across EU bookkeeping and computerisation. This system would, in principle, create a situation for taxable persons within the EU identical to the one that prevails in the member countries. In spite of the potential benefits of such a tax system, it was criticised on the grounds that it would be bureaucratic and costly.

In practice, however, the existence of widely diverging rates of tax and tax exemptions may expose the system to the risk of fraud and evasion. The EU was aware that some fraud and evasion already existed, but the scale of such distortions after the removal of fiscal frontiers and the introduction of the euro would increase without tax harmonisation. Therefore, a minimum standard VAT rate of 15 per cent on most goods became a legal obligation in the EU from October 1992.

It is relatively understandable for Britain (as well as Ireland and Greece) to oppose this type of tax alignment since cross-border shopping is not a common feature in those countries as they have no common land frontier with the rest of the EU. However, for Austria, the Benelux countries, France and Germany, where cross-border shopping is common, it is easy to accept such arguments.

A move towards the origin principle (collection of tax during production) would require a system for redistribution of revenues (refunds) from the country where the goods were produced and taxed to the one where they are consumed. The effect of such a system would be as if the tax had been levied on consumption. Although there were concerns in some member countries because of the need to find alternative employment for thousands of customs officers, the fiscal frontiers between EU countries were removed in 1993. This was the most visible benefit of the implementation of the Single European Market.[27] Consumers are now free to purchase goods in any EU country and bring them home with very few restrictions, provided that the imported goods are only for their personal consumption. There are, of course, exceptions, but only two: the purchase of new cars is taxed in the country of registration, while mail-order purchases are taxed either at the rate applying in the country of destination or at the rate in the seller's country (depending on the seller's annual sales volume in the country of destination).

Border tax adjustment without border controls was preserved in the EU. The former border controls were shifted by the interim system (introduced in 1993) to exporting and importing firms (centralised costs were replaced by decentralised costs in firms). The transitional system was extended in 1997 for an indefinite period, because EU countries were and still are unable to agree on the final shape of the VAT system based on the principle of origin. This system replaced time-consuming tax controls and payments at the EU internal borders with a demanding centralised reporting system carried out by the companies themselves. The final system will allow firms to pay VAT in the country of origin, as if all EU member countries were a single country. The burden of redistribution of VAT revenue will then fall on the member states. This would be advantageous to businesses as they would not have to differentiate between domestic and intra-EU sales. None the less, there will be two problems. First, a clearing house system will have to redistribute revenue around the EU as countries that export a lot will benefit from the system, while those that import a lot will lose. Second, the origin-based tax system will enhance the need for a higher harmonisation of VAT rates. In the meantime, the current transitory system seems to be operating quite well. This will, of course, be taken into account during the reassessment of the tax system.

This gradual approach was extremely difficult to implement. EU member states showed little enthusiasm in practice for the move towards the origin system. There is a reluctance to move towards a greater degree of harmonisation of VAT rates even though this is a precondition for the definitive system. Bearing in mind the potential and actual resistance concerning tax harmonisation, the European Commission has a patient long-term goal of origin-based taxation based on small steps, relating simplification, modernisation and administrative cooperation among member countries.

Table 3.2 illustrates differences in VAT rates in the EU, candidate countries, Switzerland, the US and Japan. The lower rates apply to food, clothing and other essential items. Portugal has lower rates in its autonomous regions. Ireland and Britain use the zero rate for food, books and children's clothing. The other countries generally apply an exception with credit (which comes down to the same thing as a zero rate) to exports and supplies assimilated to exports, such as supplies to embassies, to ships leaving the country and the like. In Ireland and Britain these supplies are also covered by the zero rate.

The EU rules assert that goods should be taxed at between 15 and 25 per cent, except for a series of commodities that carry reduced rates. In order to simplify the EU's maze of VAT rates, the European Commission proposed a plan (in 2003) that would require Britain and Ireland, which have zero VAT rate on children's clothes and shoes, to apply VAT on these goods. Otherwise, this would distort the Single European Market. The British Treasury declared that it would use the veto to block this plan if necessary as one of the election promises was to keep a zero rating on these goods.

A broad-based VAT can be criticised on the grounds that it is regressive. The reason for the regressive impact of VAT in the EU can be found in the structure of national demand. Consumption to which VAT applies usually embraces a relatively higher proportion of the GDP in the less-advanced member countries than in the richer ones. Other components of demand, such as investment, which is presumably higher in the more advanced countries, are not burdened by VAT. The low-income segment of the population can be helped by transfer payments. This can make VAT directly progressive. Zero rating, exemptions and multiple rates do not always directly assist the low-income group, which is the target population.

The EU conducted a wide-ranging survey in the second half of the 1980s. About 20 000 businessmen from 12 EU countries were asked to rank the biggest barriers to free trade. The most damaging of all were overt obstacles. Different national technical standards, administrative and customs formalities were at the top of the list, while differences in rates of VAT and excise duties were at the bottom of the list of eight barriers (Emerson et al., 1988, pp. 44–6).

Table 3.2 *VAT rates in the EU(25), candidate countries, Switzerland, the US and Japan in 2003*

Country	VAT rate (%)
1. Austria	10, 20
2. Belgium	6, 12, 21
3. Denmark	25
4. Finland	8, 17, 22
5. France	2.1, 5.5, 19.6
6. Germany	7, 16
7. Greece	4, 8, 18
8. Ireland	4.3, 13.5, 21
9. Italy	4, 10, 20
10. Luxembourg	3, 6, 12, 15
11. Netherlands	6, 19
12. Portugal	5, 12, 19
13. Spain	4, 7, 16
14. Sweden	6, 12, 25
15. United Kingdom	5, 17.5
16. Cyprus	5, 15
17. Czech Republic	5, 22
18. Estonia	5, 18
19. Hungary	12, 25
20. Latvia	9, 18
21. Lithuania	9, 18
22. Malta	5, 15
23. Poland	3, 7, 22
24. Slovakia	14, 20
25. Slovenia	8.5, 20
26. Bulgaria	20
27. Romania	19
28. Turkey	1, 8, 18
29. Switzerland	2.4, 3.6, 7.6
30. United States	no VAT, state and municipal taxes approximately 4–19%
31. Japan	5 (including local tax)

Source: International Bureau of Fiscal Documentation (2003).

EXCISE DUTIES

Excise duty is a type of indirect tax that is levied for the purpose of raising public revenue. It is applied in almost every country to tobacco, spirits and liquid fuels. Excise duties are also applied in some countries to coffee, tea, cocoa, salt, bananas, light bulbs and playing cards. These duties are levied only once, usually at the stage of production or import. Another property of excise duties is that they are generally high in relation to other taxes.

While the VAT is proportional to the value of output, an excise duty may be based either on the *ad valorem* principle (retail or wholesale price) or it may be a specific tax. Within the EU, tobacco products are subject to both. There is a specific tax per cigarette and an *ad valorem* tax based on the retail price of the cigarettes concerned (Kay, 1990, p. 34).

Table 3.3 presents the rates of excise duties in the EU member countries. There is a wide variety in charges that come from excise duties among the countries. This difference is due to the various choices of fiscal and health authorities. If the difference in excise duties among countries exceeds the costs of the reallocation of resources or transport, it will have a distorting effect on the geographical location of resources or pattern of trade. The difference in the excise duty on 1000 litres of petrol of €210 between high-duty Germany and low-duty Austria is significant when one bears in mind that it costs just a few euros to transport this amount of fuel by pipeline.

The VAT is calculated on the price of a good that includes the excise duty. Any change in the excise duty will produce differences in the VAT revenue. Hence the need for a certain harmonisation of excise duties too. In the US, each federal state has its own liquor duty. Liquor and cigarettes should bear the national tax authority stamp. Only the nationally stamped goods can be purchased legally within a state. Import for personal consumption is unlimited, while bulk intra-EU commercial transport and trade in these goods without the proper tax clearance is forbidden and punishable. The harmonised rates proposed by the European Commission should be viewed only as a yardstick, as it would be extremely difficult to try to unify excise duties throughout the EU member countries (it would be like 'waiting for Godot').

The goods that are subject to excise duties are normally stored in bonded warehouses that are controlled by the public authorities. Once the goods are taken out for consumption, the excise duty is levied. If the goods are exported, the excise duty is not charged upon the presentation of a proof of export. The importing country of these goods controls the import at the frontier where it establishes liability for excise duty. This ensures that excise duty is charged in the country where the goods are consumed. After the creation of the Single European Market, which removed tax and other internal frontiers, the wide divergence in excise duties would distort trade,

Table 3.3 Excise duties in the EU(15) countries in 2001 (in euros)

Country	Excise revenue GDP	Excise revenue Total tax revenue	Pack of 20 cigarettes	Beer 1l[a]	Wine 1l[b]	40% spirits 0.75l[c]	Unleaded as % of petroleum 1l[d]
Denmark	5.6	11.0	3.29	0.62	0.95	11.09	0.54
Luxembourg	5.0	12.0	1.41	0.01	0.00	3.12	0.37
Finland	4.7	10.1	3.03	0.29	2.35	15.14	0.56
Portugal	4.6	13.5	1.51	0.17	0.00	2.51	0.48
Ireland	4.5	13.8	3.97	0.19	2.73	8.29	0.51
Greece	4.4	11.9	1.70	0.01	0.00	2.72	0.32
UK	3.6	10.0	5.60	0.19	2.50	9.50	0.79
Sweden	3.5	6.8	2.70	0.15	2.26	15.45	0.48
Netherlands	3.5	8.3	2.07	0.25	0.59	4.51	0.61
Italy	3.5	8.0	1.54	0.01	0.00	1.94	0.52
France	2.9	6.4	2.71	0.03	0.03	4.35	0.57
Spain	2.8	7.9	1.33	0.01	0.00	2.22	0.43
Germany	2.8	7.3	2.29	0.00	0.01	3.91	0.62
Austria	2.7	6.2	1.96	0.02	0.00	3.00	0.41
Belgium	2.4	5.2	2.09	0.02	0.47	4.98	0.49
EU average	3.8	9.2	2.48	0.13	0.79	6.18	0.51

Notes:
a. The agreed minimum excise duty is €748 per hectolitre degree Plato of finished product.
b. The agreed minimum excise duty is €0 per hectolitre.
c. The agreed minimum excise duty is €550 per hectolitre or €1000 per hectolitre of pure alcohol.
d. The agreed minimum excise duty is €278 per 1000 litres.

Source: Cnossen (2001, p. 502).

because of a real danger of fraud and evasion. The White Paper proposed as a solution a linkage system for bonded warehouses for products subject to excise duties and the approximation of these charges in the EU.

6. Future challenges

Indirect taxes are already harmonised to an extent within the Single European Market. Direct tax systems, on the other hand, require only limited harmonisation and can generally be left to individual EU countries. However, there is a general consensus across the EU that cooperation is needed to remove harmful tax competition.

The impact of the potential tax competition; high international mobility of capital and certain TNCs; and integrated international production has not yet been fully grasped by many tax authorities. Divergent tax rates on highly portable luxury and expensive goods may not be sustained. Hence, there is a trend away from taxing these goods and towards taxing the consumption of petroleum, spirits and tobacco. However, different taxes and their rates may remain on non-tradable goods and real property.

In order to deal with harmful tax competition, the European Commission proposed several measures that may introduce certain bases for increased tax coordination between the member countries. These include the following:

- a code of conduct for business taxation, in parallel with a European Commission notice on state aids in the form of taxation measures;
- the elimination of distortions in the taxation of capital income;
- the elimination of withholding taxes on cross-border interest and royalty payments between companies; and
- the elimination of significant distortions in the area of indirect taxation.

The European Commission's strategy for the future was revealed in a Communication (COM(97) 464) which was approved by the Council of Ministers in 1997. The Commission has a code of conduct for business taxation. It seeks to introduce a coordinated approach to harmful tax competition and to promote a system of employment-friendly taxation. This was important as there was a trend which revealed an increasing tax burden on labour (particularly the least skilled and the least mobile). In addition, larger firms were better placed and equipped to take advantage of tax competition between countries.

The code of conduct for business taxation is not a legally binding document. It is, however, rather comprehensive as it includes a review and monitoring process. The code helps to prevent and overcome economic distortions and an erosion of tax bases within the EU. Member countries agreed to respect principles of fair competition and to refrain from harmful tax competition.

A number of disparities in the area of VAT and the tax treatment of energy products should be removed in order to prevent the risk of harmful tax competition. Among the changes proposed, the European Commission aspires:

- to modify the status of the VAT committee (regulatory committee);
- to exempt from VAT those transactions in gold that are made for investment purposes (such transactions are still taxed when used for industrial purposes);

- to review the taxation of passenger transport;
- to revise the rates applied to energy products; and
- to establish the FISCALIS programme of cooperation between member states against fraud in the area of indirect taxation.

In 2000, in order to remove the competitive disadvantage of EU firms involved in e-commerce[28] relative to foreign (principally US) competitors, the European Commission proposed a set of ideas. These include a request to a foreign supplier with annual sales of over €100 000 in the EU to be registered in an EU member country; sales of EU firms abroad would be VAT free; sales within the EU to consumers would be according to the principle of origin (does not need trans-border tax adjustment), while on-line sales among EU firms would be according to the principle of destination.

The case for the unitary method of taxation may gain certain additional support in the future. The expansion of integrated international production (TNCs) and an increased international mobility of factors, capital in particular, are reaching the point at which the taxation of business founded on the unitary method may be superior to the arm's-length method of taxation. This topic could be discussed interminably. Progress in international tax matters, including attempts to approximate, harmonise or unify tax systems, takes a very long time indeed. The reason for this is simple: the jealously protected sovereign national tax privileges.

There is a pressing need to make progress in the field of taxation and to ensure more effective coordination of tax policies. This is relevant for further development of the Single European Market, ways and means to enable industry to compete on the world market, and the need to reduce the level of unemployment and challenges brought by e-commerce. The issue of harmful tax competition, which threatens to reduce revenues, to distort tax structures and to interfere with spatial and sectoral location of investments, should be kept relatively high on the EU policy discussion agenda. Additional challenges in the tax field refer to taxation in the light of an ageing population, the social expenditure necessary for the care of the aged and the fight against fraud and irregularities.

7. Conclusion

Most national tax systems are deeply rooted in an era when economies were largely closed and when international capital movements were small or non-existent. The national tax authorities could tax income and business with little regard for what goes on in other countries. The contemporary system of integrated international production, economic integration, high degree of capital mobility and 'globalisation' changed all that. Increasingly, it matters what is going on at home, as well as abroad. There are at least three reasons for this:

- *Income of TNCs*: A large part of trade within many TNCs represents intra-firm trade. TNCs may manipulate (transfer pricing) the costs of their intra-firm transactions in order to have their income taxed where it is most favourable for the corporation. Certain TNCs may be sensitive to tax and subsidy incentives, hence they may move the location of their business.
- *Personal income*: It is estimated that income earned from foreign investment and savings (profit, dividends and interest) is growing exponentially. National tax authorities were not always able to track this individual income as much of it may come from tax havens. This income tends to be unreported or underreported to the national tax authorities. Recent moves towards the exchange of information among EU countries may significantly reduce tax evasion.
- *Sales taxes*: Open borders, advertising, access to information, the internet, mail ordering, electronic payments, smaller size of many goods, lower cost of transport, increased travel and the like all increase international purchasing, especially of goods that are expensive and easily portable. Lower sales taxes and the refund of paid taxes on these goods if exported add to the consumer's decision to purchase internationally.

The benefits that accrue from the elimination of fiscal frontiers in the EU refer to the following gains. The investment decisions of firms are improved as the tax system increases the degree of certainty in relation to the situation where every country manages its own taxes. A removal of tax posts at frontiers saves resources and, more importantly, increases the opportunities for competition and, consequently, improves prospects for a superior spatial location of production. Of course, some facilities for random anti-terrorist, health, veterinary and illegal immigration checks may be necessary. Finally, harmonisation of the tax system would enhance the equalisation of prices and lower the distortions due to different systems and rates of taxation.

Tax competition may tempt governments to offer tax concessions (lower taxes) and provide tax incentives (subsidies) in order to lure TNCs to relocate their operations. Potential (short-term) losses in tax revenue may be compensated or more than compensated in the medium term. The expectation is that if 'all goes well', TNCs can employ local labour and purchase locally produced inputs. Salaries of the employed will be taxed, as well as goods and services purchased by these salaries, and there would be less expenditure on unemployment benefits and so on.

A country (or group of countries) that frequently changes its (their) fiscal systems may be regarded as a potentially risky location(s) for investment. This may provoke a reduction in the inflow and an increase in the outflow of capital to the relatively more politically stable and economically growing destinations. Complete unification of fiscal systems, however, may not be a prerequisite for the smooth functioning of an EMU. The US is the best example in support of this argument. The federal states in the US have differences in their respective tax systems. This system has functioned relatively satisfactorily without any tax posts between the states for a number of decades. However, these differences in the tax systems are relatively minor. There is a significant degree of harmonisation among tax systems in federal units. There is also a high labour mobility in the US. If certain local or state taxes change (increase), this may easily provoke an outflow of labour and management from that location. Such a swift response does not exist in Europe. Therefore, the local European or state authorities could comfortably retain relatively high and distinct taxes without fearing that people (but not companies) would go elsewhere. In addition, operation of firms within clusters makes firms relatively less sensitive to taxes. This provides the local authorities with opportunities to tax them more heavily than would otherwise be the case.

A genuine Single European Market requires a certain degree of harmonisation of indirect taxes among its member countries. Otherwise, member governments would have to accept substantial diversions in revenues. It is widely believed that a difference in sales tax of up to 5 per cent could introduce distortions that may be acceptable among the integrated countries and that these differences would not bring unbearable budgetary problems. However, the problem arises when the national budgets have different trends regarding their deficits. Alterations in the national tax systems in such situations can bring serious political difficulties.

As for the possibility of a significant degree of harmonisation (or, in an extreme case, unification) of fiscal systems in the EMU, there are certain grounds for pessimism. A tax policy is one of the most fundamental national sovereign rights. Recall Britain's vigorous opposition to the inclusion of fiscal matters in the majority-voting issues in the Single European Act and onwards. The achievement of national goals within a fiscal policy does not necessarily coincide at all times with those of other partners. Although the eurozone may agree on the basic objectives, their achievement may be left to the member countries which may sometimes wish to use different and potentially conflicting instruments. None the less, the sophisticated market-led approach (bottom-up) to integration in tax matters that came from the

Single European Act (a removal of fiscal frontiers) might compel national tax authorities to align their tax rates and systems. Otherwise, other things being equal, businesses that are sensible to taxation may move to and settle in the countries where the tax treatment is most favourable. This bottom-up approach by the EU is a significant shift from the earlier policy proposals that argued in favour of full tax harmonisation (top-down).

The public is sensitive to general changes in tax systems. Full fiscal harmonisation in the EU may require an increase in taxes in some countries (for example, Latvia and Lithuania) while it may require their decrease in others (for example, Austria and Spain). In the low-tax countries there is an opposition to tax increases, while in the high-tax countries, there is a fear of revenue losses. Therefore, a partial fiscal harmonisation (only agreed taxes) might be a good first step for those who argue in favour of harmonisation. One of the issues not dealt with in the Single Market Programme was that very little has been done in the area of tax approximation. Harmonisation of fiscal systems of the countries that are in the EU, and especially in the eurozone, requires caution, gradualism and, more than anything else, the political will which economic theory cannot predict.

Tax harmonisation (averaging) may not bring gains either to developed or to backward regions or countries. While this harmonisation may reduce the tax revenue of the authorities in the former group, at the same time it makes backward regions less attractive for investment. As this provides certain arguments in favour of tax competition, one must note the effects of harmful tax competition for internationally mobile business activities. If there is a lack in transparency regarding tax provisions and in their application (in favour of non-residents), and if there is a lack of exchange of information between national fiscal authorities, then such tax competition may have a harmful effect on the allocation of resources. The role of international agreements is to end such practices.

There is also the ever-important question: why are taxes not coming down in the EU? There are several possible answers. First, economic integration is not yet complete. This situation may remain for quite some time to come. Second, technology has improved, and made trade in goods, communication and transport cheaper. However, there are still costs involved in overcoming the problems of distance. The third aspect may be linked with ideology. The end goal of the radical right may include the objective to end taxes on all income that comes from capital (ownership) and to replace them with taxes on wages (earned income) only. Such an approach to taxes is resisted in Europe.

A gradualist type of tax integration that allows for a certain degree of competition (public choice approach) may be preferred to a holistic unification or harmonisation. In any case, tax issues are very sensitive and many may agree, overtly or covertly, that tax matters ought to remain a matter for unanimity in the EU in spite of the fact that this may require many years of arduous work.

8. Budget of the European Union

INTRODUCTION

Together with the law and its enforcement, the budget, its revenue and expenditure, is one of the most essential instruments that an economic and/or political organisation may employ to fulfil its role. The budget should cover not only administrative costs, but also dispose of funds for intervention in the economy. Otherwise, the role of such an organisation may be limited to mere consultation and, perhaps, research of certain issues. The budget of most international organisations covers only their administrative expenses. A rare exception is the EU, which returns and redistributes about 95 per cent of its receipts back to the member countries. The budgets of the member countries reduce their expenditure for their own interventions in the fields where the EU has competence and where it intervenes.

In 1970 the EU budget amounted to €3.6 billion or €19 per inhabitant. In 2003, the EU budget stands at €98 billion or €258 per inhabitant or €0.7 per day. Yet this is 'only' 1.1 per cent of the combined GDP of the 15 member countries of the EU. Following enlargement in 2004, the EU(25) budget of €105 billion would mean an EU expenditure of €232 per inhabitant a year or €0.6 a day.

PRINCIPLES

The EU budget is subject to certain general principles. All EU expenditure must be presented in a single document (principle of *unity*). According to the principle of *annuality*, the budget operations relate to a given budgetary year which coincides with the calendar year. This eases the control of the work of the EU executive branch. The principle of *equilibrium* requires that the budget must be in annual balance (Article 268 of the Treaty of Rome) and must be wholly financed from own resources (Article 269). Deficit financing or taking loans to finance the possible deficits are outlawed. Specific budgetary revenue may not be assigned or linked to a particular expenditure (principle of *universality*). Finally, the principle of *specification* requires that expenditure has to be specified. A precise purpose has to be given to each outlay in order to prevent any confusion between appropriations.

As already seen in the chapter on monetary integration (Chapter 2), the objective of the Stability and Growth Pact (1997) is to keep the eurozone on track by means of a sustainable fiscal policy. This was needed to stabilise the debt/GDP ratios at reasonable levels following years of rising public debt. If one or several governments borrow recklessly, no limits on borrowing would give them a chance for a free ride in the eurozone. As a result, all eurozone countries could pay a price for such irresponsible national spending policy, as interest rates could increase throughout the zone. Therefore, the reasoning behind the pact was to shield the ECB from national pressures to reduce debt through inflation.

The absolute and relative size of the EU budget is, however, quite small in relation to its share of the joint GDP of the member states, as well as in relation to the potential impact on the large-scale macroeconomic life of the EU. As such, it differs from the national budgets since the EU budget plays a significant role neither in economic stabilisation, nor in allocation of resources (apart from agriculture). In addition, its potential stabilisation role is jeopardised by the annuality principle.

Even though there is a principle of annuality, the EU sometimes engages in multiannual financial operations. These operations are continuously expanding. Therefore, the dual requirements are reflected in the advent of two distinct appropriations:

- The *payment* appropriations cover expenditure (to the limit entered in the current annual budget) that results from the commitments undertaken in the current financial year and preceding financial years.
- The *commitment* appropriations refer to the total cost (ceiling) in the current financial year of the obligations that are to be carried out over a period of more than one financial year. The commitment appropriations are larger than payment appropriations.

The Treaty of Rome (Article 272) sets two types of EU budgetary outlays: compulsory and non-compulsory expenditures. The distinction between the two is basically political, so it was often a source of conflict between the European Parliament and the Council of Ministers. A vague definition of the two kinds of expenditure was drafted in 1982 by a joint declaration of the European Commission, the Council of Ministers and the European Parliament, which stated that compulsory expenditure from the budget is obligatory for the EU in order to meet its obligations. This refers both to the internal and external tasks that stem from the treaties and other acts. All other expenditure is non-compulsory.

The Council of Ministers has the last word on compulsory expenditure, while the European Parliament decides on the non-compulsory outlays. The Parliament may increase the amount of non-compulsory expenditure by amending the draft budget. The maximum rate of increase in relation to the preceding fiscal year depends on the trend of the GDP increase in the EU, average variation in the budgets of the member states, and trends in the cost of living, as well as on approval by the Council. Before the drafting of a new budget, the presidents of the three institutions have a 'trialogue' meeting to determine the grouping of the new budget chapters and the ones for which the legal basis might have changed.

PROCEDURE

Article 272 of the Treaty of Rome lays out the budgetary procedure (sequence of steps and deadlines) that should be respected by the European Commission, the Council and the European Parliament. The prescribed budgetary procedure begins on 1 July and ends on 31 December of the year preceding the budget year in question. In practice however, from 1977, the procedure has started much earlier. The sequencing of the annual budgetary procedure is as follows:

- The European Commission is to prepare and send to the Council and Parliament the *preliminary draft budget* by 15 June. It does so by compiling the requests of all spending departments according to the EU's needs and political priorities for the coming year. The Commission also arbitrates between conflicting claims on the basis of the priorities set for the year in question. The preliminary draft budget can be amended in order to allow for the inclusion of new information that was not available prior to June.
- The Council conducts its first reading of the preliminary draft budget and on this basis and after a conciliation meeting with the Parliament establishes the *draft budget* before 31 July. This draft budget is sent by mid-September to the Parliament for the first reading.
- The European Parliament conducts its *first reading* of the draft budget during October. It may amend the non-compulsory expenditure by the absolute majority of its members. Modifications in the compulsory expenditure require an absolute majority of votes cast. The Parliament is supposed to pass the amended draft back to the Council by mid-November for the second reading.
- After the conciliation meeting with the Parliament, the Council conducts its *second reading* of the draft budget during the third week of

November. The draft budget is altered following the amendments (for the non-compulsory expenditure) by the Parliament or proposed modifications regarding compulsory expenditure. Unless the entire budget is rejected by the Parliament, this is the stage when the Council determines the final amount of the compulsory expenditure. The amended draft budget is returned to the Parliament around the last week of November for the second and final reading.

- As the Council decides on compulsory expenditure, the Parliament spends most of its time in reviewing the non-compulsory outlays. For that part of the budget, the Parliament may accept or refuse the proposals of the Council. The budget is *accepted* (before the New Year) and could be implemented when the Parliament approves it by a majority of its members. Three-fifths of the votes cast must be in favour.
- As certain unforeseen and exceptional events may take place during the year when the budget is implemented, the European Commission is entitled to propose *amendments* to the ongoing budget. These changes are subject to the same procedural rules as the general budget.

EXPENDITURE

The budgetary crises of the 1980s prompted the EU institutions to reconsider budgetary procedure and discipline. The budget was sometimes balanced by accounting tricks dubbed 'creative accounting'. Certain payments were deferred until the following year, when it was expected that the financial conditions would improve. As part of the reform in 1988 and in order to ensure budgetary discipline and to improve the budgetary procedure, the European Parliament, the Council and the European Commission ought to agree in advance on the main budgetary priorities in the forthcoming medium term. The objective is to institute a binding medium-term financial framework for EU expenditure known as the 'financial perspective'.

The financial perspective shows both the maximum amount and the structure of foreseeable EU outlays. A reference point for the budgetary expenditure was the financial perspective from 1988 to 1992. The subsequent agreements covered seven-year periods, 1993–99 and 2000–06. Tough negotiations started on the post-enlargement financial perspective, 2007–13, even before the eastern enlargement in 2004.

The financial perspective differs from indicative financial programming in that the ceilings are binding on the parties to the Interinstitutional Agreement. The financial perspective marks the maximum amount of payment appropriations for the various chapters of EU expenditure. It is not a multiannual budget. The reason is that the usual annual budgetary procedure still applies in order to determine the actual level of expenditure (but up to the ceiling provided by the financial perspective). The three institutions agree to respect the annual expenditure ceiling for each expenditure item. The ceilings, however, need to be sufficiently large in order to allow for the flexibility necessary for budgetary management. The ceiling may be revised in either direction, but that depends only on unforeseen events (such as German reunification, the violent disintegration of the former Yugoslavia or aid to Rwanda) that took place after the Interinstitutional Agreement was signed.

The 1988 reform of the budget had three additional aspects:

- The total own resources of the EU budget were not linked to the VAT contribution. Instead, resources needed to cover the budgetary expenditure had a ceiling in appropriations for payments. This overall ceiling was fixed for each year from 1988 to 1992 as a percentage of the Union's GDP (for example, 1.15 per cent in 1989 and 1.2 per cent in 1992). The new ceilings gradually increased from 1.20 to 1.27 per cent in the period which ended in 1999.
- The budgetary discipline, as a shared responsibility of the European Commission, the Council and the Parliament, was increased. Its major objective was to check farm expenditure. The means to achieve this is a guideline that may not increase by more than 74 per cent of the annual rate of growth of EU GDP.
- The coordination and increase in effectiveness of the three structural funds (the European Agricultural Guarantee and Guidance Fund: EAGGF; the European Regional Development Fund: ERDF; and the European Social Fund: ESF). The objectives included the adjustment of regions whose development was below the EU average, structural conversion in the regions hit by industrial decline, the fight against long-term unemployment, the occupational integration of young people, the adjustment of farming structure and the development of rural areas.

The European Council in Berlin (1999) decided to keep the EU budget ceiling at a level that does not exceed 1.27 per cent of the total EU GDP in the period of the new financial perspective, 2000–06.[29] This means that the enlargement-related expenditure must fit within this limit set for 'own resources'.[30] This (or any other) fixed rate may be disputed as it may not fulfil the allocation, or the stabilisation, or the redistribution tasks in an EMU. As for the total annual aid that a member country may receive from the EU budget, this was limited to 4 per cent of the national GDP.[31] This was a political compromise, as are most solutions in the EU. In addition, the Council decided to link the national contribution to the EU budget to the member country's ability to contribute (GDP).[32] Economically successful EU members would have to pay more as they can afford more.

A new emphasis in expenditure includes the financing of the trans-European transport, telecommunications and energy networks. Priority would be given to the cross-frontier links between the national networks. As for external action, the EU will pay attention to emergency aid (primarily to the countries in the vicinity), as well as loan guarantees.

Outlays from the EU budget have expanded and diversified remarkably since its inception. Table 3.4 presents the financial perspective for 2000–06. As far as the annual expenditure is concerned, the CAP disposes of half of the entire budget. Hence, in relative terms, expenditure on all other various economic activities and policies may not be highly concentrated. Structural funds of the EU include the ERDF, the ESF, the Guidance Section of the Agricultural Fund and, from 1993, the Cohesion Fund. Outlays on transport and fisheries are also included in this chapter. The share of structural funds in 2003 is 33 per cent of the budget. A notable feature of the components of this chapter is that their shares are continuously rising in the general budget over time. The (ab)use of structural funds may become a serious stumbling block in the future, just as agricultural expenditure has continued to be for decades.

Administrative operations cost the EU only 5 per cent of its budget, while the rest of the budget is redistributed mostly to the member countries. This distinguishes the EU from other international organisations, since elsewhere the budget is used mainly for administrative expenditure.

The total size of the EU annual budget may not be all that large if compared with the annual national government expenditure on particular activities. For example, the EU budget in 2003 was €98 billion. During the same year, out of its annual budget of €659 billion (£456 billion), the British government spent €104 billion (£72 billion) on the National Health Service and €85 billion (£59 billion) on education. At the same time, out of its budget of €272 billion, the French government spent €69 billion on national education, research and the young. The German federal government in the same period spent €82 billion on health and social security out of its budget of €248 billion.

Audit of EU expenditure has been provoking a number of controversies. For the eighth year in a row, the Court of Auditors was able to certify that only 5 per cent of EU expenditure was legal and regular (this concerns mainly internal administration). The remaining 95 per cent of outlays did

Table 3.4 EU budget according to the financial perspective 2000–06

Appropriations for commitments	Current prices					2003 prices	
	2000	2001	2002	2003	2004	2005	2006
1. AGRICULTURE	41 738	44 530	46 587	47 378	46 285	45 386	45 094
Agricultural expenditure (except rural development)	37 352	40 035	41 992	42 680	41 576	40 667	40 364
Rural development and supporting measures	4386	4495	4595	4698	4709	4719	4730
2. STRUCTURAL OPERATIONS	32 678	32 720	33 638	33 968	33 652	33 384	32 588
Structural funds	30 019	30 005	30 849	31 129	30 922	30 654	29 863
Cohesion Fund	2659	2715	2789	2839	2730	2730	2725
3. INTERNAL POLICIES[1]	6031	6272	6558	6796	6915	7034	7165
4. EXTERNAL ACTION	4627	4735	4873	4972	4983	4994	5004
5. ADMINISTRATION[2]	4638	4776	5012	5211	5319	5428	5536
6. RESERVES	906	916	676	434	434	434	434
Monetary reserve	500	500	250				
Emergency aid reserve	203	208	213	217	217	217	217
Guarantee reserve	203	208	213	217	217	217	217
7. PRE-ACCESSION AID	3174	3240	3328	3386	3386	3386	3386
Agriculture	529	540	555	564	564	564	564
Pre-accession structural instrument	1058	1080	1109	1129	1129	1129	1129
PHARE (applicant countries)	1587	1620	1664	1693	1693	1693	1693
APPROPRIATIONS FOR COMMITMENTS – Total	93 792	97 189	100 672	102 145	100 974	100 046	99 207

199

Table 3.4 (continued)

Appropriations for commitments	Current prices					2003 prices		
	2000	2001	2002	2003	2004	2005	2006
APPROPRIATIONS FOR PAYMENTS – Total	91 322	94 730	100 078	102 767	99 553	97 659	97 075
Appropriations for payments as % of GNI	1.10%	1.10%	1.12%	1.10%	1.04%	1.00%	0.97%
Available for accession (appropriations for payments)			4397	7266	9626	12 387	15 396
Agriculture			1698	2197	2652	3172	3680
Other expenditure			2699	5069	6974	9215	11 716
CEILING, APPROPRIATIONS FOR PAYMENTS	91 322	94 730	104 475	110 033	109 179	110 046	112 471
Ceiling, payment as % of GNI	1.10%	1.10%	1.17%	1.18%	1.14%	1.12%	1.12%
Margin for unforeseen expenditure	0.17%	0.17%	0.10%	0.09%	0.13%	0.15%	0.15%
Own resources ceiling	1.27%	1.27%	1.27%	1.27%	1.27%	1.27%	1.27%

Notes:
1. In accordance with Article 2 of Decision No. 182/1999/EC of the European Parliament and of the Council and Article 2 of Council Decision 1999/64/Euratom (OJ L 26, 1.2.1999, p. 1 and p. 34), EUR 11 510 million at current prices is available for research over the period 2000–02.
2. The expenditure on pensions included under the ceiling for this heading is calculated net of staff contributions to the pension scheme, up to a maximum of EUR 1100 million at 1999 prices for the period 2000–06.

Source: European Commission (2000), *The Community Budget – The Facts in Figures.*

not receive a positive statement of assurance 'due to the incidence of errors found'.[33]

REVENUE

The EU budget was financed by the national contributions of member states until 1970. After that year, the EU got its 'own' resources, including customs duties, agricultural levies and a budget-balancing resource of up to 1 per cent of the VAT base (the base was increased to 1.4 per cent in 1985). While customs duties are an obvious revenue item of the EU budget, the rest comes from the national treasuries according to a formula which is beyond most human understanding.

Own resources of the EU budget represent a one-time tax revenue allocated to the EU. They accrue automatically to the EU without any need for additional decisions by national governments. A reform of finances in 1988 changed and expanded own financial resources of the EU. These resources are:

- customs duties;
- agricultural, sugar and isoglucose levies;
- VAT resources;
- the fourth resource; and
- miscellaneous revenue.

Table 3.5 presents the EU budget revenue in 2003:

- *Customs duties* and agricultural levies are the 'natural' proceeds of a customs union. Customs duties that are applied on imports of goods from non-member countries represent 11 per cent of revenue. Their relative impact is diminishing over time because of EU enlargements, preferential trade agreements and because of continuous reduction of tariffs by the GATT/WTO. This trend may be partly compensated by an increase in the volume of trade with external countries, but recession can reduce the level and scope of economic activity and, consequently, reduce imports.
- *Agricultural levies* (1.5 per cent of the budget revenue) are variable charges applied on imports of farm goods included in the CAP and that are imported from third countries. They are a changeable source of revenue for they depend on the volume of imports, which relies in part on weather conditions and partly on the trade concessions that the EU offers to foreign partners. Another element in this fluctuation

Table 3.5   The EU(15) budget revenue in 2002 and 2003

Type of revenue	2002 € million	2002 %	2003 € million	2003 %
1. Agricultural duties and sugar levies	1419.4	1.5	1426.4	1.5
2. Customs duties	10300.7	10.7	10713.9	11.0
3. Regularisation of collection costs for 2001	−2037.9	−2.1	–	–
4. VAT	22601.2	23.6	24121.3	24.7
5. Fourth resource	46605.0	48.7	59403.9	60.9
6. Miscellaneous and surpluses from previous years	16768.0	17.6	1837.4	1.9
Total	95656.4	100.0	97502.9	100.0

Source: European Commission, General Budget of the European Union for the Financial Year 2003.

is that world market prices for agricultural goods frequently change. The EU is becoming increasingly self-sufficient in a number of agricultural products of the temperate zone, hence there is a reduction in demand for imported farm goods from this geographical zone. Sugar and isoglucose levies are charges on producers that are supposed to make them share the financial burden of market support for production and storage.

- *The VAT contribution* includes 25 per cent of the revenue. It is calculated for each member country by the application of a uniform rate of 1.4 per cent to the national VAT base. This base for calculation may not exceed 55 per cent of the national GDP.
- *The 'fourth resource'* is closely related to a country's ability to pay. This revenue item provided 61 per cent of the EU budget. Together with the VAT resources, it is the only dynamic component of the budgetary revenue as it is derived from the application of a rate to the GDP of each member country. It is an additional source as it is calculated during the budgetary procedure in order to top up the difference between the budgetary expenditure and (insufficient) revenue that accrues from other sources.
- The fifth revenue item is negligible relative to the total budget. It covers *miscellaneous revenue* such as deductions from the salaries of EU civil servants, fines and possible surpluses from preceding years.

CHALLENGES

The EU budget expenditure and revenue were not related either to the EU need to influence economic life in the EMU (agriculture is the only exception) or, until recently, to the relative economic wealth of the member countries. Instead of singling out economic areas that need to be influenced at the EU level, and then creating the necessary funds, the EU still continues to pick up economic policies (areas for intervention) that can fit into these limited funds.

It should never be forgotten that it is neither the absolute nor the relative size of the budget that matters. What matters is the size of funds that are necessary to change certain behaviour in the desired direction. In some cases, the amount of funds can be tiny. For example, in the development of SMEs, a simple freedom of establishment, certain tax incentives and loan guarantees (underwriting risk) can do the job. In others, such as agriculture, infrastructure or adjustment out of obsolete industries, the amounts required to change behaviour in the desired way can be enormous.

When the member countries of the EU agree to pursue a common policy, one can also expect that the means for carrying out that policy may also be transferred upwards towards the EU institutions. The problem is that the member countries take the EU as the appropriate plane for the conduct of common policies in certain cases, but they are quite unyielding (Britain is not an exception here) when new funds have to be created. Reforms of the EU budget were resisted by the regions and countries that benefit from the present structure (mainly the agricultural regions in the north and the less-developed ones in the south). An increased expenditure on economic activities (other than agriculture), without extra funds, can jeopardise the current distribution of costs and benefits. Without the ability to increase or substantially reorganise spending, the EU should continue to endeavour to coordinate its own expenditure with that of the member countries.

The European Council in Copenhagen (2002) and previously in Brussels (2002)[34] reconfirmed its Berlin (1999)[35] decision that the ceiling for enlargement-related expenditure set out for the years 2004–06 must be respected. That is to say that the total EU expenditure must fit into own resources that are limited to 1.27 per cent of the combined EU GDP of all member countries. Therefore, the EU has very limited room for manoeuvre to enlarge its funds.

Sapir et al. (2003) proposed that the EU has to use its funds in a more astute way than was the case in the past. Around a half of the EU budget should be spent on growth-stimulating activities such as research, higher education, infrastructure projects and institution building in the new Central and East European member countries. The only way to do this and to remain within the current budgetary limits is to scrap the CAP and regional funds. No wonder that such suggestions were highly controversial and were subsequently rejected. In any case, these thoughts contributed to a wide-ranging debate about the future direction of the EU.

A formal obligation to contribute to the EU budget exists for every member country. The disequilibrium between the payments to and receipts from the EU budget brought tensions between Britain and the rest of the EU for quite some time.[36] These issues may have certain nominal relevance for the day-to-day (unpleasant) political debates. None the less, it must be remembered that economic integration is not an enterprise with short-term or, even, long-term clear financial balances (*juste retour*). Rather, integration is an undertaking that offers a longer-term security promise to employ resources and potentials of the participants in a superior way than would be the case otherwise. Therefore, a country that is a net contributor to the budget should not be seen as a loser from the integration venture (for example, Germany), but rather as a participant that is gaining elsewhere: a secure, unrestricted and long-term free access to partner-country markets for its goods and services. These are the principal gains from country integration.

The EU budget started to be financed from 'own resources' in 1970, three years before Britain joined the group. As a country that had a significant part of its foreign trade with non-EU countries, Britain was an important contributor to the EU budget (customs proceeds). Britain had a very small agricultural sector, hence it was not a significant receiver of EU funds. In addition, certain British regions were below the EU average level of development. Once all this was compounded, Britain emerged as a significant net contributor to the EU budget. The ERDF was created in 1973, partly in order to direct certain EU funds to Britain. None the less, the British net budgetary position continued to worsen.

The Conservative Party took office in 1979 and made a big to-do about this disproportionate contribution to the EU budget as a result of the workings of the CAP. The argument was that Britain failed to get a 'fair share' of the EU budget because of its small agricultural sector. Mrs Thatcher said: 'I want my money back'. After a long and acrimonious process, Britain obtained an annual 'rebate' (abatement) at the European Council in Fontainebleau (1984).[37] It was calculated on the basis of a formula related to EU expenditure in Britain and the VAT-based portion of the British contribution to the EU budget. This rebate was paid each year in the form of reduced VAT contribution in the following year.[38] This settlement was advantageous to the Council of Ministers because the European Parliament was not involved with the revenue side of the picture – recall that the Parliament has authority only over the expenditure part of the EU budget.

CONCLUSION

The EU budget absorbs only slightly more than 1 per cent of the combined GDP of its member countries. Compared with the national budgets (with the exception of agriculture) it plays only a minor role in the redistribution of income and allocation of resources. Its role in economic stabilisation has never existed. The influential MacDougall Report (1977) noted that in federal states such as the US and Germany, federal spending was in the neighbourhood of 20–25 per cent of GDP. Such an increase in EU spending cannot reasonably be expected in the near future. In the pre-federal stage of the EU, a budget that absorbs 5–7 per cent of the combined GDP (without transfers for defence) could have an impact on economic stabilisation and an evening of regional disparities. Such a budget might be able to influence social (unemployment, education, health, retirement), regional and external aid policies in an EMU. Resources might be found either in the transfer of funds from the national budgets and/or in an increase in the 'fourth' budgetary resource. The problem is that the member countries are still very reluctant to increase the budgetary powers of the EU. The controversial Stability and Growth Pact is institutionally preventing them from increasing expenditure beyond prescribed and monitored limits. If the EU gets more resources for its budget, the total public expenditure in the EU, compared with similar uncoordinated outlays of member states, may be reduced because of the economies of scale. A budget with increased resources may represent a built-in stabiliser for macroeconomic management. In addition, transfers among regions may enhance economic convergence and strengthen the cohesion of the EU.

In contrast to a variety of revenue sources employed to fill the national budgets, the EU budget is financed from a narrow range of sources. On the expenditure side, there is a high concentration of resources in one area: agriculture. This contrasts with the much-diversified public expenditure in member countries. However, the possibility of changing such a pattern of EU revenue still remains in the hands of member countries and is left to their (un)willingness to enhance the powers of the EU. If there are no rapid changes in the structure of national and EU expenditure, the EU Lisbon (2000) aspirations to become 'the most competitive and dynamic knowledge-based economy in the world capable of sustainable economic growth with more and better jobs and greater social cohesion' by 2010 will be a forlorn pipe-dream.

The EU has a strong indirect means of controlling a significant part of public expenditure in all member countries: EU competition policy. State aids absorb a sizeable chunk of the national budgets. Control of these outlays does not require extra expenditure from the EU budget.

One may expect that the EU(25) budget will remain at the heart of interest and controversy in the future. What may take place is reform, or rather restructuring (in relative terms), within the framework of the existing budget. Increased contributions to the EU budget according to the level of national wealth or the principle of ability to pay should be further encouraged.

Even before the eastern enlargement in 2004, very tough, complicated and controversial negotiations and horse-trading started to define the new financial perspective for the 2007–13 period. The European Commission proposed to spend €1000 billion over the seven-year period (1.24 per cent of the EU GDP). Major increases in spending would be in areas such as research and transport and other networks in order to boost the competitiveness of EU output and meet the Lisbon target by 2010. The net contributors to the EU budget (France, Germany, Austria, Britain, Sweden and the Netherlands) argue in favour of a budget equal to 1 per cent of the EU(25) GDP. In any case, in 2004 the EU entered into a much more difficult and complicated phase of integration than most people imagine.

Notes

1. 'Federal' is taken here in its widest possible meaning.
2. Public authorities may be involved in the supply of goods and services that free markets may not supply at all or may not supply in adequate quantity, quality, geographical location or on time. This public involvement may either be indirect through taxes and subsidies or direct when the government steps in, produces and supplies certain goods and services itself because of their importance (defence, security, fire fighting, statistics, weather forecasts and so on).
3. By offering preferential tax treatment to transnational corporations, governments may change/improve their competitiveness in relation to other countries or regions.
4. Allocation of resources is production efficient if all producers face the same tax for the same good or service. It is consumption efficient if all consumers face the same tax for the consumption of the same good or service.
5. This implies the expectation that integration is a positive-sum game for everyone.
6. For example, the Roman Catholic cantons formed a league (*Sonderbund*) in 1847. The federal government considered that this was a violation of the constitution. In the civil war of the same year, the league was defeated by the federal government and disbanded. The constitution of 1848 greatly increased federal powers. In 1874 a modified constitution completed the development of Switzerland from a group of cantons to a unified federal state. However, the local communes and cantons still enjoy considerable autonomy in Switzerland. For example, it is the communes within the Swiss cantons that grant individuals Swiss citizenship.
7. Helvets were a tribe that lived in pre-Roman times in what is now known as Switzerland.
8. The Vatican began to employ Swiss mercenaries at the beginning of the 16th century. Their bravery was obvious in 1527 when Charles V of Spain devastated the city. Some 147 Swiss guards died in the fight, but Pope Clement VII was saved. The Swiss guards have been guarding popes ever since. The Vatican *Cohors Helvetica* currently numbers 107.

9. Napoleon was a regular client of Swiss banks.
10. Justinian's Code 5.59.5.2. This Code (AD 528) became the principal source for Roman law.
11. The Hohenzollerns were a dynasty of German rulers, descended from a family of counts from Swabia from the 11th century. They were named after their ancestral castle, Zollern (later Hohenzollern), located near Hechingen, Swabia (now Baden-Württemberg). The Hohenzollerns ruled Prussia and united Germany until the end of the First World War.
12. This type of rule also applies in EU budgetary affairs.
13. Prussia and France became involved in a complicated diplomatic argument over the succession to the throne of Spain. The Spanish government offered the crown to a Hohenzollern (Prussian) prince. The government of Louis Napoleon objected strongly and even began to make certain military threats. The French ambassador to Prussia had a meeting with King William I. The report of this meeting was sent by telegram to Bismarck – the famous Ems Telegram. Bismarck rephrased it in such a way that if it was made public, it would offend both France and Prussia. He sent it to the newspapers and waited for the inevitable reaction. On 19 July 1870 France declared war on Prussia, but on 2 September France admitted defeat. Bismarck had triumphed.
14. Alaska, Arizona, California, Colorado, Connecticut, District of Columbia, Illinois, Indiana, Iowa, Kansas, Massachusetts, New Hampshire, New Jersey, New York, Ohio, Rhode Island and West Virginia. Because of controversy regarding the unitary system of computation of corporate profits, some states are considering abandoning this system.
15. Swiss companies do not have to publish their results unless they are listed or subject to special regulatory duties (for example, banks). One explanation is that they do not need to have a commercial purpose. They can exist for idealistic reasons (for example, to promote fair trade with developing countries) or they may distribute their profits by way of salary or bonuses to limit the withholding tax of 35 per cent on dividends or distribution of accumulated profits on liquidation.
16. Regarding the profitability of Swiss firms, for example, the most astonishing fact 'is the large share of firms with zero rate of return. Nearly half of Swiss firms does not report any rate of return' (Feld and Kirchgässner, 2001, p. 5).
17. This assumes that country A grants either an exception or a full foreign-tax credit.
18. The average level of corporation tax in the 30 richest countries in the world fell from 37.5 per cent in 1996 to 30.9 per cent in 2003 (*Financial Times*, 1 May 2003).
19. Estimates about tax evasion are exceptionally unreliable, but German savers alone are thought to have 'hidden' about €300 billion in the low-tax countries (*Financial Times*, 3 June 2003).
20. In the complex overall EU bargaining in 2003, in return for agreement on this tax matter, Italy demanded and got concessions regarding milk production.
21. Switzerland is estimated to handle one-third of all the money held in private accounts in offshore financial centres. The Swiss Banking Federation claims that Switzerland implemented tough legislation to monitor criminal and terrorist funds (*Financial Times*, 3 December 2003).
22. Switzerland will tax interest earned by EU citizens on their bank accounts in Switzerland, with 75 per cent of the proceeds going to the account holders' national tax authorities while the rest would stay with the Swiss authorities to cover running costs.
23. There is also a problem of inflation. Depreciation may be calculated according to historic costs, but how should capital gains be taxed to reflect inflation? The arrival of the euro eliminated this problem for the 12 eurozone countries, while the other countries remain quite tough on inflation.
24. Cnossen (1995) provides a survey of options for the reform of corporate taxes in the EU.
25. For example, language, seniority, xenophobia, social and family ties, as well as propensity to stay in the birth place and pure choice.
26. The EU adopted a far-reaching, but partial, move towards the origin principle for final consumers (but not for firms). Since 1993, taxation occurs in the place where a good is purchased, rather than where it will be consumed.

27. Apart from making life and travel easier for EU residents, the business community saves too. They were spared the preparation of some 60 million customs and tax documents a year. The abolition of border checks represents a saving of about €8 billion a year to the EU member states (*Business International*, 15 July 1991, p. 237). In 1988, the EU introduced the Single Administrative Document to replace some 30 documents that were required in order to allow goods to move within the EU. This document was not required for internal trade after 1993, but it is used for goods that cross an EU external frontier.
28. The solution to the problem of taxation of e-commerce may include two approaches. The first would be to harmonise taxes on a worldwide basis. The second would be to increase 'policing' of transactions on the internet. They both have weak points. The first is politically not feasible, while the second may be publicly undesirable. In any case new technologies demand new forms of international fiscal cooperation and a certain reduction in national fiscal sovereignty. Governments struggle to maintain their tax receipts in the light of a potentially expanding underground economy (the one that is not taxed). However, new electronic technologies may enhance, rather than weaken, government tax-collecting capacity. The peril that the e-economy presents is not the erosion in the public tax base, but rather the erosion in privacy. It seems that more transparency in our lives may be the price to pay for living in a complex contemporary society.
29. Regarding budgetary outlays, cereal subsidies would be cut in two steps by 15 per cent; beef prices would be reduced by 20 per cent in three stages (beef farmers would receive direct payment to compensate for 85 per cent of their losses); while the decision on the most contentious area of dairy products was delayed until 2005.
30. European Council, Berlin 1999, Presidency Conclusions, §16 and Table B.
31. European Council, Berlin 1999, Presidency Conclusions, §46.
32. European Council, Berlin 1999, Presidency Conclusions, §67.
33. *Financial Times*, 6 November 2002.
34. European Council, Brussels 2002, Presidency Conclusions, §10.
35. European Council, Berlin 1999, Presidency Conclusions, §16 and Table B.
36. Britain won an arrangement in 1984 enabling it to obtain a refund from the EU budget.
37. 'He said to his brothers, "My money has been put back; here it is in the mouth of my sack!" At this their hearts failed them, and they turned trembling to one another, saying, "What is this that God has done to us?"' Genesis 42:28.
38. The British rebate was worth €4.6 billion in 2004. Britain could not have foreseen that two decades following the Fontainebleau deal, this rebate would be partly funded by the poor countries from Central and Eastern Europe (*Financial Times*, 4 February 2004).

> And let them gather all the food of those good years that are coming, and store up grain under the authority of Pharaoh, and let them keep food in the cities. Then that food shall be as a reserve for the land for the seven years of famine which shall be in the land of Egypt, that the land may not perish during the famine.
>
> Genesis 41:35–6

4 Common Agricultural Policy

1. Introduction

During the past decades, agriculture has been a statistically shrinking economic sector in the developed market economies. The share of agriculture in the GDP of the EU(15) was 2 per cent, while its share in the region's employment was 4 per cent[1] in 2002. There were about 14 million farmers at the time of the creation of the EU(6) in 1957. Half a century later, the number of people directly employed in agriculture, forestry, hunting and fishing was a little over 6.7 million. If one adds the dependent family members to those that work in the farm sector, the number of people that rely in the EU(15) on this sector for their livelihood is about 30 million. The eastern enlargement brought into the EU 3.8 million people employed in the farming sector in 2004. This is an increase of more than half.

The customs union (common commercial policy) and the Common Agricultural Policy (CAP) were the first genuine economic policies in the EU. Later came the competition policy, as well as the monetary policy, but only for eurozone countries. For a long time the CAP was described as one of the greatest achievements in the EU's economic integration and also, perplexingly, as its weakest link.

This chapter is organised as follows. Section 2 explains why agriculture is a very special economic activity, at least in Europe. Sections 3 and 4 cover the objectives and the implementation of the CAP, respectively. Section 5 examines the operation and consequences of the CAP on self-sufficiency, farmers, consumers and external countries. Because of the persisting debate, reforms of the CAP are considered in Section 6. The Common Fisheries Policy is presented in Section 7, and Section 8 concludes.

2. Distinctiveness of agriculture

Governments have been intruding in farm production ever since Joseph advised Pharaoh to hoard grain during the seven years of abundance for the seven years of famine (Genesis 41:17–37).[2] In Europe, for example, Corn Laws were introduced in Britain in several stages since 1436. That was the time when landowners dominated parliament. Landowners wanted to protect their profits by imposing duty on imported corn. The consequence was an expansion of relatively inefficient domestic production and an increase in the price of bread. Following four centuries of protection of landowners' profit, a liberal movement, supported by the growing number of industrialists and compounded by bad harvests and famine prompted parliament to repeal these laws in 1846. Generally, trade in farm goods was free. The countries on the continent followed the British liberal example shortly afterwards. Farm business prospered as there was a growing demand for meat in the cities. This lasted only some three decades. The war between Germany and France (1871), as well as recession, forced most countries to abandon liberal trade in farm goods, which sounded the knell for the only exposure of the agricultural sector to free trade.

Since the creation of the CAP the share of agriculture in EU GDP has declined. In addition, the relative share of those employed in agriculture and their absolute number has also diminished. In that case, why does agriculture command such a prominent position in the economic and political life of many countries, as well as in the EU? The answer to this question can be found in a combination of the following elements:

- One of the basic and oldest reasons for the special attention given to the agricultural sector of the economy is strategic. Governments supported domestic food production in order to ease the situation in the country in the event of war, crisis, foreign economic blockade and natural disasters. Linked to this consideration is the fact that farmers are scattered all around the country and that the peasants (at least used to) have larger families in order to get cheaper labour. In the event of war, this segment of the population could make a valuable contribution both to manpower and to the coverage and surveillance of the national territory. In modern times, farmers are part of the population that bothers to vote. Therefore, each political party must take into account the concerns of the powerful farm lobby.[3]

- If one assumes that the national population is able to satisfy the basic needs for food, as is the case in the developed market economies, then price elasticity of demand (E_{dp}) for food is less than 1 (equation (4.1)). Such price inelasticity makes the price (p) of food fall if there is an increase in the quantity (q) supplied.

$$E_{dp} = \frac{\Delta q/q}{\Delta p/p} = \frac{\Delta qp}{\Delta pq} < 1. \quad (4.1)$$

One may find here a difference between farm and manufactured goods and compare potatoes and cars as representative products of the two sectors. If the price of French potatoes falls on the German market, then the German farmers would be able to sell their potatoes on the domestic market only if they reduce the price of their potatoes to match the price (other things being equal) of their French competitors. If, however, Renault slightly lowers the price of its cars in the German market, one cannot expect a corresponding increase in the German demand for Renaults and a matching fall in the demand for Volkswagens. The reason for such a state of affairs and in the behaviour of consumers is that most farm goods are standardised, while manufactured goods carry with them a number of psychological attributes such as status, taste or past experience.

- The relative price of food in the developed market economies is not only on the decline because of the low price elasticity of demand, but also because of the low income (y) elasticity of demand (E_{dy}) that is less than 1 (equation (4.2)).[4]

$$E_{dp} = \frac{\Delta q/q}{\Delta y/y} = \frac{\Delta qy}{\Delta yq} < 1. \quad (4.2)$$

- Agricultural production depends on natural conditions. These include not only biological cycles, but also climate, droughts/floods, fires, earthquakes, diseases and pests. On the one hand, the impact of some of these factors diminishes over time because of irrigation, drainage, mechanisation, fertilisers, pesticides, herbicides, vaccines, antibiotics, glasshouses, genetic engineering and artificial selection.

However, a disturbance of the natural cycle can be detrimental, such as giving hormones to calves in order to accelerate their growth, which could make the meat unfit for human consumption. Recall the 1996 'mad cow disease'[5] frenzy in Britain and elsewhere, the slaughter of cattle and the subsequent EU ban on imports of British beef. Similarly, the use of chemicals may be unfriendly to the environment.

The biological cycle is often a limiting factor in farm production. For example, if one year a farmer sows wheat and, then, unexpectedly there is an increase in the demand and price for maize, the farmer's switch to maize production can take place only during the next sowing season. The situation is, however, different in most of the manufacturing industry. In oil refineries a relatively simple turn of the handle can alter the processing of crude oil from the production of unleaded petrol into the production of diesel. This simple 'turn of the handle' is not possible in agricultural production. If capital is invested in a particular product, it may not be withdrawn easily or swiftly without a significant loss.

- Agriculture is not only a producing economic sector, it is also a significant consumer of goods and services. The farm sector purchases machinery, transport equipment, chemicals, construction material, fuel, energy, insurance, legal services and the like. In addition, a part of R&D in the manufacturing sector has a specific farm dimension. At the same time, the price of farm goods (food) influences the price of labour that all sectors have to pay. This is most obvious in the production of lower-end goods and services.

- Agriculture plays a role in the conservation of the environment and of the human habitat. There is a distinct demand for the preservation of the so-called 'idyllic' peasant life, particularly in countries where only a small segment of the population makes a living in the farm sector. In addition, an excessive use of chemicals may degrade the quality of the environment. Agriculture is also a big polluter of the environment. Therefore, many public bodies and a number of private firms are devoting increasing attention to the conservation of the environment.

- The prices of most of the temperate-zone farm goods on the world market reflect only a part of the planet's production. In most cases those prices are not only highly volatile, but also distorted. For some goods such as temperate-zone fruits, vegetables, beef or wine, there is hardly any 'world market' at all.

Taken together, the above elements can provide the answer to the question of why the agricultural sector attracts special and disproportionately large attention in the economies of the developed market economies relative to its direct contribution to GDP and employment.

3. Objectives

During negotiations (1956) on the creation of the EU, France insisted on the inclusion of agricultural goods in the customs union. What the internal free trade offered to German manufacturers, the CAP was to offer to French farmers. This 'deal' was agreed between the two major negotiators. In addition, the CAP united the country with a large farm output (France) and the one with high prices for farm goods (Germany). Article 3(e) of the Treaty of Rome requires the introduction of a common policy in agriculture (and fisheries) and it has a special title on agriculture (Articles 32 to 38).

Article 33 lists five *objectives* of the CAP:

- the CAP is 'to increase agricultural productivity by promoting technical progress and by ensuring the rational development of agricultural production and the optimum utilisation of factors of production, in particular labour';
- it has 'to ensure a fair standard of living for the agricultural community, in particular by increasing the individual earnings of persons engaged in agriculture'. 'A fair standard of living' is, however, not defined. It could mean an equalisation of average individual incomes in agriculture and manufacturing;
- the CAP has 'to stabilise markets';
- it has 'to assure the availability of supplies'; and
- the supplies have to 'reach consumers at reasonable prices'. However, these 'reasonable prices' are not defined by the Treaty of Rome.

Article 34 refers to the permitted measures and forms of the CAP. In order to attain the objectives of the CAP, there needs to be a common organisation of farm markets. The *measures* to attain the goals of the CAP may include the regulation of:

- prices;
- aids and funding;
- storage; and
- external trade.

Depending on the good, a common organisation of the market would take one of the following three *forms*:

- common rules on competition;
- compulsory coordination of the various national market organisations; and
- a European market organisation.

The European Commission is charged by the Treaty of Rome to 'submit proposals for working out and implementing the common agricultural policy, including the replacement of the national organisations by one of the forms of common organisation' (Article 37). In addition, one of the objectives of the EU is to contribute to the harmonious development of world trade and progressive abolition of restrictions on international trade (Article 131). Article 174 refers to the issue of environment. It accepts the precautionary and 'polluter pays' principles. Environmental protection ought to be integrated into the definition and implementation of other EU policies. Article 4 obliges the EU to adopt an economic policy which is based on the 'principle of an open market economy with free competition'. According to the Treaty of Rome, agricultural products mean 'the products of the soil, of stockfarming and of fisheries and products of first-stage processing directly related to these products' (Article 32). Although farm products also include fish, the fisheries policy in the EU has developed independently. It is outlined in Section 7.

The common organisation of the market introduced by the CAP is in essence a price policy for a large number of temperate-zone agricultural goods. It encourages production and, at the same time, 'taxes' consumption.[6] The CAP is not, however, a single compact policy, but rather a combination of different rules for different agricultural products.

The CAP has two dimensions, internal and external:

- *Internally*: the CAP is to ensure a determined price level on the EU domestic market. If the price of a farm good falls below the intervention price (the level under which EU intervention is compulsory), the excess supplies must be purchased by the intervention agencies in unlimited quantities[7] in order to keep the internal EU price of the good at the guaranteed minimum level.
- *Externally*: the CAP maintains the lowest level of prices for imports of farm goods. This threshold price protects the internal EU farm market both from foreign competitors and from fluctuation of prices in the external market. At the same time, the EU subsidises exports of internal surpluses of farm goods abroad. This policy became a

stumbling block in international trade negotiations and created a number of frictions in international trade. In fact, the CAP is the most obvious example of an inward-oriented sectoral integration arrangement that has resulted in trade diversion.

The outcome of the CAP was a high degree of self-sufficiency or surpluses in most of the temperate-zone agricultural products. In addition, many argue that the overall costs of the CAP were quite high, not only in terms of misallocation of resources and frictions in international trade, but also in terms of complex administration and degradation of the environment.

Farming, particularly in continental Europe, is on the one hand part of the social structure, a deeply rooted way of life in the region that has survived for several thousands of years. There is a relatively high degree of national self-sufficiency in the production of food, as well as highly protectionist and interventionist national institutions. On the other hand, the pattern of certain types of farming in relatively new countries and nations such as the US, Canada or Australia is different. Large-scale farming was started there by the European immigrants just a few centuries ago. It is basically linked with the commercial use of a relatively unlimited quantity of land. That's it. In Europe, however, this commercial activity is most intimately and deeply connected to national social structure, traditions, countryside and biodiversity. Free trade and liberal competition principles applied to agriculture can benefit only transnational corporations (TNCs), governments that worry only about the short-term interests and producers that do not care about the sustainable production. To apply these principles in Europe without conditions would be disastrous for the deeply rooted European social and other features. Hence, the strong support of many European countries for national farming interests, in spite of certain financial costs and tensions with certain foreign countries.

4. Implementation

The establishment of a customs union for manufactured goods is simpler than for the farm commodities. A customs union that deals solely with manufactured goods needs only an elimination of tariffs and quotas (the assumption is that there are no other non-tariff barriers: NTBs) on internal trade, an establishment of rules on competition, as well as an introduction of the common external tariff. To introduce a similar arrangement for farm goods is a much more formidable task. This is not only because of the natural significance and character of the production process, but also because of the general need and political desire to keep a part of the population in the farm business.

The six founding member countries of the EU had a strong political determination to implement the integration provisions of the Treaty of Rome. This made negotiations about the shape and direction of the CAP relatively easy in Stresa (Italy) in 1958. A common objective was to preserve and strengthen family farming as the keystone of European agriculture. The CAP started to be implemented in 1962. It was a gradual process which was expected to collect the receipts from the import levies in sufficient quantity to finance the CAP outlays. Later on, however, an increase in domestic output reduced imports and, consequently, receipts from variable import levies. Hence, the tax proceeds from import levies were insufficient to cover EU expenditure on the CAP.

Following the provisions of the treaty, although with some delay, Walter Hallstein, the president of the European Commission, submitted to the Council of Ministers the final version of the proposal on the CAP in 1964. At the same time he asked the Council to accept the proposal unanimously or to accept the resignation of the European Commission. The national interests of the member countries were overridden by common ones, hence the proposal was accepted. That was the first and only time that the European Commission so convincingly achieved this. The CAP became fully operational in 1967.

Prior to the introduction of the CAP, the member countries of the EU practised different and often complicated support and intervention systems in agriculture. These support systems could be classified in five basic groups:

- *Market control*: This was common in the founding six member countries of the EU. In this system, the government guarantees to purchase a certain quantity of farm goods at a determined (high) price. If the supply of the good is over and above the guaranteed limit, the administration may purchase the excess supply at (lower) market prices. In addition, if production is above the agreed quota, the authorities may charge these producers a penalty.
- *Direct income payments*: In order to maintain a certain level of standard of living, farmers receive payments from the chancellor of the exchequer without any relation to the quantity of their production. Sweden practised a similar system.
- *Deficiency payment*: In this system there is a free market determination of prices of farm goods. However, the government guarantees prices that are higher than those on the domestic market. The

difference between the (lower) market price and the (higher) guaranteed price is covered by transfers from the budget to the farmers. Britain used this system of support before it entered the EU in 1973. At that time, British food prices were about 30 per cent lower than those in the EU. After entry, Britain abandoned this system as a part of the *acquis communautaire*. This change was not as hard as it may appear, since an abandoning of the original system was on the way in Britain for some time because of the need to reduce public expenditure. While the price-support system demands control at the external border, the deficiency-payment system requires control both at the external border and at the level of individual farms.
- *Variable levies on imports*: In this system the administration sets a threshold price for imports of farm goods and charges a variable levy on imports. This variable levy is equal to the difference between the lower and fluctuating 'world market price' and the higher domestic threshold price. The system may be combined with quotas.
- *Other policies*: These include and refer to subsidies such as those for exports, capital investments or R&D.

Compared with the system of free trade where the consumers have freedom of choice and where they opt (other things being equal) for the cheapest source of supply, none of the above systems gets a pass mark. None the less, the direct-income payments system seems to introduce least distortions, but the real problem is where to find resources for its operation.

The EU selected the system of variable levies and quotas for imports for the CAP 'market organisation'. France would get free access to the EU farm market and the system would be supported by price policies, rather than by income payments. The established system has three basic principles:

- there is a common market organisation for agricultural goods that may circulate freely in the EU, prices are the same throughout the EU and administrative and health standards are harmonised;
- there is an EU preference for domestically produced farm goods over imported ones; and
- there is financial solidarity regarding the cost of the CAP among the EU member countries.

The CAP is operated through national customs and intervention agencies, and it is financed through the common EU budget.

5. Operation and consequences

PROTECTION OF THE INTERNAL MARKET

The CAP covers almost the entire farm production in the EU.[8] The only significant agricultural commodity that is beyond its scope is the potato. Although there are certain differences in the systems of protection/intervention for various goods, the basic idea is generally the same. It is exemplified in the case of wheat.

Figure 4.1 illustrates the CAP market organisation and the support-price system for wheat. The policy rests on three different types of prices: the target price, the threshold price and the intervention price:

- The *target price* is the price of wheat in Duisburg (Germany), the region where cereals are in shortest supply in the EU. This is the highest possible price in the EU and it includes the costs of transport and storage.
- Imports into the EU are forbidden below the *threshold price*. The threshold price is calculated on the basis of target price. Costs of transport and distribution from the frontier (Rotterdam) to the region with the greatest shortage of wheat (Duisburg) are subtracted from the target price in order to determine the threshold price. This price is applied in all ports through which imports enter the EU.
- If there is an increase in the internal EU production and supply of wheat, the internal price falls. The *intervention price* is the minimum price that the EU guarantees to the domestic producers. This price is about 8 per cent lower than the target price. Until the proposed reforms of the CAP in the 1970s and 1980s, the intervention agencies were obliged to purchase an unlimited quantity of the domestically produced good if it conformed with specified standards.

These prices are set once a year (usually in April) by the Council of Ministers and they are valid for the following 12 months. The difference between the CIF price and the intervention price represents the protection and aid that the CAP gives to the domestic producers relative to the foreign suppliers. There is no a priori knowledge about the cost of the CAP at the time the prices are set. Falling world cereal prices, drought or a generous harvest may easily upset EU farm expenditure.

When the EU imports wheat from abroad, the difference between the price at which goods are imported at CIF Rotterdam and the threshold

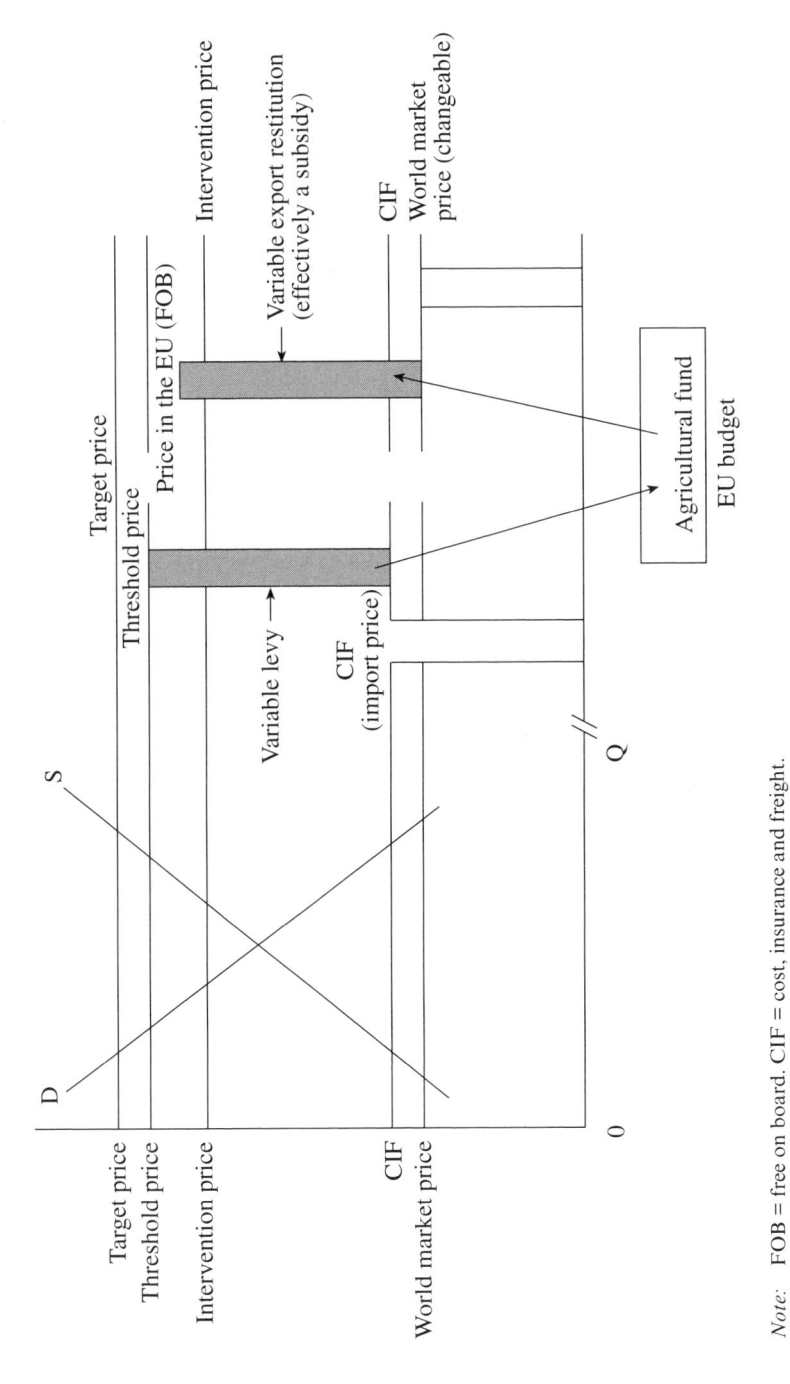

Figure 4.1 The CAP market organisation and price support system for wheat

Note: FOB = free on board. CIF = cost, insurance and freight.

price is bridged by a *variable levy*. This levy is calculated on a daily basis as the CIF price may constantly change. Such a system ensures that imported wheat always enters the EU at a fixed threshold price. Receipts from variable levies form a part of the receipts of the general budget of the EU. On rare occasions, as happened in 1973–74, when the price of cereals on foreign markets is higher than the threshold price, the EU applies the variable levy for exports of the goods abroad.

The CAP made the EU self-sufficient in most of the agricultural goods it covers. There were, in fact, substantial surpluses of farm goods in the EU. Therefore, the EU exported a part of those surpluses abroad. As the prices for these goods are generally higher in the EU than abroad, the EU hands out *variable refunds* (subsidies) for exports. The role of these refunds is to bridge (reduce) the difference between the target price and the lower price on the 'world market'. As prices on foreign markets fluctuate, the refunds are calculated daily and are paid from the EU farm fund. These refunds are similar to the inverse version of the variable levies charged on imports of agricultural goods to the EU.

The grains management committee meets every Thursday in DG Agriculture to decide the weekly export tender for grains (with subsidies). Representatives from member states and the European Commission agree on the volume of export licences and the level of subsidy (apologies, 'export refund') for that week. Tender speculation is very common before, during and after this decision-making process and can significantly move prices on world cereals markets. Whenever there is a distribution of handouts, there are possibilities for abuse and bribery. The police may raid the European Commission's premises without warning. For example, the police raided the offices of the DG Agriculture in Brussels on 15 October 2003, and a few arrests were made. This was part of a large operation in Belgium, France and the Netherlands into alleged price fraud, corruption and persistent insider trading in cereals markets. The allegations were that certain cereals companies were tipped off about grain prices two hours before they were officially available.[9]

The above analysis reveals that the implementation of the CAP rests on two pillars. The first is the intervention price, while the second includes variable levies for imports into and variable refunds for exports of farm goods from the EU. About 70 per cent of the entire farm output of the EU (cereals, milk, sugar and meats) benefited, in general, from this type of market organisation. The next 25 per cent of EU farm production (eggs, poultry and select fruits and vegetables) profited only by protection from cheap imports. The rest of the agricultural business (olive oil, tobacco, cotton, hops and a few others) receive a certain fixed subsidy from the EU.[10]

MONETARY COMPENSATORY AMOUNTS

The prices of farm goods were set in the common accounting units and then converted into the national currencies of the member countries. During the time when the rates of exchange were fixed, there were no problems regarding such conversion. However, the French franc devalued and the German mark (DM) revalued in 1969, which changed price parities for agricultural goods in the EU market. The introduction of fluctuating rates of exchange brought the 'green rates of exchange' for the prices of farm goods covered by the CAP. The 'green' rates were set by the Council of Ministers, at least once a year, in order to stabilise domestic output prices.

In order to avoid the disequilibria in the internal farm trade, the EU introduced monetary compensatory amounts (MCAs). Some argue that agriculture is an economic sector 'just like the others' (manufacturing and services). There is nothing special about its exposure to exchange market fluctuations. If market stabilisation is necessary, then the MCAs depend on the difference between the central and the 'green' rates of exchange. Once an EU country *revalues* its currency, it hands out a compensatory amount on its exports of farm goods in order to give it a subsidy.[11] The objective is to give the same amount of national currency per unit of output to the home producers as was the case prior to revaluation. The same country charges a tax on imports of farm commodities from partner countries in order to preserve the balance of relative prices of farm goods in the EU. Without MCAs, the country with the highest intervention prices would be flooded with farm goods from the EU partner countries, which would distort trade flows. If an EU country *devalues* its currency, the procedure is reversed. Exports are taxed with a compensatory amount, while imports are subsidised.

The MCAs represent taxes and subsidies on imports and exports in intra-EU farm trade. They have, in effect, split the EU agricultural market into a group of national markets that were 'divided' by a special system of taxes and subsidies on imports and exports. In fact, this introduced a variant of the system of multiple exchange rates in the internal market for agricultural goods. Because of such splintering of the market, the 1985 Cockfield Report (*Completing the Internal Market*, Point 38, p. 12) requested the abolition of MCAs.

This complex system of trade barriers hinders competition among farmers in the EU. MCAs gave artificial support to the output of farmers who live in countries with strong currencies and they hindered output in other countries. Wherever there are taxes and subsidies such as the MCAs, there is a temptation for fraud. For example, when the Belgian franc was weak in the early 1980s, Belgian farmers were smuggling their pigs and cows into the Netherlands, where they concealed the origin of their merchandise. The Belgians later imported pork and beef from the Netherlands and pocketed an import subsidy of €300 per tonne. Similar contraband exchanges existed between Northern Ireland and the Irish Republic, as well as elsewhere.[12]

The system of support for farm prices was modified in 1984. The added switchover system more or less linked the CAP prices to the DM. Hence, revaluations of the DM have not led to a larger gap between Germany's 'green' and market rates. Instead, a revaluation of the DM led to a rise in the ECU(€) value of CAP prices. This has, in turn, increased prices in other member states. The switchover system was potentially inflationary and protectionist. A positive development was that exchange rates were relatively stable during the 1980s. New MCAs could come from parity changes. As this was rare, the attention of policy makers was directed towards the dismantling of MCAs. By the beginning of the 1990s, almost all MCAs had been dismantled. However, the currency instability following that period worked against the elimination of this system of 'support'.

The system for the support of prices of farm goods was revised in 1993. The key element was a system that automatically adjusted green rates with the market rates of exchange. The MCAs became unnecessary, as small variations in the exchange rates are thought to be irrelevant in disrupting internal trade flows. As the reform was founded on the assumption of stability in the exchange markets, the events in 1992 brought frequent changes in the CAP prices and green rates. From August 1993, EMS margins of fluctuation were widened from ±2.25 to ±15 per cent (effectively a free float). Large fluctuations of DM and corresponding CAP prices could take place. As the switchover system can be prompted only by the official realignments in the EMS, a revaluation of the DM may not cause the realignment in prices, that is, CAP prices in Germany may be reduced without compensation under the switchover system. Hence, Germany (and the Netherlands) demanded a modification in the system that would activate it even by fluctuations in the exchange rates. Britain was against such a proposal. None the less, the automatic mechanism was altered at the end of 1993. The alteration permitted gaps of up to 5 per cent between CAP prices among the member states (von Cramon-Taubadel and Thiele, 1994, pp. 264–5).

The removal of border controls at the end of 1992 was the consequence of the full implementation of the Single Market Programme. Hence, the impossibility for the continuation of MCAs. An agreement was reached in December 1992, at the last minute, on how to proceed after the Single European Market was in place. The 'green rates' would continue to apply, but the European Commission was authorised to change them as required to avoid the necessity of MCAs. The agricultural ministers agreed in 1995 to introduce a 'dual green currency system', one for direct currency payments, and the other for price support payments. This was intended to protect the income of farmers in countries where currency revaluations endanger the value of CAP prices in national currencies. The principal components of the agreement included three items. First, in countries in which revaluations took place before the end of 1995, there would be a freeze in the rates for payments of aid for reforms such as set-aside land, until the end of 1998. Second, compensation payments for farmers in countries whose currency revalued was limited to a period of three years and it is due to decline during that period. Third, member states were permitted to pay farmers a flat aid from the national budgets to compensate for the losses suffered because of the movements in the exchange rates in 1994 and 1995. Half of these payments would come from the EU budget. The entire aid is to be given over a period of three years and is supposed to decline during that period. In addition, farm prices were unpegged from the DM in June 1995. The introduction of the euro and the general stability in the exchange rates in Europe ousted all these complications.

EUROPEAN AGRICULTURAL GUIDANCE AND GUARANTEE FUND

The European Agricultural Guidance and Guarantee Fund (EAGGF) was created in 1964 in order to help the running of the CAP. This fund disposed of almost €45 billion in 2003 (Table 4.1). The EAGGF has two sections, one for guarantees and the other for guidance:

- The *guarantees* section, 93 per cent of the EU expenditure on the CAP in 2003, covers outlays that include intervention on the EU market for farm goods, it gives refunds for exports of agricultural goods abroad and it finances food aid to third countries.
- The *guidance* section of the EAGGF disposes of a modest amount of finance relative to the other section. Outlays cover expenditure relating to structural policy. Expenditure usually co-finances 25 per cent (exceptionally up to 65 per cent) of the costs linked with the alteration in the structure of production within a designated area. The change in the structure of production refers to costs that include the provision of infrastructure, vocational training and modernisation.

Although the total direct cost of the CAP is relatively high in budgetary terms, the daily cost of the CAP per EU(15) consumer was €0.35 in 2003.

Table 4.1 Select CAP budgetary expenditure, 1999–2003 (€m)

Item	1999	2000	2001	2002	2003
EU budget	79 249	77 879	101 051	95 656	96 991
Total CAP expenditure	45 267	41 903	45 642	47 242	47 945
EAGGF – Guarantee	39 540	40 467	42 083	44 230	44 780
Plant products	26 739	25 812	26 713	27 349	26 176
Animal products	9 440	9 275	9 558	10 860	13 099
Rural development	2 588	4 176	4 364	4 595	4 698
EAGGF – Guidance	5 580	1 387	3 509	2 957	3 123
Charges under the CAP	2 391	2 395	1 973	1 893	1 902
Ordinary levies	1 187	1 198	1 133	1 122	1 173
Sugar levies	1 204	1 197	840	771	729

Source: European Commission, DG Agriculture (2003).

As this is a relatively small amount,[13] the consumers were not able or, rather, not interested in organising a consumer lobby that would strongly present their case in the EU.

In addition to the EU expenditure on the CAP, there are also charges under this policy. The most significant are levies on imports of farm goods (major source of receipts) and those on sugar. None the less, these charges cover only a relatively small part of the total expenditure. The coverage ratio was only 5 per cent in 2003.

The EAGGF guarantee section outlays per commodity (Table 4.2), were concentrated on a few commodities. Well over a third of expenditure was allocated to arable crops in 2002 and 2003. That was followed by beef/veal (19 per cent), milk products (6 per cent) and olive oil (5 per cent). EU intervention in the purchase of other farm products involved a relatively lower amount of funds. One of the major problems of the CAP since its inception was linked to refunds (read subsidies) for exports of EU agricultural goods to third countries. That has constantly created frictions with other international exporters of agricultural goods. Storage of agricultural goods also consumes a noted share of EU farm expenditure.

STRUCTURE OF AGRICULTURAL PRODUCTION

Whenever a government guarantees (unlimited) purchases of a certain good at a specified price that covers the local costs of production and offers profit, and when there is a protection against imports, then one can produce

Table 4.2 EAGGF Guarantee expenditure by select products in 2002 and 2003 (€m)

Product	2002 (€m)	EAGGF (%)	2003 (€m)	EAGGF (%)
Arable crops	17 916	40.5	19 790	37.5
of which refunds	80		104	
of which storage	283		206	
Beef/veal	8 095	18.3	8 404	18.8
of which refunds	488		534	
of which storage	522		29	
Milk products	1 912	4.3	2 672	6.0
of which refunds	977		1 568	
of which storage	3		135	
Olive oil	2 366	5.3	2 341	5.2
of which refunds	–		–	
of which storage	14		–	
Sheepmeat/goatmeat	672	1.5	1 805	4.0
of which refunds	–		–	
of which storage	–		–	
Wine	1 392	3.1	1 381	3.8
of which refunds	25		25	
of which storage	76		79	
Sugar	1 401	3.2	1 482	3.3
of which refunds	1 190		1 257	
of which storage	16		–	
EAGGF	44 230		44 780	

Source: European Commission, DG Agriculture (2003).

everything everywhere, no matter how expensive it may be. The CAP guaranteed the purchase of the home-produced selected agricultural goods that conformed with the specified quality standards, which boosted the production of farm goods in the EU.

The CAP market organisation was predominantly to support the income of farmers. Structural issues such as technical modernisation, size of holdings and employment in agriculture were left to the national authorities. National expenditure in the farm sector supplements that of the EU. This expenditure included subsidised loans, tax exemptions, social security and other subsidies. The EU gave incentives for the increase in the agricultural production, while at the same time, it assumed responsibility for the purchase of farm output and the disposal of excess supplies. The financial solidarity that came with the CAP made possible the externalisation of the cost of national investments in agriculture.

Subsidisation of the farm sector is not an exclusive feature of the EU. Other OECD countries subsidise their agriculture too. In some instances, and depending on the indicator, that support is much higher than is the case in the EU (Table 4.3). Compared with the 1986–88 period, 2000–02 was characterised by a relatively lower overall level of support. However, the total support to agriculture remains high. Producer support estimate (PSE) indicates the annual monetary value of gross transfers from consumers and taxpayers to agricultural producers. The higher the PSE, the lower the efficiency of farm production. The farm sector of the OECD countries received €249 billion in 2002 in this type of assistance. There has been a slight decline in assistance since 2000, but the volume was higher than during the 1986–88 period, when it was €219 billion.

In relative terms Switzerland was the country that assisted farming most in 2002, with a PSE of 75 per cent. However, other countries followed closely: Norway (71 per cent), Korea (66 per cent) and Japan (59 per cent). The PSE for the EU was 36 per cent, while for the US, it was 18 per cent.[14] The accession countries in Central and Eastern Europe had a lower PSE than was the case in the EU. Australia had the lowest support involvement in agriculture among countries presented in Table 4.3. As far as the total support estimate per capita is concerned, the OECD average was €300 in 2002. Both the EU and the US were above that average, €323 and €336, respectively. However, this assistance in Switzerland was €811, in Norway €673, in Korea €471 and in Japan €464. On average, the Central and East European accession countries assisted less than the EU. Assistance by the Czech Republic was €123, while in Hungary it was €198. Poland and Slovakia assisted much less, €66 and €76, respectively. In the OECD countries the assistance per full-time farmer was €11 000 in 2002. Norway's support was more than four times this average, at €47 000.

Agricultural exports are fundamental to the American economic system, as well as an important long-term strategic tool. The US has been in the forefront of the struggle against agricultural protection in the EU and Japan, and insisted on having agriculture at the heart of the Doha Round. The US sensibly cut farm subsidies in the 1996 Farm Bill. However, the 2002 US Farm Bill demolished the spirit and letter of such intentions. The bill authorised $180 billion in farm subsidies over the next ten years and increased the level of federal US subsidies by 70 per cent. This would not only violate the limits on farm subsidies agreed during the Uruguay Round, but also ensure that US farmers would receive subsidies that are three times the European level. At the same time the EU struggles to rationalise and scale down its €45 billion annual farm budget. The great significance of this change in the US is twofold. First, it came at a time when there was widespread protest in the US against the budget deficit. Second, the US is allegedly a country that preaches free trade.[15] As such, one may question the real US intentions to negotiate and to further liberalise trade within the Doha Round.

As a result of the CAP and its 'market organisation', there was a commitment by the EU to purchase and dispose of farm goods through its executive agencies. Figure 4.2 presents the consequences of fixing prices and guaranteeing purchase. Suppose that in the market for wheat SS and DD represent supply and demand curves, respectively. Equilibrium in the market is at E and the market-clearing price is $0P_e$, while the corresponding quantity of output is $0Q_e$. If the price is fixed above the market-clearing level, for instance, at $0P_h$ and if the government guarantees purchase, then the demand curve acquires a kink and becomes DD_h. As the supply curve is unchanged, equilibrium is at point E_h. The free market purchase of wheat is $0Q_2$, quantity Q_2Q_e presents a reduction in consumption, while Q_eQ_3 is hyperproduction. Triangle 'a' illustrates welfare loss for the consumers, while triangle 'b' stands for a misallocation of resources. Suppose that a lower level than $0P_e$ is used to fix the price, for instance $0P_l$. Equilibrium is at point E_l, the quantity consumed is $0Q_1$, while quantity Q_1Q_4 stands for a shortage. The example with the fixing of prices above the equilibrium level conforms with the price distortions that are induced by the CAP, while the fixing of prices at the level below the equilibrium, for example, represents the case with rents (and shortage of apartments).

Shares of member states in the total agricultural output of products that are subject to the CAP market organisation and those that are outside the EU 'market organisation' in 2001 are given in Table 4.4. The largest producers of farm goods in the EU are France, Italy, Germany, Spain and Britain in declining order. These five countries jointly produced three-quarters of the entire EU farm output. Being large countries in the region, their hefty shares do not come as a surprise. The Netherlands is a relatively small country in the EU, but it contributed over 5 per cent to the total EU farm output. Hence, even a small and highly efficient country received relatively large benefits from the CAP.

Some of the Central and East European countries that are the new members of the EU are significant producers of farm goods. In this group of ten countries, Poland produced more than half of the entire output in 2001, and Poland and Hungary together produced over 70 per cent (Table 4.5). If the output in the Czech Republic is added, then these three countries produced well over 80 per cent of the entire agricultural output in this group of countries.

The commodity structure of the EU(25) farm output for 2001 is given in Table 4.6. The striking feature of the output structure was relatively high concentration on a few products. Of the 22 commodities that are subject to

Table 4.3 Estimates of support to agriculture in billions of euros, share of PSE[a] in this support, total[b] support to agriculture as a share of GDP and total support per capita in euros in select OECD countries

Country	1986–88	2000	2001	2002
European Union (€bn)	86.7	96.1	98.0	106.8
% of that PSE	40.0	34.0	34.0	36.0
Total support as % of GDP	2.7	1.3	1.3	1.3
Total support per capita €	296.0	288.0	299.0	323.0
Support per full-time farmer €000	9.0	16.0	16.0	18.0
Czech Republic (€bn)	1.1	0.6	1.0	1.1
% of that PSE	31.0	17.0	23.0	28.0
Total support as % of GDP	4.4	1.3	1.7	1.7
Total support per capita €	109.0	69.0	106.0	123.0
Support per full-time farmer €000	3.0	4.0	6.0	8.0
Hungary (€bn)	0.7	1.1	1.1	1.6
% of that PSE	16.0	22.0	19.0	29.0
Total support as % of GDP	2.5	2.6	2.4	2.9
Total support per capita €	71.0	135.0	142.0	198.0
Support per full-time farmer €000	1.0	4.0	5.0	7.0
Poland (€bn)	1.2	2.2	2.4	2.2
% of that PSE	11.0	15.0	15.0	14.0
Total support as % of GDP	2.2	1.4	1.4	1.3
Total support per capita €	36.0	63.0	69.0	66.0
Support per full-time farmer €000	0.0	1.0	1.0	1.0
Slovakia (€bn)	0.4	0.4	0.3	0.3
% of that PSE	28.0	25.0	16.0	21.0
Total support as % of GDP	4.2	2.0	1.3	1.6
Total support per capita €	94.0	81.0	56.0	76.0
Support per full-time farmer €000	2.0	3.0	3.0	4.0
Other countries				
Australia (€bn)	1.2	1.0	0.9	0.9
% of that PSE	9.0	5.0	4.0	4.0
Total support as % of GDP	0.8	0.4	0.3	0.3
Total support per capita €	94.0	76.0	67.0	89.0
Support per full-time farmer €000	3.0	3.0	2.0	3.0
Canada (€bn)	5.2	4.5	4.4	4.9
% of that PSE	34.0	19.0	17.0	20.0
Total support as % of GDP	1.7	0.8	0.8	0.8
Total support per capita €	248.0	195.0	191.0	204.0
Support per full-time farmer €000	10.0	11.0	11.0	12.0

Table 4.3 (continued)

Country	1986–88	2000	2001	2002
Japan (€bn)	44.3	58.7	50.7	46.6
% of that PSE	61.0	60.0	59.0	59.0
Total support as % of GDP	2.3	1.4	1.4	1.4
Total support per capita €	246.0	577.0	503.0	464.0
Support per full-time farmer €000	12.0	28.0	24.0	22.0
Korea (€bn)	10.8	21.1	18.6	19.2
% of that PSE	70.0	67.0	63.0	66.0
Total support as % of GDP	9.3	4.8	4.6	4.5
Total support per capita €	286.0	515.0	456.0	471.0
Support per full-time farmer €000	7.0	27.0	23.0	24.0
Norway (€bn)	2.5	2.5	2.4	2.8
% of that PSE	70.0	68.0	67.0	71.0
Total support as % of GDP	3.4	1.5	1.4	1.5
Total support per capita €	673.0	602.0	582.0	673.0
Support per full-time farmer €000	26.0	38.0	39.0	47.0
Switzerland (€bn)	4.8	4.9	5.0	5.4
% of that PSE	76.0	72.0	72.0	75.0
Total support as % of GDP	3.9	2.1	2.0	2.0
Total support per capita (€bn)	872.0	752.0	761.0	811.0
Support per full-time farmer €000	31.0	32.0	32.0	34.0
United States (€bn)	38.4	53.9	57.7	41.9
% of that PSE	25.0	22.0	23.0	18.0
Total support as % of GDP	1.4	0.9	1.0	0.9
Total support per capita €	259.0	366.0	382.0	336.0
Support per full-time farmer €000	15.0	22.0	23.0	17.0
OECD (€bn)	219.2	263.0	253.3	249.2
% of that PSE	38.0	32.0	31.0	31.0
Total support as % of GDP	2.3	1.3	1.2	1.2
Total support per capita €	270.0	311.0	303.0	300.0
Support per full-time farmer €000	9.0	12.0	11.0	11.0

Notes:
a. PSE indicates the annual monetary value of gross transfers from consumers and taxpayers to support agricultural producers.
b. Total expenditure also includes the spending of other policies related to agriculture.

Source: OECD (2003a).

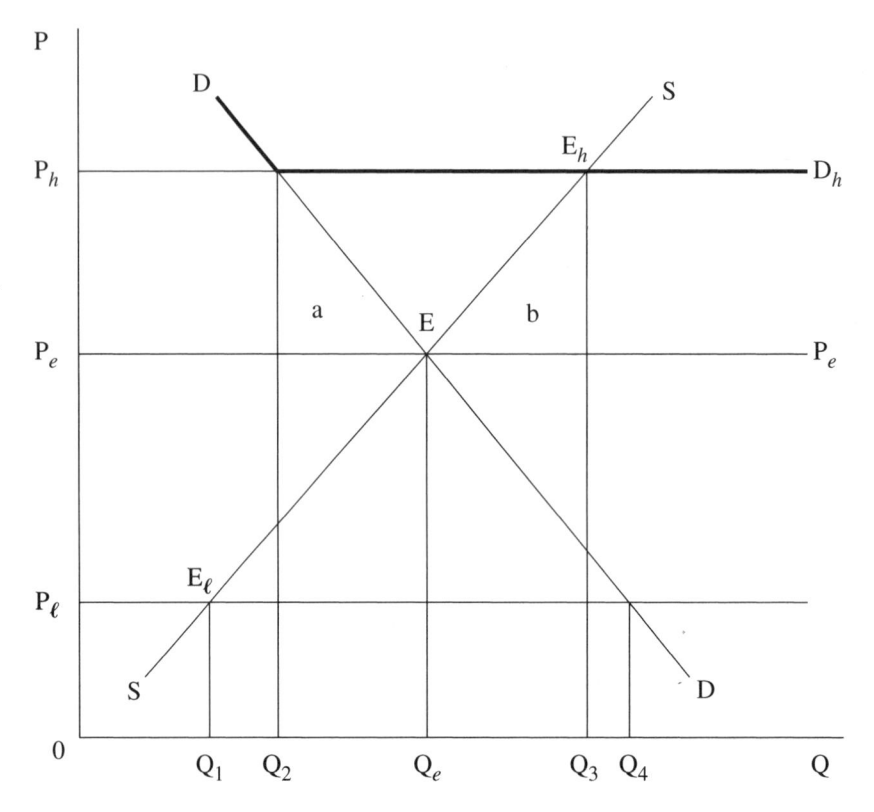

Figure 4.2 Consequences of fixing and guaranteeing prices

the CAP 'market organisation' only three products (milk, cattle and pigs), comprise 34 per cent to the total farm output, while 19 others contribute most of the rest. Because of the climate, the production of the 'three commodities' is concentrated in the central and northern countries of the EU.[16] The share of the southern countries in the production of these goods was much smaller. None the less, the contribution of the southern countries was pronounced in the output of fresh fruits and vegetables. The Central and East European countries have a relative concentration of output in the 'three northern products'.

SELF-SUFFICIENCY

Self-sufficiency is the ratio of domestic consumption to domestic output. Apart from vegetables and potatoes, the original six EU member states were not self-sufficient in farm products at the time of the creation of the EU. As a direct consequence of the CAP market organisation, as well as progress in technology, the EU reached a high degree of self-sufficiency in almost all temperate-zone agricultural products (Table 4.7). Greatest self-sufficiency exists in cereals, sugar and milk-based[17] products. The only 'deficit' in the EU internal production is in fresh and citrus fruits, as well as in maize. This means that the concessions in trade (quotas) that the EU offers to foreign exporters for all other farm goods has a heavy political dimension.

One must not forget the context of the situation when the original CAP was created (end of the 1950s). There was a huge need to increase agricultural production in the EU to meet the needs of the population (there was a food shortage at that time).[18] However, farmers respond to business signals like any other entrepreneur. Once they start to produce not for consumers, but because of guaranteed purchases, this causes market surpluses of goods. The consequence under the CAP market organisation is a withdrawal of those goods from the market and their eventual destruction, for example, the 'butter mountain' cycle. Milk produced by cows is processed into butter to profit from the intervention price, and hundreds of millions of tonnes of butter are stockpiled. When the shops are fully stocked, the European Commission transports and stores the surplus throughout Europe at enormous cost and waste of energy. After 24 months the butter is unfit for human consumption. Such butter is then processed into cheap fodder for calves. The cycle is complete – but only after two years of industrial processing, storage and transport in refrigerated trucks with enormous financial losses.[19]

There have been substantial surpluses of farm goods, and the EU has had to dispose of them in several controversial ways. Milk is sometimes distributed free of charge to schools in order to supply the children with the nutrients necessary for growth, as well as to foster the habit of consuming milk from an early age, rather that of consuming various addictive 'junk drinks' that have a questionable or negative impact on health. Butter is sold at privileged (lower) prices to hospitals, army and humanitarian organisations, while the general public can rarely enjoy those prices. Cake manufacturers and bakeries might sometimes procure butter at privileged prices in order to reduce the competitive pressure from other fats such as margarine. A portion of the surpluses is donated to poor or crisis-ridden countries as humanitarian aid. Finally and most importantly, surpluses are exported to third countries with refunds (read export subsidies). Surpluses of farm goods cannot be freely distributed or constantly sold at reduced prices to domestic consumers. If that were the case, internal EU prices would fall and the whole CAP intervention system would collapse. As part

Table 4.4 Individual member states' shares in agricultural production in 2001 (%)

	Belgium	Denmark	Germany	Greece	Spain	France	Ireland
1	2	3	4	5	6	7	8
Products subject to EU – market organisations							
Wheat[1]	1.4	4.7	21.4	3.4	7.6	31.6	0.6
Rye[1]	0.7	6.1	77.4	0.8	2.8	2.4	–
Oats[1]	0.6	4.6	17.0	1.8	11.7	8.1	1.4
Barley[1]	0.8	9.4	26.9	0.7	10.3	21.7	2.2
Maize[1]	0.1	–	9.0	6.9	14.6	36.5	–
Rice[1]	–	–	–	5.4	31.2	4.2	–
Sugarbeet	5.5	3.0	22.6	3.2	8.0	23.3	1.6
Tobacco	0.4	–	3.5	44.3	10.3	9.0	–
Olive oil	–	–	–	24.3	36.9	–	–
Oilseeds[1]	0.2	1.4	25.3	0.2	10.9	38.7	–
Fresh fruit[2]	1.8	0.1	3.9	9.5	31.9	16.2	0.1
Fresh vegetables[2]	3.7	0.6	6.6	7.9	19.4	15.2	0.9
Wine and must	–	–	6.2	0.3	4.7	52.5	–
Seeds[3]	2.3	8.9	16.0	1.0	–	26.8	–
Textile fibres	1.5	–	–	85.0	–	12.4	–
Hops	2.0	–	82.4	–	–	3.6	–
Milk	2.4	3.7	22.7	2.3	6.0	19.2	3.8
Cattle	3.6	1.5	12.2	1.1	7.9	29.1	6.8
Pigs	5.5	9.9	22.8	1.2	17.0	12.4	1.2
Sheep and goats	0.1	0.1	3.9	13.6	28.3	15.6	6.5
Eggs	2.7	1.6	19.7	3.5	13.4	15.2	0.6
Poultry	2.4	1.7	8.9	1.3	12.7	27.0	1.2
Subtotal	2.5	3.2	15.3	4.5	13.4	22.5	2.1
Products not subject to EU – market organisations							
Potatoes[1]	5.5	1.9	16.7	5.2	9.0	19.8	1.2
Agricultural services	0.4	3.3	14.7	0.0	4.1	28.2	3.5
Other	2.9	3.6	18.0	1.7	8.7	21.5	1.7
Subtotal	2.8	3.4	17.4	1.8	8.0	22.4	1.9
Grand total	2.6	3.2	15.7	4.0	12.3	22.5	2.1

Notes:
1. Including seeds.
2. The products listed in Article 1 of Council Regulation (EC) No. 2200/96 on the new market organisations.
3. Excluding cereal and rice seeds, oilseeds, the seeds of protein plants and seed potatoes.

Source: European Commission, Eurostat (Economic Accounts for Agriculture).

Common Agricultural Policy 233

EU(15)=100
(%)

Italy	Luxembourg	Netherlands	Austria	Portugal	Finland	Sweden	United Kingdom
9	10	11	12	13	14	15	16
12.1	0.1	0.8	1.5	0.5	0.6	2.1	11.7
0.1	0.1	0.3	3.8	0.8	1.7	2.7	0.4
7.6	0.1	0.1	2.4	1.2	19.5	15.2	8.7
3.7	0.1	0.6	2.1	0.1	3.8	3.1	14.5
25.3	0.0	0.7	3.7	3.2	–	0.0	–
53.2	–	–	0.0	6.0	–	–	–
9.5	–	7.1	2.9	0.3	1.2	2.8	9.1
30.6	–	–	0.1	1.8	–	–	–
38.0	–	–	0.0	0.8	–	–	–
10.1	0.1	0.1	2.0	0.4	0.8	0.7	9.2
25.3	0.0	2.7	1.4	4.3	0.2	0.2	2.2
23.6	0.0	9.0	0.8	3.8	0.8	0.6	7.2
29.7	0.2	–	3.0	3.4	–	–	–
5.7	0.0	32.2	0.1	–	0.3	0.6	6.1
0.0	–	0.3	0.1	–	0.0	–	0.6
–	–	–	1.1	–	–	–	10.9
10.5	0.2	9.3	2.3	1.7	2.6	2.6	10.7
13.4	0.2	3.9	2.5	1.3	1.1	1.8	13.6
9.7	0.1	9.0	2.7	2.0	1.0	1.3	4.2
6.4	0.0	1.7	0.5	2.9	0.0	0.3	20.0
16.2	0.1	7.6	2.4	1.6	0.8	2.0	12.7
15.3	0.0	6.1	0.7	3.9	0.8	0.8	17.3
15.7	0.1	5.3	1.9	2.2	1.2	1.5	8.5
7.2	0.0	13.7	0.8	2.0	1.1	2.0	13.7
11.1	0.1	19.2	1.5	0.1	1.7	1.1	10.9
14.2	0.1	14.3	1.9	2.2	2.1	2.1	5.0
12.9	0.1	15.0	1.7	1.8	1.9	2.0	7.0
15.1	0.1	7.3	1.9	2.1	1.4	1.6	8.2

Table 4.5 Individual candidate countries' shares in agricultural production in 2001 (%) $CC(10) = 100^4$
(en %)

1	Czech Republic	Estonia	Cyprus	Latvia	Lithuania	Hungary	Malta	Poland	Slovenia	Slovakia
	2	3	4	5	6	7	8	9	10	11
Products subject to EU – market organisations										
Wheat[1]	19.5	0.5	–	1.8	4.3	17.8	0.0	48.4	1.3	6.4
Rye[1]	3.4	0.7	–	2.0	3.7	1.9	0.0	86.2	0.1	2.0
Oats[1]	2.6	1.1	–	1.4	1.3	2.3	0.0	90.7	0.1	0.5
Barley[1]	25.4	2.7	–	2.4	8.1	13.4	0.0	40.4	0.8	7.0
Maize[1]	6.3	0.0	–	0.0	0.0	64.9	0.0	16.9	3.8	8.1
Rice[1]	0.0	0.0	–	0.0	0.0	100.0	0.0	0.0	0.0	0.0
Sugarbeet	15.8	0.0	–	2.7	6.4	14.9	0.0	54.6	0.9	4.7
Tobacco	0.0	0.0	–	0.0	0.0	24.1	0.0	68.9	0.0	7.1
Olive oil	–	–	–	–	–	–	–	–	–	–
Oilseeds[1]	30.4	1.3	–	0.4	1.8	27.4	0.0	29.9	0.3	8.5
Fresh fruit[2]	4.6	0.6	–	0.7	0.5	28.1	0.4	58.4	3.7	3.0
Fresh vegetables[2]	4.2	0.7	–	1.1	5.1	25.0	2.8	53.8	1.7	5.7
Wine and must	0.0	0.0	–	0.0	0.0	–	0.0	0.0	100.0	0.0
Seeds[3]	24.9	0.0	–	4.3	0.0	29.7	0.0	41.0	0.0	0.0
Textile fibres	36.1	0.0	–	14.7	0.0	0.9	0.0	48.4	0.0	0.0
Hops	78.2	0.0	–	0.0	0.0	0.1	0.0	21.7	0.0	0.0
Milk	13.3	3.0	–	2.8	5.2	13.3	0.4	52.7	4.1	5.3

Cattle	14.8	2.0	—	3.1	6.5	9.2	0.5	47.5	11.5	4.9
Pigs	11.5	1.3	—	1.2	2.6	19.1	0.4	57.5	2.0	4.4
Sheep and goats	0.5	1.1	—	1.1	2.3	60.4	0.0	12.0	11.0	11.5
Eggs	9.3	1.5	—	3.0	3.6	20.2	1.2	52.3	2.5	6.3
Poultry	9.5	0.6	—	0.7	2.5	30.5	1.0	46.5	4.1	4.5
Subtotal	12.3	1.4	—	1.7	3.7	20.3	0.5	51.8	3.2	5.1
Products not subject to EU market – organisations									
Potatoes[1]	6.9	1.6	0.0	3.3	6.2	8.3	0.9	68.4	1.5	2.7
Agricultural services	4.1	3.0	0.0	0.8	1.9	28.9	0.0	50.9	2.0	8.4
Other	8.9	1.6	—	2.9	7.4	16.3	0.6	51.7	6.1	4.4
Subtotal	7.6	1.8	—	2.7	6.3	15.8	0.6	56.3	4.2	4.5
Grand total	11.5	1.4	—	1.9	4.1	19.5	0.6	52.6	3.4	5.0

Notes:
1. Including seeds.
2. The products listed in Article 1 of Council Regulation (EC) No 2200/96 on the new market organisations.
3. Excluding cereal and rice seeds, oilseeds, the seeds of protein plants and seed potatoes.
4. CC(10) without Cyprus.

Source: European Commission, Eurostat (Economic Accounts for Agriculture).

Table 4.6 Share of products in agricultural production in 2001 (%)

	EU(15)	Belgium	Denmark	Germany	Greece	Spain	France
1	2	3	4	5	6	7	8
Products subject to EU – market organisations							
Wheat[1]	5.9	3.2	8.6	8.1	5.1	3.7	8.3
Rye[1]	0.4	0.1	0.7	1.7	0.1	0.1	0.0
Oats[1]	0.4	0.1	0.6	0.5	0.2	0.4	0.2
Barley[1]	2.8	0.8	8.3	4.9	0.5	2.4	2.8
Maize[1]	2.3	0.0	–	1.3	4.0	2.8	3.8
Rice[1]	0.3	–	–	–	0.4	0.8	0.1
Sugarbeet	1.6	3.4	1.5	2.3	1.3	1.0	1.6
Tobacco	0.4	0.1	–	0.1	4.6	0.3	0.2
Olive oil	1.8	–	–	–	11.2	5.5	–
Oilseeds[1]	1.8	0.1	0.8	2.9	0.1	1.6	3.1
Fresh fruit[2]	6.2	4.3	0.3	1.5	14.9	16.0	4.5
Fresh vegetables[2]	7.6	11.0	1.3	3.2	15.1	12.0	5.1
Wine and must	5.0	–	–	2.0	0.4	1.9	11.7
Seeds[3]	0.4	0.3	1.0	0.4	0.1	–	0.4
Textile fibres	0.4	0.2	–	–	8.7	–	0.2
Hops	0.1	0.0	–	0.3	–	–	0.0
Milk	14.5	13.4	16.7	21.0	8.5	7.0	12.4
Cattle	9.1	12.6	4.1	7.1	2.5	5.9	11.7
Pigs	10.2	21.7	31.3	14.8	3.0	14.1	5.6
Sheep and goats	2.0	0.1	0.1	0.5	6.8	4.6	1.4
Eggs	1.8	1.9	0.9	2.3	1.6	2.0	1.2
Poultry	4.3	3.9	2.3	2.5	1.4	4.5	5.2
Subtotal	**79.3**	**77.4**	**78.4**	**77.2**	**90.4**	**86.6**	**79.5**
Products subject to EU – market organisations							
Potatoes[1]	2.5	5.3	1.5	2.7	3.3	1.8	2.2
Agricultural services	3.2	0.5	3.4	3.0	0.0	1.1	4.1
Other	14.9	16.8	16.7	17.1	6.3	10.5	14.2
Subtotal	**20.7**	**22.6**	**21.6**	**22.8**	**9.6**	**13.4**	**20.5**
Grand total	100.0	100.0	100.0	100.0	100.0	100.0	100.0
Value in €m	282 407.5	7 317.2	9 092.7	44 369.1	11 184.5	34 705.2	63 550.0

of the reform package, the cost of handling surpluses in the future may fall on the national, rather than the EU budget.

Once such a high level of self-sufficiency has been reached, attention needs to be paid to the other dimensions of the agricultural sector, for example, the protection of the environment. A widespread use of fertilisers, herbicides, insecticides and pesticides could increase farm output in the short run, but may downgrade soil and have adverse effects in the medium and long terms for health, life and the environment. There needs

Ireland	Italy	Luxembourg	Netherlands	Austria	Portugal	Finland	Sweden	United Kingdom
9	10	11	12	13	14	15	16	17
1.6	4.7	3.3	0.7	4.7	1.4	2.6	7.9	8.5
–	0.0	0.2	0.0	0.7	0.1	0.4	0.6	0.0
0.3	0.2	0.6	0.0	0.5	0.2	6.0	4.1	0.4
3.1	0.7	3.1	0.2	3.1	0.1	7.9	5.7	5.0
–	3.9	0.3	0.2	4.5	3.6	–	0.0	–
–	1.1	–	–	–	0.9	–	–	–
1.2	1.0	–	1.5	2.4	0.2	1.4	2.8	1.8
–	0.8	–	–	0.0	0.4	–	–	–
–	4.6	–	–	–	0.7	–	–	–
–	1.2	1.0	0.0	1.9	0.4	1.1	0.8	2.0
0.3	10.4	1.3	2.3	4.6	12.8	0.7	0.8	1.7
3.4	11.9	0.4	9.3	3.1	13.7	4.4	3.1	6.7
–	9.8	9.9	–	7.8	8.0	–	–	–
–	0.1	0.2	1.6	0.0	–	0.1	0.1	0.3
–	0.0	–	0.0	0.0	–	0.0	–	0.0
–	–	–	–	0.0	–	–	–	0.1
26.4	10.1	34.8	18.5	17.5	12.0	27.9	23.9	18.9
29.8	8.1	21.1	4.8	11.7	5.7	7.6	10.4	15.0
5.9	6.5	7.3	12.5	14.4	9.6	7.3	8.7	5.2
6.2	0.8	0.3	0.5	0.6	2.8	0.0	0.3	4.8
0.5	2.0	1.8	1.9	2.3	1.4	1.0	2.3	2.8
2.6	4.4	0.5	3.6	1.6	8.0	2.4	2.3	9.1
81.3	82.4	86.1	57.7	81.5	81.9	70.9	73.9	82.4
1.5	1.2	0.8	4.7	1.0	2.3	2.1	3.2	4.2
5.4	2.4	2.9	8.5	2.5	0.1	4.1	2.4	4.3
11.9	14.0	10.1	29.1	15.0	15.7	22.9	20.5	9.2
18.7	17.6	13.9	42.3	18.5	18.1	29.1	26.1	17.6
100.0	100.0	100.0	100.0	100.0	100.0	100.0	100.0	100.0
5878.8	42630.2	256.6	20650.2	5356.9	5944.0	3841.9	4401.4	23228.8

to be greater concern for the impact of farming on the environment (soil, air and water), as well as on the health and growth of plants and animals (not to mention humans) in the future.[20]

Most of the damage to the environment over the past several decades, for example, in Britain did not come from urbanisation or road building, but rather from the CAP. Subsidies encouraged huge monocultures in arable farming, which have been responsible for the destruction of biodiversity in species-rich areas. Instead of the usual practice of ploughing winter stubble

Table 4.6 (continued)

	CC(10)[4]	Czech Republic	Estonia	Cyprus	Latvia	Lithuania
1	2	3	4	5	6	7
Products subject to EU – market organisations						
Wheat[1]	8.8	14.9	2.9	–	8.6	9.1
Rye[1]	1.7	0.5	0.9	–	1.8	1.5
Oats[1]	1.9	0.4	1.5	–	1.4	0.6
Barley[1]	3.0	6.6	5.5	–	3.8	5.8
Maize[1]	2.7	1.5	0.0	–	0.0	0.0
Rice[1]	0.0	0.0	0.0	–	0.0	0.0
Sugarbeet	2.2	3.1	0.0	–	3.3	3.5
Tobacco	0.2	0.0	0.0	–	0.0	0.0
Olive oil	0.0	0.0	0.0	–	0.0	0.0
Oilseeds[1]	2.8	7.5	2.6	–	0.6	1.2
Fresh fruit[2]	5.2	2.1	2.2	–	1.9	0.6
Fresh vegetables[2]	6.0	2.2	2.7	–	3.6	7.4
Wine and must	0.3	0.0	0.0	–	0.0	0.0
Seeds[3]	0.1	0.2	0.0	–	0.2	0.0
Textile fibres	0.0	0.1	0.0	–	0.2	0.0
Hops	0.1	0.8	0.0	–	0.0	0.0
Milk	14.9	17.2	30.6	–	22.5	18.6
Cattle	3.9	5.0	5.5	–	6.5	6.1
Pigs	18.1	18.0	16.3	–	12.0	11.4
Sheep and goats	0.3	0.0	0.2	–	0.2	0.2
Eggs	3.7	3.0	3.9	–	5.8	3.2
Poultry	6.9	5.7	3.0	–	2.5	4.2
Subtotal	82.6	88.5	77.9	–	74.7	73.4
Products subject to EU – market organisations						
Potatoes[1]	4.9	3.0	5.5	–	8.8	7.5
Agricultural services	2.5	0.9	5.2	–	1.1	1.1
Other	10.0	7.7	11.4	–	15.4	18.0
Subtotal	17.4	11.5	22.1	–	25.3	26.6
Grand total	100.0	100.0	100.0	–	100.0	100.0
Value in €m	28 038.5	3 231.8	402.6	–	522.9	1 157.5
EU(15) = 100	9.9	1.1	0.1	–	0.2	0.4

Notes:
1. Including seeds.
2. The products listed in Article 1 of Council Regulation (EC) No. 2200/96 on the new market organisations.
3. Excluding cereal and rice seeds, oilseeds, the seeds of protein plants and seed potatoes.
4. CC(10) without Cyprus.

Source: European Commission, Eurostat (Economic Accounts for Agriculture).

Hungary	Malta	Poland	Slovenia	Slovakia	Bulgaria	Romania	Turkey
8	9	10	11	12	13	14	15
8.0	0.0	8.1	3.3	11.3	9.2	10.1	–
0.2	0.0	2.8	0.0	0.7	0.1	0.0	–
0.2	0.0	3.2	0.1	0.2	0.2	0.5	–
2.0	0.0	2.3	0.7	4.1	2.3	1.8	–
9.1	0.0	0.9	3.1	4.4	3.7	14.6	–
0.1	0.0	0.0	0.0	0.0	0.1	0.0	–
1.7	0.0	2.3	0.6	2.1	0.0	0.2	–
0.2	0.0	0.2	0.0	0.2	1.9	0.1	–
0.0	0.0	0.0	0.0	0.0	0.0	0.0	–
4.0	0.0	1.6	0.3	4.8	2.8	1.7	–
7.4	3.6	5.7	5.6	3.1	6.6	5.6	–
7.7	29.4	6.1	3.0	6.8	14.0	8.9	–
0.0	0.0	0.0	7.5	0.0	0.0	1.7	–
0.1	0.0	0.1	0.0	0.0	0.1	0.1	–
0.0	0.0	0.0	0.0	0.0	0.1	0.0	–
0.0	0.0	0.0	0.0	0.0	0.0	0.0	–
10.1	11.4	14.9	17.9	15.6	13.3	12.4	–
1.8	3.2	3.5	13.2	3.7	5.2	3.7	–
17.7	12.9	19.8	10.6	15.8	15.7	8.8	–
0.9	0.0	0.1	0.9	0.6	4.9	1.3	–
3.8	7.8	3.6	2.7	4.6	2.8	3.8	–
10.7	12.4	6.1	8.4	6.2	4.3	5.1	–
85.9	80.6	81.3	78.1	84.4	87.0	80.4	–
2.1	7.8	6.4	2.3	2.7	2.6	5.7	–
3.6	0.0	2.4	1.4	4.1	6.0	1.1	–
8.4	11.6	9.9	18.2	8.8	4.4	12.9	–
14.1	19.4	18.7	21.9	15.6	13.0	19.6	–
100.0	100.0	100.0	100.0	100.0	100.0	100.0	–
5471.2	157.1	14745.0	943.1	1407.3	3240.0	10707.1	–
1.9	0.1	5.2	0.3	0.5	1.1	3.8	–

Table 4.7 *Self-sufficiency in select agricultural products in 1999/2000 (%)*

	EU(15)	Belgium	Denmark	Germany	Greece	Spain	France
1	2	3	4	5	6	7	8
1999/00							
Cereals							
Total cereals (excl. rice)	116	54	116	121	75	83	221
of which:							
Total wheat	120	63	118	125	81	68	218
Rye	154	32	266	171	97	110	131
Barley	124	49	109	123	60	109	266
Grain/maize	96	15	0	78	74	62	240
Total milled rice	–	–	–	–	–	–	–
Potatoes	98	172	93	101	84	78	100
Sugar	128	162	263	149	63	81	210
Fresh vegetables	–	126	–	40	107	147	–
Fresh fruit (excl. citrus fruit)	–	77	–	20	120	121	–
Citrus fruit	–	–	–	–	125	266	–
Wine	109	0	0	56	116	147	122
1999							
Milk products							
Fresh milk products (excl. cream)	123	102	113	–	93	103	98
Whole-milk powder	370	647	132	–	–	400	2250
Skimmed-milk powder	247	170	286	–	–	103	646
Concentrated milk	179	–	136	–	–	55	0
Cheese	34	362	96	–	–	116	422
Butter	116	122	78	–	131	89	919
Margarine	–	–	–	–	–	–	–
Eggs	103	–	89	75	96	107	10291
Meat[1]							
Total meat[2], of which:	107	–	347	87	54	106	113
Total beef/veal	103	–	115	116	25	100	113
Pigmeat	110	–	490	85	41	112	106
Poultrymeat	109	–	214	66	79	94	152
Sheepmeat and goatmeat	83	–	29	47	82	103	47
Oils and fats							
Total oils and fats	–	26	–	61	–	–	73
of which:							
Vegetable	–	2	–	53	–	–	66
Cutting-room fat	–	65	–	123	–	–	109

Notes:
1. Excl. offal.
2. Including cutting-room fat.

Source: European Commission (Eurostat).

Common Agricultural Policy 241

Ireland	Italy	Luxembourg	Netherlands	Austria	Portugal	Finland	Sweden	United Kingdom
9	10	11	12	13	14	15	16	17
75	80	93	21	106	29	92	130	110
52	75	94	29	131	9	60	120	118
0	80	133	28	94	58	43	118	109
123	66	95	24	119	9	94	141	121
0	90	40	0	88	45	0	0	0
–	–	–	–	–	–	–	–	–
67	79	69	147	86	75	88	90	89
183	109	0	152	138	9	61	109	67
68	126	–	–	60	128	51	40	–
11	132	–	–	68	47	8	8	–
0	94	–	–	0	82	0	0	–
0	153	57	0	107	71	0	0	0
90	–	83	104	105	101	99	98	–
–	–	159	106	150	84	102	108	–
–	–	34	120	109	100	104	88	–
–	214	0	100	102	–			
–	–	224	82	86	104	87	63	–
80	–	153	88	125	121	112	92	–
–	–	–	–	–	–	–	–	–
91	102	–	225	81	100	114	98	95
335	76	–	241	110	80	101	95	83
1 148	62	–	160	140	58	93	79	66
190	67	–	283	107	77	102	101	76
108	108	–	221	–	97	–	–	90
265	56	–	105	79	69	45	52	104
–	63	–	0	73	–	–	–	32
–	50	–	0	69	20	–	–	34
–	103	–	0	122	–	–	–	82

into the ground in the spring, farmers tended to burn off the stubble to grow a second crop. In addition, subsidy-supported monoculture and intensive farming were responsible for the massive disappearance of hedgerows which previously housed a large variety of birds, insects and plants, transforming parts of the English countryside – East Anglia, for example, turned into a 'green desert'.

CONSEQUENCES FOR PRINCIPAL PLAYERS

Farmers

The best answer to whether the CAP market organisation helps a farmer to begin agricultural production, remain in it or leave farming altogether would be to consider the situation when there was no CAP. Such a comparison would, however, be difficult and full of pitfalls. None the less, there are certain ways, albeit full of methodological pitfalls, to compare wages in different sectors. Most of the farmers live in the countryside where rents are lower than in urban areas. Many of them are also engaged in another gainful activity.[21] Farmers were sometimes said to live poor, but die rich. Residents in the cities have higher outlays for clothes and footwear, as well as for transportation relative to farmers who may live close to their farms. A relatively new feature is that many people leave urban areas and prefer to live in the countryside.

A graphical illustration of the income of farmers is given in Figure 4.3. DD and SS present demand and supply, respectively, for a farm good subject to the CAP 'market organisation'. Free-market equilibrium is at E, but if the CAP fixes price at P_h, then the new equilibrium is at E_h. If quantity is multiplied by price, the income of farmers equals rectangle $0P_hE_hQ_h$. In a free market situation the income of farmers would equal a smaller rectangle $0P_eEQ_e$. The difference between the two rectangles is the shaded area that equals income subsidies that EU farmers receive as a consequence of the CAP market organisation.

According to a Eurostat 1999–2000 survey[22] 58 per cent of 6.8 million farmholdings in the EU were relatively small (up to 5 hectares). These holdings were mostly located in Greece, Italy and Portugal. The largest holdings of more than 100 hectares represented 3 per cent of all EU holdings. Most of them were in Britain (17 per cent of holdings). The used area in the EU was 127 million hectares, with an average size of 19 hectares for each holding. Glasshouses included 2 per cent of the EU holdings (11 per cent in the Netherlands and 6 per cent in Belgium), while 2 per cent of the holdings practised organic farming (11 per cent in Sweden and 9 per cent in

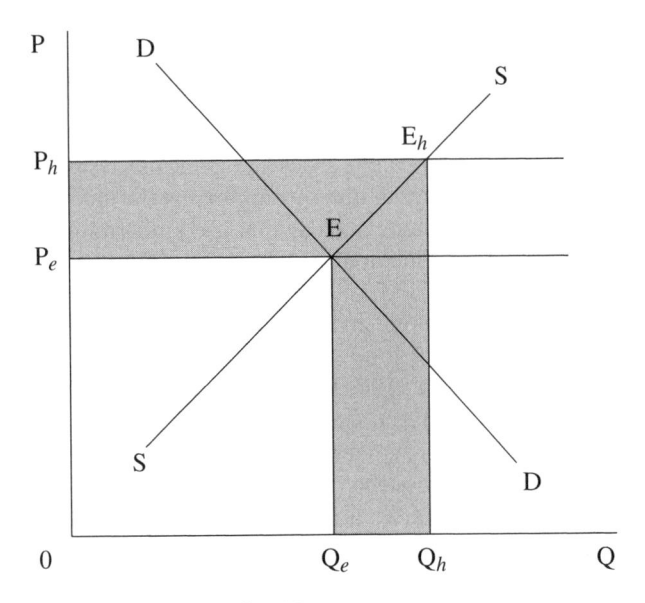

Figure 4.3 Income of farmers in the EU

Austria). Fifty-four per cent of holdings and 55 per cent of the farming were located in less-favoured or mountain areas. Single holders held 96 per cent of the holdings, while the rest was held by a legal entity (a company).

The general farm support provided by the CAP is in a sense one-sided. It favours output in the northern regions of the EU where production is large scale, takes place on large farms and is based on goods of animal origin and on certain cereals. In the southern regions, however, there is a predominance of crops that do not have such a large share in the CAP expenditure as 'northern' products. In addition, they are produced on small farms. Therefore, the owners of large farms in the north of the EU derive the greatest benefits from the CAP. This structure of farm support is far from the goal of ensuring 'a fair standard of living for the agricultural community'.

Consumers

One of the achievements of the CAP was the security of food supplies from domestic production (self-sufficiency). If the origin of farm commodities is ignored, then the security of food supplies could be achieved more cheaply. For example, agricultural goods could be purchased abroad where they are cheaper compared with prices in the EU. The outlays for storage in the EU would be the same for an identical quantity of goods, but there would be a saving equal to the difference in the value of the stored goods, as the ones purchased in the foreign markets are cheaper than those available from EU domestic production.

The CAP system of variable levies and guaranteed purchases at specified prices for agricultural goods aims at supporting the income of farmers. The deficiency-payment system, such as that used in Britain prior to EU entry in 1973, supports the income of consumers. The CAP system not only increases the cost of food and taxes (national contributions to the EU budget), but also increases production expenditure, as a part of wages is influenced by the cost of food.

One of the objectives of the CAP, as specified by the Treaty of Rome, is that supplies have to 'reach consumers at reasonable prices'. However, the treaty does not define 'reasonable prices'. 'Reasonable prices' change their meaning, not only across the different income groups of consumers, but also over time. There is statistical evidence that the prices of farm goods in the EU have been increasing at a slower rate than the incomes of consumers. None the less, one may not infer from these relative changes that consumers were supplied at 'reasonable' prices. The prices of agricultural products subject to the CAP 'market organisation' are on the same level as the highest ones for farm goods. These are the prices that prevail on the German market, a country that is one of the wealthiest in the EU. In addition, there is a weak correlation between the price of agricultural goods at the farm gate and the retail price of food for final consumers (the base good passes through a chain of transformation, value is added, in addition to the costs of marketing and distribution). Hence, a comparison between the two prices is subject to a great deal of methodological difficulty.

The CAP has created social problems too. The groups of the population with the lowest incomes (the poor, the sick, the students and the retired) have relatively the highest expenditure on food. One can find here one of the greatest controversies of the CAP: the income transfer from poor consumers to rich farmers. In fact, the major beneficiaries of the CAP include large farmers;[23] those who transport, store and trade in surplus products; and all bureaucrats (mostly in the national offices) who deal with the CAP.

The CAP-generated incentives to produce farm goods have in certain instances provoked fury. In the search for higher profit and cost reduction, producers have sometimes disregarded the safety of the agricultural product. Cancer-causing dioxins, hormones, antibiotics and other dangerous substances are found in food destined both for human and for animal consumption. Landless breeding was stimulated by cheap imported soya from the US and manioc from South Asia. Cows are locked in stables located close to the ports where these unlimited imports were arriving. In addition, these herbivores were transformed into carnivores as they were fed animal-based products. The consequences of such a forced conversion have been enormous and well documented with the arrival of BSE. Are genetically modified organisms a dream come true or the beginning of a nightmare? Is genetic code manipulation going a step too far by adding and exchanging genes between plants and animals, between viruses and conventionally edible organisms? In this complex situation would it be preferable to adopt a precautionary principle because it is better to be safe than sorry? The more the focus groups learn about these 'engineered' crops, the less they like the idea of planting them.[24] The EU demands that all items containing genetically modified organisms must be well tested and clearly labelled, their sources must be traceable and their impact on health and the environment constantly monitored.

A serious problem for the general operation of the EU arose in 1996, when the EU banned the export of British beef and its derivatives because it feared the spread of the human equivalent of 'mad cow disease' (BSE).[25] In retaliation, the British government decided to block EU business by a policy of non-cooperation. These kinds of tactics had not been seen in the EU since 1965, when General de Gaulle pursued an 'empty chair' policy. There was much hot air for a few years until a compromise deal was struck. The ban was lifted on certain conditions and Britain resumed its cooperation in the work of the EU. BSE was the most expensive disease that has ever struck the European cattle herd. Its cost to the EU governments and especially to farmers (loss of animals and a reduction in their value) would total €92 billion.[26]

Yet another crisis erupted when foot-and-mouth disease was diagnosed in spring 2001 in Britain. Of almost 4 million slaughtered animals, 95 per cent of them were healthy. The estimated revenue cost of destroying these animals was more than £2.5 billion. They could have been vaccinated, as was the case in the similar situation in the Netherlands. At a time when one can fly and go to the Moon, it would have been easy and relatively cheap to vaccinate the animals. The government's claim that 'vaccinated meat would be unsaleable and unexportable' did not hold water. At the very same time it was reported that the 'Defence Ministry is Britain's biggest importer of Argentine beef'. Meat from Argentina, where foot-and-mouth disease is endemic, was both exported and eaten by British soldiers. 'Nothing in the entire history of the common agricultural policy has been so crazy.'[27]

External Countries[28]

Protecting the income of farmers in the EU is achieved, among other ways, by restricting competition from third countries in the EU market. This is done by the employment of an efficient and flexible system of variable levies on imports of agricultural products. None the less, the EU is at the same time the largest importer of agricultural commodities in the world. On the export side, the EU is (together with the US) the largest exporter of farm items. As such, it influences the quantity, location and structure of international production, prices and trade in farm goods.

The EU has an undisputed impact on the price of farm goods because of its large share in the world trade in these commodities. When exporting farm commodities abroad, the EU applies a refund (subsidy) that bridges the difference between the higher prices for farm goods prevailing on the EU internal market and the lower prices at which those goods are sold to foreign partners. If one defines dumping as sales of domestic goods to foreign partners at prices below those on the domestic market (minus the sales tax) and/or at prices below the costs of production, then the CAP system of refunds represents a textbook example of dumping. Such sales distort international specialisation, because more-efficient producers than those in the EU are denied export markets, as well as sales. Until the conclusion of the Uruguay Round, however, trade in agricultural goods was outside the scope of the GATT. Thus, little could be done about EU farm-trade policy.

Table 4.8 presents the EU trade in agricultural products in 1999–2001. The principal EU imports include fruits, vegetables and oilseeds. Those are the goods in which the EU has the biggest deficit in trade and the lowest level of self-sufficiency. The principal export items include beverages, spirits, dairy products, meat and cereals, which are also the items that have the most obvious degree of self-sufficiency.

The principal suppliers of agricultural goods to the EU in 1999–2001 were the US and Brazil (Table 4.9). They were followed by Argentina, Turkey, Australia, New Zealand and China. On the export side and during the same period, the main customer countries for EU farm exports were the US, Japan, Switzerland and Russia (Table 4.10). The total annual EU exports agricultural goods was about €60 billion. The annual EU imports of farm goods was also about €60 billion. On balance the EU has always had a deficit in trade in farm goods. The size of this deficit was changing every year which is the consequence, in part, of the nature of farm production. However, the EU had considerable bilateral surpluses in farm trade with principal customer countries.

In spite of relatively substantial imports and exports (€62 billion and €60 billion, respectively, in 2001) of agricultural commodities and food by the EU, imports would be higher and exports lower if the EU were without the CAP market organisation. Subsidies and increase in productivity (supported by relentless technical progress) transformed the EU from a net

Table 4.8 EU(15) trade by agricultural product (CN chapters), 1999–2001 (€m)

EU(15)
(Mio ECU-EUR)

Codes CN	Products	Imports 1999	Imports 2000	Imports 2001	Exports 1999	Exports 2000	Exports 2001	Balances 1999	Balances 2000	Balances 2001
1	2	3	4	5	6	7	8	9	10	11
01	Live animals	625	874	955	813	974	856	188	100	−98
02	Meat and edible meat offal	2 609	2 993	3 550	3 743	3 943	3 829	1 133	949	279
04	Dairy produce; eggs; natural honey	1 045	1 141	1 317	4 244	5 086	5 063	3 199	3 945	3 746
ex.05	Other products of animal origin	781	872	831	344	409	347	−437	−462	−484
06	Live plants and floricultural products	1 016	1 216	1 258	1 187	1 408	1 505	171	192	247
07	Edible vegetables, plants, roots and tubers	2 483	2 706	2 883	1 212	1 305	1 459	−1 271	−1 400	−1 423
08	Edible fruit and nuts; peel of citrus fruit or melons	7 848	8 104	8 750	1 375	1 681	1 923	−6 473	−6 423	−6 826
09	Coffee, tea and spices	5 439	5 395	4 288	763	814	841	−4 676	−4 580	−3 447
10	Cereals	1 472	1 673	1 921	2 308	3 039	2 278	836	1 366	356
11	Products of the milling industry; malt; starches	82	76	77	1 398	1 598	1 742	1 316	1 522	1 664
12	Oilseeds and oleaginous fruits	5 096	5 513	6 266	1 035	943	864	−4 061	−4 570	−5 402

Table 4.8 (continued)
EU(15)
(Mio ECU-EUR)

Codes CN	Products	Imports 1999	Imports 2000	Imports 2001	Exports 1999	Exports 2000	Exports 2001	Balances 1999	Balances 2000	Balances 2001
1	2	3	4	5	6	7	8	9	10	11
13	Lac; gums, resins, other vegetable saps and extracts	394	468	465	559	577	597	166	109	132
14	Vegetable plaiting materials, other products of vegetable origin	117	135	152	15	18	16	−102	−117	−136
15	Animal or vegetable fats and oils	2636	2362	2376	2620	2704	2469	−16	342	92
ex.16	Meat preparations	579	671	744	484	572	520	−95	−99	−224
17	Sugars and sugar confectionery	1408	1401	1560	1920	2379	2622	512	978	1062
18	Cocoa and cocoa preparations	2225	1887	2233	1395	1627	1825	−830	−261	−408
ex.19	Preparations of cereals, flour or starch	478	558	608	2829	3242	3700	2351	2683	3092
20	Preparations of vegetables, fruit or nuts	3132	3379	3180	1833	2108	2276	−1299	−1271	−904
21	Miscellaneous edible preparations	978	1159	1242	2858	3183	3549	1880	2024	2307

22	Beverages, spirits and vinegar	2 597	3 118	3 714	10 543	12 010	12 678	7 946	8 892	8 964
ex.23	Residues and waste from the food industries	3 992	5 024	5 781	1 526	1 754	1 791	-2 466	-3 271	-3 990
24	Tobacco and manufactured tobacco substitutes	2 420	2 577	2 572	2 627	2 716	2 641	208	139	69
01–24	TOTAL agricultural products – Chapters 01 to 24	49 453	53 304	56 721	47 632	54 091	55 391	-1 821	787	-1 330
Others	Other agricultural products included in the Uruguay Round	4 247	5 401	5 419	3 640	4 377	4 758	-607	-1 024	-661
TOTAL	TOTAL – AGRICULTURAL PRODUCTS	53 701	58 705	62 140	51 272	58 468	60 149	-2 428	-237	-1 991
01–99	TOTAL – ALL PRODUCTS	779 825	1 033 436	1 028 014	760 192	942 044	985 331	-19 633	-91 391	-42 683

Sources: European Commission: Eurostat and DG Agriculture.

Table 4.9 EU(15) trade in agricultural products, according to principal supplier countries, 1999–2001 (€m)

No.	Main supplier countries (based on 2001)	Imports 1999	Imports 2000	Imports 2001	Corresponding exports 1999	Corresponding exports 2000	Corresponding exports 2001	Trade balance 1999	Trade balance 2000	Trade balance 2001
1	2	3	4	5	6	7	8	9	10	11
1	United States	7 385	8 399	8 032	8 996	10 493	10 756	1 611	2 094	2 724
2	Brazil	5 529	6 730	7 993	542	659	605	−4 987	−6 071	−7 389
3	Argentina	3 315	3 560	3 501	226	242	179	−3 089	−3 318	−3 322
4	Turkey	1 996	1 921	2 207	806	1 015	757	−1 190	−906	−1 451
5	Australia	1 610	1 953	2 170	873	885	963	−737	−1 068	−1 208
6	New Zealand	1 677	1 805	2 035	116	128	126	−1 561	−1 677	−1 909
7	China	1 612	1 990	1 997	751	733	591	−861	−1 257	−1 406
8	South Africa	1 233	1 325	1 622	414	367	355	−819	−958	−1 267
9	Switzerland	1 351	1 405	1 507	3 358	3 488	3 724	2 007	2 083	2 217
10	Poland	1 082	1 235	1 475	1 617	1 899	2 049	535	664	574
11	Ivory Coast	1 484	1 305	1 405	201	181	221	−1 283	−1 124	−1 184
12	Hungary	1 101	1 191	1 326	482	607	706	−619	−583	−620
13	Thailand	1 096	1 240	1 286	325	444	414	−771	−796	−871
14	Canada	1 041	1 217	1 200	1 245	1 530	1 587	203	313	386
15	India	1 082	1 272	1 178	271	152	179	−811	−1 120	−1 000
16	Indonesia	1 303	1 423	1 151	252	365	304	−1 051	−1 059	−847
17	Chile	796	815	999	113	118	110	−683	−697	−888
18	Colombia	1 079	1 050	952	85	133	146	−994	−917	−806
19	Israel	785	893	896	515	583	635	−270	−310	−260
20	Malaysia	800	745	869	238	317	341	−562	−428	−528

21	Costa Rica	796	859	854	36	50	54	−760	−810	−800
22	Kenya	689	718	711	46	50	44	−644	−668	−667
23	Morocco	696	639	673	461	666	534	−234	27	−140
24	Ecuador	555	577	645	21	33	34	−534	−545	−611
25	Ukraine	215	332	553	190	263	281	−24	−69	−272
	Total of 25 countries (A)	32922	36201	39205	958	1081	1206	578	588	660
	Total of third countries (B)| 53701	58705	62140	51272	58468	60149	−2428	−237	−1991
	% A/B	61.3	61.7	63.1						

Source: European Commission: Eurostat and DG Agriculture.

Table 4.10 EU(15) trade in agricultural products, according to principal customer countries, 1999–2001 (€m)

No.	Main client countries (based on 2001)	Exports 1999	Exports 2000	Exports 2001	Corresponding imports 1999	Corresponding imports 2000	Corresponding imports 2001	Trade balance 1999	Trade balance 2000	Trade balance 2001
1	2	3	4	5	6	7	8	9	10	11
1	United States	8 996	10 493	10 756	7 385	8 399	8 032	1 611	2 094	2 724
2	Japan	3 689	4 205	4 262	128	166	173	3 561	4 039	4 088
3	Switzerland	3 358	3 488	3 724	1 351	1 405	1 507	2 007	2 083	2 217
4	Russia	2 848	2 725	3 346	256	447	465	2 592	2 278	2 881
5	Poland	1 617	1 899	2 049	1 082	1 235	1 475	535	664	574
6	Canada	1 245	1 530	1 587	1 041	1 217	1 200	203	313	386
7	Saudi Arabia	1 504	1 779	1 479	12	9	9	1 492	1 770	1 470
8	Norway	1 238	1 325	1 429	284	307	318	953	1 018	1 112
9	Hong Kong	1 062	1 347	1 377	62	72	57	1 000	1 274	1 320
10	Czech Republic	958	1 081	1 206	380	493	547	578	588	660
11	Algeria	981	1 171	1 196	22	24	20	959	1 147	1 176
12	Australia	873	885	963	1 610	1 953	2 170	−737	−1 068	−1 208
13	South Korea	767	937	929	40	54	40	727	882	889
14	United Arab Emirates	744	812	782	90	132	144	654	680	638
15	Turkey	806	1 015	757	1 996	1 921	2 207	−1 190	−906	−1 451
16	Taiwan	655	766	739	50	54	62	606	712	677
17	Hungary	482	607	706	1 101	1 191	1 326	−619	−583	−620
18	Mexico	442	640	694	355	438	454	87	203	240
19	Israel	515	583	635	785	893	896	−270	−310	−260
20	Singapore	556	692	614	74	79	68	483	613	545

21	Brazil	542	659	605	5 529	6 730	7 993	−4 987	−6 071	−7 389
22	China	751	733	591	1 612	1 990	1 997	−861	−1 257	−1 406
23	Nigeria	272	403	579	222	154	246	49	250	333
24	Libya	393	448	577	3	9	10	390	438	566
25	Morocco	461	666	534	696	639	673	−234	27	−140
	Total of 25 countries (A)	35 756	40 888	42 113	26 165	30 009	32 090	9 591	10 879	10 023
	Total of third countries (B)	51 272	58 468	60 149	53 701	58 705	62 140	−2 428	−237	−1 991
	% A/B	69.74	69.93	70.01						

Source: European Commission: Eurostat and DG Agriculture.

importer to a net exporter of a number of individual farm products. The foreign countries that are hardest hit by the CAP are important food producers and exporters of goods that compete with the products covered by the CAP 'market organisation'. They include the US, Australia, New Zealand, Brazil and Argentina.[29] As such, the CAP hinders unimpeded international division of labour and specialisation. The CAP adversely affects the countries that export farm goods, while those that are food importers benefit from the EU-subsidised exports of farm goods. This is the main reason why an international and united front of developing countries against the CAP has never been established.

Prior to the Uruguay Round the EU and other countries could continue with their policy in the field of agriculture as they chose to suit their own domestic interests. The principal achievement of the World Trade Organisation (WTO) during the Uruguay Round was to include agriculture within the scope of its coverage. However, major constraints on the CAP were not really introduced. None the less, the Uruguay Round set up a certain framework for the handling of trade in agricultural commodities. Countries know what they are allowed and not allowed to do in four areas:

- *Market access*: WTO member countries should establish a minimum market access for imports corresponding to 5 per cent of domestic consumption.
- *Tariffication*: Various domestic tariff and non-tariff protection measures in agricultural trade should be converted into tariffs and reduced by at least 15 per cent (for sensitive commodities), but the unweighted average of these reductions should be 36 per cent. The intention was to negotiate a reduction of these tariffs in future rounds of WTO negotiations. During the 1986–88 base period for tariffication, world prices for agricultural commodities were the lowest in decades. Hence the new tariffs provided a very high level of tariff protection.
- *Domestic support to agriculture*: This needs to be reduced by 17 per cent.[30]
- *Export competition (subsidies)*: This should be reduced by 36 per cent.[31]

All this was a considerable achievement for the Uruguay Round, even though the immediate quantitative impact on trade in agricultural goods was at best limited. The reason is that the new framework for trade was tailored very generously (Tangermann, 1999, p. 1157). The Uruguay Round also introduced a 'peace clause' which sheltered the EU and US agricultural regimes (subsidies) from the WTO legal challenge until the end of 2003. It remains to be seen whether these regimes will be legally challenged in the future.[32]

6. Reforms

After the setting up of the CAP market organisation and the display of its trade-diverting effects, together with its large budgetary expenditure, it became obvious that the CAP had to be reformed. The first reform was proposed by the commissioner, Sicco Mansholt, in 1968. The Mansholt Plan encompassed a set of proposals that should have changed the shape of the CAP by 1980. The plan suggested an increase in the size of holdings, their specialisation and modernisation, the withdrawal of 5 million hectares of land from farming for afforestation and recreational purposes, as well as a reduction in the number of those employed in farming in the EU(6) from 10 million in 1968 to 5 million in 1980. This would be achieved by an early retirement system for older farmers and the retraining of others.

There were various reasons why the Mansholt Plan was not accepted, including: a 'mechanical' approach to the agricultural sector; there were no annual rates at which the change had to take place; it was too radical and hence politically dangerous to implement; and it did not consider what might take place after 1980. This plan was much more radical than its successors, which were more modest in their aims, as the European Commission 'learned the lesson' from the Council's rejection of the proposals for an extensive overhaul. None the less, the Mansholt Plan was an early taste of how the CAP might be changed.

In spite of the rejection of the Mansholt Plan, the European Commission continued with its aspirations to reform the CAP. These attempts, although on a less ambitious scale, were embodied in the various papers from 1973 to 1985, which were often much more analytical than original regarding the reform. The ideas about reforms coincided with a period of big change in the international market (two oil crises). A restructuring of the economy featured high on the agenda, while a substantial reform of the CAP was left for another time. In addition, once established, the CAP has demonstrated its strong resilience to profound change.

There was, however, a good opportunity to alter the CAP after the first EU enlargement in 1973 when Britain, Denmark and Ireland joined the group. As a large importer of food, Britain would be a net contributor to the EU budget. Therefore, the expectation was that this would prompt Britain to favour a reduction in the CAP price support. In addition, the enlargement made the EU an important player in the world market for agricultural goods. However, the CAP remained basically unaltered. As a result, self-sufficiency in most of the goods covered increased, and EU farm expenditure doubled between 1975 and 1985.

Throughout the 1980s, the CAP was in continuous crisis. This was not only because of the growing surpluses in all major farm products, but also because of a rapid increase in expenditure. Being aware of the problem, the EU implemented various measures during that decade but these had only a very limited impact on the alleviation of the major CAP problems of costs and surpluses. The measures included *co-responsibility levies*. These levies on the production of sugar had existed since the start of the CAP. Their goal was to make producers of sugar bear a part of the CAP expenditure on this commodity, as well as to reduce production. In practice, the burden of the levy was passed on to the consumers. *Guaranteed thresholds* on cereals reduced support prices for the year to come if production surpassed the agreed level. However, the pre-set production quotas were set at relatively high levels so their actual impact was quite limited. The experience with *marketing quotas* for milk was similar. *Product diversification*, such as conversion of production from milk to beef, also had limited results, as did the *subsidies to domestic consumption*, with the addition of fraud in the distribution of funds.

The first real reform of the CAP since its inception took place in 1992 with the MacSharry Plan (after the commissioner, Raymond MacSharry). The amendments to the CAP were not as profound as many economists would have liked. In addition, its coverage of farm products was limited. The reform was not directly linked to the Single Market Programme, but rather to internal financial strain and to external events (the inclusion of agriculture in the Uruguay Round). The main features of the MacSharry reform include reduction in prices for cereals and beef in order to bring them closer to the levels that prevailed on the world market, as well as the use of compensatory payments, subject to the reduction in the number of livestock and the area under cultivation in the 1993–96 period. The goal was to shift the CAP from the support and control of prices on the internal market to direct payments to farmers as a compensation for lower prices. The specific points of MacSharry's reform include:

- Intervention prices for most of the products to be reduced by 33 per cent. Farmers to receive compensatory payments if they set 15 per cent of the (productive) cereal land aside. Smaller farmers to receive compensation without conditions.[33] This element decouples output levels from compensations. If farmers set aside[34] 15 per cent of their land, this would not be translated directly into an identical drop in output, but rather to a smaller one. This is because the farmers would

not set aside their most productive land.[35] Compensation would be paid from the EU budget. However, this type of common financing would be phased out and passed on to the national governments and budgets over a period of ten years. The national fiscal authorities would be entitled to continue making such handouts, but these must follow the EU competition rules.
- Intervention prices for beef and veal to be reduced by 15 per cent. The major fall in the prices for beef and veal would come from a fall in feed prices.
- Elimination of price support for oilseeds and protein crops.
- Intervention prices for butter to be reduced by 15 per cent.
- Few changes in the systems for the production of pigs, poultry, wine and sugar.
- Compensation for the early retirement of farmers over 55 years old.
- A farm environmental package was expected to aid chemical-free production and the use of land for the protection of nature, afforestation and leisure.

The MacSharry reform was supposed to introduce at least two kinds of gain to the EU. First, a reduction in prices would diminish incentives to overproduce and, second, a fall in prices would eliminate the part of the tax that is paid by consumers. The problem with this reform was that it benefits farmers that have below-average yields, while it offered a disincentive to those who are farming efficiently. In fact, the reform 'penalised' large and efficient farmers.

The reform was presented by the EU as an exclusively 'internal' matter. It was, however, a big concession to the Uruguay Round partners. Following a long stalemate in negotiations, the MacSharry reform was enough to get the Uruguay Round re-started. Some of the negotiating partners, such as Japan, thought the reform went too far, while others, such as the Cairns Group, considered that it offered little. In short, the farm deal of the Uruguay Round required a conversion of NTBs affecting agricultural products into tariff equivalents (tariffication) and their reduction by 36 per cent over six years; tariffs should be prohibited from increases in the future; new NTBs should not be introduced in the future; domestic subsidies should be lowered by 20 per cent; and direct export subsidies should be reduced by 36 per cent during the 1995–2000 period. *If* prices fall and *if* the domestic EU production drops and *if*, at the same time, domestic demand increases, then the reform might bring some gains to the foreign exporters.

Agenda 2000 was to contribute to the reform of the EU and to prepare it for its eastern enlargement. It also referred to the European model of agriculture for the 21st century. The definition (or a wish list) has the following three dimensions:

- *Economic*: Agriculture should be competitive and gradually able to face world competition without excessive subsidies. Market balance needs to be improved.
- *Social*: The agricultural community should have a stable income and a reasonable standard of living. This social dimension needs to offer a diversification of income sources for farm households.
- *Environment*: Production should be environmentally friendly. Output should be of high quality, safe and of the kind the consumers want.

In addition, the future European model of farming should include the following elements:

- Agricultural production should not be oriented only towards the quantity of output. It should also maintain the rich European tradition and countryside (including rural communities).
- Policy making in agriculture should be simplified and more understandable. The distinction between what the EU does and what member countries do needs to be made clear.
- Expenditure for the CAP ought to be in line with what is justified by the services it provides and what society at large expects from the agricultural sector. Budgetary constraints have to be taken into consideration when setting a certain policy.

Following the MacSharry reform, along the lines of *Agenda 2000*, as well as the Uruguay Round commitments, the European Council in Berlin (1999)[36] brought the next real reform of the CAP. To put the Council's conclusions regarding the CAP and enlargement in simple terms, the reform had two prongs: first, the total annual EU expenditure for the CAP in the financial perspective for the seven-year period 2000–06 was limited to about €42 billion; second, the intervention price for cereals was to be reduced by 15 per cent.[37] The motivation and objective of these decisions was not only to limit the domestic EU farm output, but also and perhaps more importantly, to send an early and clear signal to the accession countries to curb their hope that the EU would finance a potential expansion of their agricultural production.

A further reform of the CAP represents one of the most serious challenges for the EU. It would have consequences for the EU internal operation, for external economic relations and for enlargement. A reform plan, proposed in mid-2002, would break the link between intervention and production. Farm subsidies would be linked to rural conservation. In addition, export subsidies would be significantly reduced. However, this attempt to reform the CAP was deferred by France (with Germany's support) until 2006 when the new financial perspective is to be finalised. In addition, Britain, Germany, the Netherlands and Sweden are particularly concerned about future farm spending. These countries would like to see a certain reform of the CAP before the EU offers potentially generous subsidies to farmers in the accession countries. This is important as the EU(15) has about 7 million farmers. The eastern enlargement in 2004 added to this number a further 3.8 million. The lobbying and voting power of farmers in the enlarged EU would increase in theory, but in practice it may be difficult to organise them because of their different interests and priorities. In any case, enlargement without a reform of the CAP could not be affordable for the EU(15).

France and Germany were the moving force behind the European Council in Brussels (24–25 October 2002). The deal brokered at this Council established the 'adjustment' (limit) of future CAP payments in the light of the forthcoming enlargement. From 2006 total CAP subsidies would have a ceiling. This would keep payments static at current levels during the 2007–13 period with the possibility of a modest inflation-proof amount of 1 per cent per year. In real terms, these payments would almost certainly be on a steady decrease. Subsidies to farmers in new member countries would be limited to only 25 per cent of those paid to farmers in the EU(15) in 2004. However, the payments to farmers would be gradually brought into parity in 2013. EU(15) farmers would lose from this deal over the coming decade. Since the influential French lobby would be hard hit, France has made a significant enlargement-related concession. Farmers in the new member countries should have no illusions about hefty subsidies from Brussels, but most others would gain: EU consumers and potential exporters to the EU.

The EU has always been and will continue to be a tough negotiator in the farm-trade negotiations. However, in the wake of the September 2003 Cancun (Mexico) ministerial meeting of the Doha Round of negotiations, the EU agreed in June 2003 on a radical, perhaps the most comprehensive and long-term reform of its €45 billion CAP since its introduction. The main aspects of this reform include:

- de-linking (decoupling) between subsidies and production. EU farmers would receive a single subsidy independent of the quantity of food they produce. This should encourage efficiency in farm production, focus output on quality, rather than mere quantity (response to intervention) and reduce intensive farming that damages

the environment. However, this may push farmers towards welfare and/or into becoming state employees;
- the payment would be linked to the respect of environment, food safety, as well as animal and plant health;
- a 'modulation', that is, reduction in direct payments for bigger farms;
- a financial discipline to warrant that the agricultural budget is fixed (not overshot) until 2013; and
- intervention price for butter would be reduced by 25 per cent over four years.

These alterations and concessions were insufficient to give the Doha Round ministerial meeting an incentive to continue negotiations. However, many, many others were not interested in the success of the Cancun meeting. None the less, these changes in the CAP will have a long-term impact on the agricultural sector in the enlarged EU(25). It remains to be seen whether the Cancun débâcle will be used as a pretext to reverse or slow down the CAP reforms. In addition, if certain WTO members use the expiry of the peace clause in 2004 to start challenging the US and EU farm subsidies, the potentially dozens of WTO panels could make things more difficult than they already are and the entire concept of the WTO may be in great peril.

7. Common Fisheries Policy

Fishing was not a significant economic activity in the original six EU member states. Article 32 of the Treaty of Rome includes fish in the definition of agricultural products, and this is the only primary legal source for this policy in the EU. The fisheries industry is distinct, not only because of changes in the volume of the catch, but also because the catch is heterogeneous and perishable. It is also linked with regional issues, as those employed in this industry are in areas on the periphery of the EU.

The Second World War interrupted many fishing activities. The consequence was the flourishing of marine fauna, giving the impression that the seas and oceans were inexhaustible. Fishing fleets were expanding, which led to overfishing and a failure to replenish certain species of fish. By the 1960s, the growth rate of the catch was starting to slow down, and it was time for a reappraisal of the fisheries. Hence, the EU began to develop its Common Fisheries Policy in the mid-1960s. France was the principal proponent of this policy as its fisheries industry was highly protected. It wanted to preserve certain EU safeguards for domestic fishermen.

The approaching 1973 enlargement of the EU with Britain, Denmark and Ireland[38] would double the Union's catch of fish. This was a hot topic and speeded up the debate about the fisheries policy. The European Council adopted the European Commission's proposal in 1970 to introduce the Common Fisheries Policy. Although the policy was created, it did not become a reality until more than a decade later in 1983. The thrust of the policy was the rule of equal access to EU waters by the Union's fishermen and a free internal market for fish. This was very hard for Norway to accept. The European Commission delivered a new set of proposals for the revision of the policy in the mid-1970s. These included the protection of halieutic resources by setting the quotas for the total allowable catches, which would not be defined by commercial, but rather by biological rules, that is, there should always be a minimum stock of fish in the sea to maintain reproduction levels.

In the meantime, the UN Convention on the Law of the Sea (1982) gave international legitimacy to an exclusive economic zone of 200 miles around coastal countries. As a result, fish stocks fell under the authority of the coastal countries, which are in charge of managing the sea's resources. If this is done in a rational way, it may provide a permanent and significant contribution to the supply of food.[39]

After lengthy negotiations, in particular with Denmark, the Common Fisheries Policy took off in 1983. It covers wider issues than just who fishes, where and how much. The policy is based on the following principles:

- *Non-discriminatory access* to the fishing waters for EU fishermen. However, there is a 12-mile exclusive zone for fishermen from the coastal countries, while the balance up to 200 miles is open to EU fishermen.
- *Conservation* of fish resources because fishing stocks are dwindling. Based on scientific advice on the state of stocks the total allowable catches are calculated for various species at the end of each year. Then the total allowable catches are divided up among the EU countries in the form of quotas according to historic fishing patterns and the needs of each fishery-dependent area.
- Within the EU *market organisation* and support, the European Commission sets the guide price and when the price falls below the predetermined withdrawal price, supplies may be withdrawn from the market.
- *Modernisation* of the fisheries industry includes not only the replacing of existing boats and reducing overcapacity, but also assistance to fish farming and vocational training in the areas where fishermen lose jobs.

- In its *relations with the outside world*, the EU intends to institute international bilateral and multilateral agreements about fishing and common conservation measures in the deep seas.

Although the policy has been implemented and Spain and Portugal[40] have made a smooth entry into the system, the policy has not yet had a deep impact on the industry compared with the one the CAP had on farming. Overfishing is still a problem.[41] For the policy to operate properly, there needs to be a 'policing' of the arrangements. Surveillance standards vary markedly from one country to another. Hence, the EU established its own Fisheries Inspectorate, which is supposed to check the enforcement agencies of the member countries.

The EU has had a new fisheries policy since 2003. It was introduced because of persistent overfishing, and the stocks of several species, such as cod, are on the verge of collapse. The changes introduced by the new policy include:

- longer-term conservation measures instead of annual ones;
- reducing a chronic overcapacity of the fishing fleet and matching it with the fishing possibilities. Phasing out aid to fishermen to replace or modernise fishing vessels, while keeping aid to improve security and working conditions on vessels;
- application of rules and control should be more effective. The same holds for sanctions for rule violators; and
- involvement of stakeholders, in particular fishermen, in the policy making. Fishermen and scientists need to share their expertise and to take a greater part in policy management.

These are relatively new changes, which ought to prove themselves in practice and over time as, for example, aid for the improvement of security and working conditions on vessels may free private funds from these activities for the modernisation of vessels.

8. Conclusion

Let us recall here again that farming, particularly in continental Europe, is a part of the social structure, a deeply rooted way of life in the region that has survived for several thousands of years. There is a relatively high degree of national self-sufficiency in the production of food, as well as highly protectionist and interventionist national institutions and policies. Elsewhere in the world, the pattern of certain types of farming in relatively new countries and nations such as the US, Canada, Argentina or Australia is different. Large-scale farming was started there by European immigrants just a few centuries ago. It is basically linked with the commercial use of a relatively unlimited quantity of land. In Europe, agriculture has a multifunctional character. This commercial activity is most intimately and deeply connected to national social structure, traditions, mentality, lifestyle, countryside and biodiversity. To apply free trade principles in Europe without any conditions would be disastrous for the deeply rooted European social and biological scene.[42] No, or very little, production would be profitable in the EU at 'world market prices'.[43] European society as it has been known for thousands of years could perish. Europe could be open to intimidation. Hence, the strong support of many European countries for national farming interests in spite of certain financial costs.

As agriculture is historically a very special economic and social activity in Europe, it may be unfair to assess the accomplishments and effects of this sector by employing free trade criteria. The CAP market organisation replaced the various national farm-support systems that existed prior to the establishment of the EU. In spite of the controversies created by the CAP, the objectives of farm policy in the EU, as given in Article 33 of the Treaty of Rome, were largely met. The possible exception may be the protection of the income of small farmers mainly located in the south of the EU. The implementation of the CAP brought with it several problems. These include not only highly concentrated and excessively large expenditure from the EU budget, disputes in trade, 'discrimination' between northern and southern products and large and small farmers, but also surpluses in many agricultural goods. These excess supplies are not cyclical, but rather structural.

Because of all these difficulties, the EU has tried to reform the CAP on many occasions. The problem was that those 'reforms' were merely attempts to partially adjust a CAP which is full of arbitrary elements based on political compromises. There has never been any intention to dismantle the CAP.[44] That would be politically too explosive. Hence, the past reforms were directed more to the partial alteration of the form, rather than the substance, of the CAP.

The real reform of the CAP since its inception was started by MacSharry (1992), but it still observed the historical spirit of the CAP.[45] Although it was not presented officially in such a way, it was carried out under external pressure (Uruguay Round). The reform that profoundly altered the spirit of the CAP started in 2003. The desire and motive was to adjust the CAP before the eastern enlargement of the EU and as a result of the Doha Round negotiations. Subsidies were decoupled from farmers' production.

264   *The economics of European integration*

Direct compensation payments were introduced irrespective of the quantity of output. In the (distant) future, if there is a new WTO agreement, the CAP may be more and more subject to WTO rules, including those on competition and subsidies.[46]

Notes

1. More than a quarter of the farm managers and holders have another gainful activity (Eurostat 2003. 'Structure of agricultural holdings in the EU', Statistics in Focus, Theme 5-16/2003).
2. Meddling with agriculture was well known to the Sumerian civilisation (southern Iraq). In order to increase yields the Sumerians irrigated heavily. However, irrigation in a dry and hot climate slowly but surely increased a build-up of salt in the soil. Rising salinity caused the Sumerians to replace wheat by barley which can grow more easily in such salty conditions. Later on, even barley could not tolerate the rising quantity of salt. Hence, the Sumerian civilisation disappeared around 1800 BC.
3. The entire territory of Finland is located above the line at which Sweden found that farming was problematic. The frontier of Finland with Russia is 1200 km long. It is hardly policeable. Therefore, one way of keeping the frontier regions populated is to offer subsidies to the agricultural sector.
4. An elasticity of substitution between certain food items may be pronounced. Examples include margarine and butter or beef and veal. As income increases, the diet pattern may change in favour of higher-quality and more-expensive consumption items.
5. Mad cow disease or BSE (bovine spongiform encephalopathy).
6. At the time of the introduction of the CAP, prices for food were relatively high. In addition, consumers had vivid memories about the scarcity of food during the Second World War. Hence, there were no protests when the CAP was introduced.
7. This was the case before the original CAP started to be reformed.
8. The CAP market organisation covers 22 products (see Table 4.6).
9. *Financial Times*, 15 and 16 October 2003.
10. In dealing with the same basic price, but for different commodities, the EU uses different terms. This introduces confusion. For example, the target price for beef and veal is called the *guide price*, while for tobacco, it is the *norm price*. Pork, poultry and eggs are considered to be processed cereals. Producers in foreign countries have access to cereals cheaper than those available in the EU. During the determination of the *sluice-gate price* (the threshold price) the EU takes into account the low prices for cereals available from foreign exporters. The *basic price* for pork is tantamount to the target price. The function of the threshold price is played by the *preference price* for fruits and vegetables.
11. As the DM was revaluing, the MCAs were protecting the income of German farmers.
12. *The Economist*, 18 February 1984, p. 56.
13. One should not forget that there are national subsidies of various kinds to the farm sector that may roughly equal those given by the EU. National subsidies are particularly generous in the field of social security benefits.
14. The US uses, among other policy instruments, the Export Enhancement Program and voluntary export restraint arrangements to support domestic production. The research service of the US Department of Agriculture has one of the largest collection of economists in the world. However, the highest-paid agricultural economists are not found in those countries with a vibrant farm sector, but rather in Brussels or Tokyo, where there is a dynamic 'farm-subsidy industry' (*The Economist*, 'A survey of agriculture', 12 December 1992, p. 9).

15. The real reason for this policy change was to do with politics. President George W. Bush is prodigal in farm expenditure because of the forthcoming elections. The 2002 Farm Bill would help him to win votes in the 2004 elections in the prairie belt, just as tariffs on the imports of steel may help him to win votes in Ohio, Pennsylvania and West Virginia (*The Economist*, 11 May 2002, p. 16).
16. About a quarter of the largest farm producers in the EU receive up to three-quarters of all CAP-induced support. The high level of support has tended to be capitalised in the value of land and it has stimulated capital- rather than labour-intensive farm production (Sarris, 1994, p. 115).
17. The missing data from Table 4.7 for cheese in Germany, Greece, Italy and Britain would significantly change the result and show a very high degree of EU self-sufficiency in cheeses in 1999/2000. For example, the self-sufficiency in cheese in Germany was 1686 per cent and in Italy 1068 per cent in 2000/2001.
18. *Bulletin Quotidien Europe*, 25 June 2003, p. 3.
19. *Bulletin Quotidien Europe*, 14 February 2001, p. 3.
20. The impact of the CAP on the environment is considered in chapter on environment policy.
21. More than a quarter of the farm managers and holders have another gainful activity (Eurostat [2003]. 'Structure of agricultural holdings in the EU', Statistics in Focus, Theme 5-16/2003).
22. Eurostat (2003). 'Structure of agricultural holdings in the EU', Statistics in Focus, Theme 5-16/2003.
23. Because of the bias of the CAP towards 'northern' farm products, about 80 per cent of CAP outlays goes to about 20 per cent of farmers (*European Economy*, 1994b, p. 27). One undesirable outcome of the CAP is that the largest 25 per cent of farms take almost 70 per cent of the subsidies (*Financial Times*, 17 April 2001, p. 14).
24. *Financial Times*, 'The popular verdict on GM crops,' 25 September 2003.
25. A series of articles in the *Lancet* point to the fact that there will be serious concern about BSE for quite some time in the future.
26. *Financial Times*, 30 September 2003.
27. Simon Jenkins, 'This wretched cult of blood and money', *The Times*, 23 May 2001 and Simon Jenkins, 'You must vaccinate or be damned, Mr Gill', *The Times*, 1 August 2001.
28. See also the chapter on EU trade policy (Chapter 7).
29. Most of the lightly protected countries that export farm products met in Australia in 1986. The circle was called the Cairns Group, after the town where the meeting took place. The purpose of the group is to keep farm trade high on the agenda of the Uruguay and, later, the Doha Round of trade negotiations. In spite of the relative smallness of these countries, their combined farm output is the largest in the world.
30. The MacSharry Reform reduced this support in the EU.
31. The EU continues to have a problem here. This is the constraint that may provoke internal reforms in the CAP.
32. Cotton, rice, dairy products and sugar are high on the list of potential targets.
33. Large farmers in Britain opposed such discrimination.
34. 'Set aside' is a euphemism for paying farmers not to grow crops. This policy has many drawbacks as it is expensive to administer, and also requires constant checking by inspectors and satellites. Whenever there is a disbursement of funds for similar purposes, the system is prone to abuse. For example, a random check of Italian inspectors of farms in Sardinia in 1995 uncovered various irregularities. In one case, a farmer collected the cheque and sold his land to five different buyers. He was later shot dead by the police in a shooting incident.
35. Statistically, the average output per unit of cultivated land may increase.
36. European Council, Berlin 1999, Presidency Conclusions, §§19–24.
37. This reduction took place in two equal steps of 7.5 per cent in the marketing years 2000/01 and 2001/02.
38. Norway was also negotiating EU entry, but later on the voters rejected the deal because of the fisheries policy.

39. The developing countries are the major beneficiaries of the new system.
40. The entry of the two countries doubled the EU fleet.
41. The EU fishing fleet had 96 000 vessels in 2000. Greece had the largest fleet (19 700), followed by Portugal (18 800), Italy (17 700) and Spain (16 700). Norway and Iceland had fleets of 13 000 and 2000, respectively. The average age of the fleets was 21 years. The oldest was that of Spain (27 years).
42. According to estimates by the European Commission, if the EU opened its agricultural sector to free trade, 80 per cent of EU food companies would disappear, while most of the landscape would revert to the wild (*Bulletin Quotidien Europe*, 9 September 2003, p. 3).
43. The exceptions are perhaps highly specialised, sophisticated, expensive and sought-after gourmand foods that are under constant attack from imitators.
44. It took over 40 years to build the CAP.
45. Although imperfect, relatively recent reforms of the CAP (limited expenditure) made the 'butter mountains' and 'wine lakes' a thing of the past.
46. Perhaps the EU and other rich countries in Europe and Japan may be allowed to keep certain national agricultural organisations and a certain (minimum or maximum) level of output, provided that they do not use their economic might to dump any surpluses on the markets of other countries.

> Do you not know that in a race all the runners run,
> but only one gets the prize?
> Run in such a way as to get the prize.
> 1 Corinthians 9:24

5 Competition Policy

1. Introduction

The classical theory of international economic integration (customs unions) assumed that the static effects of resource reallocation occurred in a timeless framework. If one wants to move this theory towards reality, one must consider dynamic, that is, restructuring, effects. These restructuring effects often have a spatial dimension. In addition it is generally accepted that markets are imperfect. Externalities such as economies of scale and product differentiation (goods or services are very close, but not perfect substitutes for each other) introduce imperfections in competition in the market. When a market has such a structure, regionalism/integration may find its justification. The rationale is that integration extends the market, hence there are potentials for the reduction in the market power of firms. This can have a positive impact on competition, productivity and innovation, it may reduce prices and, hence, increase welfare on average.

The old, static, neo-classical rules of economics require significant modification. Information technology, the rapid pace of innovation, fast-changing technology and uncertainty generally characterise the modern economy. A fast and easy information flow has reduced many of the past barriers to business. In addition, innovative activity has significantly changed the extent and character of the modern economy. The Middle Ages in Europe (5th to 15th centuries) offered only a few important inventions, such as horseshoes, the horse collar (that is, one that did not half-throttle the animal as soon as it started to pull with any significant force), windmills, the fork and underwear. The only constant feature in the modern dynamic economy is an ever-accelerating pace of innovation and change, in particular the improvement and reduction in cost of already existing goods and services.

Instead of considering only trade in commodities, dynamic models analyse resource allocation across time and space. The static effects of integration on the geography of production have their most obvious and profound influence in the period immediately before and following the creation of, for example, a free trade area or a customs union. Gradually, after several years of adjustment in the spatial distribution of production and consumption, the dynamic effects increase in importance and become dominant. These effects push technological constraints away from the origin and provide the group with an additional integration-induced 'growth bonus'.

Demand is constantly changing not only because of variations in tastes and needs of consumers, but also because of their sophistication and fickleness. Production and trade flows do not remain constant over time and space. They evolve and alter over time. Changes in the equilibrium points in the standard partial equilibrium model are presented as instantaneous moves. However, such shifts may not always be possible. Delays in reaction on the part of countries and consumers in a customs union could be caused by their recourse to stocks or to other barriers such as sunk costs. Hence, they do not immediately need to purchase those goods whose price has decreased as a consequence of integration or to alter the geography of production. They may also have some contractual commitments that cannot be abandoned overnight without a penalty. Finally, buyers may not be aware of all the changes: in the past the spread of information was relatively slow and sometimes incomplete, while in the period of mass media, the Internet and other means of communication, consumers may be swamped with information that some of them may not be able to handle, select, analyse and digest (fast).

Until the 19th century, state intervention in the economy was almost negligible; markets remained spatially disconnected in terms of production because of imperfect information and relatively high trade costs. The Internet has eliminated the constraint of the lack of timely information. A time lapse between the implementation of a policy change (integration) and its favourable effects may include an initial period of economic deterioration in certain industries which may be followed by improvements due to the J-curve effect. The Internet permits some industries that were previously constrained by high costs of collecting information, communication and transactions to be reconfigured. Clients may increase their bargaining power. The challenge to firms is how to translate these new opportunities into profits. As more and more firms accept and implement new Internet-based technologies, the Internet will be neutralised as a source of advantage. In this situation the initial core competences and advantages of firms would became even more important.

This chapter considers competition policy, and is structured as follows. Section 2 deals with the different strands of competition policy, including monopoly; other types of market structure, conduct and performance; innovation; specialisation; and returns to scale. Their source, importance and interrelations are related to efficiency in production and have an impact on the spatial and sectoral location of production. In Section 3, competition policy in the EU is presented in terms of deals among firms that restrict competition, abuse of the dominant position on the market and state aids. Finally, Section 4 speculates about the need for and possibility of introducing multilateral rules for competition.

2. Competition, efficiency and location

BACKGROUND

The early literature about the spatial location of firms was obsessed with the geometrical shape of market areas in an idealised landscape or with the ideal production site, given resources and markets. It ignored the crucial issue of market structure. This was like putting the cart before the horse or 'doing things in the wrong order, worrying about the details of a secondary problem before making progress in the main issue' (Krugman, 1992, p. 5).

One of the most important functions of competition is the exchange of information. In theory, free market competition provides everyone with the widest opportunities for business and produces the best sectoral and spatial allocation of resources. By so doing, competition both improves efficiency in the use of factors because of their constant reallocation and, something which is often forgotten, introduces a permanent instability into the system. This conclusion has been accepted by neo-classical economic theory as a truth. It has provided the intellectual backing for competition (antitrust) policy. However, while competition may create lucrative opportunities and gains, it may also be the source of problems and concerns such as risk and uncertainty. The objective of this policy is that markets attain and maintain the flexibility needed to promote initiative, innovation and constant improvement in the allocation of resources. The final intention and goal is, of course, to maintain and raise living standards. Hence, what matters in theory is how to play the competition game, rather than who wins or loses. In practice, however, politicians, members of the public, firms and lobbies are quite concerned about the winners.

Competition policy is a combination of two irreconcilable forces. On the one hand, there is an argument for the (spatial) concentration of business, which rationalises production and enables economies of scale. On the other hand, there is a case for an antitrust policy,[1] which prevents monopolisation, protects individual freedom and rights and, through increased competition, increases welfare. The challenge for governments is to achieve and maintain a dynamic balance between these two tendencies. They need to keep the best parts of each of the two opposing tendencies, profit from the harmonious equilibrium between the two, avoid excessive regulation that interferes with the freedom to contract which may impair competitiveness, and employ competition policy as a tool to increase the standard of living.

Although there is a strong relation between trade and competition policy, they work in different domains. Trade policy enlarges markets and encourages competition by easing market access. It permits countries to gain because they specialise in what they produce comparatively well. Competition policy handles and eliminates distortions of competition such as abuse of market power. This policy is a blend of economic, political and legal judgements. Monopoly as such is not on the whole illegal because technology (excessively high sunk costs) sometimes does not allow for competition. However, the abuse of the monopoly power is normally outlawed. Competition policy aims to prevent this abuse (rules of behaviour and reduction in entry barriers), as well as to punish it if this takes place.

The concept of 'competitiveness' was criticised by Krugman as redundant and dangerous.[2] This criticism is based on the close relation between productivity and competitiveness. In spite of the fact that world trade is larger than ever before in absolute terms, the US total exports of goods and services was 'only' 9.3 per cent of its GDP in 2002. 'The growth rate of living standards essentially equals the growth rate of domestic productivity – not productivity relative to competitors, but simply domestic productivity' (Krugman, 1996c, p. 9). As for the danger in using the term 'competitiveness', former US president Bill Clinton stated that each nation is 'like a big corporation competing in the global marketplace'. This is the same as saying that the US and Japan are competitors in the same way as Coca-Cola competes with Pepsi (Krugman, 1996c, p. 4). Firms are rivals over a limited pool of potential profits. What distinguishes states from firms is that one firm may absorb another, which is not possible in normal circumstances in the case of states. In addition, states may introduce protectionist measures (international disintegration). Such an option is not open to firms. Countries are not firms. They cannot be driven out of all businesses. However, countries can be driven out of some lines of business, which may have permanent effects on trade and the geography of production. States produce goods that compete with each other but, more importantly, states are each other's export markets and suppliers of useful things. David Ricardo taught us in 1817 that international trade is *not* about competition, but rather about mutually beneficial exchange. The purpose of trade is imports, not exports. Imports give a country the opportunity to get what it wants. Exporting is a toll that a country must 'suffer' in order to pay for its imports (Krugman, 1996a, p. 120). Hence, the gain is not in the goods given or sold, but rather in the ones that are received or imported. Ricardo's ideas were as much misunderstood two centuries ago as they are today.

Strong equilibrating forces ensure that a country can sell goods (have a 'competitive' output) in world markets. David Hume pointed out 200 years ago that in the case of the gold standard a country that imports more than it exports experiences a drain of gold and a fall in the money supply. Prices and wages fall, and as a result goods and labour in that country become cheap so that they become attractive to foreign buyers. Thus, the deficit in trade is corrected. In the modern world, with no gold standard, deficits are usually corrected not by the depreciation of prices and wages, but rather through the depreciation of national currencies (Krugman, 1996a, pp. 89–90).

New policy approaches to competitiveness take a pragmatic view. They have three basic elements (Jacquemin and Pench, 1997, pp. 8–12):

- an emphasis on the efficient use and accumulation of factors as determinants of long-term economic performance;
- recognition of the importance of the international dimension of economic performance; and
- an appreciation of the relevance of social cohesion (unemployment benefits, pensions, health insurance, labour market regulations), which provides opportunities for trust, cooperation and stability that are not available in more divided societies.

One ought to be careful about pushing liberal, as well as international competition policies too far and without conditions. The reasons include the fact that non-price competition such as brand-name or product differentiation may protect producers; non-tradable goods and services include a large chunk of local, regional or state GDP; and certain business organisation practices such as vertical agreements may, if unchecked, actually obstruct market access. The US is an example of a country that has perhaps the strongest declared commitment to liberal competition (another matter is how this declared commitment is applied in practice). However, principal industries such as telecommunications, energy and transport were highly regulated. This reveals, explains and proves that free competition may unleash innovation and improvements, but at the same time if unconstrained it may also bring unfavourable effects.[3]

Regional integration widens markets for the participating countries, hence one of its first dynamic effects is in the field of competition. Competition encourages firms to perform profitably in open markets. Thus, the EU has its own rules for market behaviour. These refer to the restriction of competition, abuse of the dominant position and state aids. The Single European Market, completed at the end of 1992, increased the importance and merit of competition policy.

MONOPOLY

In a perfectly competitive market, the marginal revenue (MR) curve of a firm is a straight line (Figure 5.1). No firm can influence the market price. Each firm is a price taker.[4] Hence, the MR curve of every firm equals the market price. In a simple model with linear demand, cost and revenue curves, the MR curve passes through the horizontal axis 0Q (representing the quantity produced) at point E. At this point, MR is zero. To the left of E on the horizontal axis, MR is positive and in moving from 0 to E, total revenue increases. To the right of E on the same axis, MR is negative, and in moving from E to Q, total revenue decreases. At E, total revenue is maximum.

The market structure of a monopolistic industry is at the opposite extreme from perfect competition. Entry into such an industry is costly, risky and time-consuming, although potentially highly profitable in the short and medium terms. Whereas in a state of perfect competition no firm has any power whatsoever over the market price, a monopoly (exclusive) supplier has the power to influence the market price of a good or a service if there are no substitutes. To counter such conduct, governments may choose to intervene and prevent/rectify such non-competitive behaviour. This can be done by regulation of the behaviour of monopolies and/or by liberalisation of imports.[5] A monopolist which wanted to maximise total revenue would never supply a quantity bigger than 0E.

With constant returns to scale, average costs are constant, hence the average cost (AC) curve is horizontal. The consequence of this simplification is that marginal costs (MC) equal AC. This enables the point to be found at which profit is at its maximum if the demand curve is DD. It is maximised at point M, where MR = MC. At that point, a monopolist produces $0Q_m$ and

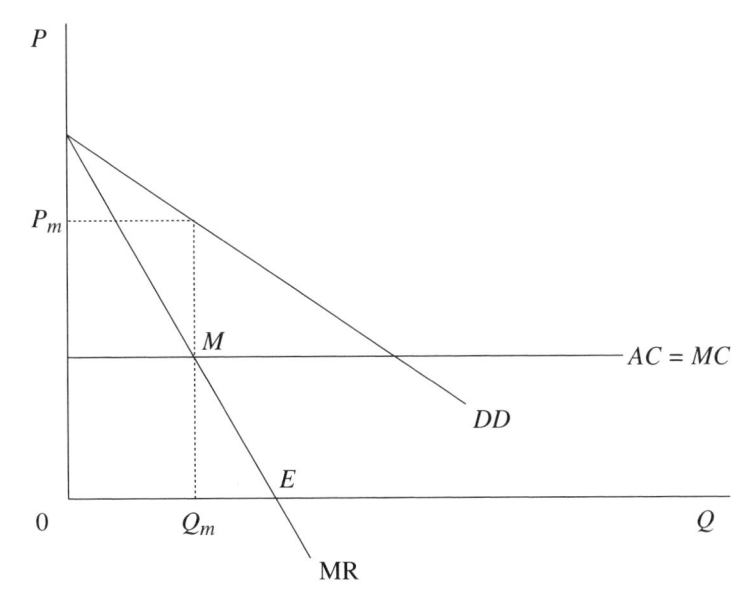

Figure 5.1 Welfare effects of a monopoly

charges price $0P_m$. The quantity produced is smaller and the price charged by the monopoly is higher than in the case of perfect competition.

This is an obvious, although very simple, example of how a monopoly (or a cartel) undermines the welfare of consumers and allocates resources in a suboptimal way from a social standpoint. In addition, if left alone, there is no pressure on the monopoly to do anything about the situation. Such a safe and secure life does not encourage the monopoly to innovate and increase efficiency as would be the case with free competition. A secure life could make a monopoly innovation-shy in the longer term. However, in the short term the opposite may occur. If a firm thinks now that an innovation may bring it a monopoly power in the medium and long terms, such a firm would be tempted to venture into a process that may lead to innovation. If successful, this may bring inertia, less flexibility and reluctance to adjust in the longer term.

Rigidities can be found not only on the part of firms. Labour, in particular labour unions, may pose obstacles and slow down the innovation process. Machines, it can be argued, may destroy jobs. If, however, this were ever true, it may be correct only in the short term. The response of the Luddites in the early 19th century to the introduction of looms and jennies was to destroy them. Technological progress, increased productivity and alternative sources of employment, often requiring a superior skills profile, more than compensate for any supposed short-term social loss. Only those who are reluctant to adjust to the new situation suffer. Although technology has advanced rapidly in recent centuries, unemployment has not risen with it. Increases in productivity, output and job openings have risen together over the long term.

If a monopoly exists, one should not rush to the conclusion that its presence *per se* leads to economic inefficiency. It is possible that in industries with high entry barriers, enormous sunk costs and economies of scale (for example, the aerospace industry), a single efficient producer may sell the good or a service at a lower price than would be charged by many inefficient producers in the same industry. In such cases it may not be a smart move to break up a concentrated industry. The authorities would be better taxing the excessive profits of firms in such industries and/or making sure that they are reinvested. If the market grows sufficiently, then the authorities need to encourage other, potentially efficient and profitable, producers to enter the same kind of business.

Policies intended to increase competitiveness sometimes produce unexpected results. During the 1950s, the US government wanted to break up large and powerful corporations. One such corporation was AT&T. Little attention was paid during the debate to the position of Bell Labs and the fact that it had played the major part in innovation in telecommunications over the preceding century. Deregulation of the industry prohibited the US telephone operating companies from making phones or switching equipment. As a result, US exports grew moderately, while imports exploded (Lipsey, 1992b, p. 295).

Five computer companies accused Microsoft of unfair business practices in the US in 1998. The court found in 2000 that Microsoft, the world's biggest software company, was guilty of antitrust violations and of monopolistic behaviour in the software market. This is another case that has generated a lot of hot air. The judge decreed that Microsoft should be split into two companies: one to develop and produce the operating system (Windows) and the other that would be involved with the application packages (Office, Internet Explorer and so on). The real outcome could be the creation of two monopolies instead of one! At the heart of the debate is the issue of capacity to innovate. There was a risk that Microsoft would limit the ability of third parties to innovate. The problem with splitting the company is that numerous operating systems and applications may emerge. However, the potential for customer confusion that could result may be exaggerated, as there is a strong commercial incentive to maintain compatibility. In addition, Microsoft was charged with exhibiting monopolistic behaviour such as operating exclusion contracts and increasing sales by raising the prices of older versions of software after the launch of a new version.

Microsoft duly appealed against such a judgment and argued that regulators have no right to meddle or determine which features software companies should bundle into their products in order to increase their functionality. This is particularly important in a dynamic and highly innovative industry. While bundling may bring certain gains, it also makes it harder for competitors to offer innovative services. One may immediately ask several questions:

- Is it smart to have (or drive) an innovative firm to spend on legal issues as much as it spends on R&D?
- In the 'new economy' based on and driven by knowledge, a firm that innovates gains a temporary monopoly power. Another firm with a superior product that creates a new temporary and 'fragile' monopoly replaces this firm. Hence, the new economy may have more (fragile) monopolies than the 'old economy'. If such dynamics encourages innovation and improvement, consumers can benefit. Should one encourage such market dynamics or not? When should regulation step in? How?
- Where is the balance between innovation and standardisation (which may choke innovation)?
- Where is the balance between intellectual property rights and wider public interest?
- How does all this affect the long-term interests of the consumers?

There are no sound data for a thorough cost–benefit analysis in such cases. Data are also missing to assess long-term interests of consumers in an industry that is at the frontier of innovation. This requires a very fine judgement and anyone who is confident of providing a clear-cut answer risks ridicule. Solving such issues may not easily fit into predetermined charts and models. Those that handle competition policy should also rely on their finer instincts. In any case, the basic principles and instincts in this area should include a preference for competition over monopoly, pluralism and spread over concentration, as well as new entrants over incumbents.

The appeals court in the US confirmed the earlier ruling that Microsoft was a monopoly, but it rejected the remedy of breaking up the company. A settlement was reached with the Department of Justice in 2001. Microsoft had to: allow PC makers to replace some parts of Windows by alternatives made by other firms; reveal certain codes to ensure that software written by other firms operates smoothly; have its operation monitored by an (enigmatic) three-man committee of experts.[6] As a declared monopoly, Microsoft is vulnerable to legal actions in the future.

The US case against Microsoft was because the company wanted to do away with competitors such as Netscape (do you still remember it?). The European Commission is also investigating Microsoft. The case is linked with the bundling of Media Player in the Windows XP operating system, as well as the smooth/rough link between PCs and servers that run Windows (users have to have a choice regarding which server to install). Microsoft's position is that consumers want products with more features. This brings better and easier interoperability, and also, Microsoft may argue, lower prices. In addition, if Media Player is unbundled from Windows, then this may put an end to such queries as: should one take out printer drivers, graphics, spellchecker, Internet browsers and so on. On the other hand, if Microsoft produces all that is required, where is the place for other firms?

As the European Commission found in 2004 that Microsoft abused its near-monopoly market position, the company faced a fine of €497 million. Some allege that this initial fine took into account Microsoft's global operations.[7] Microsoft's legal battle against this ruling may last about five years. Therefore, certain Microsoft's competitors may not survive to see its conclusion. In the meantime, market situation may change, hence there may be serious doubts and little evidence that the case against Microsoft could have favourable effects on competition and on consumers. It is also a difficult task to provide evidence on what would have happen had the European Commission let Microsoft enjoy its near-monopoly position.

The American procedure in antitrust cases is carried out in courts that permit open challenge of the arguments. The same procedure (at least initially) in the EU takes place behind closed doors in the European Commission, which acts as prosecutor, judge, jury and executioner. The complex history of the Microsoft case in the US courts reveals that there is no consistency in the principles applied even without a single legal system. Therefore, if there are various regulators in the world, they ought to harmonise principles and practices. Even a global competition authority may be a good option to be considered.

The obvious causes of ineffectiveness of antitrust policy include the following ones (Crandall and Winston, 2003, p. 23):

- The excessive duration of court cases. The particular issue that is focused on may easily evolve into something different over time. By the time the case is resolved, it may become of little relevance.
- Difficulties in formulating effective remedies.
- Difficulties in ascertaining which potentially anticompetitive act or instance may jeopardise consumer welfare.

- Rapid change in technology, intellectual property and dynamic competition relentlessly increases challenges of formulating and implementing effective antitrust policy.
- Political influences on which antitrust cases are initiated, settled or dropped.

It is sometimes argued that it is quite costly to trade intangible technology assets at arm's length because 'it is a combination of skills, equipment and organisation embodied in people and institutions as much as in machinery and equipment' (Sharp and Pavitt, 1993, p. 147). If an inventor fears that his/her patent rights[8] are not sufficiently protected (enforcement, length of the patent right, level of penalties), he/she will keep the innovation secret or be disinclined to participate in R&D in the future. A part of the innovation process may lean towards outcomes that may not be easily imitated. A conflict between static and dynamic efficiency in production, as well as between the welfare of producers and consumers, is obvious. As technology becomes older and is no longer at the core of the business activities of the innovator, it becomes more likely that the innovator will disseminate the technology, intellectual property rights, goodwill and know-how through licensing.

The appropriation of returns from innovation is not a major problem if the innovator is a non-profit institution such as a research institute, university or a government. Non-profit-making innovators are most likely to make their findings public and, in fact, may be disseminated immediately. It was estimated for 2000 that out of the $265 billion (2.7 per cent of GDP) invested in the US in R&D in that year, 68 per cent was financed by the business community (most of the balance came from the federal government), while 75 per cent of R&D was carried out by private firms (Teich, 2003).

The problem of appropriation arises when there is a conflict between public interest in the spread of information and knowledge and private interest in holding and employing that knowledge for lucrative purposes. If private knowledge acquired through risky investment of resources is not protected, at least for some period of time, there will be little incentive to generate innovations that drive efficiency and, hence, contribute to future growth. A sound knowledge-based economy demands a strong protection of intellectual property.

An analysis by Levin et al. (1987) of alternative ways of protecting the competitive (monopolistic) advantages of new and improved processes and products found that patents are the least effective means for appropriating returns. Lead time over competitors,[9] a fast-track learning curve (unit costs of production fall as output increases over time) and sales/service effort were regarded by the surveyed firms as providing better returns than patents. Firms may sometimes refrain from patenting products or processes to avoid revealing the facts or details of innovation because of the possible disclosure of information to competitors and imitators. At the same time, firms have every incentive to advertise the benefits of new or improved products and disseminate them to consumers. Therefore, secrecy about innovation is both difficult and undesirable. It may be better to be concerned about the creation of future business secrets than to worry about the protection of existing ones.

Additional profits can accrue from the production of complementary assets (cameras and films; recorders and tapes/discs). Therefore, not only innovation and manufacturing (technological leadership), but also, and equally important, distribution and after-sales service (commercial leadership) are of great advantage in capturing markets and profits.[10] In the fields of cameras, audio and video goods (and some segments of the car market) Japanese companies have virtually ousted most of their international competitors and changed the international geography of production in these industries[11] through an uninterrupted tide of technical improvements and distribution/service networks.

The benefits of increased competition will materialise only if firms compete and do not collude to avoid competition. Competition stimulates innovation. It may, in turn, bring new technologies with large sunk costs, geographical concentration of production and other entry barriers. If this is the case, then neither unfettered markets nor monopolies (oligopolies) should be ignored. Otherwise, consumer welfare would be distorted and allocation of resources may take place in a suboptimal way from a social standpoint. Hence, there is a need for a competition policy, not only in the market of a single country, but also in a much larger area. This area is generally limited by the geographical space where economic cycles are in step. The rule of law, based in part on economic theory, may modify market distortions both in single countries and in integration groups.

CONCEPT

One of the most obvious initial effects of international economic integration is the improvement in efficiency in the use of factors due to increased competition in the geographically enlarged market. In this context, competitiveness of firms has two aspects: national and international. In both cases, a competitive *firm* is one that is able to make a profit without being protected and/or subsidised. This means that the output of a firm (goods and/or services) is in demand and is produced at the right time, in the right quantity and quality, as well as being superior to the output of most of its competitors. The goods and services of a *country* are internationally competitive if they are able to withstand free and fair competition on the world market while, at the same time, the country's inhabitants maintain and increase their standard of living on average and in the long term.

There are three concepts related to competitiveness:

- *Cost competitiveness* addresses the difference (that is, profit) between the price at which a good is sold and the cost of its production. If a firm is able to reduce the costs of production by reducing input prices, innovation and/or organising production and marketing in a more efficient way that is not available to its competitors, it may improve its relative profit margin.
- A firm has a *price-competitive* product if it matches other firms' products in all characteristics, including price. This type of competitiveness can be improved if the firm unilaterally reduces the price of its good (other things being equal) and/or upgrades its attributes and provides a better service.
- *Relative profitability* exists when there is the possibility of geographical price discrimination (for example, between domestic and foreign markets). The different profit margins in these markets indicate relative profitability.

The measurement of the competitiveness of an integrated group of countries includes the intra-group trade ratio (intra-group export/intra-group import) and extra-group trade ratio (extra-group export/extra-group import). In addition, the competitiveness of an integrated country's economic sector (or industries within it) may be measured in the following two ways.

- *Trade specialisation index* (TSI). This provides details about the integrated country j's specialisation in exports in relation to other partner countries in the group. If this index for good i is greater than 1, country j is specialised in the export of good i within the group. TSI (equation (5.1)) reveals country j's comparative advantage within the group. The conceptual problem with this approach is that the structure of exports may vary because of a change in domestic consumption that may not alter either the volume or the composition of domestic output.

$$TSI = \frac{X_{i,j}/X_{ind,j}}{X_{i,g}/X_{ind,g}} \quad (5.1)$$

where:

$X_{i,j}$ = export of good i from country j to the partner countries in the integration group;

$X_{\text{ind},j}$ = total industry exports to the group from country j;
$X_{i,g}$ = intra-group exports of *good i*;
$X_{\text{ind},g}$ = total industry exports within the group.

- *Production specialisation index* (PSI). This is identical to the TSI, except that export (X) variables are replaced by production (P) ones. PSI shows where country j is more specialised in production than its integration partners. This index reveals country j's production advantage as well as its domestic consumption pattern.

Interpretation of both the TSI and the PSI may be distorted if the production and export of good i in country j is protected/subsidised. The revealed 'advantage' would be misleading, as in the case of exports of farm goods from the EU because of the Common Agricultural Policy.

Goods that are produced and traded by a country may be categorised by their economic idiosyncrasies. There are five, sometimes overlapping, types of goods (Audretsch, 1993, pp: 94–5):

- Ricardo goods have a high natural resource content. These commodities include minerals, fuels, wood, paper, fibres and food.
- Product-cycle goods include those that rely on high technology and where information serves as a crucial input.[12] This group includes chemicals, pharmaceuticals, plastics, dyes, fertilisers, explosives, machinery, aircraft and instruments.
- R&D-intensive goods include industries where R&D expenditure is at least 5 per cent of the sales value. These are pharmaceuticals, office machinery, aircraft and telecom goods.
- High-advertising goods are the ones where advertising expenditures are at least 5 per cent of the sales value. These include drinks, cereals, soaps, perfumes and watches.
- Goods that are produced by high-concentration industries include tobacco, liquid fuels, edible oils, tubes, home appliances, motor vehicles and railway equipment.

Audretsch (1993, pp. 95–6) made a geographical comparison of these five types of goods. The comparison was for the 1975–83 period among the rich Western countries (mainly the OECD), poor Western countries (mainly the South European countries) and then the centrally planned countries of Central and Eastern Europe. The findings were as follows:

- In 1975, Western countries had a comparative disadvantage in the Ricardo goods while the other two groups had a comparative

advantage. By 1983, Central and East European countries, together with the rich Western countries, were exhibiting a comparative disadvantage in Ricardo goods, reflecting their inability to compete with resource-rich developing countries.
- The rich Western countries have a constant comparative advantage in product-cycle, R&D-intensive and advertising-intensive' goods over the other two groups of countries.
- Rich Western, as well as Central and East European, countries have a competitive advantage in highly concentrated industries over the poor Western nations.

Whereas competition in goods is more or less global, competition in many services is localised. A large part of competitive activity in manufactured goods has a price component; competition in many services has, predominantly, a non-price dimension. Reputation and past experience of services often play a crucial role in choosing a supplier for a certain type of service. Local providers of some services, as well as those with a good (international) reputation, have a specific market power. Local market influence on producers of goods is in most cases non-existent as goods may be (easily) traded across space. Because the service industries are generally subjected to a lower degree of competitiveness than the manufacturing industries, and as a result of legislation designed to consumers, administrative regulation in the services sector is quite high.

The competitiveness of a country's goods and services may be increased through depreciation of a home currency and/or by a reduction in wages. The simplest way to increase competitiveness, however, is to increase productivity. Developing, intermediate and advanced countries trade more or less successfully all over the world, but their standard of living depends on their productivity. However, the ability to trade depends only on the ability to produce something that is wanted by consumers, while the rate of exchange ensures that exports can be sold. This was the message of David Ricardo in the early 19th century and is as important (and as little understood) today as it was in Ricardo's time (Lipsey, 1993c, p. 21).

The new theory of trade and strategic industrial policy (initiated in the early 1980s) argues that, with imperfect competition, there are no unique solutions to economic problems.[13] The outcome depends on assumptions about the conduct of economic agents. There is a strong possibility that in a situation with imperfect competition firms are able to make above-average profits (rents). Intervention in trade, competition and industry may, under certain conditions, geographically redistribute these rents in favour of domestic firms. This shift is the main feature of strategic trade policy. Hence, there is an assumption about the 'strategic interdependence' among firms. This means that profits of one firm are directly affected by the individual strategy choices of other firms and such a relation is understood by the firms (Brander, 1995, p. 1397). The strategic trade policy of beggar-thy-neighbour ('war' over economic rents) does not occur in the situation of either pure monopoly or perfect competition. This policy may look like a zero-sum game, where everybody loses in the long term through a chain of retaliations and counter-retaliations. However, 'countries that would otherwise compete with each other at the level of strategic policy have an incentive to make agreements that would ameliorate or prevent such rivalries' (Brander, 1995, pp. 1447–8).

There is, potentially, at least one good reason for intervention.[14] With externalities, spillovers and geographical clustering of production, governments may find reasons to protect some growing, often high-technology industries that depend on economies of scale. These are the industries for which accumulated knowledge is the prime source of competitiveness and whose expenditure on R&D, and employment of engineers and scientists is (well) above the average for the economy. Sunk costs and R&D may be funded by governments, as the positive effects of introducing new technology are felt throughout the economy and beyond the confines of the firm that introduces it. The whole world may benefit, in some cases, from new technology whose development was supported by government intervention. For example, spaceships had to be equipped with computers, which needed to be small and light. A spillover from the development of this kind of equipment was the creation of personal computers. Therefore, the new theory goes, with externalities and under certain dubious conditions (no retaliation, well-informed governments[15]), intervention may be a positive-sum game where everyone potentially gains in the long run. Critics of the new theory have not been able to prove it wrong, but argue that it is not necessarily correct. In fact, what is not understood is that the new theory provides only a programme for research, rather than a prescription for policy (Krugman, 1993b, p. 164).

MARKET STRUCTURE

A market for a good or a service is said to be contestable if there is a smooth entry and exit route for a firm. The number of firms in the market should be 'sufficient' to prevent a single firm or group of firms from increasing prices and making rents (super-normal profits). Relative ease of entering the business would prevent the incumbent firms from charging exorbitant prices. The opportunity of making high rents would immediately attract new entrants. Geographical extensions of the market (economic integration) reinforce potentials for pro-competition market behaviour.

Imagine a situation with two identical countries A and B, one good X and no trade. Assume also a monopoly in country A, and free competition in country B in the market for the same good. One can reasonably expect that prices for good X are lower in country B. If one now introduces free trade between the two countries, country B would export good X to country A. This example shows that a pure difference in market structure between the countries may explain the geographical location of production and trade, even though the countries may have identical production technologies and factor endowments. This crucial aspect has been overlooked by the classical theory of spatial economics.

Competition policies may be classified according to the structure–conduct–performance (SCP) paradigm. The thrust of the SCP paradigm is that performance in a defined market depends on the interaction between the structure of the market and the conduct of buyers and sellers in it.

- *Structure* refers to the organisation of production and distribution, that is, which enterprises are permitted to enter into which business activities. It determines the number and size of buyers and sellers; product differentiation; and relationships (horizontal and vertical integration) between buyers and sellers.
- *Conduct* describes how firms behave in their business. This refers to the competitive strategy of suppliers such as (predatory) pricing, innovation, advertising and investment.
- *Performance* refers to the goals of economic organisation such as efficiency, technological progress, availability of goods and full employment of resources.

The most common indicator of market structure or the degree of competition is the proportion of industry output, sales, investment or employment attributable to a subset (usually three to ten) of all firms in the industry. It shows the force of the competitive pressure on the incumbents. If this ratio is relatively high, then it illustrates that market power is concentrated in relatively few firms.

It is, however, important to be cautious when dealing with these ratios. While an employment concentration ratio may indicate a monopoly situation, a sales concentration ratio may not. Competitiveness is linked not only to market shares, but, as a dynamic phenomenon, to the relative growth of productivity, innovation, R&D, size and quality of the capital stock, mobility of resources, operational control, success in shifting out of declining lines of business, education of management, training of labour, incentives and so on. These ratios do, however, provide a useful, if second-best, barometer of the oligopolistic restriction of competition.

The Hirschman–Herfindahl index (HHI) is an alternative and more complete measure of market structure than the concentration ratio. It is increasingly being used in the public fight against oligopolies.

$$HHI = \sum_i S_i^2 \times 100. \qquad (5.2)$$

The HHI (equation (5.2)) is the sum of squared market shares of each firm in the defined market. It is between 0 and 100. The index is 100 when there is a monopoly, while it is relatively small in competitive industries. The HHI takes accounts of all firms (that is, both their absolute number and relative difference in size) in the defined market, whereas the concentration ratio accounts only for a select number of firms in the same market. Antitrust lawyers still place much weight on the HHI. However, economists are increasingly sceptical about its value. Although some economists use the HHI as an initial screening tool, it is more useful to consider how easy it is for new and efficient firms to enter the target market. New firms are attracted to enter an industry by the potential for new profit lures. Estimates of the ease and likelihood of new firms entering an industry are inevitably highly speculative.

Integration may provoke several scenarios regarding market structure. On the one hand, an increase in industrial concentration may arise from firms' decision to take advantage of economies of scale and intra-industry production linkages. Economies of scope[16] may also increase geographical concentration because they favour diversified firms which are often large. On the other hand, smaller firms may benefit, as in Japan or in Germany, because they may be included in the network of large ones. In addition, reduced trade costs make it easier for smaller firms to penetrate into the markets of partner countries. This may reduce concentration.

Firms compete through product differentiation, innovation, quality, R&D, advertising and special close links with suppliers, clients and various institutions, as well as on price. The exceptions are, of course, raw materials and certain standardised semi-finished goods. In spite of trendy talk about the 'global economy' and the diminishing role played by specific geographical locations for business, competitive advantages are often heavily local. These gains come from the clustering of highly specialised knowledge and skills and the existence of rivals, sophisticated customers and institutions in a specific geographical area (Porter, 1998a). Even though many of these advantages are external to individual firms, they are internal to the cluster in which they locate their operations.

Major changes in the capacity of a firm that are linked to high sunk costs do not happen frequently. It is, however, more difficult to test the impact of non-price rivalry such as competitors' R&D, innovation, design activities and non-technical matters such as management and marketing than their prices. It also takes longer to retaliate in these areas than to change prices (Schmalensee, 1988, p. 670).

INNOVATION

The process of technological change is driven by several factors, including the following five:

- the existence of unexploited lucrative opportunities for the solution of problems such as the transformation of electricity into sound or light into electricity;
- it is stimulated by changes in government regulation such as changes in technical and safety standards (including concerns about the environment) and trade policy;
- the change in prices (relative scarcity) of raw materials, energy, labour or transport and communication;
- supplying clients with the toughest demands may set in motion the innovation process. Search for a challenge and rivalry, rather than staying away from them inspires innovation. The same holds for regular contacts with research centres; and
- a change in consumers' needs, tastes, sophistication and fickleness. Increases in income and decreased working time increase the demand for leisure and entertainment. At the same time, more stressful work takes its toll on workers' health, increasing demand for medical and rehabilitation services.

Innovation is the principal activity for economic growth. It brings new ideas, enlarges the stock of knowledge that in turn enhances productivity. Patents are linked with innovation as they provide the means to reward someone that comes up with a worthy commercial idea.

The innovation process has four distinct, but interrelated phases:

- *invention*: discovery of something new which can 'work';
- *innovation*: translation of invention into commercial use;
- *spread*: diffusion in the market; and
- *absorption*: learning from clients and conversion into a public good.

If, because of a change in circumstances (for example, integration), firms innovate (that is, realise their technological, organisational and control potentials and capabilities to develop, produce and sell goods and services) and introduce new technologies and new goods/services in order to maintain or improve their market position, then efficiency overall may increase. From a given set of resources one may expect to achieve more and/or better-quality output. This directly increases national welfare on average. In fact, for a small or medium-sized country, integration enables economic development and progress at a lower cost than does autarky. There is, however, an opposing force. When there are market imperfections, such as economies of scale and externalities, firms make rents.[17] Free competition leads to concentration and agglomeration, which may reduce competition in the future. The new theory of trade and strategic industrial policy holds that there may be fierce competition even among a few firms. Examples include the aircraft industry, the long-distance telephone call market and the Japanese market for electronic goods (largely confined to half a dozen domestic conglomerates). Technical innovations prompt legal and policy innovations. The telephone business, for example, was for a very long time considered to be a 'natural monopoly'. Nowadays, it is a highly competitive industry.

Innovation changes the mix of factors that are used in the production and/or consumption of goods and services. Usually, an innovation brings a reduction in the quantity of factors needed to produce a good or service, as shown by an arrow in Figure 5.2. This makes output cheaper and, consequently, more competitive. Suppose that the production of a good requires two factors, f_1 and f_2. If production requires, per unit of output, 0A of factor f_1 and 0B of factor f_2, then the resource required to produce the good is represented by rectangle 0ACB. Innovation normally reduces the area of rectangle 0ACB (note the direction of the arrow). However, the market receptiveness to take up new products depends on the cost, convenience in use, as well as culture. If, however, one factor, such as oil or some other raw material, suddenly becomes scarce, innovation may reduce the consumption of that factor, but disproportionally increase (at least temporarily) the requirement for the other factor. Hence, in such a special case, the area of the rectangle 0ACB may increase as the result of innovation.

Economic integration opens up the markets of the integrated countries to local firms. It is reasonable to expect competition to have a positive effect on innovation, but what are the effects of such a process in the long term?

- If innovation *spreads* geographically, and if it increases competition, then competition and innovation reinforce each other.
- If, however, innovation becomes *centralised* over time and space because it is costly, uncertain and risky so that only a few large firms can undertake it, then geographical extension of markets would have a positive effect on innovation only in the short term.

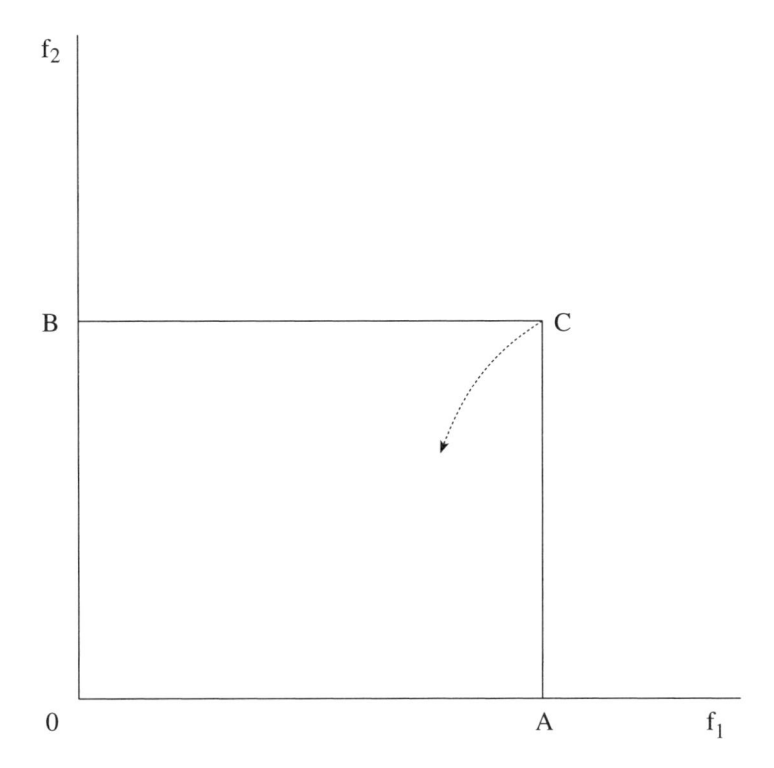

Figure 5.2   Effects of innovation on the use of factors

It is therefore necessary to ensure that immediate positive effects continue in the long term (Geroski, 1988, pp. 377–9). In order to maintain the 'necessary' level of competition within the integrated area, the countries involved may decide to reduce the level of common external tariff and NTBs.

The impact of competition is not restricted to prices and costs. Competition also yields other favourable effects. It stimulates technical progress, widens consumer choice, improves the quality of goods and services and rationalises the organisation of firms. It is important to remember that firms seldom lose out to competitors because their product is overpriced or because their production capacity is insufficient; rather, they lose because they fail to develop new products and production processes as well or as quickly as their competitors (Lipsey, 1993a, p. 18). If a firm does not make its own product obsolete through innovation, some other entrepreneur will. The 'prospect theory' of psychology explains that the individuals are more hurt by a loss than they are encouraged by gains of equal size, that is, fear of loss is often more powerful than the expectation of gain.

The innovation process is sometimes accidental, but always uncertain and risky. It is often linked with serendipity.[18] For example, in 1970, Spencer Silver, a research chemist at 3M, was working in the area of adhesive technology. His goal was to produce the strongest glue on the market and his reputation was ruined when he developed a product that was quite the opposite. He did, however, discover that his new glue could be used again and did not leave any traces on the surface to which it was applied. He tried for a decade to find an application for his glue, but there was no interest at 3 M. However, Silver had a friend, Arthur Fry, who was a singer in his local church choir. Every Sunday he inserted slips of paper into his hymnbook to mark the pages of the hymns to be sung during the service. And every Sunday the slips would fall out as he opened the book. Fry remembered Silver's 'futile' invention and applied it to the slips of paper, which stayed in place. A year later, in 1981, 3 M started producing the now omnipresent Post-it notes (Hillman and Gibbs, 1998, p. 183).[19]

As a result of relentless innovation, techniques that are used in the production process change constantly. But innovation changes not only the method of production of goods and services, but also our values and the way we live. For example, Hollywood films changed how we lived and worked, how we saw the world, even how young people courted (in cars, away from the eyes of parents and chaperones). Or the short-message system (SMS) on mobile phones altered the nightlife of the young, as well as single persons throughout the world. These changes can be minor or revolutionary. Lipsey (1993b, pp. 3–4) described four levels of innovation:

- *Incremental innovation*: a series of changes, each small, but with a large cumulative effect.
- *Radical innovations*: major but discontinuous changes such as the development of a new material (for example, plastic), a new source of power or new products (aircraft, computer or laser).
- *Changes in the technology system*: changes that affect an economic sector and industries within it, such as the changes that occurred in the chemical and related industries in the nineteenth century.
- *Technological revolution*: innovations that change the whole technoeconomic paradigm.[20]

Innovation is an important economic driver. It will be the basis of competition in the future and will continue to affect the location of production. In the field of personal computers, for example, the greatest competition is no longer between assembly companies such as Compaq, IBM and Toshiba, but between companies operating in the area of added value, such as microprocessors, dominated by Intel, and operating software, where Microsoft, through its Windows program, reigns supreme. Market advantage for critical elements of the system is often held in the form of intellectual property (Borrus and Zysman, 1997; Zysman and Schwartz, 1998, p. 409).

There is, however, no simple answer to the question of whether international economic integration (extension of the market) stimulates or prevents innovation. There are two opposing views. First, a monopoly organisation has a secure market for its output. It can anticipate reaping normal or super-normal profits (rents) from any innovation. It is therefore easier for such a firm to innovate than one that does not have such market security. On the other hand, with no competitive pressure, a monopolist company may not feel the need to innovate. The sense of long-term stability fosters a conservative way of thinking that may restrict innovative activity. Monopolists may not wish to 'rock the boat' and can prevent or delay the implementation of innovations of their own production or developed by others.

The huge increases in income and living standards that have been seen over the past 250 years, particularly in the West, are the consequence of several factors. At the end of the 17th century there was a strong convergence between the theoretical understanding of science and the application of that knowledge. A critical mass of knowledge in the fields of mathematics and mechanics was accumulated and applied to the understanding of atmospheric pressure and the invention of the steam engine. This provided the foundation for a technological revolution that resulted in a 150-year period of radical innovation in the areas of transport (rail and water), textiles, mining, tools, metallurgy and food processing.

Most inventions originated in a small group of countries, and this group has remained relatively stable over a long period of time. There is a clear geographical localisation of innovation activities. During the Industrial Revolution, Britain led the way, joined by Germany, the US, France, Switzerland and Sweden in the second half of the 19th century. Membership of this select group of countries has been stable for over a century. The only major newcomer to the group was Japan just after the Second World War, although a few newly industrialised countries, such as South Korea and Taiwan, have joined this exclusive club.[21]

Patents may be used as a helpful proxy of innovation. The available data from the US Patent and Trademark Office (Tables 5.1 and 5.2, respectively) reveal that more than half of all patents granted in the US (1977–2001) are domestic in origin.[22] This means that the US is the most innovative economy in the world. It attracts and rewards creative individuals. A warning sign for the EU about a serious brain-drain is that '40 per cent of the research community in the US are European graduates'.[23] The rest of the patents are highly concentrated on a relatively small group of 11 countries which

Table 5.1 Number of patents granted by date of patent grant, 1 January 1977 to 31 December 2001

	Pre-1988	1988	1989	1990	1991	1992
Total	772 237	84 439	102 690	99 220	106 842	107 511
US origin	456 779	44 729	54 759	52 977	57 789	58 791
Foreign origin	315 458	39 710	47 931	46 243	49 053	48 720
Japan	109 346	16 989	21 106	20 743	22 402	23 164
Germany	68 384	7 546	8 613	7 862	7 984	7 605
France	24 869	2 792	3 299	3 093	3 249	3 282
United Kingdom	27 722	2 754	3 278	3 017	3 049	2 632
Canada	14 321	1 643	2 124	2 087	2 304	2 218
Taiwan	1 450	536	688	861	1 096	1 253
Switzerland	13 845	1 299	1 420	1 347	1 448	1 294
Italy	9 713	1 173	1 425	1 498	1 388	1 446
Sweden	9 639	891	926	885	831	727
Netherlands	8 012	899	1 163	1 046	1 075	974
South Korea	341	126	183	290	449	586
Australia	3 817	486	586	517	571	497
Belgium	2 845	328	377	352	366	371
Austria	3 192	351	412	423	388	403
Israel	1 559	249	339	311	321	350
Finland	1 817	239	251	315	343	381
Denmark	1 909	208	261	204	285	275
China, Hong Kong SAR	668	104	134	151	209	159
USSR	3 050	97	162	177	182	67
Spain	896	132	148	148	185	149
Norway	1 093	137	141	119	119	121
South Africa	940	107	143	122	111	101
Hungary	1 094	94	130	93	86	89
New Zealand	584	70	75	65	50	60
Ireland	271	47	71	61	61	61
Singapore	52	8	22	16	25	35
Mexico	447	45	41	34	42	45
Brazil	280	37	39	45	66	43
China P. Rep.	48	48	52	48	52	41
Russian Federation						
India	123	14	15	23	24	24
Luxembourg	289	38	39	27	42	36
Czechoslovakia	589	33	34	39	27	18
Argentina	224	18	23	19	19	23
Venezuela	130	20	23	20	25	24
Poland	260	8	14	17	8	5
Others (125)	1 639	144	174	168	171	161

1993	1994	1995	1996	1997	1998	1999	2000	2001	Total
109 890	113 704	113 955	121 805	124 146	163 209	169 146	176 084	184 051	2 548 929
61 221	64 345	64 510	69 419	69 922	90 701	94 090	97 014	98 663	1 435 709
48 669	49 359	49 445	52 386	54 224	72 508	75 056	79 070	85 388	1 113 220
23 411	23 517	22 871	24 059	24 191	32 118	32 514	32 923	34 890	464 244
7 186	6 989	6 874	7 125	7 292	9 582	9 895	10 822	11 894	185 653
3 155	2 985	3 010	3 016	3 202	3 991	4 097	4 173	4 456	72 669
2 521	2 469	2 681	2 674	2 904	3 726	3 900	4 090	4 356	71 773
2 231	2 380	2 447	2 638	2 817	3 537	3 678	3 925	4 063	52 413
1 510	1 814	2 087	2 419	2 597	3 805	4 526	5 806	6 545	36 993
1 198	1 244	1 187	1 192	1 179	1 374	1 390	1 458	1 557	32 432
1 453	1 361	1 242	1 385	1 417	1 821	1 686	1 967	1 978	30 953
742	800	914	971	970	1 346	1 542	1 738	1 935	24 857
944	998	894	886	895	1 382	1 396	1 410	1 494	23 468
830	1 008	1 240	1 567	1 965	3 362	3 679	3 472	3 763	22 861
470	564	548	566	568	830	832	859	1 031	12 742
377	392	419	516	561	755	718	756	796	9 929
340	316	359	387	393	408	505	537	632	9 046
358	388	432	525	577	820	792	836	1 031	8 888
311	341	387	453	468	629	695	649	769	8 048
261	313	314	334	432	500	588	509	556	6 949
182	220	248	247	261	373	413	548	620	4 537
67	57	12	16	4	6	3	1		3 901
184	172	168	187	193	308	265	318	340	3 793
127	130	138	150	157	232	246	266	282	3 458
101	109	127	116	114	132	127	125	137	2 612
62	48	51	43	25	52	39	38	61	2 005
51	54	60	78	109	145	134	136	160	1 831
59	52	59	88	78	81	104	139	166	1 398
44	59	61	97	100	136	152	242	304	1 353
50	52	45	46	57	77	94	100	87	1 262
59	61	70	69	67	88	98	113	125	1 260
53	48	63	48	66	88	99	163	266	1 183
3	38	99	118	112	194	185	185	239	1 173
30	28	38	37	48	94	114	131	179	922
41	44	34	27	42	46	35	55	48	843
15	20	15	9	10	9	5	10	7	840
25	37	32	32	38	46	46	63	58	703
34	28	31	30	26	29	39	32	28	519
8	9	8	16	11	19	20	13	16	432
176	214	180	219	278	367	405	462	519	5 277

Table 5.1 (continued)

	Pre-1988	1988	1989	1990	1991	1992
Ownership:						
US corporations	341 627	33 913	41 401	39 268	42 887	44 043
US government	12 821	848	977	1 064	1 272	1 225
US individuals	121 962	11 895	14 960	15 091	16 234	15 650
Foreign corporations	248 526	32 681	39 395	37 995	40 324	40 930
Foreign government	3 838	454	448	427	473	474
Foreign individuals	43 463	4 648	5 509	5 375	5 652	5 189

Source: US Patent and Trademark Office (2002). *TAF Special Report: All Patents, All Types January 1977–December 2001.* Washington, DC.

Table 5.2 Percentage of patents granted by date of patent grant, 1 January 1977 to 31 December 2001

	Pre-1988	1988	1989	1990	1991	1992
Total	100	100	100	100	100	100
US origin	59	53	53	53	54	55
Foreign origin	41	47	47	47	46	45
Japan	14	20	21	21	21	22
Germany	9	9	8	8	7	7
France	3	3	3	3	3	3
United Kingdom	4	3	3	3	3	2
Canada	2	2	2	2	2	2
Taiwan		1	1	1	1	1
Switzerland	2	2	1	1	1	1
Italy	1	1	1	2	1	1
Sweden	1	1	1	1	1	1
Netherlands	1	1	1	1	1	1
South Korea						1
Australia		1	1	1	1	
Belgium						
Austria						
Israel						
Finland						
Denmark						
China, Hong Kong SAR						
USSR						
Spain						
Norway						
South Africa						

1993	1994	1995	1996	1997	1998	1999	2000	2001	Total
46 093	48 750	49 049	53 541	55 304	72 359	75 934	78 822	82 077	1 105 068
1 234	1 310	1 083	960	974	1 039	999	961	985	27 752
16 100	16 527	16 813	17 415	16 285	20 766	20 540	20 352	18 843	359 433
41 078	41 540	41 353	44 191	45 641	61 425	64 225	68 060	74 032	921 396
442	300	250	260	278	258	164	108	97	8 271
4 943	5 277	5 407	5 438	5 664	7 362	7 284	7 781	8 017	127 009

1993	1994	1995	1996	1997	1998	1999	2000	2001	Total
100	100	100	100	100	100	100	100	100	100
56	57	57	57	56	56	56	55	54	56
44	43	43	43	44	44	44	45	46	44
21	21	20	20	19	20	19	19	19	18
7	6	6	6	6	6	6	6	6	7
3	3	3	2	3	2	2	2	2	3
2	2	2	2	2	2	2	2	2	3
2	2	2	2	2	2	2	2	2	2
1	2	2	2	2	2	3	3	4	1
1	1	1	1	1	1	1	1	1	1
1	1	1	1	1	1	1	1	1	1
1	1	1	1	1	1	1	1	1	1
1	1	1	1	1	1	1	1	1	1
1	1	1	1	2	2	2	2	2	1
					1			1	0
									0
					1			1	0
									0
									0
									0
									0
									0
									0
									0
									0

294   *The economics of European integration*

Table 5.2   (continued)

	Pre-1988	1988	1989	1990	1991	1992
Hungary						
New Zealand						
Ireland						
Singapore						
Mexico						
Brazil						
China P. Rep.						
Russian Federation						
India						
Luxembourg						
Czechoslovakia						
Argentina						
Venezuela						
Poland						
Others (125)						
Ownership:						
US corporations	44	40	40	40	40	41
US government	2	1	1	1	1	1
US individuals	16	14	15	15	15	15
Foreign corporations	32	39	38	38	38	38
Foreign government		1				
Foreign individuals	6	6	5	5	5	5

Source: US Patent and Trademark Office (2002). *TAF Special Report: All Patents, All Types January 1977–December 2001*. Washington, DC.

includes in descending order: Japan, Germany, France, Britain, Canada, Taiwan, Switzerland, Italy, Sweden, the Netherlands and South Korea. As far as total ownership of patents is concerned, 79 per cent belong to companies. The European Council in Lisbon (2000) set a new strategic goal for the EU to become 'the most competitive and dynamic knowledge-based economy in the world capable of sustainable economic growth with more and better jobs and greater social cohesion'[24] by 2010 seems to be quite a challenging and ambitious task. There are a few tough competitors for this position.

Why is this? What happened in these (Western) countries at the end of the 17th century and was allowed to continue undisturbed? Why did it not happen before? What prevented the Islamic world from continuing its innovative course after the 13th century or what prevented China from doing so after the 15th century? Evidence to support theories about these

1993	1994	1995	1996	1997	1998	1999	2000	2001	Total
									0
									0
									0
									0
									0
									0
									0
									0
									0
									0
									0
									0
									0
									0
									0
42	43	43	44	45	44	45	45	45	43
1	1	1	1	1	1	1	1	1	1
15	15	15	14	13	13	12	12	10	14
37	37	36	36	37	38	38	39	40	36
									0
4	5	5	4	5	5	4	4	4	5

issues is still imperfect and highly controversial. None the less, several overlapping factors may, in combination, provide a partial explanation.

- Willingness and readiness to accept and live with the change (*values*) are one element. Continuous change and adaptation is essential to make a population and state wealthier. However, this 'greed' needs to be coupled with investments and displacement of the mentality of self-sufficiency.
- *Politics* steps in when there is resistance to change. All societies have tried to resist change at one time or another, but this is inevitably self-damaging and in vain. For example, ancient China looked with suspicion at new ideas introduced by foreigners. Indeed, the country's rulers often banned such innovations. In Florence, in 1299, bankers were forbidden from using Arabic numbers. And in Danzig (Gdansk)

in 1579, the City Council, afraid of unemployment, ordered Anton Müller, the inventor of the ribbon loom to be drowned.
- In the successful countries, *institutions* that provided a favourable environment for innovation and growth were created. In Britain, for example, the Magna Carta of 1215 gave subjects the right to their own property. They were protected from the Crown, which until then had been entitled to seize property at random. In contrast, arbitrary confiscation continued to be common in the Muslim world and in Asia. In the West, rulers quickly learned that a tax on property was more profitable than random confiscation as tax proceeds continue to accrue indefinitely. The outcome was a social system that promoted innovation and growth more than any previous system. In modern times it has almost eliminated the gap between frontline science and applied technology.
- The size of the *local market* (remember that integration increases the size of the market),[25] competition and supply of skills are important ingredients in the complex links between technological opportunities and entrepreneurial decisions. R&D plays a crucial role in the innovation process as it sustains a supply of knowledge.
- Another possible explanation for the relative constancy of countries that innovate most is that innovation reflects the *cumulative* and interrelated nature of acquired knowledge. Once it exists, knowledge does not cease to exist, and discovery builds on discovery. Innovation also reflects a change in technological capabilities and economic incentives.[26] It is related not only to the creation and absorption of new knowledge, but also to its adaptation, extension and control within an innovation-friendly environment. Taken together, this provides strong grounds for the creation of dynamic comparative advantages, certain irreversibilities[27] and economic growth[28] of firms and nations as success breeds the potential for further success. The higher the levels of accumulation of knowledge and capital stock, the greater are the benefits of technological progress[29] and vice versa. The law of diminishing returns does not apply to the accumulation of knowledge (Lipsey, 1994). This is also reflected in the export performance of those countries, as well as in differences in labour productivity. Innovation is concentrated in a few firms in industries with high entry barriers such as aerospace, chemicals, automobiles, electric and electronic industries, while it is spread among many firms in machinery and the production of instruments (Dosi et al., 1990).

Empirical studies show that monopolisation or concentration is not the main reason for innovation. Cumulative (clustered) knowledge enabled

Germany to excel in the fields of chemicals and high-quality engineering, Britain in pop music and publishing, Italy in fashion and design and the US in computer software, aeronautics and the cinema. But innovation is also to be found in industries that are less concentrated and where there are no significant barriers to entry. New entrants may have greater motivation to test and develop new products and technologies than well-established firms.

In many industrialised countries, the average size of firms is becoming smaller, not bigger. This reflects increased demand for more custom-made goods, produced in smaller batches, utilising production factors that can be readily switched to various alternative uses. But this is only on average. The industries with the most advanced technology are often the most geographically concentrated, highly profitable and the largest. Modern technology is increasing the importance of capital, especially human capital.[30] Krugman (1996a, pp. 13–14) found statistical evidence from the US economy that the 'really high value-added' industries (in relation to the number of employees) are cigarette manufacturing and petrol refining, whereas the so-called 'high-technology industries' such as aircraft and electronics turned out to be roughly about average. However, one has to remember that high-technology industries have important externalities and linkages for the whole economy, although the number of computers a nation has is somewhat less important than how and for what purpose they are used, for example playing Tetris or Solitaire or organising inventories, production, transport and distribution. Another problem is that most computers are used in the services sector (finance, accounting and health care) where it is hard to measure output.

It is one thing to invent or discover new or improved goods or services (product differentiation) and/or uncover a new way to produce or market already existing goods and services and quite another to exploit that success commercially. The electric dynamo was invented in 1881, but it took firms four decades to reorganise plants to take advantage of the flexibility in production offered by electric power. The basic videocassette recorder (VCR) technology was the result of an invention by Ampex in the US in the 1950s. Philips, a Dutch company, produced the first VCR aimed at the consumer market in 1971, several years before Sony introduced its Betamax model. Soon after, other Japanese manufacturers entered the market, and before long they came to dominate the international market for (home) video equipment. To avoid a repeat experience, Philips took a different tack after inventing compact discs and developed the final technology jointly with Sony. Hence, the geography of innovation and the geography of production need not coincide. The microprocessor was invented in 1971, but firms are still learning how to make best use of it. One of the reasons for this situation is due to Moore's law,[31] which refers to the doubling of chip performance about every 18 months.

In a similar vein, commercial jet technology was a British invention. Rolls-Royce was the first producer. This led to the production of the first jet transport aircraft. Later, the US took the lead (with Boeing and McDonnell-Douglas), which was, subsequently, seriously challenged by the European Airbus (a consortium of government-supported British, German, French and Spanish firms). Government support of the Airbus provoked a sharp reaction from the US (which ignored the fact that US aircraft producers were generously subsidised through defence contracts). This led to the GATT Agreement on Trade in Civil Aircraft (1979). While 'supporting' the civil aircraft programmes, the signatories 'shall seek to avoid adverse effects on trade in civil aircraft' (Article 6.1). This is a statement that offers a number of different interpretations.[32] As such, it was insufficient to calm down tensions in aircraft trade. A Bilateral Agreement (1992) between the US and the EU was supposed to introduce a framework for all government 'involvement' in the development of commercial aircraft with 100 seats or more. However, it did not take account of past damage. The deal did not eliminate, but merely constrained, subsidies (for innovation and R&D). It set quantitative limits on both direct and indirect (military) subsidies for the development of new aircraft. The permitted limit for the direct subsidy for the development cost of a new aircraft was set at 33 per cent. Identifiable benefits from indirect subsidies were limited to 4 per cent of each firm's annual sales (Tyson, 1992, p. 207).

A positive effect on innovation (creation of technology) in the EU was expected to come from the operation of the Single European Market. A deepened regional market would stimulate competition and provide an incentive to innovation that would further promote competition for the benefit of the consumers. If corrective measures (in support of trade, competition or industrial policy) were added, they would not necessarily violate a liberal trading system in the long term. They would simply add an adjustment mechanism to the already highly imperfect and suboptimal market situation.

Perfect competition (perfectly contestable market) is based on zero entry and exit costs in an industry. This eliminates inefficient firms from a market, but at the same time rewards the efficient ones. Joseph Schumpeter called this process 'creative destruction'. Competition is not driven by changes in prices, but rather by innovation and introduction of new products. If equilibrium is ever achieved, it is at best a short-term and temporary event. If inter-country factor mobility is allowed for, the supply of factors (labour, capital, land, technology, organisation and entrepreneurship) increases. This 'pluralism' backs innovation in technology, goods, services, organisation and control. Competition probably operates best when a firm believes that it is in a process that is leading it towards becoming a monopolist (at best) or an oligopolist (at least). However, consumers may suffer in a monopolistic or oligopolistic industry structure. This can be redressed somewhat if oligopolistic firms introduce the most efficient innovations as rapidly as perfectly competitive firms would and if governments prevent such a market structure from behaving in a non-competitive way.

Small open economies inevitably have to rely on various foreign technologies. Such countries often do not have the necessary resources to develop basic technologies for all lines of production. If this situation is regarded as detrimental, then economic integration may increase the pool of resources (human, technological and financial) for innovation and the development of new technologies, products and inputs, which may mitigate the potential disadvantage of smallness and isolation. Such pooling started in the EU in the mid-1980s with a series of R&D programmes.

In a relatively well-integrated area such as the EU, one would expect the prices of similar goods in different countries to be similar, owing to competition and trade. The stronger the competition and the larger the volume of trade, other things being equal, the smaller the price variation. Pre-tax prices of the same good would be expected to vary only as a result of differences in the cost of transportation, handling, insurance and, to some extent, marketing between countries. However, this expectation is not borne out in reality. The EU was aware of the barriers to competition other than tariffs and quotas (NTBs), so it created the Single European Market in 1993.

Various regional factors prevent full equalisation of prices. Some geographical areas may have small markets for certain goods and services (for example, parasols in Finland and antifreeze in Greece). So, in order to do business there, firms may price their goods relatively higher. In this case market presence may be a much more important public policy and private business objective than requiring price homogenisation in all markets. Or, for example, differences in taste or special requirements regarding the basic ingredients of a product (for instance, chocolate) may cause the price of a good to vary. And, if there are local substitutes, foreign suppliers may modify the price of their goods. Some goods (such as wine) may be regarded as luxuries in one country and taxed accordingly, but regarded as basic necessities in another country. This widens the price gap for the same good in different countries, and sometimes even in different regions of the same country. In a perfectly competitive market (with free entry and exit) for a good, free competition ensures equality of prices and drives profits to zero. In imperfectly competitive markets there is scope for price variation and, therefore, for profits.

The problem of innovation and new technology not resulting in an obvious and measurable increase in output is known as the 'productivity paradox'.

Some argue that there is no technological revolution and that computers are not productive: a personal computer that is 100 times more powerful than one made ten years ago is not proportionately more productive. Others argue that decades must pass before the fruits of technological breakthroughs can be discerned. Yet others insist that there are benefits, but that standard statistical tools are inadequate to measure them. This is most obvious in the services sector. How can the output of a bank be measured? Has the economy become so complex and fast-changing[33] that it has become unmeasurable? If this is so, it is harder and harder to regulate it, and to tax it.

SPECIALISATION AND RETURNS TO SCALE

From the vantage point of production, it might be expected that economies of scale would require some level of standardisation that would restrict product variety and consumer choice. Standards are technical regulations that specify the characteristics of goods. They deal, in general, with safety, health and environmental protection. Standards can be quite different in different countries. So, if there is a common *ex ante* trust among trading partners, these national standards may be mutually recognised among them at no cost. However, if this trust is missing, harmonisation of standards among them may be a solution, but it brings *ex post* costs to firms.

It can be difficult and time consuming to harmonise standards in an integrated area for trade and competition purposes. For example, it took 11 years for the EU to agree on the technical standards for mineral water. This and other examples from the 1970s are clear proof that such an approach will never result in a genuine single market in the EU. Hence, the EU opted for the mutual recognition of national standards in the short and medium terms. The EU strategy for the longer term is an evolutionary convergence of minimum standards towards best-practice rules. This places traders in different countries on an equal footing and eliminates the disadvantages to some of them that accrue from NTBs.

Trade in general, and intra-industry trade in particular, could increase choice (product variety) in countries compared with autarky. Product differentiation could reduce export opportunities for small open economies such as Austria, Belgium or Switzerland. These countries have little influence on foreign tastes and tend to enjoy comparative advantages in semimanufactured and standardised goods (Gleiser et al., 1980, p. 521). However, participation in the Single European Market assisted in the attraction of a large inflow of FDI to countries such as Belgium, Ireland and Spain. A strong presence of TNCs shifted the trade structure of these countries towards differentiated products. Hence, the original standard-goods specialisation hypothesis does not apply in these cases (Sleuwaegen and de Backer, 2001, p. 395).

In the field of consumer durable goods, for example, the market in the US and Japan is dominated by one or two brands and the manufacturers are able to take advantage of economies of scale. In the EU the situation is quite different. Almost every country has its own producer of consumer durables, but the American and Japanese formula for the spatial distribution of production cannot easily be replicated because of diverse and deeply rooted national preferences. While Britons like to load their washing machines from the front, the French prefer to do so from the top. The Dutch prefer high-powered machines that can spin most of the moisture out of the washing, whereas the Italians prefer low spin speeds and allow the southern sun to do the drying. This situation affects the geography of production and protects against competition from third-country suppliers, but also restricts competition from within the EU, as each producer is prevented from following a pan-European production and marketing strategy. This may be, perhaps, a blessing. Otherwise if all is homogenised, then Europeans would look uniform and 'identical' as was the case in China during the Maoist Period (1949–76) or harmonised in taste as is by and large the case in the US (with certain clear exceptions, cities, towns and settlements in the US look almost the same).

In the case of relatively new goods and services, however, consumers' preferences are identical in different countries. A certain degree of standardisation, even unification is possible, even necessary. It is likely that French cheese producers are going to look for the same qualities in a mobile phone, photocopier or a fax machine, as do Italian wine exporters. Thus, for example, common corporate governance, accounting, company or banking laws and standards could be quite useful throughout the EU and beyond. Business accounts were once simple and short, while shareholders trusted the management of a company not to mislead them. Then accountants started to prepare accurate and detailed financial statements that were totally misleading. Such practices of financial engineering (cooking the books) ended up in several huge financial scandals which include Enron (2002) in the US and Parmalat (2003) in the EU.

If in the EU harmonisation of standards means that they continue to rise, then the overall level of regulation and costs of production will increase. Southern, Central and Eastern European countries will find it increasingly difficult to withstand international competition and will grow at a slower pace than the rest of the EU. As growth falls, demand for protection increases. Alternatively, if, for example, some types of labour regulation are allowed to vary in member states and the framework of mutual recognition is maintained, then the northern EU countries could abolish some laws and the Southern, Central and Eastern European countries would grow rapidly. EU growth would continue at a substantial rate, which would permit the implementation of a liberal trade policy. The ultimate irony is that only the latter course would allow northern EU countries to pay high wages and sustain a heavy social expenditure (Curzon Price, 1991, p. 124).

Although the Single Market Programme (1985–92) removed many NTBs to internal trade in the EU, others still persist and make it imperfect. Before the era of the Single European Market, the major obstacles to internal trade included physical border controls, technical barriers (standards and product/service regulations), public procurement,[34] different intellectual and industrial property laws, state aids and fiscal barriers, as well as obstacles to the mobility of labour and capital. The Single Market Programme made a distinction between what had to be harmonised and what could be left to mutual recognition. While EU standards are being developed, the guiding principle should be mutual recognition of national standards. EU standards are being developed on a large scale, about 1000 of them a year. However, too many national regulations are still being produced, making it as hard as ever to reach a truly homogeneous Single European Market (Curzon Price, 1996a).

More than a decade after its establishment in 1993, the Single European Market is not yet delivering its full benefits to consumers and firms. This is most obvious in services that account for over 70 per cent of EU GDP.[35] For example, the EU did not get rid of internal barriers in areas that include fiscal measures in financial services (tax on savings, investment income tax and death duties), slot allocations in air transport or in advertising. Belgian electricians have to pay three times the Belgian rate to register with the Luxembourg authorities for a one-day job or Austrian bakers require eight different licences if they want to set up business in Italy.[36] The Single European Market may be weakening. So may be the chance to turn the EU into the world's most competitive knowledge-based economy by 2010. Hence, the European Commission intends to be more active in tearing down barriers in the services sector.

Various attempts to harmonise diverse goods at EU level created a public furore in some countries. Examples include the fuss over prawn cocktail crisps in Britain; the permissible level of bacteria in cheese in France;[37] small apples in Denmark; the use of other than durum (hard) wheat for pasta in Italy; the application of other than the *Reinheitsgebot* (of 1516) purity rule for brewing beer in Germany; and the removal of the tilde (~) from computer keyboards in Spain. Each year every EU country produces thousands of new regulations on new technologies and products. Every one that relates to the smooth operation of the internal market must be submitted to the European Commission. As each one carries a possible seed of conflict, it must be treated with caution, and, following implementation, monitored constantly and carefully otherwise the genuine Single European Market may disappear. Thus, Decision 3052/95 (adopted in 1995 and implemented in 1997) provides an improved procedure to deal with the remaining obstacles to the free movement of goods in the Single European Market. The decision obliges member states to notify the European Commission of individual measures preventing the free movement of a model, type or category of a product that has been made or sold legally in another country.[38] The purpose of the measure is to encourage member states to think twice before making any exception to the EU system of mutual recognition.[39]

The neo-classical theory of international trade argues that countries should specialise in the production of those goods and services for which they have a comparative advantage. Modern theories question this line of reasoning: the international geography of production, specialisation and trade are affected by other factors as well. Economies of scale stimulate specialisation in production for a narrow market niche but on a wide international market. This may entail only the reallocation of resources within a single industry or sometimes within a single company. Modern 'footloose' industries are not linked to any particular geographical region by inputs such as iron ore or copper. Thus, a country's comparative advantage can be created by deliberate actions of firms, banks and/or governments.

Returns to scale have not been thoroughly studied in the theory of economic integration because it is difficult to model them. Therefore, one should be very careful about using classical theory either to describe what is likely to happen in a customs union or as a guide to policies that will ensure that such a union or other type of integration fulfils its expectations. It is also important to bear in mind that a substantial part of production is linked with economies of scope rather than scale. While economies of scale imply a certain level of standardisation in tastes and production, economies of scope deal with the diversity in tastes, products and processes. Economies of scope allow firms such as Benetton to respond swiftly to changes in the supply of inputs and shifts in demand because they come from the common control of distinct, but interrelated production activities. For example, the same kind of fabric and sewing machines can be used in the production of various goods. Similarly, the same type of aircraft can be used for cargo and for passenger transport.

INTRA-INDUSTRY TRADE

Although increased competition offers potential gains from both more efficient industrial and geographical allocation of resources in production and increased consumption, there is no guarantee that these gains will be achieved in practice. If a government takes this view and believes that domestic production will be wiped out by foreign competition, then it may pursue a policy of protection on the grounds that it is better to produce something inefficiently at home than to produce nothing at all. This disastrous scenario has not been borne out in reality. The very existence of the EU, which has continued to expand in size, as well as in scope and depth, is the best example of a positive scenario. Most firms in the EU countries have not been put out of business because of competition from firms in partner countries. Instead, many of them have continuously increased their business in the long run. They have specialised in lines of production that satisfy distinct demand segments throughout the EU. This fact cannot be explained by the classical theories. The 'awkward fact' is that trade takes place in differentiated products (Eaton and Lipsey, 1997, pp. 228–9). Strong advertising campaigns create awareness about 'differences' among what are basically very similar and easily substitutable goods (for instance, cars, printers, fax and photocopying machines, T-shirts, skis, soaps, toothpastes, TV sets, painkillers, breakfast cereals, refrigerators, trainers, cigarettes, bicycles or audio-, video- or DVD-recorders and cassettes and discs). This phenomenon is known in theory as intra-industry trade.[40] Generally, product differentiation tends to dominate product specialisation in the internal trade of the EU.

There are also other examples that support the thesis of a smooth intra-industry adjustment in trade and geography of production. Successive rounds of negotiations within the GATT reduced tariffs. The ensuing intra-industry adjustments in trade and specialisation among developed countries were relatively smooth. Contrary to the expectation of the factor endowment theory, intra-industry adjustment prevailed and carried fewer costs than would have been the case with inter-industry adjustment. If it is feared that foreigners will eliminate domestic firms through competition, exchange rates can act as an important safety-valve to prevent this happening and ease the process of adjustment to the new situation.

Inter-industry trade between countries basically reflects differences in national factor endowment. This type of trade brings efficiency gains through resource allocation, as well as benefits that come from the supply of a new set of different products. Intra-industry trade, on the other hand, is associated with product differentiation. Consumers benefit from this type of trade through increased variety of closely substitutable goods and services, as well as through increased competition of products made with increasing returns of scale.

As incomes have risen, consumers are no longer satisfied with identical or standardised goods. They demand and pay for varieties of the same basic good, often tailored to their individual needs and tastes. The larger is the variety of demanded and available goods and services, the smaller is the importance of economies of scale. Intra-industry trade refers to trade in differentiated commodities. It occurs when a country simultaneously exports and imports goods (final or semi-finished) that are close substitutes in consumption. Differentiation of goods begins when various characteristics are added to the basic good or component, backed up by strong R&D and advertising campaigns. Thus, gains from trade in differentiated goods may arise through an increase in consumer choice (not necessarily through lower prices only).

The variety of goods produced in a country, the new theory suggests, is limited by the existence of scale economies in production. Thus, similar countries have an incentive to trade. Their trade may often be in goods that are produced with similar factor proportions. Such trade does not involve the major adjustment problems that are commonly found with more conventional trade patterns (Krugman, 1990a, pp. 50–51). In fact, one of the most distinctive properties of the liberalisation of trade in the EU was an increase in intra-industry trade coupled with modest adjustment costs (Sapir, 1992, pp. 1496–7).

At the heart of neo-classical international trade and customs union theory is the analysis of two goods only. Therefore, it cannot satisfactorily account for preference diversity and intra-industry trade. The neo-classical theory's 'clean' model of perfect competition is not applicable here. The potential for intra-industry trade increases with the level of economic development, similarity in preferences (tastes), openness to trade and geographical proximity, which reduces the costs of transport, marketing and after-sales service.

A significant portion of trade among developed countries is intra-industry. In this case, variety may be preferred to quantity, so that some proportion of trade is attributable not only to differences in factor endowment, but also to different national preferences (tastes). This is the case in the EU. The response of successful firms to such business challenges is to find a specialist market niche and to employ economies of scope, rather than scale.

In an 'early' example of intra-industry trade, Linder (1961, p. 102) noted that ships that brought European beer to Milwaukee took American beer back to Europe. Although lacking a formal theory, the examination of international trade flows by Grubel and Lloyd (1975) noted that an important part of these flows was within the same industry classification.

Finger (1975) believes that intra-industry trade is an anomaly due to the definition of new products and processes and statistical sorting of data. However, Loertscher and Wolter (1980, p. 286) demonstrated that intra-industry trade between countries is not a statistical fabrication, but a real phenomenon. This type of trade between countries is likely to be strong if:

- they are both relatively highly developed;
- the difference in their level of development is small;
- they have large national markets;
- the barriers to trade are low;
- there is a high potential for product differentiation;
- entry in narrow product lines is obstructed by significant barriers (sunk costs); and
- transaction costs are low.

Research shows that incentives to intra-industry trade are similar levels of per capita income and country size, product differentiation, participation in regional integration schemes, common borders, as well as similar language and culture. Negative influences on this type of trade are exerted by standardisation (reduction in consumer choice), distance between countries (which increases the cost of information and services necessary for trade in differentiated goods) and trade barriers that reduce all trade flows (Balassa and Bauwens, 1988, p. 1436).

Intra-industry trade is relatively high among developed countries. It refers to trade within the same trade classification group. One may, therefore, wonder whether intra-industry trade is a statistical aberration rather than an authentic phenomenon. In addition, it may be argued that two varieties of the same product are not always two distinct goods. The criteria for data aggregation in the Standard International Trade Classification (SITC) are similarity in inputs and substitutability in consumption. These criteria often contradict each other. Many of the three-digit groups in the SITC include heterogeneous commodities. For example, SITC 751 (office machines) includes typewriters, word-processing machines, cash registers and photocopying machines, whereas SITC 895 (office and stationery supplies) includes filing cabinets, paper clips, fountain pens, chalk and typewriter ribbons. On these grounds one could conclude that intra-industry trade is a pure statistical fabrication. However, this is not so in reality. If one studied trade groups with more than three digits, differences could and would appear. The index of intra-industry trade (IIT) in a country is represented by the ratio of the absolute difference between exports and imports in a trade classification group to the sum of exports and imports in the same classification group:

$$IIT = 1 - \frac{|X_i - M_j|}{X_i + M_j}. \qquad (5.3)$$

The intra-industry trade index (equation (5.3)) is high and is equal to 1 for complete intra-industry specialisation (a country imports and exports goods in a group in the same quantity). This is a sign of a geographical spread of an industry. The index is low and equals zero for complete inter-industry specialisation. Such spatial concentration of production is usually the result of high entry barriers and economies of scale. However, the index does not distinguish between cross-hauling of final output and intra-industry trade that is the consequence of production sharing within an industry. It does not distinguish between quality-differentiated trade in goods either. In any case, intra-industry trade increases welfare because it extends the variety of available goods to the consumers. As there is no evidence of large adjustment costs to this type of trade, one may conclude that intra-industry trade makes everyone better off.

The *ex ante* expectation that trade liberalisation and integration could shift the IIT index closer to 1 (suggesting a geographical spread of production) in the case of developed countries has been investigated in numerous studies.[41] Among the EU countries, the IIT index was highest in 1987 for France (0.83), Britain (0.77), Belgium (0.77), Germany (0.76) and the Netherlands (0.76) and lowest in Portugal (0.37) and Greece (0.31), implying that these two countries had a high inter-industry specialisation (*European Economy*, 1990b, pp. 40–41). None the less, various statistical results regarding the significance of intra-industry trade may be called into doubt. For example, if there are strong centripetal (agglomeration) forces in high-technology or chemical industries because of economies of scale and production linkages, the IIT index should be low. However, 'average intra-EU IIT in high-tech products has been higher than the overall mean for most of our sample period, which indicates above average geographical dispersion of these sectors' (Brülhart, 1998b, pp. 328–9). This is an indication that additional theoretical and empirical work needs to be done in this field (Brülhart, 1998a, p. 790).

Some goods belonging to the same classification group may be perfect substitutes and have identical end uses (for example, plates). However, plates can be made of china, glass, paper, plastic, wood, metal or ceramic. Every type of this end product requires totally different and unrelated factor inputs and production technology. Other examples include tableware, furniture, clothing and so on. These differences among goods that enter a single SITC group may not be important for statistical records, but they are often of crucial importance to consumers. Demand for a variety of products increases with a rise in income. Higher income gives consumers the opportunity to express variety in taste through, for example, purchasing different styles of clothing. Economic integration may change consumers' preferences as the choice of goods available before the formation of a customs union or reduction in tariffs may be quite different.

Integration in the EU increased intra-industry trade within this group of countries, whereas integration in the former Council for Mutual Economic Assistance (CMEA) had as its consequence greater inter-industry trade (Drabek and Greenaway, 1984, pp. 463–4). Preferences in the centrally planned economies are revealed through plan targets and are different from those in economies in which market forces demonstrate consumer preferences. In market economies, competition takes place among firms, whereas in centrally planned economies competition occurs among different plans offered to the central planning body. A free trade area between the US and Canada (1987) was not expected to alter crucially the pattern of trade between these two countries. One reason was that the last step in the reduction in tariffs agreed during the Tokyo Round of the GATT negotiations took place in 1987. After this reduction, trade between the US and Canada became largely free: 80 per cent of all trade was duty free, while a further 15 per cent was subject to a tariff of 5 per cent or less. Another reason was that consumer tastes are more similar in North America than between countries in the EU.

The fact that a large part of trade among developed countries is intra-industry may lead to the conclusion that the Heckscher–Ohlin (factor proportions) theory of trade is not valid. Intra-industry trade is not based on differences in factor endowments among countries. Countries tend to specialise and export goods that are demanded by the majority of domestic consumers. It is this demand that induces production, rather than domestic factor endowment. Countries have a competitive edge in the production of these goods and thus gain an advantage in foreign markets, while they import goods demanded by a minority of the home population (Linder, 1961). The US, Japan and Germany have the greatest comparative advantage in goods for which their home market is relatively big. These are standardised goods for mass consumption. There is, however, one major exception. The major market for German dyes is the British textiles industry (and to a lesser extent that in the US). The German domestic market for dyestuffs is relatively small (Nelson, 1999, p. 12). However, Toyota has achieved world leadership in passenger cars, even though its domestic market is smaller than that of General Motors. The size of the domestic market in this case became less significant than the technological competitive advantage.

An important analytical question is whether factor proportions (Heckscher–Ohlin) or economic geography (determined by economies of scale and market access) is more important to predict trade within industries. Limited research found that in the case of Sweden, it turned out that the answer was both. A large domestic market, as well as plentiful endowment of human capital increases the quality of exports (Greenaway and Torstensson, 2000, p. 277).

Petrus Verdoorn suggested that the principal difference in manufacturing between US and European firms is not so much the size of firm/plant as the length of the individual production run. The range of processes carried out in the same factory is much smaller in the US than in Europe (Hague, 1960, p. 346). Compared with plants in the same industry, production runs in the US are several times larger than in Europe, even when the plants are owned by the same TNC (Pratten, 1971, pp. 195, 308–9; 1988, pp. 69–70). On the other hand, even in the most-efficient developed countries, manufacturing is often carried out in factories of quite moderate size. Differences in plant productivity are best explained by (1) inappropriate labour relations, in particular where many thousands of workers need to be employed together; (2) inadequate level of technical training; and (3) an unsatisfactory incentives structure (Prais, 1981, pp. 272 ff.). In support of one of these arguments (1), it has been found that the number of strikes increases exponentially with plant size (Geroski and Jacquemin, 1985, p. 174).

Because of a larger and more homogenised market, which required large production runs, labour productivity in the manufacturing industries in 1986 was some 50 per cent higher in the US than in Germany. This figure may overstate the difference in productivity between the two countries as it makes little allowance for the high quality of German manufactured products (Pratten, 1988, pp. 126–7). For example, a preoccupation with large quantities of output and economies of scale rendered the taste of standard American chocolate, for a European, appalling.

Intra-industry trade may be described in terms of monopolistic competition and product differentiation. Perfect competition is not a realistic market structure, so perfect monopolistic competition is the most perfect market structure in a situation with differentiated goods (Lancaster, 1980). Armington's assumption states that products in the same industry, but from different countries, are imperfect substitutes (Armington, 1969, p. 160). In other words, buyers' preferences for different(iated) goods are independent. Armington's assumption, however, overestimated the degree of market power of a particular producer.

Three main findings stem from the data presented in Table 5.3. First, intra-industry trade is relatively high in the EU. Second, there was a convergence of levels of intra-industry trade across countries between 1961 and 1990. The countries with the lowest initial levels of intra-industry trade experienced sharp increases over this period. Third, intra-industry trade in

Table 5.3 Intra-industry trade within the EU by member country, 1961–92

Country	1961	1967	1972	1977	1985	1988	1990	1992
Belgium–Luxembourg	0.51	0.56	0.49	0.57	0.56	0.57	0.58	0.60
Denmark	0.30	0.37	0.41	0.44	0.42	0.44	0.43	0.47
France	0.60	0.69	0.67	0.71	0.68	0.67	0.67	0.72
Germany	0.47	0.56	0.57	0.57	0.60	0.59	0.61	0.68
Greece	0.02	0.06	0.08	0.10	0.15	0.15	0.16	0.15
Ireland	0.22	0.28	0.36	0.45	0.40	0.38	0.38	0.41
Italy	0.44	0.56	0.57	0.56	0.52	0.51	0.51	0.51
Netherlands	0.54	0.57	0.59	0.59	0.60	0.62	0.61	0.67
Portugal	0.04	0.10	0.13	0.14	0.24	0.25	0.30	0.31
Spain	0.10	0.16	0.29	0.38	0.47	0.56	0.57	0.60
UK	0.51	0.67	0.65	0.71	0.62	0.59	0.64	0.68
EU	0.48	0.56	0.57	0.59	0.58	0.58	0.59	0.64

Notes: Unadjusted Grubel and Lloyd indices calculated from SITC five digit statistics from OECD for SITC sections 5–8.
Average of eleven countries, weighted by values of intra-EU manufactured imports and exports.

Source: Brülhart and Elliott (1999, p. 106).

manufactured goods in the EU grew consistently in the 1960s and early 1970s and then stabilised, but it resumed its increasing trend between 1988 and 1992. However, it is important to bear in mind that the SITC was revised twice in this period, in 1978 and in 1988. Thus, it is not possible to conclude that the upward trend in intra-industry trade in the EU is slowing down. In addition, it appears that the Single Market Programme, contrary to the *ex ante* predictions, 'did not entail an increase in inter-industry specialisation' (Brülhart and Elliott, 1999, pp. 106–9). It could be concluded that the increase in intra-industry trade in the EU is evidence that economic integration did not produce a geographical concentration of production in select EU regions or countries.

Further data show that between 1968 and 1990 specialisation increased in Denmark, Germany, Greece, Italy and the Netherlands. A significant increase was recorded in Belgium, Britain, France, Portugal and Spain between 1980 and 1990. Data indicate that there was either a fall in specialisation or no noteworthy change in Britain, Portugal and Spain between 1968 and 1990. The most likely explanation is that, before joining the EU, these countries had relatively high trade barriers that protected production for which there was no national comparative advantage. Entry into the EU eliminated administrative trade barriers and reduced trade costs. However, in all countries, specialisation increased over the 1980–90 period.

'So with integration, specialisation may initially fall during structural adjustment and then increase. This would explain why Spain, Portugal, and the UK, which were all late joiners to the EU, show a fall in specialisation when comparing 1968–1990, and an upward trend starting in the late 1970s and early 1980s' (Amiti, 1999, p. 579).

Each country's geography of production became different from the rest in the group. Although this reallocation of resources has obvious benefits that come from specialisation, the snag is that specialised countries may react in a different way to asymmetric shocks and require diverse policy instruments to counter them. Therefore, in the light of the eurozone and eastern enlargement, there is a strong need for the creation of EU policy tools to counter such obstacles to the smooth operation of the Single European Market.

Instead of taking goods themselves as the basis for analysis, 'address models' of goods differentiation take characteristics that are embodied in commodities as their starting point (Lipsey, 1987a). A computer is a good that can be considered as a collection of different attributes, such as memory, speed, printing, graphics and the like. Figure 5.3 illustrates two characteristics of a set of goods (computers).

Each good (computer) A, B and C, has a certain combination of characteristic S (speed) and characteristic M (memory). Each good is defined by its location in the continuous space of characteristics, hence it has a certain 'address'. Consumer preferences are defined by characteristics, not goods. Some consumers prefer memory over speed, whereas others prefer the opposite. Under the assumption that all three goods in Figure 5.3 have the same price, let a consumer have tastes embodied in the indifference curve II. This consumer maximises utility by purchasing good B. Each good in this model has close and distant neighbours. There are many goods and many consumers. Every consumer attempts to attain his or her highest indifference curve. This gives rise to intra-industry trade. Address models of localised (monopolistic) competition can be an important factor in explaining intra-industry trade and, hence, contribute to the explanation of the location of production.

All general explanations of trade in differentiated goods refer only to final goods traded among developed countries. In addition, intra-industry trade is affected by imperfect product markets (monopolisation) and by consumer demand for a variety of goods. Economies of scale can be another important factor in explaining trade in differentiated goods.

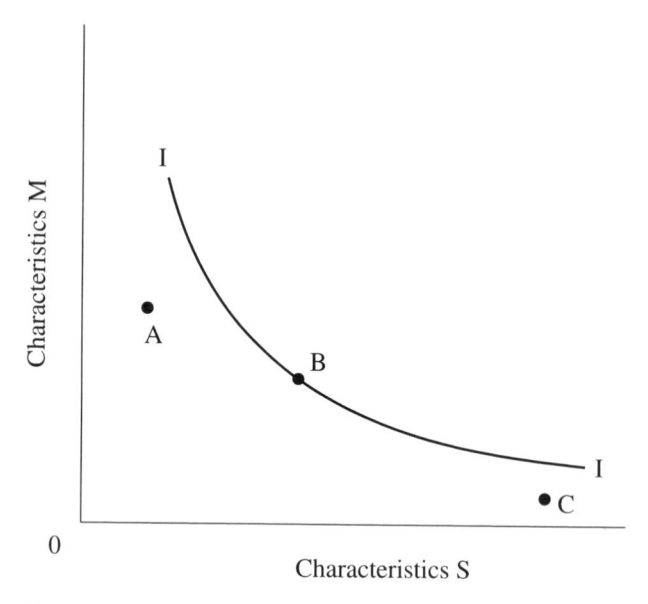

Figure 5.3   Characteristics of computers

Countries with a similar endowment of factors will still trade. Imperfect information about goods on the part of consumers might have had an impact on intra-industry trade in the past, but this aspect is rapidly diminishing as the Internet, global advertising and other methods of disseminating information worldwide gain importance.

The Heckscher–Ohlin theory gives students the impression that the factor proportions theory of trade is orthodox. Linder's theory tends to be less rigorous and thus has not made the same impression on students. None the less, Leamer (1984) found evidence which supports the classical theory, while Greenaway and Torstensson (2000) found that both factor proportions and economic geography variables appear to be important in determining trade within industries. Linder's research does not reject the factor proportion theory, but rather it asserts that factor proportion is not the only cause of trade. One may conclude that the factor proportions theory determines geographical location of production (specialisation) and trade *among* different SITC classification groups, while economies of scale and diversity in tastes determine the geography of production and trade *within* SITC classification groups. As most changes in demand take place *within* certain clusters of goods, this is a sign that changes in technology are important driving forces of trade and (re)allocation of production.

3. European Union

INTRODUCTION

Competition policy is one of the foremost economic policies of the EU. It is also an area where centralisation of authority makes full sense. The European Commission has special responsibility for the proper operation of competition in the EU because it 'handles' a much larger number of firms than any member country. The European Commission's approach to this policy is based on strict rules. Basic rules (including exceptions) in EU competition policy can be found in the Treaty of Rome and the rulings of the Court of Justice.

In essence, there should be no barriers to internal trade and competition in the EU. Freedom of movement for goods, services, people and capital (four freedoms) are contained in Article 3(c) of the Treaty of Rome. The EU does not tolerate any discrimination on the grounds of nationality[42] (Article 12). 'The internal market shall comprise an area without internal frontiers in which the free movement of goods, persons, services and capital is ensured' (Article 14). This provision was intended to abolish NTBs on internal trade and ensure the most liberal competition rules for EU residents. Freedom of movement of goods is elaborated in Articles 23–31.[43] Free movement (and establishment) of persons, services and capital is regulated by Articles 39–60. As for national tax provisions, they must not discriminate against goods that originate in other member states of the EU (Articles 90–93). In addition, Article 157 requires both the EU and its member states to ensure the necessary conditions for competitiveness of the EU industry.

Competition rules are founded on the assumption that the concentration of (private) economic power within monopolies, oligopolies, cartels or other market structures that have similar negative effects on consumers need to be outlawed and/or regulated and monitored. Individual economic freedom needs to be fostered through the rules of market competition. The objective of this approach is to allocate factors among sectors and space according to the criteria of efficiency and, hence, contribute to an increase in the average standard of living.

In 1985, the EU accepted a technical blueprint, known as the Single Market Programme,[44] which outlined 282 measures for the attainment of the genuine Single European Market by the end of 1992. Its founding principle was the removal of NTBs to internal trade in the EU. The move from a fragmented to a genuinely integrated market can produce some of the most striking results of economic integration. The Single Market Programme was meant to increase competition and increase the competitiveness of EU goods and services compared with exports from the US, Japan and the newly industrialised countries. The programme removed border controls, introduced mutual recognition of standards, established a single licence and home country autonomy over financial services and opened national public procurement contracts to suppliers from other EU member countries.

The principal gains of the Single European Market come not from the reduction in the costs of internal EU trade, which is a result of the removal of NTBs, but rather from the longer-term dynamic benefits of increased competition on the expanded internal market. This was supposed to stimulate economies of scale, removal of X-inefficiency, exit of the weakest and growth of the strongest firms, innovation and breakdown of collusive behaviour. The anti-competitive market behaviour of various local monopolies is largely checked. Competition in the EU could, however, be furthered if EU internal liberalisation were coupled with external trade liberalisation. There are at least two arguments for additional external opening of the EU in order to deepen competition. First, intra-EU trade is mostly in differentiated products (intra-industry). Second, an element of intra-EU trade takes place between subsidiaries of a single TNC. Extra-EU competitive pressure is necessary to ease such an oligopolistic structure and increase the competitiveness of both traditional and new-growth industries (Jacquemin and Sapir, 1991).

Monetary union is expected to help businesses to eliminate the risk and costs associated with currency fluctuations. The elimination of this distortion of competition, trade and investment will contribute to the reduction in intra-EU trade costs. The existence of the euro will guide the EU economy towards a greater price transparency that will ease and motivate expansion in intra-EU trade. The whole process will lead towards a downward convergence in prices.

Here we shall concentrate on the rules that govern the actions of firms and governments to prevent them from reducing competition in the Single European Market and, hence, have an impact on spatial distribution of production. Two articles of the Treaty of Rome govern the actions of *firms*. Article 81 refers to restrictions on competition, while Article 82 prohibits the abuse of a dominant position. *Governments* may also jeopardise the process of competition. This is the case with state aids (subsidies). Article 87 regulates this issue. The European Commission must be notified of all cases of aid above a certain level so that it can examine its legality and compatibility with the goals of the EU.

There were 321 new cases of breaches of Articles 81 and 82, respectively, (Figure 5.4) in 2002. The volume and dynamics of closed cases are presented in Figure 5.5. In addition, there were 613 new cases[45] of violation of Article 87 that were referred to the European Commission in 2002. This all

Competition policy

[Bar chart showing values for 1997–2002:
- 1997: 499 total (Notifications 221, Complaints 177, Cases opened 101)
- 1998: 509 total (Notifications 218, Complaints 192, Cases opened 101)
- 1999: 388 total (Notifications 162, Complaints 149, Cases opened 77)
- 2000: 297 total (Notifications 101, Complaints 112, Cases opened 84)
- 2001: 284 total (Notifications 94, Complaints 116, Cases opened 74)
- 2002: 321 total (Notifications 101, Complaints 129, Cases opened 91)
Legend: Notifications, Complaints, Cases opened on Commission's own initiative]

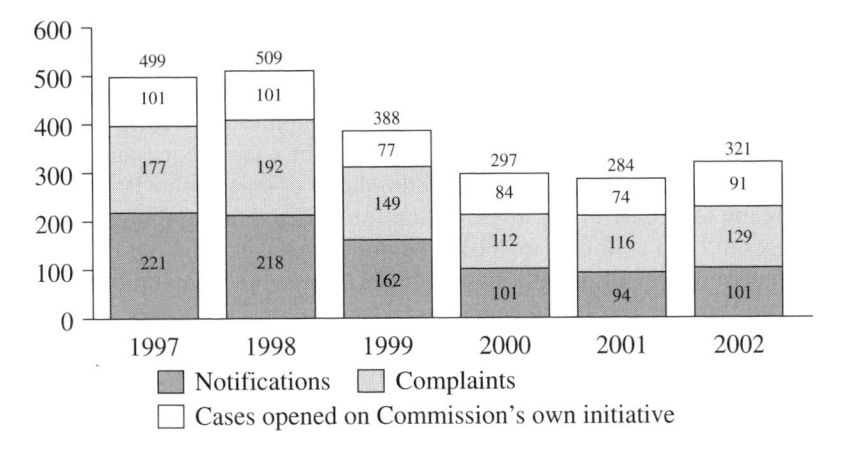

Source: European Commission (2003).

Figure 5.4 New completion-related cases, 1997–2002

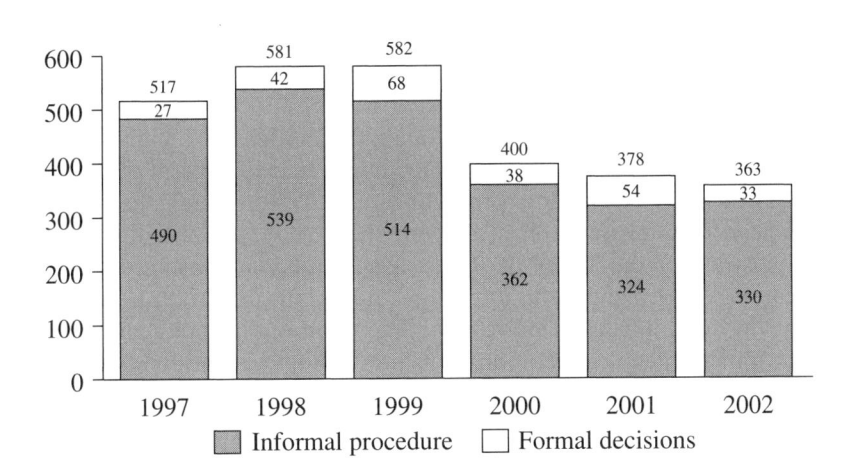

[Bar chart showing values for 1997–2002:
- 1997: 517 total (Informal procedure 490, Formal decisions 27)
- 1998: 581 total (Informal 539, Formal 42)
- 1999: 582 total (Informal 514, Formal 68)
- 2000: 400 total (Informal 362, Formal 38)
- 2001: 378 total (Informal 324, Formal 54)
- 2002: 363 total (Informal 330, Formal 33)
Legend: Informal procedure, Formal decisions]

Source: European Commission (2003).

Figure 5.5 Closed completion-related cases, 1997–2002

indicates that the European Commission is quite active in the policy area of market competition.

In order to implement its duties as the guardian of the Treaty of Rome, the Council of Ministers issued Regulation 17/62 (1962). The European Commission has the right to request relevant information from all enterprises, their associations and member states. If the information is not provided, the Commission may impose a daily fine of up to €1000 until the information is provided. The European Commission is also empowered to investigate the case. This includes 'dawn raids' (unannounced early-morning visits) to the premises of the parties involved in a case. For example, the European Commission 'raided' mobile phone companies in Britain and Germany as a part of an investigation into price fixing on international charges in both countries in 2001. The police may also raid the European Commission's premises without warning. This was the price fraud, corruption and insider trading in cereals markets case of 15 October 2003 (see Chapter 4 on the CAP).

One of many examples occurred in 1995, when inspectors raided the offices of Volkswagen and Audi in Germany, as well as the premises of their Italian distributor Autogerma. Inspectors may examine books, accounts and business records, take copies and ask questions, although the approval of the visited party is required as the investigators are not permitted to use force. As the information obtained may disclose business secrets, the European Commission must use it exclusively for the purpose of the case in question. The 'dawn raids' on various VW premises found that the company was threatening to end contracts with 50 dealers who were selling to non-Italian residents, and in fact had already done so in 12 cases.

If an infringement of the rules is found, the European Commission may fine the culpable party/parties. The maximum fine is 10 per cent of the total annual turnover of the enterprise concerned. When setting the fine, the European Commission considers both the gravity and the duration of the violation of the Treaty of Rome. Aggravating circumstances include repeated infringements, refusal to cooperate and the role of the head of the company in the infringement. Attenuating conditions include a passive role in the infringement, cooperation in the proceedings and termination of the infringement following intervention by the European Commission. In 1998, the Commission fined VW €102 million. The size of the fine reflected the duration of the felony (which began in 1987 and continued until 1993 in spite of repeated warnings). A look at the fines imposed by the European Commission shows that these have been increasing over time. The guilty parties may appeal against decisions of the European Commission to the Court of First Instance. A further appeal may be brought before the Court of Justice.

The European Commission found that 13 manufacturers of vitamins participated in cartels that allocated sales quotas, fixed and increased prices, as well as set up a system to monitor and enforce their agreements. Eight companies, led by Hoffmann-La Roche and BASF, were fined €855 million in total in 2001. The Hoffmann-La Roche portion of the fine, €462 million, was one of the biggest ever imposed on a single company by the European Commission.

RESTRICTION OF COMPETITION

It is increasingly risky and costly to develop a new good, service, technology or organisational and control competence. The same is often true for entering a new market. Thus, sharing costs and risk, as well as achieving economies of scale, is a major incentive for firms to form various types of partnership. Article 81 of the Treaty of Rome prohibits 'as incompatible with the common market' all explicit or implicit, as well as horizontal or vertical agreements (collusion) among firms that may have a negative impact on internal EU trade 'and which have as their object or effect the prevention, restriction or distortion of competition within the common market', unless authorised by the European Commission. Private practices that restrict competition according to this article include:

- direct or indirect fixing of prices and other trading conditions;
- limitation or control of production, markets, technical development or investment;
- sharing of markets;
- application of dissimilar conditions to equivalent transactions with different clients; and
- tying unconnected transactions into contracts.

It has been recognised for quite some time, at least in the smaller countries in Europe, that there is a need for some spatial concentration of business. Hence, Article 81(3) itemises the exemptions from the general EU rules of competition. Its application is often based on political compromises, hence the potential danger (uncertainty) that comes from the lack of transparency. An agreement, decision or practice may be declared as compatible with the common market if it contributes to an improvement in the production or distribution of goods, or to the promotion of economic or technical progress, 'while allowing consumers a fair share of the resulting benefit'. In addition, to be exempt from the standard rules of competition, the restrictive agreement must be necessary for the accomplishment of the desired business end (the appropriateness principle).

If some kinds of business practice occur frequently and are generally compatible with the rules of competition, if certain conditions are fulfilled, the European Commission may grant a *block exemption*. For example, Commission Regulation 2659/2000 block exempts categories of R&D

agreements between competing firms. This regulation replaced an earlier block exemption (Regulation 418/85). It belongs to a new type of block exemption regulation that moves away from the former approach of looking primarily at contractual clauses in favour of a greater regard to the actual market power of the parties. The block exemption therefore works with a market share threshold that is set at 25 per cent (combined market share of all parties to an agreement). Beyond these market shares, R&D agreements are not automatically prohibited, but have to be assessed individually. In this context, the Commission guidelines on horizontal cooperation agreements provide orientation to undertakings. However, 'hardcore' restrictions (price fixing, output limitation or allocation of markets or customers) remain prohibited. Other areas where block exemptions are in place include specialisation agreements, vertical restraints (distribution agreements), technology transfer agreements, as well as a certain number of sector-specific block exemptions.

Manufacturers in the EU constitute a powerful lobby with a large influence on economic policy. For example, car producers have been exempt (Article 81(3) of the Treaty of Rome) from the full rigour of competition since 1985 (Regulation 123/85). The rationale put forward by the car lobby, and accepted by the European Commission, was that cars are a unique type of consumer good: they are specialised items that require individual attention and after-sales service, there is an impact on the environment and road safety. Thus, cars are sold through tightly controlled exclusive dealerships and, as far as possible, serviced using only original spare parts (consumers benefit from the specialised knowledge of dealers, and service engineers, which should improve safety). In addition, producers control geographical market segmentation and regulate the quantity and prices of cars sold. Although there is little competition between retailers of the same type of the car, there is still solid competition among different producers of cars. Despite receiving such favour from the European Commission, car manufacturers have failed to fulfil their part of the bargain, that is, to allow consumers to shop around within the EU for the best deals. There are still significant differences in prices for the same type of a car among the member countries of the EU and guarantees are not honoured throughout the region. The consumers pay the cost of this uncompetitive behaviour in higher car prices and reduced choice.

In 1995, for instance, prospective buyers from Austria flooded into Italy to buy cars because identical models were as much as 30 per cent cheaper there (partly due to the depreciation of the lira). The Italian car dealers refused to sell cars to non-nationals. In other countries, dealers also often refuse to sell cars to non-nationals or discourage them from purchasing cars by quoting excessively long delivery times, various surcharges or warnings that after-sales service would not be honoured abroad. In spite of all these problems, in 1995 the block exemption was extended for a further seven years (Regulation 1475/95). The new terms allowed multidealership as a means of avoiding 'exclusive' dealership. However, this is a largely futile gesture as the second franchise had to be on different premises, under different management and in the form of a distinct legal entity. The British Consumers' Association sent a protest to the European Commission signed by 20 000 people saying that they were being 'ripped off' by the dealers.[46] This is not easily ignored and as the exemption has not brought tangible benefits to the consumers.

The European Commission changed the car dealership regime from October 2002. Under the new regime (valid until 2010) car dealers, even supermarkets, may sell cars from any manufacturer, negotiate and offer service with any service provider of their own choice, as well as open sales outlets anywhere in the EU. Car services may order spare parts from any supplier, not only from the ones that are selected by the car manufacturer. The new regime was founded on worthy intentions, as it is supposed to have some influence on the shape of the EU car market and bring certain gains to the consumers. However, massive changes in the EU car market are not expected. The entrenched local dealers and their knowledge of local clients' needs would still provide an effective entry barrier to the local market. Compounded with differences in taxes, the homogenisation of car prices in the EU will remain a pipe-dream.

Although there has been some reduction in price differentials for the same model of car in the EU over the past decade, price differences for the same car among EU member countries remain and are not likely do disappear soon. The 'normal' rules of competition do not apply in this important market. The car market remains a 'black hole' in the Single European Market, which formally started in 1993. Although the gap in pre-tax prices for cars has narrowed somewhat, it is still considerable, about 20 per cent on average across the eurozone countries. For the best-selling models in the small and medium-sized car market segments price differentials can be as much as 29 per cent for a VW Golf in 2003.

Examples of uncompetitive behaviour may be found elsewhere. Perfume producers have a similar right to license only upmarket shops to sell their products. And, after all, could or should competition laws force Burger King outlets to sell McDonald's hamburgers and vice versa?

A 1998 study of 53 homogeneous products in the eurozone by Lehman Brothers found that, on average, prices varied among countries by 24 per cent. This is twice as much as in the US.[47] Regional tastes differ. The Dutch eat much more yoghurt than others in the EU. Hence, the price of the same type of yoghurt is relatively lower in the Netherlands than in other EU member countries. Marketing methods and client convenience also have an impact on prices. Hence, ice cream or a soft drink may cost twice as much at a petrol station or on a beach than if bought in a packet of six in a supermarket. Prices will always differ by a margin that may include transport costs and differences in tax rates, but consumers tolerate small differences. The single currency (the euro), as well as Internet shopping and the competition that it introduced, are expected to lead to a convergence of prices, and those sellers that do not adjust will lose business. However, those that cater to the local market with specific regional tastes and preferences may not be affected to a large extent by increased competition.

There are objective factors that may explain a lack of price convergence and price disparities among different markets in an integrated area. They include the following:

- *Structural factors*: transport costs, type of good (perishable or not), consumer preferences, quality of good and the existence of branded and own-label products.
- *Behavioural factors*: business strategies of firms such as running distribution or market-sharing agreements.
- *Policy factors*: taxes, subsidies, permissions, quotas, standards that favour local firms, as well as other NTBs.

The EU ousted most of the policy-related factors from the Single European Market and it monitors and manages the behavioural ones. None the less, there are still differences in taxes and structural factors that will continue to have a negative impact on price convergence in the Single European Market even on homogeneous products (for example: sugar, washing powder or certain dairy products) which is entirely based on differences in prices.

The merger/acquisition control procedure of the EU has seven, often overlapping, steps. They are pre-notification discussions, notification, investigation, negotiation, decision, political evaluation and judicial scrutiny. The strength of the EU procedure in comparison with the past and with other jurisdictions is that it is:

- fast (the majority of cases are resolved within a month);
- flexible (pre-notification discussions resolve the question of the necessary background information for the decision); and
- a 'one-stop shop' (the European Commission is the single body in charge of receiving notifications, investigations and decisions).

The European Commission may approve a merger, clear it with conditions or block it. Although the EU procedure is simple, it has one (at least) major weakness: its lack of transparency. The European Commission has considerable discretionary room for manoeuvre in the decision-making process.[48]

Exemptions from the competition rules of the EU are possible under Article 81(3) of the Treaty of Rome. To obtain an exemption, the firms involved need to demonstrate that the benefits of the deal outweigh the anti-competitive effects. The firms need to prove to the European Commission that the deal improves production and/or distribution of goods/services and that it promotes technological progress. In addition, a 'fair share' of the resulting benefits must be passed on to consumers.

In the past, the procedure for clearance was quite long, typically taking up to two years to obtain an exception. However, since 1993, in the case of any deal (principally, but not exclusively, joint ventures) between firms that has implications for the structure of an industry, the parties must receive a consenting or a warning letter within two months of the mandatory notification of the European Commission about such an agreement. The first examples included an approved joint venture between Olivetti and Canon (1987) for the development and production of printers and fax machines. The justification for this exception was the avoidance of duplication of development costs and the transfer of technology from Canon (Japan) to Olivetti (Italy). The joint venture by Asea Brown Bovery (ABB) for the development and production of high-performance batteries was also approved on the grounds that it brings innovation, reduces dependence on imported oil and, indirectly, improves the quality of life of consumers. In 1991, however, a merger between Aérospatiale and Alenia/de Havilland was prohibited on the grounds that the merged company would enjoy a dominant position in the worldwide market for medium-sized (40–59 seats) turbopropelled aeroplanes.

Competition rules apply not only to the written and enforceable deals among undertakings, but also to tacit ones such as concerted practices. The 'dyestuffs' case (1969) is an example of this. On three occasions in the 1960s (1964, 1965 and 1967), the biggest EU producers of aniline dyes increased their supply prices by identical margins with a time lag of only a few days. Professional organisations from the textile and leather industries complained to the European Commission. The ten firms charged denied the existence of any gentleman's agreement and argued that in a closely knit industry each producer follows the price leader. None the less, the Commission had enough circumstantial evidence of collusion to find the parties involved guilty of price fixing and to fine them a total of €0.5 million. The firms involved in this case were BASF, Bayer, Hoechst and Cassella Farbwerke Mainkur (Germany); Francolor (France); ACNA (Italy); ICI (Britain); and Ciba, Sandoz and Geigy (Switzerland). The Court of Justice upheld the decision of the Commission on the grounds that the national markets for dyestuffs were fragmented and that synchronised price rises did not correspond to the normal conditions of the market. One of the important issues that came out of this anti-cartel case was that the Commission and the Court applied the EU competition rules on an extraterritorial basis. British and Swiss enterprises were party to the gentleman's agreement, and although at that time neither Britain nor Switzerland was a member of the EU, the companies involved were fined for non-competitive market behaviour. The principle that was established in this case was that each firm must independently determine its business policy in the common market.

EU competition legislation may be applied to firms that are located and/or do business anywhere in the world. Acceptance, adoption, implementation and enforcement of the EU competition rules is one of the key conditions that must be accepted by any country that wants to join the EU. In order to avoid a potential problem regarding competition in the EU market, two Swiss companies, Ciba-Geigy and Sandoz, requested that the European Commission 'clear' their domestic Swiss merger to form Novartis. The Commission considered over 100 affected markets. As this extraterritorial merger was predominantly of a complementary nature, it was approved in 1996. And in 1998, the Commission approved the merger of two Swiss banks, UBS and SBS. These cases provide further proof that there is a need for an internationally or, perhaps better to begin with, regionally accepted common set of minimum rules in the area of competition policy. These rules would oust, or reduce, the use of unilateral and extraterritorial competition policy instruments.

There was a big fuss in the EU about a purely American acquisition when Boeing bought McDonnell-Douglas in 1997.[49] Although the American authorities and the European Commission investigated the same market, they came to different conclusions. This was in spite of the bilateral European Commission/US Government Competition Agreement (signed in 1991, approved in 1995) to exchange information, coordinate procedures and consult on cases and remedies. The limits of bilateralism were exposed by this case. *The Economist* reported that there was 'the lethal cocktail of politics, national champions and defence interests' (26 July 1997, p. 62). In addition, the two competition regimes have different economic rationales, principles, legal forms and institutional contexts. They are not likely to see all cases in an identical way (Cini and McGowan, 1998, p. 207). None the less, Boeing recognised the jurisdiction of the European Commission when it filed details of the merger. The European Commission accepted the deal subject to some minor concessions by Boeing. However, there are encouraging examples of cooperation between the EU and US authorities, such as a joint investigation of Microsoft in 1995.

Competition policy requires skilful handling in any scheme that integrates countries. Breaking up a price-fixing cartel is obviously a competition issue. However, deciding how many large chemical or car companies the EU should have is a political question which shapes the geography of production. There should be some control over mergers with an EU dimension. All industries in the EU use mergers and acquisitions in their business strategy. This was most pronounced in the second half of the 1980s when firms were faced with the possibility of a genuine Single European Market from the early 1990s.[50] One tool of the programme was the elimination of unnecessary regulation (NTBs) that was splintering national markets for goods, services and factors in the EU. The business community responded to this challenge with mergers, acquisitions, strategic alliances, joint ventures and networking, all with the aim of consolidating their position in the new, frontier-free and highly competitive market. Such a business policy had an indirect positive effect on standardisation. The European Commission tolerated it because it believed that it would increase efficiency.

After a flurry of merger activity in the second half of the 1980s, reaching a peak in 1989/90 (when much restructuring took place), concentration activity decelerated (Table 5.4). By late 1992, when the Single European Market was operational, the business structure and operation had been clarified. The volume and dynamics of merger notifications and final decisions during 1996–2002 is given in Figure 5.6.

Table 5.4 Mergers and majority acquisitions, 1987–93

Year outside	National mergers[a]	EU internal[b]	EU international[c]	International EU[d]	EU[e]
1987/88	2 110	252	499	160	114
1988/89	3 187	761	659	447	310
1989/90	3 853	1 122	655	768	356
1990/91	3 638	947	550	729	376
1991/92	3 720	760	497	605	326
1992/93	3 004	634	537	656	381

Notes:
a. Deals among firms of the same country.
b. Deals involving firms from at least two different member states of the EU.
c. Deals in which EU firms acquire firms of non-EU origin.
d. Deals in which the bidder is from outside the EU and acquires one or several EU firms.
e. Deals in which there was no involvement of EU firms.

Source: XXIIIrd Report on Competition Policy 1993 (Brussels: European Commission, 1994).

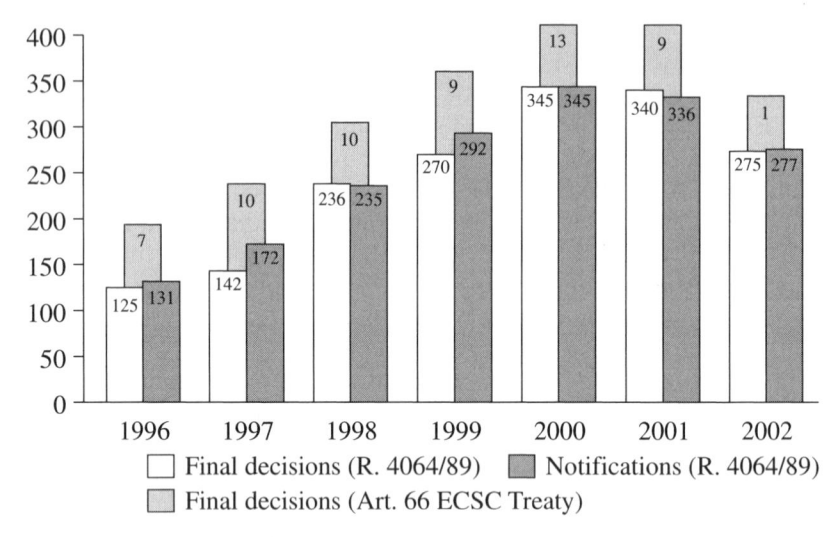

[Figure: bar chart showing Final decisions (R. 4064/89), Notifications (R. 4064/89), and Final decisions (Art. 66 ECSC Treaty) for years 1996–2002. Values: 1996: 125, 131, 7; 1997: 142, 172, 10; 1998: 236, 235, 10; 1999: 270, 292, 9; 2000: 345, 345, 13; 2001: 340, 336, 9; 2002: 275, 277, 1.]

Source: European Commission (2003).

Figure 5.6 Mergers: number of notifications and of final decisions, 1996–2002

Most mergers and acquisitions occurred around 1990 in the manufacturing industry and, especially, in paper manufacturing, followed by the food and drink,[51] sugar-based production and chemicals industries. This is explained by the removal of NTBs in internal trade. The metal-based production industries (mechanical and electro-based engineering and vehicles) also experienced a relatively high level of concentration activity. Suppliers of public goods in these two industries consolidated with the intention of sharing R&D costs and thus withstanding potentially strong competition. Wholesale distributors reacted to the elimination of NTBs by concentration of their activities. The same was true for the providers of financial services.

The major motive for mergers and acquisitions throughout the period of observation was to strengthen market position, followed by the development of commercial activities (market expansion) and rationalisation of business (*European Economy*, 1994a, p. 20). The objective was to prepare for intensive competition in the Single European Market. Companies in Britain, Germany[52] and France were the most favoured targets for intra-EU mergers. At the same time, firms from these three countries were the most active buyers of companies in the EU. None the less, the EU concentration in manufacturing was still 12 per cent below that in the US in 1993 (*European Economy*, 1996, p. 119). Parent companies from Britain, Germany and

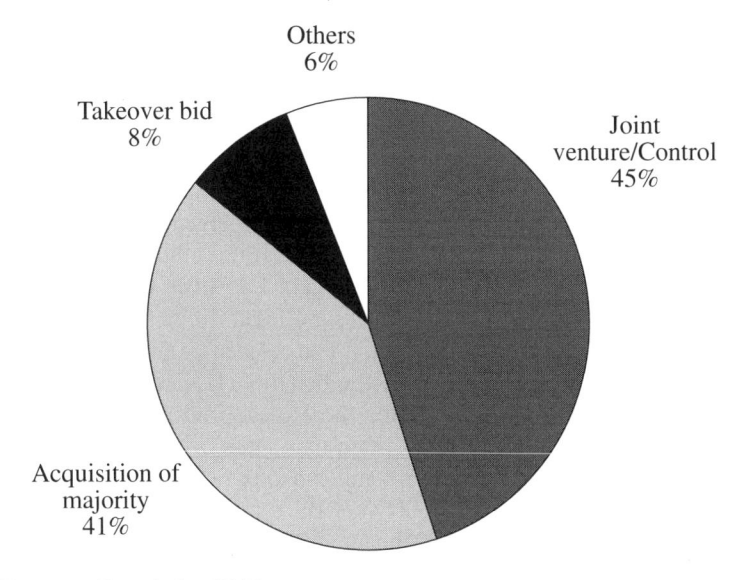

Source: European Commission (2003).

Figure 5.7   Mergers: breakdown by type of operation, 1993–2002

France (the 'trio') were also active in purchasing non-EU firms. While British firms preferred to purchase companies in North America, German and French parent firms distributed their non-EU purchases evenly among North America, Western (non-EU) and Eastern Europe. As for non-EU acquirers of EU firms, North American buyers were most active in the EU trio, followed by Switzerland, Sweden and Japan.

A new trend in inter-firm relations that has emerged is that firms operating in the low- and medium-technology sectors use mergers and acquisitions in their business strategy, whereas those in high-technology industries employ cooperation and collaboration (joint ventures). This is a divergence from the historical pattern of inter-firm relations, as firms have traditionally tried to protect their knowledge and experience in manufacturing and marketing. The high costs of developing new and upgrading existing technologies has made it pragmatic to share the high costs of R&D. As far as the actual type of merger operation was concerned, joint ventures (45 per cent of cases) and majority acquisitions (41 per cent of cases) were practised most in the EU in the 1993–2002 period (Figure 5.7).

In a competitive market, mergers and acquisitions are thought to bring at least two efficiency gains: a reduction in management costs and a reduction in transaction costs. These benefits need to be weighed against the possible costs that accrue from the potential inefficiencies that may be the consequence of concentration. If the expected efficiency gains are not realised and do not outweigh the disadvantages, the new merged enterprise may suffer as a result of differences in corporate cultures (in Germany engineers run firms, in Britain accountants, in Italy designers), inflexibility and poor coordination of business functions.

A number of studies examining full legal mergers in various countries in the EU have found no evidence of substantial efficiency gains. Nor were economies of scale significant. Mergers had little or no effect on post-merger profitability. There was no significant difference in the returns per share three years after the merger.[53] The costs of changes in business organisation were often greater than the benefits claimed by the promoters of takeovers. The main reasons for these disappointments include the high prices paid for target firms as often managers overestimate own ability to run them or they pursue personal reasons other than maximisation of shareholder value, overestimation of the business potential of the acquired firm and mismanagement of the integration process with the acquired firm (Jacquemin, 1990a, pp. 13–14; 1990b, p. 541; Jacquemin and Wright, 1993, p. 528; UNCTAD, 2000, p. 138; Pautler, 2001, p. 53). This is most obvious in the cases of mergers of firms in the production of steel or cars, as well as in airlines.

McKinsey, a management consultant company, reviewed 160 mergers in the 1992–99 period and discovered that only 12 of the merged groups succeeded in lifting growth above the trends before the merger, the other 148 failed.[54] Other studies, such as Dickerson et al. (1997, p. 359) found no evidence that acquisition in Britain had a net beneficial effect on company performance if measured by profit criteria. In fact, this impact was detrimental and systematic. Perhaps company growth through internal investment, rather than a merger, may offer a superior profit growth rate. In a study of Fortune 500 takeovers (1981–95) in the US, Trimbath (2002) found that most of them (more than two-thirds), resulted in increased efficiency measured by cost per unit of revenue. The editorial article in the *Financial Times* 'Merger mania' (29 October 2003) stated:

> The prospect of investment bankers pocketing millions for 'advising' clients to do what turns out to be a very lousy deal is unappetising. Several academic studies published in the past couple of years have suggested that two-thirds of deals fail. The criteria include revenue growth, share price performance and meeting the targets set when transaction was announced.

With this in mind, further research, analysis and evaluation are required in the area of mergers and acquisitions.

In general, shareholders in acquired firms are likely to benefit from a merger, but investors in the acquiring firms are likely to lose out. There are also problems in creating a new management culture in the merged company, whereas cost savings and new economies of scale can be negligible. This does not mean that all mergers and acquisitions have been failures, but it does mean that all claims about the splendid future of the merged company need to be taken with a pinch of salt. Business gurus, management consultants and investment bankers have reached the same conclusion: less than half of all mergers add value in the medium term.[55] Thus, some conglomerates sell off parts of their business that are not at the core of their activity in order to raise money for acquisitions in their main business area and to simplify their operations. Others expand and diversify their business activities and brands. Chocolate bar companies enter the ice-cream market. Harley-Davidson or Levi's entered the after-shave lotion market. Easy Jet went from cheap air transport to businesses that include rent-a-car, Internet cafes, holidays, gifts and insurance. Virgin expanded from low budget air transport to entertainment, clothing, drinks and books. McDonald's is varying its normally uniform menus to meet national tastes. Coca-cola was founded as a company in 1892, and remained a one-product company for almost a century. Now it manages a portfolio of over 200 brands, most of them local.[56] Smith & Wesson (the US producer of the most powerful handgun, the Magnum) started offering on its online catalogue[57] items that include furniture, salsa bowls, bed and bath items, as well as ice buckets. Smith & Wesson targets, apologies, directs, a part of its business strategy towards middle-aged homeowners. In any case, mergers and acquisitions are not necessarily wrong business strategies, but they are very risky.[58]

Despite promises of reduction in costs, economies of scale and the creation of 'champions' to counter foreign rivals, mergers were used as defensive business policy instruments. The rationale that led to the large wave of mergers in the US (and Britain) during the 1960s and 1970s proved to be unfounded. Instead of supporting adjustment, mergers obstructed it by protecting firms from competitive pressure. This was reflected in the relatively slow response of some US firms to oil crises and to Japanese competition in certain industries during the 1980s, as well as competition from China from the start of the new millennium. Firms in the EU would be wise to avoid any repetition of the US experience. The presence in the EU of Japanese and US TNCs with their advanced technology and business organisation and control in some lines of manufacturing industry, as well as the 'flight' of certain domestic firms towards China, may be the principal motivators to the EU domestic firms to restructure their business and become more competitive.

A tidal wave of mergers and acquisitions in the EU was prompted by the need to restructure segmented industries and liberalise capital markets (exploiting restructuring and financial know-how from the US), as well as by the Single European Market. The volume of mergers and acquisitions relative to start-up investments raises serious questions regarding competition (because of the reduction in the number of independent firms and an increase in the potential for collusion) in the Single European Market. Mergers and acquisitions are a global phenomenon. However, so is competition, so anxieties about the effect of the location and structure of merged businesses on competition is to some extent offset by the expansion of 'global' over regional or national competition, as well as by the fact that there has been some restructuring of business of the acquired firms (European Commission, 1998, pp. 144–5).

One result of the numerous mergers and acquisitions is that the degree of concentration in the EU has risen compared with the pre-Single Market Programme era. This may *increase* price competition on the internal EU market and abroad through rationalisation of production and economies of scale. At the same time, an increased concentration (oligopolies) of business may *restrict* competition. Therefore, the EU introduced an important legal instrument for the *ex ante* control of mergers in 1990.[59]

The EU needs a sound competition policy to prevent pan-EU oligopolies (corporate fortresses) replacing national ones and eliminating the competitive pressure that comes from open markets. Revised merger legislation (designed to simplify the regulatory burden on merging companies) that came into force in 1998 gives the European Commission a say in any merger with an EU dimension (smaller mergers are under the control of national competition authorities). This is the case if:

- annual worldwide turnover of the new (merged) company is above €2.5bn (the general threshold);
- in each of at least three member states the combined turnover of all of the companies concerned is above €100m;
- in each of these three member states the aggregate turnover of each of at least two companies involved is over €25m;
- the aggregate EU-wide turnover of at least two involved firms is more than €100m.

The decisive determinant according to these thresholds is *turnover*, not the country of domicile/nationality of the parent enterprise.[60] If the proposed merged company could occupy a dominant position that would restrict competition (the new firm could, for example, increase prices by 10 per cent without losing market share), the European Commission has the authority to stop the deal. However, the European Commission has not so far blocked any deal that would result in the merged firm having a market share of less than 40 per cent. Thus, the purpose of the Merger Control Regulation is to prevent *ex ante* the creation of unwanted market behaviour that comes from the abuse of dominant position in the Single European Market. The implementation of the policy has, however, some arbitrary aspects such as estimating the market strength of potential entrants or remaining competitors, determining substitutes and defining the product or geographical market. In any case, the refusal rate of mergers and acquisitions by the European Commission has been less than 1 per cent of the total notified deals.

A number of firms do have as their aim worldwide market dominance and, as a result, merger and acquisition deals are getting bigger and more complex. This increases the workload on the European Commission's limited resources to the possible detriment of the merits of the system: predictability and speed. That the system needs to be reformed is obvious, the question is should the time allowed for decisions be extended, thus compromising a basic tenet of the system, or should the European Commission be empowered to handle only the biggest deals and leave the rest to the national courts (and 'punish' smaller merger deals with a set of national jurisdictions)?

In the light of the eastern enlargement and with the intention of reducing bureaucracy and increasing the effectiveness of enforcement action concerning agreements between undertakings that restrict competition, as well as abuses of dominant positions, the EU implemented in 2002 the most comprehensive antitrust reform since 1962. The Council's Regulation 1/2003 is applied from May 2004 (it replaced Regulation 17/62). The substance of Rome Treaty Articles 81 and 82, respectively, is unchanged. The reform simplified the way in which the antitrust rules are enforced in the EU. The compliance burden for firms is reduced, as the notification system for agreements between firms to the European Commission no longer exists. The European Commission and the national competition authorities are able to focus their resources in the new situation on the fight against those restrictions and abuses that are most harmful to competition and consumers.

The reform places a greater responsibility on firms. They will have to assess themselves whether their deal restricts competition and, if so, whether it fulfils the conditions of the exception rule in Article 81(3). This may create some uncertainty. However, this task for enterprises is alleviated by block exemption regulations (regulations introducing a presumption of legality for agreements that fulfil the specific conditions set out therein) which are maintained in the new system. The European Commission has also published extensive guidelines on the application of Article 81. Where unusual questions arise, firms may ask guidance from the European Commission in individual cases. Guidance from the European Commission together with the body of case law of the EU Court of Justice and the European Commission's case practice should also give sufficient substance to the national competition authorities and national courts to apply the EU antitrust rules in a consistent way. The national courts may always ask the European Commission for information or opinion. The national competition authorities are linked to the European Commission through a newly created network of authorities (European Competition Network). Where they apply Articles 81 or 82, respectively, they are obliged to inform the Commission at different stages of the procedure. In addition, the investigation powers of the European Commission are extended, as the Commission may interview any person who may have useful information for the case under investigation, and it may also enter any premises where business records may be kept (including private residences).

DOMINANT POSITION

If a firm has or achieves a dominant market position, it may significantly affect competition and the geography of production. The dominant market position may be secured in several ways, including the following five:

- Firms may have innovative skills and competences not only in products (goods/services), but also in management, control and firm-level planning. They may make risky investments in R&D, production and/or marketing that their competitors do not have the nerve for. Such first-mover advantages that are in line with the rules may result in dominance of the market and supernormal profits (Microsoft's MS-DOS and Windows, Sony's Playstations, as well as Nintendo's Game Boy are obvious examples). The life cycle of products is shortening all the time, hence the importance of innovating. In fact, most firms compete by continually assuming quasi-monopolistic positions that are based on innovation of various kinds.[61] In spite of continuous innovations by Microsoft, the most valuable user assets (personal files) are transferable from one Microsoft system to another. Apple, a competitor, failed to realise this in time, allowing Microsoft to achieve a near-monopoly. The classical view that firms are only an input conversion mechanism does not reflect the contemporary world. In addition to their input conversion and value-adding functions, firms are also involved in learning-by-doing and innovation activities. Geographical concentration in industries with various entry barriers may occur as a direct consequence of a firm behaving

efficiently. A policy that promotes R&D among firms in the EU may provide them with a better basis for oligopolistic competition at home and abroad and to face up to foreign rivals, mainly from Japan and the US.
- The dominant position in the market could be attained through mergers and acquisitions. This is typical in English-speaking countries.
- A firm may achieve or protect its dominant position through anti-competitive business practices. Examples of this include exclusive dealerships and predatory pricing. However, exclusive dealerships do not always reduce welfare, for example compared with the situation of free entry and exit among dealers/retailers, permanent and exclusive dealership (including after-sales service) might be a superior and welfare-increasing solution.
- The dominant position can be captured and maintained through a competitive and risky pricing policy. If economies of scale and learning result in a significant fall in prices as output increases over time, a risk-loving firm (for example, Texas Instruments in the 1960s and 1970s) may choose to set current prices on the basis of the expected (low) costs of production in the future. Alternatively, prices may be based on the average cost of production over the life cycle of the product.
- Yet another way in which firms come to dominate a market is through the granting of a licence by public authorities. Examples can be found in 'natural' monopolies such as public utilities (water, gas, electricity, rail transport, postal services and the local telephone service). In these industries, the minimum efficient scale is so large that a single firm is necessary to serve the entire national market.

From the outset one should be less concerned about the existence of a dominant firm (Microsoft) than about how the dominant firm 'plays the game'. Many people forget that Microsoft competes with Microsoft (Windows XP competes with Windows Millennium Edition, which competes with Windows 98, which competes with Windows 95). If the price of the new version is too high, consumers will stick to the old computer software. However, Microsoft may increase the price of the old versions when the new one is launched on the market in order to boost sales of the new version.

Article 82 of the Treaty of Rome refers to the issue of the dominant position in a market. It does not prohibit a dominant position (monopoly or monopsony) *ex ante*, but rather forbids the *abuse* of it. This has only an *ex post* effect. In order to determine whether an infringement of the EU market has taken place, the European Commission looks at three factors:

- the existence of the dominant position;
- its abuse (in pricing or control of production, distribution or servicing); and
- the negative effect on trade among the member countries.

Large firms are permitted by the Treaty of Rome to enjoy market dominance, but they are forbidden to exercise it. This is somewhat naive! Whoever yields the power will behave as a monopolist, the temptation is irresistible. In any case, the legal framework recognises that there is a need for some level of concentration in some industries for reasons of efficiency. It is inevitable for the attainment of the efficient scale of production, in both home and foreign markets. Otherwise, protected and inefficient national firms, which have higher production costs than foreign competitors, would continue to impose welfare losses on consumers. This is why many/most European countries have relaxed their antitrust policies. Otherwise, small domestic firms could be protected only at a high cost and with a diminution of production efficiency. Concentration (geographical agglomeration) of production is a potential barrier to foreign competition on the home market and a springboard for penetration into foreign markets.[62]

The growing concentration of the semiconductor equipment and materials industries by a few Japanese enterprises created a strategic threat to both commercial and defence interests. For example, because of the concerns of the socialist members of the Japanese Parliament in 1983, the Ministry of International Trade and Industry (MITI) reportedly ordered Kyocera (a domestic manufacturer of high-technology ceramic products) not to take part in contracts to sell ceramic nose cones to the US Tomahawk missile programme (Graham and Krugman, 1995, p. 118). In another example, Nikon, one of only two Japanese suppliers of some kinds of semiconductor-producing machinery, withheld its latest models from foreign customers for up to two years after making them available to Japanese clients (Tyson, 1992, p. 146). The 'explanation' put forward was that the 'regular' customers needed to be served in a better way and before the others. The behaviour of IBM was similar. This firm has also refused to sell its components to other clients (Sharp and Pavitt, 1993, p. 144).

STATE AIDS

In the neo-classical economic model, perfect competition can be undermined by protection and subsidy. The distinction between the two distortions is subtle. On the one hand, tariff and non-tariff *protection* allow protected suppliers to charge higher prices in the local market than would be the case with free imports. Such protection provides an 'implicit subsidy' paid directly from consumers to producers. On the other hand, *subsidies* go to domestic producers not directly from consumers, but rather from taxpayers to the government and then to producers. The two types of 'support' have the same objective: to support a certain national (inefficient) production geography as resources are kept in or shifted into import-substituting industries. Where the two instruments differ is in transparency and the method of supplying funds to the selected industries or firms within them.

Those that accept that the market functions efficiently, use this argument as a case against subsidies (state aids). Although such an argument applies in many instances, there are other situations in which the neo-classical theory does not hold. In a situation with imperfections such as externalities (R&D or pollution), economies of scale, multiple equilibria, imperfect mobility of factors and sunk costs, intervention may be justified. Therefore, industrial and regional policies may be used as justifications for the existence of state aids.

A key element in the EU competition policy is a unique control of state aids. Subsidies may distort competition and efficient allocation of resources (geography of production). Article 87 of the Treaty of Rome recognises this issue and regulates it.[63] It prohibits any aid that distorts or threatens to distort competition among member countries. This means that Article 87 does not apply to aid given as support to firms or for the production of goods and services that do not enter intra-EU trade (local consumption), or aid for exports outside the EU (regulated by Article 132). The European Commission accepted a transparent approach to subsidies and publishes *Surveys of State Aid in the EC*. It also expects its trading partners, particularly candidate countries, to follow suit.

There are, however, a few exceptions to the general rule of incompatibility of state aids. Article 87 states that aid that *is* compatible with the treaty is of the kind given on a non-discriminatory basis to individuals for social purposes, as well as aid to regions affected by disasters. Aid that *can be* considered compatible with the treaty is the kind given to projects that are in the EU's interest and aid for regional development in the 'areas where the standard of living is abnormally low' (for the purpose of social cohesion in the EU). The Council of Ministers (based on the proposal from the European Commission) has the discretionary right to decide that other aid may be compatible with the EU rules. This includes aid to SMEs,[64] conservation of energy, protection of environment, promotion of national culture or alleviation of serious disturbances in a national economy. If an industry comes under competitive and/or restructuring pressure, the European Commission considers the social and other impact of such an adjustment according to the guidelines of 1979. The European Commission may permit aid under conditions that are based on principles that include:

- *temporariness* (a clear time limit);
- *transparency* (the amount of aid has to be measurable);
- *selectivity* (aid is supposed to be given to firms and industries that have a reasonable chance of standing on their own after the restructuring period); and
- *appropriateness* (aid has to match the basic needs of the assisted firm/industry to operate during the restructuring period,[65] after which the assisted firm/industry has to become economically viable on its own).

In order to ease the workload and concentrate on the large and potentially the most damaging cases, the European Commission introduced a *de minimis* rule in 1992. According to this rule, governments are not required to notify the Commission of aid that does not exceed €100 000 over a period of three years. The European Commission holds that such aid does not distort competition. In addition, aid linked to environmental issues may be allowed if it enables an improvement in conditions beyond the required environmental standards. The Commission takes the same favourable view regarding aid to SMEs as long as they contribute to social stability and economic dynamism.

Article 87, as well as EU court practice, provides the European Commission with a wide discretionary margin in the decision-making process. None the less, the Commission employs two criteria:

- *Compensatory justification*: To 'clear' aid as compatible with the rules, aid has to conform with goals set out in Article 87 and it must be proven that, without state aid, free markets would not be capable of accomplishing the same end.
- *Transparency*: Each aid programme has to be justified and its effects measurable. Member states must notify the Commission about the form, volume, duration and objectives of aid.

If, two months after the notification, the European Commission has not made an explicit decision, aid is regarded as tacitly accepted. The European Commission may decide 'not to raise objections', which means that the application is preliminarily approved, but the Commission needs further information in order to reach a final decision. The Commission can open up the procedure (Article 88) and ask the parties concerned to submit their comments. The European Commission then makes a final decision on the compatibility of aid with the EU rules.

Article 87 does not define state aid. None the less, the European Commission and the Court of Justice interpret aid in a broad sense. They take it to mean any favour given by a government in a form that includes subsidies, special public guarantees, supply of goods or services at preferential conditions and favours regarding credit terms offered to one or more firms or their associates. Loans and guarantees given by the state or its agency do not necessarily constitute aid. The aid element exists only when such injections of funds are offered on conditions that are superior to the ones prevailing on the market.

Some governments still attempt to disguise industrial aid as regional aid. This is difficult to detect if the aided company makes a loss. R&D support can similarly be abused. 'Support' to the manufacturing and services sectors needs to be in the R&D stage otherwise foreign competitors, mainly from the US, would complain that EU subsidies are distorting international competition. Any EU member state can finance basic and applied research in the private sector according to agreed sliding scales.[66] The Commission's framework on state aid for R&D of 1995 outlined several criteria for the compatibility of such aid with the Single European Market. They include the following:

- There is a distinction between 'industrial research' and 'pre-competitive development activity'. The closer to the marketplace for final goods, the more aid is likely to distort competition.
- State aid for R&D should create an incentive for the recipient firm to carry out R&D *in addition to* what it would undertake in the normal course of its business operation. (Now, prove that?)
- Aid for 'industrial research' may be up to 50 per cent of the cost, whereas aid for 'pre-competitive development' may be up to 25 per cent of the cost. None the less, there are special additional bonuses of 10 per cent for projects that involve SMEs, of 15 per cent if the project is a priority under the EU R&D programme and up to 10 per cent if R&D is undertaken in regions eligible for regional aid.
- Maximum aid for R&D in the EU (allowable under the GATT Agreement on Subsidies and Countervailing Measures) is 75 per cent for 'industrial research' and 50 per cent for 'pre-competitive development activity'.
- Member states have to notify the European Commission about all individual aid packages for projects exceeding €25 million where aid exceeds €5 million.

The State-aid Department of the European Commission has a staff of about 80 officials responsible for monitoring state aid and carrying out other tasks in the field. They cannot be expected to examine every instance of state aid, especially as every region in each member country has staff (which often significantly outnumber the Commission's) to dispense aid. Therefore, the European Commission's priority is to prevent the most anti-competition aid programmes.[67] The Commission has to ensure that aid is given to the most disadvantaged regions and that it is compatible with the Treaty rules. If it is not, then it may request that such aid is repaid to the state. This was the case in 2003 when the European Commission decided that Electricité de France (the state-owned power group) must repay about €1 billion. All these formidable issues linked to competition are increasingly becoming a paradise for lawyers.

The new multisectoral framework on regional assistance for large investment projects entered into force in 2004. This included a limited notification obligation for large projects balanced by a significant reduction in tolerable aid levels. According to this framework, the actual aid that a large project can receive matches the aid ceiling set in the regional aid maps, which is then automatically reduced in accordance with the scale set in Table 5.5. For example: in an area with a regional aid ceiling of 20 per cent, a project with an eligible investment cost of €80 million can obtain up to €13 million in aid; that is, €10 million for the first €50 million of investment, plus €3 million for the remaining €30 million of investment.

A 'cohesion bonus' can be granted to large projects co-financed by the EU structural funds. For such projects, the acceptable aid intensity calculated under the above scale will be multiplied by a factor of 1.15. In so doing, this system will take into account the significance of these large co-financed projects for the economic and social cohesion of the EU.

Projects still have to be notified and assessed individually if the intended aid is higher than could be obtained by a €100 million project. If such a project reinforces a high market share (less than 25 per cent), or increases capacity in a non-growing sector by more than 5 per cent, aid will not be authorised.

Table 5.5 Public aid scale

Size of the project	Adjusted aid ceiling
Up to €50 million	No reduction. 100% of regional state aid ceiling
Between €50 million and €100 million	50% of regional state aid ceiling
Exceeding €100 million	34% of regional state aid ceiling

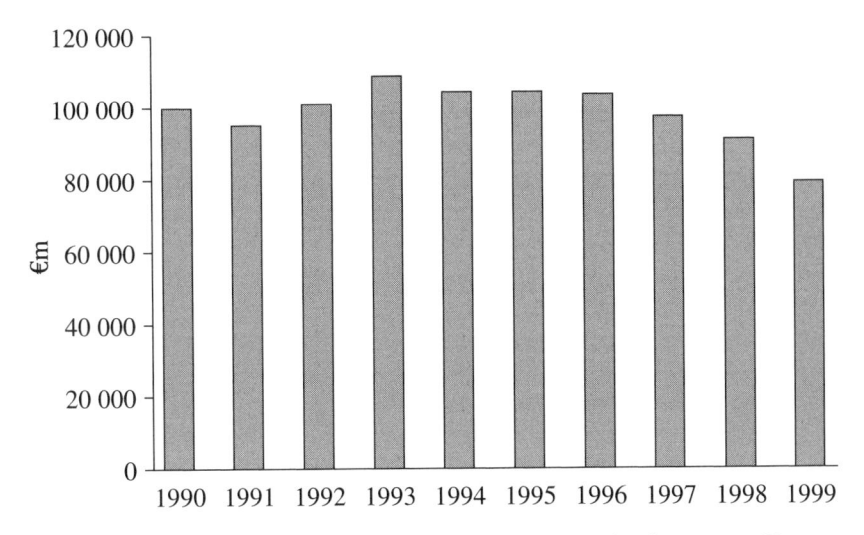

Source: European Commission (2001). *Ninth Survey on State Aid in the European Union.* Brussels, 17 July 2001, COM (2001) 403 final.

Figure 5.8 Overall state aid in the EU, 1990–99

The European Commission has approved public aid (subsidies) for many purposes. This was, usually the case when they serve the common interest of the EU. Such derogations from Article 87 include support to regional development, R&D, SMEs, training, savings in energy and protection of the environment. Figure 5.8 presents the dynamics of state aids in the EU(15) during the 1990s. State aid peaked during the 1993 recession (the year when the Single European Marked started its first year of operation) and then, slowly but clearly, declined as the eurozone has strict limits for public expenditure.

Table 5.6 provides data on annual averages and trends in the overall volume of state aid granted by the EU(15) member countries in the 1995–97 and 1997–99 periods, as well as the distribution of aid per beneficiary area. Although there was a predictable downward trend in the volume of granted aid during the period of observation, average annual aid remained massive, at €90 billion at the end of the period of observation, and it was concentrated on rail transport and manufacturing.

The available data demonstrate that there were still large disparities in both overall national aid and in per capita aid. Germany, France and Italy had the largest volume of state aid in the economy, even though per capita state assistance was the highest in Luxembourg and Finland. Least interventionist in per capita terms were Greece and Britain. In terms of overall aid per capita, the relative difference between the most interventionist

Table 5.6 Overall national state aid in the EU: annual averages, 1995–97 and 1997–99 in constant prices (1998) (€bn)

	1995–97	1997–99
Overall national aid of which:	102.0	90.0
Agriculture	15.2	14.0
Fisheries	0.3	0.3
Manufacturing	35.8	27.6
Coal mining	8.2	7.6
Transport	35.4	32.0
of which rail transport	33.7	31.5
Services	5.0	5.4
Employment	0.8	0.9
Training	1.7	2.2

Source: European Commission (2001). *Ninth Survey on State Aid in the European Union.* Brussels, 17 July 2001, COM (2001) 403 final.

country, Luxembourg, and the most liberal, Greece, was 4:1. The reduction of the EU average annual aid of €102 billion (1995–97) to the average of €90 billion (1997–99) was principally due to the reduction of aid in Germany and Italy (Table 5.7). The most interventionist EU(15) state in terms of share of GDP that was spent on aid was Finland (1.74 per cent), while the least interventionist was Britain (0.6 per cent) during 1997–99 (Table 5.8). Transport and manufacturing each received on average in the EU(15) about a third of all state aid (Table 5.9).

Owing to the strict public expenditure conditions imposed by the eurozone, the presumption was that state aid would continuously diminish in the EU. Tables 5.10 and 5.11, respectively, confirm this expectation. Even though general public assistance diminished, it was still well over €21 billion in 1999. In terms of aid per person employed in manufacturing, the former East Germany was the most assisted (subsidised) area. In terms of aid per person employed in manufacturing, the ratio between the most interventionist, Ireland, and least interventionist, Portugal, was 9:1 (Table 5.12). Regional policy objectives were the principal reason for state intervention in the EU manufacturing sector. This objective included over half of the entire assistance. R&D and assistance to SMEs were the only other two notable motives for intervention (Table 5.13). Although public aid in the EU(15) declined in general terms, it remained massive throughout the 1997–99 period. This 'price' for maintaining certain production geography in the national economies of the member countries was paid out mostly through grants and tax exemptions (Table 5.14).

Table 5.7 State aid per capita in the EU member states: annual averages, 1995–97 and 1997–99 in constant prices (1998) (€)

	Annual averages 1995–97		Annual averages 1997–99		Population in millions
	In € million	€ per capita	In € million	€ per capita	
Austria	2 389	296	2 180	270	8
Belgium	3 285	322	3 152	309	10
Denmark	1 575	297	1 681	317	5
Germany	32 228	393	26 716	326	82
Greece	1 584	151	1 305	124	11
Spain	6 801	173	6 086	155	39
Finland	2 292	445	1 994	387	5
France	17 989	306	17 829	304	59
Ireland	698	189	1 065	288	4
Italy	18 523	322	13 605	236	58
Luxembourg	140	330	218	514	0
Netherlands	2 739	175	3 159	202	16
Portugal	1 557	156	1 535	154	10
Sweden	2 000	226	1 792	203	9
United Kingdom	8 519	144	7 569	128	59
EU(15)	102 319	273	89 885	240	375

Source: European Commission (2001). Ninth Survey on State Aid in the European Union. Brussels, 17 July 2001, COM (2001) 403 final.

Table 5.8 Overall national aid in the EU member states in per cent of GDP, in euros per person employed and in per cent of government expenditure, 1995–97 and 1997–99 in constant prices (1998)

	In per cent of GDP 1995–97	In per cent of GDP 1997–99	In euros per person employed 1995–97	In euros per person employed 1997–99	In per cent of total government expenditure 1995–97	In per cent of total government expenditure 1997–99
Austria	1.32	1.16	610	550	2.37	2.15
Belgium	1.55	1.41	880	830	2.94	2.76
Denmark	1.07	1.08	599	622	1.80	1.90
Germany	1.73	1.39	864	712	3.49	2.85
Greece	1.55	1.21	416	338	3.37	2.70
Spain	1.40	1.17	493	416	3.21	2.80
Finland	2.22	1.74	1 103	914	3.76	3.21
France	1.46	1.38	790	772	2.64	2.55
Ireland	1.08	1.36	517	706	2.72	3.75
Italy	1.80	1.28	838	607	3.41	2.56
Luxembourg	0.94	1.31	633	912	2.12	3.04
Netherlands	0.84	0.90	373	406	1.69	1.90
Portugal	1.68	1.56	342	326	3.73	3.50
Sweden	0.99	0.84	492	436	1.50	1.35
United Kingdom	0.72	0.60	324	280	1.63	1.47
EU(15)	1.43	1.18	656	563	2.82	2.44

Source: European Commission (2001). *Ninth Survey on State Aid in the European Union.* Brussels, 17 July 2001, COM (2001) 403 final.

A general downward trend in state aid reflects not only the application of competition rules in the EU, but also a reduction in public expenditure and budget discipline 'forced' by the Maastricht criteria for the EMU. Reduction in state aid is a pro-competition move in the EU. This is an encouraging trend as this type of assistance to businesses and regions is one of very few policy instruments available in the presence of EMU. Reliance on competition policy within the Single European Market will continue to stimulate market-led restructuring and more efficient spatial allocation of resources. However, this has important policy implications for the new EU member countries, as they still need substantial assistance to catch up with the ever-expanding *acquis communautaire*. Budgetary restrictions could provoke internal EU(15) political problems. One can

Table 5.9 Overall national aid in the EU member states: breakdown according to main sectors, 1995–97 and 1997–99 (%)

	Agriculture and fisheries		Manufacturing		Coal		Transport		Services		Employment and training	
	1995–97	1997–99	1995–97	1997–99	1995–97	1997–99	1995–97	1997–99	1995–97	1997–99	1995–97	1997–99
AU	51	46	20	22			27	30	1	2	1	1
B	8	8	25	21			64	67			3	4
DK	17	15	41	39			32	31	2	2	9	14
D	7	6	41	37	16	18	35	37	1	1		1
GR	11	14	43	41			47	45				
E	18	20	31	25	16	18	26	24	1	1	8	12
FIN	78	74	17	21			2	2	0	1	3	2
F	20	17	23	26	4	5	37	34	16	17		
IRL	16	17	38	45			24	13	11	15	11	10
I	9	13	56	42			31	39	4	5		2
LUX	23	14	34	21			43	64	1	1		
NL	34	37	22	18			44	44	1	1		
P	13	20	12	12			19	7	45	53	10	7
S	14	19	18	23			54	51	4	5	10	2
UK	19	18	18	19	13	8	35	35	3	3	11	17
EU(15)	15	16	35	31	8	8	35	36	5	6	2	3

Source: European Commission (2001). *Ninth Survey on State Aid in the European Union*. Brussels, 17 July 2001, COM (2001) 403 final.

Table 5.10 State aid to the manufacturing sector in the EU: annual values, 1995–99 in constant prices (1998) (€m)

	1995	1996	1997	1998	1999
EU(15)	38 749	35 039	33 537	27 559	21 592

Source: European Commission (2001). *Ninth Survey on State Aid in the European Union.* Brussels, 17 July 2001, COM (2001) 403 final.

Table 5.11 State aid to the manufacturing sector in the EU: annual values, 1995–99 in constant prices (1998)

	1995	1996	1997	1998	1999
In per cent of value added	2.8	2.6	2.4	1.9	1.5
In euros per person employed	1 287	1 171	1 121	910	716

Source: European Commission (2001). *Ninth Survey on State Aid in the European Union.* Brussels, 17 July 2001, COM (2001) 403 final.

Table 5.12 State aid to the manufacturing sector in the EU member states: annual averages, 1995–97 and 1997–99 in constant prices (1998)

	In per cent of value added 1995–97	In per cent of value added 1997–99	In euros per person employed 1995–97	In euros per person employed 1997–99	In million euros 1995–97	In million euros 1997–99
Austria	1.4	1.3	685	696	473	478
Belgium	2.1	1.7	1 237	1 003	826	657
Denmark	2.6	2.6	1 429	1 453	642	655
Germany	3.4	2.4	1 592	1 211	13 144	9 808
Old *Länder*	–	–	431	437	2 914	2 913
New *Länder*	–	–	6 854	4 820	10 230	6 896
Greece	5.5	4.3	1 093	876	677	537
Spain	2.5	1.7	841	567	2 117	1 548
Finland	1.7	1.6	937	968	394	424
France	1.9	2.0	1 090	1 235	4 141	4 651
Ireland	1.3	2.0	1 075	1 683	263	477
Italy	5.0	2.7	2 025	1 108	10 350	5 694
Luxembourg	2.3	2.1	1 464	1 380	48	45
Netherlands	1.1	1.0	561	530	595	571
Portugal	0.9	0.9	185	193	183	192

Table 5.12 (continued)

	In per cent of value added		In euros per person employed		In million euros	
	1995–97	1997–99	1995–97	1997–99	1995–97	1997–99
Sweden	0.9	1.0	490	557	364	418
United Kingdom	0.7	0.6	357	322	1 558	1 408
EU(15)	2.6	1.9	1 193	916	35 775	27 563

Source: European Commission (2001). *Ninth Survey on State Aid in the European Union.* Brussels, 17 July 2001, COM (2001) 403 final.

already hear voices saying: 'Why should we subsidise the new member countries when we have unsettled domestic problems and when we make unprecedented efforts to reduce domestic expenditure still further because of the eurozone?'

4. Conclusion

The real discussion about markets and competition need not be about operational and practical details on how genetic engineering or nanotechnology should develop. Those are important issues, but nobody knows the answer. The real matter for debate should be the nature of the market economy. Should it be based on the pluralism of the market or should it be based on the wisdom of individual businesspeople? While there may be arguments that support both propositions, the historical evidence may tilt policy makers towards the first suggestion.

Relatively small countries that are in the process of development employ industrial/trade policies that may not always be competition friendly. Relatively large and developed countries value competition quite highly. As spatial agglomeration of business in some industries increases, there is a tendency to tighten antitrust policy and maintain a certain level of competition in the Single European Market. Increased competition would, in most cases, without doubt exert downward pressure on prices and costs. This outcome would enable economic growth with a reduced inflationary pressure. However, it is not clear how this would happen in practice. Competition may reduce the prices of goods and services or it may increase output but keep prices constant. In this case, a reduction in prices would be offset by an increase in demand. The most likely outcome in practice would

Table 5.13 *State aid to the manufacturing sector in the EU member states: breakdown according to sector and function, 1997–99 (%)*

Sector/objectives	AU	B	DK	D	GR	E	FIN	F	IR	I	LUX	NL	P	S	UK	EU 15
Horizontal objectives	62	66	92	29	4	38	74	48	65	22	37	83	65	59	39	37
Research and development	33	19	25	13	0	14	37	25	3	5	10	26	6	21	9	14
Environment	11	1	37	1	0	1	1	1	0	0	5	14	0	22	0	2
Small and medium-sized enterprises	14	23	2	13	3	16	16	6	1	12	22	4	12	9	22	12
Commerce	0	1	5	0	1	0	10	3	1	0	1	4	0	0	7	1
Energy saving	1	0	22	2	0	2	9	1	1	0	0	29	5	7	2	2
Rescue and restructuring	3	1	0	0	0	4	0	13	0	4	0	0	3	0	0	3
Other objectives	0	21	0	0	0	2	0	0	60	1	0	6	39	0	0	2
Particular sectors	3	0	6	5	3	40	10	10	1	5	0	3	18	0	1	7
Shipbuilding	0	0	6	3	1	28	8	6	0	3	0	3	6	0	0	5
Other sectors	3	0	0	2	1	13	2	4	1	2	0	0	12	0	0	2
Regional objectives	35	34	2	67	93	22	16	42	34	73	63	14	17	41	61	56
Regions: Article 87(3)a	6	0	0	59	93	6	0	15	34	71	0	0	17	0	17	42
Regions: Article 87(3)c	29	34	2	8	0	16	16	27	0	3	63	14	0	41	44	14
Total	100	100	100	100	100	100	100	100	100	100	100	100	100	100	100	100

Source: European Commission (2001). *Ninth Survey on State Aid in the European Union.* Brussels, 17 July 2001, COM (2001) 403 final.

Table 5.14 *State aid to the manufacturing sector in the EU member states, breakdown according to type of aid instrument, 1997–99 (%)*

	Group A Grants	Group A Tax exemptions	Group B Equity participation	Group C Soft loans	Group C Tax deferrals	Group D Guarantees	Total
Austria	77	0	0	18	0	5	100
Belgium	72	17	5	4	1	1	100
Denmark	56	35	0	7	0	2	100
Germany	60	11	0	21	1	5	100
Greece	97	1	0	2	0	0	100
Spain	91	0	2	7	0	0	100
Finland	88	2	1	8	0	0	100
France	30	47	13	8	0	2	100
Ireland	30	58	8	0	0	5	100
Italy	64	33	1	3	0	0	100
Luxembourg	94	4	0	2	0	0	100
Netherlands	64	20	0	5	8	2	100
Portugal	85	4	2	9	0	0	100
Sweden	70	16	2	12	0	0	100
United Kingdom	97	1	0	1	1	0	100
EU(15)	61	22	3	11	1	3	100

Source: European Commission (2001). *Ninth Survey on State Aid in the European Union.* Brussels, 17 July 2001, COM (2001) 403 final.

be that competition would produce a blend of benefits that accrue from increase in output and decrease in prices.

The Single European Market enhanced the dynamic process of competition through an easing of market segmentation and, somewhat paradoxically, by increasing concentration in some businesses. This concentration permitted the employment of economies of scale and an increase in technical efficiency in production. In addition, it enhanced R&D through a joint sharing of high costs.

A change in global competition and the perception of a relative diminution of competitiveness in the EU at the turn of the 1980s in comparison with the US in the computer and aerospace industries, Japan in cars and consumer electronics and certain developing countries in textiles and clothing, as well as a potential loss in a number of other industries, were among the driving forces that brought about the Single European Market.

Businesses reacted to the Single European Market by consolidating, through mergers and acquisitions, as well as through joint ventures. An increase in internal EU competition through the elimination of internal barriers gave the EU the opportunity to benefit from the so far unexploited economies of scale that would, over time, reduce the costs of production and increase global competitiveness, not only in manufacturing, but also in services. All of this would provide an additional boost to investment and the growth of the EU's economy. Hence, not only innovating firms and those that use state-of-the-art technologies, but also consumers are able to reap rewards in terms of opportunities provided by increased competition. The dynamic labour segment might gain from the integration process, as trade and competition would determine not whether there were jobs, but rather what kind of jobs are available.

The ways forward in the short and medium terms should reflect three ideas (Jacquemin and Pench, 1997, p. 38):

- developing key EU factors for the long-term growth and attraction and anchoring of footloose economic activities;
- deepening of market integration; and
- finding international points of reference (benchmarks) for comparison in order to determine the degree of success.

Binding multilateral competition rules would both do away with distortions in competition and promote an efficient spatial and sectoral allocation of resources on a global scale. These rules would restrain the behaviour of *firms* in the same way that binding international trade rules curb the behaviour of *governments*. These rules would also prevent bilateral conflicts in competition matters. However, binding international competition rules will not be introduced in the near future. Almost half of WTO member countries do not have competition laws, while other member countries have diverse competition values and apply competition laws in different ways (the US seldom allows exceptions, whereas they are quite common in the EU); yet another group of countries values its sovereignty so much that it is unwilling to accept another international bureaucratic superstructure. Because of its large and relatively closed economy, the US has been applying competition policy with a greater vigour than was the case with other developed countries with smaller and more open economies. A number of countries are opposed to a strong and vigilant supranational authority and dispute settlement system (as is the case in the EU and the US) because it would prejudice their sovereignty. If a country suspects that the gist of its national competition model is not going to be adopted in the international arena, that country may wish to remove this issue from the list of its priorities. Even though they have limits (recall the Boeing/McDonnell-Douglas case), bilateral agreements are a provisional reaction to and way out of the difficulties in competition matters. Although the speedy adoption of multilateral competition rules is unlikely for a host of reasons, the issue needs to be put and kept on the international agenda for discussion.

Notes

1. Competition policy does not protect individual competitors, but rather the process of competition.
2. See Dunning (1995) and Krugman (1995a) for further discussion.
3. Deregulation of the power generation in California 'led to one of history's great policy disasters: energy companies drove up prices by creating artificial shortages. This plunged the state into a crisis that ended only after much of its electricity supply was locked up in long-term contracts' (Krugman, *New York Times*, 19 August 2003). A deregulated electricity market to work 'properly' requires at least three preconditions: (1) a robust transmission system; (2) a watchdog agency to prevent and punish price manipulation; and (3) the watchdog agency must not be an agent of the very companies that it is supposed to police (Krugman, *New York Times*, 2 September 2003).
4. Hayek criticised the neo-classical model, which is based on perfect competition, in the following way: 'But I must be content with thus briefly indicating the absurdity of the usual procedure of starting the analysis with a situation in which all the facts are supposed to be known. This is a state of affairs which economic theory curiously calls "perfect competition". It leaves no room whatever for the activity called competition, which is presumed to have already done its task' (Hayek, 1978, p. 182).
5. Liberalisation of imports has the strongest impact when exchange rates are stable. Volatility in the exchange rate market may loosen the grip of this policy instrument.
6. These three men will be software experts, not lawyers. The Department of Justice and Microsoft would each select one member, and those two would select the third one. Their role is to notify only the Department of Justice (not the public or the industry) about their findings. The department may use the dossier by this committee for another court case.
7. *Financial Times*, 22 March 2004.
8. *Patent* rights exist to protect an individual's codifiable innovation and knowledge, whereas *trademarks* protect the reputation of a firm. Other knowledge that comes from learning through trial and error is largely unprotected because it may not be put into 'blueprints'.
9. Lead time advantages over competitors was most frequently used protection method in the EU (Eurostat, 2004, 'Innovation output and barriers to innovation', Statistics in Focus, Theme 9-1/2004, p. 3).
10. The importance of after-sales service varies depending on the good. This service is non-existent for soaps and detergents, but it is essential for printing presses, on-line printers or photocopiers.
11. Self-satisfaction and a lack of real local competition contributed to the German camera industry being driven out by the Japanese (Porter, 1990b, p. 169).
12. Timely, correct and cheap information is becoming a crucial input in the decision-making process. A banker who is handling large funds over his PC terminal is a long way from the British general, Sir Edward Pakenham, who lost the battle of New Orleans and his life on 8 January 1815, fifteen days after the Treaty of Gent ended the war, but several days before the frigate arrived at his headquarters with the news about the end of the war (Lipsey, 1992b, p. 288).

13. The neo-classical doctrine relies on an elegant, but unrealistic, assumption that markets are perfect. Without such a hypothesis, there is no case for the optimality in resource allocation.
14. If there is no retaliation, the 'optimal tariff' may be another reason for intervention. This is the case when a (large) country (or a group of countries) is strong enough to influence the world prices of the goods it trades. This country can reduce the world demand for the good in question by imposing or increasing tariffs. The price of the affected good falls, hence the tariff-imposing country tilts the terms of trade in its favour.
15. Because of asymmetric information, firms may have certain incentives to mislead the government.
16. Economies of scope are the outcome of the need for flexible (innovation-driven) methods of production. This is because the total production costs of manufacturing two separate goods may be higher than the costs of producing them together. A single firm can reduce average costs of production of two or more goods or services that share a common input without complete congestion. Identical technology can be employed for the production of differentiated output.
17. Rents are proceeds that are surplus to what is necessary to cover the costs of production and yield an average return on investment. They are due to barriers to entry such as large sunk costs, economies of scale, externalities, advertising, regulatory policies, distribution and service networks, asymmetric information, as well as consumer loyalty to a certain brand.
18. Serendipity is the faculty of making happy and unexpected discoveries by accident.
19. Viagra, the most widespread medicine against male impotence, is another example of serendipity. Dr Ian Osterloh experimented with viagra during the early 1990s with the aim of finding a painkiller for those that suffer from angina pectoris. This is a dangerous disease, the paroxysms of which are characterised by sudden and severe pain in the lower part of the chest, towards the left side, with a feeling of suffocation and threat of impending death. Pfizer, the pharmaceuticals company, was ready to give up on the project. However, certain male patients who were using this medicine during the research phase reported that following its consumption their virility got a boost. The rest is generally known. A medicine sought after for four millennia was found thanks to serendipity.
20. 'Schumpeterians' point to five long waves in modern history: (1) 1780–1840, steam power drove the Industrial Revolution; (2) 1840–90, the introduction of railways; (3) 1890–1930, the introduction and production of electric power; (4) 1930–80, cheap oil and cars; and (5) information technology.
21. While R&D and innovation activities in the US are led mainly by the military and double-use industries where demand is limited, in other countries these activities are more consumer related, that is, they are directed towards the development of goods and services for which demand exists everywhere. In addition, R&D is chiefly mission oriented towards major problems in countries such as the US, France and Britain. In countries such as Germany, Japan, Sweden or Switzerland, R&D is directed more towards the solution of practical problems.
22. Regarding the industry structure, patents are concentrated in pharmaceuticals, chemistry, molecular biology, semiconductor device manufacturing, optics, measuring and testing related devices, as well as telecommunications.
23. G. Parker, 'Brussels points the finger at lax states', *Financial Times*, 21 January 2004.
24. European Council, Lisbon 2000, Presidency Conclusions, §5.
25. Apart from the integration of separate markets, other supporting adjustment devices include deregulation and privatisation.
26. The era of imaginative individuals as major sources of innovation was the 19th century and earlier. To fly to the Moon involves the work of a large team of experts.
27. These irreversibilities include savings in factor (including energy) inputs per unit of output.
28. Economic growth may be propelled (among other elements) by the following three components (or by their combination): investment in capital and/or human resources, trade and technological change.

29. The time it takes for national income per capita to double in the early stages of industrialisation has fallen dramatically. In Britain it took about 60 years to do so after 1780, in Japan some 35 years after 1885, in Brazil 18 years after 1961 and in China 10 years after 1977. The main reason is technological progress. Countries are able to purchase foreign technology to make their home factors more productive.

    There is also another dimension to new technology. While it was an increase in the physical capacity to influence the environment and to produce goods that brought about the Industrial Revolution in the 19th century, the current industrial revolution has a more qualitative dimension. Lipsey gave us a note of caution when he compared present-day England with that in the Elizabethan era: 'It took 400 years for England to develop from that stage to its present one. To do the same elsewhere in half of the time of 200 years would be a tremendous achievement; to aspire to do it in 25 or 50 years may be to court disaster' (Lipsey, 1992a, p. 755).

30. 'The great majority of innovations did *not* come from formal R&D (even in organisations such as Du Pont . . . which had strong in-house R&D facilities). Most . . . came from production engineers, systems engineers, technicians, managers, maintenance personnel and of course production workers' (Freeman, 1994, p. 474).

31. Gordon Moore was the co-founder of Intel.

32. International agreements are usually ambiguous. This allows diplomats to interpret them at home in their own favour. Conversely, constitutions and other domestic laws are (supposedly) clear. This is because domestic politicians want the voters to understand them in order to win their votes.

33. 'The idea that we are living in an age of dramatic technological progress is mainly hype; the reality is that we live in a time when the fundamental things are actually not changing very rapidly at all. . . . The slightly depressing truth is that technology has been letting us down lately' (Krugman, 1998b, p. 104). This may be the truth if one remembers the constant maintenance necessary for PCs. The only new good that altered people's lives on a larger scale during the 1990s was the mobile phone. The Internet is the only major service that has done the same in the same period. However, there is a continuous stream of small improvements in already existing goods.

34. The total value of the public procurement market in the EU(15) was about 16 per cent of the EU GDP in 1998 (Sapir et al., 2003, p. 15).

35. As far as business services are concerned, the principal barriers to offering them in other EU countries include the need to work in the local language, local traditions and track record, distance factors and excessive costs to set up a local operation (European Commission, 2001, 'Barriers to trade in business services, Final report, Centre for Strategy & Evaluation Services, p. vi). It may be quite tough to overcome some of these obstacles.

36. *Financial Times*, 5 May 2003.

37. *Lait cru* (unpasteurised milk) contains many bacteria. However, some (many) consumers prefer cheese made from such milk because of its special taste. For example, Camembert made from *lait cru* is more expensive than other types of Camembert. If the EU bans unpasteurised cheeses, then jobs will be at risk and many consumers will be affected. There are many interests at stake. Unpasteurised cheese provoked an outbreak of food poisoning that claimed several victims in Switzerland in the early 1990s. Such cheeses were banned for some time afterwards, but slowly returned to the market.

38. If a country such as Germany sets higher standards than other EU countries, it could enforce those standards with trade restrictions. The purpose of Decision 3052/95 is to prevent such behaviour.

39. For a dissenting view about harmonisation, see Krugman (1997, p. 120), who argues that 'the demand for harmonisation is by and large ill-founded both in economics and law; realistic political economy requires that we give it some credence, but not too much'.

40. A large part of intra-industry trade is in parts and components.

41. See the surveys by Greenaway and Milner (1987) and Greenaway and Torstensson (1997).

42. This refers to the subjects that belong to the EU.

43. An exception to the general freedom of movement of goods is possible only in the case when such movement jeopardises public morality, security and the health of humans, animals or plants (Article 30).
44. This programme is also known as the White Paper, the Cockfield Report or the 1992 Programme.
45. This number does not include cases that relate to agriculture, fisheries, transport and coal.
46. *Financial Times*, 12 May 2000, p. 1.
47. *The Economist*, 28 November 1998, p. 87.
48. A special and still unresolved issue refers to takeovers by foreign firms. If the foreign buyer comes from a country with relatively cheap capital (low rate of interest) relative to the country of the target firm, such an acquirer has an advantage over other potential buyers that have access to financial markets that charge higher interest rates. If the authorities in the country of the target firm want to retain domestic ownership of such a business, they could restrict takeovers by foreign firms and/or give subsidies to the domestic acquirers. A much more effective policy than such direct interference in business would be to keep the domestic macroeconomic policy in order and, hence, have a domestic capital market competitive with the international one.
49. At the beginning of 1997, Boeing's share of the world market was 64 per cent, Airbus's was 30 per cent and McDonnell-Douglas's was 6 per cent. In Europe, the corresponding figures were Boeing 31 per cent, Airbus 37 per cent and McDonnell-Douglas 2 per cent (*Bulletin Quotidien Europe*, 23 May 1997, p. 10).
50. If to start a business requires overcoming substantial sunk costs, then mere deregulation and the Single European Market may not be enough. Further measures (such as subsidies) may be necessary to provide an investment impetus to firms.
51. The degree of concentration was much lower in the food and drink than in the chemical industry. It was higher at the national than at the EU level because of the barriers to trade (European Communities, 1991, p. 227).
52. Privatisation in the former East Germany accounted for a part of the merger and acquisition activity in Germany.
53. This result was similar to those obtained in many studies on mergers in the US.
54. W. Hutton, 'What Europe can teach Uncle Sam', *The Guardian*, 29 April 2002.
55. *The Economist*, 9 January 1999, p. 13.
56. *Financial Times*, 27 March 2003, p. 13.
57. http://www.crossingsbysw.com/pages/home_decor.
58. Europe has 40 battery producers compared with five in the US, 50 tractor makers while America has four and 16 firms building railway engines, whereas the US has two (*The Economist*, 23 January 1999, p. 67). Some firms think that they may prosper better if they become huge through mergers and acquisitions.
59. Another important tool for the control of dominance in the EU market and for enhancing competition was the conclusion of the Uruguay Round in 1994. After ratification, this deal further liberalised international trade, increased competition and, hence, modified/limited the non-competitive behaviour of the concentrated EU industries.
60. These thresholds also apply to firms that originate outside the EU.
61. If competitive firms want to keep their lead, they need to follow developments not only in their own industry, but also in unrelated, but potentially competing, ones. Examples of 'learning-by-watching' may be found in the disappearance, almost overnight, of the market for cine cameras after the appearance of video cameras, the seismic shift in the market for mechanical watches after the invention of digital ones, and the move from dot matrix to laser printers or fibreoptics that evolved independently of telecommunications technology.
62. A refusal to supply goods or services was taken to be an infringement of Article 82. In the United Brands case (1976) the European Commission found that United Brands, the major supplier of (Chiquita) bananas to most of the EU countries, abused its dominant position by refusing to supply green bananas to Olesen, a Danish ripener and distributor. Although Olesen had taken part in an advertising operation with one of United

Brands' competitors, the Court found that the reaction of United Brands to competitive threat was excessive and, hence, abusive. The discontinuation of the banana supply was a significant intrusion into the independence of small and medium-sized enterprises. United Brands was fined €1m by the Commission. The Court reduced the fine to €0.85m.
63. This article, however, neither outlaws nor discourages state ownership of enterprises.
64. EU guidelines for state aid for small and medium-sized enterprises (1992) state that these firms (defined as having fewer than 50 employees) may receive support of up to 15 per cent of investment cost. Enterprises with 50–250 employees may receive the same aid up to 7.5 per cent of their investment cost, while larger firms may get the same only in the assisted regions of the EU.
65. In the case of steel, shipbuilding or textiles, restructuring often means a reduction in production capacity.
66. A special type of public aid is in the form of public purchases. In Italy, for example, a law required that 30 per cent of contracts be awarded to firms based in the southern part of the country. The EU Court of Justice ruled in 1990 that such a law violated the public procurement directives. In other countries such as France or Germany there is no explicit buy-national law. None the less, publicly owned enterprises (railways, PTT) are 'expected' to prefer home-made goods and services to foreign ones.
67. The biggest state-aid case that came before the European Commission was the $9.4 billion rescue package for Crédit Lyonnais, the French state-owned bank. It was approved in 1995 (*Financial Times*, 27 July 1995, p. 13). The cost soared to $16.9 billion in 1998 (*Financial Times*, 7 May 1998, p. 2), while the total cost to French taxpayers was $30 billion (*Stratfor*, 16 July 2002). One cannot avoid the impression that the approval by the European Commission did not have a political motivation. In addition, the Commission failed an important test. It should have requested a bigger reduction in the bank's business.

> But this I say: He who sows sparingly will also reap sparingly,
> and he who sows bountifully will also reap bountifully.
> 2 Corinthians 9:6

6 Industrial Policy in Manufacturing and Services

1. Introduction

Explicit industrial policy as a part of overall economic policy did not attract the attention of research interests in the industrialised countries with market-based economies until the mid-1970s. This can be explained by the underlying economic developments. During the 1960s and early 1970s the industrialised countries experienced relatively fast economic growth with low rates of both inflation and unemployment. The prices of raw materials were stable and relatively low, while labour was able to move without major disturbances from agriculture to the manufacturing and services sectors. Excess demand for labour was met by a steady inflow of labour from abroad. This period was also characterised by sporadic government intervention to influence the national geography of production in the manufacturing and services sectors. Relatively free markets were operating smoothly without significant disruption. During this period, the GATT was active in the lowering of tariffs.

The 'golden 60s' were followed by a period whose principal characteristics were the result of a sharp increase in the price of oil in 1973. This triggered rises in inflation, unemployment and a deceleration in the rate of growth throughout the world. International competition increased sharply because suppliers were fighting in shrinking markets. It seemed that the free market system and the entrenched geography of production were not capable of coping satisfactorily with this situation. There developed an awareness of a need for alternative strategies (that is, based on intervention in manufacturing, services and trade) to cope with the new situation. Industrial policy could be seen as a supply-side response to market imperfections. Discussion was less about the formation of capital and more about its sectoral, industrial and geographical allocation and use. It was also more about economic adjustment policy than industrial policy (a term disliked by both politicians and neo-classical economists).[1] None the less, the gloves were off in the debate about industrial policy in the developed market economies.

This chapter is structured as follows. Various industrial policy issues such as its definition, its rationale, intervention, instruments, selectivity and small and medium-sized enterprises (SMEs) are discussed in Section 2. This is followed in Section 3 by a consideration of underlying principles of EU industrial policy, its evolution, importance and variety, technology policy and possible ways ahead. Additional analysis (Section 4) is devoted to the character and significance of services in general and in the EU in particular. The conclusion (Section 5) offers a list of forms and means that should be included in any respectable industrial policy.

2. Industrial policy issues

MEANING

An industry is usually taken to mean a group of firms that produce the same or similar kinds of good (or service) and which compete in the same market. The literature on modern industrial policy started its development in the early 1980s, and various definitions of industrial policy were proposed. Before surveying a selection of these, it is helpful to recall the difference between competition and industrial policy. The former is directed towards the freeing of market forces, while the latter seeks to channel them (Geroski, 1987, p. 57). In addition, industrial policy may sometimes have strong anti-competitive results, such as the need for the functional and spatial concentration of business to achieve economies of scale and a reduction in trade costs.

Some definitions of industrial policy are specific and selective. Industrial policy can be defined as coordinated targeting. This is the selection of parts of the economy, such as firms, projects or industries, for special treatment (targeting), coupled with a coordinated government plan to influence industrial structure in defined ways (coordination) (Brander, 1987, p. 4). Industrial policy implies policies that relate to specific industries, such as the correction of restrictive business practices (Pinder, 1982, p. 44). Industrial policies can be those government policies that are intended to have a direct effect on a particular industry or firm (McFetridge, 1985, p. 1). Industrial policy is aimed at particular industries (and firms as their components) in order to reach ends that are perceived by the government to be beneficial for the country as a whole (Chang, 1994, p. 60). This definition does not, however, distinguish between the short- and long-term perspectives. Different policies need to be employed to achieve efficiency if the timescale changes.

Other definitions of industrial policy are broad, often overloaded, and include many areas of public policy. For example, 'industrial policy includes all government actions that affect industry such as domestic and foreign investment, innovation, external trade, regional and labour policies, environmental features and all other aspects' (Donges, 1980, p. 189). 'Industrial policy can be any government measure or set of measures used to promote or prevent structural change' (Curzon Price, 1981, p. 17). Industrial policy may mean all measures that improve the economy's supply potential: anything that will improve growth, productivity and competitiveness (Adams and Klein, 1983, p. 3).

Another look at industrial policy can take it to mean a government policy action that is aimed at or motivated by problems within specific sectors. These 'problems' presumably occur in both declining and expanding (manufacturing or service) industries. The solutions to these problems are not necessarily sector specific, although that is a possibility (Tyson and Zysman, 1987a, p. 19). Initiation and coordination of government activities in order to influence and improve the productivity and competitiveness of particular industries or the whole economy is industrial policy (Johnson, 1984, p. 8). Industrial policy can be defined as the set of selective measures adopted by the state to alter industrial organisation (Blais, 1986, p. 4). Another definition states that its focus has been on the ideal relation between governments and markets. 'Industrial policy need not be equated with national planning. It is, rather, a formula for making the economy adaptable and dynamic' (Reich, 1982, pp. 75–9). 'The term industrial policy describes that group of policies whose explicit objective is to influence the operation of industry' (Sharp and Shepherd, 1987, p. 107). 'An industrial policy implies intervention by a government which seeks to promote particular industries in some way. This may be either to stimulate production and growth of an industry's size or to promote export sales' (Whalley, 1987, p. 84). This definition does not, however, include government influence on the decline of and exit from an industry. 'Industrial policy may be equated with intervention employed to cope with market failures or a price system that affects the allocation of resources' (Komiya, 1988, p. 4). 'All acts and policies of a government that relate to industry, constitute industrial policy' (Bayliss and El-Agraa, 1990, p. 137). The World Bank defines industrial policy as 'government efforts to alter industrial structure to promote productivity-based growth' (World Bank, 1993, p. 304). It is not clear whether this means that aid to ailing industries lies outside the scope of industrial policy. 'Industrial policy includes all actions that are taken to advance industrial development beyond what is allowed by the free market system' (Lall, 1994, p. 651). Industrial policy may also mean 'a set of public interventions through taxes, subsidies and regulations on domestic products or factors of production that attempt to modify the allocation of domestic resources that is the consequence of the free operation of market forces' (Gual, 1995, p. 9).

Industrial policy may mean different things for various countries at different times. Developing countries look at industrial policy as a means of economic development. They may favour some industries over others. Once these countries become developed, industrial policy may be directed towards fostering free competition. In the former centrally planned economies, industrial policy meant planning and imposing production and investment targets in each sector and industry within it.

Industrialised countries have had implicit industrial policies for a long time. They are embodied in trade, competition, tax, R&D, standardisation, education, regional, transport, environment, public procurement and other policies that have derived effects on the industrial structure. This is due to the interdependence of economic policies within the economic system. Therefore, some countries have joint ministries of industry and international trade. This is the case, for instance, with the British Department of Trade and Industry (DTI) and the Japanese Ministry of International Trade and Industry (MITI), although there are differences in the powers and role in the economy between the two ministries.

In most-developed countries the period after the Second World War was characterised by reductions in tariffs, as well as measures to prevent the demise of declining industries. However, governments' industrial policies may be a simple continuation of the old protectionism by more sophisticated means (Pinder et al., 1979, p. 9). Governments' tax and transfer policies have their impact on demand. This affects the structure and spatial location of manufacturing production, that is, where new employment is created, attracted or kept. By direct production and supply of public goods and services, as well as through public procurement, governments influence, at least in part, the geography of production of their economies. Other government policies, such as foreign policy, have no direct effect on the size of the economic pie in their country. However, they can influence industrial structure, its geographical distribution and employment. This is the case when governments ban the export of (high-technology) goods abroad.

Three (non-mutually exclusive) broad types of industrial policy are macroeconomic, sectoral and microeconomic orientation. Macroeconomic orientation is least interventionist because it leaves the operation of industries and firms to market forces. Policy orientation simply improves the general economic climate for business. Sector-specific orientation becomes relevant when market failures affect certain industries. It tries to amend the particular market shortcoming. Microeconomic orientation of industrial policy may direct a government to act directly towards specific firms or industrial groups (Jacquemin, 1984, pp. 4–5).

There are another three broad types of industrial policy: market oriented, interventionist or mixed. The first type (market oriented) fosters competition and free markets. The second (interventionist) policy may be conducted as in the centrally planned economies. In practice, industrial policy is most often a mixture of the first two. Most countries may be classified as 'massaged-market economies'.[2] The issue that most often differs between countries is not whether or not they intervene, but rather the degree and form of intervention in industry.

Industrial policy may also be described as adjustment prone or adjustment averse. Adjustment-prone industrial policy stimulates adjustment of various industries to enter into new production, remain competitive or ease the exit from selected lines of production. Adjustment-averse industrial policy is the policy of protection, which impedes changes in an economy by preserving the status quo.

The level of industrial policy can be general or specific. The choice is between discrimination and non-discrimination. The degree of intervention should be as high as possible. This means that it needs to be general, that is, available to every industry and enterprise. Once the policy is put in place, the market is perhaps the best tool to fine-tune the economy, to create and to exploit unforeseen opportunities, as well as to select the firms or industries that should take advantage of the employed policy instruments. Market forces may prevent players from the inefficient employment of resources. The policy should be tailored to suit local needs (industry or firm) in cases where there are no externalities. In addition, it should be used with care because governments are not infallible and may well make the wrong commercial choice, as was the case with the French and British Concorde project.

A critical definition of industrial policy states that it is 'the label used to describe a wide-ranging, ill-assorted collection of micro-based supply-side initiatives that are designed to improve market performance in a variety of mutually inconsistent ways. Intervention is typically demanded in cases with market failures and where major changes need to be effected quickly' (Geroski, 1989, p. 21). To formulate a definition of industrial policy may be as difficult to describe as a Chinese dish. 'One US Supreme Court Justice tried to find a definition of pornography and said: "You know it when you see it, but you can't define it"; so it may be with industrial policy' (Audretsch, 1989, p. 10).

Various economic policies have their impact on industrial policy. Not only trade policy, but also social, education, regional, energy, transport, health, environment and other policy areas all have a strong spatial impact. Hence, most definitions of industrial policy include, at least implicitly, the need for a stable economic environment and coordination of various economic policies. Only then can specific targeting of industrial policy make its full contribution to economic growth and improvement in productivity and competitiveness, the final objective being an increase in the standard of living. On such grounds, broad definitions of industrial policy may embrace all of these facets. Hence, industrial policy is an economic policy that shapes a country's comparative advantage. Its objective is to influence the change in national economic structure (reallocation of resources among sectors, industries, professions and regions) in order to enhance the creation and growth of national wealth, rather than to distribute it.

RATIONALE

The classical economic model based on free trade and perfect competition predicts that *laissez-faire* is universally beneficial and costless. However, the new theory of strategic[3] trade and industrial policy has shown that intervention can sometimes play a useful role in mitigating the shortcomings of market imperfections and can alter the national and international geography of production. In general, economic adjustment (industrial, sectoral, professional and geographical reallocation and use of resources) is prompted by factors that include an increase in GDP and its distribution, as well as by changes in demand, technology, market structure, tastes, needs, prices, foreign competition and marketing, all of which contribute to a potential increase or loss in current competitiveness. In addition, environmental constraints and a rapidly ageing population also contribute to economic adjustment. This process is not smooth, or easy or costless or fast, hence the need for an industrial policy.

The creation of wealth used to depend in the distant past to a large extent on the local availability of natural resources.[4] As the economy evolved, wealth creation started to depend more on physical assets (mainly equipment and finance). Prosperity of the modern economy and competitiveness of output depend not only on the physical, but also and increasingly on intangible assets such as knowledge, information processing, as well as on organisational and control potentials and capabilities.

Instead of relying on inherited and natural advantages, industrial policy may help in the conscious shaping of a country's comparative advantage through the supplies of trained labour and educated management with a specific profile (engineers versus ethnographers), tax, infrastructure, public purchase and R&D policies. One thing, however, has to be clear from the outset. Both intervention (action) and *laissez-faire* (non-intervention) have an impact on the structure of industry and, hence, on the geography of production. The challenge for a government is to achieve, maintain and profit from the best balance between the two approaches. That, however, is not at all easy.

Countries in the EU and the US responded to the circumstances prevailing during the 1970s primarily by protectionism. Along with other industrialised countries, they realised that the solution to lagging productivity, recession, deteriorating export performance, increasing market penetration for manufacturing goods from developing countries and reallocation of some manufacturing activities outside the developed world may be found in policies that affect the structure and development of national industry. None the less, inadequate economic performance is not a sufficient condition for the justification of industrial policy. The question is not whether the economy is operating (un)satisfactorily, but rather whether an industrial policy might have achieved a better result than a free market system (Adams, 1983, p. 405). Any policy has to be tested according to the gains and losses that it creates in a dynamic context.

Once free markets lose credibility as efficient conductors of an economy, the introduction of intervention (various economic policies) seems inevitable. The question then is 'How can the government intervene in the most efficient and least harmful way?'. The choice might be between leaving the economy to imperfect entrepreneurs and the possibly even riskier strategy of having it run by imperfect governments (Curzon Price, 1981, p. 20). However, there is no strong a priori reason why an economy run by imperfect governments should be at greater risk than one run by imperfect entrepreneurs. Both of these are second-best (suboptimal) solutions.

Risk taking (entrepreneurship) has always been a significant engine of economic growth albeit the benefits achieved are accompanied by attendant dangers. The costs of adjustment are borne principally by those that are weak or powerless. Thus, governments have often followed a defensive policy with the objective of securing employment in the short term and evading social tensions, at least during their term in office. The socialisation of risk in the form of various economic policies may make life safer in the short run, but it also prevents both free operation of individual entrepreneurial activity and an even greater increase in the economic pie in the future. This process may be seen as bowing to the public's desire to see a happy marriage between progress and stability (Blais, 1986, p. 41). Interestingly, however, in Britain rescuing a declining industry (coal) to protect jobs proved not to be the safe route to re-election for the government during the 1970s. Taxpayers and consumers are not unaware of the costs of such a rescue. However, in many countries strong trade unions in declining industries can still mobilise a strong lobbying influence. Those who have full confidence in the operation of a free market system would say that the market will take care of itself. Why bother to change those things which will happen anyway? This school of thought fails to take account of a number of serious market imperfections.

The most influential reasons for intervention may be found in the loss of a competitive position, the management of expansion of new and the decline of old industries, the handling of industries subject to scale effects and externalities, and attracting footloose industries (Lipsey, 1987b, p. 117). Fostering strategic manufacturing and services industries with strong forward and backward links to the rest of the economy can be a very attractive policy goal. These industries supply external or non-priced gains to the rest of the economy. Growing industries such as semiconductors, electronics or telecommunications have a much more profound spillover effect on the economy than do the furniture or clothing industries.

Technologies that are 'critical' for a large country's competitiveness and/or defence include those that deal with new materials, energy sources and environment; biotechnology and pharmacy; manufacturing, including production of tools; information gathering, communications, data processing and computers; and transportation and aeronautics, including navigation. Because of large sunk costs and economies of scale, small and medium-sized countries do not have the means, or indeed the necessity (if they can acquire them through trade), to develop all or most of these technologies and make them commercially viable. What these countries may do instead is to select a 'critical' mass of 'critical' technologies or parts of them (for example, components, basic chemicals) and try to excel in those market niches, as is the case with Switzerland, Austria, the Benelux and Scandinavian countries.

Another classification of the reasons for an industrial policy groups them into three broad categories: respectable, false and non-economic (Curzon Price, 1990, pp. 159–67).

- *Respectable* arguments include market failures because, in practice, a perfect competition model does not always lead to a stable equilibrium. However, the problem is that a market failure such as wage rigidity or monopolies can frequently be traced to a previous intervention by the government. Another pretext for intervention is domestic distortions. A uniform rate of value-added tax (VAT) would have a neutral effect on the consumption of goods or services in a country, but a reduction in VAT on food, for example, may cause some resources to shift to that industry at a time when the telecommunications or data-processing industries could have made better use of them. Infant industries provide a good excuse for intervention, but the problem is that there are many old 'infants' that may never become self-sustaining. One can also build an intellectually respectable case for industrial policy based on positive externalities and spillover effects (Krugman, 1993b, pp. 160–61).[5] These include benefits arising from the establishment of common technical standards for the production and/or operation of goods, for example, in the telecommunications industry. However, mistakes can be costly if governments target the wrong industry, for example, computers in France, Concorde (Britain and France) and petrochemicals and aluminium in Japan before the first oil shock.[6] The process may become overpoliticised and subject to strong lobbying as in the case of public goods that everyone wants and consumes, although these goods may be produced at a loss.

- The first *false* argument in favour of intervention is the issue of employment. Employment subsidies used to prolong the life of jobs in declining industries are often implemented at the expense of growing industries that may need them to expand operations and which could provide more and better jobs in the future. Likewise, proponents of the balance of payments argument for intervention tend to forget that resources that move into the protected industries may come from those industries with better export opportunities. Hence, a drop in imports may provoke a fall in exports.
- *Non-economic* arguments may be quite strong. It is often hard to dispute the issue of national security. This is a political process that confounds the predictive abilities of an economist. The problem is that it may be pushed to the limit in the case of industries that can be labelled as essential for national defence. In general, 'smart bombs' and electronic and nuclear weapons counteract the national security argument for intervention. Long-term supply contracts from allies and stockpiling may be considered prior to intervention. Social arguments for intervention, focused on the redistribution rather than the creation of material wealth, such as regional development or the protection of the environment and culture, may have some non-economic weight during any discussion about intervention.

The relative shares of the manufacturing industry and agriculture in GDP and employment have been declining continuously in industrialised countries over the past decades. In 2003, the GDP of the EU(15) was accounted for predominantly by services (70 per cent), with the rest distributed between manufacturing (27 per cent) and agriculture (3 per cent).[7] Hence, the process of deindustrialisation leads countries to a post-industrial society. These countries are better called service rather than industrialised economies, because manufacturing industry is a statistically 'shrinking' sector in relation to services. Some manufacturing jobs from developed countries have geographically relocated to the developing world.

One has to be very cautious with generalisations. Many services (about half) are directly linked to the manufacturing of goods, such as transport, finance, telecommunications, maintenance and other business services including everything from cleaning offices to business consultancy and advertising. Such services are not directly aimed at individuals for their personal consumption. If they are included in manufacturing and agriculture, then the relative share of these sectors in the national economy is significantly increased. In fact, they are most intimately linked with each other. In regions with few services, manufacturing industry performs below its potential. Hence, the relation between manufacturing and services is not one way. New manufacturing technologies require new, better and/or more services, while services (such as R&D) may create new manufacturing technologies that may, in turn, create demand for services and so on. Profound changes in the structure of manufacturing and services have blurred the distinction between the two economic sectors.

A relative increase in the demand for services and growth in this sector was made possible by an increase in the productivity of the manufacturing sector. This has made more resources available for the services sector of the economy. Increased productivity results in a reduction in the price of manufactured goods, leading to an increase in disposable funds for the consumption of services. This makes industrial policy in manufacturing and services interesting for consideration.[8]

The MIT (Massachusetts Institute of Technology) Commission on Industrial Policy has studied the importance of manufacturing. From a study of the US economy, the commission drew the following conclusions (Dertouzos et al., 1990, pp. 39–42):

- In 1987 in the US, imports of goods and services were ten times higher than exports of services. It is necessary to manufacture and export goods in order to pay for imports. The more resources are reallocated to services, the lower the chance of balancing the balance of payments.

- Moving resources from the manufacturing industry into services causes a shift from a sector with relatively high productivity growth to one with lower growth.
- Almost all R&D is carried out in the manufacturing sector.
- National defence depends on the purchase of a great amount of manufactured goods. If a country starts to depend on foreign suppliers, national security may be placed in jeopardy.

THE ROLE OF THE GOVERNMENT

The standard comparative advantage and factor proportions theories of international trade may be satisfactory for the explanation of trade in primary goods. However, they are less satisfactory in explaining trade in industrial goods. Manufacturing can be seen as a collection of industries with no factor abundance base. On those grounds it is difficult to explain why the US exports computer software, why France exports perfumes while Japan exports copiers, cameras and VCRs, or why the Swiss export chocolate, chemicals and watches.

A country's comparative advantage not only depends on its geographical resource endowment, but is also shaped over time by the actions of both businesses and government. Government economic policies may affect comparative advantage over time by influencing the quantity and quality of labour, capital, incentives and technology. Comparative advantage in manufacturing industries is not an unchangeable condition of nature, but often the outcome of economic policies that affect incentives to save, invest, innovate, diffuse technology and acquire or 'import' human capital (as was the choice during the 1960s and will be the case from 2010 for several decades).

Until the 1970s, market imperfections and multiple equilibria were at the margin of orthodox economic analysis, but these imperfections are at the heart of the analysis of the new theory of trade and industrial policy. A country's size, regional disequilibria, skill, mobility and unionisation of labour, R&D, sunk costs, economies of scale, competition and bankruptcy laws are just a few imperfections. To ignore them is to fail to realise that their effects can be mitigated by economic policy (Tyson, 1987, pp. 67–71). In the field of manufacturing, a government has at its disposal several policy instruments. These include trade policy (tariffs, subsidies and NTBs) that may reduce competition and antitrust policy that increases it; preferential tax treatment; non-commercial loans and loan guarantees as a support to risk capital; exports, insurance and other subsidies; public procurement;

support for education and vocational retraining; assistance to workers to improve their professional and geographical mobility; and the provision of public or publicly financed R&D.

Free competition within an economic union brings costs of adjustment to which governments, voters and citizens are not indifferent. It is often forgotten that increased competition brings benefits in terms of economic restructuring. The costs of adjustment are often highly concentrated on the (vociferous) few and are usually temporary, whereas the benefits are dispersed over a long period of time and throughout the society, but in relatively small instalments to everyone. In the real, second-best and imperfect world, there may be enough scope for both market mechanism and select intervention (economic policy).

The role of governments as organisers of national economies is coming under increasing inquiry. Governments can play several roles in economic activity, including:

- setting general economic and political stability;
- initiation;
- supervision;
- ownership of assets; and
- arbitration.

In spite of general agreement about the need to reduce the extent of public intervention in the allocation of resources in a national economy, it is a fact that the countries that have had the most impressive economic achievements during the past two decades are those whose governments exerted a strong and positive influence over all facets of commercial affairs (Dunning, 1994b, p. 1). The actions of governments, markets and firms are not substitutes for one another, but they do need to be mutually supportive. Instead of being obstacles, they need to be structured in such a way as to support and facilitate the actions of the others. This is a formidable task indeed.

A general reduction in tariffs and NTBs, as well as economic integration, may increase a country's market. However, free markets often fail to take a long-term view of society's needs when making structural adjustments. Such adjustment (the transfer of resources from declining to growing industries) is not necessarily a swift, cheap and smooth process. In addition, it is a risky operation, as the future of expanding industries is not secure in the long term. If (a big if) astute adjustment policies (intervention) can facilitate these shifts and if this stimulates the new use of resources by providing incentives and support to the private businesses to adjust to the new situation, then intervention may have a certain justification.

One can make predictions about the model of economic adjustment based on the characteristics of a country's financial system. First, if this system relies on capital markets that allocate resources by competitively established prices, the adjustment process is company led. The allocation decisions are the responsibility of firms, as is the case in the US. Second, in a credit-based financial system where the government is administering prices, the adjustment process is state led (such as the past experiences of Japan and France). Finally, in a credit-based system where price formation is dominated by banks, the adjustment process can be considered as negotiated. An example can be found in Germany (Zysman, 1983, p. 18).

A common view of the world holds that firms play Cournot–Nash games against all other players (each firm decides on a course of action, for example, optimising output, on the assumption that the behaviour of the other firms remains constant), whereas governments play the Stackelberg game (the agent knows the reaction functions of all others) against firms and Cournot–Nash games against other governments (Brander and Spencer, 1985, p. 84). Unfortunately, these are all games that can produce relatively unstable equilibria and fluctuations in prices. In contrast, collusion among the players would lead to a relatively stable (Chamberlin) solution.

JUSTIFIED INTERVENTION

The key question in the debate on industrial policy (the relationship of states and market) still remains: can imperfect governments make the shift of resources any better than imperfect markets? The answer is 'generally not', but this does not mean that market solutions are always superior to other ones. Just as the dangers of market failure are often exaggerated, so are the competencies of governments. None the less, in some cases a government's intervention (policy) may fare better than a free market solution. Here are some examples of situations in which intervention may be justified.

First, the time horizon in which private markets operate is relatively short. They may not foresee countries' long-term needs in the face of changing circumstances, capabilities and opportunities with a high degree of accuracy. Japanese manufacturing is financed to a large extent by bank credits, whereas US industry uses this source of finance to a much lesser extent. This means that managers of Japanese firms who ask their bank manager for a loan can justify the request on the grounds of the profits that will accrue when 'their ship comes in'. Managers in a comparable American firm in a similar situation must be sure that they can see the funnel of the ship in the distance. Hence, US industrial production is in general much more affected by the short-term interests of shareholders than is Japanese industry. The major goal of Japanese and German bank and enterprise managers is to try to ensure a firm's long-term competitive position in the market and thus some of them tend to look favourably on risky investments such as the commercialisation of new technologies. In contrast, the US system favours readily measurable physical (mergers and acquisitions) over intangible assets such as education or R&D. In spite of such a theoretical observation, the US is in practice the world leader in new technology and its application.

Government policy can shift this short-term perspective towards longer-term economic considerations. However, less than perfect foresight can lead banks into bad loans, which can culminate in financial crisis, as occurred in the developing countries during the 1980s or in Japan at the end of the 1990s. Japan and the newly developed countries such as Korea had been held up as examples of a successful manufacturing-led development path based on intervention. These Asian countries were delivering 'good news' for a long time over 1970s and 1980s. Much of the credit for these achievements went to government planners who 'knew what they were doing'. However, when serious regional crises emerged in the late 1990s (essentially because of lightly regulated banking, which was subject to severe moral hazard problems), the truth was revealed: they didn't know. Sceptics argue that Japan and Korea would have had an ever-steeper growth curve had it not been for selective intervention. Given macroeconomic stability, equilibrium and a stable exchange rate, high and stable savings and investment rates, an enterprising spirit, a respectable level of education, relatively competitive labour markets and relatively liberal trading system were more than enough to stimulate even faster growth. The contribution of selective intervention was negligible or harmful (Pack, 2000, p. 51).

Second, in a different case, risk-averse governments may countenance stockpiling in order to cushion the effect of a possible crisis. Private markets may not have the inclination and/or funds to do the same in the long term. A government may estimate the cost of this kind of risk in terms of GDP that would be sacrificed in the case of an unexpected reduction in the availability of certain inputs.

Third, governments may wish to keep some facilities for the home production as a bargaining chip to use with foreign suppliers while negotiating prices of long-term supply contracts. This should deter foreign monopolies from charging monopoly prices.

Fourth, market forces are quite efficient in allocating resources among producers and allocating goods and services among consumers in simple and static settings. Much of the power of markets in these circumstances emerges from the fact that prices convey all the necessary information to participants in the market. This enables them to act independently, without explicit coordination, and still reach a collectively efficient solution. It is possible that markets can, at least in principle, solve simple and static problems in a remarkably efficient way, but it is not entirely surprising to learn that the free market game is less successful in more demanding circumstances with market imperfections. Adjustment problems occur because of the unsatisfactory operation of the market/price game viewed from the long-term vantage point. It is the aim of forward-looking intervention to set the economy on the road towards the desired long-term equilibrium.

Fifth, basic research provides significant positive externalities (spillovers) throughout the economy. These social gains are in most cases difficult for private markets to grasp because the private risks and costs may be very high and the benefits uncertain. In addition, without interventions, such as patents and other intellectual property rights, free markets cannot guarantee sufficient pecuniary returns to the private risk-taking innovator. The outputs of successful basic research fuel technological progress in the country. In most countries, such research is funded in full or in part by the government either directly (subsidy) or indirectly (tax relief). Governments and private businesses share the risk.

Sixth, industrial policy may ease economic adjustment in a more efficient and equitable way than free market forces. This policy may provide support for R&D, education and training, for geographical and professional mobility of labour, investment subsidies, protection and other support such as that for the improvement of infrastructure during the early fragile period of a new industry. Free market forces fail to do so. As for adjustment and exit from ailing industries, government policy may offer unemployment benefits, vocational training and early retirement schemes. Industrial policy can, to an extent, both anticipate and shape these changes. It can be involved either directly in picking the winners/losers or indirectly by creating the business environment in which firms can make choices in a potentially successful and desirable way.

Seventh, agriculture is a sector in which every government intervenes. Because of the impact of weather conditions and biological cycles, free market forces cannot achieve the reliability of supply and stability of incomes of the farm population relative to the labour force in other sectors. In addition, governments seek to secure the domestic supply of farm goods in circumstances of war, as well as protecting the landscape and environment.

The eighth reason for the introduction of an industrial policy is that this policy may be able to respond, with various internal and external (retaliatory) measures, to the economic policies of other countries. Left alone, market forces may take advantage of foreign policies in the short term, but if the long-term strategy of foreign competitors is to undermine the importing country's home production by means of predatory pricing in order to create an international monopoly, then the long-term effect may be detrimental to the importing country's welfare. An industrial policy may be a suitable response because it can change the possible free market outcome.

INSTRUMENTS

Tariffs (trade policy) have historically been the most important instrument of industrial policy. After a number of rounds of multilateral reduction in tariffs under the auspices of GATT/WTO, the use of this instrument has been restricted in scope and reduced in power. However, other methods of intervention have developed. Some of these represent protectionist pressures against adjustment, while others are adjustment oriented. They include:

- subsidies for exports, production, education, R&D and investment;
- NTBs;
- tax, exchange rate and credit policy;
- public purchases;
- price and exchange controls;
- regulation of the market (such as licensing);
- technical and other standards;
- direct production by the state;
- provision of infrastructure; and
- competition and concentration policy.

The most benign intervention is the kind that does not harm other businesses and sectors. The most effective instruments of such an industrial policy include macroeconomic stability, education and the provision of infrastructure. Low inflation, a stable exchange rate and slightly positive real rates of interest may be the best tools of such an industrial policy. Savings will increase and entrepreneurs will have the chance to observe and shape their future with a relatively high degree of accuracy. Well-educated managers and a well-trained workforce (investment in human capital as a created factor) provide the economy with the most valuable assets capable of solving problems. Moreover, in many cases, private businesses are not interested in investing in infrastructure (sewage systems, roads, bridges and so on), so the government needs to step in.

Subsidies may be a distorting instrument of industrial policy. They may diminish incentives for the advance of profitable firms if they are always taxed in order to provide the government with revenue to subsidise inefficient enterprises. A subsidy that stimulates the introduction of new capital may distort a firm's choice of technologies. This is relevant for firms that use capital and labour in different proportions. If a firm has to pay the full cost of capital it might choose another technology. A one-off subsidy to investment may help a firm buy time and adjust to an unexpected change in technology or demand (its fickleness and sophistication). If the value of subsidies and other favours is smaller than the value added in the given industry, then subsidisation may be justified (but determining this can be quite difficult and uncertain). If subsidies are provided on a permanent basis for the protection of employment to an industry or firm, then there is no incentive for the management to perform as efficiently as in those enterprises or industries where market criteria dominate. A permanently subsidised industry or firm is a very likely candidate for nationalisation.

Sufficient subsidies will always maintain output (in ailing industries) at a level that would be unsustainable in free market conditions. Emerging industries, where investment risk is quite high, have to offer the prospects of relatively higher rewards than elsewhere in the economy in order to attract factors. Gains in productivity in these new businesses may be able to cushion increases in pecuniary rewards to investors without increases in prices. However, faced with the possibility of higher wages in one industry, trade unions may press for increases in wages elsewhere in the economy. Without increases in productivity, the result may be an increase in prices throughout the economy. None the less, the industries that use new technologies and in which productivity is higher than elsewhere in the economy may be one step ahead of other businesses in this race.

The policy of shoring up a 'dying' industry for an excessively long period of time is like moving forwards but looking backwards. It may be preferable to compensate redundant labour rather than continue to shore up ailing firms. Compensation to redundant labour needs to be provided by the public authorities because the whole society benefits from the process of industrial change and adjustment. Shareholders of dying firms should not be compensated for the depreciation in the value of their shares. They should channel their funds into the growing businesses that need fresh capital for expansion, not to those that are declining and do not need it according to free market criteria (Curzon Price, 1981, pp. 27–9).

In contrast to industries that use ageing technologies, emerging ones require venture capital: they may be quite small, numerous, unstable and have an uncertain future. When they are in trouble their voice may not be heard as loudly as that of declining industries. Investment in emerging firms is risky because many of them collapse before they reach maturity. However, these firms are the greatest propelling agents of a modern economy. Although many of them disappear from the market, many others stay and new ones are created. A high birth rate of new firms is the best indication of the vitality of a system which creates opportunities, so that many new enterprises may be started and the risk accepted. Alfred Marshall drew an analogy between the forest (industry, sector or the whole economy) and the trees (individual firms). Trees may grow and decay for individual reasons, but what is important for the economy is that the forest grows.

Entrepreneurs (sometimes seen as 'maniacs with a vision') often have genuine ideas, but many of them do not have the necessary knowledge about how to run a business. Some of them may know, but cannot persuade those with funds to support their projects. Why is this so? Reasons include a number of cultural factors (risk lovers or risk-averse investors) and the lack of knowledge and understanding to recognise and seize the opportunity. For example, a century ago a man went to a Belfast bank and asked for a loan to start a company. He explained to the bank managers that his invention was a mechanical horseless device that would replace horses in ploughing. This was too risky for the bank as it could not foresee that the enterprise would be a commercial success. Hence this man, whose name was Ferguson, went to Canada. He met another man by the name of Massey, they teamed up, and the rest of the story is generally known. Massey Ferguson became one of the major world producers of tractors and agriculture-related machinery. The moral of this story is that one needs to recognise and seize the opportunity. *Carpe diem.*

All protectionist measures offered to an industry should be conditional, otherwise the problems of the industry can be exacerbated. If the protected industry is a declining one, then its adjustment may be postponed or reversed by production or employment subsidies. This increases costs to society in the long term because the desired change (transfer of resources from low- to high-profit industries) does not take place. The adjustment policy needs to be of limited duration. It should involve both public funds and private capital, as well as make the cost of action as transparent as possible. In addition, the recipients of assistance should be expected to develop comparative advantages prior to the termination of that help. Market processes should be encouraged and managerial practices improved.

It has been argued, not without dispute, that protectionism did not cost the US economy any more than the trade deficit did. The real harm done by protectionism (reduction in the efficiency of production because of a fragmentation of markets, as well as prevention of specialisation and economies of scale) is more modest than was usually assumed in the case of the US. The major industrial nations suffer more, in economic terms, from the relatively unattractive problems for economic analysis such as 'avoidable traffic congestion and unnecessary waste in defence contracting than they do from protectionism. To take the most extreme example, the cost to taxpayers of the savings and loan bailout alone will be at least five times as large as the annual cost to US consumers of all US import restrictions' (Krugman, 1990b, p. 36). The reasons why protectionism features relatively highly on the public agenda can be found in politics and symbolism. Politically, free trade offsets economic nationalism, while symbolically free trade is a cornerstone of liberal democracies. In addition, those involved in protected businesses, such as agriculture and manufacturing industries that employ ageing technologies, tend to vote in large numbers, unlike the rest of the population.

Direct subsidies for R&D or indirect subsidies in the form of public procurement are powerful instruments for the support of industries that introduce new technologies or new goods and services. The volume of demand and its structure provides the most important incentive for production. This is also crucial for the strategic industries, whose activities provide external and non-priced gains through linkages and externalities to the rest of the economy (examples include the machine-tool industry, biotechnology, pharmaceuticals, computers, telecommunications and data-processing).[9] If start-up costs create a barrier to entry into a strategic industry, the government may step in and help out. If the governments of other countries are subsidising their strategic industries, the case for intervention by the domestic government can look very persuasive. In the early unstable phase of the introduction of a new production technology, good or service, a secure government demand provides a powerful impetus for the firm to develop the product and open new markets. If this production does not become self-sustaining within a specified period of time, then it may never become profitable and resources that may be allocated for protection may be used elsewhere in the future with a greater efficiency in improving competitiveness.

The costs of subsidies need to be considered before intervention. A subsidy to one firm is a tax on others. If there is the chance of high returns in the future, such a tax might be worth bearing, but the gains are impossible to judge in advance. Once a government starts handing out subsidies, demands for more aid may go on expanding without end. At that point, political power, rather than 'economic sense', determines who gets what and where. The long isolation of an industry from market forces may remove the incentive to respond swiftly to signals that come from competition in international markets.

When affording protection to an industry, it must be on the condition that the schedule of protection/intervention will be revised downwards over time. Protection that is not temporary and selective may create serious adjustment problems and increase costs in the future. The strategy of selection and the transitory nature of protection may provide a limited adjustment period to an industry by mitigating the full impact of international competition. This programme does not ensure the existence of inefficient industries and firms, but rather their adjustment and exit from declining industries. The self-liquidation of protection is perhaps the only way of keeping up the incentive to adjust. If adjustment programmes offer funds to firms, then this must be under the condition that these funds are spent on specified activities. Technical advisory boards that represent a wide community should oversee adjustment programmes (Tyson and Zysman, 1987b, p. 425).

Public intervention in many countries has primarily, but not exclusively, been directed towards 'problem' industries. These have usually been agriculture, coal, steel, textile and footwear industries. However, there appears to be growing interest in intervening in emerging industries where technology changes fast. Intervention in this case takes the form of providing or subsidising innovation and R&D, special tax treatment of new technologies (tax holidays and subsidies), training of labour, education of management, government procurement and provision of infrastructure, as well as more general instruments such as planning, policy guidelines and exchange of information.

Many of these instruments may be applied to a single target simultaneously, and may sometimes be in conflict. If the objective is to increase efficiency, then competition and concentration may be conflicting. Many industries may not operate efficiently without a certain degree of concentration dictated by minimum efficient economies of scale. So, this has to be accepted. Small countries usually do not have very restrictive antimonopoly laws, because efficient production in the home (unprotected) market and possibly even abroad often allows the existence of only one efficient production unit. Countries such as France foster a policy of concentration and efficiency, whereas others such as the US, because of the huge home market, have strong anti-monopoly legislation that favours free (internal) competition. Inward-looking industries whose production technologies in the declining phase of their life cycle traditionally lobby in every country for protection, whereas the emerging industries, which are oriented to the widest international market, support free trade.

SMALL AND MEDIUM-SIZED ENTERPRISES

It was a strongly held belief in Europe during the 1960s that large American-style companies were the key factor in the economic growth of a country. These enterprises may, among other things, spend substantial funds on R&D and increase the international competitiveness of their output. Hence, mergers and acquisitions were encouraged. That policy left Europe with a number of slumbering industrial giants, ill-equipped to face the challenges of the 1970s and 1980s (Geroski and Jacquemin, 1985, p. 175). However, experience has shown that those countries that spend most on R&D do not necessarily have the highest rates of growth. It was also realised that SMEs,[10] largely forgotten or pushed to the outskirts of traditional economic analysis, are important players in economic revival and employment. Subsequently, the policy that strongly encouraged mergers and acquisitions was abandoned. It is recognised that, per unit of investment, more jobs are created by SMEs than by large companies. This may be one of the outcomes of the business policy of (large) firms that want to avoid conflicts with organised labour. Product differentiation demands production on a smaller scale and decentralisation of business. This is radically different from the prevailing theoretical expectations during the 1960s.

An expansion of SMEs started after the first oil shock (1973). However, jobs created by SMEs often have the disadvantage of being relatively less secure than those in large firms. Being small, these firms need to be flexible if they want to withstand competition. Flexible SMEs often use hit-and-run tactics in their business, linked with low sunk costs, as they can react faster to new business opportunities than more rigid, large firms. 'Small is beautiful' when one wants to move and change, but it is not so 'beautiful' when you want to attract a risky investment. SMEs are often less able than large companies to behave 'strategically' and do not have as much lobbying power. This is because SMEs are vulnerable to actions of large firms and government policy. Large firms may also have a much larger capacity to deal with uncertainties and international crises than SMEs. Despite this, SMEs are necessary for the balanced growth of an economy, as they provide links among various subsectors. In general, neither large businesses nor SMEs can be efficient in isolation. They both need each other. Big businesses may use specialised SMEs as subcontractors and buffers against fluctuations in demand.

Whereas industrial policy deals with selected industries, policy on SMEs deals with firms of a specific size in all industries. The aim of SME policy is to rectify market imperfections that may work to the disadvantage of smaller firms (uncertain future, high risk, potential isolation, low asset value although not necessarily of 'low quality'). This policy also exploits the positive aspects of relative smallness, such as organisational flexibility, fast and smooth flow of information, product differentiation and custom-made goods and services.

When a large corporation operating in a declining industry closes down a plant in a city dependent on that industry, the first reaction of the government is often to offer subsidies to large new corporations to settle there. However, industrial rhinoceroses attracted by such subsidies usually remain loyal to the area only as long as the carrot lasts. If it is not certain that the incentives (subsidies) will last until the end of the investment/production programme, firms will not be attracted to the area. Risk-averse enterprises may in this situation request larger incentives and/or invest only in projects with relatively high rates of return.

Locally created jobs can be found in the development of SMEs. Of course, SMEs may not create enough jobs in the short term to make up for the loss of jobs in a geographical area where a large corporation has closed down. However, in the past ten to twenty years, SMEs have accounted for more than half of new jobs in some countries, such as the US. In the EU, SMEs are expected to flourish. About 20.5 million SMEs in 2000, were employing about 80 million people (two-thirds of all those employed) in the EU.[11] SMEs are often very efficient because, in spite of their size, they can achieve economies of scale by specialising in a very specific market segment and addressing the entire EU rather than a local or national area (assuming demand for their output exists there). Large Italian firms such as Fiat, Olivetti and Pirelli dominate the domestic market in their industries, but outside Italy these firms have a (very) modest share of world markets. In contrast, Italian firms in industries dominated by SMEs, such as footwear and clothing, are often world leaders (Porter, 1990a, p. 445).

A policy of support for SMEs is quite different from one that fosters the development of a few national champions that are easy to control. Until the 1980s, the EU countries generally regarded SMEs as unstable and marginal firms. Although it is true that many SMEs have a much shorter lifespan than large firms (many SMEs disappear from the market before they reach maturity), new ones are continually being created. This is not a worrying sign, but rather an indicator that the economic system is healthy and conducive to trying out new business opportunities. Since the mid-1980s, the EU approach towards SMEs has changed. Many industrial policy programmes now support this type of enterprise. SMEs are of vital importance when a market is in the process of opening and deepening, as was the case with the Single Market Programme. Euro-Info centres act as 'marriage' agencies for SMEs, brokering the establishment of business networks among such firms. This evolutionary and cumulative process needs for its sustenance an educational system that supplies businesses with employees proficient in the skills required. None the less, the EU needs be much more explicit in its industrial policy towards SMEs. Hence, it has been decided that the European Investment Bank (EIB) should in future support SMEs to a much greater degree than in the past.

Spain has traditionally been a relatively closed economy; hence, it is interesting to explore the impact of the Single Market Programme (market opening) on Spanish SMEs. Although the economy was protected, exporting was widespread among Spain's SMEs even before Spain joined the EU in 1986. Jarillo and Martínez (1991) surveyed a sample of SMEs three years after Spain's entry into the EU, by which time the Single Market Programme was in full swing. They found that:

- almost all SMEs were exporters even when the Spanish economy was still relatively isolated from the rest of the world;
- the costs of production were declining as a competitive advantage, whereas design, style and superior technology were assuming increasing importance;
- two-thirds of the SMEs were exporting to the EU even before 1986; and
- some SMEs saw the Single Market Programme as a threat (the group of firms for which international activities were secondary to their main business in Spain), while none saw it as a new opportunity as access to the EU market had been almost free since the mid-1970s.

Hence, the Single Market Programme was perceived by Spanish SMEs as a 'bad thing' or as a non-event! In spite of that conclusion, there is a large gap in our knowledge of the relationship between economic integration and the behaviour of SMEs.

The opening up and deepening of the internal EU market prompted by the Single European Market brought several advantages to SMEs, including:

- the rationalisation of distribution networks;
- cheaper and fewer inspections of conformity standards;
- diversification of suppliers;
- more efficient stock controls; and
- savings in time and cost of transport.

In addition, the European Council in St. Maria di Fiera (2000), Annex III, accepted the European Charter for Small Enterprises. According to this charter (which supports the Lisbon strategy for the future of the EU economy), SMEs must be considered as a main driver for innovation, employment as well as social and local integration in Europe. Policy action towards SMEs should include:

- education and training for entrepreneurship;
- cheaper and faster start-up;

- better legislation and regulation;
- availability of skills;
- improving online access;
- more benefits from the Single European Market;
- taxation and financial matters;
- strengthening the technological capacity of small enterprises;
- successful e-business models and top-class small business support; and
- development of a more effective representation of SMEs' interests at EU and national levels.

However, not everything in the garden is rosy. Many SMEs do not fully understand the operation of the Single European Market. They may be familiar with the concept, but relatively few understand the conditions under which they can use the 'CE' (conformité européenne) mark, which shows that the good was produced in the EU and that it meets EU standards. Future EU policy regarding SMEs needs to take account of the following issues:

- easing access of SMEs to financial resources (this was the major weakness of SMEs and is supposed to be mitigated by the new policy orientation of the EIB);
- incentives to individuals to become entrepreneurs;
- a simple and clear regulatory climate in which to start up small businesses;
- opening up of public contracts to SMEs;
- incentives for advice and technology transfer to SMEs;
- stimulation of innovation in SMEs; and
- modification in education and training beyond basic formation in order to assist the unemployed to become entrepreneurs.

DIVERSIFICATION AND REALLOCATION OF RESOURCES

The promotion of adjustment of some industries does not always go smoothly. Some ailing industries are well-established, relatively large employers of labour with a strong political lobby. This is often the case with the steel industry. However, some steel firms undergo adjustment quite successfully. Such was the case with the US Steel Company, which closed 13 steel-making units and diversified out of steel. The company invested funds in a shopping centre in Pittsburgh, Pennsylvania, and a chemical business in Texas. Steel-making came to account for only 11 per cent of US Steel's operating income (Trebilcock, 1986, p. 141). Other steel companies prefer a quiet life. They neither innovate nor compete, but they are able to mobilise powerful political forces and government policy instruments (for example, tariffs, quotas, NTBs, subsidies) in order to resist adjustment (contraction in output and labour redundancies).

The response of a number of US firms to shocks such as an increase in labour costs during the 1970s and 1980s was to stick to the same technology, but to invest abroad where labour costs are lower. In contrast, the response of Japanese firms to the same shock was to change technology and increase productivity. In addition, some Japanese TNCs operating in the US increased the US content of their goods over and above the domestic content of their US counterparts in the same industry. A number of US firms wanted to compete with Japanese TNCs in the home market not necessarily on the basis of productivity, but rather on the grounds of low labour costs. Thus, many US firms started either to source heavily from abroad (developing countries) or to geographically relocate their labour-intensive operations there or both. Japanese TNCs operating in the US increased productivity, so that, for example, by the mid-1980s colour TVs sold in the US by domestically owned firms had less local content than those made by Japanese competitors. In 1987, cars produced in the US by Honda had a local content of over 60 per cent. This was expected to increase to 75 per cent over the following ten years (Graham and Krugman, 1995, pp. 79–80).

The newly industrialised countries have substantially increased their competitiveness in traditional industries such as steel, shipbuilding and textiles. China has become highly competitive in certain parts of mass market electronics. Their output position is irreversible in the medium and, perhaps, long term. These industries cannot be recovered in the developed market economies on the grounds of reductions in wages. Such a policy would involve a waste of resources, as trade unions would resist cuts in wages to meet the level of wages prevailing in the newly industrialised countries which have productivity at a level similar to that in developed market economies.

When economic adjustment is spread over a number of years, it may appear to be easier and less costly per unit of time. Some 'breathing space' for structural change (slowing down the attrition or keeping ailing industries alive) may be achieved, but this argument is not always valid. First, the damage to the rest of the economy is greater the longer a depressed industry is allowed to last and, second, there is no evidence that prolonged adjustment is any easier to bear than quick surgery. Even direct costs may turn out, in practice, to be higher (Curzon Price, 1981, p. 120).

PICKING THE WINNER/LOSER

The new theory of trade and strategic industrial policy found, in contrast to the neo-classical theory, that some manufacturing and service industries may be relatively more 'important' to an economy than others. These are the industries with economies of scale, numerous forward and backward linkages and non-priced spillover effects (externalities) on the rest of the economy. Privileges to these industries *may* create a new irreversible competitive advantage for a country.

It needs to be clear from the outset that the findings of the new theory are not prescriptions for economic policy, but rather an agenda for further research (Krugman, 1993b, p. 164). A selective industrial policy goes hand in hand with a policy of picking a winner (creating a national champion) or a loser (bailing out). Industries are established or maintained in or removed from certain geographical locations. This process has always been difficult and risky and has demanded considerable and costly information. If this were not so, then you would probably not read this book, but rather look at the stock market report, and invest and increase the value of your assets by several zeros daily. Today's winner, if wrongly chosen and requiring permanent subsidies may become tomorrow's loser. When intervening, it is important to have reasonable aims and it is preferable to use policy tools in an indirect way and be ready to withdraw from the project if undesirable events occur, in order to prevent even greater damage and losses.

The preference for picking the winner most often occurs in those countries whose domestic market is small and unable to support the competition of several firms operating at the optimum level of efficiency. In theory, national free market policies can be fostered in large countries, such as the US, which can leave market forces to select the best suppliers. Smaller countries usually have to rely on selective policies, which are potentially riskier. They have to make the best use of the limited amount of available resources. These resources have to be concentrated on selected industries (specialisation). Such an industrial and trade policy may be termed 'cautious activism', which should not be taken to mean protectionism.

Whereas France relies on a relatively centralised model of the economy, Germany has fostered a decentralised model. However, these two countries have achieved a similar level of economic success (de Ghellinck, 1988, p. 140). When picking the winner, a government chooses between supporting emerging industries and propping up ailing ones (protection of the existing structure which is adjustment averse). The balance between the two depends upon both the power of the industries involved and the aims of the government.

The policy of singling out certain industries or firms for special treatment inevitably means ignoring the problems of all the others. The 'neglected' businesses may be at a relative disadvantage because they cannot count on direct support from the state if they happen to be in need. In addition, they are taxed in one way or another in order to provide funds for the public support of the 'privileged' businesses. This drains funds for investment in the promising enterprises. Such a policy has a strong impact on the geography of production.

Neglecting emerging and expanding industries with strong positive externalities can reduce the inclination of entrepreneurs to take risks and jeopardise the growth of the economy in the future. If a government cannot formulate the basic structural objectives of national economic policy, then the politically strongest segment of business will seize it.[12] Policy will be formulated in a hurry in response to the political pressures of the moment, with the likely outcome of protecting troubled industries. Independence, resistance to business pressures and clear economic objectives on the part of government remove extemporisations in economic policies. If this were not the case, a country's industrial policy would be an instrument for supporting obsolete industries and a brake on expanding ones (Tyson and Zysman, 1987a, p. 22). The history of trade and industrial policy (just look at the GATT rounds of negotiations) reveals how hard it is to combat the entrenched interests of producers.

Output grows fastest in emerging industries. These industries do not necessarily create a significant number of direct jobs but, as a result of linkages and other externalities, they have good potential to create indirect jobs. There has, however, been a notable technological improvement in declining industries such as textiles and steel. Thus, the distinction between the two kinds of industry is mostly for analytical purposes, as there are no industries with obsolete production technologies, but rather firms (within those industries) that employ ageing technology. An astute government may note that the industries are no longer sharply divided into 'good' and emerging industries such as electronics and 'bad' and declining ones such as shipbuilding as was the case in the 1970s and 1980s. In fact, it has become apparent that there is to a large extent a 'global' structure of manufacturing whatever the industry. In these circumstances, the law of supply and demand will always locate the lowest value-added part of the production chain in the geographical area with the lowest wages. In these circumstances, a smart option for the risk-averse developing country may be to choose first to establish a 'good declining industry', rather than an uncertain expanding one. Of course, the potential consequence of this type of expectation and choice may be a decline in the standard of living relative to countries that have gone for a different development model and are successful (?!) in its implementation.

Targeting (selection or welfare ranking) is linked to four basic issues:

- *which* industries or firms should receive support;
- *what* kind of support should be provided;
- *where* they are located; and
- *how long* the assistance should last.

The industries that are singled out for 'special treatment' are usually those that are significant employers and those that have important externalities or strong lobbying power. In addition, if private markets do not favour risky investments, such as the development of alternative sources of energy, then governments may also single out such investments for special treatment.

If domestic regulations regarding safety standards are stricter and more costly to implement than abroad, then, other things being equal, this may place home firms at a disadvantage relative to foreign competitors. Such a case may be used as an argument for demanding some national public 'support' and international involvement in these affairs in order to enforce foreign competitors to adhere to a similar level of environment protection. This issue was important during the eastern enlargement of the EU.

Political reasons such as national defence and pride may influence decisions about support for certain industries. Assistance should cease as soon as the beneficiary becomes profitable; or once it becomes obvious that this will never happen (governments are on the whole known to be unwilling to slash subsidies when there is evidence of failure as happened during the Concorde project); or after the expiration of the specified period of assistance.

Japan is thought to be an example of a country that has reaped the fruits of conscious targeting of certain manufacturing industries for several decades. As a result it has stayed one step ahead of its competitors regarding new technologies in the targeted industries.[13] During the 1960s, the target industries were steel and shipbuilding because of their significant externalities. Another target was the toy industry. During the 1970s the targets were machine tools and cars. The target for the 1980s was electronics (photocopiers, computers, audio and video equipment). For the 1990s it was the semiconductor industry. This may be taken as an example of the shaping of comparative advantage in a dynamic context for a specified, relatively limited, period of time. Japanese 'targeting' was first and foremost an information-collecting, interpretation and transmission process which helped the individual firms to make investment decisions. Japan emphasised intervention in technological *areas* that created a large bilateral trade surplus with the US, rather than intervention in *firms*.

However, in spite of the success in high-technology industries, average living standards in Japan are below those in the US or the EU. Part of the explanation may be found in the relatively high proportion of Japanese national resources that are devoted to stagnant industries compared with in the US.

Targeting has not always been successful, for a variety of reasons. During the 1960s, MITI selected steel and shipbuilding as the 'winners'. Intervention (support) was relatively heavy. At that time, Japanese corporations faced an identical business choice and also opted to invest in these industries, although this would have happened even without government intervention. Japan then targeted the production of aluminium and petrochemicals, a choice that was subsequently proven by the first oil shock to be mistaken. In contrast, MITI was opposed to the promotion of the car industries (nor was electronics on the priority list) during the 1960s as the US and Europe were at that time ahead of Japan in this area. In spite of official opposition to the expansion of the industry, private enterprise continued to invest and was successful without public support (if one leaves aside the relatively closed domestic market). The private policy was right and yielded positive results for some decades to come. If left alone, private businesses may sometimes find superb solutions. Throughout the 1990s, Microsoft was the prime example of such development in the US (which ended up as a global monopoly). However, it is impossible to know in advance which company of today and tomorrow from which industry and in which location will replicate the success of Microsoft.

During the 1990s, Japanese industrial policy was transformed. Increased emphasis was given to deregulation and privatisation in the economy together with safeguarding of the traditional consensus-building spirit. As for the targeting of 'high-growth industries', the evidence that is emerging does not reveal Japanese success in this area. 'Targeting was actually more prevalent in the uncompetitive Japan, while a large proportion of the competitive industries had no government targeting' (Porter, 1996, p. 88). Since the mid-1990s, China has fostered a policy of big national champions in certain parts of manufacturing. These champions (for example, TCL in television sets and mobile phones) dominate the domestic market and try to capture a share of the global one.

Elsewhere in the developed market economies, the policy of targeting has not always gone so smoothly. After the Second World War, industrial policy relied partly on the unorganised labour that was flowing from agriculture and abroad into the manufacturing industry. This situation has changed. Trade unions try to organise labour. This may influence (that is, postpone) economic adjustment, even though it may be to the long-term detriment of the economy.

France is a country that is keen to create large and efficient firms that can compete in international markets. It is less concerned with domestic competition. France's Interministerial Committee for the Development of Strategic Industries decides on the key industries, defines the strategy and picks a firm to be national champion to implement that programme. The implementation method takes the form of a contract between the government and the chosen firm. Unfortunately, however, the French government has not always had perfect foresight. Misjudgements were made in very costly projects such as Concorde and computers. The Concorde project was a technological success and an engineer's delight. The project started in 1962 when fuel was cheap and when air travel was for the elite. However, Concorde consumed a large amount of fuel, it was too noisy and there were tradeoffs between speed and passenger comfort. The air travel market has significantly changed over the past four decades. Flying is a mass market. Most passengers travel for fun, not for business. Hence, Concorde was a commercial failure and was finally grounded in 2003.

The French strategy for computers was to try to build large mainframes in order to compete directly with IBM, rather than to begin with small computers or peripheral equipment and learn by doing over time. This was too ambitious for the relatively undeveloped French firms to cope with, so the effort failed. The mistake might have been avoided if government industrial policy makers had consulted more with private experts. Private firms also make mistakes, but they are less likely to ignore market forces and the various choices that they offer (in particular when using their own or shareholders' funds) than government officials who use taxpayers' money and who are often subject to various political pressures and their own re-election goals. This was the main reason why Japanese targeting was more successful than French targeting. The early French mistakes, however, were not in vain. During the Airbus[14] project, the government learned to select the segment of the market for which demand would be high. It also tied customers by early purchasing of aircraft parts in exchange for orders (Carliner, 1988, p. 164).

Direct targeting of particular industries or firms has not been a striking feature of US industrial policy. This system was conceived and established in such a way as to foster, in principle, individual freedom, not to discriminate among firms or industries. The only exceptions are agriculture and steel, as well as sporadic bailouts of firms such as Lockheed (1971) or Chrysler (1979). Government consumption on all levels, however, creates a big overall demand pull to the economy owing to a huge general expenditure and the budget deficit. As a part of public expenditure, defence-related[15] and selective public procurement indirectly influences the development and expansion of high-technology industries with a significant impact on private consumption. For example, NASA (US National Aeronautics and Space Administration) demanded computers for spaceships. Those computers had to be small in size and powerful in scope. The industry provided such computers. Once they were commercialised, personal computers flooded the market throughout the world. Hence, the argument that the US government does not intervene in the economy does not hold water. In special situations (for example, during the Second World War), the US had an explicit industrial policy.[16] In addition, the US has become the major producer of food in the world as a consequence of calculated economic and other policies that embraced various (including credit) subsidies.

Human capital and human resource management are key factors in increasing a country's comparative advantage in a situation of rapidly changing market conditions and technology (which reduces the need for unskilled labour). Basic choices, such as the education of ethnologists or engineers, singers or mathematicians, lawyers or designers, influence a country's geography of production and competitiveness of its goods and services. Macroeconomic policy may support, in an important way, the creation of comparative advantage, but it is human capital (properly organised, valued and continuously educated) that presents the major lever in the enhancement of a country's competitive advantage.

One has to bear in mind that there is a big redistribution of income: from those less skilled (or less fortunate) towards those with many skills. This takes place among regions within each country, but also on an international scale.[17] 'Old' rules, where real wages go hand in hand with an increase in productivity, no longer apply. High productivity no longer warrants high wages. With high international mobility of goods and capital there is always somebody elsewhere in the world willing to do the same job for less money (Krugman, 1996b).

During the 19th and early 20th centuries, bright British pupils were steered towards the classics in Oxford and Cambridge, while technical subjects were reserved for the less gifted. The situation was the reverse in France, Germany and Japan. After the Second World War, British industry began to recruit widely from the universities. A career in industry, even if a fifth choice after callings at the Foreign Office, the BBC, academia or the Church, became socially acceptable for the sons (and increasingly the daughters) of the Establishment (Sharp and Shepherd, 1987, pp. 83–4; Porter, 1990a, p. 115).

Some may argue that government planners and other public officials in Japan, France and Germany may be more competent and sophisticated than managers in private firms in these countries. The best and most ambitious students aspire to government service. In North America, society has a different attitude. Many people look on government jobs as inferior to those in the private sector because, among other things, they are less well paid. It is not surprising to find that Japan, France and Germany have an 'open and direct' industrial policy, while the US and Canada do not, at least not overt industrial policies. Nevertheless, shoddy economic policies in these two countries might be easily amended if civil servants were given a freer hand by the system (Brander, 1987, p. 40).

3. European Union

RATIONALE

The grounds for the introduction of an industrial policy in the EU can be identified in at least seven related areas:

- If uncoordinated, national policies introduce a wasteful duplication either of scarce resources for R&D or investment in productive assets of suboptimal capacity. If minimum efficient economies of scale demand access to a market that is wider than the national one, then there is a case for a common EU approach to the issue. Some competition in the diversity of R&D, ideas and production is necessary because it can be a source of creativity. None the less, the authorities need to strike a harmonious balance between competition and coordination, in order to profit from both of them. Hence, a certain degree of coordination of industrial policies at the EU level contributes to the efficiency of the policy.
- A common or a coordinated industrial policy in a large and expanding EU market may wield a deeper (positive or negative) impact on the economy than any isolated national policy can, no matter how big the national market of a member country.
- With a free mobility of factors in the EU, any disequilibria in a national economy may first provoke an immediate and a massive outflow or inflow of capital and, afterwards, of other factors if the disequilibria are not corrected. If a government wants to cool down the economy by increasing the rate of interest, the result may be the opposite from the desired one. High rates of interest will provoke a large inflow of foreign hot capital and the economy may become 'overheated'. The eurozone eliminated this danger for the participating countries. Therefore, the deeper the integration in the EU, the less effective are national macroeconomic policies that are pursued in isolation. A common or coordinated EU policy in such circumstances is more effective than the sum of national ones.

- Although EU firms are rivals on the EU internal market, they are allies in competition against firms from third countries both in the world and in the Single European Market. If national economic policies used to tackle the same problem are different and have undesirable and unwanted spillover effects on the EU partner countries, then there are grounds for the introduction of a common industrial policy of the EU.
- Another argument may be found in the 'unfair' trade and industrial practices of foreign rivals. An EU industrial policy may act as a countermeasure.
- No matter how disputed in theory, concern about employment always carries weight in daily politics.
- Last, but not least, there is a case for externalities that create market failure (the difference between private and social benefits). When there are undesired spillover effects across the frontiers of a single country from, for example, large investments in certain businesses that pollute, then the appropriate response to such events can be found in a common EU policy.

In spite of the arguments in favour of an EU industrial policy, one should not be misled into thinking that this is a substitute for national policies. On the contrary, national and EU policy should be complementary. In fact, EU policy needs to apply only to those areas where it has the potential to be more beneficial than national policies (the principle of subsidiarity). In general, policies at EU level need to be as general as possible, while those with a local dimension need to be custom-made and specific. There has to be coordination between the EU and national/local policies in order to avoid the implementation of conflicting instruments even when there is agreement about the major goals to be attained.

One of the principal aims of the Treaty of Rome was to increase the competitiveness of domestic firms relative to the US at the time of the creation of the EU (1957). The intention was to locate new and expand existing industries in order to take advantage of the economies of scale that would be provided by an enlarged EU market. It was primarily the expansion of domestic demand that stimulated the development of both the US and, later, Japan. Competitiveness was created in these two countries on the basis of the secure, even protected, large domestic market. In comparison with the US and Japan, no member state of the EU could claim to have a large domestic market. The EU was conceived, among other things, to redress this 'disadvantage'.

Before the establishment of the EU, small European countries' industrial policy was often defensive (for example, subsidies to protect employment) rather than aggressive (for example, risky entry into new industries). In the 1960s relatively weak anti-merger laws created the potential for the establishment of large European corporations which could, it was thought at that time, successfully compete with their US and Japanese rivals. However, the problem was not merely in the size of firms in the EU. Fragmented by NTBs, the internal market of the EU had as a consequence economic rigidity that shielded many national firms from both EU-internal competition and the necessary adjustment. The outcome at that time was that in certain manufacturing industries, relative to the US and Japan, the EU came close to being a 'manufacturing museum'.

Protectionism has been the instrument of EU industrial policy in spite of the costs and postponement of adjustment. Resistance to abandoning obsolete technologies and industries permitted others, most notably Japan, to gain the competitive edge and penetrate the EU market with many high-technology goods. EU manufacturing has valuable attributes in industries where the growth of demand is slow. Competitive advantage is relatively smaller in the expanding manufacturing industries. Without domestic restructuring, and with the exception of German, Dutch and some firms from a few other countries, foreign TNCs that are located in the EU and that operate in the expanding industries may be among the first major beneficiaries from the Single European Market. If the instruments of protection and cartelisation (for example, in the coal and steel industry) are not coupled with other tools of industrial policy (for example, contraction of obsolete industries or assistance for a limited time for the introduction of new technologies), then such a policy will be ineffective from the resource viewpoint. It may be pursued by those who choose to do so and who can afford to be wasteful.

EVOLUTION

The first attempt to introduce a 'real' industrial policy in the EU dates back to 1970. The European Commission's *Memorandum on Industrial Policy* (the Colonna Report) aimed to shape the structure of EU industry and to set priorities for a common action. As there was no strong legal basis for the introduction of a common industrial policy in the Treaty of Rome, the report restricted itself to ambitious general statements and five recommendations:

- The report foresaw the creation of a single EU market (such as the US) based on the abolition of internal barriers to trade.
- It required the harmonisation of legal and fiscal rules that would ease the establishment of enterprises throughout the EU.

- It envisaged the creation of a European Company Statute. Although the EU had existed for more than a decade, firms were very slow to merge businesses across national boundaries. As TNCs were perceived to be important vehicles for improvements in competitiveness and technology relative to foreign rivals, there was a need for the support (intervention) of intra-EU mergers and acquisitions. The absence of EU corporate law presented a serious problem. Large national corporations that tried to merge at the EU level, such as Fiat–Citroën, Agfa–Gevaert, Dunlop–Pirelli or Fokker–VFW, soon gave up. A notable exception is Airbus Industrie (set up in 1970). The pan-EU TNCs that survived to 'adolescence' were those (Philips, Shell, Unilever) that existed long before the establishment of the EU.
- Changing demand conditions create a need for economic adjustment. This adaptation could be achieved smoothly if there was an encouragement of geographical and occupational mobility of labour and upgraded business management.
- The final recommendation was an extension of the EU solidarity regarding foreign competition, R&D and finance.

Consideration of the report ran into difficulty, as there were two opposing views. On the one hand, Germany did not want any interference in industrial policy at either the national or the EU level. On the other hand, France was in favour of coordinating national economic policies. Other countries sided with one or other of these views.

The next step in the shaping of EU industrial policy was a *Memorandum on the Technological and Industrial Policy Programme* (the Spinelli Report) in 1973. Basically, it was a scaled-down version of the Colonna Report. The new report argued in favour of the exchange of information, the coordination of national R&D policies, joint R&D projects and the elimination of national technical barriers. The broad strategy did not fully succeed because of different economic philosophies among the member countries. After the oil crisis the member countries pursued nationalistic industrial policies and were not very interested in a joint approach to the issue. In fact, they passed on to the EU the adjustment of the problem industries (steel, shipbuilding, textiles and in some cases even cars) via trade, social and regional policies, while keeping the management of expanding industries under national control. During this period there was only some coordination of technical standards and joint actions in R&D.

A profound step towards the elimination of NTBs in internal trade, competition and, hence, industrial policy came with the introduction of the programme *Completing the Internal Market* (the Cockfield Report) of 1985. This supply-side-oriented 'technical' programme had 282 industry-specific legislative proposals for the elimination of NTBs, as well as a timetable for their implementation by the end of 1992. The adoption of the Cockfield White Paper (1985) and the Single European Act (1987) provided the EU with the means to implement the Single Market Programme. The objective was the achievement of a genuine single internal market through the adoption, implementation and enforcement of 282 measures (directives). This was the outcome of the political determination of the member states to eliminate NTBs on internal trade and change their 'atomised' industrial policies. The EU tried to employ its resources in a more efficient way by a reduction in physical, technical and fiscal barriers to internal trade (elimination of X-inefficiencies).

The classical integration method (elimination of tariffs and quotas) in the EU exhausted its static effects at the end of the 1960s. A new approach, the ousting of NTBs, favoured full factor mobility. It was implemented in order to create a genuine frontier-free internal market in the EU. The stress was on a change in the rules, rather than on additional funds. The creation of a homogeneous internal market, such as that in the US, which benefits from enormous economies of scale, was not expected. The Europeans have, on average, far more refined and deeply rooted tastes, hence they value and benefit from variety and wide choice. They demand and are often ready to pay for superior quality and diversity. The aim of the Single Market Programme was simply to improve competition and market access to diverse national, regional and local markets, as well as to introduce flexible and large-scale modes of production where appropriate.

The abolition of customs duties and quotas in the EU benefited only those industries that serve *private consumers*. There is also another market, that for goods and services consumed by *governments*. Industries that employ new technologies failed to serve the entire EU market for these goods and services, as well as to profit from economies of scale because of the existence of NTBs. These national industries compete for public funds and orders. This is why EU firms tended to cooperate more with partners in the US or Japan than among themselves. By entering into a joint venture with a Japanese firm, an EU enterprise made up for its technological gap without forgoing the protectionist shield and/or privileges in the form of public procurement, major export contracts, tax relief and R&D accorded by the state (Defraigne, 1984, p. 369). Another explanation is that EU firms were interested in forming partnerships with firms that were market or technology leaders regardless of their nationality, origin or geographical location (Narula, 1999, p. 718). The outcome of such a policy was that EU standards for high-technology goods were non-existent, and relatively large and protected national corporations, which were not very interested in intra-EU industrial cooperation, were created. These firms were unable to respond swiftly to changes in the international market. An obvious example of this sluggishness was the relatively slow adjustment to the oil shocks.

EU company law was required to help meet the objectives of the Treaty of Rome regarding the harmonious development of economic activities in the Union. Thus, the European Commission proposed the European Company Statute in 1989. The arguments in favour of the statute include the elimination of the difficulties that come from the current national tax systems for those firms that operate in several EU countries. Business in the entire EU market would be made simpler if the firms were incorporated under a single code of law. The absence of this statute was estimated to cost the business community €30 billion a year.[18] The case against the statute is that increased interference by the EU may jeopardise national sovereignty.

The European Commission was not without further ideas on industrial policy. The 1990 Bangemann Communication on *Industrial Policy in an Open and Competitive Environment* had, basically, the following three proposals. First, industrial policy needed to be adjustment friendly. This has to take place within the framework of a liberal trade policy. Second, EU industrial policy has to be in accord with other common policies. They need to reinforce one another. Third, difficulties within industries or regions need to be settled by the employment of horizontal measures. The means for the achievement of these ideas should include an improvement in the operation of both the internal market and the international market, as well as the creation of an investment-friendly environment for risk taking in the EU.

The 1993 Delors White Paper, *Growth, Competitiveness, Employment*, aimed to prepare the EU for the 21st century. Its major stated goal was a reduction in unemployment. This was to be achieved, among other means, by an ambitious wave of investment from various sources into the following areas: €400 billion over 15 years into transport and energy in trans-European networks; €150 billion until the year 2000 into telecommunications; and €280 billion over 12 years into environment-related projects. The Council of Ministers did not support the project and budgetary austerity measures cast it aside.

Following a Council of Ministers resolution (1992) calling for an overall analysis of the effectiveness of measures taken while creating the Single European Market, the European Commission undertook a profound analysis of the entire set of economic policies in the EU. The Monti Report (1996) was followed by 39 volumes of background studies published by Kogan Page in 1997–98 under the title *Single Market Review*. They were split among six headings: manufacturing, services, dismantling of barriers, trade and investment, competition and economies of scale, and aggregate and regional impact of the Single European Market. The full impact of the Single Market Programme could not be fully predicted as the effect of the removal of some NTBs (technical barriers) on the geography of production and welfare would be fully felt only in the longer term. However, the report gave directions for the preservation of the Single European Market and the implementation of the eurozone from 1999.

The impact of the opening up of the Single European Market is most obvious in highly regulated (and hence fragmented) industries such as pharmaceuticals. A major regulatory change in the EU took place with the establishment of the European Agency for the Evaluation of Medicinal Products in 1995. As a result, this traditionally local government-controlled industry changed significantly. The Single European Market altered the business practices of firms in the pharmaceuticals industry in seven ways:

- *Market authorisation*: National regulatory authorities that control the introduction of new products at different rates affect not only the location of production and trade, but also the health and life of patients. To change this, the European Agency for the Evaluation of Medicinal Products became the single decision-making body in the EU in 1995. However, pharmaceutical firms still have the choice of following a centralised procedure that leads to a single authorisation for the entire EU (this procedure is mandatory for products derived from biotechnology) or a decentralised procedure based on mutual recognition of national marketing authorisations. It seems obvious that firms will tend to locate in the country with the least regulatory delay and then make use of the principle of mutual recognition to market their products throughout the EU. The result is that pharmaceutical companies are no longer required to follow the sometimes archaic regulations of a single authority, but can 'shop around' to find the most flexible one which will give the fastest approval and enable speedy market launch of the products. Biotechnology, an area that arouses tremendous hope for the future expansion of business and at the same time fear of the new and unknown, is unified at the EU level. This gives security to customers in the Single European Market.
- *Dependence on domestic market*: Before 1995, more than 60 per cent of pharmaceuticals produced in France, Germany, Greece, Italy, Portugal and Spain were sold to the domestic market. This was the consequence of preferential government procurement from local firms, insistence on local R&D and local content requirements. Since the opening up of the EU market, firms selling primarily to their national markets have been in jeopardy: in the pharmaceuticals industry it is no good being a large fish in a small pond. Even in the US, large domestic manufacturers have experienced a dramatic fall in

their market share, and in the EU 'globalisation' is the only means of survival. This can be achieved by internal growth, alliances and cooperation with other firms or through acquisitions. A lack of preferential treatment (market deepening that came from the Single Market Programme) was a wake-up call to these companies to start sharpening their competitiveness, which had suffered from earlier government protection.

- *Parallel trade*: In 1974, the EU Court of Justice ruled in favour of parallel importation (*Centrafarm v. Sterling Drug*), that is, the purchasing of drugs in a low-price market and their repackaging and diversion to other markets. The principle is that medicinal drugs are permitted to move freely from one country to another if the importing country provides a marketing authorisation. As long as drugs are priced differently in different EU countries, this type of trade will continue to exist. This 'temporary situation' will disappear with full market unification. With rising pressure on their health budgets, governments are encouraging these forms of competition and 'price reduction'. At present, prices in southern European countries are usually lower, hence most of this trade is going northwards. The introduction of the euro in 1999 marked the beginning of the process of a greater price transparency. Combined with Internet shopping, consumers can find out almost instantly where to buy the cheapest medicines. There is great potential for parallel imports. However, an emerging trend is for TNCs to treat the EU as a unified market and to sell new drugs at the same price throughout the EU.

- *Regulated prices*: The price of drugs varies between EU countries for many reasons: price control schemes, variation in the costs of production, variable exchange rates, differences in reimbursement systems, transfer pricing, patent status, package sizes, rebates and taxes. The difference in price between the cheapest and most expensive country may be as much as tenfold! The Single European Market is bringing a slow convergence in drug prices, but progress is slow and many of the distortions mentioned will continue to be present for some time. The introduction of the euro has been the principal factor in bringing price harmonisation throughout the EU. New drugs are registered centrally and are sold at the same price across the Single European Market. Previous obstacles such as exchange rates are disappearing and firms look at the EU member countries as one economic entity. This is the only weapon in the business community's armoury if it wants to enjoy undisturbed presence in all regions.

- *Expenditure for R&D*: Competition will stimulate innovation. R&D for new drugs directed at the regional and global market will increase.

R&D in the pharmaceuticals industry has always been mission oriented, regardless of integration.
- *Rationalisation of operation*: Producing a drug involves the manufacture of the active substance and, subsequently, the conversion of this ingredient into different dosage forms. The former has been centralised in the EU, whereas the latter has been decentralised. Many plants are not benefiting from economies of scale as they are operating at between one-third and one-half of their capacity. Overcapacity in the pharmaceutical industry is estimated to be 40 per cent worldwide. Plant closures and alteration in the geography of production are imminent, partly because of new manufacturing methods and partly as a consequence of market opening in the EU, which will bring benefits in the form of economies of scale. At the same time, firms are being attracted to move location within the EU by regional benefits (subsidies) aimed at reducing unemployment in the subsidy-giving region. It is fast becoming irrelevant whether company headquarters or manufacturing capacities are based in Germany, France or Spain, for example. Aventis, the largest European pharmaceutical company, formed by the merger of Hoechst and Rhône–Poulenc Rohrer, has its headquarters in Strasbourg and has adopted English as the common language of communication across the company.
- *Mergers and acquisitions*: There are still many opportunities for consolidation in the pharmaceutical industry when compared with, for example, car manufacturing. Consolidation of the industry is expected to accelerate in the next few years. During the mid-1990s the largest pharmaceutical company in the world commanded less than 5 per cent of the total world market. Expect to witness in the coming years fast growth of companies in this industry as they strive to achieve synergies, cut costs, obtain bigger R&D budgets and reach a bigger 'critical mass'. Examples of this trend so far include the purchase of Syntex by Hoffmann–La Roche and the mergers of Hoechst and Rhône–Poulenc Rohrer into Aventis, Ciba Geigy and Sandoz into Novartis, Astra and Zeneca, and Glaxo Wellcome and Smith Kline Beecham. This trend will continue and, in addition to major US mergers, such as that between Pfizer and Warner Lambert, one may expect to see more transatlantic mergers, such as that between Pharmacia and UpJohn. This consolidation is resulting in R&D departments big enough to develop new drugs, as well as the ability to produce medicines in the most efficient way unhindered by local differences that were previously limiting factors in the growth of the pharmaceutical industry in the EU.

As another step in the development of its industrial policy, the European Commission approved a communication, *Industrial Policy in an Enlarged Europe*, at the end of 2002. This was an attempt to define this important policy area in the light of eastern enlargement. The EU industrial policy has to take into account the requirements of other policies (economic, social and environment), but it also needs to attend to the needs of the manufacturing industry itself. The consistency, dynamic interaction and balance among these policies and their objectives is not simple and easy to find, implement and maintain as there are no magic solutions. The document recognises the importance and weight of the services sector in the economy, but it acknowledges that the manufacturing industry is the source of EU prosperity. It also rejects the flawed view that manufacturing will no longer play a key role in the knowledge-based information and services society.

The EU manufacturing industry is in many segments modern and competitive in spite of a slight relative reduction of EU manufacturing in international trade over the past decade (the principal rivals suffered even more from the arrival of new actors such as China and other developing countries). The weak element in EU manufacturing *vis-à-vis* principal rivals is productivity. Even though investment in computers and information technology was substantial, productivity gains are still slow in coming.

Two key factors of industrial competitiveness deserve particular attention in the EU according to the 2002 communication:

- *Knowledge and innovation*: There is a need for more and better efforts in education, vocational training and R&D to put the available accumulated knowledge at the disposal of industry. This is nothing new, but it has to be signalled repeatedly. New technologies, including electronics and bio- and nanotechnology, have to be developed, as do the skills and know-how to use them. The number of patents in the EU is much smaller than is the case in the US. However, the EU fares very well in other high, medium and mature industries. In order to counter the negative developments, the European Commission is addressing one of the roots of the problem: a lack of investment in R&D. It wants to increase the current average level of investment of 1.9 per cent of GDP to 3 per cent of GDP in order to match the US and Japanese investment of 2.7 and 3 per cent of GDP, respectively. One ought to bear in mind that one area where the EU lags behind particularly is R&D financed by the private sector.[19] Every sector and activity needs to be constantly initiating, refining and improving its products, services and processes. The conditions to stimulate vigorous innovation have to be in place.

- *Entrepreneurship*: This is the capacity and will to take risks and grow new, bigger or different businesses. A (large) number of Europeans continue to be too reluctant to bear entrepreneurial risk, too readily satisfied with limited growth of businesses and too reluctant to acknowledge and reward the social contribution of risk takers. They ought to be encouraged to change this behaviour.

Competitiveness, as the ability of the economy to provide its population with high and rising standards of living and high rates of employment on a sustainable basis, is at the very heart of the ambitious goals set for the EU by the European Council in Lisbon (2000). Achieving these goals depends in large part on the ability of the EU to develop new profitable competences (and put them in practice) and where it already has them, they ought to be maintained and advanced. There are a few tough competitors for the position of 'the most competitive and dynamic knowledge-based economy in the world'. The EU has to innovate and, as seen in the chapter on competition (see Chapter 5), the omens are not very encouraging. Political declarations ought to be translated more forcefully into action in the EU. Important barriers to entrepreneurship in the EU do not come mainly from the barriers to entry, although administrative obstacles are present. To start up a firm in the US, time is counted in days. To do the same in the EU countries, time is counted in months. Key administrative barriers in the EU countries come from impediments to adjusting and expanding. Job-protection laws discourage firms from new hiring.

A recent attempt to regulate a part of the manufacturing industry refers to chemicals. The European Commission maintains that various chemical substances are responsible, at least in part, for the increase in the number of allergies and other illnesses over the past decades. These chemical substances range from ingredients in cosmetics to substances that retard flames in furniture. Therefore, in 2003 the Commission proposed an overhaul of the way in which the chemical industry is regulated, by shifting the burden of safety testing from governments to the industry. About 100 000 chemicals that already existed in 1981 and that were unaffected by various subsequent directives will have to be tested for their safety. The industry strongly objects to such proposals, which would cost it €2.3 billion according to the European Commission, and more than ten times that amount according to the industry.[20] Animal rights campaigners also protest against this proposal as millions of animals would be killed needlessly since companies would have to replicate tests to obtain approval for the same product. It is doubtful whether such ambitious proposals will be furthered in the immediate future, even though the European Commission claims that total health benefits of the legislation may be as high as €50 billion over 30 years.[21]

TECHNOLOGY POLICY

Since the 1960s, some of the major factors determining industrial structures in the developed market economies have included changes in technologies, foreign competition, environmental issues, changing employment patterns and an ageing population. With this in mind, the European Commission was initially more concerned with industries in crisis. However, from the 1980s it started to become more involved with the industries and technologies of the future. These are those that have strategic importance for the competitiveness of goods (and services) in the internal, as well as external markets. Therefore, during the mid-1980s the EU introduced various technology-push programmes with the aim of creating and sustaining leadership in the market. In designing these programmes, the European Commission has to balance the interests of the DG Competition, which advocates *laissez-faire*, and the other DGs, which favour policy intervention. These programmes have (indirectly) resulted in the technology policy of the EU. The technology policy is necessary because of significant technological spillovers throughout the economy.

Until the mid-1980s, the form and direction of R&D in the EU fell within the remit of national governments (with the notable exception of the European Atomic Energy Community: Euratom). The model for the national approach was to some extent Japanese experience of public support to industries from MITI in the form of exchange of information, cooperation and partial funding of R&D projects. A change came with the Single Market Programme. The legal basis for the EU action in R&D came in 1987 via the Single European Act (Title VI). Although there had been previous initiatives, the member governments decided for the first time to contribute significant funds for R&D to EU programmes. According to the revised Treaty of Rome, the EU will strengthen its scientific and technological bases and encourage competitiveness at the international level (Article 163). The European Commission and the member states are supposed to coordinate policies and programmes carried out at the national level (Article 165). The EU needs to adopt a multiannual framework programme for its R&D projects (Article 166). The EU may cooperate with third countries or international organisations to implement its long-term R&D programme (Article 170).

One goal of the EU is to strengthen links between research institutes and entrepreneurs throughout the EU in order to transform the long-held perception in Europe that science (that is, R&D) is culture, whereas in the US it is business. However, in the US there is another factor that encourages a fast reaction to changing technologies. Vigilant financial markets in the US often look favourably on certain risky (short-term) investments by innovative firms. This ethos of support for such innovation, still missing in Europe, forces American firms to adjust rapidly to shifting markets and changing technology. This explains a sizeable part of the difference between the US and EU in terms of commercial exploitation of the results of R&D.

In circumstances in which strong national elements still dominate, the EU should endeavour to coordinate national policies, promote cooperation in R&D and production, and support the flexibility of the industrial structure. Coordination of national policies regarding declining industries should avoid an integration-unfriendly beggar-thy-neighbour mentality. In the light of the (irreversible) changes brought about by the Single European Market and the eurozone, expanding industries (those in which production technology is changing) should introduce common EU standards that facilitate large-scale production and an increase in competitiveness. The objective is to avoid the creation of incompatible standards, as happened with the PAL and SECAM television systems. During the 1990s, the European Commission and national governments spent heavily (it turned out to be a waste) on the development of analogue high-definition television (HDTV), which was rendered obsolete by the advance of digital technology. It would have been far more preferable for the Commission and governments to improve the R&D environment than to target possible technology winners.

The EU's dependence on third-country suppliers of high-technology goods arises for several reasons. On the supply side, EU investment in R&D is lower than in the US and Japan; the EU also allocates fewer human resources to R&D and there are often delays in putting into production and marketing the results of R&D. On the demand side, national 'attitudes' (for example, buy domestic) may limit the potential demand for high-technology products in EU countries, making it difficult for EU high-technology manufacturers to achieve the necessary economies of scale. European firms are less receptive to new products than their US and Japanese rivals, there is a lack of strong links between producers and consumers, and there is inadequate training in new technologies (Jacquemin and Sapir, 1991, pp. 44–5).[22] Various EU technology programmes are intended to redress this situation.

Philips and Thomson led the lobby of EU companies in the early 1980s pressing national governments for the completion of the Single European Market as the principal cure for countering the (past) Japanese ability to be always a few steps ahead in the business game in higher and high-technology. The Round Table of European Industrialists (rent seekers) was successful in eliciting support from governments for the Single Market Programme. When the US announced the 'Star Wars' project in 1983, EU industrialists started to worry. First the Japanese took over a large part of the market for consumer electronics, then the Americans seemed to be *en route* to domination of the market for advanced industrial goods. Subsequently, the Round Table, created in 1983, pushed for the creation of a transnational industrial policy in the form of EU support for high-technology research projects. In spite of budgetary restrictions, the big EU industrialists were successful again (Curzon Price, 1993, pp. 399–400).

Implementation of EU policy in R&D takes the form of five-year framework programmes[23] which were introduced in 1984. The purpose of these medium-term instruments is to integrate and coordinate all assistance/aid for R&D in the EU.[24] The programmes lay down objectives, priorities and the budget for EU-sponsored R&D. By distributing funds to selected research projects, the EU sets guidelines for specific R&D programmes. Based on the findings of the FAST (Forecasting and Assessment in Science and Technology) programme,[25] the EU introduced about 20 publicly supported programmes for industrial cooperation among the EU firms in the R&D stage. Most of the programmes would be beyond the financial capability and will of the participating countries to finance alone. These programmes include the following 'winners':

- A dozen renowned information technology firms from Britain, France, Germany, Italy and the Netherlands wanted to pool resources, share risk and attract subsidies from the EU (although this begs the question of why leading-edge companies should need to form cartels and seek such support). None the less, the pressure group they formed (the Round Table) lobbied both national governments and the Commission to adopt the European Programme for Research in Information Technology (ESPRIT) to try to 'correct market failures' in R&D. The European Commission was receptive to the idea and together with the Round Table won approval from the national governments. The EU adopted the programme, that is, picked a winner, in 1984. Under the auspices of ESPRIT, the EU funds half of the cost of any project that is in line with the EU terms of reference and that is supported by two or more firms from different EU countries. The other half of the funds has to come from the participating firms and national sources. Eligible projects must be in the field of pre-competitive R&D. So far, the Commission has refused to subsidise joint production in order to avoid criticism from the US about subsidies. Indeed, the Commission has tried to argue that it does not operate a large-scale industrial policy at all, but rather a series of R&D programmes (Curzon Price, 1990, p. 178).
- Research and Development in Advanced Communication for Europe (RACE) is a spillover programme from ESPRIT. Its aim is to advance

the telecommunication network in Europe in the future by means that include standardisation and coordination of national telecom services.
- Basic Research in Industrial Technologies in Europe (BRITE) aspires to revitalise traditional industries in the EU. This is to be achieved through the introduction of new technologies in these industries although it is not always obvious what is 'strategic' about the industries. Perhaps the concern here is more about employment than anything else. Public money is spent on projects that financial markets find unattractive.
- The Biotechnology Action Programme (BAP) is small relative to its 'strategic' potential in the future.
- European Collaborative Linkage of Agriculture and Industry through Research (ECLAIR) is like the BAP: relatively small, but with great potential for finding solutions regarding food in the future. It contributes to the establishment and reinforcement of intersectoral links between agriculture and manufacturing.
- The European Research Cooperation Agency (EUREKA) was established by 17 countries (from the EU and EFTA) on the initiative of the French in 1985. Its formation was a response to the American Strategic Defense Initiative ('Star Wars'). Its objective is the development and *production* of high-technology goods. It is not confined to pre-competitive R&D as the other programmes are, and other countries may be included in some of its programmes. EUREKA is, however, *not* an institution of the EU. It has a small secretariat in Brussels and has gained popularity in the business community.

Inter-firm strategic alliances in the development of technology in the EU increased sharply during the 1980s. In addition, the European Commission became quite heavily involved in projects on a cost-sharing basis. Over 70 per cent of private (largely non-subsidised) strategic technology alliances were formed to exploit joint R&D of new core technologies in informatics, new materials and biotechnology. A major field of cooperation was in information technologies, with over 40 per cent of all strategic technology alliances falling into this area (Hagedoorn and Schakenraad, 1993, p. 373). A comparison between established 'private' cooperation in R&D and cooperation sponsored by the EU found that they are very similar. In fact, 'subsidised R&D networks simply add to already existing or emerging private networks and merely reproduce the basic structure of European large firm co-operation' (Hagedoorn and Schakenraad, 1993, p. 387). This being the case, it is difficult to understand why leading and large firms in the EU need subsidies! If the 'official' network largely reproduces the already existing 'private' one, then it is surely largely redundant. The financial resources consumed in promoting cooperation might be better used elsewhere (for instance, on programmes that are not in the field of informatics such as biotechnology or education or infrastructure).

The question of whether replication of R&D networks is the result of a powerful lobby or whether it is necessary to accelerate R&D in the private sector because of significant externalities remains to be answered. Decisions taken at the EU level are easy targets for special lobbies as they are too far removed from the public to monitor. The co-decision procedure between the Council of Ministers and the European Parliament introduced by the Maastricht Treaty was an attempt to overcome this drawback. Although it is a step in the right direction, there is still a danger that EU technology policy may become just a sophisticated new form of protectionism.

The Sixth Framework Programme (2002–06) disposes of €17.5 billion. It aims to contribute to the creation of a true 'European research area' as a kind of an internal market for science and technology. It fosters scientific excellence, competitiveness and innovation through the promotion of better cooperation among relevant actors at all levels. This recognises the fact that economic growth increasingly depends on research and innovation, and that many of the present and foreseeable challenges for industry and society can no longer be solved at the national level alone. It is hoped that the Sixth Framework Programme is the financial instrument that will make the European research area a reality.

Past framework programmes have helped to develop a culture of scientific and technological cooperation between different EU countries. The programmes have been instrumental in achieving good research results. This has not, however, created a lasting impact on greater coherence at the European level. The Sixth Programme has therefore been redefined and streamlined with the following objectives:

- concentration of EU efforts on fewer priorities, particularly on areas where cooperation at European level presents clear added value;
- moving towards progressive integration of activities of all relevant participants working at different levels;
- promotion of research activities designed to have a lasting (structural) impact;
- support of activities that will strengthen Europe's general scientific and technological basis; and
- use of the scientific potential of accession countries preparing for EU entry for the benefit of European science at large.

The priorities of the Sixth Programme include:

- life sciences, genetics and biotechnology for health (€2.2 billion);
- information society technologies (€3.6 billion);
- nanotechnology, multifunctional materials and new production processes (€1.3 billion);
- aeronautics and space (€1.1 billion);
- food quality and safety (€0.7 billion);
- sustainable development, global change and ecosystems (including energy and transport research)(€2.1 billion); and
- citizens and governance in a knowledge-based society (€0.2 billion).

Earlier framework programmes have mainly been implemented through cooperative research projects. In most cases the end of a given research project meant the end of the consortium of research partners. In many cases projects did not reach the necessary 'critical mass' to have a real, structural and long-lasting impact either in scientific or in industrial or economic terms. To help solve these problems and to work towards the creation of the European research area, two new instruments have been designed in the Sixth Framework Programme:

- *networks of excellence* in different countries aim to integrate activities of network partners (universities, research centres and firms); and
- *integrated projects* are projects of substantial size, designed to help build up the 'critical mass' in objective-driven research with defined scientific and technological aims and applications.

A great deal of public money has been poured into R&D over the past decade in the EU, but the results have been very slow in coming. Of course, the effects of fundamental R&D cannot be predicted with a high degree of accuracy. As public funds are limited, and as the results of R&D are more important than the origin of the work, companies from foreign countries may take part in the R&D projects of the EU on a case-by-case basis, but without any financial help from the Commission. Production everywhere in the world is becoming more and more 'globalised'. Thus, forcing cooperation in R&D only within the EU may squander taxpayers' money. 'Global' production requires an open (global) industrial and trade policy system.

A changed and improved new industrial strategy of the EU and its member states needs to take into account first and foremost the crucial role played by the development of human capital in the long-term competitiveness of the economy. The creation of a prosperous learning society has to give priority to the creation of human capital, especially skills that create, spread, absorb and extend new technology in production, organisation, marketing and control. In addition, there may be a need for selective intervention in the form of subsidies, promotion of cooperation and information exchange during the pre-commercial phase of R&D projects that may give (oligopolistic) advantages to EU producers relative to foreign rivals. The EU has invested in the past in industries in which there is a high risk of failure and where Japan, the US and in recent times even China are strong. Part of the reason for the relative failure of electronics in the EU during the 1970s is the fact that domestic firms were sheltered from foreign competition. In contrast, in areas where the EU faced global competition, for example commercial aircraft (Airbus), the EU achieved a considerable degree of success.

The growth of knowledge currently doubles every three to four years.[26] This stimulates and drives knowledge-based societies to be involved in a 'war without shooting'. This competition is most obvious among Europe, North America and the Far East. If deemed appropriate, selective intervention in new technologies needs to be aimed at those expanding industries in which EU businesses already have or could create internal resources. This means that EU efforts and funds should be focused not on the replication of industries in which the US,[27] Japan[28] and China[29] are strong (cooperation with them may be a better choice), but primarily where there are grounds for the development of genuine EU technologies and comparative advantages. These may be the development of new production technologies for relatively traditional industries such as food, textiles and furniture, as well as for several high-technology industries such as mobile phones, chemicals and pharmaceuticals, biotechnology, heavy electrical machinery and equipment and super-fast trains, where the EU excels.

Not only now, but also in the coming decades, there will be an increased overlap between mechanical, electronic, chemical, medical and biotechnology industries. The EU has a reasonable chance of remaining the leader in some of these fields. This may be aided by the problems in the Japanese economy, which became apparent at the end of the 1990s. However, there are many dangers in this area. Although there have been important scientific achievements in genetic engineering (for example, cloning of animals), these achievements are often associated with serious ethical, moral, social and religious questions. In addition, serious negative side-effects may emerge from biotechnology and genetic engineering, as was the case with 'mad cow disease'[30] in Britain in 1996 and beyond.

OUTLOOK

The competitiveness of a country's goods and services on the international market in modern times is often much more created than inherited. The leader in some lines of production cannot be sure that this position will endure in the long run. Competition is threatening firms from all sides. Being on top is no longer a state, but rather a process. Therefore, one can find scope in the EU for industrial cooperation and risk sharing. It could be established both in the pre-commercial and during the commercialisation stages of R&D. In this way, inefficient duplication or multiplication of R&D would be eliminated and resources saved and redirected elsewhere. However, the creation of knowledge is not enough to keep a country at the competitive edge. That knowledge needs to be applied in practice with commercial success. Here the US fares much better than the EU. The US system and culture offers wide opportunities to start and restart promising businesses. If sound profit-making ideas fail (for whatever reason) in Boston, there are further chances in Seattle or San Francisco. The Americans treat past business failures like battle scars – as something to be worn with pride. In Europe, the situation is different. If your business start-up fails, you can forget another one for a while, unless you cross the Atlantic.

The elimination of most NTBs on internal EU trade as a result of the Single Market Programme has had its greatest impact on 'sensitive' businesses, and this will continue to be the case. These businesses are those that were protected by high NTBs and which experienced large price distortions, for example, the production of goods that are publicly procured either in the high-technology sector (for example, office machines, telecommunications and medico-surgical equipment) or in traditional manufacturing sectors such as electrical and railway equipment, pharmaceuticals, wine and boilermaking. Businesses protected by relatively modest NTBs will also continue to be affected by market liberalisation and deepening. These include motor vehicles, aerospace equipment, basic chemicals, machine tools for metals and textiles and sewing machines.

Some outsiders feared that the Single European Market would lead to the creation of 'Fortress Europe' as a result of a combination of intra-EU liberalisation and an increase in the existing level of external protection. However, the EU has no such plan, nor would it serve its long-term interests. If the word 'fortress' was mentioned, it was only as a potential bargaining chip with major trading partners. It was expected that the Single Market Programme would lead, among other things, to increased competition and efficiency, which would reduce prices in the EU. Therefore, even without any change in the existing level of nominal protection, the real level may rise.

Any additional increase would be neither necessary nor desirable. On the contrary, increased efficiency prompted the EU to reduce the level of trade protection in the Uruguay Round deal. None the less, the Single Market Programme has influenced the timing and extent of external FDI in the EU. Many foreign TNCs entered the EU in order to become 'internal' residents of the EU prior to full implementation of the Single Market Programme. They wanted to pre-empt any potential moves towards the creation of an EU fortress from the start of 1993.

Potential changes in the rules of origin and local content may, however, discriminate against 'internal' goods with a relatively high external import content. This may be reinforced by a discriminatory application of testing procedures and standards. A fortress mentality may be introduced in the EU through the social(ist) over-regulation of labour issues. If this is done in the future, it could provoke protectionist winds that would make the security of current jobs more important than the long-term efficiency and adjustment of the economy.

Customs union (phase I in the EU's integration) offered an incentive to economic life, but its effect was spent by the end of the 1960s. Something novel and more radical was needed. Phase II is represented by the formation of the genuine Single European Market, with an unimpeded flow of goods, services and factors, in 1993. This provided the EU with a new momentum. The member countries decided to reintroduce the principle of majority voting (except for fiscal issues, national border controls, working conditions and environmental issues) in order to ease the procedure to implement the Single European Market. In 1999, phase III of the integration process, the eurozone, reinforced earlier achievements in integration and removed all possible internal exchange rate variations for participating countries.

The EU member countries realised that the cost of failing to integrate (that is, a 'non-Europe') was too high to be ignored. An EU without internal frontiers (at least for residents of the member countries), as envisaged in the White Paper, could increase GDP in the EU by up to 7 per cent and create 5 million new jobs, if accompanied by supporting national policies (Emerson et al., 1988, p. 165). The 'costs' of these real gains are more freedom for business and less regulation. The opponents of the Single Market Programme were not able to create a more attractive and feasible economic strategy and ultimately gave up the attempt to do so. Only inefficient businesses or those that failed to compete and adjust would lose out in the new situation. As the Single Market Programme (1985–92) was not accompanied by a chain of bankruptcies throughout the EU, this is an indication that the business sector has absorbed the change without any serious and negative shocks. However, the Single Market Programme was merely the first step. One has to bear in mind that the Single Market Programme was merely a medium-term strategy. The Maastricht Treaty rearranged the decision-making process in the EU and set the 'agenda' for the eurozone.

Tables 6.1 and 6.2 show annual percentage changes in, respectively, real GDP growth rate and real gross fixed capital formation (investment) in the EU(15) and candidate countries in the 1990–2004 period. Also shown for comparison are the same indicators for the US, Japan, Switzerland and China. Although the actual figures differ for each country in the EU, economic cycles show a certain degree of synchronisation. The most obvious example is 1993, when most of the EU countries were in recession. That was the first year of the Single European Market in the EU. However, it would be unfair to blame negative macroeconomic trends on the failure of the Single Market Programme. Integration is, after all, no more than an instrument to *support* general national macroeconomic policies. If the policies are right, integration can contribute to their reinforcement. It is still too early to draw any definitive conclusions about the impact of the eurozone, introduced in 1999, on growth. Gross fixed capital formation (investment) shows business interest in the future. A change in this indicator in one period of time may provide signals about the business confidence and the growth rates of output and GDP in the next period. Although the two economic indicators shown in the tables differ among EU countries, the common feature is that their interrelation is almost always strongly positive (signs of slight synchronisation of cycles).

Well, 1992 has come and gone, and the single currency was introduced in the eurozone in 1999, but still the economies of the EU countries have not shown any great expansion despite widespread predictions of the beneficial effects of the Single European Market. There was even a recession in 1992. Has something gone wrong? Perhaps not. Economic integration, including the operation of the Single European Market and the eurozone, is an ongoing process. The Single European Market is not a project that has clear deadlines after which one may measure the overall effects with only a small margin of error.

Research on the effects of the Single European Market suffers from an identification problem. It is a common shortcoming of all studies that deal with the effects of international economic integration. It is hard to know which changes in the economy and the reaction of enterprises are due to the Single European Market and which would have happened anyway. For example, external changes include imports of improved foreign technology (software programs to manage production, inventories, transport and distribution) or 'globalisation' of business and competition. It may take another decade or so until all the effects of the Single Market Programme are fully absorbed by the economies of the EU. Then, this would all be mixed with the enlargement effects. Perhaps, and again only 'perhaps', the biggest

Table 6.1 Real GDP in EU(15), accession and other select countries, 1990–2005 (percentage change over preceding year)

Country	1990	1991	1992	1993	1994	1995	1996	1997	1998	1999	2000	2001	2002	2003*	2004*	2005*
Austria	4.7	3.3	2.3	0.4	2.6	1.6	2.0	1.6	3.9	2.7	3.5	0.7	0.7	0.9	1.9	2.5
Belgium	3.1	1.8	1.5	−1.0	3.2	2.4	1.2	3.6	2.0	3.2	3.7	0.8	0.7	0.8	1.8	2.3
Finland	−0.3	−6.3	−3.3	−1.1	4.0	3.8	4.0	6.3	5.3	4.1	6.1	0.7	1.4	1.4	2.5	2.7
France	2.6	1.0	1.5	−0.9	2.1	1.7	1.1	1.9	3.4	3.2	3.8	1.8	1.0	0.1	1.7	2.3
Germany	3.2	2.8	2.2	−1.1	2.3	1.7	0.8	1.4	2.0	2.0	2.9	0.6	0.2	0.0	1.6	1.8
Greece	0.0	3.1	0.7	−1.6	2.0	2.1	2.4	3.6	3.4	3.6	4.2	4.1	3.5	4.0	4.1	3.4
Ireland	8.5	1.9	3.3	2.7	5.8	9.9	8.1	10.9	8.8	11.1	10.0	5.7	3.3	1.6	3.7	4.8
Italy	2.0	1.4	0.8	−0.9	2.2	2.9	1.1	2.0	1.8	1.6	2.9	1.8	0.4	0.3	1.5	1.9
Luxembourg	5.3	8.6	1.8	4.2	3.8	1.3	3.7	7.7	7.5	6.0	8.9	1.0	0.1	1.2	1.9	2.8
Netherlands	4.1	2.5	1.7	0.9	2.6	3.0	3.0	3.8	4.3	4.0	3.3	1.3	0.2	−0.9	0.6	2.0
Portugal	4.0	4.4	1.1	−2.0	1.0	4.3	3.5	3.9	4.5	3.5	3.5	1.7	0.7	−0.8	1.0	2.0
Spain	3.8	2.5	0.9	−1.0	2.4	2.8	2.4	4.0	4.3	4.2	4.2	2.7	1.9	2.3	2.8	3.3
Denmark	1.0	1.1	0.6	0.0	5.5	2.8	2.5	3.0	2.5	2.3	3.0	1.0	1.7	0.8	2.0	2.3
Sweden	1.1	−1.1	−1.7	1.1	4.2	4.0	1.3	2.4	3.6	4.6	4.4	0.8	1.6	1.4	2.2	2.6
UK	0.8	−1.4	0.2	2.5	4.7	2.9	2.6	3.4	2.9	2.4	3.1	2.0	1.6	2.0	2.8	2.0
EU(15)	2.5	1.4	1.2	−0.3	2.8	2.5	1.7	2.6	2.9	2.8	3.4	1.6	0.9	1.3	2.0	2.3
Cyprus	7.6	0.6	9.8	0.7	5.9	6.1	1.6	2.5	5.0	4.8	5.2	4.1	1.8	2.0	3.8	4.5
Czech R.	–	−11.6	−0.5	0.1	2.2	5.9	4.3	−0.8	−1.0	0.5	3.2	3.6	3.6	2.8	3.9	3.0
Estonia	–	–	–	–	−2.0	4.3	3.9	9.8	4.6	−0.6	7.1	5.0	3.5	4.9	5.1	5.0
Hungary	–	–	−2.1	−0.6	2.9	1.5	1.3	4.6	4.9	4.1	5.2	3.8	3.5	3.7	4.1	3.4
Latvia	–	−10.4	−34.8	−14.9	0.6	−1.6	3.9	8.4	4.8	2.8	6.8	7.7	5.0	5.5	6.0	5.7
Lithuania	–	−5.7	−21.2	−9.8	6.2	4.7	7.0	7.3	5.1	−3.9	3.8	5.9	4.0	4.5	5.0	6.0

Malta	6.3	6.3	4.7	4.5	5.7	6.2	4.0	4.8	3.4	4.1	6.1	−0.8	2.5	3.1	3.7	3.4
Poland	–	−7.0	−33.9	3.8	44.5	7.0	6.0	6.8	4.8	4.0	4.0	1.1	1.4	2.5	3.7	4.8
Slovakia	–	–	–	6.2	5.1	6.5	5.8	5.6	4.0	1.3	2.2	3.3	3.6	3.7	4.5	4.3
Slovenia	–	−8.9	−5.5	2.8	5.3	4.1	3.8	4.6	3.8	5.2	4.6	3.0	3.0	3.4	3.7	3.7
Bulgaria	–	–	–	–	–	–	–	−5.6	4.0	2.3	5.4	4.0	4.0	4.5	5.0	5.5
Romania	–	–	–	–	–	–	–	−6.0	−4.8	−1.1	1.8	5.2	4.5	4.9	5.0	5.1
Turkey	9.3	0.9	6.0	8.0	−5.5	7.2	7.0	7.5	3.1	−4.7	7.4	−7.4	3.7	3.7	4.5	5.0
Switzerland	3.7	−0.8	−0.1	−0.5	0.5	0.5	0.3	1.7	2.4	1.5	3.2	0.9	−0.2	−0.4	1.4	–
United States	1.8	−0.5	3.0	2.7	4.0	2.7	3.6	4.4	4.3	4.1	3.8	0.3	2.5	2.8	3.8	3.3
Japan	5.2	3.3	1.0	0.3	1.0	1.9	3.4	1.8	−1.1	0.1	2.8	0.4	0.1	2.6	1.7	1.5
China	–	8.0	13.6	13.4	12.6	10.5	9.7	8.8	7.8	7.1	8.0	7.5	8.0	8.0	8.2	–

Note: *Estimates and projections.

Source: UNECE (2003), Eurostat (2003) and The Economist Intelligence Unit (2003).

Table 6.2 Real domestic gross fixed capital formation in EU(15), accession and other select countries, 1990–2002 (percentage change over preceding year)

Country	1990	1991	1992	1993	1994	1995	1996	1997	1998	1999	2000	2001	2002
Austria	6.2	6.6	0.6	-0.9	4.6	1.3	2.2	2.0	3.9	2.1	5.9	-2.2	-2.6
Belgium	8.5	-4.2	1.0	-2.5	0.4	3.4	0.9	7.2	3.0	4.3	4.1	0.5	-2.8
Finland	-4.6	-18.6	-16.7	-16.6	-2.7	10.6	8.4	11.9	9.3	3.0	3.9	4.0	-1.6
France	3.3	-1.5	-1.6	-6.4	1.5	2.0	—	-0.1	7.0	8.3	7.7	2.3	0.1
Germany	9.0	9.8	4.5	-4.4	4.0	-0.6	-0.8	0.6	3.0	4.1	2.5	-5.3	-6.4
Greece	4.5	4.2	-3.5	-4.0	-3.1	4.1	8.4	6.8	10.6	6.2	8.0	5.9	7.3
Ireland	13.4	-7.0	—	-5.1	11.8	15.3	16.8	18.1	14.8	14.0	7.0	-0.4	0.8
Italy	4.0	1.0	-1.4	-10.9	0.1	6.0	3.6	2.1	4.0	5.7	6.5	2.4	-2.2
Luxembourg	3.4	15.8	-15.1	20.6	—	-1.5	3.9	12.6	11.8	14.0	-6.3	5.9	-2.7
Netherlands	2.5	0.4	0.7	-3.2	2.1	3.9	6.3	6.6	4.2	7.8	3.5	-0.8	-3.3
Portugal	7.6	3.3	4.5	-5.5	2.7	6.6	5.7	13.9	11.5	7.3	4.7	0.1	-3.4
Spain	6.5	1.7	-4.1	-8.9	1.9	7.7	2.1	5.0	9.7	8.8	5.7	2.5	1.5
Denmark	-2.2	-3.4	-2.1	-3.8	7.7	11.6	3.9	10.9	10.0	1.0	10.7	5.6	2.3
Sweden	0.2	-8.6	-11.6	-10.3	6.6	9.9	4.5	-0.3	7.8	8.2	6.6	0.8	-1.6
UK	-2.6	-8.2	-0.9	0.3	4.7	3.1	4.7	6.9	12.8	0.6	1.9	0.3	-4.0
EU(15)	4.3	1.0	-0.3	-5.7	2.6	3.2	2.1	3.3	6.5	5.3	4.7	-0.1	-2.4
Cyprus	-2.8	-1.6	16.2	-12.8	-2.5	-1.7	7.4	-4.5	8.0	-1.4	4.1	2.5	3.5
Czech R.	—	—	—	—	—	19.3	3.7	-1.2	-10.1	0.3	4.7	6.2	-0.1
Estonia	—	—	—	—	5.3	6.4	14.8	27.4	1.5	-11.1	19.3	14.5	12.0
Hungary	—	—	—	—	—	—	14.7	4.1	8.4	6.9	10.2	3.5	5.5
Latvia	—	—	—	—	—	—	1.9	9.3	48.5	16.8	24.7	19.7	7.6
Lithuania	—	—	—	—	—	—	19.3	18.3	6.8	-8.5	2.4	32.8	0.9

406

Malta	17.9	–	–0.2	11.1	8.5	17.8	–8.4	–4.5	–3.4	4.0	17.3	–11.4	–5.1
Poland	–	–	–	–	–	–	12.9	13.8	8.0	21.4	2.1	–13.4	–4.0
Slovakia	–	–	–	32.1	–8.8	17.2	34.5	1.2	5.9	–22.3	–0.6	4.1	–
Slovenia	–	–	–	–	–	–	–	–	–	–	–4.3	0.9	3.9
Bulgaria	–	–	–	–	–	–	–	–	–	–	–	–	–
Romania	–	–	–	–	–	–	–	–	–	–	7.4	–	–
Turkey	15.9	0.4	6.4	26.4	–16.0	9.1	14.1	14.8	–3.9	–15.7	16.9	–31.7	–4.5
Switzerland	3.8	–2.9	–6.6	–2.7	6.5	1.8	–2.4	1.5	4.5	2.7	5.8	–5.2	–6.1
United States	–1.8	–6.9	6.5	8.1	9.1	6.1	9.3	9.6	11.4	7.8	6.1	–3.8	–2.0
Japan	8.1	2.3	–2.4	–2.8	–1.5	0.7	6.4	0.9	–3.9	–0.9	2.7	–1.5	–5.5
China	–	–	–	–	–	11.0	15.0	9.0	14.5	14.3	10.4	10.4	15.5

Source: UNECE (2003), Eurostat (2003) and The Economist Intelligence Unit (2003).

effect on the economies of the EU has already taken place, at the end of the 1980s. Some support for this thesis can be found in the fact that business concentration deals peaked in 1990. It needs to be borne in mind that the Single European Market was *a*, rather than *the* reason for change.

In spite of 'grand' expectations regarding employment and growth at the start of the Single Market Programme, as expressed, for example, by Emerson et al. (1988), in practice the benefits have been much more modest, although not negligible. It has been estimated that the programme created between 300 000 and 900 000 jobs, with an extra increase in EU income of 1.1–1.5 per cent over the 1987–93 period (European Commission, 1997c).

Direct intervention in the manufacturing industry by the EU was primarily aimed at declining industries such as steel, shipbuilding and textiles during the 1970s and early 1980s. After 1985, the major emphasis of the policy changed. The EU became much more involved in the expanding high-technology industries through its R&D and technology policies. This should not be taken to mean that the EU is no longer concerned with obsolete 'industries', or that it was not interested in the support and development of advanced industries in the past. On the contrary. EU involvement with both types of manufacturing industries existed in the past, and it continues in the present. What changed was only the order of priorities. None the less, high on the agenda for the future are the following priorities:

- promotion of investment into intangible assets;
- fostering the information society and life-time learning;
- backing good corporate governance;[31]
- advancement of industrial cooperation;
- paying special attention to services, SMEs, energy, bio- and nano-technologies;
- strengthening of competition; and
- modernisation of public intervention.

4. Services

ISSUES

Goods are tangible assets and, as such, are readily defined; the same cannot be said of services. Services have numerous recipients: an individual in the case of a haircut, education, entertainment or transport; a legal entity such as a firm or government in the case of banking or construction; an object such as an aeroplane in the case of guidance, defrosting, repairs or other airport services; or goods in the case of transport and storage. Some services can be provided to more than one recipient. For example, banking, insurance, transport, telecommunication, leasing, data processing and legal advice could be offered to individuals, businesses and governments.

In general, the services sector in the developed market economies contributes more than half to both GDP and employment (about 70 per cent in the EU(15) in 2003). The share of the economy occupied by services has been continuously increasing. This tendency to deindustrialisation has resulted in a shift of emphasis towards the services sector as one of the key solutions to the problems of unemployment and growth. Employment in the manufacturing sector has been declining in the EU since the 1980s, whereas employment in the services sector has been constantly expanding. In 2002, out of 158 million people employed in the EU(15), 43 million (or 27 per cent) were employed in the manufacturing sector, while 110 million (or 70 per cent) were employed in the services sector. Newly created jobs in the services sector more than compensated for job losses in manufacturing. Production of almost all services takes place in every country. However, the same is not true for the manufacturing of cars, lorries, aircraft or steel. This is the direct consequence of high tradability of goods and restricted tradability of services. Hence, the alleged importance of the creation of new jobs in the services sector.

Notwithstanding its importance and impact on the economy, the services sector has been largely neglected in economic analysis. Classical economists such as Adam Smith and Karl Marx neglected services as the residual sector of the economy on the grounds that it does not have durable properties and no facility for physical accumulation or trade. The production and consumption of services is simultaneous and requires a degree of mobility of factors. Therefore, the classical economists turned their attention towards the manufacture of physical goods. In addition, rules relating to trade in services were not negotiated for a long time. However, as world trade in services was constantly increasing, it came as no surprise that services were included in the Uruguay Round Accord and in the WTO. World trade in services was over $1540 billion in 2002. This represented a quarter of the $6240 billion trade in goods during the same year.

The services sector of an economy changes its structure and location over time. The traditional services (such as transport, law, medicine, banking and insurance) are enriched by the new and fast-growing ones (such as telecommunications, information, data processing, engineering and management consultancy).

On the 'technical' side, services differ from other economic activities in at least five ways (Buigues and Sapir, 1993, p. xi):

- The production and consumption of services occur at the same time and at the same location. Therefore, they are regarded as non-tradable as they cannot be stored. Because of a relatively low level of internationalisation, the right of establishment (FDI) is essential for the provision of services abroad. Although services account for over two-thirds of the GDP in the EU, their share of total trade is about 20 per cent. This epitomises the non-tradable nature of many services. On the other hand, services account for over half of all FDI in the EU. Internationalisation of services is lowest in distribution, road transport and construction, average in telecommunications, financial and business services; and relatively high in air transport and hotel chains.
- The quality of services cannot easily be ascertained in advance of consumption. Non-price competitive factors such as reputation often play a key role during the decision-making process by consumers. This is important in longer-term relations such as in financial services. Experience plays a part even in one-off relationships in some cases and places.[32]
- Governments in all countries intervene in services more than in other economic activities, because of market failures. These include imperfect competition in a number of services; asymmetric information between providers and consumers (sellers potentially know more about a service, such as an insurance policy, than do buyers); and externalities. Positive externalities are to be found frequently in the services sector, such as in telecommunications or the Internet. In these areas the value for one user increases with the total number of all users. A negative externality may be found, for example, in financial services, where the failure of one bank may cause problems for others (Sapir, 1993, p. 27). Public intervention influences entry, operation, competition and exit from the sector. Regulation is high and competition low in financial services, air transport and telecommunications. Thus, these industries are served by only a few large companies. Reputation plays a major role in finance and economies of scope are important in air transport, while in telecommunications there are relatively large sunk costs and economies of scale (in most countries a single public firm used to provide the service until the mid-1990s). Competition tends to be higher and regulation easier in road transport, business services, construction and hotels.
- Debates about the (in)ability of the government to intervene (in) efficiently to correct market failures, as well as changes in technology, contributed to an ebb in deregulation in the services sector first in the US at the end of the 1970s, then in Britain during the early 1980s,

which subsequently spread to the rest of Europe. All this was also supported by the results of the Uruguay Round.
- Services are characterised by a relatively slow growth of labour productivity. Their rate of productivity growth during the 1970–90 period was half of what it was in the manufacturing sector. There are at least two explanations for such development. First, competition in services is obstructed by a high degree of regulation and, second, the substitution of capital for labour is more limited in services than in manufacturing. Technological innovations, however, increased labour productivity in telecommunications and air transport during that period.

Differences between services and other economic activities are not confined to the 'technical' side. There is also a social dimension:

- in the 1990s, half of employees in the service sector were women. This is in sharp contrast with the manufacturing sector, in which women account for only one in five jobs;
- there are many more part-time employees in the services sector than in manufacturing;
- temporary contracts are increasing in the services sector;
- there is a relatively high level of non-employees;
- labour unions are not strong in the services sector except in transport and telecommunications; and
- SMEs are the dominant type of business organisation in most service industries.

There are other reasons that make the analysis of services tricky. One is a lack of any profound theory or definition. Services were defined as:

- *indivisibles* because they disappear in the very moment of their production; or
- *unstorables* because they perish as they are produced. Services could be bought and sold, but they could not be *'dropped on the foot'*; or
- *non-tradables* and *non-transportables* because of their above two properties; or
- *the residual sector* of the economy as it does not belong to agriculture, or to mining or to the manufacturing sector.

A wide definition of services states that 'a service is a change in the condition of a person, or a good belonging to some economic unit, which is brought about as a result of the activity of some other economic unit' (Hill, 1977,

p. 317). Without a proper definition, the measuring unit is lacking. Trade statistics list thousands of items for goods, but record only a handful of services (making analysis quite difficult). This reflects the fact that goods have a very high degree of tradability, whereas the tradability of services is low. Hence, the production of services is much more geographically dispersed than is the production of goods. Although many services are not tradable, progress in information and telecom technology has made many services eligible for international trade. Nevertheless, trade in many services is not recorded. For example, the service part of a good, such as repair and regular maintenance of a car, may be incorporated in the total price of traded goods.

Services may have the following general dimensions:

- *producer*: finance, accounting, consulting . . .
- *distribution*: transport, trade, advertising . . .
- *social*: government, health, security, old-age . . . and
- *personal*: entertainment, restaurants, hotels . . .

This classification is relevant if one wants to employ certain policy instruments to influence the development of the targeted dimension. But even here one may encounter classification, and then policy-related problems. Where to put insurance, marketing, education or postal services?

Apart from transport, financial and telecommunication services, in principle, entry into and exit from a service industry is relatively cheap and easy. However, there are regulatory barriers to such (dis)orderly operation in the service businesses. TNCs release few data on their internal trade in services, whereas other establishments in the sector only reluctantly make this information public, as this can endanger their competitive position. In addition, information can be easily, swiftly and cheaply distributed, which jeopardises property rights. Such a lack of hard statistical information makes trade in services difficult to study.

It is easier to sell goods than services in foreign markets. While barriers to trade in goods can be eliminated at the border, problems for the suppliers of services usually start once they pass the frontier control. Provision of services often requires the right of establishment and national treatment of enterprises. Providers of a service frequently need to be physically present in order to provide a service to their customers.

Impediments to trade in services are not found in the form of tariffs. The principal obstacles can be found in two classes of barriers that may be theoretically obvious, but they may often be blurred in practice:

- *market access*: regulation of the entry of foreign service providers in the national market (prohibitions, bilateral and regional preferential

agreements, local content rules, travel and residency restrictions, recognition of qualifications and experience, standards, insurance and obligatory deposits); and
- *national treatment*: this shows whether a foreign provider of a service is treated the same as the domestic one in the same situation (taxes, subsidies, charges for public services, buy domestic obligations and campaigns, exchange controls).

Experts may enter and settle in foreign countries, but their qualifications and licences may not be recognised by the host authorities. Public authorities regulate the supply of services to a much higher degree than they do the production of goods. They often regulate public shareholding, quality and quantity of supply, rates and conditions of operation. Fiscal incentives are often given more easily to firms in the manufacturing industry than to those in the services sector. Because of the wide coverage of regulation of industries in the services sector, an easing or a removal of control of the establishment in services can have a much greater impact on trade and investment than would be the case in the trade and production of goods.

More than a decade after its establishment in 1993, the Single European Market is not yet delivering its full benefits to consumers and firms. This is most obvious in services. Belgian electricians need to pay three times the Belgian rate to register with the Luxembourg authorities for a one-day job or Austrian bakers need eight different licences if they want to set up business in Italy.[33] The Single European Market may be weakening. So may be the opportunity to turn the EU into the world's most competitive knowledge-based economy by 2010. Hence, the European Commission intends to be more active in tearing down barriers in the services sector.

Small and open countries that are net importers of goods may prefer not to rely on their domestic manufacturing industry, as this might not operate on an efficient scale. These countries may choose to develop service industries to create proceeds to pay for imports of goods. Thus, the Netherlands has developed trade and transport, Austria tourism, Norway and Greece shipping, while Switzerland and Luxembourg are highly specialised in financial services.

Services and the jobs that they create may be broadly classified into two groups:

- those that require high skills and pay (such as business, financial, engineering, management, consulting and legal advice); and
- those that are geared to consumer and welfare needs.

The suppliers of services in this second group receive poor training, have a high turnover and low pay (such as jobs in shops, hotels and restaurants). Economic development in its post-industrial phase should be aimed at the creation of jobs in the former group, rather than the latter (Tyson, 1987, p. 79).

EUROPEAN UNION

Articles 43–8 of the Treaty of Rome grant the right of establishment to EU residents, freedom to supply services throughout the region and freedom of movement for capital. Article 86 states that public enterprises and those with special or exclusive rights to provide services of general economic interest 'shall be subject to . . . the rules on competition, in so far as the application of such rules does not obstruct the performance, in law or in fact, of the particular tasks assigned to them'. Compared with trade in goods, these rights have not yet materialised in practice on a large scale. The major reason for this situation is the existence of various national restrictions (NTBs). In fact, about half of the 282 measures that came from the Single Market Programme related to services such as finance, transport and telecommunications. It was in the financial services (banking and insurance) that the Single Market Programme advanced most swiftly. This was partly due to the impressive changes in technology (data processing and telecommunications services) and partly a result of international efforts to liberalise trade in services under the auspices of the WTO.

One could ask whether the changes prompted by the Single Market Programme had the same effects on services as they had on manufacturing. A more apposite question is whether the programme had an impact on the geographical location of services in the EU, as could have happened with manufacturing. In the case of some services that are tradable because of data processing and telecommunications technology, such as accounting, there was some centralisation and reallocation of business. For most others, significant changes are not expected in the short and medium terms. Skilled accountants are able to move around the EU and offer their services, but the Greek islands (tourism) will remain where they are.

The still-evolving legislative framework for the single EU market in services is based on the following four principal elements:

- *Freedom of establishment*: Enterprises from other EU countries may not be discriminated against and must receive national treatment in the country of operation. This is important in the services sector because of the need for direct contact between the providers and consumers of services. A single licence is required for the provision of services throughout the EU. This means that a firm that is entitled to provide services in one EU country has the same right in another EU country. The country that issues such a licence is primarily responsible for the control of the licensed firm on behalf of the rest of the EU.

- *Liberalisation of cross-border trade in services*: This element increases the possibility of cross-border provision of services without the actual physical establishment of the business in the host country. A gradual inclusion and a full permission for cabotage (internal transport service within a country) was one of the key changes. Cabotage in EU air transport was fully liberalised in 1997, and in road transport in 1998.[34]
- *Harmonisation of the national rules*: This eases the trans-border establishment of business and the provision of services. This is relevant for telecommunications (technical standards) and financial (solvency) services.
- *Common rules of competition*: Restrictive business practices, abuse of the dominant market position and state aid are forbidden or strictly regulated.

Financial services deal with promises to pay. In a world of developed telecommunication services, these promises can move instantaneously all around the globe. Customs posts do not matter in this business. None the less, restrictive rights of establishment may limit the freedom to supply these services. Traditionally, monetary power was jealously protected and saved for domestic authorities. This has changed in recent decades. International mobility of capital can hardly be stopped, therefore countries try to make the best use of it. Financial services not only generate employment and earnings themselves but also, and more importantly, the efficient allocation of resources and the competitiveness of the manufacturing sector depends on a wide choice of efficient and low-cost financial services.

As a result of the First Banking Directive (1977), EU-resident banks are free to open branches throughout the Union, but this is subject to host-country authorisation. Foreign banks cannot compete successfully with local banks, as the costs of establishment differ widely among countries. In addition, foreign banks may be excluded from certain services (securities) which are reserved for local residents. The Second Banking Directive (1989) brought a major breakthrough in the EU banking industry as it introduced the single banking licence. From 1993, member countries of the EU accepted the home-country control principle, as well as a mutual recognition of each other's licensing rules for the banks.

The European Parliament approved a plan in 2002 to unify the EU financial markets ambitiously set by 2005. The intention is to standardise rules for corporate accounting, reporting and oversight in order to allow for greater financial market consolidation and to avoid risks such as those that emerged with the Enron and Andersen corporate scandals in the US in 2002 and Parmalat in the EU in 2003.

Full harmonisation of the banking laws in the EU countries is, however, neither easy nor necessary. Banking laws among the states in the US differ, but this has never been a major handicap to the economic performance of the country. As financial services become globalised, the challenge to the EU and its member countries is to adjust to this change and remain competitive, become mature or lose out to other competitors. In the event that third-country banks wished to benefit from the Single European Market, the Second Banking Directive asked for reciprocal treatment. However, it subsequently became evident that this would be an unrealistic provision in relation to US banks. These banks are not allowed to enter into certain financial operations (such as securities) across the boundaries of federal states. It would be unreasonable to give EU banks operating in the US more favourable treatment than domestic US banks and/or to expect the US to change the domestic rules because of a different regulation in the EU. In the end, the reciprocity provision did not apply to subsidiaries of US banks that were established in the EU prior to 1 January 1993.

The *insurance* business is very special and complex indeed. There are few homogeneous products and there is usually a long-term relation between the parties. If a consumer purchases a bottle of Scotch whisky, he/she still has the pleasure of consuming this drink even if the producer goes out of business. The same is not true for an insurance policy. Control of the insurance business is exercised by regulating entry into the business. Insurers in the EU are granted the general right to establish (locate operations in another partner country), but they are often permitted to solicit business only through local agencies. This is particularly true for compulsory insurance.[35] The rationale for such restrictions can be found in the protection of consumers' interests because of the asymmetric information between the seller and the buyer (the seller may know much more about the policy than the buyer),[36] but it can be employed for the protection of local businesses too. Where a sound case for the protection of local consumers ends and where a barrier to trade in the insurance business and protection of the local industry begins is difficult to determine. Buyers of an insurance policy may appreciate the benefits of relatively tougher regulation, but may not wish to accept the higher costs involved.[37]

Progress in the EU was faster in the non-life than in the life insurance business. The directive (1988) on the freedom to supply non-life insurance distinguished between two kinds of risks. Mass risks (commercial risks) and large risks (transport, marine, aviation) are covered by the home-country regulation of the insurer, whereas personal insurance is covered by national regulations in the country where the policyholder resides. Integration in the insurance business in the EU has not advanced as much as in the field of banking. EU insurance companies are allowed to compete only under the host-country rules, which significantly reduces the opportunity for real competition. In fact, the insurance industry is barely affected by the 'globalisation' of business. Highly protected national insurance markets would require a great deal of harmonisation before real competition could take place and before a 'single EU insurance passport', introduced in 1994, could have a greater impact. The benefit of this 'single passport' is subject to harmonised solvency margin requirements and regulatory supervision among countries.

As part of the implementation of the Single European Market, personal insurance policies have been sold and advertised freely in the EU since 1994. This is not to say that insurers and consumers had reason to rejoice. One reason for this is that national tax treatment still favours local companies. These firms have a wide network of tied agents that may not be easily and swiftly replicated by foreign competitors. Another reason is national restraints on the sale of certain types of policies. For example, Italy banned the sale of kidnap insurance because of the concern that it would encourage abductions. The European Commission advocates equal treatment and access for men and women to goods and services. Therefore, in 2003 it proposed to abolish the use of sex as a determining factor in the evaluation of risk. Insurers argue that women live longer than men and if the insurance industry is deprived of such distinct treatment, the ability to assess risk would increase insurance premiums for women for products such as car insurance.[38]

Uncoordinated national laws can no longer provide the basis for future developments of financial services in the EU. This is increasingly important in the light of increasing globalisation and a loss of an EU-specific dimension in business, especially in banking. If the EU wants to preserve or even increase the existing amount of business and employment that goes with it, it is crucial that it fosters the development of an open and efficient market for financial services. Consumers will gain a wider choice, and better-quality and cheaper financial services, which is essential for the competitiveness of the manufacturing industry and the smooth operation of the whole economy.

The Debauve case (1980) dealt with advertising, and showed how complicated cases could be in the services sector. Belgium prohibited advertising on TV. None the less, cable TV programmes that originated in other countries without such restrictions and which were marketed in Belgium contained advertising messages. The issue was whether the government of Belgium had the right to ban advertising on channels received in the country, but which originate in other countries. The EU Court of Justice concluded that, in the absence of the EU action, each member state would regulate and even prohibit advertising on TV on its territory on the grounds of general interest. The question here is what was the 'general interest' in this case? A typical argument for regulation would be the protection of consumers (viewers). An increase in the choice of channels would not be against the interests of the viewers regardless of whether foreign programmes contain advert breaks. Therefore, the argument that an improvement in the welfare of those in Belgium who wished to watch foreign channels was increased by the ban cannot hold water (Hindley, 1991, p. 279). If Belgian viewers watch foreign programmes (with or without advertising), they will watch fewer domestic channels. Hence, support for the public financing of domestic TV will decrease. An additional reason for the Belgian policy was the protection of the advertising revenue of the local newspapers.

One of the fastest-growing industries in the services sector is *telecommunications*. This is due to the profound technological changes that have taken place since the 1960s, which include communication via satellite, microwaves and digital technology. New goods and services, such as fax machines, electronic mail and mobile phones, also appeared. A total of €450 billion has been invested in the EU information industry. The natural monopoly argument for the provision of long-distance, as well as local services has vanished.

The EU policy in the telecommunication field was slow and late to appear. During the mid-1980s, the EU was concentrating its efforts on R&D and common standardisation. Subsequently, the aim of having an open network was translated into a directive in 1990. In addition, public contracts that exceed €0.6 million in the industry must be transparent and officially published. Directive 96/19/EC introduced full competition in the telecommunications market in 1998, although Greece, Portugal and Spain were allowed a few years' grace. This means that EU consumers have the right to have a phone connected, access to new services, have services of a specified quality and benefit from new methods of solving problems between the consumer and the provider of the service. The obvious benefit was an increase in the number of telecommunication services (often free access to the Internet, huge growth in mobile telecommunications) and a sharp decline in the price of these services.

Business services have high rates of growth too. They include accountancy, auditing, legal, R&D, information, data-processing, computing and various engineering and management consultancy services. Different technical standards, licensing of professionals and government procurement of services represent barriers to the free supply of services throughout the EU. A liberal treatment of these services may reduce their costs and increase the efficiency of business. In a world undergoing continuous changes in technology, markets, laws and so on, consultants who manage to stay at least one step ahead of their clients will survive.

Trade in professional services still faces significant obstacles. The domestic regulation in the accounting business, for instance, is burdened with limits. They commonly include the following restrictions and requirements:

- qualifications (education and experience);
- recognition of diplomas and certificates (professional competence);
- transparency regarding activities;
- standards for the quality of service (protection of clients);
- professional ethics and insurance/deposit requests;
- obligatory membership in local professional associations;
- limitations in the scope of business;
- control and ownership restrictions;
- residency requirements; and
- limits regarding the nationality of staff employed.

OUTLOOK

The policy of the EU towards services should be founded on three major freedoms: the freedom to establish business (geographical or spatial liberty); the freedom to offer services; and the freedom to transfer capital. Deregulation in the services sector increased competition, which reduced costs for consumers, increased opportunities and improved the competitive position of the entire economy. Apart from partial deregulation, the promotion of the development of the EU-wide service industries needs to be encouraged. Initial steps towards this objective include recognition of qualifications, a single insurance licence and the opening up of government procurement over a certain (small) threshold to all EU suppliers.

Opening up market for trade and foreign investment in services brings at least two distinct benefits for the domestic economy:

- the competitiveness of the entire economy depends on a free access to efficient services; and
- opening the domestic market for trade in services is the principal means to warrant the efficient operation of the services sector. This method permits (1) an improvement in efficiency because of

competition and (2) makes available services that otherwise may not be available locally.

Although the general interests of a member country do not always conform with the overall interest of the EU, the EU Court has often been reluctant to question national stances. This has limited the effectiveness of Articles 49–55, as well as Article 86 of the Treaty of Rome. While the Cassis de Dijon case was applied to internal trade in goods, the application of the same principle to services is waiting for 'better times'. The relatively 'soft' stance of the EU regarding restrictive agreements and abuse of dominant position in services cannot easily be explained only by the properties of services; one also needs to add the influence of entrenched businesses, lobbies and the public protection of specific interests. None the less, it is slowly being realised that regulation that limits competition prevents, rather than stimulates, efficiency in services such as telecommunication, transport and finance.

More than a decade after its establishment in 1993, the Single European Market is not yet delivering its full benefits to consumers and firms. This is most obvious in services that account for over 70 per cent of EU GDP. In order to avoid the weakening of the Single European Market, as well as the chance of transforming the EU into the world's most competitive knowledge-based economy by 2010, the European Commission identified in 2002 a set of barriers that impede the free movement in services. These are barriers that deal with the following stages of the business process:

- establishment of the service provider (authorisation, declaration, qualifications of staff);
- use of inputs necessary for the provision of services;
- promotion;
- distribution; and
- after-sales phase (professional liability, insurance, guarantees, maintenance).

The European Commission intends to be more active in tearing down barriers in the services sector and to have a Single European Market for services by 2010.

As the provision of most services has a local character (because many of them are non-tradable), there will be no big change in the geographical location of their production. Local incumbents have established and operate strong retail networks, and their own reputation (accounting may be an exception) may act as an additional barrier to entry. Because of this aspect of services, national regulation may remain dominant in many industries within the services sector in the future. The structure of ownership, however, may change as local firms enter into the network of large TNCs in the industry. Nevertheless, one should not exaggerate the potential expansion of TNCs in the services sector as most mergers and acquisitions in the sector have a strong national dimension. An international, that is, EU, dimension in the services sector is growing in the insurance industry. Assicurazioni Generali, the biggest insurer in the EU by market capitalisation, earned two-thirds of its premium income from outside Italy, while a third of its equity is reckoned to be in the hands of foreigners.[39]

The impact of the Single European Market on the changing geography of production is much more obvious in the manufacturing sector than in services. This is the consequence of a much higher degree of tradability of goods than is the case with services. The impact on services may not be immediately obvious. It will take a long time to materialise. The Single European Market brought certain benefits to the consumers of services. The most obvious are in telecommunications. However, large-scale benefits may be absent because of important barriers that include the reputation of the already established service firms, past experience, excess capacity and cultural differences. It may be wrong to expect that the genuine internal market will cause an equalisation of prices of services throughout the EU. Prices will only tend to converge because of increased competition. None the less, some price differentials will persist because of differences in productivity and taxation, as well as the needs and preferences of the local markets.

Some trends are, however, obvious. There is a general trend for the share of services in the economy to expand, while that of the manufacturing industry shrinks. In addition, the services sector of the economy is more spatially dispersed (because of limited tradability) than the manufacturing sector. As personal income increases, there is a disproportional increase in demand for services. At the same time, many manufacturing industries are farming out various services (from cleaning to accounting and design) and relying on external specialist firms to provide them. Finally, as manufacturing in the EU undergoes some degree of spatial reallocation, this will have an impact on the location of services, which may follow their clients in the manufacturing sector.

5. Conclusion

Consideration of the various problems that arose during the creation and implementation of an industrial policy in the manufacturing and services sectors of a country has given an insight into the magnitude of the problems facing the introduction of schemes across integrated countries. There is at least one forceful argument that favours the introduction of an industrial policy. The neo-conservative school argues that a free market system is the best existing method for solving economic problems. However, this cannot be accepted without reservations. Neither the economic performance of the US prior to the New Deal nor contemporary economic performance in the most successful industrialised countries such as Germany, Japan or Sweden supports this view. Strategic government intervention and comprehensive social welfare programmes, rather than free markets, have been the engines of economic success throughout the advanced industrial world (Tyson and Zysman, 1987b, p. 426). In fact, according to this view, free markets were often no more than 'fine-tuning' policy choices of the government.

A country with a flexible policy towards manufacturing industry in response to market signals (such as Japan during the 1960s and 1970s) or one that shapes the market (France during the 1950s and 1960s or China during and after the 1990s) is better able to adapt to changes than a country that largely resists such changes (such as in Britain in the case of coal and steel production during the 1970s). Industrial policy that ignores market signals and that supports industries with obsolete technologies introduces confusion over future developments and increases the cost of inevitable change. These costs may be much higher in the future than they were in the past because of social rigidities and rapid changes in technology. The success of an industrial policy may be tested by its effectiveness in shifting resources from industries that use ailing technologies, not by how effective it is in preventing this adjustment. However, the problem is that even the most sophisticated national or international institutions and think-tanks do not know exactly what will happen in the future (recall the debt crises in the 1980s, and the impact of Microsoft on the economy).

A policy of picking a winner (a strategic industry with important externalities) *ex ante* may propel the economy of a country in the future. This may have a favourable outcome for the country or the EU if the choice is correct, if this policy is coordinated with the suppliers of inputs and if it is limited to a defined period of time in which the national champion is expected to become self-reliant. The other interventionist approach of rescue (*ex post*) may simply postpone the attrition of the assisted industry and increase the overall costs of change to the society.

The shift out of industries that use obsolete production technologies and into modern ones seems easy in theory, but can be quite difficult, costly and slow in practice. This is, of course, a matter of political choice. The inability to do something is different from an unwillingness to do it. During the 1980s, the EU opted for the creation of the Single European Market as the environment that favours change. None the less, its direct industrial policy is in many respects a set of R&D policies coupled with public procurement. Other dimensions of industrial policy are implemented within the domain of competition, trade, regional, education and monetary (stability) policies. It is to be hoped that the 'social dimension' in the future of the EU will remain only as a set of non-obligatory standards and aspirations that will not mislead the EU into the complacency that would kill the urge for continuous change and adjustment for the better.

Britain and Spain were behind the ambitious Lisbon (2000) goal for the EU. This rests on the liberal ideas of deregulation that would make the EU economy more flexible and dynamic. Other EU countries did not quite realise what they agreed to. The European Councils usually set political targets which include deadlines. This is generally a clear-cut part of the exercise. However, it takes much longer for the European Commission and the national governments to jointly legislate and implement policies (most governments try to protect their national interests). If the principal competitors such as the US (because of the huge budget and trade deficits) or China (because of distortions in the economy) slow down, the EU may feel less urgency in making painful reforms in its structured labour and product markets.

The shaping of an industrial policy in every country requires detailed data about the available factors, competition, externalities, changes in the production and management technology, and policies of the major trading partners, as well as about the tax, legal and political environment. Even then, industrial policy prescriptions should be taken with a pinch of salt. At the time when Britain was industrialising, the textile industry was the leader in technology. The capital required to start up a textile firm was much smaller than that required to build a steel mill, which was the leading manufacturing industry when Germany started to industrialise. The problems of development had to be solved by government incentives (intervention) and bank loans. Modern industries require not only capital investment (in many cases this entails reliance on banks) but also, and more importantly, investment in highly qualified personnel. Education policy is always shaped to a large extent by government.

There are justifiable reasons for pessimism about the ability to create and implement an effective and coherent industrial policy in a decentralised country or a group of integrated countries. Many agents and issues need to be taken into account during the decision-making process about uncertain events. Numerous agencies have an impact on industrial policy, including ministries of trade, finance, social affairs, education, regional development, energy, environment, transport, technology, defence and foreign affairs. Most of these departments exist at the federal, regional and local levels. There are also labour unions, banks, industrial associations and non-governmental organisations. They all have diverse and often conflicting goals. The complexity of coordination, communication, harmonisation and control of all these players increases exponentially with their number. In spite of all these organisational difficulties, the rewards are worthwhile.[40] However, while numerous agents may, of course, be a source of creativity, in practice they often turn out to be a source of disagreement over the distribution of instruments of industrial policy. The interaction of all these players has an amalgamating effect on the national industrial policy. To reconcile all these diverse demands is a great political challenge.

Luckily, some evidence from the cases of Japan (1960–90) and Germany may serve as partial examples to other countries in the shaping of national industrial policies. The crucial property of a promising industrial policy is that if it cannot be organised centrally then it ought to coordinate measures taken at lower levels. Without a consensus about the basic objectives of industrial policy among the major players and their commitment to these goals, such a policy will not come about. Exchange of views, mutual understanding, trust, support and, finally, an agreement about the goals and means of industrial policy between governments at all levels, business community and labour are essential elements of its effectiveness.

While the EU creates conditions for competition, its member countries implement their own national industrial policies. The divergence in industrial policy philosophies among the member countries and a lack of funds has prevented the EU from playing a more influential role. The variety of uncoordinated national policies has introduced confusion and uncertainty regarding the future actions of the EU. Until the member countries take advantage of a vast Single European Market, they may not profit from the potentials for an increase in the competitive edge in a number of manufacturing industries primarily *vis-à-vis* the US, but also Japan, China and some newly industrialised countries. If it attempts to be durable and successful, an EU industrial policy will require the agreement of the member states about their objectives and policy means. A new philosophy by the European Commission regarding industrial policy is based on the idea that this policy needs to offer primarily a stable macroeconomic environment. The eurozone epitomises this policy stance. In addition, various research programmes are should provide an input into the EU industry's competitiveness.

If there are any 'golden rules' for a respectable industrial policy, they should include the following elements:

- The policy should not harm other parts of the economy.
- The policy needs to be continuous and stable.
- The policy instruments should reinforce one another.

- Inflation needs to be low, rates of interest positive and exchange rates stable. In such an environment incentives exist for savings and investment.
- Public borrowing needs to be small in order to give the private sector better opportunities for obtaining investment funds.
- If necessary, intervention needs to be general and offer support to industries, rather than individual firms within them.
- There always needs to be an element of choice among various courses of action, as well as the flexibility to respond to crises and opportunities.
- If certain support (such as subsidies, tariffs or quotas) is offered, it should have a timetable, be transparent and be of limited duration, after which it has to be withdrawn.
- There needs to be a reference to investment in human capital. Well-trained labour and an educated management are the most valuable created assets that an economy can have. The policy needs to create a 'learning society' that supports and rewards the acquisition of new skills and promotes the flexibility needed for adapting to constant changes in the economy and technology.[41]
- Measures to ease the adjustment frictions are often a necessary element in an industrial policy. Emphasis needs to be on all industries (including traditional ones) that use modern technologies.
- A relatively easy international transfer of production from one location to another within a liberal trading system has to be borne in mind. National location-specific advantages (clusters and networks) for the production of specific goods and services need to be cultivated.
- The policy should not neglect the creation of SMEs, which form valuable links throughout the economy, not only with large firms, but also with producers and consumers.
- There needs to be a consensus among the major players (employers, employees and the government) in the economy about the global economic goals and means for their achievement. These players should also be committed to the achievement of the agreed goals. This implies that the long-term vision of the goals needs to be realistic.
- Innovation in general, and faster innovation than others, in particular, ought to be matched by education and training that would make the labour force able to exploit profitable new opportunities.
- Public support to R&D and innovation should increase the exchange of information among the interested parties.
- As private capital is generally uninterested in investment in certain types of infrastructure, the government needs to step into this field on its own and to stimulate public–private partnership.

Although industrial policy is wider than trade or competition policy, the boundaries between them are blurred. Whether an industrial policy increases national GDP compared with what would happen without it can be debated for a long time without a solution to satisfy everyone. A promising industrial policy should neither shield expanding industries from competition for an excessively long period of time nor prevent the attrition of declining industries for ever. It ought to facilitate the movements of factors from industries that employ obsolete technologies to industries that use modern technologies.

Industrial policy has to be well coordinated at all levels of government with other economic policies that affect the manufacturing and services sectors. Without successful communication, harmonisation and coordination, intervention in industry will be similar to the work of a brain-damaged octopus. This holds both for single countries and for schemes that integrate countries. None the less, traditional behaviour is sometimes hard to change in reality, even though the need for change is recognised. The EU has chosen the Single European Market and the eurozone as paths to create conditions for change according to market criteria of efficiency. It is up to the economic agents to take advantages of these opportunities.

Certain results from such a choice have begun to emerge. The industrial structure of the EU countries became more specialised from the early 1980s than was the case before. This confirms the theoretical expectations of both the standard, neo-classical and the new theory of economic integration. A new pattern of industrial production is emerging in the EU. The major features of this process of divergence in the economic structure of the EU(15) countries include the following (Midelfart-Knarvik et al., 2000, pp. 46–7):

- The process is slow and does not provoke great adjustment costs.
- There was a certain convergence among the geography of production in the EU countries towards the EU average during the 1970s, whereas since the early 1980s countries have tended to diverge from the EU average. This is a general sign of increased national specialisation in the EU. The most remarkable national change in the geography of production was the spread of relatively high-technology and high-skill industries to the EU peripheral countries (Ireland and Finland).
- Not all industries follow the same path as a reaction to economic integration. Some of them concentrate, while others spread (contrary to the expectations of neo-classical theory). Several forces, therefore, drive such changes in the structure of production. Strong functional intra-industry linkages (high share of intermediate goods from the same industry and/or the need for a large pool of highly skilled

labour and researchers) stimulate agglomeration. Weak functional linkages acts as an incentive to the spread of production.
- While 'economic integration' has made the US geography of industrial production more similar (less specialised) since the 1940s, integration in the EU had as its consequence growing disparity (increasing specialisation) in manufacturing production. This slow process in both regions shows no sign of abating. The unquestionable driving force for this is still not known.
- The slow change in the geography of production has not provoked major adjustment costs in the EU. If this continues, and if it is associated with production linkages and comparative advantages, there will be long-term benefits for everyone.
- Availability of highly skilled and educated workers and engineers is becoming an increasingly important determinant of industrial location.
- Agglomeration tendencies towards the central locations have become more pronounced for industries that use many intermediate inputs.
- High returns to scale are becoming weaker as centripetal (agglomeration) forces.

Notes

1. The EU has always conducted an industrial policy, but its intensity and the cover name was different: state aid, technical standards, company law, competition policy, Single European Market, trade protection, social policy and protection of the environment. In addition, the European Commission changed the name of its DG for Industrial Policy to Enterprise DG.
2. Lipsey (1993a, p. 21) first used the term 'massaged-market economies'.
3. 'Strategic' is not taken here to have any military sense, but rather refers to businesses that have important forward and backward links with other industries, as well as strong and positive externalities (spillovers) on the rest of the economy.
4. Abundant natural resources may often be a problem for a country, not a benefit. A discovery of resources attracts gamblers, opportunists and crooks such as Francisco Pizzaro (Latin America), Robert Clive (East India Company) or Cecil Rhodes (South Africa). These resources provoke or contribute to civil wars: Angola, Congo or Nigeria. Elsewhere, abundant oil reserves and exports as is the case in Saudi Arabia, Bahrain or Kuwait keep local wages too high to permit the local development of the manufacturing industry. Foreigners from less-well-off countries fill jobs in services in these countries. However, certain countries that are exceptionally poor in natural resources such as Switzerland, Austria or Japan are highly developed and among the wealthiest in the world. They base their prosperity on the most important resource: human capital.
5. There is a growing awareness that *most* external economies apply at a regional or metropolitan level, rather than at an international one. Therefore, the fear that external economies would be geographically dissipated abroad is mostly wrong (Krugman, 1993b, pp. 161, 167).
6. Firms also make mistakes and wrong choices. IBM, for example, misjudged the commercial worth of the haloid copying technology it was offered. This technology became the foundation of Xerox.

7. Services employed 69 per cent of the EU(15) labour force in 2001, while the shares of manufacturing and agriculture were 27 and 4 per cent, respectively (Eurostat, 2003).
8. Akio Morita, the chairman of Sony Corporation, argued that 'an economy can be only as strong as its manufacturing base. An economy that does not manufacture well cannot continue to invest adequately in itself. An economy whose only growth is in the service sector is built on sand. Certainly, the service sector is an important and growing economic force. But it cannot thrive on its own, serving hamburgers to itself and shifting money from one side to another. An advanced service economy can thrive only on the strength of an advanced manufacturing economy underlying it . . . The notion of a postindustrial economy that is based principally on services is a dubious one' (Morita, 1992, p. 79).
9. New technologies are less and less sector or industry specific. The same holds for modern firms. Many of them cannot be easily classified in a group of enterprises that belongs to only one industry or sector.
10. A common definition of an SME uses the number of employees as the determining factor. Small enterprises are taken to be those with up to 25 employees, while medium-sized ones have up to 250 workers.
11. European Commission (2003). *SMEs in Focus: Main Results from the 2002 Observatory of European SMEs*, Observatory of European SMEs 2002, p. 4.
12. Groups that lobby in Brussels include 400 trade associations, about 300 large firms, 150 non-profit pressure groups, 120 regional and local governments and 180 specialist law firms (*The Economist*, 15 April 1995, p. 26). Together, they have about 10 000 lobbyists, and their number has been steadily rising since the start of the Single Market Programme because of its implication for business (*European Voice*, 17 February 2000, p. 8). A very high concentration of lobby services in Washington, DC, made, in some cases, a collection of some (private) interests stronger than those of the government.
13. A lack of natural resources made Japan invest in the development of human and technological capital.
14. Airbus was established in 1970. It is a publicly sponsored consortium of British (British Aerospace, 20 per cent), French (Aérospatiale, 37.9 per cent), German (Deutsche Airbus, 37.9 per cent) and Spanish (CASA, 4.2 per cent) enterprises. It was established without the involvement of the EU and under the French law as a *Groupement d'Intérêt Economique*. The purpose of Airbus is to produce great aeroplanes, fight for orders and please clients well before thinking about dividends. The conception of this company is different from Boeing's. As such, Airbus makes no profits or losses in its own right. This means that the accounts of the group were available only to the four shareholders. Unlike Boeing's accounts, which are accessible to the public, Airbus's accounts were concealed from the public and the profit disguised in the accounts of its shareholders. It is, therefore, difficult to assess the commercial success of the best-known consortium in Europe. Why then does Boeing not pressure the US administration to do something about this? As about half of the value built into Airbuses is of US origin, the producers of these components have a strong lobbying power in Washington, DC, and could counter the potential actions of Boeing.

In 2001, 30 years after its creation, Airbus formally became a single integrated company, thus passing another major milestone in its history. The European Aeronautic Defence and Space Company (EADS) was the consequence of the merger between Aérospatiale Matra (France), Daimler Chrysler Aerospace (Germany) and Construcciones Aeronauticas (Spain) and BAE Systems (Britain). They all transferred their Airbus-related assets to the newly incorporated company and, in exchange, became shareholders in Airbus with 80 and 20 per cent, respectively, of the new stock.
15. One may think of wars with Korea, Vietnam, Iraq, Yugoslavia and Afghanistan.
16. The policy goal was to acquire the production of war materials. There was little concern about antitrust laws, international competitiveness or competing national objectives (Badaracco and Yoffie, 1983, p. 99). Governments have always affected industrial development through trade policy, public procurement, taxes and subsidies, as well as provision of public goods.

17. One has, however, to remember extreme cases which are not very numerous, but exist everywhere. The most highly paid people are not always highly educated. Many pop singers or sportspeople (often very poor speakers) have a poor education. However, one cluster of educated people that is being paid most are managers and lawyers (in the countries where law means something).
18. *Single Market News*, February 1996, p. 13.
19. *Bulletin Quotidien Europe*, 7 February 2003.
20. *Financial Times*, 29 and 30 October 2003.
21. *Financial Times*, 14 October 2003.
22. In the US, small, high-technology firms sell as much as half of their output to the federal government and benefit from R&D support. In contrast, public procurement in Europe is effected through a small number of large national suppliers. This suggests that fostering of a free entry and mobility within flexible industries may be a superior policy choice than supporting a few giants that react to changes with some delay (Geroski and Jacquemin, 1985, p. 177).
23. Nobody in the European Commission uses the term 'five-year plan'. That would remind many of the five-year plans in the former centrally planned economies of Eastern Europe.
24. The First Framework Programme (1984–87) disposed of a budget of €3.7 billion, the Second (1987–91) had a budget of €6.5 billion, the Third (1991–94) was allocated €8.8 billion, the Fourth (1994–88) received €13.1 billion, while the Fifth (1998–2002) had €14 billion.
25. FAST is a shared-cost programme involving a number of research and forecasting centres in the EU. It is an instrument for studying future developments, as well as the impact and social uses of science and technology.
26. *European Voice*, 13 November 2003, p. 15.
27. Software, aerospace, telecommunications, advance materials, semiconductors, biotechnology and defence technology.
28. Electronics and cars.
29. Lower-end mass market consumer goods.
30. Even a layperson would acknowledge that cows were created as herbivorous animals and should not be expected to eat meat products!
31. Good corporate governance is essential to avoid scandals and bankruptcies as their consequences always fall on the shoulders of the employed, shareholders and sometimes taxpayers.
32. Do you remember your first (or for that matter even your second or third) taxi ride from the airport in a Central or South European country as a foreigner? If you have not yet experienced this pleasure, be assured it is one you will remember. In particular the rate that you will pay.
33. *Financial Times*, 5 May 2003.
34. In spite of the liberty to offer transport services in other EU member countries, cabotage still represents a negligible part of the EU road transport market. In 2001, cabotage represented 0.7 per cent of total road freight transport. This issue and transport services are discussed in the chapter on transport policy (see Chapter 13).
35. The number of road traffic accidents per motor car or per inhabitant is different among countries. Hence, there is a variation in risk. Therefore, differences in insurance premiums among countries will remain in spite of increased competition.
36. 'As patriotism is the last refuge of scoundrels (according to Dr Johnson), the welfare of widows, orphans, and the incompetent is the last refuge of supporters of regulation. Individuals free to make their own decisions will indeed make mistakes. Even if potential buyers are clearly informed of the regulatory regime, some will not understand its significance. Even if large amounts of information are available on that significance, some will not bother to obtain it . . . Protection of the foolish against error provides a rationale for almost infinite extension' (Hindley, 1991, pp. 272–3).
37. Everyone may appreciate the benefits of a car such as a BMW or a Mercedes. It is quite another thing, however, whether consumers are willing to pay or have the means to pay for such a motor car. A small Fiat may be the ultimate limit for many of them.

38. *Financial Times*, 2 November 2003.
39. *Financial Times*, 10 March 2003.
40. Without the highest degree of coordination one would not be able to fly to the Moon and return safely to the Earth.
41. Education may be a subsidised input for which the business sector has not paid the full price. None the less, countervailing duties cannot be introduced by foreign partners as education often takes a long time and cannot be easily and directly valued as is the case with other subsidies, such as those for exports.

> I pray that in all respects you may prosper
> and be in good health,
> just as your soul prospers.
> 3 John 2

7 Trade Policy

1. Introduction

The Preamble to the Treaty of Rome states that the EU desires to contribute to the progressive abolition of restrictions on international trade by means of a common commercial policy. Internal trade in the EU would be free of all customs duties and quantitative restrictions and there will be a Common Commercial Policy (Article 3). The EU is ready to contribute to the harmonious development of international commerce and to lower barriers to trade (Article 131).

Probably the most important provision of the Treaty of Rome regarding trade is that the Common Commercial Policy is based on uniform principles, in particular regarding tariff rates and trade arrangements with third countries (Article 133).[1] In the case of economic difficulties, the European Commission may authorise the affected member state(s) to take the necessary protective measures (Article 134).[2] There are two other safeguard provisions in the treaty. Article 30 allows member states to prohibit or restrict trade or the transit of goods that jeopardise public morality, policy or security, or endanger the health or life of humans, animals or plants. There is also an agreement to associate the non-European countries that have special (read: ex-colonial) relations with the EU (Article 182).[3]

The associated countries would be given the same treatment in trade as the members of the EU (Article 183). The EU may conclude association agreements with a third country, group of countries or an international organisation (Articles 300 and 310). Article 95 refers to the establishment and operation of the internal market. Save for fiscal, free movement of persons and rights of employees, the earlier principle of unanimity is replaced by one of qualified majority in the decision-making process. The EU is also authorised to impose uniform sanctions against third countries (Article 301 and 60).[4]

This chapter includes not merely the external trade policy of the EU, but also general external economic relations with the exception of FDI, which is considered in the chapter on capital mobility (Chapter 9). This chapter is structured as follows. It starts with an outline of the basic theory of customs unions and preferential trading areas that are the origin of the theory of international economic integration (Section 2) and reasons for international economic integration (Section 3). Section 4 provides an overview of the role of the World Trade Organisation (WTO) in international trade. Non-tariff barriers (NTBs) are presented in Section 5. Section 6 provides a thorough examination of EU trade relations, with an overview of EU imports and exports followed by the presentation of trade issues with the principal trading partners: the US, EFTA, Central and Eastern European countries, Japan and the developing countries. The structure of preferred partners in trade is presented in Section 7 and Section 8 concludes. The EU has taken certain bold steps to liberalise trade with its foreign partners, but it also has the means (NTBs) to step back from such commitments when the internal or external economic situation is unfavourable.

2. Theory of customs unions[5]

INTRODUCTION

All types of international economic integration have always provoked interest because they both promote and restrict trade at the same time. Trade is liberalised, at least partly, among the participating countries, while it is also distorted with third countries as there are various barriers between the integrated group and the rest of the world. On these grounds the analysis of international economic integration including preferential trade agreements is delicate, complex and often speculative. It is a set of theoretical experiments that try to simplify and portray the economic process. However, this ought to be tested against evidence. A customs union is the type of integration that has received the most attention in research and is the most rigorously developed branch of the neo-classical theory of economic integration and preferential trading areas. This section is limited to an analysis of the essentials of the static and dynamic models of customs unions. Let us first discuss a few basic concepts.

TYPES

If trade is impeded by tariffs, quotas, NTBs and obstacles to factor mobility, then consumption in an integrated area is potentially higher than the sum of the consumption of individual countries which are potential partners for integration. International economic integration removes, at least partly, these and other distortions to trade, competition, investment and, possibly, factor mobility. In this sense, international economic integration between at least two countries can be of the following seven theoretical types:

- A *preferential tariff agreement* among countries assumes that the tariffs on trade among the signatory countries are lower in relation to tariffs charged on trade with third countries.
- A *partial customs union* is formed when the participating countries retain their initial tariffs on their mutual trade and introduce a common external tariff on trade with third countries.
- A *free trade area* is an agreement among countries about the elimination of all tariff and quantitative restrictions on mutual trade. Every country in this area retains its own tariff and other regulation of trade with third countries. The bases of this agreement are the rules of origin. These rules prevent trade deflection which is the import of a good from third countries into the area by country A (which has a relatively lower external tariff than the partner country B) in order to re-export the good to country B. None the less, production deflection is possible if the production of goods that contain imported inputs is shifted to countries that have lower tariffs if the difference in tariffs offsets the difference in production and trade costs.
- In a *customs union*, participating countries not only remove tariff and quantitative restrictions on their intra-group trade, but also introduce a common external tariff (CET) on trade with third countries. The participating countries take part in international negotiations about trade and tariffs as a single entity.

- In a *common market*, apart from a customs union, there exists free mobility of factors of production. Common regulations (restrictions) on the movement of factors with third countries are introduced.
- An *economic union* among countries assumes not only a common market, but also the harmonisation of fiscal, monetary, industrial, regional, transport and other economic policies.
- A *total economic union* among countries assumes union with a single economic policy and a supranational government (of this confederation) with great economic authority. There are no administrative barriers to the movements of goods, services and factors, hence prices are equalised net of transport costs.

Table 7.1 presents select theoretical types of international economic integration arrangements. The process of integration does not necessarily have to be gradual from one type to another. The establishment of any of these types depends on the agreement among the participating countries. Spontaneous or market integration is created by actions of transnational corporations (TNCs), banks and other financial institutions, often without the involvement of their parent governments, while formal or institutional integration seeks an official agreement among governments to eliminate select or all restrictions on trade and factor movements in their economic relations (Panić, 1988, pp. 6–7). There is substantial historical evidence to support the argument that the formal (*de jure*) approach to integration seeks a spontaneous (*de facto*) way, and vice versa. The decision about entering into a customs union or any other type of integration has always been political. The question to abandon part of national sovereignty

Table 7.1 Types of international economic integration

Policy action	Type				
	Free trade area	Customs union	Common market	Economic union	Total economic union
Removal of tariffs and quotas	Yes	Yes	Yes	Yes	Yes
Common external tariff	No	Yes	Yes	Yes	Yes
Factor mobility	No	No	Yes	Yes	Yes
Harmonisation of economic policies	No	No	No	Yes	Yes
Total unification of economic policies	No	No	No	No	Yes

regarding taxation of trade (all in a customs union, a part of that in a free trade area) is made by politicians. The EU was, after all, not established in 1957 in order to liberalise trade, but rather to exclude the possibility of war between France and Germany. Economic integration was just a means for the achievement of that political goal.

An interesting case occurred following the establishment of a free trade area between Canada and the US in 1988. There were moves to include Mexico in the North American Free Trade Agreement (NAFTA). If the US were to enter into a bilateral free trade deal with Mexico, and then conclude similar arrangements with other (Latin American) countries, that would create the hub-and-spoke model of integration (which was undesirable for Canada and other countries involved). The US, as the regional hub, would have a separate agreement with each spoke country. As such, the US would reap great advantages from negotiating individually with each partner country, as well as being the only country with a tariff-free access to the markets of all participants. This would further enhance the US locational advantages for foreign direct investment (FDI). Therefore, Canada decided to be involved in the free trade deal with Mexico in order to avoid the negative consequences of the hub-and-spoke model of integration.

The tariff system may discriminate between commodities and/or countries. *Commodity discrimination* takes place when different rates of import duty are charged on different commodities. *Country discrimination* is found when the same commodity is subject to different rates of duty on the basis of country of origin. Lipsey (1960, p. 496) defined the theory of customs unions as a branch of tariff theory which deals with the effect of geographically discriminatory changes in trade barriers. However, while this is true in the static sense, in a dynamic setting a customs union may be, among other things, a means for economic development.

The efficiency criterion used most often in economics is that of Pareto optimality. An allocation of resources is said to be Pareto optimal if no other feasible allocation exists in which some agents would be better off (in a welfare sense) and no agents worse off. By a judicious definition of welfare, the Pareto-optimal allocation is that allocation which best satisfies social objectives. Pareto optimality is achieved exclusively in the state of free trade and free factor mobility (the first-best solution), so that other states, in which there are distortions (tariffs, subsidies, taxes, monopolies, externalities, agglomerations, differentiated goods, minimum wages, local content requirements, to mention just a few), are suboptimal.

It is highly likely that the Pareto-optimal allocation cannot be achieved because of one or several distortions. Can a second-best position be attained by satisfying the remaining Pareto conditions? The theory of the second best answered in the negative (Lipsey and Lancaster, 1956–57). In the presence of distortions, if all the conditions for Pareto optimality cannot be satisfied, then the removal of some of the distortions does not necessarily increase welfare, nor does the addition of other distortions necessarily decrease it. One suboptimal situation is replaced by another suboptimal situation. Welfare may remain unaffected, increased or decreased.[6] This implies that there can be no reliable expectation about the welfare effect of a change in the current situation. The theory of the second best has a disastrous effect on welfare economics. However, Lipsey (1960) was not discouraged enough to be prevented from writing a seminal article on the theory of customs unions.

The intuition behind the neo-classical theory of customs unions is the proposition that the potential consumption of goods and services in a customs union is higher than the sum of the individual consumption of the potential member countries in the situation in which trade among these countries is distorted by tariffs and quotas. In this situation one should, at least partly, remove these impediments.

STATIC MODEL

Assumptions

A static model of the theory of customs unions considers the impact of the formation of a customs union on trade flows and consumption in the integrated countries. The classical (orthodox or static) theory of customs unions relies on a number of explicit and implicit assumptions. This model makes theoretical consideration easier, but it also simplifies reality to the extent that the policy recommendations should be considered with great care. None the less, many things can be learned from the consideration of extreme cases.

Assume that there are only three countries. Country A, a relatively small country in relation to the other two, forms a customs union with country B. Country C (which may represent all other countries in the world), is discriminated against by the customs union by means of a common external tariff. A relatively small number of states in this abstract model provides the possibility of a relatively higher analytical power in the model. Tariffs are levied on an *ad valorem* basis in all countries. Rates of tariffs are the same both for final commodities and for inputs, so that the rate of nominal protection equals the rate of effective protection. The assumption of equal rates of tariffs prior to integration removes the possible dispute about the initial level of the CET. Tariffs are the only instrument of trade policy and there are no NTBs. The price of imported goods for home consumers (P_{mt}) is composed of the price of an imported good (P_m) and tariff (t):

$$P_{mt} = (1 + t)P_m \qquad (7.1)$$

where $t = 0$. State intervention exists only at the border and trade is balanced. Free or perfect competition, exists in markets for goods, services and factors. Perfect competition (or complete equality of opportunity) exists in all economies, but for the existence of tariffs.

Production costs per unit of output are constant over all levels of output. To put it more formally, production functions are homogeneous of degree one, that is, to produce one more unit of good X, inputs must be increased by a constant proportion. Costs of production determine the retail prices of goods. Producers in an industry operate at the minimum efficient scale at the production possibility frontier. Countries embark upon the production of certain goods on the basis of the prices (relative abundance or scarcity) of home factors.

The theory of customs unions refers to the manufacturing sector: a fixed quantity of factors of production is fully employed. There are no industry-specific factors such as special human and physical capital, entrepreneurship and the like. In a dynamic model these specific factors can be transformed in the medium and long runs, but this would require adjustment costs which are ruled out in the static model. Mobility of factors is perfect within their home country, while commodities are perfectly mobile between the integrated countries. This means that TNCs are ignored. There are no trade costs (transport, storage, insurance and banking).

All countries have access to the same technology and differ only in their factor endowments. Economies are static with constant expectations. This is to say that rates of growth, technologies, tastes, and propensities to consume, save, import and invest, are given and unchangeable. There are no new goods, no innovation and no depreciation of the capital stock. All goods and services are homogeneous, that is, consumers do not have a preference for the consumption of goods and services from any particular supplier. They decide upon their purchases exclusively on the basis of differences in price. All goods and services have unit income elasticities of demand, that is, every increase or decrease in income has a proportional change in demand for all goods and services in the same direction. This means that demand is 'well behaved'. Non-tradable commodities do not exist. There is no intra-industry trade or 'cross-hauling', that is, a country cannot both export and import identical goods or close substitutes. There are no inventories. All markets clear simultaneously. Such equilibrium must be both sustainable and feasible, that is, firms can neither profitably undercut market price nor make losses.

In this model there is no uncertainty. Firms and resource owners are perfectly informed about all markets while consumers are fully familiar with goods and services. This assumption was relevant in the past, but the existence of the Internet put the economies close to a situation of full, timely and perfect information. Fiscal (taxes and subsidies) and monetary (rates of exchange, interest, inflation and balance of payments) operations are ruled out. Finally, a country that is not included in a customs union is assumed not to retaliate against the integrated countries.

The above assumptions are highly restrictive. However, they greatly simplify the analysis so that the essential properties of the model can be understood without too much effort. A simple story told within this model does not necessarily mean that it is a naive story. The objective of the following analysis is to make a point, rather than to be realistic.

Partial Equilibrium Model

International trade comes as a response to causes that are based on national differences in the following essentials:

- factor endowments (factor proportions);
- demand (size, sophistication and fickleness);
- home market effect;[7]
- production functions (technology and efficiency);
- economies of scale;
- growth rates and increase in income;
- income distribution;[8]
- market structure and competition;
- production and factor taxes;
- rates of exchange;
- change in tastes;
- agglomeration and clustering of production;
- trade costs; and
- demographic factors.[9]

These basic reasons for trade are tackled in economic theory in several ways, but the principal models are two: the classical (or neo-classical) and the new (strategic) theory of trade. The basic features of these two models are briefly outlined in Table 7.2.

The partial equilibrium model of trade deals with the market for a single good. Suppose that three countries produce the same commodity, but with varying levels of efficiency: their production functions differ. This model, is described in Table 7.3. Country C has the lowest unit cost of production,

Table 7.2 Trade theory models

Aspect	Classical trade theory	New (strategic) trade theory
Assumptions	Given factor endowments Technology given No entry barriers Static model Trade based on costs, i.e. supply potentials Considers trade in goods Factors are mobile within a country, but not between countries There are no trade costs Theoretical ideas: sound, clear and straightforward	Economies of scale High fixed costs (entry and exit barriers) Innovation in production, organisation and control Technology constantly changing Trade is based on demand, i.e. 'love of variety' Intellectual property Dynamic and evolutionary model Accumulation and upgrading of factors which magnify output potential (cumulative causation) Path dependence and non-ergodicity Considers trade in goods and services Both national and international mobility of factors are constrained The target of the theory is moving (nature of production and trade changes fast because of multiple equilibria) Existence of trade cost Theoretical ideas: an incomplete and unsystematic collection of various ideas and common themes that discount the weight of tariffs and trade creation and trade diversion effects
Trade barriers	Transparent Tariffs and quotas	Non-transparent Standards and their implementation Customs and administrative procedures Government intervention: NTBs, public procurement, taxes, subsidies, public monopolies, local content rules, etc.

Table 7.2 (continued)

Aspect	Classical trade theory	New (strategic) trade theory
Specialisation	Absolute advantages Comparative advantages Homogeneous goods	Man-made comparative advantages (periodically short-lived) Goods and services are differentiated Widening in varieties of goods and services High-quality goods with after-sales service Clusters and agglomerations
Competition	Perfect Many small suppliers First-best situation Prices	Imperfect A select number of suppliers that may influence prices within their (narrow) market niche Second-best situation Price and non-price
Trade policy	Liberal Exceptionally 'infant industry' protection	Interventionist, but selective and (presumably) diminishing over time
Trade pattern	Inter-industry Highly specialised Set of traded goods is both complete and fixed	Intra-industry Not totally specialised (full specialisation is only within a given and narrow product niche) Trade pattern in developed countries is as wide as ever
Adjustment costs	In theory: none (all markets clear at once) In practice: significant	Weak if related to product differentiation and changes in varieties within the same commodity group Significant if related to economies of scale, innovation, launching of an utterly new production or a cluster
Welfare effect of trade	Favourable for all participants Higher steady state comes instantly	Highly uncertain Some may gain a lot, others may lose a lot Always changing Higher steady state comes after unpredictably long time

Table 7.3 Unit cost of production of a commodity in euros

Country	A	B	C
Unit cost of production	60	50	35

hence this country will become the world supplier of this commodity in the free trade situation. Suppose now, that country A wants to protect its inefficient domestic producers from foreign competition for whatever reason. Tariffs are an available means of protection which have distortionary effects.[10] The most important effect is that they move the country away from free trade towards autarky. Gains from specialisation are sacrificed because resources are diverted away from the pattern of comparative advantage. In addition to reducing potential consumption, tariffs redistribute income in favour of factors which are used in production in the protected industry and decrease the possibility of their more efficient employment elsewhere in the economy. If country A wants to protect its home production of this good it must levy a tariff. This tariff of, for example, 100 per cent, not only increases the price of the imported commodity to country A's consumers, but more importantly, it shifts consumption away from imports towards country A's domestic production. In these circumstances, country A could increase domestic consumption of this good if it enters into a customs union with either of the countries in this model. Table 7.4 presents prices of the imported commodity with the tariff on country A's market.

If country A forms a customs union with country B, then consumers in country A could import the good from country B at a cost of €50 per unit, rather than buy it from domestic suppliers at the cost of €60 as before. Hence, they are better off than with a non-discriminatory tariff. If country A creates a customs union with country C, then country A's consumers are in an even better position compared to a customs union with country B. Now, they purchase the good at a unit price of €35. In both cases, consumers in country A are better off than in the situation in which they were buying the domestically produced good. The final effect in both cases is welfare-increasing trade creation as the cost of trade is reduced.

The formation of a customs union encourages *trade creation* as the result of a shift from a dearer to a cheaper source of supply. Other things being equal, this is a potential move towards free trade because a less efficient protected domestic supplier is replaced by a more efficient foreign one. Country A gives up the production of a good in which it has a comparative disadvantage in order to acquire it more cheaply by importing it from a partner country, so trade is created. This welfare-improving effect

Table 7.4 *Price of an imported commodity in euros with the tariff in country A*

Import duty (%)	Price of a commodity from	
	Country B	Country C
100	100	70
50	75	52.5

depends crucially on the assumption that the freed domestic resources can find alternative employment elsewhere in the economy. If in addition to trade creation 'internal' to the customs union there appears an increase in imports from third countries ('external' to the customs union) due to increased growth, as was the case in the EU, the situation is described as *double* trade creation.

Suppose now that prior to the formation of the customs union, the duty on imports was 50 per cent in country A. Table 7.4 shows that in this case the supplier of country A would be country C. Country A's domestic industry offers this good at a unit price of €60, country B at a price of €75, while country C is the cheapest source of supply at €52.5. If, instead, country A enters into a customs union with country B and if the CET for the commodity in question is 50 per cent, then country A would purchase this good from country B. In this case country A pays €50 per unit to country B, while at the same time, a unit of the good from country C costs €52.5. The outcome in this case is *trade diversion*.

Trade diversion works in the opposite way from trade creation. The cheapest foreign supplier is changed in favour of a relatively dearer customs union partner. Due to the CET, business is taken away from the most efficient world producer and production and trade in this commodity are reduced. This creates a global welfare loss. Trade within a customs union takes place at a protected (higher) level of prices. A higher union level of prices relative to the international one brings benefits to internal exporters. Importers lose as they pay the partner country suppliers a higher price per unit of import and their country forgoes tariff revenue which is not levied on intra-union imports. Trade creation and trade diversion are often called 'Vinerian effects' after Jacob Viner (1950), who first introduced the terms and provoked discussion and research into the issues of customs unions and international economic integration.

The net static welfare effect on the world depends on which of the two Vinerian effects dominates. It may be positive, negative or neutral. There is no a priori general statement about the final effect. The second-best nature of preferential trading and creation of customs unions make it hard to gauge the final welfare effect. Some consider regional preferential trading to be stepping stones (building blocks) towards universal free trade, while others worry that they embody stumbling blocks on the same route. Hence, the favourable attitude of the General Agreement on Tariffs and Trade (GATT) (Article XXIV) towards customs unions and free trade areas as trade liberalising moves cannot be accepted without reservation.

The principal economic policies in the EU such as the Common Commercial Policy (customs union) or the Common Agricultural Policy (CAP) are mostly shaped according to the interests of the domestic producers. The interests of consumers are largely neglected. Hence, the possibility of a potentially trade-diverting bias in the EU should not come as a surprise. None the less, the mounting role of the European Parliament in the EU structure may increase the influence of consumers in the EU decision-making structure.

Trade diversion may be more beneficial than trade creation for the consumption in country A, which gives preferential treatment to select suppliers. This is because country A does not sacrifice home production. The source of benefits is anticipated trade creation since, by assumption, bilateral trade flows must balance. The comparison here is between trade creation and the autarkic volume of domestic production. An integrating country will not benefit from trade creation unless it increases its exports to the partners (as compared to the pre-union level) which from a partner's point of view can represent trade diversion (Robson, 1987, p. 52).

Suppose that country A and country B form a customs union and that trade flows among countries A, B and C have the following patterns:

- If country A alone produces this good, but does so inefficiently, then the choice between domestic production and imports from country C depends on the level of the CET.
- If both countries in the customs union produce the good, but inefficiently, then the least inefficient country will supply the customs union market subject to the protection of the common external tariff.
- If neither country in the customs union produces the good, then there is no trade diversion. The cheapest foreign supplier supplies the customs union.
- If only one country in the customs union produces the good in question, but in the most efficient way, then this country will supply the market even without a common external trade protection.

By offering a joint level of protection, the CET may promote a more efficient allocation of resources within the customs union.

The influence of international economic integration on trade flows is illustrated here by two examples. When Britain joined the EU in 1973, the share of its imports from other EU partner countries significantly increased over a decade. Trade between Mexico and the US doubled over the five years that preceded the creation of NAFTA in 1994. Even the announcement and preliminary negotiations about a serious integration deal had a positive impact on the volume and direction of trade (and investment) in the region.

Patterns of consumption change following the creation of a customs union. *Inter-country substitution* occurs when one country replaces the other as the source of supply for some good. *Inter-commodity substitution* occurs when one commodity is substituted, at least at the margin, for another one as a result of a shift in relative prices (Lipsey, 1960, p. 504). The latter occurs, for example, when country A imports from the customs union partner country B relatively cheaper veal which replaces at least some of the pork produced in country A and at least some of the chicken which is imported from country C, and when consumers in a customs union replace a part of demand for theatre and opera by relatively 'cheaper' stereo, video and other entertainment equipment.

Figure 7.1 illustrates the effects of a tariff and a customs union on economic efficiency for a single good in country A's market. SS represents country A's domestic supply curve, similarly, DD shows the domestic demand curve. Country B's supply curve is BB, while country C's supply curve for the same good is CC. Both foreign countries can supply unconditionally any quantity of the demanded good at fixed prices. Both foreign supply curves are flat (perfectly elastic). This is a consequence of the smallness of the country in our example. This country cannot exert influence on its terms of trade, but in a customs union with other countries this is likely to change. Prior to the imposition of a tariff, at price 0C home demand for the good is $0Q_6$. Domestic producers supply $0Q_1$ while country C supplies Q_1Q_6.

Suppose that country A introduces a tariff on imports such that the price for domestic consumers is 0T. Now, country A can expand domestic production from $0Q_1$ to $0Q_3$ and curtail home consumption of the good from $0Q_6$ to $0Q_4$. The government collects tariff revenue equal to $CT \times Q_3Q_4$.

Let us assume that country A, which imposed a non-discriminatory *ad valorem* tariff on imports, enters into a customs union with country B. The price of imports from country C with a CET of CT is 0T. Country B will supply country A's market. Country A's inefficient production contracts from $0Q_3$ to $0Q_2$ while consumption increases from $0Q_4$ to $0Q_5$. *Trade expansion* due to the creation of the customs union equals the sum of the reduction in home production Q_2Q_3 and the increase in home consumption Q_4Q_5. Country A's government does not earn any tariff proceeds from imports of the good from the customs union partner, country B. Trade

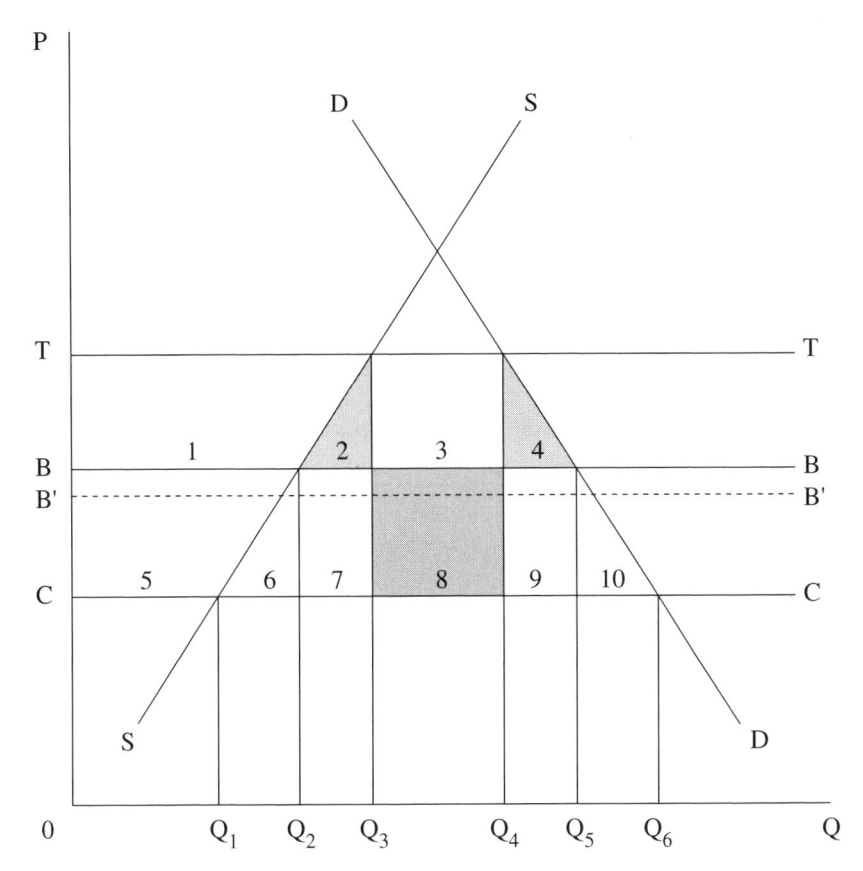

Figure 7.1 Effect of a tariff and customs union on production and consumption in country A

expansion inevitably effects rationalisation in production. This takes place through an improved deployment of existing factors, increased size of production units (reallocation of resources within sectors). One of the responses of firms in the EU to the Single Market Programme was a big wave of mergers and acquisitions around the year 1990. The consequences of these rationalisations are in theory decreased unit costs of goods and services, as well as increased standards of living on average.

Trade expansion effects, however, should not be overemphasised. The downward adjustment of domestic tariffs to the CET need not result in an increased trade expansion effect in a customs union. This alignment will first lead to a reduction to 'normal' levels of the profit margins of the protected domestic producers. If there is excess capacity in the protected industries, a possible increase in the domestic demand which comes as a consequence of the fall in price will be met first by the country's own production (if it exists), rather than through imports. Thus the trade expansion effects due to the creation of a customs union will not be as large as would be suggested by the difference in tariffs before the creation of a customs union and after it. Therefore, the scope for trade diversion is, indeed, smaller than it may first appear. It is simply the potential for an expansion in trade and competition that does this good work for consumers, as well as producers, in the long term.

Consumers' surplus is defined as the difference between the consumers' total valuation of the goods consumed and the total cost of obtaining them. It is represented by the area under the demand curve and above the price that consumers face. Any decrease in price, other things being equal, increases consumers' surplus. Country A's consumers benefit when their country enters into a customs union with country B in relation to the situation with an initial non-discriminatory tariff. Their gain is given by the area $1 + 2 + 3 + 4$ in Figure 7.1. These consumers are, however, worse off in comparison to the free trade situation in which country C is the supplier. This loss is given by the area $5 + 6 + 7 + 8 + 9 + 10$. Domestic producers lose a part of their surplus in a customs union compared to the situation with a non-discriminatory *ad valorem* tariff (area above SS up to the price 0B which they receive). This is represented by area 1. From the national standpoint, area 1 nets out as part of both the consumers' gain and the producers' loss. Country A loses tariff revenue (area 3) which it collected in the initial situation. Hence, the net gain for country A is area $2 + 4$.

The formation of a customs union has increased trade and consumption in country A in comparison to the initial situation with a non-discriminatory tariff. In the situation prior to the formation of a customs union, country A imports the good from country C, pays for it an amount equal to $Q_3Q_4 \times 0C$ and collects revenue equal to the area $3 + 8$. After the formation of a customs union, area 3 is returned to consumers in the form of lower prices for the good, while area 8 represents a higher price charged by the customs union partner country. The return of area 3 to the consumers may be regarded as Hicksian compensation. When tariffs change, compensation is seldom paid. Hence, demand curve DD may be regarded simply as an approximation to the compensated Hicksian demand curve. It is important to note that country A pays, for the same amount of imports Q_3Q_4, a higher price to the customs union partner ($Q_3Q_4 \times 0B$) than was paid to the country C suppliers prior to the customs union formation. The country has a greater outflow of foreign exchange and does not collect revenue which it had done when it had imposed a non-discriminatory tariff on imports from country C. The outflow of foreign exchange from country A was equal to

$Q_3Q_4 \times 0C$, while area 3 + 4 illustrates the transfer from consumers to producers within the home country.

The net welfare effect of the creation of a customs union in country A depends on the relative size of the Vinerian effects; trade creation (area 2 + 4) minus trade diversion (area 8). Instead of a *revenue-generating* obstacle to trade (tariff) a government may introduce *cost-increasing* barriers (various technical standards and tests) whose effect may be a reduction in trade. (Let the effect of the NTBs be BT in trade with country B.) If the set of NTBs is removed, the effect on domestic consumers and producers would be the same as in the situation when the tariff was removed. The government, which has never earned direct revenue from the set of non-tariff regulations, would lose nothing. The social gain from reducing these barriers is area 2 + 3 + 4. This internal market opening took place in the EU under the name the Single Market Programme.

If one introduces dynamics into this model, in the form of increasing returns to scale, country B, as the customs union supplier of the good, faces an increased demand. Production would become more efficient and the price might fall from 0B to 0B'. This enhances trade creation and decreases the size of the trade diversion effect.

Figure 7.1 belongs to the family of standard microeconomic partial-equilibrium analytical tools. Unfortunately, they all deal with only a part of the business cycle, that is, with the first third of the cycle when demand rises. Other cases, such as stagnation or reduction in demand, are seldom considered.

Protection

The choice by country A to protect its industry may be questioned from the outset. There are at least two good reasons to object to trade restrictions in the medium and long terms in particular in the developed countries:

- First, new barriers to trade can provoke retaliation from foreign countries where domestic exporters already have an interest or intend to penetrate.[11]
- Second, and more subtle, if intermediate goods exist, all trade barriers raise the price of imported inputs. Therefore, they act as a tax on exports.[12] With the tariff, country A employs more resources in an industry in which it does not have a comparative advantage (although it may develop it).

Bearing in mind the assumption that the amount of resources is fixed and stepping out shortly from the partial equilibrium model, the fact is that resources are diverted away from business activities in which this country may have a comparative advantage. If a home industry is not competitive, a tariff may save jobs in this business in the short term. This may, however, lead to reduced activity in other home industries. If the uncompetitively produced home good is an input in other industries, their export performance may be at risk and investment reduced. The overall end result is increased unemployment and a lower standard of living in the longer term.

Policy makers can easily identify jobs that are saved by various forms of protection, but do not easily recognise the adverse consequences of this protection, hence the need for a general equilibrium model. Through protection in the long term, resources are wasted on inefficient production. Everybody loses except the government (because of increased revenues) and the protected industry in the short term. The problem in the short run is that the general equilibrium consequences of a given policy cannot be easily quantified. This policy of import substitution as opposed to a policy of export promotion and openness may be substantiated only on the grounds that foreign markets for country A's exports are closed.

The national security argument for tariffs can also be questioned. Trade-affected industries lobby for protection. This plea does not take into account the fact that industrial decline rarely, if ever, implies the actual demise of an industry. Possible nuclear warfare, long-range cruise missiles and 'smart' bombs remove a part of the classical national security argument for protection. Risk-averse governments may consider stockpiling and/or guaranteeing supplies of goods and services from allies before imposing a tariff (Tyson and Zysman, 1987a, p. 41). Apart from security of supply, there are other reasons why a country may wish to preserve at least part of (a declining) domestic industry which is exposed to international competition. The opportunities for domestic production increase bargaining power in negotiations about the long-term supply contracts with foreigners. In addition, if the cost situation changes in the future, some domestic research and development (R&D), as well as production capacity, may be a good starting point for regaining competitiveness.

The infant industry and similar arguments of learning by doing for protection state that entrants to an industry suffer losses while they acquire know-how, suppliers, customers, trained labour and the like in the period of infancy, so they need protection. It takes time for a firm to become profitable. Everybody knows that. If bankers, investors and entrepreneurs are not prepared to accept short-term losses as their investment towards long-term gains without government intervention, this is a clear indication that the market does not consider the enterprise to be viable, and so does not deserve tariff protection.

A free trader would argue that every firm profitable by market criteria does not need to be protected. If the infant industry argument is to make sense, then there must be some evidence of market failure, either in capital markets (entrepreneurs cannot obtain adequate loans), or labour markets (such as inadequate training or fluctuations in the labour force) or some evidence that the production structure warrants protection. For example, increasing returns to scale or other positive externalities that require a certain level of protection during the initial, but limited time period. These market failures may be corrected by economic policy (intervention). However, there are many old infants. What starts as an infant industry argument for protection turns into an employment protection argument. Finally, old infants are often nationalised at continuous cost to the taxpayers (Brander, 1987, p. 19). If a government bails out a declining industry and/or firm and creates a precedent, this produces expectations that the cost of poor business management will be socialised. This may be one of the main sources of the adjustment difficulties in the 'problem' industries in the developed countries.

Is There a Superior Policy to the Creation of a Customs Union?

One ought to ask always whether there are superior alternative policies for a country to the creation of a customs union. Unilateral, non-discriminatory reductions in import tariffs may look to be a better policy than the formation of a customs union. It seems preferable to obtain exclusively trade creation as a result of unilateral tariff reductions, than to create a customs union which causes both trade creation and trade diversion (Cooper and Massel, 1965, pp. 745–6). Such an argument cannot be accepted without serious reservations. A customs union offers something which is not offered by a unilateral reduction in tariffs. That is, an elimination of tariffs in customs union partner countries. A unilateral reduction in tariffs exaggerates the price reduction effects on consumption, while it eliminates the possibility of penetration into the markets of customs union partners.

The necessity of tariff bargaining with foreigners, so important to domestic exporters, was left out of the picture in the earlier analysis. In addition, various barriers to trade with the non-union member countries were neglected (for example, transport costs). If such barriers are present, then a redirection of trade towards customs union partners may not introduce (large extra) costs. On the contrary, it may bring certain savings in the form of lowered transport charges. Hence, this model questions, from an efficiency viewpoint, the desirability of a wide preferential-trading system such as the old British Commonwealth, where transport costs downgraded the commercial opportunities that were offered by preferential trade. Given the elimination of tariffs in the markets of customs union among partner countries and reduction in obstacles to trade such as transport costs, the gains that come from the non-preferential unilateral tariff reduction need not be greater than the beneficial effects that arise from the creation of a customs union (Wonnacott and Wonnacott, 1981). Reciprocal deals draw in obligations of several countries, hence they may have greater standing than mere unilateral concessions.

Bilateral trade deals can offer returns that might not be realistically expected through multilateral negotiations. In the case of free trade deal between Canada and the US, these gains include (Lipsey and Smith, 1989, pp. 319–21):

- the complete elimination of tariffs on goods that meet the stipulated rules of origin;
- a number of NTBs are eliminated, while the use of the rest is seriously restricted;
- most commercial services are covered by the agreement;
- a number of specific trade disputes were settled;
- there is a liberal and stable bilateral FDI regime;
- any US legislation that concerns Canada must be discussed bilaterally before it is passed; and
- if there is a dispute, the complaining country may elect to use either the GATT/WTO or the bilateral mechanism.

The likelihood that Canada would obtain such pathbreaking and powerful trade-liberalising measures through multilateral negotiations in the foreseeable future is very slim. Therefore, this bilateral deal was chosen as a much faster path to achieve this goal.

In spite of trade diversion costs of a customs union, the terms of trade of member countries might turn in their favour, so that, on balance, each member country may be better off than in the unilateral tariff reduction case. The classical approach to the theory of tariffs is mistaken. This approach, on the one hand, finds gains in the replacement of domestic goods for cheaper foreign goods, while on the other hand, the expansion of domestic exports does not bring gains in this model to the exporting country (except possible improvement of the terms of trade), but rather to the foreigners (Johnson, 1973, p. 80).

Suppose that transfer payments between countries are allowed for. Then any customs union (or preferential trading area) is potentially favourable for all countries considering participation, since they can be compensated for losses when they join. This means that customs union among countries can be extended to $n+1$ countries. By expansion, this implies that there is an incentive to extend the customs union until the whole world is included, until free trade prevails throughout the world. Preferential trade blocs can be constructed in such a way that welfare of the outside countries is unaffected (Kemp and Wan, 1976). For example, a 'deeper' integration within the EU caused 'wider' integration in Europe. A market deepening, Single Market Programme triggered membership requests from European countries that were previously happy to be outside the EU. Once a group enlarges, the cost to non-members of staying out of the club may increase. Hence, there is a domino effect (Baldwin, 1995a, p. 46). If there are no entry costs and no strong political objectives, this process may lead to universal free trade.

While Viner questioned the overall welfare effects of the creation of a customs union, Kemp and Wan seem to bring back the pre-Viner perception that customs unions are always welfare-improving devices. The Kemp–Wan smooth scenario, perhaps among the most elegant reasoning in international economics, is often interpreted in a way that relates to two post-integration elements: the level of tariffs and the volume of trade with outsiders. If both are unaffected by integration, or better, if these tariffs are in the post-integration period at a lower level, while trade and investment with outsiders increase, it is supposed that integration was globally beneficial and welcome. While such interpretations may make certain sense in the short run, if one wants to get a fuller picture about welfare effects, then one must consider changes in terms of trade between the customs union and the non-members.

The general Kemp–Wan argument hinges on the supposition that the integrated countries are open and that they welcome new entrants, and also rests on the absence of political obstacles to integration. The possibility either of blocking any new enlargement or making the entry costs excessive (without full, direct or indirect compensation) puts this neat scenario into question.

Incentives to join a free trade agreement exist even without compensatory transfers among the participating countries. The reason is that the group may turn its terms of trade with the rest of the world towards own advantage (against the non-members). Third countries may face shrinking markets, hence their domestic producers lobby to join the group. As the group enlarges, this provides inducements to others to join. The bigger the group becomes, the stronger the influence it may exert on its terms of trade with the rest of the world. In theory, the group enlarges until it covers the whole world.

Such reasoning may lead to the classical pre-Viner proposition that a customs union is a step towards free trade. This conclusion depends on the existence of inter-country transfers within the customs union. This is a severe restriction and the greatest weakness of this approach. The more countries there are in a customs union, the greater will be the potential demand and need for compensation. If compensation schemes are adopted in reality, they are often the products of political bargaining, not purely the outcome of the economic impact of integration. These schemes are too complicated and they never compensate in full (compensation schemes are never perfect) which limits the actual size of a customs union. This leads to the conclusion that non-economic reasons play a prominent role in economic integration. The experience of the EU, its creation and enlargements illustrate that political considerations play a major role in integration.

General Equilibrium Model

A partial equilibrium model considers the market for a single good. It assumes that all prices other than that of the good in question are fixed. A general equilibrium model considers all markets. All prices are variable and competitive equilibrium requires that all markets clear. All markets are connected by a chain of inputs and substitutes, information, technology, mobility of factors and goods, income (if one spends more on something, less will remain for other things) and so on.

Consideration of the general equilibrium model will start with the 3×2 model. In this case there are three countries, A, B and C, as well as two goods (markets) X and Y, respectively. Lipsey (1957 and 1960) was the first to study these cases in a customs union framework. The model included full specialisation and constant costs. A small country A imports good X from country C which is the foreign supplier with the lowest price.

Consider a case illustrated in Figure 7.2, where substitution in consumption is allowed for by smooth and convex indifference curves. There are three countries, A, B and C, and two goods, X and Y, respectively. In the free trade case, country A trades with country C and achieves indifference curve II. Suppose now that country A introduces a non-discriminatory tariff on imports. The relative price in country A is now AT.

Suppose that this tariff does not give enough incentive to home entrepreneurs to embark upon production of good X. Country A achieves the indifference curve I_1I_1 with equilibrium at point G. If the government either returns all tariff proceeds to consumers or spends the entire amount in the same fashion as the consumers would have otherwise done, then the equilibrium should be on line AC (as country C is the best foreign supplier). The equilibrium point is at point K, which is the point where the line T_2 (parallel to AT which illustrates compensation of consumers) intersects with terms of trade line AC. The extent of the rightward shift in the terms of trade line depends on how much people are willing to import at these prices and, hence, the volume of tariff revenue to be returned to them. T_2 is deliberately drawn in such a way that K and L lie on the same indifference curve. The tariff has changed the structure of production and relative prices. Consumption of the home good increases, while imports and exports decrease.

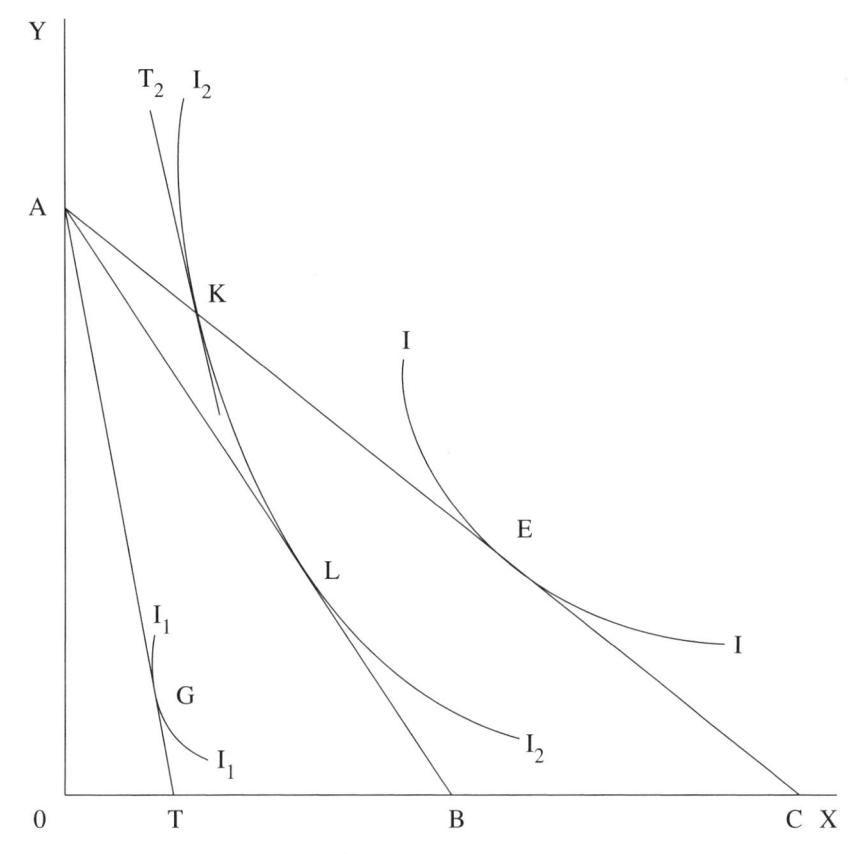

Figure 7.2 Welfare in a trade-diverting customs union

Suppose that country A forms a trade-diverting customs union with country B. The terms of trade line with country B is illustrated by line AB. Suppose that K and L lie on the same indifference curve I$_2$I$_2$. The formation of a customs union has not changed country A's welfare, although the structure of consumption has changed. If the best situation is at point E, then the formation of a customs union for country A is a move from one suboptimal position K, to another suboptimal position L. Country A is indifferent. If country A obtains in a customs union terms of trade which are worse than 0B/0A, then country A is worse off than in the situation with a non-discriminatory tariff. If country A, however, obtains terms of trade which are better than 0B/0A, then a trade-diverting customs union can be welfare improving for this country. Hence, the classical statement that trade diversion is always a bad thing is rejected.

DYNAMIC MODEL

Introduction

The classical theory of customs unions assumed that the static effects of resource reallocation occurred in a timeless framework. If one wants to move the theory of customs unions towards reality one must consider dynamic, that is, restructuring, effects. Many accept the proposition that markets are imperfect and that there are externalities such as economies of scale and product differentiation that make competition imperfect. When market structure is like this, regionalism/integration can be justified, as markets may be extended, deepened and secured, and because the market power of individual firms may be reduced. This may have a positive impact on competition, productivity, innovation and a reduction in prices.

Instead of considering only the possibility of trade in commodities, dynamic models analyse the possibility of resource allocation across time. The static effects of international economic integration have their most obvious and profound influence in the period immediately following the creation of, for example, a customs union.[13] Gradually, after some years of adjustment, the dynamic effects will increase in importance and become dominant. These dynamic influences, which also include accumulation effects, push further technological constraints and provide the group with an additional integration-induced 'growth bonus'.

Trade flows do not remain constant. In fact, they evolve and alter over time. Changes in the equilibrium points in, for example, Figure 7.1 are described as instantaneous. Such shifts in equilibrium points, however, may not always be possible. Delays in reaction on the part of countries and consumers in a customs union could be caused by their recourse to stocks. Hence, they do not immediately need to purchase those goods whose price has decreased as a consequence of the formation of a customs union. They also may have some contractual commitments that cannot be abandoned overnight. Finally, buyers may not be aware of all the changes. Up to the 19th century, state intervention was negligible, but markets remained disconnected because of imperfect information and relatively high transport costs. The Internet has, however, eliminated the constraint of the lack of timely information. A time lapse between the implementation of a policy change (the creation of a customs union) and its favourable effects may include an initial period of economic deterioration in certain industries which may be followed by improvements due to the J-curve effect.

Consideration of dynamic, that is, restructuring effects is limited here to economies of scale, specialisation and the terms of trade. The impact of opening up markets on increased competition was covered in the chapter on competition policy, (see Chapter 5).

Specialisation and Returns to Scale

Returns to scale refer to the relation between input requirements and output response with its impact on costs. Economies of scale comprise a number of things, from simple technical scale, to phenomena such as processing complex information; direction, control and improvement of independent activities; and experience. If a firm's output increases in the same proportion as its inputs, then that firm's technology exhibits constant returns to scale, or, one may say, a firm has constant marginal costs. If a firm's output increases by a greater proportion than inputs, then this firm's technology has increasing returns to scale or it enjoys decreasing marginal costs (or increasing marginal product).[14] If a firm's output decreases by a smaller proportion than input requirements, then the firm suffers from decreasing returns to scale or increasing marginal costs.

Suppose that a firm uses a set of inputs X in the production of a good Y. Constant, increasing and decreasing returns to scale may be defined for homogeneous production functions. A function is homogeneous of degree k if:

$$f(tx_1, tx_2) = t^k f(x_1, x_2) \tag{7.2}$$

$t > 0$ and k is constant. If the set of inputs X is increased by t, output is increased by t^k: $k = 1$ implying constant returns to scale; $k > 1$ increasing returns to scale; and $0 < k < 1$ results in decreasing returns to scale.

The pure theory of international trade is concerned mostly with perfect competition. In a situation in which the minimum efficient scale is relatively large, only a few firms can survive simultaneously. Competition in such markets is not perfect. When internal markets are enlarged by international economic integration or opened up by market-deepening projects such as the EU's Single Market Programme which increase competition, firms might expand their production and specialise in order to achieve lower production costs per unit of output (economies of scale).

The existence of internal NTBs was in many cases the cause of unexploited economies of scale in the EU. An empirical study of potential economies of scale in the EU industry reported that in more than half of all manufacturing industries, 20 firms of efficient size could co-exist in the EU, whereas the largest national markets can support only four each. The EU internal market offers the potential for efficiency and competition. Twenty efficient firms are more likely to ensure effective competition than only four firms (Emerson et al., 1988, p. 18). This finding ignored the logic behind the role of concentration in modern industries and the contribution which a few oligopolies, exploiting economies of scale and carefully monitored by appropriate regulatory authorities, can and do make to economic welfare. Besides, there may be fierce competition even among these four firms. Just take a look at competition in the EU and US long-distance telephone-call business or the fierce competition among a few Japanese electronic conglomerates both in the domestic and international markets. In addition, relatively high diversity of tastes in EU countries can make the achievement of output in large production runs unnecessary and unprofitable, contrary to the US where the internal market is very homogenised.

Changes in technology exert a continuous pressure on plant efficiency. Hence, the minimum efficient size of plant changes over time. Large-scale production is attractive and profitable only if there is secure access to a wide and growing market. It is reasonable, therefore, to assume that firms which operate on a wide market are more likely to be closer to the minimum efficient plant size than those which act within a more restricted framework. However, recent developments in technology are diminishing the classic scale economies associated with mass production in large plants. In response to an increase in income and to changes in demand, modern technology increases the role of smaller, but highly specialised or flexible, plants.

Economies of scale are largest in transport equipment, electronics, office machines, chemicals and other manufactured products. These are the industries in which demand has the highest growth and where technology changes fast. The common element in these industries is the vast investment required to produce even a small amount of output.[15] Advanced technology is not necessary for increasing returns to scale, but such returns to scale are frequently found in high-technology industries. In addition, these industries are under continuous pressure from international competition. Industries with relatively smaller returns to scale are those with a stagnant demand and relatively low technology content. They include the food, textile, clothing and footwear industries. The problem with the EU's manufacturing sector is that a significant part of its export specialisation has for a long time been in industries with relatively stagnant or declining demand and relatively weak economies of scale, while the US and Japanese producers and exporters have specialised in goods produced by industries with strong economies of scale. This was especially true during the 1980s.

Adam Smith pointed out that specialisation is limited by the extent of the market. A customs union increases the market area for firms in the participating countries, hence it opens up opportunities for specialisation. A country may gain from economies of scale which form an independent source for trade. If countries trade, they may gain not only from the exchange of goods and services, but also from specialisation and a wider choice of goods. Trade increases the bundle of available goods and services in relation to what is available in autarky. Specialisation and alteration in the output mix in a country may take full advantage of its factor endowment. This holds not only for economic integration, but also for strategies to open up and deepen the internal market, as was the case with the EU Single Market Programme. It was hoped that the long-term impact of the programme, together with additional instruments, would rectify the EU's comparative disadvantage in comparison with the US, Japan and a few other countries in certain industries. Later on came the Lisbon (2000) declaration.

Economies of scale may be internal to individual firms. They may also be external to these firms when the whole industry grows and when all the firms in that industry enjoy the fruits of such growth. For example, networking (phones or cyberspace exchange of data) is the consequence of economies of scale. The peculiarity of economies of scale is that they are not consistent with perfect competition. With imperfect market structure all welfare outcomes are possible (but not necessarily desirable). A perfectly competitive firm takes the price for its output as given. A firm with increasing returns to scale in such a market will find it profitable to produce one more unit of output since it can do so at less than the prevailing price. Thus, it would tend to increase output until it dominates the market, while efficiency may set the price for its output.

Consider the case in Figure 7.3, which illustrates the impact of economies of scale on price in the exporting country A. The vertical axis shows the price in country A for good X. Increasing returns to scale are implied by the downward-sloping AC_a curve. The producer of this good has a monopoly position in the domestic market. There is no producer in country B, but this country has a tariff on imports of good X for fiscal reasons. Domestic demand in country A is represented by the curve D_a and the demand for the product in country B is represented by the curves D_b and $D_{b'}$. The former is the demand curve incorporating a tariff in country B on imports of good X, while the latter reflects demand for this good if no tariffs were levied.

The initial equilibrium in this market is represented by the intersection of the joint demand curve D_{a+b} and the AC_a curve as implied by the monopoly position of the country A producer. If countries A and B enter into a customs union, then the tariff on imports of good X into country B will be eliminated, increasing the demand for this good. Thus, the curve representing demand in country B is $D_{b'}$ and the joint demand in the customs union is $D_{a+b'}$. Faced with this increased demand the producer in country A will expand output. With increasing returns to scale this output expansion lowers the marginal and average costs of production and leads

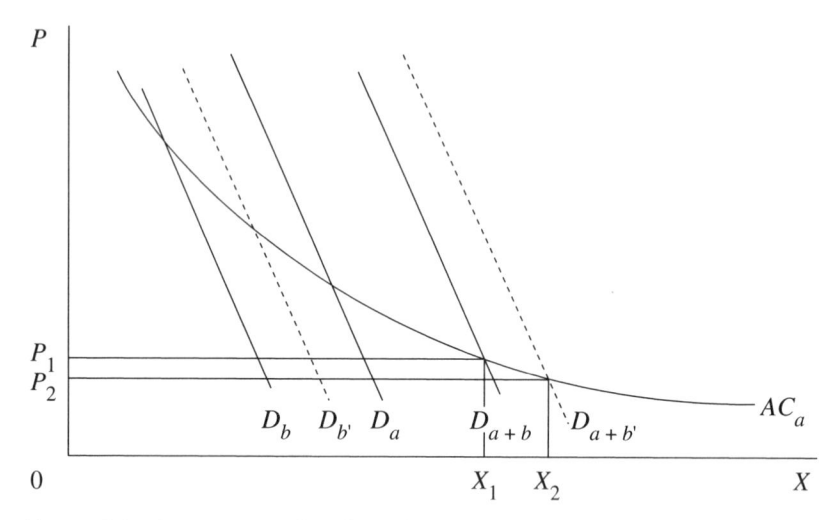

Figure 7.3 Economies of scale and their impact on price in the exporting country

to a fall in the equilibrium price from P_1 to P_2. The elimination of the tariff has an unambiguously positive effect: all consumers can purchase a greater quantity of good X at a lower price and profit to the producer has increased.

The above result is called the *cost-reduction effect* (Corden, 1984, p. 123). It is distinct from trade creation since the existing supplier reduces price for the good X. There is an additional effect: suppose that there was an initial tariff on imports of good X but it was insufficient to induce domestic production of X in country A. After the creation of a customs union with country B, the market area for country A is increased. Costs of production may fall, hence production of good X may begin in country A, replacing imports into both customs union partners from country C. For country A this is *trade suppression*, while for country B this represents trade diversion. While learning by doing, country A may become a more efficient producer of good X than country C, so in the longer run, this policy may pay off. The country in which production with increasing returns to scale occurs gets double gains (employment and increased production). Governments in the customs union may cooperate in order to evenly distribute the industries with increasing returns to scale, otherwise they may end up in an investment subsidy war to attract such industries.

In perfectly contestable markets price equals marginal cost (firms just cover production costs of the last unit and profits are zero). Economies of scale introduce imperfection into the market system, since firms set prices at average cost and make profits. Therefore, economies of scale lead to more specialisation compared with the situation with constant returns to scale. The existence of these firms with economies of scale is protected by barriers to entry and exit which increase risk, costs and delays to a newcomer relative to the incumbent. Barriers to *entry* in an industry include:

- high human and capital requirements (sunk costs necessary to achieve minimum efficient scale of output);
- product differentiation and consumer preferences;
- indivisible production technology (a strong close spatial presence of suppliers and consumers is necessary);
- externalities (linkages);
- R&D;
- regulation (environment, product quality, permissions, accounting, standards, intellectual property rights);
- marketing (access to distribution network, exclusive dealership);
- advertising needs and costs;
- reaction by market incumbents (predatory pricing and excess capacity in the existing firms to discourage any new entry);
- trade and industrial policies (tariffs, quotas, NTBs, domestic content requirements);
- organisational complexity; and
- availability of staff.

Barriers to *exit* include:

- past sunk costs (not yet depreciated);
- durable specialised assets that cannot be sold easily;
- regulation (bankruptcy law, labour settlement, cost of dismantling facilities, for example, nuclear power plants);
- public bailout (otherwise medium-sized towns may disappear);
- new trade protection;
- strategic business decision by a diversified firm to save the facility for the future; and
- emotional attachment to the facility by the managers and owners.

After a certain level of output some costs, such as depreciation of equipment, can increase disproportionately in relation to output, but they can be partly offset by a reduction in costs that accrues from increasing returns to scale. For example, the ends of the blades on a very large turbine move at a speed that can be close to that of sound. At such a speed, 'metal fatigue' increases disproportionately in relation to a turbine's capacity. Beyond a certain level of rotation speed, the costs in all engines based on revolution increase more than the returns. A strike in a firm with increasing returns to scale technology may have a profound impact on the profitability of a firm. However, the threat of competition or of removing barriers to imports may mitigate the distortion imposed by trade unions.

Returns to scale have not been thoroughly studied in the theory of customs unions because it is difficult to model them. Therefore, one should be very careful about using classical theory either as a description of what is likely to happen in a customs union or as a guide to policies that will ensure that such a union fulfils its expectations. Another important fact is that a substantial part of production is linked with economies of scope rather than scale. While economies of scale imply a certain level of standardisation in tastes and production, economies of scope deal with product or process diversity. Economies of scope allow firms such as Benetton to respond swiftly to changes in the supply of inputs and shifts in demand because they come from the common control of distinct, but interrelated production activities. For example, the same kind of fabric can be used in the production of various goods.

Economies of scale are coupled with market imperfections which allow various welfare outcomes. Distortions, such as deviations from marginal cost pricing or the existence of barriers to entry and exit, mean that the creation of a customs union (or for that matter any other type of international economic integration) does not necessarily either improve or worsen welfare. With economies of scale and other distortions, the welfare effects of customs union creation and pattern of trade are much more affected by government policy than they are in the neo-classical theorists' world of comparative advantage and factor proportions.

Terms of Trade

A number of people commonly and intuitively think and worry that the emergence of new competitors can reduce real income in the incumbent economies. Others argue that this is a positive development. An expansion of markets brings success and wealth to everyone. Both of these intuitions are mistaken. Growth in other countries may either aid or hurt the home country. This effect depends on the home country's bias in terms of trade:

$$T = \frac{P_x}{P_m}. \tag{7.3}$$

The terms of trade (T) is the ratio: the price of a good a country exports (P_x) divided by the price of a good it imports (P_m). It is the ratio of the quantity of imports that may be obtained in trade for a certain quantity of exports or, alternatively, it is the relative price of imports to exports.[16] An increase in the terms of trade increases a country's welfare, while a decrease in this ratio reduces welfare. If a country experiences a growth, strongly biased towards its export good X, then if other things are equal, the relative price of good X is decreasing. In this situation, the country has to export more of this good X for the same quantity of imported good Y. Export-biased growth tends to worsen a growing country's terms of trade to the benefit of the rest of the world. The reverse is true for the import-biased growth.

Although terms of trade provide an intellectually 'justified' basis for intervention, this has not featured significantly in many of the arrangements to integrate countries. If home demand for good X is elastic, then the home country's tariff on imports may reduce both consumption and imports of this good. If this country can act as a monopsonist it may turn prices on the international market in its favour which improves its terms of trade (at least in the short term). The same powers may be wielded by a customs union. Third countries may lose on two accounts: first, there is a loss in exports through trade diversion; and second, third countries have to increase their effort in exports to the customs union in order to mitigate the impact of adverse terms-of-trade changes.

If a customs union is large enough to influence its terms of trade on both the export and import sides (externalisation of integration), then the customs union sets the international prices for these goods. Other countries, supposedly small ones, which are price takers for the standardised goods, must accept prices which prevail in the customs union less the CET and less the cost of transport if they want to sell in the customs union market. However, even relatively small countries are able to influence their terms of trade if they have specialisation in industries that are monopolistically competitive. A big customs union may exercise its monopoly and monopsony powers at the expense of third countries' consumers who pay domestic tariffs and producers who pay the customs union's external tariff if they want to export there.[17]

Monopoly power is not without its disadvantages. If a customs union is large enough to influence prices on international markets then, in the absence of offsetting changes in the rest of the world, an increase in the customs union's supply of good X simply decreases the price of that good. On the side of the customs union's demand for good Y from abroad, an increase in demand will increase the price of good Y. The greater the demand in the customs union for good Y and the greater the supply of good X and the greater the trade of the customs union, the greater will be the deterioration of the customs union's terms of trade. With both monopoly and monopsony powers, as well as without changes in the outside world, the customs union is made worse off by its desire to increase trade. This situation may be called an *immiserising customs union*.

The terms-of-trade effects of a customs union not only have an external dimension. There is also an internal significance. Trade flows among the member countries are affected too. The integrated partners are not only allies in their relations with third countries, but also competitors in the customs union's internal market. The elimination of tariffs and quotas on trade in a customs union has a direct impact on internal trade and prices. A union member country may gain from an improvement of customs union terms of trade with third countries, but this gain may be reduced by worsened terms of trade with the customs union partner countries.

The countries that are in a customs union may experience a shift in productivity due to increased competition and the rapid introduction of new technologies. If one excludes all demographic changes, then any increase in labour productivity has the direct effect of increasing real income under the assumption of unchanged quantity and velocity of money. This has a direct impact on the terms of trade because prices of home goods fall.

The bargaining power of those countries that have entered into a customs union is greater than the power they exert as individuals prior to entering the customs union. The EU countries use this 'weapon' in trade relations and negotiations with both the US and Japan and others. The Association of South-East Asian Nations (ASEAN) is another example of an 'integrated' group that is able to extract concessions in trade from foreign partners that are superior to those that would be available to the individual member countries. What matters however, is not the absolute, but rather the relative size of the union against its trading partners. The improvement in the terms of trade is not only the principal effect, but also one of the major goals of the integration of trade in manufactures in Western Europe. The reason for the official silence on the issue is the possible charges by the injured trading partners (Petith, 1977, p. 272). The statement that improvement in terms of trade (beggar-thy-neighbour) is the major goal of integration in trade in manufactures in Western Europe is hard to reconcile with what is happening in practice. Neither firms nor governments think in these terms, although the potential for the employment of a 'fortress' mentality as a bargaining chip is there.

The EU is often advised by third countries, especially the US, to adopt more liberal trade policies and to resist the temptation to create a 'Fortress Europe'. This was most obvious during the years of the creation of the Single European Market (1985–92). The capacity and willingness of the EU to accept such advice depends, at least in part, on similar actions by its major trading partners: the US, Japan and, increasingly, by newly industrialised countries such as South Korea, China (and Taiwan), as well as Brazil.

3. Why countries integrate

Economic integration may increase the average welfare of consumers in the involved countries in many different direct and indirect ways. The problem is that the benefits accrue to everyone in relatively small instalments and only in the medium and long terms. Some of these gains include:

- secure access to the market of partner countries;
- increased investment opportunities as expectations may be established with an increased degree of security;
- improved efficiency in the use of resources;
- an elimination of trade barriers reduces the cost of trade;
- increased competition on internal market puts a downward pressure on prices;
- facilitation of exchange of technical information;
- competition forces firms to implement new ideas and technologies;
- due to the enlarged market, producers may better exploit and benefit from economies of scale;
- potential for coordination of certain economic policies in order to increase their effectiveness;
- improved bargaining position with external partners;
- research and innovation may be stimulated because of tougher competition on a larger market and a possibility to share fixed costs in such a market environment;
- market of the integrated group provides more opportunities for a wider range of goods and services that can be offered to consumers, hence there is an improvement in individuals' utility function; and
- reduction in X-inefficiency which moves the production activities of firms closer to best-practice business organisation.

However, one must always bear in mind that international economic integration is never more than a useful *supporting* tool to sound domestic macro- and microeconomic policies and that it cannot act as their replacement. If these domestic policies are not healthy, integration cannot be their substitute.

The traditional (static) model of customs unions considered the effect of a reduction in tariffs on trade and welfare. It concluded that the lowering or elimination of tariffs increased competition which could lead to an improvement in welfare. The new theory pays attention to the dynamic effects of integration. With economies of scale and imperfect competition, there are no unconditional expectations that all countries will gain from integration, even less that they will gain equally. In the absence of adjustment policies, such as industrial, regional, cohesion and social policies, integration may impose costs on some countries, rather than give them benefits. It may take decades to reach a new, higher and stable steady state. Therefore, cooperation among countries regarding the distribution of gains and losses is a necessary condition for successful integration. In any case, integration profoundly changes the economic structure of participating countries which must modify, and even abandon, the established domestic monopolies and autarkic traditions.

The theory of a customs union is based on a large number of restrictive assumptions, so the technical modelling may be far from realistic. Various restrictions in a customs union, such as the prohibition on factor movements or coordinated fiscal and monetary policies, can be overcome in common markets and economic unions.

The theory of customs unions studies extreme cases and is intuitive in nature. All analyses are suggestive rather than definitive and conclusive. Yet another difficulty stems from the fact that this theory includes simultaneously both free trade within a customs union and protection against third countries in the form of the CET (and NTBs). A customs union reduces tariffs on trade among some countries, so it may seem beneficial in relation to a situation where each country applies its own system of tariffs. In a customs union, tariffs are removed on the internal trade, but a CET is erected. One distortion is replaced by another, so regarding the final effect on welfare, all outcomes are possible. If free trade is the first-best policy, then a customs union is, at best, a second-best situation. Hence a universal prescription for the success of a customs union may not be found. None the less, our effort was not in vain, as many things may be learned from the analysis of extreme and second-best cases.

Dynamic effects are extremely hard to model and quantify rigorously. It is, for example, difficult to predict the exact impact of competition on technological innovation. Modern trade barriers are more obscure and complicated to negotiate and enforce than was the earlier case with pure tariffs and quotas. These are intuitive issues, but important for economic integration and its direction.

There is still a question of why integration takes place in reality. Estimates of trade creation and trade diversion that could contribute to the explanation of why integration takes place at all have been disappointingly small in most studies. In addition, the literature has been slow to develop quantification of dynamic effects of integration. Hence, the hard quantitative explanations for economic integration were missing. Therefore, the rationale for the creation of integration schemes in real life was found in non-economic motives.

One has to recall two things. First, the major goal of European integration was to protect peace by ensuring, through economic means, that war between France and Germany would be impossible. Integration was a tool, not an objective in itself. Second, the important wave of theoretical contributions to the theory and measurement of international economic integration came only *after* the signature of the Treaty of Rome (1957).

Why do international economic integration and preferential trading agreements take place at all? The answer to this question has several components and dimensions:

- first and foremost, countries integrate in order to secure access to markets of partner countries;
- they also want to secure and solidify domestic market-oriented reforms;
- trade barriers can be adapted according to preferences of the involved countries;
- trust among the participating countries. A relatively small number of participants may create cosy relationships, make monitoring and enforcement of the deal easier, while friendly positive cooperation within the group may potentially help the exchange of favours, mutual agreement and perhaps settle disputes more quickly and efficiently than is the case in multilateral institutions. A large group of countries may have many conflicting objectives;
- opening up for trade is about greater competition which weakens and reduces the power of vested interests and monopolies. This gives opportunities to many firms, rather than to a select few. This, in turn, creates additional opportunities for growth;
- these agreements can be employed as a bargaining tool; and
- terms-of-trade effects and gains to exporters provide benefits from preferential trading agreements that are not available from unilateral trade liberalisation policies.

Given these seven motives, it is not necessary to resort exclusively to non-economic reasons for economic integration.

International economic integration increases the potential for significant international improvement in economic welfare. The countries have to organise themselves, that is, adjust individually and collectively, to reap these gains. Specialisation and increase in the export potentials in order to pay for the imports are necessary conditions for success. In addition, adjustment policies must be well thought out. Unfriendly policies can cancel out all the beneficial effects which accrue from an improved access to a larger market.

In the world of rapid change in technology and conditions in the market, a country may not be sure that its current comparative advantages will be secured in the future. So, a country may wish to secure markets for the widest variety of its goods and services as a hedge against abrupt changes in the trade policy of its partners. International economic integration is an uphill job, but may be an attractive solution to such a problem.

Integration can be a risky enterprise for a small country in relation to protectionism in the short run. However, a defensive policy of protection may generate the economic decline of a small country in the long run. Few countries could accept this as their long-term goal. Integration may be a way out of this scenario. A willingness to cooperate with partner countries on the issue of the distribution of costs and benefits that accrue from the creation of a customs union and the settlement of disputes is of great importance for the smooth and beneficial operation, as well as for the survival of a customs union. International economic integration may be subject to various disputes. Most of them stem from the existence of NTBs. An effective dispute settlement mechanism is a necessary condition for the adhesion of the scheme.

Discrimination in trade has not gone away. There is still a long way to go before genuine multilateral liberal trade has been achieved. Integration may assist, complement and ease multilateral trade:

- if trade and investments are free within the group;
- if common external barriers to trade are made transparent and not increased relative to the pre-integration situation (GATT Article XXIV);
- if the group reduces its external barriers to trade, investment and factor mobility;
- if the group is not closed and if it expands;
- if the internal rules (competition, origin and so on) are clear and friendly (not bureaucratic); and
- if there is an effective and reliable dispute settlement mechanism.

Integration is a tool that only supports (rather than replaces) a sound domestic macroeconomic economic policy and structural reforms. Inappropriate domestic fiscal (taxation that distorts the economy), monetary and exchange rate policy will prevent the domestic private sector from being internationally competitive.

An inevitable question has always been: are regional trading arrangements good or bad for world welfare? The answer to this question depends on the answer to a related question: is regional economic integration assisting (building block) or damaging (stumbling block) the multilateral trading system? Some reply yes, others reply no. This is the consequence of the value judgements within the 'second-best' world. Even though most of the past international integration schemes were on a rocky road (indeed, many of them disappeared, particularly in the developing countries), in general terms they tended to increase trade, rather than to restrict it. Hence, this may be taken at first sight to be an economically beneficial effect.

The current wave of interest in integration which started in the 1990s is different from the largely unsuccessful attempts to integrate countries during the 1950s and 1960s, with a notable exception in Europe. The new integration initiatives are founded on a different basis:

- Almost all countries credibly decided to accept and implement market-based reforms and outward-oriented economic policy. They became open and welcomed FDI.
- Integrated international production created and extended by TNCs and huge international flows of FDI are features of the modern economy. This was the case to a very much lower degree during the 1950s and 1960s.
- The successive GATT/WTO rounds of trade negotiations have almost eliminated tariffs and quotas as important obstacles to trade on a multilateral basis.

It is, however, true that on the negative side, the new regional integration initiatives may generate trade diversion. The founding fathers of the GATT/WTO exempted free trade areas and customs unions from the most favoured nation (MFN) clause, but they did not predict a proliferation of these agreements that may fragment the world trading system. There were about 250 notified free trade areas in 2003. Many are being negotiated. If they continue to proliferate, the world trading system may soon have 300 of them. Big countries such as the US may break coalitions in the developing world by offering bilateral trade deals. Bilateral or regional deals may divert attention from the multilateral path. However, the US entered into free trade deals with Israel, Canada and Mexico during the Uruguay Round (1986–94) without reducing its commitment to the final multilateral deal. Similarly, the US entered into free trade arrangements with Chile and Singapore in 2004 during the Doha Round. It is feared that regional trading blocs may turn hostile and cause a collapse in the world economy because of various conflicting interests, including the pressure from the well-entrenched rent-seeking special lobbies. What if the simplicity of non-discriminatory multilateral trade is replaced by complex internal rules of origin that are not in accord with the others?

In the real world, bilateral or regional trading agreements may be a response to tremendous and uncertain resource costs related to multilateral negotiations and deals. It may be simpler, faster, cheaper and more tangible to put into practice a regional integration deal, than to wait an interminable time for an uncertain multilateral trade arrangement and its benefits. The choice that policy makers face is not between multilateral agreements and economic integration, but rather between a potentially beneficial economic integration with select partners or no such arrangement at all. Whether regional economic integration can evolve into multilateral liberal trade cannot be proven. Integration may, however, start this process. The bottom line may be that the new integration programmes are the outcome of the success of multilateralism, not its failure (Ethier, 1998, p. 1161).

4. World Trade Organisation and international trade

TRADE NEGOTIATIONS

Various rounds of trade negotiations under the auspices of the GATT have an important impact on world trading arrangements in the long term. Negotiations, however, during distinct rounds may take almost a decade. In addition, there is usually a transition period of another decade, so the impact of trade concessions that each round brings is felt only in the distant future by another generation.

Experience has shown that real and substantial negotiations take place only among a select number of negotiators. So far, these have been the US and the EU. Japan appeared as the third major negotiator in the late 1960s, but the basic negotiations still take place between the EU and the US. A number of (developing) countries have shown little interest in negotiations, at least in the past. They were free riding since the MFN clause extended to them all the concessions that were exchanged among the three major players. There is an increasing influence by the developing countries on negotiations. In fact, the openness of the markets of the developed economies for trade and FDI in the future will increasingly depend on similar concessions being offered by the developing countries (at least the newly industrialised ones).

The international trading system is in its eighth round of tariff negotiations (Table 7.5). Attention will be given here only to the most recent ones. The Dillon Round of trade negotiations brought a relatively modest reduction of tariffs. A more significant step took place during the Kennedy Round when tariffs on manufactured goods were reduced by 35 per cent on average. Unlike the earlier round which reduced excessive protection, this one cut deeper into protection. It provoked a serious structural adjustment of the economies, at least in the developed world. During this round the US wanted to include

Table 7.5 *GATT/WTO rounds of trade negotiations*

Round	Year	Participating countries	Subject
1. Geneva	1947	23	Tariffs on manufactured goods
2. Annecy	1949	13	Tariffs on manufactured goods
3. Torquay	1950–51	38	Tariffs on manufactured goods
4. Dillon	1959–62	26	Tariffs on manufactured goods
5. Kennedy	1963–67	62	Tariffs, on manufactured goods, antidumping
6. Tokyo	1973–79	102	Tariffs, on manufactured goods, NTBs
7. Uruguay	1986–94	125	Tariffs, on manufactured goods, NTBs, services, intellectual property, textiles, agriculture, dispute settlement, creation of WTO
8. Doha	2001–05(?)	149	Agriculture, services, intellectual property rights, trade and investment, competition rules, public procurement, electronic commerce, environment

trade in farm goods in negotiations, as at that time, a fifth of the US exports into the EU were agricultural goods. The EU has proven its bargaining power, as it resisted those pressures and protected the CAP. The Tokyo Round reduced tariffs on manufactured goods by a third on average. The inclusion of farm goods and NTBs in negotiations was a big success. None the less, the results of the round in these new areas remained small.

It is widely accepted that the Dillon, Kennedy and Tokyo rounds of trade negotiations were attempts by the US and other developed market economies to reduce the discriminating effect that came from the creation and enlargement of the EU. Theory predicted that a customs union increases its clout in dealings with the outside world. The outcome of these rounds was that the average tariff decreased from 11 per cent at the time of the introduction of the CET in the EU to 7.5 per cent after the completion of the Tokyo Round reductions (Yannopoulos, 1988, pp. 26–7). One could have argued that the pace of multilateral trade liberalisation during the 1960s and beyond, as well as the extension of GATT/WTO coverage of new areas such as services, agriculture and NTBs would have been delayed without European integration. Hence, European integration provided a favourable environment for general multilateral liberalisation of trade.

THE URUGUAY ROUND

The Uruguay Round of trade negotiations had a very ambitious agenda. Hence the reason for numerous standstills during negotiations. The developed countries wanted to update the GATT system by the inclusion of new areas such as trade in services, intellectual property rights or trade related investment measures (TRIMs).[18] In addition, there were a proliferating number of grey areas that required a certain international structuring. These included market-sharing deals such as orderly marketing and voluntary export-restriction agreements.[19] There was also a desire to include trade in textiles and agricultural goods in the deal. The new GATT rules were expected to introduce an 'insurance policy' regarding security and predictability about market access in future.

A word should be said here about international trade in agricultural commodities. The EU was generally in favour of a liberal international trade regime for manufactured goods, unlike the temperate agricultural products. However, the root of the GATT/WTO problem regarding trade in agricultural goods was the initial US demand to exclude these goods from the GATT. The US had succeeded in weakening the original GATT rules that applied to trade in farm goods during the 1950s. It wanted to preserve its domestic autonomy in handling a highly interventionist and protectionist farm policy after the Second World War. When the EU and Japan applied own farm policies, which was allowable because of the earlier American action in the GATT, the US and other exporters of temperate agricultural goods found their farm exports to be restricted by the EU and Japan. Thus, the US Congress' solution to the American problems of the 1940s and 1950s (that is, to exclude agriculture from the GATT) served as an impediment to worldwide liberalisation of trade in farm goods (Lipsey and Smith, 1987, p. 6). Perhaps the US and others have learned a lesson from this example for trade policy in the future.

'Stickiness' of certain policy decisions is not only the prerogative of the US. The EU, for example, added a Protocol on the Banana Import Regime to the original Treaty of Rome in 1957, and it took the EU 36 years, two GATT panels and pressure from trading partners to alter it in 1993. The final settlement of this distorted EU import regime may come in 2006, almost half a century after the introduction of the policy. The moral is that policies need to be crafted carefully at the start. Once they are introduced (such as the CAP), it is hard to change or to eliminate them.

The basic principles of the GATT – non-discrimination, reciprocity,[20] transparency, enforcement and the impartial settlement of disputes – were originally conceived to ameliorate international trade at the border. At the time of the creation of the GATT (1947), border measures were, perhaps, the most important protectionist instruments. As tariffs were reduced over time, grey-area measures expanded, which shifted protectionist techniques. Protection now takes place not at the border, but within the domestic market once goods and services cross the border. The Uruguay Round was a sign that the multilateral trading system was seeking ways and means to address these new challenges.

The Uruguay Round deal established the World Trade Organisation in 1995. The WTO is the only multilateral institution that can curb the operation of large trading blocs. It is an 'umbrella' organisation for the GATT, the General Agreement on Trade in Services (GATS) and the Agreement on Trade Related Intellectual Property Rights (TRIPS). The major results of the Uruguay Round can be summarised as follows:

- Tariffs on industrial goods are to be reduced by a little more than a third (38 per cent). This would decrease the average tariff on industrial goods in the developed market economies from 6.3 to 3.9 per cent in 1999. Such a reduction is supposed to enhance competition and increase efficiency in the employment of resources.
- The US and the Cairns Group[21] were able to push trade in agricultural goods very high up the agenda. Trade in farm goods was earlier subject to little 'international discipline'. While the EU and Japan argued against changes in the past rules, the US wanted a complete liberalisation by the year 2000. The compromise included a partial liberalisation in farm trade: (1) All NTBs should be converted into tariffs (tariffication). This tariffication may produce very high, even prohibitive, tariff rates of 200–500 per cent *ad valorem*. (2) These tariffs are to be reduced by 36 per cent on average by 2001 in the developed countries, while in the developing countries, the average reduction should be 24 per cent by the year 2005. (3) Production and export subsidies in the farm sector should be reduced. Developed countries will have to reduce export subsidies (the value of budgetary outlays) by 36 per cent over six years, while the corresponding figure for the developing countries is 24 per cent over a period of ten years. Although, the establishment of a full international framework for trade in farm goods will take quite some time, the current deal provided the framework for

further negotiations, as well as the first step on the road towards a more stable and predictable trade in farm goods.
- Developed market economies should reduce their 'support' to the farm sector by 20 per cent, and developing countries by 13.3 per cent. Subsidies that are not directly related to production are exempted. These include environmental protection, regional development, structural adjustment and income support.
- In the textile trade, average tariffs should fall from 15.5 to 12.1 per cent. The average tariff protection may still look high, but it will take over the protective measures from quotas, which is a positive achievement. A renegotiation of the Multi-Fibre Agreement (MFA)[22] was of vital importance for developing countries. The arrangement included a gradual coverage of trade in textiles by the MFN clause by 2005. The elimination of quotas for the imports of textiles is a welcome event for a number of countries throughout the world that may export to the EU. However, most of them worry that China, with its cheap textiles, may possibly make the biggest inroad into the EU market and wipe out their competitive advantages.
- The Kyoto Customs Convention (1973) on the determination of rules of origin is vague. As it is not applied by the US, its practical value is limited. The WTO is to draft rules of origin that would be applicable to all of its members. This creditable task of harmonisation, intended to increase certainty in trade relations, may run into problems as it is difficult to predict the progress in the preparation, acceptance and implementation of new rules.
- Regarding technical standards, the EU in its internal trade implements mutual recognition of national standards. The WTO requires that trading partners follow international standards.
- Article VI authorises the use of antidumping duties if the injured country proves that domestic producers are (potentially) harmed by such imports. Predatory pricing (through dumping) falls on the profit of firms. This practice is subject to antidumping duties. Export subsidies, however, cause the outflow of public funds. This practice is subject to countervailing duties.[23] The GATT outlaws export subsidies (Article XVI), but these are not the only subsidies that distort trade. A subsidy is defined as a financial contribution by a government or any public body. Such a financial contribution includes a direct transfer of funds, potential transfers of funds such as loan guarantees, discriminatory public procurement, forgoing of revenue by tax authorities and public provision of goods or services. The WTO has even entered into *domestic* economic policy, since any WTO member state can start an action if a foreign subsidy injures a domestic

industry. If a domestic subsidy is an aid package to a disadvantaged region, for research and pre-competitive activities or ecological matters, an action under the auspices of the WTO cannot be called. However, what if the opaque subsidies are 'sold' as permitted ones?
- Temporary safeguards are allowed under Article XIX of the GATT Charter if there is a sudden and serious injury or potential injury to domestic industry from an unexpected surge in imports. This provision continues to be important. For example, a sudden fall in the exchange rate of the dollar helps US exporters. This may cause concern to importers. However, if increased quality and productivity is at stake, such as Japanese cars or electronics, then, instead of trying to increase domestic productivity and penetrate the Japanese market, the US and the EU restrict the entry of Japanese goods into their domestic markets. According to the Uruguay Round provisions, all peripheral measures such as voluntary export restraint agreements are ruled out. Other NTBs need to be eliminated within a period of four years after the entry into force of the Uruguay deal.[24] As there is the possibility of introducing safeguards without retaliation for a period of three years, this leaves the door open to potential abuse of those rules. Safeguard measures, however, would not apply against a good originating in a developing country if its share of imports in the country of destination is 3 per cent or less.
- The new organisation, the GATS, is to provide a forum that will take charge of liberalisation: trade in services. The deal introduces the MFN principle in trade in services and member states have to provide market access and national treatment in specific service industries. A regulatory framework would increase certainty in world trade in services over $1540 billion in 2002. This represented a quarter of the $6240 billion trade in goods. Previously, trade in services was referred to as 'invisible' transactions. In spite of the numerous MFN exceptions the inclusion of services into the negotiations agenda is one of the greatest achievements of the Uruguay Round.
- Together with the deal regarding services, the major novelty of the Uruguay Round was the arrangement on intellectual property rights. Although these are regulated by several conventions and by the World Intellectual Property Organisation, the WTO is to introduce an additional element for the protection of these rights: enforcement through the WTO dispute settlement system.
- An efficient and impartial settlement of disputes should enhance the role of the WTO, revive multilateralism and prevent the implementation of unauthorised and whimsical unilateral measures introduced by an individual member country. If the informal settlement of a

dispute through bilateral consultations is not successful, then there is a dispute settlement panel that may issue a verdict. Panels usually take at least six months to deliver a verdict, which may be contested before the standing Appellate Body (this procedure may take a year or more). After its decision, the injured party may request compensation. If there is no agreement on the settlement with the perpetrator, the injured party may impose sanctions. If applied strictly, this dispute settlement system is supposed to eliminate the unilateral retaliation measures, as practised mostly by the US.

The simple post-Uruguay Round average[25] EU tariff protection is rather low. For 2002, it was estimated to be 6.4 per cent. However, this average conceals the fact that the average tariff on imports of manufactured goods is 4.1 per cent, while the same average tariff on imports of agricultural goods is 16.1 per cent. Tariff peaks within these groups of goods are the highest for meat, dairy products, cereals, textiles and clothing (WTO, 2002, p. 29). Tariffs and NTBs reveal that the most highly protected are often the labour-intensive industries in the EU.

The level of trade protection can be measured in different ways. Three indicators are of particularly important:

- the average tariff rate;
- the ratio of tariff duties paid to total imports; and
- the ratio of tariff duties paid to all *dutiable* imports.

The last indicator is superior to the first two in demonstrating the average protection in the EU. In general, the EU level of protection throughout the 1990s was about 14 per cent. This, however, hides the selectivity of protection as the averaging process erodes tariff peaks. In order to get a fuller picture of EU protection, one has to add various technical regulations and public procurement, as well as subsidies for production and export. If these costs of protection of goods and services in the EU are taken together, it is estimated that it amounts to 7 per cent of the entire EU(15) GDP which is equal to the Spanish GDP. In addition, if one combines the effect of higher prices for consumers and relatively few jobs saved, the average annual cost per job saved in the EU is astronomical: €220 000. This is ten times the EU average annual wage in the protected industry. If saving EU jobs is the policy goal, there are much more efficient and cheaper ways to do the job than by trade protection (Messerlin, 2001, pp. 40–41). This reveals the strength of a few, concentrated rent-seeking vested interests in the EU, as well as the cost paid by most EU consumers. It is hard to orchestrate the voice of consumers, if they are dispersed and paying a bit more per good purchased.

The Uruguay Round of tariff negotiations brought the most profound changes in international trade negotiations in the past century. There is a legal framework for trade in important new areas (agriculture, services) that were earlier beyond the scope of the GATT. Estimates of the global increase in income put it at about $213 billion a year, which is roughly 1 per cent of the annual world product (Cline, 1995, p. 11). Is this not too little to justify such a big fuss?

Estimates of the potential gains from the implementation of the Uruguay Round were generally based on the classical assumption that a set of traded goods is both complete and fixed. In such a case, the gains from trade liberalisation (elimination of tariffs and other barriers to trade) appear to be quite small. Prices in the economy could be changed by government (tariff) intervention, so the quantity of produced and traded goods would change, but the list of the manufactured and traded goods would remain the same.

Suppose now, that the list of goods in production and trade can be expanded. The neo-Schumpeterian economic model assumes that there are no limits for the introduction of new goods and services in an economy. Assume, in addition, that the introduction of a new commodity requires a large amount of fixed costs.[26] This is especially true in the case of the developing countries. Perfect competition and free trade exclude (major) fixed costs from consideration. Once the fixed costs are included in the picture, their presence is often used as a justification for government intervention. When important fixed costs enter the model, a substantial amount of the good needs to be sold in order to make a profit. In such a case, a tariff on the good in question may reduce demand. If such a reduction in (international) demand is important, then the commodity may never appear on the market. Losses from such a development or gains in the reverse case cannot easily be estimated, at least, not yet. In any case, if the new goods are left out of consideration, then this kind of analysis may bring substantial underestimates of the welfare cost of trade restrictions (Romer, 1994).

The major beneficiaries of gains that come from trade liberalisation would be the EU and the US, because they are the largest international traders and they have, perhaps, the biggest distortions in trade. The final package deal of the Uruguay Round was supposed to satisfy all parties. On the one hand, the developed market economies obtained from the deal some regulation of trade in services and protection of intellectual property rights. On the other, the developing countries and transition economies found gains in the reduction of tariffs and the ousting of NTBs, as well as the liberalisation in trade in textiles and farm goods. They, or some of them, will be able to increase their exports of textiles and farm goods.

A relatively free trade is not necessarily always the best policy that benefits everyone and everywhere. TNCs continue to shape trade liberalisation plans and agendas within the WTO to an unacceptable level. This creates international trade disputes by powerful companies that influence and manoeuvre national governments in order to obtain certain advantages for themselves. It is uncertain and doubtful whether the benefits obtained in this way are valuable and favourable to everyone in international economic integration.

THE DOHA ROUND

The Doha Round, which started in Qatar in 2001 (officially expected to finish in 2005), is different from previous rounds. Following fast expansion of membership, of the 149 countries that take part in negotiations, over 100 are developing countries. This group of developing countries can no longer be ignored by the principal negotiating parties: the US, the EU and Japan. In addition, the borders of trade policy are growing blurred. The old 'technical' trade issues such as tariffs and quotas, as the primary subject of negotiations, are being replaced by highly charged political, difficult social and sensitive emotional issues. Politicians labelled Doha the 'development' round. Even though this term was not defined, it was often used as a carrot to persuade many hesitant and leery developing countries to support the start of the round.

Negotiations in the Doha Round have never been expected to be easy as they are entering uncharted and potentially troubled waters. According to the Doha Work Programme the principal negotiating areas are the following:

- *Agriculture*: World trade in agricultural goods is riddled with tariffs, NTBs and distortions unknown to trade in other goods since the Great Depression and protectionism of the 1930s. Even though their agricultural population is shrinking, the developed countries spend about $300 billion a year in subsidies on farming. The Uruguay Round introduced agriculture into the WTO. It laid down foundations for future negotiations about market access and subsidies. The 17-member Cairns Group[27] is ready to fight for increased market access into the EU and Japan. The EU wants the Doha Round to have a strong development connotation. Yet it still restricts the market access that poorer countries so desperately seek for their farm goods. Both the EU and the US are deeply entrenched in subsidising the domestic farm sector. They both have serious political constraints on reducing these subsidies. Although there are signs of a certain flexibility, this needs to be translated into a negotiating offer.

- *Services*: The services sector of the economy contributes more to worldwide economic growth and employment than any other sector. Therefore, an increased legal confidence and certainty to service providers and consumers is of vital importance for investment. The US and EU are eager to request further advances in market access for services.
- *Intellectual property*: Weak law protection provides opportunities for the manufacturing and use of counterfeit and copied goods and technologies that avoid royalty payments. The US depends on strong intellectual property rights and integrity to fuel its economic strength. The moral rights of authors, inventors and so on must be respected; such people should be rewarded for their inventions and innovations, as well as for taking risks. The problem arises once the lawful production or reproduction has taken place. There are different costs of production in different locations in the world. Should the intellectual property argument be used as a protective device? The EU also wants to enlist the WTO to protect its gastronomic treasures. It wants to have a stronger protection in the form of 'geographical indicators' for food and drinks such as Chablis, Champagne, Cognac, Gorgonzola and Parma ham only for the original regional producers. Interestingly, it is not poor countries that produce imitation champagne or abuse the Parma ham brandname, but the US, Canada, Australia, New Zealand, Brazil and Argentina.[28]
- *FDI*: Negotiators will try to formulate rules for the protection of FDI.[29] They will focus on definitions, transparency, non-discrimination, development provisions, balance of payments safeguards, consultation and settlement of disputes.
- *Competition rules*: Action is necessary to prevent conflicts between national antitrust authorities; to avoid the use of national competition rules as a means to check imports; and to ensure a global regulatory and monitoring system. The problem is that about a half of WTO members do not have national competition law, so it may be difficult to agree on multilateral competition rules. However, certain uncontested international standards would lay the foundations for putting this item on the WTO agenda in the future. Negotiations relate core principles, transparency, non-discrimination and procedural fairness.
- *Public procurement*: Negotiations are limited to transparency aspects.
- *Electronic commerce*: The WTO rules treat goods and services differently. Goods are subject to tariffs, while services are not. However, trading by electronic means blurs the difference between a good and a service. A shipped CD with music from one country to another is trade in a good. However, if the contents of the same CD

are sent by electronic mail from one country to another, does this represent trade in goods? This cannot be dropped on your foot. How should the electronic sale of dubious investment schemes or finance by e-mail from 'faithful friends' in Nigeria and other countries be treated? In any case, there is a moratorium on duties on electronic transmissions.
- *Low-cost prescription drugs*: A WTO agreement on the supply of essential low-cost medicines to poor countries has been blocked by the US. The developing countries dominate the WTO in terms of number of members. They accuse the US administration of siding with the US drugs companies (because of hefty campaign donations) against the world's poor and sick.
- *Environment*: Negotiations are related to the link between WTO rules and specific trade obligations set in multilateral environmental agreements; labelling for environmental purposes; as well as on the protection of dolphins against nets that are used to catch tuna; and restriction of imports of shrimps that are caught by nets that also catch turtles.

A serious obstacle to the Doha Round is time. The round is officially expected to conclude its work in 2005. If one recalls that it took eight years to complete the Uruguay Round in which the negotiated issues were less contentious and also that there are some 30 new participants, the omens are not favourable.[30]

Two tough farm trade negotiators, the EU and the US, jointly tried to reinvigorate the stalled negotiations a month before the September 2003 Cancun (Mexico) ministerial meeting of the Doha Round of negotiations. The good news was that the two largest trading parties issued a joint proposal to liberalise farm trade. However, the bad news was that the common plan contains only broad principles on farm tariff reductions (a single mathematical formula to reduce all tariff rates), but without any specific figures or target dates. This gave the EU and the US considerable room for manoeuvre, while it gave very little substance to other countries to evaluate the proposal. As such, this platform had difficulty attracting the attention of the main groups of WTO countries (principally Australia, Brazil, Canada and India), who question the real desire of the EU and the US to compromise. The Cairns Group and developing countries deem that such a platform falls short of what is necessary to liberalise farm trade. The platform does not propose the elimination of either farm export subsidies or the 'peace clause' which sheltered agricultural trade policies and subsidies from legal challenge in the WTO until the end of 2003. If certain WTO members use the expiry of the peace clause in 2004 to start challenging the

US and EU farm subsidies, the potentially dozens of WTO panels could make things more difficult then they already are and the entire concept of the WTO may be in great peril. Cotton, rice, dairy products and sugar are high on the list of potential targets. Yet another serious problem is the retaining of substantial tariffs and subsidies on 'sensitive' products, because each country defines them differently. These sensitive products include beef, dairy products, sugar and certain fruits and vegetables in the EU; sugar citrus fruits and cotton in the US; and rice, wheat, barley, sugar beet, beef and pork in Japan.

These proposals were insufficient to give the Doha Round ministerial meeting an incentive to continue negotiations in Cancun. None the less, the agreed changes in the CAP in June 2003[31] will have a long-term impact on the agricultural sector in the enlarged EU(25) until 2013. It remains to be seen whether the Cancun débâcle will be used as a pretext to reverse or slow down the CAP reforms.

It became common to blame the tacit alliance of two groups of countries for the failure[32] of the Cancun meeting. The first includes France (EU), which prevented a fair deal in agriculture. The second includes Brazil and India (with several other developing countries), which were against a substantial and general liberalisation of trade. The tacit alliance of these two groups brought them success in Cancun, even though the world as a whole might have lost. Such an interpretation of the Cancun events may be too simplistic. In spite of public declarations, there were many, indeed very many other countries at the negotiating table that were not eager to reach a deal. Real reasons for the failure of the Cancun meeting include:

- Stubbornness and brinkmanship in negotiations by both developed and developing countries.
- The US angered four very poor African states which complained about the $3.3 billion annual subsidy to domestic American cotton producers (who enjoy powerful support in Congress). These subsidies have been depressing world prices for cotton, which in turn put poor African cotton farmers out of business. American negotiators proposed that these African countries should diversify away from dependence on the exports of cotton. In addition, they gave vague promises about multilateral development aid. 'The US uses subsidies to deprive poor countries of comparative advantage. Then it tells them that they have to find other kinds of business.'[33]
- US general policy has moved away from multilateralism and international organisations, which are perceived as politicised, slow and cumbersome. As such, they only impede fast unilateral US actions.
- Developing countries fear competition from China.

- General fatigue from excessive and relentless 'globalisation' pressures.
- Non-government organisation (NGOs) irresponsibly raised developing countries' expectations to an unrealistic level.

Negotiations within the WTO (and its predecessor the GATT) have always been complex, fragile and interminable, and a mixture of pressure, threats, bullying, intimidation, buy-offs, dubious promises, brinkmanship and strange compromises. The failure of the Cancun meeting showed the outer limits of liberalisation of the touchy issue of agriculture, at least for the time being. Even though there are limitations to the coverage and influence of the WTO, it continues to be a useful international organisation because of the following two factors. On the one hand, member countries use the WTO to extract concessions from prospective member countries. China, for example, was forced to introduce a number of reforms. The next big catch may be Russia.[34] On the other hand, there are certain permitted WTO enforcement instruments that include a tit-for-tat exchange of threats. If there is a clash in trade, countries may threaten to introduce punitive tariffs. The enforcement mechanism is slow, cumbersome and imperfect, but a potential punitive threat became a useful and effective tool to settle disputes, particularly by large countries.

Is it sensible to force complex rules of competition, FDI and transparency in public procurement on poor countries that may not be able to honour them? Or should there be a two-speed WTO? One, advance group of countries (consisting perhaps of OECD countries) would spearhead the opening up of national markets, while countries from the other group would follow when they feel that they can. But would this be a corrosive step backward regarding multilateral liberalisation, which is enshrined in the WTO's basic principles? Or would this simply be a recognition of the actual situation and an attempt to deal with it in a structured way in order to avoid the Cancun-type rift and paralysis? Would the WTO be marginalised if its member countries seek solutions in a complicated spaghetti-type maze of bilateral or regional deals burdened by multiple standards and rules of origin?

By starting the Doha Round, governments have declared their willingness to negotiate a more liberal multilateral trade regime. But this is only a promise. A declaration. The reality is that the EU already has some 30 free trade and special customs agreements. The US has free trade deals with Canada, Chile, Mexico, Israel, Jordan and Singapore, while there is a long list of candidates and potential candidates for such deals (mainly, but not exclusively, for political reasons) throughout the world. If, however, the Doha Round cannot handle new issues satisfactorily, it seems possible that the regional trade organisations and various bilateral deals may take their own, potentially uncoordinated, path.

The US trade deficit is not provoked by foreign malice; its primary reason may be the rapid growth in the US, combined with sluggish growth elsewhere. This de-synchronisation of economic cycles in the world economy may continue to provoke tensions in trade. A global institution such as the WTO may not always be able to solve this problem. Regional institutions may be better able to synchronise economic cycles within their confines. In any case the US should be persuaded that it would get something more from the outcome of the Doha Round than a bigger trade deficit.

It is convenient and common to blame foreigners during turbulent economic times. An often considered first reaction is to introduce trade restrictions. Policy makers may take a wrong-headed approach and regard trade as a zero- or even a negative-sum game. When many participants look at trade in this same way, they feel no necessity to back down. This method of handling economic troubles culminated in the Great Depression during the 1930s, and the vital role of the WTO is to prevent this happening again. Until the Uruguay Round of trade negotiations the topics for negotiation were tariffs and quotas on manufactured goods. Now they embrace services, farm goods, NTBs, environment and health which together with an increased number of negotiating countries creates new challenges, difficult choices, but also potentials for favourable economic rewards in the long term.

The politicians should explain the situation to the business sector and the general public and convince them that trade liberalisation increases access to markets; that liberalisation supported by sound domestic economic policies contributes to growth and higher living standards; that trade liberalisation is not a favour to others, but rather to the domestic entrepreneurs and consumers in the long run; as well as that the winners generally greatly outnumber the losers both in the medium and long terms.

5. Non-tariff barriers

INTRODUCTION

The GATT was quite successful in achieving a continuous reduction in tariffs on industrial goods during the post-war period. Unfortunately, at the same time, NTBs have flourished and eroded the beneficial liberalising effects of tariff cuts. NTBs are all measures other than tariffs that influence international trade. They affect trade and the geography of production. Some of them are overt (quotas), while others fall into a grey area such as the application of technical standards or rules of origin. Although they are costlier in terms of resource efficiency and they do not create customs revenue, they have increased because the GATT/WTO do not permit a unilateral introduction of new tariffs, while at the same time domestic pressure groups and vested interests may be quite successful in eliciting protection. NTBs are strongest in the 'sensitive' commodity groups and services. In fact, the use of NTBs may determine which commodity groups are sensitive. The implementation of the Treaty of Rome eliminated tariffs and quotas on internal trade in the EU in 1968. The elimination of NTBs, was the task of the Single Market Programme (1985–92).

Whereas tariffs, like transport costs, increase the price of a good, NTBs act like import quotas, but do not generate revenue for the government. Currently, NTBs present the most important and dangerous barriers to trade, fragmenting markets and production more severely than tariffs have ever done. Tariffs were, on average, reduced under the auspices of the GATT/WTO to relatively low levels, so that they now play a relatively minor role in the protection of the economic inefficiency of a country. None the less, national administrations try to obtain short-term political gains through protectionism at the expense of long-term economic benefits. Hence, NTBs are and will be high on the agenda for all future international moves to liberalise trade.

Consideration of NTBs has always been difficult. One reason for this is the creativity of their instigators, but another, more important, reason is the lack of data. Administrations either do not record the use of NTBs, or do so only partly. It comes as no surprise that the reported impact of NTBs can lead to considerable underestimations. Our classification of NTBs is presented in Table 7.6.

Table 7.6 Non-tariff barriers

Principal group	Type
1. Government involvement in international trade	Subsidies (production, exports, credit, R&D, cheap government services)
	Public procurement (local, regional, central)
	State monopoly trading
	Exchange rate restrictions
	Embargoes
	Tied aid
2. Customs and administrative entry procedures	Customs classification
	Customs valuation
	Monitoring measures (antidumping and countervailing duties)
	Rules of origin
	Consular formalities

Table 7.6 (continued)

Principal group	Type
	Trade licensing
	Deposits
	Compulsory insurance with the local insurers
	Compulsory unloading and storage
	Calendar of import
	Administrative controls
	Inadequate institution to appeal against decisions by the customs
3. Standards	Technical
	Health
	Safety
	Environment ('green standards')[a]
	Lack of recognition of international standards
	Inspection, testing and certification
	Abusive sampling practices
	Packing, volume, weight and labelling[b]
	Registration of patents and brand names (and lack of it)
	Pirated goods
4. Others	Quotas (tariff-free ceilings)
	Local content and equity rules
	Tax remission rules
	Variable levies
	Bilateral agreements
	Buy-domestic campaigns
	Voluntary export restriction agreements
	Self-limitation agreements
	Orderly marketing agreements
	Multi-Fibre Agreement
	Lack of transparency and ambiguous laws
	Cartel practices
	Precautionary principle
	Permission to advertise

Notes:
a. Recycling at least a part of the product (e.g. paper, plastic, glass, electrical appliances or computer hardware) may be a 'green' requirement. However, recycling paper requires a lot of chemicals (which are partly released into the environment) and energy. Would a request to plant more trees be a superior choice?
b. Labelling in itself is not a panacea. It ought to have an easily understandable message. However, should it be a positive or a negative statement? For example: 'meat from an animal that *was* fed with genetically modified organisms' *or* 'meat from an animal that *was not* fed with genetically modified organisms'?

The greatest criticism of NTBs is their lack of transparency. Hence, they are prone to abuse and need to be monitored closely, which increases firms' administrative costs. As an economic policy instrument, tariffs are a blunt weapon against which markets can defend themselves through adjustment measures. In contrast, NTBs circumvent market forces and, hence, introduce greater distortions, risk and uncertainty. NTBs therefore prevent efficient spatial and industrial location of resources, investment and specialisation.

ANTIDUMPING

If a government observes that a good is or is likely to be suddenly imported into its country in large quantities, it may introduce an antidumping tariff. Foreign exporters can circumvent this barrier by changing the geography of production. For example, they may move the final, often screwdriver, stage of production to the tariff-imposing country. To counter this action, the home authorities may request that the goods produced domestically must have a certain local content in order to obtain preferential treatment. Once the original supplier of the good meets this requirement, the local authorities may go further, as was the case with the EU control of imports of Japanese integrated circuits (microchips). Chips that are only assembled in a country are not considered to originate in that country. The EU non-preferential rules of origin link the origin of microchips to the place where the diffusion process takes place. Assembly and testing come after the diffusion process and they add to the final value of the chip approximately as much as diffusion.

There are two reasons for this decision by the Commission regarding rules of origin for integrated circuits. First, the rules demand that a part of the manufacturing process takes place in the EU, which requires an inflow of FDI and the creation of high-quality local jobs in the EU. Second, the intention was to support EU producers of microchips, some of whom carry out diffusion in the EU while assembly and testing takes place in non-EU countries where labour costs are lower. In this case, the EU defined the origin of the good as the place where the 'most' (rather than the 'last') substantial production process took place. Origin is determined by where R&D takes place and by the location of capital equipment used in the production of such goods, rather than by the place of transformation of goods. According to these rules, Ricoh photocopiers, which are made (well, assembled) in California, originate not in the US, but rather in Japan because that is where essential parts such as drums, rollers, side plates and other working equipment originate. Having declared the origin of these machines to be

Japan, the EU has an arsenal of NTBs to curtail imports of these goods from the US. This has provoked tensions in EU trade with the US.[35]

The EU has a so-called 'sunset' clause that applies to antidumping duties. Antidumping measures apply for 'only' five years unless there is a review in which dumping and injury are again established (Regulation 2026/97). There is no sunset provision in US antidumping laws, which can last almost indefinitely, as exemplified by the fact that they have been applied to Japanese colour TV sets for 30 years. In addition, the scope of the measures has been expanded to cover liquid crystal display, as well as projection television (Belderbos, 1997, p. 425).

A firm may avoid antidumping actions by changing production geography (relocating production). A new plant may be located either in a third country or in the country that has imposed antidumping duties (tariff jumping). However, the European Commission and the US Department of Commerce have the right to include third-country exports within the scope of an antidumping measure. For example, during the 1989–90 period, nine Japanese fax plants were established in the EU even though there were no antidumping investigations. Some of these firms explicitly stated that fear of antidumping measures was their major reason for investing and location in the EU (Belderbos, 1997, pp. 434–4). However, once established in the EU, these firms can sell at any price they want (below the production costs or below the prevailing prices on the local market). They are not allowed to discriminate or segment the market and they may not follow predatory pricing policies. The EU rules on competition may prevent this.[36]

After virtual elimination of tariffs and quotas through multilateral negotiations, the GATT-sanctioned antidumping trade protection devices are becoming the principal barriers to trade at the start of the 21st century.[37] If a firm sells a product abroad at the price that is below that at which it sells in its home market, this constitutes dumping. The injured country may introduce a duty. Both dumping and injury are necessary conditions to impose an antidumping duty. This idea seems neat, but to apply it in practice may be difficult and controversial.

- *Dumping*: What if a country produces and exports a good that is not sold at home? How should this principle be applied if, say, the Chinese produce and export each year millions of artificial Christmas trees for the EU and US markets and do not sell these products at home because there is no market there? Which arbitrary method should be used to determine the domestic Chinese price for Christmas trees?
- *Injury*: To determine injury to the domestic industry may be even more open to random whims and abuse by the 'injured' industry and investigating government. What measure should be used? An increase in the

volume of imports? Changes (reduction) in the domestic production? Market share? An increase in the domestic unemployment? All of these? In what proportion?

Ambiguity of rules and discretion in determining injury present considerable problems. The most contentious issue relates to cumulation whereby the investigating authority adds all imports from all countries under investigation and assesses their combined injury impact on the domestic industry. This cumulation is in use in the EU, as well as in the US, Canada and Australia. In the EU, in 45 per cent of cases in which defendants agreed to increase their prices in order to bridge the dumping (injury) order, no injury would have been found if the European Commission had not aggregated imports from the countries under investigation (Tharakan et al., 1998, p. 335).[38]

The number of antidumping duties or antidumping cases (there are hundreds of them, mainly in the developed countries although India and China also use them) is not something that matters most as an NTB. The biggest problem and discouragement to trade, investment, innovation, economies of scale and reduction in prices to consumers may result from the serious possibility of being harassed by the authority of a country that imports the good in question. This country may apply ambiguous rules and use them in an unorthodox way with the intention of sheltering inefficient domestic producers. The exposure to such risk cannot be quantified. The investigated suspect (foreign producer) has, at his/her own expense, to provide the inspectors with all operating details, including a full list of the costs of production. The result is that the 'injured' country's industry obtains all important details about foreign competitors for free.

The existence of antidumping measures may endanger and reduce all expected gains from trade that may result from multilateral free trade. This situation in international trade may prevail for quite some time. The way out of it may be to create, apply and enforce multilateral rules to determine dumping and injury. To start with it may be possible to construct a counterfactual situation of a case to try to ascertain and separate effects. In addition, cumulation may be eliminated, save for the case where there is collusion among exporters.

PUBLIC PROCUREMENT

Government at all levels (local, regional and central) is an important consumer of goods and services. It can use its procurement policies either to protect home business (SMEs in particular, as is the case in Germany) and employment or to influence the geography of production and support young industries during the first fragile steps in order to help the creation of a country's comparative advantage. Public procurement can also be employed as an instrument to implement regional policy and aid to the disadvantage of certain population groups (for instance women and minorities).

An open public procurement market in the EU is seen to be one of the major potential benefits that EU firms may exploit. The EU-wide competitive tendering directives require the publication of all tender notices above a certain (rather low)[39] financial threshold in the *Official Journal of the European Community*. Coupled with compliance with EU technical standards and a reasonable time for the submission of the offer, together with transparent award criteria, this increases the fairness of the bidding and award procedure. The low threshold is intended to avoid understating the value of the contract in order to evade open tendering. The threshold may need to be increased. On the one hand, it may not be attractive enough for the non-national companies, while on the other, it is quite costly for local authorities to put work out to tender.

The European Commission may exclude foreign firms from the public procurement market if EU enterprises do not have reciprocal access to public contracts in the countries from which these firms originate. In spite of this, there is a chance of inertia (read 'buy domestic'). A public authority could subdivide a large public contract into a series of small ones and thus avoid the obligation to advertise and award the business locally.

The annual EU(15) public procurement market for goods and services was 16 per cent of the combined GDP of member countries or over €1350 in 2000. Yet the value of public procurement contracts advertised in the *Official Journal of the European Community* was only 2.4 per cent of total EU GDP in the same year (WTO, 2002, p. 46). Suppliers from other EU countries win, on average, 10 per cent of public procurement contracts; however, in Germany, which is the most restrictive country in this respect, other EU countries account for only 5 per cent of public contracts. The countries most receptive to foreign EU suppliers are the smaller ones, such as Ireland (32 per cent), Finland (28 per cent), Denmark (26 per cent) Greece (26 per cent) and Portugal (21 per cent).[40] These data suggest that only those countries that lack indigenous industrial capacities of their own seem prepared to source outside their domestic economies.

TECHNICAL STANDARDS

Goods eligible for tariff and quota-free trade in all integration arrangements are those that are produced by countries within the group. The exceptions are the products that endanger public morality, public security and order, as well as human, animal or plant life or health. An important NTB can be found in the guise of technical standards (a set of specifications for the production and/or operation of a good). Technical standards are different from tariffs in that they increase production and operation costs, while tariffs have an additional revenue-generating effect for the government. The real intention of these standards as hidden barriers to trade is in many cases to protect the national producer despite the long-term costs in the form of higher prices that come from lower economies of scale, poorer technical/energy efficiency and reduced competition.

One of the best-known examples of an NTB operating within an integrated group arose in Germany in 1979. Germany banned the importation of a French fruit-based liqueur, Cassis de Dijon, on the grounds that liqueurs consumed in Germany should have an alcohol content of at least 25 per cent, and that of Cassis de Dijon was 5 per cent less than this norm. The German administration wanted to protect the domestic consumers as they may buy this 'weaker' drink thinking that it is 'strong'. In addition, weak spirits may be better tolerated by consumers. Hence the administration wanted to reduce consumption in order to protect public health. This case was considered by the EU Court of Justice, which ruled that the ban on liqueur imports was not legitimate. The implications of this ruling are of paramount importance: any goods legally produced and traded in one member country cannot be banned from importation in partner countries on the grounds that national standards differ. The ruling opened the way to competition in all goods manufactured in the EU, with the exception of those that could jeopardise an important national interest.

Where differences in national standards do exist, consumer protection is assured by the addition of a warning on the product. However, this ruling is not in itself sufficient to guarantee a uniform market throughout EU and a concomitant increase in competitiveness. To achieve a uniform market requires harmonisation, with all its attendant disadvantages of excess regulation, reduction in choice and the long time required for its implementation. The Cassis de Dijon case was cited as a precedent when the EU forced Germany in 1987 to open its market to beers from other EU countries despite the fact that some beers do not comply with the German beer purity law (*Reinheitsgebot*) of 1516, which specifies that beer must be composed only of water, barley, hops and yeast. This decision has not, as feared, endangered Germany's beer production. Many other national laws define, in particular countries, what, for example, can be sold as pasta, sausage or lemonade. In any case, since the Cassis de Dijon case in 1979, mutual recognition (and standardisation) has been the cornerstone of the Single European Market.

Following a six-year legal battle, the European Court of Justice ruled in 2003 in favour of the *Associazione Prosciutto di Parma* in the case against the British ASDA Stores Ltd (owned by the US retail giant Wall Mart). The judges upheld the *Associazione's* request to stop slicing and packing the hams in-house and selling the result as Parma ham. The ruling does not affect Parma ham sold at delicatessen counters, which is sliced in front of the client. The pre-packed and sliced ham sold on supermarket shelves must be cut in the region of origin, otherwise the reputation and authenticity of the ham may suffer. The *Associazione* has about 200 producers of ham in Parma. It controls the whole process of production including slicing and packaging. This guarantees the quality and genuineness of this popular and expensive product.[41] The ruling also applies to *Grana Padano* (Parmesan) cheese, another prime gastronomical product.

Italian cuisine is highly appreciated and is becoming hugely popular throughout the world. However, this great popularity and market created a fertile ground in which many cheap imitations may flourish. There are about 600 foods and 4000 wines that enjoy the protection of EU law. In order to be protected against cheap imitations, they must pass rigorous checks to maintain quality. These goods may be luxuries, but their annual market is €40 billion. Consumers also show interest in the protection of originality and quality of food. A carefully regulated and supervised system would eliminate a host of food scares from dioxin in chicken to mad cow disease.

The European Commission drafted a plan in 2004 to introduce a 'Made in the EU' label on all products. This is supposed to promote European origin as a mark of distinction. In addition, the specific origin mark ignores the existence of global production chains. Brand experts criticised this plan on the grounds that consumers have few positive associations with the EU. Some governments asked the Commission to abandon this proposal. Distributors and consumers rightly want specific information about the origin of goods they sell, buy and consume. In this regard, they prefer to see, for example, a 'Made in Germany' stamp on tools or 'Made in Italy' label for clothes or shoes. Or, if they buy whisky, they think of Scotland, not of the EU.[42]

Many examples of NTBs arise from the application of standards, and this has a direct impact on the location of production. Belgium allows margarine to be sold only in oval containers, while square ones are reserved for butter. The standard width of consumer durables in the EU countries is 60 centimetres, but in Switzerland it is a few centimetres less. A bylaw of the City of London stipulates that in taxis gentlemen must be able to sit comfortably in an upright position with their hats on. While in Britain it is illegal for lifts to have a stop button, the same button is obligatory in Belgium. In the Netherlands, beer can be sold only in returnable bottles, whereas the German standard for a beer container is non-returnable bottles. None of these technical specifications has a crucial impact on the protection of life and health. Their final effect is to reduce competition and increase prices to the consumers. Trade policy is one detail that easily escapes the scrutiny of voters whereas small, but well-organised manufacturing lobbies may wield a strong influence on government attitudes in trade and industrial policy.

In order to protect the integrity of the French language against an invasion of foreign words, the French government tried to insist that a French word should be used on the package of a particular good that is sold in France: *pétales de maïs* instead of 'cornflakes'. However, according to the 1995 EU law, if a good that is legally sold on the Single European Market has a clear and unambiguous photograph together with a name in an 'easily understood language', it is not necessary to translate the name of the good into the language of the country in which the good is sold.

In order to deal with various standards, the EU has adopted three different approaches:

- *Mutual recognition*: National regulation in other member states is recognised as equivalent.
- *Harmonisation of standards (old approach)*: Various technical standards for vehicles, food or chemicals had to be harmonised in detail and were mandatory. It is not surprising that this was a rather slow approach, not only because of the thorough technical work involved, but also because of the required unanimity in the Council of Ministers.
- *The new approach*: The EU sets only the essential characteristics of the good (minimum important requirements). The industry can have a greater degree of freedom to satisfy it and to be innovative.

Harmonised standards are essential in some areas, such as safety, health and the environment, whereas mutual recognition (an agreement to acknowledge diversity) may be an interim solution for traded goods until harmonisation is implemented. In any case, a long-term advantage of harmonisation is that firms will have to comply with only one set of rules instead of up to 25 different sets. This may increase the gains that can be achieved from economies of scale. However, this only makes sense when the market for a good or a service extends to more than one member state. For example, although consumer preferences for relatively new goods such as VCRs, fax and photocopying machines, printers, CD-ROMs, computers and mobile phones are similar throughout the EU, there are widespread differences in the markets for foodstuffs and beverages, with preferences often strictly local.[43] In such cases, a potential EU standard that does not embrace these distinctions may do more harm than good. The member states of the EU are, however, obliged to notify the European Commission in advance about all draft regulations and standards. If the Commission or other member states find that a new standard contains elements of a barrier to trade, they may implement remedial action as allowed under Articles 30 or 94 of the Treaty of Rome.

RED TAPE

Another imaginative NTB is illustrated by the Poitiers case. In autumn 1982, the French government wanted to protect the home market from imports of Japanese VCRs. There was, however, no indigenous production of VCRs. The domestic manufacturer, Thomson, simply imported Japanese VCRs and distributed them under its own name. Just before Christmas 1982, the French government decreed that all Japanese VCRs should undergo a customs inspection in the town of Poitiers in order to ensure that instruction manuals in French accompanied them. Poitiers is in the middle of France, far from all main ports of entry for these goods; its customs post was staffed by only eight officers and was not well equipped. This decision increased costs (transport, insurance, interest, delays) and reduced the quantity of imported and sold VCRs to 3000 units a month. Such a measure might make some sense in a situation where a government wanted to restrain rising consumer expenditure that was causing a short-term drain on the balance of payments. In such instances, however, a more appropriate measure might be an excise duty or high sales tax. The moral of this tale is that the time to protect against the importation of goods whose efficient manufacturing depends on economies of scale and a steep learning curve is before external suppliers have captured most of the domestic market. The attention that this case attracted in the media was considerable, leaving the French government 'no other choice' than to revoke the measure. After Christmas, of course! A supplementary tax 'replaced' the Poitiers customs clearance procedure in January 1983.

JAPANESE CARS

Japan feared in 1952 that small Italian cars would make substantial inroads into its market. Therefore, Japan initiated an import quota deal. According to this arrangement, the number of Japanese cars that could be imported from Japan directly into Italy was set to be 2800 passenger cars and 800 all-terrain vehicles per year. When the situation changed and the Japanese became highly competitive in the production of cars, this NTB rebounded on Japan.[44] Since 1987 the European Commission has refused to support Italy's attempts to invoke Article 134[45] to block indirect imports of Japanese cars through other EU countries. Hence, imports of Japanese cars have soared.[46] Other EU countries had annual 'caps' on the imports of Japanese cars. For example, the 'cap' for Japanese cars in the French market was about 3 per cent, while in Britain it was about 10 per cent of domestic sales. A tacit limit to the market share achieved by Japanese car producers in the German market was about 15 per cent. The result is a lose–lose situation. On the one hand, consumers lose as they have to pay more for both domestic and imported cars and, on the other, the location of the EU car industry is postponing its inevitable structural adjustment and potentially losing its competitive edge relative to the Japanese. The governments of the EU countries simply bow to the short-term interests of powerful domestic manufacturing lobbies.

The EU and Japan concluded a 'car deal' in 1991. The EU offered the Japanese an increase in market share from 11 per cent in 1991 to 17 per cent (including Japanese cars manufactured in the EU) until 2000, when all quotas disappeared. Unfortunately, the parties placed different interpretations on the deal. The EU argued that the maximum number of Japanese cars either imported from Japan or produced in Japanese plants in the EU is based on forecasts of market growth and, if the market grows less than forecast, it had the right to renegotiate the deal. The Japanese interpretation of the deal was that the EU has committed itself not to restrict the sale of Japanese cars in the EU. In any case the accord shows that the EU is keen to increase competition and efficiency in the EU car industry. Another accord between the EU and Japan of 1995 is intended to simplify EU exports of cars and commercial vehicles to Japan through the mutual recognition of vehicle standards, as well as allowing Japanese inspectors (who issue certificates to imported cars) to work in Europe. From 2000, the EU protection of its car industry relied mostly on tariffs, standards, as well as market entry and distribution costs.

PRECAUTIONARY AND PREVENTION PRINCIPLES

As already stated, all goods legally produced in the EU may be freely traded throughout the EU unless they endanger public morality or the life or health of humans, animals and plants. This freedom may be challenged in practice by two principles that can sometimes act as NTBs:

- *Precautionary principle* refers to a proactive regulatory method. According to this principle, there are specific cases that are linked to

a certain exposure to danger and risk. They concern products, technologies or activities. Although a hazard may not yet be scientifically documented beyond reasonable doubt, it can plausibly be anticipated according to the accumulated experience. Even though there is a lack of definitive scientific knowledge, one must react now (prohibit or regulate heavily), before the arrival of a potential hazard. Although it may have certain justification following grave hazards and dangers such as BSE, this principle may be badly manipulated and abused by rent-seeking vested interests. This principle has been on the books since 1958 when the US Congress enacted an amendment to the Food, Drug and Cosmetic Act. Any new additive to food is presumed unsafe until its safety had been demonstrated through scientific procedures. 'The US statute places the burden of proof on the manufacturer and requires that foods containing new additives be presumed unsafe until proven safe. But in the case of GM foods, the US turned the law on its head and insists they must be presumed safe until proven not to be.'[47] From the 1980s, Germany was very active in introducing environment-related legislation based on this principle. The French court invoked the principle in 1998 when it suspended the sale of three genetically modified corn varieties. The EU may apply this principle in practice, but action should be proportional[48] to the potential risk and non-discriminatory, as well as subject to review and change in the light of new scientific findings. The EU lifted this six-year long ban in 2004 because of the pressure from the US through the WTO.
- *Preventive (reactive) principle* applies in the situation when the mischief has already occurred and when there is a need to prevent or curtail the repetition of the known type of harm and damage.

France invoked the precautionary principle in 1999 to maintain its unilateral ban on the imports of beef from Britain. This was a direct challenge both to the principle of the free movement of goods and to the authority of the European Commission, which after several years had lifted its ban on exports of British beef, which had been imposed because of BSE.

The precautionary principle touches on several sensitive and emotional issues (health, food safety, environment) and can provoke fierce protests from consumer groups. Although the precautionary principle is not (yet) enshrined in EU law, its political significance is that it may be applied at any point. If the application of the principle were to proliferate to any great extent, this would signify the end of the Single European Market for the goods involved.[49] The goal of the newly established European Food Safety

Authority (2002) is to provide scientific input into the EU decision-making procedure.

RULES OF ORIGIN

Liberalisation of trade and FDI with third countries potentially increases both trade with those countries and the share of foreign inputs in domestically produced 'hybrid' goods.[50] Rules of origin in general, and the minimum local content requirement in particular, are used as NTBs to prevent goods with a high external content from receiving preferential treatment in the internal trade of the EU. However, it is increasingly difficult to determine the 'nationality' of some goods, for example, cars. Countries throughout the world are free to use rules of origin as policy measures, as they are not yet regulated by the WTO. As a result, practice varies considerably, causing difficulty for both producers and traders.

The present EU rules of origin are based on the Community Customs Code (CCC) established in Regulation 2913/92 and its implementing provisions established in Regulation 2454/93. Article 23 of the CCC relates to goods produced in a single country. According to Article 24, goods whose production involved more than one country are deemed to originate in the country where they underwent their last substantial processing or working, provided that this processing or working was economically justified, took place in an undertaking equipped for that purpose, and that its working or processing results in a new product or represents an important stage of manufacture. The WTO intends to draft new standards for the determination of origin that will be universally applicable. Until it does so, the EU will continue to determine the origin of the goods according to the above legal provisions and in accordance with the Kyoto Convention (except for the provisions on which a reservation has been expressed by the EU).

Yet another complication in the calculation of added value and the shares of different countries in the final origin of a good is presented by fluctuations in the rates of exchange. For example, what rate of exchange should be used to calculate added value: the rate prevailing on the date of importation of inputs or the rate on the date when the final good is exported into the EU? A case in point arose in the export of ballpoint pens (made from American components) from Switzerland to France in 1983. The EU Court of Justice decided in favour of the date of importation.

Controversies about origin were for a long time confined to trade in goods, but are now relevant to trade in services too. What determines the 'nationality' of traded services? Many are based on wide international networks. None the less, certain criteria are emerging, including place of incorporation, location of headquarters, nationality of ownership and control, and the principal place of operation and intellectual input.

Rules of origin are responsible for many controversies, heated debates and tensions in international trade. In a supposedly 'globalised' international economy where TNCs are increasingly involved in foreign production, rules of origin make less and less sense. They are associated with distortions in investment decisions and reduction in international production and trade, and generally do more harm than good.

TRADE-RELATED INVESTMENT MEASURES

A trade-related investment measure (TRIM) is a new name for the 'old' performance requirement. The UNCTC (1991a) provided a survey of TRIMs. It was found that local content requirements are more common than regulations regarding exports or employment. Although TRIMs exist in both developed and developing countries, they are more common in the developed world. They are usually concentrated in specific industries, such as car-making, chemicals and computers. This study of 682 investment projects found that in 83 per cent of cases, TRIM requirements (such as local sourcing, exporting) would have been undertaken anyway, that is, not only were TRIMs intruding in the mix of inputs in the production process, but they were also redundant.

IMPACT OF NON-TARIFF BARRIERS ON THE EU

NTBs contribute to an increase in costs that accrue from the non-competitive segmentation of the market. They encourage import substitution and discourage rationalisation of investments. The anticipated benefits that would come from their elimination include increased competition, with its parallel effects of improved efficiency, increased gains coming from economies of scale and a consequent reduction in unit costs of production for an enlarged market, as well as increased specialisation. The outcome of this process would be an increase in average living standards.

A study by Emerson et al. (1988) illustrated the possible benefits that could accrue, under certain conditions, from the completion of the Single Market Programme (1985–92). The total EU(12) GDP in 1985 (the base year for most estimates) was €3300 billion. The private and public sector firms in Emerson et al.'s study estimated the direct cost of frontier formalities to be 1.8 per cent of the value of goods traded in the EU, or about €9 billion, and the cost of identifiable barriers, such as technical regulations, to be 2 per cent of total costs, or about €40 billion. Liberalisation of public procurement would bring gains of €20 billion, while liberalisation of the supply of financial services would save a further €20 billion. Gains due to economies of scale would reduce costs by between 1 and 7 per cent, yielding an aggregate cost saving of €60 billion. A downward convergence of presently disparate price levels could bring gains of about €40 billion under the assumption of a much more competitive and integrated EU market. The estimate of gains offered by the surveyed companies ranged from €70 billion (2.5 per cent of EU GDP), to €190 billion (6.5 per cent of EU GDP). The one-time gains for the 1988 EU GDP would give a range of €175–255 billion. At the time, these figures seemed likely to be underestimates as they excluded important dynamic effects on economic performance such as technological innovation and the introduction of new goods and services, which is difficult to model and predict. There was no widespread opposition to the completion of the Single European Market, because opponents to the plan could not offer an alternative strategy that would make up for the losses forgone from preserving the status quo.

The analysis of Emerson et al. was based, in part, on shaky assumptions. Hence, there were those who disagreed with their conclusions because of their *underestimation* of the effects of the Single Market Programme. Baldwin (1989) believed that one-off gains would be translated into a substantial 'medium-term growth bonus'. Others disputed Emerson et al.'s conclusions because they thought that the expected results were *overestimates* by a factor of two or three (Peck, 1989, p. 289). A communication from the European Commission provided an *ex post* assessment of the impact of the Single Market Programme (European Commission, 1997c, pp. 5–6). Its findings included:

- solid evidence of the positive effects of the Single Market Programme;
- growing competition between firms in both manufacturing and services;
- an accelerated pace of industrial restructuring;
- a wider range of products and services available to public sector, industrial and domestic consumers at lower prices, particularly in newly liberalised services such as transport, financial services, telecommunications and broadcasting;
- faster and cheaper cross-frontier deliveries resulting from the absence of cross-border controls on goods;
- greater inter-state mobility of workers, as well as students and retired people;
- between 300 000 and 900 000 more new jobs created than would have been the case without the programme;

- an extra increase in EU income of 1.1–1.5 per cent over the 1987–93 period;
- inflation rates 1.0–1.5 per cent lower than would have been the case otherwise; and
- an increase in economic convergence and cohesion between different EU regions.

The above quantitative findings are (for whatever reasons) more in accord with the expectations by Peck (1989) than in line with any other *ex ante* estimation.

Several arguments may be put forward to explain these relatively 'small' results, including the following two:

- Although the Single Market Programme was 'formally' implemented and the Single European Market introduced from 1993, the process of 'digestion' of all changes and opportunities still needs additional time. In spite of the large wave of (defensive) mergers and acquisitions around 1990, the exploitation of new opportunities for output and business in an enlarged market (free of NTBs) needs more time, perhaps a decade or two. This is relevant both for the manufacturing sector and, even more important, for services.
- The reunification of Germany and related adjustment difficulties have affected the economic performance of the EU.

Evidence regarding the effects of integration, in particular the Single Market Programme, is sometimes conflicting. For example, Neven (1990) concluded that the programme was relatively unimportant to the northern EU member countries since they have already exploited most of the potential for large-scale production. Alternatively, Smith and Venables (1988) and Emerson believed that the potentials for economies of scale were significant throughout the EU. This divergence shows that there is not a complete understanding of the determinants of trade and production patterns in the EU, which suggests that the analyses of integration will remain speculative, at least in part.

6. The European Union in world trade

OVERVIEW

As the EU is the principal international trading bloc, it has a profound effect on the world economy. In 2002 (Table 7.7), EU(15) merchandise exports

Table 7.7 Value of world trade in goods by region in 2002 ($bn)

Region	Exports	Imports
Western Europe	2 648	2 644
European Union(15)	2 441	2 438
Excluding intra-EU trade	938	931
Intra-EU trade	1 502	1 507
Transition economies	309	297
Eastern Europe	145	176
Russian Federation	107	60
North America	946	1 431
United States	694	1 202
Latin America	351	355
Asia	1 610	1 457
Japan	416	336
Developing Asia	1 114	1 033
China	326	295
Africa	139	133
Middle East	236	183
World total	6 240	6 501

Source: WTO, Press/337, 22 April 2003.

represented 15 per cent of world exports,[51] while the same share for the US and Japan was 11 and 7 per cent, respectively. On the import side, the EU(15) was the destination of 14 per cent of world imports, while the same share for the US and Japan was 18 and 5 per cent, respectively. The above data show that the EU is strongly linked to and interdependent with the world trading system.

The EU is also the most important actor in world trade in services. In 1990, the share of the EU in world trade in commercial services was 27 per cent, compared to the US share of 'only' 16 per cent and Japan of 10 per cent. In 2002,[52] world exports of services was $1538 billion, while world imports of services was $1522 billion. The share of the EU in the world exports of services during that year was 44 per cent, while its share in world imports was 43 per cent. The corresponding share for US exports was 17 per cent and for imports 14 per cent, while for Japan, the shares were 4 per cent (exports) and 7 per cent (imports).

Figures 7.4–6, respectively, show the developments in the EU current account, total external trade in goods and in services, as well as balances over the 1992–2001 period. While the EU current account and the EU trade in goods had a largely similar trend regarding balances, the EU has always

Trade policy 499

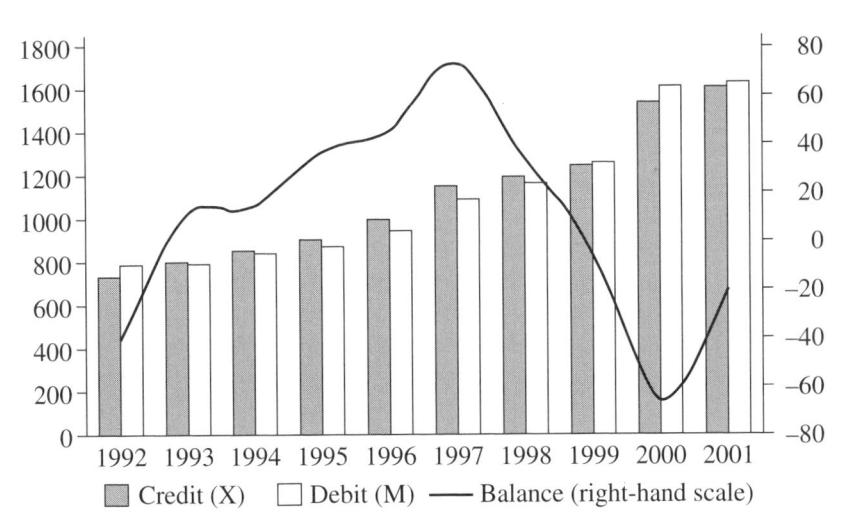

Figure 7.4 Extra-EU current account, 1992–2001 (€bn)

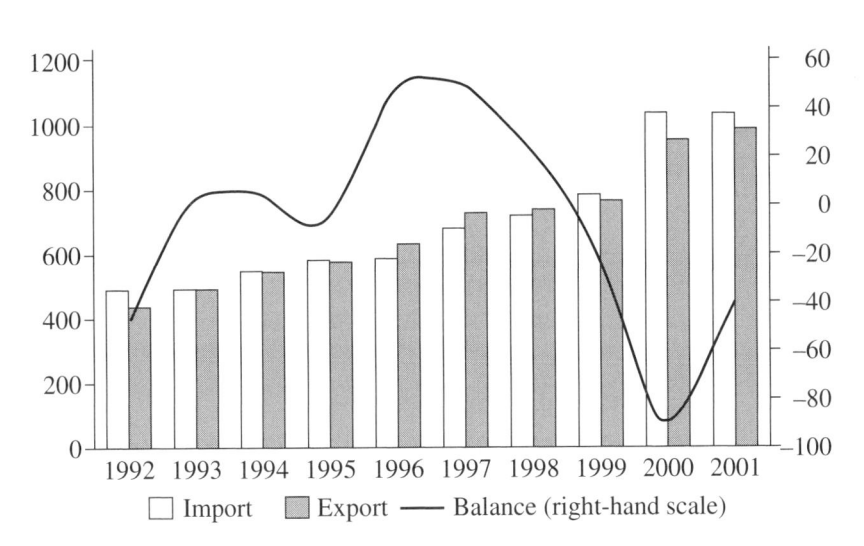

Source: Eurostat (2003).

Figure 7.5 Total EU external trade in goods, 1992–2001 (€bn)

Source: Eurostat (2003).

500   *The economics of European integration*

Source: Eurostat (2003).

Figure 7.6   EU external trade in services, 1992–2001 (€bn)

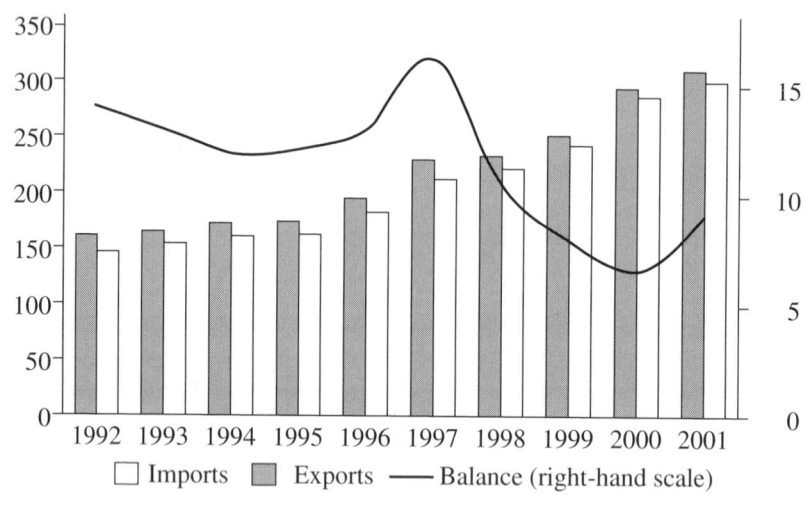

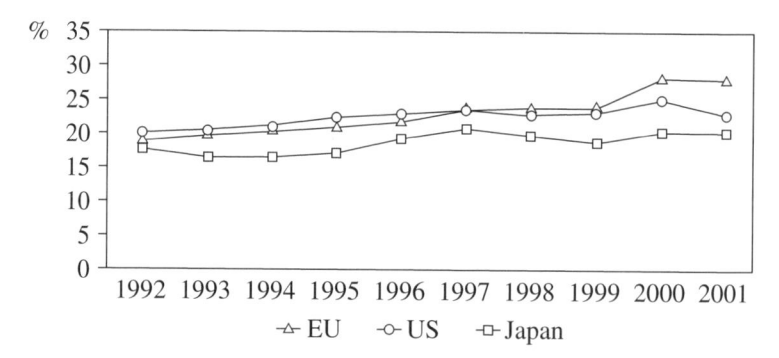

Source: Eurostat (2003).

Figure 7.7   Degree of openness of the EU, the US and Japan, 1992–2001

had a persisting surplus in trade in services. The principal EU export services that contributed to this surplus include financial, air transport, construction, insurance and computer, and information services. This clearly reveals the competitive strength and points to services industries that the EU may wish to foster further in the future. On the import side of trade in services, the EU has deficits in royalties, licence fees and travel. Figure 7.7

presents the degree of openness (the share of exports plus imports in the GDP) in the EU, the US and Japan. This indicator shows that the EU has become more 'open' to external trade than the US since the end of the 1990s, and that it has been more open to trade than Japan throughout the period of observation, 1992–2001.

It is often forgotten, however, that the mere balance of trade does not show a country's gain (or loss) from trade. What matters for the gains from trade to materialise is the volume, rather than the balance of trade. The larger the volume of trade, the larger the international impact on competition and allocation of resources. Bearing this in mind, the EU fares well.

IMPORTS

The principal partner in EU imports has been the US. In 2000 (Table 7.8), the US share in EU imports was 19 per cent. The EFTA countries, with a 10 per cent share in EU imports, were the principal group exporter to the

Table 7.8 Merchandise imports (extra-EU trade) by region and country, 1995 and 1998–00 (€bn and %)

Description	1995	1998	1999	2000
Total extra-imports	545.1	710.5	779.8	1 026.8
		(Per cent)		
America	27.3	28.4	27.7	26.3
United States	19.0	21.1	20.6	19.2
Canada	2.1	1.8	1.7	1.8
Other America	6.2	5.5	5.3	5.3
Brazil	2.0	1.9	1.7	1.7
Europe	28.0	26.2	27.3	27.5
EFTA	12.8	10.7	10.8	10.4
Switzerland	8.0	6.9	6.9	5.8
Norway	4.7	3.6	3.8	4.4
Eastern Europe	11.9	12.1	13.2	14.2
Russian Federation	3.9	2.7	3.3	4.4
Poland	2.2	2.3	2.3	2.3
Czech Republic	1.7	2.1	2.2	2.1
Hungary	1.4	2.1	2.3	2.1
Other Europe	3.2	3.4	3.3	2.9
Turkey	1.7	1.9	1.9	1.7

Table 7.8 (continued)

Description	1995	1998	1999	2000
Asia	33.5	34.1	35.2	35.2
Middle East	4.5	3.4	4.1	5.0
Saudi Arabia	1.6	0.9	1.1	1.6
Israel	0.9	1.0	1.0	1.0
East Asia	26.8	28.6	29.1	28.3
Japan	10.0	9.2	9.2	8.3
China	4.8	5.9	6.4	6.8
Chinese Taipei	2.4	2.7	2.8	2.8
Korea, Rep. of	2.0	2.2	2.4	2.4
Malaysia	1.7	1.7	1.7	1.7
Singapore	1.6	1.7	1.6	1.6
Thailand	1.2	1.3	1.3	1.2
Hong Kong, China	1.3	1.3	1.4	1.1
Indonesia	1.1	1.3	1.1	1.1
South Asia	2.2	2.1	2.0	1.9
India	1.4	1.4	1.3	1.2
Oceania	1.4	1.5	1.3	1.2
Africa	8.6	7.2	7.3	8.2
Sub-Saharan Africa	3.4	2.6	2.4	2.4
Other Africa	5.2	4.6	4.9	5.8
Algeria	0.9	0.7	1.0	1.6
South Africa	1.4	1.3	1.4	1.4
Libyan Arab Jamahiriya	1.1	0.8	0.9	1.3
Other areas n.c.s	1.3	2.7	1.3	1.6

Source: WTO (2002).

EU. Switzerland alone contributed 6 per cent to EU imports, while Central and Eastern Europe (without Russia) contributed 10 per cent. One also needs to note the relative shares of EU imports held by Asian countries. Japan contributed 8 per cent, and China 7 per cent. The relative share of sub-Saharan African countries was on the decline during the period of observation.

As far as the commodity structure of EU imports is concerned (Table 7.9), the principal single import item is machinery and transport equipment (38 per cent) followed by mineral fuels and lubricants (14 per cent of imports). There was a shift in the product composition of EU imports over time. Manufactured goods in EU imports regularly displaced food, raw materials and primary products. The principal reasons for these changes could be traced to the energy- and resource-saving technologies, changes in

Table 7.9 Leading merchandise imports (extra-EU trade) by SITC Rev.3 category, 1997–00 (€m and %)

SITC	Description	Value (€ million) 1997	1998	1999	2000	Share of total (per cent) 2000
	Total imports	670 529	712 370	776 707	1 026 792	100.0
33	Petroleum, petroleum products and related materials	65 383	47 208	61 211	121 261	11.8
77	Electrical machinery, apparatus and appliances, n.c.s	49 803	54 418	61 201	92 124	9.0
75	Office machines and automatic data processing machines	45 393	53 990	59 993	71 175	6.9
84	Clothing and accessories	38 645	40 925	43 619	50 915	5.0
76	Telecommunication and sound recording and reproducing apparatus	22 792	26 357	32 130	48 326	4.7
78	Road vehicles	29 953	36 827	42 913	48 220	4.7
79	Other transport equipment	25 412	30 598	37 539	43 371	4.2
89	Miscellaneous manufactured articles, n.c.s	27 869	29 693	32 256	39 004	3.8
71	Power generating machinery and equipment	19 441	23 350	27 141	34 735	3.4
74	General industrial machinery and equipment	18 201	20 790	22 875	28 538	2.8
66	Non-metallic mineral manufactures, n.c.s.	16 752	16 362	19 947	25 877	2.5
68	Non-ferrous metals	16 826	17 801	17 257	25 357	2.5
87	Professional, scientific and controlling instruments	14 490	16 011	17 695	22 838	2.2

Table 7.9 (continued)

SITC	Description	Value (€ million) 1997	1998	1999	2000	Share of total (per cent) 2000
51	Organic chemicals	15 073	15 551	16 471	19 861	1.9
65	Textile yarn, fabrics, made-up articles, n.c.s.	15 480	16 370	16 012	18 799	1.8
69	Manufactures of metals, n.c.s	12 330	14 036	14 941	18 175	1.8
34	Gas, natural and manufactured	12 461	10 797	10 189	17 714	1.7
54	Medicinal and pharmaceutical products	10 747	12 614	14 907	17 558	1.7
72	Special industry machinery	11 925	13 253	14 348	17 394	1.7
67	Iron and steel	9 289	12 302	10 159	14 475	1.4
28	Metalliferous ores and metal scrap	11 993	11 384	10 575	14 066	1.4
0.5	Vegetables and fruit	12 291	12 617	13 511	13 896	1.4
0+1	Food, beverages and tobacco	48 161	49 637	50 082	54 472	5.3
2+4	Crude materials, animal and vegetable oils and fats	42 621	42 293	40 201	49 894	4.9
3	Mineral fuels, lubricants and related materials	84 795	64 854	77 925	147 612	14.4
5	Chemicals	51 220	55 186	58 590	70 672	6.9
7	Machinery and transport equipment	227 827	265 511	303 995	391 125	38.1
6+8	Paper, textile, iron and steel, clothing accessories, etc.	195 841	210 626	223 586	278 033	27.1

Source: WTO (2002).

relative prices and the high degree of self-sufficiency in temperate-climate farm goods (mainly as a consequence of the CAP).

EXPORTS

The geographical structure of merchandise exports is similar to the same composition of imports. The principal EU export market in 2000 was the US (Table 7.10), which accounted for a quarter of all EU exports; EFTA

Table 7.10 Merchandise exports (extra-EU trade) by region and country, 1995 and 1998–00 (€bn and %)

Description	1995	1998	1999	2000
Total exports	572.8	733.3	759.9	937.5
	\multicolumn{4}{c}{(Per cent)}
America	26.9	31.0	33.1	33.5
United States	18.0	21.7	24.1	24.7
Canada	1.8	2.0	2.2	2.2
Other America	7.1	7.4	6.8	6.7
Brazil	2.0	2.1	1.9	1.8
Mexico	0.8	1.3	1.4	1.5
Europe	28.9	31.8	30.9	30.5
EFTA	12.1	11.3	11.6	10.5
Switzerland	9.0	7.8	8.3	7.6
Norway	3.0	3.3	3.1	2.7
Eastern Europe	12.0	15.1	14.2	14.4
Poland	2.7	3.8	3.8	3.6
Czech Republic	2.0	2.3	2.4	2.6
Hungary	1.5	2.3	2.4	2.5
Russian Federation	2.8	2.8	1.9	2.1
Other Europe	4.7	5.4	5.2	5.6
Turkey	2.3	2.9	2.7	3.2
Asia	31.0	24.4	25.1	25.8
Middle East	7.2	6.8	6.7	6.6
Israel	1.7	1.5	1.7	1.7
Saudi Arabia	1.5	1.6	1.3	1.3
United Arab Emirates	1.1	1.2	1.3	1.3
East Asia	21.6	15.9	16.6	17.4
Japan	5.7	4.2	4.7	4.8
China	2.6	2.3	2.5	2.7
Hong Kong, China	2.8	2.3	2.1	2.2
Korea, Rep. of	2.2	1.2	1.5	1.7

Table 7.10 (continued)

Description	1995	1998	1999	2000
Chinese Taipei	1.8	1.7	1.7	1.7
Singapore	1.9	1.5	1.6	1.6
South Asia	2.2	1.7	1.8	1.9
India	1.6	1.3	1.4	1.4
Oceania	2.4	2.1	2.3	2.1
Australia	1.8	1.7	1.8	1.7
Africa	9.0	7.9	7.4	7.0
Sub-Saharan Africa	3.6	2.7	2.5	2.4
Other Africa	5.4	5.2	5.0	4.6
South Africa	1.5	1.4	1.3	1.2
Other areas n.c.s	1.9	2.7	1.2	1.1

Source: WTO (2002).

and Central and East European countries together absorbed 30 per cent; Switzerland alone was the destination of 8 per cent; Japan received 5 per cent; and China was the destination for 3 per cent. It is interesting to note a continuous decline in the share of sub-Saharan Africa as a destination for EU exports during the period of observation.

Machinery and transport equipment were the principal EU export items (47 per cent of total exports) (Table 7.11). As this was also the major import item, this reveals a relevance of intra-industry trade. Chemicals also featured high in EU exports (14 per cent).

INTRA-EU TRADE

The most important effect on trade that results from economic integration is an expansion in the size of the market and an increase in the security of access to a group of otherwise separate national markets. Internal trade of a group of integrated countries is often taken to be one of the first indicators of the extent of their integration. The EU (and NAFTA) were the exceptions among the market-based integration groups regarding the volume of internal trade. Intra-EU exports (see Table 7.7) was 62 per cent of total trade in 2002 (the corresponding share for imports was 62 per cent), up from 36 per cent in 1958.

The establishment of a full customs union in the EU in July 1968 eliminated tariff and quantitative restrictions on internal trade. That was a year and a half before the target date set in the Treaty of Rome.

Table 7.11 Leading merchandise exports (extra-EU trade) by SITC Rev. 3 category, 1997–00 (€m and %)

SITC	Description	1997	1998	1999	2000	Share of total (per cent) 2000
	Total exports	720 446	731 577	759 798	937 471	100.0
78	Road vehicles	65 578	68 107	69 516	87 515	9.3
77	Electrical machinery, apparatus and appliances, n.c.s.	51 527	53 903	56 747	74 771	8.0
74	General industrial machinery and equipment, n.c.s.	45 949	47 269	45 677	52 138	5.6
79	Other transport equipment	36 424	39 309	41 568	50 374	5.4
72	Machinery specialised for particular industries	46 325	44 175	40 631	48 297	5.2
76	Telecommunication and sound recording and reproducing apparatus	27 233	28 045	31 352	43 451	4.6
89	Miscellaneous manufactured articles, n.c.s.	29 821	29 805	31 582	38 014	4.1
71	Power-generating machinery and equipment	29 081	32 776	31 850	38 455	4.1
54	Medical and pharmaceutical products	23 165	26 794	30 410	35 043	3.7
51	Organic chemicals	20 259	20 270	24 610	31 612	3.4
75	Office machines and automatic data processing machines	19 474	21 418	24 039	31 138	3.3
66	Non-metallic mineral manufactures, n.c.s	24 035	22 572	25 064	30 881	3.3
33	Petroleum, petroleum products and related materials	14 870	12 141	14 591	27 302	2.9
87	Professional, scientific and controlling instruments	17 664	18 490	19 912	24 294	2.6
65	Textile yarn, fabrics, made-up articles, n.c.s	20 143	20 256	20 092	23 331	2.5
69	Manufactures of metals, n.c.s	18 231	19 369	19 278	21 960	2.3
67	Iron and steel	19 050	17 699	14 962	19 410	2.1
64	Paper, paperboard and articles of paper	13 580	13 445	13 810	16 988	1.8

Table 7.11 (continued)

SITC	Description	Value (€ million) 1997	1998	1999	2000	Share of total (per cent) 2000
84	Clothing and accessories	13 881	14 103	13 690	15 854	1.7
57	Plastic in primary forms	9 896	9 150	9 730	12 384	1.3
0+1	Food, beverages and tobacco	45 863	43 498	43 498	49 681	5.3
2+4	Crude materials, animal and vegetable oils and fats	15 573	14 317	15 244	18 475	2.0
3	Mineral fuels, lubricants and related materials	16 993	13 888	16 460	30 160	3.2
5	Chemicals	92 934	95 261	106 464	127 932	13.6
7	Machinery and transport equipment	330 342	343 725	352 034	436 625	46.6
6+8	Paper, textile, iron and steel, clothing accessories, etc.	203 481	202 019	205 988	250 977	26.8

Source: WTO (2002).

Compared with the pre-1957 period, tariffs presented an important part of the final price of traded goods. As there were few NTBs, there was a strong and positive impact on an increase in internal trade and economies of scale. The goods that were affected most from this internal trade liberalisation were passenger cars, chemicals (including pharmaceuticals), tyres, office machines and home electrical equipment. However, the expansion of internal trade in the EU as an integration-prone development needs to be clarified further. The increase in the relative share of internal trade is due partly to the enlargement of the EU, and partly to commercial and other EU policies.

THE UNITED STATES

Introduction

As there are no preferential trade agreements between the US and the EU, the US is placed next to the bottom of privileges in trade that the EU offers to its external partners. The US treats the EU in trade relations no differently. The framework for trade between the two principal partners was essentially set by the GATT/WTO. In spite of these 'low-level' concessions in trade, as a single country, the US has continuously been the major single foreign supplier of the EU. In 2000, 19 per cent (€197 billion) of EU external imports came from the US. On the exports side, the US has always been the major exports outlet for the EU. In 2000, 25 per cent (€232 billion) of EU exports to third countries went to the US. Figure 7.8 shows a relatively large and increasing volume in merchandise trade between the EU and the

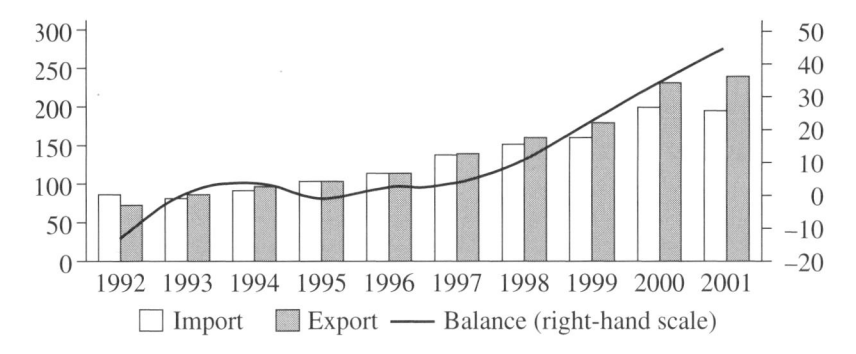

Source: Eurostat (2003).

Figure 7.8 EU trade in goods with the US, 1992–2001 (€bn)

US during the 1992–2001 period. As far as the balance in this trade is concerned, the EU has had an increasing surplus from the mid-1990s.

Problems

Agriculture is the economic sector that has constantly created tensions in trade relations between the EU and the US since the early 1960s. This situation is likely to continue for quite some time in the future. A Byzantine EU banana import regime provoked another problem in EU–US trade relations (see below).

The introduction of the CAP (not forbidden under international law) had two consequences that led to conflicts in trade relations between the two partners. First, it introduced domestic subsidies in the EU that artificially increased domestic production of farm goods and, hence, reduced imports. Second, excess domestic production of farm goods created surpluses that were exported abroad with hefty export subsidies. The access of US exporters of farm goods to third markets (Mediterranean countries) has been put in danger by the EU farm policy. The entry of Greece, Spain and Portugal to the EU further reduced farm export outlets to the US. During 1979–80, the US provided 47 per cent of total farm imports to Portugal, 28 per cent to Spain and 13 per cent to Greece (Yannopoulos, 1988, p. 118). These strong tensions in the past were on the brink of becoming 'trade wars'. The Doha Round has agriculture on its agenda. It remains to be seen what will be the outcome of difficult and uncertain negotiations.

The question of *food safety and genetically modified organisms* has raised a number of issues. The US (together with Canada and Argentina) is in favour of liberal trade in hormone-treated animals and genetically modified organisms. Following food-safety panics and concerns, the EU is exercising caution and has expressed hostility to this liberal approach in such a controversial matter. Even consumers in much of the developing world are leery.[53] The EU has tight rules on this type of trade, in particular since 1998 when the approval of genetically modified food became very difficult. The strict EU labelling and traceability rules of 2003 require that genetically modified organisms must be kept separate from the 'non-engineered' crops. The US objection is that this EU policy is costly to implement.

The Americans find it hard to understand and accept the attitude in the EU regarding genetically modified food because it is 'unfriendly with scientific progress' which 'could relieve hunger, raise farm productivity and improve the environment'.[54] However, they have soon forgotten, or deliberately ignored, the fact that the Bush administration seriously curbed federal funding for stem-cell research in 2001 as the official concession to pressure by the domestic conservative religious groups.[55]

The desire of American biotechnology firms to introduce the 'terminator gene' in their genetically modified grains is highly controversial. Such genes would make output sterile from a reproductive standpoint. Farmers would be forced to buy new seed from the biotechnology firms every year. US farmers would not notice much difference compared to the current situation in which they buy new hybrid seed each year. However, farmers in the developing countries who run their farms marginally above the subsistence level view this as another big step towards economic domination by and dependence on foreigners.

Following scares and anxieties provoked by BSE and other diseases, the EU and its consumers are very cautious about allowing these types of 'engineered' goods on its market, to the dismay and annoyance of the US. The Americans propose that consumers should have the freedom to choose between the products. Many Europeans fear that once in, these genetically modified products can easily poison the entire food chain. This EU policy, which was at odds with the WTO rules during 1998–2004, forbade, for example, the US exports of maize to Spain and Portugal, worth about €200 million a year.[56] Even though the EU ban was lifted in 2004, this will not open the floodgates to genetically modified food ('Frankenfood') in Europe for reasons that include consumer preferences and labelling of these products.

In 2003, the EU amended its legislation regarding the hormone-treated beef import ban in order to satisfy the US, Canada and the WTO. The ban remained in force, as it was fully backed by scientific evidence undertaken by the EU Committee on Veterinary Health. Studies have proven the risks and dangers of hormones that are widely used in North American beef production. One of the six hormones banned by the EU was found to be a cancer-inducing substance, while the other five also posed a health risk. Therefore, the sanctions were no longer necessary.[57] As the US was not convinced by the EU move in October 2003, the EU will seek a new WTO ruling on this case. This would just add to a long and growing list of transatlantic trade disputes that are awaiting a decision and resolution.[58] In any case, the US was not immune to food security frenzy. BSE was detected in America at the end of 2003, which dealt a hard blow to the American beef consumption and exports.

Banking is another bone of contention between the two partners. A single banking licence permits a bank that is legally instituted in one EU country to operate freely in any other. In order to allow foreign banks to benefit from this advantage, the EU requires for reciprocal treatment (in particular in the establishment of subsidiaries) in the country of origin of the bank in question. There are, however, certain financial activities in the

US that are not granted to US banks. The US would not permit foreign (EU) banks to engage in financial operations in the US market that are not allowed to domestic banks. One needs to distinguish between strict reciprocity in which all practices are the same in either country and reciprocity of national treatment. Under *strict reciprocity*, the home authorities would have to administer different regulations to each class of foreign firms determined by the origin of (the majority) of its owners. A reasonable application of this system is hardly possible. If *national treatment* is applied, then foreign banks are allowed to engage in the same businesses that are permitted to the local banks.

So much for the 'sins' of the EU. In its smug self-perception, the US still sees and portrays itself as the most open major trading nation in the world. This may not easily and directly correspond to reality. The first and the major concern of the EU in its economic relations with the US, is *unilateralism*[59] in American external economic relations. Unilateralism has always been epitomised by the lack of confidence and discontent of the US with WTO rules and dispute settlement procedures. The multilateral trading system may be placed in great jeopardy by the continued resort to unilateral retaliation measures because of the vicious circle of retaliation and counter-retaliation. No other important EU trading partner has similar unilateral legislation. Such measures increase uncertainty, potentially reduce economic interaction with the US and seriously question the WTO dispute settlement system as a freely negotiated and agreed multilateral framework.

The US intends to secure and improve access for its goods, services and investment in foreign markets through sector-specific[60] negotiations with foreign countries. These arrangements, according to some in the US, need to cover structural barriers that are still outside the scope of the WTO and they should be supported by a credible threat of retaliation. A widely disputed 'enforcement' tool is Section 301 of the US trade law (1974) and its modification, Super 301 (1988),[61] which epitomise the weakening of the US commitment to multilateralism in international trade relations.[62] The controversy about these legal means of promoting 'aggressive unilateralism' in international trade relations has provoked a heated debate both in the US and abroad.

This policy is unilateral because the US is allowed to define its own register of unfair trade practices employed by foreigners. These include a number that are not specifically outlawed by the WTO. Hence, the US may determine independently whether a foreign partner is 'guilty of unfair trade practice' and request direct negotiation with US representatives, instead of arbitration by a multilateral organisation. The policy is also aggressive as the US may threaten to impose retaliation measures in order to pursue its objectives (Tyson, 1992, pp. 255–8).[63] The US would disregard international trade rules and act as an investigator, prosecutor, jury, judge and executioner, all at the same time.

Instead of listing foreign countries and their unfair trade practices, the renewed Super 301 has a 'milder and less insulting form'. The renewed Super 301 requires the US trade representative to list only the practices that present barriers to trade. The implementation of the Uruguay Round dispute settlement mechanism would limit the use of Super 301 legislation. The Clinton administration extended the 301 until the end of 2001, but the Bush administration decided not to renew it once it expired in 2001.

The American trade policy is a model of hypocrisy. Whenever a domestic lobby is unhappy about imports of foreign goods, the US casts aside all national free trade principles and flexes its negotiating muscles in order to try to control trade. The US needs to be reminded that bilateral deficits primarily indicate differences in savings rates, private and public expenditure, productivity and the comparative advantages of countries.

Another problem is the *extraterritorial* enforcement of US legislation. The case in question is the Cuban Liberty and Democracy Solidarity Act or Helms-Burton Act (1996). This was one of the latest legal initiatives since 1962 when the US introduced a trade embargo on Cuba. If a foreign company invests in the confiscated US (including Cuban–American) property in Cuba, US citizens may file lawsuits for damages. In similar vein, the Iran and Libya Sanctions Act (1996) provides for sanctions against foreign companies that invest more than $20 million in the development of petroleum or gas resources in Iran and Libya. Because of Libya's 'cooperation' in the area of disarmament, this ban was lifted in 2004. Linked to unilateralism, this issue puts at risk the sovereignty of partner countries. In addition, it may lead to enormous legal complications. If the declared objective is to create a (free) negotiated multilateral trading system, then one country should not force and impose its standards on others, no matter how noble they are.

Next is the *national security* consideration. The US continues to bolster its trade and FDI barriers using national security arguments. In certain circumstances, the argument for national security may be valid, in particular following the attack on 11 September 2001. Every country has the right to defend itself against terrorism and foreign attack. The Exon-Florio Amendment to the Defense Production Act (1988) authorised the US president to investigate the impact on national security of any merger, acquisition or takeover that may result in foreign control of certain US industry. What bothers the EU is the vague and scarcely defined notion of 'national security'. Such an ambiguous term and a lack of transparency provide a fertile soil for the multiplication of various 'protectionist mushrooms'. There is controversy regarding protectionism in the US.

Supporters of protectionism argue: how protectionist can a country be that had a merchandise trade deficit of $452 billion in 2000; $427 billion in 2001; $484 billion in 2002 and $491 billion in 2003, while its current account deficit was $410 billion in 2000; $393 billion in 2001; and $503 billion in 2002? Any response to this question must take into account that these events regarding the American deficit in trade are principally the result of purely domestic American developments (not the 'wickedness' of foreigners). These domestic reasons include: relatively high growth in the US, expanded public expenditure together with a fall in tax receipts due to tax cuts, disequilibria between savings and expenditure, as well as sluggish growth in other countries.

Public procurement is another general problem. The Buy America Act (1933) and strong lobbying by the US industry introduced practice that discriminates or even excludes foreign firms from that lucrative market at both federal and state levels. Basically the procured goods should have at least 50 per cent of US local content. Executive Order 10582 (1954) allowed procuring agencies to reject foreign bids either on national interest or national security grounds. However, the Agreement on Government Procurement (Annex 4b of the Uruguay Round Final Act, 1994)[64] provided waivers from many Buy America provisions, but actual implementation may produce legal uncertainties. The EU is particularly interested in contracts linked to federal aid administered by the US Department of Transport. These include mass transport and airport improvement, precisely where the EU industry is competitive. It is expected that this annual market would grow to $35 billion in 2005 (European Commission, 2002b, p. 31). As far as major defence equipment is concerned, there is a requirement that it is to be produced on US soil (like the British Harrier jets) in addition to national preference.

Another issue is *high tariffs* for certain imported goods. Although the Uruguay Round reduced the overall tariff burden for exports into the US, certain tariffs still remain high. Tariff peaks are the highest for textiles and clothing (32 per cent), footwear (48 per cent), jewellery (13 per cent), ceramics and glassware (38 per cent) and trucks between 5 and 20 tons (25 per cent). High tariffs (25 per cent) are also applied in America on imports of two-door multipurpose vehicles. Although the US Court of International Trade ruled in May 1993 that these vehicles are passenger cars to which a tariff of 2.5 per cent is to be applied, the US government has appealed against that ruling.

Tax legislation may have negative effects on trade and FDI. This legislation includes different reporting requirements (subsidiaries of foreign TNCs have to report in a different way from the domestic American companies). Certain states in the US assess corporate taxes on the basis of an arbitrary unitary method. The proportion of income to be taxed is calculated in such a way that it may give rise to double taxation. There is also a luxury and 'gas-guzzler' tax on cars imported from the EU.

According to the WTO Panel findings in 2001, the US Foreign Sales Corporation (FSC) is an illegal export subsidy scheme, which has to be changed or abolished. It provides tax relief for income earned abroad by a subsidiary of an American TNC. This benefits big exporters such as Boeing and Microsoft. The US claimed that the FSC tax exemption was to avoid double taxation. This was not upheld as FSCs are typically established in tax havens such as Barbados, Guam and the Virgin Islands where no income tax is paid at all.[65] The WTO entitled the EU to introduce annual trade sanctions against imports from the US worth $4 billion. This is the biggest ever retaliation authorisation by the WTO. In 2003, the WTO approved a list of 1800 US products targeted by the EU for retaliation. The EU hit list selected American products that would be hardest hit in electorally sensitive areas. Tariffs would be imposed on products from textiles (hurting North Carolina) to Tropicana juice (wounding Florida). The EU would wait to apply these approved sanctions by March 2004. This pressure made the US Senate Finance Committee pass legislation in 2003 that would abolish the FSC and replace it with a 3 per cent tax cut for producers located in the US.[66] This bill was unacceptable to the EU as it has a three-year transition period to enable the gradual withdrawal of existing tax breaks.

For the first time in the history of transatlantic trade relations the EU imposed trade sanctions on US goods on 1 March 2004. The EU chose to be rather careful with the application of sanctions (in the form of tariffs) not to antagonise the US. Sanctions were not applied on politically sensitive products such as citrus fruit or textiles. Instead, they were applied on fairly 'inoffensive' goods such as jewellery, honey, paper, nuclear reactors, roller skates, toys and refrigerators. The EU sanctions could affect US exports worth €290 million in 2004. However, the tariffs were designed to rise gradually by 1 per cent each month (to increase economic pain for US exporters) until they affect US exports worth €533 million a year (which is far below the WTO approved volume of imports eligible for sanctions).[67]

The WTO panel found in 1997 that the EU was in breach of rules because of its banana imports regime. The EU subsequently altered this regime. However, the US threatened to retaliate in 1999 with 100 per cent tariffs even before the WTO delivered its finding about the new regime.[68] This threatened $520 million worth of annual trade with the EU on account of its banana and hormone-treated beef imports regimes. However, the WTO authorised US annual punitive tariffs on EU goods worth $117 million. The US tariff retaliations were on British, Italian, French and German exports, but not on Danish and Dutch ones as these two countries did not support the EU banana import regime. The retaliation affected goods such as feta cheese, biscuits, candles, handbags, speciality pork, coffeemakers and cashmere sweaters and pullovers. This would harm EU producers who have nothing to do with fruit, as well as US consumers who would find their favourite European goods excessively expensive. These American sanctions were suspended in 2001, after a US–EU agreement on the distribution of EU import quotas. Both the US and the EU would like to avoid a very harmful cycle of retaliations and counter-retaliations that can easily get out of control.

Another problem arises with *multiplicity of standards*. These reduce the potential economic and technical links among partners and diminish the benefits from economies of scale in fragmented markets. The EU and the US are engaged in consultations in order to advance cooperation and reduce potential conflicts in this area. The EU–US Mutual Recognition Agreement (MRA) of 1998 covers the mutual recognition of evaluation of conformity to each other's industrial standards. It covers trade in medical products, medical equipment, telecommunication equipment and recreational craft. These goods can be automatically sold in each other's market without having to go through a second round of costly verification in the importing country. There is a possibility of extending the coverage of the MRA to other products. The significance of the MRA is not only that it deals with technical detail, but more importantly that it ensures market access for important tradable goods in the 21st century. The problem is that the MRA has not yet been fully implemented in the US (electrical and electronic equipment).

Intellectual property rights (moral rights to authors) have already provoked several disputes between the two partners. Regarding patents, the US applies the 'first to invent' principle, while the rest of the world applies the 'first to file' principle. The first to file principle fixes the exact moment in time when the priority right to a patent is established. This is not the case with the US system. The US principle creates problems not only for the EU, but also for domestic American companies that try to obtain a patent right in the US. In addition, the US legislation permits American producers to use certain European geographical denominations on the US-made goods. For example, American wine producers are permitted to use names such as Burgundy, Champagne, Chablis, Chianti, Malaga, Porto or Rhine Wine, which may mislead consumers and damage the reputation of the genuine European wine producers.

National treatment is one of the basic pillars of liberalisation in the world economy. However, this type of treatment for foreign TNCs operating in the US is still not complete. Conditional national treatment in the US takes several forms. It is linked to reciprocity with the home country of the TNC;

in some cases there are performance requirements (employment); and there are certain tests if a subsidiary of a foreign TNC meets certain criteria in order to receive public subsidies. An example is the American Technology Pre-eminence Act (1991) designed to assist the private sector to engage in R&D in high-risk technologies that would not otherwise be started without public support. If the US continues to press for conditional national treatment, this may jeopardise the free flow of FDI from the EU into the US.

The next problem concerns the application of US *countervailing duties* and *antidumping measures*. The US Antidumping Act (1916) is inconsistent in several aspects with US obligations under the relevant WTO agreements. According to the EU, in the application of countervailing duties the US did not follow reasonable procedures and methodology. As a result, the EU had to ask the WTO Panel about the issue. As for the antidumping measures, they are allowed by the WTO, but their restrictive effect on trade needs to be kept to a minimum. Following the WTO Panel findings, the US Senate introduced a bill in 2002 that would repeal the 1916 Act, and this is still pending in the US Congress.

In March 2002, US President Bush introduced a 'safeguard measure' in the form of an increase in tariff of up to 30 per cent on ten steel product groups. After inconclusive consultations, the EU together with Brazil, China, Japan, South Korea, Norway, New Zealand and Switzerland entered into a dispute settlement procedure against this American protectionist measure. The WTO Panel found in July 2003 that the US measure was not taken as a result of unforeseen developments; in most of the ten steel products, imports have not increased (there was no serious injury); and the US has excluded imports from Canada, Israel, Jordan and Mexico from the tariff, while those imports have been included in the injury investigation. This is inconsistent with the WTO rules because of the lack of parallelism. To counteract the US measure, the EU has a retaliation hit list of US goods 'for the suspension of concessions'.

The WTO Panel ruling allowed the EU to introduce punitive tariffs of between 8 and 30 per cent on $2.2 billion worth of annual imports from the US unless the American tariffs were withdrawn before 15 December 2003. Faced with such a serious threat, the US backed down on 3 December 2003.[69] 'President George W. Bush said the tariffs, which he imposed in March last year and which had been due to last three years, had achieved their purpose by helping US producers consolidate and regain competitiveness.'[70] Thus, the American offenders unlawfully protected and mollycoddled their home steel producers, their illicit safeguard measures had a positive impact[71] on the domestic manufacturers (but detrimental to efficient foreigners and domestic consumers) and, ultimately, they were let off scot-free. One must observe and recognise that the general WTO trade-dispute settlement system, as shown in this case, is imperfect, but it may be better than none.

In the fields of *agriculture, telecommunications* and *insurance*, the Uruguay Round Agreement has brought some relief and market access is improved. However, there are still obstacles to sales in the US market. For example, because of unjustified (according to the European Commission) US phytosanitary measures, the export of Spanish clementines was suspended from November 2001. Estimated losses in EU (Spanish) exports of clementines to the US for the 2001–03 period were about €200 million. The US continues to maintain an aggressive export policy for farm goods through various subsidies. The US Farm Security and Rural Investment Act (2002) greatly increased the distorting effect of farm subsidies. Entry barriers are still important in the areas of mobile telephony (lack of access to frequencies, lengthy administrative procedure and investment restrictions). Even though there is an increasing convergence between the EU and the US in financial services, prompted, in part, by a number of acquisitions, the US insurance market is splintered because of different state licensing and operation requests.

Last, but not least, are the direct and indirect *support* measures that the US offers to its domestic shipbuilding and aircraft industries. For example, the US applies a 50 per cent *ad valorem* tax on non-emergency repairs to domestically owned ships outside the US. In addition, the Merchant Marine Act (1920) (known as the Jones Act), restricts shipping between US ports to the US-flagged and US-made ships. As such, this pushed freight rates to between twice to four times what they would be under free trade.[72] The act also effectively closed the US market to imports of high-speed catamaran passenger and car ferries. As for the US aid to the domestic civil aircraft industry, the EU estimated that it was up to $2 billion (which includes FSC to Boeing of $291 million) in 2000 (European Commission, 2002b, p. 47).

Compliance with WTO dispute settlement recommendations ought to be prompt. Both partners, however, have a poor record on this matter: the EU with respect to its import system of bananas, and the US on the subject of the FSC and the revoking the 1916 Antidumping Act.

Conclusion

To look only at trade relations between the EU and the US may not give a full picture about economic relations between the two partners. A number of American TNCs have operated in the EU for several decades. They have concluded that the most favourable way to take advantage of the EU market opportunities is to locate, produce and market there, rather than to export. The creation of the Single European Market aimed to enhance EU competitiveness of the EU-based firms. This would benefit all TNCs that are operating in the EU, which would, of course, harm certain exporters in the US, unless they adjust to the new situation. Finally, economic relations between the EU and the US would be shaped in the future more by the (sectoral) commercial interests of the partners and their local vested interests, than by the political and strategic aspects of their 'special' relations.

In spite of the serious problems and rows in trade relations, the glue that binds transatlantic economic relations is FDI. The total stock of FDI that American and EU TNCs held in each other's market amounted to more than $9000 billion in 2002. Although this may not be an assurance that the two economies will grow together in step, it may give some indication that they will not drift apart to a very large extent.

It is a well-known fact that in the long run economies can only grow together, not at each other's expense. In this respect the possible problems in transatlantic economic relations are twofold. First, the US has huge budgetary and trade deficits. The time will come when this continuing situation will need to be reverted, which will be when foreigners stop lending about $500 billion a year to the US. Throughout 2003 the US required $1.5 billion a day of foreign capital to finance its widening current account deficit. Second, the problem on the EU side is not so much economic, as institutional. The EU with 25 member states will increase its internal management complications by attempting to streamline policy making and reforms. Rapid reactions EU to problems and challenges may suffer.

EFTA

European Economic Area

One of the most striking features of economic relations between the EU and EFTA was that it was without tensions. One needs to view in that light the creation of the world's largest free trade zone, the European Economic Area (EEA), which came into being on 1 January 1994 (one year behind schedule). The EEA consisted of 18 developed market economies with 372 million people. What the EEA did in practice was to extend the Single European Market for manufactured goods and services to the six (Austria, Finland, Iceland, Liechtenstein, Norway and Sweden) of the seven[73] EFTA countries. Apart from Switzerland, the six EFTA countries adopted the EU competition rules and they were included in the EU market for public procurement.

As a group, EFTA has been the major trading partner of the EU. Its share in EU merchandise imports was 18 per cent (€11 billion) in 1970, while its share in EU exports of goods was 26 per cent (€14 billion) in the

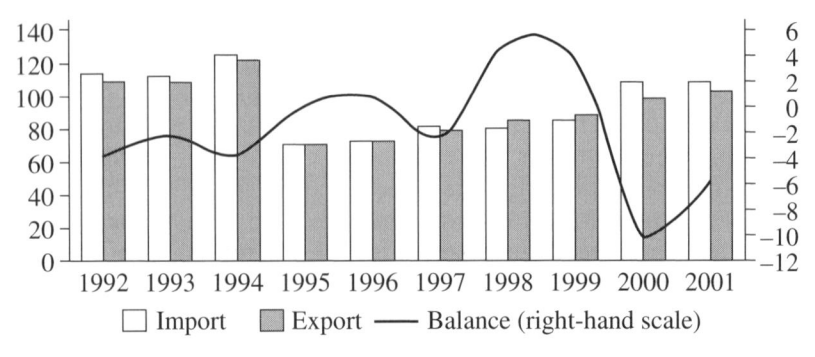

Figure 7.9 EU trade in goods with EFTA, 1992–2001 (€bn)

same year. In 2000, the EFTA countries' share in EU imports was 10 per cent (€107 billion), while the share in EU exports was 10 per cent (€98 billion). Relative shares in trade between the EU and EFTA should be treated with caution, bearing in mind that many EFTA countries left this trade association to join the EU from 1973. Figure 7.9 presents the volume and balance of EU trade with EFTA countries during 1992–2001. Even though EFTA countries are small in geographical terms, and even though the EFTA membership diminished in 1995 when Austria, Finland and Sweden joined the EU, the 'rest' of the original EFTA countries are a significant EU partner in merchandise trade.

The EEA was originally envisaged to be a kind of waiting room which would keep the EFTA countries 'out' of the EU for (quite) some time, at least until the provisions of the Maastricht Treaty were absorbed in the EU. The EFTA countries that take part in the EEA are subject to EU laws without the political clout to influence them. Hence, five (Austria, Finland, Liechtenstein, Norway and Sweden) of the seven EFTA countries applied for full membership of the EU. Austria, Finland and Sweden approved the arrangement in national referendums and entered the EU on 1 January 1995. Norway's voters, however, declined to join the EU, just as they had done in 1972. So, what is the longer-term value of the EEA? Would an EFTA that consists of Iceland, Liechtenstein, Norway and Switzerland (not a member of the EEA) be a viable trade organisation?

The EEA was inspired by the Single Market Programme which was expected to create a genuine Single European Market for the free movement of goods, services, capital and people. The EFTA countries were concerned about their competitive position in the Single European Market after 1992. Their trade conditions could worsen unless an arrangement with the EU could be found. Hence, the first contacts between the EU and EFTA about a change/improvement in their economic relations date from 1989. The agreement on the establishment of the EEA between the EU and EFTA was signed in May 1992. One of its objectives was to contribute to the creation of conditions for the eventual reunification of all the European nations in the (distant) future.

The agreement on the EEA is comprehensive.[74] It includes, first and foremost, four basic freedoms of movement (for goods, services, capital and people). Agriculture, fisheries and common financial policies are not covered.[75] Second, come horizontal policies, a catch-all title for a variety of areas such as environment, R&D, education and consumer policy. Last, are the legal and enforcement provisions. Areas that are beyond the scope of the agreement are the eurozone, common defence and foreign policy, as well as EU moves towards political union. An interesting feature of the agreement is that, in general, it did not have a transition period. The *acquis communautaire* was applied without delay, except in a few specified cases. Let us briefly consider the major features of the agreement.

Free Movement of Goods

Trade between the two groups of countries was initially hampered by the existence of various tariffs and NTBs (quantitative restrictions and technical standards were the most prominent). After the departure of Britain, Denmark and Ireland from EFTA, and their entry into the EU in 1972, all EFTA countries concluded bilateral free trade agreements for manufactured goods with the EU. It is curious that the EU did not treat the EFTA countries as a unit – hence the bilateral approach.

The 1972 agreements eliminated most of the tariffs and the NTBs. The EEA Agreement introduced a new dimension into relations between the EU and EFTA, as EFTA was recognised by the EU for the first time as a unit. The EEA Agreement abolished all the remaining obstacles to trade in manufactured goods between the partners. The Cassis de Dijon principle (1979) applies to trade in the EEA. This means that all the goods that are legally produced and traded in one of the EEA countries would be freely accepted for imports and sale in the other EEA countries. The exceptions include those that are hazardous to the health and life of humans, animals, plants and environment, as well as not in the consumer interest.

Free Movement of Persons

Citizens of the EEA enjoy unrestricted freedom of movement within the area. Their residence may depend on employment in the relevant country.

Special provisions cover retired people and students. With the exception of certain jobs in the public sector, workers and self-employed persons have the right to be employed throughout the EEA. They may not be discriminated on the basis of their nationality regarding employment, pay or other working conditions. Social security benefits obtained in any EEA country may be both accumulated and freely transferred within the group. This was a big concession that was granted by the EFTA countries. As a rule, the EFTA countries may be the receiving countries for labour that originates in the EU. They often have significantly higher average income than EU countries, hence they would be the preferable destination for a labour force that is willing to migrate.

Free Movement of Services

More than half of those employed in the developed market economies are in services. An important accomplishment of the EEA is that it grants full freedom for the provision of services throughout the area. As such, it goes beyond the traditional free trade arrangements, which usually limit themselves to a free trade in manufactured goods only.

Liberalisation in the supply of financial services (banking, insurance) in the EEA is supposed to increase competition and bring gains to consumers. Single licensing would ease the establishment of branches and subsidiaries in the EEA. A bank that is authorised to operate in one EEA country may establish its operation in any other EEA country without asking for a prior licence in the other EEA host country. The home country that has given the first permit is in charge of supervising the whole (EEA) operation of the financial institution.

Transport services have long been protected in the EU. The EEA introduced non-discriminatory access in its transport market. To support the new freedom in the transport market, EEA participants agreed to harmonise their technical standards (weight of vehicles, dimensions and so on).This is all expected to increase competition and benefit consumers, not only through lower prices, but also through a wider choice, higher efficiency and improved safety.

Free Movement of Capital

Linked with the freedom to supply services is a full liberalisation of capital mobility in the EEA. This is meant to enhance the efficiency of industries by extending choice and lowering the cost of capital. This freedom is an important achievement of the EEA. It also aims to eliminate exchange controls and freedom for FDI. As real estate investment has been the most restrained form of FDI in the EFTA countries, they were given some time to fully comply with these rules. A standard escape clause regarding restrictions on capital movements applies in the EEA too. A country may introduce controls if the domestic capital market and/or balance of payments are in danger.

Institutions

In order to ensure the smooth and efficient operation of the EEA, there was an agreement to establish the following seven institutions:

- the Joint Committee, to exchange information among partners and to take decisions (it holds monthly meetings);
- the Council, which is the highest political body as it comprises the EEA ministers and the European Commission, to give political guidance to the EEA by consensus (it meets twice a year);
- the Standing Committee, to receive information from various expert groups to assist countries in reaching a common position in the EEA Joint Committee;
- the Surveillance Authority, to ensure that the EEA is properly implemented by EFTA, while the same role in the EU would be performed by the European Commission;
- the Court, together with the EU Court of Justice, to safeguard the correct operation of the EEA agreement;
- as there is no transfer of sovereignty to the EEA in the form of legislative powers (the parliaments of the EFTA countries have the right to approve new legislation), the EEA Joint Parliamentary Committee would be an important forum for the discussion of parliamentary matters; and
- the Consultative Committee, which comprises members of the EU Economic and Social Committee and the EFTA Consultative Committee, to consider EEA social and economic matters.

Conclusion

Although small in economic and geographical terms, the EFTA countries practise a more liberal trade policy (imports of cars, for example) than the EU. These countries have a highly specialised economic structure. The Single European Market, which was supposed to increase the specialisation of EU producers, brought little, if any, gains to EFTA countries as they are already highly specialised and have free access to the EU market for manufactured goods. The per capita income in EFTA is higher than the average in the EU. The value of the EEA is that the EFTA countries convinced the EU that they can be a trustworthy and stable economic partner through thick and thin.

The EFTA countries had an interest in staying out of the EU since they did not have to accept the EU common external tariff which is at a higher level than their own tariffs on external trade. Participation in the EU could, potentially, bring some losses in trade with external partners to the EFTA states. In addition, the EFTA countries did not have to take part in the controversial CAP which in some cases offers smaller subsidies per farmer than is the case in the EFTA countries (for example, Norway and Switzerland). The cost of staying outside the EU would include sacrificing the chance to influence the shaping of economic policies of the new generation in the EU. However, this view is based on the assumption that small countries are in reality being consulted and, more importantly and optimistically, that their opinion is (highly) respected. This discussion of the EU trade arrangement with EFTA was necessary as it could present one of the possible ways in which relations between the EU and Central and Eastern Europe could develop in the future.

CENTRAL AND EASTERN EUROPE

Background

The relative share of countries from Central and Eastern Europe in world trade has been on the decline for quite some time. This share reached 8 per cent in 1988. These countries conducted about 50 per cent or more of their trade within their integration scheme, the Council for Mutual Economic Assistance (CMEA) before its formal demise in 1991. The economic shift towards a market-based economic system and a decentralised decision-making process enabled the transition countries to take advantage of being fully included in the international trading system. However, success in integrating the transition economies into the international trading system depends on at least two factors: the first is the transformation of their economic system towards a market-based one; the second hinges on the openness of Western markets for goods and services from transition countries.

One of the significant features of the transition process is a change in the direction of trade. After the collapse of the CMEA, transition countries redirected their trade westwards in a relatively short period of time, in particular towards the EU. Although a change in the pattern of trade took place, a portion of goods released from CMEA trade could not easily find market outlets in the EU, because they do not always satisfy the quality, quantity, design, environment, safety and other standards that prevail in the EU. In addition, goods that may be potentially important as export items for transition countries are often regarded as 'sensitive' in the EU.

Initially, transition countries were at the very bottom of the EU pyramid of preferences. Only Romania and the former Yugoslavia benefited from the EU generalised system of preferences (GSP). Other transition economies were facing every trade obstacle for exports to the EU – hence the Soviet policy of keeping friendly countries in the camp, not only through political and military means but also through economic ties, was lavishly assisted by the trade policy of the EU.

In order to curtail the technological capabilities of the (then) socialist countries, the West established the Coordinating Committee on Multilateral Export Controls (COCOM), whose objective, during and after the Cold War, was to prevent the transfer of high technology to socialist countries which would enhance their military power.[76] As that was not necessary after the collapse of socialism, COCOM was replaced by the Wassenaar Agreement[77] which includes Russia. The secretariat of the new organisation started work in Vienna in 1996. The purpose of this body is to control and prevent trade in technology for atomic, chemical and bacteriological weapons, in particular, to areas of tension and countries such as Iraq, Iran, North Korea and Libya that may abuse them.

EU trade with the Central and East European countries was relatively small until the mid-1970s. After that period it increased to 12 per cent (€55 billion) of EU imports and 12 per cent (€48 billion) of EU exports in 1989 the last pre-transition year. In 1990, owing to the transition-induced sharp deceleration in economic activity in the East, trade fell sharply. In that year the share of EU imports from these countries was only 7 per cent (€31 billion), while the share of EU exports fell to 7 per cent (€28 billion). After the initial shock, the relative share of EU imports from Central and East European countries recovered to reach 14 per cent (€146 billion) in 2000, while the share of EU exports to these countries increased to 14 per cent (€135 billion) in the same year.

Links

For a very long time there were no formal links between the EU and the transition countries which was one of the obstacles to trade liberalisation between the two economic groups. The two opposing economic blocs and systems were discriminating against each other. There was little that the East was able to offer to the West in return for MFN status in trade, and this situation continued until the end of the Cold War in 1989. However, the transition process introduced a significant change. From piecemeal assistance and trade concessions, eight transition countries entered the EU as full members in the new situation in 'just' 15 years. The transformation began with the EU granting the GSP, over trade and cooperation agreements, to the association agreements in order to culminate in full membership in 2004. Interest in supporting the transition economies in their reform efforts was amplified by the fact that the EU has an unprecedented opportunity to reshape Europe and make it a better and safer area.[78]

As late as 1989, but as early as the start of the transition process, trade relations between the two regions started to 'normalise'. The G-7 and the EU took the first step to assist transition countries in their reform towards a market-type system, as well as to regulate relations in 1989. It was a unilateral decision to grant GSP and to curtail certain quantitative restrictions on trade with transition countries. Subsequently, most of the transition economies were removed from the list of state-trading countries.

The second step in the formalisation and normalisation of economic relations between the two groups was the conclusion of trade and cooperation agreements with those transition countries that did not have them.[79] Albania, the Baltic states and Slovenia conducted trade with the EU on the basis of such agreements, which provide for reciprocal MFN treatment and trade concessions, remove specified quantitative restrictions and aim at a further liberalisation of mutual trade. This type of agreement was concluded between the EU and the former Soviet Union in 1990. After the disintegration of the Soviet Union, in 1992 most of the newly independent states accepted the obligations of the agreement.

In order to coordinate Western aid to Hungary and Poland in their transition process to a market-based economic system, political pluralism and democracy, the EU started a PHARE (Poland, Hungary: Assistance for Economic Restructuring) programme in 1989. Assistance from this programme was later extended to Albania, the Baltic states, Bulgaria, the Czech Republic, Romania, Slovakia and Slovenia. The PHARE programme aimed at an improvement in access to markets, promotion of investment, adjustment in the farm sector, food aid, environmental protection and vocational training. Its focus was the development of and support to the private sector in the transition countries.

Association Agreements

The following step in the liberalisation of economic relations brought association agreements (Europe agreements) between the EU and select transition countries. Short of full membership, EEA and ACP (African, Caribbean and Pacific) deals, these agreements[80] are supposed to be the

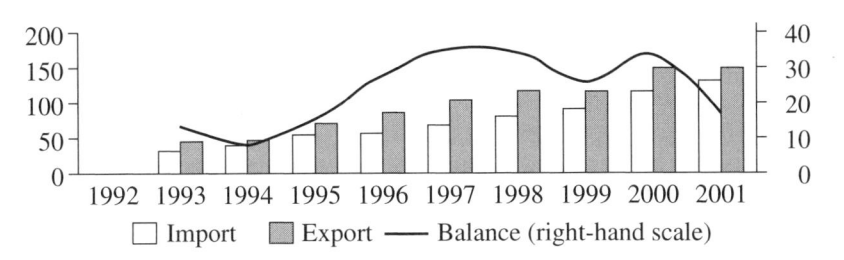

Figure 7.10 EU trade in goods with candidate countries, 1993–2001 (€bn)

most favourable arrangements that the EU can offer to foreign countries. The agreements mention in the Preamble the possibility of full membership for transition countries in the EU in the future. As a result of the increased openness on both sides, trade has been continuously increasing between the EU and candidate countries from 1993 (Figure 7.10).

Different agreements offered to transition economies reflect the extent of the reform process achieved in these countries. Although the need to aid transition countries through trade concessions is recognised and some actions were taken to create free trade areas between the EU and certain transition countries, there were NTBs that seriously hindered exports from transition economies to the EU. This is most obvious in goods in which transition countries have a comparative advantage, such as steel, textiles, clothing, bulk chemicals and farm products.

Association agreements between the EU and Hungary, Poland and the former Czechoslovakia[81] rewarded these countries' transition efforts and achievements, and these countries enjoyed the fastest ever climb on the EU pyramid of trade privileges.

The agreements were asymmetric, as the EU removed all quotas, while the elimination of tariffs is supposed to take place over a period of up to five years. The concessions to the transition counterparts also included a slower pace of tariff elimination of up to nine years. There are provisions that refer to trade in 'sensitive' commodities. In textiles, for example, tariffs are to be eliminated within six years, while the existing quotas should disappear in five years. At the end of the ten-year transition period there would be no special treatment for textiles in trade among these partners. The association agreements eliminated national quotas for trade in iron and steel. In agriculture, there are only reciprocal concessions for select goods.

Other major provisions of the association agreements refer to political dialogue among partners (this does not cost the EU budget anything), as well as safeguard measures. During times of recession and when jobs are at stake, there is an increased pressure on the authorities to introduce protectionist measures against foreign suppliers. The agreements stipulate that if EU producers are seriously injured, or if there are dangerous developments within an EU industry that jeopardises economic activity in the EU, then the EU has the right to undertake (unspecified) safeguard measures.

Association agreements introduced an element of stability into otherwise potentially volatile trade relations. An important point is that the EU accepted certain bold and liberalisation-prone steps even in trade in sensitive goods. The agreements offered some vision for economic relations in the future. This view is supported by a general view that concessions in trade may be the most effective way in which the West can help transition countries in their difficult, but in the longer term rewarding, transition process.

The transition process in economies and in politics does not progress in all transition countries at the same pace. Most of the countries that emerged from the former Soviet Union are the ones that lag behind the Central European transition economies. Therefore, the EU intends to conclude partnership and cooperation agreements with most of the former Soviet countries. This type of accord would offer more than the usual trade and cooperation agreement, but it falls short of the benefits offered by association agreements. One bargaining problem is that Russia wants to be treated as if it were a WTO member country. The EU cannot accept this. Before Russia joins the WTO, the EU has offered the countries of the Commonwealth of Independent States the TACIS (Technical Assistance for the Commonwealth of Independent States) programme which is similar to the PHARE programme offered to the Central and East European countries.

South-eastern Europe

After the violent disintegration of the former Yugoslavia, the EU wants to ensure peace, stability and economic prosperity in south-eastern Europe. This region includes Albania, Bosnia and Herzegovina, Croatia, the former Yugoslav Republic of Macedonia, as well as Serbia and Montenegro. As the main motivator for reforms the EU has offered stabilisation and association agreements to these countries. The final point of reforms is full membership of the EU.

In 2000, the EU granted autonomous trade concessions to the five countries in the region. As a consequence of this EU move, 95 per cent of regional exports enter the EU duty free. Stabilisation and association agreements are tailored to the circumstances of each country. The two such agreements with Croatia and the former Yugoslav Republic of Macedonia cover a number of issues from trade liberalisation over political dialogue and legal approximation to industry, energy and the environment. The general EU objective in the region is to establish reciprocal free trade areas between the EU and the countries in south-eastern Europe. A network of bilateral free trade agreements ought to pave the way to full integration with the EU. In addition, these countries need to adopt similar behaviour towards one another as now exists between the EU member states. Hence, the common purpose of these agreements is to put these countries on the road to full membership of the EU.

Conclusion

A plethora of agreements that the EU had with the Central and East European transition countries (before their entry) offered an improved access to the EU market. Those technical agreements were a paradise for lawyers and consultants. This variety of arrangements might have complicated life. However, eight Central and East European countries advanced rapidly in their transition process, as well as towards full membership of the EU. These countries signed accession treaties in 2003 to become full members of the EU on 1 May 2004. This enlargement is the subject matter of Chapter 14.

JAPAN

There are no preferential trade arrangements between the EU and Japan, just as in the EU–US case. Regarding privileges, Japan is, together with the US, next to the bottom of the league as far as trade concessions from the EU to third countries are concerned. In fact, Japan is often at the heart of various NTBs that the EU imposes or intends to impose. Overt and covert treatment of the Japanese by the EU tends to be similar.

Despite low-level preferences in trade, Japan is after the US, the most important single trading partner of the EU. In 2000, 8 per cent (€85 billion) of EU imports from third countries came from Japan. Compared with 1970, when the share of Japan in the EU imports was 3 per cent (€2 billion), that represents an enormous increase in nominal terms. On the exports side in 2000, Japan was the destination for 5 per cent (€45 billion) of the EU merchandise exports. The EU has always had a negative trade balance with Japan – in 1970, the deficit was €0.7 billion; it reached €40 billion in 2000 and €31 billion in 2001. This deficit has been the focus of trade disputes between the EU and Japan. Figure 7.11 presents the volume and balance of trade in goods between them in the 1992–2001 period.

□ Import   ▪ Export   —— Balance (right-hand scale)

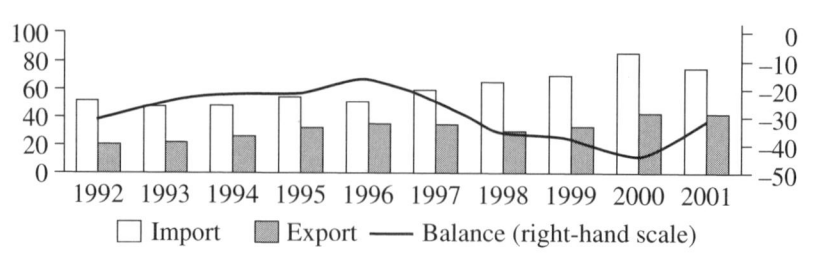

Source: Eurostat (2003).

Figure 7.11 EU trade in goods with Japan, 1992–2001 (€bn)

Access to goods, especially those targeted by Japanese industrial policy like cars, electronics and machine tools, has enormously benefited consumers in the EU. This has had a positive spillover effect on the acceleration of the restructuring of those industries in the EU. The problem is that in tackling the enormous trade deficit with Japan, the EU often stresses protectionism rather than domestic industrial adjustment and increases in exports to Japan. This EU policy may introduce frictions in trade with the US on two fronts. First, Japan may shift more of its exports to the US and, second, the output of Japanese companies that operate in the US may be regarded by the EU as being Japanese, rather than American, in origin.

It is inevitable that sooner or later Japan is going to become a mature creditor country. That is, one that takes more earnings each year from its past foreign investment than it invests abroad. At that point, Japan would shift from being a net exporter to a net importer. Once the Japanese seek to repatriate their foreign investment income, demand for the yen would increase and make it more expensive. This, in turn, would make it easier for foreigners to sell in Japan. Such a scenario depends, however, on the savings behaviour of the Japanese and many aspects of the Japanese economic policy (Lipsey and Smith, 1986, p. 12). When this happens, protectionism may partly recede in the EU and in America. This is all in the long term. In the meantime, the EU and the governments of its member countries are hard pressed by the short-term problems of employment and structural adjustment, as well as by elections. Following the Asian financial crises of the late 1990s, Japan's share in EU trade has declined slightly.

It is true that Japan has to be very much more receptive to EU merchandise. Japanese business organisations and their internal relations on the one hand, and their relations with the Japanese government on the other, comprise the major barrier to entry into the Japanese domestic market. Overt impediments to trade may be relatively easy to identify and could be challenged by WTO rules. There are, however, covert structural barriers in the Japanese market which fall outside WTO rules. This may be remedied by enforceable multilateral regulations on competition, which may ease restrictive business practices and policies that offer Japanese companies a preferential advantage in the domestic market (Tyson, 1992, p. 83).

Japan is not necessarily the only guilty party for a trade deficit that creates frictions in trade. The importing countries, in particular the US, need to put their economies in balance and reduce domestic budget deficits which have a strong impact on the balance of trade. Even if all the Japanese barriers to trade were eliminated overnight, the budget deficits of the importing countries would remain. Japan would still have a trade surplus.[82] Exports from Japan are concentrated in several groups of goods in which Japan excels. Exports from the EU and the US are much more diversified and often compete with the developing countries in the Japanese market.

Knowing that the creation of the Single European Market could have negative effects on the Japanese TNCs, many of these companies decided to relocate in the EU in order to become local 'residents' before 1993. This was most obvious in the late 1980s when the Japanese TNCs feared the possible creation of a 'Fortress Europe' that would discriminate against foreigners. These protectionist worries were not the only ones that prompted a surge of Japanese FDI in the EU. The Single European Market demanded it. A frontier-free EU offers possibilities for reaping the economies of scale, so there was an incentive to take advantage of that opportunity. An entry of foreign firms may prompt other domestic EU enterprises to adjust to the new situation and increase competitiveness.

DEVELOPING COUNTRIES

Introduction

The EU has advanced formal trade relations with a very heterogeneous group of developing countries. This is most pronounced in relations with a select group of ACP developing countries. This group consisted of 79 developing countries in 2004 with a population of more than 500 million. The main EU import commodities from this group are mineral fuels and precious metals and stones. In spite of relatively generous preferences in trade, the ACP countries' share in EU imports was 4 per cent in 2000 (approximately as much as Norway alone), while their share in EU exports was also 4 per cent in the same year. South Africa and Nigeria are the principal EU trading partners that contribute to half of all EU trade with the ACP group.

From Colonies to Yaoundé

With the exception of Luxembourg, all the founding member states of the EU have a colonial legacy. The association of colonies was one of the most difficult issues during negotiations on the creation of the EEC in 1955–56. France and Belgium insisted on the inclusion of the (then) colonies in the community-to-be. On this issue, as well as most of the others, France called the tune. France did not want the CET to be applied to trade with the Francophone countries in Africa. In addition, at that time, Algeria was considered to be part of France.

France was giving substantial aid to its own colonies (mainly in Africa) and wanted the community-to-be, in particular Germany, to share that burden. France accepted Germany's requests for free trade (a customs union), only after Germany accepted the French demands regarding the association of colonies and the special arrangements for agriculture. The European Development Fund (EDF) was created with initial resources of $581 million. All countries of the 'six' contributed to the EDF according to the allocated quota (France and Germany had a quota of 40 per cent each) to assist the development of the associated external territories.

The fourth part of the Treaty of Rome (Articles 182–188) relates to the association of the non-European countries and territories with which 'the six' had 'special relations'. The deal signed with the Associated African States[83] and Madagascar (AASM)[84] referred to the 1958–63 period. Preferences offered by the EU to the AASM were: the gradual elimination of tariffs on imports to the EU on the basis of reciprocity, financial aid from the EU, secured access to the EU market and guaranteed prices (higher than those on the world market) for the exports of the traditional tropical products. Temperate agricultural commodities were not included in the deal as the EU farm policy was in the process of formation.

With decolonisation, many African states became independent. New and more formal types of legal instruments were necessary to link the EU and an increasing number of 'overseas countries and territories' with which the EU countries had 'special relations'. The former colonial powers intended to retain economic (and political) influence over their ex-colonies in order to prevent Soviet intrusion into that region. They linked the newly independent states (former colonies) to the EU, not under Articles 182–8, but under Article 310 of the Treaty of Rome. After negotiations, the agreement on trade and aid was concluded in Yaoundé, Cameroon (Yaoundé Convention) between 18 African states (south of the Sahara) and Madagascar on one side, and the EU on the other.

In Yaoundé I (1964–69), the EU gave preferences in trade and development aid to developing partner countries. On the one hand, France and the formerly associated countries wanted to formalise the already existing preferences and, on the other hand, Germany and the Netherlands wanted to extend preferences to all developing countries in order to avoid selective discrimination among countries in the developing world. The objective of Yaoundé I was a free entry of imports of manufactured goods from the 18 countries to the EU under the principle of reciprocity and non-discrimination between the six; guaranteed prices for tropical agricultural products coupled with free access to the EU market; and, finally, an increase in aid from the EU (the EDF disposed of $730 million).

During the negotiations (1968–69) to renew the Yaoundé Convention, the partners had the same intentions as those that prevailed during the Yaoundé I period. The only important change that Yaoundé II (1969–75) introduced was an increase in the amount allocated to the EDF ($900 million) and the possibility for the developing partner countries to obtain $100 million loans for industrialisation from the European Investment Bank (EIB).

When assessing the Yaoundé conventions, it is important to note the doubling of the absolute volume of trade between the partners from $933 to $1817 million between 1958 and 1969, respectively. The relative share of the Yaoundé countries in the total EU imports, however, decreased from 5.5 per cent (1961) to 3.2 per cent (1971). At the same time, EU exports to the group fell from 5.5 to 3.4 per cent in the same period (Coffey, 1982, p. 15). In spite of preferences in trade to the group of developing countries, these trends show a relative increase in EU trade with other partners. In part, these changes are also due to the relative increase of prices for industrial goods and the relative fall of prices of primary commodities at the time.

Lomé Agreements

Introduction
The Yaoundé conventions were directed almost exclusively at the former French colonies. After the British entry into the EU in 1973, Britain wanted to include its own former colonies from Africa, Asia, the Caribbean and the Pacific, to the EU (Yaoundé-type) preferences. No less important was concern about the unsatisfactory trends in trade between the Yaoundé countries and the EU that was not mitigated by the two conventions. All this turned attention to alternative ways of regulating relations between the EU and select developing countries, for example, to

stabilising developing countries' exports earnings and diversifying the economic structure (industrialisation).

Provisions and impact

Forty-six ACP countries negotiated a new and wider agreement with the EU in relation to the preceding ones. The objective was to introduce dialogue, partnership and contractual predictability. The ACP countries exist as an organised group only in relations with the EU. The agreement known as Lomé I was signed in 1975 in Lomé, the capital of Togo. Lomé I (1976–80) has had three extensions so far: Lomé II (1980–85), Lomé III (1985–90) and Lomé IV (1990–2000). Later deals incorporated several changes and amendments in the first agreement. The two most relevant features that led to the renegotiations of Lomé I were the following: first, most of the participating African states stagnated in their development during the Lomé I period; second, Africa is vulnerable to economic influences over which it does not have control such as fluctuations in the price for primary commodities. The number of developing countries that have entered the chain of Lomé agreements expanded from 46 (Lomé I) to 58 (Lomé II) over 65 (Lomé III) to 70 in Lomé IV.

Lomé IV deals with a number of areas from agriculture to the environment to culture. The core of the EU and ACP cooperation, however, may be found in the areas of trade, financial aid and special facilities (Stabex and Sysmin). Lomé IV was concluded for a ten-year period (1990–2000), split into two five-year subperiods. It maintained the major terms of the previous Lomé deals with certain updates. One is the introduction of a human rights 'suspension clause'. If any of the essential human rights are violated in the ACP country, the EU may suspend development aid.

Almost all (99.5 per cent) goods that are exported by the ACP countries to the EU have free access (no duties or quotas) to the EU market. The EU has not asked for reciprocity from the ACP for these preferences in trade. None the less, these concessions may be misleading regarding the generosity of the EU. They refer to goods that are currently exported, but they do not refer to the products which might be exported after the (industrial) development of the ACP states. As for the rest of the ACP goods (0.5 per cent), they represent products that directly compete with the farm commodities covered by the CAP. A relatively generous nominal non-tariff treatment of imports from the ACP countries in the EU market conceals the fact that almost two-thirds of the ACP exports would enter the EU tariff free, anyway.

The developments of the EU trade in goods and the EU trade deficit is represented in Figure 7.12. In spite of relatively favourable trade treatment in the market of the EU compared with most other trading partners, the

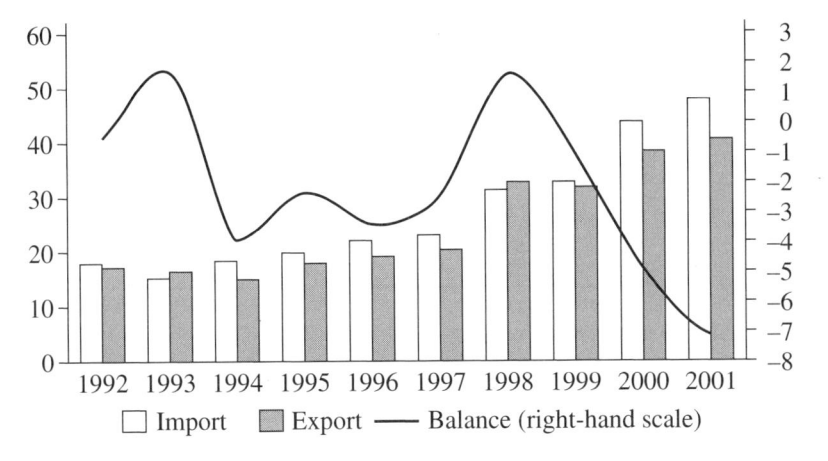

Figure 7.12   EU trade in goods with ACP countries, 1992–2001 (€bn)

share of the ACP countries in the EU imports and exports was, generally, on a steady decline (Table 7.12). The share of the ACP countries, as a proportion of EU imports from other developing countries was also shrinking. This took place in spite of the fact that they have not been subject to fully blown competition from other, in particular Asian, developing countries, which shows that other, non-preferred, developing countries were doing much better in the EU market than the select ACP group. The non-ACP group of developing countries diversified their economic structures and widened and upgraded the composition of their exports.[85] In addition, the increase in relative importance in the EU trade of other developing countries was due to changes in the relative price of crude oil since the early 1970s.

The principal EU import goods by value were oil (24 per cent) and diamonds and gold (20 per cent) in 2000. Hence oil and precious metals and stones contributed to almost half of all EU imports from ACP countries. Ten key EU import items (oil, precious metals and stones, wood, ores, fruit, nuts, cocoa, coffee, tea and fish) from the ACP group are basic commodities with little value added. Together these commodities make up about 70 per cent of all ACP exports to the EU. Prices of many of these basic products are subject to sharp fluctuations on the world market which create instability in export earnings. This is unconducive to the attainment of macroeconomic stability and development objectives in the ACP group. Roughly two-thirds of all EU imports from the ACP group come from only seven countries (South Africa, Nigeria, Ivory Coast, Cameroon, Angola,

Table 7.12 *EU trade with ACP countries including South Africa in 1980, 1990 and 2001 (€m and %)*

Imports	1980	1990	2001	Exports	1980	1990	2001
€ million	28 590	27 864	47 514	€ million	23 293	22 716	40 007
Share of EU total %	10.4	6.4	4.6	Share of EU total %	11.5	5.8	4.1
Trade balance	−5 297	−5 148	−7 507				

Source: Eurostat (2003).

Mauritius and Ghana). With its share of 20 per cent, Britain is the main destination for the EU imports from the ACP group. Next come France (16 per cent), Spain (14 per cent) and Germany (13 per cent).

The major EU export items to the ACP countries were mechanical and electrical machinery, ships and road vehicles. These four major export items represented half of all EU exports to the ACP countries. Prices of EU exports tend to be stable. The principal destination countries for EU exports in the ACP group are similar to those for EU imports.

The reasons for such a weak performance in trade by ACP countries in spite of substantial openness for trade by the EU can be found in the structure of domestic production and market in these countries. A highly heterogeneous group of ACP countries has on average a very small domestic market. This influenced the structure of production and the weak impact of economies of scale. Consequently, costs of production in the manufacturing sector are high. Trade concessions given to the ACP developing countries may not fully compensate for this structural cost disadvantage relative to other developing countries. In addition, single commodities such as cocoa, coffee, bananas, petroleum, sugar or timber often dominate in the export structure of ACP countries. There is also a lack of products with high value, many of which would enter the EU without any obstacle. Hence, the EU concessions in reality applied only to about a third of all exports from ACP countries. In addition, production of competitive goods and trade depend to a large extent on adequate infrastructure. Power supply, telecommunications, electronic data interchange and transport links and capacity are poor, in particular in Africa.

The reasons for such unfavourable developments in ACP exports to the EU include a high concentration of ACP countries in the production and exports of traditional tropical agricultural products, as well as a weakness in the productivity and quality of the manufactured goods compared with those from Asia and Latin America. In addition, both the EU and its member states initially promote industrialisation in ACP countries, but they restrict imports of the products of these industries as soon as the ACP countries become competitive on the world market. An example of this policy was the earlier EU warning to Mauritius to accept the 'voluntary export restraint agreement' for textiles.

The Lomé deals offered to the ACP group a preferential duty-free access for goods to the EU market, without formal reciprocity. The EU has the right to introduce safeguard measures in case of the need for 'external financial stability'. The EU considers the ACP countries as a single group, which is very important with regard to the origin of the goods exported to the EU. The GSP offers preferences to each developing country, however, the developing countries are not taken to be a single unit. In that respect the Lomé arrangement has an advantage over the GSP.

Financial aid
The aid package that was offered to the ACP countries by the EU during the first half of the duration of the deal (1990–95), disposed of €12 billion. Allocated resources for the 1996–2000 period were €14.6 billion.[86] Most of that amount (61 per cent) was reserved for the programmable aid. This included national and regional indicative programmes, as well as support for structural adjustment. The national indicative programmes of each ACP country referred to the development programmes and projects that are planned. Similar programmes existed at a regional level. A novel feature introduced by Lomé IV is that there is a direct reference to the environmental (drought, desertification) impact of the financed projects. Most of the rest of the funds represented non-programmable aid that was granted to ACP states on a case-by-case basis. These include Stabex and Sysmin (see below), risk capital, emergency aid and assistance to refugees.[87] Although there was a substantial nominal increase in the available funds for the first five years of Lomé IV over Lomé III (over 40 per cent) if one considers the increase in the number of ACP countries and their population together with inflation, the real growth in the available resources (if there was any) was quite small.

The feature that represented an entirely new point in relations between the north and south was the system for the Stabilisation of Export Earnings from Agricultural Commodities (Stabex).[88] It was introduced in Lomé I and upgraded in the agreements that followed. If a country exports a small number of primary commodities and if the price of these commodities fluctuates on the international market, the exporting country has changes in export earnings. The EU introduced Stabex in order to stabilise earnings of the ACP countries that come from the exportation of tropical agricultural commodities. The intention of the EU was to inject into the economies of the ACP countries an amount of funds that would be received from the EU market if unexpected circumstances (a decrease in price) had not occurred. An ACP country is eligible for the stabilisation of export earnings (receipt of funds) if:

- an eligible export commodity contributed at least 5 per cent to the total export earnings of all goods to all destinations (in the case of least-developed, landlocked and island ACP countries, the corresponding threshold is 1 per cent); and
- the export earnings were decreased by 4.5 per cent of the reference level[89] (for the least-developed countries the threshold is 1 per cent).

A transfer from Stabex is meant to stabilise export earnings. However, the destabilising element is a long lag between the fall in export earnings and the actual transfer, as well as a shortage of Stabex funds.

Stabex disposed of €1.5 billion during 1990–95[90] and €1.8 billion during 1996–2000. The number of tropical agricultural commodities that are covered by Stabex was extended from 29 (Lomé I), to 44 (Lomé II), Lomé III covered 48, while Lomé IV covered 49 basic agricultural and fishing products that ACP countries export to the EU.[91] The list included almost all ACP agricultural export commodities, so one could not expect a large expansion of it in the future. The bulk of all transfers (over half) went on the support of only a few commodities such as oils and fats (groundnuts and related products such as groundnut oil) and tropical beverages (coffee and cocoa). Such a high concentration of the disbursements of funds, however, was not the intention of the Stabex founders. The funds received from Stabex may be spent either in the sector that recorded the loss of export earnings or in other (farm) sectors for the purposes of diversification. The recipient ACP country is obliged to send a report to the European Commission on the use of the transferred funds within a year. Failing that, the Council of Ministers may suspend the application of decisions on subsequent transfers until the ACP state has provided the required information.

The Compensatory Financing Facility introduced by the IMF in 1963 was to finance the fall in the developing countries' export earnings from primary products. The fall in export earnings eligible for financing has to be the consequence of circumstances beyond the control of the developing countries. This might look, at first sight, similar to the Stabex scheme. However, there are crucial differences between the two systems. The IMF gives support in dealing with the balance of payments problems in general. It takes into account the general situation of the balance of payments of the country. Stabex, on the contrary, considers only the specific commodity fall in export earnings. The amount of funds that can be received from the IMF is limited by the country's quota, while transfers from Stabex are limited by the funds that are allocated to it by the EU.

Cotonou Agreement

Once the Uruguay Round concessions are put into full effect (2005), this would end three decades of privileged access of ACP countries to the EU market. The ACP countries would face the global market conditions as they are. The EC–ACP relation should take another path. The Cotonou Agreement, signed in Cotonou (Fiji) in 2000 replaced the last Lomé Convention after it expired. The new deal is the biggest North–South cooperation framework, relating to a 20-year partnership between the EU and, at the time of signing, 71 ACP states. There is free access to the EU market for all industrial goods originating in ACP countries. A new feature in the Cotonou Agreement is that reciprocity in trade concessions will start in 2008.

The Cotonou Agreement will run until 2007, when it will be replaced by a new type of deal: economic partnership agreements, negotiations for which started in 2002. These new agreements will deal with political issues, cooperation in the economic domain and trade, as well as development aid. It is likely that the new agreements will take the form of agreements between the EU and groups of neighbouring ACP countries (hub-and-spoke integration). The ACP countries will have to open their markets for imports from the EU in the 2008–20 period. If an ACP country does not wish to do so, it will benefit from the new EU GSP which will be announced before 2005.

The agreed financial framework for the 2000–06 period disposes of €13.5 billion in aid plus €1.7 billion in loans from the EIB. The considerable and unused resources from previous funds of €10 billion[92] are also made available to the ACP countries. The EU insisted on the norms of civil society. Violations of sensitive issues such as human rights, democratic principles, rule of law and good public governance (no corruption), could lead to the suspension of aid. The Cotonou Agreement abandoned the Stabex and Sysmin schemes. Even under Lomé IV, the emphasis gradually moved from income compensation to structural reforms. The Cotonou deal finalised this transition towards the support of development objectives (and fight against poverty) in ACP countries.

Everything but Arms

One of the latest and most highly publicised unilateral and 'groundbreaking' EU initiatives concerning least developed countries is called 'Everything but Arms' (2001). The EU offered to eliminate all tariffs on all imports originating in the 48 least-developed countries (39 of them are ACP countries), but arms and ammunition. There are only a few exceptions: fresh bananas, rice and sugar. Tariffs on these three goods will be eliminated according to a special schedule until 2006 for bananas and until 2009 for rice and sugar. All this is no doubt generous – completely free access by 2009. But compared to the already prevailing situation, that is, under the Cotonou deal, developing countries already have an 'everything but arms' free access to the EU market. So who can benefit from the offer? The nine non-ACP developing countries: Afghanistan, Bangladesh, Bhutan, Cambodia, Laos, Maldives, Myanmar, Nepal and Yemen. Can this be considered a radically new departure from the EU development–aid policy? And of course, banana, sugar and rice lobbies in the EU are also beneficiaries (Curzon Price, 2002, p. 9).

Trade in Bananas

Bananas are one of the world's most traded fruits. The international market for bananas is of great importance for the developing countries that export them. World imports of bananas were worth $5.8 billion in 2001. Compared with other imported fruits in the same year, it was below the trade in green coffee ($6.3 billion), but more than imports of either oranges ($2.6 billion) or cocoa beans ($2.6 billion).[93] As an agricultural product, banana cultivation is generally confined to the tropical developing countries, which are mainly situated in Latin America, the Caribbean, Africa and certain Asian countries such as the Philippines. Major banana consumers are the industrialised countries in the temperate zone. Bananas are also produced in the EU in Crete, as well as in overseas departments such as the Canary Islands, Guadeloupe, Madeira and Martinique. As EU domestic production does not satisfy internal demand either by quality or quantity, bananas are imported from abroad – EU imports represented one-third of world imports of bananas in 2001.

Prior to 1993, the EU had several distinct regimes for the import of bananas. Belgium, Denmark, Ireland, Luxembourg and the Netherlands imported bananas predominantly from Latin America, and the only border measure was the 20 per cent *ad valorem* tariff. Germany has always had a tariff-free quota for banana imports from all sources. Britain, France, Greece, Italy and Portugal limited imports by licence and other quantitative restrictions, while Spain had a closed domestic market.

The objective of the Single European Market was to increase competition, widen choice and reduce prices for goods and services in the EU market. This means that all overseas goods that enter the EU need to circulate freely in the internal market. The rules of this market should also be applied to the EU internal market for bananas. This meant that the previous national import systems had to be abandoned in favour of a common one. Regulation 404/93 introduced a common market organisation for bananas in July 1993.

The new EU banana imports regime that entered into force in 1993 had two basic purposes: to create a single internal market for bananas and to secure access to the EU market for bananas from the ACP countries. The EU domestically produced bananas (Crete, Canary Islands and the French Overseas Departments) have a general annual quota of 854 000 tonnes. Each producing region has a specific quota derived from the quantities produced in the best year prior to 1991. The basic features of this Byzantine import system include the following provisions:

- *Quota 1*: A general annual tariff-free quota for the traditional imports from the ACP countries is 857 700 tonnes, which is about 15 per cent more than the situation prior to 1993.
- *Quota 2*: Imports from ACP countries over and above the traditional level are non-traditional imports. They face a specific tariff of €100 per ton.
- *Quota 3*: Imports from all other countries, mainly from Latin America (the 'dollar area bananas') have an annual EU quota of 2.1 million tonnes (following the entry of Austria, Finland and Sweden, the quota was increased to 2.5 million tonnes).[94] This quota was roughly equal to EU imports of bananas prior to 1993. These imports face a specific tariff of €100 per tonne.
- *Above Quota 3*: Any annual EU imports over and above the 2.5 million tonnes quota face a duty of €850 per ton (for ACP countries, it is €750 per ton).

Detailed specifications on conditions of trade in general, such as quantity, quality, preferences, charges, penalties and so on reduce uncertainty. However, such managed trade removes one problem (uncertainty), but introduces another one (too much certainty or rigidity). It distorts market signals and (mis)leads entrepreneurs down blind alleys (Curzon Price, 1994, p. 3).

The European Commission issues import licences for bananas according to previous levels of imports. Although the licences are issued free of charge, there is a secondary market for them among traders who experience an excess or drop in demand. The Framework Agreement (1994) allowed the four exporting countries to have export licences. Hence, in order to export to the EU, traders must obtain both export and import licences. EU importers must import at least 30 per cent of bananas from ACP countries.

The new EU banana imports system introduced equity regarding the treatment of the domestic consumers, although at potentially higher prices, at least in Germany. As for the producers of bananas, the system is inefficient. The EU import quotas favour preferential suppliers (ACP) over the domestic consumers (Read, 1994, p. 232). The efficient and highly competitive 'dollar area' producers of bananas, both regarding price and quality, are handicapped by the new EU system. The EU may divert some production of bananas from the 'dollar area' into the ACP countries, not on the grounds of efficiency, but on the grounds of the discriminatory administrative preferences. At the same time, the favoured ACP countries may have certain medium- and long-term costs, as their inefficient production structure is being supported and extended in time. This may postpone structural adjustment of their economies for the future, when the cost of such reallocation of resources may be much higher.

In any case, the EU system for the imports of bananas will be subject to alterations in the future. Domestic consumers may be reluctant to pay more and get lower-quality bananas from the inefficient (marginal) sources than would be the case if they were able to acquire bananas from the 'dollar area' suppliers. In their fight against the 'special relations' of the domestic administration with the preferred countries, the domestic consumers may get support from the giant TNCs such as Castle & Cooke, Del Monte and United Brands and the government of their parent country (US), which have strong interests in the 'dollar area' countries.

This complicated banana regime cost EU consumers an estimated $2.3 billion a year. However, currently only $0.3 billion reaches the target developing countries, the rest 'disappears' in the distribution process (Borrell, 1994, p. 24). One could interpret the cost of this policy as a readiness by EU consumers to give aid to ACP producers. If that is so, a better policy for both the EU and ACP producers would be to accept a free trade in bananas and offer half of the cost of the EU policy to ACP countries in outright grants.

The EU import regime for bananas was so restrictive that four principal banana producers in Latin America – Ecuador, Guatemala, Honduras and Mexico – together with the US, requested intervention by the Dispute Settlement Panel in the WTO in 1996. The next year's ruling was that the EU violated the WTO obligations and authorised sanctions on $117 million worth of imports from the EU. The US tariff retaliations were on British, Italian, French and German exports, but not on Danish and Dutch ones as these two countries did not support the EU banana import regime. The real American motives to introduce retaliatory sanctions in 1998 against the EU were highly suspicious as the US grows almost no bananas. Its stance is dictated by a strong vested interest and lobbying power by Chiquita Banana.[95]

Faced with serious pressure and in breach of the WTO obligations, the EU introduced a new transitory regime based on tariffs and quotas for the 2001–05 period. This regime would be replaced by a wholly tariff system from 2006. After a serious eight-year row over the EU banana imports regime introduced in 1993, the EU and the US agreed in 2001 on a new EU regime that refers to Quota 3. EU quotas had been distributed on a country basis; now they are distributed to operators (companies). Traditional banana 'operators' have 83 per cent of the quota, while non-traditional 'operators' have 17 per cent – what a victory for free trade principles!

The EU import regime for bananas creates production, market and price distortions; it wastes resourses; it brings trouble, WTO intervention and trade sanctions to the world trading system; and ultimately it does not help those that it has assisted for almost half a century. This aid provided no incentives to change the current structure of production, and EU consumers bear the cost of the regime – estimates for the year 1995 are in the range of €1.2 to €1.9 billion (Messerlin, 2001, p. 324). Most of this goes to banana distributors in the EU, while the real producers in the poor ACP countries receive only about 10 per cent of the estimated total cost. Would it not be better and more effective to give this amount directly to the protected and inefficient banana producers in the impoverished ACP countries to help them to start up something else? That is, production of something legal and profitable, not cocaine, marijuana or opium. Is it not time to recognise openly that this type of EU aid has failed? The past EU aid in the banana business was much more of a problem in itself, than it was a solution.

Have the Lomé and Cotonou Conventions Benefited the ACP Countries?

If the ACP countries have been continuously marginalised with regard to EU trade relations over the past several decades, the question is, were the Lomé arrangements of any advantage to the beneficiary countries? Although there is no counterfactual world that would disclose what would have happened without the Lomé deals, terms of trade would have been much worse for the ACP countries without the Lomé regime. The Lomé deals could have supported trade and development of the ACP countries only if these countries had a sufficient manufacturing capacity to take advantage of the offered opportunities. Failure to process primary goods and add value is the chief cause of the relative decline of the ACP countries in imports to the EU (Cosgrove, 1994).

Concluding the discussion on EU relations with the ACP countries, one must concede one crucial fact. The Lomé and other preferential deals were not offered to the ACP countries either because of economic efficiency or because of altruism. Rather, the deals were offered to the ACP countries, even at a certain cost to the EU, because the beneficiary countries were 'natural' targets for the intrusion of communist interest at the time. The Lomé scheme was a product of the Cold War.[96] After the disappearance of the Soviet zone of influence and the Cold War, has the reason for Lomé also vanished (Curzon Price, 1994, pp. 4–5)? Apparently it has, as there is no clear evidence that the beneficiary countries really gained from the various concessions. The older and more complex the system becomes, the more administrative resources it absorbs. Many working hours were lost by firms, by customs, by forgers of origin certificates, by checkers of these forgeries and so on. If those countries had been offered MFN treatment, the new system would have been more efficient from the resource-allocation point of view, as well as cheaper to run (Curzon Price, 1996a, pp. 73–4). The post-Cold War era was replaced by the period of 'globalisation' which shaped and directed economic relations between the EU and developing countries. New aspects such as democracy, human rights, environmental standards, rule of law, social standards (trade unions, child labour, right to strike) and good governance have entered the formal relations between the EU and ACP states.[97]

In general, and in spite of big words, tens of billions of euros in aid and significant nominal concessions in trade, almost half a century of EU policy towards the developing countries has produced few tangible longer-term benefits for these countries. In fact, some developing countries that did not have preferences in trade with the EU grew faster than those that had such preferences. A topic for a long and heated theoretical debate and econometrical research is whether there is an inverse relationship between economic growth and the availability of preferences in trade.

The ACP countries are no longer a high priority on the EU agenda. Economic adjustment (reallocation of resources) relies principally on domestic resources and capabilities. A degree of support from international organisations including the EU, may be the best answer to the enormous economic and social problems in the ACP countries. Putting aside the Lomé preferences that produce, after all, only a marginal effect on the beneficiaries, the ACP, as well as other developing countries, may wish to place more emphasis on the WTO and multilateralism in the future, as there is an obvious risk of 'donor fatigue'.

Since the Second World War, Africa has received in aid more than any other continent, yet it has remained impoverished. Aid has promoted urbanisation and impoverished agriculture. Latin America and South-east Asia were largely ignored; they have their problems, but these are less acute than is the case in Africa.

Apart from general political statements about its interest in the ACP, particularly African countries, the future substantial focus of the EU interest in this group of countries is highly uncertain. Cuts in public spending

Trade policy 545

in the EU can reasonably be expected in the future. This would affect ACP countries too. In spite of grand talk about 'globalisation', the focused priority of the EU in the future is to absorb the East European countries; to create a stable, peaceful and prosperous neighbourhood in the EU-rim countries in Europe and in the Mediterranean region. This would all add to the pressure on developing countries to make internal market reforms that would stimulate diversification based on local entrepreneurship within a stable and predictable environment for thriving private business and investment (domestic and foreign), with the objective of enhancing competitive production and growth. This could assist in the mitigation of a huge accumulated debt problem in ACP countries. FDI and trade liberalisation should be the principal policy tools, while foreign aid need play only second or third fiddle. Foreign aid ought to be directed towards the creation of a respectable local economic and social environment.

Trade with China is an important issue (Figure 7.13). China is a developing country without preferential access to the EU market such as that enjoyed by the ACP countries. None the less, China has developed its export industry in such a way that it has become one of the principal trading partners of the EU. China has a persisting surplus in trade with the EU. Since 2000, China has been closing in on Japan with respect to its share in EU trade. In addition, the EU intends to foster special and good relations with China, which is why China was invited to take part in the EU Galileo satellite navigation system in 2003.

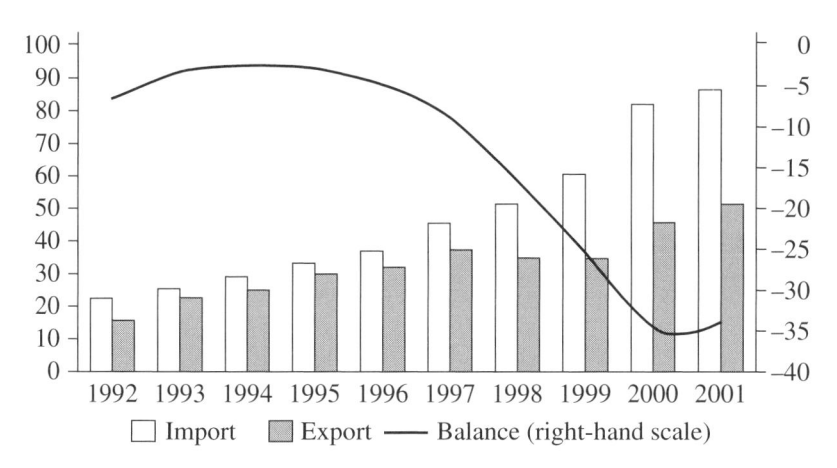

Source: Eurostat (2003).

Figure 7.13 EU trade in goods with China (including Hong Kong), 1992–2001 (€bn)

GENERALISED SYSTEM OF PREFERENCES

Just like the Yaoundé and Lomé conventions, the GSP was a product of the Cold War. Negotiations on the GSP took place under the auspices of UNCTAD during 1964–71. The GSP were supposed to offer two solutions. First, the domestic market of many developing countries is too small for the internationally competitive operation of a number of manufacturing industries. The GSP had to stimulate exports from the developing to the developed countries and increase the flow of funds to the developing partners through trade (indirectly), rather than through aid and loans (directly). Second, the intention was to counterbalance the preferential trade agreements between the EU and the select group of the developing countries (Yaoundé group).

The scheme is *generalised* because it is granted to the developing countries by most industrialised ones, and because it includes all industrial (manufactured and semi-manufactured) goods, as well as specific processed agricultural commodities. It is *preferential* because the exported goods from the developing countries enjoy an advantage over similar exports from the industrialised countries. Commodities that have undergone only limited processing (inputs) are charged lower duties than finished goods. The more sophisticated the commodity, the higher the effective tariff protection. The developing countries consider that such a tariff structure in the advanced countries makes industrialisation and exporting from developing countries difficult. The developing countries have always asked for a preferential tariff (and non-tariff) treatment for their industrial products and components in exports to the advanced countries. What the GSP offered to the developing world is a tariff-free treatment (up to a certain quota) of manufactured exports. At the same time, the developed countries charge customs duties on identical imports from other developed countries. The GSP offers preferences to the developing countries that are equal to the difference between the preferential (lower) GSP tariff and the 'standard' tariffs charged on imports of the same manufactured commodities from the developed countries. A continuous reduction in tariffs under the auspices of the GATT/WTO that are charged under the MFN clause, led to the devaluation of preferences in trade that the GSP offers to the developing countries.

One of the basic rules of the WTO is that the participating countries must, in general, extend to each other the most favourable terms negotiated with any other single partner (MFN clause). The only exception is when the preferential terms are the result of an agreement to form a free trade area or a customs union (Article XXIV). The reasons for the exception of the GSP from the WTO rules was a recognised need to increase the export earnings of developing countries and to support their industrialisation and modernisation.

The EU introduced GSP in 1971, Japan followed suit during the same year, while the US did the same in 1976. In general, most of the OECD countries grant GSP preferences. The beneficiary countries were, until relatively recently, all of the developing countries. Unfortunately, the GSP is not a single consistent generalised system offered by donor countries. Rather, it is a myriad of individual schemes offered by each donor country. The GSP is not a contractual agreement like the Cotonou deal. It is a preference that is granted, and can also be modified, unilaterally. All developing countries ought to receive, in principle, preferences in trade from the developed countries without reciprocity.

The application of GSP has many restrictions. The GSP does not generally apply to trade in farm, textile and leather goods. The US and Japan have excluded textile products from their GSP, while the EU has included these goods into its own GSP, but only to those developing countries that accept the 'voluntary export restraint agreement'. The duration of the EU GSP was ten years. However, this period was insufficient for most of the developing countries to industrialise and develop, and therefore it was extended.

Every year the EU reviews its GSP and determines the import quota for each commodity covered by the scheme. Once the quota is used in full, the EU applies a tariff on further imports. The level of the quota is determined in relation to the 'sensitivity' of the good. The producer's lobby in the EU is able to move some 'non-sensitive' and 'semi-sensitive' commodities into the group of 'sensitive' commodities and decrease the GSP quota accordingly.

The EU has two priorities regarding GSP for the 1995–2005 period. First, as a tool of development, the GSP needs to be directed towards the neediest, that is, poorest countries. This means that the EU will implement 'graduation', a programme of transfer of preferential margins from relatively advanced to poorer developing countries. This is to avoid the problem of a high concentration of beneficiary exporting countries supplying a large share of the total GSP exports. Over half the benefits of the GSP in 1983 accrued only to four relatively advanced beneficiary countries: Hong Kong, South Korea, Taiwan and Brazil (Karsenty and Laird, 1986, p. 10).[98] The purpose of graduation is to enlarge export opportunities for the least-developed countries.[99] However, the cut in the MFN tariffs erodes this potential benefit. In addition, another objective was to dilute a high concentration of GSP benefits on a few relatively advanced developing countries. As such, the graduation programme is not trade, but development oriented. Second, as an instrument of economic development, the GSP needs to take into consideration broader objectives, such as social and environmental concerns. None the less, the new ten-year scheme would not introduce extra benefits to the developing countries over and above those reached in the Uruguay Round combined with the existing GSP.

A country that wants to receive GSP treatment from the EU has to submit a certificate of origin showing that the whole or a substantial part of the value was added (production and/or transformation) in the exporting country. The EU grants a cumulative origin principle to the ACP countries, as well as to some of the integration schemes of the developing countries (ASEAN and the Andean Pact). The majority of the developing countries did not get any benefit from the GSP since they did not have the commodities (industrial base) to help them take advantage of the GSP.

A serious problem with the GSP is its complexity. It is sometimes so complicated that the system itself can represent an NTB. During business negotiations, neither exporters from the developing countries, nor the EU importers know whether the GSP will be implemented. This is because data about tariff-free quotas may not be readily available, which introduces an element of instability.

Overall, the developing countries have had, at best, only modest trade (and development) gains from the GSP. Tariffs by the EU and other GSP sponsors are at a relatively low level. Hence, the margins of preference and a limited commodity coverage of the GSP do indeed offer relatively small advantages in trade to the developing countries. An estimate for 1983 concluded that imports by the GSP donor countries from the beneficiary developing countries were only 2 per cent higher than they would have been otherwise (Karsenty and Laird, 1986, p. 9). If such a situation in trade and development does not change, the developed countries may soon face a choice between an increase in the importation of goods from the developing countries or an inflow of immigrants from the same source.

Although the second EU GSP scheme expired at the end of 1990, its application was extended until the end of 1994, pending the outcome of the Uruguay Round negotiations. A new EU GSP scheme for manufactured goods was put in place in 1995. The new scheme has four features:

- The quotas on GSP imports from the previous system were completely replaced by tariff modulation. Duties on imports of very sensitive products (textiles and clothing) would be reduced by 15 per cent, the reduction for sensitive products is 30 per cent, while for nonsensitive ones it is 65 per cent.
- The EU will apply the policy of graduation. GSP would be reoriented towards low- and medium-income countries which so far have had little benefit from the system.
- An additional margin of preference would be granted to countries that comply with certain labour (freedom of association, minimum-age

employment, collective bargaining) and environment standards (forest management).
- GSP may be withdrawn if there is a violation of human rights in the beneficiary country.

The immediate benefits of the new GSP system are that it is much simpler to operate than previous ones, and it abolished disruptive quotas.

The current EU GSP (1995–2004) awards tariff reduction preferences in three ways: (1) *modulation*: tariff concessions vary according to the degree of import 'sensitivity' of the good, (2) *graduation*: least-developed countries have trade preferences almost the same as those given to the ACP countries, while countries that reach a certain level of development measured by GDP per capita are excluded from GSP. This happened in 1998 when Hong Kong, Singapore and South Korea were excluded from EU GSP as they each have GDP per capita over $8000; and (3) *incentives*: if a developing country meets social and environmental standards ('green premiums'), the EU may improve tariff benefits.

ECONOMIC RELATIONS WITH OTHER DEVELOPING COUNTRIES

EU contractual relations with the Mediterranean countries are much less comprehensive than those with the ACP group. The Mediterranean countries are, together with the transition countries of Eastern Europe, the EU's closest neighbours. One of the major stumbling blocks in trade relations was the fact that the Mediterranean countries produce similar agricultural commodities (wine, olive oil, citrus fruits, vegetables) to the ones produced in southern Europe, in particular Greece, Italy, southern France, Spain and Portugal, as well as textiles.

In the late 1960s the EU concluded trade agreements with Greece, Turkey,[100] Israel, Tunisia, Algeria and Morocco, but it was only in 1973 that the EU introduced its global strategy towards the Mediterranean countries. The reasons for this late start were, on the one hand, France's insistence on relations with the select group of the developing countries (ACP) and, on the other, Dutch and German objections to such selectivity. As for Italy, there was a problem that agricultural production would be jeopardised by a more liberal treatment of imports from the southern Mediterranean countries.

Bearing in mind its special historic, economic, political and strategic interest in the Mediterranean region, the EU delivered its 'global strategy'. The main features of this policy were proposals to create a free trade area in industrial goods between the EU and each country in the Mediterranean region, industrial cooperation, technical and financial aid, as well as concessions in farm imports to the EU that do not interfere (much) with the CAP. The most striking feature was that the EU wanted free trade in industrial goods, while on the other hand, did not either allow for a free movement of labour or permit free trade in agricultural goods in which the Mediterranean countries have comparative advantages.

Countries included in the global strategy were the Maghreb countries (Morocco, Algeria and Tunisia), Mashreq countries (Egypt, Jordan, Lebanon and Syria), Israel, Libya, Turkey, Cyprus, Malta and the former Yugoslavia. Greece, Spain and Portugal were included before their entry into the EU in 1981 (Greece) and 1986 (Spain and Portugal).[101] The EU offered these countries duty-free access for their manufactured goods, various concessions in imports of agricultural commodities, EU grants and loans from the EIB.

So far the EU has concluded two generations of agreements with the Mediterranean countries, ranging from non-preferential treatment, to cooperation to association. The main features of these deals are EU concessions in trade. The EU and Cyprus concluded negotiations in 1987 on the creation of a customs union. This was the first such agreement between the EU and an outside country. In 1995, the EU concluded association agreements with Israel, Morocco and Tunisia. Similar agreements are in preparation for a few other countries.

A grand conference took place in Barcelona in 1995 between the 12 Mediterranean and EU(15) countries which was supposed to strengthen peace and prosperity in the region, as well as bring free trade in manufactured goods across the Mediterranean by 2010. In addition, the EU offered an aid package of €4.7 billion and loans from the EIB. However, the basic objectives of such moves by the EU were two: first, to create the economic and social conditions that prevent emigration from southern Mediterranean countries into the EU; and, second, to address the threat of militant Islamic fundamentalism. Time will tell if this move by the EU has been too little, too late.

In spite of various good intentions, talks, meetings, declarations, hopes and promises, EU private investors are not much interested in southern Mediterranean countries. There is little real 'cultural dialogue' and the EU fears a flood of illegal immigrants. In addition, since the fall of the Roman Empire and the arrival of Islam, confrontation has been common, while harmony in the Mediterranean has been rare. As far as most of the 12 Mediterranean countries are concerned, they should reform their tax system in order to profit more from the offered opportunities. They would have to reduce reliance on import duties as a source of public revenue and introduce a sales tax instead. This may be a bitter pill for many countries to swallow.

The EU is very dependent on the imports of Middle Eastern oil. The vulnerability of the EU in this regard was obvious during the Yom Kippur war of 1973. The EU aims to secure oil supplies through Euro-Arab dialogue. This dialogue has a very strong political element, derived from the Arab states. If Arab countries unite in their relations with the EU, they will be able to win important concessions from the EU in the short run. However, due to deep-rooted divisions and hostilities among the Arab countries about the general issue of who is going to lead the Arab world, this outcome is far removed from reality. Apart from Morocco and Tunisia, most other Arab countries' major export item is oil, which enters the EU duty free.

Until the British entry into the EU (1973), the Commonwealth countries enjoyed tariff preferences on the British market. After the British entry, the EU concluded cooperation agreements with countries in the Indian sub-continent: Bangladesh, India, Nepal, Sri Lanka and Pakistan. These agreements provide for reductions in tariffs, consultation and an exchange of information. However, the countries were excluded from the Lomé deals, not because they were more developed relative to other ACP countries, but because they were comparatively large countries with a sufficient manufacturing capacity to present a competitive threat to the EU manufacturers. The EU signed a similar agreement with ASEAN[102] in 1980 which was aimed at the promotion of trade, technical cooperation and a stimulation of investment in the ASEAN region. China is also a beneficiary of an agreement from this family. EU agreements with countries in Latin America are relatively recent in origin. The EU intends to penetrate the huge markets of the countries in the 'Green Continent'. In doing this, the EU needs to bear in mind the strategic interests of the US in the region. Beneficiaries of agreements with the EU are the Andean Pact,[103] MERCOSUR[104] countries, Mexico and a number of Central American countries. The deals often offer 'special' treatment for exports of sugar, jute and cocoa products from countries such as Bangladesh, India and Sri Lanka.

DEVELOPING COUNTRIES: A RECAP

EU trade policy towards developing countries has two basic elements: concessions and aid. The EU depends on imports of raw materials, so it needs secure supplies and good export outlets for its manufactured goods. Hence the need for the development of cooperation with developing countries. None the less, trade had lost a lot of relevance for EU relations with the ACP countries.

The development cooperation policy of the EU was very selective regarding preferences in trade and aid. This policy was Afrocentric (especially sub-Saharan Africa). The Lomé deals included initially (only) half of all developing countries. None the less, many of the ACP countries are among the poorest countries in the world and they obtained certain preferences in trade and aid. Because of the eastern enlargement and proximity of the transition economies of Eastern Europe, the EU is shifting its trade and aid focus eastwards. There is a kind of donor fatigue with the countries of the south as decades of preferences in trade and about €30 billion of aid to the ACP region produced little positive result. In fact, the lone-wolf development policies of the 'Asian tigers'[105] proved to be much more productive than the policies of mollycoddling through preferences in trade and aid. Therefore, it should come as no surprise that many developing countries would be well advised to help themselves in future, as there will be little direct aid available. Trade is neither a panacea for all economic illnesses, nor a replacement for a sound domestic economic policy. Trade only offers opportunities for competition to participants, it reduces the power of vested interest. Possibilities to trade offer the poor much more than aid and debt relief. This should not be a cause for much concern (one may even be indifferent to such a change) as there is little, if any, evidence of the impact of aid on economic growth and efficiency. Of course, a certain level of aid will always be necessary, but only for disaster relief and for a small group of the poorest and neediest countries.

The EU policy towards the select ACP developing countries is embodied in the Cotonou Agreement and a chain of previous Lomé deals. However, the developing countries that remained out of such preference agreements did better in trade and exports to the EU than the ACP countries. The EU continues to import raw materials from ACP countries, while ACP countries import industrial commodities from the EU. Lomé and Cotonou have not changed these trends. This may have led some observers to look at the Lomé conventions and the Cotonou deal as a failure. However, this conclusion may not be fully substantiated as certain ACP countries expanded the range of goods in exports. Although relations under these special deals were deemed to be of equality and interdependence, they turned out to be a system of unilateral preferences and aid to the ACP countries from the EU.

France has succeeded in keeping out of special EU deals with Asian countries that were former British colonies. The EU can offer the GSP and cooperation agreements to the developing countries which are not included in the Cotonou deal. The EU has concluded various trade agreements with countries in the Mediterranean, the Indian sub-continent, ASEAN and Latin America. The ACP countries and France would like to see the Cotonou agreement as a permanent means of EU–ACP cooperation. The

ACP group would like to receive larger funds from the EU and its member countries. At the same time, the ACP countries would not welcome an expansion in the Cotonou membership since this would mean a loss of their position in the EU market.

The EU helps the development of industrial activity in the developing countries, but as soon as exports from these countries become competitive, the EU imposes import restrictions (the best example was the Multifibre Agreement). Probably the most suitable way to help developing countries would be to grant certain preferences in trade for a limited period of time. This could be coupled with a particular, conditional aid package in order to develop entrepreneurship in the developing countries. Since the middle of the 1990s the EU has forcefully pursued a policy of replacing non-reciprocal preferences for the developing countries in the Mediterranean, Latin America and with South Africa, by bilateral free trade agreements.

The Lomé agreements and the new Cotonou deal were as much praised as criticised. They were condemned because they do not cover all developing countries and because they do not solve the problem of trade in textiles and temperate agricultural commodities. Stabex is, without any doubt, the most important innovation in the economic relations between the North and the South. None the less, its coverage of export commodities is limited and its budget was often short of funds. The EU started introducing human rights clauses in its trade deals with external countries. If these clauses are violated, the EU reserves the right to suspend its concessions.

The Single European Market and the EU eastern enlargement may have little direct effect on the developing countries. If they bring an acceleration of economic growth in the EU, that may have a potential spillover effect on an increase in imports by the EU from the developing countries. In fact, this has taken place regarding imports from certain Asian developing countries. The biggest impact of the Single European Market on the developing countries may not necessarily be traced in trade, although the developing countries may be adversely affected in the short run by the new EU standards (environment, for example) that could be met only at relatively high costs. The greatest effect may be found in investment diversion. No matter how small those flows were/are to the developing countries, they may be diverted both to the EU because of the growth effects, and to Central and Eastern Europe.

Apart from some agricultural commodities, the EU is more or less an open market for the commodity exports from the developing countries. The paradox is that the most successful exporters have been the developing countries that suffered the highest EU exports restrictions. This suggests that the EU border protection was a relatively small barrier to the developing countries' exports. Bigger obstacles were unfavourable domestic conditions and policies in the developing countries such as distorted exchange rates, inadequate incentives and poor infrastructure.

7. Preferred partners

The agreements that the EU offers to its external partners have several common features, but two are particularly striking. First, as a rule, deals basically refer to liberal, even free trade regimes for manufactured goods. Agricultural goods are generally excluded from coverage, although there may be select (reciprocal) concessions. Second, if partners are on a lower level of economic development than the EU countries (developing countries or transition countries, but not EFTA), the EU offers asymmetric deals.

A formidable collection of preferential and regional trade agreements by the EU is presented in Tables 7.13 and 7.14, respectively. While these lists

Table 7.13   EU preferential trade agreements

Parties to regional trade or preferential trade agreements with the European Union, and beneficiaries of EU preferential arrangements, in force as of April 2002

Europe Agreements: Bulgaria, the Czech Republic, Estonia, Hungary, Latvia, Lithuania, Poland, Romania, Slovakia, Slovenia

Association Agreements: Cyprus, Malta, Turkey

Stabilisation and Association Agreements: Former Yugoslav Republic of Macedonia (FYROM), Croatia

Euro-Mediterranean Association Agreements: Israel, Morocco, the Palestinian Authority, Tunisia

Cooperation Agreements (Euro-Med Association Agreements concluded, but not in effect, or under negotiation): Algeria, Egypt, Jordan, Lebanon, Syria

Other Free Trade Agreements: Denmark (Faroe Islands), Iceland, Liechtenstein, Mexico, Norway, South Africa, Switzerland

Other Customs Unions: Andorra, San Marino

Association of Overseas Countries and Territories (OCT): *Anguilla*, Antarctica, Aruba, British Antarctic Territory, British Indian Ocean Territory, British Virgin Islands, Cayman Islands, Falkland Islands, French Polynesia, French Southern and Antarctic Territories, Greenland, *Mayotte*, *Montserrat*, Netherlands Antilles, New Caledonia, Pitcairn, *Saint Helena, Ascension Island, Tristan da Cunha*, South Georgia and the South Sandwich Islands, *St. Pierre and Miquelon, Turks and Caicos Islands, Wallis and Fortuna Islands*

Table 7.13 (continued)

Parties to regional trade or preferential trade agreements with the European Union, and beneficiaries of EU preferential arrangements, in force as of April 2002

EU–African, Caribbean and Pacific (ACP) Partnership: *Angola*, Antigua and Barbuda, Bahamas, Barbados, Belize, *Benin, Botswana, Burkina Faso, Burundi,* Cameroon, *Cap Verde, Central African Republic, Chad, Comoros,* Congo, Cook Islands, *Dem. Rep. of Congo,* Côte d'Ivoire, *Djibouti,* Dominica, Dominican Republic, *Equatorial Guinea, Eritrea, Ethiopia,* Federated States of Micronesia, Fiji, Gabon, *Gambia,* Ghana, Grenada, *Guinea, Guinea-Bissau,* Guyana, *Haiti,* Jamaica, Kenya, *Kiribati, Lesotho, Liberia, Madagascar, Malawi, Mali,* Marshall Islands, *Mauritania,* Mauritius, *Mozambique,* Namibia, Nauru, Nigeria, Niue Islands, Palau, Papua New Guinea, *Rwanda,* St. Christopher and Nevis, St. Lucia, St. Vincent and the Grenadines, *Samoa, São Tomé and Príncipe, Senegal,* Seychelles, *Sierra Leone, Solomon Islands, Somalia,* South Africa, *Sudan,* Suriname, Swaziland, *Tanzania, Togo,* Tonga, Trinidad and Tobago, *Tuvalu, Uganda, Vanuatu, Zambia,* Zimbabwe

Autonomous Trade Measures for the Western Balkans: Albania, Bosnia-Herzegovina, the Federal Republic of Yugoslavia, Kosovo

Generalised System of Preferences (GSP) only: *Afghanistan,* Argentina, Armenia, Azerbaijan, Bahrain, *Bangladesh,* Belarus, *Bhutan,* Bolivia, Brazil, Brunei Darussalam, *Cambodia,* Chile, People's Republic of China, Colombia, Costa Rica, Cuba, East Timor, Ecuador, El Salvador, Georgia, Guatemala, Honduras, India, Indonesia, Iran, Iraq, Kazakhstan, Kyrgyzstan, Kuwait, *Lao People's Dem. Rep.,* Libyan Arab Jamahiriya, Malaysia, *Maldives,* Moldova, Mongolia, *Myanmar, Nepal,* Nicaragua, Oman, Pakistan, Panama, Paraguay, Peru, Philippines, Qatar, Russian Federation, Saudi Arabia, Sri Lanka, Tajikistan, Thailand, Turkmenistan, Ukraine, United Arab Emirates, Uruguay, Uzbekistan, Venezuela, Vietnam, *Yemen,* American Samoa, Bermuda, Bouvet Island, Cocos Islands, Cook Islands, Gibraltar, Guam, Heard and McDonald Islands, Macao, Norfolk Island, Northern Mariana Islands, United States Minor Outlying Islands, Tokelau Islands, Virgin Islands (USA)

Note: Least-developed countries in *italics.*

Source: WTO Secretariat, based on DG Trade (2001), in WTO (2002).

---

demonstrate a variety of concerns and EU preferences about relations with various trading partners, they also show that the EU ought to run parallel multiple trading regimes in the international trading environment. While this may assist in the process of aid to the preferred partners, it may also complicate the spirit of general liberal trade relations.

Table 7.14 *EU regional trade agreements, 2002*

Party	Goods		Services	
	Entry into force	Examination reference	Entry into force	Examination reference
I. Customs unions				
Andorra	1 July 1991	WT/REG53/	n.a.	n.a.
Malta[a]	1 April 1971	L/3665, 19S/90	n.a.	n.a.
San Marino	1 December 1992	n.a.	n.a.	n.a.
Turkey[a]	31 December 1995	WT/REG22/	n.a.	n.a.
II. Free trade areas				
Bulgaria[b]	31 December 1993	WT/REG1/	1 February 1995	Pending
Croatia	1 March 2002	notification pending	n.a.	n.a.
Cyprus[a]	1 June 1973	L/4009, 21S/94	n.a.	n.a.
Czech Republic[b]	1 March 1992	WT/REG18/	1 February 1995	Pending
Denmark (Faroe Islands)	1 January 1997	WT/REG21/	n.a.	n.a.
Estonia[b]	1 January 1995	WT/REG8/	12 June 1995	Notification submitted
Former Yugoslav Republic of Macedonia	9 April 2001	WT/REG129/	n.a.	n.a.
Hungary[b]	1 March 1992	WT/REG18/	1 February 1994	WT/REG50
Iceland[c]	1 April 1973	L/3902, 20S/158	1 January 1994	Pending
Israel[d]	1 June 2000	WT/REG124/	n.a.	n.a.
Latvia[b]	1 January 1995	WT/REG7/	12 June 1995	Notification submitted
Lithuania[b]	1 January 1995	WT/REG9/	12 June 1995	Notification submitted
Liechtenstein[c]	1 January 1973	L/3893, 20S/196	1 January 1994	Pending

Mexico	1 July 2000	WT/REG109/	Pending
Morocco[d]	1 March 2000	WT/REG112/	n.a.
Norway[f]	1 July 1973	L/3996, 21S/83	n.a.
Palestinian Authority[d]	1 July 1997	WT/REG43/	n.a.
Poland[b]	1 March 1992	WT/REG18/	1 February 1994	WT/REG51/
Romania[b]	1 May 1993	WT/REG2/	1 February 1995	Pending
Slovak Republic[b]	1 March 1992	WT/REG18/	1 February 1995	WT/REG52/
Slovenia[b]	1 January 1997	WT/REG32/	10 June 1996	Notification submitted
South Africa	1 January 2000	WT/REG113/	n.a.
Switzerland[c]	1 January 1973	L/3893, 20S/196	1 January 1994	Pending
Tunisia[d]	1 March 1998	WT/REG69/	n.a.
III. Non-reciprocal access to the EU market			
Algeria[f]	1 July 1976	L/4559, 24S/80	n.a.
Egypt[g]	1 July 1977	L/4660, 25S/114	n.a.
Jordan[g]	1 July 1977	L/4559, 24S/80	n.a.
Lebanon[f]	1 July 1977	L/4663, 25S/142	n.a.
Syria[f]	1 July 1977	L/4661, 25S/123	n.a.

Notes:

a. Association agreement, forerunner to possible accession.
b. Europe agreement, forerunner to possible accession.
c. European Economic Area (EEA).
d. Euro-Mediterranean association agreement.
e. Seven bilateral agreements of EEA type.
f. Euro-Mediterranean association agreement under negotiation.
g. Euro-Mediterranean association agreement signed but not entered into force.
n.a. Not applicable.

Source: WTO Secretariat; DG Trade (2001), 'EC Regional Trade Agreements' [Online] Available at http://europa.eu.int/comm/trade/pdf/ecrtagr.pdf (1 November 2001), in WTO (2002).

```
                    /\
                   /EU\
                  /────\
                 /EEA (EFTA)\
                /────────────\
               /     ACP      \
              /────────────────\
             / Association agreements \
            /──────────────────────────\
           /   Mediterranean countries   \
          /──────────────────────────────\
         /              GSP                \
        /──────────────────────────────────\
       /               MFN                   \
      /──────────────────────────────────────\
     /        Non-members of the WTO          \
    /──────────────────────────────────────────\
```

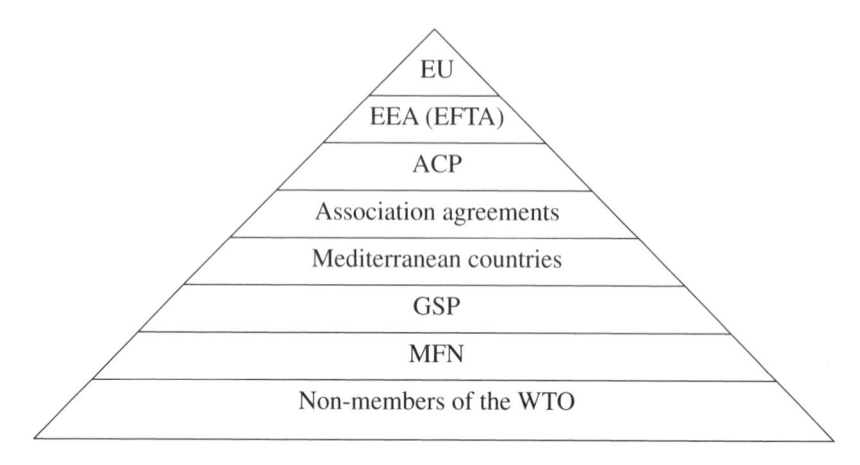

Figure 7.14   The EU pyramid of privileges in trade around 1990

A far as third countries are considered, the EU offered the most favourable trade treatment to those EFTA countries that take part in the EEA (Figure 7.14). 'Below' the EEA partners came the ACP countries (Cotonou Agreement), then come the countries with association agreements (transition economies and several Mediterranean countries). Further down are countries that are privileged under the GSP, and then the countries that are offered MFN status. At the very bottom of this pyramid of privileges in trade were countries that were not members of the WTO.

This pyramid of trade privileges with the EU was in existence until the end of the 1980s. It crumbled following the fall of the Berlin Wall when a new set of trade arrangements with Central and East European countries emerged. Within a brief period they moved from the very bottom to the very top of 'preferred' countries. Hence, a complex 'spaghetti bowl' of trade deals replaced the old EU pyramid of privileges (Figure 7.15). In any case, through this 'bilateral way' the EU entered into the role of a regional hub, while most of the other partners are the trade (and investment) 'spokes'. The spaghetti bowl is further seasoned with the formidable entry process of transition countries and deals with Mediterranean and Latin American countries. If all this looks complicated, difficult and confusing, that is because it is.

8. Conclusion

The external trade policy of the EU is founded in general on liberal principles. Trade is taken to be beneficial, not because it creates jobs, but rather

Trade policy 559

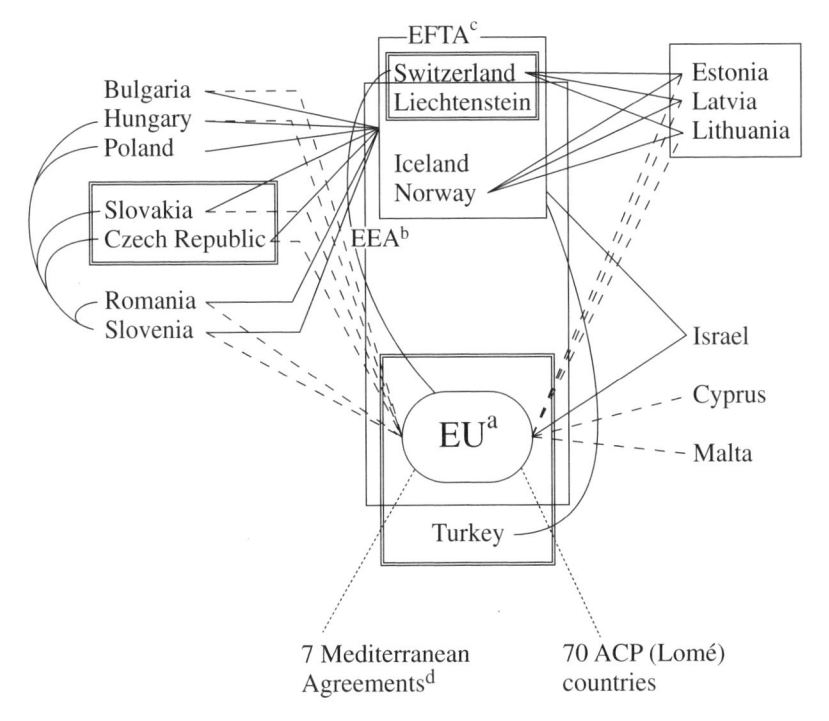

Notes: Does not include countries of the former Soviet Union other than the Baltic countries.
a. European Union comprises Austria, Belgium, Denmark, Finland, France, Germany, Greece, Ireland, Italy, Luxembourg, Netherlands, Portugal, Spain, Sweden and United Kingdom.
b. European Economic Area.
c. European Free Trade Association.
d. Algeria, Egypt, Jordan, Lebanon, Morocco, Syria, Tunisia.

⊂⊃ EU Single Market.
—— Customs unions.
—— Free trade areas.
-------- EU association agreements.
·········· Non-reciprocal agreements.

Source: Snape (1996, p. 392).

Figure 7.15 Preferential trade agreements of the European Union in 1996

because it improves the allocation of resources which stimulates growth. So much for the declared trade philosophy. In practice, the EU has taken important liberalising steps, even in sensitive areas. However, the problem is that these bold steps have been confined only to select countries. The EU has considerable discretionary power to differentiate (even discriminate) among its trade partners by offering or not offering different types of trade and other agreements. Although member countries of the EU are members of the WTO, which promotes multilateralism, the EU 'rewards' its foreign friends with special bilateral trade agreements.

The EU has a passion for preferential (that is, discriminatory) trade agreements, which were often used as carrots and sticks in trade relations. Almost 80 ACP developing countries (mostly former colonies) benefited from ACP conventions that offered trade concessions and aid from the EU. These conventions had a negative effect on the beneficiary countries. ACP exporters were ensured of access to the EU markets so they did not lobby their own governments to open domestic markets as a quid pro quo for access to foreign markets. The domestic political engine (export lobbies) behind trade liberalisation was destroyed. To make things worse, just before independence,

> [S]ubsidiaries of EC firms constituted the core of the modern industrial sector in ACP countries, and became the major beneficiaries of growing ACP protection – enjoying considerable monopoly rents when things were still going well, end benefiting from subsidies granted by the ACP host countries (and often financed by EC member-state aid funds) when things turned bad. (Messerlin, 2001, p. 204)

International trade liberalisation in the post-1960s, as well as extension of the GATT and later the WTO into new areas such as services, could have been slower in the absence of the 'challenge' posed by the evolution of the EU (Blackhurst and Henderson, 1993, p. 412). Krugman reached a similar conclusion (1995b, p. 181). None the less, there are certain reasons to suppose that the impact of the EU on the multilateral trading system has not been entirely benign (Winters, 1994, p. 602).

The EU trade policy is sometimes under strong pressure from vested interests and lobbies that frequently and forcefully demand protection. Farmers are the most obvious example, followed by both manufacturers (whose output), and trade unions (whose jobs) are 'jeopardised' by a surge of foreign imports (steel, for example). Their influence is strong during recessions. There are constant opportunities to employ 'temporary' safeguard measures as allowed by both the Treaty of Rome (Article 120) and the GATT (Article XIX). This introduces uncertainty in trade relations. However, consumers are becoming more and more aware of the cost of protection.

Most of the recent international conflicts in commerce among the major trading partners (the EU, the US, Japan and the newly industrialised countries) can be found in trade in specific goods. These deal with industrial policy and free competition (antidumping, standards, subsidies, origin, market access, public procurement), intellectual property rights and TRIMs. Most of these conflicts arise in relation to high-technology and farm goods. These goods and many fast-growing and lucrative services linked to them (telecommunications or data processing, for example) encompass an ever-growing share in international trade and provide supernormal profits (rents) to those that are ahead of other competitors. Being ahead of the others provides the opportunity to set standards that may prevail long into the future. As the manufacturing of the goods and the production of services is based on market imperfections (economies of scale, sunk costs, R&D), frictions in trade in such goods may not be excluded in the future, unless there is a reliable and effective conflict resolution mechanism that the WTO is supposed to provide.[106]

The principal trading countries and blocs may wish to consider moving away from preferential trade deals towards multilateral WTO agreements in the future. Preferential (bilateral) trade deals are often made with countries that include efficient world producers of certain goods. As such, they exert the same adjustment pressure and costs on the EU producers as do the WTO deals. However, these preferential deals do not bring with them the widest market access for EU goods and services, as do WTO agreements.

In conclusion, David Hume wrote in his essay 'Of the jealousy of trade' in 1752 a message that is at least as relevant today as it was during his time and even much earlier (see the opening quotation in this chapter from 3 John 2):

> I will venture to assert, that the increase of riches and commerce in any one nation, instead of hurting, commonly promotes the riches and commerce of all its neighbours; and that a state can scarcely carry its trade and industry very far, where all the surrounding states are buried in ignorance, sloth, and barbarism.... I shall therefore venture to acknowledge, that, not only as a man, but as a British subject, I pray for the flourishing commerce of Germany, Spain, Italy and even France[107] itself. I am at least certain, that Great Britain, and all those nations, would flourish more, did their sovereigns and ministers adopt such enlarged and benevolent sentiments towards each other.

Notes

1. Common instruments of EU commercial policy include the common external tariff, quantitative restrictions, customs valuation regulation, rules of origin, antidumping and countervailing policy, common trade arrangements with external countries and measures to counter the violation of intellectual property rights.
2. Article 115 in the original Treaty of Rome referred to a similar issue. The removal of internal border controls achieved by the Single European Market rendered Article 115

ineffective. In any case, the authorisation of actions (most of them referred to trade in textiles) based on this article were in a steady decline during the 1980s. From over 300 authorisations in 1980, the number had more than halved by the end of the decade.
3. One of the crucial French demands during the negotiations that led to the signature of the Treaty of Rome was an association of its overseas territories. France was a big colonial power at that time and wanted its colonies, predominantly in Africa, to get preferential status in trade with the EU. At the same time, Germany and Italy wanted to secure their traditional suppliers for bananas and coffee. So, a liberalisation of trade within the EU coexisted with 'special' trade relations with select external countries.
4. The examples include countries such as Haiti, Iraq, Libya and Yugoslavia.
5. This section gives no more than a brief outline of the basic theory of customs unions. For a broader treatment of the issue, see Baldwin and Venables (1995), Baldwin (1997), Jovanović (1998a), Robson (1998) and Panagariya (2000).
6. There are difficulties in explaining to the general public that half a loaf of bread in certain cases may be worse than none.
7. Countries tend to specialise and export goods for which they have a relatively large domestic market. It is this domestic demand or 'home market' effect (Linder, 1961; Krugman, 1980) that induces production, rather than domestic factor endowment. The response by firms to strong local demand for a product is so powerful that it leads this country to export that product. Countries have a competitive edge in the production of these goods and thus gain an advantage in foreign markets, while they import goods demanded by a minority of the home population. The factor endowment or comparative advantage model would not predict the home market effect. However, economic geography would predict such effects. The US, Japan and Germany have the greatest comparative advantage in goods for which their home market is relatively big. These are standardised goods for mass consumption. Empirical investigation by Davies and Weinstein (2003) found support for the existence of home market effects, as well as for the role and importance of increasing returns in determining the production structure for the OECD countries.
8. Income may be distributed to a small part of the population (landowners or owners of capital), who may easily spend it on imported luxury goods and services. This may prevent the establishment of industry in their area or country. If income is predominantly distributed in favour of a large number of families that demand home-made goods and services, this may have a strongly positive impact on the location of firms in the domestic market.
9. Ageing population and retirement patterns influence trade. The old demand health-related goods and services. A significant number of retired Germans move to Spain to enjoy a milder climate and a lower cost of living. They have specific demands that have a partial influence on trade.
10. Quotas are another instrument, but this one makes it pointless for producers to compete against each other. Quotas are more harmful than tariffs because their impact on rising prices to consumers is hidden. Hence, they may spread without check.
11. In general, EU integration has benefited third countries. The major exceptions are the countries that specialised in temperate agricultural goods covered by the CAP (Sapir, 1992, p. 1503). The Single European Market has been trade creating both for the EU and for external producers (European Commission, 1997b, p. 3). Hence, there was no need for retaliation.
12. This is part of the reason why highly protected countries, such as those in Eastern Europe before the transition period had, in general, a poor export performance in Western markets.
13. For the countries that enter an already existing customs union, this effect starts the moment there is a serious promise, announcement and possibility of full entry.
14. When there are significant scale and learning economies, risk-loving firms have incentives to set current prices not on current costs, but rather on the costs they expect to achieve in the future once full economies of scale are reached.

15. The first disk that Microsoft produced with Windows 2000 cost Microsoft about half a billion dollars. The second disk cost them three to four cents, just the cost of reproducing the first one. The cost of the third was three to four cents, and so on. Start-up costs are immensely high (Arthur, 2002, p. 2).
16. *Barter* terms of trade are measured by how many units of domestic good have to be exported to pay for one unit of imports. *Factorial* terms of trade are measured by how many hours of foreign labour can be paid by exporting the output of one hour of domestic labour.
17. Alternatively, the government may offer subsidies. In this case, foreign taxpayers foot the bill.
18. A TRIM is a new name for the 'old' performance requirements.
19. These grey-area measures insulate users from exchange rate fluctuations. Hence, market signals get distorted.
20. The developed market economies granted the developing countries an exception from reciprocity. Although this might have been a concession given to the developing world, in some cases, indeed, this 'concession' excluded the developing countries from negotiations about certain trade issues. As these countries 'graduate' in their development process, as the newly industrialised Asian countries have done, there is an understandable demand that there needs to be an exchange of concessions between the developing countries and the developed market economies. This has, in fact, taken place, during the Uruguay Round.
21. The Cairns Group includes countries that are significant exporters of agricultural products.
22. The formal name of the MFA is the Arrangement Regarding International Trade in Textiles. This waiver from GATT rules started as a short-term trade measure, at the request of the US, with restraints on trade in cotton textiles in 1961. It was subsequently broadened to include wool and man-made fibres, hence the name MFA. There were about 30 countries involved in these bilateral deals, which all ended in 1994. Since then, WTO rules have applied.
23. Countervailing duties are the trade devices of strong partners (antidumping duties are too, but to a lesser extent). Tariffs and quotas are available to all countries. Opponents of the use of countervailing duties in the US have urged Canadian firms to start countervailing cases against the US, in order to show that the Americans also subsidise. Canadian enterprises responded that if they do that, the Americans will find some other way to retaliate against them (Lipsey, 1991, p. 100).
24. NTBs have continuously irritated international trade relations. The most striking manifestation of international concern about the reduction of NTBs can be found in the extended scope of the Uruguay Round of tariff negotiations beyond the 'traditional' GATT agenda. On the regional scale the EU White Paper (European Communities, 1985) and the subsequent Single European Act (1987) aimed to complete the internal EU market and create an economic area without frontiers. For EU residents, of course. This ambitious programme intended was to eliminate or reduce substantially NTBs that hinder the free creation and operation of economic activities in the EU.
25. The simple average of all tariffs takes no account of the relative importance of different weights of goods in imports.
26. The introduction of a new good depends not only on fixed costs and expected benefits, but also on substitution and complementarity with those goods that already exist on the market.
27. Fourteen member countries in the Cairns Group are developing countries.
28. *Bulletin Quotidien Europe*, 10 September 2003, p. 4.
29. Developing countries are highly suspicious about these rules. After the failure of the Multilateral Agreement on Investment under the auspices of the OECD in 1998, developing countries look at this issue as a plot by the developed world that wants to place the burden of protection on the developing countries, without adequate compensation (for example, a liberal treatment of migrant workers from the developing countries).

30. Before Doha, the US was pushing hard the issue of workers rights' (freedom of association, child labour, labour in prison camps and so on). The developing countries were suspicious about this. They regard this issue as a back-door attempt to legitimise protection. In addition, children are often forced to work because their parents' income is insufficient to cover the family needs. Their parents ought to have better paid jobs. This is a case for a more liberal trade regime in relation to the developing countries' exports, rather than more restrictions. If the parents cannot generate enough income, children may be forced to work. If the children cannot go to school and if they are directly or indirectly forbidden to work by the WTO rules, what is the alternative – theft or child prostitution, perhaps?
31. See Chapter 4 on the CAP.
32. As there were no violent demonstrations (as in Seattle in 1999) to blame for the failure of the meeting, the WTO member countries have only themselves to blame.
33. Guy de Jonquieres, 'Crushed at Cancun', *Financial Times*, 15 September 2003.
34. A big obstacle in dealing with Russia is domestic energy prices, which are about one-fifth of the price prevailing on the EU market. Russia may easily be accused of granting indirect subsidies to the entire economy. However, as the largest producer and exporter of natural gas, Russia has a 'natural advantage' that may allow lower prices. Interestingly, nobody censures Italy or Spain about indirect subsidies that come from access to the southern sun, which provides a natural advantage in the production of fruit and vegetables, and also reduces heating costs throughout the economy. Nobody accuses them of unfair competition.
35. Canon invested over $100 million and located a new production facility for photocopiers in the US, rather than build it in China or Malaysia where the production costs are lower. The reason was a special NAFTA rule of origin for copiers which requires 80 per cent of local value added (UNCTAD, 1999b, p. 15).
36. A comparative study of antidumping actions in the US, EU, Canada and Australia concluded that 90 per cent of imports that were unfairly priced according to antidumping rules would be found to be fairly priced under corresponding domestic rules of competition (UNCTAD, 1999b, p. 17).
37. If a government of one country subsidises exports, then another country has the right to introduce countervailing duties. As governments of at least two countries are involved, this dispute often becomes visible.
38. Another complication presents the practice of 'zeroing'. Goods priced above home market prices are ignored for the calculation of average dumping margin. Therefore, the final antidumping duty is inflated.
39. Public procurement contracts that surpass certain thresholds must be advertised in the *Official Journal*. The directives operate within many different thresholds. For example, the threshold for public works is €5 million, supply contracts for various goods and services all have different thresholds which are about €0.2 million. There are, of course, loopholes. For example, certain public works may be split into a number of smaller ones that are below the limit. Another way of avoiding EU scrutiny is to underestimate the value of the procured goods and services. The supply of military goods is excluded from these rules.
40. *Financial Times*, 10 May 2000, p. 2.
41. The *Associazione* exported to Britain more than 6 million packets of pre-sliced Parma ham in 2002 (*The Independent*, 21 May 2003).
42. *Financial Times*, 11 January 2004 and 4 February 2004.
43. In 1999, 54 per cent of all EU products followed EU standards, another 28 per cent followed international standards, while the remaining 18 per cent of products were covered by national standards. In 1987, the share of national standards was 72 per cent (direct communication from the European Commission).
44. It was the US demand to exclude agriculture from the agreement that resulted in the formation of the GATT. This resulted in a later backlash against the US in farm trade with the EU and Japan.
45. Old Article 115.

46. Between 1989 and 1991, the annual imports of Japanese cars into Italy more than doubled from 10 000 to 22 000 (*Financial Times*, 5 August 1991).
47. S. Druker, 'America's hypocrisy over modified produce', *Financial Times*, 18 May 2004, p. 19.
48. Yes, proportional. This may be perfect in theory, but how to ascertain it in practice?
49. There was little that the European Commission could do against the French unilateral action. This was not because of the fear of protests in France, but because it would take up to two years to settle the dispute in the European Court of Justice. 'If the Commission cannot bring the "offenders" into line fast, its confidence can be seriously damaged. Therefore, a change in the EU rules is necessary that would provide the Commission with the necessary instruments for a quick reaction' (*European Voice*, 28 October 1999, p. 11).
50. An example is cars produced by Nissan in Britain. France limited imports of Japanese cars to 3 per cent of the domestic market and claimed that the Nissan Bluebird cars produced in Britain were Japanese in origin. An earlier informal guideline stated that Japanese cars produced in the EU would receive preferential (domestic) treatment in the EU market if local EU content was at least 60 per cent. In 1988, France proposed an increase in this threshold to 80 per cent. Currently, in order to qualify for national treatment in the EU, the produced (assembled) cars must have 60 per cent of local (EU) content.
51. This share excluded the intra-EU(15) trade. If trade among EU member countries is included, then the EU share in world trade would increase to 39 per cent.
52. WTO, Press/337, 22 April 2003.
53. In order to alleviate food crises in Africa in 2003, the US offered food aid containing genetically modified organisms. This was, however, rejected by several African countries. The US accused the EU stance for worsening the food crises in Africa. (*Financial Times*, 18 August 2003).
54. F. Williams, 'EU may face ruling on biotech food curbs', *Financial Times*, 18 August 2003.
55. *Financial Times*, 'Faith in science,' 22 July 2003.
56. The US continues to maintain an aggressive export policy for farm goods through various subsidies. The US Farm Security and Rural Investment Act (2002) greatly increased the distortionary effect of farm subsidies.
57. *Financial Times*, 15 October 2003.
58. *Financial Times*, 19 October 2003.
59. Political considerations for the introduction of protection in the US are presented in Finger et al. (1982).
60. Contrary to such selective reciprocity, which inspires the creation of regional trading blocs, the WTO stands for a broad-based exchange of concessions in international trade relations.
61. Super 301 was designed to provide a quick response retaliation and to send strong signals to foreign partners. This was a reaction to the long and costly delays common in the application of Section 301.
62. Another anti-multilateral signal that the US is sending is a resort to bilateral deals in trade relations.
63. In general, most of the recent frictions in international trade come from conflicts in trade in specific goods, rather than from the conduct of global policies that distort trade. In that light, the polemic about the 301 legislation raised three basic issues: has the US the right (legal/moral) to circumvent the WTO rules and to prosecute, judge and retaliate unilaterally? What would be the consequences if other countries follow a similar unilateral path? Do small trading partners have any chance of refusing to 'negotiate' in such circumstances? Is this a version of the old 'gunboat diplomacy'?
64. This agreement liberalised about $100 billion worth of procurement opportunities on both sides of the Atlantic (European Commission, 2002b, p. 37).
65. Boeing's financial statement for 2001 shows that the FSC benefit amounted to $222 million which represented about 8 per cent of Boeing's net earning in the same year (European Commission, 2002b, p. 45).

66. The bill is complicated by a provision that the US companies may repatriate as much as $400 billion of foreign earnings at a corporate tax rate of 5.25 per cent instead of the normal 35 per cent (*Financial Times*, 27 October 2003).
67. T. Buck, 'Sad day as EU puts sanctions on US goods', *Financial Times*, 1 March 2004.
68. To concentrate only on the EU banana imports regime in this case is to miss the point. The real reason for such an excessive American reaction was mounting US deficit in trade. The US protectionist lobby was looking for a scapegoat.
69. One must not discount the impact of the forthcoming presidential election cycle in the US. The products that would be hit by WTO-authorised trade sanctions by the EU, Japan, Brazil, South Korea, China, New Zealand, Norway and Switzerland come from the states that would have a big impact on the election outcome.
70. E. Alden, G. de Jonquieres and M. Sanchanta, 'US scraps its tariffs on imports of steel', *Financial Times*, 4 December 2003.
71. One could argue that this positive impact may be only in the short run. However, one could also argue that protection measures in the most developed and the most dynamic economy in the world are not necessary at all, since measures do more harm to dynamism than good.
72. *The Economist*, 'Survey of World Trade', 3 October 1998, p. 14.
73. Switzerland does not take part in the EEA, primarily because it feared a large inflow of foreign labour. Liechtenstein entered the EEA in 1995, but had to renegotiate its customs union with Switzerland, as the EU was afraid that Swiss goods would enter the EEA through Liechtenstein without restrictions.
74. The agreement has about 129 articles, amounting to about 1000 pages, supplemented by over 1400 EU laws (on 12 000 pages). This is the application of the *acquis communautaire* in practice. As a matter of comparison, the original Treaty of Rome (1957), which created the EEC in 1958, has a little less than 250 pages in spite of all its annexes and protocols.
75. Although farm goods are the chief exception to the free movements of goods agreement in the EEA, they are not fully excluded. Both the EU and EFTA are committed to liberalise trade in farm goods in the spirit of WTO arrangements.
76. The goods whose trade was monitored by COCOM fell into three categories: nuclear-related exports, conventional weaponry and dual-use (civil or military) goods and technologies.
77. Wassenaar is a suburb of The Hague.
78. As a reminder, the share of transition countries in imports of the EU in 1993 was 8 per cent (roughly the share of Switzerland alone). On the exports side, the fraction of transition economies was 8.7 per cent, which was roughly the same as the share of Switzerland (8 per cent) and similar to that of Austria (6 per cent) alone.
79. Trade and cooperation agreements entered into force for Hungary in 1988, Poland 1989, former Czechoslovakia 1990, while for Bulgaria and Romania it was in 1991.
80. Europe agreements were signed with Hungary, Poland and the former Czechoslovakia in 1991. The interim agreements entered into force in 1992. Bulgaria and Romania concluded association agreements in 1994, while the Baltic states did the same in 1995 and Slovenia in 1996.
81. After the dissolution of Czechoslovakia in 1993, the two successor states renegotiated their original agreement with the EU.
82. On a purely commercial level, foreign firms have demonstrated a relative lack of sales efforts in Japan. This does not refer just to sales and marketing staff (few non-Japanese sales managers speak Japanese), but also and more importantly, goods created for the US market (passenger cars or bulky home appliances such as fridges) are not commercially successful in Japan.
83. These were the African states south of the Sahara.
84. Mauritius joined the original AASM group of 18 countries in 1972.
85. Sharp criticism of the ACP group came from the secretary-general of the ACP group, Edwin Carrington, who said: 'We of the ACP have talked a lot, philosophised a lot, we have studied a lot, we have met a lot. We have not done much else' (*The Courier*, March–April 1990, pp. 18–19).

86. Lomé I disposed of €3.4 billion, Lomé II had €5.7 billion, while Lomé III offered ACP countries €8.5 billion.
87. Apart from aid through the EU, member states have their own bilateral aid programmes. In some instances, such as in France, one of the determining factors for the allocation of aid is which language is spoken in the beneficiary country.
88. A similar system, called Sysmin, existed for mining products. It was introduced in Lomé II.
89. The reference level is calculated on the basis of average export earnings during the period of six preceding years less the two years with the highest and lowest figures.
90. The Stabex disbursed €382 million during Lomé I, €557 million during Lomé II and €925 million during Lomé III.
91. Important commodities for the Lomé countries that are not included in the Stabex list are sugar, tobacco, citrus fruit and beef.
92. The complex procedure for the disbursement was partially responsible for this amount of unused funds in the past.
93. FAO Database 2003. http://apps.fao.org/page/form?collection=Trade.CropsLivestock Products&Domain=Trade&servlet=1&language=EN&hostname=apps.fao.org&version=default.
94. As a result of the Second Banana Panel in the GATT (1994), the Framework Agreement between the EU and four exporting countries (Colombia, Costa Rica, Nicaragua and Venezuela), these four exporting countries were allocated half of the 2.5-million-tonne quota.
95. 'Big TNCs in Latin America devastated land with their large plantations and increased their power through large donations to the US government' (*The Guardian*, 8 April 1999).
96. The US has always publicly argued in favour of a free multilateral trading system. The Lomé and similar deals ran contrary such an ideal. The US, however, was silent about them because of strategic considerations. None the less, in spite of a strong Cold War-influenced preference in trade towards select developing countries, France (and Belgium) would argue in favour of retaining certain trade preferences for their former colonies.
97. These are all laudable and necessary points. However, in the situation of excessive poverty and foreign debt, diseases, drought, instability and uncertainty, during the first EU–Africa Summit in Cairo (2000) an African delegate commented: 'We need water pumps, not democracy' (*The Economist*, 8 April 2000, p. 48).
98. The key products that benefited from the GSP treatment were those based on labour, rather than capital-related technologies. The major ones were perambulators, toys, sporting goods, footwear and telephones.
99. For example, Hong Kong, Singapore and South Korea 'graduated' in the EU GSP plan. Hong Kong, South Korea, Singapore and Taiwan 'graduated' in the US GSP scheme.
100. Upgrading trade arrangements with Turkey in the second half of the 1990s to a customs union may benefit more exporters from the EU than from Turkey. Most trade barriers against Turkish goods by the EU were eliminated many years ago.
101. One should note that Jordan and Portugal were included in this strategy, although geographically they do not border the Mediterranean Sea.
102. Brunei, Cambodia, Indonesia, Laos, Malaysia, Myanmar, the Philippines, Singapore, Thailand and Vietnam.
103. Bolivia, Colombia, Ecuador, Peru and Venezuela.
104. Argentina, Brazil, Paraguay and Uruguay.
105. Other examples include Japan, China and Switzerland.
106. An analysis of trade conflicts in high-technology industries is provided by Tyson (1992).
107. One does not have to be an independent observer to note that as far as France itself is concerned, this has always been quite an effort for an Englishman, and vice versa.

> A man's steps are of the LORD;
> How then can a man understand his own way?
> Proverbs 20:24

8 Spatial Location of Production and Regional Policy

1. Introduction

Where economic activity will locate in the future is one of the most important and challenging questions in economics. Progress in technology, changes in demand and moves towards a liberal economic policy create new challenges for theorists, policy makers and business executives. As a number of economic activities became 'footloose' and highly mobile, one of the most demanding and intricate questions in such a situation is where firms and industries would locate, relocate or stay.

Regional policy dealing with the spatial location of production, as a part of the EU Cohesion[1] Policy, affected the daily life of almost half of the 380 million people who lived in the EU(15). It affects even more people out of the 456 million in the EU(25). The EU regional policy involves various subsidies and development projects, including infrastructure, training and support to SMEs, in order to ease and remedy regional disparities. The objective and intention is to strengthen the output potential of the disadvantaged locations and regions, as well as to reinforce the unity (cohesion) with diversity of the EU.

Annual expenditure from the EU structural funds[2] was about 30 per cent (this is second to the EU expenditure on agriculture) of the overall EU budget of €100 billion during the 2000–06 financial perspective. As a result, European integration has a direct and significant impact on a substantial number of EU citizens and businesses. The importance of the EU regional policy ought to increase in the future at least because of two crucial developments:

- *Eurozone*: Member countries can no longer deal with national economic problems using policy instruments such as interest rate, inflation, excessive deficit-financed expenditure or changes in exchange rate. Potential national balance of payments disequilibria became regional disequilibria in an EMU. Hence, one of the policy instruments to deal with such problems is regional policy.
- *Eastern enlargement*: Eight Central and East European countries plus Cyprus and Malta joined the EU in 2004. Other countries may also join the group in the future. The eastern enlargement has highlighted regional disparities in the EU. Thus, the EU(15) will continue to assist (as much as the political will and resources permit during the 2007–13 financial perspective) the Central and East European EU countries. This assistance will be necessary for quite some time to come in order to ensure that these countries adjust well and with least disturbance to the EU membership.

Various theoretical and policy-oriented aspects that affect the location of production, as well as regional policy, such as competition, industrial and trade policies or the choice of spatial location of foreign-owned firms (TNCs), have been encountered in other chapters of this book. The purpose of this chapter is to present the issues related to the spatial location of firms and industries, the impact of economic integration and the EU regional policy. The chapter is structured as follows. Section 2 examines the issues relating to the location of firms and industries. Section 3 provides a brief survey of the theoretical foundations of how firms and industries fit and stay in a certain geographical space. A simplified explanation of the creation of cities and clusters is given in Sections 4 and 5, respectively. The role of historical lock-in effect and expectations is the subject matter of Section 6. Section 7 explores examples of how wars influence the location of production. Theoretical considerations about location of production are dealt with in Section 8. Section 9 outlines the theory of regional policy. Sections 10 and 11 consider, respectively, objectives and instruments of a regional policy. The impact of economic integration on regions is covered in Section 12. Various aspects of regional policy in the EU are discussed in Section 13. The conclusion (Section 14) is that the EU(25) should pay attention to regional and cohesion matters for three reasons. First, in an EMU (eurozone), balance of payments disequilibria are replaced by regional disparities. Second, eastern enlargement deepened the regional problem. Third, there is a constant need for the coordination on all levels of government of various policies that have a regional impact.

2. Issues

Spatial economics (geography of production, that is, the spatial relation among economic units) has been separately analysed as a sub-branch of a number of subjects within economics. It has, however, been treated with different intensity and depth within those research disciplines. Contributions are scattered widely across fields which include: microeconomics, planning, development, economic geography, regional science, urban economics, location theory, industrial organisation, international trade,[3] foreign direct investment, transport economics, business economics, innovation studies, public finance, price theory, imperfect competition, labour economics, environment and resource economics. The common research denominator in all these fields was the spatial dimension, which was seen as an opportunity, a medium for interactions and a limitation. As a multidisciplinary research field, spatial economics has integrated these previously separate research areas. This is in line with the new trend in science which includes merging various methods in research.

In this complex situation, the crucial questions for research, business decisions and economic policy are the following:

- Where will economic activity locate in the future?
- Does international economic integration encourage agglomeration, clustering, spatial concentration of industries, adjoint locations of linked productions and 'thick' market effects? Or, alternatively, does agglomeration encourage economic integration?
- Does this cause convergence or divergence in the geography of production in the participating countries?
- Does this induce convergence or divergence in income in the participating countries?
- How do these forces interact?
- What is the role of public policy (intervention)?
- What will be the properties of economic adjustment (spatial and sectorwise reallocation of resources) to the new situation?
- Where will the 'hot spots' be for the location of business?
- Who will benefit from these developments?

The spatial location of a firm is an issue only in the situation with market imperfections. Without market imperfections such as transport cost (so that location matters), the production location decision becomes irrelevant. This is to say that without market failures, firms may split into units of any size and operate in all locations without any cost disadvantage. Recent empirical research found 'that the degree of production indeterminacy is greatest when trade barriers and trade costs are relatively low' (Bernstein and Weinstein, 2002, p. 73).

While considering feasible locations for its business in the situation with market imperfection, a firm may either prefer the spatial location with the lowest-cost production function and ignore the demand side; or emphasise demand/revenue and neglect everything else. In practice, neither of these choices necessarily offers the optimal location in terms of profit. Therefore, when considering possible locations for its business, a firm studies both options simultaneously. The firm attempts to maximise profit, taking into account the operating cost 'penalty' linked with alternative geographical locations.

In the distant past, the resource endowment of a specific location, together with the available technology, was the principal determinant of location for the manufacturing industry. In the new situation, in which most determinants for the spatial location of firms and industries are mobile and man-made, the location determinants for (footloose) industries include considerations about:

- *Costs and prices*: availability, substitutability, quality and prices of inputs (raw materials, energy, labour); cost of market access (trade costs); economies of scale; utility costs; infrastructure; transport cost of inputs and output; earlier sunk costs in other locations (not yet depreciated); availability of investment funds; and cost of the project.
- *Demand*: its real and potential size, its growth and consumer preferences.
- *Organisation and technology*: input–output production links; externalities; competition and market structure; location decisions of other competing or supplying firms; technology and the speed of its change; and local R&D resources and capabilities.
- *Policy-related factors*: incentives; taxes; subsidies; public procurement; permissions; and mandatory or voluntary unionisation of labour.
- *Social factors*: system of education of management and training of labour; brain drain; income distribution; general quality of life; and retirement patterns.

Hence, the decision about the location of a firm or an industry is a complex, uncertain and risky task. It comes as no surprise that the national or regional production geography does not always change very quickly.

3. Theories of location

The study of the location of production (spatial economics) has a long, although somewhat meagre history (Krugman, 1998a, p. 7). In spite of the general interest, there is no consensus in the literature about the factors that influence the location of new businesses. The problem was noted, for example, by Ohlin who wrote that 'the theory of international trade is nothing but *internationale Standortslehre*' (teaching about international location) (Ohlin, 1933, p. 589). In the same vein, Isard wrote that 'location cannot be explained without at the same time accounting for trade and trade cannot be explained without the simultaneous determination of locations. . . . trade and location are the two sides of the same coin' (Isard, 1956, p. 207).

A country's or a region's level of income and its structure of production (size, scope and variety of firms and industries) depend on at least two factors. The first includes a country's endowment of primary and derived stock of factors such as land, labour, capital, infrastructure, technology, as well as production, organisation, entrepreneurial and control skills and competences. The other element is how the country or region interacts with the external environment; in particular, the extent, level and form of its access to the international market for goods, services, capital and knowledge.

Let us now turn to the principal theories of firm location. Acknowledging the arbitrary character of our classification and its limits, we shall look into the issue of how and where firms and industries locate in space, without paying attention to the origin, control and ownership of the firm. The issue of (foreign) ownership and control (TNCs) is considered in the chapter on capital mobility (see Chapter 9).

A starting point in location (spatial) theory and economic geography is the national endowment of primary factors of production. Adam Smith and David Ricardo referred to the geography of production and spatial economics in an indirect way. A country specialises in the production of a good for which it has an absolute advantage in production. Hence, according to Smith, an *absolute advantage* determines the geographical location of production. Ricardo's argument is similar, but in his model a country specialises in the production of goods for which it has a *comparative advantage* in production. Regarding land, the fertile areas are put into cultivation first, while less productive land enters use only as demand for agricultural goods increases.

The models by Smith and Ricardo depend on constant returns to scale and on the assumption that competitive prices guide spatial resource allocation. Hence, free trade allows countries to gain, because they specialise in production that they carry out comparatively well. Such an assumption is challenged by the view that there are in reality important market distortions such as monopolies, externalities (pollution), controlled prices and rigid wages that do not tell the truth about social costs. As such, they send wrong price signals and may lead to the conclusion that trade liberalisation may make matters even worse! Thus some argued that protectionist policies were required for:

- the security of jobs, as was the case during the 1930s and ever since; or
- the safeguard of infant industries, as during the 1950s; or
- rent shifting in oligopolistic markets, as during the 1980s; or
- the safety of the environment, as is currently the case.

In addition to these classical models, the standard neo-classical *factor endowment* or *Heckscher–Ohlin* model refers to locational fundamentals. The national endowment of factors (land, capital and labour) and their relative proportion decides the location of production. A relatively abundant national factor of production (compared with other factors) determines what a country produces and exports. Conversely, a country will import goods whose production requires factors that are scarce in the national economy. Considering cases of 'localisation' of industry in one or a few countries, Ohlin (1933, p. 133) simply argued that 'it must be shown that costs of production on the basis of existing factor prices are lower than in other countries: certain factors are cheaper here than abroad, which accounts for that condition'.

In an empirical study of trade patterns of over a hundred economies, Leamer (1984) confirmed that the factor endowment model can explain these trade patterns rather well. This model elegantly assumes that there are no specific factors and that production functions are identical in all countries. As such, it does not give the answer to the whole issue, for it cannot explain intra-industry trade. This type of trade, which includes a large part of trade among developed countries, is not based on differences in factor endowments among them.

The factor endowment model has been one of the two principal single-cause models in dealing with specialisation, trade and spatial location of production. The other principal approach takes account of differences in technology, economies of scale and learning by doing. It was conceived by

Krugman (1979, 1980) and later developed and expanded both by him and by a host of others. In a nutshell, a variety of causes including history, expectations and changes in technology (not only factor endowment as before) influence a country's specialisation, geographical location of production and, hence, trade patterns. Differences in technology and increasing returns to scale change productivity levels. This in turn alters the bases for specialisation, spatial location of production and trade patterns. In the case where there are both increasing returns to scale and transport costs, there is an incentive to concentrate production. By spatially concentrating production near its largest market, a firm can both profit from economies of scale and minimise transportation costs. Economies of scale have a stronger impact on the location of modern, knowledge-based production than was the case before the Industrial Revolution.

While one cannot dispute the importance of factor proportions for the location of production and some processing of primary resources, this approach cannot explain the location of footloose industry. In addition, this model does not consider market structure, economies of scale, demand conditions or trade costs. The Heckscher–Ohlin theory is not capable of explaining the location of an industry in regions with high mobility of factors such as the US or in countries with a broadly similar endowment of factors (France and Germany). A common feature in the standard trade theory is that it considers states, while it utterly ignores firm or regions, that is, the distribution of economic activity within a country. This gap is filled by spatial economics.

In their survey of trade theory, Leamer and Levinsohn (1995, p. 1363) stated that 'one rather awkward assumption that cries out for change is that of equal numbers of commodities and factors. After all, we really don't know how to count either'. The existence of more goods than factors, economies of scale, multiple equilibria, trade costs and differences in technology present the principal obstacles for predicting the location of production and specialisation.

Harris (1954) argued that manufacturing firms tend to locate in places where they have favourable access to the market. He showed that the industrialised US regions were also the areas of high *market potential* (a large market attracts producers). The idea is that firms choose to locate in regions that have good market access. However, this access is good in areas in which many other firms already exist and have chosen to settle. There is a self-reinforcing, snowball or herding effect in which the size of the market attracts still more firms. The underlining feature of this approach is, like in most models of spatial economics, that it is based on some kind of economies of scale that rely on a spatial concentration (agglomeration) of certain production activities. Such agglomeration economies represent increasing returns in spatial form.[4] In the case of France, Crozet et al. (2004, pp. 50–51) found that firms from Belgium, Germany and Switzerland initially preferred to locate their operations in the frontier regions, near their home market. However, as time passed by and as they learned how to operate in France, it became more important to be physically closer to final demand and less relevant to be in locations that share common attributes with the home country.

Countries tend to specialise and export goods for which they have a relatively large domestic market. It is this domestic demand or 'home market' effect (Linder, 1961; Krugman, 1980) that induces production, rather than domestic factor endowment. The response by firms to strong local demand for a product is so powerful that it leads this country to export that product. Countries have a competitive edge in the production of these goods and thus gain an advantage in foreign markets, while they import goods demanded by a minority of the home population. The factor endowment or comparative advantage model would not predict the home market effect. However, economic geography would predict such effects. The US, Japan and Germany have the greatest comparative advantage in goods for which their home market is relatively big. These are standardised goods for mass consumption. Empirical investigation by Davies and Weinstein (2003) found support for the existence of home market effects, as well as for the role and importance of increasing returns in determining the production structure for the OECD.

At the heart of the location theory by von Thünen (1826) are differences in land rents and land uses. This model is primarily concerned with the *location of agricultural production*. While Ricardo focuses on the difference in the fertility of land, von Thünen studies how different agricultural lands around a city (marketplace) bid for various uses. The model assumes a given isolated city (one consuming centre) and surrounding agricultural hinterland, homogeneous land surface, free and costless mobility of labour and identical tastes at all income levels. Land rents are highest in the city. From there, they steadily decline to zero at the outermost limit of cultivation (beyond that limit, land is a free good). Hence the rent in a given location totals the difference between the value of its yield minus the sum of production and transport costs. Under the above assumptions the model explains the kind of crop that would be grown at places with different distances from the market. In other words, farmers decide on the type of production (expensive to transport vegetables and cheap to transport grain) by taking into account land rent and cost of transport. As transport costs and yields differ among crops, the result is a spontaneous development of concentric circles of production around the city. Land is allocated among different crops in a(n) (optimal) way that minimises production and transport costs of different crops.

Von Thünen's model is based on careful study of farming practices in northern Germany in the early 19th century. Such distribution of farmland is less obvious in the modern more intricate world, but there are certain remnants around large urban centres such as dairy production and gardening. This early model, however, does not consider the role played by economies of scale. There is no answer to the question whether vegetables can be shipped in both directions: towards the city (in exchange for cloth) and towards the outmost limits of cultivation (in exchange for grain). The model is, therefore, suitable for the analysis of a pre-railroad and a pre-industrial society.

The problem in von Thünen's model is to find which good to produce in the given location. In the optimal plant site model by Weber (1909) the branch of industry is given, so the problem is to find the spatial location for production. Weber's model takes the spatial location of markets, raw materials and population as given and assumes that there can be only one location for production. The objective of an individual producer is to minimise the combined costs of production and delivery. When the production costs are independent of location, the locational problem relates to the minimisation of transport costs for inputs and output.[5] This is the key condition in the decision-making process about the location of a firm. However, when there are key resources that are used on a large scale in certain industries and that are highly localised, this may affect the location of manufacturing industry. These industries would be attracted to locate near resource sites. Hence, this case is 'out of step' with the spatial uniformity and the underlying principle of central-place location for some, but not for all kinds of manufacturing. The problem with this approach to the location of new firms is, however, that the initial, static locational needs of a firm may change over time as the firm, industry, technology, consumers' needs, income and tastes, or markets change and evolve. There is also the possibility of a historical accident which can be coupled with the economies of scale, lock-in effect and agglomeration. Moses (1958) extended Weber's work and integrated location theory with the theory of production. This allowed investigation of the relation between substitution of inputs and geographical location of a firm.

Geographical remoteness can be a handy scapegoat to some, who may use it to explain why peripheral regions are marginalised in economic and certain social terms. Hummels (1999) argues that geographical factors remain an important determinant of both trade and location. He suggests furthermore that trade composition patterns and direct investment decisions can be sensitive to changes in the relative cost of different transport modes and information transfer. His proposition that international transportation costs have not declined significantly receives some support from Finger and Yeats (1976), who demonstrate that with the process of tariff liberalisation overseen by the GATT/WTO the effective rate of protection from transport costs exceeds that from tariff barriers for many commodities. It is, however, a shallow justification for many industries. Innovations in transport and communication technologies have made these costs rarely the most important determinant for the location of business. In addition, the cost of 'transport disadvantage' on exports is already included in the local factor prices. Hence, a peripheral location is not an insurmountable obstacle for a number of businesses as demonstrated in the cases of countries such as Japan, Australia, New Zealand, Finland or Ireland.

Christaller (1933) wanted to clarify and explain the rationale for the number, size and spatial distribution of cities. The analysis of this geographer is based on the idea of market threshold and transport distance. He suggested that cities form a *hierarchy of central places*. This hinges on the supposition that larger cities can sustain a wider variety of activities relative to smaller (low-order) cities and villages. Economies of scale are the source of such uneven distribution of production. The consequence of Christaller's model is that if there exist economies of scale, then the size of the market matters for the location of business. The concern here, therefore, is about the most 'national' product, below which are other products. The hidden idea in this model is based on the minimisation of transport costs by rational consumers that make multipurpose trips. In spite of its obvious value for the analysis of urban growth and distribution of services, this rigid application of the impact of market size neglects the consequences of unequal distribution of natural resources, changes in technology and negative externalities that come from agglomeration.

Developing the central-place theory and the issue of how the economy fits into space further, the economist Lösch (1940) started with a useful, but most unrealistic assumption, that there is a perfectly even distribution of raw materials and population. He starts his consideration of the economic landscape with a 'local' good and seeks to *minimise transport costs* for a given density of central places. In such a space, centres specialise in different products, hence there is a diversification of economic landscape. An efficient pattern of central places would have the shape of nested hexagonal (honeycomb) market areas with no empty corners.[6] This means that certain economic activities can be done only at a restricted number of locations. It was subsequently demonstrated that there is a wide range of geographical configurations of firms. The spatial arrangements that can satisfy the equilibrium condition include squares, rectangles and regular and irregular hexagons (Eaton and Lipsey, 1976, p. 91). Even though based on unrealistic assumptions, the model of central places need not be disregarded out of hand. A coherent general equilibrium model found certain justification for the central-place theory (Krugman, 1993a, p. 298).

While the background theory in Christaller's model of central places is implicit, Lösch's separate approach made it explicit. When they seek to find synchronised locations for many kinds of goods and services they use different arguments. Lösch's model is more appropriate for the analysis of the manufacturing sector, while Christaller's hierarchies are more relevant for the tertiary sector (retail services). In any case, it would seem that Christaller and Lösch deal with planning problems, rather than with considerations of market results.

The theory of central places points to the factors that need to be examined during the decision-making process about the location of an industry or a firm. These factors are sources of supply, intersections of traffic routes and the centre of gravity.[7] In order to reduce inaccuracy in such 'technical' process (suitable for the centrally planned system) one needs to consider additional elements that are parts of a market-based economy, including actions of other functionally related firms, competitors, consumers and government policies.

The classical German location theory dealt with the locational decisions of firms which are in essence reduced to two issues: homogeneous distribution of natural resources over a flat space and optimum cost of transport. This literature was obsessed with the geometrical shape of market areas in an idealised landscape or with the optimal production site with given resources and markets. It ignored the crucial issue of market structure and competition. This was 'doing things in the wrong order, worrying about the details of a secondary problem before making progress in the main issue' (Krugman, 1992, p. 5). Organisational issues such as institutional reality and policies were put aside. Institution-free theoretical models avoid the problem of the impact of various policies on the location or reallocation of firms and industries.

Perroux (1950, 1955, 1961) introduced a predominantly intuitive concept of *growth poles* in spatial economics. The idea was discussed in the context of controversy between balanced and unbalanced regional growth during the 1950s. Geographical agglomeration, significant production linkages (with the key industry) and strong human contacts are necessary for the growth of a pole. A firm is located in a space consisting of poles. Each pole has both centrifugal and centripetal forces. Hence, each pole has its zone of influence (it attracts and repulses firms) and interacts with other poles. If, however, a certain pole does not have a degree of flexibility and adaptability to new technologies and changes in the market, it will stagnate and decline. For instance, France selected eight urban areas and bolstered their growth during the 1960s in the expectation that such a policy would counteract the growth of Paris. Hence, the policy of spatial concentration of investments was diluted over time as it was coupled with political snags. Many other national 'areas' exerted pressure to be included in the select group of geographical poles for special treatment. The evaluation of the policy of growth poles is beset by difficulties, as it was not vigorously implemented in practice.

Multiple equilibria create a situation for welfare ranking and set up many temptations to try to pick winners. The selection problem, however, remains unresolved. Hence a small historical accident (chance, arbitrariness)[8] remains the unique deciding factor that counts heavily in deciding the location (Arthur, 2002, p. 6). If governments want to tip markets towards a preferred solution, then it is timing and, to an extent, instruments that are crucial. There is only a narrow window of opportunity during which the policy may be effective. Otherwise, governments with their limited knowledge, instruments and resources try to stabilise artificially a 'naturally' unstable and evolving process.

Arthur (1989, 1990a, 1994a, 1994b) argued that certain models of production geography give weight to differences in factor endowment, transport costs, rents and competition. In such cases, the pattern of production locations is an equilibrium outcome. Hence, in these models history does not matter. The locational system is determinate and predictable (Arthur, 1994a, pp. 49–50). However, if one takes increasing returns and multiple equilibria into consideration, the new model has four properties that cause serious difficulties in analysis and policy making (Arthur, 1989, pp. 116–17):

- *Multiple equilibria (non-predictability)*: *Ex ante* knowledge of firms' preferences and potentials of technologies may not be sufficient to predict the 'market outcome'. The outcome is indeterminate.[9]
- *Potential inefficiency*: Increasing returns (*i*-activities) may uplift the development of technology with inferior long-run aptitude as firms make irreversible investments under uncertainty.[10] Basically, a superior technology may have bad luck in gaining early adherents. For example, the American nuclear industry is dominated by light-water reactors as a consequence of the adoption of such a reactor to propel the first nuclear submarine in 1954. Engineering literature asserts, however, that a gas-cooled reactor would have been a superior choice (Arthur, 1989, p. 126). If the claim by engineers is that Betamax is a technically superior system for video recorders, then the market choice (around 1980) of the VHS did not represent the best outcome. Similar arguments could be used for the triumph of DOS over Macintosh during the mid-1980s. In addition, the 'qwerty' arrangement for the typewriter keyboards was designed in the 19th century. Its name refers to the first six top-line letters. Even though it has repeatedly been shown that this distribution of letters was suboptimal, the 'qwerty' system continues to be the standard for keyboards.

- *Inflexibility*: Once an outcome such as a dominant technology begins to surface it turns out to be more 'locked in' and persist for a long period of time. In order to replace an entrenched product or technology, the new one must be very much superior to the existing one. It must significantly increase the convenience in use to the consumers, it has to be available at a price that takes into account three factors: culture (openness to change); investment of capital and time (learning) into the new good or service (once people learn to use something, they do not want to switch easily); and convenience in use. VCRs were introduced during the 1970s. It took three decades to replace them by DVDs and full replacement is not yet finished.
- *Path dependence (non-ergodicity)*:[11] Small, unpredictable, random and arbitrary events (chances and accidents), path dependence and economies of scale in a non-ergodic system may set in motion mutations in economic structures and irreversibly decide the final outcome. These events are not normalised, or averaged away, or forgotten by the dynamics of the system. There is no homeostasis (habitual return to the initial equilibrium).

In this model history matters, but the system's dynamics, increasing returns, multiple equilibria, lock-in effect and path dependence generate theoretical and practical limits to predicting the future spatial location of an industry with a high degree of certitude.

The probability of the location of an industry resulting from a historical accident is shown in highly stylised, graphical form in Figure 8.1. If the distribution of potential locations of an industry is concave (Figure 8.1a), with a single minimum and a corresponding single outcome, the location is not influenced by a historical chance. This type of distribution is exemplified by the mining and steel-making industries, which are normally located close to their source of raw materials. If, however, the distribution is convex (Figure 8.1b), with two minima, then there are two potential outcomes, each resulting in a different location which may depend on the historical chance. The third case represents a sphere in which there are n solutions for the location of footloose industries (Figure 8.1c). Hence, multiple equilibria make policy analysis conceptually difficult. This type of distribution is exemplified by corner shops, bakeries and petrol stations. However, firms in most industries need to be close to one another (that is, they tend to agglomerate and create towns and cities), not only to be close to common suppliers of inputs, but also to foster competition and to facilitate exchange of information, which can be hampered if firms are spatially dispersed.

If agglomeration forces based on increasing returns are unbounded, then

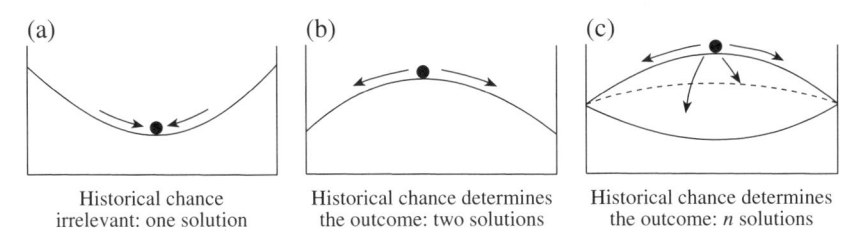

Figure 8.1 Concave (a), convex (b) and spherical (c) distributions of potential industry locations

a single geographical location monopolises the industry. Which region is selected depends on its geographical attractiveness and the historical accident of firm entry, in particular early preferences of first entrants. If, however, agglomeration forces that come from increasing returns are bounded, then various regions may share the industry as if agglomeration economies are absent (Arthur, 1990b, p. 249). Locations with a large number of firms cast an 'agglomeration shadow' in which little or no settlement takes place. This causes separation of an industry. Agglomeration occurs at a certain level of trade costs, while at another level of these costs, the spread of activities takes place. With bounded agglomeration economies, neighbouring locations cannot share the industry, but sufficiently separated regions can. In France, for example, Lyon lies between Paris and Marseille. Bounded agglomeration economies caused separation and dispersion. Again, 'which locations gain the industry and which become orphaned is a matter of historical accident' (Arthur, 1990b, p. 247).

4. Cities

It may be astute to recall Plato's discussion about the location of cities or city-states written in 360 BC in *Laws* (Book IV).[12]

> Then there is some hope that your citizens may be virtuous: had you been on the sea, and well provided with harbours, and an importing rather than a producing country, some mighty saviour would have been needed, and lawgivers more than mortal, if you were ever to have a chance of preserving your state from degeneracy and discordance of manners. But there is comfort in the eighty stadia; although the sea is too near, especially if, as you say, the harbours are so good. Still we may be content. The sea is pleasant enough as a daily companion, but has indeed also a bitter and brackish quality; filling the streets with merchants and shopkeepers, and begetting in the souls of men uncertain and unfaithful ways-making the state unfriendly and unfaithful both to her own citizens, and also to

other nations. There is a consolation, therefore, in the country producing all things at home; and yet, owing to the ruggedness of the soil, not providing anything in great abundance. Had there been abundance, there might have been a great export trade, and a great return of gold and silver; which, as we may safely affirm, has the most fatal results on a State whose aim is the attainment of just and noble sentiments: this was said by us, if you remember, in the previous discussion.[13]

Urbanisation is one of the important features of modern society. One of the reasons for this development is a declining share of labour relative to capital in agriculture. Footloose industries are less reliant on natural inputs than other types of manufacturing and service industries. In some cases they may place more emphasis on the proximity to final markets which further adds up to the urbanisation trend. Another incentive for urbanisation comes from the dependency of many manufacturing and service operations on access to public services, in particular in the countries that are known for intervention. Because of this, lobbyists cluster in politically significant cities such as Brussels or Washington, DC because that is the geographical location where decisions are made and subsidies distributed.

In the dim and distant past the creation of wealth largely depended on the local availability of natural resources. A mix of geographical, economic and historical factors shaped industrial development and the location of firms, industries and cities. However, as the economy evolved, wealth creation came to depend more on the accumulated physical assets (mainly equipment and finance).[14] The prosperity of the modern economy depends not only on the physical, but also and increasingly on intangible assets such as knowledge,[15] information-processing potentials and organisation capabilities.

Even though cities were initially created to reduce transport and communication costs for people and their goods and ideas (to eliminate physical space between people and firms), many other factors were quite accidental.[16] The most attractive spatial locations for setting up cities, industries and businesses included: a crossroads, the mouth of a river, safe natural harbours,[17] defendable hilltops, places with ample fresh water and rich soil, and dry cool highlands (free of malaria-carrying mosquitoes).

In the past, the location of a firm or a city was influenced both by the endowment of immobile local resources and by flows of mobile factors.[18] Once the development of a business activity starts in an area and if the economic system is flexible, this area attracts (gravity) other business activities to the region. This model of uneven development is based on the possibility of meaningful multiple equilibria in the presence of external economies. The point is evident: with external economies, the return to resources in a certain industrial activity is higher, when more resources are committed to it (Krugman, 1991a, p. 651). The property of a modern firm is high mobility in its search for profitable opportunities, not only within its region or country, but also internationally. For a footloose firm, the advantages of one location in relation to others are much more man-made than subject to resource endowments.

According to the analysis of spatial economics by Fujita et al. (1999, p. 131), cities exist because firms locate at a cusp in the market potential function made by a concentration of other firms. Cities form because a growing and spreading agricultural population makes it beneficial for producers to form new cities. The size of the cities differs (there is a hierarchy) because of differences in industrial externalities and transport costs. Finally, natural advantages (that is, the existence of harbours) help as they create natural cusps in market potential. In addition, Arthur (1994b, p. 109) argued that the observed pattern of cities cannot be explained only by economic determinants without considering chance events. They are also the result of the places where immigrants with certain skills landed, where the politicians decided to build railways and canals or where trains stopped for the night.

Those cities that were based on educated and skilled labour have grown faster than comparable cities with less embodied human capital over the past century. Firms in such cities are more productive than elsewhere where labour is less skilled. In addition, cities based on skilled labour and management adapt better to shocks. Accumulated knowledge and talents allow easier adaptation to changes, challenges and opportunities. In addition, the lifestyle in such cities may be more attractive to some people than elsewhere. Some three-quarters of the US population lives in the 100 km wide coastal belt which includes the Great Lakes and the St. Lawrence Seaway.

New possibilities and changes such as the use of the Internet permit modification in working time and place of work for select professions. Certain key employees can work at home in the environment that they may enjoy best (presumably non-congested countryside). In this situation, certain office space is liberated in cities which may turn into areas for entertainment.

Why are cities of different sizes? Henderson (1974) argued that there is a trade-off between economies of agglomeration of industries specific to that city and general diseconomies (negative externalities) such as costs related to commuting and high rents which (apart from pollution) do not depend on the structure of the local industry. The optimum city size depends on the maximum welfare of participants in the economy. It does not make much sense to put industries without spillovers (steel production and publishing) in the same city. However, it does make sense to locate the steel and textile industries in close proximity as they employ, respectively, mostly male and mostly female labour. Cities need to be specialised in one or a few industries with related external economies. These external economies, however, vary a great deal across industries. Because of strong links internal to the industry, a financial centre may do best if it includes virtually all financial institutions. The same is not true for the textile or food industry. Hence, the optimal size of a city depends on its role (Fujita et al., 1999, p. 20).

Although Henderson deals with spatial aspects, this type of model is surprisingly 'aspatial', because it does not say much about the actual location of a city, either in space or relative to other cities. In addition, national trade policy can influence the size of a city as exemplified by Mexico City. The Mexican import-substitution policy had, as its unintended byproduct, the expansion of the capital city because of production linkages and economies of scale. Once Mexico started to open its economy during the 1980s, there was a relocation of certain firms away from Mexico City, mainly towards the northern frontier.

5. Clusters

Industrial clusters often determine what a country exports. Their success often establishes the competitive position of a country's goods and services on the international market. Prior to the Industrial Revolution, high transport costs splintered production into many units throughout space. The Industrial Revolution reduced the cost of transport, but brought high fixed costs that contributed to the development of new and the expansion of existing agglomerations.

A promising point of departure for the analysis of clusters is to consider two basic forces which, through their tension and interplay, influence the spatial distribution (concentration or spread) of firms: the centripetal and centrifugal forces that also help to explain the agglomeration and dispersion forces of the 'core–periphery'[19] development model:

- *Centripetal forces* promote agglomeration. They concentrate production and employment in specific geographical areas. These 'snowball' or herding forces include: economies of scale, forward and backward linkages in production, trade costs, increasing returns in transport, concentration of firms and consumers, existence of suppliers, limited spread of information and embodied knowledge, as well as a 'thick' labour market (especially for certain skills so that employers can find

workers and workers can find jobs). Centripetal forces take the production system towards the equilibrium.
- *Centrifugal forces* push the other way and test whether the equilibrium is stable. These dispersion (comparative advantage) forces discourage further spatial concentration of business. They favour a geographical spread of firms and include factor immobility, regional or international wage differentials, relative amount of land rents, competition for factors and consumers, commuting costs, pollution, congestion, traffic accidents, crime, infectious and other diseases, sewage and waste disposal.

The final result depends on the balance between these two forces, on what factors are mobile and what immobile, on barriers to the reallocation of resources, on demand and its change and on public policy. In essence, three outcomes are possible. First, economic activity may spread so that each region becomes specialised in a certain activity. This type of clustering does not mean polarisation as is exemplified in North America. The US economy is less geographically polarised than Europe. Second, activity may agglomerate in core regions, leaving others without production potentials and without people. Finally, a long-run polarisation may split the country or an economic grouping into advanced regions with high incomes and low unemployment and depressed regions with low income and high unemployment (Braunerhjelm et al., 2000, pp. 29–30).

A concentration of functionally related business activity within a relatively small area (agglomeration; thick market effects; benefits of co-location; and non-ergodicity) provides firms with collective gains that would not be available if the firms operated in a remote place. These shared benefits or externalities are different from those that are created within and available to a single firm. In essence, clusters create economies that are external to individual firms, but internal to a network of firms in a cluster, which are exchanged and enriched in a non-market way. Hence, a great deal of an individual firm's competitive advantage is outside it, but inside the location where it operates.

A firm locates in an area where there are firms from the same or related industry (in a cluster) because:

- it has production links with other firms;
- it may benefit from the already existing pool of suppliers;
- there are services such as finance, information, consulting and maintenance;
- there may be a pool of trained and experienced labour;
- firms may reduce the cost of transport;

- there may be a concentration of consumers (proximity to the major growing markets is often the most important reason for the selection of a particular location); and
- they may jointly negotiate contracts with transporters and organise export promotion boards and the like.

Manchester (England) in the 19th century provides an example of such a cluster specialising in textile manufacturing. Subsequently, the manufacture and repair of looms, and bleaching, dyeing and finishing facilities also located there. In the course of time, the town set up a technical college in order to train people for the manufacture of machinery, textile design and other skills related to the local industry. All this was supported by marketing organisations such as the Cotton Exchange (Smith, 1981, pp. 60–61). It was a similar story with Reutlingen in Germany. However, even the most recent industries rely on the 'old rule' of geographical concentration (clustering), which is why there is a Silicon Valley in California or a Route 128 in Boston (because of the existence of the best universities in the vicinity).

A more recent example of similar developments in the manufacturing of surgical instruments and certain sports goods can be found in the town of Sialkot (Pakistan), which leads the world in its export of surgical instruments and hand-sewn footballs. This success, as well as of all other clusters, is based on two factors: first, a demand-driven approach and, second, competition based on collective efficiency (Schmitz, 1998, p. 6). An example of a joint action can be found in the surgical-instruments manufacturing cluster in Tuttlingen (Germany). This cluster produced joint publications on various topics of common interest, including booklets on: quality requirements in the surgical-instrument-making industry; a guide on the correct use of the instruments; and a guide providing customers arriving in Tuttlingen with a list and profile of firms that produce such instruments.

Technical advances in transportation, information technology, organisation and control of production and distribution reduce production time and costs. They 'do away' with distance. 'Globalisation' (integrated international production) creates possibilities for dispersing production and ownership. In such circumstances already established locations face tougher times anchoring income-generating activities. At the same time, strong centripetal forces ensure that certain spots remain 'sticky places in slippery space' (Markusen, 1996, p. 293). Spatial barriers for the location of businesses are becoming less important, but capital is more sensitive to the choice of location.

Until the 1960s, it seemed to be more efficient to move people to jobs by migration. The footloose element of many modern industries supports production in relatively small and flexible units. Hence, there is an arbitrary and uncertain element (multiple equilibria) in the location of firms that have a footloose industrial character. Locations that are close to consumers save in transport costs of final output, while other locations may save in the cost of production. Due to costs of inputs, economies of scale and forwarding outlays, one business may favour peripheral locations, while another's preference may be for locations nearest to the consumers.

A cluster is a relatively large group (a critical mass) and system of formal and informal functionally related specialised firms, knowledge, skills and competences, as well as specialised institutions (standards-setting bodies, schools, universities, research institutes, trade associations), in a particular geographical location. This functional relation among firms may be downstream (suppliers), horizontal (competitors and collaborators), upstream (clients) and/or through the circulation of accumulated knowledge, skills and competences by means of personnel turnover.

Clusters, as spatially limited business incubators, are a part of the new industrial order called 'alliance capitalism', in which continuous collaboration and networking with related knowledge and experience-rich firms are sources of competitiveness. It is also associated with the complex and dynamic 'new economy' based on knowledge and continuous innovation, as firms that operate in clusters are usually innovative. In addition, a vibrant dialogue is constantly taking place among all players in a cluster. The reason why this view fails to define a clear geographical boundary for a cluster is because the structure of a cluster may change over time. Nor does it refer to the specific industrial boundary of a cluster, as this may overlook the complex relationship among different industries that support one another's competitiveness.

Agglomeration and the spatial clustering of firms and industries are motivated by efficiency considerations within a network. They are based on economies of scale in production and transportation, as well as on transaction costs. For example, the Massachusetts General Hospital in Boston is among the largest in the world in terms of R&D funds. Industrial managers are attracted to the R&D department of the hospital because all the specialists and all the needed knowledge are 'within 20 minutes walking' (Lambooy, 1997, p. 298). This cluster of more than 400 firms linked to medical devices is invisible as it is concealed in business categories such as electronic equipment and plastics products.

Agglomeration does not only apply to private businesses. Bearing in mind the complexity of action and need for a fast response to changing and uncertain events, Simon Jenkins has noted that 'Britain is a centralised state. Two thirds of the top 100 powerful people in Britain work within 300ft of the Prime Minister and Chancellor of the Exchequer' (*The Times*, 11 December 2002).

Marshall (1890) considered the issue of why it is beneficial for producers from the same industry to be located together. He offered three basic reasons why producers concentrate (form a cluster):

- *Knowledge spillovers*: Proximity eases exchange and spread of information.
- Advantages of *thick markets for specialised skills*: Firms may easily find the necessary labour and workers may get promotion or work if the current employer does poorly. There is no need to create the human capital from scratch. The 'mysteries of trade' (craft secrets) are no mysteries at all as they are 'in the air' and children learn many of them unconsciously from their parents (*vertical cultural transmission*).[20] Knowledge, experience and values are 'stored'. In addition, tacit knowledge and shared culture of beliefs and practices is difficult to transfer without labour mobility.
- Backward and forward *linkages* associated with large markets: Links may clarify and explain a part of the concentration story only if there are economies of scale. Otherwise, a firm would set up a separate production unit to serve each distinct market. A concentrated industry provides a market for specialised local suppliers of components, as well as private and public suppliers of various services (institutional thickness).

These economies, external to individual firms in a cluster, but internal to a network of firms in a cluster, are essential, but not sufficient to explain the basic reason for the strength of firms in a cluster. Conscientiously pursued joint action and horizontal and vertical cooperation by firms in a cluster (sharing equipment, developing a new product, various consortia) enhance collective efficiency and improve the competitive advantage of the participating firms. When there is a problem (market failure), it can be resolved by government intervention and/or by private self-help (as was the case in Sialkot, Pakistan)[21] (Schmitz, 1999, pp. 468–70). However, relations between firms in a cluster may take different forms. Take a look, for example, at shoe-producing clusters in Italy and Mexico. While cooperation is more common in Italy, market rules prevail in Mexico.

There are, however, additional reasons for the spatial clustering of firms and industries. They include the following:

- because of the changed situation in competition and technology, the past arm's-length and hierarchical organisation of a firm can be

replaced by a flexible network of business organisation in a cluster. Inter-firm competition is based on innovation;
- firms may reduce transaction costs;
- the presence of one firm/industry creates direct or indirect market for another firm/industry. One industry output is used exclusively as another industry's input (tyres and cars);
- firms use common services (marketing, storage, accounting, repair, transport);
- two industries use a common resource;
- firms may create entry barriers;
- labour markets of two unrelated industries may be complementary: one industry (metal or car assembly) uses male labour, while another (textile or food processing) employs female labour;
- firms use common social infrastructure (schools, health, roads); and
- the more potential firms that can use the infrastructure, the more likely that infrastructure will be built. Each user in a cluster assists other users in this situation, hence the fixed cost of an infrastructure project (such as educational and training centres, power plant, railway or airport) can be recovered and the project can come close to profitability. These are relatively standard projects, hence the government can readily be involved as specific local knowledge is not always essential for the success.

The presence of a relatively large concentration of demanding consumers in an agglomeration, coupled with technologies with economies of scale and agglomeration forces, can bring certain economic advantages through the interrelationship of functionally connected, as well as competing firms. Competition forces firms to employ state-of-the-art technology, hence there are no low-technology industries, but only low-technology firms within various industries.

The clustering of firms selling identical goods (competitors) such as ice cream on the beach was thought to be welfare inefficient from a social standpoint (Hotelling, 1929, p. 53). However, the clustering of firms often occurs in response to consumers' desires to make comparisons between goods (for example, in shopping malls). Consumers usually visit more than one store prior to making a purchase. Department stores often demand that certain space is made available in shopping malls to small shoe and clothing retailers, to assure clients that the offered goods are balanced by other competitive offers (that is, that a minimum differentiation exists) for comparison. Clustering of *identical* firms can serve a socially-useful purpose because they lower transportation costs (Eaton and Lipsey, 1979, pp. 422–3). The same holds for the clustering of *heterogeneous* firms.

A rational consumer would connect purchasing activities such as search, purchase and transport. Multipurpose shopping assists in the lowering of shopping costs (Eaton and Lipsey, 1982, p. 58).

If the firms are similar, they seek comparable if not identical features for the spatial location of business. If this is true, then the outcome may be a cluster in such an industry. For example, the US film industry started a century ago in California, around Los Angeles. The companies were all looking for comparable locational features such as dry weather and excellent daylight conditions. Although modern filming and lighting technology does not depend on natural light at all, the clustering of the film and entertainment industry in California continued. Homogeneous initial needs of firms created the film cluster rather than the input–output production relations. Hence, functional production links and agglomeration economies are not a necessary condition to create a cluster.

In spite of a few global TV stations such as the BBC or CNN and newspapers such as the *International Herald Tribune* or electronic media, most of the stories that editors publish or broadcast are still local. The proximity of firms in the same industry increases both the visibility of the course of action of competitors and the speed of the spread of information. 'Popular luncheon spots are patronized by executives from several companies, who eye each other and trade the latest gossip. Information flows with enormous speed' (Porter, 1990a, p. 120). This 'cafeteria effect' breaks the spatial boundaries to information flow and gives incentives for the creation of matching improvements by other firms in the cluster. It also offers a partial confirmation that there is a spatial limit to knowledge spillovers. Information may be freely available notwithstanding distance, but the charge for the spread of embodied knowledge, in particular tacit, complex, changeable and 'sticky', increases with the distance.[22]

The high speed of information diffusion is one of the major strengths of clusters. Entrepreneurs often prefer to enter or stay in a cluster even though they may be able to appropriate a higher return on their innovation elsewhere. The reason for this preference is that the firms in the cluster are not only providers of information, but also recipients (Schmitz, 1999, p. 475). In the fields where technology changes often, personal contact may be the preferred way of communication rather than the less timely sources such as professional journals, fairs and conferences. 'Human capital accumulation is a *social* activity, involving *groups* of people in a way that has no counterpart in the accumulation of physical capital' (Lucas, 1988, p. 19). This all supports progress in technology (creation of knowledge).

Personal contacts and informality are essential for the exchange of tacit knowledge:

> *Tacit knowledge*, as opposed to *information* . . . can only be transmitted informally, and typically demands direct and repeated contact. The role of tacit knowledge . . . is presumably the greatest during the early stages of the industry life cycle, before product standards have been established and a dominant design has emerged. (Audretsch, 1998, p. 23)[23]

> Companies that have gone furthest towards linking their global operations electronically report an increase, not a decline in the face-to-face contact needed to keep the firms running well: with old methods of command in ruins, the social glue of personal relations matters more than ever. (*The Economist*, 30 July 1994, p. 11)

Such a durable social network that shortens the learning curve, informality in contacts and local embeddedness are essential to identify user requirements, proper installation, operation and service of the product.[24] A phrase 'you know what I mean' among members of a professional group in face-to-face communication can transmit a lot. The same holds in relations between suppliers and their clients. Therefore, operation of firms within clusters makes firms relatively less sensitive to local taxes. This provides the local authorities with opportunities to tax them more heavily than would otherwise be the case.

The principal key of success in clusters of related firms in northern Italy ('Padania') is their ultra-specialisation and family-run type of business. Relatives support one another in business so there is no need for supervision, they constantly upgrade skills and they have opportunities for invention. Common values and local consensus is preserved. This reduces the possibility for business sclerosis, so common in large, vertically organised firms. For example, in Lumezzane (near Brescia) which produces two-thirds of the national output of bottle openers: one family specialises strictly in the production of the corkscrews, another has expertise in covers and so on. A similar situation can be found in Cadore (near Austria) regarding the production of spectacles. In general, company strategy is friendly with rapid changes, customised products and niche marketing.

A summary of properties of such industrial districts would include (Garofoli, 1991a, p. 52):

- a high level of division of labour between the firms and closer input–output relations;
- a high level of specialisation which stimulates accumulation of knowledge and introduction of new technologies;
- a high level of skills of workers as a result of a very long-term accumulation of knowledge at a local level;

- a large number of local competitors which leads to the adoption of 'trial and error behaviour' and a fast imitation process;
- efficient local informal (and formal) system for the exchange of information; and
- an increased emphasis on face-to-face relations.

The following elements could also be added: entrepreneurs; innovators; financial institutions with venture capital; and client demand.

The growing importance of intangible assets, particularly intellectual capital together with complexities and changeability of information and uncodified knowledge, increases the importance of knowledge externalities (spillovers) and frequent face-to-face contacts among the relevant players. They need to exchange uncodifiable knowledge, to be involved in interactive learning, to have feedback and suggestions, as well as to have a dialogue about risk and changing situation in the market and technology. Clear-cut, routine and simple activities based on codified and standardised knowledge can be managed and controlled from a distance. They can easily be located in regions with lower wages. However, successful handling of more elaborate activities still requires a high degree of exchange of information and face-to-face contacts.[25] This is highly important in complex activities with little or no codified knowledge and where market changes and uncertainty require a fast response (contracts are incomplete). 'Knowledge is the most important resource and learning is the most important process' (Pinch and Henry, 1999, p. 820).

Knowledge externalities are among the key reasons for the existence and success of clusters. Hence, clusters may also be seen as networks for information gathering, fact processing and network production places. 'Almost every internationally successful Italian industry has several if not hundreds of domestic competitors. Frequently, they are all located in one or two towns. . . . Where domestic rivalry is absent Italian firms rarely succeed internationally' (Porter, 1990a, p. 447). Toyota in Japan, for example, is cultivating suppliers in its own back yard. Toyota independent suppliers are on average 94 km away from its assembly plants. They make nine deliveries a day. By contrast in North America, GM's suppliers are on average 683 km away from plants they serve to which they make fewer than two deliveries a day. One of the results is that Toyota and its suppliers keep inventories that are a quarter the size of GM's.[26] While a just-in-time delivery and logistics method may be technically possible, organisationally feasible and financially desirable for a firm, an area that asks for further research includes the environmental and social costs of this type of logistics. The just-in-time delivery method is often linked with half loads and more transport journeys than are the more traditional delivery methods.[27]

The existence of competitors in the vicinity serves a useful business and social purpose. If one imagines a cluster in the shape of an input–output matrix for information, then the direct and indirect functional relations are 'diffused' through rows and columns. Competition increases productivity, which is the key ingredient of prosperity. Firms do not pursue every opportunity to ruin rivals. This is contrary to the standard story in every introductory economic textbook.[28] Every firm in a cluster perceives its survival, growth and success in terms of collective growth. These firms learn and prosper collectively. The learning process in a cluster is not only interactive, but also cumulative as it persists over time (once it exists it does not cease to exist, experience and discovery builds on experience and discovery). Turnover of labour, technical staff and management among these firms reinforces the transfer of tacit knowledge, cross-fertilising research, collective learning process and regional competitive advantage.

The underlying general operations within a cluster can be seen from another example:

> New York City's garment district, financial district, diamond district, advertising district and many more are as much intellectual centers as is Columbia or New York University. The specific ideas exchanged in these centers differ, of course, from those exchanged in academic circles, but the process is much the same. To an outsider, it even *looks* the same: A collection of people in similar activities, each emphasizing his own originality and uniqueness. (Lucas, 1988, p. 38)

Continuous and straight dealings among players allow tacit and accumulated knowledge to be exchanged within a network of players. Social closeness in such cases may be equally, if not more, relevant than the geographical proximity.

Established locations can be vulnerable to 'technological lock-in' in certain cases. New ideas may need new space. 'When IBM developed its own personal computer, the company located its fledgling PC capacity in Boca Ratton, Florida, way outside of the manufacturing agglomeration in the North-east Corridor' (Audretsch, 1998, p. 24). This is an example of a bifurcation point. In addition, certain industrial regions may become victims of own past success. Institutional sclerosis, vested interests of large firms, labour unions and public authorities may oppose changes and adjustment to new circumstances. For example, the German Ruhr region was led into the 'trap of rigid specialisation' (Grabher, 1993, p. 275). The Belgian Walloon region is in the same situation. However, it is sometimes overlooked that in certain cases new footloose industries often create own conditions for growth. For example, new environment-related industries are emerging in the Ruhr (the connection may be the solution of the pollution problem).

In addition, there is little technological continuity between the textile machinery complex in New England of the 19th century and the current electronics cluster (Boschma and Lambooy, 1999b, p. 394).

The existence of a good university or a research institute is not enough by itself for the overall economic success of an area. During the period of central planning in the former Soviet Union, Akademgorodok (near Novosibirsk) was essentially a town full of research institutes financed by the Soviet Academy of Sciences. It remained an 'isolated island' as it has not developed functional links with industries. During the centrally planned period, the Soviet enterprises depended primarily on the respective ministries and the central plan.

Sophia-Antipolis was developed in a vacant space at the end of 1960s in the south of France. It did not develop around an established university as was the case in Cambridge. Much time and effort, such as the establishment of the University of Nice, was necessary to create the necessary links among the high-technology firms in the Sophia-Antipolis cluster. In general, it is hard to find any plan of action or best practice to promote a cluster that could have an instantly recognisable success. However, there is a rare general agreement on one point: to have a commercial success, one needs to build on already existing competences in the target location.

The cluster of high-technology firms around Cambridge (England) offers a different story. The common tacit code of behaviour among the high-technology firms in the region includes trust and cooperation. The cluster is based on two local 'collective agents'. They are Cambridge University and consulting firms in R&D. In contrast to most other British universities which have formally regulated links with the industry, Cambridge has rather liberal rules governing such links. In fact, faculty members are allowed to work part-time in the private sector. All this had a strong and positive spillover effect on the regional cluster of high-technology firms.

There is also the view put forward by Porter, that

> [C]lusters often emerge and begin to grow naturally. Government policy had little to do with the beginning of Silicon Valley or the concentration of mechanical firms around Modena, Italy. Once a cluster begins to form, however, government at all levels can play a role in reinforcing it. Perhaps the most beneficial way is through investments to create specialized factors, such as university technical institutes, training centres, data banks, and specialized infrastructure. (Porter, 1990a, p. 655)

In fact, many governments impeded the 'natural' development of clusters on behalf of regional policy and subsidised firms to locate in areas with high unemployment and without supporting infrastructure (rather than to encourage migration of labour from these regions).

Until the 1960s, it was thought that production costs were not sensitive to regional location. It is therefore not surprising that firms located in such areas became white elephants, demanding subsidies to continue operations later on. The importance of endogenous technological change came to be appreciated only in the following decades, so the policy of regional decentralisation became suspect (Bekar and Lipsey, 2001, p. 1). However, universities have always been established in cities, where there were many children and students. Only relatively recently have universities become established in the countryside.

Governments and big TNCs often have nothing to do with the establishment of clusters (Silicon Valley, clusters in Italy, City of London financial district), which were created out of 'thin air'.[29] However, governments support their growth through the provision of education, infrastructure, tax policy, public procurement, as well as through sponsoring R&D.[30] All this should build on existing local specialties and competences, rather than create entirely new ones. The private sector needs to lead the process, while the government needs to play a flexible catalytic role as a one-size policy does not fit all clusters. There may not be a mechanical transfer of policy instruments from one cluster to another. Positive experiences from other clusters ought to provide more a source of inspiration and less a prescription for a general action.

Papageorgiou (1979) demonstrated that agglomerated firms can achieve higher aggregate profit and lower prices per unit of output and generate more demand than more dispersed firms. In addition, firms located in a cluster tended both to introduce more innovations and to grow faster than more isolated firms (Beaudry et al., 2002, p. 191). Relative to the rest of the economy, clusters could have higher productivity and higher profitability, and they may create more new jobs and new firms. On the cost side, land rents tend to increase in and around clusters and so does pollution and congestion. Labour costs can inflate, while institutions and specialisation may suffer from a path-dependence and lock-in effect which may be unconducive to adaptation to changes in technology which is not directly related to the specialisation in the cluster, but may easily alter the structure of general demand.

6. History and expectations

BACKGROUND

As already noted, the Heckscher–Ohlin theory is inadequate to provide the reason for the location of an industry in regions with a high mobility of factors (US) or in countries with a broadly similar endowment of factors (France and Germany). Patterns of regional specialisation and location of firms and industries are often created by a historical accident. Ohlin noted that 'Chance plays a significant part in determining the localisation of industry . . . A different distribution of inventions would have caused a different localisation' (Ohlin, 1933, p. 137). More recently, Krugman wrote: 'I at least am convinced that there is a strong arbitrary, accidental component to international specialization; but not everyone agrees, and the limitations of the data make a decisive test difficult' (Krugman, 1992, p. 9). In any case, evolutionary dynamics is based to a large extent on chance.

When there are multiple equilibria, various spots for the location of business are substitutable *ex ante* ('putty'). After the investment is made, these locations cannot be easily substitutable for quite some time ('clay'). Once a business is established at a specific geographical location, it is then 'locked in' through learning, path dependence, sunk costs, circular and cumulative causation effects (for examples of this putty–clay locational model, see Appendix 8A1). In this sense 'history matters in a way that it does not in neo-classical theory' (Eaton and Lipsey, 1997, p. xxv). Two questions are relevant here:

- Are there inherent differences among locations that create predestination for certain activities?
- How can a small historical accident, a chance (something that is beyond the prior knowledge of an investor), alter the economic fate of an industry, region or a country?

Meaningful multiple equilibria exist when firms make independent profit-maximising decisions about output, prices and location. Sources of this multiplicity are pecuniary externalities that originate in (large) fixed costs and imperfect competition. The question is, which equilibrium gets established? Will it be stable in the long run? Since a particular space has only a limited influence on the location of new economic activity (especially footloose industries), what are the options for policy makers in this situation?

On the one hand, there is a belief that the choice is basically resolved by history. Past events set preconditions that move the economy from one steady state to another. This reasoning, found in the traditional literature, argues that history matters because of increasing returns and lumpiness (inseparability) and activity-specific knowledge and capital goods (Eaton and Lipsey, 1997, pp. x–xi). The same idea is also behind promotional campaigns or 'location tournaments' (David, 1984) among countries to attract international footloose capital (TNCs). The idea is that once an activity starts in a place, it perpetuates itself and related businesses gravitate towards it. However, this 'self-reinforcing aspect of foreign investment begins to operate only after a certain development threshold has been reached' (Wheeler and Mody, 1992, p. 71). This is to say that spillovers on the local economy are not a direct consequence of the location of a TNC. Gains that come from these externalities can be achieved only if the local firms have taken on, or can be motivated to take on, new (foreign) technologies and skills. The structure of the local economy, attitude of the private sector and policies of the government that promote change play a key role. In addition, there is evidence in the case of the US foreign investors that 'past investment in the country was a strong predictor of new investment. That persistence was attributed to the favourable effects of agglomeration' (Mody and Srinivasan, 1998, pp. 780–81).

There is, on the other hand, a view that the choice of equilibrium is determined by expectations. This observation is based on the belief 'that there is a decisive element of self-fulfilling prophecy' (Krugman, 1991a, p. 652). Let us consider both these views in turn.

HISTORICAL LOCK-IN EFFECT

The non-linear probability theory can predict with some certitude the behaviour of systems subject to increasing returns. Suppose that balls of different colours are added on a table. The probability that the next ball will have a specific colour depends on the current proportion of colours. Increasing returns occur when a red ball is more likely to be added when there is already a high proportion of red balls (Arthur, 1990a, p. 98). Equilibrium depends on the initial point and later arrivals. Hence, history as a series of (random) arrivals sets the final result.

The national rate of growth of capital stock (without FDI and foreign loans) depends on home savings and investment. Suppose now that one region/country initially accumulates more capital than the other does. In the following period both regions grow, but the one with more capital grows faster than the one with less capital. As manufacturing capital grows, the relative prices of manufacturing goods fall. After a certain period of time, there is a point where the lagging region's industry cannot compete internationally and it begins to shrink. Once this process begins, the new theory of trade and strategic industrial policy suggests that nothing can stop agglomeration for a long time. Economies of scale may drive prices down in the capital-abundant region and at the same time the lagging region's manufacturing industry disappears. In this model, relatively small beginnings can have large and irreversible final consequences for the manufacturing structure of a country, its trade and competitiveness of its output (Krugman, 1990a, pp. 99–100).

The dynamics of capital accumulation ensures that the region that starts with a higher capital stock than the other regions, ends up with a dominant industrial position. If this is reinforced with a learning process and cumulative causation (strong internal production links where extension of one activity increases the profitability of others), then the existing pattern of comparative advantage is reinforced over time even if the overall structure of the economy has changed. This process-dependent development adds new layers of firms and industries onto the inherited production structure. If output is concentrated within a relatively small area, firms can benefit from economies of scale and linkages (growth of one activity increases the profitability of other). If this area is close to a larger market, there are additional benefits in the form of lower trade (including transport) costs. Hence, the current state of the economy determines its future shape.

The investment decisions and trade policy of a country in the current period will have an impact on the shape of the national economy in the future periods. For example, at the end of the 19th century, Argentina and Sweden were relatively comparable backward farming-based economies. At about the same time, Argentina invested in the education of lawyers and priests, while Sweden invested in the education of engineers. The impact of such choices (coupled with other economic policies) on the material standard of living between the two countries is obvious.

Once the structure of an economy becomes unsustainable, there are certain critical branching points (bifurcations), at which the qualitative behaviour of the economy changes. New production geography either evolves or is triggered. This history-dependent development can follow different paths, hence it is unpredictable. A long period of stability is broken up by an event of change (equilibrium is punctuated). For example, nearly all big cities are ports. However, it is a long time since New York or Boston ceased to be primarily harbour cities. One may find examples of punctuated equilibrium elsewhere. In biology, for instance, many species (crocodiles, crabs, turtles or monotreme animals) remain stagnant for a very long period. However, there are crucial, relatively brief and unpredictable moments (bifurcations) when new species arrive and old ones disappear. These include a change in climate 64 million years ago caused by a meteor colliding with the Earth, which provoked enormous volcanic activity and fires, water and the atmosphere were polluted, while smoke and dust prevented the penetration of heat from the Sun. Hence a very large part of life on Earth was frozen, burned, starved or suffocated. This change in climate caused the extinction of the dinosaurs.[31]

More than a century ago, Alfred Marshall spelled out the idea of 'backward-looking dynamics' (or 'external economies' in the modern jargon). In his analysis, factors of production are moving towards those industries in which they earn the highest current rate of return. If there are several meaningful equilibria in which the returns would be equalised, then the initial conditions determine the outcome. History matters, together with factor endowment, tastes and technology (Krugman, 1991a, pp. 653–4).

Marshall also described the concentration of specialised industries in particular localities in the following way:

> When an industry has once chosen a locality for itself, it is likely to stay there long: so great are the advantages which people following the same skilled trade get from near neighbourhood to one another. . . . if one man starts a new idea it is taken up by others and combined with suggestions of their own; and thus becomes the source of yet more new ideas. (Marshall, 1890, p. 332)

Contemporary jargon refers to these processes as 'externalities of innovation'.[32]

Somehow similar 'first-mover advantages' (to use the term from the analysis of competition) may be found in biology as many elements of the past can be found long after their functions were lost. For example,

> [E]mbryonic birds and mammals still have gill arches, which have been useless for 400 million years. Why are the vestiges not eliminated by natural selection? The usual answer is that baupläne and the vestiges are developed early in the embryo and hence are most difficult to modify than features that develop later. The genetic programs controlling embryonic development were formed in the early days and have been frozen ever since. (Auyang, 1998, p. 195)

A similar example can be found in the appendix in the human body. However, a question immediately comes to mind: why cannot newly created adaptive features also be frozen?

One of the chief causes for the localisation of industries can be found in the physical conditions of the area. Metals producers located either near mines or close to sources of cheap energy. First-rate grit (for grindstones) was found near Sheffield, England, therefore it also became the place for the manufacture of cutlery. Another reason for the localisation of production has been the presence of a royal court. In the Middle Ages many rulers in Europe were constantly changing their place of residence (partly for sanitary reasons). They frequently invited artisans from distant places and settled them in a group near the royal court. Once the court left, if the town survived, in many cases it continued the development of a specialised industry (Marshall, 1890, pp. 329–30).

Thus, cities often began to develop around royal courts and bishops' sees (concentration of consumers). Later on, the administrative, defence and educational dimension of towns and cities reinforced their function as consumers, but industrial production also started evolving in the cities. Today, many cities produce more value added than they consume.

Recent research has provided some evidence that general government policy can indeed influence the location of firms and industries. Since 1947, a number of manufacturing industries in the US migrated to southern states because of the wish to escape unions. This was, however, only one of the reasons for the change in the location of certain businesses in the US. Others included innovation and change in transport (substitution of truck-haulage for rail freight which contributed to a spread in production), as well as the advent of air conditioning that 'made the climate in the South relatively more attractive than the climate in the North' (Holmes, 1998, p. 670).

Firms cluster together in order to benefit, among other reasons, from the availability of a close network of suppliers. They usually, but not necessarily, cluster in locations with a large local demand. This demand will be large in the areas where most producers chose to locate (a process of circular interdependence or cumulative causation). 'There is a degree of indeterminacy in the location of activities – firms locate where they do because of the presence of other firms, not because of underlying characteristics of the location' (Venables, 1996a, p. 57).[33] For example, there are about 600 tanneries in Arzignano (Vicenza, Italy), most of which employ just a few dozen workers. However, the region produces 40 per cent of Europe's leather supply. The area around Vicenza not only soaks, dyes, stretches, stamps, cuts and ships material used for Gucci handbags, Louis Vuitton luggage, Nike sneakers and BMW car seats, but also produces gold chains, clothing and machine tools, many of them for export. The major problem of a small or a medium-sized enterprise is often not in its 'smallness', but rather in its isolation which is eased in a cluster.

In such an indeterminate situation should one search for answers to the questions on the geography of production elsewhere? Should it be outside standard economics? Should it be in non-linear dynamics (popularly known as chaos theory) which examines unstable behaviour with multiple dynamic equilibria, lock-in effects, bifurcations and extreme sensitivity to initial conditions; or in self-organisation (spontaneous appearance of order)[34] so common in complex systems; or in the new evolutionary economics[35] that has open frontiers, maintains an interdisciplinary dialogue and considers the role of history, technical change, institutions and development of human capital; or in evolutionary biology (evolution and hybridisation)[36] or elsewhere?

'Organisms are vulnerable, but they are not passive; they dig holes, build dams, modify the environment, and create their own niches of survival. Thus organisms and their environment interact, and together they form an ecological system that is better treated as a whole' (Auyang, 1998, p. 61). Similarly, the effects of externalisation are also pronounced in economics. Consumers' tastes and institutions, both public and private, interact, evolve and alter over time. Consumers, for example, in similar situations make different choices (recall the diversity of breakfast cereals, painkillers, cigarettes, chocolate bars, T-shirts, shoes, cars, cameras or bicycles). Hence, complex systems keep on moving from one pseudo-stable situation to another.

EXPECTATIONS

Resources move gradually from one location and/or industry to another in response to differences in current earnings. If this shift is only gradual, then there must be certain barriers that increase the cost of the move. If there are costs, then the resource owners will be interested in expected returns in the future, rather than in current returns. However, future returns also depend on the decisions of owners of other factors and their expectations about future earnings. For instance, when a new technology is introduced, multiple equilibria cause expectations of potential action from competitors. In this model, expectations (rather than history) determine the future shape of the economy.

A river may, over centuries, enrich its bed and reinforce the work of natural forces over time. However, a strong earthquake (a bifurcation point) may instantaneously ruin such a long history. Such was the case with the mechanical cash registers that were made obsolete by digital ones. Subsequently, optical scanners that read bar codes replaced digital cash registers. These changes were all based on totally different technologies.

Other examples may be found in an almost overnight disappearance of the market for film cameras after the appearance of video cameras; the redressing of the market for mechanical watches after the invention of digital and quartz ones; a shift from dot matrix to bubble jet and laser printers; or fibre optics that evolved independently of the telecommunication technology. A good encyclopaedia has always been a must if parents wanted their children to be well educated. A door-to-door salesman of *Encyclopaedia Britannica* has been replaced by Microsoft's cheap CD-ROM encyclopaedia Encarta, first produced in 1993. In addition, Amazon is taking business from real-world retail booksellers. A new product (or service) has to be vastly superior to the well-established product, be it in convenience of use, price, size, shape and/or speed in order to remove the entrenched product from the market. Innovation is threatening firms from every side, hence the lock-in effect is not for ever. High business concentration of a cluster/town on a single line of production can leave it highly vulnerable to external shifts in demand and technology. Rational entrepreneurs should let bygones be bygones. Being a key player and staying on the top is not a state, but a process.[37]

Even though they may be important, one may not wish to give an absolute value to external shocks. For example, the nuclear bombs dropped on Hiroshima and Nagasaki in 1945 had no long-run impact on the size of these two cities. 'Within the space of just 20 years, they recovered from the devastation to return to their former place in the constellation of the cities' (Davies and Weinstein, 2002, p. 1283). Similarly, the impact of the bombardment of German cities during the Second World War on the place of the city in the economy and its growth was significant, but temporary (Brakman et al., 2002, p. 28). There may be a stronger resilience to shocks in the locational fundamentals than one might expect a priori.

A clear example of how expectations shape the national geography of future production can be found if one considers the case of debt in the developing countries.[38] In the 1980s, these countries found themselves unable to repay huge debts owed to the big international banks. Had they all gone into default together, they would have threatened the global economic system. US Secretary of Treasury Nicholas Brady developed a scheme for refinancing this debt, with the International Monetary Fund (IMF) playing the role of the financial policeman of developing countries by linking lines of credit to severe austerity programmes. This was taken to be a victory for the IMF and international institutions. It could have been, but only the short run.

During the 1970s, the world saw a massive increase in the price of oil and other internationally traded commodities. The conventional wisdom (expectation) was that commodity prices would only go higher. The Club of Rome and other similar observers of history pointed out that the world was running out of scarce resources. The world was compared to a space ship: resources were being exhausted by growing populations and intensified industrial use. It followed that the price of commodities such as oil, copper and wheat could only increase. If this were the case, a rational expectation was that the best business area to invest in was commodities. Correct?

The primary producers of commodities were developing countries that lacked manufacturing capability, but controlled natural resources so much demanded by the industrial world. Any sane investor in the 1970s knew that investing in industries that purchased raw materials was foolish, while investing in production of raw materials was smart. So everyone, particularly the international banking community and the World Bank, began investing billions of dollars in ventures designed to produce raw materials in developing countries such as Mexico, Nigeria and the Philippines. As the crucial commodity such as oil was expected to cost 40, 50 or even 100 dollars a barrel in the future, the cost of production was not a critical element in decision making about investment. The price of commodities was going up and it was important to get into this business early. All of the technocrats simply knew this and the entire international economic system became skewed towards investing and lending to commodity producers in the developing countries.

As a consequence of the above process, the inevitable happened. It turned out that while the world may have a finite amount of oil or copper, there were still huge untapped reserves and progress to be made in technology (which saves on the use of resources). When these megaprojects in the developing world started operating, the price of commodities collapsed. When prices fell below the cost of production, projects went bankrupt because of unsustainability. The outcome was the debt crisis. Nicholas Brady and the IMF stepped in to rectify the trouble. The debt crisis, arising from a belief in commodity scarcity, led to an avalanche of investment decisions that has left a legacy of misery. The simplistic and linear projection of the future in which commodity producers dominated industrial commodity consumers was rendered false by the collapse in commodity prices and made irrelevant by another phenomenon in the early 1980s, which is related to Microsoft and similar companies that came out of nowhere.

Microsoft, and the endless number of other software and related companies that appeared during the 1980s, altered the equation that had obsessed the World Bank and most other serious economic thinkers. The emergence of computing technologies and 'brain imports' in the US meant that it was possible to increase economic growth without having a similar increase in commodity consumption. Microsoft and creators of ideas, after all, produce wealth without consuming commodities in proportion to growth.

A sharp increase in productivity[39] based on knowledge and innovation is at the heart of the new economy. Investments by US firms in shorter-lived assets such as information and communication technology (supposedly important contributors to an increase in productivity) were very high during 1995–2000. After 2000, these investments shrank, but productivity growth accelerated. What is the reason for such growth? Are studies about productivity flawed? These studies may arbitrarily include or exclude depreciation. They may also assume that new computers have a direct and full impact on production from day one. In reality, however, it takes quite some time to master new equipment.[40] Or, are invisible and intangible activities such as formal and informal computer-related training and reorganisation of business methods more important than measurable investments in new equipment which show only the tip of the iceberg? These intangible assets helped American companies produce more output with fewer production workers. As far as Europe is concerned, it had the worst performance in industries that are heavy users of information and communication technology, especially retail trade (where the US productivity is growing strongest which is obvious in retail chains such as Wal-Mart).[41] In addition, the US energy consumption in 1997 and 1998 was almost unchanged, while the US economy grew by 9 per cent during those two years.[42] Those economies that are successful in reducing energy consumption per unit of output can, comparatively, benefit a lot from increases in the price of energy in the future; competitors that have not made similar adjustments will suffer.

The extraordinary growth of the US economy has many causes. There is no doubt that the persistent growth of productivity in the US is due to the improvement in efficiency introduced by computing and 'brain imports'. Even Federal Reserve Chairman Alan Greenspan has acknowledged this, while also recognising that it is hard to calculate the impact. This much is apparent. At a time when productivity should be falling, inflation and interest rates soaring and the economy moving towards recession, growth in productivity (driven by the effects of computing, as well as new ideas) is maintaining a long-term growth trend.

At the start of the 1980s, Japan produced cars and cameras at lower prices, smaller in size and of better quality than the US. Two decades later the ability to produce cars, copiers and cameras is much less interesting than the ability to write software. The structure of production has changed almost beyond recognition. The hardware that runs a web server is much less valuable than the immaterial intellectual property that resides on the server. Perhaps the Japanese industrial targeting was superior during the age of fax machines, while the US liberal (unplanned) economic system and alert financial markets that force firms to adjust rapidly to shifting markets and changing technology are more appropriate for the age of the Internet (Krugman, 2000, p. 174). To put it bluntly, the Japanese bet on hardware, while the Americans bet on software. The decoupling of value from physical production, its shift to intellectual production, is a millennial shift whose full meaning will not unfold for many generations.

The firms that will define the next twenty years of economic history and production geography are probably completely unknown to anyone today. Uncertainty and risk are very high and the way forward is not always clear. Therefore, it is very difficult to know with a high degree of confidence where the world's economy is really going. Profound changes that occur little by little (such as the transformation in the economy and in our lives that was brought about by Microsoft) may be noticed only long afterwards. Therefore, the greatest danger is in 'linear thinking': the belief and expectation that what exists today will also exist tomorrow, but with a higher degree of intensity.

7. War and the location of firms

Unexpected political events (chance, accidents) such as wars, their start, intensity and length cannot be predicted by everyone with a high degree of certitude. None the less, wars decisively influence the development, expansion, location, dislocation and spread of certain industries. There are numerous examples that support such arguments. For instance, as a latecomer in the colonial era and because of post-war(s) external sanctions, Germany had the 'incentive' (was forced by events) to produce various chemicals as substitutes for natural inputs that were not available either in their colonies or through 'normal' trade. Self-sufficiency has often been of vital national importance. Germany's success was remarkable as the country developed world-leading chemical[43] and related industries such as pumps, sophisticated precision measurement and control instruments. Let us consider other examples:

- After the First World War there was a recession in Seattle (Washington). The economy of the region was based on fishing, production of timber and ship/boat building. At about the same time, demand for aircraft (made of wood) started to emerge. Seattle had unemployed boat-builders and other inputs: workers had the skills to make wooden boats, they could easily build a fully covered boat (the body of an aeroplane), and they also knew how to fix a propeller – all of which led to the emergence of Boeing. The US recognised the huge potential of airmail on a large scale, large purchases of military aircraft and high demand for fast travel, which in turn provided domestic producers with early incentives to lower production and learning costs per aircraft as compared with foreign competitors.
- The first commercially successful motor scooter, the Vespa, was produced by the Italian company Piaggio in 1946, although the idea for it was conceived during the Second World War.[44] During the war, Piaggio, at Pontandera, near Pisa, made aircraft engines. After RAF bombing destroyed the factories, warehouses and roads at the site, it became difficult and tiring to get around the site on foot. The company owner, Enrico Piaggio, asked one of his engineers, Corradino d'Ascanio to design a simple and economical two-wheel personal vehicle. D'Ascanio built the prototype using his imagination, the leftovers from small two-stroke motors used to start the aircraft engines, aircraft wheels (note the shape of wheels on a Vespa when you next see one) and whatever else he could find in the warehouse (or what remained of it), such as metal sheets. The vehicle also incorporated a shield on each side to protect the rider's legs from injury. The prototype

was ready within a few weeks and once in production, the Vespa became an immediate hit. It was extremely popular and fashionable in the 1950s and 1960s and was rediscovered by another generation in the 1990s because of increasing traffic congestion in cities.
- The Swiss chemical and heavy industry enjoyed certain benefits during the world wars. On the one hand, as German industry did not have access to the international market, Swiss entrepreneurs filled the gap where they could. On the other hand, the Swiss benefited from the inflow of funds, talents and invalidation of German patents by the Allies.
- US Caterpillar relocated abroad during the Second World War in order to service machines that were used by the US Army. Following the war, the machinery that remained abroad had to be serviced. Hence, Caterpillar became an international company on a larger scale. Coca-Cola also followed the US Army during the Second World War to keep up the morale of the soldiers, and also remained abroad. Mars Bars were also distributed to armed forces all around the world during the war.[45]
- Sialkot is a provincial town in the Punjab, Pakistan. It had a military garrison and a mission hospital during the British period a century ago. This created a demand for repair and, later on, production of surgical instruments, tennis rackets and footballs. The area had had a local tradition of producing swords and daggers for several centuries. When the military technology changed, the need for surgical instruments from the local hospital provoked a demand for scalpels. Later on, around the time of the Second World War, the supply of surgical instruments became a necessary adjunct to the war. Technology and experts were brought from Britain in order to support the production of those goods. Currently, a core of about 300 family-run firms (almost all have less than 20 employees) in Sialkot produce a range of 2000 surgical instruments. Together with firms in Germany, they are major world exporters of such instruments. As Sialkot has no airport and as it is located more than 1500 km from the nearest sea port, a private self-help initiative created the Sialkot Dry Port Trust which 'brought the port to Sialkot'. The trust offers a range of collective services such as customs clearance, warehousing and transport. The success of this, as well as all other clusters is based on two factors: first, the demand-driven approach and, second, competition based on collective efficiency. However, the situation in Sialkot is not perfect: the infrastructure is still rather undeveloped; the power supply is inadequate; communications are poor; and roads are ankle deep in mud during the monsoon season. In addition, health and

safety standards are insufficient and child labour is a serious problem in Sialkot's football-making industry (Nadvi, 1998).
- Italian motor car racing companies such as Alfa Romeo, Ferrari and Lancia dominated the market in the period immediately after the Second World War. Within several years, however, a cluster of small firms from around Oxford became another dominant world player. There were several fortuitous events that prompted this evolution. First, there was a huge surplus of abandoned airfields in southern England after the war. Second, Mercedes withdrew from motor racing in 1955 after an accident in Le Mans in which 183 spectators were either killed or injured. This left room for the British racing car builders. Third, large and vertically integrated manufacturers such as Ferrari and Porsche built cars for their own racing teams, while the British were selling cars to anyone who wanted to buy them. Even though the British were not winning races, they dominated the starting grids with the sheer number of cars. Fourth was the ban on cigarette advertising on British TV in 1965. Tobacco companies became sponsors of motor racing, doling out vast sums of money in return for having their logos displayed on racing cars. Pinch and Henry (1999) argue that although the success of the British constructors may have been influenced by a few accidents, it was only to a small extent. Other more important causes such as accumulated knowledge, its circulation through the companies by means of transfer of personnel, as well as skilled labour, are the origins of the British success. The British have a tradition of expertise in engines and lubricants, aerodynamics and composite materials. In particular, the national aerospace industry was bigger and more sophisticated after the war than that in Italy. According to Pinch and Henry, this would probably have encouraged the production of racing cars even without the Mercedes crash or the money from cigarette manufacturers.
- Another example of the impact of war on the change in the spatial distribution of production emanates from the end of the 'Cold War' around 1990, when huge defence cuts badly damaged the military aerospace cluster in southern California.

8. Wrapping up the theory of location

A century or even half a century ago, economic theory looked at the location of firms and industries in a rather technical and deterministic way. Subjects and causes were separated from objects and effects, and everything ended in equilibrium. Parts of modern spatial economics and the new geography of production consider the location of firms in an evolutionary way, where the state of equilibrium is only a temporary special case and everything is in an unstable organic process of change.

Where a firm or an industry should locate is not a question that has a straightforward answer. Rich nations fear the relocation of firms and industries to low-wage nations; poor nations worry that the production of goods and services will migrate to developed countries; while small countries are concerned that businesses will move to large countries. In an age of business 'globalisation', one might expect the importance of firm location to be diminishing. Some argue that distance is 'dead' in terms of production and business because of the astonishing changes in communications and computers. 'Time zones and language groups, rather than mileage, will come to define distance' (Cairncross, 2001, p. 5). But this may be relevant only for certain manufacturing and services activities that are simple, routine and have codified knowledge. However, local proximity (clusters) of firms that produce similar, competing and/or related products together with supporting institutions still matters for complex activities, with no or lightly codified knowledge and where market changes and uncertainty require a rapid reaction. Economies of scale, activity-specific backward and forward linkages (indivisible production), accumulated knowledge, innovation, lock-in effects, the existence of sophisticated customers and a fall in transportation costs play relevant roles in the protection of clusters and the absolute advantage of certain locations. 'Global' competitiveness often depends on highly concentrated 'local' knowledge, capabilities and a common tacit code of behaviour which can be found in a spatial concentration (a cluster) of firms. Hence, successful managers must often think regionally and act locally.

The neglect of spatial economics (geography of production) in mainstream economic theory was not because this research field was uninteresting, but rather because the issues were traditionally regarded as intractable. Ricardo's comparative advantage model provided insufficient answers to the problem. New research tools such as increasing returns, production linkages (presence of intermediate goods and services), multiple equilibria (with centrifugal and centripetal forces) and imperfect competition were introduced into the field of spatial economics in the early 1990s. These methodological tools also helped to explain why firms form clusters. Such new developments did not mean the birth of a new subject. Spatial economics has always been important. Even though the ever-increasing demand for quantitative vigour is making considerations more difficult, the introduction of new analytical tools assisted spatial economics in finding its proper place in mainstream economics and becoming a hot research topic.

The new economic geography differs from the traditional model in several important dimensions. The new model makes a case that production specialisation in a given locality is based not only on certain comparative advantages, but rather on a self-reinforcing lock-in effect, path dependence, accumulated knowledge, agglomeration, clustering and linkages (indivisible production). In addition, while the traditional models reason that a reduction in trade costs among locations favours local specialisation, the new economic geography claims that the effect on local specialisation is ambiguous. The final outcome is industry specific and depends on the functional intra-industry production linkages, market structure, consumer preferences (homogeneity of tastes) and factor market (availability and mobility of factors and flexibility in prices). In general, the choice of location for a new investment or a new firm that produce tradable goods and services depends on a complicated interplay of at least three elements: factor intensity; transport intensity; and each in relation to the already established firms and their activities and (re)actions. Remote places do not necessarily need to be poor locations for firms as their remoteness is already reflected in their factor prices (Venables and Limão, 2002, pp. 260–61).

As a reaction to trade liberalisation and economic integration, various industries follow different paths. Depending on the functional intra-industry production links, some industries concentrate (reinforcing absolute advantages of certain locations), while others spread. This is contrary to the expectations of neo-classical theory, which predicts that all industries will be affected in the same way. Different forces, therefore, propel such changes in the spatial structure of production. Strong functional intra-industry linkages (high share of intermediate goods from the same industry and/or the need for a large pool of highly skilled labour and researchers) stimulate agglomeration. Where these functional linkages are weak, this acts as an incentive to spread production.

Ultimately, one can reason that there is an important lacuna in our understanding of spatial economics. It is little wonder that there are many disagreements and perhaps only four theoretical agreements:

- first, if one wants to start a new activity in a specific location, one has to build on already existing expertise and specialisation of that location;
- second, if one wants to use policy intervention to influence the location of firms, this is most effective only very early in the process;
- third, economies of scale and functional linkages in production have a certain impact on the location of firms and industries; and
- last, success or failure of a region or a policy sometimes depends on uncontrollable factors and events that are located outside regions themselves.[46]

The analysis of spatial economics depends on special assumptions. It is often a detective-type study and a collection of particular cases. Generality is often abandoned for discovery. This is not surprising as spatial economics is simultaneously charged with some of the most difficult problems in economic theory: multiple equilibria, economies of scale, externalities, imperfect competition (which kind?), linkages and path dependence. None the less, many useful things can be learned from exceptional cases. The examination of the issue is still elastic and highly suggestive (in particular how a historical accident may shape the production geography) rather than conclusive, convincing and general. A coherent theory of the subject is not yet in sight. However, there are various approaches that contribute to the raising of new questions and understanding of the issue. This leaves the topic subject to further theoretical and empirical analysis.[47]

9. Regional policy

A region may be more easily discerned than defined. The definition of a region depends on the problem that one encounters. A region is a geographical phenomenon with distinct borders with others, but it also has political, governmental and administrative features and is an ethnic and social concept with human and cultural characteristics. A region is also an economic concept defined by its endowment factors, their combinations and mobility. Therefore, a region can be defined in theory as a geographical area that consists of adjoining particles with similar unit incomes and more interdependence of incomes than between regions (Bird, 1972, p. 272). A region of a country or an economic union may be thought of as an open economy.

There are many causes of regional disequilibria, including (Vanhove and Klaasen, 1987, pp. 2–7):

- market rigidities (such as relatively low mobility of factors);
- geographical factors;
- differences in the availability of resources;
- education of management and training of labour;
- regional economic structure (in some regions industries with ageing technologies, in others industries with modern technologies);
- institutional factors such as the centralisation of public institutions (Paris is an obvious example); and
- national wage setting in spite of differences in productivity and labour market conditions across different regions.

Regional disparities adopt numerous forms. They include not only differences in income levels per capita, rates of growth or rates of unemployment, economies of scale, externalities, output and consumption structures, productivity and access to public services, but also the age structure, population density and the pattern of migration.

The controversy regarding the definition of the 'regional problem' remains. However, several factors together may provide an insight into the issue. These elements include:

- different regions may grow at uneven rates for a long period of time. This provokes government intervention to reduce that problem;
- intervention may aim to equalise consumption or GDP per capita among different regions;
- a government may wish to create an equal access of the population to an adequate level of public goods and services; and
- public authorities may be interested in having a spatially stable distribution of economic activities and population in order to avoid negative externalities.

Regional policy is basically aimed at influencing economic adjustment in the four (theoretical) types of regions:

- Regions in which agriculture accounts for a relatively high share of production and employment. These are usually underdeveloped rural areas with relatively low levels of income, high levels of unemployment and poorly developed infrastructure.
- Regions whose former prosperity was founded on industries that are now in decline, such as coal, steel, shipbuilding or textiles. These are the regions that failed to keep pace with changes in technology and were unable to withstand external competition (in some cases because of earlier excessive protection). In the case of recession, labour in these regions is the first to be made redundant.
- Regions with a high concentration of manufacturing and resulting congestion and pollution problems. There are benefits from the joint use of goods and services available in these areas. Regional policy may, however, try to reduce the existing congestion (concentration) and pollution and/or prevent their further increase.
- Frontier regions, which are far from the strongest areas (poles of growth) of a country's or union's economic activity.

Jobs can be located in regions where there are people with suitable qualifications, training and experience. Therefore, regions with unskilled labour cannot be expected to attract any significant number of industries that use modern technologies. By definition, these industries require trained labour and educated management. The location of business near large and/or growing markets saves transport costs. If returns to scale were constant, as neo-classical theory assumes, this could tend to equalise factor owners' rewards in different regions. With economies of scale and other market imperfections (the situation with multiple equilibria), these tendencies may increase rather than decrease regional disequilibria.

Convergence in the level of development among different regions is not a self-sustaining process. It is easier during an economic recovery than during recession. Lagging regions/countries usually have a higher proportion of both 'sensitive industries' and public enterprises than prosperous ones. Therefore, they may be hit harder by a recession and budgetary restrictions (no subsidies and public purchases) than other regions.

The *convergence* or *neo-classical* school of thought regarding regional matters did not consider either market imperfections such as economies of scale, sunk costs and externalities or institutions that set the organisational environment. This school argued that the 'regional problem' and the spatial location of economic activity are not problems at all. Free trade and unimpeded factor mobility would produce a smooth spatial dispersion of people, skills, technology and economic activity. This would equalise factor earnings and living standards in all regions and countries. Apart from transport costs, it should not matter where a tradable good or service is produced. Hence, the spatial location of output is no more than an operational detail. This is because transport, communication and other trade costs have been declining over time because of innovation and increases in productivity. The peripheral regions and countries are expected to gain from trade liberalisation and integration in terms of an increased relocation of industries and trade. Ultimately, there would be a full equalisation in factor prices.

The neo-classical one-sector growth models based on exogenous technological progress anticipate economic convergence among regions. This expectation based on comparative advantages depends on the starting conditions (including the endowment of factors). However, different regions may have different long-run growth rates because of a different starting situation. As technological progress in this model is exogenous, developing countries should grow faster than the developed ones. If, however, technological progress is endogenous, then the convergence school does not give a clear prediction about growth rates and patterns.

This liberal (non-interventionist) attitude in the field of regional policy in the market economies had a certain validity until the economic crisis of the 1930s. With free trade, perfect allocation and use of resources,[48] intervention in regional policy is not necessary because markets clear and bring the economy to equilibrium. Such a convergence approach was not validated by time and experience. In spite of expectations about convergence, even the *laissez-faire* governments may consider it necessary and beneficial to intervene as the adjustment process may take too long to be politically acceptable.

The new spatial economics emphasises potentially growing disparities, rather than convergence among regions and countries. This *divergence* school of thought offered theories that refer to the growing discrepancy among regions. Explanations are based principally on economies of scale.[49] Together with the new geography of production (spatial economics), divergence theories consider market imperfections and institutions that set rules which streamline liberties and behaviour.[50] This moves theoretical concepts closer to reality. The list of new assumptions includes economies of scale, high fixed costs, trade and adjustment costs, entry and exit barriers,[51] constrained mobility of factors, transport costs, externalities, multiple equilibria, path dependence, the multiplier effect, cumulative causation,[52] non-ergodicity and inflexibility. If applied to intermediate production, these forces can combine and influence one another in such a complex way that their behaviour becomes fickle. They can produce most unpredictable outcomes regarding locations of firms and industries. In many cases history, chance and expectations set the final outcome.

Production and trade in goods are increasingly becoming elaborate and difficult. They depend heavily on sophisticated information and services that are included in the final good and its price. Internal trade within each TNC may account for a large part of the total trade. Hence, national and international markets become more and more incomplete and tough to manage. In addition, the listed new elements that consider divergence theory exert a strong influence on the location of production, trade and *absolute* advantages (which widen regional gaps), while *local comparative* advantages may play a less important role. In this case, competition, liberalisation and economic integration generate concentration (or increase the attractiveness of the already developed areas), they generate economic divergence and widening of regional gaps, not economic convergence among regions and countries.

Given that spatial concentration is the most striking feature of the geography of production, there is clear evidence of some kind of increasing returns to scale (Krugman, 1992, p. 5). New technologies in select industries may overcome some of the obstacles to the spread[53] of production, but not much. Hence, the pattern of regional specialisation and trade can be arbitrary and potential gains from specialisation and trade are likely to be ambiguous.[54]

A lack of R&D, innovation and acquisition and employment of new technological knowledge may be among the principal causes of slow growth in less-developed regions and countries. This weakness may be partially eased by the two-way labour mobility from developed to weaker regions and vice versa. A one-way migration of labour would only depopulate weaker regions, while it could create overcrowding in the prosperous areas.[55] However, *structural* disparity among the regions does not necessarily mean that there is an *income* disparity between them. If there are two regions and if each region specialises in a different output activity, then economic structure among them would change, even though the incomes in both regions may still remain comparable.

In a simple model, the allocation of manufacturing between two regions determines the difference in real wages between them. Let the horizontal axis represent the share of manufacturing workers residing in region 1 and let the vertical axis show the difference in real wages between the two regions in per cent. Figure 8.2 shows how various transport costs influence the curve that relates the regional manufacturing population to real wages. Transport costs are taken to epitomise all costs of doing business across geographical space. With high transport costs there is little interregional trade. Regional wages depend mainly on the local conditions in the labour market. If there is an increase in the regional labour supply, competition reduces wages. With low transport costs, there is much interregional trade. A firm can have a superior market access if it is located in the region with a higher concentration of workers (consumers). It can also afford to pay higher wages. These higher wages increase the purchasing power as the workers have better access to consumer goods. As the number of residents/workers

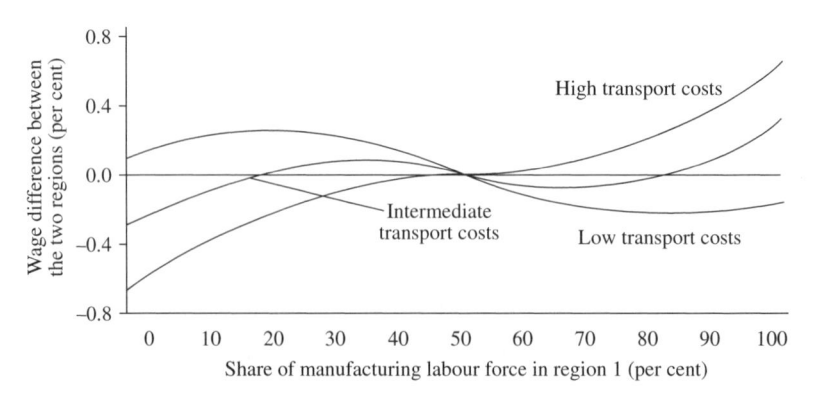

Figure 8.2   Relation between regional manufacturing populations and real wages with varying transport costs

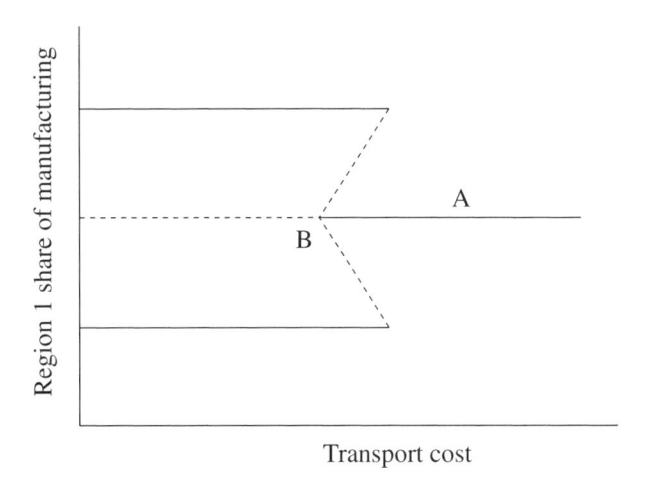

Figure 8.3   Transport costs and equilibria

increases in the region, real wages increase in the same direction. With intermediate transport costs, there is some evening out between centrifugal and centripetal forces (Krugman, 1999, p. 95).

Figure 8.3 shows the situation in which the workers move to the region that offers higher real wages measured by the share of manufacturing labour force in region 1. A set of equilibria depends on transport costs. Solid lines specify stable equilibria, while broken lines show unstable equilibria. If an economy starts with high transport costs, then there is an even distribution of manufacturing between regions 1 and 2, respectively. Point A represents this situation. Then suppose that there is a reduction in transport costs and that the economy reaches point B. At this point the process of concentration of manufacturing in one region starts. The economy would spontaneously organise itself into core–periphery geography (Krugman, 1999, p. 96). A relatively high interregional labour mobility is a feature of the US economy, but not within the EU. However, 'agglomeration can be generated equally well by interplay between the location decisions of firms in industries that are linked through an input–output structure. Thus, even without labour mobility, there may be forces leading to agglomeration of activity at particular locations in an integrating region' (Venables, 1996b, p. 356).

Even in a next to perfectly homogeneous world, production activities will tend to cluster, not least because of a different endowment of resources and because of economies of scale. In these circumstances, government intervention in the form of various policies (industrial, regional, competition, trade, technology and/or education) may find some justification.[56] If policies mattered, then one would find an abrupt change in production activity when crossing the (national) frontiers at which policies change. The policy is generally aimed at developing or enhancing the regional or national production potential, competences and capabilities through a (supposedly) superior allocation and use of resources from the national standpoint. The objective of such intervention is to influence the spatial distribution of economic activity, as well as to create and redistribute wealth in order to ease and, eventually, solve the 'regional problem'.

Governments intervene in regional matters mainly for the following three reasons:

- *Equity*: This is a strong social motive based on public pressure on the government to try to achieve and maintain a 'proper' balance, as well as an 'orderly' geographical distribution of national wealth and access to the public in different regions.
- *Efficiency*: This is a desire to employ, sustain and increase national economic potentials and capabilities.
- *Strategic behaviour*: This gives public authorities a chance to shape comparative advantages and influence the output potential and capabilities of the country.

In the 1960s, the regional problem was usually tackled with supply-side subsidies for the provision of infrastructure and the reallocation of various (public) manufacturing and service industries. Foreign competition, in particular from the newly industrialised countries, placed in jeopardy a number of industries that failed to adjust. As there had been little success with earlier approaches to the regional problem, and coupled with austerity programmes in public finances, there was a major change in national regional policies from the 1980s. Outright subsidies were reduced or removed and the policy was supplemented by a system intended to make the lagging regions more self-reliant (support to indigenous development). This included the development of human resources, the attraction of private investors (in particular foreign ones) and the provision of technical services.

There is a great deal of uncertainty regarding the impact of international economic integration on regional matters. One thing, however, should be mentioned here. Having a 'peripheral' location is not an irreversible economic disadvantage. Its impact can be mitigated and even reversed, as has been successfully shown by countries such as Ireland and Finland (or Australia and Japan). What matters most for the competitiveness of a country's goods and services on the international market is the efficient creation of, employment of and reward to the most precious economic factor: human capital.

Regional policy was neglected in the EU before its first enlargement in 1973. This was followed by a period of interest in an active regional policy.

However, enthusiasm for this policy waned in the 1990s as there were few obvious positive results from intervention. Public intervention in regional issues is still a highly controversial issue. Is there or is there not a self-equilibrating process among the regions in the long term? Is intervention (regional policy) necessary or not? Hence, can regional policy work at all?

National governments introduced regional policies in order to promote growth in weak regions. The policy was based on the assumption that market failures exist. The instruments of the policy included investment aid, direct investment by the state, wage subsidies, tax allowances, licensing and the provision of infrastructure and services. However, since the 1990s, the emphasis of regional policy has moved away from the attraction of extra-regional investment and general subsidies, primarily towards the development of endogenous regional growth and human resources. The national regional policy was transformed in most EU(15) countries into an enterprise and entrepreneurship development policy.

The situation regarding regional policy at the EU level has been ambivalent. On the one hand, cohesion is becoming a leitmotif of European integration, hence EU involvement in this issue. On the other hand, market liberalisation and an active regional policy (intervention) do not go hand in hand. Since an automatic market-led adjustment mechanism operates too slowly to be politically acceptable, EU structural funds for regional development and social issues emphasise supply-side intervention. They provide assistance to infrastructure, training and structural adjustment.

Intervention in the form of a regional policy is not a simple task as there are constant changes in technology, taste, competition and demography over time. In spite of intervention in regional affairs over the past decades, a trend appeared during the 1990s in many EU countries towards abandoning or easing regional policies. However, at the EU level, intervention in regional affairs remained fervent, but with questionable results.

10. Objectives and justification

Regional policy is intervention by the state in order to influence the 'orderly' distribution of economic activity and to reduce social and economic differences among regions. It was usually a reactive (*ex post*) policy that primarily tried to reduce the existing regional disparities, rather than a policy that primarily prevented the creation of new regional disequilibria.

Trade liberalisation and/or economic integration can easily provoke a country's economic adjustment (geographical, sectoral and professional reallocation of resources). Enhanced competition may force certain regions to embark upon a painful, but potentially rewarding, alteration in the structure of the geography of production (transfer of resources from unprofitable into profitable economic activities). The politicians in the affected regions often blame integration or trade liberalisation for adjustment 'pains'. However, this objection may not always be justified. The most basic reason for a painful adjustment process is often earlier protection. A policy of long and excessive sheltering of the domestic economy reduces the reaction time of local enterprises to international structural pressures and opportunities and, hence, increases the cost of adjustment in the future. Adjustment costs and 'pains' are always present, but the potential benefits from such a change may more than compensate for the effort.

Relatively low wages may attract investment into a region; however, there may be at the same time some agglomeration and concentration tendencies in other regions. If wages are set at a national level, this may act as a structural barrier that works against the lagging regions. In this case, the lack of flexibility in the level of wages among regions despite relative differences in productivity and in the labour market conditions means that the less-developed areas are unable to respond to this situation by reduced wage costs. One cannot know in advance where the balance will tilt. Some developed regions may become more developed, while some less-developed regions/countries may become poorer (if nothing is done to alleviate the situation), but other less-developed regions may move to the group of advanced ones.

The objectives of a regional policy are various, but their common denominator is that they aim to employ the regions' unemployed or under-employed resources and potentials, to locate new ones, to attract missing factors, as well as to increase output and incomes. In congested or polluted areas, this policy restricts the expansion of firms and stimulates exit from the region. In the developing countries, the primary concern is economic development. This is most often coupled with regional imbalances, but their solution is not as high on the agenda as increases in economic potentials and capabilities. In areas of economic integration, the problem of regional (in)equalities is of great concern. Countries are reluctant to lag behind their partners for any length of time. This is of great concern in an EMU, where there are no balance of payments disequilibria, but rather regional disparities. Depressed regions/countries can no longer resort to devaluation as there is a single currency, while advanced regions/countries will not always be willing to finance regional disequilibria without proof that there is structural adjustment and improvement taking place in the regions assisted. With this in mind, a regional policy can be justified on nine counts.

The first justification for a regional policy (intervention that is supposed to assist in the process of economic adjustment), in contrast to free market adjustment, can be found in the structural deficiencies of regions. These include market rigidities, conditions of access to the market and the structure of output. When such imperfections exist, a free market system is 'unable' to achieve a satisfactory equilibrium from the social standpoint in the short and medium terms, so there may be a need for intervention in order to enhance the creation and use of the regional income-generating potentials and capabilities.

Regional imports consists of goods and services. In France, for example, most of the country's regions purchase financial, insurance, legal and other services from Paris. This is not easily quantified. A reduction in a region's exports, for instance, may be obvious from the outset. Regional solutions to these disequilibria are inhibited by rules of competition and by the existence of a single currency. Hence, the second 'justification' for regional intervention in an economic union.

The third reason for intervention may be found in the employment of factors. The neo-classical theory of international trade usually assumes free and full international mobility of factors, which ensures full employment. However, even Adam Smith noted that a man is the most difficult 'commodity' to transport. During recession, the employment situation is tough everywhere, therefore the potential advantages of some regions that are abundant in labour are removed. Reduced mobility of labour prevents the equalisation of discrepancies in economic unions.

Suppose that economic space consists of core and a periphery. In the case when there are market imperfections, there is a general agreement in theory that at one point in time the core region is likely to dominate the periphery. The disagreement is about the nature, extent, evolution, effects and duration of the core–periphery relation over time.[57] If there is growth in one region, this may create conditions for even higher growth in the same core region and increase inequalities among regions (polarisation or backwash effect). This may, however, also act as a 'locomotive' for development in other peripheral regions as there may be increased markets for food, economies of scale and innovation in other regions (spread effect). In order to adopt the idea that there are benefits from the spread effect, one must assume that there is a complementarity between the regions in question and ignore the fact that the spread effects operate in an asymmetrical way throughout space.

In a situation closer to reality and which includes economies of scale, large sunk costs, externalities and other market failures, adjustment does not happen according to a relatively smooth neo-classical expectation. The regional absorption capacity of new technologies requires an industrial and general culture that incorporates continuous learning, adaptation, spread and development of human capital, as well as flexibility. Therefore, the introduction of new technologies is often uncertain and quite risky, which is why some technologies diffuse quite slowly among the regions. The reallocation of resources induced by the spread effect works at a (much) slower pace than may be politically acceptable, hence the need for intervention.

The fourth rationale can be found in the 'need' for compensation. Two forces created by economic integration affect regional development. The first one, specialisation, leads the backward regions to specialise in labour-intensive production according to their comparative advantage. The second force includes economies of scale, externalities and path dependence. This can lead to a divergence in regional incomes. As integration extends the size of the market, firms take advantage of economies of scale and externalities. The Single Market Programme provided incentives for the concentration of industries with strong internal links. In the case of other regions, the programme reduced trade costs, hence there are potentials for a spread of other industries that may benefit the EU periphery, where labour costs are lower. However, if this does not happen, or takes place very slowly, there is a possibility that some regions may actually be damaged by integration if there are no instruments for compensation, which is another justification for a regional policy.

Subsidies may be one of the tools of a regional policy. However, the distribution of subsidies is always subject to political pressures and mismanagement. The final disbursement of subsidies often reflects more the balance of political powers than the comparative (dis)advantage of a region. At the end of the process, regional policies implemented in such a way may do more harm than good if they diminish local incentives for adjustment and flexibility or, at best, they may have a dubious effect. None the less, public policies in the backward regions, such as support for education, infrastructure and selected public goods, as well as aid for SMEs in the form of loan guarantees for the start-up of a business, have the potential to assist regional development.

The fifth reason for intervention may be found in the improved allocation of resources. When the market is imperfect, free market forces usually direct capital towards already developed regions in the short and medium terms. Private investors tend to maximise the speed of the safe return of their invested funds and to minimise investment in infrastructure. Thus, it is understandable why they direct their funds towards already advanced regions. These tendencies of agglomeration (adjoint locations of linked productions), where the developed tend to become more developed while the underdeveloped remain at best where they are, have significant private benefits, but also social costs and benefits. A society may reap the benefits of large-scale efficient production. However, if private entrepreneurs are not impeded in their decision making by government policy, the geographical location of their business may introduce significant social costs such as pollution, congestion and traffic jams in some regions and unemployment and increased social assistance in others.

The sixth reason for intervention may be found in the improvement of stabilisation (macroeconomic) policy. Regional differences in rates of unemployment may reduce the opportunities to control inflation and introduce a stabilisation policy. The reduction of inflation in some regions may increase unemployment in others. This may not always be the desired outcome. Diversified regions with a variety of employment opportunities will be able to adjust in a less painful way than specialised regions with entrenched market rigidities.

The seventh justification for the introduction of a regional policy is that it may reduce public expenditure in the assisted region in the long run. Public support to firms to locate in certain regions may propel economic activity towards these regions. Unemployment may drop, reducing welfare payments and in the long term increasing tax receipts that may be spent on something else. In addition, 'employment' in public administration used to provide a shelter for the unemployed. Such artificial employment may be reduced or even eliminated once the private sector (with superior wages and career prospects) starts thriving in the assisted region.

The eighth rationale for intervention is that although regional policy is targeted at regions with some disadvantage (underdevelopment, unemployment, obsolete technologies and output structure, congestion or pollution), the benefits of a regional policy are not confined to the assisted area. Other regions, through externalities, enjoy part of the benefit. The beneficial effects of a regional policy extend beyond the assisted area itself, which is why the Germans and Swedes have an interest in helping out the Poles or Estonians. In general, integration may be reinforced, unwanted migration of labour may be prevented, factors may be employed in a superior way and there are important non-economic gains.

Finally, apart from the above arguments for regional policy, which mostly deal with 'economic' efficiency, there are political grounds which are at least as important as the economic ones. Solidarity, tolerance and perception of a common future are the core of any social community. The mitigation of economic disparities among the constituent regions may be the necessary reason for the unity of a state or an economic union. This is relevant as the costs and benefits of international economic integration tend to be unequally spread among the participating countries in a situation with market imperfections and multiple equilibria. Arguments of equality require the solution and/or mitigation of intolerable or growing differences in the distribution of wealth among the population which lives in different regions. The national political system does not always take fully into account the needs of backward regions. For example, the national system of setting wages may significantly reduce the wage-cost advantages of many regions, whereas welfare expenditure can contribute to a greater regional equilibrium. Complete equalisation in the standards of living in different regions is neither possible nor desirable because it may reduce incentives for change and improvement. What is needed in regional matters is a continuous adjustment of regional development within commonly agreed guidelines, as well as the protection of the standard of living accepted as desirable by the group.

Regional intervention may be quite costly. In addition, there may be an inefficient replication of effort at various levels of government. Therefore, one may use the coordination argument in favour of an EU regional policy. The EU is best placed to coordinate various national and regional actions, to improve their efficiency and to collect and transfer resources from the prosperous to the weak regions of the EU.

The goals of regional policy, such as balanced growth, equal shares of social and cultural progress of the society, solidarity, regional distinctiveness and stability, are vague and may not be accurately measured. Specific objectives such as job creation, reduction in unemployment, improved housing and development of infrastructure introduce fewer problems in quantification. Care has to be given to select policy tools in order to ensure that the regional policy does not evolve into protection of the present economic structure; rather it needs to assist in continuous structural adjustment of the regions.

11. Instruments

Instruments of regional policy are often directed towards entrepreneurs and factor owners. They can be employed either directly (for example, support of existing technologies or shifting towards new technologies or business activities) or indirectly (for example, improvement in infrastructure). Their joint effects may alter and increase employment, investment and output in the assisted regions, at least in the short term.

The dilemma of the state may be whether to stimulate regional development through private investment, to invest directly in production and infrastructure for which there is no interest in the private sector and/or to stimulate public–private partnership. The available policy tools include those that provide incentives and disincentives to firms to move and to locate in or out of specific geographical regions. Major instruments include:

- subsidies: regional allocation of capital, investment, infrastructure, output, social security and income/wage;
- vocational training;
- public procurement and provision of goods, services and infrastructure;
- reduction in interest rates;
- tax concessions;
- decentralisation of government offices, education and health services;
- reductions in energy and public transportation costs;
- free locations;
- licences for the location of business; and
- trade protection.

As seen from this short list, the choice of policy tools is rather limited. The secret of success in this situation is not the wide range of instruments, but rather their astute combination and application.

If offered, cash grants may be preferred to reduced tax liabilities as regional policy instruments. Grants apply horizontally and directly to all firms, whereas reduced tax liabilities help only those that are profitable. Trade restrictions are not the wisest instruments of a regional policy. The costs fall on the whole economic union, but they bring benefits to one or only a few regions.

Disincentives for regional expansion in congested areas are a relatively novel feature. In Britain, for example, they appeared in the form of industrial development certificates that had to be obtained prior to expansion or location in non-assisted regions. However, after the second oil shock, as unemployment increased, these certificates were abandoned as an instrument of regional policy. In France, for instance, there were certain constraints on the expansion of manufacturing and service industries in the Paris region. They included a special tax on office floor construction and authorisations for large-scale investments.

The policy of moving workers to jobs views the regional problem as being exclusively one of unemployment. It ignores the fact that other problems in a region may be worsened further by this 'forced' mobility of labour. The productive sector of the population moves out of the region while the consuming sector remains in it. The local tax base may not be able to provide sufficient funds to cover the costs of local health care, schools and other social services. The overall situation may be worsened by the multiplier effect. In advanced regions that receive the migrants, new disequilibria may be created. The additional population increases congestion and rents for a certain type of housing, which may reduce the quality of life there. Education and training are often emphasised as key elements in the solution to the unemployment problem. Although they are necessary, they are not sufficient conditions to fight unemployment. Creating new jobs also requires investment and increased flexibility in the labour markets.

Unemployment rates may be one of the most telling indicators of regional variations. If labour mobility is relatively low, then the movement of jobs to workers may reduce regional disparities in unemployment. An argument against this is that it may increase costs, as alternative locations may not be optimal for the efficient conduct of business. However, as more industries become footloose, these costs to firms may diminish. Improvements in infrastructure, including the training of labour and the education of management together with the spread of timely information, help the location of footloose industries which are at the beginning of their product cycle in the assisted regions.

12. Impact of integration

GAINS

Economic integration may increase the average welfare of consumers in the involved countries in many different direct and indirect ways. The problem is that the benefits accrue to everyone in relatively small instalments and only in the medium and long terms. Some of these gains include:

- secure access to the market of partner countries;
- increased investment opportunities as expectations may be established with an increased degree of security;
- improved efficiency in the use of resources;
- an elimination of trade barriers reduces cost of trade;
- increased competition on internal market puts a downward pressure on prices;
- facilitation of exchange of technical information;
- competition forces firms to implement new ideas and technologies;
- due to the enlarged market, producers may better exploit and benefit from economies of scale;
- potential for coordination of certain economic policies;
- improved bargaining position with external partners;
- research and innovation may be stimulated because of tougher competition on a larger market and a possibility of sharing fixed costs in such a market environment;

- the market of the integrated group provides more opportunities for a wider range of goods and services that can be offered to consumers, hence there is an improvement in individuals' utility function; and
- reduction in X-inefficiency which moves the production activities of firms closer to best-practice business organisation.

However, one must always bear in mind that international economic integration is never more than a useful *supporting* tool for sound domestic macro- and microeconomic policies and that it cannot act as their replacement. If these domestic policies are not healthy, integration cannot be their substitute.

REALLOCATION OF RESOURCES AND ADJUSTMENT COSTS

Economic integration affects welfare through increases in product variety and consumption. It was assumed, along the lines of a neo-classical model, that adjustment of production (shifts from unprofitable into profitable activities) is instantaneous and costless. This is a significant weakness of the model. External shocks such as changes in technology, trade liberalisation and economic integration have an immediate impact in the form of increases in efficiency and income. The new employment of labour may be generated at a later stage. Adjustment to these shocks may require both time and government intervention. Gains from shifts in production and trade as a consequence of integration should be reduced by the cost of the adjustment needed to obtain net welfare effects of integration.

Adjustment costs (the social price for change) may be quite high in the uncompetitive economies. Think of the 'pain' and length of time needed for the transition economies of Central and Eastern Europe to change to a market-type economic system. However, if these countries protect themselves from external trade for too long, such a policy can become an additional obstacle to adjustment. Adjustment costs are borne both by individuals and by society. Private adjustment costs include a reduction in wages, losses in the value of housing and a depreciation of the value of firms' capital. Social costs include lost output from unemployed capital and labour.

The common external protection may discriminate against imports from third countries in such a way that these external economies may adjust swifter than would otherwise be the case. In order to avoid the common external protection, the governments of those countries may, among other things, respond by shaping their geography of production and comparative advantage in higher lines of manufacturing to gain a competitive edge in advanced products and export them to the integrated group of countries. The dynamic models are not as simple, smooth and straightforward as classical models of trade and investment, but they are much closer to real life.

Experience in the EU, its enlargements, EFTA and successive rounds of tariff reductions under the GATT/WTO have shown that geographical and industrial adjustment takes place relatively slowly and smoothly over a long period of time. In the case of the EU these costs were so much smaller than expected, that the elimination of tariffs has advanced at a faster pace than anticipated in the Treaty of Rome. There were intra-industry adjustments, rather than inter-industry ones. The disastrous scenario of throwing home firms out of business on a large scale has not materialised at all. The buffer against such a scenario, as well as the means for the mitigation of adjustment costs may be found in increased capital mobility and flexible rates of exchange. However, one has to add that the period of the 1960s was characterised by relatively high growth rates and near full employment, which helped the adjustment process.[58]

If freeing trade does not produce pain in the form of pressure and adjustment costs, it probably produces no gain either. The 'compulsory' reallocation of resources is a source of gains. The adjustment cost is a finite, one-time investment. The gains from improved resource allocation present a continuous flow over time. Therefore, there are reasons to believe that the 'pain' is much exaggerated (Curzon Price, 1987, p. 16). Trade liberalisation accelerates competition in participating countries. For this reason, the expectation that international economic integration is beneficial in the long run can be accepted with considerable confidence. Economic adjustment and the alteration in the geography of production is a necessary condition if countries want to maintain the growth of the economy in circumstances of high-risk choices where technology and the situation in the market changes fast. They will have to learn how to live with change in order to reap gains from such a strategy.

Adjustment costs associated with shifts among economic activities, include a need for a reallocation of labour. Positions will be lost in some business activities and geographical areas, while they will be created in others. Structural funds for social, regional and industrial issues can act as built-in stabilisers which help the initial losers to recover.

An economic policy of non-interference with market forces has obvious advantages because competition and efficiency are stimulated, consumers' tastes are satisfied and there is a reduction in the costs of government administration and intervention. On the other side of the coin, government intervention may be required because markets are imperfect, firms seldom take into account social costs of production (externalities) and adjustment, and market forces may increase inequality in the regional distribution of income. However, intervention meant to smoothe adjustment problems can develop into a deeply rooted protectionism which over time increases costs to everybody. Hence, neither a pure market system nor a paramount government intervention can take account of all private and social costs and benefits of adjustment. While intervention may solve major economic issues, market forces may be more successful in the fine-tuning of the economy.

A country's comparative advantage and geography of production are dynamic concepts. They shift over time. Countries may not be sure that their current production advantages will remain unchanged in the future. International economic integration may be a reliable way for a country to secure wide markets for home goods/services and to obtain sources of supply in the future. Geographical proximity of the partner countries ensures that gains from trade, specialisation and a wider choice of goods are not wasted on transport costs.

CLUSTERS

The production geography of the US is particularly interesting to examine as it is a country without important internal borders and it is so big that it may serve as an example for economic comparison with an integrated Europe. Even a superficial look at the US production geography reveals a high concentration of industries. For example, the following industrial clusters come to mind:

- aviation around Seattle;
- finance on Wall Street;
- insurance in Hartford (Connecticut);
- pharmaceuticals in central New Jersey;
- medical equipment in Minneapolis;
- electronics in the Silicon Valley and Boston's Route 128;
- advertising on Madison Avenue in New York City;
- optics-related industries in Rochester (New York);
- cars around Detroit;
- paints and coatings in Cleveland (Ohio);
- entertainment in California;
- office furniture in western Michigan;
- orthopaedic devices in Warsaw (Indiana);
- hosiery and home furnishings in North Carolina;
- carpets in Dalton (Georgia);

- wine in Napa Valley (California);
- shoes in Massachusetts; and
- gambling in Las Vegas and Atlantic City.

Development and growth histories differ between Europe and the US. While the US developed, industrialised and grew as an economy under constant, but integrated territorial expansion, the same process took place in Europe behind barriers of trade protection, state support and different languages and cultures. As a result, the US has a number of highly developed and specialised regional clusters throughout the country, whereas the same type of specialisation is much less obvious in Europe (Storper et al., 2002, p. 103). European clusters that come to mind include: production of knives in Solingen, watches in Geneva and the Swiss Jura, financial services in London, fashion garments and motorcycles in northern Italy, carpets in Kortrijk (Belgium), pleasure in Paris, flowers in Holland, sex/prostitution[59] in Amsterdam and food manufacturing in York. However, the European car industry has never created a cluster similar to Detroit. A select list of clusters in Italy and Germany is given in Appendix 8A2.

Once the concentration of business becomes too high, there may be negative externalities for work and private life such as pollution, sewage and waste disposal problems, congestion, allergies, crime and an increase in the price of land and rents. This may have an impact on the spread and decentralisation of businesses and their shift to other regions as firms may wish to leave the 'threatened' regions. However, the EU has on average a much less concentrated manufacturing geography and much more segmented markets than the US, because of various NTBs which increase trade costs. The goal of the Single Market Programme (1985–92) was to eliminate all barriers on internal trade. Hence, if this takes place, the expectation was that the EU industries and its geography of production could resemble those in the US. One should not be deceived that the EU will ever have a homogeneous market like the one in the US. Most things and the ways of doing things (culture) in the US are alike throughout the country (for example, food, customs, services, what towns and settlements look like). In the EU, for instance, citizens have distinct national consumer preferences for food and drink. This will persist. In addition, the EU countries have a range of national policies regarding health, safety, social issues and worker representation.

A lesson for the EU is that the Single Market Programme (integration deepening) provided opportunities for a concentration of production in certain hot spots, as well as for rationalisation of business operations. Amiti (1998, 1999) found evidence that this took place in the manufacturing industries which include industrial chemicals, petroleum, textiles, plastics, iron and steel, machinery and transport equipment. These are all industries that are subject to economies of scale and that have a high proportion of intermediate inputs in final production. Hence, this provides some support to the arguments of the new theory of spatial economics. In the 1976–89 period, geographical concentration increased in 30 of 65 recorded industries, concentration fell in 12 industries (the biggest fall was in the manufacturing of concrete for construction), while there was no significant change in the geographical concentration in other industries (Amiti, 1999, p. 580). Midelfart-Knarvik et al. (2000) found that 'between 1970/73 and 1994/97, the general trend towards spatial dispersion is reflected in 29 out of 36 industries' (p. 30) and that there is an 'impression of a spreading out of European manufacturing activity' (p. 30). On the other hand, a study by the European Commission observed that an 'examination of data offers mixed evidence for the contention that the single market is leading to a geographical concentration' (p. 67) and that there is 'little evidence of concentration occurring in the EC' (European Commission, 1998, p. 69). Hence, this topic demands further research.

PRODUCTION GEOGRAPHY: WITH TRADE BARRIERS

International economic integration may influence the geography of production in several ways. There are three in particular, which were neglected in the earlier analysis because of non-linear analytical complications that result from externalities and because they deal with trade costs (Fujita et al., 1999, p. 251):

- With high transport costs and high trade barriers (or autarky), each country is likely to have manufacturing to supply its local consumers.
- With low or no transport and trade costs (free trade), the world gets 'smaller' and markets larger, forward and backward linkages (presence of tradable intermediate goods) dominate and there are possibilities for footloose manufacturing to agglomerate in a single country or a single location (American outcome). There is no need for producers and consumers to be in vicinity as trade is costless. Firms move to the lowest-cost locations.
- With intermediate transport costs concentration becomes possible and necessary. Costs of production may differ among countries depending on country size (market) and economies of scale. Firms in a smaller or peripheral country that produce tradable goods on

average depend more on foreign trade than do firms in larger countries. Therefore, if trade is liberalised, firms from the small country may gain more than firms from large countries. However, firms from large country may exploit economies of scale and have lower costs of production and prices of output than the firms in a small country. Once trade is liberalised and trade costs fall, firms from the large country may capture a large part of the small country's market. Then comes a period of adjustment. Certain firms may relocate in search for low-cost immobile factors (land, labour) and larger markets. In small countries such as Austria, Switzerland or Luxembourg, firms may successfully adjust and penetrate niche markets in a large country.[60] Although the national production geography (distribution of industries) is altered, this does not mean that there will be a divergence in national per capita income. Each country may have a cluster of industries that supply the entire integrated market. However, this case brings with it a range of stable and unstable equilibria (European outcome).

Suppose that transport costs in the real world have a declining path over time. This is a relatively reasonable assumption from the time of Ricardo. One may observe a trend in the narrowing of the income gap between the advanced countries (North) and certain developing countries (South). 'Declining trade costs first produce, then dissolve, the global inequality of nations' (Fujita et al., 1999, p. 260). The problem is that industrialisation and economic development is not a uniform process. It takes place in a series of waves. Labour-intensive industries are the first ones to leave the industrialised country because of high wages there. The less labour-intensive industries that move at a later stage, do so possibly more rapidly than the earlier movers. Usually upstream industries move first and create potentials for forward and backward production links in the target country which facilitates entry of firms from other downstream industries.

PRODUCTION GEOGRAPHY: REDUCTION IN TRADE BARRIERS

There is, however, an initiative that may help out the lagging regions in an integrated area. Suppose that the initial reduction of barriers to the movement of goods, services and factors in a common market spurs an inflow of factors to already industrialised areas where they benefit from economies of scale and various externalities. If all barriers to internal trade and factor movements are eliminated or become insignificant, firms may benefit from economies of scale and externalities in other (less-advanced or peripheral) regions where the variable costs of production are potentially lower than in the centre of the manufacturing or service activity (Krugman and Venables, 1990, p. 74; Venables, 1998, p. 3). In this case, the less-developed region or a country that takes part in a common market is likely to benefit on two accounts:

- it gets firms that benefit from economies of scale; and
- the former regional production structure that was typified by a lack of open competition is altered.

Kim confirmed this type of reasoning for the manufacturing industry in the US during the 1860–1987 period. Industry specialisation rose substantially prior to the turn of the 20th century. At about the same time, the US was developing its transport and communication network in order to become a fully integrated economy. During the inter-war years, the level of regional specialisation 'flattened out', but then fell substantially and continually between the 1930s and 1987. Economic integration made the US regions less specialised today than they were in 1860 (Kim, 1995, pp. 882–6). This trend of dispersion of industries and increasing similarity in the US continued throughout the 1990s (Midelfart-Knarvik et al., 2000, p. 44). As we shall see later, economic integration in the EU made the industrial structure in the member countries more specialised and less similar.[61]

In theory, economic integration may, but not necessarily will, bring greater benefits to the regions/countries that lag in their development behind the centre of economic activity. However, if production linkages (forward and backward) are strong (meaning that production is indivisible) and *internal* to an industry such as in chemicals or financial services and imperfect competition prevails, economic integration would trigger agglomeration (clustering) tendencies. If the linkages are not limited to a relatively narrow industry group, but are strong *across* industries and sectors, integration would produce agglomeration tendencies in select spots. If labour is not mobile, the whole process would tend to open up new and widen the existing regional wage differentials (Venables, 1996a). Although this may produce deindustrialisation tendencies in the peripheral regions, it does not mean that integration is not desirable. For instance, education and regional policies increased the attractiveness of Spain as a location for various manufacturing industries, discovered by the EU and foreign investors. This was particularly obvious following the Spanish entry into the EU in 1986. Integration of Mexico with the US shifted many manufacturing industries from the area of Mexico City northwards, along the border with the US. This took place not only because there was a growing demand in the US, but also because of the general trade liberalisation policy in Mexico. Once the economy turns outwards, internal production linkages weaken and firms have less incentive to stay in the congested hub.

If costs of trade are high, industries tend to disperse. When this cost is reduced, agglomeration can take place as demand in distant places can be met by exports. When these trade costs approach zero (as is the case in writing computer software in Bangalore, India or data entry in Manila and the use of the Internet), footloose production may be dispersed and located according to the availability of the specific resource inputs.[62] Globalisation of certain industries (integrated international production) reduces the weight of physical proximity between various production units, as well as between producers and consumers. However, in industries that have strong internal links such as those based on new knowledge (innovation activities are still highly clustered in the world), financial services or chemicals, there is a strong propensity to cluster in spite of 'globalisation' of other businesses.

Deepening of economic integration in the EU through the elimination of NTBs during the introduction and after the establishment of the Single European Market, reduction in the cost of transportation and the eurozone may diminish motives for regional and national self-sufficiency. However, integration may also stimulate agglomeration tendencies and reinforce the core–periphery problem. Production in the EU may resemble that in the US where industrial output (both in manufacturing and in services) is concentrated in distinct geographical locations. Hence, if this takes place in the future, internal EU trade among its member countries will no longer be intra-industry, but rather inter-industry in nature. Further reduction of trade costs in the EU may lead to further concentration of production, which is subject to the economies of scale in the already existing core locations, while the periphery may specialise in the manufacturing production that does not depend on scale economies. This provides support to the arguments of the new economic geography and trade theories (Brülhart and Torstensson, 1996; Amiti, 1999).

Industry characteristics set the locational response to lower trade costs. Industries that have significant economies of scale and important intra-industry links have a hump-shaped relation between integration and concentration. When there are high trade costs, trade production is dispersed so industrial concentration is low; as these costs are lowered and reach intermediate level, there is an increase in industrial concentration; as trade costs fall to low levels, there is a decrease in concentration (spread) as industries start to respond to factor markets.[63] These industries are metals, chemicals, machinery and transport equipment. Industries that are not strongly based on economies of scale (textiles, leather and food products) have a monotonously increasing path towards concentration as trade cost decrease because of integration (Forslid et al., 2002, p. 293). This kind of reasoning and regional compensation funds of the group may be used to convince the adversely affected peripheral regions to tolerate the difficult period of transition that may follow trade liberalisation and economic integration (Puga and Venables, 1997, p. 364). Similar arguments may be used in the Central and East European EU member countries.

If indigenous entrepreneurs are flexible, then the regional geography of production can be altered within a large integrated area without substantial external assistance or even without a separate regional currency. A clear example is the conversion of New England's production geography from the production of shoes and textile in the 1960s (coupled with relatively high unemployment) to an economy based on 'high technology' and low unemployment in the 1980s.

Centripetal forces may explain relatively low indices of intra-industry trade (agglomeration, clustering) in industries subject to high economies of scale. Conversely, relatively high indices of intra-industry trade (in 'labour-intensive' industries) may suggest the spread of industries. In the case of the EU, Brülhart (1998b, pp. 340–41) suggested that in the 1980–90 period:

- there was no further concentration of already clustered industries that are subject to increasing returns in the central regions;
- there was further concentration of textile-related industries at the periphery; and
- there were certain indicators of spread of 'high-technology' industries towards the periphery.

Others, however, argue that the outcome may be reversed from the one just described and that an active regional policy is necessary particularly in an EMU. Emigration of people would discourage an entry of new businesses into such a region. That trend would further weaken the economic position of the region in question. None the less, such a vicious circle has not taken place in the EU. Even though there are severe problems regarding data, particularly regarding the 1950s and 1960s, one may discover certain trends. What seems likely to be the case in the EU is that regional disparities were slowly narrowing until the early 1970s. This was followed by a decade-long period of widening the regional gaps, and then a mixture of stabilisation and widening of regional gaps between member countries ever since. It is not yet clear what prompted the halt in the convergence process after the 1970s. This does not mean that specific regions are irrevocably affixed to a specific position in the regional rank order. Evidence is available that there is quite a lot of switching over from one position on the regional rank to another (Armstrong and de Kervenoael, 1997, p. 41; Midelfart-Knarvik et al., 2000).[64]

The economic history of integrated states such as the US points to the fact that integration is associated with regional convergence which predominates over economic divergence in the long run. This process is rather slow, about 2 per cent a year, but it is sustained over a long period (Barro and Sala-i-Martin, 1991, p. 154). General, but very slow regional convergence has been confirmed by the literature, however, a poor region can expect the gap between its initial level of income and the aggregate to be reduced by only 30–40 per cent at the outside (Canova and Marcet, 1995, pp. 1 and 24). Armstrong (1995, p. 149) found that the convergence rate between 1970 and 1990 was only 1 per cent a year, which is half the rate estimated by Barro and Sala-i-Martin.

In a critical survey of the new geographical turn in economics, Martin found that regional convergence is remarkably similar across the US, the EU, Canada, Japan China and Australia and stated that 'the observed rate of regional convergence is very slow, about 1–2% per annum, and considerably lower than predicted by the simple neoclassical growth model' (Martin, 1999, p. 72). In any case, there are endogenous growth factors (increasing returns) at work and regional policies based on pure transfers of funds are not working unless linked with structural changes and factor mobility.

Carrington (2003, p. 382) argued that growth in each region depends not only on its own characteristics, but also on those of the regions that comprise the neighbourhood to which it belongs (adjoining regions). Applying spatial econometrics to 110 regions of the EU(15), it was found that during the 1990s, two opposing forces were exerting their influence across the EU(15). While regions did converge at a rate of about 2 per cent, neighbourhoods of regions diverged at an almost equal rate, leaving a net effect of convergence considerably smaller than the one previously reported in the literature.

The vast majority of EU countries 'experienced a growing difference between their industrial structure and that of their EU partners' (Midelfart-Knarvik et al., 2000, p. 9). These growing divergences in the geography of national production may be the consequence of two factors:

- One comes from the *importance of history*. This is when countries initially have industries that grow at different rates. Hence a country with a higher proportion of high-growth industries becomes increasingly more specialised than the average or the rest of the group.
- The other factor is the *differential change*. This is when countries move out of a certain type of production and into another.

Midelfart-Knarvik et al. (2000, p. 6) found that over 80 per cent of the change in the EU during 1980–97 was due to the 'differential change', while the rest came from the amplification of the initial differences. The most striking feature of this process was a change in the industrial structure of Ireland and Finland. New high-technology industries and the ones subject to increasing returns to scale were established in these two countries.

The impact of integration on individual industries can also be looked at in the following way. Midelfart-Knarvik et al. (2000, pp. 19–22) divided industries into five groups and observed their concentration in the 1970/73 and 1990/97 periods. The results of the analysis were as follows:

- *Concentrated industries that remained concentrated over time*: motor vehicles, aircraft, electrical apparatus, chemical and petroleum products. These are the industries with high increasing returns to scale, and which depend on high/medium technology and have a high share of inputs from their own industrial group. In this group, Germany reinforced its position in motor vehicles, to the detriment of Britain and France. In the aircraft industry, Britain, France and Germany remained dominant. However, there was a slight reduction in the shares of Britain and Sweden, while Belgium, France and Spain had slight increases. Britain, Germany and France remained dominant in chemicals, but Britain reduced its share in the petroleum and coal industries.
- *Concentrated industries that became less concentrated*: beverages, tobacco, office and computing machinery, machinery and equipment, and professional instruments. This group of industries relies more on inter- rather than intra-industry linkages, relatively high labour skills, but lower returns to scale than the previous group. A spread of these industries was pronounced in the 1991–97 period. Germany saw a reduction in its dominance in this group. The same trend was also noted for Britain and France. Ireland and Finland were the biggest gainers in this industrial group, but Austria, Italy, Portugal, Spain and Sweden also gained.
- *Dispersed industries that became more concentrated*: textiles, apparel, leather products, furniture and transport equipment. Relatively low technology in this group has low returns to scale and so are the requirements regarding labour qualifications. Britain, France and Germany reduced their shares in this group, while the southern EU countries exhibited growing shares. In the transport equipment, however, Germany increased its share by 10 per cent, while Britain and Spain had a combined decrease of 7 per cent.
- *Dispersed industries that remained spread*: food, wood products, paper and products, printing and publishing, metal products, non-metallic

minerals, and shipbuilding. There were no obvious changes in the group. National differences in taste and culture explain such developments for most industries in this group.
- *Residual group*: footwear, industrial chemicals, drugs and medicines, petroleum refineries, rubber and plastic products, pottery and china, glass and products, iron and steel, non-ferrous metals, railroad equipment, and other manufacturing. This medium concentrated group did not change much. The only significant change was in drugs and medicines, which became less concentrated. Production spread from Germany and Italy towards Britain, Denmark, Ireland and Sweden.

The change in the production structure data in the EU found certain support in the change in the structure of EU trade. Trade data support the finding that there was a decrease in specialisation during the 1970s. However, the picture is mixed from the beginning of the 1980s. The growing specialisation revealed in the production data is not reflected in the change in the structure of trade. The main reason for this discrepancy is the growing volume of intra-industry trade (Midelfart-Knarvik et al., 2000, p. 12). In addition, trade data may not be a suitable substitute for the production records. The structure of trade may change as a response to changing demand without any change in production. If there is a change in domestic tastes, then the domestic producers may sell goods on the home market rather than make extra efforts to sell abroad. The structure and volume of trade are altered in this case, while there may be no change in the composition of the domestic output.

Compared with the pre-Single Market Programme, the EU 'problem regions' saw an improved economic performance in the period following the completion of the Single European Market. This improvement was obvious in terms of growth in both employment rates and growth in gross value added (European Commission, 1997d, p. 5). Concerns that the Single Market Programme would lead to a concentration of economic activity in the 'core' EU countries were not realised. There has been only a limited spread of economic activity to the 'peripheral' EU countries which enjoy certain cost advantages (European Commission, 1998, p. 145). This is consistent with the view that as costs of trade fall for products of certain industries, the periphery may became more attractive for investment as the returns on the capital are greater. However, this development in the EU may also be the consequence of the impact of regional aid (European Commission, 1997d, p. 34).

One of the outcomes of the Single European Market was that certain clusters of firms and industries in the EU became a bit more visible. Relatively high geographical concentration of related firms in relatively small areas eased exchange of information. Following these changes, Frankfurt, London and Paris are now the areas that create jobs faster than the rest of the national economy. However, the problem is in the regions outside a large metropolitan area which still seem to remain 'poor'. Success, like many other things, also appears to cluster.

13. European Union

INTRODUCTION

International economic integration brings multiple equilibria and may, in some cases, aggravate the situation of already weak and peripheral regions in comparison with previous circumstances. This is recognised in part by the existence of national and EU regional policies. None the less, having a peripheral location does not mean that a country is destined to have a poor economic performance. The accumulation and efficient employment of human (and physical) capital is the most important factor in a country's economic performance. Although countries such as Finland, Sweden, New Zealand, Australia and even Japan and South Korea have relatively unfavourable geographical locations regarding major transport routes, the irreversibility of their 'peripheral' geographical position is mitigated and more than compensated for by the accumulation and efficient employment of their national human and physical capital. The expansion of infrastructure and further development of human and physical capital alleviated Spain's location at the fringe of the EU. It is expected that the Central and East European countries will do likewise in the future.

The regional policy of an economic union can be justified at least on the grounds of solidarity, unity, harmonisation of national regional policies and the (re)distribution of wealth within the group. Policy coordination at the central level is defended on the grounds that it prevents clashes of different national regional policies with common objectives. The policy needs to ensure, at the very least, that the existing regional problems are not made worse by economic integration, otherwise the less-developed regions/countries will have no incentive to participate in the project.

EVOLUTION

The evolution of the regional policy of the EU can be divided into four broad phases. Regional issues did not feature highly on the agenda among the original six member countries. During the late 1950s and 1960s, only Italy gave weight to the regional problem because of its southern part (Mezzogiorno), which is why regional policy in the EU was practically nonexistent until 1973. Following the entry of Britain, Denmark and Ireland in that year, the situation changed. The second phase in the development of the regional policy began after the first enlargement of the EU. Britain was particularly interested in the inclusion of regional issues in the EU. The first tool to implement the policy was the European Regional Development Fund (ERDF). The entry of Greece in 1981, and Spain and Portugal in 1986, increased the desire and need for an EU regional policy. This policy mainly gave benefits to the EU-rim countries (Britain, Greece, Ireland, Italy, Portugal and Spain), just as the CAP favours the 'northern' countries.[65] The third phase started with the reform of policy and the ERDF in 1988. The fourth phase is linked with two events: the creation of the eurozone in 1999 and the eastern enlargement of the EU in 2004.

Following the first enlargement of the EU, the new regional conditions of the EU were officially analysed for the first time in the *Report on the Regional Problems of the Enlarged Community* (the Thomson Report) (European Communities, 1973). The report identified two types of regions in the EU that have problems. First are the farming regions that are located in the periphery of the EU. The Italian Mezzogiorno and Ireland fit into this group. In both regions there is a relatively high long-term structural unemployment and dependence on farming. The second type of problem regions are those that have a high proportion of regional output and employment in industries with obsolete technologies and those with declining demand. These problem regions have a slow rate of shifting resources out of such industries and technologies, as well as a relatively high level of long-term structural unemployment. Some regions in Britain fall into this group. A renegotiation of the British entry and concerns by Italy and Ireland led to the creation of the ERDF in 1975 under Article 308[66] of the Treaty of Rome. However, the ERDF only provides resources for regional development that are *additional* to those available from national funds.

REGIONAL DISCREPANCIES

Differences in economic development among regions exist in every country, but at the EU level they seem much larger. Less-developed regions in one country may have different characteristics from less-developed regions in others, including large variations in income. In addition, congestion in southern Italy is greater than that in the south-west of France. Table 8.1 presents GDP per capita in the EU(15) and 13 candidate countries at

Table 8.1 *GDP per capita at current prices (€) in the EU(15) and candidate countries in 2002 and 2003*

Country	2002	2003*
Luxembourg	50 190	51 240
Denmark	34 180	35 140
Ireland	33 090	33 710
Sweden	28 650	29 520
United Kingdom	28 040	26 190
Netherlands	27 540	27 880
Austria	27 110	27 670
Finland	26 860	27 490
Germany	25 590	25 880
Belgium	25 170	25 640
France	24 840	25 170
European Union(15)	*24 060*	*24 220*
Italy	21 690	22 380
Spain	17 170	18 160
Cyprus	15 000	–
Greece	12 910	13 950
Portugal	12 470	12 700
Slovenia	11 700	12 240
Malta	10 380	10 690
Czech Republic	7 660	7 840
Hungary	6 780	7 210
Estonia	5 070	5 450
Poland	5 230	4 900
Slovak Republic	4 670	5 300
Lithuania	4 230	4 490
Latvia	3 820	3 730
Turkey	2 750	2 900
Romania	2 230	2 270
Bulgaria	2 110	2 280

Note: * Estimates.

Source: Eurostat (2004).

market prices in 2002 and 2003 in order of decreasing level. This comparison of the relative difference in GDP per capita among countries at current prices may well overestimate the real difference between advanced and weak countries (or regions). The difference within the EU between Luxembourg, the richest country according to this indicator, and Portugal, apparently the least developed, is 4:1. For comparison, on this criterion the difference between Luxembourg and Bulgaria would be 22:1, while the EU(15) average GDP per capita in 2003 was ten times higher than in Bulgaria.

A useful device for overcoming part of the problem associated with the inter-country comparison of GDP at market prices can be found in the use of current purchasing power standard (PPS). This statistical indicator is based on the relative prices of a basket of representative and comparable goods and services. The PPS represents more adequately the real level of the local purchasing power, and it often gives significantly different results from the ones given in current euros, in particular during times with volatility in exchange rates. The PPS is not affected (in the short term) by fluctuations in the exchange market. This problem has disappeared in the case of the countries in the eurozone. Significant differences between data given in current euros and those in the PPS are assigned to differences in price levels in the member countries. If prices in an individual member country are higher than the EU average, then the GDP per capita is higher in current euros than according to the PPS. The reverse is true for the countries whose GDP per capita in current euros is below the EU average. In these countries, the PPS gives a higher value than the GDP in current prices.

Table 8.2 provides data in descending order on the differences in GDP per capita in the EU(15) and 13 candidate countries in 2002 and 2003 in order of decreasing level. This kind of presentation changes, to an extent, the picture of the relative wealth of countries in comparison with Table 8.1. According to this indicator, the difference in average real income between the richest EU country, Luxembourg, and the poorest, Portugal, was only 2.8:1. These measures are an indicator of differences in the level of economic development, whereas disparities in unemployment rates may be an indicator of a relatively poor capacity to adjust to various economic shocks. Differences between the two measures also have implications for the regional problem as they show that local output is below its potential. The ratio between average EU(15) GDP and that in Bulgaria as measured by the PPS is 3.8:1, which is much less dramatic than the difference expressed in current prices.

There are regional differences within countries too. These discrepancies may be capable of dividing the EU. The objective of the EU is to mitigate existing and prevent the creation of new regional imbalances. Even though there are methodological difficulties, the new ranking indicators by Eurostat give data and ranks for 2000.[67] This reveals that the most developed regions in the EU(15) were Luxembourg, Valle d'Aosta (Italy), Trentino-Alto Adige (Italy), Vlaams Brabant (Belgium) and Inner London. This is a different ranking from the one that offers the regional per capita GDP: Inner London, Brussels, Luxembourg, Hamburg and Île de France. The most backward regions by both indicators were Peloponnisos (Greece), Açores (Portugal) as well as a number of other regions in Greece and Portugal.

Table 8.2 *GDP per capita at purchasing power standard (€) in the EU(15) and candidate countries in 2002 and 2003*

Country	2002	2003*
Luxembourg	45 490	45 230
Ireland	30 140	29 500
Denmark	27 480	27 730
Netherlands	27 050	26 740
Austria	26 930	27 100
Belgium	25 880	26 060
United Kingdom	25 000	25 460
Finland	24 800	24 790
Italy	24 570	24 780
Germany	24 650	24 760
Sweden	24 540	24 670
France	24 660	24 570
European Union(15)	*24 060*	*24 220*
Spain	20 280	20 710
Slovenia	17 710	18 010
Cyprus	17 360	17 760
Greece	15 840	16 540
Portugal	16 470	16 230
Czech Republic	15 280	14 660
Hungary	13 420	14 150
Malta	12 000	–
Slovak Republic	11 340	11 890
Estonia	10 020	10 590
Lithuania	9 410	10 030
Poland	9 550	9 890
Latvia	8 460	8 950
Romania	6 080	6 610
Bulgaria	5 940	6 390
Turkey	5 500	5 600

Note: * Estimates.

Source: Eurostat (2004).

In a comparison of worker productivity and per capita income, Paci (1997) found that European workers are becoming more similar as differences in their productivity are diminishing. However, European citizens are becoming less equal as disparities in per capita income are not diminishing. Therefore, the EU and national governments have much work to do in order to assist the weaker regions to increase the standard of living of their population (Paci, 1997, p. 630).

ACTION

Regional policies that are carried out at a local level by the member states and their regional authorities can have an advantage over EU regional policy because the local authorities may be better informed about local needs and problems. On the other hand, the EU is better placed to coordinate regional, as well as other national policies. In addition, the EU may contribute its own resources and introduce common priorities and standards, and it may take into account regional interests when it reaches certain policy decisions. The EU has to ensure through the use of the rules of competition that the member governments do not distort competition by a 'subsidy war'. Normally, the EU puts a ceiling on the permitted subsidy per establishment and/or a job created in various regions.

Established in 1975, the ERDF allocated its expenditure to the member states in fixed quotas as compensation to the countries that contributed more than average to the EU budget. These national quotas were set according to the following four criteria:

- the national average GDP per capita had to be below the EU average;
- the assisted region had to have an above-average dependence on farming or a declining industry;
- there had to be structural unemployment in and/or emigration from the region; and
- EU policies (such as free internal trade) had to have had a detrimental impact on the region.

In other words, to obtain EU funds, the governments of the member states had to submit regional projects to the EU to meet the allocated financial quota and to commit certain funds themselves to these projects. The EU had no leverage on the selection process. It simply reacted to national initiatives. There was also a minuscule non-quota section of the ERDF, which absorbed only 5 per cent of the resources. The EU was able to use these funds freely. This situation came in for much criticism and the ERDF was reformed in 1985.

The reformed ERDF divided its funds among the EU member states by indicative ranges instead of fixed quotas as was the case previously. A government is guaranteed to receive the minimum of the range over a period of three years only if it has submitted a sufficient number of suitable projects.

The projects submitted are evaluated according to criteria that are consistent with the EU priorities and objectives. The intention is to stimulate a greater number of applications in order to increase competition among various proposals. ERDF support may be up to 55 per cent of public expenditure on regional projects; in addition, it is allowed to co-finance programmes and it may prop up the development of indigenous potential in regions. The ERDF also attempts to mobilise local resources because it is increasingly difficult to attract private investment from wealthy to poor regions. Additional attention is devoted to the coordination of both member countries' regional policies and EU policies that have an impact on regions (agriculture, trade, environment, for example).

A further modification of EU regional policy followed the Single European Act (1987) and the entry of Spain and Portugal, which deepened the EU regional problem. The act introduced a new Title into the Treaty of Rome on Economic and Social Cohesion. Article 158 requests the promotion of a harmonious development in the EU and 'reducing disparities between the level of development of the various regions'. Article 159 requires the coordination of economic policies among the member countries and authorises the EU to support those actions and other objectives through structural funds. Apart from these grant-awarding funds, loan-awarding institutions such as the European Investment Bank (EIB) and the European Coal and Steel Community are also involved in regional projects.

Special regional problems emerged in the EU in 1986 after the entry of Spain and Portugal. Therefore, during the preparations for this enlargement, the EU introduced the Integrated Mediterranean Programme in 1985. The goal of this coordinated programme was to help the Mediterranean regions of the EU (Greece and the southern regions of Italy and France, with a combined population of about 50 million) to adjust to competition from the two new member countries. The programme disposed of €4.1 billion in grants and €2.5 billion in loans over a period of seven years. It integrated all available sources of finance on the levels of the EU, national, regional and local authorities. In addition, it coordinated other policies of the EU. The programme was aimed not only at adjustment of agricultural production (olive oil, wine, fruit, vegetables), but also at the adjustment of existing and the creation of new SMEs. Alternative employment for jobs lost in agriculture was to be found in services (tourism) and SMEs. Apart from the border regions of Finland, the largely 'unnoticed' entry of three developed countries (Austria, Finland and Sweden) in 1995 has not introduced new regional distortions in the EU.

The modification of regional policy and the ERDF took place in 1988 following the southern enlargement of the EU. It had one basic objective: to improve the coordination of various structural funds in order to support the Single Market Programme. The 1988 reform introduced the following six basic *principles*:

- member countries are to submit plans according to priority objectives;
- there needs to be a partnership between the administration at the local, regional and national level;
- EU measures play only an additional role;
- there needs to be compatibility with other EU policies such as competition and environment;
- different EU policies need to be coordinated; and
- resources need to be concentrated on the least-developed regions.

At the same time, five priority *objectives* of the regional policy included:

- promotion of the development of the backward regions (Objective 1);
- economic adjustment and conversion of the production structure in the regions that were affected by a large-scale industrial decline (Objective 2);
- a fight against structural unemployment (Objective 3);
- the promotion of youth employment (Objective 4); and
- structural adjustment in agriculture, in particular in the regions affected by the reform of the Common Agricultural Policy and fisheries (Objective 5a) and promotion of development in rural areas (Objective 5b).

Another decision in the reform package was to more than double the resources of structural funds from €6.3 billion in 1987 to €14.1 billion in 1993.[68] None the less, these funds had to be only additional regional expenditure to that undertaken by national governments. The objective was to ensure that structural policy was a tool with a real impact, to move from an informal project to multiannual programme financing, to increase the predictability of the policy (as the funds were allocated for a period of five years) and to increase partnership with authorities that are involved in regional policy at all levels of government. In practice, all these tasks were quite bureaucratic; the methodology for the designation of regions that had to receive assistance permitted a high degree of political influence, so the coverage of the assisted areas was wider than originally planned, and support was less concentrated (Bachtler and Mitchie, 1993, pp. 722–3).

The provisions that regulate the operation of the structural funds were revised in 1993. The main thrust of the 1988 reform was, none the less, preserved. Alterations included only a simplification of the decision-making procedure and its greater transparency; the planning period over which the structural funds operate was extended to six years (1993–99); the resources for the 1994–99 period totalled €144.5 billion; and there was the inclusion of a few new regions that are eligible for the assistance.

As always when there is a disbursement of funds, the European Commission has to be careful. It has to find a balance between, on the one hand, its aim of having effective policies that do not introduce distortions that may be damaging for the EU in the long term, and subsidy-seeking regions and firms on the other. To be eligible for EU assistance, a disadvantaged region has to have per capita GDP of 75 per cent or less of the EU average. In reality, the application of this official ceiling is quite 'flexible' as aid has also been given to regions with an average income that is 80 per cent of the EU average. As a result, half of the EU(15) population of one of the richest and most-developed regions in the world became eligible for assistance because of the relative drawbacks of the region in which they live.

The regional policy of the EU is simply a supranational policy that is additional to, rather than a partial replacement of, various national regional policies. Its first shortcoming is that the ERDF is modest in relation to regional needs. It should not be forgotten, however, that the regional policy of the EU, and particularly its Cohesion Policy, is relatively new although it is improving over time. In 2000, structural funds accounted for 35 per cent of the entire EU budget. The attempt to reduce disparities between rich and poor countries in the EU is great in circumstances of relatively slow growth and cuts in expenditure. National governments also act as a brake on the development of regional policy, as they prevent, in some cases, greater involvement of the EU in their own regional affairs. A greater degree of coordination of national economic policies may avoid dissipation of scarce EU funds, which may result in help to the rich in the relatively less-developed regions to the detriment of the poor in the developed ones.

It could appear that there is a tendency to redirect structural spending from rural to urban areas. Regional problems are starting to concentrate in the urban areas of the problem regions. The principal beneficiaries of economic integration in the EU are urban areas in the central regions. This process has also created disadvantages in urban areas and in *other* regions of the EU. This is because the EU is a heavily urbanised group of countries.

The impact of the Single European Market on regional disequilibria in the EU is ambiguous. There is an identification problem. First and foremost, one needs to answer difficult questions: what are the short- and long-term effects of the programme on the regions, and what is the impact of the changes on the regional disequilibria that would have happened on their own? If the longer-term effects of the Single European Market include the liberalisation of EU trade, then output may continue to be concentrated in the already advanced regions in order to benefit from positive externalities (this implies a fall in output and wages in the less-advanced regions). However, internal trade liberalisation may reallocate some EU production activities towards the periphery in order to take advantage of lower wages and other production costs there. As the outcome is uncertain in a situation with market imperfections and multiple equilibria, the effects of the Single European Market on the regions will continue to be debated for quite some time in the future.

Traditional forms of national regional policy started to change and to decline in importance from the early 1990s in most of the EU member countries.[69] Denmark, for example, abolished all regional development grants and loans in 1991. The Dutch have restricted their regional assistance to a relatively small part of the country in the north. Owing to budgetary constraints, France had to scale down its regional aid. Germany has severely curtailed regional policy in the western part of the country, while placing priorities in the new eastern *Länder*. Even the less-developed countries such as Greece or Ireland have had to be careful with their regional expenditure because of the restrictions that originated in recession. The new spirit of national regional policies in the EU countries includes (Bachtler and Michie, 1993, pp. 721–2):

- reduction of the importance of regional policy in the northern countries;
- transfer of responsibilities to regional and local levels;
- automatic aid replaced by discretionary assistance; and
- increased involvement of the European Commission in regional matters, in particular through the rules on competition.

Contemporary regional policy also includes the local development of producer services. This feature was gradually incorporated into regional policy only in the second half of the 1980s. None the less, the creation of jobs in new manufacturing businesses, their extension in existing ones or relocation of businesses still account for the major part of regional intervention. The European Commission may authorise investment aid of up to 75 per cent net grant equivalent in the least-developed regions. The same limit is 30 per cent in other areas where aid is allowed. The upper limit for aid in the least favoured areas is intended to increase the competitiveness of these regions in attracting private investment. In practice, the country that has such regions within its confines may face severe budgetary problems and lack the necessary funds to finance projects in these areas. Hence, the impact of this concession is significantly eroded. In any case, a relatively high proportion of the allowed aid of up to 75 per cent may seriously question the degree of commercial risk borne by the private firm (Yuill et al., 1994, p. 100).

EU regional policy is governed by six key principles (Armstrong, 1996, pp. 194–6):

- coordination of various EU policies and funds;
- partnership with member state governments, regional and local authorities, private businesses and banks;
- multiannual and multiproject programming;
- subsidiarity: policy should be carried out at the lowest possible level of government;
- concentration of assistance on the priority objectives; and
- additionality: the EU regional policy should be additional to, rather than a replacement for, national or regional or private expenditure.

The objective of *Agenda 2000* was to offer an overall medium-term plan (2000–06) for the future of the EU. It wanted to prepare the EU for the new millennium when the EU was preparing to enlarge eastwards. As far as regional policy is concerned, for reasons of efficiency and visibility *Agenda 2000* merged earlier objectives for the structural funds into two regional objectives and one pan-EU objective (European Commission, 1997a, pp. 22–5):

- *Objective 1*: Backward regions with per capita GDP of 75 per cent of the EU average or below. This covers about 20 per cent of the EU(15) population.
- *Objective 2*: Rural and urban reconversion regions. Economic and social restructuring in areas undergoing economic change in manufacturing and services, declining rural areas, urban areas in difficulty and crisis-hit areas depending on fisheries. This covers about 18 per cent of the EU(15) population.
- *Objective 3*: Development of human resources in regions not covered by Objective 1 or 2. This supports training, education and employment.

The 2000–06 financial perspective allocated €213 billion to structural funds to disburse over seven years. *Agenda 2000* also reduced the percentage of the EU(15) disadvantaged population covered by Objectives 1 and 2 from 51 per cent to 35–40 per cent. This is much more in line with the intention to concentrate EU resources on those areas that really need them. In addition, candidate countries were allocated as a pre-accession aid €45 billion for the 2000–06 period. However, the level of annual assistance to a candidate country cannot exceed 4 per cent of that country's national GDP. This shifting of funds eastwards has aroused some hostility towards such developments as the beneficiary regions and countries (Spain, France) in the EU(15) feel that they are losing out to the eastern regions. Therefore, there are certain moves, particularly by the net contributors to the EU budget, to scale down regional expenditure during the period that will cover the 2007–13 financial perspective.

It is apparent that the European Commission is exerting increasing influence in EU regional matters, mainly through competition rules and funds with an impact on regional markets. National governments also conduct regional policies; however, they are becoming increasingly selective and are making sure that the policy provides value for money. In addition, outright general assistance to the regions is being replaced by transparent grants for capital investment.[70]

There is concern among member countries that the European Commission relies heavily on quantitative indicators in the designation of areas for assistance and that it does not take sufficient cognisance of the specific circumstances of each area. For example, unemployment data in rural areas may hide the 'real' regional problem, as there may be a high level of emigration from those areas. Unemployment rates that are below the national average do not reflect a buoyant local economy, but rather a lack of local job opportunities. The quantitative approach by the European Commission may be justified on the grounds that it must be impartial. The Commission can be questioned in its work by the European Parliament or by the Court of Justice, so it must be able to give reasons for its actions. Although quantitative criteria play an important role in the first phase of the consideration of the problem by the European Commission, the second phase of analysis provides for a greater flexibility and consideration of other, more qualitative elements (Yuill et al., 1994, pp. 98–100).

Three factors account for most of the inequalities in regional levels of income. They deal with differences in: total factor productivity, employment level and the share of agriculture in regional income. The suggested regional policy, based on the experience of Ireland from the mid-1980s, relates to the market-oriented approach as 'the best conduit to sustained economic growth and fast convergence in per capita income' (Boldrin and Canova, 2001, p. 211).

In spite of substantial regional expenditure by the EU, Boldrin and Canova (2001) showed that neither convergence nor divergence was taking place among the EU(15) regions during the 1980–95 period. The adopted and implemented regional policies, as well as substantial public resources channelled to less-developed regions do not appear to enhance the capacity of these regions. These funds only redistributed income among regions. With no prospects for change and if income distribution is the principal concern, such transfers will be necessary on a continuous basis. Therefore, there was no evidence that the adopted policies of redistribution of income were the most appropriate. As most regions were growing at a fairly uniform rate, these policies reflected internal political compromises which have little effect on fostering economic growth and convergence in the EU (Boldrin and Canova, 2001, pp. 211 and 242).

In spite of substantial expenditure on regional matters by the EU during the 1980s and 1990s, regional inequalities have not narrowed during this period, and by some measures have even widened. 'Income differences across states have fallen, but inequalities between regions within each state have risen. European states have developed increasingly different production structures' (Puga, 2002, p. 400). A similar observation came from Midelfart-Knarvik and Overman (2002, p. 333) who noted that despite the fact that the EU(15) spent about a third of its overall annual budget on regional matters, there was an increasing regional inequality. If the EU regional policy and instruments were successful on the country level, they were less so on the subnational plane.

ONE CASE: MEZZOGIORNO[71]

Since the early 1950s, Italy has implemented a range of inconsistent regional policies that have failed to enable the Mezzogiorno to catch up with the rest of the Italian economy to any great extent.[72] Public intervention started after the Second World War with the development of a regional infrastructure. Poor transport links may have 'protected' local industries in the backward regions of southern Italy. The building of the *Autostrada del Sole* led to a chain of bankruptcies in the local food, textiles and clothing businesses because of a fall in trade costs compared with the rest of the country. The Mezzogiorno started to 'import' cheaper goods from elsewhere in Italy, hence the previously protected local businesses suffered.

Towards the end of the 1950s, the major infrastructure was built, but it was not sufficient to attract firms to invest in the south. At that time regional policy started to offer hefty financial and fiscal incentives to businesses that wanted to locate their activities in the Mezzogiorno. In the late 1960s, public enterprises increased their role in the production geography of the south. At the same time, wage subsidies were employed as a means of industrial policy. In 1968, a national wage agreement laid down a common wage throughout the country. This introduced a major rigidity in the economy of the Mezzogiorno. Private firms abstained from hiring because of wage costs that were not linked to productivity. The south lost wage flexibility to respond to shocks, while public enterprises were overmanned. This type of economy was vulnerable to shocks, as was exemplified in the early 1970s after the increase in the price of oil (Braunerhjelm et al., 2000, p. 72).

The policy reaction to such geography of production was support to SMEs. However, this policy change came too late to be effective. The gap between the north and the south began to grow again from the mid-1970s. During the 1980s, Italian regional policy was restricted to income support (public employment and pensions). Growing taxes and continuous transfers to the Mezzogiorno were frustrating the north of the country. In addition, the European Commission requested the removal of wage subsidies to firms in the south as they were distorting competition.

Dissatisfaction with previous regional policies carried out since the 1950s, pressure from the northern regions and involvement of the European Commission in regional and competition affairs contributed to the introduction of Law 488 in 1992. This law effectively abolished special intervention (*intervento straordinario*) for the Mezzogiorno and extended the coverage of the policy (grant-based support) to the centre-north of Italy. This means that regional policy in Italy is no longer tantamount to a policy directed at the southern part of the country. The abolition of this special treatment for the Mezzogiorno may be considered as one of the most significant developments in regional policies during the past four decades.

One of the policy tools that was used to support industrialisation in the region was law provisions that required public corporations to direct the majority of their investments towards the south. These firms were regarded in the receiving area more as providers of jobs (hence, as supporters of the local demand) than as contributors to the growth of the national economy. As such, a relatively low efficiency of investment in the Mezzogiorno comes as no surprise at all. Because of these 'results' there was growing pressure for a reconsideration of the public policy towards the south, as well as open opposition to the policy from the northern regions of the country.

During the first half of the 1950s, GDP per capita income in the south of Italy was about 55 per cent of that in the north and centre of the country. In the second half of the 1980s the equivalent figure was 57 per cent. In spite of this, the Mezzogiorno cannot be described as a 'poor' region, particularly in terms of consumption. Large transfers of resources from outside the region support the artificially high levels of consumption. Therefore, the Mezzogiorno may be described as a structurally dependent economy (*European Economy*, 1993, pp. 21–2).[73]

The source of the regional problem of the Mezzogiorno lies not necessarily in a lack of funds or infrastructure, but rather in the non-material sphere. One of the major obstacles can be found in the absence of an 'entrepreneurial culture'. In addition, a survey of TNCs that already operate in or have considered investment in the Mezzogiorno revealed that the major obstacles to foreign investors include the existence of criminal organisations and political factors. A lack of infrastructure featured highly only for those TNCs that have not yet established their branches there. Factors that contributed to the attractiveness of the Mezzogiorno included the availability of relatively low-cost labour (both quantity and quality), the availability of land, as well as various public incentives to locate business operations there.[74]

14. Conclusion

A country or economic union in which there are differences in the levels of development and/or living standards among constituent regions that do not have at least a tendency towards equalisation cannot be regarded as having a well-integrated economy. Therefore, all countries and economic unions have a certain commitment to reduce regional disequilibria for a few economic and, more importantly, a variety of non-economic reasons. The objectives of EU regional policy are to diminish existing and prevent new regional disparities.

If a regional policy is to be effective, then the authorities at all levels of the government have to coordinate their activities in order to influence decisions about the allocation of resources (location of economic activity). In spite of these coercive powers, the regional policies of countries have had relatively limited positive achievements. It should therefore come as no surprise that the achievements of the regional policy of the EU, which often relies more on rules of competition, persuasion and on certain funds than on coercion, are scant indeed.

Regional policy has been based on a number of compromises, to the detriment of the purity of principles. Previous attempts to shape regional policy relied mainly on the alleviation of transport and communication costs through the expansion of infrastructure, as well as the mitigation of agglomeration disequilibria. More recently, attention has shifted towards a greater self-reliance for those regions that are lagging in development, as well as the enhancement of enterprise competitiveness in these regions.

Statistical evidence and various surveys of past actions offer little testimony that the EU regional policy had any significant effect. In the case of France, for example, Crozet et al. (2004, pp. 28, 51), found that French and EU regional policy investment incentives and structural funds did not have any significant impact on investors. Elsewhere, the growth of clusters and regions such as northern Italy or Baden-Württemberg was not based on any public action, but rather on inside elements. Public action in regional matters as took place in the Mezzogiorno had a very limited success and occasionally could have been harmful.

Enterprise policy and the policy of macroeconomic stability are gradually being used instead of regional policy to tackle the regional (spatial) problems of a country. The new regional (development) policy ought to change the traditional intra- and interregional relations of dependence and hierarchy. This type of rigid structural organisation of firms, industries and institutions (state commands, taxes and shelters; big firms are protected; small and new firms are tolerated but not highly encouraged; while the family ties and 'old boy' networks connect everything) ought to be replaced by structures that are open for contacts based on affinity, support and perception of common growth and positive-sum games. This new policy ought to include the following features:

- assistance to innovation and permanent learning;
- aid to increase flexibility to face and adapt to challenges;
- reduction in the traditional financial regional support;
- emphasis on SMEs, business 'incubators' and start-ups of new firms;
- backing of the producers' services; and
- coordination with other policies.

The critics of this policy stance believe that the two policies lack the firmness needed to have a direct influence on a given spatial problem.

In contrast to the decentralisation and trimming down of national regional policies, EU regional policy has continued to widen its coverage and scope. It is, however, hard to determine the point at which regional policy distorts competition beyond the interest of the EU. Hence, uncertainty over regional policy will continue in the future. There are many arbitrary elements in the policy, as well as special cases. EU regional policy has revealed its limitations. It is still Byzantine in its complexity. A solution to the regional development problem, as well as to achieving some balance among various regions, is an urgent, difficult, but highly rewarding challenge for the EU(25). Instability in regional policy at national and EU levels seems likely to continue. It is possible that the trend to decentralise the creation and implementation of national regional policy will continue in the future. However, there is a danger in the expansion of regional incentives that compete with one another.

The question, however, arises as to whether regional policy increases or decreases market imperfections. In the second-best world, all answers are possible, but not always desirable. If the costs of such a policy are less than the benefits it brings, then the policy is justified. The rationale for a regional policy that basically redistributes income (equity) must be found in solidarity among regions that constitute countries and/or the EU, as well as the fact that the area of benefit is larger than the assisted region.

Demand, technology and supplies of factors often change. Regions that fail to adjust continuously to the new challenges and opportunities remain depressed and weak. One of the broad objectives of regional policy is to help the redistribution of economic activity among different regions. Its impact cannot be measured easily as it is not a simple task to construct a counterfactual world that would specify what would have happened without this policy. The difference between the actual and counterfactual situation may be attributed to regional policy.

As the Central and East European countries brought serious regional disequilibria into the EU, cohesion will remain one of the major long-term issues in the EU(25). Hence, there are at least three major arguments in favour of the EU regional policy in order to preserve unity with diversity in the EU(25):

- In the absence of policy instruments such as tariffs, NTBs, devaluation or changes in rates of interest, regions that are not able to adjust as fast as the rest of the EU face increases in unemployment and decreases in living standards. In this situation, there is some case for the demand for short-term fiscal transfers at the EU level to ease the adjustment process. The possibility of such transfers in unforeseen cases ought to be permanent in an EMU (eurozone). Otherwise, when in need, the regions that are in trouble may not be sure that other partner countries will provide resources on a case-by-case basis. The eurozone may not be able to operate efficiently in the long term without an effective regional policy. However, there is high uncertainty regarding the size of the EU(25) structural funds during the 2007–13 period. There are serious political pressures to limit and to scale down the overall EU budgetary expenditure.
- Coordination of national regional policies, as well as other principal economic policies at the EU level can avoid self-defeating divergent regional programmes that are taken in isolation.
- Footloose industries, multiple equilibria, economies of scale and externalities do not guarantee that integration will bring an equitable dispersion of economic activities. Some direction for economic adjustment and allocation of resources in the form of regional policy may be necessary.

Regional policy is another facet of social policy. Hence, the EU faces difficult political choices regarding regional policy. Challenges in this area include the eastern enlargement, monetary union, continuous unemployment, structural change and international competition. Obstacles to a stronger influence in this policy area come from the eurozone restrictions in the monetary and fiscal fields, lack of a federal EU system of transfer of funds, slower growth and little internal migration of labour. However, one has always to bear in mind that the amount of funds at the disposal of a particular policy is not always what matters most. What matters is the amount of funds that is necessary to change a particular type of behaviour in the desired direction. The amount of funds and their astute use to change certain types of behaviour will continue to be a matter for debate long into the future.

Appendix 8A1 Examples of the putty–clay locational model

Relatively modest initial differences between countries or the humble beginnings of an industry or a firm in a region can have irreversible effects for a specific location or region. Even if two or more potential locations are identical, then the case may be 'solved' by chance. Hence, it may be impossible to predict where a cluster will emerge. But once the industry starts developing, the process of circular interdependence or cumulative causation cuts in and may continue for a long time, even if the structure of the economy has changed. For example, there are interesting stories of why certain firms/industries come to be located where they are today:

- For centuries Basle was an important trading and banking city because of its favourable geographical position. For instance, the Rhine is navigable from Basle. This supported trade and later production specialisation in the textile industry. In neighbouring France, the national patent law of 1844 protected materials, not the production process. Hence, the patent of 1859 gave the inventor of the red aniline dye (fuchsine), used for dying textiles, a virtual monopoly to produce it in the country. A few months following the granting of this patent (monopoly to produce), another Frenchman invented a completely different method for producing the same red dye. However, the law prohibited him from producing this protected dye in France, even though the domestic demand was larger than supply. Hence, he went abroad to Switzerland which, like many other countries, did not have patent laws. Basle was the preferred location because it was a trading and banking centre, electricity and salt were available in the vicinity, one could 'safely' unload arsenic in the Rhine, transport and forwarding infrastructure was readily available and the oldest Swiss university, founded in 1460, was located there. Physician and alchemist Paracelsus (1493–1541), a precursor of homeopathy, lectured on the link between medical and chemical events, which freed medical thinking. Hence, Basle was a prime and open location to start production of something new. At the same time in France, the (monopolist) producer of the dye, mollycoddled by the system, did not invest further in R&D or improvements in production techniques, while the competitive market structure in Switzerland motivated firms to increase production efficiency. The price of the dye in Switzerland was less than half the price in France, hence smuggling into France became significant. This French monopoly subsequently collapsed (Weder, 1995). Production of pharmaceuticals emerged, almost by chance around 1880, when the curative effects of dyes became apparent. The Swiss dye industry could not compete with its German counterpart either on scale of output or on access to raw inputs. Therefore, the Swiss specialised in high-value-added market segments of medicines, pesticides, herbicides, perfumes and flavourings. Highly sophisticated medical and health-care services and equipment followed their expansion throughout the country. Strong incentives came from an inflow of talents and the invalidation of German patents by the Allies following the two world wars, as well as a government policy in education and through the support of R&D. As a relatively small country, Switzerland had to export from the outset. It became specialised and highly competitive in an industry that is not based on natural resources.

- Towards the end of the Middle Ages, Genevan goldsmiths and jewellers were renowned for their skills, the splendour of their products and their knowledge of precious metals. They were 'expected' to become involved in the new watchmaking industry that started to appear in France, Flanders, England and Germany around 1500. However, the Genevans were so prosperous that they were uninterested in the emerging industry. Nevertheless, two chance events prompted the abrupt appearance of watchmaking in Geneva. First, in 1541, Jean Calvin issued an edict against luxury, pleasure, elegant clothing and 'useless jewellery'. This limited the activities of the Geneva jewellers and goldsmiths and virtually ended their craft 25 years later when their activities were even more restricted. Second, at about the same time, the persecuted Protestant Huguenots from France and Flanders found sanctuary in Switzerland (Basle, Geneva and Zurich). Some of these refugees brought with them watchmaking knowledge and experience, one of whom was Charles Cusin who settled in Geneva in 1574. As watches performed a 'useful' function, Geneva's jewellers and goldsmiths learned how to make quality, stylish and durable watches in order to find a new source of income. Once the number of watchmakers increased, they organised themselves in a guild in 1601. Most of the production was sold outside the country as few Swiss were able and willing to afford such watches. None the less, production flourished and the city became congested with watchmakers. It became increasingly difficult and time consuming to obtain a master watchmaker's licence, so many of the apprentices moved to other locations. They mostly clustered in the Swiss Jura (Nyon, Neuchâtel, La Chaux-de-Fonds, Bienne and Basle). In contrast to Geneva, light regulations permitted the production of parts to be farmed out to the peasants in the mountains, who had limited sources of income, especially during the long winters. These watches were, of course, less sophisticated and cheaper than the ones produced in Geneva, but they found a niche in the marked and production expanded. In spite of changes in time measurement technology and hard times during the 1970s and 1980s, the Geneva watchmaking cluster for stylish and the Jura cluster for standard watches weathered the storm, justified their label 'Swiss made' and retained 'global' dominance (Bumbacher, 1995).

- Sassuolo (near Bologna, Italy) is, perhaps, the world capital in the production of ceramic tiles. Pot making started there in the 13th century. Production of ceramic tiles for street names and house numbers began in the 19th century. Immediately after the Second World War, there were only a few ceramic tile producers in the area. The post-war reconstruction created a boom for all building materials including Italian ceramic tiles. Tiles did well on the market because in the Mediterranean climate ceramic tiles were cool in warm weather, because wood was scarce and dear, and because the Italians prefer natural materials to vinyl and carpeting. The principal raw material was kaolin (white) clay. The region was abundant in red clay, hence the white had to be imported from Britain. The equipment kilns and presses were imported (mainly from Germany) in the 1950s and 1960s. From the mid-1960s, the local entrepreneurs learned how to modify the imported equipment for the use of the regionally available red clay. In the 1970s, the Sassuolo area manufacturers became very competitive suppliers of kilns and presses, and they began to export them. A relatively saturated domestic tile market in 1980s provided the incentive to export ceramic tiles all around the world. Producers were successful in responding quickly to the changing design and other demand conditions which gave them the competitive edge (Porter, 1990a, pp. 210–25).

- Modena (Italy) is an important hub for translations from and into many languages. This area has long been well known for the production and export of agricultural machinery. As the machinery required instruction manuals in various languages, such publications were initiated in Modena; once established, the industry developed and expanded.
- Provided that profitability is maintained, personal factors (that is, whims) can play a role in firm location decision. For example, the establishment of car production factories in Detroit and Oxford, as in each case the founder of one of the major manufacturers (Ford and Morris, respectively) was born there. Incidentally, Bill Gates, the founder and chairman of Microsoft was born in Seattle. Fashion-producing firm Hugo Boss is located in Metzingen (Germany) because Hugo Boss was born there and he wanted to contribute to the development of his home town. Metzingen is situated very close to Reutlingen (near Stuttgart) and there is quite a significant textile industry in the area. Now, not only is there Hugo Boss production and a huge Hugo Boss outlet in Metzingen, but others have also established enterprises there, such as Escade and Bally. Hilti, a tools maker, is located in Liechtenstein because its founder Martin Hilti was born there. Nowadays, it has been known for golf-addicted entrepreneurs and business executives to search for locations for their businesses that are close to good golfing facilities.
- Policy changes such as the passage of anti-union statutes in the southern states of the US gave certain manufacturing firms the incentive to leave the northern part of the country. This process was supported by another unrelated event: the advent of air conditioning, which made the southern climate more attractive for living and working in than that in the north of the country.
- St. Martin's Court is a short street near the English National Opera in London. The street is full of sellers of second-hand books and prints. Potential customers go there because they expect to find a number of shops with a wide range of second-hand books, while shop owners locate there because they expect to welcome a stream of clients. A similar reasoning explains the cluster of theatres around Leicester Square and the location of restaurants in Soho. During the Renaissance, Florence was the centre for art in Italy. The clients who lived there were sophisticated, they appreciated art and were able and willing to pay for it. At the same time the artists needed such clients. The densest art expertise in the world can be found along a one-kilometre-long stretch that connects New Bond Street, Old Bond

Street and St. James's Street in London. The combined turnover of the auction houses Christie's, Sotheby's, Bonhams and Phillips is the largest in the world. In addition, in the same area there are 15 top art dealers. They all tend to flourish during troubled times: periods of calm and political stability have been disastrous for their business, while unpredictable crisis, death, divorce and sorrow are their best friends.

Krugman (1996b) draws an interesting analogy between clusters and the natural evolution process:

> The general attitude of evolutionary theorists seems to be that the nature can often find surprising pathways to places you would have thought unreachable by small steps; that over a few hundred thousand generations a slightly light-sensitive patch of skin can become an eye that appears to be perfectly designed. . . . [Imagine] a group of frogs sitting at the edge of a circular pond, from which a snake may emerge . . . and that the snake will grab and eat the nearest frog. Where will the frog sit? . . . if there are two groups of frogs around the pool, each group has an equal chance of being targeted, and so does each frog within each group – which means that the chance of being eaten is less if you are a frog in the larger group. Thus if you are a frog trying to maximize your choice of survival, you will want to be a part of the larger group; and the equilibrium must involve clumping of all the frogs as close together as possible.

Does this remind you of the principle of agglomeration? Unlike changes in biology, real-world entrepreneurs are smart and often radically change their behaviour within a short period of time in response to opportunities for business.

Appendix 8A2   Clusters in Italy and Germany

Italy is an often quoted example of a country with distinct manufacturing clusters. A select group of those clusters include the following:[75]

- motorcycles in Bologna [2370];
- electronics, mainly alarms for cars in Varese [100];
- jewellery in Valenza Po [1400] (Alessandria); Vicenza [1100]; Arezzo [1300] (Florence);
- spectacles in Cadore [930] (Belluno);

- textiles and clothing in Sempione [3900] (Varese);
- textiles around lake Como; Prato [8481] (Florence); Olgiatese [2614] (Varese); Biella [1300] (Piedmont); Valdagno (Pisa);
- clothing in Val Vibrata [1150] (Pescara); Empoli (Florence); Treviso;
- female underwear in Castel Goffredo [280] (Mantova);
- silk in Comasco [2600] (Como);
- wool in Biella;
- knitwear in Carpi [2054] (Modena);
- shoes in Fermo, Montegranaro, Porto Santelpidio, Sanbenedetto, San Benedetto del Trono (Ancona); Lucca, Santa Croce Sull'Arno [1749] (Pisa); Ascoli [3100]; Riviera del Brenta [886] (Padova);
- sports footwear in Montebelluna [623] (Treviso); Asolo (Treviso);
- tannery in Arzignano [600] (Vicenza) and Solofra (Naples);
- ceramic tiles in Sassuolo [199] (Bologna);
- marble in Apuo-Versiliese [1161] (Carrara);
- taps and valves in Alto Cusio [300] (Novara);
- furniture in Brianza Comasca Milanese [6500] (Milan); Cantù [7200] (Milan); Alto Livenza [2000] (Udine); Poggibonsi [1294] (Siena); Bovolone-Cerea [3000] (Verona);
- kitchens in Pesaro [1200];
- chairs and tables in Udine [1200];
- wood machinery in Rimini [1345];
- agricultural machinery in Modena [100];
- foodstuffs in Parma [215];
- saucepans and valves in Lumezzane [1008] (Brescia);
- packaging machinery in Bologna; and
- accordions and other musical instruments in Castelfidardo [400] (Ancona).

Clusters in Germany include:

- steel in Dortmund, Essen and Düsseldorf;
- locksmiths' products in Velbert;
- cutlery in Solingen;
- surgical instruments in Tuttlingen;
- chemicals in Leverkusen, Frankfurt and Ludwigshafen;
- jewellery in Pforzheim;
- cars in Wolfsburg, Stuttgart, Munich, Ingolstadt, Neckarsulm and Regensburg;
- machine tools in Stuttgart;
- pens and pencils in Nuremberg;
- printing presses in Heidelberg, Würzburg and Offenbach;

- optics in Wetzlar; and
- tool-making in Remscheid.

Notes

1. Economic and social cohesion is defined as 'overall harmonious development' (Article 158 of the Rome Treaty). As cohesion is defined in such a vague way, it can mean different things to different people. It can also mean different things to the same person at various points in time. Does 'overall harmonious development' mean equalisation of income; or equalisation of opportunities; or providing an incentive to remain in the EU?
2. Guidance Section of the Agricultural Fund, European Regional Development Fund, European Social Fund, Cohesion Fund and Financial Instrument for Fisheries Guidance.
3. Trade theory has not come to grips with multiactivity firms and multiplant production as was the case with the theory of industrial organisation.
4. The question with agglomeration economies is which geographical spot is going to dominate in production? The analytical difficulty with agglomeration is that it introduces multiple equilibria.
5. In the case with one market and two deposits of resources, the optimal firm location would fall inside the triangle area which links these three different spots.
6. If one imagines a geometrically even distribution of centres across a flat and homogeneous surface and the corresponding circles (representing ranges of goods) around them, then if one wants to cover all the space with circles, there would be an overlap between the two adjoining circles. If one draws a straight line between the points where the two adjoining circles intersect, one would get a hexagonal market space of identical size around each centre without empty corners, as consumers would purchase goods from the cheapest (nearest) producer.
7. Paris and Madrid have a relatively central geographical location in France and Spain, respectively. The same holds for Munich in Bavaria. In 1998 the capital of Kazakhstan was transferred from Almaty to Astana precisely because the latter city lies at the intersection point of major North-South and East-West transport routes.
   One of the reasons why Peugeot-Citroën announced in 2003 that it intends to invest and to locate a large (€700 million) car assembly factory in Trnava, Slovakia (over alternative locations in Poland, the Czech Republic and Hungary) is that this country has good access to transport links and that it is 'in the centre of Europe' (R. Anderson, M. Arnold and J. Reed, 'Peugeot to build new plant in Slovakia', *Financial Times*, 15 January 2003). The factory would start production of about 300 000 small cars from 2006. The management intends to be closer to fast-growing markets in the EU accession countries and to profit from wage rates that are a fifth of the rates paid in the EU(15) for similar industrial operations.
   In 2004, Hyundai selected Slovakia over Poland (known for the aggressive reputation of its labour unions) to build a €700 million car assembly plant in Zilina. This is Hyundai's first car assembly plant in Europe. It would assemble 200 000 cars a year (potentially 300 000 from 2008). The reasons for the decision to locate in Slovakia include wage costs (a quarter of the prevailing rates in Western Europe); half the car ownership levels of Western Europe; laws that made labour market flexible; reduced corporate and income taxes; existing network of suppliers (expected to expand further); and membership of the EU. As Volkswagen already produces cars in Slovakia (Bratislava), this 'tiny' (5.4 million people) central-European country becomes one of the European motor giants. The three Slovak car plants could produce over 800 000 cars a year from 2006. That would make the highest per capita car production in the world (R. Anderson and J. Cienski, 'Hyundai picks Slovakia for new €700m car assembly plant', *Financial Times*, 3 March 2004).
   Slovakia may produce about 900 000 cars a year from 2008. The automotive industry

8. contributes a quarter to the manufacturing output and a third to exports (this will increase to a half once the two plants are completed). The problem may be in the increasing unbalance in the Slovak industrial structure. Although Slovakia may be the victim of its own success, some of the neighbouring countries that lost out to Slovakia (Poland, for example) may like to have such 'troubles'.
8. Marriages (chances or historical accidents) of the Habsburgs created the Austro-Hungarian Empire, which altered the economic space in Central and Eastern Europe.

   In addition, the spread of certain products is based on a chance. For example, in 1519 the Aztec king Montezuma offered Hernando Cortez a chocolate drink. Know-how about chocolate was passed on to Spain. When the 14-year old Spanish princess Ann of Austria, daughter of Spanish king Philip III, married in 1615 her peer Louis XIII of France, the Spanish hosts served chocolate to the European nobility. Ann of Austria brought in her wedding basket some chocolate to the French court. That was one way how chocolate crossed the Pyrenees. At about the same time, the Inquisition in Spain instigated another. The fleeing Jews came to Bayonne (France) and established cocoa processing plants there. Some of them went also to the Low Countries.
9. Murphy et al. (1989) discuss multiple equilibria with respect to the process of industrialisation, postulating that a certain critical mass of industries may have to be involved in order for industrialisation to be successful. A parallel could be drawn with location theory, and a role for government policy to aid the 'take-off' of a particular location, and encourage firms to move to the location.
10. Positive feedback economics may also find parallels in non-linear physics. For example, ferromagnetic materials consist of mutually reinforcing elements. Small perturbations, at critical times, influence which outcome is selected (bifurcation point), and the chosen outcome may have higher energy (that is, be less favourable) than other possible end states (Arthur, 1990a, p. 99).
11. An ergodic system (a pendulum, water in a glass) ultimately returns to its original state, regardless of the disturbances between the starting and ending points in time.
12. http://classics.mit.edu/Plato/laws.html.
13. http://classics.mit.edu/Plato/laws.4.iv.html.
14. During past centuries, the colonial powers obtained natural resources from their colonies. In many cases they prevented the development of manufacturing industry in the colonised countries in order to secure those 'outer markets' for the exports of the manufactured goods from the colonial master. Thus local competition was eliminated and if any development of manufacturing activity took place it was usually in port cities and was limited to primary processing.
15. It is difficult to trace knowledge flows, because they are invisible and do not leave a paper trail by which they can be measured and tracked. Hence a theorist may assume anything about them (Krugman, 1992, pp. 53–4). Certain traces such as quotations in professional journals may be found, however.
16. An Italian saint prompted the creation of Brasilia, Brazil's capital in 1883. He promised great bounties if the interior of the country, mostly Amazon jungle, was developed. In 1891, a new constitution called for the move. A foundation stone was laid in 1922, but only in 1957 the new capital city project got under way 900km inland. This was a utopian experiment in modern urbanism that was intended to stimulate leaps in the development process. What turned out is a pedestrian-unfriendly city which misses a human touch. It is packed with (monstrous) concrete government buildings in various states of decay. Or another example: Washington D.C. was created in 1790s when President George Washington picked a swamp for the permanent seat of the US government. 'It's not quite so bad now, but . . . once the city's cubicle-dwellers flee to the suburbs, Washington can feel as empty as a bad high-school dance' (K. Iskyan, 'Trading places – What drives a country to switch its capital city?', *Slate*, 1 March 2004.
17. Landlocked countries such as Chad, Mali or Niger have a geographical disadvantage that increases the cost of trade. However, Austria, Switzerland and Luxembourg may offer examples showing that the situation for landlocked countries is not hopeless.
18. Relevant factors that influence agglomeration tendencies for producers include the avail-

ability of raw materials, energy, labour and capital, while for consumers they include the availability of jobs and education, as well as climate and surroundings.
19. A core region may be taken to mean one that has capabilities and potentials to create, attract and employ resources and ideas. A periphery region may be taken to be one that has its economic path determined chiefly by the developments in the core region(s).
20. Learning from teachers is called *oblique transmission*, while learning from the members of one's professional group is *horizontal transmission*.
21. See section 7 on war and the location of firms.
22. Audretsch and Feldman (1996) found evidence that the US industries in which new knowledge spillovers are relevant (semiconductors and computers in California; pharmaceuticals in New Jersey) have a greater propensity to cluster innovative activity than industries where these spillovers are less important. Bottazzi and Peri (2002) reported that the benefits of R&D in generating innovation were extremely localised.
23. Information is simple structured and unstructured data. Knowledge is the capability to process those data, to analyse and evaluate them and, possibly, to deepen and extend them. Tacit knowledge is something that is within a knowledgeable person, but something that one cannot put in a manual.
24. Personal contacts, face-to-face communication, proximity and trust with a partner are emphasised by Kleinknecht and ter Wengel (1998, pp. 645–6), Porter and Sölvell (1998, pp. 445–6), Sternberg and Tamásy (1999, p. 374), Gordon and McCann (2000, p. 520), Porter (2000a, p. 262), Crafts and Venables (2001, p. 32), Henderson et al. (2001) and Venables (2001, p. 24), but were also well known to Perroux (1955, p. 317 and 1961, p. 152).
25. Do you know anybody who learned to cook a good French or a Chinese dish merely by reading a cookbook?
26. *Fortune*, 8 December 1997, p. 43.
27. It has been estimated that empty trucks travelled about 60 billion kilometres in the EU at an approximate annual cost of €45 billion. A better organisation of transport could radically reduce these figures (*European Voice*, 29 January 1998, p. 15).
28. Even though Siemens is a dominant firm in the Munich high-technology cluster, it does not threaten or absorb SMEs in the cluster, but rather develops ties with SMEs that are characterised by collaboration (Sternberg and Tamásy, 1999, p. 375).
29. The emergence of a cluster may be based on a historical accident such as the existence of certain skills or raw materials or a crossroad. Its evolution may enter into the second phase with the agglomeration of firms and the arrival of externalities that may have cumulative features. The next step in the growth of a cluster may include creation of supporting bodies such as business associations and knowledge-related institutions (schools and research centres). The next stage includes the spread of non-market relations. Firms and institutions create and maintain the spirit of strong non-market collaboration which is external to individual firms, but internal to the cluster. Such clusters may be highly specialised and may have success with their output on the market. However, they may easily become victims of their own success. They may fall into a 'trap of rigid specialisation' in the final period in their life. They may be locked in their own technology, specialised output and spirit. If there is another, competing and new good, service or technology elsewhere, which is in demand, then the cluster may decline and disappear.
30. Public policy and administrative areas in which the authorities collect statistics are usually not the same as clusters, which is why it is hard to determine the exact economic significance of clusters with a high degree of reliability.
31. It is also likely that dinosaurs came into being following an earlier meteor impact 251 million years ago.
32. Because of the availability of wood, Sweden developed its huge pulp and paper industry. Strong links with the suppliers contributed to a similar success for the machinery involved in the production processes.
33. 'Japanese business firms operating in Germany have an unexplainable attraction to Düsseldorf rather than Frankfurt' (Beckmann, 1999, p. 61).
34. Think of the theatre when the audience applauds. Soon the audience will spontaneously

Regional policy 663

35. start clapping at the same tempo. Such self-organisation occurs when many initially uncorrelated actions lock into one another's rhythm and create a strong collective group.
35. Mainstream economics deals with decision making within given structures. Evolutionary economics is concerned with decision making and long-term changes of the structure. See the classical article on the issue by Boschma and Lambooy (1999a).
36. Information in the physical world is transmitted via flows of particles such as electrons or photons and density gradients. In the social world (and to a lesser extent in the biological) 'there are the controls of information flows from the exercise of the *principle of optimum loss of detail* and use of *near-decomposability* within hierarchical structures – and even more so within the intricate interconnections of complicated hierarchical structures that may be embodied in an heterarchical model conceived by a human mind' (Isard, 1996, p. 357). Even though there are difficulties in applying biological analogies to social phenomena, they were widely used in the analysis of firms. The examples include the 'life cycle' theory of the firm, 'viability' of the firm and 'homeostasis' (habitual return to the initial equilibrium) (Penrose, 1952).
37. Australians were prevented from selling their wines under French names such as champagne, chablis or claret. So they simply rebranded their products as sparkling wines, cabernet sauvignon and chardonnay. The French were subsequently forced to rebrand obscure labels with varietal names to compete with the Australians on the British market (*Financial Times*, 28 July 2003).
38. 'IMF's Camdessus misses the point', *Stratfor*, 15 November 1999.
39. Increased productivity (growth in output per hour) is the basis for an increase in living standards and economic progress in the long term.
40. The performance of computer chips doubles every 18 months (Moore's law). However, this does not mean that the impact of computers on productivity follows this trend in a linear way. It depends who uses computers, how, when and for what purpose: management of stocks or computer games.
41. R. Gordon, 'America wins with a supermarket sweep', *Financial Times*, 19 August 2003.
42. *The Economist*, 19 August 2000, p. 9.
43. The German chemical industry was based on domestic deposits of salt and coal, as well as skills.
44. The first of many attempts to produce a small, economical runaround vehicle early in the 20th century resulted in the Auto-Ped. Introduced in New York in 1915, this looked like a child's scooter: it had no seat and there was a platform for the rider to stand on. A two-horsepower motor gave the Auto-Ped a maximum speed of 55 km/h.
45. In an attempt to eliminate textile waste during the Second World War, the US government reduced by one-tenth the amount of fabric allowed for women's swimwear. The chain of events that resulted in the ever-decreasing amount of material necessary for the bikini was set in motion.
46. Coalmining regions weakened and declined when liquid fuels started to be used as principal sources of energy.
47. Topics for further research include: spillovers, externalities and linkages as they are so poorly understood; local interactions; monopolistic competition; cross-fertilisation with industrial organisation and urban economics, trade and growth; cost–benefit analysis that can include linkages; services as research was mainly concentrated on the manufacturing sector; the speed of (exponential?) weakening of the effect of spillovers and information relative to distance, especially in developing countries; and agglomeration and spread of innovative activities.
48. The tacit assumption is that there are no transport and adjustment costs.
49. Sources of economies of scale include very high set-up or sunk costs (in fixed capital and R&D); learning effects (the more people learn how to use one Microsoft program, the easier it is for them to learn and adjust to other programs); and network and coordination effects (the more people use mobile phones or electronic banking the greater is the utility of that to all network users).
50. Institutional organisation, social regulation and political intervention may have a

significant influence on the location of production.
51. Entry and exit barriers include: huge sunk costs (in project investment and advertising), economies of scale, product differentiation (for example, local market demands a specific brand name drink), access to distribution channels, R&D, regulation (product quality), marketing, restriction of access to complementary assets and structures (such as a computer reservation system for tickets), reactions of competitors such as predatory pricing, exclusionary pricing, as well as trade, competition and industrial policies.
52. Cumulative causation mixes causes and effects of an event. They are combined in a chain reaction that is increasingly circular, snowballing, herding or perpetually accumulative. This type of self-reinforcement has different labels in economics which include: economies of scale, path dependency, virtuous and vicious circles, as well as threshold effects. The sources of this process are large sunk costs, learning, and network and coordination effects.
53. Income distribution also affects the location of production. If, for example, income is distributed to a small segment of the population (landowners or owners of capital) who spend it on imports of luxury goods and services, there may not be a spread of development of industries in their area or country. If, however, income is distributed in favour of a large number of families that demand domestically produced goods and services, this may have a positive impact on the location of firms and industries closer to the domestic market.
54. See Brülhart (1998a) for a brief survey of theoretical strands.
55. Evidence from the EU shows that the strongest internal labour mobility took place during the 1960s and the beginning of the 1970s; it came to a halt during the 1990s. However, intra-EU capital mobility increased during the 1980s and has remained strong ever since. Even domestic labour mobility within countries such as Italy was reduced. Labour used to move northwards on a larger scale during the 1950s and 1960s. Not any more. Southerners may easily be overqualified for simple jobs offered in the north of the country, the cost of living is higher in the north and there is also the attraction of the 'southern way of life'.
56. A strategic industrial (and trade) policy is based on a number of assumptions that include next to perfect information and forecast, as well as on the policy of non-retaliation by the foreign partners.
57. Is the core–periphery relation based on the purchase of goods by the core region from periphery? Or outflow of capital from the core region to the periphery? Or migration of labour (and capital) from the periphery region to the core? Or is there a mix of these possibilities?
58. The shipbuilding industry in Britain and Spain was in decline as it failed to specialise in a market niche as the Finnish industry has (icebreakers), it was not able to match the production costs in Korea and it lacked the potential for diversification existing in Japan. But this is the story from only one industry. One should never generalise the situation in the whole economy from a single industry case study.
59. This has always been an urban 'activity' because cities 'sell' anonymity and limited tolerance.
60. Casella (1996) discusses the case of reallocation of resources and gains from an enlargement of a trade bloc in small and large countries that already belong to that bloc. She showed that smaller EU countries gained more from the entry of Spain and Portugal into the EU than the large EU countries.
61. Storper et al. (2002, p. 103) argued that the US had a number of highly developed and specialised regional clusters throughout the country; the same type of specialisation is much less obvious in Europe.
62. There are, however, certain limits to this type of 'offshoring' and migration of such services jobs towards the developing countries. Tastes and needs change, markets are fickle, hence there will always be the necessity for a certain local presence, close to consumers. It may be difficult to service such consumers and markets in the EU from Bombay.
63. Spain as a peripheral country attracted a relatively large number of foreign investors.

64. Does this mean that there is a need for a more active cohesion policy in the EU? 'Not necessarily. We still lack evidence on whether existing cohesion policies have been effective in reducing growing regional disparities in the EU' (Midelfart et al., 2003, p. 865).
65. Federal countries such as the US, Canada, Australia or Switzerland have different regional policies from that of the EU.
66. This is the 'catch-all article'.
67. Eurostat (2003), 'How rich are Europe's regions', *Statistics in Focus*, Theme 1 – 06/2003.
68. The European Coal and Steel Community has exerted its own influence on regions that are involved in the coal, iron and steel industries. Loans were given for the retraining and redeployment of workers, as well as for a modernisation of the industry. The EIB has been giving loans for projects in the less-developed regions of the EU.
69. Britain changed its regional policy in 1980. The most important features of this alteration were the following three elements. First, the regional disequilibria started to be seen as a *regional*, rather than a *national* issue, one that had to be resolved by indigenous development rather than by a transfer of resources and business activity from elsewhere. Second, direct subsidies for employment were replaced by a system of regional aid programmes based on employment creation through improved competitiveness. Third, the policy became increasingly reliant on employment cost-effectiveness (Wren, 1990, p. 62).
70. Regional support started to include producer services and incentives for the introduction of innovations such as licences or patents.
71. The Mezzogiorno (a synonym for the southern geographical region relative to the central region of a country) is the area south of Lazio. The population of this region is 21 million.
72. Regional policy in Ireland, another formerly backward EU country, was consistent for over four decades. The policy emphasised the role of markets, selected electronics and pharmaceuticals for special treatment, invested in infrastructure (telecommunications) and more than anything else invested in education (creation of human capital).
73. A very similar situation developed in Germany following the *Anschluss* of 1989. During the first decade after reunification, a 'total net resource transfer of about 750 billion € has been transferred to the east' (Sinn and Westermann, 2000, p. 7).
74. *Business Europe*, 31 May 1991, p. 3.
75. The list is based on data for 1996; if available, the number of related firms in the cluster is given in square brackets; and a bigger city in the vicinity or province is given in round brackets. Source: 'Quanti sono i distretti industriali in Italia?', *Newsletter Club dei Distretti Industriali* no. 9, November 1998, Club dei distretti industriali Prato, p. 9.

> Does the eagle mount up at your command,
> And make its nest on high?
> Job 39:37

9 Capital Mobility

1. Introduction

The spatial distribution of production is shaped not only by actions of national firms and governments, but also by decisions, customs and practices by foreign-owned (controlled) firms, as well as organisations that impose international rules. Some preferential trading or integration agreements such as common markets permit the free movement of factors among member countries on the condition that factors originating in partner countries are not subjected to discrimination. The promotion of geographical and sectoral factor mobility results in more efficient allocation of resources from the group's standpoint. These improvements in the locational advantages of the group for business are due to the free internal factor flow from low- to high-productivity locations and businesses within the common market. In this situation, factors respond to signals that include demand, higher productivity and higher returns within the group.

This chapter is devoted to the mobility of capital and is structured as follows. Section 2 considers the relation between factor mobility and trade. The following sections examine the principal issues related to FDI (Section 3), TNCs (Section 4), intervention (Section 5), and TNCs and international economic integration (Section 6). Section 7 discusses the nature, evolution and significance of flows in the EU, and Section 8 concludes.

2. Factor mobility and trade

Let us start by assuming a model that consists of two countries A and B, two final goods X and Y and two factors of production K and L. Suppose further that factor mobility is perfect within each country, but prohibited between countries. If there are no barriers to trade and no distortions, if technology is the same and freely accessible to both countries, if production functions are completely homogeneous, if both goods are produced in both countries and isoquants intersect only once (there is no factor intensity reversal), then free trade in goods will in theory equalise both relative prices in goods and relative factor prices and their returns in each country.[1] This stringent situation is illustrated in Figure 9.1.

In the figure X_a represents the unit isocost line (the combination of factors which keeps output constant) for good X in country A (production

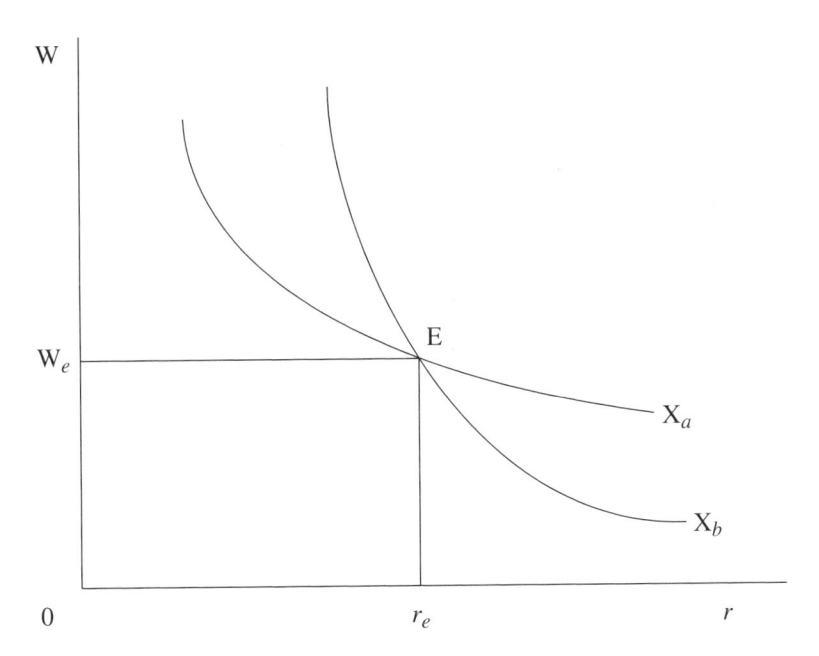

Figure 9.1 Equalisation of factor prices

of which is relatively labour 'intensive'), while X_b describes the same cost line for good X in country B, where its production is relatively capital 'intensive'. Equilibrium occurs at point E, where factor prices are equalised through trade at levels $0r_e$ for capital and $0W_e$ for labour. In this model trade is a substitute for factor mobility.

The exclusion of balance of payments adjustments from comparative statistics implies that the adjustment process between the two distant points in time has worked well and that the balance is in equilibrium. However, in reality, such a process may last for up to a generation (recall the eastern enlargement of the EU). Thus, a static model, which usually neglects the adjustment process, can hardly be justified. If capital accumulation, economies of scale and economic growth are included in the consideration, they produce different results in the long term from the straightforward static model.

Free international trade in goods and factor movements are prevented by the existence of various barriers. In this framework, according to one view, commodity movements are still a substitute for factor movements. An increase in trade restrictions stimulates factor movements, while an increase in barriers to international factor mobility enhances trade in goods (Mundell, 1957, p. 321).

So far it has been assumed that technology is the same in both countries. This is, however, not always the case. Differences in technologies among countries enhances, rather than reduces, the opportunities for international capital mobility. Some developing countries export raw materials in return for FDI, which enables them to produce and later export manufactured goods (Purvis, 1972, p. 991). When technologies differ, factor mobility may increase the volume of trade, rather than reduce it. Factor mobility and commodity movements may act in this case as complements.

If factor mobility leads to a reduction in the volume of trade in goods, then factor movements and trade in goods are substitutes. This is the case when there are differences in the prices of goods between countries. If labour moves from country A, where good X is dearer, to country B, where this good is cheaper, this decreases the demand for and price of good X in country A and increases demand and price in country B until the two prices are equalised. If relative differences in factor endowments are not the only basis for trade, international mobility of factors and trade may stimulate each other and become supplements (Markusen and Melvin, 1984).

The factor price equalisation theorem anticipates that free trade will have as its consequence parity of wage levels among countries. This need not always be the case. Migration is a necessary condition for the equalisation of wages if the majority of labour in both high-wage countries and low-wage countries is employed in the production of non-tradable goods. In this case, free trade is not a sufficient condition for the equalisation of wages between the countries involved.

Substitutability between trade in goods and mobility of factors (the Heckscher–Ohlin model) may be the exception, rather than the rule. If countries are quite different in relative factor endowments and with weak economies of scale, then individuals who draw their income from factors that are relatively scarce end up worse off as a result of trade. If countries are similar and trade is mostly motivated by economies of scale (intra-industry trade), then one might expect to find that even scarce factors gain (Krugman, 1990a, p. 80).

If there is a free geographical mobility of factors, then countries become relatively well endowed with the factors used 'intensively' in the production of export goods (Markusen, 1983, p. 355). International mobility of factors and trade are often taken to be complements, rather than substitutes. A high mobility and concentration of factors (designers in northern Italy, chemical engineers in Basle, financial experts in London and New York or computer scientists in California or Boston) will create an additional comparative advantage, which will, in turn, enhance trade. 'Globalisation' of international business and the integrated international operations of TNCs contribute to this situation. This is most obvious in the EU, where an expansion of intra-group FDI and TNC operations has accompanied a high level of intra-group trade.

In the manufacturing industry, access to foreign markets by horizontal TNCs is a choice between exporting and investing abroad. The decision depends on factors such as economies of scale, the cost of the project, trade costs, trade regime, competition and the like. In this case, trade and FDI (foreign production) are substitutes. Vertical TNCs, by contrast, aim to profit from location of plants in different countries. Depending on local circumstances, these affiliates specialise in different phases in the production process and send (sell) each other inputs, components and final goods. In this case, FDI and trade are complements. In services, however, trade and FDI can be expected to have a complementary dimension. A foreign presence (right of establishment) in the services sector is normally expected to increase trade.

If FDI is a response to trade barriers, then FDI acts in a trade-replacing way. If, however, FDI is an efficiency-seeking investment (developing natural resources), then it operates in a trade-promoting way. In any case, there is some evidence that FDI has increased trade in the EU (van Aarle, 1996, p. 137). An extensive survey of the impact of the Single Market Programme on FDI in the EU found strong evidence that FDI and trade are complementary (European Commission, 1998, p. 1).

Theoretical considerations about substitutability or complementarity between trade and FDI lost their significance in the light of new considerations about the spatial location of firms. This is reinforced by the fact that high-technology exports are the principal foreign exchange earners for the developing countries.[2] The issue is: what are the underlining conditions that make specific locations advantageous for particular business activities? This holds for both domestic and foreign firms.

3. Foreign direct investment

GENERAL CONSIDERATIONS

The theory of preferential trade explores the effect of integration on the location of production, structure of trade and changes in welfare. Little attention has been devoted to the geographical origin of ownership of firms. This gap is bridged by the theory of FDI, which studies locational advantages for investment in different countries, competitive advantages of firms that originate in different countries, as well as the interaction between firms, local natural and government resources and capabilities in the contexts of spatial distribution of economic activities and economic integration.

Entrepreneurs view a country's preferential trading and integration arrangements as long-term economic indicators and firm facts, unlike changes in prices, which may reflect only a temporary situation on the market. Entrepreneurs may form expectations with a higher degree of certainty. Hence, TNCs may locate a part of their production in such an expanding area and increase FDI by the creation of 'tariff factories'.

The creation of tariff factories within an integrated area is a strategy that TNCs pursue, not to take advantage of their efficiency or to employ a foreign resource (resource efficiency), but rather to benefit from (or avoid) the shield provided by the common external tariff and NTBs. This could be one of the reasons why Japanese TNCs were eager to establish a presence in the EU prior to 1993 and the full implementation of the Single European Market. They wanted to become EU residents and thus circumvent the potential threat of a 'Fortress Europe'. In addition to such an *investment creation effect* (a strategic response of foreign firms to potential trade diversion), new prospects for improved business without tariffs and quotas on trade within the (protected) region may prompt local firms to rearrange production facilities within the group. This may produce the *investment diversion effect*. This strategic response of firms to trade creation may have as its effect an increase in FDI in some countries in the group and a decrease in FDI in others.

Foreign direct investment reflects the goal of an entrepreneur from country A to acquire a lasting interest (including management) in an asset in country B. FDI is much more than plain capital. FDI includes technological, managerial, marketing and control knowledge and capabilities; it also includes a network of contacts that may be available only internally through TNCs. One should bear in mind that more than a third of world trade today is within the same company.[3] In principle, FDI asks for freedom of establishment and, if possible, national treatment in foreign markets. This distinct type of international capital flow has a strong risk-taking and, often, industry-specific dimension. FDI is often the result of decisions by TNCs. Therefore, FDI may be a part of a proxy for the investment and location activities of TNCs (bearing in mind that TNCs may control operations abroad simply by issuing licences).

Capital moves among countries in the form of portfolio and direct investment. Portfolio investment is most often simply a short-term movement of claims that is speculative in nature. The main objectives include an increase in the value of assets and relative safety. This type of capital mobility may be prompted by differences in interest rates. The recipient country will probably not wish to use these funds for investment in fixed assets and structures that must be repaid in the long term, so these movements of capital may be seen by the recipient country as hot, unstable and 'bad'. Volatility of portfolio investment complicates their analysis. The large number of portfolio investments, made in many cases by brokers, obscures who is doing what and why.

INTERNATIONAL FIRM: THEORY

Ownership and control of the firm was neglected in the analysis by an implicit assumption that these do not matter or by the supposition that all assets and structures are domestically owned. The presence of TNCs increases the mobility of capital, expands the availability of information and new products, widens marketing and trade networks, changes competition structure and alters substitution of labour for capital. A TNC has different locational considerations from a comparable national firm engaged in the same type and scale of activity. A tendency is that strictly national firms expand where they already are, while TNCs enter where they think they may profit from access to the largest and growing market, availability and favourable costs of inputs, transport and/or taxes and subsidies. TNCs have 'organisational capital', that is, a common set of rules, practices, routines and values, which help them overcome various barriers through an internal network while operating in different geographical, social, legal and other environments.

There are at least eight basic theories that explain certain aspects of why firms engage in trans-border business activities and become TNCs.[4] First, the motivation to control foreign firms may not come from the need to employ assets and structures in a prudent way in foreign markets, but rather to remove competition from other enterprises. Hymer (1976) advocated such a *market-power* approach by TNCs. Reuber (1973, pp. 133–4) argued in a similar vein that long-term strategic factors for FDI include the desire to eliminate competitors from foreign markets, to be within a protected foreign market, to secure a low-cost source of supply and to lock in the target country to a specific technology for a long time. Such a longer-term strategic view overshadows possible short-run variations in the profitability of FDI.

The problem with this argument is that most of the TNCs (measured by their number) are small and medium sized. There were about 64 000 parent firms with about 870 000 foreign affiliates in 2002 (UNCTAD, 2003, p. 23). This shows that to become a TNC, a firm need not be a monopolist or an oligopolist at home and try to exercise that power abroad. If there is strong competition in the market for differentiated goods and services and if there is a high degree of substitutability between products (perfumes, soaps, watches, clothing, vehicles, passenger air transport on certain lines, to mention just a few examples), then the market-power argument for the transnationalisation of business is weakened.

Second, while the market-power model excludes potential rivals from competition, the *internalisation* theory holds that an arm's-length relation among individual firms is in some cases less efficient (for example, trade in technology) than an intra-firm cooperative association. Profits may be maximised by means of an efficient and friendly intra-firm trade in intermediaries that eliminates sometimes excessive transaction costs (middlemen, exchange rate risk, infringement of intellectual property rights, bargaining costs) which occur when the business is conducted through the market. In these circumstances a hierarchical organisation (an enterprise) may better reward parties in the longer term, as well as curb bargaining and incentives to cheat, than markets and external contractors. The share of intra-firm exports by parent firms in the total exports of their home country was 31 per cent in the case of the US TNCs in 1998, while the same share in the case of Japanese TNCs was 38 per cent (UNCTAD, 2002, p. 153). In addition, more than a third of world trade in 2003 was within the same company.[5] Payments of about 80 per cent of fees and royalties for technology 'take place between parent firms and their foreign affiliates' (UNCTAD, 1997, p. 20). This is an indication that TNCs play a key role in disseminating technology around the world (at least in the locations where they operate).

The importance and volume of intra-firm trade and various special alliances among firms reveal the fact that markets are (becoming) incomplete. As such, they may be hard to put in order according to free trade principles and objectives. Therefore, absolute advantages of a country or specific locations within it (clusters) may dominate and outweigh comparative advantages in their relevance for the location of production, FDI and, consequently, structure, volume and direction of trade.

While Reuber and Hymer conceive TNCs as vehicles for reaping monopoly profits and for the internalisation of pecuniary externalities, the internalisation model looks at TNCs as a mode of business organisation that reduces transaction costs and internalises non-pecuniary externalities. This model of FDI may be convincing in some cases, but it may not explain the structure and location of all FDI flows. In addition to the internalisation possibilities, there ought to be ownership-specific and locational advantages for FDI.

Excessive internalisation leads firms to diversify into unrelated technologies. This may provoke an increase in costs of production as they venture into businesses that are outside their core competence. Mastering new technologies diverts time, efforts and funds from further specialisation in the core business competence. Therefore, buying from other specialised firms (outsourcing), rather than producing certain goods and services in-house may be the preferred course of business action on the way to achieve and maintain greater degree competitiveness.

Markusen (1984) tried to integrate TNCs into general equilibrium trade models and locational patterns of firms that horizontally or vertically integrate across national borders. Intangible assets, as sources of multiplant economies, are often firm, rather than plant specific. They include organisation, management, control, R&D, advertising, marketing and distribution. Many of these activities are centralised (finance) and present a 'joint input' across all production units. A TNC avoids replication of these activities that would be necessary if these units operated as independent national firms. This brings a 'technical' advantage to a TNC. However, if these advantages are transformed into market power, then the welfare effects of TNCs may not be clear. In any case, a firm will operate in two or more countries and become a TNC if trade costs are sufficiently high relative to the disadvantage that comes from fixed costs that are linked to the operation of two or more plants (Markusen and Venables, 2000, p. 221).

Third, the *eclectic paradigm* (Dunning, 1988, pp. 42–5; 1999, pp. 1–3) explained the trans-border business activities of TNCs as a joint mix and interaction of three independent factors:

- In order to locate production abroad and be commercially successful, a TNC must have or control internationally mobile income-generating *ownership*-specific (O) advantages, assets, structures, capabilities or skills. These firm-specific advantages include tangible

and intangible advantages such as better technology, brand name, access to wide markets, monopoly, competence of managers, ability to innovate and so on that are superior to the ones that are available to local firms (including other TNCs) in the potential target country. This is to say that a firm needs to operate either on a different production function from other firms or that it operates at a different point on the same function.
- *Locational* (L) (non-mobile) advantages refer to the comparative or location-specific advantages of the target country. They refer both to the geographical distribution of resources and to those created by the government.[6]
- There must be opportunities for the *internalisation* (I) of ownership-specific advantages (management and quality control, protection of property rights, avoidance of uncertainty of buyers and so on). It should be in the interest of the firm to transfer these advantages abroad within its own organisation, rather than sell the right to use these advantages to other firms located in the country of intended production. Fixed exchange rates or a single international currency provide a degree of stability necessary for longer-term business planning with a high degree of confidence.

The eclectic paradigm claims that the exact mix of the OLI factors facing each potential investor depends on the specific context. If a firm possesses or controls ownership-specific advantages, then it may use licensing in order to penetrate foreign markets. If it has both ownership-specific and internalisation advantages, such an enterprise may use exports as a means of entering foreign markets. Only when a firm is able to take *simultaneous* return of OLI advantages, will it employ FDI as a means of locating and operating in foreign markets. This model, however, does not apply to diversified and vertically integrated TNCs (Caves, 1996, p. 5).

Fourth, the *product-cycle* model reasons that mature (and, perhaps, environmentally unsound) lines of production of goods (there is no explicit reference to services) are passed on to developing countries (Posner, 1961; Vernon, 1966). Such spatial reallocation of production is based on the experience of Anglo-Saxon firms and depends a lot on low factor costs.

The product-cycle argument as the major explanation for the location of business abroad and with a rather vague timetable for this spread of production cannot pass the test of recent developments. Asian firms, however, do not replicate this pattern of location of production abroad on a large scale. The Japanese auto companies invested at home and in the US and Europe at about the same time for a similar type of production. There is a heavy concentration of FDI in developed countries (65 per cent of the world stock), while the majority of developing countries are relatively neglected in FDI flows. In addition, countries start investing abroad at a much earlier stage of their development than before. The newly industrialised countries and many other developing countries are already investing abroad. In many cases these investments are in the developed world. Such developments may be prompted by the desire:

- to be present in the developed countries' markets (closer to wealthy customers);
- to be near the source and cluster of the principal technological developments in manufacturing, distribution, management and already existing infrastructure (to have a foreign 'listening and learning post');
- to participate in R&D programmes;
- to avoid the dangers of protectionism in target countries;
- to win public contracts; and
- to exploit the strength of the host country's domestic currency.

Fifth is the *follow-your-leader* hypothesis. Oligopolists are risk minimisers. They would like to protect their own market position and avoid destructive competition. Therefore, they typically try to minimise risk and follow each other into the new (foreign) markets (Knickerboker, 1973, p. 100). A study of timing of FDI by US TNCs in manufacturing seems to support this snowball or 'herd behaviour'. The Japanese TNCs in automotive and consumer electronic industries were 'following their domestic leader' when they located their manufacturing facilities in the EU and the US during the 1980s and 1990s. This type of investment location behaviour is quite relevant during the opening phases of new markets. If a TNC has no previous experience in a certain new market, then the actions of competitors in that market may be quite informative. Examples of this 'herd behaviour' are the actions of TNCs in China and to an extent in Eastern Europe from the start of the 1990s.[7] In addition, mergers and acquisitions[8] 'mania' of the 1990s in the EU and the US show how asset seeking by one TNC may be followed by others.

Such 'catastrophic' relocation of industry as a result of the predicted behaviour of rival firms is one feature of the core–periphery model, one of the key new economic geography models. It is postulated that when trade costs lie in a certain range all firms in an industry may relocate *en masse*, although this would not be the optimum strategy for an individual firm were it to relocate on its own.

While relatively low labour costs in China could have been the reason to start to locate certain operations there at the start of the 1990s, things have changed. It was reported that China's Pearl River delta attracted $1 billion of FDI a month. Microwave ovens are produced in Shunde. Just one of its giant factories produces 40 per cent of the global output of microwave ovens. Shenzhen produces 70 per cent of the world's photocopiers and 80 per cent of the artificial Christmas trees. Dongguan has 80 000 people working in a single factory making running shoes for the world's teenagers. Flextronics is a Singapore electronics maker that produces for Microsoft, Motorola, Dell and Sony. The manager of its Chinese plant in Doumen said that 'It is a myth that companies are coming here just for the cheap labour. It is the efficiency of the supply chain that drives them here as more and more of worldwide demand is consolidated in this area'.[9]

Sixth, the competitive international industry model for the location of business abroad refers to oligopolistic competition and rivalry within the same industry. This is basically *exchange of threats* (tit-for-tat strategy) to business moves by foreign rivals (Graham, 1978). Large firms keep an eye on the actions of their rivals, that is, they act strategically (pay attention to the likely reaction of their competitors to their own actions). What Texaco does in Europe, Shell will (try to) do in the US. Competition is not 'cut-throat', but rather 'stable' among several oligopolies. Other examples of this rivalistic trend include FDI in the manufacturing of cars and tyres or supply of services such as hotels and advertising. SMEs such as gas stations in the middle of nowhere may act independently in their business. However, SMEs in a cluster keep a vigilant eye on the actions of the competitors.

Seventh, is the *diversification of portfolios* model of foreign investment (Brainard and Tobin, 1992). This approach considers uncertainty. Fluctuations in the rates of return on capital invested in various countries introduce an element of risk. This inconvenience may be reduced by a diversification of portfolios.

Firm-specific assets and exchange rates may be the eighth basic reason for FDI. Suppose that there is a target firm in the US with an innovation (a firm-specific asset) that can make the acquiring firm's assembly line 10 per cent more productive (10 per cent more output for the same level of input). If a US firm wants to acquire the target firm, then a change in the rate of exchange makes no difference as its gains will continue to be denominated in dollars. If, however, the acquiring firm is in Japan, the gains will be denominated in yen. A depreciation of the dollar relative to the yen will increase the Japanese firm's reservation bid, while the US firm's bid would remain unchanged. It is more likely that the Japanese firm would acquire the asset in this situation.

The actual evidence about this taking place is rather mixed. The price of US assets need not matter, only the rate of return: when the dollar depreciates, both the price of a US asset and its rate of return will go down. Blonigen (1997) found a connection between exchange rate movements (weak dollar) and higher levels of Japanese acquisitions in the US in industries which involve firm-specific assets. This refers to the Japanese acquisitions in the US during 1975–92. However, in their analysis of relations between exchange rate movements and FDI flows from the US to 20 countries during the 1980–95 period, Chakrabarti and Scholnick (2002, p. 19) found that devaluation in the preceding year does not have a robust positive impact on FDI flows.

In addition to the above basic theories on why firms locate abroad, three other dimensions are relevant for coming to grips with the issue: cost minimisation, available technology and taxes. First, Kravis and Lipsey (1982, p. 222) argued that the location of foreign affiliates of TNCs is decided on the basis of *cost minimisation*. However, the intensity of this determinant varies from industry to industry. Second, Yamawaki (1993, pp. 19–20) did not dispute the importance of a relative difference in factor costs, but the *availability of technology* in the target country is an additional and equally important factor for the location of Japanese FDI in the EU. A Japanese TNC from a certain industry decided to locate in the EU country which has a certain advantage over other EU countries in the same industry. Britain is preferred by the Japanese TNCs for the location of production of cars and electrical/electronic equipment, Germany for precision instruments and machinery, Belgium for stone, glass and clay products, while TNCs from the chemical industry prefer Germany, the Netherlands, Spain and France (Yamawaki, 1993).

Third come differences in *taxes and fiscal incentives*. While there are many 'tax havens' that attract quite a few firms (mainly from finance) and many countries offer different fiscal incentives to firms in order to attract them, is this enough by itself? Are tax incentives a bit more than 'corporate welfare'? Should countries enter into a 'locations tournament'? Politicians usually use only three reasons to justify a local incentive programme: jobs, jobs and jobs!

The importance, influence and evidence of taxes on the location of firms is still controversial. Investors may avoid locations that offer financial incentives as evidence of a region's non-competitiveness. Limited survey information reveals that fiscal variables matter little regarding business location. However, business executives often lobby hard for fiscal incentives. One can understand that attitude as firms have no incentives to forgo such direct and indirect subsidies, even if they do not affect location decisions to a significant degree (Wasylenko, 1991). This was a confirmation of the results of an earlier study by Carlton which found that tax variables usually have a 'very small and always statistically insignificant' (Carlton, 1983, p. 447) impact on locational choice.

Mody and Srinivasan (1998, p. 795) found that corporate tax rates do not have a major influence over FDI either by the American or by the Japanese

TNCs. In another case in France, Crozet et al. (2004), found that foreign investors were not sensitive to investment incentives. In addition, French and EU regional policy investment incentives did not have any significant impact.

A study of the effect of the elimination of a tax on paper for printing news (which accounted for about half of the production costs) in the Netherlands in 1869 revealed that this assisted in the creation of new newspaper firms. Two-thirds of these new entries took place in cities that already had other newspapers, while the other third occurred in provincial towns that previously did not have a newspaper. Even though a tax cut played an important role, the principal reason for this type of location of firms was the size and growth of the local market. Hence, there is no basic difference in the rationale for a firm's location between a century and a half ago and now (Pfann and van Kranenburg, 2002).

Although many surveys give state and local taxes a low ranking on the list of location determinants, many locations in various states within the US can be close substitutes. In such a situation, even a small difference in production costs can play a key role for a particular decision about the location of business (Bartik, 1991, p. 8). As far as FDI by American firms was concerned during 1984–92, they have become more sensitive to differences in host-country taxes towards the end of that period (Altshuler et al. 1998).

This continues to be a controversial research area. There is a lack of consensus as the results of academic literature on the issue are still mixed. High(er) taxes may be preferred to low taxes by firms if the tax proceeds are used to finance local services useful for the business sector. In any case, high-quality infrastructure is preferred by foreign investors to tax incentives. Transfer pricing and tax deductions in the home country provide other ways to minimise the tax burden on profit (Wheeler and Mody, 1992, pp. 71–2).

'The economic desirability of locational incentives is not clear, particularly if they detract from building competitive capabilities and encourage bidding wars' (UNCTAD, 2003, p. 126). Tax incentives for investment, in particular FDI, are conventionally not recommended. This is also the stance taken by the World Bank, the IMF and international bodies that advise on tax matters. Tax incentives are bad in theory and bad in practice. They are bad in theory as they introduce distortions. Investment decisions by entrepreneurs are made differently from the case without the special tax stimulus. They are bad in practice because of their ineffectiveness: tax considerations are rarely the principal determinant for the location of FDI. They are also inefficient as their cost may well exceed any benefit that they may bring.[10] They are difficult to administer as there is a lack of transparency and they are subject to abuse and corruption[11] by the 'old boys' club'. Finally, they are not equitable as they benefit certain investors, but not others (Easson, 2001, p. 266). If various incentives are offered only to foreigners, then there is a possibility for 'round-tripping'. Domestic capital leaves the country in order to return in the guise of FDI, in order to profit from better treatment in the home country. This has been the case in Russia from the early 1990s.

In spite of the above arguments, tax considerations have recently become an increasingly important factor for the location of investment. Why is this so? Why are tax incentives becoming more and more generous? Tax considerations do not feature highly in the initial decision by TNCs to invest abroad. However, once this decision is reached, differences in taxes between regions of the target country or differences among countries tend to play a significant role.

More than 100 countries worldwide offer tax incentives for FDI. The type of incentive that is most commonly employed is the tax holiday, which is the worst in almost every respect. Administration of these incentives is amazingly complicated; there are opportunities for abuse and avoidance; they may attract only short-term FDI to benefit from the tax holiday while it lasts; and (particularly in the developing countries) they are often beyond the capacity of tax administration to manage and monitor. Therefore it is not surprising that tax incentives are often inefficient and ineffective (Easson, 2001, p. 375; Tanzi and Zee, 2000, p. 316).

The optimal solution to the issue of these enticements may include an international agreement among countries to eliminate all tax incentives for investment (or to limit them in a uniform way). In the absence of such an agreement, and according to the prisoner's dilemma concept, few countries would risk acting in this way unilaterally.

In the situation with market imperfections there is no single theory or model that can provide a completely satisfactory answer to each issue related to trans-border investment activities of the firms. Motives for foreign production are different and they change over time in response to changes in the market, technology, needs, tastes, sophistication, management strategy, actions of rivals and economic policy. However, if taken together, these theories may provide useful elements for an understanding of the issue.

GLOBALISATION

Liberalisation in the national and international economy is a policy choice of *governments*, primarily in the developed world. It is linked with privatisation and downsizing of the activities of the public sector and the expansion of the activities of the private sector. *Globalisation* of the economy and production is a fact. It is the outcome of the behaviour of *firms* (TNCs), their organisation, changing technology in production and distribution, control and finance, as well as economies of scale and takeovers. In part, it is also the consequence of a change in the behaviour of consumers (fickleness and declining loyalty to national producers and certain national products)[12] and liberalisation of national and international economies for trade, production and finance.

As a process primarily driven by technology and actions of TNCs (power is shifted from states to firms),[13] globalisation lacks two important components: transparency and accountability.[14] This process deals with the change in the geography of (integrated international) production and consumption as it reduces the importance of proximity to inputs or markets. It widens boundaries and deepens space for the geographical location of production and consumption because of the declining costs of getting goods and services to the market. A rapid expansion of FDI is the key component of this process. Capital market liberalisation and increased capital mobility have radically reduced the influence of governments in the monetary sphere. However, governments have gained increased control in other areas. For example, computers and information technology have greatly increased potential for data collection and processing, and consequently control over firms and citizens which is relevant for tax and other purposes.

Regionalisation is increasing in importance in the world economy. This was exemplified in the inability of 135 member countries of the WTO to agree even on the agenda for the 'Millennium Round' of global trade negotiations that took place in Seattle in 1999. Well-organised, vociferous and strong worldwide protests by environmentalists, farmers, enemies of genetically modified food and big business, labour unions, anti-capitalists and animal rights activists exacerbated the problems of that meeting and many others that followed. Therefore, the creation of integrated global economic policies is likely to be a very hard task for quite some time to come. It seems that the regional approach to economic problems will call the tune at least in the medium term.

The rapid international expansion of TNCs made them the most visible feature of globalisation. Being foreign, making sometimes visible and highly publicised mistakes and often being big, TNCs are easy targets for NGOs which can run successful campaigns to disgrace a mighty TNC. A number of NGOs are relatively small players who would like to 'punch above their weight' because of the urgency of the matter.[15] Examples of their campaigns include valid targets such as land mines, HIV/Aids or poverty and third world debt. NGOs increased public awareness and pushed through agreements on the control of 'greenhouse gases' in the United Nations Conference on Environment and Development, the 'Earth

Summit' in Rio de Janeiro in 1992. They also helped in torpedoing the Multilateral Agreement on Investment in 1998 and created much ado in Seattle in 1999 (and many other subsequent meetings), which contributed to the failure to start a new WTO round of global trade negotiations before the meeting in Doha in 2001. No matter how justified the reasons for the campaign, these 'civil society' protestors against global capitalism demonstrated that the tide of globalisation could be checked and even turned back.

The anti-globalisation movement is moving beyond its radical, protest-driven even anarchist legacy (which might have worked against it) towards a movement with a concrete agenda. Rock-throwers, like the Luddites (1811–16) who destroyed factory machines, were ineffectual and irrelevant in the long term. The strategy of the anti-globalisation movement is to address four weaknesses of the globalisation process: a lack of legitimacy, a lack of accountability, a lack of organisation and a lack of transparency. The idea is not to be against globalisation, but rather to put limits on it. The question is what kind of 'globalisation' is desirable and how to achieve it? The World Social Forum (Porto Alegre, Brazil) has made valiant attempts to put hundreds of disparate groups under one umbrella. The forum recommends a range of activities from limiting the power of TNCs to adding new responsibilities and regulatory powers to the established international organisations such as the UN, the International Labour Office and the World Health Organisation. In this way the anti-globalisation movement may be able to gain more leverage on the national and international scene.

The anti-globalisation campaigners have shown that governments are not powerless. The authorities can just as easily dismantle old trade and investment barriers, as they can introduce new ones. New technology, in particular the Internet, telecommunications, computing and data processing can offer some of the greatest economic opportunities ever for increasing living standards in all countries. Governments and the national elite in all countries (due to incompetence or indifference) have failed to explain this. However, the process needs to be coupled with balanced policies both in the rich and the poor world. Even though global economic integration may be the best end point for the future of the world economy for the proponents of globalisation, it is more likely that other outcomes may be chosen in the future. Globalisation may be favourable for economic efficiency, but it can be harmful for social goals.

Apart from a partial integration of international production, globalisation brings risks and disruptions. Volatile capital flows, speculative attacks on currencies, financial crises and unpredictable reallocation of jobs are obvious examples of the increased economic and social vulnerability of many countries, in particular in the developing world. To wrap up the issue,

Henry Kissinger called globalisation 'another name for the dominant role of the United States'.[16]

The vogue term 'globalisation' has not yet been well or clearly defined. Hence, this fuzzy, but powerful metaphor is overused, often abused and very often misleading. For some it basically refers to the choices and strategies, as well as the shape, extent, direction and significance of activities of TNCs. 'Globalisation has been defined in business schools as the production and distribution of products and services of a homogeneous type and quality on a worldwide basis. Simply put – providing the same output to countries everywhere' (Rugman and Hodgetts, 2001, p. 333).[17] 'Thanks' to al-Qaida many realised that globalisation goes well beyond links that bind TNCs, producers, traders and bankers. For others, globalisation is linked with and invigorated by new technologies in communications and information processing. It is a sum of techniques that are at the disposal of private players and states. Yet for others, globalisation is an incentive to the reform process in economic strategy in many countries as outward-looking economic models replace inward-looking and TNC-hostile economic policy approaches. Others look at globalisation as a process that alters interactions among agents across space; still others equate globalisation with economic integration.[18]

The Internet symbolises the borderlessness brought about by globalisation. Physical presence in a specific location is not necessary. In the invisible continent of cyberspace, the users are 'everywhere and nowhere' at once. They use the Internet as a meeting place, a market, a distribution device, a library, and the like. This alters the geography of production, at least for certain products. People spend more time working at home or 'on the road', hence certain office space (in congested cities) is vacated. However, one does not need to give an absolute value to globalisation. In spite of this process, localisation and clusters still matter. Firms that went furthest in 'globalisation' report that face-to-face contact is essential for the smooth organisation of business within the firm and marketing outside it. In addition, just try telling someone who wants to enter the EU or North America from outside that this is a 'borderless world'. Borders continue to matter a great deal as people from different locations are prevented from crossing them without a cumbersome, costly and uncertain administrative procedure.

The Internet is based on communication and data that are located in computers that exist in the real world. Initially, this parallel universe of pure data existed everywhere freely in a 'lawless' world. The Internet was breaking down barriers and eliminating physical distance. However, computers exist in an identifiable geographical space. If they can be located together with their users, then they are subject to law. Now governments are increasing their control over cyberspace. For example, France prohibited the sale of Nazi memorabilia on the Internet; Iran banned access to immoral or anti-Iranian information; while South Korea prohibited access to gambling websites. There is also increased international police cooperation in combating child pornography, or computer viruses and hackers that attack major computer networks. Hence, borders are being created in the Internet. Even though the economic impact of geographical distance is being reduced, the local economic geography is retaining its strength.

The imposition of 'global' standards may have its justification for relatively new and standardised goods and services such as copiers, fax machines, computers, mobile phones or better medicines, otherwise communication and exchange of information might be difficult and costly. However, the imposition of such standards for traditional goods (for example, food) with the exception of health and the environment may not be easily justified. If needs and tastes for certain types of food are strongly locally specific (even the thickness of pizzas throughout Italy differs) why should one favour or impose global Pizza Hut type standards?

John Gray of the London School of Economics claimed that people are losing faith in globalisation, and that:

> [L]ed by the United States, the world's richest states have acted on the assumption that people everywhere want to live as they do. As a result, they failed to recognise the deadly mixture of emotions – cultural resentment, the sense of injustice and a genuine rejection of western modernity – that lies behind the attacks on New York and Washington . . . The ideal of a universal civilisation is a recipe for unending conflict, and it is time it was given up.[19]

It is not that the people who live outside the Western world cannot adopt a liberal attitude, rather that there are social, cultural and institutional barriers that prevent a fast transfer of Western values, culture and institutions elsewhere. One must also consider the choices of the 'recipients'. Do they really want and need what is exported or 'imposed' on them?

There was a faulty premise and a vision that all people are culturally homogeneous in that they think, act and most of all, shop alike (or like Americans); that there exist institutional bases for political democracy; and that citizens are aware of their duties to one another and to the state. Checks and balances are mixed; there is mistrust *vis-à-vis* the government and state administration which has is often deeply rooted in dictatorship, authoritarian and bureaucratic conduct, as well as in corruption. Without a very long-term reform, education and trust-building, any attempt to transfer 'global' (social) standards quickly would fail, and fail miserably, in many parts of the world. It should not be forgotten that 'it took 400 years for England to develop from that stage to its present one. To do the same elsewhere in half the time of 200 years would be a tremendous achievement;

to aspire to do it in 25 or 50 years may be to court disaster' (Lipsey, 1992a, p. 755).[20] Local differences tend be stubborn. Until the world becomes homogeneous, adaptation towards local preferences and capabilities will be necessary. Globalisation problems, which appeared in the form of concerns over progress in the WTO or in the Multilateral Agreement on Investment illustrate signals of regional (triad: US, EU and Japan) or even local power.

It is true that the greatest and matchless advantage of free markets and globalisation is that they give free choice to consumers. Economic interactions are voluntary, so consumers are free to choose, for example, between local and global goods and services. But, this is only on the surface. If global products are advertised aggressively by large TNCs, including campaigns that are often beyond the financial capacity of local competitors, then the 'free choice' by consumers may be restricted and the local producers (and certain dimensions of the local culture) may be damaged. Critics of such unchecked global capital movements say that global TNCs put 'profits before people'. When these TNCs 'start talking about how they will no longer put profits first, people (rightly) think they are lying'.[21]

Another cost of globalisation can be found in the examples of countries such as Mexico, Thailand, Indonesia, South Korea and Russia, which suffered financial crises in the second half of the 1990s. Without the exposure to global capital markets, the crises would not have developed as they did. Critics of this view argue that these countries would not have experienced such rapid development prior to the crisis without such exposure. In any case, one ought to be fair and observe that certain 'global tendencies' were already present, well before the current wave of globalisation. For example, there was (for whatever reason and by whatever means) a spread of certain European languages outside Europe; a spread of Islam in Africa, Asia and Europe; and a spread of Christianity in Latin America.

Trade and foreign investments (globalisation) are partners, not adversaries of social agendas, but they ought to be coupled with effective national and international institutions that ease adjustment problems (such as the polluter-pays principle). Globalisation may bring adjustment costs in the affected industries and labour markets, but this may be only transitory. The gradual opening up of markets in Japan during the 1970s, and later in South-East Asia during the 1980s and in China during the 1990s, demonstrates that as a country grows wealthier, it ceases to be competitive in the production of labour-intensive goods. Such a country becomes an importer of these goods and concentrates its production on higher value-added activities.

Child labour, begging, theft and prostitution in poor countries would certainly decline if globalisation opened advanced countries' markets to the products made by the children's parents. Even though globalisation spreads symbols of highly dubious value such as Coca-Cola, McDonald's, MTV,

Halloween and chewing gum,[22] it also spreads basic values such as the rights of women and children. However, it is unfortunate that the latter takes place at a much slower pace. A still unresolved problem is that under globalisation human rights may sometimes be more important than state sovereignty.

The debate about globalisation is often about jobs (social dimension). Supporters argue that it is beneficial and that it creates jobs, while critics argue the opposite and say that jobs migrate to trading partners and competitors. Certain segments of labour in all countries are suspicious of globalisation, as they no longer perceive the national government as a guaranteed protector of their concerns against external threats. To counter these fears, the best long-term policy response may be to advance the possibilities for education and training, as technical progress has a strong bias against unskilled workers.

As far as firms are concerned, efficiency-seeking enterprises, particularly some TNCs, search for seamless and wide international markets regarding trade and investment. On the one hand, the *globalisation* of economic activity is making national frontiers less divisive than ever before.[23] Such worldwide economic integration and integrated international production of goods and services whereby competitors are in one another's backyard are made possible by the expansion of information and telecommunication technologies.[24] This process is sometimes inverted, on the other hand, by the spread of *regionalism* pushed by relatively inefficient firms and governments that are driven by short-term election interests, even though the conditions for a relatively successful integration process, such as that in Western Europe, may be largely absent.

Regional integration (a second-best solution) may be a promising form of supranational governance in areas where there is a strong case for coordination and harmonisation of national policies. Integration may resolve conflicts through positive cooperation within a cosy group but, if pushed to the limit, it may undermine multilateral (first-best) trade and investment systems and fragment the world economy into conflicting regional blocs. Regionalism and multilateralism (globalisation) need not necessarily conflict. If the regional blocs cooperate and if they adopt liberal external trade and investment policies, the outcome may be an overall welfare improvement. The pace of international trade liberalisation since the 1960s, as well as the extension of the GATT into new areas such as services and agriculture, might have been much slower in the absence of challenges posed by the progress in integration in the EU. The debate should not be between regionalism and multilateralism, but rather between liberalism and interventionism (Blackhurst and Henderson, 1993, p. 412).

It is often forgotten that the spirit of 'globalisation' does not bring anything essentially new. The need is for more freedom for trade in goods and services and for capital mobility (FDI). The economic role of national frontiers declines as national economies merge in a single 'global' unit. In a nutshell, the idea is to return to the essentials of the system that was prevailing before 1914. 'Re-globalisation' may be a more appropriate term.

An enlarged market is an important gain for efficiency-seeking firms in a small country. In a situation without integration, foreign countries can simply threaten a small country that they will introduce protectionist measures or 'sanctions' against it (the US frequently makes such threats to many countries). Such a warning can seriously undermine the quality of all economic decisions in a small country. Integration enhances and secures market access for partner countries, as well as increases the potential for long-term competitiveness of a small country's goods and services. A common market may eliminate or harmonise national incentives to foreign TNCs to locate in partner countries (which were previously subject to countervailing duties). It also mitigates non-economic considerations, such as political pressures on third-country investors to locate in a particular country.

Transnational corporations behave like other firms: they primarily follow the opportunities for maximising profit while staying within the law. Size and growth of the local market, including privileged access to international markets (instead of mere differences in the cost of labour), are the most prominent motivators for their trans-border business operations. In addition, in a situation where market liberalisation became a widely accepted policy choice, there is an increase in the importance of created assets and structures (technology and ability to create it, business culture, capability to organise and control production and marketing, communications infrastructure, marketing networks) as determinants for FDI. These are why 65 per cent of the activities of TNCs were located in developed market economies (measured by the stock of FDI in 2002) (UNCTAD, 2003). In spite of the talk about 'globalisation,' on average, a significant part of the output of affiliates is still sold on the local market.[25] In this situation the developing countries and those in transition face very tough competition to attract TNCs.

Foreign investors will locate their activities in a country that offers the most favourable cost mix of operation (production and marketing), provided that this factors well into the longer-term vision of potential profit. FDI can be made simpler by regionalisation of the world economy and international economic integration. However, integration/regionalisation is only a supporting tool for the tendencies that bring about international business globalisation. Modern competitive firms are usually TNCs that 'globalise' their business in the search for seamless and extensive markets. Therefore, an increasing share of domestic output even in the developed countries is under the control of foreign TNCs. The same holds for an increasing share of foreign output of domestic TNCs. Strong FDI relations may exist even though the countries or groups of countries are not formally integrated. Just take a look at the example of two-way FDI flows between the US and the EU.

The glue that binds transatlantic relations together is not principally trade, but FDI. Large global interpenetration of FDI reduces the possibility that regional arrangements may turn into closed blocs. A 'hostage population' of TNCs may reduce the fear of retaliatory measures. Extensive FDI links between the US and the EU helped reduce any potential conflict between the two partners regarding market access. The same is not yet true of Japan. It is hoped that Japan will mature as a foreign investor in future and that potential conflict with that country will be defused.

TRANS-BORDER BUSINESS ACTIVITIES

There are four main types of trans-border business activities that are conducted by TNCs: market seeking, resource based, rationalised and strategic asset seeking (Dunning, 1999, pp. 3–4):

- *Market-seeking* (demand-oriented) investments search for new markets, but they replace trade. They are influenced by the relative size and growth of the foreign market in which the investment is made, the relative costs of supplying that market through imports or local production, as well as the relative advantage of engaging in direct local production or licensing.
- *Resource-seeking* (supply-oriented) FDI is motivated by the availability and cost of both natural resources and labour in the target location. As the products of such investments are often exported abroad, the economic climate in foreign markets, changes in technology, transport costs and barriers to trade influence the attractiveness of such investment to TNCs.
- *Rationalised investments* seek efficiency. Like resource-based investments, they are complementary to trade. Their attractiveness is found in cost considerations. They are influenced by the ease with which intermediate or final products (linked to economies of scale and specialisation) can be traded on the international market. A case in question is the US loss of competitiveness as a site for labour-'intensive' production. The domestic US enterprises from this area of manufacturing locate abroad (Mexico and Asia).

- *Strategic asset-seeking* FDI is aimed at protecting and augmenting the existing ownership-specific advantages by the investing firm. Alternatively, such FDI may be aimed at reducing the advantages of competitors.

4. Transnational corporations

INTRODUCTION

Any firm that owns, has a lasting interest in or controls[26] assets and structures in more than one country can be called a TNC. It is a wider concept than FDI since it includes non-equity business participation in another country. FDI is often the result of decisions by TNCs. Therefore, FDI may be a relatively good proxy for the investment activities of TNCs. A note of caution has to be added, however. TNCs may control trans-border business operations by non-equity involvement such as licensing. In the case of licensing, a TNC must be assured that the goods or services provided conform with the original quality standards.

Investment activity is one of the most sensitive indicators of a country's economic climate. What exactly it indicates, however, is not always clear. Increases in investment may indicate the emergence of new business opportunities, interest in the future, reactions to international competition and response to increasing cost pressures. In any case, sluggish investment activity, as during the 1970s, is an indication of rough economic times (Schatz and Wolter, 1987, p. 29).

The stock of FDI in a national economy indicates what proportion of the home economy is owned/controlled by foreign firms. The total world inward *stock* (the production potential) in 2002 was estimated to be $7.1 trillion (Table 9.1). The spatial distribution of the stock of FDI is asymmetrical. In 2002, 65 per cent of FDI stock was located in developed countries. This is confirmation that FDI activity is strongest among comparable, mainly highly developed, countries.

Inflows of FDI reflect the ability of a country to attract FDI (national location-specific advantages). The EU was the major target for FDI. Worldwide *inflows* of FDI in 2002 were $651 billion. This was 'only' a half of the flows in 2000, when the flows had a peak of $1.4 trillion (Table 9.2). The principal factor behind this decline was slow economic growth throughout the world, as well as weak prospects for recovery in the short term. FDI flows are a strongly cyclical phenomenon. The remarkable exceptions from the generally declining tendency were China (huge and

Table 9.1 FDI inward stock in the world, the EU, the US, Central and Eastern Europe, developing countries and China, 1990, 1995 and 2000–2002 ($bn)

Host-country/region	1990	1995	2000	2001	2002
World total	1954.1	3002.1	6146.8	6606.8	7122.5
EU(15)	748.7	1136.4	2240.5	2418.1	2623.9
US	394.9	535.5	1214.2	1321.1	1351.1
Central and Eastern Europe	2.8	40.2	129.2	155.7	187.9
Developing countries	551.5	920.4	2029.4	2173.8	2339.6
China	24.8	137.4	348.3	395.2	447.9

Source: UNCTAD (2003).

Table 9.2 Annual FDI inflows in the world, the EU, the US, Central and Eastern Europe, developing countries and China, 1997–2002 ($bn)

Host-country/region	1997	1998	1999	2000	2001	2002
World total	481.9	686.0	1079.1	1392.9	823.8	651.2
EU(15)	127.9	249.9	475.5	683.9	398.4	374.4
US	103.4	174.4	283.4	314.0	144.0	30.0
Central and Eastern Europe	19.0	22.5	25.1	26.4	25.0	28.7
Developing countries	193.2	191.3	229.3	246.0	209.4	162.1
China	44.2	43.5	40.3	40.8	46.8	52.7

Source: UNCTAD (2003).

growing potentials of the local market and possibilities to export to third countries) and Central and East European countries (imminent entry of the EU).

Outflows of FDI mirror the willingness and capacity of a country's firms to enter and stay in trans-border business activities. The principal world sources of FDI during 1997–2002 were the EU countries (Table 9.3).

The sectoral distribution of FDI reveals that the industries that are absorbing the largest slices of FDI are those dominated by high-technology and highly qualified personnel. They also have higher than average expenditure on R&D relative to sales. The reasons for such a distribution may be found in the excessive transaction costs of arm's-length contacts through the market, so internalisation of these links within a firm seems to be a better business choice. In addition, they include those that benefit from

Table 9.3 Annual FDI outflows in the world, the EU, the US, Canada, Japan and Switzerland, 1997–2002 ($bn)

Host-country/region	1997	1998	1999	2000	2001	2002
World total	477.0	683.2	1 096.5	1 200.8	711.4	647.4
EU(15)	220.9	415.4	731.1	819.2	451.9	394.1
US	95.8	131.0	209.2	142.6	103.3	119.7
Canada	23.1	34.5	17.2	46.6	36.6	28.8
Japan	26.0	24.1	22.7	31.5	38.3	31.5
Switzerland	17.7	18.8	33.3	44.7	17.3	11.8

Source: UNCTAD (2003).

strong economies of scale in the production of (sophisticated) intermediary goods; their output of final products is highly differentiated; and their production is sensitive to information.

A drive towards a reciprocal treatment of FDI with Japan (or any other country) may not be highly productive. It is generally accepted that TNCs bring benefits that potentially more than compensate for the possible costs and concerns. The EU is, after all, the major world source of FDI, so the demand for a reciprocal treatment may be counterproductive. The principle of reciprocity in FDI often means the aligning of regulations upwards (reciprocal treatment in trade is often different as it levels down trade provisions).

DETERMINANTS

Large companies are in most cases TNCs. They are not directly or completely accountable to any government, but rather have their own ethos. Chauvinism regarding the location of business (personnel matters are a different issue) is alien to international firms, for their business decisions are not likely to be based on either ideological or nationalistic grounds (Rubin, 1970, p. 183). The most crucial determinants of FDI are the relative difference in returns and profit maximisation in the long run, market presence, availability of resources, expectations of growth in demand and political stability. These determinants for the location of an affiliate may be more important than a country's participation in a regional economic bloc.

Table 9.4 summarises investors' motives and determinants for FDI in the target location. It is obvious that the issue is rather complicated. Therefore,

Table 9.4 *Investors' motives and determinants for FDI in the target location*

Investors' motive	Determinants in the target location
1. Market	Size of private and public demand Its growth (current and prospective) Access to regional (integration) and global markets Local, regional and country consumer needs, tastes, sophistication, preferences and fickleness Market structure (competition, openness, protection) Exercise market power (becoming a monopolist) Actions by competitors: follow your leader (snowball or 'herding behaviour') or exchange of threats (tit-for-tat strategy among oligopolists) Demanding clients
2. Resources	Mobility of resources Raw materials Skilled labour and educated management System of education Brain drain Unskilled labour (low cost) Available technology (production functions) Innovation and R&D capabilities and potentials Infrastructure Inputs including supporting services Available capital at favourable rates Organisation of labour (voluntary or mandatory labour unions) Work habits (Japanese TNCs sometimes prefer to locate in rural areas as they mistrust urban workers because of their 'different' work habits and mobility)
3. Efficiency	Cost of resources (listed under point 2) adjusted for productivity where appropriate Cost and easiness of operation (transactions, trade, transport, communication, etc.) Efficiency of the supply chain Trade and marketing networks Logistics Points at the product cycle and production function
4. Others	Existence of clusters Macroeconomic and other stability Incentives (subsidies and taxes) and concessions

692   *The economics of European integration*

Table 9.4 (continued)

Investors' motive	Determinants in the target location
	Rules, regulations and policies (FDI entry and protection, mergers and acquisitions, competition, labour, tax, trade, NTBs, etc.)
	Pressure by the government in the target country to locate there
	Movements in exchange rates
	Investment promotion and friendliness (helpfulness during considerations about FDI, entry, operation and exit)
	Dispute settlement system
	Establishment of a listening, learning and monitoring post
	Culture (way of doing business, openness, corruption, red tape, languages spoken, etc.)
	Quality of life

forecasting FDI flows is tough and uncertain, as determinants are complex, highly changeable from case to case and not always measurable.

Transnational corporations behave like other market-oriented firms: they primarily look for opportunities to make a profit. Thus they compare current and expected profits at home and abroad. The principal motivators for FDI and trans-border business activity are summarised in Table 9.4, and just a few will be mentioned here. The size and rate of growth of a local market in the target country is approximated by income, its growth and by privileged access to regional and international markets. This was the most prominent general motivator for trans-border business operations. Depending on the industry, the availability of resources (including the cost of labour adjusted for productivity) were relevant too. Other motivators, although recognised, were less important. This is because of the strong impact of the real market size on the minimum efficient scale for production.

As the general level of protection of the national market declines due to liberalisation (there is no need to jump over national tariff barriers) and as various types of economic integration proliferate around the world, the mere size of the national market continues to be important, but other motivators are gaining in significance and strength. The local availability of technical, managerial and organisation (networking) knowledge and capabilities including innovation and the existence of clusters become prominent motives for FDI. Seeking, enhancing and protecting such strategic assets and structures became a prominent motivator for FDI. This is linked with high skills, education and experience of labour in the target location. Such labour and management is expensive everywhere. This means that low wages (adjusted for productivity) cease to be a sufficient determinant for FDI.

Where market liberalisation is a widely accepted policy choice, created assets (technology and ability to create it, business culture, capability to organise and control production and marketing, communications infrastructure and marketing networks internal and external to firms) are increasingly important determinants for FDI. This is why most activities of TNCs are geographically located in developed market economies (measured by the stock of FDI).

Neo-classical theory cannot predict with absolute certainty the geographical location of activities resulting from capital mobility within a common market. TNCs that use complex technologies do not worry about tariffs and quotas. They are concerned, rather, with domestic regulations such as environmental standards.[27] A degree of government intervention may influence the spatial location of TNCs, with important implications for the future distribution of output and trade.

Some goods and services must be adapted in order to meet local needs (for example, food). Locating at least a part of the production process near the place of consumption may do this more cheaply. Other reasons for FDI instead of, or together with, exporting include taking advantage of a range of the host country's incentives such as financial incentives (subsidies, reduced taxes), tariff protection, exemption from import duties, public purchases and granting monopoly rights. Other motives include market pre-emption, increase in market power, as well as the empire-building ambitions of firms.

The literature based on surveys and case studies suggests that government strategies such as tax incentives and industrial policies have little, if any, effect on the location of industry. All studies are aware of the difficulties in ascertaining the impact of public policy measures on the location of production. Public policies have mixed effects on the location of firms: on the one hand, higher taxes increase the operating costs of firms; on the other, higher taxes in some areas may be used to pay for better public services, such as education or infrastructure, that support the operation of firms (Smith and Florida, 1994, p. 31).

In a survey of 30 TNCs covering 74 investment projects in cars, computers, food processing and petrochemicals, many TNCs revealed that government incentives were not an issue and, where they existed, simply made an already attractive country for the location of business operations even more attractive. Investment decisions were made on the grounds of economic and long-term strategic conditions regarding inputs, costs and markets. Overall, incentives are not an important factor in the set of elements that determine inward FDI. Once the decision is made to invest in the target country (or region), the incentives may have an impact on the exact choice of location within the target country (UNCTAD, 1998, pp. 103–4).

As for the geographical origin of the TNCs, most of them originate in countries with decentralised political systems such as the US, Britain and the Netherlands, which have the longest history of transnationalisation of national economic activity. In these countries, the TNCs and the state foster relations of complementarity. In centralised states, the administration does not want to share power with any enterprise; however, this has changed in past decades, particularly in France.

If producers and government in a big country A make a credible threat to close its market to exporters from a small country B, then one of the options for country B is to establish 'fifth column' production in country A. This would preserve country B's market share in country A's market. If overheads are covered in country B's home market, then its firm in country A may sell on a marginal cost basis. Many European and Japanese TNCs have concentrated on breaking into the US market and become 'US nationals' in order to avoid unilateral and whimsical US economic sanctions and easy changes in the American trade regime. Making immediate profit from such an investment has played a secondary role, at least in the short term. A similar observation in the EU was the flurry of non-EU TNCs that settled in the EU prior to the full implementation of the Single Market Programme at the end of 1992.

The success of Japanese firms in reducing the labour content of the final output is one of the factors contributing to the expansion of their FDI into relatively high labour cost areas such as North America or the EU. High labour productivity can make up for higher wages. This is why the most significant part of all activities by TNCs takes place in a select group of developed countries. Relatively low nominal wages do not necessarily equal low labour costs – labour productivity should be taken into consideration. In addition, low or declining wages may mean a (local) shrinking market. If this were the case, and if TNCs are interested in the local market, this may act as a deterrent to FDI. Despite the advantage of cheaper labour in Italy, Greece and Portugal, relative to the central and northern EU countries in the 1960s, labour outflow from, rather than capital inflow to, southern Europe was the equilibrating force at that time.

Foreign direct investment is a tool used by enterprises that want to exploit long-term profit-making opportunities abroad. Before embarking upon FDI, an enterprise compares alternative geographical locations at home and at various places abroad. If investing abroad seems to be the more promising option, then the enterprise has to make sure that it possesses or can obtain certain mobile income-generating firm-specific advantages in production or transactions that could enable it to operate profitably in the foreign environment. These advantages include exclusive or privileged access to specific assets and structures, as well as better organising and control capabilities for both production and transactions.

Local firms have several advantages over foreign ones. These include:

- a better knowledge of local consumer and supplier markets;
- they do not have the costs of operating at a distance;
- they often receive favours from the government;
- they do not operate in a different, often hostile, language, tax, legal, exchange rate, social and political environment; and
- TNCs may sometimes have some disadvantages in the eyes of certain local politicians in target countries as they are foreign and, often, relatively large.

Therefore, TNCs bear these elements in mind when deciding about the location of their affiliates. They consider whether they have enough advantages over other firms or whether they may create the capacity to overcome these obstacles. A difficulty for TNCs may be that they have to attract key managers and technicians from the headquarters to a foreign subsidiary. This may require both higher wages for such personnel and higher allowances for their families. TNCs that extract and export natural resources are at risk of becoming a target for nationalisation. If a TNC wants to operate in such a geographical and social environment, it must have or control special advantages. These special and mobile advantage over its domestic competitors include a superior technology and management (a TNC ought to operate on a different production function or at a different point on the same production function than domestic firms), a well-known brand name or, especially important for services, access to markets and quality control. For these reasons, it is no surprise that TNCs are often more profitable and successful than local competitors in the same industry.

While firm-specific income-generating and mobile advantages are a necessary condition for FDI, they are not a sufficient condition. If trade were free, firms could simply use their advantages by exporting instead of producing abroad. Various market imperfections limit the size of the market for free trade and, hence, justify FDI. These include tariffs and NTBs, differences in factor prices, sunk costs and after-sales service. Therefore, an enterprise with a specific and mobile income-generating advantage considers a number of different possibilities and restraints at various foreign locations before settling abroad.

LINKAGES OF TRANSNATIONAL CORPORATIONS

Targeting some key productive activities that have significant linkages with the rest of the economy requires some form of government intervention. Japan's decision to target steel, shipbuilding and toys in the 1950s and 1960s was highly profitable. This choice turned out to be questionable in the 1970s, so Japan turned to cars and machine tools. The Japanese have chosen electronics as their target industry in the 1980s and 1990s (Tyson, 1987, p. 70). This target became obsolete from the 1990s as software overtook hardware in importance, and in this industry the US leads.

In the past the selected industries have had important spillover effects throughout the economy. Telecommunications affect the dissemination of information, computers have an impact on data processing, while transportation equipment and logistics affect the size of the market. As a result of these linkages, private returns from these industries are smaller than social returns. The targeting and location, in a common market or any other type of integration, of key industries that may have significant linkages with other industries or partner countries may have important and long-term beneficial spillover effects on the group. Various linkages between the operation of TNCs and the growth process are presented in Figure 9.2.

When a firm wants to locate and produce abroad it does not necessarily need to export capital. A firm may rent capital abroad rather than purchase or build a production unit. Instead of using its own funds, a firm may borrow in its home, host country's or a third country's financial market. In the case of fixed exchange rates, countries may enter into an 'interest rate war' in order to attract capital into their economies. Integrated capital markets with harmonised rates of interest and mobility of capital may prevent this outcome. While labour markets are most often regional (in Europe), capital markets were national and, with liberalisation, they are becoming international.

Neither firms nor governments depend on savings in their home markets. Interest rates and demand for funds in one country are affected by money (short-term) and capital (long-term) markets in other countries because of the links among financial markets. Of course, this holds if there is confidence in foreign borrowers. Small countries are interest rate takers, so that even the national housing (non-traded good) market feels the impact from foreign markets by means of changes in interest rates. Free international mobility of capital prevents the independent conduct of monetary policy. If a country lowers interest rates in relation to third countries, then capital will flow abroad. This also destabilises the exchange rate if all else is equal. In addition, if a country increases interest rates (in relation to foreign countries) in order to curb the domestic inflation, if other things are constant, capital will flow into the country. The supply of money increases, hence inflation is the

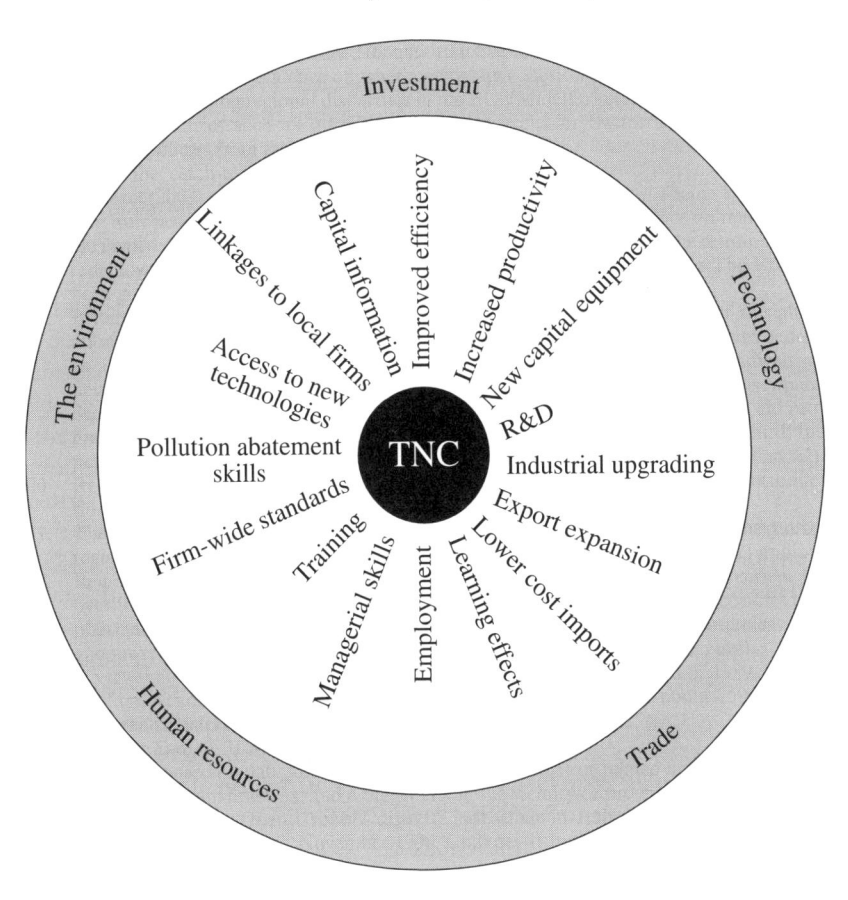

[Figure: Circular diagram showing TNC at center, surrounded by spokes labeled: Linkages to local firms, Capital information, Improved efficiency, Increased productivity, New capital equipment, R&D, Industrial upgrading, Export expansion, Lower cost imports, Learning effects, Employment, Managerial skills, Training, Firm-wide standards, Pollution abatement skills, Access to new technologies. Outer ring labeled: Investment, Technology, Trade, Human resources, The environment. Below: Host economy]

Source: UNCTAD (1992, p. 247).

Figure 9.2   Transnational corporations and the growth process

consequence. Free international mobility of capital introduced during the 1990s, at least among the developed market economies, a self-policing international market device that controls the 'correctness' of national monetary policy and its conformity with the 'best practice'. In this situation, the role and the existence of the IMF became largely unnecessary and irrelevant, and in the cases of IMF loans that kept certain corrupt and bankrupt regimes in the developing countries afloat, this role could easily have been harmful.

Financial markets may sometimes favour large companies and countries and discriminate against small ones. Large companies and countries provide greater security that the funds will be returned and interest paid. A large stock of assets provides this confidence. These markets may discriminate against risky investments such as seabed research, new sources of energy or materials and the like. By integrating capital markets, small countries may mitigate the effect of their relative disadvantage.

The electronics industry in Taiwan has benefited from a geographical variety of foreign investors (mainly from the US and Japan). These TNCs provided education for managers and training for workers, improved the efficiency and quality of production and created stable markets and production and marketing links with local suppliers. These initiatives provided a solid foundation for the creation of an indigenous electronics industry in Taiwan, which evolved with global standards. Mexico's misfortune in the electronics industry was that it received FDI only from declining US component makers and assemblers. This was coupled with a lack of integration with the domestic Mexican electronics industry. Crediting the Taiwanese government for the success of its industry and blaming the Mexican government for its failure would be too simplistic (Lowe and Kenney, 1999, p. 1439).

There are a few arguments that support a thesis that Japan and South Korea would have experienced superior growth trajectories had it not been for selective intervention. Given macroeconomic stability, equilibrium and a stable exchange rate, high and stable savings and investment rates, an enterprising spirit, a respectable level of education, relatively competitive labour markets and a relatively liberal trading system were more than enough to stimulate even faster growth. The contribution of selective intervention was negligible or harmful (Pack, 2000, p. 51).

Economic and business intuition, as well as theory accepts the existence of favourable spillover effects of TNCs on local businesses. *Ex ante* expectations are that TNCs would increase local employment, exports, tax revenue and that some knowledge would spill over into the local economy through movement of labour or by means of purchase orders. However, clear empirical evidence about the actual nature and magnitude of these effects is still to be ascertained. This sheds another doubt on the wisdom of offering (financial) incentives to TNCs to locate in a specific area. Görg and Strobl (2001, p. F724) found that the results about the presence of spillovers are mixed, while Görg and Greenaway (2002, pp. 14–16) found that there is little robust empirical evidence on the existence of spillovers. In a similar survey of spillovers in the host economies, Blomström and Kokko (2003, p. 14) found that the results from a number of case studies about the presence of spillovers seem to be mixed. If these spillovers have an impact on the adjoining firms, these effects depend on the adequate, even comparable, technological level of local firms to absorb them and on host-country policies. Spillovers are largely in the form of transfer of knowledge and ways of fitting into the production network, which is neither obvious nor easy to measure (R.E. Lipsey, 2002, p. 50).

What is the reason for such negative or neutral effects? Answers to this question can be found in the fact that affiliates of TNCs may outcompete the domestic firms and shift demand away from the local competitors; there are time lags in the learning process by the domestic firms and adjustment to the presence and demand of TNCs; and TNCs may guard their internal advantages and prevent leaks to local firms. Even though there is controversy about spillovers, there is a consensus in the literature in this respect: the national economic policy regarding investment should be general and available to all firms (notwithstanding their origin), rather than specific and targeted towards a select type of investment.

TRANSFER PRICING

Foreign ownership and control of domestic output potentials is often seen by the general public as a burden on the domestic economy that is brought by TNCs. A more serious argument against the operation of TNCs is that they behave in the market of the host country in an anti-competitive way through various business practices such as predatory pricing, monopolisation or transfer pricing.

One argument against TNCs used by host countries concerns their internal (transfer) pricing system.[28] TNCs internalise intermediate product and service[29] markets. Prices in trade among different sister enterprises are arrived at by non-market means.[30] For example, GlaxoSmithKline develops, produces and sells drugs in a global market. It conducts R&D in seven countries, manufactures in 38 and sells in 191. It may not be meaningful to ask what part of worldwide profits is made in Britain, as if the same profits were made in transactions among independent national firms. TNCs prosper precisely because this is not the case.[31] In addition, if transfer of technology is measured by international payments of royalties and fees, then about 80 per cent of payments are undertaken on an intra-firm basis (UNCTAD, 1997, p. 20). By doing so, TNCs may shift profits out of countries with relatively high taxes to those with the lowest corporate taxes (tax avoidance)[32] or they may oust competition by cross-subsidising product lines. In order to shift profits, vertical TNCs may overprice imports of inputs and underprice exports.[33] This pricing system may distort both the efficient spatial location of production (resource-wise) and flows of trade.

One way to control operations of the TNCs in the host country could be to ask that the internal pricing system treats the parent and its subsidiary as if they were two separate companies. The enforcement and control of this request may be seriously endangered if there are no substitutes for these internally traded goods and various (headquarters) services. Another solution may be to harmonise fiscal systems in countries where TNCs operate. None the less, a note of caution needs to be added. Transfer pricing is probably used much more commonly than TNCs are willing to admit, but much less frequently than is supposed by outsiders (Plasschaert, 1994, p. 13). In any case, transfer pricing is not widespread in small and decentralised TNCs or in TNCs that operate in competitive markets.

Internalisation of intermediate goods or services markets within TNCs is not always done with the primary goal of avoiding taxes on corporate profits. Another possible reason is to maintain high quality in the supply of goods and services, as local or external suppliers may not necessarily be able to maintain the high quality and timely delivery standards required by the TNC. None the less, fiddling with transfer pricing is more widespread in the developing countries than in the developed world. The balance of payments position of developing countries often drives them to control flows of foreign exchange. Strict controls may induce TNCs to manipulate the internal pricing in order to protect and/or increase profits. The developing countries are not well equipped either to detect or to control manipulation of the internal prices of TNCs.

RESEARCH AND DEVELOPMENT

A potential case in the host country against TNCs is that TNCs rely heavily on the R&D of their parent companies and that their head office charges for their services in a way that might not be controlled by the host country. This can make both subsidiaries and host countries too dependent on foreign R&D and technology. Is this really the case?

When General Electric acquired Tungsram, a huge and renowned Hungarian light bulb company in 1990, it closed down Tungsram's R&D department. However, when it was realised that the light source research was so strong in Hungary, General Electric resumed and reinforced this Hungarian research in 1994. Some empirical research in Canada found that the subsidiaries of TNCs undertook more R&D than domestic Canadian firms (Rugman, 1985, p. 468). In another example, European lift manufacturers undertake their R&D of lifts for tall buildings in their US subsidiaries because there are so many skyscrapers there.

While there is historical evidence that most R&D takes place in the headquarters of TNCs, this is no longer necessarily the case on a large scale. There are many instances of foreign subsidiaries having developed technologies that have benefited the parent firm. For example, a US TNC such as IBM had research breakthroughs in superconductor technology in Switzerland; Hoffmann-La Roche (Switzerland) developed important new pharmaceuticals such as librium and valium in New Jersey (US); Toshiba made advances in audio technology in its British laboratory; and Matsushita's R&D facilities for air-conditioners are in Malaysia. However, for a solid conclusion, more evidence at a much more disaggregated level is needed. Affiliates of foreign TNCs in the US look much like the domestic US firms: there are no particular signs of headquarters effects (Graham and Krugman, 1995, pp. 73–4, 119).[34]

The geographical spread of R&D activities carried out by TNCs is driven by several factors, including:

- the available sophisticated and experienced local R&D staff;
- desire to enhance the existing and acquire new competences;
- the need to adapt output to the needs, preferences and requests of the local market;
- subsidies or pressure from the host government to establish local R&D facilities; and
- the possibility of establishing a 'listening and learning post' in the host country.

However, an international spread of locations for R&D does not mean, as seen in the chapter on competition policy (Chapter 5), that the innovation process has also followed this 'global' trend.

A small country often does not have the necessary resources for large-scale basic research compared to a big and developed country. By importing technology a small country may have access to the results of a much larger volume of R&D wherever it is carried out. It can be both complementary and supplementary to R&D already undertaken in the domestic economy. Relying on the domestic operation of foreign-owned TNCs may be a superior economic policy choice for a risk-averse (poor and small) country than being dependent on foreign supplies of the same good produced elsewhere. Technology transfers from abroad and domestic efforts in education and endeavours to master new technology are like the blades of a pair of scissors: their joint effect is greater than the impact of either one alone (Pack and Saggi, 1997, pp. 94–5).

Inter-firm strategic alliances in the development of technology in the EU increased sharply during the 1980s. In addition, the European Commission became heavily involved in projects on a cost-sharing basis. Over 70 per cent of private (largely non-subsidised) strategic technology alliances were related to joint R&D of new core technologies in the fields of informatics, new materials and biotechnology. A major field of cooperation was in information technologies, as over 40 per cent of all strategic technology alliances were in this field (Hagedoorn and Schakenraad, 1993, p. 373).

A comparison between established 'private' cooperation in R&D and cooperation sponsored by the EU found that the two forms are very similar in the case of leading enterprises. In fact, 'subsidised R&D networks add to already existing or emerging private networks and merely reproduce the basic structure of European large firm co-operation' (Hagedoorn and Schakenraad, 1993, p. 387). This being the case, it is difficult to understand why leading and large firms in the EU need subsidies! If the 'official' (EU-sponsored) spatial network largely reproduces the already existing 'private' one, then it may be redundant. Financial resources could have been used elsewhere (for instance, to fund programmes that are not in the field of informatics, such as biotechnology or education or infrastructure). Is such replication of R&D networks the outcome of the lobbying power of powerful firms or is it necessary to accelerate R&D in the private sector because of significant externalities?[35] Perhaps such waste of scarce public money will be checked in the future by WTO rules on subsidisation.

There is a tendency to reduce the risks and costs of R&D within TNCs. Over 70 per cent of international strategic technology alliances between companies from the EU and NAFTA are focused on R&D (Hagedoorn, 1998, p. 184). This may be an important incentive for mergers and acquisitions in the pharmaceuticals industry (the major reason is still the very fragmented nature of the pharmaceuticals industry compared with car manufacturing). High risk and uncertainty, as well as excessive R&D costs drive firms to centralise these functions (usually in their country of origin). Another reason is the exploitation of host countries' incentives to R&D (subsidies, tax breaks, secure contracts). In this case, the basic research remains in the headquarters, while subsidiaries undertake applied development according to local demand, regulations and incentives. It is often forgotten that many firms that create knowledge are neither TNCs nor large (for example, in the areas of computer hardware and software). The only condition for their creation in certain locations is that they operate in a competitive environment, which is often lacking in small countries.

HOST COUNTRIES AND TRANSNATIONAL CORPORATIONS

The greatest power of TNCs stems from their high international mobility to enter and exit from an industry. TNCs can act as spatial capital arbitrageurs. They may borrow in countries where the rate of interest is lowest and invest in countries where they expect the highest returns. TNCs may spread overheads and risk among their subsidiaries. These enterprises also extend control over international markets. If a subsidiary is producing final goods, then other parts of a TNC may increase export components to this subsidiary.

Many TNCs create sophisticated and complicated technologies. They avoid the transfer of this technology through the market in order to prevent competitors from copying it. The longer the technology gap with imitators, the longer the TNC can behave like a monopolist. Thus, a TNC usually transfers technology only among its subsidiaries.

Relations between TNCs and host countries may sometimes be quite tense. Mining is an industry that requires a huge amount of investment before commercial exploitation. Different countries often compete and offer incentives for FDI and effectively engage in a 'locations tournament' (David, 1984). At this stage a TNC has the strongest bargaining position. When TNCs locate their operations in host countries they may, for example, react to changes in the host country's tax system or interest rates quite differently from domestic firms, which may not be able to withdraw from the home market. Thus, TNCs may become a threat to the host country's national economic policies. To counter this danger, the common market member countries should coordinate and harmonise their policies regarding competition, capital mobility and TNCs.

If TNCs produce final goods in host countries and if they import raw materials and components from countries which are outside the common market instead of purchasing them from the local suppliers, then they may jeopardise the process of integration within a common market. The external dependence of the area may increase instead of being reduced. Where the member countries of a common market or other type of international economic integration compete among themselves for FDI in the absence of an agreed industrial policy, it is unreasonable to expect the operation of the TNCs to result in an optimal spatial allocation of resources (Robson, 1983, p. 32). This has happened in the Caribbean region.

A large amount of investment may, however, keep a TNC as a hostage of the host country. These sunk costs with limited or no 'salvage value' may represent a barrier to exit from the host country. In this case, the host-country government can show the TNC who is boss. The host governments may renegotiate the deals with the TNCs. This kind of danger may induce the TNCs to borrow predominantly on the host-country's financial market and transfer from elsewhere only the technical and managerial expertise. A possible closure of a subsidiary in the host country would be at the cost of some local jobs in both the subsidiary and supplying firms. The affected local workers and their families may lobby in favour of the interests of the TNC, which may find allies among industries in the host country. As long as TNCs purchase from them, both subsidiaries and local firms may work together in lobbying the government for protection, subsidies, tax breaks and procurement agreements.

A serious threat to the market structure of a host country may be introduced by a TNC. It may monopolise the whole domestic market and by predatory pricing prevent the entry of domestic firms to the industry. It may introduce technologies that use relatively more of the resources in short supply (capital) and relatively less of the component that is abundant (labour) in the host country.

As far as wages are concerned, there is overwhelming evidence that TNCs in all kinds of countries pay relatively higher wages to labour of a given quality than local firms do. The reasons for such wage policy include the following elements (R.E. Lipsey, 2002, pp. 21, 29):

- TNCs may be forced to offer higher wages by host-country regulations or by home-country pressures about 'fair pay';
- local labour may prefer domestic firms and it ought to be compensated to overcome this preference;
- if TNCs bring certain proprietary technology, they may wish to reduce labour turnover. By offering higher pay they may retain labour, hence they may reduce technology leaks to domestic firms;
- TNCs may wish to find and attract better workers and managers. More knowledgeable local firms may identify, get and keep these workers without this wage premium; and
- certain TNCs operate in higher-wage industries of the economy. They hire highly educated managers and sophisticated workers.

Differences in wages may also be due to the fact that the home firms do not value sufficiently a resource that is in short supply. Vacancies in the domestic firms may be filled by less-well-trained labour, which may have an adverse effect on the growth of production in the host country. Although technologies used by the TNCs in the host countries may not be the most up to date, they can be superior to those which are currently in use in developing countries (environmentally sound technologies are an obvious example).

Transnational corporations may have an adverse impact on the allocation of resources in the host country if their operation accounts for a significant proportion of production, employment, purchases and sales. Thus, the operation of TNCs may have a greater influence in certain segments of industry in developing countries than in developed countries. This state of affairs demands a coordinated approach towards TNCs by the regional groups in the developing world, as was the case with the controversial Decision 24 (1970) in the Andean Pact.[36] It also requires the establishment and enforcement of a common industrial policy. This can be supported by the regional development banks and/or by joint planning. Openness to and participation in an integrated network of international production of TNCs will contribute to the growth potential of the developing countries.

This analysis suggests that the TNCs do not pay much attention to the overall needs of the host countries. This is true. However, it is not a duty of TNCs to meet the social needs, including the infrastructure needs, of the host country. Nobody forces host countries to accept TNCs. The fulfilment of these social demands is the role of the host country's government. In the presence of unemployed resources, inflation, foreign and budgetary debt, famine and underdevelopment, any hard currency investment is welcome. Any attempt by the host government to restrict the entry and operation of TNCs may dry up this thin trickle of capital inflow. Host countries sometimes behave (or used to) as if they want FDI funds, but not the foreign investor to handle them. Unfortunately, the developing countries are those that most need these investments. TNCs often ask what will happen after they invest and start production: would the utility companies increase prices? Would the employees request an immediate increase in wages? Would the consumers demand bigger loans as the TNC is a large, successful and rich company?

In order to increase local embeddedness, some TNCs involve themselves in local communities through sponsorship of local sporting and cultural events, and even education and training. Whether this is a calculated public relations ploy (as in the case of some Japanese and German TNCs that operate in Britain) to avoid criticism or a real and deep commitment towards the local communities remains unanswered (Dicken et al., 1995, p. 41).

Economic adjustment in the developing world may be facilitated by the presence of TNCs. These corporations have the know-how, the ability to raise funds and the widespread marketing channels that help export growth. They may create and maintain relevant spillover effects such as linkages with local firms that may prompt the creation of new local firms and the restructuring of existing ones.

The local content[37] requirements for locating FDI in a particular country may be criticised on the grounds that they distort investors' input choices, stimulate suboptimal input mixes and potentially increase prices. In a survey of 682 projects, it was found that in 83 per cent of cases in which there was a requirement to accomplish the objectives of trade-related investment measures (TRIMs) such as local sourcing and exporting, the firms planned to do so anyway (UNCTC, 1991a, p. 4). That is to say, TRIMs were redundant.

Certain companies, such as Nike and Wal-Mart, have sourcing structures that are more geographically spread than their sales. Nike, for example, sources 99 per cent of its products offshore (principally from China and

South-East Asia). However, most of its sales (52 per cent) are in its home US market (Rugman and Verbeke, 2003, p. 14).

Local content requirements were often used in the past as means to promote, even force, linkages between TNCs and local firms. Others with the same policy objective included trade (export performance) and foreign exchange balancing demands. However, over the past few decades, most countries have strategically altered their economic policies from the general protection of domestic firms to widespread openness. In addition, the WTO 1995 TRIMs Agreement (Article 2) requires the phasing out of TRIMs.[38] While there might be certain initial successes in the forging of linkages with the local suppliers, forced requirements on a TNC's affiliate may jeopardise the efficient technology mix in the production. As such, this can easily endanger the efficiency in the production process, lower competitiveness and reduce incentives for other TNCs to come and locate in that country. A far superior and sophisticated policy that can be employed by the governments to foster links and spillovers between the local industry and affiliates of TNCs is to provide information about the local business environment, to act as a matchmaker with the local firms and to upgrade the technology level of the local firms through education, training and finance.

In many developing countries, mineral resources, including oil, are the property of the state. It is the government that negotiates terms of entry with TNCs. In manufacturing, the role of the government is somewhat less pronounced. In this case, the government usually sets general terms of entry, performance and exit from an industry. While the developing countries, as a rule, regulate the conditions for entry of TNCs with greater scrutiny, industrialised countries control their exit and the possible consequences regarding job losses and the environment.

It is popularly argued that TNCs invest most often in fast-growing manufacturing industries such as electronics and medicine-related industries. These industries thus 'fall into foreign hands', possibly giving foreigners undue influence in the host country and interfering with sovereignty. An example was when the US introduced a ban on the export of technology for the gas pipeline from the then USSR to Western Europe in the early 1980s. Many subsidiaries of US TNCs in Western Europe were affected by this decision. It is much harder for a host country to influence the parent country of a TNC through a subsidiary.

In spite of allegedly lower environmental standards in the developing countries, a large-scale transfer of polluting business activities to these countries has not taken place, at least not on a large scale. This is the consequence of the constant focus of TNCs on the developed countries and the adherence of TNCs to the application of environmental standards (often the same as in their home country) that are superior to those prevailing in the host developing country.

As noted earlier, modern technologies complicate the employment impact of FDI. Modern technologies substitute capital for labour. A *'greenfield'* investment (building a new factory) is an attractive business option when blending existing assets and structures with others is undesirable and costly. Investors can tailor-make the production site, and manufacturing and management techniques to suit their particular needs. Previous management habits and labour relations are not inherited. This type of investment increases employment in the host country if it does not put domestic competitors out of business.

A *takeover* (merger and acquisition) of an existing firm is a preferred business choice if the cost of a greenfield entry exceeds the cost of a takeover. The investor may immediately start production, but this does not add to the national output capacity in the host country at the time of entry (this is just a transfer of ownership). This is a fast way to enter rapidly changing markets, and hence, in general, a more common way to enter foreign markets than through a greenfield investment. This holds particularly for entry into the developed market economies. Takeovers do not necessarily increase employment and may reduce it if the merged firm rationalises the existing activity. A foreign-located subsidiary may begin as a unit for marketing of the final good. If it develops further, it may become a product specialist, which may increase employment (direct and indirect) of a particular type of labour. However, one has to remember that employment is determined by demand for final goods and services.

Takeovers (mergers and acquisitions) provide means for the 'external' growth of TNCs. They are attractive to TNCs that have wide international marketing networks and are tempting to sellers who are interested in penetrating the widest possible market. This is enhanced if the acquired (or merged) enterprise is not linked to any industrial group, which helps to avoid conflicting interests. This is why the Anglo-Saxon enterprises dominate cross-border mergers and acquisitions in Europe. TNCs may also grow 'internally' through subsidiaries. Mergers and acquisitions are, however, virtually unknown in Japan.

Transnational corporations treat their business in different countries as a single market operation. Therefore, their financial service is always centralised (or confined to a very limited number of locations) as this may best meet the needs of the corporation as a whole.[39] The financial service represents the backbone of the control of overall corporation operation and efficiency. This is most pronounced in the case where ownership-specific advantages of a TNC are generating high returns. Other operations such as employment, wage and labour relations are always decentralised within

TNCs. Labour markets are local and often highly regulated, so decentralisation of these issues is the optimal policy for TNCs. Rapid international mobility and multiplant coordination and control of a growing part of business activities are among the greatest advantages of TNCs over other firms. For example, Nike (an American 'producer' of sports goods) keeps its R&D in Oregon, but subcontracts the actual manufacturing of clothes and shoes in more than 700 factories in 50 countries, principally in Asia.[40] If wages increase in one country, Nike simply moves production to another.

BENEFITS AND CONCERNS

Estimates of the potential gains from economic integration and operations of TNCs are generally based on the classical assumption that the set of traded goods is both complete and *fixed*. In such a case, the gains from trade and FDI appear to be quite small. Prices in the economy could be changed by government (tariff) intervention, so the quantity of produced and traded goods would change, but the list of the manufactured and traded goods would remain the same.

Suppose now that the list of goods is *expandable*. The neo-Schumpeterian economic model assumes that there are no limits for the introduction of new goods and services in an economy. Let us assume, in addition, that the introduction of a new commodity requires a large amount of fixed costs.[41] This is especially true in the case of the developing countries. Perfect competition and free trade exclude (major) fixed costs from consideration. Once the fixed costs are included in the picture, their presence is often used as a justification for government intervention. When important fixed costs enter the model, a substantial volume of the good needs to be sold in order to make a profit. In such a case, a tariff on the good in question may reduce demand. If this reduction in (international) demand is important, then the commodity may never appear on the market. Losses from such a development or gains in the reverse case may not be easily estimated, at least, not for the time being. In any case, if the new goods are left out of consideration, then this kind of analysis can bring substantial underestimates of the welfare cost of trade restrictions (Romer, 1994). These new goods and services are usually brought (to the developing countries) by TNCs.

Integrated countries may obtain certain benefits from the trans-border business activity of firms. These gains, specific to the operation of TNCs within the area, include not only *tangible* resources (for example, transfer of capital on more favourable terms than could be obtained on capital markets, tax receipts, economies of scale, sourcing of inputs from local suppliers and employment) that are provided at lower cost than through the market, but also various *intangible* assets and structures. These intangible assets include new technologies in production, management and control of assets and structures that make the existing resources more productive; positive externalities in production through linkages;[42] international marketing networks that can overcome barriers for exports into foreign markets; new ideas; clustering of related firms; training of labour; and competition. The pecuniary element of these spillovers is quite difficult to measure and could easily escape the attention of a non-economist. Other issues include monopolisation, restrictive business practices, increased sourcing from the parent country with a negative impact on the balance of trade, transfer pricing, transfer of profits abroad and spatial polarisation of economic activity. All these elements affect the spatial allocation of resources in a way that is not always favourable to either the integrated country or the whole group.

Despite a relative academic hostility, public sensitivity, polemics against foreignfirms that export home resources and some official anxiety about the operation of TNCs, the situation has changed since the 1980s. All countries in the world welcome TNCs. There is a tendency towards convergence in the national rules regulating FDI. Apart from some screening, these countries provide TNCs with various incentives which include the provision of infrastructure, subsidised loans, tax exemptions, export incentives, opportunities for complete ownership and exemptions from duties. However, these countries have to bear in mind that they compete with other possible locations (and countries), hence there is a tendency towards liberal and converging national systems relating to TNCs. The growing and wide markets in the US and EU are still the most preferred locations for TNCs. If other regions want to attract TNCs, then, ideally, they should have some 'unique selling point' that TNCs cannot find in Europe or North America.

Apart from these drawbacks, host countries experience significant gains and thus welcome the arrival and operation of TNCs. These corporations may bring in new technology that is superior to existing domestic technology. This has the effect, in the host country, of increasing output capacity, jobs and tax proceeds, as well as resulting in savings in unemployment benefits and perhaps also creating exports. TNCs enter into growth industries and provide technological expertise that would otherwise be missing. Some TNCs produce brand-name drinks or cigarettes, whose consumption is subject to excise duties. Governments may need or want these proceeds and therefore become an ally of the TNCs. Barriers to entry, such as huge initial capital investment in an industry, can be overcome with TNC input. When the host country's policy is to promote exports or substitute imports, then TNCs may fill part of this role.

One major incentive to persuade TNCs to locate their operations in a country or an integrated region is to offer them a stable macroeconomic environment and a growing market. International economic integration provides this opportunity. Other carrots include tax holidays, subsidies, tariff protection and secure public purchases. In the medium and longer terms, the best policy is to influence the supply of educated local labour (a created factor) as an additional incentive to TNCs to select the country for the location of their operations.

Potential benefits and concerns from the location of TNCs in a national economy may not be measured directly and in the short term. None the less, many of them can be listed as in Table 9.5.

Table 9.5 *Potential benefits and concerns that bring TNCs to the target country/location*

Benefits	Concerns
1. Investment may add to the capital formation and production capacity of the country. This may stimulate growth of the target country	• Flow of FDI is volatile • Capital may be raised on the local market so there is no inflow of fresh capital • Mergers and acquisitions relate only to the transfer of ownership. Only greenfield investment adds to the capital formation • If higher productivity of a TNC affiliate is achieved at the expense of lower productivity of domestic firms, there may be no implications for aggregate growth • Most FDI goes to financial services (the EU case). This does not bring a direct and large-scale improvement in the manufacturing industry in the target country • TNCs may exert strong lobbying pressure and may demand incentives such as subsidies and tax holidays. Such benefits and 'locations tournaments' among countries may introduce important opportunity costs, unnecessary waste of scarce public funds and serious distortions in the national economy regarding spatial and industrial location of resources. This creates disadvantages to local firms. Incentives to TNCs may be difficult to administer • Foreigners own and control domestic assets and structures. The domestic industry falls into the hands of foreigners, hence these firms may behave in a different way from

Table 9.5 (continued)

Benefits	Concerns
	the domestic firms in identical situations • TNCs repatriate profits abroad instead of reinvesting them in the location where they were made
2. TNCs may transfer new technology, knowledge, experience, skills and ideas in production, management and control (human and organisational capital embedded in TNCs). This is also linked with economies of scale and improved efficiency. TNCs may also develop local innovation activities and transfer certain R&D activities if there exist local knowledge, experience, skills and/or subsidies	• TNCs may transfer out-of-date and polluting technologies • A TNC may close local departments and concentrate R&D activities in its headquarters. The country in which the affiliate is located may be put in a long-term dependency position regarding technology • TNCs may introduce technologies that use more resources that are in short supply (capital) in the target country and relatively less of the locally abundant resource (labour) • TNCs may develop and employ sophisticated technologies in order to prevent easy copying. They may keep this technology internal to the firm to retain as long as possible their position of monopolists in their respective businesses. Spillovers to the local industry do not take place • TNCs pay higher wages in order to attract and keep better workers. The domestic industry is left with other workers. There is no transfer of knowledge to local firms • Excessive internalisation of business may diversify the affiliate into unrelated technologies (outside the core competence). This may reduce the competitiveness of its output
3. TNCs may create, develop, expand and upgrade spillovers and links with the local economy	• Spillovers and links depend on the technological capacity of the local economy to accept them. The closer the technological capacity of the local firms to a TNC affiliate, the greater the potential spillover • Literature surveys such as Görg and Strobl (2001), Görg and Greenaway (2002), Blomström and Kokko (2003) and R.E.

Table 9.5 (continued)

Benefits	Concerns
	Lipsey, (2002) found only mixed evidence about the existence of spillovers in the local economy
4. TNCs employ local labour and contribute to an increase in the local skills	• A takeover (merger or acquisition) of a local firm transfers only the ownership. There is no immediate change in employment. If the new owner rationalises production, employment may be reduced • A greenfield entry may increase employment, but if the affiliate puts local competitors out of business, the level of employment may change in the target country • TNCs often offer higher wages, hence they attract the best workers and managers. The local firms may be left with a lower quality of labour • TNCs pay higher wages to keep the best workers and managers to prevent the leakage of knowledge to the local economy • Local trade unions may demand higher wages throughout the economy. These increases may be over and above productivity, which may jeopardise the competitiveness of the country's output • TNCs may use technologies that employ factors that are in short supply locally (capital) • If labour unions demand 'too much', a TNC may threaten to move its affiliate elsewhere
5. TNCs may stimulate competition and force local competitors and suppliers to upgrade their business	• Restrictive business practices such as monopolisation of the market, predatory and transfer pricing may hamper the expansion of existing and development of new local firms • TNCs may crowd out local firms from the local capital market • Various public concessions and subsidies offered only to TNCs create distortions that damage local firms

Table 9.5 (continued)

Benefits	Concerns
	• Unethical and criminal practices (for example, bribery, 'campaign contributions', improper accounting, false billings and statements) may create huge corporate failures such as Enron (2002) in the US or Parmalat (2003) in Italy with business consequences reverberating throughout the world
6. TNCs offer access to a wide international manufacturing, marketing and trade network. They include the target country in this well-established network that may stimulate exports. More than a third of world trade today is within the same company. Some of these important 'internal' TNC markets may be infiltrated only through affiliates	• Affiliates may produce only for the local market at a suboptimal scale of production • Affiliates do not buy inputs in the local market, but import them from other affiliates. This may increase imports (rather than exports). Transfer pricing may jeopardise the balance of payments position
7. TNCs pay taxes and contribute to the tax revenue in the host country	• Transfer pricing may diminish local tax receipts • Tax avoidance may do the same • Various tax incentives may degrade the effect of taxes collected

NATIONAL AND INTERNATIONAL REGULATION

The basis of the OECD Declaration on International Investment and Multinational Enterprises (1976) and the OECD Guidelines for Multinational Enterprises (1986) (both revised in 2000) is the principle of national treatment of foreign companies. This principle means that, provided national security is not jeopardised, TNCs have the same rights and obligations as domestic companies in similar situations. This does not put all foreign suppliers on an equal footing in the importing country market (which is what the MFN clause does), rather it refers to the treatment of foreign suppliers in comparison with domestic ones.

Resource-rich and prosperous countries such as Canada may exercise the greatest leverage on TNCs.[43] Canada's experience is one of the most interesting examples of control of TNCs. It is relevant, as a significant part of the economic integration between Canada and the US has an FDI dimension.

Both Canada and the US are signatories to the OECD Declaration. In 1973, a few years before this declaration was delivered, Canada established the Foreign Investment Review Agency (FIRA) to survey inward FDI. This move was a reaction to a relatively large share of foreign ownership of Canadian industry. One could argue that much of the foreign ownership of the host-country industry can be attributed to the level of the host country's tariffs, taxes, subsidies and other incentives. TNCs overcome tariff obstacles by locating 'tariff factories' in the host country. FIRA's intention was not to stop FDI in Canada, but rather to allow FDI only if it resulted in beneficial effects to Canada. The criterion upon which FIRA evaluated both the takeovers of existing Canadian firms and the establishment of new businesses included expanded exports, use of Canadian resources, increase in investment, employment and productivity, as well as compatibility with the national industrial and other economic policies.

FIRA's rejection rate of 20 per cent was an important barrier for certain investors and was high compared with rates of some 1 per cent in other countries that used a similar screening process (Lipsey, 1985, p. 101). This caused many firms to withdraw their requests in order to avoid uncertain and costly application procedures, while other firms that might have been potential investors have not even applied. At the beginning of the 1980s, FIRA's rejection rate was reduced. The Conservative government transformed FIRA from a nationalistic authority aimed at increasing Canadian ownership in domestic industry into an organisation for the attraction of FDI and in 1984 renamed it Investment Canada. The fear of too much foreign capital had given way to a fear of too little (Lipsey and Smith, 1986, p. 53).

Access to growing national and international markets and a stable macroeconomic environment are major incentives for locating of FDI in some geographical areas. However, a stable, predictable and transparent legal situation also encourages FDI as it lowers risk and potentially increases profits. There are global rules that regulate international trade in goods (WTO), but as yet there are no such rules regarding FDI. A complex set of bilateral[44] and some regional treaties regulate FDI. The coverage of these rules is not full. In addition, many governments offer incentives to attract FDI. Diversity in the treatment of FDI in bilateral deals and the possibility of a sudden reversal in the liberalisation trend in times of crisis (Asia 1997–98) create a need for a multilateral treaty.

The OECD drafted a Multilateral Agreement on Investment (MAI) with the aim of providing a sound legal environment, including open markets, based on the principle of non-discrimination between domestic and foreign investors. In addition, there would be instruments for dispute settlement among all involved parties (various combinations of public and private players) and enforcement of decisions.

In spite of grand expectations, the MAI project got into serious trouble and was put aside in 1998. The critics argued that the exclusive OECD 'club' of then 29 countries did not take into account the needs of the developing countries. Another criticism was that the MAI gave excessive power to TNCs regarding protection of the investment, transfer of funds, right of establishment and MFN treatment. These criticisms are relevant if one bears in mind that India still remembers the moment when the first ships of the East India Company arrived at the port of Surat. The company came to India as a trader in 1608 and ended up virtually owning the country.

The national legal system that regulates FDI in most OECD countries is well developed. Hence, the MAI was of little real significance for these developed countries, even though most of the FDI activity in the world is within the OECD group. The drafters' intention was to lure the emerging players in the FDI flows to join the agreement. However, few developing countries were ready and willing to sign a deal that they did not shape (exchanging concessions such as domestic market opening for FDI in return for the opening of OECD markets for agricultural goods and migration of labour). Some critics saw the MAI as a tool of neo-colonialism. However, the work on the MAI was not in vain since it raised an important issue. Perhaps it will have better luck in the future possibly within the WTO, which has a wider membership (about 150 countries), dispute settlement instruments and experience in handling difficult negotiations.

5. Intervention

If market imperfections permit rents (above-average profits), then the governments of the integrated countries may wish to intervene. The larger market of an integrated area may be better able to absorb the cost of intervention owing to the spread of such costs than would be the case for individual countries acting alone. For instance, a simplified (prisoner's dilemma) example is presented in Table 9.6.

Suppose that there are just two firms capable of producing aircraft: British Aerospace in Britain and Aérospatiale in France. Assume also that,

Table 9.6 Profit in the aircraft industry without intervention

France \ Britain	Production	No production
Production	−3; −3	10; 0
No production	0; 10	0; 0

because of sunk costs, R&D and economies of scale, only one firm can produce aircraft efficiently (profit-wise) within the EU and that public authorities prefer to purchase domestically made goods. The numbers in Table 9.6 then show the profit of the two firms. If there is no intervention by the government, the firm that moves first captures the market and makes a profit. If both produce, both lose; if neither produces, there is neither gain nor loss. If only one country has the ability to produce aircraft, the government of the other may then try to persuade a foreign TNC to locate its production within the confines of its borders, thus putting the potential competitor from the partner country out of business. This possibility for a geographical location of production is a strong case for a joint treatment of TNCs by the integration groups.

Now suppose that there is no domestic producer of aircraft in Britain and that the domestic government decides that it may be sensible to have aircraft production located at home and to move first to strategically and irreversibly pre-empt any other player.[45] The reasons may include employment, export and prestige, but also, and more importantly, various externalities, including obtaining the leading edge in one of the high-technology industries and also national pride. Some early movers sustain their position for decades. For example, Procter & Gamble, Unilever and Colgate have been international leaders in washing powder production since the 1930s. With this in mind, the government decides to invite Boeing to come and locate its production in Britain. As bait, it offers various subsidies and protection to capture the aircraft market in the integration arrangement with France. The major reason for the subsidy is not simply to increase export sales, but rather to improve the terms of trade and secure rents for the home firm, a cluster of related domestic enterprises and, finally, for the country itself. Of course, such a policy may have a significant balance of payments effect in the medium and long terms. Hence, the structure of markets and the operations of TNCs matter for the spatial distribution of production.

The neo-classical model deals with the given and perfect resources and capabilities, whereas the new theory studies market imperfections, multiple equilibria and government intervention in a dynamic set-up. This new approach tries to suppress market constraints and to push economic frontiers outwards. It considers economies of scale, externalities, differentiated products, changing technology and FDI. These are all features of modern manufacturing. The new theory questions the proposition that free markets may successfully take advantage of the potential benefits in the new situation. Such an approach is different from the neo-classical one, in which TNCs were, by definition, excluded from consideration. The assumption in free markets is that there are no grounds for trans-border business activities as the spatial and sectoral allocation of resources is perfect and full (first-best solution). The new theory explains why countries can trade not only when their resource endowments and production capabilities are *different*, as in the neo-classical situation, but also when their resource endowment and production capabilities are *identical*. The case in question is the intra-industry trade (that is, intra-EU trade in cars).

One thing, however, ought to be clear from the outset. The new theory does not replace the neo-classical one. It considers only market imperfections that can be mitigated by intervention, which may introduce an adjustment instrument into an already highly imperfect situation. Table 9.7 shows what would happen to the profits of the two aircraft producers if the British government subsidised its (foreign owned/controlled) firm with monetary units that equal 5. If the firm located in Britain decides to produce, it will always have an advantage over its non-subsidised French rival.

When market imperfections exist, the British government can influence the geography of production (spatial location of resources and specialisation). None the less, if the choice of national champions is to be a good one, the government should be competent and well informed, otherwise the result may be costly commercial failures, such as the Franco-British Concorde project or computers in France. Many governments in East Asia have intervened successfully in their economies. However, governments in many East European and developing countries have intervened much more, and yet have singularly failed to achieve the economic successes seen in East Asia. In any case, intervention is facilitated when the number of potentially competing firms is small and production output is standardised.

Table 9.7 Profit in the aircraft industry with intervention

France \ Britain	Production	No production
Production	−3; 2	10; 0
No production	0; 15	0; 0

Engineering comparative advantages of countries and firms are becoming more important in modern footloose industries and are eroding, to an extent, inherited comparative advantages. For example, trade within the EU is to a large extent of an intra-industry character. It is much more driven by economies of scale than by the 'classic' comparative advantages of those countries. If pushed to the limit, a national reaction to a monopoly in a foreign country is the creation of a national monopoly. That is fighting fire with fire (Curzon Price, 1993, p. 394).

In order to intervene/subsidise in an intelligent way, governments need a great deal of information that is quite costly to obtain: information not only about current and potential future technology and demand, but also about the strategies of other governments and TNCs. If they choose wisely, strategic policy can be a superb device. In practice, a subsidy in one country may provoke retaliation in another in the form of a subsidy or a counter-balancing duty. The retaliation and counter-retaliation cycle makes everyone worse off. Integration may offer some advantages to developing countries in such a situation. It may inspire these countries to negotiate the distribution of strategic industries within the area or attract TNCs in order to maximise positive externalities and reduce unnecessary subsidies. The basic argument for the government's involvement may be that without intervention in the area, and owing to imperfections, there may be *underinvestment* in a strategic industry. If, however, intervention is not well managed, *overinvestment* may be the consequence.

The simple model of strategic investment, industrial and trade policy is based on the expectation that the subsidised home production of a tradable good or service shifts monopoly profits (rents) to the home country and to the firms owned/controlled by it. These profits should be over and above the cost of the subsidy. If the domestic firms are affiliates of foreign TNCs, then the effect on the home country's welfare may be uncertain. No matter what the circumstances are, the expectation that profit shifting may enhance the home country's welfare holds *only* when foreign countries do not retaliate against domestic subsidies. A cycle of retaliation and counter-retaliation would make everyone worse off. In addition, when there is a liberal treatment of FDI, bilateral trade deficits may give off misleading signals. For example, if Japan (or any other country) invests in China in order to take advantage of relatively low labour costs and to export output to the US, the bilateral deficit in trade between the US and Japan may shrink, but the overall US trade deficit may increase because of extra US imports from China.

Governments need to bear in mind that general favours (subsidies) handed out to domestic firms may trickle out to foreign beneficiaries located within the confines of the jurisdiction of the government. A more effective policy may be to use subsidies to develop and upgrade the skills of domestic human capital as footloose capital is increasingly attracted by, among other factors, created factors such as the local availability of skilled, highly trained and experienced labour and management.

In advanced countries such as the US, the constituent parts may compete with one another by offering substantial grants (and grant equivalents) in order to attract world-scale manufacturing projects. The size of these grants is increasing. In 1984, Michigan offered state and local incentives worth $120 million (equivalent to $14000 per job) to attract Mazda; in 1986, Indiana offered $110 million ($51000 per job) to Subaru-Isuzu; in 1989, Kentucky offered $325 million ($108000 per job) to Toyota (UNCTC, 1991a, pp. 73–4); in 1983, Alabama gave $252 million ($168000 per job) to Mercedes-Benz; and North Carolina handed out $130 million ($108000 per job) to BMW. In spite of strict rules of competition, countries in the EU are sometimes allowed to dispense 'incentives' to TNCs to settle within their confines. Britain gave $89 million ($29675 per job) to Samsung in 1994, while France granted $111 million ($56923 per job) to Mercedes-Benz and Swatch in 1995 (UNCTAD, 1995a, p. 18). In 1996, Dow Chemicals received a subsidy of $6.8 billion for an investment in the petrochemical industry in Germany ($3.4 million per job), and in 2000, Alabama gave an incentive package worth $158 million to Honda to locate a $400 million assembly plant that would employ 1500 workers ($105333 per job)(UNCTAD, 2002, pp. 204–5). These kinds of subsidies and participation in location tournaments are well beyond the financial capabilities of developing countries.

The self-reinforcing aspect of FDI begins to operate only after a certain level of development. The developing countries 'which are already doing well in these categories do not need location tournaments. The others are not likely to profit from them' (Wheeler and Mody, 1992, p. 72). The ability of the developing world to attract FDI depends on many factors that these countries cannot control. They need to try to stabilise their macroeconomic and political situation, improve the quality and quantity of human capital and infrastructure, liberalise trade and investment policies, actively promote their advantages to the business community and study potentials for integration or preferential trade with other (neighbouring) countries. Such a policy approach would stimulate domestic private investment and growth. It could also be argued that they might wish to pursue such policies even if they had little effect on FDI.

In an examination of annual FDI flows (1960–90) towards the major integration groups in the developing world, Jovanović (1995) found no difference in FDI flows before and after the creation of the integration group. The national economic (and political) situation played a much more important role for the attraction of FDI than did participation in the integration deal. This conclusion was later reconfirmed by Blomström and Kokko (1997, p. 39). In considering the situation in Ireland, it was found that 'recent FDI growth has taken place at a time when the relative value of Ireland's incentives has been eroded. This erosion stems both from domestic reductions in incentives and from the increasing use of regional incentives elsewhere in the EU. This may suggest that incentives are necessary but not sufficient to attract internationally mobile investment' (Braunerhjelm et al., 2000, p. 85).

6. Transnational corporations and international economic integration

Many business activities entail high costs, uncertainties and risk as they face rapid changes in technology, demand and needs, so the operation of such activities in relatively small markets may not be commercially viable from an efficiency point of view. Worldwide free trade may not be achieved in the short or medium term (if ever), so international economic integration or preferential trade may be an attractive second-best policy option. Such integration, although to an extent an inward-looking strategy, widens/pools the markets of the participating countries. Larger and growing markets provide greater confidence than relatively smaller ones to both domestic and foreign investors.

Domestic markets in most countries are so small that even a high degree of protection of growth-propelling manufacturing industries and services aimed at supplying the local market may not be viable in terms of efficient employment of resources. By supplying a larger market provided by the integration arrangement, participating countries may increase production, capacity utilisation, employment and investment; reduce vulnerability to external shocks; capture economies of scale; improve bargaining positions in international markets; and increase average standards of living. These results should be viewed in comparison with the situation in which all countries act alone under heavy domestic protection.

The production and distribution of goods and services in an integrated area is not the sole prerogative of domestic firms, but can also be carried out by TNCs and their affiliates. This consideration adds an extra element to the theoretical analysis that brings it closer to the real world, but it also introduces some analytical drawbacks to the pure and simple theoretical models. In an early work, Mundell (1957) argued that, within the Heckscher–Ohlin theoretical model, trade in goods and trade in factors may substitute for each other. Markusen (1983) has shown that the operations of TNCs (flow of factors) are complementary to international trade, rather than substitutes, and that Mundell's proposition may describe only a special case.

Foreign direct investment is the result of market imperfections, as in a free trade situation the spatial and sector-wise allocation of resources is perfect and there are no grounds for FDI. None the less, TNCs are a source of powerful internal enterprise-created links that may contribute to the integration of national economies. Countries should aim to set realistic objectives in relation to integration or preferential trade: to determine how TNCs fit into the picture, to structure their entry, operation and exit and to negotiate deals. In addition, if the integrated countries master the production of goods and services to such an extent that it increases their international competitiveness, then firms within the area may expand abroad and themselves become TNCs. They may increase the employment of home resources and enter new markets beyond the confines of the market of the integrated area.

Suppose that a monopolist TNC exports a good to a group of integrated countries protected by a common binding quota. If the TNC also decides to locate within the integrated area, it may choose to produce there any quantity of the good it wishes. In such a case, the integration scheme (as a whole, but not necessarily every part of it) may benefit significantly as there is additional employment of domestic factors and domestic consumers also gain because the price of the good may fall. In another case, if local firms are competing with a TNC in the home market, the location of the TNC within the integrated area may benefit both consumers (price falls) and resource utilisation as domestic firms must become more competitive if they want to remain in business. If such a process works well, then there is no justification for restrictions on the operation of foreign TNCs in an integrated area (be it in the developed or developing world).

An arrangement that integrates countries may improve the terms of trade of the group with the rest of the world. If the price of a good or service that is imported to the group falls after integration, then such an arrangement increases the rents of the scheme to the detriment of those previously made by foreign firms. Suppose that country A and country B integrate. If a TNC outside the integration scheme that produces good X is located in country B prior to integration and continues to operate there after the regional arrangement is formed, then the price of good X may fall as a result of either competition in the integrated market or the increased efficiency that comes from economies of scale. If country A starts importing good X from country B, then country A experiences other benefits in addition to the stimulation of trade. The rents of the TNC dwindle, whereas the surplus of country A's consumers rises. In this case country A experiences the so-called *foreign profit diversion effect*. If another TNC in country A were to produce good Y, which is then exported to the partner country B after integration, country A experiences the opposite effect of *foreign profit creation effect* (Tironi, 1982, pp. 155–6).

Foreign profit creation/diversion effects are of vital importance to integration schemes whose economic structures are dominated or influenced by TNCs. This may be the case in countries that are involved in the 'globalisation' of international business, as well as in many developing countries. If such countries integrate, then TNCs are mostly interested in favourable foreign profit creation effects. Consider two countries contemplating integration, each of which has in its market a TNC that manufactures the same undifferentiated good. If the leverage of the two TNCs on decision making is significant in the two countries, then the TNCs may collude and undermine the integration efforts.

Governments usually respect the opinions of the business community, especially if the business has a significant effect on the welfare of the country. Hence, in some cases, TNCs may even play off one government against another and continue with an inefficient (from a resource allocation point of view) but, for them, profitable production.[46] This is one reason why the integration arrangements of developing countries may include provisions that refer to TNCs. None the less, the policy of an integrated area towards TNCs depends on the basic objectives of the group. If the basic objective of the group is an increase in employment, then ownership of the firms is irrelevant. FDI is, after all, an investment. If the goal of the group is to shift rents towards the integrated countries, then it matters who is the owner of the manufacturing and services production and marketing units.[47] In reality, however, governments are not totally indifferent to who owns 'national' assets and structures.

If the integrated market of the (developing) countries is still small enough for the establishment of a cluster of related suppliers, then the major beneficiaries may be TNCs that assemble goods and/or perform only limited (usually final) manufacturing operations. Such a tendency may be enhanced when the integrated countries have relaxed rules of origin for goods that qualify for liberal treatment in internal trade. Although the internal trade of the group increases, so does the extra-group import content of the traded goods. Broad regional deepening of production linkages does not take place. Estimates of the potential increase in trade should refer to the dual pattern of trade (imports of components from abroad and export of finalised goods within the group) and discount the gross increase in internal trade of the region. Instead of the expected relative reduction in the dependency on external markets, integration on such terms may have the completely opposite effect.

The governments of potential host countries may compete with one another in offering subsidies to TNCs to entice them to invest and locate in their country. In this game, the principal winners may be the TNCs themselves as their bargaining power is enhanced. One outcome may be that TNCs locate in more than one country, supply the local protected market and engage in parallel production on a scale that is suboptimal from a resource allocation point of view, while these countries lose interest in the integration process. Such a strategy requires a common competition policy, a joint industrialisation programme and coordinated treatment of TNCs by countries in the group, otherwise the links with the suppliers from the local economy and integration partner country may be superficial. Integration may lead to a production structure that is dominated by firms alien to the integrated group and in which potentially positive absorption and spread of changes in the market (created by the involvement of TNCs) by the local enterprises fails to take place.

Transnational corporations have an interest in promoting integration among developing countries with small markets, but only in countries where they have not been involved before integration. In medium-sized and large developing countries, the position of TNCs may be quite different. TNCs may in fact attempt to prevent integration among countries of this size. The primary concern of TNCs may not be efficiency in production, but rather the likely reactions of other TNCs, as well as the avoidance of conflicts (UNCTAD, 1983, p. 12).

7. European Union

ISSUES

Free capital mobility largely results in the loss of national monetary independence. For example, all else being equal, an increase in a member country's interest rate relative to those in the outside world, intended to slow down the economy and curb inflation, would have the result of increasing the domestic money supply. Many TNCs would invest funds in that country in order to profit from higher rates of interest. The reverse situation, of a country lowering its interest rates with the intention of stimulating economic activity by cheap loans, would lead to a decrease in available funds as TNCs would transfer financial resources to countries with higher rates of interest (Panić, 1991, p. 212). It is unlikely that national firms would be able to influence exchange rate policy to the same degree and as fast as TNCs. However, this does not mean that TNCs render government policies irrelevant. The governments of large countries still have significant autonomy to pursue policies in the national interest for two reasons. First, they have more self-sufficient economies than small countries and, second, the size of their market is such that TNCs do not want to be excluded from it. Hence, TNCs will be careful not to irritate the host government (Panić, 1998, pp. 273–4).

The establishment of the European Economic Community, as phase 1 in the integration process, stimulated TNCs from the US to invest and later expand activities in this region during the 1960s and 1970s. The implementation of the Single Market Programme (phase 2 in the integration process) and the completion of the Single European Market was expected to increase investment of Japanese TNCs in the EU. However, the realisation of this expectation also depended, in part, on the evolution of the tariffs and NTBs in the EU. The establishment of the eurozone in 1999 as phase 3 in the EU integration process may reinforce the attractiveness of the EU as a location for FDI. This expectation was supported by a relative decline in the value of the euro relative to the dollar in the first year of its operation.

While phase 1 in the integration process eliminated (among other things) tariffs on internal trade, the objective of phase 2 was to eliminate NTBs on internal trade, which was expected to increase efficiency of production (rationalised investments), reduce transaction costs, increase competition and demand and harmonise standards. This required some adjustments of internal production in the EU. The rationale for the existence of 'tariff factories' was removed. Thus, investment in production that avoided internal EU barriers was significantly reduced or even eliminated. In any case, phase 2 was expected to increase the operation and investment of TNCs originating in the EU, as well as cooperative agreements and strategic alliances between them. An additional effect would be investment creation. In the longer term, it was thought that European TNCs could become like those in the US and take full advantage of economies of scale. Europeans generally have more demanding and sophisticated tastes than American consumers, and demand differentiated goods (one need go no further than Italy for examples of this behaviour). Hence, large-scale production of homogenised goods, as occurs in the US, has never been expected in the EU. The objective of phase 3 in the EU integration process is to 'level the monetary playing field' for the countries that take part in the eurozone and to remove all exchange rate risks that jeopardise competition, trade and investment. Eastern enlargement as phase 4 in the integration process widens the EU market to cover 25 countries and makes the EU a more attractive location for FDI.

Foreign TNCs initially feared that the EU would create a 'Fortress Europe' whose aim would be to protect the home market through the Single

Market Programme. Some of them rushed to establish themselves in the EU before the potential 'discrimination' took place. Target enterprises in the EU became overvalued to the extent that other locations, most notably in the US, began to appear more attractive. Despite this, the EU continued to be an interesting location for FDI, as foreign TNCs were also hoping to enter into strategic alliances with EU firms.

Fragmentation of production in various EU countries had as its result a replication of various group functions. The primary impact of the Single European Market on TNCs located in the EU was through increased competition. TNCs were led to coordinate production in their subsidiaries in order to profit from economies of scale. Horizontally integrated TNCs such as 3M responded to the deepening of integration in the EU by specialisation of production in their plants. 'Post it' notes are made in its British plant, while scotch tape is produced in its German unit. Previously, 3M produced a wide range of 'sticky' goods in each country in order to serve predominantly the local market. Vertically integrated TNCs such as Ford responded to the new opportunities by vertical specialisation. Differentials and gearboxes are produced in France, while engines are made in Spain. A further restructuring of the company, announced in 2000, ended production in Belarus, Poland and Portugal, and concentrated output in Germany, Spain and Belgium.[48] In addition, there emerged a special kind of relation among the competing firms. A removal of NTBs on internal trade and liberalisation of public procurement 'forced' inter-firm specialisation in similar goods. For example, ICI (Britain) specialised in marine, decorative and industrial paints, while BASF (Germany) did the same in automobile paints (Dunning, 1994a, pp. 296–7).

In spite of the potentials for the concentration of production that were provided by the Single European Market, the Japanese (and the US) car-producing TNCs continue to spread locations for production in the EU, rather than simply aim to concentrate production to employ economies of scale (Ando, 1998, p. 23). Although the Japanese began by assembling cars in Britain, they are now starting to settle their new production activities elsewhere in the EU (Toyota plant in France).

EVOLUTION

The Defense Production Act (1950) in the US and its amended Section 721, known as the Exxon–Florio amendment (1988), give the US president the right to block mergers, acquisitions or takeovers of domestic firms by foreign TNCs when such action is likely to jeopardise national security. If a merger, acquisition or takeover has security implications, it has to be notified for clearance with the Committee on Foreign Investment in the United States (CFIUS) which implements the Exxon–Florio provisions. Japan has few formal barriers to inward FDI. None the less, the real obstacles to FDI in Japan are not found in the legal sphere. They exist as a cost of 'doing business in Japan', such as close and strong informal links among businesses, tight labour markets, language barriers and difficulties in obtaining the necessary data.

Unlike the US, the EU does not have a common policy regarding FDI. Only Article 43 of the Treaty of Rome gives the right of establishment to businesses throughout the EU for the nationals of any member state. Of course, articles that refer to the issues that include competition, taxation, environment, industry and social issues also refer to FDI. In any case, the EU has the lowest barriers in the industrialised world to inward FDI (OECD, 2003b, p. 169). The obstacles mainly included personnel restrictions, local content requirements and government procurement.

The impact of the creation of the EU on the attraction of FDI from the US was at the centre of early studies of the relationship between integration (or, as it was then called, 'tariff discrimination' introduced by the EU and EFTA) and FDI. The expectation was that the spatial location of FDI would be influenced by integration, and in particular that the establishment of the EU would lure TNCs there. Scaperlanda (1967, p. 26), in examining the American FDI trend in Europe between 1951 and 1964, found that the formation of the EU(6) did not attract a large share of American FDI. FDI from the US to the EU(6) since 1958 has amounted to $3.5 billion, compared with $4 billion to non-EU European countries over the same period. Factors such as familiarity with the country in which the investment was to be located, differences in the application of technology and the financial liquidity to fund foreign investment had a greater effect on the spatial distribution of FDI than the creation of the EU(6). In addition, the American TNCs were more interested in the French market than in the EU(6).

Instead of calculating the FDI trend for the whole 1951–64 period, merging 'before' and 'after' EU effects (as did Scaperlanda) and masking investment shifts rather than revealing them, Wallis (1968) divided the period of analysis into two subperiods. The share of the American FDI in the EU(6) moved along a continuous and increasing path in the 1951–64 period with a kink in 1958. Before 1958, the EU(6) share increased by 0.7 per cent a year, whereas after 1958 the average annual increase was 2.7 per cent. An increase in the US FDI in Europe was also observed in the following way: 'Fifteen years from now it is quite possible that the world's third largest industrial power, just after the United States and Russia, will not be Europe, but *American industry in Europe*. Already, in the ninth year of the Common Market, this European market is basically American in organisation' (Servan-Schreiber, 1969, p. 3).

D'Arge (1969, 1971a, 1971b) attempted to determine the impact of European integration on American FDI in the EU and EFTA. The effect of the formation of a trading bloc on the location of FDI may follow three patterns:

- a one-off (intercept) shift in trend;
- a gradual increase in trend (slope shift); or
- a combination of the other two.

The data showed that, in the case of EFTA, there was a positive intercept shift (a one-off effect), while in the period following the creation of the EU(6) there was a combination of shifts in both slope and intercept.

Scaperlanda and Reiling (1971) found that European integration had no significant effect on US FDI flows in this region: FDI flows to the EU(6) and EFTA were similar after 1959, although it had been expected that the EU would attract more FDI than EFTA did. However, it is important to remember that at that time the major beneficiary of US FDI was the UK, which was a member of EFTA, but not the EU(6). Thus, early studies of the impact of integration on FDI do not give a clear picture of the effect of integration on FDI.

Clarification of the situation came later with evidence that, in the case of American FDI in the EU(6), size and growth of the market played an important role (Goldberg, 1972, p. 692; Scaperlanda and Balough, 1983, p. 389). However, Culem (1988) argued that FDI is not in direct competition with domestic investments. A foreign country may be desirable in its own right because it has a specific factor (not available at home) that is necessary for the production process, or because an external outpost may be better placed to monitor developments in foreign markets or because the foreign government has exerted political pressure to locate there. Culem found that 'the size of the European market does not appear to exert any attraction on U.S. direct investments' (1998, p. 900).

Econometric modelling of FDI is a formidable task as FDI flow is a cyclical phenomenon, while determinants are complex, changeable over time and space and not always measurable. The results of models depend greatly on the assumptions made, so the conclusions can only be tentative. None the less, there is general support for the hypothesis that tariff discrimination, regionalism and integration influence FDI. However, this cannot be translated into a statement that an x per cent change in tariffs will induce a y per cent change in FDI. Therefore, strong policy recommendations on the basis of such models would be reckless (Lunn, 1980, p. 99).

Recent studies report that the net effect of integration has been to increase both internal EU and third-country investment in the EU. The elimination of import duties on internal EU trade encouraged non-EU investors to locate in the EU (Dunning and Robson, 1987, p. 113), while the elimination of NTBs (Single Market Programme) and widening of the internal market prompted both EU and third-country TNCs to invest.[49] An increase in the FDI activity following the start of the Single Market Programme in 1985 has been confirmed not only by Eurostat statistics, but also by studies including those by Aristotelous and Fountas (1996, p. 579), Dunning (1997, p. 13), Jovanović (1997a, pp. 324–9; 1998a, pp. 158–64; 2001a, pp. 239–52), European Commission (1998) and Clegg and Scott-Green (1999, p. 612).

The Single Market Programme prompted TNCs to rationalise their operations in the EU. Hence, the absence of any reference to TNCs in the influential official reports generated by the Single European Act, such as Emerson et al. (1988) and Cecchini (1988), comes as a surprise. The assumption in those reports seems to be that international specialisation and trade is carried out by firms whose operational facilities are confined to a single country. The growth and predominance of TNCs in most areas of economic activity made this kind of analysis inappropriate (Panić, 1991, p. 204).

Britain has always been a relatively attractive location for TNCs, although its economic performance relative to other EU major economies has often been poor. What is the reason for this interest? Regional incentives are no more generous there than in the rest of the EU.[50] One reason for its appeal that is often cited is the commonality of the English language, although large TNCs are able to afford to ease and overcome the language barrier. Another reason that is sometimes put forward is that a presence in Britain can serve as a springboard to the rest of the EU, but this could equally apply to other EU member states. Britain scores well in the following essentials:

- the labour force can be highly competent and experienced, but relatively low paid (compared with other major EU countries, in particular during the periods when the pound is low as was the case at the end of the 1970s) and because of relatively low add on costs (social charges);
- a relatively large and open domestic market;
- a favourable industrial and educational infrastructure;
- social and political stability; and
- once clusters of TNCs were established, they started to act as a magnet for other TNCs to locate in Britain ('snowball effect').

Japanese TNCs have not been reluctant to invest in Britain. However, they prefer to build new factories in rural areas rather than take over existing plants. They also prefer takeovers to joint ventures. Where Japanese TNCs have a clear comparative advantage they generally prefer 'greenfield' entry (the preferred way to locate). One advantage of this is that previous managerial habits and labour relations are not inherited. In addition, such sites are often in depressed areas which attract subsidies. Greenfield locations enable Japanese TNCs to introduce their own technology, work practices and management style, with high productivity (Ford and Strange, 1999, p. 124). In Britain, Japanese TNCs were not always attracted to existing clusters, but created new ones. In industries where their comparative advantage is weaker, Japanese TNCs are more likely to form alliances and joint ventures.

In the US, Japanese investors tend to prefer locations (states) where labour unionisation is low. This has less to do with saving on labour costs and more to do with the Japanese organisation of production. Japanese manufacturing plants often require fewer job categories than is the case in their American counterparts. Labour unions are perceived as impediments to flexible production practices. In some cases, Japanese TNCs prefer to locate in rural areas as they mistrust urban workers because they perceive that these workers have developed 'bad work habits' and because they have greater mobility (Woodward, 1992, pp. 696–9). In addition, Japanese TNCs in the car industry offer relatively high wages in order to ensure the development of higher levels of human capital and workforce stability. This is in sharp contrast to the hypothesis in the earlier literature that TNCs predominantly seek locations for their investment in the areas where they can profit from low wage costs (Smith and Florida, 1994, pp. 29–30, 39).

Yamawaki (1993, pp. 19–20) argued that the decision about the location of production depends not only on factor costs, but also on comparative advantage in technology in the target country. A Japanese TNC from a particular industry invests in the country that already has a comparative advantage in the same industry over its counterparts in the EU partner countries.

Spatial choice of location of Japanese TNCs has the following policy implications for the countries that consider the location of these TNCs as an astute policy choice (Ford and Strange, 1999, pp. 133–4):

- Japanese TNCs are attracted to areas with a cluster of manufacturing industries in which they operate and where there exists a high density of previous Japanese FDI;
- a highly educated and innovative workforce attracts Japanese TNCs, with consequent policy implications for education and R&D;

- labour market flexibility and low level of labour unionisation are preferred by the Japanese TNCs. This may be a stimulus to labour market reform; and
- Relatively low wages are also an attractive factor for Japanese TNCs.

FLOW OF FOREIGN DIRECT INVESTMENT

Table 9.8 summarises internal EU FDI outflows per investor country during the 1992–2001 period. FDI outflows were steadily increasing from €33 billion in 1992 to a peak of €687 billion in 2000. As was the case with the global world FDI flows, owing to the economic slowdown internal FDI flows declined to €251 billion in 2001. The largest investors were Germany, Belgium/Luxembourg,[51] France, the Netherlands and Sweden.

The destination of internal EU FDI flows is given in Table 9.9. These flows were concentrated in Britain, Belgium/Luxembourg, France, Germany, the Netherlands, Spain and Sweden. Apart from Spain, these countries were at the same time major internal investors in the EU. Internal flows of FDI in the EU, therefore, suggest a trend towards agglomeration.

Before the start of the Single Market Programme, endogenous EU firms generally had a primarily national orientation, whereas foreign-owned TNCs (mainly American) had a pan-European business perspective. The removal of NTBs that came with the Single Market Programme was, among other things, aimed at addressing this disequilibrium in European business operations. It had an obvious and positive impact on internal FDI flows from 1985. EU internal FDI flows became more important than outflows from the EU to third countries in the 1990–96 period. Another interesting observation is that the southern countries such as Greece and Portugal (but also Denmark) were initially left out of the internal EU flows of FDI, but began slowly to catch up in the course of the 1990s.

The EU countries were investing not only within their group, but also outside of it. Data on external EU FDI outflows are given in Table 9.10. The US and EFTA countries have always been both major locations (targets) for FDI from the EU and, at the same time, major sources of FDI coming into the EU (Table 9.11). This evidence supports arguments about agglomeration tendencies in FDI. It is interesting to note that favourable trade and cooperation together with prospects for the full entry of the EU were incentives for an ever-increasing flow of FDI from the EU to the candidate countries. Hence, the possibility of EU accession contributed to the changing geography of production in the region.[52] The principal EU

Table 9.8 Intra-EU(15) FDI flows, 1992–2001, per EU investor country (€m)

Investor EU country	1992	1993	1994	1995	1996	1997	1998	1999	2000	2001
European Union (15 countries)	32 714	37 231	39 358	43 163	44 723	61 284	122 720	347 856	687 461	250 908
Eurozone (EUR(11) up to 31.12.2000 / EUR(12) from 1.1.2001)	–	–	–	–	40 393	49 383	93 433	235 961	572 100	216 543
Belgium–Luxembourg	6 737	6 302	5 357	6 489	7 943	7 866	12 229	118 447	201 185	53 936
Denmark	541	843	3 053	2 587	208	1 860	1 320	7 356	28 169	5 295
Germany	1 400	1 093	4 262	5 572	4 634	7 279	19 712	43 155	206 961	30 238
Greece	–	–	–	–	–	–	–	–	1 155	1 641
Spain	4 300	6 963	5 446	3 784	3 590	4 719	9 493	7 551	27 807	20 163
France	8 212	7 803	9 341	11 646	13 152	14 279	20 934	35 384	40 328	49 827
Ireland	–	–	–	–	–	–	–	2 807	36 763	12 432
Italy	1 501	2 528	1 467	2 567	2 274	2 224	2 117	2 500	8 382	10 194
Netherlands	–	5 987	1 616	5 104	2 822	7 058	12 833	22 019	28 865	24 792
Austria	–	–	–	387	2 920	1 090	3 471	775	7 900	4 702
Portugal	1 168	1 070	681	390	691	1 187	586	187	6 193	5 686
Finland	221	538	826	206	776	1 112	9 508	3 137	7 716	2 931
Sweden	196	1 264	2 378	853	2 205	5 092	12 950	47 948	12 797	10 436
United Kingdom	3 011	–428	1 259	1 344	1 256	4 861	14 865	56 581	73 240	18 634

Source: Eurostat (2003).

Table 9.9 Intra-EU(15) FDI flows, 1992–2001, per recipient EU country (€m)

Destination	1992	1993	1994	1995	1996	1997	1998	1999	2000	2001
European Union (15 countries)	48 222	40 711	53 593	53 787	63 013	76 119	131 986	342 406	588 233	175 773
Eurozone (EUR(11) up to 31.12.2000 / EUR(12) from 1.1.2001)	–	–	–	–	50 653	55 939	108 012	280 854	352 243	170 738
Belgium–Luxembourg	7 332	2 675	866	6 671	2 347	5 930	16 778	112 942	158 640	54 009
Denmark	1 460	297	2 212	998	1 614	2 460	3 280	6 835	17 338	4 497
Germany	9 929	10 022	8 558	17 292	17 202	11 306	22 611	58 058	5 467	–11 226
Greece	–	–	–	–	–	–	–	–	1 932	233
Spain	234	1 584	474	827	1 634	3 826	5 241	10 983	23 683	15 249
France	11 891	6 012	10 345	9 014	11 626	15 597	20 246	66 103	104 602	54 795
Ireland	–	–	–	–	–	–	–	145	–663	2 315
Italy	2 464	4 732	3 201	3 601	3 732	5 667	5 183	1 443	9 088	22 273
Netherlands	–	6 840	9 102	5 927	11 482	8 415	17 163	29 436	33 210	15 737
Austria	–	–	–	411	437	750	1 282	896	3 472	11
Portugal	462	77	163	416	184	681	958	–1 854	2 703	6 263
Finland	87	1 983	3 418	691	1 952	2 545	18 154	2 702	12 041	11 080
Sweden	–69	1 192	2 655	1 214	663	1 305	9 519	7 192	22 130	1 096
United Kingdom	6 364	4 421	5 090	5 017	9 580	16 340	11 021	47 526	194 591	–558

Source: Eurostat (2003).

Table 9.10 EU(15) FDI flows to third countries, 1992–2001, per target destination (€m)

Destination	1992	1993	1994	1995	1996	1997	1998	1999	2000	2001
European Union (15 countries)	17 670	24 377	32 386	46 022	46 992	85 460	198 669	276 977	373 998	207 308
EFTA (CH, IS, LI, NO)	1 525	1 692	8 265	1 928	3 831	8 307	21 563	8 864	63 997	15 773
13 Candidate countries (BG, CY, CZ, EE, HU, LV, LT, MT, PL, RO, SK, SI, TR)	–	–	2 882	5 533	5 581	6 936	10 508	11 643	17 840	14 488
United States	6 956	13 856	9 772	24 581	17 275	36 113	119 130	176 929	175 757	98 491
Japan	420	–1 172	735	853	2 159	513	384	8 491	6 852	9 045

Source: Eurostat (2003).

Table 9.11 EU(15) inward FDI flows from third countries, 1992–2001 (who invests in the EU) (€m)

Origin	1992	1993	1994	1995	1996	1997	1998	1999	2000	2001
European Union (15 countries)	22 907	20 775	22 132	37 934	32 422	39 773	86 983	89 531	126 010	96 743
EFTA (CH, IS, LI, NO)	3 309	1 913	5 450	7 261	6 307	3 984	16 361	7 078	16 509	−2 167
13 Candidate countries (BG, CY, CZ, EE, HU, LV, LT, MT, PL, RO, SK, SI, TR)	–	–	473	199	118	140	404	326	946	1 532
United States	12 424	10 886	11 722	24 332	20 630	21 416	47 880	65 278	59 686	66 882
Japan	1 858	1 599	1 340	1 540	459	2 614	2 779	−1 942	9 661	3 437

Source: Eurostat (2003).

investor outside the EU was Britain, followed by France and Germany (Table 9.12). Other important investor countries were the Netherlands, Spain and Belgium/Luxembourg.

In general terms, the EU, together with the US, was the major target for the location of FDI from third countries. The principal foreign (third-country) investor in the EU was the US (Table 9.11), followed at a large distance by EFTA. Japan also invested in the EU, but its investment was much less than FDI by EFTA. Yamada and Yamada (1996) reported that the principal goal of Japanese investors in the EU was to avoid emerging protectionism. The EU candidate countries invested modestly in the EU, predominantly in trade-related services.

Earlier data on FDI flows demonstrate that that intra-EU FDI flows became very important from 1989. A comparison of total FDI flows in Tables 9.8 and 9.12 shows that EU investors invested more within the EU than outside it in almost every year during the period of observation (1992–2001). Previously, regional integration was only one factor that influenced FDI flows from the EU countries within and out of the EU. While the liberalisation of internal EU trade had a strong impact on trade integration, a study of FDI flows shows that before 1989 and during 1995–98, integration was stronger on the global plane than within the EU.

Thomsen and Nicolaides (1991, p. 103) argued that the Single Market Programme had its greatest influence not on the *quantity* of FDI in that period in the EU, but rather on its *timing*. Such an argument should be viewed with caution. The Single Market Programme has the potential to affect (enhance) the long-term growth prospects of the EU. In addition, the programme changed the EU business regime and created advantages additional to the already existing EU specific locational advantages. Hence, the long-term level of inward FDI in the EU is higher than it would have been otherwise (European Commission, 1998, p. 96).

The geographical distribution of incoming FDI in the EU in the 1992–2001 period is given in Table 9.13. The principal location in the EU for external investors was Britain, followed by Belgium/Luxembourg, France, the Netherlands and Germany. Again, there was a certain spatial clustering of FDI in the 'core' EU countries. In addition to these countries, external investors were also interested in Spain and Sweden. Spain can provide a useful example for other EU-rim countries including the countries in Central and Eastern Europe. With its improved infrastructure, unimpeded access to the EU market and relatively abundant well-qualified and cheap (according to EU standards) labour force, it provides an attractive springboard for external TNCs that are

Table 9.12 Extra-EU(15) outward FDI flows per EU investor country, 1992–2001 (who invests outside the EU) (€m)

Origin	1992	1993	1994	1995	1996	1997	1998	1999	2000	2001
European Union (15 countries)	17 670	24 377	32 386	46 022	46 992	85 460	198 669	276 977	373 998	207 308
Eurozone (EUR(11) up to 31.12.2000 / EUR(12) from 1.1.2001)	–	–	–	–	50 684	62 914	115 135	157 534	314 968	191 944
Belgium–Luxembourg	698	1 333	151	2 379	3 994	890	6 035	11 259	78 329	41 680
Denmark	269	779	1 123	1 345	371	1 240	120	4 956	9 069	5 500
Germany	4 425	3 830	5 929	10 924	18 040	22 435	51 636	40 271	46 278	59 566
Greece	–	–	–	–	–	–	–	–	368	464
Spain	727	937	2 977	2 353	2 771	7 248	11 680	28 517	35 661	15 820
France	2 628	4 381	8 976	5 379	11 263	14 159	18 452	41 291	80 202	31 500
Ireland	–	–	–	–	–	–	–	3 838	4 297	2 228
Italy	1 910	1 442	1 101	783	932	3 704	5 605	1 735	4 066	2 681
Netherlands	–	2 978	3 035	4 827	10 892	10 541	16 777	22 753	45 718	33 063
Austria	–	–	–	543	858	617	824	1 537	2 629	2 694
Portugal	67	6	76	115	425	806	1 403	4 440	5 065	1 736
Finland	290	177	251	369	699	1 182	1 172	1 897	12 733	520
Sweden	729	127	685	3 392	–396	5 264	5 509	5 466	10 014	3 930
United Kingdom	504	4 704	2 634	11 604	–3 281	15 528	77 697	109 024	39 570	5 934

Source: Eurostat (2003).

Table 9.13 EU(15) inward FDI flows from third countries, 1992–2001 (who receives FDI from third countries) (€m)

Destination	1992	1993	1994	1995	1996	1997	1998	1999	2000	2001
European Union (15 countries)	22 907	20 775	22 132	37 934	32 422	39 773	86 983	89 531	126 010	96 743
Eurozone (EUR(11) up to 31.12.2000 / EUR(12) from 1.1.2001)	–	–	–	–	20 382	19 622	33 817	61 826	75 406	68 086
Belgium–Luxembourg	1 998	2 899	1 658	2 229	1 792	3 123	6 331	15 315	38 631	23 990
Denmark	243	582	1 076	609	397	610	4 387	3 340	6 852	2 494
Germany	658	2 087	2 444	5 503	4 115	3 937	2 773	13 636	8 425	8 936
Greece	–	–	–	–	–	–	–	–	95	77
Spain	2 065	1 087	2 371	1 023	1 786	919	1 049	7 241	12 921	3 702
France	4 096	2 647	4 495	7 013	4 984	5 702	4 942	6 514	3 994	5 869
Ireland	–	–	–	–	–	–	–	5 523	−19 344	−5 802
Italy	940	673	416	1 112	515	1 039	208	1 091	2 980	1 912
Netherlands	–	272	2 231	3 658	6 646	1 298	16 179	11 791	26 524	28 522
Austria	–	–	–	171	112	323	−295	585	751	339
Portugal	317	227	376	117	−43	350	1 497	−17	113	104
Finland	221	181	244	152	−265	144	244	104	370	−11
Sweden	397	1 002	1 716	8 351	1 314	2 876	1 522	5 370	8 280	2 715
United Kingdom	8 756	7 904	2 398	8 592	9 415	16 581	47 209	18 991	35 422	23 448

Source: Eurostat (2003).

interested in operating in a pan-EU market. The noted enthusiasm of external investors in Spain points to a relative spread of external FDI in the EU.

It has already been mentioned that there was a degree of concentration of FDI in the 'core' EU countries. This was in spite the fact that these countries did not (always) have the highest rates of growth. Greece, Ireland and Portugal had higher rates of growth than Britain. However, in spite of this growth and increasing integration, the size of an individual country market may still be a very important determinant for the location of FDI. The highest-growth countries are not always the principal locations for FDI.

Data for the industry distribution of intra-EU(15) FDI in the 1992–2001 period are presented in Table 9.14. Internally, EU investors were primarily interested finance related services, transport, telecommunications, real estate and business-related services. Within the non-services side of the economy, they were also interested in general manufacturing, petroleum, chemicals, transport equipment and mechanical products.

The distribution of incoming FDI from third countries among sectors and industries in the EU(15) in the 1992–2001 period is presented in Table 9.15. EU services received by far the largest share of FDI from third countries. Finance-related services, real estate, transport and trade were the principal target industries for this type of FDI in EU. Office machinery and transport equipment were the major targets for FDI within the manufacturing sector.

These data permit only cautious conclusions about the impact of the Single European Market and the eurozone on the spatial concentration of extra-EU FDI in EU manufacturing. In the car-making industry, Britain became a less attractive proposition for FDI, while Spain became more so. In the electrical equipment manufacturing industry, Germany became the preferred location for FDI, in particular for the higher-value-added operations. However, it is still a moot analytical point whether inward FDI brings to the EU high-value-added employment and technology or low-level, tariff-jumping assembly work (European Commission, 1998, p. 141). In addition, a high concentration of FDI on finance provokes a question: how big an impact has FDI had on the EU manufacturing industry?

Outflow of FDI from the EU(15) to third countries in the 1992–2001 period is given in Table 9.16. Finance-related services, real estate and business-related services were the principal targets for EU investors in third countries. There was also interest in general manufacturing, as well as in electricity, gas and water. Again, there is a certain clustering of FDI on select industries within the services sector.

Table 9.14 Distribution of internal FDI outflow from EU(15) to other EU countries per destination sector/industry, 1992–2001 (€m)

Destination	1992	1993	1994	1995	1996	1997	1998	1999	2000	2001
Agriculture and fishing	49	33	−24	0	−869	−43	121	−964	43	26
Mining and quarrying	743	615	231	884	683	1 368	1 948	704	−2 009	10 249
Manufacturing	16 680	11 270	19 695	8 613	19 975	22 639	40 047	103 176	53 505	−7 331
Food products	–	–	3 642	−136	1 500	2 567	3 733	9 542	7 829	−1 398
Textiles and wearing apparel	–	–	–	–	–	–	–	149	300	485
Wood, publishing and printing	–	–	–	–	–	–	–	812	703	6 629
Total textiles and wood activities	–	–	2 558	2 256	2 492	2 878	5 676	961	1 004	7 114
Manufacture of chemicals and chemicals products	–	–	–	–	–	–	–	33 756	9 334	−7 592
Total petroleum chemical, rubber, plastic products	–	–	5 419	310	6 799	7 396	8 513	42 214	16 530	−19 827
Metal products	–	–	–	–	–	–	–	4 036	1 347	2 584
Mechanical products	–	–	–	–	–	–	–	26 771	2 101	−646
Total metal and mechanical products	–	–	2 500	1 027	3 073	7 510	2 546	30 810	3 448	1 936
Total office machinery, computers, RTV, communication equipment	–	–	865	−225	2 826	8	8 185	−113	4 921	−574
Total vehicles and other transport equipment	–	–	2 936	2 016	2 505	−511	4 354	453	13 780	5 375
Electricity, gas and water	172	523	670	231	552	2 313	2 893	5 830	3 054	14 214
Construction	318	82	573	756	534	785	537	1 167	1 143	1 294

Table 9.14 (continued)

Destination	1992	1993	1994	1995	1996	1997	1998	1999	2000	2001
Trade and repairs	3 885	3 077	3 783	3 989	7 403	8 873	9 157	16 641	20 642	21 907
Hotels and restaurants	1 108	70	552	1 282	2 050	173	432	−110	−463	−511
Transport, storage and communication	657	567	1 234	1 520	3 115	5 335	1 444	12 398	245 444	7 898
Land transport	–	–	–	–	−71	−770	−932	−712	−955	712
Sea and coastal water transport	–	–	–	–	254	996	501	−88	943	105
Air transport	–	–	–	–	784	2	406	593	−310	462
Total land, sea and air transport	–	–	–	−110	966	227	−25	−206	−320	1 282
Telecommunications	–	–	–	1 605	2 060	4 912	1 043	11 252	235 964	5 860
Financial intermediation	18 647	18 136	12 145	18 863	15 337	11 744	43 510	124 886	185 614	73 604
Monetary intermediation	–	–	–	5 169	4 085	2 812	21 132	12 694	34 491	7 744
Other financial intermediation	–	–	–	7 798	9 598	8 472	11 256	97 573	145 630	55 683
Insurance and activities auxiliary to insurance	–	–	–	5 776	1 389	395	8 629	4 634	5 072	7 765
Total other financial intermediation and insurance	–	–	–	13 574	10 987	8 870	19 884	102 206	150 705	63 446
Real estate and business activities	5 020	4 620	9 694	9 812	9 427	18 920	29 700	79 307	71 718	51 154
Real estate	–	–	–	726	260	1 481	3 514	2 702	3 571	2 242

Computer activities	—	—	—	211	453	541	654	1986	3271	525
Research and development	—	—	—	225	23	118	276	65	530	162
Other business activities	—	—	—	8441	8246	16465	22875	65461	63029	41555
Total computer, research, other business activities	—	—	—	8877	8716	17124	23808	67514	66826	42243
Other services	723	468	581	1177	1399	3480	394	2481	10145	7525
Not allocated	220	1250	4459	2229	4833	530	1803	−3110	−602	−4257
Sub-total	48222	40711	53593	53787	62805	76116	131986	342406	588233	175773
Miscellaneous manufacturing	—	—	—	—	—	2791	7041	19309	5994	43
Miscellaneous transport, storage and communication	—	—	—	—	—	196	426	1352	9800	758
Miscellaneous financial intermediation	—	—	—	—	—	63	2494	9987	418	2415
Miscellaneous real estate in business activities	—	—	—	—	—	315	2379	9091	1320	6670

Source: Eurostat (2003).

Table 9.15 Distribution of FDI inflow from third countries per destination sector/industry in the EU(15), 1992–2001 (€m)

Destination	1992	1993	1994	1995	1996	1997	1998	1999	2000	2001
European Union (15 countries)	22907	20775	22132	37934	32422	39773	86983	89531	126010	96743
Agriculture and fishing	105	−49	71	17	−280	143	48	35	26	−9
Mining and quarrying	752	655	1873	1246	−536	−855	836	1262	−1368	10582
Manufacturing	8333	7855	5331	14620	6529	11436	20105	27062	−15611	9650
Food products	–	–	790	824	−651	−605	729	2633	−4488	−1198
Textiles and wearing apparel	–	–	–	–	–	–	–	983	–	–
Wood, publishing and printing	–	–	–	–	–	–	–	1567	–	–
Total textiles and wood activities	–	–	826	2331	794	793	1572	2551	2459	2608
Manufacture of chemicals and chemicals products	–	–	–	–	–	–	–	−631	−15108	4573
Total petroleum, chemical, rubber, plastic products	–	–	1364	8412	3517	4441	1860	2838	−16577	5039
Metal products	–	–	–	–	–	–	–	2626	−4734	−96
Mechanical products	–	–	–	–	–	–	–	1880	−3368	−963
Total metal and mechanical products	–	–	487	439	−159	3456	2533	4499	−8104	−1057
Total office machinery, computers, RTV, communication equipment	–	–	435	1832	1094	1385	10070	3200	4092	4413
Total vehicles and other transport equipment	–	–	165	−112	1727	1420	937	9383	4260	−722
Electricity, gas and water	404	144	−35	2662	1354	3371	1054	992	2641	378

Construction	−25	417	79	−216	2 277	846	−21	501	−624	−580
Trade and repairs	2 760	2 763	2 757	2 079	5 096	3 829	−1 896	5 476	9 950	2 556
Hotels and restaurants	284	202	64	119	475	623	426	−39	1 303	599
Transport, storage and communication	604	606	311	−7	549	2 444	9 275	4 209	15 295	4 164
Land transport	—	—	—	—	21	303	65	199	46	447
Sea and coastal water transport	—	—	—	—	93	742	30	6	−43	12
Air transport	—	—	—	—	290	61	358	119	122	311
Total land, sea and air transport	—	—	—	6	400	1 109	450	320	121	769
Telecommunications	—	—	—	130	−57	492	7 166	3 050	15 090	2 718
Financial intermediation	5 614	5 633	4 708	4 732	8 834	5 013	34 860	27 694	39 049	46 786
Monetary intermediation	—	—	—	1 489	1 212	3 567	2 440	789	−4	266
Other financial intermediation	—	—	—	4 220	5 692	−158	30 070	23 898	36 156	43 740
Insurance and activities auxiliary to insurance	—	—	—	−975	1 874	1 334	2 383	3 101	2 955	2 569
Total other financial intermediation and insurance	—	—	—	3 245	7 566	1 178	32 449	26 999	39 115	46 310
Real estate and business activities	2 807	3 306	5 227	9 275	6 895	11 167	20 890	18 891	42 133	17 150
Real estate	—	—	—	1 349	898	222	1 020	560	1 130	2 351
Computer activities	—	—	—	284	300	192	1 887	1 771	3 138	635
Research and development	—	—	—	193	536	28	761	474	−8	559
Other business activities	—	—	—	7 387	4 559	10 370	17 166	15 480	35 855	15 492
Total computer, research, other	—	—	—	7 864	5 390	10 590	19 813	17 725	38 979	16 683

Table 9.15 (continued)

Destination	1992	1993	1994	1995	1996	1997	1998	1999	2000	2001
business activities										
Other services	302	61	464	364	1034	1695	1100	226	2100	623
Not allocated	967	−818	1282	1152	1954	68	306	3221	31116	4842
Sub-total	22907	20775	22132	37934	32396	39776	86983	89531	126010	96743
Miscellaneous manufacturing	–	–	–	–	–	545	2405	1959	2746	568
Miscellaneous transport, storage and communication	–	–	–	–	–	843	1658	839	84	678
Miscellaneous financial intermediation	–	–	–	–	–	268	−29	−94	−61	210
Miscellaneous real estate in business activities	–	–	–	–	–	356	57	606	2024	−1884

Source: Eurostat (2003).

Table 9.16 Distribution of FDI outflow from EU(15) to third countries per destination sector/industry, 1992–2001 (€m)

Destination	1992	1993	1994	1995	1996	1997	1998	1999	2000	2001
European Union (15 countries)	17 670	24 377	32 386	46 022	46 992	85 460	198 669	276 977	373 998	207 308
Agriculture and fishing	37	12	138	27	−1 643	163	183	87	105	188
Mining and quarrying	−248	455	1 906	487	1 072	7 225	49 168	2 822	14 414	−2 717
Manufacturing	7 475	7 444	16 825	19 579	17 764	32 124	64 219	64 060	75 180	64 000
Food products	–	–	1 572	2 038	1 278	3 075	5 974	9 598	17 629	21 343
Textiles and wearing apparel	–	–	–	–	–	–	–	758	1 578	1 410
Wood, publishing and printing	–	–	–	–	–	–	–	1 110	9 510	1 928
Total textiles and wood activities	–	–	2 434	1 939	1 495	2 059	5 635	1 872	11 082	3 339
Manufacture of chemicals and chemicals products	–	–	–	–	–	–	–	2 049	13 016	17 798
Total petroleum, chemical, rubber, plastic products	–	–	6 884	6 874	7 880	10 173	5 217	17 612	14 799	25 887
Metal products	–	–	–	–	–	–	–	2 700	4 319	1 322
Mechanical products	–	–	–	–	–	–	–	5 104	4 717	3 467
Total metal and mechanical products	–	–	1 752	2 678	1 748	5 223	3 156	7 799	9 037	4 791
Total office machinery, computers, RTV, communication equipment	–	–	2 435	333	642	774	4 338	4 064	7 869	−2 827
Total vehicles and other transport equipment	–	–	−1	1 831	291	5 703	33 640	11 176	6 323	6 314
Electricity, gas and water	−185	155	455	951	807	3 057	6 102	29 676	37 340	−956
Construction	128	554	557	352	1 098	773	694	1 370	2 732	844

Table 9.16 (continued)

Destination	1992	1993	1994	1995	1996	1997	1998	1999	2000	2001
Trade and repairs	1 114	2 022	−1 688	1 501	7 085	5 108	5 759	2 823	13 342	16 209
Hotels and restaurants	438	263	412	−242	−176	−863	1 404	334	1 139	3 259
Transport, storage and communication	761	−430	−139	2 936	2 218	3 285	5 141	86 639	18 918	31 407
Land transport	–	–	–	–	−439	74	441	5 253	614	553
Sea and coastal water transport	–	–	–	–	559	−56	77	649	−816	−1 842
Air transport	–	–	–	–	−314	−292	−84	502	17	−236
Telecommunications	–	–	–	1 843	2 054	2 084	3 405	79 116	19 132	29 566
Financial intermediation	5 706	7 063	3 136	10 153	9 960	22 992	39 764	55 067	124 042	45 020
Monetary intermediation	–	–	–	2 810	2 000	5 316	11 278	19 091	21 517	13 535
Other financial intermediation	–	–	–	6 284	5 247	7 288	23 434	27 804	80 404	26 541
Insurance and activities auxiliary to insurance	–	–	–	1 152	2 452	9 890	3 510	7 684	18 835	3 577
Total other financial intermediation and insurance	–	–	–	7 436	7 699	17 175	26 943	35 488	99 236	30 120
Real estate and business activities	827	4 262	2 859	7 554	8 362	10 132	22 252	13 842	53 819	29 575
Real estate	–	–	–	259	792	−523	479	1 329	2 337	2 634
Research and development	–	–	–	218	283	58	93	194	501	966
Other business activities	–	–	–	6 807	6 170	9 084	18 341	10 026	40 683	17 535
Total computer, research, other business activities	–	–	–	7 212	6 753	10 091	21 545	11 648	49 115	24 754

Other services	682	248	−400	808	−148	786	2 436	4 275	5 481	−6 037
Not allocated	935	2 329	8 325	3 284	3 300	690	1 548	15 982	27 489	26 515
Sub-total	17 670	24 377	32 386	46 022	46 933	85 463	198 669	276 977	373 998	207 308
Miscellaneous manufacturing	–	–	–	–	–	5 118	6 259	11 938	8 440	5 155
Miscellaneous transport, storage and communication	–	–	–	–	–	1 472	1 302	1 123	−26	3 368
Miscellaneous financial intermediation	–	–	–	–	–	501	1 542	487	3 289	1 365
Miscellaneous real estate in business activities	–	–	–	–	–	564	228	865	2 367	2 187

Source: Eurostat (2003).

8. Conclusion

As FDI touches issues such as ownership of land and real estate, direct employment and taxes, it is a more politically charged issue than trade. A popular perception, based on shoddy economics, is that the export of goods is beneficial for a country and, therefore, needs to be supported, whereas (some) imports are perceived to be dangerous as they might jeopardise the national output and employment potential.[53] FDI is, however, treated in a different way. Outflows are being deterred, as there is a fear that exporting capital means exporting exports and exporting jobs, while inflows are welcomed.

With protection and subscale operations by TNCs, the host country may end up worse off than if it had never received FDI. Such a situation may create a vicious circle of adverse signals and harmful incentives. The penalties in terms of lost opportunities are high, but so are rewards for successes in attracting TNCs into well-structured projects. If TNCs operate at full scale in a reasonably competitive environment, they may provide the host economy with the 'usual list' of benefits such as capital, technology and management know-how (Moran, 1998, pp. 155–6).

Capital mobility has its costs and benefits. If these effects are desirable, they should be stimulated, otherwise they should be regulated, controlled and taxed. Simultaneous inflow and outflow of FDI in integrated countries is possible and quite likely. This was confirmed in the case of the EU. However, FDI flows and the consequent geography of production may be significant even without formal integration – just look at transatlantic FDI flows. TNCs primarily follow the opportunities for making profits in large and growing markets in the long term. Therefore, regional economic integration is *a*, rather than *the* cause of FDI.

The relative loss of the international competitive position of the EU in relation to the US, Japan and the newly industrialised countries (in several lines of production) in the 1970s and 1980s has increased both interest in and the need for strengthening the competitiveness of EU companies. These TNCs are the key actors in improving the international competitiveness of goods made and services provided in the EU. Ambitious and well-funded public research programmes in the EU may assist the domestic firms first to catch up and later to improve their position *vis-à-vis* their major international competitors if astutely linked with the production resources and potentials, as well as domestic and foreign demand.

American investors in the EU were market seeking in the 1950s and 1960s. The same was true of Japanese FDI in the 1970s and 1980s. As EU consumers were not able to purchase what they wanted because of NTBs, Japanese TNCs invested in the EU in order to satisfy an existing and growing local demand. TNCs from both source countries have always looked at the EU market as a single unit. Their advantages over local EU enterprises included, in some cases, not only a superior capability to innovate products and technologies and manage multiplant production and supply, but also a willingness, experience and ability to serve consumers from a local base, rather than through exports, which was the favourite method of operation of many national firms in the EU.

There is, however, at least one difference between Japanese and American FDI in the EU. Nearly half of Japanese FDI was concentrated in banking and insurance in the early 1990s. At the same time, more than half of American FDI was in the manufacturing industry, while about a third was in financial services. Therefore, Japanese FDI has relatively less impact, at present, on EU manufacturing industry than the American TNCs (Buigues and Jacquemin, 1992, p. 22; European Commission, 1998, p. 3). This focus by Japanese investors may come as a surprise as Japan has the advantage in electronics and cars. A concentration of Japanese FDI in financial services (relying on human, rather than physical, capital) both in the EU and the US is, however, a partial reflection of Japanese balance of payments surpluses and the appreciation of the yen at that time. However, from 1994, the interest of the Japanese TNCs shifted predominantly towards the Pacific Rim countries.

In order to avoid weakening the competitive position of EU firms in global markets, the EU may follow two courses, although employing a mix of the two has its attractions. First, the EU may increase protection of domestic firms against foreign TNCs through various NTBs (although the use of TRIMs is outlawed by the 1995 WTO Agreement). Second, the EU may open its domestic market and encourage foreign, in particular high-technology, TNCs to locate their manufacturing operations in the EU. As widely argued, EU firms in certain manufacturing industries are less efficient than their counterparts in the US and Japan. If the EU were to adopt and maintain a liberal economic policy and EU firms were to adjust and withstand competition from foreign TNCs, then they may, in relative terms, gain more from market liberalisation than their foreign competitors.

The incomplete internal market in the EU was the major cause of a suboptimal production structure in the region prior to 1993. All economic agents, including TNCs, behave as welfare-maximising units in the long term, subject to the prevailing conditions. These private agents should not be criticised for actions that may be in conflict with public objectives. The start of the Single European Market, which included the removal of NTBs, assisted in a rationalisation of production and enhanced the location-specific advantages of the EU. The introduction of the eurozone in 1999 removed internal EU exchange rate risks and consolidated earlier achievements in integration, at least for the participating countries. Coupled with eastern enlargement (2004), this will continue to increase both the size and the growth of the EU market, which could, in turn, further increase investment expenditure in the region in the longer term.

An extensive survey of the impact of the Single European Market on FDI found strong evidence that FDI and trade are complementary (European Commission, 1998, p. 1). Concerns that the Single European Market would lead to a concentration of general economic activity into the 'core' EU countries were not justified. In fact, there has been a limited spread of economic activity to the 'peripheral' EU countries which enjoy certain cost advantages (European Commission, 1998, p. 145).

As one of the major players in the international capital mobility scene, the EU would like to see multilateral rules for FDI. Even though there are multilateral agreements that deal with specific 'technical' FDI issues such as TRIMs or dispute settlements or with sectoral matters such as services (GATS), there is no overall multilateral agreement on investment. However, FDI issues are discussed within the WTO. The future multilateral agreement may include the following elements:

- Foreigners would have the right to invest and operate competitively in all sectors of the economy; only a few exceptions to the general rule may be allowed.
- There should be no discrimination of foreign investors based on their origin. A 'stand still' commitment would prevent the introduction of new restrictions.
- There should be a 'roll-back' principle to gradually eliminate national (or group) measures that run counter to the liberalisation of FDI rules.

Notes

1. Various regional factors prevent full equalisation of prices. Some geographical areas may have small markets for certain goods and services (for example, parasols in Finland and antifreeze in Greece). So, in order to do business there, firms may price their goods relatively higher. In this case, market presence may be a much more important public policy and private business objective than requiring price homogenisation in all markets within the EU. Or, for example, differences in taste or special requirements regarding the basic ingredients of a product (for instance, chocolate) may cause the price of a good to vary. And, if there are local substitutes, foreign suppliers may modify the price of their goods. Some goods (such as wine) may be regarded as luxuries in one country and taxed accordingly, but regarded as basic necessities in another country. This widens the price gap for the same good in different countries, and sometimes even in different regions of the same country.

2. Exports of high-technology products by developing countries in 2000 amounted to $450 billion. This is $64 billion more than exports of primary products or $140 billion more than medium-technology exports (UNCTAD, 2002, p. 145).
3. *Financial Times*, 25 May 2003.
4. In an early study, Weber (1909) offered two basic reasons why firms 'go to produce abroad'. The primary determinant is the achievement of lower labour and transport costs, while the secondary element is the benefit of large-scale production.
5. *Financial Times*, 25 May 2003.
6. For example, over a certain period of time governments may change the availability, quality and cost of the domestic factors. The disposable tools for this policy include training of labour and education of management, R&D, science, transport and communication infrastructure and tax policies.
7. 'Japanese companies follow each other', said a senior adviser at the Czech investment promotion agency. 'As soon as there is a big famous investor, the others start to consider the possibilities.' The principal reason for the location in the Czech Republic is geography (rather than relatively low wages). Another important reason for the Japanese TNCs is a tradition in technical universities and the electronic industry ('Electronic giants go for Czech launchpad', *Financial Times*, 10 June 2003).
8. In a *merger* two or more firms decide to pool their assets to form a new company. In this process one or more companies diappear completely. An *acquisition* does not consitute a merger if the acquired company does not disappear. Mergers are relatively less frequent than acquisitions.
9. J. Kynge and D. Roberts, 'The Pearl river delta is attracting $1bn of investment a month amid one of the fastest bursts of economic development in history', *Financial Times*, 4 February 2003.
10. How should one measure these benefits? What should be measured? Should it be done in fiscal terms? Or in social terms?
11. 'Jack Straw, foreign secretary, has let it be known that he intends to turn a blind eye to some of the requirements of two-year-old legislation banning UK businesses from bribing foreign officials. . . . From one perspective, his stance can be viewed as pragmatic realism. So-called facilitation payments are exempted by the US Foreign Corrupt Practices Act, a model of its kind, and are not explicitly outlawed by the anti-bribery convention negotiated by members of the Organisation for Economic Co-operation and Development. . . . the borderline between "facilitation" payments and bribes aimed at winning business by underhand means is only loosely defined legally and fuzzy in practice. . . . None the less, his partial and retrospective interpretation of the law sounds curious from a politician who, as home secretary, boasted of being "tough on crime"' ('De minimis non curat Straw', *Financial Times*, 20 February 2004).
12. One should not accord an absolute value to the decline of consumer loyalty to local brands. Regional, rather than 'global' strategies in certain food and health-care products may offer a superior business outcome. However, there was a certain 'global success' by, for example, Coca-Cola, which succeeded in replacing a part of the consumption of milk and healthy natural fruit juices for an artificial and sweet liquid that has a questionable impact on health and weight.
13. It was the church that once determined our life, then the state and now it is corporations. Governments court firms (TNCs) to come and locate within the confines of their control. Critics say that the protection of the vulnerable in society or safeguarding of the environment is weakened, even that it is left to the mercy of big businesses. This may be the case in certain lines of production, but it all depends on specific circumstances. In some cases the regulatory framework facing TNCs was strengthened, while in others it was loosened.
14. The same holds for the increase in the power of special influence groups such as NGOs. Do these unelected groups of people, with sometimes questionable accountability, represent a risky shift of power towards special vested interests? Or do they represent a move towards the new 'civil society' (does anyone know how to define this type of society)? Why does the general public sometimes believe more in these organisations, which often lack resources for rigorous analysis, than in governments?

15. NGOs often consider that it may be better to be just about right and make a big fuss now in order to put an issue on the policy agenda, than to wait a long time for firm scientific evidence and miss the political opportunity.
16. H. Kissinger, 'Globalisation: America's role for the millennium', *Irish Independent*, 13 October 1999.
17. Uniformity and homogeneity in the modern world may be a heavy price to pay for the new or 'better' standardised things we consume. This introduces an ever-present potential for the neo-communist danger that everyone eats and drinks the same, is dressed the same, uses homogeneous (perfectly substitutable) goods and services and ends up or is forced to, perhaps, even think 'the same'. If someone is not 'in step' with these global developments (no matter what their democratic appearance and sugar-coating), well, then . . . the concerned may 'court trouble' from the central 'politburo'!
18. 'Globalisation is no more than an (admittedly ugly) name for the process of integration across frontiers of liberalising market economies at a time of rapidly falling costs of transport and communications' (M. Wolf, *Financial Times*, 3 October 2001, p. 15).
19. *The Economist*, 29 September 2001, p. 14. The reference here is to the attacks of 11 September 2001.
20. Institutional elements such as clear property rights are very important for foreign investors. However, the mere transfer of these solutions from the developed countries elsewhere is not a sufficient condition for a successful economic performance. For example, while Russia has introduced a system of private property rights, China guarded the general socialist legal system. None the less, domestic and foreign investors regarded China as a promising location for investment and this country became one of the prime locations for investment. There was a strong credibility that investments would be protected. In contrast, this credibility was lower in Russia in spite of the property rights system. Hence, this was one of the reasons why Russia continued to score much lower than China as a location for investment.
21. *The Economist*, 'A survey of globalisation', 29 September 2001, p. 4.
22. One thinks of the particular menace of chewing gum for the cleanness of elevators and chairs.
23. Increased international mobility of factors, increased international intra-firm transactions, expanding international cooperative arrangements between firms, the increasing importance of knowledge, as well as a reduction in transport and communication costs, support the process of globalisation and are constituent parts of it. In these circumstances, individual actions of national governments may not increase global welfare (pollution is an example) and certain supranational rules may be necessary in order to deliver more beneficial outcomes.
24. Trade is relatively more concentrated within regions than FDI. This suggests that trade plays a more prominent role in intra-regional integration arrangements, while FDI has a greater influence on global integration (UNCTAD, 1993, p. 7).
25. 'Over 90 per cent of products produced in each of the triad regions is sold within that region. There is no global car. . . . well over 90 per cent of MNE manufacturing is intra-regional rather than global' (Rugman, 2002, p. 5).
26. Control may not be easy to define in all circumstances. A 51 per cent ownership of a firm is a clear sign of full control. However, in some cases 20 or even 10 per cent ownership is sufficient for the control of a firm if other shareholders are widely dispersed and unorganised.
27. According to research carried out by the location division of Ernst & Young, firms now appear to accept higher costs of production in return for high environmental standards. 'Regions that sell themselves on the basis of relaxed environmental legislation may soon find their approach counterproductive' (*Business Europe*, 12 March 1997).
28. Intra-company pricing refers to transactions among related units of the same firm. Not every manipulation of transfer prices increases the overall profits of the entire company, as these extra revenues stem from sales to outside customers (Plasschaert, 1994, p. 1).
29. Trade in services is expanding. Monitoring internal prices for services is a much more

complex task than inspecting the same prices for goods by the employment of free market criteria.
30. Firms are reluctant to comment and release data on their internal prices. Hence, there is a black hole in this area of research.
31. *Financial Times*, 26 January 2004.
32. Tax avoidance, unlike tax evasion, does not involve breaking any laws, but rather making the best use of positive regulations. In practice, the difference between the two is often ambiguous.
33. Transfer of profits out of the country takes place when TNCs do not find the country in question a promising geographical location for the reinvestment of earnings. Such a transfer may send a warning signal to the local government that something is wrong in the economy and that something needs to be done about it.
34. TNCs that come from the US and operate in the EU reported an annual R&D of almost $2500 per employee in 1989. In contrast, Euro-affiliates of Japanese TNCs reported R&D per employee of about $725 in the same year (Gittelman et al., 1992, p. 18). The reasons for the difference include a relatively strong headquarters effect, as Japanese FDI in Europe is a fairly novel phenomenon compared with FDI from the US. American TNCs have been present in Europe on a larger scale since the 1950s. In addition, Japanese TNCs may be more involved in the EU in relatively mature manufacturing industries and services where R&D expenditure is not as high as in other activities.
35. Decisions taken at the EU level are easy targets for special lobbies as they are far from the public gaze. The co-decision procedure between the Council of Ministers and the European Parliament introduced by the Maastricht Treaty tried to ameliorate this shortcoming. This is a step forward compared with the past, but there is still a danger that EU technology policy may become a sophisticated new form of protectionism.
36. One of the most widely cited attempts to introduce a common policy towards TNCs in the groups that integrate developing countries was Decision 24 (1970). This was the first attempt by an integration group of developing countries to develop and implement a policy towards TNCs. It should be mentioned at the outset that the aim of Decision 24 was not to obstruct FDI inflows into the region. On the contrary, the member countries wanted to encourage such inflows, but in a structured way that would benefit members and increase economic efficiency within the region. In addition, they wanted to increase the bargaining power of home firms in relation to foreign TNCs in order to promote equitable distribution of gains from FDI.

The thrust of the complicated and controversial Decision 24 was the regulation of FDI and transfer of technology. It permitted the establishment of national screening and registration bureaus; outlawed new FDI in utilities and services; prohibited an annual reinvestment of corporate profit of more than 5 per cent without approval; allowed the annual transfer of profits of up to 14 per cent; and compelled TNCs to disclose all data that relate to the transferred technology, including data on the pricing of inputs. In addition, the expectation from the divestment stipulation (the most polemic feature) imposed on TNCs was a gradual reduction in foreign ownership of local assets, national capital accumulation and a basis for the development of local technology (Mytelka, 1979, p. 190).

Foreign investors loudly criticised Decision 24 as an unfriendly measure, but in practice they took a more pragmatic and longer-term approach. In spite of stringent conditions for FDI, the flows to the region did not decrease; on the contrary, in some cases they even increased. In order to enhance the inflow of FDI in the region the group replaced Decision 24 by the more liberal Decision 220 in 1987. This move introduced a set of common rules for FDI, but gave independence to the member states in the implementation of the policy. Decision 220 was replaced in 1991 by Decision 291, which offered national treatment of FDI. The intention of the group was to remove obstacles to FDI and promote a free inflow of capital to the region.
37. Local content usually means 'national content' (value added within a country) or value added within the group such as the EU or NAFTA.
38. Article 4 of the same agreement allows only temporary derogations from this obligation to developing countries.

39. For example, Pirelli (Italy) coordinates and guarantees its global financial duties from a Swiss affiliate which is in charge of finance for the whole corporation. The US affiliate of Siemens (Germany) transmitted daily financial data to headquarters, which is in charge of global financial management (UNCTAD, 1993, p. 124).
40. *Financial Times*, 7 March 2002, p. 8.
41. The introduction of a new good depends not only on the fixed costs and expected benefits, but also on substitution and complementarity with the goods that already exist on the market. Of course, real demand for the new good or service must be or needs to be created.
42. Linkages with the local suppliers (local embeddedness) depend on the choice of the TNC and the existence of the suitable local firms with which a TNC can do business.
43. Investment in natural resources has three distinct features. First, the geographical location of non-renewable resources is not mutable; second, investments require huge amounts of capital which is linked with significant economies of scale; and, third, processing of minerals is linked with a considerable consumption of energy.
44. By the end of 2002, 2181 bilateral investment treaties and 2256 double taxation treaties had been signed (UNCTAD, 2003, p. xvi).
45. According to one influential view, no matter what a government does to influence competitiveness and increase exports in the short term would still cause the adjustment of the exchange rate and factor prices in the long term (Johnson and Krauss, 1973, p. 240). The new theory disputed such an approach and argued that, in the presence of increasing returns to scale, externalities and the economies of learning, the policy of the government does matter. Such a policy may, if handled properly, bring irreversible advantages for the country in question.
46. In the situation where TNCs do not dominate in the economy of a country or an integrated group of countries, then, of course, their impact may be marginal. The situation, however, in virtually all present-day regional groupings of developing countries is that TNCs play a dominant role (Robson, 1987, p. 209).
47. Educated management and a trained labour force (domestic human capital) is what matters for the country, rather than ownership of the business (Reich, 1990). Tyson (1991) disagreed with such a view and argued that ownership still mattered. This view is, however, opposed to the traditional and declared US stance that favours free trade and free flow of capital (the application of this in practice was discussed in the chapter on trade policy – see Chapter 7).
48. *Financial Times*, 13 May 2000, p. 1.
49. Yannopoulos (1990) surveyed the diversity of views expressed in the debate on the effect of European integration on FDI.
50. Government incentives influenced TNCs such as Ford to make new investments in the north-west of the country and Wales. Honda, Nissan and Toyota benefited from public grants as they settled in regions with unemployment problems. However, those allowances were equally available in Britain to other firms from the EU or third countries, whether they were from car production or other industries.
51. One has to be careful when interpreting the data for a country such as Luxembourg (or Switzerland). Such countries often act only as intermediates for the inflow and outflow of funds.
52. A similar development occurred in the case of Mexico and the US before the creation of NAFTA.
53. Through trade a country acquires useful things from abroad. Therefore, imports are a gain, rather than a cost. To pay for imports, the country has to 'send' its useful goods and services abroad. In these terms exports are a cost, rather than a gain!

> Lord, we do not know where You are going,
> and how can we know the way?
> John 14:5

10 Mobility of Labour

1. Introduction

Mobility of labour or labour responsiveness to demand has long been a significant facet of economic life. Labour has not only moved among regions and countries, but also among economic sectors. In the late 1950s, agriculture employed about 20 per cent of the labour force in most industrialised economies. Half a century later, agriculture employs about 4 per cent of the labour force in these countries.

The theoretical assumption that labour has a greater degree of mobility within a country than among countries may not always be substantiated. Inter-country mobility of labour between Ireland and other developed English-speaking countries was, perhaps, much greater than internal Irish labour mobility. None the less, labour mobility should not always be taken in its 'technical' meaning of pure movements of persons from place A to place B. One has to bear in mind that these people are moving with their skills, knowledge, experiences and organisational competence.

Outside of common markets,[1] international labour migration is characterised by a legal asymmetry. The Universal Declaration of Human Rights (1948), Article 13, denies the right to the country of origin to close its borders to bona fide emigrants. This country may not control the emigration flows according to its interest. The country of destination, however, has an undisputed right to restrict the entry of immigrants, although this is not explicitly mentioned in the Declaration. In these circumstances migration flows are primarily determined by demand in the receiving countries. So, the personal will and readiness to move is a necessary condition for labour migration, but it is not a sufficient one.

This chapter is structured as follows. Sections 2 and 3 consider the costs and benefits of labour migration for countries of origin and countries of destination, respectively. Section 4 deals with labour mobility in the EU (legal framework, migration data and waves, and the EU response). Section 5 concludes that labour migration, in particular immigration, will be high on the EU agenda of priorities over the coming decades because of demographic trends in the EU and imminent labour shortages that may last several decades.

2. Country of origin

If political instability and economic problems (push determinants) overcome the propensity to stay in the homeland (pull factors), then there are several reasons for the international migration of labour. The most significant include the possibility of finding a job which may be able to provide conditions for better living, as well as improved conditions for specialisation and promotion. Most immigrants to the EU worked prior to migration, although unemployment was a factor that influenced 'push' towards emigration.[2] In these complex conditions migrants act as utility-maximising units subject to push and pull forces.

In general, an emigration pattern has a few phases. Initially, men migrate individually in search of a (better) job and education or in order to escape persecution. Then, gradually, comes a phase which involves women because of family reunification.

The migration of labour has its obstacles. They can be found both in receiving countries and in countries of origin. Socio-psychological obstacles to migration can include different culture and languages,[3] national historical experiences (wars, occupation), rules for the recognition of qualifications, as well as variations in climate, religion, diet and clothing. Such barriers to migration were high in the 19th century for intra-European mobility of labour, which was one of the reasons why Europe was a source of significant emigration at that time. In addition, socio-psychological obstacles may be part of the reason why Japan has almost closed borders for legal immigration. Economic obstacles include lack of information about job openings, conditions of work, social security, legal systems, systems of dismissal (last in, first out) and the loss of seniority. During recession and unemployment periods there may be nationalistic, racial and religious tensions between the local population and immigrants. Some political parties and certain trade unions may lobby against immigration, as well as for driving immigrants away.

Countries of origin have significant losses in manpower. Migrants are usually younger men who are prepared to take the risk of moving. These regions may then be left with a higher proportion of women and older people. Potential producers leave while consumers remain behind. Countries of origin lose a part of their national wealth which was invested in the raising and education of their population. If the migrants are experienced and educated, then their positions may often be filled by less sophisticated staff. The result is lower productivity and lower national wealth.

The brain-drain argument is not always convincing. Many of those who migrate cannot find appropriate jobs in their home countries. The physician who leaves Ghana is one thing – Ghana needs more medical services. An astrophysicist from Congo is quite another. Congo has few laboratories, radio-telescopes or powerful computers; expertise in this field cannot be deployed and so it makes sense for this skilled person to go abroad and possibly send some money back to his country of origin. However, if computer engineers emigrate from Mozambique, there is no point in this country importing computers, and without the import of new technology it will remain backward indefinitely. If the migrants return after a (long) period abroad, some of them may be old and/or ill, so they become consumers. This might all reduce the local tax base and increase the cost of social services to the remaining population.

Apart from these costs, countries of origin can obtain certain short-term gains from emigration. This movement of labour reduces the pressure which is caused by unemployment and reduces the payment of unemployment benefits (if they exist). Possible remittances of hard currency can reduce the balance of payments pressure, and if migrants return they can bring with them certain new skills and (hard currency) savings which can help them to obtain or create better jobs. This can help the development efforts of the country. One should not forget a potential inflow of pension funds.

If some countries do not produce exportable goods, then they have to export labour services (if other countries want to accept that) in order to pay for imports. However, there is an asymmetry in the perception of labour mobility. When the rich north wants to send workers abroad, then that counts as trade in 'services'. When the poor south wants to do the same, it is regarded as 'immigration'.

The volume of possible remittances depends on the number of migrants, the length of their stay, and incentives. The World Bank estimated that the annual volume of remittances in the world by migrants to their families at home is at least $80 billion.[4] The shorter the stay of migrants abroad, the higher the probability that they would transfer or bring back all their savings to their home country. During short stays abroad, their aim is to earn and save as much as possible. If they stay abroad for a longer period, then they may wish to enjoy a higher standard of living than during relatively short stays, thus reducing the volume of funds which may potentially be remitted to their country of origin. If the country of origin offers incentives for the transfer of these funds by way of attractive rates of interest, rate of exchange, allowances for imports and investment, as well as if there is an overall stability, then there is a greater probability that some funds would be attracted.

3. Country of destination

The supply of local labour and the level of economic activity determine the demand for foreign labour in the country of destination. A country may permit an inflow of foreign labour, but this country must be aware that these people come with all their virtues and vices. Foreign workers may face both open and hidden conflicts with the local population. The host-country population may dislike foreigners because they take jobs from the domestic population,[5] they bring their customs, increase congestion, depress wages and send their savings abroad, to mention just a few reasons. In certain cases, such as the migration of retired persons from Scandinavia to Spain or from Canada to Florida, this should not be regarded as migration that is in response to wage differentials. These migrants do not work – they spend and enjoy their life savings, and create a permanent demand for certain services and jobs for the locals.[6]

The country of destination gains obvious benefits from immigration. Migrants are a very mobile segment of the labour force. Once they enter a country, they are usually not linked to any particular place. Mobility of local labour in the EU is quite low.[7] There are various reasons for this, including: relatives and friends living nearby; spouses with jobs that they do not want to leave; children are well settled in local schools; and because they enjoy living in their home, which may still be mortgaged.

In general, the country of destination may acquire labour which is cheaper and whose training has not been paid for by the domestic taxpayers. Migrants increase demand for housing and goods, they pay taxes (which may exceed what they receive in transfer payments and public services) and take jobs that are unattractive to the domestic workforce at the offered rates. These jobs include low-paid and often tedious work in mines, foundries, construction, garbage collection, cleaning, hotels, restaurants and so on. Migrants compete for these vacancies with the local youth and women who may have reduced opportunities for work. While offering lower wages for these jobs, countries of destination may partially reduce the price of inputs (labour) and partially increase competitiveness of their tradable goods and services, at least in the short run.

There are no language barriers to the movement of local labour within the home country. Migrant workers may not know the language of the host country, making it difficult for them to participate in the local social life. The only place where they can express themselves as creative beings is in production, with the result that these workers may sometimes work more quickly and efficiently. This may provoke clashes with the local workers as new production norms may be increased. Migrants may leave after a while, while the locals may be tied by those norms for a long time. Employers may sometimes prefer to conclude direct agreements with migrant workers rather than employ local labour. Migrant workers may not only be working for lower wages than the domestic labour in the absence of legal protection, but also they can be dismissed with fewer repercussions for the employer. Alternatively, the permits of foreign workers' might not be renewed.

The mobility of migrant labour within the country of destination has an impact on the national equalisation of wages. Of course, every new wave of immigration depresses the wages offered to earlier immigrants. Foreign labour that is legally employed need not necessarily be cheaper than local labour as there is legislation requiring the payment of fair wages to all. However, foreign labour is more easily controlled and manipulated by management.

The impact of labour immigration on the local labour market in the destination country has always provoked certain interest. This is particularly true for the traditional destination countries such as the US, Canada and Australia. For example, there is a well-known case of a sudden inflow of refugees from the Cuban port of Mariel to Miami (Florida) in 1980. Within just a few months 125 000 people arrived, increasing Miami's labour force by 7 per cent. However, employment and wages among the local population including the unskilled labour remained virtually unaffected.[8] Surveys of studies about the relation and impact of immigrants on the wage rates and native unemployment in the US found no significant effects (Leamer and Levinsohn, 1995, p. 1360; Simon, 1996, p. 130).[9] Such findings question the widely held view that wages, just as almost everything else on the

American market, are flexible. Analyses of similar effects in Europe are rather limited. A study of the impact of immigrants on the local wages in Britain,[10] the Netherlands[11] and Norway[12] found very small effects (Hartog and Zorlu, 2002, p. 25). This finding would also support the widely held view that wages are quite rigid in Europe.

4. European Union

LEGAL FRAMEWORK

The original Treaty of Rome had only a few provisions that relate to immigration. Article 39 provides for the freedom of movement of workers within the EU. It also abolishes any discrimination among workers who are citizens of the member states. In addition, Article 18 provides the citizens of the EU with an unrestricted right to move and reside within the territory of the EU. Title IV Visas, Asylum, Immigration and Other Policies Related to Free Movement of Persons was introduced into the original Treaty of Rome by the Treaty of Amsterdam (Articles 61–9 of the Treaty of Rome). There is a requirement to establish progressively an area of freedom, security and justice; to introduce common measures for controls while persons are crossing external borders of the EU; and to eliminate all such controls for people (be they EU or non-EU nationals) crossing internal borders within the EU. Britain and Ireland got an opt-out from this provision (Article 69). There is also a requirement for the harmonisation of measures regarding legal and illegal immigration, refugees and asylum.

MIGRATION WAVES

Following the Second World War, the migration of people in Europe had four distinct phases:

- The first phase was the period from 1945 to the early 1960s. People moved because of the adjustment to the situation following the end of the war, as well as because of the process of decolonisation. For example, 12 million ethnic Germans were forced to leave Central and Eastern Europe. Most of them settled in Germany. Colonial powers such as Britain, Belgium, France and the Netherlands were affected by return migration from European colonies and the inflow of workers from former overseas territories. There were over a million

French residents of Algeria who resettled in France during and after the Algerian war of independence.
- The second phase of the movement of people had an overlap with the preceding one. It lasted from 1955 to 1973. Labour shortages in certain EU countries led to openness for immigration. Labour from Italy, Spain, Portugal, Greece, Turkey, former Yugoslavia, Morocco and Tunisia was migrating northwards, mainly, but not exclusively, to Germany and France. About 5 million people moved northwards during this period.
- The third period from 1973 to 1988 was characterised by restrained migration. Following the first oil price shock and the related economic crises and social tensions, the recruitment of foreign labour stopped abruptly. Policies that encouraged return migration were not working. The foreign population in the EU was, however, increasing as family members were joining workers who were already in the EU. In addition, these new residents had high fertility rates.
- The fourth phase started in 1988. It was linked with the dissolution of socialism, economic transition and ethnic wars. Hundreds of thousands of refugees and asylum seekers, as well as economic immigrants moved to the EU countries. Germany alone received 1.5 million new immigrants in 1992 (Zimmermann, 1995, pp. 46–7).

A fifth stage of labour movement may start around the year 2010. Demographical trends and imminent labour shortages in the EU may provoke labour migrations towards the EU for decades to come.

CONSEQUENCES

Conventional wisdom states that an abolition of barriers to international migration of labour would bring an increase in labour flow in relation to the previous situation. This hypothesis could be tested in the case of the EU. The total number of intra-EU migrants of the original six member countries was about half a million prior to 1960, which increased to a little over 800 000 in 1968. This volume of migrant workers remained almost constant until the early 1980s and since then it has decreased to 650 000 migrants. All other intra-EU migrations were national (from southern to northern Italy or from western regions of France into Paris), rather than inter-state. The inevitable conclusion is that the creation of the EU has not significantly changed intra-EU labour migrations. While intra-EU trade increased, the intra-EU migrations decreased. Trade and the migration of labour were substitutes (Straubhaar, 1988).

The explanation for a greater migration of labour from third countries rather than within the EU can be found in part in the differences in production functions and barriers to trade among countries. The more similar the structure and the level of development between countries and the lower the barriers to trade, the greater will be the substitution effect between trade and labour migration. This also explains the migration of labour from Italy just after the creation of the EU, as well as the subsequent reduction in this flow.

The explanation for the decline in intra-EU labour mobility during the 1980s can also be found in significant improvements in the state of their local economies. Labour migration from Italy has slowed down since 1967. The same has happened in Greece since the early 1970s. Similar tendencies can be observed in the cases of Spain and Portugal since the mid-1980s. In addition, traditional countries of emigration such as Italy or Greece became targets for significant legal and illegal immigration. North Africans and Albanians were entering Italy clandestinely, while Greece was a target for a similar migration by the Albanians. A certain number of Bulgarians, Serbs, Poles and Russians entered Greece legally, but stayed on after their permits expired.

An interesting fact is Italy's transition over the past three decades from a net exporter to a net importer of non-European, mainly Mediterranean, illegal labour. Illegal immigrants work in and contribute to the growth of the informal economy. Costs of labour are both lower and more flexible in the black economy. This encourages firms to shift resources from the legal economy to the informal one. However, the technology available is less efficient in the underground economy. Hence, illegal immigration makes possible a transfer of capital (and labour) towards the informal economy. This may be favourable for the firms that avoid tax obligations, but it is damaging for the economy as a whole (Dell'Aringa and Neri, 1989, p. 134).

Recessions now rarely affect only one country. During times of economic slowdown the unemployed in the EU stayed in their country of origin. This was because the chances of finding employment abroad were smaller than at home. If there were some gaps between supply and demand in the labour market, labour migration from third countries was closing them, rather than internal EU flows. Reduced EU internal labour migration was due to a trend which was evening up the income and productivity levels among the original six member countries, as well as the growth in the other EU countries that created domestic demand for labour. Hence, the expectation that the creation of a common market would significantly increase long-term intra-group migrations of labour was refuted in the case of the EU.

There is also a special type of international mobility of labour which is often overlooked. Many TNCs stipulate that their employees must circulate and spend time in various affiliates in order to keep the corporation internationally and personally integrated. Staff often move at regular intervals. Although this is recorded in statistics as international mobility of labour, it occurs within the same firm.

DATA AND TRENDS

Exact data on the flow of migrants are deficient. There is a conservative guess that illegal immigrants into the EU(15) number 500 000 a year.[13] Therefore, Table 10.1 presents an approximation about stock data of the labour force by broad groups of citizenship in the EU in 2002. Just a brief look at the structure reveals the fact that the majority of migrants in the EU were non-EU nationals. Migration of labour can be a significant feature even if countries are not formally integrated.

Immigration into the EU has been the principal source of population growth over the 1990s. In absolute terms migration is highest in recent years in Italy, Britain and Germany. These countries together accounted for more than 60 per cent of the total net immigration in the EU.[14] The net inflow of migrants added 0.2 per cent a year to the EU population during the second half of the 1990s. Most of the immigrants were non-EU nationals. The vast majority of them (about 40 per cent) were young, under the age of 30. The non-EU nationals that were emigrating from the EU were older than those immigrating into the EU. This could be expected as those persons were returning after working or studying in the EU. Given the low and declining rate of natural increase in the EU population, net immigration added about 80 per cent to the population growth. Immigration could assume rising importance in the years to come as the growth of the working-age population in the EU slows down and comes to a halt around 2010. Given the persistent slowdown in the rate of natural increase of the population means that the population growth in the EU over the coming 10–20 years is likely to be determined almost entirely by the scale of immigration.[15]

Non-EU nationals represented about 4 per cent of the population living in the EU in 2000. EU nationals living in another EU member state accounted for an additional 1.5 per cent of the EU population.[16] Migrants from Central and Eastern Europe were concentrated principally in the EU countries that are bordering their country of origin. Migrants from Africa represented about a quarter of non-EU nationals living in the EU. People from this region accounted for over two-thirds of immigrants in France and Portugal. Asians and immigrants from the Caribbean accounted for almost half of non-EU nationals living in Britain.

Non-EU nationals (in 2000) represented 9 per cent of people residing in Germany (this share includes those born in Germany) and 7 per cent in

Table 10.1 Estimates of the labour force, (employed plus unemployed populations), in EU countries by broad groups of citizenship, 2002 (thousands)

Citizenship	B	DK	D	EL	E	F	IRL	I	L	NL	A	P	FIN	S	UK
Nationals	3754.0	2662.8	33225.6	3739.5	15819.8	22562.4	1653.5	–	107.8	7838.8	3383.5	5016.2	2375.0	4164.8	27025.3
Other EU nationals	231.5	28.3	1022.4	5.3	83.2	575.2	56.5	–	71.6	124.1	59.9	12.2	8.5	86.6	501.5
Non-EU nationals	67.0	49.4	2027.0	204.1	337.7	747.5	39.9	–	8.9	156.8	291.0	104.4	22.8	95.7	810.9
No Answer	–	–	–	–	–	–	–	21756.8	–	56.7	–	–	0.1	0.7	0.5
Total	4052.5	2740.5	36275.0	3948.9	16240.7	23885.1	1749.9	21756.8	188.3	8176.4	3734.4	5132.8	2406.4	4347.8	28338.2

Source: Eurostat (2003), Labour Force Survey.

Austria. Non-EU nationals accounted in Spain, Italy, Ireland and Finland less than 1 per cent of the total resident population.

As far as the level of education is concerned, non-EU nationals living in the EU in 2000 had, on average, lower levels of education than the EU nationals. Forty-six per cent of men of non-EU nationality in the 25–39 age group had no educational qualifications beyond compulsory schooling, compared with 29 per cent of the EU nationals. Only 17 per cent of non-EU nationals had tertiary or university education, while the share of the EU nationals in this educational group was 24 per cent. The unemployment rate among men who were EU nationals in the same age group was 6.5 per cent which was significantly lower than the 15 per cent rate among the non-EU nationals. As far as women are concerned, their unemployment rates were 10 and 19 per cent, respectively. These differences in unemployment rates need not be seen primarily as the reluctance by non-EU immigrants to work compared with the EU nationals. It reflects, in part, problems regarding access to jobs that face non-EU nationals. In addition, non-EU immigrant women are faced with cultural differences and difficulties in affording childcare.[17]

Demographical trends in the EU(15) reveal that Europeans are living longer, but they are not having enough children to keep the working-age population stable between now and 2050. This is particularly relevant for the ratio between workers and pensioners. In order to maintain this balance, the EU(15) would need to 'import' about 1.6 million migrants a year.[18] According to certain scenarios presented in a UN study,[19] France would need an average of 136 000 immigrants per year in the 2010–50 period; Germany alone would need 458 000 migrants a year in the 1995–2050 period; while Italy would need to have an annual net immigration from 75 000 in 1995–2000 to 318 000 in 2045–50 with a peak of 613 000 immigrants between 2025 and 2030. There is a slight downward longer-term trend in unemployment rates in the EU countries. EU nationals may become more and more choosy about the jobs they are prepared to do. If nothing is done, the EU(25) population of about 450 million in 2004 would drop to fewer than 400 million in 2050 without immigration.[20] No matter how selective immigration policy may be, it may not solve demographical problems, but it may be a part of the solution. A growing number of potential immigrants may be found in the Middle East and north Africa, however, the fact that they are Muslims may cause friction in the receiving countries.

In theory, all EU citizens have the freedom to travel, stay and work in other partner countries. This also applies to the ten countries that joined the EU in 2004. This eastern enlargement is expected to have only a transitory impact on migration flows towards the EU(15). The annual flow of these migrants is estimated to be about 300 000, which represents 3 million people over a decade. They will go mainly to Germany and Austria (OECD, 2003c, p. 85). However, in practice, with the exception of Britain and Ireland, all EU(15) member countries apply their right to impose transitional arrangements which restrict these freedoms for the nationals from Central and Eastern Europe until 2011.

Central and East European countries will also be influenced by the general demographical trends that will be prevailing in the EU around the year 2010. In addition, as was the case in Spain and Portugal when they joined the EU, and earlier in the case of Italy, migrations flows ceased once the domestic economic situation had improved following EU entry.

RESPONSE

The reality is that geographical mobility of EU nationals within the EU is very low, with the exception of certain border regions. Cultural obstacles, including language are very important in this domain. In order to ameliorate this problem, the European Commission coordinates the European Employment Services (EURES). EURES is a European labour market network for cooperation among public employment services, trade unions and employers' associations. The goals of EURES are:

- to inform and counsel mobile workers about vacancies, living and working conditions elsewhere in the EU;
- to assist employers who wish to recruit workers from other EU countries; and
- to guide and ease the free movement of workers in the EU.

The connected job databases within EURES provide greater opportunities for job seekers, as well as a greater transparency in the EU labour market. The EU member countries realised that if they act together, they may become more efficient. Hence, they try to engage in a convergence process regarding national employment policies.

According to one proposal, an efficient EU immigration policy needs to be regulated by economic instruments. This may be based in future on two possible pillars (Straubhaar and Zimmermann, 1993, p. 233):

- The labour market should determine the volume of labour migration. There should be no legal restrictions for economically motivated migration. As soon as the migrant has a job, he or she should be allowed to enter the EU country. If the person is out of a job for a specified period (such as 6 or 12 months), the local authority may

withdraw the residence permit from that person. Migrants may be invited to purchase citizenship and pay for it over a fixed period of time.
- The authorities need to set quotas for non-economically motivated (mass) migration such as refugees and asylum seekers.

The European Commission is aware of the demographical changes and realities regarding the imminent labour shortages. Following the requirement introduced by the Treaty of Amsterdam, the common legal framework concerning the admission and conditions of stay of non-EU nationals has been put in place. The European Commission set out its strategy related to immigration, integration and employment in its Communication (2003).[21] It is expected that immigration or internal EU migrations involving the Central and East European countries will be between moderate and limited. In order to fulfil the objectives set in Lisbon, the EU should first mobilise its internal resources. Recruitment of suitable migrants may help reduce labour shortages in the short term. In the longer term (2010–30) immigration may help to ease the effects of the demographic transition. EURES should investigate how to contribute to the job mobility of non-EU nationals within the EU. Non-EU nationals will need to be more firmly integrated in the EU social inclusion process.[22] In addition, an enhanced, structured and quality dialogue ought to be developed with the countries that may be the source of immigrants. However, immigration is not the only solution to all the effects of an ageing population. Incentives to EU nationals to produce more children should also be introduced.

In spite of privatisation, the government is still an important employer in all EU countries. Therefore, many jobs may be closed to foreigners even if they are citizens of the EU partner countries. This potential obstacle to employment has been removed by the EU Court of Justice ruling that only those positions that are linked with national security may be reserved for domestic labour. It would be absurd to argue that a person loses skills, experience and knowledge after crossing a border. In order to facilitate labour mobility, in particular highly educated labour, the EU sets qualitative (content of training) and quantitative (years of study, number of course hours) criteria which must be met in order that courses should be accredited and mutually recognised.

The Bologna process on the creation of a European area for higher education started in 1999 when 29 countries signed a declaration to reform their national higher education systems. This reform should be such that an overall convergence in education emerges at the European level. The principal commitments are: to have university courses organised in two cycles (bachelors and masters); to promote mobility of students (to use credit transfers) and lecturers; and to work towards a mutually acceptable quality assurance in education. The resulting debate and reform process has moved with surprising speed, and a number of signatories have already started to overhaul their own national system of higher education. Many other countries, impressed by the declaration and the reform process, have also started to sign up.

The free movement of people is one of the cornerstones of the single market in the EU. It is also one of the visible symbols for ordinary people that European integration actually works. Therefore, most EU countries signed an accord on the free circulation of people in the small Luxembourg village of Schengen in 1985 (the deal was revised in 1990). The nub of the Schengen Agreement was to shift passport controls from internal frontiers to external EU borders, to set a uniform visa policy, to increase cooperation among the national authorities that deal with these issues, as well as to coordinate asylum policies.[23] Once in, everyone can move freely within the Schengen zone countries. However, non-EU nationals can work only in the country that gave them the visa. The curious feature regarding the Schengen deal is that until the Treaty of Amsterdam (1997) it was a convention outside the remit of the EU treaties.

The Schengen Agreement was finally put into effect in seven[24] EU countries in March 1995. In practice the introduction of the deal was coupled with many delays which included for example, the creation of the Schengen Information System, a common database for wanted people and for stolen goods. Once initiated, the system soon got into difficulty. Faced with a wave of Islamic terrorist attacks, France effectively pulled out of the main commitment of the deal in June 1995. It introduced land-border controls because of the fear of terrorism,[25] the same reason why Britain stayed out of the arrangement in the first place.

No matter how genuine these fears of terrorism, drug smuggling and illegal immigration are, the truth is that, as a rule, terrorists and drug smugglers with their illicit cargoes are not caught on borders, but rather in the actual country after tip-offs. Another setback to the spirit of Schengen came when Spain threatened to suspend the key provisions of the agreement when a Belgian court failed to authorise the deportation of two suspected Basque terrorists to Spain in 1996. In spite of these initial difficulties, the Schengen zone operation developed in a satisfactory way. Other countries joined the group, and by 2004 it had 15 members. Of the EU countries, Britain and Ireland chose to stay outside the Schengen zone; however, two non-EU countries (Iceland and Norway) joined the group.

5. Conclusion

Major labour movements took place from the Mediterranean countries into the EU during the 1960s and early 1970s. The exception was Italy which had been in the EU since its establishment. Internal labour mobility in the EU has not played a significant role in European integration in spite of relatively significant differences in average wages (and productivity) among countries. The experience of EU countries with a tradition of being the source of emigration such as Italy, Greece, Spain and Portugal is revealing. During the initial period following the EU entry there was a wave or two of emigration to the EU partner countries. However, once the economic situation improves in the sending countries, emigration slows down and eventually ceases. Meanwhile, a new type of temporary human mobility has emerged in the EU: it concerns students, lecturers and research staff supported by the EU.

The stagnating population level in the EU, combined with prosperous economic conditions in comparison with adjoining regions, will continue to create strong economic incentives for migration into the EU, especially from the year 2010.

The EU is aware of the demographical changes and realities regarding the looming labour shortages, and it is anticipated that immigration into the EU will be one of the principal challenges for the EU in the coming decades.

Notes

1. Recall that labour mobility is permitted in common markets.
2. Eurostat (2001). 'Why do people migrate?', Statistics in Focus, Theme 3-1/2001, p. 2.
3. Different languages are not always an insurmountable problem for big TNCs. Philips, ABB and SKF use English as their corporate language, rather than Dutch, German or Swedish.
4. *Financial Times*, 11 June 2003.
5. In a static world, free immigration of labour lowers (or prevents the increase of) the real wages of certain wage earners in the receiving country. This 'lump of labour fallacy' is touched upon in the chapter on social policy (see Chapter 11).
6. There is a distinction between immigration and immigrant policy. The former refers to the admission of foreigners into the receiving country. An immigrant policy deals with the treatment of resident foreigners.
7. It is estimated that labour is almost three times more mobile among the federal states in the US if compared with labour mobility within individual EU states. There are some good reasons for the American geographical rootlessness. The US is a very homogenised country indeed. If one pushes this to the limit, no matter where you go within the US, the structure of the supply of goods and services is almost identical. Language is the same, while most American cities, towns and settlements look similar. This may be one of the most important reasons why the majority of Americans move so easily and so often.
8. *The Economist*, 1 November 1997, p. 98.

9. If allowed to work, immigrants may be putting into the local public funds more than they take from them. They arrive when they are young, healthy and productive. They pay taxes and other contributions for many years before they receive pensions and medical care.
10. Immigration from the Caribbean countries and south Asia.
11. Immigration from Indonesia, Suriname, Antilles, Turkey and Morocco.
12. Immigrants from other Scandinavian countries, Britain and the US were employed in the oil and gas exploration and production. Immigrants from Turkey, Morocco, India and Pakistan found unskilled manual jobs.
13. *The Economist*, 16 October 1999, p. 20.
14. Eurostat (2002). 'Migration keeps the EU population growing', Statistics in Focus, Theme 3-7/2002.
15. Eurostat (2003). 'Women and men migrating to and from the European Union', Statistics in Focus, Theme 3-2/2003, p. 2.
16. Eurostat (2003). 'Women and men migrating to and from the European Union', Statistics in Focus, Theme 3-2/2003, p. 4.
17. Eurostat (2003). 'Women and men migrating to and from the European Union', Statistics in Focus, Theme 3-2/2003.
18. *The Economist*, 6 May 2000, p. 21.
19. United Nations (2000). 'Replacement migration: is it a solution to declining and ageing populations?' ESA/P/WP.160, 21 March 2000.
20. Kofi Annan, 'Migrants can help rejuvenate an ageing Europe', *Financial Times*, 29 January 2004.
21. Communication from the Commission to the Council, the European Parliament, the European Economic and Social Committee and the Committee of the Regions on Immigration, Integration and Employment. Brussels, 3 June 2003 COM (2003) 336 final.
22. Certain EU countries such as Britain, France, Ireland and Italy allow dual citizenship. Others, such as Germany or Denmark, require people to relinquish their old citizenship when becoming German or Danish. If a Turk gives up his/her citizenship, he/she has to forgo rural property rights in Turkey. This is one of the reasons why Turks in Germany are very cautious about becoming German.
23. The Dublin Convention (1990) of the EU(12) provided for a joint procedure for asylum seekers. The convention has reconfirmed the Schengen Agreement on this issue.
24. Benelux, France, Germany, Portugal and Spain. Other countries joined later.
25. The French refused to implement the agreement, using the argument that terrorists might escape the vigilance of some of their co-signatories.

> My people perish for lack of knowledge.
> Hosea 4:6

11 Social Policy

1. Introduction

The object and purpose of social policy in a country is to ensure, at least, a socially acceptable minimum standard of living for all its population. Hence, social policy goes beyond simple employment-related issues. It touches people not only when they are at work, but also when they are outside of it or without it. Social policy deals with problems which include wages, unemployment insurance, the welfare system, pensions, health, safety at work and education, as well as the professional and geographical mobility of labour. The short-run redistributive (security) goal of this policy does not necessarily conflict with economic adjustment. In the long run these two objectives complement each other. There will be no security without adjustment and no adjustment without a certain security in the long run. Social policy should not prevent the economic system from adjusting. On the contrary: it ought to stimulate shifts from low productivity economic structures to those that demand a qualified and highly productive labour and management.

The foundations of a social policy may be traced to the 19th century when the social security system was introduced. Between the two world wars, there was increased concern that economic and social risks should be shared by the whole society. After the Second World War and up to the 1970s a sustained and relatively high rate of economic growth, as well as a favourable demographic structure of the population, made possible a big increase in social policy expenditure in most developed countries. This has not involved great political costs because government budgets were able to sustain such outlays without too much trouble. Since the recession of the early 1970s, it became obvious that social expenditure was growing so expensive that it posed a threat to the adjustment of the entire economic system. This situation demanded reform. Social policy has been transformed from a safety net designed to ease economic adjustment to a concept whose role is to provide citizens with something approaching property rights or entitlements to the status quo (Courchene, 1987, pp. 8–9).

Certain attempts have been made to change the welfare state into a competition state. However, once a social system is in place, it is very hard to reform it downwards. When France tried to do that in 1995, the result was the worst wave of strikes since 1968, and the prime minister lost his job two years later. A reform of pensions was again attempted in France in 2003, but the resultant strikes brought French cities to a virtual standstill in May 2003. This illustrated trade unions' determination to resist changes in the pensions system. Similar reforms were also bitterly resisted in the same year in both Germany and Italy[1]. In a situation of continuous budgetary deficits and strict limits on public borrowing, the current welfare state system (high degree of income protection and social insurance) can no longer be afforded without reforms. Otherwise, economic adjustment will be unable to take place. The social cost of preserving current entitlement to everybody without any conditions would be endless.

An additional problem and a serious test that is looming in Europe is linked to pensions. A vast majority of pension liabilities are unfunded.[2] The ongoing burden on taxpayers is immense – an alarming fact for public spending. Demographic trends show that the 'baby boom' generation will retire *en masse* around the year 2010. The pressure on pension funds will increase significantly for several decades to come. This important and expanding imbalance will put a strain on the eurozone rules.[3]

This chapter is structured as follows. Section 2 outlines the general social policy issues. Unemployment is the topic of Section 3. Section 4 is devoted to the social policy of the EU. Specific consideration is given to the mounting legal base for this policy, its evolution and the European Social Charter. Section 5 concludes that in spite of limited powers of the EU in the social sphere, this policy has been expanding.

2. Social policy issues

Public authorities, no matter whether regional, national or at the level of the EU, are often called upon to rescue the unsuccessful. As soon as a firm, industry, region or social group perceives or encounters a difficulty, they are inclined to seek government intervention rather than attempt to solve the problem themselves. Such pressure can be quite strong. However, the budgetary situation drives all public authorities to think less about whether to reform this policy and more about how to reform social policy and its expenditure.

A society should create the conditions for the attainment of a minimum standard of living of the entire population, including the guarantee of a minimum income, but to such an extent that it neither downgrades the values and incentives to work, move and acquire new knowledge, nor impedes economic adjustment and growth. Expenditure should be coupled with the social ability to pay and should not overtax the most enterprising agents who drive the economic and social life of society. Social policy should be coordinated with other economic policies in order to increase its effectiveness. There is no dispute about these issues, whatsoever, but difficulties arise about how to achieve these goals in an 'equitable' way.[4]

The system of unemployment insurance is one of the first on the reform agenda. This system often downgrades the value of work in some societies. Short-term employment and reliance on longer unemployment insurance eligibility periods can become a tolerable way of life for some segments of the population. If workers' wages are relatively low, and unemployment benefits are at a similar level, then a proportion of this group of low wage earners may shift to the welfare-recipient segment of the population. Incentives to work, move, retrain and acquire further education may be weakened or eliminated. Unemployment benefits were created to provide a cushion against short-term difficulties when workers were in-between jobs. Hence, they are not a suitable means for the correction of structural or long-term unemployment. A reform should introduce a link between the duration and level of unemployment benefits for relatively younger and middle-age groups of unemployed and their vocational retraining and length of previous work, as well as introduce incentives for relocation.

Human capital management (employment) has to ensure that there is a balance of employment over an economic cycle; that the age, sex and qualification distribution of the employed is adequate; and that there is a passing on of knowledge and experience among employees. Part-time and fixed-term contracts, as well as the hiring of outside specialised firms may be useful and flexible methods of achieving a balance of manpower and meeting the needs of all firms, in particular SMEs.

Structural unemployment, in particular among the young and women, is an indicator of poor vocational training. This type of unemployment should not be considered in the traditional way, that is, labour is either in or out of full-time work. Training and education of this part of the population may be the most appropriate policy response.[5]

Education is another major field for reform. This is important because human knowledge services become increasingly relevant and crucial in economic life. Knowledge is the cornerstone of modern manufacturing and services industries. Hence, education should be coordinated with the needs of firms. Employers increasingly demand highly trained labour and educated management. Experience suggests that the 19th century approach by the Luddites to the introduction of new technology (that is, to destroy the new machines) and its modern version of opposing a shift to new technologies is mistaken. The countries that were most successful in creating new jobs, such as Japan (between 1960 and 1990) and the US, were also the ones that made the fastest adjustment and shift towards a knowledge-based, high-technology economy. None the less, compared to those two countries, social solidarity in the form of maintaining the income of certain social groups is higher in the EU. However, everything has its price. For a long time the EU was involved in the neutralising of unemployment instead of being involved in the creation of new jobs.

The higher education of students is expensive and is becoming increasingly so. On the one hand, top experts may be attracted to private industry, so universities should keep their offers to the brightest teachers and students relatively high. On the other hand, to maintain up-to-date libraries, computers and their software, laboratories, equipment and various consumables become increasingly expensive. Universities and their research institutes are hit hard by budgetary cuts, and may not always rely only on public funds and random donations. The only way to solve this financial problem on a more permanent basis may be to increase tuition fees. Everyone who wants post-secondary education should have free access in the first year. Those that want and are eligible to go further, may face higher tuition fees. It may be appropriate that students bear a larger share of their education costs. Students are, of course, one of the most needy groups of the population. They should be assisted by a well-endowed public system of loans with favourable conditions.

Health care and pensions are social subsystems which will be most difficult to reform. They are the subject of a great deal of attention in every society, and they have immense social value. Free access to a minimum of health care personifies one of the most fundamental values of equality in modern societies. On these grounds, the expenditure for health care, particularly in ageing societies (a pan-European feature), may not be easily reduced. Windows for reform may be found in the partial charging of medical care by those in relatively high-income groups, the extension of working age and a reduction in pensions.

3. Unemployment

Structural unemployment results from a failure of firms, labour and government policies to adapt to changing circumstances. Firms or entire industries produce goods and services that are not in demand, production costs are excessive or cannot withstand competition from abroad. Labour on the other side, fails to adjust and move from one profession or region to another. Another type, cyclical unemployment, comes from a lack of demand. Economic activity fluctuates, consumers may feel insecure at certain times, they save more and spend less, hence there is a lack of the demand that has a cyclical impact on employment. The stated objective of the EU is to make its industries more competitive and to ease the problem of structural unemployment, as well as to assist in the geographical and professional mobility of labour.

The idea that there is a fixed amount of work to be done in the world is known as the 'lump of labour fallacy'. According to this suggestion, if one worker increases the amount of work he or she does, this reduces work and job opportunities to others. In France, for example, the socialist governments sought to initiate job creation by reducing the length of the working week, early retirement schemes and the extension of vacations. The Luddite 'lump of labour' idea generally reappears each time there is a recession. If jobs cannot be created because of inappropriate policy, it is easy, politically effective and cheap to blame foreign competitors for domestic problems and failures. Hence, protection against goods that are imported from China may be demanded.

Most people would hesitate before discussing or passing judgement (if any) on matters such as asteroids, Kant's *Critique of Pure Reason*, x-ray treatment of fruit and vegetables (for example, strawberries or tomatoes) in order to keep them fresh for a longer period of time on supermarket shelves, live cells in computers or black holes in space. However, the same people will often make a snap judgement on the impact of the euro, perhaps because it directly touches them. But passengers on high-speed trains (TGV) are also affected by new and high-technology. They may comment and advise on comfort in these trains, but they would leave the design of TGVs to well-trained, experienced and sophisticated engineers.

While engineers are able to conduct various key experiments, many of which are without grave consequences, medical doctors and economists seldom do that. Such experiments are very uncertain, while consequences may be fatal. Therefore, being a simple consumer or a producer in an economy does not provide an overall picture of such a complex system. Formal education and professional experience is necessary for this – and sometimes not even that is sufficient. The Luddites and the neo-Luddites found/find it difficult to appreciate that while new technology can make certain segments of currently employed labour redundant, it may at the same time increase productivity, reduce prices and increase demand for goods, services and labour in other related and unrelated activities (leisure). It is no less easy now to demonstrate to 'them' the whole picture than it had been for Galileo.[6]

Since the 1970s, unemployment in the EU has been provoked and sustained by several factors, including:

- slow adjustment of the industry to shocks (such as the oil shocks in the 1970s);
- restrictive monetary policies introduced in order to curb the imported inflationary impact of higher oil prices;
- successful competition from the newly industrialised countries, in particular in industries that use a lot of unskilled labour;
- advances in technology that made unskilled labour redundant;
- a high level of labour unionisation and powerful labour unions;
- inadequate training of labour;
- high taxes and social charges imposed on the employment of labour;
- weak coordination among the principal EU economies; and
- the initial effect of the strict monetary policy that was introduced in the eurozone.

The eurozone aims to contribute to an increase in employment and, at the same time, keep the euro strong. This is quite a challenging task in the short and even in the medium term. So far the euro has brought pain to the employment market (low inflation that does not permit a larger-scale expansion of the economic activity), while the gain is expected to arrive at some future date. If there is no flexibility in exchange or interest rates, then the flexibility has to come from elsewhere. So far it has come from highly regulated EU labour markets that accommodate potential shocks and opportunities. This not only includes deregulation of the labour market, but also sustained education and training of labour and management as technological progress is reducing the demand for unskilled labour.

Table 11.1 outlines in a very simplified way the principal national economic models. It is obvious from this table that in addition to the accumulated experience from over two centuries of economic research and practice, there is no magic model for economic growth and, consequently, employment. Each one has good and bad points. In any case, if a magic recipe were to exist, it would include:

- first and foremost a first-rate education and incentives to lifelong learning; then
- a stable and sound monetary and fiscal policy;
- openness to trade;
- relatively low taxes;
- high savings (and investments);
- SMEs should not be put at a disadvantage; and
- the rule of law (including a certain social security net).

Table 11.2 presents annual rates of unemployment in the EU and other major countries in the 1999–2003 period. The principal lesson to be learned from the comparison of these rates is the following. National social systems are often compared. However, not many realise that in spite of the relatively generous social protection and welfare state in the EU member states, countries such as Austria, Denmark, Luxembourg, the Netherlands, Sweden or Britain have lower or comparable rates of unemployment in relation to the 'liberal' and 'easy' US.

4. European Union

LEGAL BASE

The original Treaty of Rome did not exclude social issues, but they were not mentioned often in the text. A relatively small space devoted to social policy in the original Treaty of Rome reflected the belief that the impact of social policy on the operation of the EU was not of primary importance. The EU acquired wider powers in the area of social policy with the Single European Act and the Maastricht Treaty which both amended the original Treaty of Rome. The Preamble of the revised Treaty of Rome mentions among the basic goals of the EU continuous improvements in the living

Table 11.1 Principal features of select national economic models

Model	Favourable features	Unfavourable features
1. Traditional: Formerly in Southern Europe	• Little structured regulation of the economy	• Lack of competition • Slow reaction to challenges, so modern business and industry arrive late • High taxes • Nepotism • Corruption
2. Liberal: American	• Venerates market • Strong competition • Flexible labour and product markets • Low taxes	• Low welfare benefits • Huge income disparities • Relatively meagre quality of primary and secondary education
3. Conservative: German. Created by Bismarck to obstruct the appeal of socialism	• First-rate education on all levels • Relatively narrow wage disparities • Relatively generous welfare state (pensions included) • Close relations banks–firms • Hierarchical	• Too powerful labour unions • High labour market regulation • Costly in budgetary terms during recessions • Rigid
4. Social-democratic: Swedish	• Broad welfare state combined with relatively open markets • Lifelong learning • State is to reduce market insecurity • Relatively narrow wage disparities	• Strong involvement by the state in the economy • Broad welfare state increases pressure on budget deficit during recession • High taxes
5. Others: French	• First-rate education on all levels • Relatively narrow wage disparities • Relatively generous welfare state • Hierarchical	• High taxes • Too powerful labour unions • High labour market regulation and social security taxes • Costly in budgetary terms during recessions

Table 11.1 (continued)

Model	Favourable features	Unfavourable features
		• Nepotism • Corruption
6. Dutch	• Relaxed rules on short- and part-time work • Workers accept lower pay rises in exchange for the security of work • Reduction in social security taxes • Relatively generous welfare state	• A large part of the employed are part-time workers • Huge income disparities
7. Japanese	• Lifetime employment • High quality education • Close relations banks–firms • Long-term view of investment	• Employees and firms sheltered from full effect of market forces, hence insufficient pressure to use capital efficiently

and working conditions, as well as the promotion of the highest possible level of knowledge of the people through a wide access to education. Article 2 states the objectives of the EU, which include a high level of employment and social protection, equality between men and women, as well as raising the standard of living and quality of life. Article 13 refers to the issue of non-discrimination 'based on sex, racial or ethnic origin, religion or belief, disability, age or sexual orientation'. Articles 39–42 introduce a free movement of labour among the EU countries and also guarantee eligibility for and aggregation of social-insurance benefits. Freedom of establishment, including the mutual recognition of diplomas, is contained in Articles 43–8.

Title VIII of the Treaty of Rome covers employment (Articles 125–30). EU member countries should contribute to a high level of employment and promote a skilled, trained and adaptable workforce. Hence, labour markets could be responsive to economic changes. Title XI refers to the social policy, education, vocational training and youth (Articles 136–50). Member countries are encouraged to cooperate in areas that include standards of living, vocational training, employment, social security, as well as safety and protection of health in the workplace. The EU is to support and complement actions of the member states in the fields that include working conditions, social security and information and consultation with the

Table 11.2 *Annual rate of unemployment in the EU and other major countries, 1999–2003 (%)*

Country	1999	2000	2001	2002	2003*
Austria	3.9	3.7	3.6	4.0	4.5
Belgium	8.6	6.9	6.7	6.8	8.0
Denmark	4.8	4.4	4.3	4.5	5.3
Finland	10.2	9.8	9.1	9.3	9.0
France	10.7	9.3	8.5	8.6	9.4
Greece	11.9	11.1	10.5	10.3	9.2
Germany	8.4	7.8	7.7	8.2	9.4
Ireland	5.6	4.3	3.9	4.4	4.7
Italy	11.3	10.4	9.4	9.1	8.5
Luxembourg	2.4	2.3	2.0	2.3	3.8
Netherlands	3.2	2.9	2.5	2.6	4.1
Portugal	4.5	4.1	4.5	4.5	6.7
Spain	12.8	11.3	10.6	11.2	11.4
Sweden	6.7	5.6	4.9	5.0	5.5
United Kingdom	5.9	5.4	5.0	5.1	5.0
European Union	8.7	7.8	7.4	7.6	8.1
Cyprus	3.6	3.4	3.0	3.3	4.4
Czech Republic	9.4	8.8	8.9	9.8	7.0
Estonia	6.7	7.7	7.7	6.8	8.2
Hungary	9.6	8.9	8.0	8.0	6.0
Latvia	9.1	7.8	7.7	7.6	12.0
Lithuania	10.0	12.6	12.9	10.9	11.0
Malta	5.8	5.0	5.1	5.5	7.5
Poland	13.1	15.1	17.5	18.1	20.0
Slovakia	19.2	17.9	18.6	17.5	16.0
Slovenia	13.0	12.0	11.8	10.0	9.0
Bulgaria	16.0	17.9	17.9	16.3	13.0
Romania	11.5	10.5	8.8	8.1	8.5
Turkey	7.6	6.6	8.5	10.4	10.0
Switzerland	2.9	2.5	2.6	3.1	4.0
United States	4.2	4.0	4.8	5.8	6.1
Japan	4.7	4.7	5.0	5.4	5.1

Note: * Estimate.

Sources: UNECE (2003); Eurostat (2003).

management. Equal opportunities, equal treatment and equal pay for equal work between men and women must be respected. Cooperation between educational establishments and mobility of students and teachers is also among the goals of the EU. The European Social Fund (also referred to in Article 3) is to assist workers to get employment and to increase their geographical and occupational mobility. In addition, the European Commission has to use high standards while regulating health, safety, environmental and consumer protection (Article 94).

EVOLUTION

One of the first legal documents, which the EU delivered in 1958, was the social insurance system for migrant workers who are citizens of EU member countries. The basic principles are that these workers have the same social insurance rights as workers from the host country, that social insurance contributions may be freely transferred among EU countries and that social insurance contributions will be taken in their aggregate amount.

The objective of the European Social Fund (ESF) established in 1961, is to be the main financial tool through which the EU translates its strategic employment policy aims into action. The ESF is a part of the EU structural funds.[7] It will disburse €60 billion in the 2000–07 period. The ESF is to improve employment opportunities, to contribute to raising the standard of living and to increasing the mobility of labour both between occupations and between regions. The highest priority is to be given to the easing of the unemployment problem, because unemployment has been the most important social issue in the EU since the mid-1970s.

Social policy, however, usually covers a much wider group of issues than those awarded to the ESF. Apart from the involvement in unemployment and education/training issues that are partly covered by the ESF, a 'standard' national social policy intervenes in a much larger number of issues which include health and welfare. At the beginning of its operation, the ESF was merely reimbursing half of the costs of vocational training and relocation of workers in the member countries. However, two problems were obvious: interventions were retroactive and they were concentrated in the country that had the greatest expenditure is these fields (Germany).

The ESF was reformed in 1971 when it was allowed to intervene in the field of vocational training with an emphasis on the young, under 25 years of age, and to intervene in regions with ailing industries and structural unemployment. After the reform, about 90 per cent of expenditure went on the occupational mobility of workers, while the remainder was spent on geographic mobility. The subsequent reform of the ESF in 1984 reserved 75 per cent of its resources for the training and employment of those under 25 years of age. The most disadvantaged regions were guaranteed 45 per cent of all appropriations. The ESF covers up to half of the eligible costs, but never more than the total public expenditure of the country concerned. In support of adults, the fund gives priority to women, to the long-term unemployed, the disabled and migrants from within the EU. The ESF has had a minor, but growing, role in ameliorating the EU's unemployment problem.[8]

There were about 14.5 million people unemployed in the EU(15) (8 per cent of the workforce) in 2003. A high concentration of unemployed is in the group of unskilled workers, many of whom are young. They are at the bottom of the EU pool of labour and due to their poor training they will remain unemployable. This problem may be easy to overlook while they are still young, but, once they establish their own families, they will constitute a distinct underclass. This is why the ESF has been concentrating more on the problem of youth unemployment since 1984. Incentives to vocational training, geographical mobility and flexible employment laws may represent a long-term solution to this problem. None the less, the employment policy ultimately remains the responsibility of EU member states. A coordination of national policies has begun, in particular since the Treaty of Amsterdam.

Social security benefits may have a significant impact on the level of wages. If employers are required to pay relatively high social security contributions, then they can lower wages and vice versa. Different levels of expenditure on social security contributions among countries may have an influence on competition among countries in the short run. When unemployment is relatively high and long term, various tax revenues are affected in a negative way, demand for social expenditure increases, and budget deficits are harder to cut. In addition, taxes and social security contributions on labour in the EU countries (30 to 50 per cent of labour costs) are higher than in the US or Japan. National labour markets are over-regulated in Europe. This is one of the reasons why significantly fewer new jobs (if any) are created in the EU than in the US, where the regulation of the labour market is easier. None the less, regulation is primarily at the *national*, rather than at the EU level, hence the EU need not necessarily be blamed for the failure of efforts to ease the unemployment problem. Flexibility in the labour market of the EU member countries refers principally to the newly created, replacement or part-time jobs. Those that are already entrenched in their positions are or were hardly touched by the new flexibility in the EU labour market.

The reality is that geographical mobility of labour among the EU(15) member states is indeed very low. The exceptions are certain border regions. In order to ameliorate this problem, the European Commission coordinates the EURES labour market network for cooperation among public employment services, trade unions and employers' associations.

EDUCATION

Initially, the EU has not done much about education. There was an EU programme in 1976 which aimed to promote cooperation in higher education in the region, to standardise teaching courses, to increase the access to education throughout the EU and to improve and widen the teaching of languages that are spoken in the member countries. The EU required member states to offer classes for the children of migrant workers in order to give them the opportunity to receive some education in the culture and in the language of their country of origin. Since the 1980s, the EU education and youth-exchange programmes have been expanding.

The European Council in Lisbon (2000) set a new strategic goal for the decade: to make the EU 'the most competitive and dynamic knowledge-based economy in the world capable of sustainable economic growth with more and better jobs and greater social cohesion'.[9] In order to achieve this objective, a high-quality performance of the firms should be based on the skills of their workforce. According to the European Commission, this ought to be supported by a high level of flexibility, both on the side of management and on the side of workers, their continuous education and training, involvement of workers in the life of firms they work in, as well as a high level of trust and security for employees. These general objectives are geared towards the longer run.[10] Sapir (2003) proposed that the EU should spend about half of its budget on growth-stimulating activities such as research, higher education, infrastructure projects and institution building in the new Central and East European member countries. The only way to do this and to remain within the current budgetary limits would be to scrap the CAP and regional funds. This would be in line with the Lisbon objectives. However, politicians did not accept this suggestion. Unfortunately, they have not proposed an alternative.

To carry out its intentions in the field of education, the EU has a number of action programmes. *Socrates* is the EU action programme in the field of education (2000–06). It involves about 30 European countries, and its main objective is to build up a 'Europe of knowledge'. Socrates has to provide a better response to the major challenges of the new century. It has to promote lifelong learning, encourage access to education for everybody, and help people acquire recognised qualifications and skills.

Socrates emphasises the multicultural character of Europe. It supports the education of the least-advantaged groups of people, it endeavours to counter social exclusion and underachievement at school, it promotes equal opportunities for women and men irrespective of circumstances, it includes new information communication technologies and it encourages the learning of the different European languages.

Socrates comprises eight separate programmes:

- *Comenius* is European Cooperation on School Education. It focuses on the first phase of education, from pre-school and primary to secondary school. It is directed at all members of the education community such as pupils, teachers, local authorities, parents' associations and NGOs.
- *Erasmus* is the EU programme in the field of higher education. It covers student and teacher exchanges, joint development of study programmes, thematic networks between departments across Europe and language courses.
- *Grundtvig* is aimed at enhancing the European dimension of lifelong learning. It supports a wide range of activities designed to promote innovation and the improved availability, accessibility and quality of education for adults.
- *Lingua* deals with the promotion of language teaching and learning in order to encourage and support linguistic diversity and understanding throughout the EU.
- *Minerva* seeks to promote European cooperation in the fields of information and communication technology, and open and distance learning in education.
- *Observation and innovation* of education systems and policies tries to collect descriptive and statistical data, to make comparative analysis of educational systems and policies in the EU member states and to develop methods for the evaluation the quality of education.
- *Joint actions* with other EU programmes aim to promote a 'Europe of knowledge' and focus on themes that, by their very nature, are not limited to one field alone, that is, education, training or youth policy.
- *Supplementary measures* support various activities which, though not eligible for funding under the main programmes, can contribute to achieving a programme's objectives.

Other EU programmes in the field of education include:

- The *Leonardo da Vinci* programme of lifelong learning, which promotes transnational projects based on cooperation between the various players in vocational training (for example, vocational schools, universities, businesses, chambers of commerce) in an effort to increase mobility, to foster innovation and to improve the quality of training. This programme aims at helping people improve their skills throughout their lives.

- The *Tempus* programme, which was established in 1990 to respond to the needs for higher education reform in Central and East European countries.
- The *Media* programme, which aims at strenghtening the competitiveness of the European audiovisual industry with a series support measures.
- The *Jean Monnet* project, which contributes by co-financing universities for the establishment of Jean Monnet chairs, Jean Monnet permanent courses, Jean Monnet modules in European law, European economy, political studies of European construction, and the history of European integration. The Jean Monnet project also supports the creation of Jean Monnet centres of excellence.

THE EUROPEAN SOCIAL CHARTER

The European Social Charter (1989) was controversial from the outset. It outlined basic rights of EU workers and was adopted as a political declaration by all EU member states with the exception of Britain. The Charter provides for 12 basic rights:

- to work in the EU country of one's choice;
- to a fair wage;
- to improved living and working conditions;
- to social protection under prevailing national systems;
- to freedom of association and collective bargaining;
- to vocational training;
- of men and women to equal treatment;
- of workers to information, consultation and participation;
- to health protection and safety at work;
- to protection of children and adolescents;
- to guaranteed minimum living standards for the elderly; and
- to improved social and professional integration for the disabled.

The objective of the Charter is to lay down political foundations for a minimum common legislation in the area of labour affairs. Although initially without a legal force, the Charter presented a political obligation. Most of the Charter's provisions are not disputable at all. Controversies arise regarding 'fair wages' that may be interpreted as an intention to introduce an EU-wide minimum wage; and the regulation of working hours, holidays and workers' participation which may all jeopardise the flexibility, so essential in labour markets.

Britain was not in favour of the Charter, because of a fear that the European Commission would use it as a foundation for an expansion of various proposals and for legislation in the social sphere. As such, it could impose uniformity in labour legislation on countries that have different traditions and economic structures (labour regulation in smelting may need a different model from tourism). Freedom of contract and flexibility in the labour market, important components of competitiveness, would be restrained. For example, Britain thinks that it would be better that employers and employees negotiate the length of the working week, rather than to have uniform EU-wide rules.

The adoption of the European Social Charter in 1989 by all member states except Britain marked a turning point for the EU. The following three years saw a continual struggle between Britain, which sought to retain its American-style liberal labour market as free as possible from minimum pay and working hours regulations, and the EU drive to set as high a standard as possible in order to prevent member states from undercutting one another through gaining or preserving an undue labour-cost advantage. In spite of British (Tory) opposition, the European Commission introduced all but a handful of its 47 proposals set out in its action programme.

A Social Protocol in the Maastricht Treaty (1992), from which Britain got an opt-out, licensed the EU to regulate on working conditions, employment rights for men and women[11] and workers' participation. The EU is to contribute and encourage (but not legislate) in the areas of cross-border cooperation in education, culture and health. In addition, a new employment chapter introduced in the Treaty of Amsterdam (1997) is supposed to promote (undefined) cooperation among member countries to create jobs. In addition, Maastricht's social chapter was included in the Treaty of Rome. Following the election victory in 1997, the Labour government in Britain accepted the Social Charter.

The European Commission proposes binding regulation on health and safety at work. The reason is that there are tens of thousands of workers who are killed or injured at the workplace each year. Although the objective of the EU is to support the creation of jobs, this need not be achieved at the cost of reduction in health and safety. These are areas without dispute among the member countries. Problems, however, arise with part-time employment. The European Commission intends to propose that part-time employees receive the same benefits as full-time workers. Britain is the strongest opponent of such a policy, since excessive regulation may discourage the creation of part-time jobs.[12]

European firms are finding creative ways to avoid rigid labour laws. Some of them make wage concessions in return for flexible work in shifts or they promote counter staff in shops to managers in the same vein to evade strict working-time laws.

Firms with a longer-term perspective may perceive the prospect of paying firing costs ('golden handshakes', retirement pensions and so on) as a 'tax' on current hiring. This may be a drain on profits, which causes a disincentive to take on new labour in the future. The Social Charter may add to unemployment and usher in protectionism in two ways. First, regulation has its costs in the reduction of flexibility in the labour market and the decline in competitiveness compared with countries that have a lighter regulatory burden and can make their businesses adapt, change and grow. Second, if EU regulation is adjusted upwards to the standards that prevail in the northern countries, then southern and eastern EU countries would need a transfer of funds to make up for the loss of growth. The EU commitment to free trade would be placed in jeopardy (Curzon Price, 1991, pp. 130–31).

If the social dimension of the harmonisation of labour laws includes an upward adjustment, then this would increase the costs of production in those countries with a relatively lax legislation (south and east), economic growth would suffer and there would be a demand for protection. Conversely, if member countries are left alone to set their labour laws, harmonisation through competition may produce a downward adjustment. Over-regulation of the labour market (north) would be eased, costs of production would fall, competitiveness would be enhanced and there would be positive impact on growth. It is only in this way that high wages can be sustained in the longer term with a reasonable degree of openness of the economy.

The 1994 directive required that firms with more than 1000 employees should set up consultative works councils if at least 150 of employees work in two or more EU countries. The directive affected about 1200 EU enterprises. Its objective was to improve the right of workers to be kept informed and consulted. Participation of workers in the affairs of their firms, even though it might only take the form of consultation and exchange of information, may well increase cohesion and morale and improve productivity. Certain affected enterprises such as Canon or Panasonic asserted that the councils fit neatly into their (Japanese) standards of collective responsibility. Volkswagen has a positive experience with works councils as a means of disseminating information.

In spite of these developments, firms worry about two issues related to works councils. The first is costs. The council meetings have to take place once a year. However, if mergers, acquisitions and relocations that affect employees take place, then there would need to be additional meetings. The costs to enterprises of running works councils would soar. The second issue concerns relations between works councils and trade unions. There is a fear that works councils would lead to EU-wide collective bargaining. The current degree of integration in the EU does not yet permit efficient wage bargaining on this level. Centralised wage bargaining by the EU is, however, unlikely. It is doubtful whether national trade unions would relinquish their local bargaining rights to a higher tier. In the future, it is likely that both the unions and the employers would want to keep the extent of works councils quite limited. However, the greatest peril that the works councils pose is that they may curb the development of more flexible ways of maintaining the flow of information between management and employees.

The European Commission and the European Parliament are determined to press ahead with proposals that would force EU companies that take part in cross-border mergers to have obligatory consultations with labour unions and to have their representation on the management board. Companies are lobbying hard against the extension of this 'principle of co-determination' which allows workers a powerful voice in the running of companies.[13] This reveals the problems involved in trying to harmonise EU company law without running the risk that TNCs would move elsewhere to locations with less burdensome requirements.

Besides the directive on works councils, more legislation is in the pipeline. It includes granting to part-timers the same benefits regarding pay, holidays and other rights as are given to full-time staff. Such strengthening of employees' rights represents a potential threat during times of relatively high unemployment and job insecurity. This may hit SMEs hardest (those with up to 250 employees), as they may refrain from taking on staff. One has to recall that there were about 20.5 million SMEs in 2000, employing about 80 million people (two-thirds of all those employed) in the EU.[14]

The introduction of the euro in the 12 eurozone countries is expected to have wide implications. A stability-oriented area would provide solid and transparent grounds for longer-term investments, as well as for combating cyclical unemployment. Once this is provided for, greater attention can be given to the fight against structural unemployment. In addition, the EU member states recognise that they can be more efficient if they act together.

5. Conclusion

The demand for social expenditure is almost insatiable. The expenditure for these services may be increased during periods of prosperity at lowest political cost, as was the case in the 1960s. During economic slowdowns and budgetary deficits, the social services which have mushroomed or which have become too generous or badly conceived have to be reformed. Unemployment insurance was more of an income-support instrument than oriented towards labour adjustment. This should be changed in favour of mobility of labour, in particular, that of younger people, both among occupations and regions. Sometimes it may be better to give a pension to 60-year-old workers than to provide dole money to teenagers and tweenagers. However, demographic pressures will continue to put an increasing strain on public expenditure in particular in the areas of health and pensions.

In many cases linked with the social issues (and, hence, social philosophy), the EU was long on statements, but short on action as economic constraints were not taken into consideration. The Social Action Programme of 1974, for example, called for full and better employment, improvement in living and working conditions, as well as the participation of workers and employers in the EU decision-making process through the Standing Committee on Employment. Due to economic crisis and introverted economic strategies, the programme did not have any notable achievements.

Coverage of the EU social policy is limited. Intervention has been much less of a well-organised policy and much more a mix of various social issues that the member states were willing to transfer to the EU. The 'loose' character of social policy comes from the legal provisions that are, in certain cases, aspirational rather than operational. The major concern of this policy in the EU was to alleviate the unemployment problem and, later on assistance in education. But one needs to remember that (un)employment policies and the instruments remaining to deal with the problem are still in the hands of *national* governments, not in the hands of the EU. Other aspects of the EU policy in social affairs include education, geographical and professional mobility of labour, and safety at work.

The effects of social policy may not be measured directly. Indirectly, social policy has its impact on the length of life expectancy, the reduction of illiteracy, the increase in training and the safety of workers. All this increases the production potential of a country. Average life expectancy of the EU population is increasing: in 1960, life expectancy at birth in the EU(15) was 73 years for females and 68 years for males; by 2000 it had increased to 81 years for females and 75 years for males.[15] Therefore, national social protection systems will have to be adjusted over the coming three decades because of the ageing population in the EU and the consequent increase in the demand for social care. Due to demographical changes the EU labour force will start to shrink after 2010. Part of the solution to the problem may be found in a selective immigration policy, in particular, targeted at other European countries.

Many workers prefer longer night shifts over a shorter period of time than shorter shifts over a longer period of time. If working time is regulated, then workers would lose the freedom to negotiate their working time. The need for choice and flexibility in the labour market beneficial both to employees and to employers is something that the European Commission often forgets. Uniform laws that do not provide for flexibility may put undue pressure on SMEs that not only need flexibility, but are also the major employers of labour. Moreover, SMEs also employ the most disadvantaged groups of workers such as the young and women. In addition, there is an increasing demand by enterprises for temporary workers hired from specialised firms, rather than permanent staff.

The eurozone (1999) eliminated separate national currencies for countries that participate. Without separate currencies, countries have a limited arsenal of means to adjust to sizeable economic disparities. Countries may introduce flexible wages, give incentives to mass migration and/or employ transfer payments. The German example since the *Anschluss* of 1989, has shown that wages were inflexible, mass migration was barely tolerable, while transfer payments were highly demanding. Instead of creating conditions for a greater flexibility in the labour market, one of the stated policy goals, the EU was bracing itself with the Social Charter.

The EU must adapt its welfare state social policy in order to create a competition state. Otherwise, the real danger stems from the fact that without this reform, member countries and the EU may encounter problems in the present and future with methods which were designed in and for the past times.[16] The best way to solve unemployment problems is for member states and the EU to work together towards the achievement of the common goal: greater flexibility in the labour market and an increase in economic growth. However, there is great confusion in the EU policy between the need for flexibility in the labour markets necessary for economic adjustment and mounting regulation that determines labour-related laws.

Notes

1. The first Berlusconi government in Italy fell from power when pension reforms provoked strikes in 1994.
2. It is very hard to approximate this ratio, but most research would estimate that it is about 85 per cent.
3. Pensions are becoming one of the principal economic imbalances. However, they are not as much studied as are imbalances in trade and in capital flows. The issue of pensions was considered in the chapter on monetary policy (see Chapter 2).
4. For instance, overviews of an earlier British welfare system stressed that it should be changed because it was incomprehensible, uncoordinated, unnecessarily expensive to

administer, a chief cause of unemployment, discriminatory, arbitrary, unfair, deteriorating instead of improving, that it penalised marriage and subsidised family breakup, and also de-stabilised and divided society (Courchene, 1987, p. xv). Unfortunately, at least some of these aspects of social policy are, not restricted to the British social system.

5. There is potentially substantial scope for part-time employment. For example, students or young mothers may be quite happy to work a couple of hours a day as they are not in a position to accept different types of contracts. The creation of such jobs needs to be encouraged, as they introduce flexibility both on the supply and demand sides of the market and they need not (although they may) evolve into permanent posts. Supporting flexible legal and fiscal instruments can be important incentives along these lines.

6. Galileo Galilei (1564–1642) made discoveries with his telescope in 1610 that transformed understanding of the world. However, he could not persuade the inquisitors to look through his telescope. The inquisitors believed, according to their doctrine, that what Galileo claimed to see was not there. Some 350 years after Galileo's death, in 1992, Pope John Paul II gave an address on behalf of the Catholic Church in which he admitted that errors had been made by the theological advisors in the case of Galileo. He declared the Galileo case closed, but he did not admit that the Church was wrong to convict Galileo on a charge of heresy because of Galileo's belief that the Earth rotates round the Sun.

7. The ERDF and the Cohesion Fund are the other two.

8. Only publicly authorised agencies (training agencies, trade unions and so on) may apply for allocations from the ESF, and since they play the role of both fox and hound at the same time, the scene is set for potential fraud. For example, 36 Portuguese trade union officials were charged in 1995 with setting up a fake training company in order to get subsidies. The funds received were used to pay the bills of the trade union (*The Economist*, 27 January 1996, p. 30).

9. European Council, Lisbon 2000, Presidency Conclusions, §5.

10. European Commission (2000). 'Social Policy Agenda', Brussels, COM(2000) 379 final, 28 June 2000.

11. A certain margin of preference for female applicants for jobs has been an unwritten practice in many of the EU countries. This was especially true in the northern part of the EU in spite of a 1976 directive requiring equal treatment of both sexes. The European Court of Justice ruled (1995) that job quotas were not allowed. The case in question (landscape gardening) arose when the German state of Bremen gave jobs to women ahead of equally qualified men.

12. Certain low-paid jobs in services, such as packing assistants in supermarkets, janitors or car washers, have all but disappeared in the EU, but not in the US. If European employers are required to provide such a fluctuating labour force with excessive benefits, they would prefer to relinquish these services.

13. *Financial Times*, 22 October 2003.

14. European Commission (2003). *SMEs in Focus: Main Results from the 2002 Observatory of European SMEs*, Observatory of European SMEs 2002, p. 4.

15. Longevity in biblical times is referred to in the Old Testament. For example, Methuselah lived for 969 years (Genesis, 5:27), Adam 930 (Genesis, 5:5), Abraham 175 (Genesis, 25:7), and Sarah 127 years (Genesis, 23:1).

16. This is particularly relevant for pensions.

> Then God saw everything that He had made,
> and indeed it was very good.
> Genesis 1:31

12 Environment Policy

1. Introduction

A clean and healthy environment has been taken by many to be a ubiquitous good for a very long time. The ecological system was assumed to balance itself in a more or less satisfactory way on its own (just like free markets in theory), hence there was no need for public intervention in these matters. This is why public concern about the environment was mainly limited to declarations.[1] Such an attitude has, however, changed over time. In the case of the environment, the free market does not 'get it right'. For example, a power plant may burn coal and it may use and pollute clean air and water in its production process. Suppose that this firm pays for coal, but not for the clean water and air that it consumes. Then, if there are no other restrictions, this firm would save in the use of coal, but it would be careless in the use of air and water. Free markets do not turn dross and concrete into clean nature; they do not take care of externalities such as the pleasures of enjoying the countryside. Governments can. Hence the grounds for government intervention in the field of the environment.

The formal cornerstone in the evolution of global concern about the environment was the UN Conference on Human Environment that took place in Stockholm in 1972. The conference reached an agreement on the universal responsibilities regarding the global environment and produced a large set of recommendations that would guide policies all around the world in this field. Relatively recent environmental disasters such as Seveso (Italy, 1976),[2] Bhopal (India, 1984),[3] Chernobyl (Ukraine, 1986), the cyanide spill (Romania, 2000) and the tanker *Prestige* oil spill (Spain, 2002) reminded everyone how vulnerable is the natural environment. They have also increased global awareness about the impact and damage that can be inflicted on humans, the environment and the natural balance.

This chapter is structured as follows. Section 2 considers select issues that are linked with environmental policy. Section 3 presents foundations, principles and policy initiatives in the environmental policy of the EU, as well as the impact of agriculture on the environment. Section 4 concludes that after a modest start, the environmental policy of the EU continues to expand. The EU business sector is finding that this policy is becoming quite costly, but even though the costs are increasing for the private sector, there are obvious benefits for society at large.

2. Issues

Public intervention in the field of environment and the control of pollution is limited by at least two obstacles. The first barrier to an effective public intervention rests on the imperfect information that is available to the government. For example, the administration needs data on the possible negative effects of a chemical. This information is often obtained from the affected chemical company, which has an incentive to provide incomplete, misleading or even false data to the government in order to influence the outcome of the policy in its own favour (to reduce potential costs in the event of regulation). The work of the government is made even more difficult as scientists often disagree on the acceptable or environmentally safe level of emission of pollutants. The problem is, what level of pollution can the environment and humans tolerate, and at what point do the harmful effects start? Therefore, it is often difficult for the government to set standards.

Imperfect information leads us to the second obstacle to an effective public intervention in the area of environment. As information is often deficient, public decision makers have a wide margin for discretion. Therefore, the bureaucrats are subject to lobbying. Such influence is strong from the organised and potentially affected (chemical or power-generating) industries which may often sway government decisions and laws in their favour.[4] The voice of the (unorganised) consumers and general public has been quite quiet for a long time. However, various dangers and disasters, as well as the entry onto the political scene of powerful pressure groups, has raised awareness about the environment and led to demands for intervention and regulation. All this has changed the balance of power between the business community and the general public.[5]

From 1972, the accepted basis for environmental policies in the OECD countries has been the polluter-pays principle. The Earth Summit in Rio de Janeiro (1992)[6] reaffirmed this principle, but added that states have common, although differentiated obligations. Although the polluter-pays principle may seem self-evident, its universal application may encounter problems. If producers are in the position to pass on the costs linked to environment management expenditure to their consumers, the users of goods or services are the ones that pay for those costs. While the developed countries may have the capacity, means and will to apply the principle in practice, problems arise on the side of the developing countries as they are price takers for many of their goods on the international market. In many cases they may not be able to pass on the costs to their consumers and finance the necessary compliance with international standards and demands.

Pollution is not only a regional, but also a trans-frontier, trans-regional and global phenomenon. For example, the quality of Dutch drinking water taken from the Rhine depends on substances that entered the river in the upstream countries starting from Switzerland. Similarly, there is a partial link between vehicle exhaust fumes in Britain and damage that acid rain does to the Black Forest region in Germany or in Scandinavia.

If the issue of the protection of the environment is global, then there is the need for a global action (and funds, if possible) regarding environmental issues. Examples of such global action include the Convention on International Trade in Endangered Species of Wild Fauna and Flora (1973); the Montreal Protocol on Substances that Deplete the Ozone Layer (1987); the Basle Convention on the Control of Transboundary Movements of Hazardous Wastes and Their Disposal (1989); and the Kyoto Protocol (1997) to the United Nations Framework Convention on Climate Change.

High environment-related standards may bring a potential danger of 'eco-protectionism' as a new type of NTB in international trade. Countries or their groups with relatively strict domestic environmental standards prevent or make difficult imports of affected goods produced in countries where these standards are low. There are, however, a number of valid reasons for a variation in standards among countries. They include not only differences in climate, but also level of development and population density. Countries with relatively lax environmental standards such as Malaysia, the Philippines, South Korea or Thailand have not received foreign investment in polluting industries, although one could expect that this may become the case (Charnovitz, 1995, p. 19). Foreign investors also fear that their environmental damage abroad may be challenged in courts in their country of origin.

It is sometimes alleged that compliance with environmentally sound standards may increase costs of production and, hence, jeopardise the international competitiveness of goods. Various purification gadgets and changes in technology to make the production or exploitation process cleaner cost money. However, does this put the competitiveness of a country's output in peril? A World Bank study of the impact of the environment-related expenditure on competitiveness of countries that have relatively high expenditure on those projects brought interesting results. For example, it was found that Germany, a country with strict environmental standards and relatively high national expenditure on these matters, maintained international competitiveness in environmentally sensitive goods in the 1970s and 1980s, in spite of increases in environment-related expenditure. In addition, the study found little systematic relationship between higher environmental standards and competitiveness in environmentally sensitive goods. In general, developed countries have maintained their comparative advantage in these goods (Sorsa, 1994).

International trade agreements that link countries have, for a long time, avoided environmental issues. For instance, Article 27 of the EFTA convention has as its objective an expansion of trade in fish, but without any reference to conservation. Similarly, for years the GATT promoted trade in tropical goods, but without due respect for the environment. Following the Rio Declaration (1992), future arrangements will take ecological issues into consideration. None the less, there is an unresolved issue on the global scale, which concerns the settlement of disputes. Trade arrangements deal with the settlement of commercial disputes, while environmental issues have been left aside.

3. European Union

FOUNDATIONS

The original Treaty of Rome does not lay grounds for a common EU policy on the environment. This reflects the prevailing neglect of the environmental matters at the time of its drafting. The general authority for *any* policy is, however, given in the catch-all Article 308. None the less, EU action in the field of the environment has been evolving. A few months after the Stockholm Conference, the EU Summit in Paris (1972) provided the groundwork for an EU environmental policy. The polluter-pays principle was adopted and five-year environment action programmes were launched from 1973. These programmes were initially only attempts to harmonise national legislation on the environment in order to prevent distortions in competition, but later on, they became more ambitious. Since that time the environmental dimension of the *acquis communautaire* has evolved to include 320 pieces of 'green' legislation.[7]

Together with the signing of the Treaty of Rome (1957) which set the foundations of the EU, another treaty was also signed – the one that established the European Atomic Energy Community (Euratom). The potential benefits, as well as perils of atomic energy were recognised, hence at that time the six countries wanted to impose a legal control over ownership, trade, research and employment of nuclear power. The potential negative impact of this source of energy on the environment was recognised by the treaty. Article 2 requires the establishment of 'uniform safety standards to protect the health of workers and of the general public'. In addition, Article 30 requires the introduction of basic health and safety standards linked with atomic energy.

The Single European Act (1986), Articles 130r–t, introduced a title on the environment into the Treaty of Rome. These articles were reaffirmed and some of them revised in the Maastricht Treaty (1991). They can be found in Title XIX, Articles 174–6 of the revised and consolidated Treaty of Rome. Article 6 of the consolidated Treaty of Rome stipulates that environmental protection must be integrated into the definition and implementation of other EU policies. The objectives of EU environmental policy (Article 174) include preserving, protecting and improving the quality of the environment; protection of human health; prudent exploitation of natural resources; and promotion of international measures that deal with global environmental problems. Although the polluter-pays principle is still applied (Article 175), there is provision for EU assistance if the costs of the agreed EU action fall disproportionately on the authorities of one or more member states. Common measures in the field of the environment may not, however, prevent member states maintaining or introducing more stringent national protective measures.

To realise its objectives and obligations in the field of the protection of the environment the EU can act and introduce regulatory, anticipatory, preventive and rectifying measures. Specific actions may include:

- increasing awareness of problems;
- sponsoring research;
- introducing policies;
- passing laws (introducing prohibitions, for example, for the use of certain technologies, chemical or the exploitation of resources such as

certain kinds of wood or hunting certain animals; imposing exploitation standards, for example, maximum extraction of minerals or catch of fish);
- setting minimum quality standards;
- imposing technology (for example, to ensure that pollutants are not discharged above a certain level);
- introducing measures to implement laws and policies (taxes, subsidies, deposits and refunds, for example, for beverage containers);
- setting legal liability for environmental damage;
- applying an integrated approach in all other policies (to include in the dimension of the environment);
- providing assistance; and
- acting on regional and global levels.

The task of the European Environment Agency is to monitor the state of the environment and to act as a whistle blower about approaching problems. Set up in 1990 by the EU in Copenhagen, the European Environment Agency has members that cover the whole of Europe. Its mission is to support sustainable development by providing relevant and timely information and data to policy makers and to the public, as well as to promote best practice in environmental protection.

PRINCIPLES

The EU environmental policy rests on five principles:

- *Prevention* (rather than cure): The general objective of the EU policy is to prevent all environmental damage through preventive and anticipatory action and measures. This precautionary principle is embodied in Article 174 of the Treaty of Rome. This means that even if the risk is not proven beyond reasonable doubt, but there are reasonable expectations that it may be present, the EU should consider action to avert it. All planning and decision-making processes that affect the environment such as motorways or power plants have to take into account the impact on the natural habitat in order to avoid the need for any corrective action in the future. Directive 85/337/EEC (1985) and its amendment Directive 97/11/EC (1997) list detailed criteria for the assessment of the effects of public and private projects on the environment.
- *Rectification*: If there is certain pollution it has to be tackled at its source and as promptly as possible. In cases where it cannot be entirely eradicated, it needs to be kept at the lowest possible level.

- *Polluter pays*: Prevention, cleaning and compensation for pollution and its damage to the environment should be borne, in principle, by those who cause it. The rationale for this principle is to provide an incentive not to pollute at all or, if necessary, to do it with as 'clean' technologies as possible and in the least harmful way. There is, none the less, a possibility of EU assistance if common measures to protect the environment impose unequal costs on certain countries, for example in the south or recently in the east of the EU where the previous rules and, more importantly, their application were lax.
- *Inclusion*: Environmental aspects have to be considered whenever the EU decides in the domain of all other common policies.
- *Subsidiarity*: Whenever possible, national and local authorities ought to decide their priorities and manage their responses. However, in the field of the environment an individual action may not always be appropriate. Rivers often flow through several states, animals migrate across borders and wind carries many pollutants across frontiers. Some EU action is often necessary.

Although the principles are there, their application and new eco-legislation should avoid segmenting the EU market. None the less, if the application of the spirit of the Cassis de Dijon case cannot be easily applied in the EU in environmental issues for reasons that include differences in climate or national (im)possibilities of absorbing the related costs over a short period of time, then EU eco-legislation needs to be coupled with funds and loans to those (southern and eastern) countries that are forced to implement such laws.

There are, of course, often profoundly conflicting interests in the regulation of environmental issues because firms want to reduce delays and costs of production, otherwise their competitiveness and profit may suffer. Governments must make tough political choices as they wish to preserve the environment while, at the same time, their aim is to stimulate economic growth.

In order to broaden policy instruments beyond environmental legislation, the EU countries intend to use market-based instruments such as environmental taxes. The objective is to internalise external environmental costs and to stimulate both producers and consumers to limit the environmental pressure towards responsible use of and greater respect for natural resources. In this regard, governments impose four broad categories of taxes on: energy, transport, pollution and use of resources. The most significant are taxes on energy. The idea behind this swing in taxation is to increase environmental taxes and, at the same time, to reduce taxes on labour (to combat unemployment).

Eurostat estimated that industry in the EU spent about €33 billion on environment protection in 1999.[8] Most of this was spent on investment in new equipment. Preventing pollution at the source involved half of this expenditure. Chemicals, rubber, plastics, metals, food, beverages and paper-related industries are the principal industries in terms of environmental protection expenditure. The most important protection domains are air, wastewater and waste. Austria and Germany are the EU countries that spent most on the protection of the environment if measured as a share of the GDP (0.6 per cent, each; the EU average was 0.4 per cent). Even though compliance with the EU legal duties involves costs for the businesses, these obligations create both substantial and general benefits to the society in terms of improvement in health and the environment. Expenditure related to the protection of the environment also establishes markets for environment-related goods and services. Approximately 1.6 million people or 1 per cent of the total number employed in the EU work in these industries in the EU(15).

COMMON AGRICULTURAL POLICY AND THE ENVIRONMENT

Together with trade, the CAP has been one of the oldest and most profound common policies of the EU. In essence, it set high prices for select farm products and guaranteed purchases at those prices. The production and, especially, the overproduction of farm goods may have an adverse effect on the salinisation and erosion of soil. An excessive usage of fertilisers, pesticides, herbicides, insecticides, phosphorus, minerals, nitrogen and fossil fuels pollute ground, water[9] and food with dangerous chemicals. This also reduces the number of species of plants and animals in their natural habitat. If, however, the implementation of environmental laws increases the cost of production and decreases output, the producers may (but not necessarily will) weaken their competitive position. An additional environment-unfriendly aspect is that the CAP disregards crops that were traditionally rotated, such as pulses, oats and fodder. The price policy has created a virtual monoculture that has upset the long-established farm balance. In addition, the production of milk and other animal-based goods would have generated quantities of animal manure, which is a rich source of nitrogen.

Anyone who travelled around England must have noticed the impact of the CAP on the environment and the traditional landscape. The sight of sheep and cattle grazing in fields and meadows has become less common. This was a direct consequence of the increasing intensification of livestock husbandry and a shift of land into cereal production. The bright yellow colour of the ripening crop is, however, distinctive and alien to the traditional green English landscape that has been so magnificently presented and documented over the past centuries in certain paintings by John Constable and Thomas Gainsborough.[10] In addition, the CAP price policy gave incentives to farmers to increase output and change the countryside. Ponds were drained, hedgerows uprooted and footpaths ploughed over in the quest to cultivate more land (Atkin, 1993, pp. 128–30). Many plants, birds, animals and insects disappeared.

The intention of various reforms of the CAP was to reduce farm output in the EU. A positive externality on the environment was expected. For example, there might be a drop in the use of pollutants. This would be most noticeable in the northern regions of the EU as the (large) farmers there employ chemically-based methods of production to a larger extent than farmers elsewhere in the EU. However, a fall in EU output may increase the price of some farm goods on the international market. As a consequence, there may be an expansion of agricultural output in the Cairns group and the US. Hence, the demand for polluting chemicals in these countries may increase. While there may be some improvement in the environment of the EU, there may be a degradation of the quality of the environment elsewhere in the world.

If there are cases in which farm production does not respond to incentives or when the damage to the environment is extreme, then regulatory measures may be an efficient policy instrument. Changes that are being considered by the EU in this respect include certification and registration of chemicals used in agriculture, restrictions of the chemical content in foodstuffs, as well as the dissemination of information and knowledge to traders and users of farm chemicals about their impact on the environment, food and health.

All these problems and concerns were considered, and the MacSharry Reform (1992) included the Agri-environmental Programme. It recognised both the role that farmers play in the protection of rural areas and the need to compensate for that role. The programme envisaged premiums for the employment of non-polluting methods of production (organic farming), conversion of farmland into parks, development of leisure activities, protection of the scenery, conservation of biodiversity and training in the preservation of the environment. All these activities, together with tourism, would create alternative local jobs that would compensate, at least in part, for the loss of jobs in direct farming. Member states draft their zonal programmes and then submit them to the EU for approval. Agri-tourism is growing in the EU. For instance, Parco dell'Orecchiella in Tuscany is becoming a popular destination for visitors. This provides additional business and employment in the region. Hence, the CAP's impact on the environment was not all negative.

The biggest scientific experiment ever undertaken on the environmental impact of genetically modified crops took place in Britain. This three-year government-funded project started because of serious public concerns about the overall impact and opposition to the commercial exploitation of engineered crops. The results on just one of the issues, that is, the danger to biodiversity, were published in 2003. Research on other concerns such as cross-pollination of genetically modified crops with other plants (which may create 'superweeds' or monsters) is still under way. Several genetically modified crops (sugar beet and rapeseed) reduced the number of insects such as bees and butterflies as the weeds that gave them food and shelter vanished. Lack of weed seed denied food to certain birds and animals. Modified maize, however, was less harmful for bees, butterflies and birds as farmers had to use fewer herbicides. One conclusion was that the impact of genetically modified organisms can be examined and that it can be damaging for the environment. The other one was that genetically modified organisms should be evaluated individually, just like medicines. There should not be an across-the-board acceptance of engineered organisms. Another government-sponsored report concluded at the same time that there is little demand for genetically modified products, and even less so once consumers know more about them.[11] In Belgium, scientists gave similar advice in 2004. They found that the commercial growing of genetically modified oilseed rape would be harmful to the environment. Wildlife and natural varieties would be damaged through the vertical gene-flow.[12]

In any case, there is a general finding in science that genetically modified plants and cloned animals are less fitted to survive in the environment over a longer period than organisms that have evolved naturally. The public is sceptical about the competence and commitment of government to promote and keep food safety. 'This problem is most acute in Britain, where official statements about "mad cow" disease and foot-and-mouth diseases were subsequently found to be unjustified and untrue. Rebuilding trust will be a slow process.'[13]

It ought to be clear that genetic modification is only a manipulation (production) technique. It is not an additive put into a living organism. But who benefits primarily from the process? John Kay states this clearly: 'And yet the actions of the companies that promote GM are, if possible, even more cynical and foolish. Throughout history, people have embraced new technology when it has offered better products or lower prices. But the GM seeds for which approval is sought are not nicer to eat, safer to use or cheaper to buy. They have been modified to encourage farmers to use other products made by the same companies. Why should a sceptical public support GM when the businesses promoting it are not only the principal beneficiaries but also probably the only ones?'[14] 'The Government knows that the case for authorising herbicide-tolerant GM maize is weak, but it is a sufficient fig-leaf to give the biotech companies what they want. The maize is designed to be treated with glufosinate, which is sold by Bayer, the same company that produces the seed.'[15]

POLICY INITIATIVES

As transport, agriculture, production of energy, tourism and manufacturing have an impact on the environment, a successful environmental policy should be developed, implemented and enforced by everyone, not just by the ministry of the environment. Sustainable development has to meet the needs of the present generation without compromising the ability of future generations to meet their own needs. Therefore, while it is true that the EU started with a series of action programmes[16] on the environment from 1973, these remained initially more haphazard statements of intent which had little serious impact on the substantive activities of the EU.

A striking example of this lack of consideration for environmental consequences was the Single Market Programme (1985–92). The implementation of the Single European Market went ahead without due attention to its impact on the environment until 1989. In that year an EU task force studied the environmental impact of the Single Market Programme which supplemented the Cecchini Report. The task force concluded that an increase in output would have a negative impact on the environment because an expansion in the production of goods and services (particularly transport) would increase the amount of waste and pollution. Hence, the optimistic results of the Cecchini Report had to be modified, that is, reduced by the amount of damage done to the environment.

In a consideration of a case regarding the Danish law on the packaging of drinks (the provision was that drinks should be marketed in returnable bottles), the EU Court of Justice ruled in 1988 that the protection of the environment took priority over the rules of free trade. This may be an important precedent for similar cases in the future (Weale and Williams, 1993). A shortage of raw materials and a lack of landfill sites resulted in the creation of policies for waste management and recycling. The EU directive on packaging and package waste (1994) was an attempt to harmonise national packaging laws[17] in addition it set recycling targets.

The eco-audit directive (1993) encourages industrial firms to introduce voluntarily eco-audit schemes. The objectives of these schemes are to determine how well the management and equipment is performing; verification of compliance with local, regional, state and EU environmental provisions; and minimisation of risks of pollution. In addition, the European Commission entered into voluntary environmental agreements with industry on several occasions. One agreement covered the labelling of cleaning products, while several others dealt with the reduction in the use of chlorofluorocarbons (CFCs) in different industries. However, the European Parliament is sceptical about the effectiveness of voluntary agreements as a means to achieve policy objectives.

Action programmes are the cornerstone of the EU policy and action in the field of the environment. The Sixth Environment Action Programme builds on five earlier programmes and three decades of standard setting in this policy field. The Sixth Programme, *Environment 2010: Our Future, Our Choice*, covers the 2001–10 period, and identified four priority areas for action:

- *Climate change*: A fall in the snow cover by 10 per cent since the 1960s, retreating mountain glaciers and the melting of ice in the sea have increased the sea level by 10–20 cm over the past 50 years. Many human activities are to be blamed for these developments. They include the burning of fossil fuels in power plants and various types of manufacturing and transport. The EU had a pivotal role in the conference that led to the Kyoto Protocol (1997). This has been the only international response so far to global warming. This multilateral agreement set detailed targets for the reduction in the emission of carbon dioxide (CO_2) and lessening of the 'greenhouse effect'. In order to limit and reduce emissions of CO_2, member states would grant tradable allowances to companies. The UN-sponsored review of the Kyoto Protocol in Milan in 2003 was subject to two setbacks. The US and Australia chose not to ratify the protocol, while Russia still needs to ratify it. Russia was given most credits to sell, but they were devalued by the American withdrawal. The US objection to the protocol is that it is along the lines of ever-increasing regulation. This may be true, but global warming is also increasing: summer 2003 was one of the hottest on record.[18] More than 120 countries have ratified the protocol. Their message regarding the climate protection is that there is no alternative to multilateral cooperation. If the EU implements a unilateral approach to curb greenhouse gas emissions, this may prompt industries that emit gases to move outside the EU.
- *Nature and biodiversity*: Nature and biodiversity are in danger almost everywhere and they have to be protected.
- *Health and the quality of life*: Human health problems that are provoked by the environment refer not only to allergies, asthma and infertility, but also to premature death and cancer. In this connection,

there is a need to avoid ever-growing traffic congestion, noise, air pollution and stress. Transport networks ought to be 'sustainable'. In addition, the EU requests that all items containing genetically modified organisms must be thoroughly tested and clearly labelled, their sources must be traceable and their impact on health and environment constantly monitored.
- *Preserving natural resources and managing waste*: The objective here is to reduce the use of depleted resources, through innovations and new technologies (for example, new car engines). As far as waste is concerned, the EU aims to prevent its creation primarily through better manufacturing methods and through shifting demand towards 'greener' products. Recycling[19] and recovery will be the next priority.

Management of forests is an important part of environmental policy. This should ensure that timber originates from sustainably managed forests. The idea for afforestation of farmland in the EU as part of the reform package originated in the Mansholt Plan (1968). The MacSharry Reform simply reinvigorated it. As afforestation deals with the medium and long terms, its scope and effect cannot be evaluated at present. For example, if the policy applies premiums for the alteration of the landscape with fast-growing poplars, this may result in a surplus production of soft wood which would jeopardise the position of traditional and non-subsidised growers. The local programmes need to emphasise indigenous types of forest that will increase the consumption of nitrates already in the soil, prevent erosion of land, create jobs in the timber industry, reduce surpluses of farm goods and, at the same time, beautify the local landscape. Special subsidies for chestnut and oak planting need to be high on the agenda. Although the overall benefits of such schemes are self-evident, doubtful financial pledges introduce a degree of uncertainty into their future. Unfortunately, short-sighted decision makers fail to see that programmes such as these will have to be undertaken in the future, but their cost will then be higher than it is at present.

The cyanide spill into the Tisa in Romania (2000) was the worst ecological disaster since the Chernobyl nuclear accident (1986). It polluted water and killed aquatic life in several states. This served to remind everyone about the gravity of the problem in the accession countries, the consequence of years of neglect of the environment even well after the collapse of the centrally planned system. *Agenda 2000* stated that the environment is a major challenge for enlargement.[20] The environmental dimension of the *acquis communautaire* has about 320 pieces of 'green' legislation. To implement all those laws could cost the ten Central and East European countries as much as €110 billion over a decade.[21] Without the implementation and enforcement of the 'green' legislation, the eastern countries may well be accused of 'environmental dumping' by the rest of the EU(15).[22]

4. Conclusion

Public concern and action over environmental issues has increased significantly since the 1970s. This is not only limited to local concerns such as the revitalisation of a lake or the preservation of an endangered species of birds, but it also includes global issues such as the depletion of the ozone layer and global warming.[23]

Market forces do not take into account environmental issues that are often linked with longer-term considerations. Environmental externalities, however, do become recognised, so the previous 'benign neglect' policy is evolving into an active and costly approach. Intervention in environmental affairs may be costly in the short term, but the overall pecuniary and other longer-term non-financial gains more than compensate for that shortfall. There may also be short-term direct gains from environmental programmes. Examples include benefits from savings in the consumption of energy.

Strong industrial lobbies and general reductions in public expenditure create a certain anxiety over the future extent of environmental policies. For example, the worthy goals of the EU Agri-environmental Programme may be slowed down by the lack of resources. None the less, increased public awareness, pressure and research, as well as the involvement of the producers of the environmentally related goods may provide compelling forces for the expansion of environmental policies.

Although certain important steps were taken towards the creation of an EU environmental policy, the policy remained rather vague for quite some time. However, once it was on the policy agenda, it tended to develop, just as other EU policies did. From initial declarations, the policy has become an established and quite costly part of the EU. One of the biggest problems refers to the issue of non-compliance with the EU law in this area. Another difficulty is that there are insecure funds to support the policy in cases where there is a need (eastern part of the EU). This reflects both general restraints on public expenditure and a concentration of public authorities on other more immediate short-term issues.

Demand for leisure is increasing in the EU. People are ready, willing and able to pay for a pleasant walk in the picturesque countryside or to enjoy healthy food. Care for the environment also creates jobs. Coupled with the increasing general consciousness about the conservation of a clean, healthy and sustainable environment, this policy will remain high on the EU agenda in the future.

One may find evidence of EU involvement in the area of environment protection and management since the early 1970s. Industrial emissions of toxic substances such as lead and mercury, as well as SO_2 have substantially declined. The use of many dangerous chemicals has been either banned or regulated and restricted. Better sewage and wastewater treatment has improved the water quality of rivers and lakes, and this has allowed fish to return to their old natural habitat in rivers such as the Rhine and Thames.

Notes

1. This neglect does not mean that environmental problems were neither existing, nor obvious. People, at least in Europe, were well aware of the problems for the elderly and sick created by the notorious London smog up until the 1970s.
2. Contamination around Seveso (northern Italy) was the result of an explosion in a chemical plant and the release of a cloud of trichlorophenol containing cancer-provoking dioxins.
3. Highly toxic methyl isocyanate was released from a storage tank. About 2000 people died and tens of thousands were injured.
4. The European Commission drafted a plan in 2003 to regulate the EU chemical industry and to test thousands of chemical substances that may be harmful to humans or the environment. To implement this plan would cost this industry around €7.5 billion over a decade. This plan has met with fierce opposition both from industry and from EU governments (*Financial Times*, 14 October 2003).
5. The expansion of government activities regarding environmental issues provided an incentive for the development of those industries that produce environment-related goods and services. One firm's expensive obligation is another's chance for profit. Among the principal buyers of these products are power and water-producing companies, mining and manufacturing firms (chemicals) and municipalities.
6. The 2002 Earth Summit in Johannesburg devised and launched about 300 voluntary partnerships (there were no agreements that would lead to new treaties) among governments, intergovernmental organisations, NGOs and the private sector in the areas that include management of the ecosystem, toxic chemicals, energy and access to water and sanitation.
7. Scandinavian countries together with Austria, Germany and the Netherlands form an inner EU group that is in favour of stricter environmental regulation. They even considered forming an 'eco-Schengen lobby group' in 1996. The goal would be to push for stricter environmental regulation and its faster implementation.
8. Eurostat (2002). 'Environmental protection expenditure by industry in the European Union', Statistics in Focus, Theme 8-14/2002.
9. Water drained from surface soil carries phosphates into rivers. This stimulates the expansion of algae that consume oxygen in water. This may kill aquatic life, including fish. Such pollution has been observed in many rivers in north-western Europe and in Lombardy.
10. British painters have always been fascinated (at least in the past) by two themes: the landscape and the human face.
11. *Financial Times*, 17 October 2003.
12. *Financial Times*, 28 January 2004.

13. J. Kay, 'A rich crop of cynicism, greed and mistrust', *Financial Times*, 17 March 2004, p. 19.
14. J. Kay, 'A rich crop of cynicism, greed and mistrust', *Financial Times*, 17 March 2004, p. 19.
15. J. Ruddock, 'Why are they foisting GM crops on us?', *The Independent*, 20 February 2004.
16. Action programmes refer to areas such as water and air quality, disposal of waste, chemicals and dangerous substances, noise and safeguarding of countryside and wildlife.
17. For example, Belgium applied a packaging tax, Denmark had a deposit-refund scheme, while Germany used a labelling system.
18. According to one point of view, the cost of implementing the Kyoto Protocol may exceed its benefits. Even if one assumes that climate is sensitive to CO_2 emissions, Kyoto would lower the global mean temperature by only 0.15 degrees Celsius. This is below the natural annual variation. The future price of liquid fuels is linked with high uncertainty, as is the investment cost to implement the deal. These risks are compounded by uncertainty about the possible arrival of new and cheap alternative sources of energy (*European Voice*, 20 November 2003, p. 8).
19. Most virgin paper comes from Canada and Scandinavia. Dump hilly territory is good both for trees and production of hydroelectricity. This is important from the vantage point of fuel savings. There is little difference between the production of virgin and recycled paper, but fuel for the latter comes from mostly from non-renewable sources. Here enters the issue of recycling as it catches the attention of corporate lobbyists. Governments may be requested to offer subsidies for the collection of paper that is later processed with chemicals that are dumped in the nature. This all is at the expense of Scandinavian businesses that chop and plant the trees. 'Business interests and naive environmentalists find common cause' (J. Kay, 'Thinking outside the blue box on recycling', *Financial Times*, 25 February 2004, p. 19).
20. European Commission (1997a, p. 49).
21. *European Voice*, 28 May 2003, p. 14.
22. A more detailed consideration of this issue can be found in the chapter on eastern enlargement of the EU (see Chapter 14).
23. Low-level ski resorts such as Kitzbühel (787m) in Austria could be ruined by global warming. Frozen soil (permafrost) is vulnerable to melting. This would increase the costs of anchoring and maintenance of ski lift and cable car masts.

> The highway of the upright is to depart from evil;
> He who keeps his way preserves his soul.
> Proverbs 16:17

13 Transport Policy

1. Introduction

The size of the market determines, in static terms, the opportunities for the division of labour and specialisation. Market size and its extent is, on the other hand, limited by natural and human imposed barriers to trade. The impact of natural obstacles to trade, such as distance or physical geography, could be moderated by the construction of infrastructure such as roads, railways, airports, bridges, tunnels and ports. In addition, a fall in transport costs per unit of transported good (or per passenger) reduces barriers that may exist between two or more places. International economic integration is able to mitigate or even eliminate the impact of artificial barriers to trade such as tariffs, quotas, taxes and NTBs. Developed and relatively cheap transport and communication links among states are necessary conditions for successful and profound economic integration.

There was little intervention in trade during the 19th century. None the less, markets among many countries remained detached because of relatively high costs of transport and a lack of full and timely information about opportunities for trade. Since then, heavy public investment in infrastructure, as well as advances in technology have reduced the distance between various markets.

Classical models of trade and international economic integration have excluded the space dimension from considerations (alternatively, when transport costs were included, they were assumed to be equal to zero). As increasing productivity reduces cost per unit of transported goods, that theoretical assumption was not entirely legitimate. In addition, the transport industry has a great importance and weight in the economy as it is a significant contributor to the GDP and direct and indirect employment. In a standard case, transport costs have the same effect on the final price of goods and trade as have tariffs or taxes. When the cost of transport is reduced (as with the reduction in tariffs), new trade among states may be created.

The transport industry as a part of the services sector has at least seven distinct characteristics:

- transport may contribute to an efficient allocation of resources;
- transport services play a crucial role in the successful operation of the market and competitiveness of goods and various services;
- transport services have a significant impact on the standard of living;
- there is often public intervention regarding investment in infrastructure, rates, taxes, subsidies and conditions of operation (safety, dimensions of vehicles, pollution and the like).[1] It is most pronounced in railways, the mode of transport that until recently was virtually a monopoly;[2]
- transport services are significant direct and indirect employers of labour;
- transport is a significant consumer of capital goods, energy and R&D; and
- the demand for transport services depends on the level of economic activity and income. However, the supply of these services is inelastic in the short term.

Consideration in this chapter is concentrated primarily on road transport as the most significant mode of transport in the EU. In addition, road transport is the transport mode in which the EU has made the most resolute efforts to secure the adoption of common policies. The chapter is structured as follows. Section 2 examines the legal base for the common transport policy and its significance in the EU economy, and then considers its delayed and modest evolution. The EU had and has ambitious plans and aspirations to be involved in various aspects of transport, and these are surveyed in turn. The stumbling block in the future development of this policy is the lack of full-hearted support by the national governments and the lack of massive investment necessary to finance trans-European networks and many other plans on the European Commission's agenda. Section 3 concludes.

2. European Union

LEGAL BASE

Apart from trade and agriculture, transport was the only major industry to which the original Treaty of Rome devoted a special Title. The inclusion of transport policy in the treaty was at the request of the Dutch who have a special interest in this economic activity. Articles 3 and 70 state that the creation of a common transport policy is one of the objectives of the EU. Apart from this general requirement, there are no other instructions about the nature of a common transport policy. However, the Council of Ministers is charged by Article 71 to lay down common rules for the policy. The question of aid is regulated by Articles 73 and 74. Basically, unless authorised by the European Commission, state aid is forbidden. For internal EU transport, Article 75 outlaws any discrimination regarding rates or conditions for carriage of the same goods over the same transport links on the grounds of destination or origin of goods. The Maastricht Treaty introduced a new Title: Trans-European Networks (Articles 154–6). The EU is empowered to contribute to the establishment and development of trans-European networks in transport, telecommunications and energy infrastructures in order to derive full benefit from the area without internal frontiers. The objectives include a promotion of interconnection and interoperability of national networks, as well as standardisation and cooperation with third countries on projects of mutual interest. In addition, Article 6 obliges the EU to pursue environment-friendly policies and actions.

SIGNIFICANCE

Transport is one of the most important economic activities in the EU at the start of the new millennium. It accounts annually for about €1000 billion which contributes to about 10 per cent to EU GDP. This service industry employs directly about 10 million people in the EU(15). Its impact on the EU economy is amplified by the fact that about 3 million people work in the production of transport-related equipment. In addition, the operation of and efficiency in many other parts of the economy depends on the smooth and efficient performance of transport.

Transport is an evolving and growing industry. This is not only the consequence of changes in technology (fuel-saving and environment-friendly engines, or very fast trains, or reductions in the price of air travel), but also because of the changing structure of manufacturing. New production methods reduce stocks, become flexible and depend on varied and rapid delivery services (just-in-time delivery). Shipment sizes are being reduced, but deliveries are becoming more frequent. Storage is being passed on from firms' warehouses to supply trucks. Certain firms prefer to locate away from congested urban areas, to run multisite business operations, so they depend on a reliable transport system for inputs and the delivery of goods to major markets. On the downside of this evolving approach to manufacturing, there are costs. Trucks are often empty or have half loads.[3] This may increase the consumption of energy, while traffic jams contribute to pollution, allergies, waste of time and noise. Increased professional mobility and a rise in personal income, coupled with increased holiday time, has also boosted demand for travel.

Transport is linked with a general policy controversy. Firms and consumers demand more and better transport services; they are intolerant of delays. At the same time, there is general concern about noise, accidents and the impact of transport on the environment and health. A major policy challenge is to find and maintain an optimal balance among these concerns and to create and manage a sustainable transport policy from an economic, social and environmental position. The size and importance of the transport-related part of the economy has enabled suppliers of transport services to establish contacts with and sometimes influence the policy makers. However, various NGOs also press their case, thus influencing public debate and, to an extent, the final policy outcome.

Road transport is the predominant mode of transport in the EU. In the goods transport market the share of road transport is 44 per cent, sea 41 per cent, rail 8 per cent and inland waterways 4 per cent. The dominance of road transport in the passenger market is even more pronounced. The share of road transport in this market is 79 per cent, rail 6 per cent and air 5 per cent. While helping the economy to operate smoothly, the expansion of transport has brought frustrating traffic jams, but also costly delays and damage to health and the environment. Some 7500 km (10 per cent) of the EU road network are affected by traffic jams daily. The annual cost of these jams is approximately 0.5 per cent of EU GDP. If nothing is done about this issue, this cost may double over a decade.[4] Traffic jams and delays also take place on railways, as well as at airports. The ever-increasing volume of freight transport by road in the EU and EFTA is presented in Figure 13.1 for the 1970–2000 period, while Figure 13.2 shows the same trend for road passenger transport during the same period for the same group of countries.

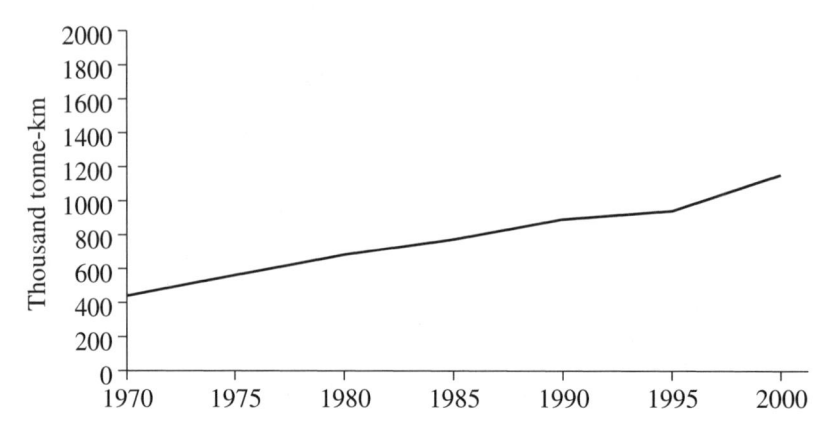

Source: UNECE database (2004).

Figure 13.1 Freight transport by road in the EU and EFTA, 1970–2000

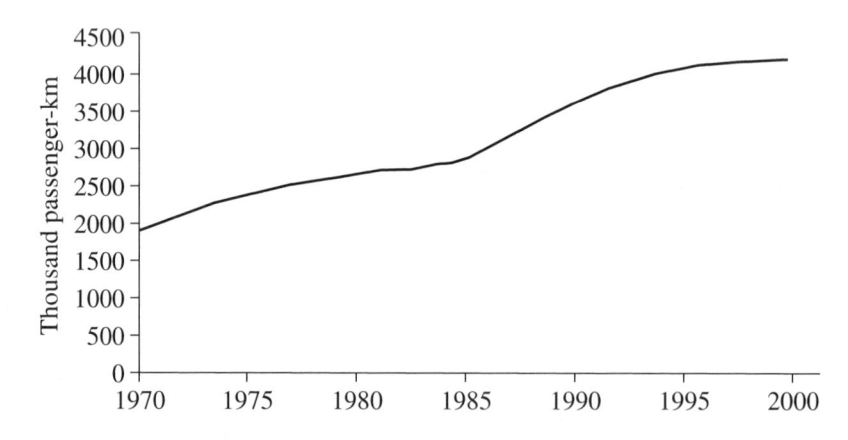

Source: UNECE database (2004).

Figure 13.2 Passenger transport by road in the EU and EFTA, 1970–2000

DELAYED LAUNCH

The Schaus Memorandum (Commission of the European Economic Community 1961) was the first attempt to introduce a common transport policy in the EU. The memorandum suggested an elimination of impediments to the creation of a common market in transport services; the national markets for transport services ought to be open; and that there should be attempts to create conditions for free competition in the provision of transport services. At a time when transport markets were highly regulated, Schaus's ideas were highly controversial and were shelved. Another attempt by the Commission to advance its transport policy was in 1973. The central element was the call to establish a system that would improve transport infrastructure, promote social progress, increase safety and reduce costs. The Council of Ministers, again, made no formal response to the proposal. The European Commission continued with its efforts to create a common transport policy and came up with a new set of proposals in 1983. In essence, these provided principles for a comprehensive internal market in transport activity. In spite of a few attempts by the European Commission to initiate the creation of a common transport policy, the EU was unable or unwilling to do so. For 30 years after the signature of the Treaty of Rome, transport policy remained under the control of national governments.

Developments in transport policy were prevented by different perceptions about how such a policy needs to be structured. Some countries, such as France and Germany, saw transport as an industry that has to contribute to wider social and regional policy objectives. Britain, on the other hand, regarded transport as a services industry that is no different from others and that should be treated accordingly. The consequence was that an EU policy has not been established.

The lack of progress regarding the creation of the common policy in transport was such that the European Parliament (supported by the European Commission) took the Council of Ministers to the European Court of Justice in 1983. The charge was that the Council of Ministers had failed to act on the basis of Article 71. The ruling of the Court of Justice (1985), confirming the charge by the European Parliament, was a landmark in the development of EU transport policy. The Council of Ministers was obliged to take the necessary measures in order to go ahead with the creation of an obligatory, but still missing, common policy within a reasonable time. Consequently, direct measures towards the creation of a common transport policy (such as an elimination of segmented national markets, phased removal of licences and the granting of cabotage[5] rights) and indirect ones (a removal of checks on internal frontiers)[6] were included in the Single Market Programme.

EVOLUTION

Following the landmark ruling of the European Court of Justice (1985) and the establishment of the Single European Market, the European

Commission tried to set out a general approach to the development of a common transport policy. Its 1992 Communication, *The Future Development of the Common Transport Policy*,[7] spells out the desired policy action for the future. There were seven major objectives:

- *Proper operation of the internal market*: This includes removing restrictions on cabotage for the EU-residing operators.
- *Intermodal competition and complementarity*: The thrust of this objective is that users have to pay the full cost of the transport service. It may be difficult to implement: for example, in urban public transport or railway lines that are servicing small, backward and distant rural areas. Such services have always been subsidised within the functions of social, regional and cohesion policies.
- *Development of trans-European networks*: This is a medium- and long-term objective. The networks are supposed to become the 'arteries through which the economic lifeblood' of the EU flows. They should become major routes along which people, goods and services flow. As such, they would further economic integration, ease communication, shrink distances and bring peripheral regions into easier and cheaper contact with central areas. In order to operate these networks efficiently, the provision of these services needs to be liberalised, they must be technically compatible and any possible bottlenecks have to be eliminated. Most of the projects, however, require massive investment. This is a major obstacle to their realisation. The expectation that the private sector will be the major investor may not be fulfilled. The very long-term nature of the projects, their sky-high costs, as well as bad experience of private sector financing of infrastructural projects such as the Channel Tunnel may be serious obstacles for the involvement of the private sector in these projects.
- *Safety*: Each year road traffic accidents cause tens of thousands of deaths and more than 1.5 million injuries on the roads of the EU. Safety improvements are a legitimate area for EU concern. A chain of directives was issued regarding the harmonisation of standards for brakes, lighting, windshields, sound levels, dimensions and weights of commercial vehicles and the like. The EU aim to promote better training of drivers, to increase awareness of the dangers of driving while intoxicated or tired, and to encourage 'calm driving'. Technical measures to reduce the high toll in human and economic terms, include improvements in the safety of vehicles and roads.
- *Environment*: Transport is responsible for about 25 per cent of the total EU emission of CO_2. This 'greenhouse gas' contributes to global warming. The target was to stabilise the EU emission of CO_2

in 2000 on the 1990 level, and a reduction in the years beyond. This would require an increase in the efficiency of fuel consumption.
- *Social issues*: The EU aimed to further the implementation of the Social Charter in the area of transport. In addition, there must be an obligatory period of rest for drivers (for example, by the introduction of the tachograph as 'the spy in the cab'), the regulation of working time and other conditions, as well as training.
- *External relations*: First and foremost, the aim of the EU was to cooperate with Switzerland on transport issues. Because of the lack of a land frontier with Greece, certain Balkan nations may be included in the list of those countries that could participate in a common transport policy.

Both large-scale and flexible modes of production require efficient and reliable transport services. Increased sophistication and a reduction in own-account transportation have redressed the demand for these services. A just-in-time delivery system (frequent, punctual and reliable shipments) was the result of sophisticated logistics which reduced storage costs. The majority of firms in the haulage industry are small or medium sized. About 95 per cent of the companies have fewer than six vehicles. This reflects the fact that the road haulage market is mainly local (Carlén, 1994, p. 89). While one-third of the total volume of all goods forwarded by road (expressed in t/km) were carried up to 150 km in 2000, the equivalent share was only 10 per cent for rail. Almost half of all goods forwarded by rail were carried over 500 km, and the equivalent share for road haulage was 23 per cent.[8] This shows the flexibility of road transport over relatively short distances and the relative importance of rail transport for longer distances. This finding suggests the existence of a spatial clustering of manufacturers in the vicinity of consumers in the EU. While in most EU countries road transport is geared towards domestic service (most obvious in Greece, Spain and Portugal), the Netherlands and Belgium direct about a half of their respective road transport services to other countries (primarily Germany) because of their ports of Rotterdam and Antwerp.

The Single Administrative Document for international transport of goods, introduced by the EU in 1988, was a significant step in the direction of improving the transport service. This document replaced some 30 documents that had been required in order to allow goods to move within the EU. The Single Administrative Document was not required for EU internal trade after 1993 because of the Single European Market, but it is used for goods that cross an EU external frontier.

The EU was relatively successful in introducing special transport permits valid for a limited time throughout the EU. However, the number of these permits was relatively small in relation to demand. The shortage of international haulage licences which were acceptable for business throughout the EU has created a black market for them. The Single European Market changed all that. International road transport in the EU was fully liberalised from 1993. Liberal rules for EU road haulage, including cabotage (from 1998), increased the potential for efficiency of transport and reduced the costs of this service to the manufacturing sector, trade and distribution.[9] There was a quota of about 30 000 authorisations (valid for two months) for cabotage in the EU. It was progressively increased until 1998, after which EU hauliers were free to pick up or deliver their cargo anywhere in the EU without any restrictions.

In spite of the freedom to offer transport services in other EU member countries, cabotage still represents a negligible part of the EU road transport market. In 2001, cabotage represented 0.7 per cent of total road freight transport. As expected, the Benelux hauliers were the most active in the EU with 52 per cent of the total. German hauliers account for a significant share (17 per cent). France and Germany were the principal countries in which cabotage took place as each of them accounted for more than a quarter of the total, but even so, only 1.6 per cent (France) and 1.1 per cent (Germany) of the total domestic transport market was 'handed over' to hauliers from other EU member countries.[10]

AIR TRANSPORT

The EU skies were open to all EU-domiciled air-transport companies in 1997. These companies are allowed to operate domestic air service (cabotage) in the EU country of their choice. In addition, they can offer air-transport services between EU countries. However, anyone who expected massive changes in this market was disappointed. Few companies started a domestic air service in other countries. Barriers to 'real' competition in this industry involve various national bilateral deals that regulate long flights to non-European destinations. Alitalia cannot operate flights between Paris and New York because the Franco-American deal does not allow for such a possibility. These bilateral deals are the result of arrangements between governments, not airlines. Hence the solution needs to be found by national administrations. None the less, tentative moves towards reshaping the EU air travel market are being made.

For a decade, the European Commission offered to negotiate transatlantic 'open skies' traffic rights with the US (the most world's most important transport market). However, the EU member states preferred to keep the current bilateral arrangements. The European Commission took these countries to the European Court of Justice in 1998 on the grounds that such a stance infringes the principle of the freedom of establishment. The ruling by the European Court of Justice (2002) was that bilateral open-sky agreements between individual EU member countries and the US were illegal under the EU rules. The European Commission was delighted about this ruling which drew a line between national sovereignty and EU jurisdiction.

The new situation would unravel the disparities in the transatlantic air-transport market, which had been fragmented by detailed bilateral intergovernmental deals since the end of the 1940s. The situation is disparate because air transport has been a principal impetus to the 'globalisation' of the world economy. These bilateral deals created rigidities, inefficiencies, financial losses and forgone consumer benefits. They also prevent companies from carrying out broad reorganisation and adjustments. The current bilateral deals are more beneficial to the US carriers than to those from the EU: they allow the American carriers to take passengers to a third country and to hop between EU states and pick up passengers, whereas the EU carriers cannot operate between the US federal states. Labour unions are opposed to this as they fear job losses. In addition, the US government subsidises the domestic carriers by demanding that US officials and cargo must travel on US aircraft. It is obvious why the US is in no rush to alter the current situation.

FUTURE PROSPECTS

The expansion of transport services resulted in the facilitation and growth in trade, more efficient production and wider choice for consumers, but it also contributed in certain cases to increased congestion and accidents, as well as environmental and health nuisances. In order to meet challenges in transport in the coming decade and to set an agenda for action, in 2001 the European Commission published the White Paper *European Transport Policy for 2010: Time to Decide*. The central features of the new set of objectives are: to restore the balance between different modes of transport and to develop intermodality; to grapple with the problems of congestion and the degradation of the environment; and to improve the safety and quality of transport. These objectives will be translated into about 60 policy measures by the end of the decade.

The transport policy White Paper formulated an action plan. The goal is to bring substantial improvements in the quality and efficiency of transport in the EU. The plan also proposed a strategy to reduce the pressure on the environment and prevent congestion. The intention is to maintain market competitiveness of goods and services produced in the EU and to increase the overall standard of living.

The proposed policy measures that would develop a transport policy for Europe's citizens would revolve around the following themes:

- *Road safety*: Each year road traffic accidents cause over 40 000 deaths in the EU(15). In 2000 alone, there were 40 812 persons killed in these accidents and more than 1.7 million injured.[11] The age group most affected are 14–25 years old. The directly measurable cost of these accidents is about €45 billion. The indirect annual cost is estimated to be about €160 billion or 2 per cent of EU GDP.[12] The European Commission would like to halve the number of fatalities in road traffic accidents by 2010.

  In addition to the already introduced directives regarding safety standards, the European Commission proposes to instigate appropriate signposting of blackspots, oppose excessive driving times, harmonise road transport penalties at a European level, and considerably increase the use of new technologies: safe new vehicles, the protection of vehicle occupants in the event of an impact, and the setting of safety standards for the design of car fronts in particular. Citizens are to be guaranteed the highest possible level of safety and this takes priority in all circumstances. This applies not only to road traffic, but also to all other modes of transport such as aviation, shipping and railways.
- *Congestion*: The European Commission proposes to put an end to current trends and shift the balance between the different modes of transport. An active policy would encourage the linking-up of the different modes and promote rail, maritime and inland waterway transport. The Marco Polo programme tries to link up different modes of transport; it includes the introduction of an integrated ticket (and luggage handling) between transport modes such as air–coach–ferry–train–urban transport–car parks.
- *Environment protection*: A wide range of measures are envisaged to develop fair charges on infrastructure which takes into account external costs and encourages the use of the least-polluting modes of transport. Sensitive areas will be defined, in particular in the Alps and the Pyrenees, which should be eligible for additional funding for alternative transport. Clean fuels and improved fuel efficiency will be promoted.
- *Taxes*: Harmonising taxes on diesel for professional use would reduce distortions of competition on the liberalised road transport market.
- *Quality of service*: The development of transport in Europe must go hand in hand with a high level of quality. The European Commission

recommends the harmonisation of working conditions, especially in road transport, and the maintenance of high-quality public services. In addition, it intends to encourage best practices to ensure a high quality of urban transport services. This would improve the use of public transport and the already existing infrastructure.

- *Passenger rights*: Air passenger rights will be reinforced. This would include compensation where travellers are delayed or denied boarding due to overbooking by airlines. The next step would be to extend passenger protection measures to other modes of transport. The European Commission has a plan that would force railway companies to compensate passengers who have suffered delays or cancellation of cross border train journeys. Among other issues, on journeys that last more than two hours on a high-speed train, a delay of one hour or more would entitle passengers to request a full refund of their tickets. Rail operators would be liable for damages arising from the delay such as the cost of theatre tickets or missed connections.
- *Major new infrastructure*: Priorities include the missing links in the trans-European networks (in particular the high-speed passenger rail network, including airport connections) and infrastructure with genuine potential for transferring goods from the roads to the railways. In 2003, the European Commission put forward a plan to complete the Single European Market by overcoming the natural barriers presented by the Alps, the Pyrenees and the Baltic sea. This plan listed 22 priority projects to be completed by 2020, at an estimated cost of €220 billion. These projects include a bridge between Sicily and the mainland; railway lines linking Budapest–Lyon, Paris–Vienna–Bratislava, Gdansk–Warsaw–Brno–Bratislava and Warsaw–Riga–Tallin, and an improvement in the existing links over the Alps and the Pyrenees. The overall cost of these priority and other projects was estimated to be €600 billion over two decades. Even though the projects were to be financed through public–private partnership, the Council of Ministers was not amenable to this idea as many national governments are struggling with deficits.
- *Galileo (radio-navigation system)*: Satellite radio-navigation technology enables everyone with a receiver to pick up signals. This technology is evolving and expanding, and new applications are constantly being discovered which offer possibilities for considerable profits. Only two countries have this technology: the US has its global positioning system (GPS) and Russia has Glonass. Both of these were developed and operated principally for military purposes. The result is that signals can be denied or jammed at any moment as happened with the GPS during the NATO attack on Yugoslavia in 1999. Signals

could be restricted to own forces in the battlefield. Because the EU does not want to risk being dependent on third countries in this respect, it is developing Galileo, it's own radio-navigation technology with a system of 30 satellites. This €3.25 billion project is expected to be operational in 2008.[13] It will offer new universal services such as location of vehicles, telemedicine and geographical information systems for agriculture.

3. Conclusion

Compared with trade policy, the CAP or policy in the area of competition, a common EU transport policy is far less developed. However, this situation is gradually changing. The EU has always been involved in the financing of transport infrastructure in one way or another, but this has been more on an *ad hoc* project-by-project basis than as part of a coherent common transport policy. The role of the EU in financing transport infrastructure could be reinforced in the future by the development of trans-European networks, in particular with the Central and East European countries.

A turning point in the creation of an effective (common) transport policy came with the Single European Market. Policy emphasis moved away from the elimination of NTBs towards the broader objective of the smooth operation of a transport system within the Single European Market. The result is a more open market, free of bureaucracy, which is helping firms to increase their efficiency in production and marketing, as well as in competitiveness. The objective of the EU is to integrate national transport networks into a coherent European transport system, to remove bottlenecks and to forge previously missing links.

It is to be expected that the European Commission will propose and carry out a more active policy in the area of transport (with the support of national governments in the Council of Ministers) on the grounds of subsidiarity, cohesion, regional development, safety, social issues and protection of the environment and health. The strategy for the coming decade spelled out in the 2001 White Paper is compounded with challenges brought about by the eastern enlargement. This would increase not only social and environmental, but also cohesion policy concerns. The desired and declared policy by the European Commission is as yet only a statement of ambitious and costly aspirations: to perform not only an economic, but also a wider social, health and environment-related function. It remains to be seen whether and how this will be approved, financed and put into operation by the member governments.

Notes

1. Public authorities often use subsidies and discriminatory rates for the transport of goods and passengers to and from select regions with certain disadvantages as aids to the development of employment in those areas.
2. A loss-making and highly subsidised train transport system was revived following the opening up of the high-speed TGV train service between Paris and Lyon in 1981. Since then, this development has boosted similar train services on the major railway routes in the EU.
3. It has been estimated that empty trucks travelled about 60 billion kilometres in the EU at an approximate annual cost of €45 billion. A better organisation of transport could radically reduce these figures (*European Voice*, 29 January 1998, p. 15).
4. European Commission (2001, p. 12).
5. Granting cabotage right to foreigners occurs when country A allows operators from country B to provide internal transport services in country A. It represents a profound move towards the full freedom to provide transport services on the internal market.
6. A Single Administrative Document, introduced in 1988, replaced up to 70 different forms that were previously necessary for lorries crossing internal frontiers in the EU. The document is also valid for EFTA countries.
7. Commission of the European Communities (1992).
8. European Commission (2003). *Panorama of Transport*. Luxembourg: European Communities, pp. 53–4.
9. The US offered a convincing example of the deregulation of inter-state transport services in 1980.
10. Eurostat (2003). 'Road freight cabotage 1999–2001', Statistics in Focus, Theme 7-7/2003.
11. In France alone, for example, there were 7720 persons killed in road traffic accidents in 2001. This is an average of 21 persons a day (UNECE, 2003).
12. European Commission (2001, p. 66).
13. China is expected to contribute about €230 million to this EU project.

> But whoever has this world's goods,
> and sees his brother in need,
> and shuts up his heart from him,
> how does the love of God abide in him?
> 1 John 3:17

14 Eastern Enlargement

1. Introduction

Eastern enlargement of the EU has been referred to throughout this book. The objective of this chapter is to look at certain specific issues. Eight countries with economies in transition,[1] the Czech Republic, Estonia, Hungary, Latvia, Lithuania, Poland, Slovakia and Slovenia, and two market economies, Cyprus and Malta, concluded[2] terms for full membership with the EU from May 2004. Bulgaria and Romania may join the EU in 2007. Turkey is mentioned and referred to here only as a potential candidate for entry negotiations.[3]

This chapter is structured as follows. It begins by looking at the economic structure of the accession countries and the entry criteria in Sections 2 and 3, respectively. The topic of general costs and benefits of EU enlargement cost and benefits is analysed in Section 4. This is followed, in Section 5, by certain reflections about the disillusionment on both sides of the story regarding the enlargement. The financial cost of the eastern enlargement for the EU is given in Section 6. Section 7 concludes that the final operational entry conditions set by the European Council in Brussels (2002) are such that this enlargement may be relatively cheap for the European Union in financial terms, but much more costly and slower for the accession countries than expected by politicians, both in the EU and in the accession countries. The reasons for this include the voting rules in the enlarged EU, self-imposed limits for the EU's expenditure and increasing standards that come from the ever-growing *acquis communautaire* that are costly to introduce, implement and enforce. The Central and East European accession countries will need to invest a lot of effort, time and funds of their own to comply with the requirements for full membership.

2. Economic structure of the accession countries

The 12 accession countries would bring 106 million additional consumers into the EU. If Turkey is included, then this number would increase to 176 million. Some of the countries are so small that the EU economy would barely register their entry. As for the level of development measured by GDP per capita in purchasing power standard (PPS), accession countries are at a far lower level of development than the EU average (Table 14.1). However, there are four distinct groups of newcomers. Cyprus and Slovenia

Table 14.1   GDP per capita at purchasing power standard and population in the EU, accession countries and Turkey in 2003

Country	GDP per capita (PPS)	Population (m)
EU(15)	24 220	380.5
Slovenia	18 010	2.0
Cyprus	17 760	0.7
Czech Republic	14 660	10.2
Hungary	14 150	10.1
Malta	12 000*	0.4
Slovakia	11 890	5.4
Estonia	10 590	1.4
Lithuania	10 030	3.5
Poland	9 890	38.2
Latvia	8 950	2.3
Romania	6 610	21.8
Bulgaria	6 390	7.8
Turkey*	5 600	70.0

Note: *Estimate.

Source: Eurostat (2003).

are in the group of relatively developed accession countries. In descending order, the other groups consist of the Czech Republic, Malta, Hungary and Slovakia (with GDP of roughly half the EU average); then come Estonia, Poland, Lithuania and Latvia. Bulgaria, Romania and Turkey (with a quarter of EU average GDP) are in the bottom group. If there were no changes in EU policy, most of the accession countries would be eligible for a large share of EU regional funds. This is particularly relevant for Poland and Romania because of their large population and relative 'backwardness' measured by GDP per capita. However, the European Council in Brussels (2002) confirmed earlier budgetary restrictions and put new limits on EU expenditure.

The economic structure of the accession countries shows that services are the predominant economic sector (Table 14.2). The same is true for the EU. However, there are concerns regarding agriculture. The contribution of this sector to the GDP in the accession countries is much higher than is the case in the EU. In Bulgaria and Romania, for example, it is 6.5 and 7 times, respectively, the EU average.

Table 14.2 Structure of GDP in accession countries, Turkey and the EU in 2001 (%)

Country	Agriculture[a]	Manufacturing[b]	Services
EU	2.1	22.3	75.6
Bulgaria	13.8	23.0	63.2
Cyprus	4.2	13.3	82.5
Czech Republic	4.2	32.8	63.0
Estonia	5.8	22.7	71.5
Hungary	4.2	28.3	67.5
Latvia	4.7	18.7	76.6
Lithuania	7.0	28.3	64.7
Malta	2.4	24.5	73.1
Poland	3.4	25.4	71.2
Romania	14.6	28.5	56.9
Slovakia	4.6	27.5	67.9
Slovenia	3.1	31.0	65.9
Turkey	12.1	23.8	64.1

Notes:
a. Agriculture, hunting, forestry and fishing.
b. Excluding construction.

Source: Eurostat (2003).

The unemployment problem in the accession countries is uneven (Table 14.3). Poland and Slovakia had unemployment rates that are more than twice as high as the EU average in 2002. The problem is that these are relatively large economies in the group of newcomers. As for the sectoral structure of employment, 45 per cent of the Romanian labour force is employed in agriculture. This is largely semi-subsistence farming and its share is more than ten times the EU average. Almost a fifth of the labour force in Poland is in agriculture (this is more than four times the EU average). 19 per cent of Poland's labour employed in agriculture contributes little more than 3 per cent to the GDP. This compares with figures of 4 and 2 per cent, respectively, in the EU(15). If farm labour in Poland migrates to cities, this may increase the productivity of Polish farming. However, if there are no new jobs in manufacturing and services sectors to absorb such an inflow, significant societal tensions may develop.

A relatively active labour market policy (safety regulation) which is the feature of the economies in the EU countries may harm the accession countries in the short term. Nobody questions the social and other features of high labour protection standards, but these standards are often expensive to implement and maintain. This may hinder the creation of new firms, as

Table 14.3 *Unemployment rate (2003) and share of agriculture in total employment (2001) in the EU, accession countries and Turkey (%)*

Country	Unemployment rate 2003	Agriculture in total employment 2001
EU	8.1	4.3
Cyprus	4.4	4.9
Czech Republic	7.0	4.6
Estonia	8.2	7.1
Hungary	6.0	6.1
Latvia	12.0	15.1
Lithuania	11.0	16.5
Malta	7.5	2.2
Poland	20.0	19.2
Slovakia	16.0	6.3
Slovenia	9.0	9.9
Bulgaria	13.0	26.7
Romania	8.5	44.4
Turkey	10.0	35.4

Sources: UNECE (2003); Eurostat (2003); European Commission (2003).

well as the protection of existing marginal jobs. The general EU labour market rigidities may slow down the painful and ongoing transition and adjustment processes in the accession countries.

3. Entry criteria

'Any European state may apply to become a Member of the Union' (Article O of the Maastricht Treaty). This is the only Maastricht Treaty based (necessary) condition for a country to be considered for full membership of the EU. In addition, there are several other sufficient, economic and political requirements for entry, which were formally defined during the European Council in Copenhagen (1993). The potential candidate country must fulfil three conditions: it must have a functioning market economy, a democratic political system and accept, implement and enforce the *acquis communautaire*.

First, apart from the Czech Republic and Slovakia, not a single transition country had a fully functioning market economy even before they became centrally planned countries (van Brabant, 1996). Entry into the EU, in particular an early entry by transition economies, could cause a serious external shock. Their economies are not yet fully adjusted to the market-based economic system and their manufacturing and services sectors are still too fragile to absorb the expensive *acquis communautaire*. Early entry into the EU without full macroeconomic stabilisation and modernisation of the output structure may be painful for them. Countries that pass through the 'transition phase' would not be able to comply with the strict rules governing competition with EU producers in most industries.[4] Transition fatigue is already apparent in these countries and is evidenced by the return of the 'recycled' communists to office.

The second condition is that the prospective entrant has a stable democratic political system. This means a multiparty parliament, rule of law and respect for human and minority rights. It also includes good neighbourly relations and no territorial disputes. With regard to the last criterion, not a single transition country passes the test, and the northern part of Cyprus is still occupied. Nor do certain EU countries fare well here: just consider Northern Ireland. However, their advantage is that they are already in the EU.

The European Union is interested in resolving pressing problems in the region. There are some signs that the prospect of EU membership may ease tensions, as happened with Hungary and Romania in 1996, Greece and Turkey in 2000 or Serbia and Montenegro with Croatia in 2003. The EU needs to assist accession countries in order to create a peaceful and prosperous neighbourhood for itself in the future. The question has not been whether Central and East European countries need to be incorporated into the EU. The question has always been the cost to the EU(15) of expanding their club, as well as how much time the enlargement would take.

The third condition relates to the *acquis communautaire* or the Community patrimony (the whole body of the established EU laws, policies and practices). The accession countries must accept, implement and enforce the existing set of rules. The belief that skilful national diplomacy and bargaining may provide better deals for the accession countries is false. Entry to the EU is just the beginning, not the end of the story. The *acquis communautaire* consists of about 80 000 pages of EU legislation. The only possibility for negotiations concerned the length of the adjustment period and, potentially, the size of funds that may help to implement it. *Agenda 2000* (European Commission 1997a), the EU's plan for action in the medium term, is clear on this point. The new EU member countries are required to apply, implement and enforce the *acquis communautaire* upon accession. In order to safeguard the EU internal competition rules, those measures that relate to the Single European Market should be applied immediately upon accession.[5] However, there may be certain transition measures for a limited period of time. Many EU companies are against any transition period that may be given to their competitors from the accession countries because they fear social and environmental dumping from the east.

The European Union is already a multispeed organisation. Countries that are in the EMU form one tier, with Britain, Denmark and Sweden forming another. Even within the EMU, large countries (France, Germany and Italy) succeeded in 2002 in persuading the European Commission to bend the rules of the Stability and Growth Pact (1996) which require eurozone countries to keep their national budgets within strict limits. As a result, the European Commission postponed the target date for achieving budgetary balance from 2004 to 2006. Another EU tier includes the countries that are members of the Schengen Agreement on the free movement of foreigners. Creating yet another tier by conceding derogations or opt-outs to the accession countries would complicate the operation of the EU and imperil free competition in the Single European Market. Hence, according to *Agenda 2000* and subsequent official statements this shall not happen.[6] An accession country's record in the implementation of existing commitments was used by the EU as one measure by which to judge the country's capacity to take on the obligations of full membership.[7]

The fourth, tacit, requirement is that an enlargement should not imperil the EU's financial resources, nor should widening of the EU risk deepening of the integration process. If there were no changes in the EU policies and if accession countries entered the unreformed EU, various early estimates stated that the annual transfers from the EU to those countries would cost the EU budget about €50 billion a year.[8] This is about half of the entire current annual budget for EU(15). The European Council in Brussels (2002) set the final operational financial rules that made eastern enlargement of the EU relatively cheap for the EU, as will be seen below.

In order to assist prospective transition countries, the European Council in Essen (1994) outlined the EU's 'pre-accession strategy'. The key element is the assistance offered to the select group of transition countries. The prospective member countries committed themselves, among other things, to approximate their legislation to that of the EU. The gap in the political, economic and social organisation and development between the EU and the potential new members has to narrow, otherwise the new members may not assume the full set of obligations and enjoy all the benefits of membership. Europe agreements, a structured dialogue and the PHARE programme are the major tools of the pre-accession strategy.[9] In addition, the European Council in Cannes (1995) endorsed the White Paper, a reference document that can guide the prospective member countries through the labyrinth of EU legislation in order to make the task of accession simpler. Additionally, in order to ease entry, the EU opened the Technical Assistance Information Exchange Office (TAIEX) in 1996, providing a one-stop shop where information and technical/legal advice on EU legislation, enforcement and infrastructure can be obtained.

All the necessary conditions for entry into the EU reveal that the Union has very high discretionary powers and flexibility to select would-be members, as well as to set the time, pace and conditions of entry.

4. Costs and benefits

ACCESSION COUNTRIES

Accession countries from Central and Eastern Europe share political, security and economic reasons for joining the EU. Politically, these countries have a still young and potentially fragile democratic system. Fragility comes from unfulfilled grand hopes that the change for the better towards a market-type democratic system can take place in a relatively short period of time and at a relatively acceptable cost. Although there is little likelihood of any immediate threat of an armed conflict in Europe (even though there are hot spots such as the Balkan peninsula, the Aegean Sea and Cyprus), there is still apprehension regarding the division of 'spheres of influence' between the West and Russia. The Central, Eastern European and Baltic states only recently obtained their freedom from the 'Eastern bloc'. They have concerns both about preserving their independence from the East and about 'losing' that independence to the West.

With regard to the economic issues, there are important gains for the accession countries from entry of the EU:

- The major benefit for the accession countries is to secure access to the huge EU market. This is particularly relevant for the goods that are politically 'sensitive' for the EU (agricultural products, textile, steel, chemicals), as the accession countries have comparative advantage in the production of these goods. Entry would mean a kind of 'insurance policy' that the EU trade regime would credibly remain open for their exports.
- The second gain would be the possibility for labour migration into the rest of the EU following the specified adjustment period. This may, however, be a two-edged sword. If the educated and the experienced leave the accession countries, the productivity in the 'accession region' would suffer and funds for the education of experts would be lost. However, a relatively tight labour market in the rest of the EU(15) would prevent such a scenario occurring. In addition, experience has shown that labour migration (wars apart) takes place chiefly when workers cannot find employment in their country of origin.
- A third benefit from entry includes access to the structural and other EU funds. All this would give an impetus to strengthen the market system (van Brabant, 1996).

Structural Aid and the Geography of Production

None of the potential gains from entry to the EU is without risk. In some cases, the costs are quite serious. Central and East European countries still have fragile economies that would be exposed to the chill wind of fierce competition in the Single European Market. Adjustment problems are well known even for relatively advanced transition economies, as evidenced by the difficulties experienced in the former East Germany after the *Anschluss* of 1989.[10] Gross annual transfers from the western part of the reunified Germany to the east were about DM 180 billion (€90 billion) during the 1990s (Table 14.4). Such massive aid to the former East Germany will be necessary for at least another five years in order to try to adjust its economy and catch up with the rest of the country. If the eastern part of the reunited Germany needs such massive annual transfers of about 4 per cent of west German GDP,[11] one shudders to think about

Table 14.4 Annual public financial transfers[a] from western to eastern Germany, 1991–99 (DM bn)

Transfer	1991	1992	1993	1994	1995	1996	1997	1998[b]	1999[c]
Gross	139	152	168	168	185	187	183	189	194
Net	106	115	129	125	140	140	136	141	144

Notes:
a. Including social insurance.
b. Partly estimated.
c. According to the draft budget.

Sources: Herausgeber BMI, *Jahresbericht der Bundesregierung zum Stand der Deutschen Einheit*. Berlin, 1998. Data for 1998 and 1999 = Bundestags-Drucksache 13/11472, p. 11.

Table 14.5 Convergence indicators for East Germany 1991, 1996 and 1998 (West Germany = 100)

Indicator	1991	1996	2000
Average monthly wages			
Gross	48.3	76.7	77.2*
Net	54.8	84.2	86.1*
Productivity			
Total economy	34.3	66.8	68.2
Manufacturing	23.9	63.6	69.5
Construction	48.8	75.7	67.8
GDP per capita at current prices	32.8	54.0	59.9

Note: *1998.

Sources: Economic Commission for Europe (1997, p. 30). Wirtschaftsdaten neue Bundesländer, Bundesministerium für Wirtschaft und Technologie. Berlin, 2001.

the volume of potential transfers that will be needed by other accession countries.[12]

There have been certain positive results during this 'catch-up' process as exemplified in the doubling of productivity (Table 14.5). However, the financial cost was immense. The question remains as to whether such massive aid will be necessary in the medium and long terms. Aid may kill local incentives to adjust and it may create a structurally dependent economy out of the former East Germany as happened with the Italian Mezzogiorno. Welfare has been increased in the former East Germany and, consequently, wages have increased above productivity. Similarly, the Italian social system prevented wages from falling to competitive levels in the Mezzogiorno. As a result, both southern Italy and the former East Germany have high unemployment and dependency on public transfers.

Bearing all these issues in mind, one may ask whether the accession countries are not, perhaps, aspiring to do too much too soon? Where are the funds to accommodate the adjustment of the Central and East European countries to come from? The Maastricht criteria for the EMU and the Stability and Growth Pact require budgetary cuts throughout the EU. The Cannes Summit (1995) allocated 'only' €6.7 billion to the PHARE programme for the 1995–99 period. Therefore, most of the funds will have to come from the accession countries themselves or from foreign loans.

As for the 2000–06 period, it has been decided to keep the spending limit for all EU activities at the current level of 1.27 per cent of the total GDP of the 15 member countries. This limit is combined with strict constraints on the national public expenditure that are related to the EMU. However, *Agenda 2000* earmarked €45 billion for the 2000–06 period (a kind of mini-Marshall plan) to be used as pre-accession aid to the accession countries. During that time, accession countries will be granted €1 billion a year as structural aid plus €0.5 billion a year for agricultural development.[13] Future negotiations about the financing of the EU(25) expenditure (financial perspective 2007–13) will be much more difficult than was the case in the past. The EU(15), in particular the eurozone member governments, will argue against an expansion of the EU budget at a time when they are making unprecedented efforts at home to cut spending in order to keep within the rules of the EMU.

In theory, economic integration may, but will not necessarily, bring greater benefits to the regions/countries that lag behind the centre of economic activity in their development. However, if production linkages (forward and backward) are strong and internal to an industry such as in chemicals or financial services, and if imperfect competition prevails, economic integration would trigger agglomeration tendencies. If those linkages are not limited to a relatively narrow industry group, but are strong *across* industries and sectors, integration would produce agglomeration tendencies in select spots. If labour is not mobile, the whole process would tend to open up new and widen the existing regional wage differentials (Venables, 1996a). Although this may produce deindustrialisation tendencies in the peripheral regions, it does not mean that integration is not desirable. For instance, education and regional policies increased the attractiveness of Spain, Finland and Ireland as locations for various manufacturing industries, as discovered by EU and foreign investors.

As for the structure of industrial geography of production in the EU and relying on the study by Midelfart-Knarvik et al. (2000, pp. 46–7), the observation is that the EU countries became more specialised from the early 1980s than was previously the case. This confirms the theoretical expectations of standard, neo-classical and new theories of economic integration. A new pattern of industrial production is emerging in the EU. The major features of this divergence process in the geography of industrial production are that this process is slow and does not provoke great adjustment costs; the most remarkable change in the geography of production was the spreading of relatively high-technology and high-skill industries towards the EU periphery (Ireland and Finland); and that the availability of highly skilled and educated workers is becoming an increasingly important determinant for industrial location.

Acquis Communautaire

Economic transition towards a market-type system is in itself a lengthy and costly process. Furthermore, to accept and to implement a continuously evolving *acquis communautaire* is costly not only for the new members, but also for the countries that are already in the EU. Being less developed, the accession countries have both a lower financial, technical and administrative capacity, and require a greater degree of reform to incorporate and 'digest' the EU rules. Many things are highly regulated in the EU. They include not only health, environment and consumer protection, but also safety at work and social standards. Many of those items do not directly increase productivity. With an out-of-date capital stock, there is a dilemma in the accession countries. Should they invest scarce capital first into upgrading output potential or do something else or both (in what proportion)?[14]

The cyanide spill in Romania (2000) was the worst ecological disaster since the Chernobyl nuclear accident (1986). It reminded everyone of the gravity of the problem in the accession countries.[15] The environmental dimension of the *acquis communautaire* has 320 pieces of 'green' legislation. To implement all those laws could cost the ten transition accession countries as much as €110 billion over a decade.[16] Table 14.6 provides information on part of these harmonisation costs that deal with water, air and waste standards in six selected accession countries. The EU would offer some financial support to these countries in order to ease the burden of meeting the entry criteria, but most of the funds would have to come from the new member countries themselves.[17] Can these costs be compensated for by the potential benefits that would come from the entry? If so, how can one measure that? How long would it take? Is such an investment justified at this moment? Public opinion polls in transition countries rank concern

Table 14.6 What would it cost six accession countries to reach the EU environmental standards? (€bn)

Country	Water	Air	Waste	Total investment (maximum)	Total per capita (maximum)
Poland	18.1	13.9	3.3	35.2	927
Hungary	6.6	2.7	4.4	13.7	1 306
Czech R.	3.3	6.4	3.8	12.4	1 427
Slovakia	1.9	1.9	1.6	5.4	760
Estonia	1.5	n.a.	n.a.	1.5	n.a.
Slovenia	n.a.	0.7	1.1	1.8	n.a.

Source: European Parliament, 'La politique de l'environnement et l'élargissement', *Fiche thématique* no. 17, Luxembourg, 23 March 1998, p. 15.

for the environment much lower than health care, education, security and the economy.

All these data reveal that a number of accession countries are not only considerably worse off than current EU members, but they still constitute a distinct structural class by themselves. The difference in income per capita, as well as investment needed to comply with the *acquis communautaire* between the accession countries and that of the EU(15) is not only structural, but also huge.

The benefit side of these investments is hard to measure and is unfortunately often forgotten. Safe water free of toxins or pollutants, pure air and secure handling of waste would contribute both to an improvement in the quality of life and savings in resources. For example, it is estimated that by cutting air pollution, all accession countries could avoid between 43 000 and 180 000 cases of chronic bronchitis and between 15 000 and 34 000 premature deaths. The cumulative value of these benefits to the accession countries until 2020 is estimated to be in the range of €134–681 billion.[18] Having to accept and implement expensive *acquis communautaire*, Central and East European member countries expect an inflow of FDI as compensation.

Even though the European Commission noted in its annual enlargement reports (2003) that accession countries have made meaningful progress in the adjustment of their economies in relation to the EU(15), serious flaws still persist. They include weaknesses in administrative capacity,[19] excessive public expenditure, underperforming judicial systems, public sector internal auditing and widespread corruption. For example, Poland, a country that presents the biggest enlargement challenge slowed down all reforms and did little to reduce its public expenditure and deficit throughout 2003. However, even the EU's administrative capacity is far from perfect. This can be seen from the annual reports by the EU Court of Auditors.

Economic and Monetary Union

The theory of international monetary integration is based on criteria which include factor mobility, openness of the economy, similar rates of unemployment, diversification of the economic structure, coordination of economic policies and comparable rates of inflation between the integrating countries (Jovanović, 1998a, pp. 170–85). The Maastricht Treaty brought conditions for the EMU that are not known in the theory of monetary integration. A sceptic might say that this is the reason why the eurozone may work! In any case, if transaction costs remain significant and if there is a danger that comes from the exchange risk, then the EMU might give stability and an additional impetus to the expansion of intra-EU trade.

Let us recall the Maastricht criteria for the EMU:

- a high degree of price stability (low inflation);
- a sound public finance position (budget deficit of maximum 3 per cent of the GDP);
- national debt of less than 60 per cent of GDP;
- no devaluation within the exchange rate mechanism for at least two preceding years; and
- the national interest rate needs to be within the 2 per cent margin of the three best performing countries.

The criteria for the EMU may create some barriers for accession to the EU. *Agenda 2000* and subsequent documents state that each accession country is required to apply, implement and enforce the *acquis communautaire* upon accession. In order to safeguard the EU competition rules, those measures that relate to the Single European Market should be applied immediately upon accession.[20] Being out of the EMU, a new member country's currency may be the target for a speculative attack on the currency market that the country may not be able to withstand.[21] The country may alter the rate of exchange. By doing so, trade flows and free competition in the Single European Market could be jeopardised. Hence the need for the accession countries to join the eurozone. The three EU(15) member countries that are currently out of the eurozone should not be taken as best precedents for the accession countries. The 'three' are already fully adjusted EU members with stable and developed economies. It would be difficult to manage the EU(25) economy if one half of the EU uses the euro while the other half does not.

If the macroeconomic situation remains stable in the future, many accession countries may not have great difficulty in satisfying most (inflation apart) of the loosely interpreted Maastricht criteria for the EMU (Tables 14.7 to 14.10).[22] All accession countries have growing economies, which is a very positive development. The problem is to maintain this positive differential growth rate over and (well) above the EU rate for a long period of time in order to catch up with the EU level of development. A relatively stable catch-up process with the EU may well require a rate of inflation that may be over and above the norms required by the EMU. This is a very real conflict between the demand for an accelerated growth and the EMU request for the stability both in prices and in the exchange rate. Long-run growth projections predict that it may take about 30 years (one generation) for most of the Central and Eastern European countries to catch up with the income levels in 'low income' EU countries (Table 14.11).[23] With average income per capita about half the EU average, Central and East European countries need continuous economic growth. For them this may be a much more important sign of economic success than an early eurozone entry.

Table 14.7 Government deficit(−)/surplus(+) in the EU, accession countries and Turkey, 1997–2004 (% of GDP)

Country	1997	1998	1999	2000	2001	2002	2003*	2004*
EU	−2.4	−1.6	−1.3	2.0	−1.6	−2.2	−2.5	−2.4
Bulgaria	−0.3	1.3	0.2	−0.6	1.7	−0.7	−0.6	−0.5
Cyprus	−5.3	−5.6	−5.0	−2.7	−3.0	−3.5	−4.0	−3.5
Czech Republic	−2.7	−4.5	−3.2	−3.3	−5.5	−6.5	−6.3	−5.9
Estonia	2.0	−0.4	−4.0	−0.4	0.2	1.3	−0.5	−0.6
Hungary	−6.8	−8.0	−5.3	−3.0	−4.1	−9.1	−4.9	−3.7
Latvia	−0.2	−0.7	−5.3	−2.7	−1.6	−2.5	−2.9	−2.6
Lithuania	−1.1	−3.1	−5.6	−2.7	−1.9	−1.8	−1.9	−2.0
Malta	−10.7	−10.8	−8.3	−7.0	−7.0	−6.1	−5.2	−4.1
Poland	−4.3	−2.3	−1.5	−1.8	−3.9	−4.2	−4.2	−4.0
Romania	−4.5	−3.2	−4.5	−4.5	−3.4	−2.6	−2.7	−2.7
Slovakia	−5.5	−4.7	−6.4	−12.8	−5.6	−7.7	−5.3	−3.8
Slovenia	−1.9	−2.3	−2.2	−3.2	−2.5	−1.8	−1.5	−1.2
Turkey*	−13.0	−12.0	−19.0	−6.0	−29.0	−13.7	−9.8	−6.9

Note: *Estimates and projections.

Sources: Eurostat (2003) and *European Economy* (2003a).

Table 14.8 National debt in the EU, accession countries and Turkey, 1997–2004 (% of GDP)

Country	1997	1998	1999	2000	2001	2002	2003*	2004*
EU	71.0	68.8	67.7	63.8	63.1	62.7	63.5	63.2
Bulgaria	105.1	79.6	79.3	73.6	66.4	53.0	52.0	–
Cyprus	57.7	60.1	56.8	54.6	55.6	58.6	61.2	–
Czech Republic	13.0	13.7	14.5	16.6	23.3	27.1	29.6	–
Estonia	6.9	6.0	6.5	5.1	4.8	5.8	5.5	–
Hungary	64.2	61.9	61.2	55.5	53.4	56.3	56.8	–
Latvia	12.0	10.6	13.7	13.9	15.7	15.2	19.2	–
Lithuania	15.7	17.1	23.4	24.3	23.4	22.7	22.9	–
Malta	51.5	64.9	60.8	61.3	66.1	66.4	66.9	–
Poland	46.9	41.6	42.7	37.2	37.3	41.8	43.3	–
Romania	16.5	18.0	24.0	23.9	23.1	22.7	23.7	–
Slovakia	28.8	28.9	43.8	46.9	48.1	42.6	41.8	–
Slovenia	23.2	25.1	26.4	27.6	27.5	28.3	27.8	–
Turkey	53.0	50.0	67.4	57.6	105.4	95.0	86.3	–

Note: *Estimates and projections.

Sources: Eurostat (2003) and *European Economy* (2003a).

Monetary policy in the Central and East European countries may gain in general credibility and stability inside the eurozone, but different growth priorities and asymmetric shocks relative to other eurozone countries may introduce tensions within the EMU. While the eurozone may serve the interest of many of the 12 participating member countries fairly well, this may not be the case for an EMU of perhaps 27 member countries. This difficulty is compounded with the Governing Council's voting system in which each participating country has one vote. A reduction in the weight of small countries in the decision making process may be necessary in the future (de Grauwe, 2002).

Agriculture

Farm gate prices in the accession countries were on average within a range of 40 to 80 per cent of the EU level which is guaranteed by the Common Agricultural Policy (CAP).[24] If the unreformed CAP prices were to apply directly in the accession countries, that would give a strong boost to output of both crop (cereals, oilseeds and sugar) and livestock production, as well

Table 14.9 Growth rate of GDP in the EU, accession countries and Turkey, 1997–2004 (% change over preceding year)

Country	1997	1998	1999	2000	2001	2002	2003*	2004*
EU	2.5	2.9	2.8	3.4	1.6	0.9	1.3	2.4
Bulgaria	−5.6	4.0	2.3	5.4	4.0	4.0	4.5	5.0
Cyprus	2.4	5.0	4.5	5.1	4.1	1.8	2.0	3.8
Czech Republic	−0.8	−1.0	0.5	3.2	3.6	3.6	2.8	3.9
Estonia	9.8	4.6	−0.6	7.1	5.0	3.5	4.9	5.1
Hungary	4.6	4.9	4.1	5.2	3.8	3.5	3.7	4.1
Latvia	8.4	4.8	2.8	6.8	7.7	5.0	5.5	6.0
Lithuania	7.3	5.1	−3.9	3.8	5.9	4.0	4.5	5.0
Malta	4.8	3.4	4.0	5.5	−0.8	2.5	3.1	3.7
Poland	6.8	4.8	4.0	4.0	1.1	1.4	2.5	3.7
Romania	−6.0	−4.8	−1.1	1.8	5.2	4.5	4.9	5.0
Slovakia	5.6	4.0	1.3	2.2	3.3	3.6	3.7	4.5
Slovenia	4.6	3.8	5.2	4.6	3.0	3.0	3.4	3.7
Turkey	7.5	3.0	−4.7	7.4	−7.4	3.7	3.7	4.5

Note: *Estimates and projections.

Sources: UNECE (2003); Eurostat (2003); and *European Economy* (2003a).

as milk. At the same time, an increase in the price of farm goods in the accession countries could provoke social tensions. These price hikes would severely hit social groups such as the retired and the unemployed, unless their income situation is improved. However, it would be difficult to convince the accession countries not to increase farm production, unless they can see clear signs that the CAP is undergoing reform prior to their entry. One thing was clear: enlargement of the EU could not easily proceed without a prior change in the CAP. A deep reform of the CAP would test the actual seriousness of the EU about enlargement.

The eastern enlargement would also introduce a practical problem of how to operate country-specific transitional arrangements. If, for example, alignment of the prices of agricultural products between the EU and Hungary takes place at a different rate from alignment of prices in Poland, it would be necessary to impose tariffs, not only between the accession countries and EU(15), but also between the accession countries themselves.

Introduced in the 1960s, the CAP was an instrument for ensuring security in food supplies and a means for the protection of income of farmers. As food shortages were eliminated, as the EU started to dispose of surpluses of

Table 14.10 Annual rate of inflation in the EU, accession countries and Turkey, 1997–2004 (%)

Country	1997	1998	1999	2000	2001	2002	2003*	2004*
EU	2.1	1.8	1.3	2.5	2.6	2.2	2.1	1.7
Bulgaria	1 082.6	18.7	2.6	10.3	7.4	5.8	4.5	4.0
Cyprus	3.3	2.3	1.1	4.9	2.0	2.8	4.3	2.2
Czech Republic	8.0	9.7	1.8	3.9	4.5	1.8	1.5	2.8
Estonia	9.3	8.8	3.1	3.9	5.6	3.5	3.5	4.0
Hungary	18.5	14.2	10.0	10.0	9.1	5.4	5.0	4.5
Latvia	8.1	4.3	2.1	2.6	2.5	1.9	2.5	3.0
Lithuania	8.8	5.0	0.7	0.9	1.3	0.4	1.0	2.5
Malta	2.6	2.3	2.3	3.1	3.0	2.5	2.7	2.4
Poland	15.0	11.8	7.2	10.1	5.3	1.9	1.1	2.3
Romania	154.9	59.1	45.8	45.7	34.5	22.5	16.0	11.8
Slovakia	6.1	6.7	10.5	12.0	7.3	3.3	8.8	7.4
Slovenia	8.3	7.9	6.1	8.9	8.6	7.6	6.0	5.5
Turkey	85.7	84.6	64.9	54.9	54.4	45.0	25.9	18.0

Note: *Estimates and projections.

Sources: UNECE (2003); Eurostat (2003); and *European Economy* (2003a).

agricultural output and as farmers' income was largely safeguarded against unfavourable developments, EU concern shifted towards food safety and protection of the environment. This last concern is of great importance, as the accession countries have a legacy of serious environmental damage.

Reform of the CAP represents one of the most serious challenges for the EU. It would have consequences both for the EU internal operation, for external economic relations and for enlargement. A reform plan, proposed in mid-2002, would break the link between intervention and production. Farm subsidies would be linked to rural conservation. In addition, export subsidies would be significantly reduced. However, this attempt to reform the CAP was deferred by France (with Germany's support) until 2006 when the new financial perspective (2007–13) is to be finalised. In addition, Britain, Germany, the Netherlands and Sweden are particularly concerned about future farm spending. These countries would like to see a certain reform of the CAP before the EU offers potentially generous subsidies to farmers in the accession countries. This is important as the EU(15) has about 7 million farmers, while Central and East European countries would bring an additional 3.8 million.[25] The lobbying and voting power

Table 14.11 Period needed to reach 75% of the EU(15) average GDP per capita

Country	Annual growth rate Assumption From 2004	Annual growth rate Average achieved 1995–2002	Period needed to reach 75% of EU GDP per capita in years
Bulgaria	5.0	0.5	40
Cyprus	3.8	3.6	1
Czech Republic	3.9	1.7	19
Estonia	5.1	4.9	23
Hungary	4.1	3.9	24
Latvia	6.0	5.6	24
Lithuania	5.0	3.9	28
Malta	3.7	3.3	25
Poland	3.7	3.9	50
Romania	5.0	0.4	44
Slovakia	4.5	3.7	22
Slovenia	3.7	3.9	7
Turkey	4.5	2.9	61

Source: European Economy (July 2003b, p. 10).

of farmers in the enlarged EU would increase in theory, but in practice it may be difficult to organise them because of their different interests and priorities. In any case, enlargement without a reform of the CAP would not be affordable for the EU.

France and Germany were the driving force behind the European Council in Brussels (24–25 October 2002) deal that brought the 'adjustment' (limit) of the future CAP payments in the light of the forthcoming enlargement. From 2006, total CAP subsidies would have a ceiling. This would keep payments static at current levels during the 2007–13 period with the possibility of a small inflation-proof increase of 1 per cent per year. In real terms, these payments would almost certainly decline steadily. Subsidies to farmers in new member countries would be limited to only 25 per cent of those paid to farmers in the EU(15) in 2004. However, the payments to farmers would be gradually brought into parity by 2013. EU farmers would lose from this deal over the coming decade, and this would hit the influential French lobby hard. Therefore, France has made a significant enlargement-related concession. Farmers in the new member countries could no longer anticipate hefty subsidies from Brussels, but most others would gain: in particular, EU consumers and potential exporters to the EU.

EUROPEAN UNION

The European Union is generally interested in enlargement for various political, security, ecological and economic reasons. Key EU values would be secured in countries that desperately want them. What, however, the accession countries would actually contribute to the EU's economy is less easy to discern. One negative organisational aspect of the enlargement process is that the EU may become cumbersome and ungovernable. The enlarged EU may turn into an extended free trade area. In addition, the entry of 12 Central and East European countries and Turkey would increase the EU population by 46 per cent, while the volume of the EU's GDP would increase only 7 per cent at current prices and 15 per cent at PPS (Table 14.12) which is roughly comparable to the Dutch GDP.

Is the 'eastern' market, with relatively cheap labour and certain possibilities for investment,[26] an opportunity or a threat for the EU? Germany and Austria fear that eastern enlargement would set off an annual inflow of more than 300 000 immigrants (OECD, 2003c, p. 85). This would

Table 14.12 *Total GDP at current prices and in purchasing power standard in the EU, candidate countries and Turkey in 2001*

Country	€ billion	€ billion PPS
Bulgaria	15.2	51.8
Cyprus	10.2	12.5
Czech Republic	63.3	126.2
Estonia	6.2	13.4
Hungary	58.0	121.0
Latvia	5.5	18.2
Lithuania	13.4	30.5
Malta	4.0	–
Poland	196.7	355.9
Romania	44.4	131.3
Slovakia	22.3	58.0
Slovenia	20.9	31.8
Turkey	164.6	357.3
13 Candidate countries	627.7	1 317.8
EU(15)	8 814.8	8 814.8
% of EU(15)	7.1	15.0

Source: Eurostat (2003).

amount to over 3 million over a decade. Workers from the accession countries would get preferential treatment in the EU labour market over others that come from non-EU countries. However, there is a five-year transition period, which may be extended for another two years, before these workers are at liberty to work anywhere in the EU. Austria and Germany are authorised to introduce safeguards in sensitive industries in certain regions. When Spain and Portugal entered the EU they had a seven-year transition period before full labour mobility was granted. However, when labour mobility became fully free, there was no large labour migration flow to the rest of the EU partner countries. In any case, there are no expectations of any significant labour migrations from Central and Eastern Europe towards the rest of the EU(25). These countries would also be affected by the general European demographic trends. This is because the citizens from the new member countries do not have the right to obtain paid employment in the EU(15) until 2009. However, at the end of the decade, the demographic trends in the new member countries are such that they would have labour shortage.

The potential economic and political gains for the EU need to be combined with at least two potential economic costs that are often mentioned.

- The first is the need to finance the adjustment of the accession countries to the *acquis communautaire* and to the Maastricht criteria for the eurozone.[27] In a situation with serious austerity measures in the EU countries, the question is, where would the funds come from? The European Council in Brussels (2002) put a cap on all EU expenditure in order to make enlargement cheap for the EU in financial terms.
- The second 'cost'(?) could come from the (potential) loss of jobs and business in the 'sensitive' manufacturing industries and in agriculture in the EU because of the penetration of goods from the east. There may be strong lobby pressure on policy makers in certain countries to slow down eastern enlargement and/or demand compensation from the EU. This second 'cost' may be exaggerated. As a result of the signing of Europe agreements, 'sensitive' manufactured goods from the accession countries now enter the EU mainly free of tariff and quantitative restrictions. The major continuing barriers are chiefly anti-dumping measures. In addition, exports of sensitive products from the accession countries to the EU have not expanded relative to other products since the 1980s. Hence, one should not expect a surge in accession countries' exports of sensitive manufactured products to the EU as a consequence of accession.

The production structure in the accession countries within each of the three broad economic sectors is very different from the prevailing structure in the existing EU(15). If the gains from trade depend on the extent of these differences, the (private) gains should be correspondingly large. Hence, a surge of 'sensitive' imports from the accession countries by the EU may be welcome. The job losses in the sensitive sectors will be more than made up for by expansion in the non-sensitive industries.[28] This approach is hotly disputed by politicians and well-entrenched lobbies, but if economists have only one thing to say about adjustment 'costs', then this is it.

The problem with such debates about the employment effect of trade liberalisation (in the countries with developed and stable economies) are based on 'a fallacy of composition, that the effect of productivity increase *in a given industry* on the number of jobs *in that industry* is very different from the effect of a productivity increase *in the economy as a whole* on the *total* number of jobs' (Krugman, 1998b, pp. 16–17). The negative impact of jobs going 'south' on a large scale has not materialised in practice and the net effect on the US job market might even have been positive.

In the medium term, southern EU countries need not fear the eastern enlargement of the EU and the potential 'exodus' of jobs to Central and Eastern Europe because of lower wages there. If there is no adjustment 'pain' for these southern countries, there may also be little 'gain' from enlargement. If firms were looking only for low-cost production locations, then China and India may be superior long-term choices than countries in Central and Eastern Europe. If relatively low wages were the only determining factor for the location of production, then the EU would already have been flooded with cheap goods from those countries. Factors such as productivity, the capital stock, size and growth of the market and stability often play a more decisive role for investors than mere differences in nominal wages. But this may change in the future in the accession countries. For example, Peugeot-Citroën announced in 2003 that it intends to invest and to locate a large (€700 million) car assembly factory in Slovakia. The factory would start production of about 300 000 small cars in 2006. The management intends to be closer to fast-growing markets in accession countries and to profit from wage rates that are a fifth of those paid in the EU(15) for similar operations. Earlier plants established by Western companies in Central and Eastern Europe were often only additions to their Western plants. This one will serve as a replacement plant.[29] Even though similar stories to this one may be repeated in the region, this 'eastern region' is still too small to impact significantly on total production and real income elsewhere in the EU.

The most important argument about the employment impact of the eastern enlargement of EU has, unfortunately, not yet made its way into the public consciousness. It has also put certain academic debates on the wrong foot. The eastern enlargement may create certain new jobs or at least keep the existing 'higher-quality' jobs in the EU. Isolated and highly publicised stories about the closure of a firm due to the enlargement are not typical for the whole EU economy. These stories need to be seen in the context of a bigger picture. Because of the start of the EMU in the majority of EU countries, the average unemployment rate over the coming years will be to a large extent at the level chosen by the European Central Bank. The ECB may pay little or no regard to the situation in the EU trade balance with the accession countries. This is important if one bears in mind that the total annual merchandise trade of the accession countries with the EU(15) in recent years is twice as much as the EU(15) trade with 'small' Switzerland alone.

Spain, France and Austria (with tacit support from a number of other countries) were cautious about the enlargement of the EU. Spain has two national fears that can be substantiated. First, there may be an inflow of cheap fruit and vegetables from the east in EU(15) which would put Spain's market share for these goods at risk. Second, expenditure from generous structural funds would be directed eastwards to the detriment of the beneficiaries in Spain. Following the EU enlargement, Spain will cease to qualify for much of the relatively generous EU regional aid that it currently receives. Indeed, Spain may even become a net contributor to the EU budget. Therefore, it has a vested interest in keeping EU expenditure under strict control. France has reservations about the overall capacity (among other things) of the accession countries to accept all the obligations that are required for EU membership.

It should be remembered that European integration started in the early 1950s, not for economic reasons, but rather to preserve peace. The political goal (through economic means) was to ensure that war between Germany and France would be impossible. The southern enlargements of the EU, although costly in financial terms, had the objective of stabilising democracy in Greece, Spain and Portugal following a period of dictatorship. Identical arguments can be used regarding the eastern enlargement of the EU. As for Cyprus, reunification of the country and a reduction in tensions in the eastern Mediterranean region may be among the goals. Stability and predictability at the eastern border is in the interest of the EU. If the EU wants to play a more prominent role in geopolitics, then eastern enlargement has to take place. Enlargement is not a charity. It is in the EU's self-interest. Ecological and certain economic factors also apply. In addition, modernisation of the Central and East European countries may create and keep certain high-technology jobs in manufacturing and services in EU(15).

5. Disillusionment

The Treaty of Nice is popularly portrayed as the act that allowed the new EU enlargement. However, the member countries of the EU(15), in particular the large member countries, preserved certain influence in the new voting structure. Nevertheless, the Byzantine voting system will put the EU(25+) on track for a train crash as far as quick action is concerned. No bloc of member countries, indeed no two blocs, would be able to force through any policy, but nearly any single bloc would have the ability to veto any policy. And there is no shortage of topics that would face harsh clashes of interest. Hence, one may predict that the basic (economic) policy structure of the EU would remain as it is.

Consideration of the issues of the timing and terms of the new EU enlargement has been highly speculative. Entry depends on the political will (and the funds) of the EU countries. However, the funds and the political will existed even when Spain and Portugal were negotiating entry with the EU during the 1980s, but their entry took several years more than expected and it was almost another decade before they got to full speed with the rest of EU. In addition, the Iberian enlargement of the EU was technically and economically much simpler than the accession of Central and East European transition countries.

The overriding goal of the EU is to safeguard the efficient operation of its Single European Market. This means that a multispeed EU needs to be avoided as much as possible. Thus, there may be a sufficiently long pre-accession period tailored to the individual conditions of each new country in order to absorb the *acquis communautaire*. This would eliminate the need for the unnecessary post-entry transition period. However, all this is highly speculative as the *acquis communautaire* will be different in the year 2004 from what it was when enlargement negotiations started. Only in 2003 the *acquis communautaire* was 'enriched' by 2348 new regulations. To make matters worse, more and tougher rules are on the horizon. It is true that most of them have a limited time duration. However, the new member countries have a race against ever-shifting goalposts. This would not be a problem for Cyprus as *Agenda 2000* does not expect any major obstacle regarding the adoption, implementation and enforcement of the *acquis communautaire* in the southern part of the country.[30]

When the EU last accepted 'poor countries' (Spain and Portugal in 1986), the European Community, as it was then called, was not a single market for goods, services, capital and labour. The EU deepened integration and the EMU was introduced in 1999. Even though Spain and Portugal were 'poor' countries, they were market economies. With this in mind, the chances of even the most advanced Central and East European countries of accepting, implementing and enforcing the *acquis communautaire* in full seem bleak for quite some time in the future.

The European Union has few incentives and limited funds to accept countries with economic structures that are significantly different from its own. Such an attitude may seem hypocritical since the West has spent almost half a century encouraging those countries to join the free market and democratic world. Accession countries also need to exercise patience. Jovanović (1997b, p. 368) argued from the vantage point of 1997, that if all goes well, that is, if all entry negotiations proceeded smoothly including ratification in all the involved countries and a post-entry adjustment period of about a decade, then it would take even the most advanced Central and East European countries some 15–20 years to become full members of the EU.

A clear message to accession countries came from the head of the European Commission's DG for Enlargement in 2000.[31] These countries should not attach too much importance to the date of accession, but rather to the essential issue: quality of the accession, that is, respect for the accession criteria. To set at that time a firm date for entry might be a mistake, as it might lock the EU in a promise it might regret. The enlargement should take place in such a way as to be beneficial both to the existing EU member countries and to the Central and East European countries. In addition, the EU has to remain strong after enlargement. The European Commission would recommend access only if the accession country can respect rights and duties from the first day of accession.[32] Such a clear and open message contributed to a drop in enthusiasm among the accession countries for rapid entry. The Convention on the Future of Europe (2002–03) on the institutional reform of the EU raised new doubts among the Central and East European countries, which feared that the accession would be made subject to new conditions or that something was being plotted against them. Expectation fatigue was taking its toll. None the less, the European Commission considered that Cyprus, the Czech Republic, Estonia, Hungary, Latvia, Lithuania, Malta, Poland, Slovakia and Slovenia would be ready for EU membership from May 2004. Bulgaria and Romania are expected to be ready for accession in 2007 (European Commission, 2002a, pp. 33–4).

Is it necessary to move so fast with the eastern enlargement? It may be true that the Central and East European countries have 'no alternative' but to join the EU. It is also true that they have survived a 'big boom' adjustment following the transition process. However, the 'big boom' was a one-time affair. Integration in the EU is a constantly evolving process. Unless the Central and East European countries are well prepared, they may face similar problems to those that Germany encountered with the absorption of the eastern part of the country.[33]

Can the accession countries repeat the relative economic and development success of Ireland? One has to bear in mind that Ireland is a relatively small country (population 3.7 million). Its story resembles those of Singapore and Hong Kong. Ireland created a business-friendly environment for new-technology firms and FDI. A relatively small amount of foreign investment could have a powerful impact on a small economy such as Ireland. In addition, over a long period, Ireland unlike Greece used EU funds for infrastructure projects of lasting value. Greece, on the other hand, lagged behind other EU countries for years following its EU entry. There is a serious concern that with Poland on board, the EU may be burdened with a much larger version of Greece for years to come.

6. Cost of enlargement

What will the financial cost of enlargement be for the EU(15)? Since *Agenda 2000* (1997) and the European Council in Berlin (1999), there has been an overall cap on the total receipts that any EU member state may get from the EU: 4 per cent of the recipient country's GDP. As the total GDP of 12 accession countries plus Turkey is rather small (7 per cent of the total EU GDP in 2001), the actual cost of enlargement for the EU need not get out of hand and should be relatively small.

The European Council in Copenhagen (12–13 December 2002) and previously in Brussels (2002)[34] reconfirmed its Berlin (1999)[35] decision that the ceiling for enlargement-related expenditure set out for 2004–06 must be respected. That is to say that total EU expenditure must fit into own resources that are limited to 1.27 per cent of the combined EU GDP of all member countries. Therefore, the EU has very little room for manoeuvre in which to enlarge its funds. During the three years from 2004 to 2006, 'of the €25.1 billion in payments for the period, €14.1 billion will be covered by new member states' contributions, so that the net cost for the EU(15) would be €10.3 billion' (*Enlargement Weekly*, 28 January 2003) Consequently, the actual annual net 'cost' of the eastern enlargement will be €3.4 billion (or less than €10 per EU(15) citizen).[36] From 2005 there will be very tough negotiations and horse-trading in order to define the new financial perspective for the 2007–13 period. If one recalls the CAP adjustment deal, full equality of the accession countries with the rest of the EU(15) will not come before 2013. Before that, the new member countries will in certain respects be second-class citizens. In any case, the EU will enter a much more difficult phase of integration in 2006 than most people imagine.

The fact that public transfers to agriculture, and on regional policy grounds, are to be limited is surely a good thing. Aid has never helped anyone in the medium and long terms. The Central and East European countries need private investment, not public aid. Many would argue that public investment is a 'good thing'. If devoted to infrastructural public goods, it can be. But much gets lost on the way. The administrative capacity of public officials in the Central and East European countries to handle projects in a new way still needs to be strengthened.[37] There are fears that a lot of EU aid goes to the general budget, allowing local ex-communists to pursue policies for which there is little or weak democratic support and accountability, as well as to prop up lost causes, rather than to assist promising projects which require assistance only in their initial phase.

The European Council in Brussels (2002) brought in two safeguard clauses; one regarding the internal market and the other in the area of justice and home affairs, of up to three years' duration after accession. These measures may be invoked even *before* accession and the 'duration of such measures may extend beyond the three-year period'.[38] Hence, the message from the European Council to the accession countries was: 'We warmly welcome you to our club. But from today we are watching you closely applying and enforcing "our" rules. Any mistake and you will pay for that. And do not forget, your dreams about big money from our kitty will remain just that. Dreams'. What an unfriendly message regarding investment, particularly private investment, in and towards the accession countries! If there is a 'mishap', the introduction of EU safeguards may easily jeopardise returns on an investment.

7. Conclusion

When full integration with the EU was first discussed at the beginning of the 1990s and when it was merely a remote possibility, everyone was enthusiastic about it. As the date of entry approached, the more this enthusiasm evaporated and serious doubts emerged. Some say that the EU carried out a promise that many now wish had never been made – at least not so quickly. The general mood is one of anxiety, rather than of celebration. The leaders failed to explain to citizens the benefits of this enlargement. Others rejoice: enlargement, as such, is a very good thing as it marks the end of the East–West divide in Europe. But, if European integration is such a profound and necessary process, can one explain why Europe consisted of 32 countries in 1990, while it now has 48? Festivities and fulsome speeches cannot, however, disguise distrust and discontent beneath the surface.

They cannot mask the sombre fact that almost all the EU(15) countries slammed the doors against the free movement of labour from Central and East European member countries.[39] Would this all play into the hands of Euro-sceptics? Would the basic geopolitical principle that nations always act in their own self-interest prevail in the EU?

Notes

1. The Czech Republic, Estonia, Hungary, Poland and Slovenia started accession negotiations on 31 March 1998, while Bulgaria, Latvia, Lithuania, Romania and Slovakia started negotiations on 15 March 2000.
2. The Treaty of Accession was signed in Athens on 16 April 2003 and subsequently duly ratified.
3. Although it has never been the public position of the EU, there are influential voices that reflect serious privately expressed anxiety of many officials that the EU is storing up trouble by embracing Turkey. The worry is that if Turkey enters the EU, then the biggest EU country could be 'south-east European'. For example, a prominent Christian Democrat in the European Parliament, Wilfried Martens, said: 'The EU is in the process of building a civilisation in which Turkey has no place'. In addition, eminent Dutch politicians have expressed doubts about the Turkish application 'because there are too many of them, and they are too poor – and they are Muslims' (*The Economist*, 15 March 1997, p. 31). Or, Valéry Giscard d'Estaing, Chairman of the Convention on the Future of Europe, said that Turkey's membership would represent 'the end of the European Union . . . Those who are pushing hardest for the enlargement in the direction of Turkey are adversaries of the EU' (*Financial Times*, 8 November 2002). The European Council in Copenhagen (2002) decided that it would decide in December 2004 whether Turkey fulfils conditions for the start of entry negotiations. However, a former senior American official declared that 'the US has done everything but slap the German government across the face in an effort to get the EU to agree to Turkish membership' (*Financial Times*, 2 February 2003).
4. 'Several commissioners, led by Frits Bolkenstein, who is responsible for the internal market, said many of the candidate countries would not be ready to withstand the pressures of competition once they joined' (*Financial Times*, 10 October 2002, p. 1).
5. European Commission (1997a), p. 52; *Bulletin Quotidien Europe*, 12 November 2001, p. 3.
6. European Commission (1997a), pp. 44, 51 and 134; *Bulletin Quotidien Europe*, 12 November 2001, p. 3.
7. European Commission (1997a), p. 45.
8. An early short survey of select studies is given by Baldwin (1995b).
9. There are concerns that the accession countries do not all have the institutional capacity to absorb the financial opportunities provided by the PHARE programme. To obtain funds (aid), the acceding country has to make reforms and submit sensible projects to the EU. As the submitted Polish projects were ill-prepared, the EU cut €34 million off the planned aid of €212 million for that country for 1998 (*The Economist*, 6 June 1998, pp. 37–8). As this was the first time ever that the EU had cut funds to a PHARE country, this sent a strong signal to the accession countries that they should undergo a serious institutional overhaul if they wanted to meet the high EU criteria.
10. The former German Democratic Republic was admitted into the EU without questions asked and there were no tests applied.
11. Economic Commission for Europe (2003, p. 37).
12. If the rules on regional aid from the EU were not changed, then such aid to the acces-

sion transition countries would transfer resources equal to 10–20 per cent of the new members' GDP. This is far more than the 3.5 per cent of GDP that Greece received in 1996 (*The Economist*, 3 August 1996, p. 28). *Agenda 2000* limited the level of annual structural and cohesion aid to 4 per cent of the recipient country's GDP (European Commission 1997a, p. 25). This was reconfirmed by the European Council in Berlin (1999) in §46. Given the relatively small size of the economies of the accession countries, this rule would strictly limit the amount they could get from the EU.

13. European Commission (1997a, pp. 25 and 53).
14. The NATO entry, completed with little public debate, may harden both the economic adjustment and the EU accession. Most of the investment in the military forces is not producing direct value added which can be consumed or exported. Investment in this sector crowds out investment in other, market-oriented sectors because of the need to coordinate and to harmonise with other NATO partners and standards. Hungary, for example, met less than a third of its NATO commitments three years after NATO entry in 1999. If Hungary is considered to be a successful country in transition, then one may question the ability of Bulgaria and Romania to meet the NATO challenge (*The Times*, 18 November 2002). If this continues, the Americans would control the still fragile democracies in the new member countries; guide political, military and other types of European integration; and be even closer to the oil-rich Caspian and Middle-Eastern regions.
15. *Agenda 2000* states that the environment is a major challenge for enlargement (European Commission 1997a, p. 49).
16. *European Voice*, 28 May 2003, p. 14.
17. Compliance with those standards refers to all member countries of the EU. For example, the privatised British water industry is expected to spend about $60 billion between 1989 and 2004 to bring its water supply network into line with EU directives (*Financial Times*, 6 October 1997, p. 18).
18. *Uniting Europe*, 10 December 2001, p. 5.
19. This may be one of the consequences of the badly underpaid officials in the public sector.
20. European Commission (1997a, p. 52).
21. When the Polish government presented its 2004 budget (€9.9 billion deficit) to parliament, the Polish zloty hit its lowest level ever against the euro (*Financial Times*, 30 September 2003).
22. Some of the Maastricht criteria were loosely interpreted as national debt was over 120 per cent of the GDP in 1997 both in Belgium and in Italy, but in 1998 both countries were permitted to enter the EMU from the start, even though the Maastricht norm is 60 per cent.
23. Also Fisher, et al., 1998, p. 28; Economic Commission for Europe, 2002, p. 183.
24. *European Economy*, 1997a, p. 8.
25. The rural working age population in Poland is growing annually by 100 000. To create alternative jobs for many existing and newly arriving farmers could be likened to pushing water uphill (*Financial Times*, 10 June 2003).
26. Central Europe received $16.3 billion in FDI in 2001. The primary beneficiaries were Poland ($7 billion), the Czech Republic ($5 billion) and Hungary ($2.4 billion) (Economic Commission for Europe, 2003, p. 93). While relatively low wages could have been an advantage for the Central and East European countries in the past, they are becoming less and less so. For example, real wages in Hungary are on a rise. This may be one of the reasons why Hungary could easily experience a net capital outflow of foreign investment in 2003. Investors are leaving for China.
27. The total direct expenditure of the EU on enlargement in the 1990–2006 period is estimated to be €69.5 billion (*Uniting Europe*, 14 July 2003, p. 7). In relative terms and over the period of 17 years this cost does not seem to be large at all compared with EU GDP.
28. With about 14.5 million EU citizens out of work in 2003, the sensitivity of the issue in the EU does not come as a surprise. A similar debate on trade liberalisation with Mexico and the creation of the North American Free Trade Agreement (NAFTA) was going on in the United States in the early 1990s. In spite of strong opposition by the US presidential candidate Ross Perot regarding the free trade agreement between the US and

Mexico and a possible loss of jobs in the American economy ('giant sucking sound' of jobs moving south (*The Economist*, 18 September 1993, p. 51)), only 117 000 Americans have applied for the benefits offered to workers displaced by the free trade agreement. If this is compared with the 1.5 million who lose their jobs each year from factory closures, slack demand and corporate restructuring (*The Economist*, 5 July 1997, p. 17), the cost of adjustment to the agreement by the US does not seem too high. Free trade with Mexico might have destroyed some jobs in the American textile industry which is 'labour intensive', but it created new ones in electronics, aeronautics or writing software.

29. *Financial Times*, 15 January 2003.
30. European Commission (1997a, p. 54).
31. *Bulletin Quotidien Europe*, 15 March 2000, p. 11.
32. *Bulletin Quotidien Europe*, 29 March 2000, p. 12; 12 November 2001, p. 3.
33. On the political side, there are still problems which include a divided Cyprus and the Beneš Decrees (1946) in Czechoslovakia under which 2.5 million Germans were deported and deprived of their property.
34. European Council, Brussels 2002, Presidency Conclusions, §10.
35. European Council, Berlin 1999, Presidency Conclusions, §16 and Table B.
36. The 'net benefit' for Spain, for instance in 2001, amounted to €7.7 billion or €192 per EU citizen (*Uniting Europe*, 23 December 2002, p. 6).
37. The European Commission confirmed in July 2003 that some of the €22 billion allocated to accession countries for the 2004–06 period may remain unused unless adequate administrative structures are set up quickly (*Enlargement Weekly*, 22 July 2003).
38. European Council, Brussels 2002, Presidency Conclusions, §8.
39. With the exception of Britain and Ireland, all EU(15) member countries have exercised their right to impose transitional arrangements which restrict freedom to work and stay for the nationals from Central and East European member countries until 2011.

> O LORD, I know the way of men is not in himself;
> It is not in man who walks to direct his own steps.
> O LORD, correct me, but with justice;
> Not in Your anger, lest You bring me to nothing.
> Jeremiah 10:23, 24

15 Conclusion

The objective of this book is to provide an introduction to the origin, evolution, operation, problems, successes, failures and possible prospects for *economic* integration in Europe under the auspices of the EU. It is timely to recall in these concluding comments that the evolution and possible prospects for the EU can fit into eight broad and sometimes overlapping periods:

- creation and growth (1957–68);
- consolidation and first enlargement (1969–73);
- 'Eurosclerosis' (1974–84);
- Euro-activism (1985–92) which culminated in the creation of the Single European Market (1993–);
- creation and maintenance of the eurozone (1999–);
- eastern enlargement and its absorption (2004–13);
- aspiration to create the most competitive and dynamic knowledge-based economy in the world (2001–10); and
- coping with problems provoked by demographical developments such as equilibrium in the labour market, pensions, immigration and public expenditure (2010–50).

In order to face current and imminent challenges, the EU is trying to change. Following the second Irish referendum in 2002, the Treaty of Nice was duly ratified. Hence, before eastern enlargement the EU(15) member countries preserved their blocking influence in the decision-making process.[1] It would be very difficult to introduce a new and controversial policy in the EU, as well as to change radically the *acquis communautaire*. Any reaction to new challenges could potentially be very slow and difficult, while the voting structure in the EU(25) makes the blocking of new initiatives relatively swift and easy. In addition, the EU(15) limited its total expenditure in advance of enlargement. Hence, the basic structure of the EU may remain as it is for quite some time in the future.

The key procedure in the EU has been that all member countries try to move together or not at all (one-size-fits-all). This was not always easy to apply even among the EU 15 member states. It does not seem to be operationally feasible in an enlarged EU. So, would 'flexibility' make the enlarged EU of almost 30 countries more manageable? Would flexibility, that is, a multispeed organisation of the EU, make it more viable? Would it strengthen or weaken the EU?

Notwithstanding political declarations and aspirations about unity, Europe, as a continent, can be divided into at least ten groups of countries that move at different 'speeds':

- The first and fastest group includes the 12 eurozone countries.
- Even within the first group there is a subgroup that includes big countries (France, Germany and, perhaps, Italy) which are able to sway events in their own way.[2] This is why smaller EU countries want a strong European Commission which would be their friend and protector against the domination of big countries.
- The third set includes Britain, Denmark and Sweden, which do not (yet) participate in the eurozone.
- The fourth circle consists of the EU countries that are members of the Schengen Agreement.
- A fifth group contains Central and East European countries, as well as Cyprus and Malta which joined the EU in 2004. The Central and East European countries have a decade-long adjustment period for agriculture ('unequal speed') until 2013.
- Bulgaria and Romania are slow-speed accession countries which have a tentative EU entry date in 2007.
- Switzerland, Iceland and Norway are cases on their own.
- Turkey has only the title of an accession country.
- Other European countries, mainly in the Balkans and east of Poland and Romania.
- There is also a group of countries that are members of NATO, those that aspire to join this organisation and those that are neutral.

Predictions about future political events are uncertain, risky, difficult and often poorly received. They are always subject to harsh criticism. Still, the EU as we have known it now is finished. The European Constitution is expected to take effect from 2009. In the meantime, the Treaty of Nice will provide guidance for the EU in the 2004–09 period. However, the exact organisational steps and directions may not be known for several years. The European Constitution will have also to be ratified.[3]

Monetary integration is a field where genuine economic integration among countries is tested.[4] Even though the creation of the eurozone (1999) was a very important step towards completing the Single European Market, the zone has always been an essentially political, rather than a predominantly economic project. Never before have so many countries entered into a monetary union with so little progress towards a political union. As long as governments are sovereign (no political union), the eurozone will be capable of breaking up. Therefore, the eurozone is the greatest achievement and the biggest risk the EU has ever taken. It is also a mission that may transform both the political and economic scenery of Europe.

The politicians in the eurozone countries succeeded in creating an EMU with the euro as an über-currency that may rival the dollar. This introduced monetary stability in economic relations among the participating countries. However, a mere EMU is not the end of the story. Fiscal harmonisation and budgetary coordination could be the next steps, as this would contribute to the full effectiveness of the stabilisation and growth policy.

The eurozone is and will be going through serious trials. The ECB will be tested in times of economic difficulty. There may be a perception that it is not able to act decisively because it has to be mindful of each component nation. In addition, budget deficits in the major eurozone countries and a flexible interpretation of rules may continue to challenge the credibility of the eurozone. This may cause a serious dent in confidence in the Stability and Growth Pact, which will be compounded by a severe test around the year 2010 and beyond with the increased demand for old-age related payments.

Following eastern enlargement, very tough, complicated and controversial negotiations and horse-trading are expected to define the new EU financial perspective that is supposed to set EU spending for the 2007–13 period. In any case, in 2004 the EU entered into a much more difficult and complicated phase of integration than most people imagine.

The shifts out of industries that use obsolete production technologies into modern ones seems easy in theory, but can be quite difficult, costly and slow in practice. This is, of course, a matter of political choice. The inability to do something is different from an unwillingness to do it. The EU opted for the creation of the Single European Market as the environment that favours change. The creation of the Single European Market enhanced the dynamic process of competition through an easing of market segmentation and, somewhat paradoxically, by increasing concentration in some businesses. This concentration permitted the employment of economies of scale in select lines of production and an increase in technical efficiency. In addition, it enhanced R&D through a joint sharing of high costs.

As far as 'unification' of the market is concerned, there is a burning question: is the EU aiming at an almost totally homogenised market, with similar tastes, preferences and lifestyles, such as the US exhibits? Apart from some noteworthy exceptions, it seems that wherever one goes in the US, there are the same types of towns and settlements, and virtually the same general style of life, work or diet. This may be the reason why the Americans are so mobile within their own country. This form of integration is not necessary or even possible in Europe. It is barely conceivable in Europe that *pasta con radicchio rosso* in Veneto or *bistecca alla fiorentina* in Tuscany should taste the same elsewhere (for example, in Wales, Lapland or Galicia), as is the case with McDonald's hamburgers in Chicago, San Diego or Tokyo.[5] There need to be various measures to preserve unity with diversity in the EU as long as people want that and are prepared to pay for it. How far one can go with integration is up to the people to decide at the ballot box, if they are given the opportunity.

A relatively large and integrated market is not a guarantee in itself that international economic integration will bring the desired economic outcomes. The evidence for this can be found in the cases of Russia and India, as well as China (perhaps until the 1990s). Contrasting evidence is supplied by the impressive experience of individualistic development of the small countries such as Switzerland, New Zealand or Singapore. A country's prosperity does not depend on its size and the availability of natural resources; much more important are human resources, as well as the political and regulatory framework.

While possible economic gains arouse substantial interest in integration, countries are also aware that there are costs of adjustment that temper the enthusiasm for integration. However, integration is not a cure for all economic ills. It is only a tool to support sound national economic policy. Integration ensures free access to an enlarged market. This creates opportunities for increased competition in an enlarged market, but its success also depends on an astute national macroeconomic policy and policies in education, R&D and investment in capital goods, as well as the willingness of firms to take both risk in and advantage of the newly created environment.

The life cycle of goods is getting shorter and the situation in the market changes rapidly. Innovation, technology and the skills of the labour force are key factors in competitiveness. Therefore, there should be more emphasis on education in Europe. This is because human capital is the most valuable asset that a country or region can have, and it is human capital that will solve problems and shape comparative advantage for and in the future.

The European Council in Lisbon (2000) set a new strategic goal for the decade: to make the EU 'the most competitive and dynamic knowledge-based economy in the world capable of sustainable economic growth with more and better jobs and greater social cohesion'.[6] This is a daunting task, but also a challenge, especially in view of the remarkable growth of the US economy over the past several years, as well as the economic expansion of China. In order to achieve this stated objective, firms' high quality performance should be based on the skills of the workforce, competence of management, as well as on the reform of the labour market. Perhaps, secure jobs for some should not be at the expense of others.

Sapir et al. (2003) proposed that the EU should spend about half of its budget on growth-stimulating activities such as research, higher education, infrastructure projects and institution building in the new Central and East European member countries. The only way to do this and to remain within the current budgetary limits would be to scrap the CAP and regional funds. This would be in line with the Lisbon objectives. However, politicians did not accept this suggestion and failed to propose an alternative – a missed opportunity.

The external trade policy of the EU is founded on liberal principles. Trade is seen as be beneficial, not only because it creates jobs, but also because it improves the allocation of resources which stimulates growth. So much for trade philosophy. In practice, the EU has taken important liberalising steps, even in sensitive areas. However, the problem is that these bold steps have been confined only to select countries. The EU has a passion for preferential (that is, discriminatory) trade agreements. The EU has considerable discretionary power to differentiate among its trade partners by offering or not offering different types of trade and cooperation agreements. Although member countries of the EU are members of the WTO, which promotes multilateralism, the EU 'rewards' its foreign friends with special bilateral trade agreements.

There is no doubt that European integration sometimes contributed to international trade liberalisation in the post-1960s period. The extension of the GATT, and later the WTO, into new areas such as services could have been slower in the absence of the 'challenge' posed by the evolution of the EU. None the less, there are certain reasons to suppose that the impact of the EU on the multilateral trading system has not been entirely benign (for example, in agriculture).[7] However, historically agriculture has been a very special social and economic activity in Europe for several millennia. Hence, it may be unfair, unnecessary and harmful to assess the needs, accomplishments and effects of this sector by employing unconditional free trade criteria.

Free market forces cannot protect the environment. Otherwise would you burn a Vermeer or a Cézanne if you were told that this may help to save non-renewable fossil fuel? Would benefits of such a foolish act be more important than the loss? Pure market forces may not encompass and value immaterial externalities such as beauty, pleasure and spiritual enrichment. Governments can protect this. Demand for leisure is increasing as people are ready, willing and able to pay for a pleasant walk in the countryside or to look at a historic building. They do the same for healthy and safe food and the environment. Care for the environment also creates jobs. Coupled with the increasing general consciousness about the conservation of a clean, healthy and sustainable environment, this policy will remain high on the EU agenda and policy action in the future. All EU policies will have to continue to pay attention to the impact of intervention on the environment.

The demand for social services and expenditure is almost insatiable. The expenditure for these services may be increased during periods of prosperity at lowest political cost, as was the case in the 1960s. During economic slowdowns and budgetary deficits, the social services which have mushroomed or which have become too generous or badly conceived have to be reformed. However, demographic pressures will continue to put an increasing strain on public expenditure in particular in the areas of health, care for the old and pensions, especially from around 2010.

Average life expectancy, one of the measures of social achievements, of the EU population is increasing. Therefore, national social protection systems will have to be adjusted over the coming three decades because of the ageing population. Due to demographical changes and realities, the EU labour force will start shrinking for decades from around 2010. A part of the solution to the problem of looming labour shortages may be found in selective immigration policy, in particular, from other European countries.

Coverage of many EU policies such as those in social, regional, taxation, environment or transport areas is still limited. These policies have been based on a number of political compromises, which have affected the purity of their principles. Intervention has been much less of a well-organised policy and much more a mix of various issues that the member states were willing to transfer to the EU. The often 'loose' character of these policies also comes from the legal provisions that are in certain cases aspirational, rather than operational, as well as because of the lack of funds.

The eastern enlargement is altering the EU almost beyond recognition. The EU is not what it was 30, 20 or even 10 years ago. From a relatively 'generous' common market (later Single European Market) regarding expenditure on agriculture and other policy areas such as cohesion, the EU has become a much more demanding and costly place to be in as far as the *acquis communautaire* is concerned. At the same time, EU spending has become tight and thrifty. Hence the 'promised land' the Central and East European countries expected from the EU at the time (1989) when they aspired to join the EU is not at all what they got at entry in 2004. None the less, the EU has an unprecedented opportunity to reshape Europe and make it a better and safer region. However, it may take the EU at least a decade or a generation to 'digest' all economic, political and organisational dimensions that the eastern enlargement brings with it.

Increased heterogeneity in the EU following the eastern enlargement will be one of the big tests for coordination of EU policies. Half of the EU is inside the eurozone, while another half is outside of it. The economy of Britain and countries in Central and Eastern Europe is structured such that they may easily be subject to asymmetric shocks relative to the eurozone. Policy coordination problems may become tough.

Some welcome the eastern enlargement as they consider that this would water down the EU into an extended free trade area. Others are depressed because they think that enlargement was done in rush, without adequately prepared candidates and without a duly consolidated EU. The cost of implementing the *acquis communautaire* is staggering, and this represents one good reason why the Central and East European countries should think again about such a relatively speedy entry. A very slow and long transition period might be the only reasonable alternative solution, but it is too late for such thoughts now. Economic integration is a highly charged political process which requires caution, gradualism and, more than anything else, the political will which economic theory may not predict.

Regarding possible future enlargements of the EU inevitable is the issue of Turkey, Russia and Ukraine. It is hard to conceive what has Sweden, Ireland or Poland in common with Turkey. In these terms, Russia and Ukraine are much more 'European' than Turkey can ever be. This is particularly important in the light of strong and repeated demands to include a reference to the EU 'Christian roots' in the Constitutional Treaty.[8] In fact, it is hard to imagine in the long term a strong, sovereign and independent Europe without Russia. With Russia in the EU, Europe can be free from any transatlantic or Middle Eastern blackmail regarding energy.[9] Apart from energy-related security and independence, so necessary for the EU because of its dependence and vulnerability, Russia may offer a huge market potential, as well as certain types of high technology.

The issue of the Turkish aspirations about full membership of the EU is highly sensitive and controversial both regarding politics and economics. An obvious peril for Turkey is that it may regard EU membership as a panacea for all domestic ills. One has to recall that Turkey has already had a functioning customs union with the EU since 1995. Hence a number of trade gains have already been in place. In any case, Turkey may be welcome to the EU, but it has to make its European identity and credentials right and clear.

The negotiation and preparation process may easily last about 15 years (if there are no political interruptions in Turkey). Apart from the Copenhagen criteria for EU entry, there are also others. Turkey is a special, indeed a very special, Euro-Oriental country. The obvious conditions are the following:

- *Genocide*: The highest-level German statesmen and politicians have explicitly and officially stated their apologies regarding genocide committed during the Second World War. The country still pays compensation to the victims. As such, Germany has passed through the moral catharsis (*Vergangenheitsbewältigung*) and is accepted in the family of countries that share common European values. Therefore, Turkey must do the same. The genocide committed by Turkey against the Armenians in 1915 left 1.5 million Armenians massacred. Turkey has to come to terms with this (as was the German case). An international commission about this issue may be a good starting point.
- *Expansionism*: Germany relinquished the expansionist nazi-type pan-German ideas that are very dangerous for peace. This is most obvious and important in the relations with Poland (German eastern border). Turkey's statesmen, politicians and government institutions must clearly and publicly renounce the pan-Turkish ideas asserted even by the latest generation of its statesmen such as Suleiman Demirel and Turgut Ozal about Turkey 'from the Chinese Wall until the Adriatic sea'. Such ambitions, dangerous for peace, introduce concerns and fears about the reestablishment of the Ottoman Empire (1350–1918). The Austrians still have strong collective memory about sufferings during the Turkish sieges of Vienna (1529–1683) and fear that this may be repeated. Many of them wonder if the 1683 victory over the Ottoman Empire was in vain. There are also perpetual Turkish claims and provocations regarding the Greek territory.[10]
- *Turkish speaking countries*: Following the dissolution of the former Soviet Union, Azerbaijan, Kazakhstan, Turkmenistan, Kirghizistan and Uzbekistan emerged as independent Turkish-speaking states. Would Turkey also bring these countries into the EU or, at least, their Turkish-speaking citizens? There are also concerns and fears in the EU about the large-scale intrusion of Muslims into Europe and a 'clash of civilisations'.
- *Cyprus*: Turkey must withdraw all occupation forces from an EU

member country. Cyprus must be recognised in its entirety. In addition, the illegally seized property in Cyprus must be returned to the original owners.
- *Kurds*: Turkey must improve the treatment of its Kurdish minority which is about 12 to 15 million strong. Calls for regionalisation and autonomy are quite strong.
- *Frontier control*: Turkey has a long frontier with countries such as Lebanon, Syria, Iraq and Iran. It is quite hard, demanding and costly to police it effectively. Turkey ought to demonstrate that it can apply, keep and implement the EU standards regarding this issue.

These are all tough and important issues that must be dealt with. In addition, by 2015 Turkey would be the most populous EU state. It would have the biggest single voting power in the EU. This would have an enormous consequence for the voting process and operation of the entire EU. The choice whether to let Turkey in or not is neither simple nor easy. Even the European Commission has publicly revealed certain divisions on the issue. Frits Bolkestein (Dutch) is against the entry of Turkey for historical, political and religious reasons. Franz Fischler (Austrian) is opposed to the entry not only because of the lack of 'long-term secular and democratic credentials' but also because the financial cost of applying even just the CAP on Turkey would not be tenable. This would cost the EU €11.5bn a year. However, Chris Patten (British) is positive about the entry and argues in favour of an increase in EU farm and structural spending.[11]

It is complex even now to create a common and coherent EU foreign and defence policy. Given the political and military weight of Turkey, this would make it inconceivable in an enlarged EU. The EU may be easily transformed into an impressively large free trade area with certain elements of policy coordination. Britain may argue that this is not a bad idea at all. One of the possible options is to offer Turkey a 'special partnership status' rather than full membership.

No real and wide public debate has yet taken place about the entry of Turkey. EU citizens (and voters) need to know what benefit Turkish entry would bring them. If the entry of Turkey is presented by the elite as a *fait accompli* without wide public debate and consultation with the people (voters), their resistance and revenge may shatter the project later.[12]

In spite of public statements by various governments that Turkey is welcome into the EU, polls reveal that the EU public shows serious discomfort about letting such a big, poor, and culturally and religiously different country into the EU club.[13] If Turkey joins the EU, then it would be hard to say 'no' to countries such as Armenia, Azerbaijan, Georgia, Moldova and, of course, to Russia and Ukraine.

Concerns that the Single European Market would lead to a concentration of general economic activity in the 'core' EU countries were not borne out in practice. On the other hand, there has been only a limited and slow, but obvious, spread of certain economic activities towards the 'peripheral' EU countries that enjoy certain cost advantages. The millennium shift of certain high-technology industries in the EU took place towards Ireland and Finland, the EU periphery. If similar tendencies continue and prevail, the Central and East European countries may hope and expect that a certain relocation of some EU industries may take place towards this 'new EU periphery'.

European integration has always been based on the political decision to secure peace and freedom in Europe. This is the purpose of the EU, although many observers seem to have forgotten it. European integration is intended to mitigate the impact of old rivalries and replace them by mutual economic advantage and social prosperity. The eastern enlargement will not bring the EU extra efficiency or growth; nor will it create new jobs. Its basic objective is to provide support to friendly countries and governments during their reform and general stabilisation process.

The US has such an awesome, unrivalled and unprecedented economic and military power since the Roman Empire that it may not need (or may easily ignore) international institutions. Such institutions merely constrain the US unilateral acts and its room for manoeuvre. The EU can exert the only substantial international pressure towards such ends, in particular as the US appears to be a 'rogue state' on issues of global warming and the International Criminal Court. If the EU collapses in dysfunctional paralysis, everyone may become poorer and may suffer. The EU is powerful enough not to be ignored, but it may be too divided to be an impressive counterbalance or an equal partner. Limits to further integration in the EU can be found essentially in national politics. Most of EU member states and nations are among the oldest in the world, they differ not only in social, legal and tax structures, but also in history and climate. Notwithstanding a plethora of differences and motivations, the connecting tissue among those countries are economic and political interests and a vision of the common future.[14]

European integration has always been in the hands of national elites, which is why the treaties on which European integration is based are complicated and incomprehensible to the man in the street. Intelligibility is a condition of democratic legitimacy. When the national elites decide to defend Europe from various challenges, in particular external ones (coming from both west and south), public enthusiasm to deepen integration and to enlarge further the EU may regain momentum. Of major importance to the national elites in the EU countries is now to reclaim popular backing for the process of European integration. Perhaps the enormous task of consolidating of the already started grand projects such as the Constitution, adjustment to the eastern enlargement, increasing competitiveness of goods and services and the settling of the eurozone may need to be EU priorities. This is already more than enough. Looking for additional high-flying ideas without ways and means to achieve them now may be better postponed for the next decade. Therefore, European integration deserves full support, but perhaps its speed is not always so important as mistakes could be made, resulting in a longer-term loss of confidence in the integration process. Dr Samuel Johnson (1709–84) would probably say that the EU is 'like a dog walking on his hind legs. It is not well done, but you are surprised to find it done at all'. *Festina lente!* (Hurry, slowly!)

The objective of this book has been, among other goals, to provoke thoughts and contribute to the debate about European economic integration. Those (few) who decided to specialise in European integration during the late 1970s and early 1980s (including the present author) were asking themselves at that time of Eurosclerosis whether their choice of subject was wise. Those who embark upon studying European integration now can at least be sure that their efforts will not be in vain for a long time to come.

Notes

1. This is particularly valid for the large member countries.
2. This has happened in 2002 when the European Commission postponed a deadline for the eurozone countries to balance their budgets from 2004 to 2006. In addition, the Council of Ministers decided in 2003 not to fine France and Germany for their repeated fiscal deficits.
3. Recall that certain EU countries have to (Ireland) or intend to (France) put the new European Constitution to a national referendum. This is a much less certain approval procedure than a vote in national parliaments.
4. This subject is challenging both for policy makers and for researchers as it combines the hardest macroeconomic issues. At the same time it is annoying as there are no *ex ante* counterfactual situations against which one may measure costs and benefits of monetary integration.
5. With apologies to the Italians for the inappropriate comparison of their cuisine with hamburgers. The intention here was simply to make a point. Le mie più sincere scuse agii Italiani.
6. European Council, Lisbon 2000, Presidency Conclusions, §5.
7. EU trade policy is sometimes under the strong influence of vested interests and lobbies that often and forcefully demand protection. Farmers are the most obvious example. They are followed by both manufacturers (whose output) and trade unions (whose jobs) are 'jeopardised' by a surge of foreign imports (steel, for example).
8. The loudest voices come from the Czech Republic, Italy, Lithuania, Malta, Poland, Portugal and Slovakia.
9. Recall that most of the oil resources in the Middle East are under the control of the US firms or the US Army.
10. One can immediately think of the islands of Imia and Gavdos.
11. *Bulletin Quotidien Europe*, 8 September 2004, p. 4 and 16 September 2004, p. 3; Q. Peel,

'The case for letting Turkey', *Financial Times*, 16 September 2004, p. 21; *Enlargement Weekly*, 21 September 2004.
12. This may happen even earlier on an unrelated issue. One ought to recall that there will be quite a few national referendums about the ratification of the Constitutional Treaty.
13. Austria, Cyprus and Greece are the most obvious examples. The Scandinavian countries attach great weight to human rights records. In addition, Ljubljana (Slovenia) is the only EU capital without a mosque.
14. If European integration is such a profound and a necessary process, can one explain why Europe consisted of 32 countries in 1990, while it now has 48?

Bibliography

Adams, G. (1983). 'Criteria for US industrial policy strategies', in *Industrial Policies for Growth and Competitiveness* (eds G. Adams and L. Klein). Lexington, MA: Lexington Books, pp. 393–418.
Adams, G. and A. Bolino (1983). 'Meaning of industrial policy', in *Industrial Policies for Growth and Competitiveness* (eds G. Adams and L. Klein). Lexington, MA: Lexington Books, pp. 13–20.
Adams, G. and L. Klein (1983). 'Economic evolution of industrial policies for growth and competitiveness: overview', in *Industrial Policies for Growth and Competitiveness* (eds G. Adams and L. Klein). Lexington, MA: Lexington Books, pp. 3–11.
Altshuler, R., H. Grubert and T. Newlon (1998). 'Has U.S. investment abroad become more sensitive to tax rates?', NBER Working Paper No. 6383, National Bureau of Economic Research, Cambridge, MA.
Amin, A. and A. Malmberg (1992). 'Competing structural and institutional influences on the geography of production in Europe', *Environment and Planning*, pp. 401–16.
Amiti, M. (1998). 'New trade theories and industrial location in the EU: a survey of evidence', *Oxford Economic Papers*, pp. 45–53.
Amiti, M. (1999). 'Specialization patterns in Europe', *Weltwirtschaftliches Archiv*, pp. 573–93.
Ando, K. (1998). 'The Single European Market and the location strategy

of foreign car multinationals', Discussion Paper No. 249, Department of Economics, University of Reading.
Aristotelous, K. and S. Fountas (1996). 'An empirical analysis of inward foreign direct investment flows in the ECU with emphasis on the market enlargement hypothesis', *Journal of Common Market Studies*, pp. 571–83.
Armington, P. (1969). 'A theory of demand for products distinguished by place of production', *International Monetary Fund Staff Papers*, pp. 159–78.
Armstrong, H. (1995). 'Convergence among regions of the European Union, 1950–1990', *Papers in Regional Science*, pp. 143–52.
Armstrong, H. (1996). 'European Union Regional Policy: sleepwalking to a crisis', *International Regional Science Review*, pp. 193–209.
Armstrong, H. and R. de Kervenoael (1997). 'Regional economic change in the European Union', in *The Coherence of EU Regional Policy* (eds J. Bachtler and I. Turok). London: Jessica Kingsley, pp. 29–47.
Arthur, B. (1989). 'Competing technologies, increasing returns, and lock-in by historical events', *Economic Journal*, pp. 116–31.
Arthur, B. (1990a). 'Positive feedbacks in the economy', *Scientific American*, February, pp. 92–9.
Arthur, B. (1990b). 'Silicon Valley locational clusters: when do increasing returns imply monopoly', *Mathematical Social Sciences*, pp. 235–51.
Arthur, B. (1994a). 'Industrial location patterns and the importance of history', in *Increasing Returns and Path Dependence in the Economy* (ed. B. Arthur). Michigan: University of Michigan Press, pp. 49–67.
Arthur, B. (1994b). 'Urban systems and historical path dependence', in *Increasing Returns and Path Dependence in the Economy* (ed. B. Arthur). Michigan: Michigan University Press, pp. 99–110.
Arthur, W.B. (2002). 'How growth builds upon growth in high-technology', *Annual Sir Charles Carter Lecture*. Belfast: Northern Ireland Economic Council.
Atkin, M. (1993). *Snouts in the Trough*. Cambridge: Woodhead.
Audretsch, D. (1989). *The Market and the State*. New York: New York University Press.
Audretsch, D. (1993). 'Industrial policy and international competitiveness', in *Industrial Policy in the European Community* (ed. P. Nicolaides). Dordrecht: Martinus Nijhoff, pp. 67–105.
Audretsch, D. (1998). 'Agglomeration and the location of innovative activity', *Oxford Review of Economic Policy*, pp. 18–29.
Audretsch, D. and M. Feldman (1995). 'Innovative clusters and the industry life cycle', CEPR Discussion Paper No. 1161, Centre for Economic Policy Research, London.

Audretsch, D. and M. Feldman (1996). 'R&D spillovers and the geography of innovation and production', *American Economic Review*, pp. 630–40.

Auyang, S. (1998). *Foundations of Complex-system Theories in Economics, Evolutionary Biology and Statistical Physics*. Cambridge: Cambridge University Press.

Bachtler, J. (1995). 'Policy agenda for the decade', in *An Enlarged Europe: Regions in Competition?* (eds S. Hardy, M. Hart, L. Albrechts and A. Katos). London: Jessica Kingsley, pp. 313–24.

Bachtler, J. and R. Michie (1993). 'The restructuring of regional policy in the European Community', *Regional Studies*, pp. 719–25.

Bachtler, J. and R. Michie (1995). 'A new era in EU regional policy evaluation? The apprasal of the structural funds', *Regional Studies*, pp. 745–51.

Bachtler, J. and I. Turok (1997). *The Coherence of EU Regional Policy*. London: Jessica Kingsley.

Badaracco, J. and D. Yoffie (1983). 'Industrial policy: it can't happen here', *Harvard Business Review*, November–December, pp. 97–105.

Balassa, B. and L. Bauwens (1988). 'The determinants of intra-European trade in manufactured goods', *European Economic Review*, pp. 1421–37.

Baldwin, R. (1989). 'The growth effects of 1992', *Economic Policy*, pp. 248–70.

Baldwin, R. (1995a). 'A domino theory of regionalism' in *Expanding Membership of the European Union* (eds R. Baldwin, P. Haaparanta and J. Kiander). Cambridge: Cambridge University Press, pp. 25–48.

Baldwin, R. (1995b). 'The eastern enlargement of the European Union', *European Economic Review*, pp. 474–81.

Baldwin, R. (1997). 'Review of theoretical developments on regional integration', in *Regional Integration and Trade Liberalization in SubSaharan Africa* (eds A. Oyejide, I. Elbadawi and P. Collier). Basingstoke: Macmillan, pp. 24–88.

Baldwin, R. and A. Venables (1995). 'Regional economic integration', in *Handbook of International Economics* (eds G. Grossman and K. Rogoff). Amsterdam: Elsevier, pp. 1597–646.

Baldwin, R. and C. Wyplosz (2003). *The Economics of European Integration*. London: McGraw-Hill.

Baptista, R. and P. Swann (1998). 'Do firms in clusters innovate more?', *Research Policy*, pp. 525–40.

Barnes P. and I. Barnes (1999). *Environmental Policy in the European Union*. Cheltenham, UK and Northampton, MA: Edward Elgar.

Barro, R. and X. Sala-i-Martin (1991). 'Convergence across states and regions', *Brookings Papers on Economic Activity*, pp. 107–82.

Bartik, T. (1991). *Who Benefits from State and Local Economic Development Policies?* Kalamazoo, MI: Upjohn Institute.

Bauer, P. (1998). 'Eastward enlargement – benefits and costs of EU entry for the transition countries', *Intereconomics*, January/February, pp. 11–19.

Bayliss, B. and A. El-Agraa (1990). 'Competition and industrial policies with emphasis on competition policy', in *Economies of the European Community* (ed. A. El-Agraa). New York: St. Martin's Press, pp. 137–55.

Beaudry, C., S. Breschi and P. Swann (2002). 'Clusters, innovation and growth', in *Multinational Firms* (eds J. Dunning and J. Mucchielli). London: Routledge, pp. 190–213.

Beckmann, M. (1999). *Lectures on Location Theory*. Berlin: Springer.

Begg, I. and D. Mayes (1994). 'Peripherality and Northern Ireland', *National Institute Economic Review*, pp. 90–100.

Bekar, C. and R. Lipsey (2001). 'Clusters and economic policy', Simon Fraser University, Vancouver, mimeo.

Belderbos, R. (1997). 'Antidumping and tariff jumping: Japanese firms' DFI in the European Union and the United States', *Weltwirtschaftliches Archiv*, pp. 419–57.

Bernstein, J. and D. Weinstein (2002). 'Do endowments predict the location of production? Evidence from national and international data', *Journal of International Economics*, pp. 55–76.

Bhagwati, J., D. Greenaway and A. Panagariya (1998). 'Trading preferentially: theory and policy', *Economic Journal*, pp. 1128–48.

Bhagwati, J. and E. Tironi (1980). 'Tariff change, foreign capital and immiserization', *Journal of Development Economics*, pp. 71–83.

Bianchi, P. (1995). 'Small and medium-sized enterprises in the European perspective', *International Journal of Technology Management* (Special Publication), pp. 119–30.

Bird, R. (1972). 'The need for regional policy in a common market', in *International Economic Integration* (ed. P. Robson). Harmondsworth: Penguin Books, pp. 257–77.

Blackhurst, R. and D. Henderson (1993). 'Regional integration arrangements, world integration and GATT', in *Regional Integration and the Global Trading System* (eds K. Anderson and R. Blackhurst). New York: Harvester Wheatsheaf, pp. 408–35.

Blais, A. (1986). 'Industrial policy in advanced capitalist democracies', in *Industrial Policy* (ed. A. Blais). Toronto: University of Toronto Press, pp. 1–53.

Blomström, M. and A. Kokko (1997). 'Regional integration and foreign direct investment', Policy Research Working Paper No. 1750, World Bank, Washington, DC.

Blomström, M. and A. Kokko (1998). 'Multinational corporations and spillovers', *Journal of Economic Surveys*, pp. 247–77.

Blomström, M. and A. Kokko (2003). 'The economics of foreign direct investment incentives', Stockholm School of Economics Working Paper No. 168, Stockholm.

Blonigen, B. (1997). 'Firm-specific assets and the link between exchange rates and foreign direct investment', *American Economic Review*, pp. 447–65.

Boldrin, M. and F. Canova (2001). 'Inequality and convergence in Europe's regions: reconsidering European regional policies', *Economic Policy*, pp. 207–53.

Bordo, M. and L. Jonung (1999). 'The future of the EMU: what does the history of monetary unions tell us?, NBER Working Paper, No. 7365, National Bureau of Economic Research, Cambridge, MA.

Borrell, B. (1994). 'EU bananarama III', Policy Research Working Paper 1386, World Bank, Washington, DC.

Borrus, M. and J. Zysman (1997). 'Wintelism and the changing terms of global competition: prototype of the future?', BRIE Working Paper No. 96B, University of California, Berkeley.

Boschma, R. and J. Lambooy (1999a). 'Evolutionary economics and economic geography', *Evolutionary Economics*, pp. 411–29.

Boschma, R. and J. Lambooy (1999b). 'The prospects of an adjustment policy based on collective learning in old industrial regions', *GeoJournal*, pp. 391–9.

Bottazzi, L. and G. Peri (2002). 'Innovation and spillovers in regions: evidence from European patent data', CEPR Working Paper, No. 215, Centre for Economic Policy Research, London.

Brakman, S., H. Garretsen and M. Schramm (2002). 'The strategic bombing of German cities during World War II and its impact on city growth', CESifo Working Paper No. 808.

Brander, J. (1987). 'Shaping comparative advantage: trade policy, industrial policy and economic performance', in *Shaping Comparative Advantage* (eds R. Lipsey and W. Dobson). Toronto: C.D. Howe Institute, pp. 1–55.

Brander, J. (1995). 'Strategic trade policy', in *Handbook of International Economics* (eds G. Grossman and K. Rogoff). Amsterdam: Elsevier, pp. 1395–455.

Brander, J. and B. Spencer (1985). 'Export subsidies and international market share rivalry', *Journal of International Economics*, pp. 83–100.

Braunerhjelm, P. and K. Ekholm (eds) (1998). *The Geography of Multinational Firms*. Boston, MA: Kluwer.

Braunerhjelm, P., R. Faini, V. Norman, F. Ruane and P. Seabright (2000). *Integration and the Regions of Europe: How the Right Policies Can Prevent Polarization*. London: CEPR.

Brülhart, M. (1998a). 'Economic geography, industry location and trade: the evidence', *World Economy*, pp. 775–801.
Brülhart, M. (1998b). 'Trading places: industrial specialization in the European Union', *Journal of Common Market Studies*, pp. 319–46.
Brülhart, M. and R. Elliott (1998). 'Adjustment to the European single market: inferences from intra-industry trade patterns', *Journal of Economic Studies*, pp. 225–47.
Brülhart, M. and R. Elliott (1999). 'A survey of intra-industry trade in the European Union', in *Intra-Industry Trade and Adjustment: The European Experience* (eds M. Brülhart and R. Hine). Basingstoke: Macmillan, pp. 98–117.
Brülhart, M. and R. Hine (eds) (1999). *Intra-Industry Trade and Adjustment: The European Experience*. Basingstoke: Macmillan.
Brülhart, M. and J. Torstensson (1996). 'Regional integration, scale economies and industry location in the European Union', CEPR Discussion Paper No. 1435, Centre for Economic Policy Research, London.
Buigues, P. and A. Jacquemin (1992). 'Foreign direct investment and exports in the Common Market', paper presented at the Japanese Direct Investment in a Unifying Europe, conference held at INSEAD, Fontainebleau, 26–27 June 1992, mimeo.
Buigues, P. and A. Jacquemin (1994). 'Foreign direct investment and exports to the European Community', in *Does Ownership Matter* (eds M. Mason and D. Eucarnation). Oxford: Clarendon Press, pp. 163–97.
Buigues, P. and A. Sapir (1993). 'Market services and European integration: issues and challenges', *European Economy Social Europe*, No. 3, pp. ix–xx.
Bumbacher, U. (1995). 'The Swiss watch industry', in *Studies in Swiss Competitive Advantage* (eds M. Enright and R. Weder). Bern: Peter Lang, pp. 113–51.
Cairncross, F. (2001). *The Death of Distance 2.0*. London: Texere.
Canova, F. and A. Marcet (1995). 'The poor stay poor: non-convergence across countries and regions', CEPR Discussion Paper No. 1265, Centre for Economic Policy Research, London.
Canzoneri, M. and C. Rogers (1990). 'Is the European Community an optimal currency area? Optimal taxation versus the cost of multiple currencies', *American Economic Review*, pp. 419–33.
Carlén, B. (1994). 'Road transport', EFTA Occasional Paper No. 49, Geneva, pp. 81–111.
Carliner, G. (1988). 'Industrial policies for emerging industries', in *Strategic Trade Policy and the New International Economics* (ed. P. Krugman). Cambridge, MA: MIT Press, pp. 147–68.
Carlton, D. (1983). 'The location and employment choices of new firms: an

econometric model with discrete and continuous endogenous variables', *Review of Economics and Statistics*, pp. 440–49.

Carrington, A. (2003). 'A divided Europe? Regional convergence and neighbourhood spillover effects', *Kyklos*, pp. 381–94.

Casella, A. (1996). 'Large countries, small countries and the enlargement of trade blocs', *European Economic Review*, pp. 389–415.

Castells, M. and P. Hall (1994). *Technopols of the World*. London: Routledge.

Caves, R. (1996). *Multinational Enterprise and Economic Analysis*. Cambridge: Cambridge University Press.

Cecchini, P. (1988). *The European Challenge 1992 – The Benefits of a Single Market*. Aldershot: Wildwood House.

CEPR (1992). *Is Bigger Better? The Economics of EC Enlargement*. London: Centre for Economic Policy Research.

CEPR (1994). *The Location of Economic Activity: New Theories and Evidence*. London: Centre for Economic Policy Research.

Chakrabarti, R. and B. Scholnick (2002). 'Exchange rate expectations and foreign direct investment flows', *Weltwirtschaftliches Archiv*, pp. 1–21.

Chandler, A., P. Hagström and Ö. Sölvell (eds) (1998). *The Dynamic Firm*. Oxford: Oxford University Press.

Chang, H. (1994). *The Political Economy of Industrial Policy*. London: Macmillan.

Christaller, W. (1933). *Die Zentralen Orte in Süddeutschland*, Jena: Gustav Fischer (translated from German by C. Baskin, *Central Places in Southern Germany* (1966), Englewood Cliff, NJ: Prentice-Hall).

Cini, M. and L. McGowan (1998). *Competition Policy in the European Union*. Basingstoke: Macmillan.

Clark, G., M. Feldman and M. Gertler (eds) (2000). *The Oxford Handbook of Economic Geography*. Oxford: Oxford University Press.

Clark, S. (2000). 'Tax incentives for foreign direct investment: empirical evidence on effects and alternative policy options', *Canadian Tax Journal*, pp. 1139–80.

Clausing, K. (2001). 'Trade creation and trade diversion in the Canada–United States Free Trade Agreement', *Canadian Journal of Economics*, pp. 677–96.

Clegg, J. and S. Scott-Green (1999). 'The determinants of new FDI capital flows into the EC: a statistical comparison of the USA and Japan', *Journal of Common Market Studies*, pp. 597–616.

Cline, W. (1995). 'Evaluating the Uruguay Round', *World Economy*, pp. 1–23.

Cnossen, S. (1986). 'Tax harmonization in the European Community', *Bulletin for International Fiscal Documentation*, pp. 545–63.

Cnossen, S. (1990). 'The case for tax diversity in the European Community', *European Economic Review*, pp. 471–9.
Cnossen, S. (1995). 'Reforming and coordinating company taxes in the European Union', paper presented at the conference Changing Role of the Public Sector: Transition in the 1990s, Lisbon, 21–24 August 1995.
Cnossen, S. (2001). 'Tax policy in the European Union: a review of issues and options', *FinanzArchiv*, pp. 466–558.
Cobham, D. (1989). 'Strategies for monetary integration revisited', *Journal of Common Market Studies*, pp. 203–18.
Cockfield, A. (1994). *The European Union: Creating the Single Market*. London: Wiley.
Coffey, P. (1982). *The Common Market and Its International Economic Policies*. Amsterdam: Europa Institute.
Commission of the European Communities (1992). *The Future Development of the Common Transport Policy*. Brussels: European Union.
Commission of the European Communities (2002). Communication from the Commission to the Council, the European Parliament, the European Economic and Social Committee and the Committee of the Regions: Joint Report by the Commission and the Council on Adequate and Sustainable Pensions. Brussels, 17 December, COM(2002) 737 final.
Commission of the European Economic Community (1961). *Memorandum on the General Lines of the Common Transport Policy* (Schaus Memorandum). Brussels: European Economic Community.
Cooper, C. and B. Massel (1965). 'A new look at customs union theory', *Economic Journal*, pp. 742–7.
Corden, W. (1972). *Monetary Integration*. Princeton, NJ: Essays in International Finance, Princeton University.
Corden, W. (1984). 'The normative theory of international trade', in *Handbook of International Economics* (eds R. Jones and P. Kenen). Amsterdam: North-Holland, pp. 63–130.
Cosgrove, C. (1994). 'Has the Lomé Convention failed ACP trade?', *Journal of International Affairs*, pp. 223–49.
Cosgrove-Sacks, C. (ed.) (1999). *The European Union and Developing Countries*. Basingstoke: Macmillan.
Cossentino, F., F. Pyke and W. Sengenberger (eds) (1996). *Local and Regional Response to Global Pressure: The Case of Italy and Industrial Districts*. Geneva: International Labour Organisation.
Courchene, T. (1987). *Social Policy in the 1990s, Agenda for Reform*. Toronto: C.D. Howe Institute.
Crafts, N. and A. Venables (2001). 'Globalization in history: a geographical perspective', Centre for Economic Performance, London School of Economics.

Crozet, M., T. Mayer and J. Mucchielli (2004). 'How do firms agglomerate? A study of FDI in France', *Regional Science and Urban Economics*, pp. 27–54.
Culem, C. (1988). 'The location determinants of direct investments among industrialized countries', *European Economic Review*, pp. 885–904.
Curzon Price, V. (1981). *Industrial Policies in the European Community*. London: Macmillan.
Curzon Price, V. (1987). *Free Trade Areas? The European Experience*. Toronto: C.D. Howe Institute.
Curzon Price, V. (1988). 'The European Free Trade Association', in *International Economic Integration* (ed. A. El-Agraa). London: Macmillan, pp. 96–127.
Curzon Price, V. (1990). 'Competition and industrial policies with emphasis on industrial policy', in *Economics of the European Community* (ed. A. El-Agraa). New York: St. Martin's Press, pp. 156–86.
Curzon Price, V. (1991). 'The threat of, "Fortress Europe", from the development of social and industrial policies at European level', *Aussenwirtschaft*, pp. 119–38.
Curzon Price, V. (1993). 'EEC's strategic trade-cum-industrial policy: a public choice analysis', in *National Constitutions and International Economic Law* (eds M. Hilf and E. Petersmann). Deventer: Kluwer, pp. 391–405.
Curzon Price, V. (1994). 'The role of regional trade and investment agreements', paper presented at the conference 'Policies dealing with the EU–LDC relations in view of the transition in central and eastern European countries', The Netherlands Economic Institute, Rotterdam, 16–17 May.
Curzon Price, V. (1996a). 'Residual obstacles to trade in the Single European Market', *Euryopa*, Institut européen de l'Université de Genève.
Curzon Price, V. (1996b). 'The role of regional trade and investment agreements', in *Transition in Central and Eastern Europe* (eds A. Kuyvenhoven et al.). Dordrecht: Kluwer, pp. 69–88.
Curzon Price, V. (1997). 'The European Free Trade Association', in *Economic Integration Worldwide* (ed. A. El-Agraa). London: Macmillan, pp. 175–202.
Curzon Price, V. (2002). 'Everything but arms', Institute of European Studies, University of Geneva, mimeo.
d'Arge, R. (1969). 'Note on customs unions and direct foreign investment', *Economic Journal*, pp. 324–33.
d'Arge, R. (1971a). 'Customs unions and direct foreign investment', *Economic Journal*, pp. 352–5.

d'Arge, R. (1971b). 'A Reply', *Economic Journal*, pp. 357–9.

Davenport, M. (1995). 'Fostering integration of countries in transition in central and Eastern Europe in the world economy and the implications for the developing countries', Geneva: UNCTAD / ITD 7, 31 October.

David, P. (1984). 'High technology centers and the economics of locational tournaments', Stanford University, mimeo.

Davies, R. and D. Weinstein (2002). 'Bones, bombs and break points: the geography of economic activity', *American Economic Review*, pp. 1269–89.

Davies, R. and D. Weinstein (2003). 'Market access, economic geography and comparative advantage: an empirical test', *Journal of International Economics*, pp. 1–23.

de Ghellinck, E. (1988). 'European industrial policy against the background of the Single European Act', in *Main Economic Policy Areas of the EEC – towards 1992* (ed. P. Coffey). Dordrecht: Kluwer, pp. 133–56.

de Grauwe, P. (1975). 'Conditions for monetary integration – a geometric interpretation', *Weltwirtschaftliches Archiv*, pp. 634–46.

de Grauwe, P. (1991). 'The 1992 European integration program and regional development policies', in *Trade Theory and Economic Reform : North, South and East* (eds J. de Melo and A. Sapir). Cambridge, MA: Basil Blackwell, pp. 142–53.

de Grauwe, P. (1994). 'Towards EMU without the EMS', *Economic Policy*, pp. 149–85.

de Grauwe, P. (1995). 'The Economics of convergence towards monetary union in Europe', CEPR Discussion Paper No. 1213, Centre for Economic Policy Research, London.

de Grauwe, P. (2002). 'The challenge of the enlargement of the Euroland', Paper presented at the conference 'EU Enlargement: Endgame Economic Issues', Jean Monnet European Centre of Excellence, University of Genoa, 15 November.

de Grauwe, P. (2003). *Economics of Monetary Union*. Oxford: Oxford University Press.

de Grauwe, P. and M. Sénégas (2003). 'Monetary policy in EMU when the transmission is asymmetric and uncertain', CESinfo Working Paper, No. 891.

de la Fuente, A. and X. Vives (1995). 'Regional policy and Spain: Infrastructure and education as instruments of regional policy', *Economic Policy*, April, pp. 13–51.

de Melo, J., F. Miguet and T. Müller (2002). 'The political economy of migration and EU enlargement: lessons from Switzerland', University of Geneva, mimeo.

Defraigne, P. (1984). 'Towards concerted industrial policies in the European

Community', in *European Industry: Public Policy and Corporate Strategy* (ed. A. Jacquemin). Oxford: Clarendon Press, pp. 368–77.

Dell'Aringa, C. and F. Neri (1989). 'Illegal immigrants and the informal economy in Italy', in *European Factor Mobility* (eds I. Gordon and A. Thirlwall). New York: St. Martin's Press, pp. 133–47.

Delors, J. (1989). *Report on Economic and Monetary Union in the European Community*. Brussels: European Community.

Demopoulos, G. and N. Yannacopoulos (1999). 'Conditions for optimality of a currency area', *Open Economies Review*, pp. 289–303.

Demopoulos, G. and N. Yannacopoulos (2001). 'Monetary unions, adjustment mechanisms and risk sharing: can market forces replace fiscal policy in the European Union?, Discussion Paper No. 135, Athens University of Economics and Business.

Dent, C. (1997). *The European Economy*. London: Routledge.

Dertouzos, M., R. Lester and R. Solow (1990). *Made in America*. New York: Harper Perennial.

Deutscher Bundestag (1999). *Jahresbericht 1999 der Bundesregierung zun Stand der Deutschen Einheit*, Drucksache 14/1825, 10 October.

Dicken, P., M. Forsgren and A. Malmberg (1995). 'The local embeddedness of transnational corporations' in *Globalization, Institutions and Regional Development in Europe* (eds A. Amin and N. Thrift). Oxford: Oxford University Press, pp. 23–45.

Dickerson, A., H. Gibson and E. Tsakalotos (1997). 'The impact of acquisitions on company performance: evidence from a large panel of UK firms', Oxford Economic Papers, pp. 344–61.

Donges, J. (1980). 'Industrial policies in West Germany's not so market-oriented economy', *The World Economy*, pp. 185–204.

Dosi, G. (1988). 'Sources, procedures and microeconomic effects of innovation', *Journal of Economic Literature*, pp. 1120–71.

Dosi, G. (1997). 'Opportunities, incentives and collective patterns of technological change', *Economic Journal*, pp. 1530–47.

Dosi, G., K. Pavitt and L. Soete (1990). *The Economics of Technical Change and International Trade*. New York: Harvester Wheatsheaf.

Dowd, K. and D. Greenaway (1993a). 'Currency competition, network externalities and switching costs: towards an alternative view of optimum currency areas', *Economic Journal*, pp. 1180–89.

Dowd, K. and D. Greenaway (1993b). 'A single currency for Europe?', *Greek Economic Review*, pp. 227–44.

Drabek, Z. and D. Greenaway (1984). 'Economic integration and intra-industry trade: the EEC and CMEA compared', *Kyklos*, pp. 444–69.

Dunning, J. (1988). *Explaining International Production*. London: Unwin Hyman.

Dunning, J. (ed.) (1993). *The Theory of Transnational Corporations (The United Nations Library on Transnational Corporations)*. London: Routledge.
Dunning, J. (1994a). 'MNE activity: comparing the NAFTA and the European Community', in *Multinationals in North America* (ed. L. Eden). Calgary: University of Calgary Press, pp. 277–308.
Dunning, J. (1994b). 'Globalization: the challenge for national economic regimes', Discussion Paper No. 186, Department of Economics, University of Reading.
Dunning, J. (1995). 'Think again Professor Krugman: competitiveness does matter', *International Executive*, pp. 313–24.
Dunning, J. (1997). 'The European Internal Market Programme and inbound foreign direct investment', *Journal of Common Market Studies*, (Part I) pp. 1–30, (Part II) pp. 189–223.
Dunning, J. (1998a). 'Location and the multinational enterprise: a neglected factor?', *Journal of International Business Studies*, pp. 45–66.
Dunning, J. (1998b), 'Globalization, technological change and the spatial organization of economic activity', in *The Dynamic Firm* (eds A. Chandler et al.). Oxford: Oxford University Press, pp. 289–314.
Dunning, J. (1998c). 'Regions, globalization and the knowledge economy: the issues stated', Rutgers University, mimeo.
Dunning, J. (1999). 'The eclectic paradigm as an envelope for economic and business theories of MNE activity', Discussion Paper No. 263, Department of Economics, University of Reading.
Dunning, J. and P. Robson (1987). 'Multinational corporate integration and regional economic integration', *Journal of Common Market Studies*, pp. 103–24.
Easson, A. (2001). 'Tax incentives for foreign direct investment', *International Bureau of Fiscal Documentation Bulletin*, (Part I) pp. 266–74; (Part II) pp. 365–75.
Eaton, C. and R. Lipsey (1975). 'The principle of minimum differentiation reconsidered: some new developments in the theory of spatial competition', *Review of Economic Studies*, pp. 27–49.
Eaton, C. and R. Lipsey (1976). 'The non-uniqueness of equilibrium in the Löschian location model', *American Economic Review*, pp. 77–93.
Eaton, C. and R. Lipsey (1979). 'Comparison shopping and the clustering of homogeneous firms', *Journal of Regional Science*, pp. 421–35.
Eaton, C. and R. Lipsey (1982). 'An economic theory of central places', *Economic Journal*, pp. 56–72.
Eaton, C. and R. Lipsey (1997). *On the Foundations of Monopolistic Competition and Economic Geography*. Cheltenham, UK and Lyme, USA: Edward Elgar.

Eaton, J., E. Gutierrez and S. Kortum (1998). 'European technology policy', *Economic Policy*, pp. 405–38.
Economic Commission for Europe (1949). 'European steel trends in the setting of the world market'. United Nations: Geneva, [E/]ECE/112 - [E/]ECE/ STEEL/42.
Economic Commission for Europe (1994). *Economic Survey of Europe in 1993–1994*. New York: United Nations.
Economic Commission for Europe (1996). *Economic Bulletin for Europe*. New York: United Nations.
Economic Commission for Europe (1997). *Economic Survey of Europe in 1996–1997*. New York: United Nations.
Economic Commission for Europe (1998). *Economic Survey of Europe 1998 No. 3*. New York: United Nations.
Economic Commission for Europe (2000). *Economic Survey of Europe 2000 No. 1*. New York: United Nations.
Economic Commission for Europe (2002). *Economic Survey of Europe 2002 No. 1*. New York: United Nations.
Economic Commission for Europe (2003). *Economic Survey of Europe 2003. No. 1*. New York: United Nations.
Economic Policy Committee (2000). Progress report to the Ecofin Council on the Impact of Ageing Populations on Public Pension Systems. Brussels, 6 November, EPC/ECFIN/518/00-EN-Rev.1.
EFTA (1993). *Pattern of Production and Trade in the New Europe*. Geneva: EFTA.
Eichengreen, B. (1993a). 'European monetary unification', *Journal of Economic Literature*, pp. 1321–57.
Eichengreen, B. (1993b). 'Labour markets and European monetary unification', in *Policy Issues in the Operation of Currency Unions* (eds P. Mason and M. Taylor). Cambridge: Cambridge University Press, pp. 130–62.
El-Agraa, A. (1997). 'UK competitiveness policy vs. Japanese industrial policy', *Economic Journal*, pp. 1504–17.
El-Agraa, A.M. (ed) (1998). *The European Union*. London: Prentice-Hall.
Ellison, G. and E. Glaeser (1997). 'Geographic concentration in U.S. manufacturing industries: a dartboard approach', *Journal of Political Economy*, pp. 889–927.
Ellison, G. and E. Glaeser (1999). 'The geographic concentration of industry: does natural advantage explain agglomeration?', *American Economic Review* (Papers and Proceedings), pp. 311–16.
Emerson, M., M. Auejan, M. Catinat, P. Goybet and A. Jacquemin (1988). 'The economics of 1992', *European Economy*, March.
Enright, M. (1998). 'Regional clusters and firm strategy', in *The Dynamic*

Firm (eds A. Chandler et al.). Oxford: Oxford University Press, pp. 315–42.
Enright, M. and R. Weder (eds) (1995). *Studies in Swiss Competitive Advantage*. Bern: Peter Lang.
Ethier, W. (1998). 'The new regionalism', *Economic Journal*, pp. 1149–61.
Euro Papers (2001). 'The economic impact of enlargement', Enlargement Papers No. 4.
European Commission (1997a). *Agenda 2000 for a Stronger and Wider Union*. Luxembourg: European Communities.
European Commission (1997b). *The Impact and Effectiveness of the Single Market*. Luxembourg: EU.
European Commission (1997c). *Trade Creation and Trade Diversion*. London: Kogan Page.
European Commission (1997d). *Regional Growth and Convergence*. London: Kogan Page.
European Commission (1998). *Foreign Direct Investment*. London: Kogan Page.
European Commission (2001). *European Transport Policy for 2010: Time to Decide*. Luxembourg: European Communities.
European Commission (2002a). *Towards the Enlarged Union: Strategy Paper and Report of the European Commission on the Progress towards Accession by Each of the Candidate Countries*. Brussels, 9 October, COM(2002) 700 final.
European Commission (2002b). *Report on United States Barriers to Trade and Investment*. Brussels: European Commission.
European Commission (2003). *European Union Competition Policy: XXXIInd Report – 2002*. Luxembourg: European Communities.
European Communities (1973). *Report on the Regional Problems of the Enlarged Community*. Brussels: European Communities.
European Communities (1985). *Completing the Internal Market* (White Paper Cockfield Report). Brussels: European Communities.
European Communities (1991). *XXth Report on Competition Policy*. Brussels: European Communities.
European Communities (1993). *The Community Budget: The Facts in Figures*. Luxembourg: European Communities.
European Economy (1989). *International Trade of the European Community*. No. 39.
European Economy (1990a). *One Market? One Money*. No. 44.
European Economy (1990b). *Social Europe*. Special Edition.
European Economy (1991). *The Economies of EMU*. Special edition No. 1.
European Economy (1993). *The Economic and Financial Situation in Italy*, No. 1.

European Economy (1994a). *Competition and Integration; Community Merger Control Policy*. No. 57.
European Economy (1994b). *EC Agricultural Policy for the 21st Century*, No. 4.
European Economy (1996). *Economic Evaluation of the Internal Market*. No. 4.
European Economy (1997a). 'The CAP and enlargement', Reports and Studies No. 2.
European Economy (1997b). 'Towards a Common Agricultural and Rural Policy for Europe', Reports and Studies No. 5.
European Economy (1998). 'Getting environmental policy right', Reports and Studies No. 1.
European Economy (2003a). 'Economic forecasts for the candidate countries Spring 2003', Enlargement Papers No. 15.
European Economy (2003b). 'Key structural challenges in the acceding countries: The integration of the acceding countries into the Community's economic policy co-ordination processes', Occasional Papers No. 4.
European Economy (2003c). 'Main results of the April 2003 fiscal notifications presented by the candidate countries', Enlargement Papers No. 17.
European Economy (2003d). 'Structural features of economic integration in an enlarged Europe: patterns of catching-up and industrial specialisation', Economic Papers No. 181.
Feld, L. and G. Kirchgässner (2001). 'The impact of corporate and personal income taxes on the location of firms and on employment: some panel evidence from Swiss cantons', CESifo Working Paper No. 455.
Finger, J., K. Hall and D. Nelson (1982). 'The political economy of administered protection', *American Economic Review*, pp. 452–66.
Finger, J. and A. Yeats (1976). 'Effective protection by transportation costs and tariffs: a comparison of magnitudes', *Quarterly Journal of Economics*, pp. 169–76.
Finger, M. (1975). 'A new view of the product cycle theory', *Weltwirtschaftliches Archiv*, pp. 79–99.
Fisher, S., R. Sahay and C. Végh (1998). 'How far is eastern Europe from Brussels?', IMF Working Paper, WP/98/53, International Monetary Fund, Washington, DC.
Fleming, M. (1971). 'On exchange rate unification', *Economic Journal*, pp. 467–86.
Folkerts-Landau, D. and D. Mathieson (1989). *The European Monetary System in the Context of the Integration of European Financial Markets*. Washington, DC: International Monetary Fund.

Ford, S. and R. Strange (1999). 'Where do Japanese manufacturing firms invest within Europe and why?', *Transnational Corporations*, pp. 117–42.

Forslid, R., J. Haaland and H. Midelfart-Knarvik (2002). 'A U-shaped Europe? A simulation study of industrial location', *Journal of International Economics*, pp. 273–97.

Freeman, C. (1994). 'The economics of technical change', *Cambridge Journal of Economics*, pp. 463–514.

Frenkel, J. (1997). *Regional Trading Blocs*. Washington, DC: Institute for International Economics.

Frenkel, J. and A. Rose (1998). 'The endogeneity of the optimum currency area criteria', *Economic Journal*, pp. 1009–25.

Friedman, J., D. Gerlowski and J. Silberman (1992). 'What attracts foreign multinational corporations? Evidence from branch plant locations in the United States', *Journal of Regional Science*, pp. 403–18.

Fujita, M. and R. Ishii (1998). 'Global location behavior and organizational dynamics of Japanese electronics firms and their impact on regional economies', in *The Dynamic Firm* (eds A. Chandler et al.). Oxford: Oxford University Press, pp. 343–83.

Fujita, M., P. Krugman and A. Venables (1999). *The Spatial Economy*. Cambridge, MA: MIT Press.

Fujita, M. and T. Mori (1996). 'The role of ports in the making of major cities: self-agglomeration and the hub-effect', *Journal of Development Economics*, pp. 93–120.

Fujita, M. and J. Thisse (1996). 'Economics of agglomeration', *Journal of the Japanese and International Economies*, pp. 339–78.

Garofoli, G. (1991a). 'Industrial districts: structure and transformation', in *Endogenous Development and Southern Europe* (ed. G. Garofoli). Aldershot: Avebury, pp. 49–60.

Garofoli, G. (1991b). 'Endogenous development and southern Europe: an introduction', in *Endogenous Development and Southern Europe* (ed. G. Garofoli). Aldershot: Avebury, pp. 1–13.

Gavin, B. (2001). *The European Union and Globalisation*. Cheltenham, UK and Northampton, MA, USA: Edward Elgar.

Geroski, P. (1987). 'Brander's "shaping comparative advantage": some comments', in *Shaping Comparative Advantage* (eds R. Lipsey and W. Dobson). Toronto: C.D. Howe Institute, pp. 57–64.

Geroski, P. (1988). 'Competition and innovation', in Commission of the European Communities, *Studies on the Economics of Integration*. Brussels: European Community, pp. 339–88.

Geroski, P. (1989). 'European industrial policy and industrial policy in Europe', *Oxford Review of Economic Policy*, pp. 20–36.

Geroski, P. and A. Jacquemin (1985). 'Industrial change, barriers to mobility, and European industrial policy', *Economic Policy*, pp. 170–218.

Gittelman, M., E. Graham and H. Fukukawa (1992). 'Affiliates of Japanese firms in the European Community: performance and structure', paper presented at the conference on Japanese Direct Investment in a Unifying Europe, at INSEAD, Fontainebleau, 26–27 June, mimeo.

Gleiser, H., A. Jacquemin and J. Petit (1980). 'Exports in an imperfect competition framework: an analysis of 1,446 exporters', *Quarterly Journal of Economics*, pp. 507–24.

Goldberg, M. (1972). 'The determinants of U.S. direct investment in the E.E.C.: a comment', *American Economic Review*, pp. 692–9.

Gordon, I. and P. McCann (2000). 'Industrial clusters: complexes, agglomeration and/or social networks?', *Urban Studies*, pp. 513–32.

Görg, H. and D. Greenaway (2002). 'Much ado about nothing? Do domestic firms really benefit from foreign investment?', CEPR Discussion Paper No. 3485, Centre for Economic Policy Research, London.

Görg, H. and F. Ruane (1999). 'US investment in EU member countries: the internal market and sectoral specialization', *Journal of Common Market Studies*, pp. 333–48.

Görg, H. and E. Strobl (2001). 'Multinational companies and productivity spillovers: a meta analysis', *Economic Journal*, pp. F723–F739.

Grabher, G. (1993). 'The weakness of strong ties: the lock-in of regional development in the Ruhr area', in *The Embedded Firm* (ed. G. Grabher). London: Routledge, pp. 255–77.

Graham, E. (1978). 'Transatlantic investment by multinational firms: a rivalistic phenomenon?', *Journal of Post Keynesian Economics*, pp. 82–99.

Graham, E. and P. Krugman (1995). *Foreign Direct Investment in the United States*. Washington, DC: Institute for International Economics.

Greenaway, D. and C. Milner (1987). 'Intra-industry trade: current perspectives and unresolved issues', *Weltwirtschaftliches Archiv*, pp. 39–57.

Greenaway, D. and J. Torstensson (1997). 'Back to the future: taking stock on intra-industry trade', *Weltwirtschaftliches Archiv*, pp. 248–69.

Greenaway, D. and J. Torstensson (2000). 'Economic geography, comparative advantage and trade within industries: evidence from the OECD', *Journal of Economic Integration*, pp. 260–80.

Grilli, E. (1993). *The European Community and the Developing Countries*. Cambridge: Cambridge University Press.

Gros, D. (1989). 'Paradigms for the monetary union of Europe', *Journal of Common Market Studies*, pp. 219–30.

Grubel, H. (1970). 'The theory of optimum currency areas', *Canadian Journal of Economics*, pp. 318–24.

Grubel, H. (1984). *The International Monetary System*. Harmondsworth: Penguin Books.

Grubel, H. and P. Lloyd (1975). *Intra Industry Trade*. London: Macmillan.

Gual, J. (1995). 'The three common policies: an economic analysis', in *European Policies on Competition, Trade and Industry* (eds P. Buigues, A. Jacquemin and A. Sapir). Aldershot, UK and Brookfield, US: Edward Elgar, pp. 3–48.

Haberler, G. (1977). 'Survey of circumstances affecting the location of production and international trade as analysed in theoretical literature', in *The International Allocation of Economic Activity* (eds B. Ohlin, P. Hesselborn and P. Wijkman). London: Macmillan, pp. 1–24.

Hagedoorn, J. (1998). 'Atlantic strategic technology alliances', in *The Struggle for World Markets* (ed. G. Boyd). Cheltenham, UK and Lyme, USA: Edward Elgar, pp. 177–91.

Hagedoorn, J. and J. Schakenraad (1993). 'A comparison of private and subsidized R&D partnerships in the European information technology industry', *Journal of Common Market Studies*, pp. 373–90.

Hague, D. (1960). 'Report on the proceedings: summary record of the debate', in *Economic Consequences of the Size of Nations* (ed. E. Robinson). London: Macmillan, pp. 333–438.

Hamilton, B. and J. Whalley (1986). 'Border tax adjustment and US trade', *Journal of International Economics*, pp. 377–83.

Hanson, G. (1998). 'North American economic integration and industry location', *Oxford Review of Economic Policy*, pp. 30–44.

Harris, C. (1954). 'The market as a factor in the localization of industry in the United States', *Annals of the Association of American Geographers*, pp. 315–48.

Harris, R. (1985). *Trade, Industrial Policy and International Competition*. Toronto: University of Toronto Press.

Hartog, J. and A. Zorlu (2002). 'The effect of immigration on wages in three European countries', IZA Discussion Paper No. 642, Institute for the Study of Labor, Bonn.

Hay, D. (1993). 'The assessment: competition policy', *Oxford Review of Economic Policy*, pp. 1–26.

Hayek, F. (1978). *New Studies in Philosophy, Politics, Economics and the History of Ideas*. London: Routledge & Kegan Paul.

Heinemann, F. (2002). 'The political economy of eastern enlargement', *Rivista di Politica Economica*, pp. 359–83.

Henderson, J. (1974). 'The sizes and types of cities', *American Economic Review*, pp. 640–56.

Henderson, J., Z. Shalizi and A. Venables (2001). 'Geography and development', *Journal of Economic Geography*, pp. 81–106.

Herin, J. (1986). 'Rules of origin and differences between tariff levels in EFTA and in the EC', Occasional Paper No. 16, EFTA, Geneva.
Hermann-Pillath, C. (2000). 'Indeterminacy in international trade: methodological reflections on the impact of non-economic determinants on the direction of trade and absolute advantage', *Aussenwirtschaft*, pp. 251–89.
Herzog, H. and A. Schlottmann (eds) (1991). *Industry Location and Public Policy*. Knoxville, TN: University of Tennessee Press.
Hill, T. (1977). 'On goods and services', *Review of Income and Wealth*, pp. 315–38.
Hillman, D. and D. Gibbs (1998). *Century Makers*. London: Weidenfeld & Nicolson.
Himphrey, J. and H. Schmitz (1996). 'The triple C approach to local industrial policy', *World Development*, pp. 1859–77.
Hindley, B. (1991). 'Creating an integrated market for financial services', in *European Economic Integration* (eds G. Faulhaber and G. Tamburini). Boston, MA: Kluwer, pp. 263–88.
Holmes, T. (1998). 'The effects of state policies on the location of manufacturing: evidence from state borders', *Journal of Political Economy*, pp. 667–705.
Hotelling, H. (1929). 'Stability in competition', *Economic Journal*, pp. 41–57.
Hume, D. (1752). *Essays: Moral, Political and Literary*, 'Of the jealousy of trade' (Part II). http://www.angelfire.com/pa/sergeman/issues/foreign/jealousy.html.
Hummels, D. (1999). 'Have international transportation costs declined?', University of Chicago, Graduate School of Business, mimeo. http://www.mgmt.purdue.edu/faculty/hummelsd/research/decline/declined.pdf.
Hymer, S., (1976). *The International Operations of National Firms: A Study of Direct Foreign Investment*. Boston, MA: MIT Press.
Isard, W. (1954). 'Location theory and trade theory: short run analysis', *Quarterly Journal of Economics*, pp. 305–20.
Isard, W. (1956). *Location and Space-Economy*. Cambridge, MA: Technology Press of MIT and London: Chapman & Hall.
Isard, W. (1977). 'Location theory, agglomeration and the pattern of world trade', in *The International Allocation of Economic Activity* (eds B. Ohlin, P. Hesselborn and P. Wijkman). London: Macmillan, pp. 159–77.
Isard, W. (1996). *Commonalities in Art, Science and Religion: An Evolutionary Perspective*. Aldershot: Avebury.
Isard, W. and M. Peck (1954). 'Location theory and international and interregional trade theory', *Quarterly Journal of Economics*, pp. 97–114.

Jacquemin, A. (1984). *European Industry: Public Policy and Corporate Strategy*. Oxford: Clarendon Press.

Jacquemin, A. (1990a). 'Mergers and European policy', in *Merger and Competition Policy in the European Community* (ed. P. Admiraal). Oxford: Basil Blackwell, pp. 1–38.

Jacquemin, A. (1990b). 'Horizontal concentration and European merger policy', *European Economic Review*, pp. 539–50.

Jacquemin, A. (1991). 'Collusive behaviour, R&D and European competition policy', in *European Economic Integration* (eds G. Faulhaber and G. Tamburini). Boston, MA: Kluwer, pp. 201–35.

Jacquemin, A. (1996). 'Les enjeux de la competitivite européenne et la politique industrielle communautaire en matiére d'innovation', *Revue du Marché commun et de l'Union européenne*, March, pp. 175–81.

Jacquemin, A., P. Lloyd, P. Tharakan and J. Waelbroeck (1998). 'Competition policy in an international setting: the way ahead', *World Economy*, pp. 1179–83.

Jacquemin, A. and J. Marchipont (1992). 'De nouveaux enjeux pour la politique industrielle de la Communauté', *Revue d'économie politique*, pp. 69–97.

Jacquemin, A. and L. Pench (1997). *Europe Competing in the Global Economy*. Cheltenham, UK and Lyme, USA: Edward Elgar.

Jacquemin, A. and A. Sapir (1991). 'The internal and external opening-up of the Single Community Market: efficiency gains, adjustment costs and new Community instruments', *International Spectator*, pp. 29–48.

Jacquemin, A. and A. Sapir (1996). 'Is a European hard core credible? A statistical analysis', *Kyklos*, pp. 105–17.

Jacquemin, A. and D. Wright (1993). 'Corporate strategies and European challenges post-1992', *Journal of Common Market Studies*, pp. 525–37.

Jansen, M. (1975). *History of European Integration 1945–75*. Amsterdam: Europa Institute.

Jarillo, J. and J. Martínez (1991). 'The international expansion of Spanish firms: towards an integrative framework for international strategy', in *Corporate and Industry Strategies for Europe* (eds L. Mattsson and B. Stymne). Amsterdam: Elsevier, pp. 283–302.

Johnson, C. (1984). 'The idea of industrial policy', in *The Industrial Policy Debate* (ed. C. Johnson). San Francisco: Institute for Contemporary Studies, pp. 3–26.

Johnson, H. (1973). 'An economic theory of protectionism, tariff bargaining and the formation of customs unions', in *Economics of Integration* (ed. M. Krauss). London: George Allen & Unwin, pp. 64–103.

Johnson, H. (1977). 'Technology, technical progress and the international allocation of economic activity', in *The International Allocation of*

Economic Activity (eds B. Ohlin, P. Hesselborn and P. Wijkman). London: Macmillan, pp. 314–27.

Johnson, H. and M. Krauss (1973). 'Border taxes, border tax adjustment, comparative advantage and the balance of payments', in *Economics of Integration* (ed. M. Krauss). London: George Allen & Unwin, pp. 239–53.

Jovanović, M. (1992). *International Economic Integration*. London: Routledge.

Jovanović, M. (1995). 'Economic integration among developing countries and foreign direct investment', *Economia Internazionale*, pp. 209–43.

Jovanović, M. (1997a). *European Economic Integration: Limits and Prospects*. London: Routledge.

Jovanović, M. (1997b). 'Probing leviathan: the eastern enlargement of the European Union', *European Review*, pp. 353–70.

Jovanović, M. (1998a). *International Economic Integration: Limits and Prospects*. London: Routledge.

Jovanović, M. (ed.) (1998b). *International Economic Integration: Critical Perspectives on the World Economy – Theory and Measurement* (Volume I). London: Routledge.

Jovanović, M. (ed.) (1998c). *International Economic Integration: Critical Perspectives on the World Economy – Monetary, Fiscal and Factor Mobility Issues* (Volume II). London: Routledge.

Jovanović, M. (ed.) (1998d). *International Economic Integration: Critical Perspectives on the World Economy – General Issues* (Volume III). London: Routledge.

Jovanović, M. (ed.) (1998e). *International Economic Integration: Critical Perspectives on the World Economy – Integration Schemes* (Volume IV). London: Routledge.

Jovanović, M. (1998f). 'Does eastern enlargement mean the end of the European Union?', *International Relations*, pp. 23–39.

Jovanović, M. (1999). 'Where are the limits to the enlargement of the European Union?', *Journal of Economic Integration*, pp. 467–96.

Jovanović, M. (2000a). 'Eastern enlargement of the European Union: sour grapes or sweet lemon?', *Economia Internazionale*, pp. 507–36. http://papers.ssrn.com/ sol3/papers.cfm?abstract_id=261059.

Jovanović, M. (2000b). 'Economic integration and location of industries', in *Economic Interests and Cultural Determinants in European Integration* (ed. B. Schefold). Bolzano: European Academy, pp. 169–204.

Jovanović, M. (2001a). *Geography of Production and Economic Integration*. London: Routledge.

Jovanović, M. (2001b). 'Why eastern enlargement of the European Union won't be fast', in *Europe: What Kind of Integration? (Europa: Verso Quale Integrazione?)* (ed. G. Casale). Milan: Franco Angeli, pp. 140–67.

Jovanović, M. (2003a). 'Spatial location of firms and industries: an overview of theory', *Economia Internazionale*, pp. 23–81. http://papers.ssrn.com/sol3/ papers.cfm?abstract_id=451800.

Jovanović, M. (2003b). 'Local vs. global location of firms and industries', *Journal of Economic Integration*, pp. 60–104. http://papers.ssrn.com/sol3/papers.cfm? abstract_id=394760#Paper%20Download.

Jovanović, M. (2003c). 'Eastern enlargement of the EU: a topsy-turvy endgame or permanent disillusionment', in *The Economics of Enlargement* (ed. F. Praussello). Milan: Franco Angeli, pp. 39–73.

Karsenty, G. and S. Laird (1986). 'The generalized system of preferences: a quantitative assessment of the direct trade effects and of policy options'. UNCTAD Discussion Paper 18. Geneva: UNCTAD.

Kay, J. (1990). 'Tax policy: a survey', *Economic Journal*, pp. 18–75.

Kemp, M. and H. Wan (1976). 'An elementary proposal concerning the formation of customs unions', *Journal of International Economics*, pp. 95–7.

Kenen, P. (1969). 'Theory of optimum currency areas: an eclectic view', in *Monetary Problems of the International Economy* (eds R. Mundell and A. Swoboda). Chicago: Chicago University Press, pp. 41–60.

Keuschnigg, C. and W. Kohler (2000). 'Eastern enlargement of the EU: a dynamic general equilibrium perspective', in *Using Dynamic General Equilibrium Models for Policy Analysis* (eds G. Harrison, S. Hougard Jensen, L. Haagen Pedersen and T. Rutherford), Amsterdam: Elsevier, pp. 119–70.

Keynes, J. (1923). *A Tract on Monetary Reform*. London: Royal Economic Society.

Kim, S. (1995). 'Expansion of markets and the geographic distribution of economic activities: the trends in U.S. regional manufacturing structure, 1860–1987', *Quarterly Journal of Economics*, pp. 881–908.

Kimura, Y. (1996). 'Japanese direct investment in the peripheral regions of Europe: an overview', in *Japan and the European Periphery* (ed. J. Darby). Basingstoke: Macmillan, pp. 13–36.

Kissinger, H. (1957). *A World Restored: Metternich, Castlereagh and the Problems of Peace 1812–22*. Boston, MA: Houghton Mifflin.

Kleinknecht, A. and J. ter Wengel (1998). 'The myth of economic globalisation', *Cambridge Journal of Economics*, pp. 637–47.

Knickerbocker, F. (1973). *Oligopolistic Reaction and Multinational Enterprise*. Boston, MA: Harvard University Press.

Komiya, R. (1988). 'Introduction', in *Industrial Policy of Japan* (eds R. Komiya, M. Okuno and K. Suzumura). Tokyo: Academic Press, pp. 1–22.

Krätke, S. (1999). 'Regional integration or fragmentation? The German–Polish border region in a new Europe', *Regional Studies*, pp. 631–41.

Kravis, I. and R. Lipsey (1982). 'The location of overseas production and production for export by U.S. multinational firms', *Journal of International Economics*, pp. 201–23.

Krugman, P. (1979). 'Increasing returns, monopolistic competition and international trade', *Journal of International Economics*, pp. 469–79.

Krugman, P. (1980). 'Scale economies, product differentiation and the pattern of trade', *American Economic Review*, pp. 950–59.

Krugman, P. (1987). 'The narrow moving band, the Dutch disease, and the competitive consequences of Mrs. Thatcher', *Journal of Development Economics*, pp. 41–55.

Krugman, P. (1990a). *Rethinking International Trade*. Cambridge, MA: MIT Press.

Krugman, P. (1990b). 'Protectionism: try it, you'll like it', *International Economy*, June/July, pp. 35–9.

Krugman, P. (1991a). 'History versus expectations', *Quarterly Journal of Economics*, pp. 651–67.

Krugman, P. (1991b). 'Increasing returns and economic geography', *Journal of Political Economy*, pp. 483–9.

Krugman, P. (1992). *Geography and Trade*. Cambridge, MA: MIT Press.

Krugman, P. (1993a). 'On the number and location of cities', *European Economic Review*, pp. 293–8.

Krugman, P. (1993b). 'The current case for industrial policy', in *Protectionism and World Welfare* (ed. D. Salvatore). Cambridge: Cambridge University Press, pp. 160–79.

Krugman, P. (1993c). 'First nature, second nature, and metropolitan location', *Journal of Regional Science*, pp. 129–44.

Krugman, P. (1995a). 'A reply to Professor Dunning', *International Executive*, pp. 325–7.

Krugman, P. (1995b). 'The move toward free trade zones', in *International Economics and International Economic Policy: A Reader* (ed. P. King). New York: McGraw-Hill, pp. 163–82.

Krugman, P. (1996a). *Pop Internationalism*. Cambridge, MA: MIT Press.

Krugman, P. (1996b). 'What economists can learn from evolutionary theorists', a talk given to the European Association for Evolutionary Political Economy, November (http://web.mit.edu/krugman/www/).

Krugman, P. (1996c). 'The Adam Smith Address: what difference does globalization make', *Business Economics*, pp. 7–10.

Krugman, P. (1996d). 'Urban concentration: the role of increasing returns and transport costs', *International Regional Science Review*, pp. 5–30.

Krugman, P. (1997). 'What should trade negotiators negotiate about?', *Journal of Economic Literature*, pp. 113–20.

Krugman, P. (1998a). 'What's new about the new economic geography', *Oxford Review of Economic Policy*, pp. 7–17.

Krugman, P. (1998b). *The Accidental Theorist*. New York: Norton.
Krugman, P. (1998c). 'Space: the final frontier', *Journal of Economic Perspectives*, pp. 161–74.
Krugman, P. (1999). 'The role of geography in development', in *Annual World Bank Conference on Development Economics 1998* (eds B. Pleskovic and J. Stiglitz). Washington, DC: World Bank, pp. 89–107.
Krugman, P. (2000). 'Can America stay on top?', *Journal of Economic Perspectives*, pp. 169–75.
Krugman, P. (2003). *The Great Unraveling*. New York: Norton.
Krugman, P. and A. Venables (1990). 'Integration and the competitiveness of peripheral industry', in *Unity with Diversity in the European Economy: the Community's Southern Frontier* (eds C. Bliss and J. Braga de Macedo). Cambridge: Cambridge University Press, pp. 56–75.
Krugman, P. and A. Venables (1995). 'Globalization and the inequality of nations', *Quarterly Journal of Economics*, pp. 857–80.
Krugman, P. and A. Venables (1996). 'Integration, specialization, and adjustment', *European Economic Review*, pp. 959–67.
Lall, S. (1994). 'The east Asian miracle: does the bell toll for industrial strategy?', *World Development*, pp. 645–54.
Lambooy, J. (1997). 'Knowledge production, organisation and agglomeration economies', *GeoJournal*, pp. 293–300.
Lambooy, J. and R. Boschma (2001). 'Evolutionary economics and regional policy', *Annals of Regional Science*, pp. 113–31.
Lancaster, K. (1980). 'Intra-industry trade under perfect monopolistic competition', *Journal of International Economics*, pp. 151–75.
Leamer, E. (1984). *Sources of International Comparative Advantage*. Cambridge, MA: MIT Press.
Leamer, E. and J. Levinsohn (1995). 'International trade theory: the evidence', in *Handbook of International Economics* (eds G. Grossman and K. Rogoff). Amsterdam: Elsevier, pp. 1339–94.
Levin, R., A. Klevorick, R. Nelson and S. Winter (1987). 'Appropriating the returns from industrial research and development', *Brookings Papers on Economic Activity*, pp. 783–820.
Linder, S. (1961). *An Essay on Trade and Transformation*. Uppsala: Almquist & Wiksell.
Lipsey, R.E. (1999). 'The role of foreign direct investment in international capital flows', NBER Working Paper No. 7094, National Bureau of Economic Research, Cambridge, MA.
Lipsey, R.E. (2002). 'Home and host country effects of FDI', NBER Working Paper No. 9293, National Bureau of Economic Research, Cambridge, MA.

Lipsey, R.G. (1957). 'The theory of customs unions: trade diversion and welfare', *Economica*, pp. 40–46.
Lipsey, R.G. (1960). 'The theory of customs unions: a general survey', *Economic Journal*, pp. 496–513.
Lipsey, R.G. (1985). 'Canada and the United States: the economic dimension', in *Canada and the United States: Enduring Friendship, Persistent Stress* (eds C. Doran and J. Stigler). New York: Prentice-Hall, pp. 69–108.
Lipsey, R.G. (1987a). 'Models matter when discussing competitiveness: a technical note', in *Shaping Comparative Advantage* (eds R. Lipsey and W. Dobson). Toronto: C.D. Howe Institute, pp. 155–66.
Lipsey, R.G. (1987b). 'Report on the workshop', in *Shaping Comparative Advantage* (eds R.G. Lipsey and W. Dobson). Toronto: C.D. Howe Institute, pp. 109–53.
Lipsey, R.G. (1991). 'The case for trilateralism', in *Continental Accord: North American Economic Integration* (ed. S. Globerman). Vancouver: Fraser Institute, pp. 89–123.
Lipsey, R.G. (1992a). *An Introduction to Positive Economics*. London: Weidenfeld & Nicolson.
Lipsey, R.G. (1992b). 'Global change and economic policy', in *The Culture and the Power of Knowledge* (eds N. Stehr and R. Ericson). New York: De Gruyter, pp. 279–99.
Lipsey, R.G. (1993a). 'Globalisation, technological change and economic growth', Annual Sir Charles Carter Lecture. Belfast: Northern Ireland Economic Development Office.
Lipsey, R.G. (1993b). 'The changing technoeconomic paradigm and some implications for economic policy', Canadian Institute for Advanced Research, Vancouver.
Lipsey, R.G. (1993c). 'Canadian trade policy in relation to regional free trade agreements: CAFTA, NAFTA and WHFTA', Canadian Institute for Advanced Research, Vancouver.
Lipsey, R.G. (1994). 'Markets, technological change and economic growth', Canadian Institute for Advanced Research, Vancouver.
Lipsey, R.G. (1997). 'Globalization and national government policies: an economist's view', in *Governments, Globalization and International Business* (ed. J. Dunning). Oxford: Oxford University Press, pp. 73–113.
Lipsey, R.G. and K. Lancaster (1956–57). 'The general theory of the second best', *Review of Economic Studies*, pp. 11–32.
Lipsey, R.G. and M. Smith (1986). *Taking the Initiative: Canada's Trade Options in a Turbulent World*. Toronto: C.D. Howe Institute.
Lipsey, R.G. and M. Smith (1987). *Global Imbalances and US Policy Responses*. Toronto: C.D. Howe Institute.

Lipsey, R.G. and M. Smith (1989). 'The Canada–US free trade agreement: special case or wave of the future?', in *Free Trade Areas and U.S. Trade Policy* (ed. J. Schott). Washington, DC: Institute for International Economics, pp. 317–35.

Lipsey, R.G. and R. York, (1988). *Evaluating the Free Trade Deal: A Guided Tour through the Canada–US Agreement*. Toronto: C.D. Howe Institute.

Lösch, A. (1938). 'The nature of economic regions', *Southern Economic Journal*, pp. 71–8.

Lösch, A. (1940). *Die Räumliche Ordnung der Wirtschaft*. Jena: Gustav Fischer (translated from German by W. Woglom and W. Stolper, *The Economics of Location* (1973). New Haven, CT: Yale University Press).

Lowe, N. and M. Kenney (1999). 'Foreign investment and the global geography of production: why the Mexican consumer electronics industry failed', *World Development*, pp. 1427–43.

Lucas, R. (1988). 'On the mechanics of economic development', *Journal of Monetary Economics*, pp. 3–42.

Ludema, R. and I. Wooton (2000). 'Economic geography and the fiscal effects of regional integration', *Journal of International Economics*, pp. 331–57.

Lunn, J. (1980). 'Determinants of US direct investment in the EEC', *European Economic Review*, pp. 93–101.

Lunn, J. (1983). 'Determinants of US direct investment in the EEC', *European Economic Review*, pp. 391–3.

MacDougall, G. (1977). *Report of the Study Group on the Role of Public Finance in European Integration*. Brussels: European Community.

Machlup, F. (1979). *A History of Thought on Economic Integration*. London: Macmillan.

Macleod, I., I. Hendry and S. Hyett (1998). *The External Relations of the European Communities*. Oxford: Clarendon Press.

Malmberg, A. (1996). 'Industrial geography: agglomeration and local milieu', *Progress in Human Geography*, pp. 392–403.

Malmberg, A., Ö. Sölvell and I. Zander (1996). 'Spatial clustering, local accumulation of knowledge and firm competitiveness', *Geografiska Annaler*, pp. 85–97.

Maloney, M. and M. Macmillen (1999). 'Do currency unions grow too large for their own good?', *Economic Journal*, pp. 572–87.

Markusen, A. (1996). 'Sticky places in slippery space: a typology of industrial districts', *Economic Geography*, pp. 293–313.

Markusen, J. (1983). 'Factor movements and commodity trade as complements', *Journal of International Economics*, pp. 342–56.

Markusen, J. (1984). 'Multinationals, multi-plant economies and the gains from trade', *Journal of International Economics*, pp. 205–26.

Markusen, J. and J. Melvin (1984). *The Theory of International Trade and Its Canadian Applications*. Toronto: Butterworths.

Markusen, J. and A. Venables (1998). 'Multinational firms and the new trade theory', *Journal of International Economics*, pp. 183–203.

Markusen, J. and A. Venables (2000). 'The theory of endowment, intra-industry and multi-national trade', *Journal of International Economics*, pp. 209–34.

Marshall, A. (1890). *Principles of Economics*. London: Macmillan.

Martin, R. (1999). 'The new geographical turn in economics: some critical reflections', *Cambridge Journal of Economics*, pp. 65–91.

Mayes, D. (ed.) (1997). *The Evolution of the Single European Market*. Cheltenham, UK and Lyme, USA: Edward Elgar.

McFetridge, D. (1985). 'The economics of industrial policy', in *Canadian Industrial Policy in Action* (ed. D. McFetridge). Toronto: University of Toronto Press, pp. 1–49.

McKinnon, R. (1963). 'Optimum currency areas', *American Economic Review*, pp. 717–25.

McKinnon, R. (1994). 'A common monetary standard or a common currency for Europe? The fiscal constraints', *Rivista di Politica Economica*, pp. 59–79.

Meade, J. (1973). 'The balance of payments problems of a European free-trade area', in *The Economics of Integration* (ed. M. Krauss). London: George Allen & Unwin, pp. 155–76.

Messerlin, P. (1996). 'Competition policy and antidumping reform: an exercise in transition', in *The World Trading System: Challenges Ahead* (ed. J. Schott). Washington, DC: Institute for International Economics, pp. 219–46.

Messerlin, P. (2001). *Measuring the Cost of Protection in Europe*. Washington, DC: Institute for International Economics.

Midelfart, H., H. Overman and A. Venables (2003), 'Monetary union and the economic geography of Europe', *Journal of Common Market Studies*, pp. 847–68.

Midelfart-Knarvik, K. and H. Overman (2002). 'Delocation and European integration', *Economic Policy*, pp. 323–59.

Midelfart-Knarvik, K., H. Overman, S. Redding and A. Venables (2000). 'The location of European industry', Economic Papers No. 142, European Commission.

Mody, A. and K. Srinivasan (1998). 'Japanese and U.S. firms as foreign investors: do they march to the same tune?', *Canadian Journal of Economics*, pp. 778–99.

Moran, T. (1998). *Foreign Direct Investment and Development*. Washington, DC: Institute for International Economics.

Morita, A. (1992). 'Partnering for competitiveness: the role of Japanese business', *Harvard Business Review*, May–June, pp. 76–83.
Moses, L. (1958). 'Location and the theory of production', *Quarterly Journal of Economics*, pp. 259–72.
Mundell, R. (1957). 'International trade and factor mobility', *American Economic Review*, pp. 321–35.
Mundell, R. (1961). 'A theory of optimum currency areas', *American Economic Review*, pp. 321–5.
Mundell, R. (1994). 'European monetary union and the international monetary system', *Rivista di Politica Economica*, pp. 83–128.
Murphy, K., A. Shleifer and R. Vishny (1989). 'Industrialization and the Big Push', *Journal of Political Economy*, pp. 1003–26.
Mytelka, L. (1979). *Regional Development in a Global Economy*. New Haven, CT: Yale University Press.
Nadvi, K. (1998). 'International competitiveness and small firm clusters – evidence from Pakistan', *Small Enterprise Development*, pp. 12–24.
Narula, R. (1999). 'Explaining the growth of strategic R&D alliances by European firms', *Journal of Common Market Studies*, pp. 711–23.
Nelson, R. (1999). 'The sources of industrial leadership: a perspective on industrial policy', *De Economist*, pp. 1–18.
Neven, D. (1990). 'EEC integration towards 1992: some distributional aspects', *Economic Policy*, pp. 14–46.
Nicolaides, P. (ed.) (1993). *Industrial Policy in the European Community*. Dordrecht: Martinus Nijhoff.
Nicolaides, P. (1994). 'Why multilateral rules on competition are needed', *Intereconomics*, pp. 222–18.
Nicolaides, P. (1999). 'The economics of enlarging the European Union: policy reform versus transfers', *Intereconomics*, January/February, pp. 3–9.
Nicolaides, P. and A. van der Klugt (eds) (1994). *The Competition Policy of the European Community*. Maastricht: EIPA.
Noël, E. (1993). *Working Together – The Institutions of the European Community*. Luxembourg: European Communities.
Norman, V. (1995). 'The theory of market integration: a retrospective view', in *35 Years of Free Trade in Europe: Messages for the Future* (ed. E. Ems). Geneva: EFTA, pp. 19–37.
OECD (2003a). *Agricultural Policies in OECD Countries*. Paris: OECD.
OECD (2003b). *OECD Economic Outlook*, No. 73. Paris: OECD.
OECD (2003c). *Trends in International Migration (SOPEMI 2002)*. Paris: OECD.
Ohlin, B. (1933). *Interregional and International Trade*. Cambridge, MA: Harvard University Press.

Ottaviano, G. (1999). 'Integration, geography and burden of history', *Regional Science and Urban Economics*, pp. 245–56.

Ottaviano, G. and D. Puga (1998). 'Agglomeration in the global economy: a survey of the "new economic geography"', *World Economy*, pp. 707–31.

Ottaviano, G. and J. Thisse (1999). 'Integration, agglomeration and the political economics of factor mobility', CEPR Discussion Paper No. 2185, Centre for Economic Policy Research, London.

Paci, R. (1997). 'More similar and less equal: economic growth in the European regions', *Weltwirtschaftliches Archiv*, pp. 609–34.

Paci, R. and S. Usai (1999). 'The role of specialisation and diversity externalities in the agglomeration of innovative activities', University of Cagliari and University of Sassari, mimeo.

Pack, H. (2000). 'Industrial policy: growth elixir or poison?', *World Bank Research Observer*, pp. 47–67.

Pack, H. and K. Saggi (1997). 'Inflows of foreign technology and indigenous technological development', *Review of Development Economics*, pp. 81–98.

Palmeter, D. (1993). 'Rules of origin in customs unions and free trade areas', in *Regional Integration and the Global Trading System* (eds K. Anderson and R. Blackhurst). New York: Harvester Wheatsheaf, pp. 326–43.

Panagariya, A. (2000). 'Preferential trade liberalization: the traditional theory and new developments', *Journal of Economic Literature*, pp. 287–331.

Panić, M. (1988). *National Management of the International Economy*. London: Macmillan.

Panić, M. (1991). 'The import of multinationals on national economic policies', in *Multinationals and Europe 1992* (eds B. Bürgenmeier and J. Mucchelli). London: Routledge, pp. 204–22.

Panić, M. (1998). 'Transnational corporations and the nation state', in *Transnational Corporations and the Global Economy* (eds R. Kozul-Wright and R. Rowthorn). Basingstoke: Macmillan, pp. 244–76.

Papageorgiou, G. (1979). 'Agglomeration', *Regional Science and Urban Economics*, pp. 41–59.

Peck, M. (1989). 'Industrial organization and the gains from Europe 1992', *Brookings Papers on Economic Activity*, pp. 277–99.

Pelkmans, J. and P. Robson (1987). 'The aspirations of the White Paper', *Journal of Common Market Studies*, pp. 181–92.

Penrose, E. (1952). 'Biological analogies in the theory of the firm', *American Economic Review*, pp. 804–19.

Perroux, F. (1950). 'Economic space: theory and applications', *Quarterly Journal of Economics*, pp. 89–104.

Perroux, F. (1955). 'Note sur la notion de "pôle de croissance"', *Économie Appliqué*, pp. 307–20.
Perroux, F. (1961). *L'Économie du XXe Siècle*. Paris: Presses Universitaires de France.
Petith, H. (1977). 'European integration and the terms of trade', *Economic Journal*, pp. 262–72.
Pfann, G. and H. van Kranenburg (2002). 'Tax policy, location choices and market structure', IZA Discussion Paper No. 499, Institute for the Study of Labor, Bonn.
Pinch, S. and N. Henry (1999). 'Paul Krugman's geographical economics, industrial clustering and the British motor sport industry', *Regional Studies*, pp. 815–27.
Pinder, J. (1982). 'Causes and kinds of industrial policy', in *National Industrial Strategies and the World Economy* (ed. J. Pinder). London: Croom Helm, pp. 41–52.
Pinder, J., T. Hosomi and W. Diebold (1979). *Industrial Policy and International Economy*. New York: Trilateral Commission.
Pitelis, C. and R. Sugden (eds) (1991). *The Nature of the Transnational Firm*. London: Routledge.
Plasschaert, S. (1994). 'Introduction: transfer pricing and taxation', in *Transnational Corporations: Transfer Pricing and taxation* (ed. S. Plasschaert). London: Routledge, pp. 1–21.
Pomfret, R. (1997). *The Economics of Regional Trading Arrangements*. Oxford: Clarendon Press.
Porter, M. (1990a). *The Competitive Advantage of Nations*. New York: Free Press.
Porter, M. (1990b). 'The competitive advantage of nations', *Harvard Business Review*, pp. 73–93.
Porter, M. (1994). 'The role of location in competition', *Journal of the Economics of Business*, pp. 35–9.
Porter, M. (1996). 'Competitive advantage, agglomeration economies, and regional policy', *International Regional Science Review*, pp. 85–94.
Porter, M. (1998a). 'Clusters and the new economics of competition', *Harvard Business Review*, pp. 77–90.
Porter, M. (1998b). 'Location, clusters, and the "new" microeconomics of competition', *Business Economics*, pp. 7–13.
Porter, M. (2000a). 'Locations, clusters and company strategy', in *The Oxford Handbook of Economic Geography* (eds G. Clark et al.). Oxford: Oxford University Press, pp. 253–74.
Porter, M. (2000b). 'Location, competition and economic development: local clusters in a global economy', *Economic Development Quarterly*, pp. 15–34.

Porter, M. and Ö. Sölvell (1998). 'The role of geography in the process of innovation and the sustainable competitive advantage of firms', in *The Dynamic Firm* (eds A. Chandler et al.). Oxford: Oxford University Press, pp. 440–57.

Posner, M. (1961). 'International trade and technical change', *Oxford Economic Papers*, pp. 323–41.

Prais, S. (1981). *Productivity and Industrial Structure*. Cambridge: Cambridge University Press.

Pratten, C. (1971). *Economies of Scale and Manufacturing Industry*. Cambridge: Cambridge University Press.

Pratten, C. (1988). 'A survey of the economies of scale', in *Studies on the Economics of Integration*, Research on the Costs of Non-Europe, vol. 2, Brussels: European Communities, pp. 11–165.

Praussello, F. (2002). 'The stability of EMU in the aftermath of the EU eastwards enlargement', paper presented at the conference 'EU Enlargement: Endgame Economic Issues', Jean Monnet European Centre of Excellence, University of Genoa, 15 November.

Prest, A. (1983). 'Fiscal policy', in *Main Economic Policy Areas of the EEC* (ed. P. Coffey). The Hague: Martinus Nijhoff, pp. 58–90.

Puga, D. (2002). 'European regional policies in light of recent location theories', *Journal of Economic Geography*, pp. 373–406.

Puga, D. and D. Trefler (2002). 'Knowledge creation and control in organizations', NBER Working Paper No. 9121, National Bureau of Economic Research, Cambridge, MA.

Puga, D. and A. Venables (1997). 'Preferential trading arrangements and industrial location', *Journal of International Economics*, pp. 347–68.

Puga, D. and A. Venables (1999). 'Agglomeration and economic development: import substitution vs. trade liberalisation', *Economic Journal*, pp. 292–311.

Purvis, D. (1972). 'Technology, trade and factor mobility', *Economic Journal*, pp. 991–9.

Pyke, F., G. Becattini and W. Sengenberger (eds) (1990). *Industrial Districts and Inter-firm Co-operation in Italy*. Geneva: International Labour Organisation.

Pyke, F. and W. Sengenberger (eds) (1992). *Industrial Districts and Local Economic Regeneration*. Geneva: International Labour Organisation.

Quah, D. (1996a). 'Empirics for economic growth and convergence', *European Economic Review*, pp. 1353–75.

Quah, D. (1996b). 'Regional convergence clusters across Europe', CEPR Discussion Paper No. 1286, Centre for Economic Policy Research, London.

Rauch, J. (1993). 'Does history matter only when it matters little? The case

of city-industry location', CEPR Discussion Paper No. 4312, Centre for Economic Policy Research, London.
Read, R. (1994). 'The EC internal banana market: the issues and the dilemmas', *The World Economy*, pp. 219–35.
Reich, R. (1982). 'Why the U.S. needs an industrial policy', *Harvard Business Review*, January/February, pp. 74–81.
Reich, R. (1990). 'Who is us?', *Harvard Business Review*, January/February, pp. 53–64.
Reuber, G. (1973). *Private Foreign Investment in Development*. Oxford: Clarendon Press.
Robson, P. (1983). *Integration, Development and Equity*. London: George Allen & Unwin.
Robson, P. (1987). *The Economics of International Integration*. London: George Allen & Unwin.
Robson, P. (1998). *The Economics of International Integration*. London: Routledge.
Rodas-Martini, P. (1998). 'Intra-industry trade and revealed comparative advantage in the Central American Common Market', *World Development*, pp. 337–44.
Romer, P. (1994). 'New goods, old theory and the welfare costs of trade restrictions', *Journal of Development Economics*, pp. 5–38.
Rose, A. (2000). 'One money, one market: the effect of common currencies on trade', *Economic Policy*, pp. 9–45.
Rosenberg, N., R. Landau and D. Mowery (eds) (1992). *Technology and the Wealth of Nations*. Stanford: Stanford University Press.
Rosenblatt, J., T. Mayer, K. Bartholdy, D. Demekas, S. Gupta and L. Lipschitz (1988). The Common Agricultural Policy of the European Community, Occasional Paper 62, International Monetary Fund, Washington, DC.
Rubin, S. (1970). 'The international firm and the national jurisdiction', in *The International Corporation* (ed. C. Kindleberger). Cambridge, MA: MIT Press, pp. 179–204.
Ruding Committee (1992). *Conclusions and Recommendations of the Committee of Independent Experts on Company Taxation*. Luxembourg: European Communities.
Rugman, A. (1985). 'The behaviour of US subsidiaries in Canada: implications for trade and investment', in *Canada/United States Trade and Investments Issues* (eds D. Fretz, R. Stern and J. Whalley). Toronto: Ontario Economic Council, pp. 460–73.
Rugman, A. (2002). 'Multinational enterprises and the end of global strategy', in *Multinational Firms* (eds J. Dunning and J. Mucchielli). London: Routledge, pp. 3–17.

Rugman, A. and R. Hodgetts (2001). 'The end of global strategy', *European Management Journal*, pp. 333–43.

Rugman, A. and A. Verbeke (1998). 'Multinational enterprise and public policy', *Journal of International Business Studies*, pp. 115–36.

Rugman, A. and A. Verbeke (2003). 'Regional and global strategies of multinational enterprises', Kelley School of Business, Indiana University, mimeo.

Sadiq, K. (2001). 'Unitary taxation – the case for global formulary apportionment', *International Bureau of Fiscal Documentation Bulletin*, pp. 275–86.

Sala-i-Martin, X. (1994). 'Regional cohesion: evidence and theories of regional growth and convergence', CEPR Discussion Paper No. 1075, Centre for Economic Policy Research, London.

Sala-i-Martin, X. (1996). 'Regional cohesion: evidence and theories of regional growth and convergence', *European Economic Review*, pp. 1325–52.

Sala-i-Martin, X. and J. Sachs (1992). 'Fiscal federalism and optimum currency areas: evidence for Europe from the United States', in *Establishing a Central Bank: Issues in Europe and Lessons from the US* (eds M. Canzoneri, V. Grilli and P. Mason). Cambridge: Cambridge University Press, pp. 195–219.

Sapir, A. (1992). 'Regional integration in Europe', *Economic Journal*, pp. 1491–506.

Sapir, A. (1993). 'Structural dimension', *European Economy Social Europe*, No. 3, pp. 23–39.

Sapir, A. (1996). 'The effects of Europe's Internal Market Program on production and trade: a first assessment', *Weltwirtschaftliches Archiv*, pp. 456–75.

Sapir, A. (2003). *An Agenda for a Growing Europe*. Brussels: European Commission.

Sapir, A., P. Buigues and A. Jacquemin (1993). 'European competition policy in manufacturing and services: a two speed approach?', *Oxford Review of Economic Policy*, pp. 113–32.

Sarris, A. (1994). 'Consequences of the proposed common agricultural policy reform for the southern part of the European Community', *European Economy*, No. 5, pp. 113–32.

Scaperlanda, A. (1967). 'The EEC and US foreign investment: some empirical evidence', *Economic Journal*, pp. 22–6.

Scaperlanda, A. and R. Balough (1983). 'Determinants of US direct investment in Europe', *European Economic Journal*, pp. 381–90.

Scaperlanda, A. and E. Reiling (1971). 'A comment on a note on customs unions and direct foreign investment', *Economic Journal*, pp. 355–7.

Schatz, K. and F. Wolter (1987). *Structural Adjustment in the Federal Republic of Germany*. Geneva: International Labour Organisation.

Schmalensee, R. (1988). 'Industrial economics: an overview', *Economic Journal*, pp. 634–81.

Schmitz, H. (1998). 'Fostering collective efficiency', *Small Enterprise Development*, pp. 4–11.

Schmitz, H. (1999). 'Collective efficiency and increasing returns', *Cambridge Journal of Economics*, pp. 465–83.

Schmitz, H. and K. Nadvi (1999). 'Clustering and industrialization: introduction', *World Development*, pp. 1503–14.

Servan-Schreiber, J. (1969). *The American Challenge*. New York: Athenaeum.

Sharp, M. and K. Pavitt (1993). 'Technology policy in the 1990s: old trends and new realities', *Journal of Common Market Studies*, pp. 129–51.

Sharp, M. and G. Shepherd (1987). *Managing Change in British Industry*. Geneva: International Labour Organisation.

Sidjanski, D. (1992). *L'Avenir Fédéraliste de L'Europe*. Paris: Presses Universitaires de France.

Sidjanski, D. (1998). *The ECE in the Age of Change*. New York: United Nations.

Sidjanski, D. (2000). *The Federal Future of Europe*. Ann Arbor, MI: University of Michigan Press.

Sidjanski, D. (2001). 'The federal approach to the European Union or the quest for an unprecedented European federalism', Notre Europe, Paris, Research and Policy Paper No. 14.

Siebert, H. (1991). 'Environmental policy and European integration', in *Environmental Scarcity: The International Dimension* (ed. H. Siebert). Tübingen: J.C.B. Mohr, pp. 57–70.

Siebert, H. (ed.) (1995). *Locational Competition in the World Economy*. Tübingen: J.C.B. Mohr.

Simon, J. (1996). 'Some findings about European immigration', *International Regional Science Review*, pp. 129–37.

Sinn, H. and F. Westermann (2000). 'Two Mezzogiornos', CESifo Working Paper No. 378.

Sleuwaegen, L. and K. de Backer (2001). 'Multinational firms, market integration and trade structure', *Weltwirtschaftliches Archiv*, pp. 379–403.

Smith, A. (1839). *An Inquiry into the Nature and Causes of the Wealth of Nations*. Edinburgh: Adam & Charles Black.

Smith, A. and A. Venables (1988). 'Completing the internal market in the European Community', *European Economic Review*, pp. 1501–25.

Smith, D. (1981). *Industrial Location – An Economic Geographical Analysis*. New York: John Wiley.

Smith, D. and R. Florida (1994). 'Agglomeration and industrial location: an econometric analysis of Japanese-affiliated manufacturing establishments in automotive-related industries', *Journal of Urban Economics*, pp. 23–41.
Snape, R. (1996). 'Trade discrimination – yesterday's problem?', *Economic Record*, pp. 381–96.
Sorsa, P. (1994). 'Competitiveness and environmental standards', World Bank Policy Research Working Paper 1249, World Bank, Washington, DC.
Stephanou, K. (1997). *Réformes et mutations de l'Union Européenne*. Brussels: Bruylant.
Sternberg, R. and C. Tamásy (1999). 'Munich as Germany's no. 1 high technology region: empirical evidence, theoretical explanations and the role of small firm/large firm relations', *Regional Studies*, pp. 367–77.
Storper, M., C. Yun-chung and F. de Paolis (2002). 'Trade and location of industries in the OECD and European Union', *Journal of Economic Geography*, pp. 73–107.
Straubhaar, T. (1988). 'International labour migration within a common market: some aspects of EC experience', *Journal of Common Market Studies*, pp. 45–62.
Straubhaar, T. and K. Zimmermann (1993). 'Towards a European migration policy', *Population Research and Policy Review*, pp. 225–41.
Swann P., M. Prevezer and D. Stout (eds) (1998). *The Dynamics of Industrial Clustering*. Oxford: Oxford University Press.
Tangermann, S. (1999). 'Europe's agricultural policies and the Millennium Round', *World Economy*, pp. 1155–78.
Tanzi, V. and H. Zee (2000). 'Tax policy for emerging markets: developing countries', *National Tax Journal*, pp. 299–322.
Tavlas, G. (1993a). 'The theory of optimum currency areas revisited', *Finance and Development*, June, pp. 32–5.
Tavlas, G. (1993b). 'The "new" theory of optimum currency areas', *The World Economy*, pp. 663–85.
Tavlas, G. (1997). 'The international use of the US dollar: an optimum currency area perspective', *World Economy*, pp. 709–47.
Teich, A. (2003). 'R&D in the Federal Budget: frequently asked questions', *AAAS Report XXVI: Research and Development FY 2002*. Washington: AAAS. http:// www.aaas.org/spp/rd/xxvi/chap1.htm.
Tharakan, M., D. Greenaway and J. Tharakan (1998). 'Cumulation and injury determination of the European Community in antidumping cases', *Weltwirtschaftliches Archiv*, pp. 320–39.
Thomsen, S. and P. Nicolaides (1991). *The Evolution of Japanese Direct Investment in Europe*. New York: Harvester Wheatsheaf.

Thygesen, N. (1987). 'Is the EEC an optimal currency area?', in *The ECU Market* (eds R. Levics and A. Sommariva). Toronto: D.C. Heath, Lexington Books, pp. 163–89.
Tironi, E. (1982). 'Customs union theory in the presence of foreign firms', *Oxford Economic Papers*, pp. 150–71.
Trebilcock, M. (1986). *The Political Economy of Economic Adjustment*. Toronto: University of Toronto Press.
Trimbath, S. (2002). *Mergers and Acquisitions: Changes across Time*. Boston, MA: Kluwer.
Tyson, L. (1987). 'Comments on Brander's "shaping comparative advantage", creating advantage, an industrial policy perspective', in *Shaping Comparative Advantage* (eds R. Lipsey and W. Dobson). Toronto: C.D. Howe Institute, pp. 65–82.
Tyson, L. (1991). 'They are not us. Why American ownership still matters', *The American Prospect*, Winter, pp. 37–49.
Tyson, L. (1992). *Who Is Bashing Whom? Trade Conflict in High-technology Industries*. Washington, DC: Institute for International Economics.
Tyson, L. and J. Zysman (1987a). 'American industry in international competition', in *American Industry in International Competition* (eds J. Zysman and L. Tyson). Ithaca, NY: Cornell University Press, pp. 15–59.
Tyson, L. and J. Zysman (1987b). 'Conclusion: what to do now?', in *American Industry in International Competition* (eds J. Zysman and L. Tyson). Ithaca, NY: Cornell University Press, pp. 422–7.
UNCTAD (1983). *The Role of Transnational Enterprises in Latin American Economic Integration Efforts: Who Integrates with Whom, How and for Whose Benefit?* New York: United Nations.
UNCTAD (1992). *World Investment Report: Transnational Corporations as Engines of Growth*. New York: United Nations.
UNCTAD (1993). *World Investment Report: Transnational Corporations and Integrated International Production*. New York: United Nations.
UNCTAD (1994). *World Investment Report: Transnational Corporations, Employment and the Workforce*. New York: United Nations.
UNCTAD (1995a). 'Incentives and foreign direct investment', TD/B/ITNC/Misc. 1, 6 April.
UNCTAD (1995b). *World Investment Report: Transnational Corporations and Competitiveness*. New York: United Nations.
UNCTAD (1996). *Sharing Asia's Dynamism: Asian Direct Investment in the European Union*. New York: United Nations.
UNCTAD (1997). *World Investment Report: Transnational Corporations, Market Structure and Competition Policy*. United Nations: New York.
UNCTAD (1998). *World Investment Report: Trends and Determinants*. United Nations: New York.

UNCTAD (1999a). *World Investment Report: Foreign Direct Investment and the Challenge of Development*. United Nations: New York.
UNCTAD (1999b). *Investment-Related Trade Measures*. New York: United Nations.
UNCTAD (2000). *World Investment Report: Cross-border Mergers and Acquisitions and Development*. United Nations: New York.
UNCTAD (2001). *World Investment Report: Promoting Linkages*. New York: United Nations.
UNCTAD (2002). *World Investment Report: Transnational Corporations and Export Competitiveness*. United Nations: New York.
UNCTAD (2003). *World Investment Report: FDI Policies for Development – National and International Perspectives*. United Nations: New York.
UNCTC (1990). *Regional Economic Integration and Transnational Corporations in the 1990s: Europe 1992, North America and Developing Countries*. New York: United Nations.
UNCTC (1991a). *The Impact of Trade-related Investment Measures on Trade and Development*. New York: United Nations.
UNCTC (1991b). *World Investment Report: The Triad in Foreign Direct Investment*. New York: United Nations.
UNCTC (1991c). *Government Policies and Foreign Direct Investment*. New York: United Nations.
UNECE (2003). *Statistics of Road Traffic Accidents in Europe and North America*. New York: United Nations.
United Nations (2000). 'Replacement migration: is it a solution to declining and ageing populations?' ESA/P/WP.160, 21 March.
van Aarle, B. (1996). 'The impact of the Single Market on trade and foreign direct investment in the European Union', *Journal of World Trade*, pp. 121–38.
van Brabant, J. (1996). 'Remaking Europe – the accession of transition economies', *Economia Internazionale*, pp. 507–31.
van Brabant, J. (2001). 'EU widening and deepening – are these goals reconcilable?', *Most*, pp. 113–41.
Vanhove, N. and L. Klaasen (1987). *Regional Policy: A European Approach*. Aldershot: Avebury.
Vaubel, R. (1990). 'Currency competition and European monetary integration', *Economic Journal*, pp. 936–46.
Venables, A. (1985). 'Trade and trade policy with imperfect competition: the case of identical products and free entry', *Journal of International Economics*, pp. 1–19.
Venables, A. (1994). 'Economic integration and industrial agglomeration', *Economic and Social Review*, pp. 1–17.
Venables, A. (1995). 'Economic integration and the location of firms',

American Economic Review (Papers and Proceedings), pp. 296–300.
Venables, A. (1996a). 'Localization of industry and trade performance', *Oxford Review of Economic Policy*, pp. 52–60.
Venables, A. (1996b). 'Equilibrium locations of vertically linked industries', *International Economic Review*, pp. 341–59.
Venables, A. (1998). 'The assessment: trade and location', *Oxford Review of Economic Policy*, pp. 1–6.
Venables, A. (2001). 'Geography and international inequalities: the impact of new technologies', London School of Economics, Centre for Economic Performance.
Venables, A. and N. Limão (2002). 'Geographical disadvantage: a Heckscher–Ohlin–von Thünen model of international specialisation', *Journal of International Economics*, pp. 239–63.
Vernon, R. (1966). 'International investment and international trade in the product cycle', *Quarterly Journal of Economics*, pp. 190–207.
Viner, J. (1950). *The Customs Union Issue*. London: Stevens & Sons.
von Cramon-Taubadel, S. and H. Thiele (1994). 'EU agriculture: reduced protection from exchange rate instability', *Intereconomics*, 6, November–December, pp. 263–8.
von Thünen, J. (1826). *Der Isolierte Staat in Beziehung auf Landtschaft und Nationalökonomie*. Hamburg: Perthes (translated from German by C. Wartenberg, *Von Thünen's Isolated State* (1966), Oxford: Pergamon Press).
Wallis, K. (1968). 'The EEC and United States foreign investment: some empirical evidence re-examined', *Economic Journal*, pp. 717–19.
Wasylenko, M. (1991). 'Empirical evidence on interregional business location decisions and the role of fiscal incentives in economic development', in *Industry Location and Public Policy* (eds H. Herzog and A. Schlottmann). Knoxville, TN: University of Tennessee Press, pp. 13–30.
Weale, A. and A. Williams (1993). 'Between economy and ecology?', in *A Green Dimension for the European Community: Political Issues and Processes* (ed. D. Judge). London: Frank Cass, pp. 45–64.
Weber, A. (1909). *Über den Standort der Industrien*, Tübingen: J.C.B. Mohr (translated from German by C. Friedrich, *Theory of the Location of Industries* (1962), Chicago: University of Chicago Press).
Weder, R. (1995). 'The Swiss dyestuff industry', in *Studies in Swiss Competitive Advantage* (eds M. Enright and R. Weder). Bern: Peter Lang, pp. 24–60.
Werner, P. (1970). *Report to the Council and the Commission on the Realization by Stages of Economic and Monetary Union in the Community*. Luxembourg: European Communities.
Whalley, J. (1987). 'Brander's 'shaping comparative advantage': remarks', in

Shaping Comparative Advantage (eds R. Lipsey and W. Dobson). Toronto: C.D. Howe Institute, pp. 83–9.

Wheeler, D. and A. Mody (1992). 'International investment location decisions: the case of U.S. firms', *Journal of International Economics*, pp. 57–76.

Winters, A. (1994). 'The EC and protection: the political economy', *European Economic Review*, pp. 596–603.

Wonnacott, P. and R. Wonnacott (1981). 'Is unilateral tariff reduction preferable to a customs union? The customs union of the missing foreign tariffs', *American Economic Review*, pp. 704–13.

Woodward, D. (1992). 'Locational determinants of Japanese manufacturing start-ups in the United States', *Southern Economic Journal*, pp. 690–708.

World Bank (1993). *The East Asian Miracle*. New York: Oxford University Press.

Wren, C. (1990). 'Regional policy in the 1980s', *National Westminster Bank Quarterly Review*, pp. 52–64.

WTO (2002). *Trade Policy Review: European Union*. Geneva: WTO.

Yamada, T. and T. Yamada (1996). 'EC integration and Japanese foreign direct investment in the EC', *Contemporary Economic Policy*, pp. 48–57.

Yamawaki, H. (1991). 'Discussion', in *European Integration: Trade and Industry* (eds A. Winters and A. Venables). Cambridge: Cambridge University Press, pp. 231–3.

Yamawaki, H. (1993). 'Location decisions of Japanese multinational firms in European manufacturing industries', in *European Competitiveness* (ed. K. Hughes). Cambridge: Cambridge University Press, pp. 11–28.

Yannopoulos, G. (1988). *Customs Unions and Trade Conflicts*. London: Routledge.

Yannopoulos, G. (1990). 'Foreign direct investment and European integration: the evidence from the formative years of the European Community', *Journal of Common Market Studies*, pp. 236–59.

Yannopoulos, G. (ed). (1991). *Europe and America, 1992*. Manchester: Manchester University Press.

Yuill, D., K. Allen, J. Bachtler, K. Clement and F. Wishdale (1994). *European Regional Incentives, 1994–95*. London: Bowker.

Zimmermann, K. (1994). 'European migration: push and pull', *Proceedings of the World Bank Annual Conference on Development Economics 1994*, Washington, DC: World Bank, pp. 313–42.

Zimmermann, K. (1995). 'Tackling the European migration problem', *Economic Perspectives*, pp. 45–62.

Zysman, J. (1983). *Governments, Markets and Growth*. Ithaca, NY: Cornell University Press.

Zysman, J. and A. Schwartz (1998). 'Reunifying Europe in an emerging world economy: economic heterogeneity, new industrial options, and political choices', *Journal of Common Market Studies*, pp. 405–29.

Select Websites

EU

A–Z Index	http://www.eurunion.org/infores/euindex.htm
Welcome page	http://europa.eu.int/index_en.htm
Policies	http://europa.eu.int/comm/index_en.htm
EU Encyclopaedia	http://www.euro-know.org/dictionary/t.html
Directorates-General	http://europa.eu.int/comm/dgs_en.htm
Europa	http://europa.eu.int/index-en.htm
Laws and policies	http://www.eurunion.org/legislat/
Laws	http://europa.eu.int/eur-lex/
Treaty of Rome	http://europa.eu.int/eur-lex/pri/en/oj/dat/2002/c_325/c_32520021224en00010184.pdf
EU summits	http://www.europarl.eu.int/summits/index.htm
History	http://www.let.leidenuniv.nl/history/rtg/res1/index.htm
European Convention	http://european-convention.eu.int/bienvenue.asp?lang=EN
Eurostat	http://europa.eu.int/comm/eurostat/
Euractiv	http://www.euractiv.com/cgi-bin/cgint.exe?1&1000=1&tmpl=index
DG Agriculture	http://europa.eu.int/comm/dgs/agriculture/index_en.htm
DG Transport and Energy	http://europa.eu.int/comm/dgs/energy_transport/ index_en.html
DG Environment	http://europa.eu.int/comm/dgs/environment/index_en.htm
DG Regional Policy	http://europa.eu.int/comm/dgs/regional_policy/ index_en.htm
DG Development	http://europa.eu.int/comm/dgs/development/index_en.htm
DG Enlargement	http://europa.eu.int/comm/dgs/enlargement/index_en.htm

Bibliography

DG Trade	http://europa.eu.int/comm/trade/index_en.htm
DG Competition	http://europa.eu.int/comm/dgs/competition/index_en.htm
DG Economic and Financial Affairs	http://europa.eu.int/comm/dgs/economy_finance/index_en.htm
DG Enterprise	http://europa.eu.int/comm/dgs/enterprise/index_en.htm
DG Finance	http://europa.eu.int/comm/economy_finance/index_en.htm
	http://europa.eu.int/comm/budget/infos/publications_en.htm
	http://europa.eu.int/comm/budget/pdf/infos/vademecum2000/en.pdf
	http://europa.eu.int/comm/budget/budget/index_en.htm
	http://europa.eu.int/comm/economy_finance/publications/european_economy/2003/ee303en.pdf
Budget	http://europa.eu.int/comm/budget/infos/publications_en.htm
European Economy and Papers	http://europa.eu.int/comm/economy_finance/publications_en.htm
Competition, aid reports	http://europa.eu.int/comm/dg04/index_en.htm
SMEs	http://europa.eu.int/comm/enterprise/enterprise_policy/analysis/doc/smes_observatory_2002_report2_en.pdf
EU Transport policy	http://europa.eu.int/comm/energy_transport/en/lb_en.html
A–Z Employment and social policy	http://europa.eu.int/comm/employment_social/az_en.htm
Communication on immigration, integration and employment	http://europa.eu.int/comm/employment_social/news/2003/jun/com2003336_en.pdf
Education programmes and actions	http://europa.eu.int/comm/dgs/education_culture/guide/liste_en.html
Structural indicators	http://europa.eu.int/comm/eurostat/Public/datashop/print-product/EN?catalogue=Eurostat&product=1-structur-EN&mode=download

R&D expenditure % GDP	http://europa.eu.int/comm/eurostat/Public/datashop/print-product/EN?catalogue=Eurostat&product=1-ir021-EN&mode=download
Dialogue with citizens	http://europa.eu.int/citizens/index_en.html
Newsletter	http://europa.eu.int/newsletter/current/index_en.htm
EU in UK	http://www.cec.org.uk/index.htm
TRADE sites:	
Trade Policy Review	http://europa.eu.int/comm/trade/wto_overview/index_en.htm
EU–US trade barriers	http://europa.eu.int/comm/trade/issues/bilateral/countries/usa/docs/ustbr2002.pdf
Statistics	http://europa.eu.int/comm/trade/goods/stats.htm
WTO Press Releases	http://www.wto.org/english/news_e/pres03_e/pr337_e.htm
	http://www.wto.org/english/news_e/pres02_e/pr288_e.htm
Ninth Survey on State Aid in the European Union	http://europa.eu.int/eur-lex/en/com/cnc/2001/com2001_0403en01.pdf
EU Annual Reports on Competition Policy	http://europa.eu.int/comm/competition/annual_reports/
EU Competition glossary	http://europa.eu.int/comm/competition/publications/glossary_en.pdf
EU Completion rules	http://europa.eu.int/scadplus/leg/en/s12000.htm

INTERNATIONAL ORGANISATIONS

UNECE	http://www.unece.org/
OECD	http://www.oecd.org/home/
	http://www.oecd.org/std/others1.htm

Agri policy evaluation	http://www.oecd.org/dataoecd/25/63/2956135.pdf
Science, Technology and Industry Scoreboard 2003	http://www1.oecd.org/publications/e-book/92-2003-04-1-7294/
Sopemi	http://www1.oecd.org/publications/e-book/8103061E.PDF
WTO	http://www.wto.org/
EBRD	http://www.ebrd.com
World Bank	http://www.worldbank.org/
UNCTAD	http://www.unctad.org/
FAO	http://www.fao.org/
	http://apps.fao.org/page/collections

OTHERS

Social Sciences Research Network	http://www.ssrn.com
EconLit	http://www.econlit.org/subject_descriptors.html
A–Z economics	http://economics.miningco.com/c/esntl.htm?PM=ss10_economics
NetEc	http://netec.mcc.ac.uk/.
Global Macroeconomics	http://www.stern.nyu.edu/globalmacro/
Economics of Networks	http://www.stern.nyu.edu/networks/site.html
Information Economy	http://sims.berkeley.edu/resources/infoecon/
Economics News	http://www.argmax.com/
ELIAMEP	http://www.eliamep.gr/
European Community Studies Association	http://www.ecsanet.org
Earthnet	http://earth.esa.int/
World Wildlife Fund	http://www.panda.org
NGOs in Brussels	http://europa.eu.int/comm/civil_society/coneccs/listedomaine.cfm?CL=en
US Patent and Trademark Office	http://www.uspto.gov/web/navaids/siteindx.htm

Index

ABB 321
ability to pay 150–51, 154, 206
absenteeism 74
absolute advantage 572, 608, 613, 673
abuse 270, 329, 331–2, 334
accountability 121
accounts 301
ACP 20, 533–9
acquis communautaire 33–5, 39, 41, 62, 68, 72, 76, 84, 217, 340, 796, 804, 823, 826–7, 832, 841, 844, 852, 857
acquisitions and mergers 320, 323–9, 331, 346, 371–2, 391, 421, 445, 702, 725
address model 311
adjustment 101, 113–14, 116, 135, 142, 146, 268, 304–5, 353, 356–7, 363, 366–7, 370–71, 449, 463, 544, 618, 625, 668, 699, 771, 817, 832, 842
ageing population 61, 134, 136, 150, 189, 357, 394, 562, 767
Agenda 2000 35–6, 41, 257–8, 647, 804, 827, 831, 834, 844, 846

agglomeration 307, 332, 427, 570, 576, 580–81, 584, 587, 597, 620, 631, 633, 658, 730, 831
agriculture 11, 14, 146, 209–64, 855–6
aid 35, 205, 218, 231, 314, 332–43, 551–2, 636, 646, 652, 810
Airbus 298, 350, 381, 386, 400, 428
Alenia/de Havilland 321
alliances 43, 45
allocation 91, 119, 132, 147, 149, 164, 181, 205, 206, 268–70, 273, 303, 311, 333, 346, 365, 435, 438, 573, 620, 625–7, 651, 666, 703–4, 709, 809
aluminium 380
Alva, Duke of 155
Amiti, M. 311, 628–9, 632
anchor currency 102
Anschluss 829
arbitrary 151, 296
Argentina 598
Armington, P. 305
Arthur, B. 563, 579, 581, 583, 597, 661
Article 81 317–30
Article 82 329–32

Article 87 332–43
Article 115 22–3, 83, 87, 561
ASEAN 462
asymmetry 113, 132, 136–7, 143, 311, 348, 410, 416, 554, 755, 757, 857
AT&T 274
Austria 31–2, 41, 42
autarky 286, 300, 441, 457, 629

baby-boom 133, 150, 772
balance of payments 90, 92, 96, 98–9, 102, 113, 668
Balassa, B. 306
Baldwin, R. 451, 496
Balkans 51–3, 62
ballpoint pens 494
bananas 350, 470, 510, 515, 540–43
Bangemann Communication 388
bank secrecy 156
Barcelona 550
bargaining 365, 401, 448–9, 451, 462, 703, 723, 827
barriers 159, 221, 268, 299, 302, 310, 313, 393, 420, 432, 464, 530, 601, 628–31, 668, 681, 726, 756, 761, 793, 808, 816, 834
  entry and exit 138, 274, 296–7, 307, 319, 330, 370, 459–60, 589, 703, 709
Bayer 802
BBC 382, 590
beggar-thy-neighbour 282, 462
Belfast 52
Belgium 59
Benetton 303, 460
Berlin Council 197, 258, 846, 849
Berlusconi, S. 133
Betamax 297, 579
bifurcation 593, 598, 600–601
bilateral 322, 346–7, 450, 467, 480, 521, 561, 816–17, 855
Bismarck, O. 48, 133, 159–60, 207
block exemption 317–19, 329
Boeing 298, 322, 350, 428, 515, 565, 605
Bologna 767
Bolsheviks 60, 141
border-tax adjustment 183
Bosnia 51, 78
Brander, J. 282

Brazil 479
bribe 220
Britain 17–20, 44–6, 162–3, 204, 237, 245, 297, 359, 533, 587, 638, 728
  and euro 134–40
Brülhart, M. 307, 310, 632–3
budget 109, 193–206
  deficit 118–19, 121, 124, 130–31, 133, 136, 141–3, 145, 191, 226, 381, 772
budgetary rebate 36, 204, 208
building blocks 443, 466
Burger King 319
Bush, G. 47, 265, 510

cabotage 415, 813–14, 816
Cairns Group 257, 265, 471, 476, 800
California 144, 165, 347
Canada 23, 104, 308, 435, 450, 477, 563, 714, 807
Cancun 259, 478–80
CAP 16, 41, 60, 138, 198, 204, 209–64, 469, 799, 859
capital controls 116–17
cars 22, 151, 183, 288, 318–19, 323, 345, 380, 491–2, 494, 604, 729
cash registers 601
Cassis de Dijon 420, 488, 521
catch-all 795
central bank 117, 120, 122, 125
Central and Eastern Europe 524–9
central place (area) 576–8
centrifugal 578, 584–5, 608
centripetal 578, 584–5, 608
Cézanne, P. 856
Chamberlin 364
champions 327, 373, 377–83
chance 579, 580, 583, 596, 605, 655, 661, 836–9
Channel Islands 170–71
chemicals 393
child labour 544, 564, 684
China 301, 327, 376, 380, 400, 472, 479–80, 485, 545, 675–6, 752, 854–5
Chiquita bananas 350
chocolate 661
Christaller, W. 577–8
Christian roots 857
cities 581–4

Clinton, W. 270
Club of Rome 602
cluster 123, 170, 282, 284, 296, 438, 584–95, 608, 627–9, 633, 651, 658, 673, 682, 729, 738, 815
CMEA 308, 524
Coca-Cola 270, 327, 684
Cockfield, A. 22, 65–6, 82, 221
Cockfield Report 386
Cohesion Fund 198
Cohesion Policy 568, 645
Cold War 4, 8, 20, 49, 525, 607
collusion 314, 364, 722
colonies 11, 95, 161, 431, 532, 562, 661, 760
Colonna Report 385
Committee of the Regions 78
common market 11–12, 434
Community method 24, 80
comparative advantage 303, 357, 362, 447–8, 562, 572, 673, 718
competition 105, 138, 214, 270–71, 281, 283, 287, 298, 328, 355, 578, 610, 619
  policy in EU 205, 267–347
  restriction of 317–30
  tax 169, 187–8, 190, 192
competitiveness 23, 270, 274, 279, 283, 313, 346, 357, 376, 393, 598, 794, 809
complacency 134, 162
concentration 283–4, 296–7, 313, 317, 323–4, 326, 328, 330, 332, 345, 350, 353, 408, 456, 574, 578, 588, 599, 613, 629, 636, 674, 738
Concorde 356, 360, 381
conduit company 169
Constable, J. 800
Constitutional Treaty 56–9, 853, 857
convergence 320, 390, 421, 496, 570, 612, 634, 649, 767
Cooper, C. 449
cooperation, enhanced 37–8
Copenhagen criteria 33, 40, 826, 858
core–periphery 584, 615, 619, 664, 675
Coreper 69
Corn Laws 210
corporate governance 408, 429
Cosgrove, C. 543
Cotonou 539

Council of Ministers 13, 67–72, 80, 130–31
countervailing duties 472, 563
Cournot–Nash 364
Court of Auditors 77, 198
Court of Justice 76, 130
creative accounting 196
credibility 131, 143
Crédit Lyonnais 351
culture 125, 177, 285, 306, 326–7, 333, 369, 398, 401, 550, 580, 588, 619, 683, 765–6
cumulative causation 439, 593, 596, 598, 600, 613, 664
Curzon Price, V. 14, 302, 354, 358–9, 368, 376, 396, 540–41, 544, 626, 718
customs union 12, 141, 158, 268, 303, 432–62

Danzig 295
Davies, R. 562, 575, 602
dawn raid 316
de minimis 334
debt
  foreign 119, 142
  national 119, 129, 131, 145
deflation 124–5
Delors Report 121
Delors White Paper 388
democratic deficit 67–8
demography 46, 133, 438, 772, 789, 841, 851
Demopoulos, G. 132
Denmark 17–20, 43, 638
derogation 35
  see also opt-out
devaluation 101–2, 107, 114, 116, 221, 618, 677
differentiation 267, 271, 297, 300, 304–6, 311, 314
discrimination 313, 435
  commodity 435
  country 435
disdain 42, 53, 120
disillusion 53–4
dispersion 421, 584–5
distortions 119, 147, 149, 152, 166, 188, 191, 270, 314, 333, 435–6, 441, 645, 678, 796

divergence 613, 634
diversification 97–8, 126, 676
Doha Round 226, 259–60, 265, 467, 476–81
dollar 110–11, 114, 122, 142, 145–6, 473, 542, 676–7
dominant position 330–32
domino effect 451
DOS 579
double signature 72
DTI 355
Duisburg 218
Duke of Alva 155
dumping 246, 472, 484–6, 805
Dunning, J. 347, 363, 673, 687, 725, 728
DVD 580
dyestuffs case 321
dynamic effects 267–8, 272, 314, 454–63, 496
dynamo 297

EAGGF 223–4
East India Company 161, 715
eclectic paradigm 673
Economic and Social Committee 77
economies of scale 22, 153–4, 267, 282, 300–303, 305, 309, 311–12, 314, 317, 326–8, 346, 447, 455–60, 497, 562, 573–4, 577, 579–80, 597, 609, 613, 620, 630–32, 653, 668, 718
ECSC 7–9
ECU 111, 114–15, 121
EDF 532
EEA 31
EEC 10–14
efficiency 278, 303, 369, 401, 435, 438
EFTA 14–15, 20, 31, 82, 93, 519–24
EIB 78, 643
Eichengreen, B. 94–5
elite 43, 53, 58–61, 120, 141, 681, 859
Emerson, M. 184, 402, 456, 495, 497, 728
emigration 154
EMS 93, 97, 110–19
EMU 27, 89–91, 105, 107, 119–28, 153, 834
Encarta 601
endowment of factors 304, 312, 438, 562, 573–4, 595
enhanced cooperation 37–8

enlargement
  Austria, Finland and Sweden 31–2, 41
  Britain, Denmark and Ireland 17–20, 638
  Eastern 35–6, 39–41, 143, 206, 569, 822–48, 851, 857
  Greece 21
  Spain and Portugal 23
Enron 301, 416
environment 212, 215, 237, 245, 258, 333, 478, 593, 792–806, 856
equalisation 133, 213
  of prices 190, 299, 421, 612, 667–9, 750
equilibrium
  general 452–3
  meaningful 596, 599
  multiple 333, 362, 439, 579–80, 582, 596, 600–601, 608, 610, 613, 637, 646, 653
  partial 268, 438–52
  punctuated 598
ERDF 197–8, 204, 638, 642–5
ergodic system, 180, 580, 661
ESF 197–8, 781
d'Estaing, V. 56
Ethier, W. 468
Euratom 13–14
euro 27, 128–9, 141–2, 223, 314
European Central Bank 27, 29, 77, 121
European Commission 13, 30, 37, 56, 64–7, 80, 130–31, 313
European Company Statute 386–7
European Council 21, 28, 75, 80
European Parliament 13, 30, 65–75
European snake 110
European Social Charter 785–8
European Union 468, 475–6, 480
Eurosclerosis 20–22
eurozone 41, 43, 45, 60, 126–7, 129–32, 134, 141–3, 169, 182, 311, 319, 337, 402–3, 569, 724, 772, 831, 834, 851, 853
'Everything but Arms' 539
evolutionary economics 600, 608, 658, 663
exchange rate 90–98, 101, 104, 107, 109, 116, 120, 124, 128, 142, 150, 304, 494
green 221

exchange of threats 676
excise duties 186–7
Exon-Florio 513, 725–6
expectation 449, 601–4, 670, 718
externalities 267, 282, 297, 356, 366, 384, 410, 454, 592, 596, 599, 610, 630, 653, 709, 716, 792, 805

face-to-face 591–2, 662, 682
factors, endowment of 304, 312, 438, 562, 573–4, 595
FDI 137–8, 169, 300, 402, 409, 435, 467, 477, 669–750
federalism 2–3, 7–8, 54–9, 83
    fiscal 152–4
Ferguson 369
financial perspective 196–9, 206, 831, 846, 853
fine 129–30, 276, 316
Finland 31–2, 41, 264, 426, 635, 832, 860
FIRA 714
first-mover advantage 330
fiscal federalism 152–4
fiscal frontier 182–3, 190
fiscal incentives 677–9, 693, 698
fiscal policy 147–54
Fisheries Policy 260–62
follow your leader 675
foot and mouth disease 245, 801
footloose 303, 346, 359, 568, 571, 574, 580, 583, 586, 593, 596, 624, 632, 653, 718–19
foreign and defence policy 46–54
'Fortress Europe' 401–2, 462, 531, 670, 724
France 381, 465, 532–3, 574, 578
Franco-German axis 44–8, 54, 58, 84
Frankfurt 123
free trade area 11–12, 14, 20, 31, 63, 147, 227, 263, 433, 443, 451, 467, 475, 543, 612, 802
Friedman, M. 103
FSC 515

Gainsborough, T. 800
Galileo 776, 791, 819
Game Boy 330
GATT 201, 246, 298, 304, 308, 443, 466, 468–81
    see also WTO

Gaulle, C. de 16–19, 82, 144, 245
Genesis 208, 209–10
genetically modified organisms 245, 493, 510–11, 680, 801, 804
Geneva 156, 655
gentleman's agreement 322
geopolitics 45
Germany 157–60, 297, 465, 574, 605, 760
Gestapo 156
globalisation 165, 190, 284, 390, 403, 417, 480, 544–5, 586, 608, 632, 669, 679–87, 722, 817
Grauwe, P. de 103, 126, 137, 145–6, 836
Gray, J. 683
Greece 21, 31–2, 846
green desert 242
green rate of exchange 221
greenfield 707, 729
Gresham's Law 109, 144
growth bonus 268, 454
GSP 525, 546–9

Hagedoorn, J. 702
Hallstein, W. 216
hard ECU 121
harmonisation 110, 141, 147, 152–3, 169, 349, 490, 796
Hayek, F. 347
Hecksher–Ohlin 308, 312, 573–4, 595, 669, 720
hedgerows 242
Heider, J. 42
Hill, T. 411
Hiroshima 602
Hirschman–Herfindahl index 284
historical accident 579, 580–81, 596, 661
    see also chance
history 579–80, 596–601, 610
Hoffmann-La Roche 316
Hollywood 288
home-market effect 438, 562, 575
Hoover 116
horseshoes 268
hub-and-spoke 435, 539
human capital 297, 309, 362, 367, 382, 400, 427, 437, 583, 590, 619, 719, 729, 754, 773, 854–5

human rights 534, 549, 685, 826
Hume, D. 271, 561

IBM 332, 427, 593, 701
IMF 697
immigration 134
immiserising customs union 462
imperfections, market 286, 333, 359–60, 362, 366, 449, 458, 571, 613, 646, 652, 695, 715, 717
import substitution 333
incentives, fiscal 677–9, 693, 698
increasing returns *see* economies of scale
indexation 96
India 479, 715, 854
industrial policy 352–427, 703, 705
infant industry 360
inflation 89, 94, 98, 103, 107, 113, 121, 123, 125–6, 135, 142, 145, 151, 367
innovation 268, 273–5, 277–8, 283, 285–300, 314, 330, 392, 608
insider trading 220
instincts 275
institutions 613
Integrated Mediterranean Programme 643
intellectual property 277, 289, 473, 477, 516
intergovernmental method 24, 80
Internet 268–9, 320, 438, 682
intervention 14, 107, 110, 113, 119, 268, 282, 353, 356–71, 400, 449, 454, 609, 613, 616–22, 650, 693, 698, 715–20, 792–4, 805
investment creation 670
investment diversion 670
Ireland 17–20, 426, 635, 638, 832, 846, 860
irreversible effects 296, 376, 377, 395, 579–80, 597, 654, 716
Isard, W. 572
Italy 297

J-curve effect 268, 454
Jacquemin, A. 271, 309, 314, 326, 346, 356, 372, 395, 749
Japan 226, 365, 379–80, 395, 400, 476, 491–2, 529–31, 604, 698
Jenkins, S. 52, 265, 587

Johnson, H. 450
Johnson–Krauss law 180, 754
Juppé, A. 133
juste retour 154, 204

Kant, E. 775
Kay, J. 801, 807
Kemp, M. 451
Kenen, P. 97–8
Keynes, J. 144
Kissinger, H. 47, 682
knowledge 296
Korea 365, 698
Kosovo 51–2, 86
Krugman, P. 47–8, 146, 269–71, 282, 297, 305, 332, 347, 349, 360, 370, 376–7, 382, 427, 560, 562, 572, 574–5, 577–8, 583, 596, 598–9, 604, 613, 615, 631, 658, 661, 669, 701
Kyocera 332
Kyoto Protocol 46, 803, 807

labelling 245, 478, 510, 803–4
lait cru 349
landscape 799–800
Le Pen, J. 42–3
learning-by-doing 131, 330, 448, 573
learning-by-watching 350
life cycle 330, 331, 371
lifts 700
Linder, S. 305, 308, 312, 562, 575
linkages 93, 95–7, 104, 170, 284, 296–7, 359, 377, 426, 571, 578, 584, 588, 594, 608–9, 620, 631–2, 689, 696–9, 705–6, 709, 721, 794, 819, 831
Lipsey, R.E. 699, 704
Lipsey, R.G. 274, 281, 287–8, 296, 304, 311, 347, 349, 359, 435–6, 444, 450, 452, 470, 530, 563, 577, 589–90, 595–6, 684, 714
liquidity trap 125
Lisbon Council 35–6, 59, 62, 205–6, 294, 393, 423, 457, 767, 783, 855
List, F. 159
lobby 270, 318, 359–60, 378, 398, 428, 448, 451, 461, 513, 560, 582, 677, 702–3, 753, 757, 788, 793, 805, 807, 841

local advantage 275, 284, 695
local content 376, 705–6, 726
location 164, 166, 169, 178, 180–81, 186, 190, 246, 284, 311–12, 328, 377, 389, 420, 435, 484, 518, 562, 568–660, 673, 677, 693, 702, 716–17, 729
location tournaments 596, 677, 703, 719
lock-in 576, 580, 593, 595–6, 597–602, 608–9
Lockheed 381
Lomé Agreement *see* ACP
London 123, 162
lone-wolf 552
Lösch, A. 577–8
Lucas, R. 590, 593
Luddites 273, 681, 774–6
'lump of labour fallacy' 775
Luxembourg Agreement 16–17, 24

Maastricht Treaty 25–30
McDonald's 319, 327, 361, 684, 854
MacDougall Report 132, 205
Macedonia 31–2, 83
Machlup, F. 4–5, 93, 99
McKinnon, R. 95, 97–8
MacSharry, R. 256–8, 800, 804
mad cow disease 212, 245, 400, 801
Mafia 95
Magna Carta 296
MAI 715
Malraux, A. 19
Mansholt, S. 255, 804
Maoist period 301
market
    failures *see* imperfections
    home-market effect 438, 562, 575
    structure 269, 282–5, 438, 574, 578, 704
    thick 570, 584–5, 588
Marshall, A. 369, 588, 599
Marshall Plan 3–6, 35, 831
Marx, K. 409
Meade, J. 89
Merger Treaty 63
mergers and acquisitions 320, 323–9, 331, 346, 371–2, 391, 421, 445, 702, 725
Messerlin, P. 46, 474, 543, 560

Mezzogiorno 146, 638, 649–51, 830–31
MFA 472
MFN 468
Miami 759
Microsoft 274–6, 288, 322, 330–31, 380, 515, 563, 603
Middle Ages 268, 599
Midelfart-Knarvik, K. 426, 629, 631, 634–6, 649, 665, 832
milk quota 88, 207
MIT 361
MITI 332, 355, 380, 394
Mitterrand, F. 43
mobility
    capital 666–750
    factors 93–5, 126
    labour 175, 755–69
monetary compensatory amount 221–3
money illusion 96–7, 101
Monnet, J. 8, 16
monopoly 151, 270, 272–8, 283–4, 298–9, 311, 313, 331, 560, 703, 707, 718, 721
Monti Report 388
Müller, A. 296
multilateral 450, 467–8, 470, 480
multiple equilibria 333, 362, 439, 579–80, 582, 596, 600–601, 608, 610, 613, 637, 646, 653
multispeed 39, 41, 852
Mundell, R. 93–4, 668, 720
mutual recognition 300–303, 314, 389, 415, 490, 779

NAFTA 435, 444
NAIRU 103–4
national interest 17, 36, 45, 48, 66, 122, 134, 145, 148
nationalisation 695
nationalism 84, 158
NATO 6, 18, 48–50, 819, 849
neo-communism 752
new economy 275, 587, 603
new theory of trade 180, 281–2, 286, 305, 357, 362, 377, 438, 463, 632, 716–17, 754
NGO 480, 680, 751
Nigeria 478

Nike 705, 708
Nikon 332
non-price rivalry 284
non-tradables 95, 126, 143, 188, 271, 409, 420, 437, 668
Norway 226
Novartis 322
NTBs 22, 215, 287, 299, 302, 313–14, 320, 323–4, 362, 387, 414, 433, 447, 466, 481–97, 563, 632, 695, 724, 730, 749, 794

OECD 15, 226, 713–15, 726, 766
Ohlin, B. 572–3, 596
oil crises 327, 352, 360, 372, 380, 386, 388, 623
Olivetti 321
one-size-fits-all 34, 39, 84, 135–6, 852
openness 40, 92, 95–7, 101, 105, 126, 468, 536, 760, 777
opt-out 17, 20, 35, 43, 57, 83, 760, 786, 827
optimum currency area 93, 95–100
origin, rules of 433, 450, 472, 484, 494–5
ostracism 87
overshooting 92
own resources 19, 197, 201, 204

Padania 59, 95, 591
Panić, M. 100, 117, 434, 723–4, 728
paper 807
parallel currencies 107–9
Pareto, W. 435
Parmalat 301
patent 277, 285, 289, 347
path dependence 580, 595, 620
pay, ability to 150–51, 154, 206
peace clause 254, 260, 478
Peck, M. 496–7
penalty 216
pensions 61, 133–4, 143, 150, 160, 772
periphery 576, 616, 620, 636–7, 831, 860
Perroux, F. 578
personal contact 590–91, 662
petrol station 320
PHARE 526, 828, 831, 848
pharmaceuticals 389–91, 701–2
Philadelphia 87

Philips 116
Phillips curve 103
photocopiers 484, 564
picking winner 377–83, 422, 579
pioneer group 38, 58
Pirelli 753
Pizzaro, F. 427
Plato 581–2
Playstation 330
Poitiers 491
Poland 660–61, 846
politbureau 67, 752
politics 20, 62, 75, 85, 91, 119, 129–30, 137, 140, 141, 322–3, 370, 452, 480, 853, 857, 860
poll tax 162–3
pollution 149, 333, 593, 793–4, 798–9, 804
Porter, M. 284, 347, 373, 380, 382, 590, 592, 594, 656
Portugal 23
Post-it notes 288
PPS 640
pre-empt 402, 693, 716
precautionary principle 245, 492–4, 797
predatory pricing 283, 331, 367, 459, 472, 485, 699
Prest, A. 152
pricing, transfer 165, 167, 699–700, 709
printers 350, 601
Prodi, R. 130
product cycle 674
productivity 473
productivity paradox 299
promise 131
prospect theory 287
protectionism 218, 301, 304, 369–71, 385, 447–9, 466, 474, 628, 735, 748
public good 360
public procurement 118, 302, 314, 349, 351, 355, 362, 367, 370, 381, 387, 423, 477, 486–7, 514, 564, 595, 623, 726
pyramid of privileges 558

qualified majority 69–71
quota 22, 147, 433, 562
qwerty 579

R&D 23, 275, 277, 280, 282, 296, 298–9, 305, 317, 324–5, 330–31, 333, 335, 337, 345, 348, 355, 361, 365–6, 386–7, 394–400, 587, 595, 700–702
region 94, 610–17
regional policy 568–660
Reinheitsgebot 302, 488
remittances 758
rents 282, 286, 289, 348, 395, 474, 560, 715, 722
reserves 105–6, 113, 144
resources, own 19, 197, 201, 204
restriction of competition 317–30
retaliation 282, 285, 438, 447, 562, 687, 718
retirement 134
Rhodes, C. 427
Ricardo, D. 271, 281, 572–3, 575, 608, 630
rigidity 141–2, 273, 610, 619, 649, 760, 817
risk 132, 288, 317, 327, 330–31, 358, 365–8, 372, 377, 400–401, 466, 572, 620, 626, 646, 681, 695, 698, 702, 720, 820, 853–4
risk-aversion 369, 373, 701
risk-loving 331, 369, 562
Robson, P. 99, 179, 703, 728, 754
rogue state 46
Roman Empire 49, 60, 63, 81, 141, 550, 860
Romer, P. 475, 708
Rose, A. 98, 137, 146
Rougemont, D. de 3, 55, 59
Roundtable of European Industrialists 22, 395
royalty 699
Ruding Committee 173
Rugman, A. 682, 700, 706, 752
rules of origin 433, 450, 472, 484, 494–5
Russia 48–9, 85–6, 480, 528, 564, 752, 803, 854, 857

Saarland 82
sanctions 129–30, 432, 515
Sapir, A. 59, 203, 305, 314, 349, 395, 409–10, 562, 783, 855
Sardinia 265

scars 401
Schaus Memorandum 812
Schengen 768, 827
Schuman, R. 8
Schumpeter, J. 298, 348, 475
Second World War 2–3, 7–8, 25, 260, 264, 605–7, 760
second-best 283, 358, 363, 435–6, 442, 464, 466, 652, 685, 720
seigniorage 104, 144
self-sufficiency 202, 215, 220, 230–31, 236–42, 246, 256, 295
serendipity 288, 348
services 281, 297, 300, 302, 324, 361, 392, 408–21, 428, 473, 477, 498, 738, 757, 809
set aside 256, 265
shock 97–8, 122, 136–7, 142, 311, 376, 602, 649, 761, 776
Sialkot 606
Sidjanski, D. 1–2, 8, 55, 81
Single Administrative Document 208, 815, 821
Single European Act 22–5
Single European Market (Programme) 23–5, 41, 60, 92, 116, 127, 141–2, 147, 169, 174, 181, 183, 186, 222, 272, 298–303, 309, 311, 313–14, 319–20, 323–4, 328–9, 335, 337, 345, 373–4, 385, 387–9, 395, 401–3, 408, 413, 416, 445, 447, 482, 488, 496–7, 620, 632, 636, 644, 669, 724–5, 728, 730, 735, 802
Single European Market Programme 813, 815–16, 820, 827, 829, 851
Slovakia 660–61, 842
SMEs 171, 181, 203, 333–5, 337, 351, 371–5, 620, 652
Smith & Wesson 327
Smith, A. 151–2, 409, 456, 572–3, 619
smuggling 221
snowball effect 574, 584, 675
social contract 46, 125
social policy 771–90
Socrates 783–4
solidarity 45, 145, 225, 621
Solitaire 297
Sony 428

Sophia-Antipolis 594
sources of law 68
sovereignty 8, 17, 34, 63, 94, 101, 120, 131, 138, 141, 148, 158, 191, 208, 346, 388, 685, 817, 853
spaghetti bowl 558–9
Spain 23, 738
spatial economics 570, 572, 574, 609
specialisation 105, 152, 246, 254, 300–303, 312, 377, 455–60, 620, 631, 808
spillovers 154, 282, 359–60, 366, 377, 384, 394, 588, 590, 592, 597, 662, 696, 698–9, 705
Spinelli, A. 2
Spinelli Report 386
Stabex 537–8
stabilisation 194
stabiliser 108, 114, 132, 136, 141
Stability and Growth Pact 60, 62, 85, 118, 129–32, 135, 141, 194, 827, 831, 853
Stackelberg game 364
standards 184, 218, 225, 275, 285, 300–302, 306, 308, 320, 355, 367, 387, 395, 402, 487–91, 549, 591, 683, 706, 794–5, 797, 803, 839
static effects 267–8, 436–53
steam engine 289
Stephanou, C. 67
Stockholm Convention 14
strategic industries 370
Stresa 216
structural funds 197–8, 568
structure–conduct–performance 283
stumbling block 466
subsidiarity 29, 33, 141, 153, 384, 648, 798
subsidy 23, 35, 82, 147, 164, 190, 220–22, 224, 226, 231, 242, 246, 254, 264, 298, 332–43, 360, 362, 367–8, 472, 616, 620, 623, 642, 645, 716, 719, 817
substitution 444
Sumerians 264
sunk costs 268, 270, 274, 282, 284, 306, 333, 359, 410, 596, 703
supranationality 8, 13, 17, 21
Sweden 31–2, 41, 134, 264, 598

Switzerland 23, 87, 96, 155–7, 170, 207, 226, 322, 359, 427, 494, 654, 854
Sysmin 537

TACIS 528
tacit deals 321, 334, 590–91, 593, 827
target 327, 360, 379–81, 674, 676, 695–6, 725, 735
tariff 18, 362, 367, 433, 441, 447
    common external 11, 18–19, 287, 433, 436, 442
    factory 670, 714, 724
    optimal 348
tariffication 254, 471
taste 285, 299–300, 303, 305, 307, 309, 311–12, 319–20, 437–8, 456, 599, 601, 617, 683, 724
Tavlas, G. 99, 106, 144
tax 94, 118, 133, 147–93, 300, 320, 677–8, 798
    avoidance and evasion 142, 166, 169, 171, 180, 182, 189–90, 699
    code of conduct 188
    competition 169, 187–8, 190, 192
    corporate/firm income/profit 142, 152, 164–74
    destination principle 178–80, 189
    direct 163–78
    double taxation 173–6, 181
    e-commerce 189, 208
    harmonisation 155, 182–3, 187, 192
    haven 190
    high 164
    indirect 178–87
    neutrality 169, 171
    origin principle 178–80, 183, 189
    passing on 167–8
    personal income 142, 175–8
    principles 147, 150–52
    ratio 150
    sales 152, 181
    unitary 165–7, 174, 189
    VAT 171, 181–5, 360
    withholding 169–71, 188
Technology Policy 394–400
technology transfer 703
tectonic changes 41
terrorism 768

Tetris 297
Thatcher, M. 162–3, 204
thick market 570, 584–5, 588
thin air 132, 595
Thomson Report 638
threats, exchange of 676
TNCs 117, 164–7, 170–74, 190, 215, 300, 309, 314, 327, 385, 402, 421, 434, 467, 475, 596, 669–750
Tocqueville, A. de 85
Toyota 592
tradables 95
trade
  costs 284, 311, 314, 433, 438–9, 581, 598, 632, 636, 673
  creation 138, 439, 441–3, 449, 464, 562
  deficit 246, 481
  deflection 443
  diversion 215, 255, 439, 442–3, 446, 449, 453, 458, 461, 464
  expansion 444–5
  free 11–12, 14, 20, 31, 63, 147, 227, 263, 433, 443, 451, 467, 475, 543, 612, 802
  inter-industry 304, 307–8, 632
  intra-firm 115, 190, 672
  intra-industry 300, 303–12, 314, 573, 632–3, 636, 669, 717–18
  new theory of 180, 281–2, 286, 305, 357, 362, 377, 438, 463, 632, 716–17, 754
  non-tradables 95, 126, 143, 188, 271, 409, 420, 437, 668
  policy 270, 283, 302, 431–561, 584
  reasons for 438
  suppression 458
  terms of 97, 348, 444, 450–51, 460–62
trademark 347
trans-European network 30, 388, 810, 814, 819–20
transfer pricing 165, 167, 699–700, 709
transfers 104, 114, 126, 132–3, 141, 145, 150, 153, 154, 450, 829
transparency 138, 321, 333–4, 480
transport 808–20
Treaty of Amsterdam 32–4
Treaty of Nice 36–9

Treaty of Paris 8–9
Treaty of Rome 12, 465
Treaty of Westphalia 84
TRIM 470, 495, 705–6
TRIP 471
Tungsram 700
Turkey 49, 549, 567, 822–3, 840, 846, 848, 857–9
Tyson, L. 298, 332, 354, 362, 371, 378, 414, 422, 448, 512, 531, 567, 696, 754

über-currency 128, 131, 141, 853
uncertainty 267, 288, 317, 329, 368, 372, 438, 541, 560, 572, 592, 620, 676, 720, 776, 807
UNCTAD 672, 678, 686, 694, 699, 719, 753
underground economy 176
UNECE 4, 8
unemployment 103, 125, 130, 135, 775–7
unilateralism 512
Uruguay Round 226, 246, 254, 256–8, 467, 470–76
US 142, 160–62, 226, 297, 301, 308, 400, 435, 467–8, 470, 475–7, 480, 509–19, 542, 563, 604, 627–8, 631, 634, 803, 817, 854–5, 860
US Department of Agriculture 264
US Farm Bill 226, 265
US film industry 590
US Steel 375

values (European and American) 85
variable levy 217, 220
variable refund 220, 224, 246
VAT 171, 181–5, 360
VCR 297, 491, 580
Venables, A. 497, 600, 609, 615, 631, 633, 673, 831
Vermeer, J. 856
VHS 579
Viagra 348
villeins 86, 162
Viner, J. 442, 447, 451
vitality 369
vitamins 316
Volkswagen 316, 319
von Thünen, J. 575–6

war 605–7
warning 130
washing machines 301
watches 350, 601
Weber, A. 576
Weinstein, D. 562, 571, 575, 602
Werner, P. 98, 110
whims 657
White Paper 22–5, 147, 182, 387, 402
windmills 268
Wolf, M. 137, 146
Wolfowitz, P. 48
Wonnacott, P. 450

World War II 2–3, 7–8, 25, 260, 264, 605–7, 760
WTO 254, 260, 264, 367, 467–81, 542, 681, 706
see also GATT

X-inefficiency 314, 387, 463
Xerox 427

Yannopoulos, G. 469, 510
Yaoundé Convention 18, 532–3
Yugoslavia 51

zollverein 82, 159